Flores Florentino

Dead Sea Scrolls and Other Early Jewish Studies in Honour of Florentino García Martínez

Edited by

Anthony Hilhorst, Émile Puech and
Eibert Tigchelaar

BRILL

LEIDEN • BOSTON
2007

This book is printed on acid-free paper.

Library of Congress Cataloging-in-Publication Data

Flores Florentino : Dead Sea Scrolls and other early Jewish studies in honour of Florentino Garcia Martinez / edited by Anthony Hilhorst, Emile Puech, and Eibert Tigchelaar.
    p. cm. — (Supplements to the Journal for the study of Judaism ; v. 122)
    Includes bibliographical references and index.
    ISBN 978-90-04-16292-1 (hardback : alk. paper) 1. Dead Sea scrolls. 2. Qumran community. 3. Judaism—History—Post-exilic period, 586 B.C.–210 A.D. 4. Christianity—Origin. 5. Dead Sea scrolls—Relation to the New Testament. I. Hilhorst, Anthony. II. Puech, Emile. III. Tigchelaar, Eibert J. C. IV. García Martínez, Florentino. IV. Title. V. Series.

    BM487.F575 2007
    296.1'55—dc22

                                                            2007036703

ISSN 1384-2161
ISBN 978 90 04 16292 1

Flores Florentino

⌄Supplements

to the

Journal for the Study of Judaism

Editor

John J. Collins
The Divinity School, Yale University

Associate Editors

Florentino García Martínez
Qumran Institute, University of Groningen

Hindy Najman
Department of Near and Middle Eastern Civilizations,
University of Toronto

Advisory Board

J. DUHAIME — A. HILHORST — P.W. VAN DER HORST
A. KLOSTERGAARD PETERSEN — M.A. KNIBB — J.T.A.G.M. VAN RUITEN
J. SIEVERS — G. STEMBERGER — E.J.C. TIGCHELAAR — J. TROMP

⌄ VOLUME 122

CONTENTS

PREFACE

In Elias Canetti's novel *Auto–Da–Fé*, the protagonist, Professor Kien, greatly enjoys the confinement in his study. On the occasion of a learned conference he sends his assembled colleagues a letter in which he wishes them a nice gathering; he himself will not attend. He is the classic example of the scholarly recluse. Florentino García Martínez is a regular resident of his study as well—where else could the stupendous output of his scholarly work, the list of which can be consulted at the end of the present volume, have been prepared? And yet, there could be no greater contrast than that between Canetti's hero and Professor Florentino García Martínez, whose proper biotope, so to speak, is the conference hall, the corridors just as much as the auditorium. And so we have already two of his qualities: his productivity in writing books, articles and book reviews, and his pleasure in meeting friends and colleagues. Two more qualities should at once be added to the record: his intelligence and his drive. Did you not quite hear what he was saying, because his words had some blend from other languages? Just listen better, for he has always interesting views to offer. Were you disturbed because some rare spelling mistake was left in his paper? Think how many more brilliant essays he produced than you will ever be able to.

There can be no question of compiling his biography here, but a rapid sketch of his life may be permitted. Born in Mochales in the province of Guadalajara, Spain, on 27 November 1942, he was educated in the seminary of Sigüenza and the University of Comillas (Santander), where he graduated *cum laude* in theology in 1967. Ordained as a priest, he taught history at a secondary school, and subsequently studied at the Pontifical Biblical Institute in Rome, where again he graduated *cum laude* in 1973. After research stays at the New York Jewish Theological Seminary, the University of Bonn, and the Hebrew University in Jerusalem, he was at the École Biblique et Archéologique Française of Jerusalem as a fellow of the Fundación Juan March from 1975 to 1979. It was in Jerusalem that he met his future wife Annie Barnet. In 1980, the late Professor Adam Simon van der Woude, the founder of the Groningen Qumran Institute as well as of the *Journal for the Study of Judaism*, won him for a position at the University of Groningen; the

close cooperation of the senior and junior scholar, resulting in a number
of remarkable publications and a theory about the Qumran origins they
christened as the "Groningen hypothesis," counts no doubt as one of
Florentino's happiest memories. Almost immediately after his arrival
in Groningen, Florentino became involved in two major journals, the
Journal for the Study of Judaism, and the *Revue de Qumran*. Beginning in
1980, he wrote numerous reviews of articles and reviews of books for
the *JSJ*, and later became its secretary in 1990, and its editor-in-chief
in 1997. For the *Revue de Qumran*, he took care of the "Bibliography"
and the "Tables" from 1981 on, and after Jean Carmignac's death in
1986 Émile Puech and Florentino became together responsible for the
journal up to the present day, the former as director, and Florentino
as secretary. Only later in his career, after having published many articles, Florentino took his doctoral degree in Groningen, once more *cum
laude*, on 27 February 1992. In 1995 he was appointed extraordinary
Professor by the Nicolaas Muleriusfonds of the University and in 2000
Ordinary Professor of Early Judaism and Dead Sea Scrolls at the Faculty
of Theology and Religious Studies of the University of Groningen. In
the meantime, Florentino and Annie married in Jerusalem; his return
to the lay status was awarded him by papal decision in 1987. In 2000,
Florentino's academic career changed course: he was invited as Guest
Professor by the Catholic University of Louvain (Katholieke Univer-
siteit Leuven), which appointed him as Ordinary Professor in 2002.
He moved then to Louvain, continuing, however, his professorship in
Groningen, on a part-time basis. In 2004 he was elected as a Foreign
Member by the Humanities and Social Sciences Division of the Royal
Netherlands Academy of Arts and Sciences (KNAW).

From his first publications up to the present ones, Florentino's
scholarly work is characterized by a few basic features. For him scholarship is an ongoing process, and his own work is one moment in this
continuum of past, present and future scholarship. There is no one else
with such a vast and thorough knowledge of the history of Qumran
research, and the notes in his work include extensive bibliographies,
or express our indebtedness to earlier scholars. He also realizes that all
scholarly work sooner or later will be corrected or improved upon by
later scholarship. Therefore he is not plagued by the desire to present
a work that is perfect in all details. Instead, he aims at participating
in the scholarly debate and shaping current and future directions of
the discipline. The qualities he admired in the work of André Dupont-
Sommer, are also those he pursues in his own work and fosters in

younger scholars: *courage et fécondité d'une pensée*. In specific cases, such as the origins of the Qumran community (the "Groningen Hypothesis") or his views on apocalypticism, Florentino has demonstrably influenced scholarship with new theses or approaches. In other cases his influence has been more subtle, showing how one should formulate questions on the basis of earlier scholarship, and answer them on the basis of the available data, and setting an example with the transparency of his approach and his lucid observations.

The present collection of essays is meant as a token of the gratitude of many colleagues and admirers for all he gave them in the field of Early Jewish Studies. The contributors are friends, colleagues and students from many countries and from different stages of Florentino's academic career. The majority of the essays are in the areas of Florentino's own scholarship and interests, including not only Qumranica, but also many other fields of Second Temple Judaism, from late biblical texts and Septuagint up to early rabbinic writings. Florentino's own polyglottism, evident from his bibliography, and his close relations with many scholars from Spain, France and Italy, is reflected in the different languages used in this volume.

It is as colleagues and as friends that we present this bouquet of essays to Florentino, and join in wishing him and Annie many more years of health and happiness.

Anthony Hilhorst
Émile Puech
Eibert Tigchelaar

ACKNOWLEDGMENTS

Thanks are due to the following persons and institutions: Nicole Tilford, MA student Religions of Western Antiquity at Florida State University, for the conscientious style-editing of virtually all the English-language papers as well as the bibliography, without whose assistance this volume would not have appeared in time; Department of Religion, FSU, for practical support; Jim Lehman, PhD student RWA at FSU, for the correction of the English of one of the contributions; Matthew Goff, for help with English; Adam Bechtel, Elijah Merrett, and Colin Womack, MA students RWA, for assisting with the indexing of this volume; Eveline van Staalduine-Sulman, for double-checking the Or 1474 manuscript of the *Targum Obadiah*; Martin Abegg for providing the new 1QH^a column and line numbers of the forthcoming 1QH^a edition (this new numbering has been used throughout in this volume); Silvana Cordero for the photograph included in this volume; Pim Rietbroek of Brill, for technical advice with regard to supralinear vocalisation; Linguist's Software for permission to use the font Hebraica II Supra; John Collins and Hindy Najman, editors of the Series Supplements to the Journal for the Study of Judaism for accepting this volume in the series and for their involvement in this project; Machiel Kleemans and Mattie Kuiper of Brill for the supervision of the production of this book and for many practical matters; Anita Roodnat for the desk-editing of this volume.

LIST OF CONTRIBUTORS

Hugo Antonissen, K.U. Leuven (Belgium)
Jesús Asurmendi, Institut Catholique de Paris (France)
Katell Berthelot, CNRS, Aix en Provence (France)
Jan N. Bremmer, University of Groningen (Netherlands)
Alessandro Catastini, Università di Roma «La Sapienza» (Italy)
John J. Collins, Yale (USA)
Luis Díez Merino, Universidad de Barcelona (Spain)
Devorah Dimant, University of Haifa (Israel)
Natalio Fernández Marcos, Instituto de Filología—CSIC, Madrid (Spain)
Peter W. Flint, Dead Sea Scrolls Institute, Trinity Western University (Canada)
Luis F. Girón Blanc, Universidad Complutense de Madrid (Spain)
Francolino J. Gonçalves, École Biblique et Archéologique Française, Jérusalem (Israel)
Charlotte Hempel, University of Birmingham (UK)
Ton Hilhorst, University of Groningen (Netherlands)
Albert L.A. Hogeterp, K.U. Leuven (Belgium)
Pieter W. van der Horst, Utrecht University (Netherlands)
Giovanni Ibba, Facoltà Teologica dell'Italia Centrale, Firenze (Italy)
Menahem Kister, The Hebrew University of Jerusalem (Israel)
Anders Klostergaard Petersen, University of Aarhus (Denmark)
Michael A. Knibb, King's College London (UK)
George H. van Kooten, University of Groningen (Netherlands)
Armin Lange, University of Vienna (Austria)
Johan Lust, K.U. Leuven (Belgium)
Gerard P. Luttikhuizen, University of Groningen (Netherlands)
Corrado Martone, University of Turin (Italy)
Hindy Najman, University of Toronto (Canada)
Étienne Nodet, École Biblique et Archéologique Française, Jérusalem (Israel)
Ed Noort, University of Groningen (Netherlands)
Donald W. Parry, Brigham Young University (USA)
Miguel Pérez Fernández, Universidad de Granada (Spain)
Antonio Piñero, Universidad Complutense de Madrid (Spain)

Mladen Popović, Qumran Institute, University of Groningen (Netherlands)

Emile Puech, CNRS, Paris (France)—École Biblique et Archéologique Française, Jérusalem (Israel)

Josep Ribera-Florit, Universidad de Barcelona (Spain)

Lautaro Roig Lanzillotta, Universidad de Córdoba (Spain); University of Groningen (Netherlands)

Jacques van Ruiten, University of Groningen (Netherlands)

Paolo Sacchi, University of Turin (Italy)

Günter Stemberger, University of Vienna (Austria)

Eibert Tigchelaar, Florida State University (USA)

Emanuel Tov, The Hebrew University of Jerusalem (Israel)

Julio Trebolle, Universidad Complutense de Madrid (Spain)

Johannes Tromp, Leiden University (Netherlands)

Eugene Ulrich, University of Notre Dame (USA)

James C. VanderKam, University of Notre Dame (USA)

Jaime Vázquez Allegue, Universidad Pontificia de Salamanca (Spain)

Luis Vegas Montaner, Universidad Complutense de Madrid (Spain)

Joseph Verheyden, K.U. Leuven (Belgium)

Géza G. Xeravits, Reformed Theological Academy, Pápa (Hungary)

ABBREVIATIONS

AAA	*Acta Apostolorum Apocrypha.* Edited by R.A. Lipsius and M. Bonnet. Leipzig, 1891–1903. Reprinted Darmstadt 1959
AB	Anchor Bible
ABD	*Anchor Bible Dictionary.* Edited by D.N. Freedman. 6 vols. New York, 1992
ABR	*Australian Biblical Review*
AfO	*Archiv für Orientforschung*
AGJU	Arbeiten zur Geschichte des antiken Judentums und des Urchristentums
AGSU	Arbeiten zur Geschichte des Spätjudentums und Urchristentums
AISG	Associazione italiana per lo studio del giudaismo
AJEC	Ancient Judaism and Early Christianity
ALGHJ	Arbeiten zur Literatur und Geschichte des hellenistischen Judentums
ANRW	*Aufstieg und Niedergang der römischen Welt: Geschichte und Kultur Roms im Spiegel der neueren Forschung.* Edited by H. Temporini and W. Haase. Berlin, 1972–
AOAT	Alter Orient und Altes Testament
AOT	*The Apocryphal Old Testament.* Edited by H.F.D. Sparks. Oxford, 1984
APOT	*The Apocrypha and Pseudepigrapha of the Old Testament.* Edited by R.H. Charles. 2 vols. Oxford, 1913
ARG	*Archiv für Religionsgeschichte*
ARW	*Archiv für Religionswissenschaft*
ASSR	*Archives de sciences sociales des religions*
ASTI	*Annual of the Swedish Theological Institute*
ATD	Das Alte Testament Deutsch
AuOr	*Aula Orientalis*
AUSS	Andrews University Seminary Studies
BA	*Biblical Archaeologist*
BAC	Biblioteca de autores cristianos
BAR	*Biblical Archaeology Review*
BASOR	*Bulletin of the American Schools of Oriental Research*
BBB	Bonner biblische Beiträge

BETL	Bibliotheca Ephemeridum Theologicarum Lovaniensium
BHQ	*Biblia Hebraica Quinta*. Edited by A. Schenker et al., 2004–
BHS	*Biblia Hebraica Stuttgartensia*. Edited by K. Elliger and W. Rudolph. Stuttgart, 1983
Bib	*Biblica*
BibOr	Biblica et Orientalia
BICS	*Bulletin of the Institute for Classical Studies*
BiOr	*Bibliotheca Orientalis*
BIOSCS	*Bulletin of the International Organization for Septuagint and Cognate Studies*
BIS	Biblical Interpretation Series
BiTS	Biblical Tools and Studies
BJb	Bonner Jahrbücher
BJGS	*Bulletin of Judaeo-Greek Studies*
BJRL	*Bulletin of the John Rylands University Library of Manchester*
BJS	Brown Judaic Studies
BKAT	Biblischer Kommentar, Altes Testament. Edited by M. Noth and H.W. Wolff
BN	*Biblische Notizen*
BNP	*Brill's New Pauly*. Edited by H. Cancik and H. Schneider. Leiden, 2002–
BOT	Boeken van het Oude Testament
BRS	Bible Resource Series
BSJS	Brill's Series in Jewish Studies
BTB	*Biblical Theology Bulletin*
ByzZ	*Byzantinische Zeitschrift*
BZ	*Biblische Zeitschrift*
BZAW	Beihefte zur Zeitschrift für die alttestamentliche Wissenschaft
BZNW	Beihefte zur Zeitschrift für die neutestamentliche Wissenschaft
CahRB	Cahiers de la Revue Biblique
CBQ	*Catholic Biblical Quarterly*
CBQMS	Catholic Biblical Quarterly—Monograph Series
CCCM	Corpus Christianorum: Continuatio Mediaevalis. Turnhout, 1966–
CCJW	Cambridge Commentaries on Jewish Writings of the Jewish and Christian World 200 B.C. to A.D. 200
CCSA	Corpus Christianorum: Series Apocryphorum. Turnhout, 1983–

CCSL	Corpus Christianorum: Series Latina. Turnhout, 1953–
CEA/SA	Collection des Études Augustiniennes. Série Antiquité
CHJ	*Cambridge History of Judaism.* Ed. W.D. Davies and Louis Finkelstein. Cambridge, 1984–
CJAS	Christianity and Judaism in Antiquity Series
CMG	Corpus Medicorum Graecorum
ConBNT	Coniectanea Biblica: New Testament Series
COT	Commentaar op het Oude Testament
CQ	*Classical Quarterly*
CQS	Companion to the Qumran Scrolls
CRAI	Comptes rendus de l'Académie des inscriptions et belles-lettres
CRINT	Corpus Rerum Iudaicarum ad Novum Testamentum
CSCO	Corpus Scriptorum Christianorum Orientalium
CSEL	Corpus Scriptorum Ecclesiasticorum Latinorum
CSHJ	Chicago Studies in the History of Judaism
DBSup	*Dictionnaire de la Bible: Supplément.* Edited by L. Pirot and A. Robert. Paris, 1928–
DJD	Discoveries in the Judaean Desert (of Jordan)
DJD 1	Barthélemy, D., and J.T. Milik. *Qumran Cave I.* DJD I. Oxford, 1955
DJD 3	Baillet, M., J.T. Milik, and R. de Vaux. *Les "Petites Grottes" de Qumrân. Exploration de la falaise. Les grottes 2Q, 3Q, 5Q, 6Q, 7Q à 10Q. Le rouleau de cuivre.* DJDJ III. Oxford, 1962
DJD 4	Sanders, J.A. *The Psalms Scroll of Qumran Cave 11 (11QPsª).* DJDJ IV. Oxford, 1963
DJD 5	Allegro, J.M. *Qumrân Cave 4.I (4Q158–4Q186).* DJDJ V. Oxford, 1968
DJD 7	Baillet, M. *Qumrân grotte 4.III (4Q482–4Q520).* DJD VII. Oxford, 1982
DJD 8	Tov, E. *The Greek Minor Prophets Scroll from Nahal Hever (8HevXIIgr) (The Seiyâl Collection I).* DJD VIII. Oxford, 1990
DJD 9	Skehan, P.W., E. Ulrich, and J.E. Sanderson. *Qumran Cave 4.IV: Palaeo-Hebrew and Greek Biblical Manuscripts.* DJD IX. Oxford, 1992
DJD 10	Qimron, E. and J. Strugnell. *Qumran Cave 4.V: Miqṣat Maʿaśe ha-Torah.* DJD X. Oxford, 1994
DJD 11	Eshel, E. et al. *Qumran Cave 4.VI: Poetical and Liturgical Texts, Part 1.* DJD XI. Oxford, 1998

DJD 12   Ulrich, E., F.M. Cross et al. *Qumran Cave 4.VII: Genesis to Numbers.* DJD XII. Oxford, 1994

DJD 13   Attridge, H. et al. *Qumran Cave 4.VIII: Parabiblical Texts Part 1.* DJD XIII. Oxford, 1994

DJD 14   Ulrich, E., F.M. Cross et al. *Qumran Cave 4.IX: Deuteronomy, Joshua, Judges, Kings.* DJD XIV. Oxford, 1995

DJD 16   Ulrich, E., F.M. Cross et al. *Qumran Cave 4.XI: Psalms to Chronicles.* DJD XVI. Oxford, 2000

DJD 17   Cross, F.M. et al. *Qumran Cave 4.XII: 1–2 Samuel.* DJD XVII. Oxford, 2005

DJD 18   Baumgarten, J.M. *Qumran Cave 4.XIII: The Damascus Document (4Q266–273).* DJD XVIII. Oxford, 1996

DJD 19   Broshi, M. et al. *Qumran Cave 4.XIV: Parabiblical Texts, Part 2.* DJD XIX. Oxford, 1995

DJD 22   Brooke, G. et al. *Qumran Cave 4.XVII: Parabiblical Texts, Part 3.* DJD XXII. Oxford, 1996

DJD 23   García Martínez, F., E.J.C. Tigchelaar, and A.S. van der Woude. *Qumran Cave 11.II: 11Q2–18, 11Q20–31.* DJD XXIII. Oxford, 1998

DJD 26   Alexander, P.S., and G. Vermes. *Qumran Cave 4.XIX. Serek ha-Yaḥad and Two Related Texts.* DJD XXVI. Oxford, 1998

DJD 28   Gropp, D., *Wadi Daliyeh II: The Samaria Papyri from Wadi Daliyeh;* Bernstein, M. et al. *Qumran Cave 4.XXVIII: Miscellanea, Part 2.* DJD XXVIII. Oxford, 2001

DJD 29   Chazon, E. et al. *Qumran Cave 4.XX: Poetical and Liturgical Texts, Part 2.* DJD XXIX. Oxford, 1999

DJD 30   Dimant, D. *Qumran Cave 4.XVII: Parabiblical Texts, Part 4: Pseudo-Prophetic Texts.* DJD XXX. Oxford, 2001

DJD 31   Puech, É. *Qumrân grotte 4.XXII: Textes araméens, première partie: 4Q529–549.* DJD XXXI. Oxford, 2001

DJD 35   Baumgarten, J.M. et al. *Qumran Cave 4.XXV: Halakhic Texts.* DJD XXXV. Oxford, 1999

DJD 36   Pfann, S.J., *Qumran Cave 4.XXVI: Cryptic Texts*; Alexander, P.S. et al. *Miscellanea, Part 1.* DJD XXXVI. Oxford, 2000

DJD 39   Tov, E., ed. *The Texts from the Judaean Desert: Indices and an Introduction to the* Discoveries in the Judaean Desert *Series.* DJD XXXIX. Oxford, 2002

DNP   *Der neue Pauly: Enzyklopädie der Antike.* Edited by H. Cancik and H. Schneider. Stuttgart, 1996–2004

DSD   *Dead Sea Discoveries*

DSSR	The Dead Sea Scrolls Reader. Edited by D.W. Parry and E. Tov. Leiden, 2004–2005
EBib	Études Bibliques
EKK	Evangelisch-katholischer Kommentar zum Neuen Testament
EncJud	*Encyclopaedia Judaica*. 16 vols. Jerusalem, 1972
EPRO	Études préliminaires aux religions orientales dans l'empire romain
ErIsr	*Eretz-Israel*
EstBíb	*Estudios Bíblicos*
ETL	*Ephemerides Theologicae Lovanienses*
FBBS	Facet Books Biblical Series
FJTC	Flavius Josephus: Translation and Commentary. Edited by S. Mason. Leiden, 1999–
FOTL	Forms of the Old Testament Literature
FRLANT	Forschungen zur Religion und Literatur des Alten und Neuen Testaments
GCS	Die griechischen christlichen Schriftsteller der ersten [drei] Jahrhunderte
GSCC	Groningen Studies in Cultural Change
HALAT	Koehler, L., W. Baumgartner, und J.J. Stamm, *Hebräisches und Aramäisches Lexikon zum Alten Testament*, Leiden, 1967–1995
HALOT	Koehler, L., W. Baumgartner, and J.J. Stamm, *The Hebrew and Aramaic Lexicon of the Old Testament*, Leiden, 1994–2000
HAR	Hebrew Annual Review
HAT	Handbuch zum Alten Testament
HCS	Hellenistic Culture and Society
HdO	Handbuch der Orientalistik
HeyJ	*Heythrop Journal*
HKAT	Handkommentar zum Alten Testament
HSCP	*Harvard Studies in Classical Philology*
HSM	Harvard Semitic Monographs
HSS	Harvard Semitic Studies
HTR	*Harvard Theological Review*
HTS	Harvard Theological Studies
HUCA	*Hebrew Union College Annual*
ICC	The International Critical Commentary
IEJ	*Israel Exploration Journal*
IOS	*Israel Oriental Studies*

ISACR	Interdisciplinary Studies in Ancient Culture and Religion
JAOS	*Journal of the American Oriental Society*
JBL	*Journal of Biblical Literature*
JBS	Jerusalem Biblical Studies
JECS	*Journal of Early Christian Studies*
JHS	*Journal of Hellenic Studies*
JJS	*Journal of Jewish Studies*
JNSL	*Journal of Northwest Semitic Languages*
JRASup	Journal of Roman Archaeology Supplement Series
JRS	*Journal of Roman Studies*
JSHRZ	Jüdische Schriften aus hellenistisch-römischer Zeit
JSJ	*Journal for the Study of Judaism*
JSJSup	Supplements to the Journal for the Study of Judaism
JSM	Journal of Semitic Studies Monograph
JSNT	*Journal for the Study of the New Testament*
JSOT	*Journal for the Study of the Old Testament*
JSOTSup	Journal for the Study of the Old Testament: Supplement Series
JSP	*Journal for the Study of the Pseudepigrapha*
JSPSup	Journal for the Study of the Pseudepigrapha: Supplement Series
JSQ	*Jewish Studies Quarterly*
JSRC	Jerusalem Studies in Religion and Culture
JSS	*Journal of Semitic Studies*
JTS	*Journal of Theological Studies*
KD	*Kerygma und Dogma*
KEK	Kritisch-exegetischer Kommentar über das Neue Testament
KlPauly	*Der kleine Pauly*
LCL	Loeb Classical Library
LD	Lectio Divina
LSTS	Library of Second Temple Studies
LUÅ	*Lunds universitets årsskrift*
McCQ	*McCormick Quarterly*
MEAH	*Miscelánea de Estudios Árabes y Hebraicos*
MH	*Museum Helveticum*
NEB.AT	Neue Echter Bibel. Altes Testament
NHC	Nag Hammadi Codices
NHMS	Nag Hammadi and Manichaean Studies
NHS	Nag Hammadi Studies

NICOT	New International Commentary on the Old Testament
NovT	*Novum Testamentum*
NovTSup	Supplements to Novum Testamentum
NRSV	New Revised Standard Version
NTL	New Testament Library
NTOA.SA	Novum Testamentum et Orbis Antiquus. Series archæologica
NTS	*New Testament Studies*
NTTS	New Testament Tools and Studies
OBO	Orbis Biblicus et Orientalis
ÖBS	Österreichische biblische Studien
OLA	Orientalia Lovaniensia Analecta
OLZ	*Orientalistische Literaturzeitung*
OTE	*Old Testament Essays*
OTL	Old Testament Library
OTP	*Old Testament Pseudepigrapha*. Edited by J.H. Charlesworth. 2 vols. New York, 1983–1985
OTS	Oudtestamentische studiën
PAAJR	*Proceedings of the American Academy of Jewish Research*
PFES	Publications of the Finnish Exegetical Society
PG	Patrologia Graeca. Edited by J.-P. Migne. 162 vols. Paris, 1857–1886
PL	Patrologia Latina. Edited by J.-P. Migne. 217 vols. Paris, 1844–1864
POT	De Prediking van het Oude Testament
PTA	Papyrologische Texte und Abhandlungen
PVTG	Pseudepigrapha Veteris Testamenti Graece
RAC	*Reallexikon für Antike und Christentum*. Edited by T. Klauser et al. Stuttgart, 1950–
RAPH	Recherches d'archéologie, de philologie et d'histoire
RB	*Revue Biblique*
RCatT	*Rivista Catalana de Teologia*
RE	*Pauly's Realencyclopädie der classischen Altertumswissenschaft*
REB	Revised English Bible
REG	*Revue des études grecques*
REJ	*Revue des études juives*
RevQ	*Revue de Qumran*
RGRW	Religions in the Graeco-Roman World
RheinMus	*Rheinisches Museum für Philologie*
RHPR	*Revue d'histoire et de philosophie religieuses*

RivB	*Rivista Biblica / Rivista Biblica Italiana*
SAPERE	Scripta Antiquitatis Posterioris ad Ethicam Religionemque Pertinentia
SBLDS	Society of Biblical Literature Dissertation Series
SBLEJL	Society of Biblical Literature Early Judaism and Its Literature
SBLMS	Society of Biblical Literature Monograph Series
SBLSCS	Society of Biblical Literature Septuagint and Cognate Studies
SBLSymS	Society of Biblical Literature Symposium Series
SBS	Stuttgarter Bibelstudien
SBT	Studies in Biblical Theology
SC	Sources chrétiennes. Paris: Le Cerf, 1943–
ScrHier	*Scripta Hierosolymitana*
SCS	Septuagint Commentary Series
SDSS	Studies in the Dead Sea Scrolls and Related Literature
SECA	Studies on Early Christian Apocrypha
SEG	*Supplementum Epigraphicum Graecum*
SEJ	Studies in European Judaism
Sem	*Semitica*
SHR	Studies in the History of Religions
SJOT	*Scandinavian Journal of the Old Testament*
SNTSMS	Society for New Testament Studies Monograph Series
SOTSMS	Society for Old Testament Studies Monograph Series
SPAW	*Sitzungsberichte der preussischen Akademie der Wissenschaften*
SPhilo	*Studia Philonica Annual*
SR	*Studies in Religion*
STDJ	Studies on the Texts of the Desert of Judah
StPB	Studia Post-Biblica
SUNT	Studien zur Umwelt des Neuen Testaments
SVTP	Studia in Veteris Testamenti Pseudepigrapha
TBN	Themes in Biblical Narrative
TDNT	*Theological Dictionary of the New Testament*. Edited by G. Kittel and G. Friedrich. Translated by G.W. Bromiley. 10 vols. Grand Rapids, 1964–1976
TGUOS	Transactions of the Glasgow University Oriental Society
ThB.AT	Theologische Bücherei. Altes Testament
ThWAT	*Theologisches Wörterbuch zum Alten Testament*. Edited by G.J. Botterweck and H. Ringgren. Stuttgart, 1970–
TQ	*Theologische Quartalschrift*

TRE	*Theologische Realenzyklopädie*. Edited by G. Krause and G. Müller. Berlin, 1977–2004
TS	*Theological Studies*
TSAJ	Texte und Studien zum Antiken Judentum
TS NS	Texts and Studies, New Series
TUGAL	Texte und Untersuchungen zur Geschichte der altchristlichen Literatur
TWNT	*Theologisches Wörterbuch zum Neuen Testament*. Edited by G. Kittel and G. Friedrich. Stuttgart, 1932–1979
UTB	Uni-Taschenbücher
VC	*Vigiliae Christianae*
VCSup	Supplements to Vigiliae Christianae
VD	*Verbum Domini*
VT	*Vetus Testamentum*
VTSup	Vetus Testamentum Supplements
WBC	Word Biblical Commentary
WMANT	Wissenschaftliche Monographien zum Alten und Neuen Testament
WUNT	Wissenschaftliche Untersuchungen zum Neuen Testament
ZAH	*Zeitschrift für Althebraistik*
ZAW	*Zeitschrift für die alttestamentliche Wissenschaft*
ZDPV	*Zeitschrift des deutschen Palästina-Vereins*
ZNW	*Zeitschrift für die neutestamentliche Wissenschaft und die Kunde der älteren Kirche*
ZPE	*Zeitschrift für Papyrologie und Epigraphik*
ZTK	*Zeitschrift für Theologie und Kirche*

L'OSTRACON DE *KHIRBET* QUMRÂN (KHQ1996/1) ET UNE VENTE DE TERRAIN À JÉRICHO, TÉMOIN DE L'OCCUPATION ESSÉNIENNE À QUMRÂN

Émile Puech

Rarement quelques mots assez maladroitement couchés sur un tesson auront autant attiré l'attention. Il s'agit de deux fragments de jarre jointifs, retrouvés sans contexte archéologique par une expédition américaine au cours de l'hiver 1996 étudiant la résistivité des sols de part et d'autre de l'affaissement qui détruisit la citerne 48,[1] soit la ligne de fracture que de Vaux attribua au tremblement de terre de 31 avant J.-C.[2] A ce sujet, les notes sur la trouvaille à l'est du long mur de la terrasse marneuse sont des plus floues. Les éditeurs écrivent que l'ostracon fut trouvé à la base du mur, du côté est, par un volontaire nettoyant la surface du sol avec sa truelle (Cross and Eshel 1997, 17), dans des sondages à la base du mur (Cross and Eshel 2000, 497), ou encore "an ostracon... which was once in the archives of the Qumran

---

[1] Strange (2001, 48 s): "In 1996 the present senior author conducted a soil resistivity survey at Qumran. Measurements of soil resistivity on either side of the subsidence in cistern 48 revealed no anomalous readings. There the crack and subsidence appear to be shallow, which suggests that this feature may not be an earthquake crack at all, even if it is a subsidence. In other words, unless the putative earthquake crack is in fact as long as the Preliminary Reports indicate, it may have been caused by the weight of the water above an underground, natural void." Mais cette remarque qui n'explique pas la réfection des murs de part et d'autre tout au long de la faille, ou ailleurs au nord, à l'ouest, au sud et à l'est du site (voir R. de Vaux, *Archaeology and the Dead Sea Scrolls* [London: Oxford University Press, 1973], 20), paraît un peu courte, et on attend un rapport de cette campagne de fouilles autre que ces quelques lignes, avec un plan des zones explorées, les tranchées et des résultats plus précis, d'autant que le fouilleur en reste à de pures suppositions "...may not be an earthquake crack at all" (p. 49). En effet, Cross and Eshel (1998, 49) donnent une autre explication: "In the spring of 1996, a small expedition... was searching for more scroll caves in the marl terrace," mais où sur cette terrasse?, c'est le flou le plus complet dans toutes les notes au sujet de cette découverte. On sait que d'autres fissures plus ou moins parallèles se sont produites à l'ouest de celle-ci et une autre juste à l'est du mur de la terrasse après la destruction du site. Au sujet de la ruine, on doit corriger une bévue qui circule dans beaucoup de travaux postérieurs, à savoir que de Vaux n'a jamais compris ni qualifié les ruines comme celles d'un "monastère ou couvent" (malgré Strange 2001, 51). Ce sont ses détracteurs qui lui attribuent cette idée contre laquelle il s'est lui-même élevé vigoureusement, voir la réponse de de Vaux à G.R. Driver (*RB* 73 [1966]: 229).

[2] De Vaux, *Archaeology*, 20.

community, and ended up in a dump outside the perimeter wall of
the site, when it was discarded by the soldiers of the Tenth Legion in
68 C.E." (Cross and Eshel 1997, 26; 1998, 51). Or, dans une réponse
à Callaway, Strange rattache ces déblais, à l'est du mur, à de Vaux
fouillant jusqu'au sol vierge au centre de la terrasse (Callaway 1997,
156).[3] Enfin, on aimerait connaître à l'aide d'un relevé topographique
précis, cet emplacement au centre de la terrasse qui aurait dû être le
dépôt des archives de la communauté au dire des éditeurs, tout comme
l'emplacement des supposés déblais nettoyés jusqu'au sol ainsi que
l'emplacement de la tranchée à la base du mur où l'objet fut trouvé
en 1996.[4]

Au dire des éditeurs, cet ostracon revêt une importance toute particulière, même en ignorant s'il s'agit d'un document juridique authentique ou d'une simple ébauche. Son intérêt viendrait de ce qu'il porte

---

[3] Voir Callaway (1997, 156 et n. 9): réponse e.mail évasive de Strange à une question de Callaway lui demandant des précisions sur la localisation de la trouvaille et des
déblais de de Vaux: "had excavated straight down into virgin soil in the center of the
terrace and dumped beside the east wall... to remove every last trace of the intrusive
soil originating from the middle of the terrace." Mais il ne précise nullement ce qu'il
entend par "in the center of the terrace." Cryer (1997, 232 et n. 3) donne encore une
autre information sur la découverte: dans un tas de terre déplacée par un bulldozer.

[4] Avant d'attribuer à de Vaux et à son équipe une quelconque négligence dans le
repérage de cette trouvaille et de bien d'autres (Callaway 1997, 157), alors qu'ils ont
répertorié pas mal de toutes petites inscriptions provenant du site, que ce soit sur plâtre,
tessons ou pierre. Murphy (2002, 383–84 et 525) indique le mur en question "11" mais
sans connaître l'emplacement de ces travaux et de la trouvaille. Depuis la rédaction de
cette note, vient de paraître une communication de J.F. Strange, "The 1996 Excavations
at Qumran and the Context of the New Hebrew Ostracon," *Qumran, The Site of the Dead
Sea Scrolls: Archaeological Interpretations and Debates: Proceedings of a Conference held at Brown
University, November 17–19, 2002* (ed. K. Galor et al.; STDJ 57; Leiden: Brill, 2006),
41–54, mais elle n'apporte aucune réponse claire sur le sujet, (p. 51) "6.9 m north of
the gap" dans "the east side of the wall," d'autant que dans ce long mur il existe trois
brèches d'une part et que, d'autre part, de Vaux n'a pas fouillé à l'est du mur mais
à l'ouest (voir dans ce même volume, la figure 1.1, relevé de Ch. Coüasnon, p. 21),
et "Since we were simply cleaning our deposits from the bottom of de Vaux's trench
along the east face of the wall... Fifth, it is interesting to speculate that the ostraca
were *in situ* in a scatter of sherds of an earlier era. The simplest explanation of how
the ostraca arrived at the context in which they were found is that they were discards
in antiquity. At this juncture, it is impossible to deduce whether this was a coherent
context untouched by de Vaux and others. How far they may have been transported
before being discarded is up for speculation. There is reason to believe that the two
halves of the large ostracon were not broken in antiquity but by visitors to the site
since 1956 who walked along the east face of the east wall in the bottom of de Vaux's
trench. Surely the ostraca and the other sherds lay more or less undisturbed for many
years after de Vaux's excavations. These ostraca and other sherds were not battered
or rubbed from transport" (54). Ces explications parlent d'elles-mêmes.

la cession par un certain Ḥonî d'un bien et d'un esclave de Ḥôlon à Eléazar fils de Naḥamani, lequel serait probablement l'intendant ou le gardien à la tête de la communauté, cession due à l'accomplissement d'un vœu ou au terme du temps de probation avant son admission dans la communauté qumrano-essénienne. L'ostracon serait un précieux témoin de la pratique de la mise en commun des biens d'une part[5] et, d'autre part, ce serait le premier acte de don fait par un juif en Israël, puisque ce genre de document dans l'antiquité ne concerne que les femmes qui ne peuvent être des héritières légales. Mais d'autres objections ont été soulevées à ce sujet: rédaction à la troisième personne non à la première, en hébreu non en araméen, absence apparente de témoins et de signatures, le sort de l'esclave Ḥisday si l'ostracon est bien en rapport avec la communauté essénienne de Qumrân où il n'y avait pas d'esclaves, une datation incertaine (première ou deuxième révolte?), mais surtout le don est dit être fait à Jéricho même et non à Qumrân, les lectures plus que douteuses de la mention de l'accomplissement d'un vœu ainsi que du terme "*yḥd*—Communauté," ligne 8.[6]

Aussi avant une quelconque exploitation de cet ostracon dans un sens ou dans un autre, il importe d'en asseoir au plus près sa lecture par un collationnement des diverses reproductions publiées,[7] puisque l'objet est devenu très difficilement lisible.

L'ostracon de Qumrân KhQ1996/1 *(voir figure 1)*

1   [(?)בשנת שתין/(ם) למ]ולאת עתו[(?)
2   [(?) בירחו נתן חני ב]ן שמעון [(?)
3   [(?)לאלעזר בן נחמן[י עבדו/מירחו
4   [את המקום הלז]ן את מקה]ה
5   [המ(י)ם הסילו<ני>ם] [(ו)את הבית
6   [(?) וא(ת)(ח)תחומי הבית ו]את הכרם [(?)
7   [(?)פה}/<וה>האנים הרמ]ונים (ה)תמרים/הזיתים[(?)
8   [(?)וכול אילן אחן]ר עצי פרי(י) [
9   [ועזבם ונ]תן לו את כול אשר]

---

[5] Hypothèse aussi vite exploitée par Flusser (1997), suite aux affirmations des éditeurs (1997, 1997a, 1997b, 1998, 2000).

[6] Lecture mise sérieusement en doute par Yardeni (1997, 1998), Callaway (1997, 159–61, 164–68), Golb (1997, 171–73), Cryer (1997), Murphy (2002, 384–85), Qimron (2003, 144–45).

[7] Cross and Eshel (1997, 19; 1998, 50; 2000, Pl. XXXIII), Yardeni (1997, 235; 1998, 44, 46–47), Golb (1997, 172), Flusser (1997, 12), en particulier celle de J. Henderson (digital enhancement).

10 לו את (>?<)מע[שה] התנובה/הכרם/השדה(?)]
11 ואתנבה/א) כו]ל (המתנה?X)
12 ובידי(?) חני זהב] וכסף x [
13 ללבבו טוב ב[מכר הלז(?)]
14 {לב/לב}<הלב> עבדו טוב] במתנה(?)]
15 שלם אל(עז)ר לח [ני כ(כר) (?)]
16 ||||[ו/ו] (?) ש(ע) ל x (המכר) הל[ז (?)]
17 [(?)]נכח[בו(?)]זהב וכסף ב[ספר (?)]
18 [(?)]במבקר ה[י]חד (?)

Traduction

1 La deuxième année *à l'acco*[*mplissement de son temps*(?),]
2 à Jéricho, a vendu Ḥonî fi[ls de (*Shiméon?*)]
3 à Eléazar, fils de Naḥamanî,[*son serviteur*/ *de Jéricho*(?)]
4 cette propriété,[*le bassin*]
5 d'eau, les canalisations,[*la maison*]
6 et les limites de la maison et[*le verger*/ *champ*(?),]
7 {*là (sont)*}/ *et* les figuiers, les grena[diers, *les palmiers-dattiers*/ *oliviers*(?)]
8 et tout aut[re] arbre[*fruitier*(?).]
9 Et il s'en est dessaisi et [il *lui*] a ve[ndu *tout ce qui est*]
10 à lui, les 'produit[s' *de (toute) la récolte*(?)]
11 et se monta le tota[l *de la vente) à x*]
12 et en possession de Ḥonî, (il y avait) de l'or[*? et de l'argent?*]
13 Concernant son cœur (il est) satisfait avec[*ce prix*/ *cette vente*(?)]
14 {Concernant(?)}<Est-ce que> le cœur de son serviteur est satisfait [*avec ce prix*/ *cette vente?*]
15 A payé *Eléazar* à Ḥ[onî *des deniers*(?) x(?)]
16 *IIII*(*I*/ *et?*) *š*(*eqels*] x (pour [cet] *achat*(?))[?]
17 [(.?.) *ont été*] *inscrit*[*s*(?)] l'or et l'argent dans[*le livre*(?)]
18 [(?)????] *par l'*intendant *de la*[*Communauté*(?).]

Commentaire

L. 1 : La lecture paraît assurée à l'exception du *mem* final très douteux de
štym qui semble devoir être lu de préférence *štyn* (mais le sens ne change
pas,)[8] et des deux lettres à la cassure, toutefois les restes de *lamed-mem*/ *ḥet*

---

[8] Cette lecture ne peut être totalement exclue à cette époque, voir *štym* et *štyn* tous
deux employés dans l'hébreu du rouleau de cuivre, 3Q15 : deux fois *štym* et trois fois
štyn. Mais une lecture *štwr y*["la destruction de J[" (Cryer 1997, 233) est exclue au
moins pour le *sens*, et déjà par le tracé à gauche de la haste du *reš* et, la ligne allant
en remontant légèrement à gauche, rien ne s'oppose à *lamed*, comparer ligne 10, *pace*
Cryer. En outre, il est hasardeux de supposer une destruction de Jérusalem en 135 à
propos de la deuxième révolte (p. 239).

(ou encore *he/nun/samek*) semblent s'imposer par les traces et le sens. En fin de ligne, on peut exclure la mention du roi Hérode (Agrippa) *lh*[(*w*)*rdws* qui donne une ligne trop courte par rapport aux suivantes en supposant un bord gauche régulier comme à droite, d'autant que le *he* est plus difficile. On devrait exclure probablement encore *ln*[*rwn qsr*, formule connue en Murabbaʿât 18 1, si, comme il semble, on a bien affaire à un document en rapport avec un (futur) membre de la communauté très peu encline à ce genre de référence, d'autant que cette lecture serait en outre bien trop courte pour la ligne. Comme la lecture *lg*[*ʾlt*- est elle aussi exclue, malgré Murphy (2002, 386–87), par le tracé à gauche de la lettre, *lh*[*rwt sywn*] reste une lecture théoriquement possible et préférable pour l'espace à *lh*[*rwt yrwšlm*] en rapport à la deuxième révolte.[9] "L'an deux" serait alors l'an 67, et de Vaux (1973, 37) signale avoir retrouvé au moins 83 monnaies frappées cette même deuxième année de la révolte. Toutefois une lecture *lm*[*wlʾt ʿtw*] "à l'acco[mplissement de son temps (de probation)]" ou une formule parallèle est tout aussi possible, et elle expliquerait bien mieux l'absence de mention de jour et de mois dans la formule introductive.[10] Mais n'attendrait-on pas, dans ce cas, de préférence la formule *bmwlʾt lw* (*h*)*šnh* (*h*)*šnyt* ou *šntym* (voir 1QS VI 21 ou 4Q259 II 3)? En effet, les Esséniens de Qumrân n'attendant pas une libération de Sion de la part des zélotes mais une intervention divine en leur faveur, il est peu probable qu'ils aient daté une telle cession de propriété d'après ce comput, aussi la deuxième possibilité paraît-elle de loin la plus vraisemblable. Quoi qu'il en soit, la formule incomplète sans la mention du jour et du mois, fait grandement douter d'avoir affaire là à un acte juridique officiel, brouillon ou pas.

---

[9] Cross and Eshel (2000, 500–501, et déjà 1997, 20) estiment possible la lecture *gimel*, et ils suggèrent encore une référence à un grand prêtre de Jérusalem ou à un prêtre 'sectaire' de la communauté, ce qui paraît assez risqué, puisque ladite communauté était coupée du sacerdoce hiérosolymitain d'une part et que, d'autre part, le sacerdoce essénien qui n'a rien de 'sectaire,'—bien au contraire, il est l'authentique selon leur formulation *hṣdq*—, peut difficilement servir de référence pour une telle datation. (On doit cesser de qualifier les Esséniens de 'secte/sectaires,' ce qu'ils n'ont jamais été, ou alors ce terme s'applique aussi aux Pharisiens et aux Sadducéens.) Mais, poursuivent-ils, si l'ostracon n'était qu'une ébauche sur un objet bon marché avant son remplacement sur papyrus pour devenir un document légal, il pourrait être de plusieurs décennies plus ancien (1998, 51–52).

[10] S. Goranson a suggéré une datation de la deuxième année du néophyte Ḥonî (Cross and Eshel 1997, 20, n. 8), mais on ignore comment il comprenait la fin de la ligne.

L. 2: Jéricho, qui désigne ici l'oasis, de préférence à la toparchie ainsi que l'estiment les éditeurs (Cross and Eshel 1997; 1998, 52), est certainement le lieu du transfert de la propriété et très probablement même le lieu-dit de la propriété. Mais rien ne prouve que l'ostracon a été écrit à Jéricho même,[11] cela d'autant plus qu'il n'a rien d'un acte juridique et légal officiel, trop de clauses font défaut. En effet, les éditeurs en ont fait un acte de donation "a deed of gift" (Cross and Eshel 1997, 21; 1997a, 39–40; 1998, 49; 2000, 501), mais cela est beaucoup moins assuré qu'ils ne le prétendent, car dans les contrats en araméen, *yhb* seul est souvent employé pour "vendre" et signifier un transfert de propriété à une tierce personne, tout comme *nadānu* en akkadien,[12] et dans ce cas-ci il ne s'agit manifestement pas d'une donation de mari à épouse. On devrait donc voir un aramaïsme dans l'emploi de ce mot dans ce plus ancien texte en hébreu relatant une cession et, en conséquence, une cession de propriété à titre onéreux, ainsi que l'explique quelque peu la suite, malgré Murphy (2002, 385). Dans ce cas, la vente a dû avoir lieu à Jéricho mais cet ostracon peut aussi bien avoir été rédigé à Qumrân. Bien qu'il soit impossible de l'affirmer, la suite semble fortement l'indiquer.

Le nom du vendeur est bien attesté par ailleurs,[13] et on doit aussi rappeler que cet anthroponyme est particulièrement connu dans la famille sacerdotale légitime des Oniades—Simonides à l'origine de l'exil à Qumrân.[14] Manque le patronyme dans la lacune à gauche. La

---

[11] Ainsi que l'écrivent Cryer (1997, 233 n. 7): "the text claims to have been written in Jericho, rather than in Qumran" et Flusser (1997, 14), mais pour Murphy (2002, 387) ce serait une ébauche de contrat à Qumrân avant son exécution à Jéricho! Contrairement à une suggestion des éditeurs (Cross and Eshel 1997, 20; 1998, 52; 2000, 501), on ne doit pas attendre une mention d'un autre toponyme à la fin de la ligne 1, Qumrân—*skkh*.

[12] Voir J. Hoftijzer and K. Jongeling, *Dictionary of the North-West Semitic Inscriptions, I–II* (Leiden: Brill, 1995), *s. v. yhb—ntn*, et Y. Muffs, *Studies in the Aramaic Legal Papyri from Elephantine, SD VIII* (New York: Ktav Publishing House, 1973), *passim*; R. Yaron, "Aramaic Deeds of Conveyance," *Bib* 41 (1960): 248–74 (254–55).

[13] T. Ilan, *Lexicon of Jewish Names in Late Antiquity. Part I: Palestine 330 B.C.E.–200 C.E.* (TSAJ 91; Tübingen: Mohr Siebeck, 2002), 377–79 n° 25.

[14] Voir É. Puech, "Le grand prêtre Simon (III) fils d'Onias III, le Maître de Justice?" *Antikes Judentum und Frühes Christentum: Festschrift für Hartmut Stegemann zum 65. Geburtstag* (ed. B. Kollmann et al.; BZNW 97; Berlin: de Gruyter, 1999), 137–58. Et on sait que les familles sacerdotales possédaient, à Jéricho, des biens, résidences secondaires, etc., voir R. Hachlili, "A Jerusalem Family in Jericho," *BASOR* 230 (1978): 45–56; eadem, "The Goliath Family in Jericho: Funerary Inscriptions from a First Century A.D. Jewish Monumental Tomb," *BASOR* 235 (1979): 31–66; eadem and A. Killebrew, *Jericho: The Jewish Cemetery of the Second Temple Period, IAA Reports 7* (Jerusalem: IAA, 1999). Voir

longueur estimée de la ligne laisserait supposer un nom de quatre à six lettres, et, à titre d'hypothèse, le patronyme *šm'wn* conviendrait ici parfaitement, voir encore une telle filiation *šm'wn br ḥwny* en 4Q348.

L. 3 : Le nouveau propriétaire se nomme Eléazar fils de Naḥamani,[15] et pour le patronyme, voir aussi Ne 7,7.[16] Un mot manque à gauche, très difficilement [*ḥywm*], puisque le quantième et le mois sont déjà absents au début du texte. On pourrait suggérer, à titre d'hypothèse, [*'bdw*], ce que rapporte la ligne 14 en fin du document, ou *myrḥw* précisant le lieu de résidence de la partie contractante comme il arrive parfois dans les contrats de vente,[17] mais ce pourrait paraître ici inutile.

L. 4 : Les éditeurs ont lu *'t ḥsdy mḥwln* "Ḥisday from Ḥolôn[" (Cross and Eshel 1997 ; 1998 ; 2000, suivis par Callaway 1997, 147).[18] Mais cette lecture pose d'énormes difficultés à commencer par celle des *ḥet* et *dalet* et aussi pour la vocalisation *ḥwln* au lieu de *ḥlwn* attendu ; aussi d'autres solutions ont-elles été proposées : *'t hmqwm hlz* (Cryer 1997, 234 "[with] this place)" et *'t hśqym hll[w* "the…[…] sacks/sackcloths[" (Yardeni 1997, 235–36).[19] Dernièrement Qimron (2003, 144–45) accepte la lecture de Cryer et comprend *'t hmqwm hlz[wbw…]* ; pour lui l'acte de donation concerne un champ ou jardin avec des arbres à Jéricho, mais cette interprétation et la restauration sont peu vraisemblables. Il est clair que, dans cette ligne, on a deux tracés de *he* et non deux *ḥet* d'une part et que, d'autre part, la lecture d'un tracé de *qof* cursif bien connu est supérieure à celle d'un *dalet* plus que difficile, comparé à

---

[15] aussi *ḥwnyh* de KhQ1313, A. Lemaire, "Inscriptions du Khirbeh, des grottes et de 'Aïn Feshkha," *Khirbet Qumrân et 'Aïn Feshkha II* (ed. J.-B. Humbert et J. Gunneweg ; NTOA. SA 3 ; Göttingen : Vandenhoeck & Ruprecht, 2003) : 341–88 (354).

[15] Ilan, *Lexicon*, 65–79 n° 163 et 198 n° 3.

[16] Une lecture *nḥ[š]ny* (Cryer 1997, 234) est de loin moins probable par les traces visibles, même restaurée comme *nḥšny[ḥw*.

[17] Voir R. Yaron, "The Schema of the Aramaic Legal Documents," *JSS* 2 (1957) : 33–61 (37). Une restauration (*hmbqr* ou *hpqyd*) ainsi que l'interprètent les éditeurs, ne se recommande pas en rapport avec les lignes 13–14.

[18] Flusser (1997, 14–15) fait de Ḥolôn le lieu de la propriété vendue et de Ḥisday un esclave non juif, hors de la communaté essénienne. Mais il n'y a pas de mention d'un esclave Ḥisday de Ḥolôn, un étranger de Moab, dont le statut découlerait de l'absence de patronyme sur cet ostracon (anthroponyme à supprimer en conséquence de la liste en Ilan, *Lexicon*, 384).

[19] Mais cette lecture est plus que difficile pour le sens dès le début de l'énumération d'une vente ou cession compte tenu de la suite du texte, et n'est donc certainement pas à retenir, ainsi que l'a bien vu Cross par la suite (Cross and Eshel 2000, 505–6), mais les arguments paléographiques donnés sont irrecevables, et la lecture *ḥlwn* qui est plus que douteuse ligne 15, ne confirme rien.

celui de la ligne 12.[20] Comme le scribe ne distingue pas toujours le *mem* médian et final, la lecture de deux *mem* est possible et bien supérieure à celle d'un *samek*. Enfin, il ne semble pas y avoir de lettre *waw* entre *he* et *lamed*, et à la cassure le tracé rectiligne convient bien mieux à *zaïn* qu'à *nun*, ce peut difficilement être un *lamed* infra-linéaire (Yardeni). En conséquence, comme les *yod-waw* ne sont pas distingués, ou du moins pas toujours, et que la longueur de la haste n'est pas distinctive ici (voir lignes 6–7), la meilleure lecture de la ligne est incontestablement '*t hmqwm hlz*[, formule attendue dans un tel document. Le démonstratif *hlz* est déjà connu en hébreu biblique : Jg 6,20 ; 1 S 14,1 ; 17,26 ; 20,19 ; 2 R 4,25 ; 23,17 ; Dn 8,16 ; Za 2,8, voir encore Gn 24,65 ; 37,19 ; Ez 36,35, et on compte une dizaine d'emplois dans les documents de la période de Bar Koseba.[21]

L. 5 : Cette ligne est une des plus difficiles à lire. Sur une suggestion de Naveh, les éditeurs ont proposé *mhywm hzh l<'>wl*[*m* "depuis ce jour et pour toujours" (Cross and Eshel 1997, 18–19, 23 ; 1998, 51–52 ; 2000, 499, 502, suivis par Callaway 1997, 147) estimant que la correction s'impose d'elle-même, tant elle est indispensable dans les actes de donation entre vifs, et ils citent divers exemples à cet effet. Mais cette lecture reste très difficile et on devrait s'assurer d'abord qu'on a bien affaire à un tel acte juridique avant de corriger le texte. Cryer (1997, 234–35) lit *ḥtwm h*[*g*]*ly*[*ḥ*] "seal of the [d]istrict (?)" en notant le difficile *ḥet* au début, le *yod* des éditeurs douteux ou même non écrit, et une lettre barrée ou effacée par le scribe, mais la lecture et le sens retenus sont plus que douteux. Yardeni (1997, 236) propose *m/t/.m/t/.ywm h…ly/w.*[sans aucune traduction. Enfin Qimron (2003, 144–45) lit *tmrym h ..lw .*[, "des palmiers-dattiers…[," le début d'une liste d'arbres. Mais cette lecture est difficile, en particulier pour *reš*. A priori deux *taw* seraient possibles ou *taw-mem*, mais *ḥet* est beaucoup plus difficile, ou alors *he* serait tout aussi possible (voir le *he* identique de la ligne 6) pour lire *hm(y)ym*.[22] En effet, le mot suivant semble devoir être lu

---

[20] Aux exemples de *qof* cités par Yardeni (1997, 236) 4Q398 2, 4Q212 C 24, voir par exemple les ostraca de Masada nᵒˢ 420 1 ; 421 7 ; 449 3 ; 451 3 ; 452 3 ; 500 ; 569 2 (Masada I), ce qui contredit l'affirmation de Cross (Cross and Eshel 2000, 505) que les ostraca ne sont pas écrits avec une extrême cursive. Mais tout dépend du scribe !

[21] Voir Y. Yadin et al., eds., *The Documents from the Bar Kokhba Period in the Caves of Letters. Hebrew, Aramaic and Nabatean-Aramaic Papyri* (Jerusalem : IES, 2002), 395.

[22] Si le premier *yod* est bien écrit, et qu'on n'ait pas affaire, comme il semble, à un défaut de la surface, on y verrait une autre influence araméenne pour le pluriel *myy*'—*myyn*, voir 4Q196 27 1 par exemple.

hsylym corrigé en *hsylw<ny>m*, avec un *samek* triangulaire et fermé. Le mot *sylwn* signifie "rigole, tuyau, conduit(e), canal" et irait bien avec le mot précédent, spécialement pour qualifier le terrain *hmqwm* à Jéricho, une oasis où courent de nombreuses canalisations pour l'irrigation à partir de la source pérenne et abondante ou à partir d'autres sources ('Aïn Dok ou le Ouadi Qelṭ). Dans ce cas, on restaurerait assez bien *ʾ(t) hmqwh]* en fin de ligne 4.[23]

L. 6: Cette ligne ne pose pas de difficulté particulière et a été lue correctement: *wʾ<t> thwmy hbyt w[* par les éditeurs (Cross and Eshel 1997, 18–19, 24; 1998, 51; 2000, 499, 503, suivis par Callaway 1997, 147). Yardeni (1997, 236; 1998, 45) propose *wʾt ḥ/twm/pwtby/wt w/y[* "and the walls(?)/coverings(?) of the house(?) of...[" sans autre explication. Cryer (1997, 235) lit *wʾt tmw hbyt w[* "and [with] its entirety, the house and[."[24] Qimron (2003, 144–45) lit *wʾt hkwtbwt w.[*, expliquant *kwtbwt* comme une des espèces de palmiers-dattiers. Cette lecture ne satisfait pas outre mesure pour le sens et reste paléographiquement bien difficile. On préfère certainement retenir la lecture des éditeurs *wʾ(t) thwmy hbyt w[* "et les limites de la maison et[." Dans ce cas, la restauration de la fin de la ligne 5 s'impose d'elle-même pour le sens et pour la longueur alignée sur les précédentes: *[(w)ʾt hbyt]* "[(et?) la maison,] et les limites de la maison et[."

L. 7: Les éditeurs (Cross and Eshel 1997, 18, 24; 1998, 51–53; 2000, 499, 503, suivis par Callaway 1997, 147) ont lu: *whtʾnym hzy[tym]* "and the fig trees, the ol[ives trees]." Et Yardeni (1997, 136; 1998, 45) lit: *wh/ʾtʾnym hd/y.[* "and the fig-(tree)s, the p(alms (?),...(?)]." De son côté, Cryer (1997, 235) propose: *wʾt ʾnws hw[ ]...* "and [with] a man, he...," lecture assez surprenante au demeurant, mais *waw-yod* sont très souvent indistincts et le *mem* 'final' paraît assuré dans la séquence, sans faire appel à un *samek* douteux pour le sens; quant au dernier *waw* on ne peut l'accepter. Qimron (2003, 144) lit: *whtʾnym hd.[* avec *dalet* douteux. La lecture fait quelque difficulté au début où on peut lire *pʾ* ou mieux *ph* suivi de *tnʾnym*, dans ce dernier cas le *he* de l'article est compris dans *p(h)htʾnym*; mais le début pourrait aussi avoir été corrigé

---

[23] La suite montre que *taw* et *he* peuvent être confondus et ne pas être toujours écrits dans la séquence *ʾt h-*, à plus forte raison *ʾt t-* d'une part et que, d'autre part, le singulier *mqwh* paraît bien préférable à *ʾt hmqw]-t m(y)ym*, avec coupure des mots d'une ligne à l'autre, sans autre exemple.

[24] Le deuxième *taw* reste difficile alors que *ḥet* est bien mieux assuré d'une part et que, d'autre part, une lecture *wʾthm*, *nota accusativi* avec suffixe pluriel, est étrange dans cette séquence suivie de *wbyt w[*.

en *wht'nym*, *waw* réécrit sur *pe* avec le calame retrempé dans l'encrier, à moins que le scribe ait voulu simplement retracer la tête du *pe*. Les deux lectures sont également possibles par le tracé et le sens, mais la correction paraît bien préférable. Le mot suivant, juxtaposé, est difficilement *hzy*[*tym*, le *yod* fait difficulté, et *reš* paraît bien meilleur que *dalet*. Dans ce cas le mot serait à lire *hrm*[*wnym*, avec des traces de *mem*, non de *taw*, à la cassure. On restaurerait alors à la fin de la ligne 6 *w*[*'t hkrm* ou *hśdh*] pour comprendre ainsi: "et[le verger/champ,] *là* (*sont*) les figuiers, les grena[diers,…]" corrigé en "et[le verger/champ,] *et* les figuiers, les grena[diers,…]"

L. 8: La lecture de cette ligne est la plus controversée depuis la publication. Cross and Eshel (1997, 18, 24–25; 1998, 51–53; 2000, 499, 503, 505–507, suivis par Callaway 1997, 147) ont lu avec assurance *wkmlwtw* (pour *kml'wtw*) *lyhd*[, "when he fulfills (his oath) to the Community [."[25] Mais Yardeni (1997, 234–37 et 1998, 45–47) conteste, avec raison, cette lecture et en propose une autre plus logique dans la séquence et surtout qui répond parfaitement au tracé des lettres sans avoir à les forcer ou à les fausser: *wkwl 'yln ḥ*[*r* "and every oth[er(?)] tree[…].". A ce sujet, la reproduction en Golb (1997, 172) ne laisse aucun doute comme d'ailleurs toutes les autres en y regardant de près et en faisant abstraction des nombreux petits points noirs dans cette région de la surface. Toutefois, cette lecture a été, à son tour, contestée par les éditeurs (Cross and Eshel 2000, 499, 503 et 505–507), mais ils sont à la peine en tentant de démontrer que leur premier déchiffrement est bien préférable: le *ḥet* de *yhd* serait unique sur cet ostracon qui, bien que différent des autres et ici le seul en écriture cursive, serait assuré; le jambage gauche du *yod* aurait été coupé et ne différerait pas beaucoup de ceux des lignes 1 et 2; le *dalet* ne peut être lu *reš*. Mais le dessin de Cross (2000, Pl XXXIII) interdit la lecture *dalet* comparé à celui de la ligne 12 et ne permet que la lecture *ḥet* contrairement à ce qui est écrit (p. 506), la tête de lettre par lui dessinée est celle de *ḥet* (lignes

---

[25] Toutefois, Cross and Eshel (1997, 25) s'empressent d'ajouter: "if the reading *lyhd* is correct—and it seems to be without serious objection (the *dalet* at the edge of the ostracon is certain)—we must suppose that the reference is to Ḥonî's fulfilling of his vow and entering the Community at Qumran, or…," (1998, 53): "Indeed, the *d* (*dalet*) is certain, and this excludes every other reasonable suggestion for interpreting this word," (2000, 506): "The final letter of the line is *dalet*." En fait, *lyhd* est une suggestion de Ḥ. Eshel. Flusser (1997, 14) comprend ainsi cette ligne: "And when he has completed [his first year as a novice] of the community." On doute fortement de ces certitudes conditionnelles à répétition.

2–3), non de *dalet* qui est de forme carrée ! Concernant le tracé du *ʾalef* lu *ḥet* par les éditeurs, on ne peut suivre Cross (2000, 506), puisqu'il est clair que la diagonale est certainement tracée en descendant (= un plein) et indépendamment ainsi que les deux autres traits comme pour le *ʾalef*, non en remontant et en suivant comme pour un *ḥet* (= un délié) ainsi qu'il est expliqué ; enfin la cassure n'a rien enlevé du tracé de la lettre qui est complète. Quant au *yod*, la forme triangulaire en accent circonflexe est un leurre, la lettre est tracée à l'aide d'un trait d'abord vertical puis à gauche à quelque 100°, comme dans plusieurs *nun* de ce scribe (malgré Cross, 2000, 507). Au sujet du mot précédent, les *mem* et *taw* des éditeurs sont impossibles : entre la tête du *waw* et le pied du *lamed*, un point noir, comme il y en a d'autres au-dessus de cette ligne, n'appartient pas au tracé des lettres, et de jambage gauche pour *mem* il n'y a aucune trace. Ce que les éditeurs ont lu *waw-taw* n'est autre que *ʾalef* au tracé habituel, le même qu'à la ligne 3, sans tête crochue au sommet du jambage droit qui touche la diagonale. Quant au grand espace entre les *yod-lamed*, il est moins grand que celui entre *ʾalef-ḥet* ou *kaf-waw* dans cette même ligne. Enfin, le mot *ʾyln* est un judéo-aramaïsme comme il y en a d'autres dans ce texte, voir ci-dessus,[26] mais le mot se coule parfaitement dans la séquence de ces lignes et peut revendiquer plusieurs parallèles (voir ci-dessous). La lecture de Cryer (1997, 235–36) *wkml*[ʾ]*w ln ʾḥz* "and when/if he completes taking possession for himself" est matériellement plus proche, mais avec des coupures différentes, de celle de Yardeni à l'exception de l'impossible *mem* et du *zaïn* inexistant, arrivant ainsi à un sens douteux et à des formes grammaticales nouvelles. On ne peut la retenir, pas plus que celle de Murphy (2002, 529 et 384–85) qui suit toujours les éditeurs à l'exception ici du *ḥet*, mais sans rien proposer. Qimron (2003, 144–45) suit purement et simplement la lecture de Yardeni.

Cette lecture, certainement la seule possible, rejoint d'autres exemples de listes d'arbres (fruitiers) dans des contrats du Désert de Juda : *ʾtrʾ dk bthwmh wbmṣrh tʾnyʾ wkl dy bh wdy ḥyʾ ʿlh* "ce terrain dans ses limites et ses bornes, les figuiers, tout ce qu'il y a et tout ce qui vit dessus,"[27]

---

[26] Voir J.T. Milik, "Parchemin judéo-araméen de Doura Europos an 200 ap. J.-C.," *Syria* 45 (1968) : 97–104 (101 ligne 8), avec aussi la mention des "palmiers" *tmrʾ*, ligne 4.

[27] Voir J.T. Milik, "Deux documents inédits du Désert de Juda," *Bib* 38 (1957) : 255–64 ; Yaron, "Aramaic Deeds," 255–56, et en particulier la vente de maison du papyrus Brooklyn 12 où l'expression *yhb wntn* revient sans cesse.

Murabba'ât 30 18 (hébreu) que je propose de lire ainsi: *hmkr hzh bthwmw byt wkrm ht'nym hzytym h's* "cette vente dans s(es) limite(s) (comprend) maison et verger, les figuiers, les oliviers, les arbres…," serait très proche de la formulation de cet ostracon.[28] Naḥal Ḥeber 44 11–13 (hébreu): *hmqwm… whmqwm… wtkl 'yln šbhm… 15–16 wtkl 'yln…* "le terrain… et le terrain… et tous les arbres qui y sont,… et tous les arbres…"[29] Naḥal Ḥeber 46 3–4 (hébreu): *tmqwm… tmqwm… tdqlym wtš'r h'yln šbhm* "le terrain… et le terrain… et les palmiers-dattiers et les arbres qui y sont."[30] Naḥal Ḥeber 2 5–6 (nabatéen): *rqq' gnt' hy klh bkl thwmyh wkl dy 'yty l… wtmryn wšqmyn w'yln klh w'syh rtybh wybyšh…* "le marécage, la plantation elle-même tout entière dans toutes ses limites et tout ce qui appartient à.., les palmiers-dattiers et les sycomores et tous les arbres et le bois vert et sec,…"[31] Naḥal Ḥeber 7 48 (araméen): *wkwt kl tmryn w'yln mbdryn dy ly bmhwz' 'l šqy'* "et de même tous les palmiers-dattiers et les arbres qui sont à moi éparpillés à Maḥoza le long des canalisations."[32]

Ces parallèles autoriseraient-ils de restaurer *(h)tmrym]* "les palmiers-dattiers]" en fin de ligne 7? Ce mot semble plus vraisemblable que *hzytym]* "les oliviers," à Jéricho,[33] toutefois ce dernier ne peut être exclu en parallèle au figuier.

L. 9: Les éditeurs (Cross and Eshel 1997, 18, 25; 1998, 51; 2000, 499–500) ont proposé de lire *ḥwny* "and Ḥonî [," suivis par Cryer (1997, 236), mais Yardeni (1997, 236; 1998, 45) lit *wng..[.* Toutefois, les restes visibles semblent devoir être lus *w'zbm wn[*, le premier mot paraît plus assuré à l'exception du *mem* ou *nun-waw* (?), et ensuite on peut hésiter entre *waw/zaïn* et *nun/kaf/*?. Le verbe *'zb* au sens de "céder, confier, laisser, se dessaisir" avec le suffixe pluriel pourrait être parallèle à *ntn* (ligne 2) et peut-être encore ici à *wn[tn* à moins de préférer *wk[wl…*, lecture qui paraît moins en situation. La formule *'zb wntn* pourrait

---

[28] J.T. Milik, *DJD* 2: 146–47, propose de comprendre "bâtisse et [sol]" en s'inspirant d'autres contrats, mais les traces correspondent assez bien à *wkrm* que je propose de restaurer ici, ligne 6 de l'ostracon de Qumrân, préférable à *wsdh*.

[29] Yadin et al., *The Documents from the Bar Kokhba Period*, 44–45.

[30] *Ibid.*, 66.

[31] *Ibid.*, 208.

[32] *Ibid.*, 86.

[33] Pline l'Ancien lui-même témoigne des palmeraies de Jéricho et de En Gaddi, *Histoire Naturelle* V 17, 73, même si les éditeurs ont cru devoir lire *hzy[tym*, ligne 7. Mais une lecture *hd[qlym* "les dattiers" suggérée par Yardeni (1997, 233, 236; 1998, 45) n'est pas possible pour le *qof* et est déjà très difficile pour le *dalet*. Ainsi, il n'y a pas de doublet pour différentes espèces de palmiers-dattiers, malgré Qimron (2003, 144–45).

correspondre à, ou du moins rappeler *zbn wyhb wrhq/wšbq* des formules juridiques araméennes de vente de propriété.[34] Quant à la fin de la ligne précédente, elle pouvait porter une expression du type *ṣ(y) pry* ou *nwtn pryw*, "arbre(s) fruitier(s)," ou autre, voir 4Q88 (Ps^f IX 10–12: *wlw' tkhš [tbw] 'wtyh 'ṣy pry bt[n]wbwtm*,[35] (voir aussi la vente de la récolte aux lignes suivantes).

L. 10: Les éditeurs (Cross and Eshel 1997, 18, 25; 1998, 51; 2000, 499–500) ont lu *lw 't hs[dy* "to him His[day(?)]" comme rappel de leur lecture de la ligne 4 *'t hsdy mhwln[*. Yardeni (1997, 236; 1998, 45) propose *ly/w 't h.[* "to me/him the...[," et Cryer (1997, 236) lit *lw't ^hX...* "to him with...," supposant le *he* au-dessus de la ligne comme appartenant peut-être à une précédente inscription. Toutefois, après *lw 't* qui est certain, la première lettre doit être *mem* au tracé comparable à la plupart des autres *mem*, et on peut hésiter à lire auparavant une correction supralinéaire: *dalet* ou plus difficilement *het* ou *he*. A la cassure la lecture est difficile: comme *qof* est exclu pour *'t (h?)mq[wm*, on peut hésiter entre *samek*[36] et *'aïn* avec *apex*, donc entre *'t (h?)m['šr* "la dî[me (de-) (avec ou sans article et donc déterminé ou construit), *'t <d>m'[* "les produits (ou l'imposition de -/ la *terumah*?)]" en rapport avec la récolte des fruits et du terrain vendu, et de préférence *'t m'[šh/y* "les produits de—," voir Hb 3,17 *m'šh zyt*, Ex 23,16 *bkwry m'šyk...'t m'šyk mn hśdh*. Cette lecture paraît recevable paléographiquement et contextuellement après l'énumération précédente. Dans ce cas, si une lecture *wn[tn lw* est acceptable, ligne 9, on pourrait compléter par *'t kwl 'šr] lw*, "et il [lui] a ve[ndu tout ce qui (est)] à lui, les 'produits'[*de (toute?) la récolte*," le *nomen rectum* pourrait alors être *htnwbh* ou un synonyme; lire donc soit *'t m'[šh (kwl) htnwbh]* soit *t m'[šh/y hkrm/śdh]*, mais le sens général est le même.

L. 11: Cross and Eshel (1997, 18, 25; 1998, 51; 2000, 499–500) ont lu *w't°°°[* "and the [" avec, comme possible à la cassure, *mem/kaf* ou *ṣade* (2000, 500) influencés alors par Yardeni (1997, 18; 1998, 45) qui a lu *w't....ṣ[* "and...[," et Cryer lit *w't XXX n...* "and [with]..." La lecture des restes est certainement difficile, mais on proposerait de lire

---

[34] Voir Muffs, *Studies, passim*, formule qui implique une compensation ou paiement.
[35] La lecture *bt[n]wbwtm* est certaine au lieu de *b°° gpnyhm* "b.. their wines," malgré les éditeurs, *DJD* 16: 103–104.
[36] Ce *samek* n'aurait pas un tracé régulier pour l'horizontale et une lecture avec *het* ne donne rien dans cette séquence.

w'tgbh/ ' kw[*l* "et se monta le to[tal (de)..]." En effet, à la cassure, seul le *kaf* répond au tracé de la lettre sans possibilité de lecture *ṣade* (un dégraissant de la pâte en surface donne la fausse impression d'une petite division de l'épaisseur du trait = un plein) avec encore des restes de la haste de *waw*. Auparavant, paraît possible *'alef* (voir ligne 4), ou mieux *he* (voir ligne 7). Entre *taw* et *'alef/he*, on lit au mieux *gimel* au trait à gauche touchant le tracé en boucle d'un *bet* du type de celui de la ligne 12 par exemple. La forme *hitpaʿel 'tgb'* de *gb'* serait un autre aramaïsme parallèle au *nifʿal* habituel de l'hébreu, "être collecté, soumis à taxes," mais le *hitpaʿel* de *gbh* est connu en hébreu "se monter/s'élever à (en parlant d'une somme)" et paraît plus satisfaisant. Le mot *kw*[*l* pouvait être suivi de *hmtnh* ou *hmkr* (voir *hmkr hzh* de Murabbaʿât 30 17) ou d'un autre substantif, mais ce ne serait pas indispensable, et enfin sans doute du prix de la vente.

L. 12 : Les éditeurs (Cross and Eshel 1997, 18, 25 ; 1998, 51) ont lu *wbyd* °°°*h*["And by the agency of[" et (2000, 499–500) "And into the hand of[," alors que Yardeni (1997, 236 ; 1998, 45) propose *wbyd'g. lh*["and in the hand(?) of... [" (avec *ʿaïn-gimel* et *lamed* en petits caractères). Cryer (1997, 236) a lu *wbyd* X *w* X *yh*... "and by the hand of..." Une lecture semble encore ici possible, tout en hésitant entre une possible rature du deuxième *yod* ou un défaut de la surface : *wbyd*(*y*?) *ḥny zhb*["et en possession de Ḥonî de l'or[." Les séquences *ḥet-nun-yod* (comparer ligne 2 et pour *nun-yod*, voir ligne 3) et *zaïn-he-bet* (boucle du *bet* à la cassure) sont assez assurées pour être retenues tandis qu'une lecture *yhb*[paraît bien plus difficile. L'expression *byd* est normalement utilisée au singulier pour signifier "dans la main de, en possession de," le scribe a-t-il fait une faute avec ou sans correction ? On ne peut répondre vu l'état de la surface d'après les seules données photographiques. Mais la lecture est attendue et le sens du texte se comprend alors assez bien dans la séquence des lignes ; *zhb*[pouvait (/devait ?) être suivi de (*w*)*ksp* et de chiffres.

L. 13 : Les éditeurs (Cross and Eshel 1997, 18, 25 ; 1998, 51 ; 2000, 499–500) ont hésité entre *lg.nn* ["to guard (?) "et *lḥ?nn*, toutefois le dessin de Cross (2000, Pl XXXIII) ne correspond pas à cette lecture. Yardeni (1997, 236 ; 1998, 45) lit *l.*[*?*]*n.*[, et Cryer (1997, 237) a lu *ll nn* "night?..." La lecture de ces restes est très difficile, aussi la proposition suivante est-elle une possibilité, d'assez grande probabilité tout de même, de rendre compte des traces encore perceptibles : *llbbw ṭwb b*[, littéralement "Concernant son cœur, il est satisfait par/avec[." Dans ce cas, les deux premiers *bet* sont un rien plus cursifs que les précédents au point de se rapprocher du tracé de *nun* médial mais très cambré, suivis de légères traces du *waw*, puis on devine assez bien le contour de *ṭet* et, à la cassure, le tracé de deux autres *bet*, et entre les *ṭet-bet* un *waw* peut être lu mais les traits sont très empâtés en cet endroit. Il semble que la formule hébraïque veuille correspondre à, ou reprendre *ṭyb lbb b-* des formules juridiques des contrats de vente en araméen.[37] Dans ce cas, *llbbw ṭwb b*[à compléter par *b*[*mkr/mhyr/dmy*(*m*) *hlz*(?)], signifie "Quant à lui, il est satisfait avec[cette vente/ce prix]."

L. 14 : Les éditeurs (Cross and Eshel 1997, 18, 25 ; 1998, 51 ; 2000, 499) ont lu *ḥsdy 'bd ḥ*[*ny ...mn*] "Ḥisday servant of Ḥ[onî (?)... from]" d'après les lignes 4 et 10, Yardeni (1997, 236 ; 1998, 45) a lu *ḥ.. 'b..*["the[...]," et Cryer (1997, 237) lit *ḥly 'bd* "illness... a servant (PN?)..." qui ne fait pas grand sens ici. Les traces ne permettent pas une lecture totalement assurée, cependant il semble que le *he* en début de ligne soit une correction sur *lamed* et, dans ce cas, une lecture *llb* ou *lbb* (voir ligne 13) *'bdw ṭwb*[*b-* serait corrigée en *hlb 'bdw ṭwb*[*b-* "Concernant le cœur de son serviteur (il est) *ou* Le cœur de son serviteur (est) satisfait[*avec ce prix*]" corrigé en "Est-ce que le cœur de son serviteur (est) satisfait [*avec ce prix* ?]." En faveur d'une telle lecture, les restes des deux *lamed* ou de *bet* corrigé en *lamed* sont encore bien visibles suivis de *bet* probable. Après *'aïn-bet* assurés, il y a de bons restes de *dalet* et de *waw*, et à nouveau de *ṭet*, *waw* et *bet* à la cassure. Une telle lecture paraît aussi attendue pour l'autre partie contractante, celle qui fait l'acquisition de la propriété cédée certainement à titre onéreux, sinon la clause n'aurait pas lieu d'être de part et d'autre. Dans ce cas, le sens de *ntn*, ligne 2, (et peut-être encore ligne 9) est bien définitivement celui de "vendre" qu'il a parfois dans les contrats, comme il a été rappelé ci-dessus. On n'a pas affaire à une donation pure et simple entre deux hommes, ainsi que l'ont compris les éditeurs et d'autres après eux, mais bien à une vente de terrain avec maison dont l'ostracon ne fait que rappeler l'acte, sans être lui-même, en quoi que ce soit, l'acte juridique et légal.[38]

L. 15 : Les éditeurs (Cross and Eshel 1997, 18, 25 ; 1998, 51 ; 2000, 499) ont lu *ḥlwn* ["Ḥolôn" pour retrouver leur lecture de la ligne 4,

---

[37] Voir Muffs, *Studies*, 30–50 pour les formules de satisfaction dans les contrats de vente en particulier.

[38] La mention de la satisfaction des partenaires ainsi que la qualification *'bdw* interdisent de voir en Eléazar l'intendant ou financier de la Communauté auquel Ḥonî aurait fait don de ses biens au terme de ses deux ans de probation, ainsi que l'écrivent les éditeurs et ceux qui les suivent.

mais ici dans une orthographe différente.[39] Yardeni (1997, 237; 1998, 45) a lu *ḥl*.["the...[," et Cryer (1997, 237) lit *ḥlwn* "a window." Il est clair que ces lectures ne font pas de sens ici et qu'il faut voir les tracés de plus près. Le premier mot semble devoir être lu *šlm* avec un *šin* assez cursif en trois traits séparés et un grand *mem* final, puis plus loin on peut distinguer des traces qui conviennent à *'alef* un peu étalé, un *lamed* assuré, des traces de lettres qui conviendraient à *'aïn* et *zaïn*, de bons restes de *reš* et enfin, à la cassure, ceux de *lamed* probable, suivi sans doute du bas de la haste de *ḥet*. On obtient ainsi: *šlm 'l'zr lḥ*[*ny* X] "a payé Eléazar à Ḥ[onî X]." Le verbe *šlm* au *pi'el* signifie "payer, rembourser (une dette)" et conviendrait parfaitement au contexte. Puis les anthroponymes sont difficiles à lire mais ils sont déjà connus des contractants aux lignes 2–3. On pourrait ensuite envisager la mention en abrégé de la monnaie, par exemple *k* pour *ksp* et/ou *k* pour *kkr*(*ym*) et peut-être un chiffre, 10/20/?.

L. 16: Seule Yardeni lit des traces de lettres de cette ligne: .*l*[. Les quelques restes pourraient se lire *waw*(?), *he/'alef*, ou trois(?) traits obliques parallèles et un ou deux autre(s) en sens opposé pour 4 (ou 5) ou un *waw*, puis *šin* probable (abréviation pour *šql*?) et d'autres traces très difficilement déchiffrables, chiffres et peut-être *'l hmkr ḥl*[*z* ou??. Il ne s'agit là que d'une proposition suggérant une séquence possible d'une lecture qui échappera toujours. Avec la fin de la ligne 15, cette ligne devait porter le prix de la vente-cession des biens ou la somme payée en espèces, somme qui a dû être vraisemblablement ensuite versée à l'intendant de la Communauté (voir ci-dessous).

L. 17: La partie droite est abîmée (dès avant l'utilisation comme ostracon?), mais à la hauteur du *mem* (ligne 15) on peut apercevoir des restes possibles de deux traits obliques et des traces ensuite qui pourraient se lire]*nkt*[*bw*] préférable à].*nt*[*n*, puisque paraît tout à fait possible ensuite la lecture *zhb wksp b*[, *he-bet* et *samek-pe* final en ligature et *bet* étant les plus probables. On aurait là la mention de l'or et de l'argent inscrits dans le livre des comptes lors de la mise en commun des biens, une fois le néophyte Ḥonî admis dans la Communauté.

L. 18: Dans la dernière moitié de la ligne, il y a des restes de *bet* ou *lamed*, puis *mbqr* qui semble de lecture assez assurée, suivi probablement de *he* sans doute pour *h*[*yḥd*, donc soit]*bmbqr* ou]*lmbqr h*[*yḥd* "]*par/à*

---

[39] Le dessin de 1997, 19 et 1998, 50 est dû à Eshel et celui de 2000, Pl XXXIII, à Cross mais ils diffèrent dans les tracés des lettres pour une lecture identique!

*l'*intendant *de la* [*Communauté.*" Même si la lecture de cette fin est difficile et désespérée, la mention de l'intendant ne peut surprendre, elle est même attendue.

L'ostracon de Qumrân KhQ1996/2 (*voir figure 2*)

Un autre tout petit fragment inscrit fut découvert avec le précédent. Il porte des restes de quatre lignes dont la dernière à un intervalle très réduit. La présentation de ce document, bien que probablement écrit par une main différente, peut aider à une datation paléographique.

Le texte :

1   בנ צדו[ק א]ל(עזר) בנ
2   בנ ש[ת חונ]י(ה) בנ
3   יהוס[פ בנ נתנ]
4   ב]ני מעי[נ

Traduction :

1   *fils de Sado*]q(?), É[*l*(*éazar*)(?) *fils de*...
2   *fils de Se*]t(?), Ḥôn[*î*(*ah*) *fils de*...
3   Jose]ph(?) *fils de* Natan[(*aël*)(?)...
4   ] *ses* [*fi*]ls, *de* 'Aï[n-...

Commentaire

L. 1 : Les éditeurs (Cross and Eshel 1997, 27 et 2000, 5008) ont lu]*q ś*[, mais le *šin* est impossible dans ce tracé, et on doit lire *'alef.* On a sans doute affaire ici à une séquence de noms propres, patronymes y compris, voir lignes 3 et 4, dont les plus fréquents à cette époque sont d'une part Sadôq et, d'autre part, É[l(éazar),[40] y compris à Qumrân, 3Q15 X 17 ; XI 3, 6,[41] et 4Q348 1, 11, 15, KhQ734 et KhQ1650,[42] l'ostracon KhQ1996/1 (ci-dessus), et un autre ostracon de Qumrân.[43]

[40] Ilan, *Lexicon*, 208s et 65–79 respectivement.

[41] Voir É. Puech, *Le Rouleau de Cuivre de la grotte 3 de Qumrân (3Q15), édition révisée* (STDJ 55 ; Leiden : Brill, 2006), *in loco.*

[42] Voir Lemaire, "Inscriptions du Khirbeh."

[43] Y. Magen and Y. Peleg, "Back to Qumran : Ten Years of Excavation and Research, 1993–2004," *Qumran, The Site of the Dead Sea Scrolls: Archaeological Interpretations and Debates*, 55–103 (72s), mais à lire ainsi en hébreu : *'ʿzr/bn yšwʿ/hbyrwty* "Eléazar fils de Jésus le beyrotin," non *br* et *hbwryt, nun* final non *reš* sans tête (voir ostracon KhQ161) et le gentilice en *scriptio plena* (voir 1 Ch 11,39).

L. 2: Les éditeurs ont lu]*t ḥw*[, mais un *he* paraît ici exclu, on a
plus vraisemblablement le ductus de *ḥet*, bien connu à cette époque,
voir en particulier KhQ161, 621, 1313, 2108 pour ce genre de tracé
ou l'inscription des Benē Ḥézîr. Et à la cassure il y a des restes du
coude du *nun*; lire donc *ḥwn*[*y* ou *ḥwn*[*yh*, tous deux bien attestés à
cette époque, voir 4Q348 15, KhQ1313, l'inscription des Benē Ḥézîr
ligne 1 et 2,[44] et le vendeur de KhQ1996/1. Le premier mot pourrait
lui aussi être lu comme le patronyme *š*]*t*, voir KhQ2109]*št*,[45] de préférence à *by*]*t* / *b*]*t* / *'š*]*t*, etc.

L. 3: Les éditeurs ont lu *yhws*]*p bn ntn*[avec un *nun* final à la cassure,
mais il y a des traces d'un coude de *nun* médial qui peut certes faire
fonction de *nun* final, voir *bn*, mais cela n'est pas certain, et on pourrait
aussi envisager *ntn*[*'l*.[46]

L. 4: Lire *m'y*[*n* non *m'yn*[des éditeurs. La restauration 'Aï[n Gaddi
est une possibilité, mais non la seule.

Il semble qu'on ait affaire à une liste de noms accompagnés des
patronymes, autre qu'un simple exercice de scribe. Cette liste pourrait
comprendre un certain nombre de prêtres, car ces noms sont bien
attestés parmi eux, mais non exclusivement, cela va de soi. Et on sait
la présence importante des prêtres dans la Communauté essénienne
de Qumrân.

Datation et Paléographie (voir figure 3)

Comme l'archéologie n'est ici d'aucun secours (voir ci-dessus), les
éditeurs (Cross and Eshel 1997, *passim*; 1998, 51–52; 2000, 497–98,
500–501) ont classé l'ostracon KhQ1996/1 dans l'écriture 'vulgaire
semi-formelle' de la période hérodienne tardive (20–68) vers le milieu
du premier siècle de notre ère, mais ils hésitent à déterminer l'année
"deux," de la première révolte ou de quelque règne, Agrippa (I ou II),
Néron ou de quelque grand prêtre. Leur analyse paléographique est
assez générale d'une part et, d'autre part, elle dépend grandement de
leur déchiffrement. Aussi de vives réactions se sont-elles manifestées.

Callaway (1997, 147–155, 163–64) qui accepte les lectures de l'édition,
lui reproche le manque de précision dans les analyses paléographiques

---

[44] Ilan, *Lexicon*, 377–79.
[45] Voir Ilan, *Lexicon*, 236–37.
[46] Voir Ilan, *Lexicon*, 198–200.

et leur partialité, sans parler de l'assurance dans des lectures capitales comme *yḥd*, et les spéculations sur le contenu et la reconstruction de tout un contexte en relation avec la Communauté qumranienne, vœu du néophyte, Eléazar le nom de l'intendant de la Communauté, l'esclave Ḥisday d'origine étrangère, etc. En conséquence, cet auteur daterait l'ostracon aussi bien de la deuxième année de la seconde révolte, en 133, puisque la graphie ne peut être qualifiée de "qumranienne" au sens habituel du terme (bien que son tableau [pp. 150–51] dépende entièrement des lectures des éditeurs) d'une part et que, d'autre part, des transactions comparables entre des personnages de même nom ont été retrouvées à Murabba'ât. En cela il rejoint Cryer (1997, 237–39) bien qu'il soit prêt à suivre maintenant, dans un post-scriptum, Yardeni mais avec une tout autre datation, c'est dire que ses critères paléographiques sont sujets à bien des interprétations.

Pour sa part, Yardeni (1997, 233) qualifie cette écriture de semi-cursive hérodienne ancienne et serait favorable à une datation vers la fin de la Période Ib de de Vaux (en 31 avant J.-C.). Elle refuse la lecture *yḥd* et un certain nombre d'autres sur lesquelles elle se fonde pour une datation paléographique différente comme le *nun* médial encore utilisé en position finale et l'orthographe de *kwl* au lieu de *kl* plus tardive. Puisque la transcription et la traduction des éditeurs ne peuvent être reçues telles quelles, elle en conclut que l'identité de ceux qui ont écrit les manuscrits de Qumrân et leur lieu de résidence ne peuvent être déterminés à partir de cet ostracon (p. 236).

De son côté, Cryer (1997, 237–39) refuse la datation des analyses paléographiques des éditeurs, car les *bet, nun, taw, qof* et la ligature, ligne 2, en particulier montreraient une indépendance totale des données paléographiques des manuscrits et des autres *ostraca* du site. Les caractéristiques relevées indiqueraient une datation vers 120 ou même plus tard, mais certainement après 68. Il en trouve la confirmation d'une part dans la langue hébraïque utilisée sur des documents comparables datant des environs de 135 et retrouvés au Naḥal Ḥeber alors qu'auparavant on emploie l'araméen et, d'autre part, dans les traces d'une occupation juive du site de Qumrân lors de la deuxième révolte, ainsi que de Vaux l'a montré. Mais indépendamment des données paléographiques qu'on peut analyser différemment, on voit mal tout de même comment on peut lire "En l'an deux de la destruction de J[érusalem]" en 135 (p. 239, voir ci-dessus) et affirmer que l'ostracon a été écrit à Jéricho (p. 233, n. 7), alors que rien ne l'indique.

Le déchiffrement présenté ci-dessus qui essaie de tenir le plus grand compte des restes de toutes les lettres et de leur tracé, donne, sans aucun doute, une lecture plus cohérente du contenu de l'ostracon. La datation de l'objet pourrait être partiellement donnée mais elle reste le seul point discutable de cet ostracon: "En l'an deux de *la li*[*bération de Sion*]" ou "La deuxième année *à l'acco*[*mplissement de son temps*]." Dans le premier cas, serait indiquée la date assez précise de la vente d'un terrain à Jéricho, en 67 de notre ère, sans indication du jour et du mois, mais certainement en automne après les récoltes du verger, ce qui, toutefois, avec l'absence de témoins en fin de texte ainsi que d'autres clauses et la forme impersonnelle, ne peut en faire un document juridique à valeur légale. Si le terrain vendu est vraisemblablement localisé dans le périmètre de l'oasis de Jéricho (voir le bassin et les canalisations), l'ostracon retrouvé à Qumrân n'est pas nécessairement écrit là-bas, il pourrait l'être un peu plus tard à Qumrân, contrairement à l'opinion de Cryer (1997, 233) et de Murphy (2002, 387), car il ne peut aucunement s'agir ici d'un brouillon avant l'acte officiel. Quoi qu'il en soit, on ne pourrait imaginer un laps de temps très grand entre la vente et ce témoignage ou rappel/mémorandum de la vente, puisque le site a été détruit l'année suivante. Dans ce cas, seule resterait possible la première révolte et on sait que Qumrân est tombé en 68 (juin?) sous l'occupation romaine (de Vaux 1973, 37–44). La paléographie de ce texte écrit certes par une main peu experte ne s'opposerait pas fondamentalement à cette indication "interne," même si elle ne la favorise pas; ce serait alors un des très rares cas où une telle précision serait donnée par la documentation épigraphique des sites de Qumrân-Feshkha.[47]

Mais dans la deuxième hypothèse de lecture de cette première ligne qui paraît de loin préférable (voir ci-dessous), l'ostracon pourrait dater quelque part dans la période II de de Vaux ou même de la Période Ib (la fin pour Yardeni). Bien des parallèles de cette écriture "vulgaire semi-cursive" se retrouvent de part et d'autre, y compris dans la période hérodienne ancienne ou même hasmonéenne, et cela vaut pour les deux ostraca trouvés ensemble en 1996. On peut comparer cette écriture à celle de l'abécédaire-exercice de scribe trouvé dans les fouilles du site,[48] à celle du bol inscrit *l'zr* gravé avant cuisson par une main un

---

[47] On donnera dans une autre occasion les lectures qui conviennent à ces textes dont la publication récente laisse beaucoup à désirer.

[48] Voir R. de Vaux, "Fouilles au Khirbet Qumrân," *RB* 61 (1954): 206–36 (229) et Pl Xa. Cet ostracon trouvé dans un trou avant l'ouverture de la tranchée A pourrait

peu plus experte,[49] ou de l'inscription tout à fait semblable sur l'épaule de la jarre KhQ2553,[50] et de l'ostracon KhQ1996/2 (Cross and Eshel 1997, 27 ; 2000, 508). L'écriture y est moins cursive que dans le contrat araméen de Murabba'ât 18, daté de 55/56 de notre ère et elle a aussi des parallèles en Murabba'ât 72 (fin du 2ᵉ siècle avant J.-C.), dans les inscriptions sur les ossuaires datés pour la plupart sur un siècle avant la chute de Jérusalem, (de 30 avant J.-C. à 70), et dans quelques inscriptions de Masada antérieures à 73 A.D.[51]

Quoi qu'il en soit des deux hypothèses de lecture de la première ligne, le *terminus ante quem* reste certainement les récoltes de la fin de l'été 67, mais sa datation paléographique peut s'étaler sur un siècle auparavant, avec une forte préférence dans la période hérodienne ancienne et même hasmonéenne tardive.

Genre et Contexte Historique

Les éditeurs (Cross and Eshel 1997, 26–28 ; 1997a, 39–40 ; 1998, 49 ; 2000, 503–505) ont hésité entre un document légal (real legal document) et une simple ébauche sur un ostracon, peut-être pour cause de pénurie de papyrus au temps de la révolte ; ils y ont lu un acte de donation

---

provenir des déblais des soldats romains lors de la réoccupation (Période III) en 68, il serait donc antérieur, mais de combien (Période II)?, ou encore d'autres déblais de la Période Ib "dans la tranchée A et probablement attribuable à la période I."

[49] Sa datation est discutée, fin de la Période Ib (voir de Vaux, *Archaeology*, 11–12 n. 1, bol appartenant au niveau inférieur) ou Période II (J.T. Milik, *Ten Years of Discovery in the Wilderness of Judaea* [London : SCM, 1959], 55 : "in a script typical of the first century of our era," mais voir F.M. Cross, "The Development of the Jewish Scripts," *The Bible and the Ancient Near East. Essays in Honor of W.F. Albright* (ed. G.E. Wright ; Garden City, N.Y. : Doubleday, 1961), 133–202 (190 n. 9), qui, avec raison, suivrait maintenant de Vaux. Les arguments archéologiques invoqués faisant fi des données ne tiennent pas, malgré J.-B. Humbert, "Some Remarks on the Archaeology of Qumran," *Qumran, The Site of the Dead Sea Scrolls: Archaeological Interpretations and Debates*, 19–39 (31 et 39), et Lemaire, "Inscriptions du Khirbeh," 356, qui l'attribuent "à la période II" contre les notes explicites du fouilleur du terrain.

[50] Voir les Notes de R. de Vaux, *Fouilles de Khirbet Qumrân et de Aïn Feshkha. I—Album de photographies, répertoire du fonds photographique, synthèse des notes de chantier de R. de Vaux* (présentées par J.-B. Humbert et A. Chambon ; NTOA.SA 1 ; Göttingen : Vandenhoeck & Ruprecht, 1994), 331 locus 124 : "Il semble que cette poterie ait été jetée là, lors du nettoyage du bâtiment après le tremblement de terre. C'était alors à l'extérieur." Dans ce cas, la jarre serait à dater de la fin de la Période Ib, reproduction dans Lemaire, "Inscriptions du Khirbeh," 367.

[51] Voir Y. Yadin and J. Naveh, *The Aramaic and Hebrew Ostraca and Jar Inscriptions*, Y. Meshorer, *The Coins of Masada (Masada I. The Yigael Yadin Excavations 1963–1965. Final Reports* ; Jerusalem : IES, 1989), 1–70 et Pl 1–59.

(*ntn*) d'un esclave, d'une propriété et de produits à la communauté de Qumrân (*yaḥad*) suite à l'accomplissement d'un vœu ou du temps de probation d'un néophyte, faisant d'Eléazar le responsable principal du *yaḥad* ou l'intendant (*mbqr*) ou le chef de la congrégation (*pqyd br'š hrbym*) en charge des biens de la communauté (1QS VI 18–29).[52] Ḥonî est le donateur qui entre dans une communauté et donne tous ses biens, esclave y compris, enregistrés sur un ostracon faisant partie des archives de Qumrân. Sans doute, la mention d'un esclave fait difficulté dans un milieu essénien au dire de Philon, *Quod omnis probus liber sit* § 79, et de Josèphe, *Antiquités XVIII* § 21, même si CD XI 12 connaît, dans d'autres groupes, l'existence d'esclaves qui, une fois circoncis, ne peuvent plus être vendus à des païens (XII 9–11). En conséquence, dans le cas présent, l'esclave aurait été libéré ou serait devenu le gardien de la propriété (1997, 26) ou encore aurait été accepté comme membre de la communauté à part entière, voir le parallèle de Ac 4,34 (2000, 506). L'usage de l'hébreu, au lieu de l'araméen ou du grec habituels dans ces documents à cette époque, serait dû à la pratique qumranienne qui usait de l'hébreu dans ses propres compositions. Toutefois ce serait le premier acte juif de donation trouvé en Israël dans lequel le récipiendaire est un homme. Enfin, la lecture du mot *yaḥad* établit un lien direct entre *Khirbet Qumrân* et les manuscrits trouvés dans les grottes avoisinantes.

Yardeni (1997, titre et 233; 1998, 44, 46) en ferait une ébauche d'acte, ou peut-être un acte de donation de Ḥonî à Eléazar, mais elle refuse d'utiliser cet ostracon comme lien entre les copistes des manuscrits et ceux qui vécurent à Qumrân (p. 47).

Murphy (2002, 385–389) en fait une ébauche de contrat ou même un acte de donation à un homme à la fin des deux ans, don en nature de produits, pas nécessairement sous forme de monnaie, exécuté à Jéricho. Et elle reproche (2002, 385), à tort à notre avis, à Cryer d'en

---

[52] Les éditeurs (2000, 505) nuancent leur première conclusion: l'ostracon "semble être soit un brouillon ou une copie d'un document légal" du fait qu'il manque les signatures des témoins (mais le bas est illisible), que la datation est bien incomplète, ligne 1, et que l'écriture sur un ostracon ne saurait être un acte original. Cette conclusion est acceptée par C. Hempel, "Community Structures in the Dead Sea Scrolls: Admission, Organization, Disciplinary Procedures," *The Dead Sea Scrolls after Fifty Years. A Comprehensive Assessment* (ed. P.W. Flint and J.C. VanderKam; 2 vols.; Leiden: Brill, 1999), 2: 67–92 (74–75), même si elle a des doutes sur certains points, en particulier le statut d'Eléazar et celui de l'esclave.

faire un acte de vente et à Callaway d'en faire un enregistrement d'une transaction antérieure, et non un acte de donation.

Il est clair maintenant que, même en l'absence d'un bon tiers à gauche qu'on peut assez bien restaurer pour le sens général,[53] l'ostracon ne peut être un acte légal de donation (a deed of gift) à un homme, ni davantage son ébauche (a draft), mais une note ou rappel/mémorandum (pour archivage?) d'un transfert de propriété qui a eu lieu à Jéricho. Ḥonî a vendu à Eléazar, son serviteur (pas nécessairement son esclave), une propriété à Jéricho comprenant maison et alentours, bassin et annexes, un verger avec des arbres fruitiers ainsi que la récolte pour une somme d'argent, vente sur laquelle ils se sont entendus et qu'Eléazar a réglée. En effet, la formule *mhywm hzh wl'wlm* étant indispensable dans un acte de donation avec une formule de renonciation de quelque droit à la propiété dans le futur, les éditeurs, convaincus d'avoir affaire à un tel acte légal, se sont crus obligés de lire à tout prix cette formule, ligne 5. Et poursuivant dans cette voie, ils étaient contraints de lire *wkmlwtw lyḥd* (ligne 8) pour l'accomplissement d'un vœu ou du temps de probation d'un néophyte d'après 1QS VI 18–23. Il y a aussi une contradiction entre une action faite (*ntn*) et le terme de l'accomplissement d'un vœu, sans parler des lectures forcées de *mhywm hzh l'wlm*. Il manquerait encore une datation précise de l'acte en jour, mois et année selon la coutume, les signatures des témoins, les limites définies de la propriété, et la formule juridique sous la dictée du vendeur (*'l py* NP) car il ne peut être le scribe, puisque le discours est à la troisième personne et au passé. Toutes ces difficultés tombent dans la nouvelle lecture de l'ostracon, ainsi que l'existence et le destin d'un esclave d'origine étrangère entrant dans la communauté.

Le genre de l'ostracon en hébreu étant mieux défini comme note ou rappel d'une vente de terrain à Jéricho, quoi qu'il en soit de la lecture difficile des dernières lignes, sa présence à Qumrân n'est plus une difficulté insurmontable pendant la période d'occupation essénienne (Périodes Ib ou II). Bien au contraire, il est le premier témoignage écrit, trouvé sur place, de la pratique essénienne de la vente des biens par le nouveau membre admis dans la communauté et, par le fait même, de la remise du prix de la vente à l'intendant des biens qui l'inscrit

---

[53] Un essai de restauration dans cette main donne 8 à 8,5 cm pour la longueur des lignes d'écriture et 9 à 9,5 cm pour la largeur de l'ostracon en supposant un bord gauche assez régulier comme celui de droite.

sur les registres à son nom. La *Règle* nous apprend qu'au terme de la première année de probation, les biens sont inscrits d'abord au nom du néophyte—*yqrbw gm 't hwnw w't ml'ktw 'l yd h'yš hmbqr 'l ml'kt hrbym wktbw bḥšbwn bydw w'l hrbym l' yw'ṣy'nw* (1QS VI 19), et qu'au terme de la deuxième année a lieu la mise en commun de sa fortune—*wbmwl't lw hšnh hšnyt ypqwdhw… yktwbw bsrk tkwnw btwk 'ḥyw ltwrh wlmšpṭ wlṭwhrh wl'rb hwnw…* (VI 21–22). Cette manière de comprendre l'ostracon ne dépend pas d'abord de l'une ou l'autre manière de lire la première ligne, mais la lecture *lm*[*wl't 'tw* (?) ou un synonyme] paraît, sans nul doute, plus satisfaisante par les traces des lettres et le sens, même si la formulation "la deuxième année" ne semble pas une reprise littérale de 1QS VI. Mais on comprend que la vente des biens par le nouveau membre n'ait lieu que la deuxième année, lors de son admission définitive dans la Communauté, car en cas de refus il retrouve sa propriété qu'il avait confiée à son serviteur et dont il n'avait pas eu à se séparer ; ce cas est quelque peu différent de celui du néophyte arrivant avec une somme d'argent en numéraire qu'il dépose et qui est inscrite en son nom dès la fin de la première année.

Cette interprétation expliquerait mieux la vente à "son serviteur," lui qui a eu l'entière charge de la propriété de son maître pendant tout son temps de probation de néophyte, au moins depuis la première année. En outre, on comprendrait aussi assez bien que, pour leur comput dans le cas d'une vente, les Esséniens n'aient jamais pensé prendre en compte les années de la libération de Sion par des Zélotes. En effet, depuis l'exil forcé du Maître de Justice, ils attendaient eux-mêmes une autre libération. Une telle attente de leur part ne devrait-elle pas aider à départager le choix entre deux possibilités de lecture de la première ligne, d'autant que, dans l'autre hypothèse, la formulation ne permet pas d'en faire un document légal et qu'elle paraît impossible pour une note interne de la communauté essénienne ? Dans ce texte rédigé à la troisième personne, le vendeur peut difficilement être l'auteur ou le copiste du texte, la finale ne permet pas de décision à ce sujet. En outre, la copie ne peut guère être l'œuvre d'un scribe entraîné comme devait l'être l'intendant de la Communauté.

Quoi qu'il en soit de ce point, le nom de l'intendant des biens de la Communauté de Sokokah-Qumrân reste inconnu, Eléazar est le nouveau propriétaire des biens de Ḥonî, devenu membre de la Communauté, et il est présenté comme le serviteur du vendeur et devait, sans aucun doute, être le premier intéressé à acheter les biens de son ancien maître ; il doit donc demeurer dans sa nouvelle propriété à

Jéricho. On connaît les liens étroits entre Jéricho et Qumrân-Sokokah, ne serait-ce que par la liste des cachettes du rouleau de cuivre trouvé dans la grotte 3 (3Q15).[54] Il ne serait pas surprenant que cet Eléazar ainsi que d'autres Jérichontins aient été des sympathisants esséniens ou un de ces Esséniens des villes et villages, comme on en connaît l'existence par les notices anciennes.[55] Enfin, la mention très vraisemblable de "l'intendant" *mbqr* en fin de texte confirmerait le genre de cet objet et renforcerait encore davantage son origine essénienne.[56]

En conclusion, la découverte de cet ostracon sur le site même et la lecture présentée ici revêtent une importance particulière en confirmant définitivement et de manière inespérée l'interprétation du site par le fouilleur, R. de Vaux. Qumrân-Sokokah doit être identifié avec le site essénien non loin du rivage du lac asphaltite dont parlent la notice de Pline l'Ancien et celle de Dion d'après son biographe Synésius. L'ostracon assure le lien manquant entre les habitants du site et des grottes environnantes, ce que déjà la situation géographique de la ruine et son rapport direct avec les grottes de la terrasse notamment indiquaient largement et clairement malgré les réticences de certains. Sokokah n'était pas un manoir, une *villa rustica* ou une villa romaine, un fortin, une forteresse,[57] un port commercial, un poste de douane, une hôtellerie-centre de pèlerinage, un hospice, un mouroir, un centre industriel de fabrication de poterie[58] ou de quelque produit de luxe (baume), une teinturie, ou autre encore, ainsi que tentent de le proposer, ces dernières décennies, les réviseurs en mal de nouveautés, mais bien

---

[54] Voir É. Puech, *Le Rouleau de Cuivre de la grotte 3 de Qumrân.* Est-ce un hasard si un nombre important de cachettes de cette liste se trouve à Jéricho et ses environs et jusque sur la voie de Sokokah-Qumrân? Ce serait aussi une des sources des trésors de la Communauté dont le Rouleau donne toute une liste.

[55] Philon d'Alexandrie, *Prob.* 76, *Apologie des Juifs*, 4–6 (= Eusèbe, *Praep. Ev.* 8, 11, 4–6).

[56] Il est possible que le bol inscrit *'l'zr* KhQ1650 trouvé dans le locus 89 ait été fabriqué à Jéricho et viendrait comme une autre confirmation, voir J. Gunneweg and M. Balla, "Possible Connection Between the Inscriptions on Pottery, the Ostraca and Scrolls Found in the Caves," *Khirbet Qumrân et 'Aïn Feshkha II*, 389–94 (392), dans la mesure où ces résultats sont quelque peu fiables mais les argiles des poteries qumraniennes n'ont-elles jamais varié?

[57] Cette qualification du site par des résistants de la deuxième révolte est loin d'être assurée en Murabba'ât 45 6, voir É. Puech, "La « Forteresse des Pieux » et Kh. Qumrân. A propos du papyrus Murabba'ât 45," *RevQ* 16/63 (1994): 463–71.

[58] Malgré Magen and Peleg, "Back to Qumran."

le principal centre essénien que de Vaux a justement identifié.[59] Il est donc tout aussi futile de rechercher le centre essénien décrit par Pline l'Ancien dans les hauteurs au-dessus de ʿEn Gaddi pour expliquer le *infra hos* de sa notice.[60]

Enfin, ce modeste ostracon est un autre document essénien attestant la pratique de la vente de propriétés et de la mise en commun des biens dans une communauté juive aux alentours de l'ère chrétienne, pratique que Luc, de son côté, décrit dans les *Actes* 2–5 aux débuts de la communauté ecclésiale de Jérusalem. Une telle pratique y est vraisemblablement due à l'arrivée d'esséniens convertis venant grossir la nouvelle communauté des croyants, l'*ekklèsia* de Jérusalem.

BIBLIOGRAPHIE DE L'OSTRACON

Callaway, P.R. 1997. "A Second Look at Ostracon No. 1 from Khirbet Qumrân." *The Qumran Chronicle* 7: 145–70.

Cross, F.M. and E. Eshel. 1997. "Ostraca from Khirbet Qumrân." *IEJ* 47: 17–28.

——. 1997a. "The "Yahad" (Community) Ostracon." *A Day at Qumran. The Dead Sea Sect and Its Scrolls.* Ed. par A. Roitman. Jerusalem: The Israel Museum, 38–40.

——. 1997b. "A New Ostracon from Qumrân." *Qadmoniot* 30/2: 134–36 [ʿivrît].

——. 1998. "The Missing Link. Does a new inscription establish a connection between Qumran and the Dead Sea Scrolls?" *BAR* 24/2: 48–53, 69.

——. 2000. "1. Khirbet Qumran Ostracon." *Qumran Cave 4, XXVI. Cryptic Texts and Miscellanea*, Part 1. *DJD* 36. Oxford: Clarendon Press, 497–507 et Pl XXXIII.

Cryer, F.H. 1997. "The Qumran Conveyance: a Reply to F.M. Cross and E. Eshel." *SJOT* 11: 232–40.

Flusser, D. 1997. "Ostracon from Qumran Throws Light on First Church." *Jerusalem Perspective* 53: 12–15.

Golb, N. 1997. "Qadmoniot and the "Yahad" Claim." *The Qumran Chronicle* 7: 171–73.

Murphy, C.M. 2002. *Wealth in the Dead Sea Scrolls and in the Qumran Community.* STDJ 40. Leiden: Brill, 383–89, 529 et Pl. II.

Qimron, E. 2003. "Improving the Editions of the Dead Sea Scrolls." *Meghillot* 1: 135–45 (144–45) [ʿivrît].

---

[59] Cette identification assure en retour la justesse des descriptions de Philon et de Flavius Josèphe concernant les Esséniens et leurs indications sur leurs habits blancs considérés comme sacrés à l'instar des prêtres au temple, malgré les remarques d'E. Tigchelaar, "The White Dress of the Essenes and the Pythagoreans," *Jerusalem, Alexandria, Rome. Studies in Ancient Cultural Interaction in Honour of A. Hilhorst* (ed. F. García Martínez and G.P. Luttikhuizen; JSJSup 82; Leiden: Brill, 2003), 301–21 (321): "the community that lived at Qumran cannot directly be identified with the Essenes described by Philo and Josephus, and there is no direct evidence that Qumranites dressed in white."

[60] Voir Y. Hirschfeld, "A Settlement of Hermits Above ʿEn Gedi," *Tel Aviv* 27 (2000): 103–55, idem, "The Archaeology of Hermits: a Reply," *Tel Aviv* 27 (2000): 286–91, et ceux qui le suivent.

Strange, J.F. 2001. "The Archaeology of Everyday Life at Qumran." *Judaism in Late Antiquity*. Éd. par A.J. Avery-Peck, et al. Part Five. *The Judaism of Qumran: a Systemic Reading of the Dead Sea Scrolls*. Volume One. *Theory of Israel*. HdO 56. Leiden: Brill, 45–73.

Yardeni, A. 1997. "A Draft of a Deed on an Ostracon from Khirbet Qumrân." *IEJ* 47: 233–37.

———. 1998. "Breaking the Missing Link. Cross and Eshel Misread the Qumran Ostracon Relating the Settlement to the Dead Sea Scrolls." *BAR* 24/3: 44–47.

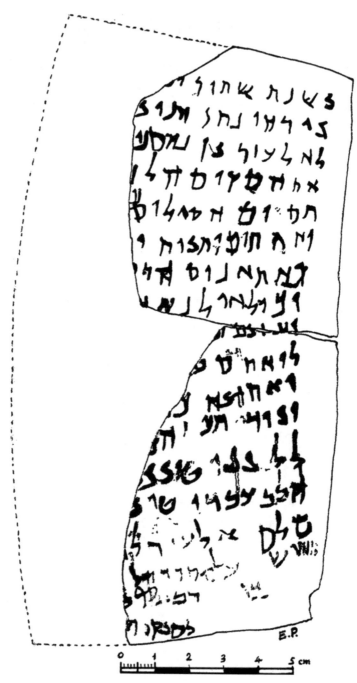

Figure 1. L'ostracon KhQ 1996/1

Figure 2. L'ostracon KhQ 1996/2

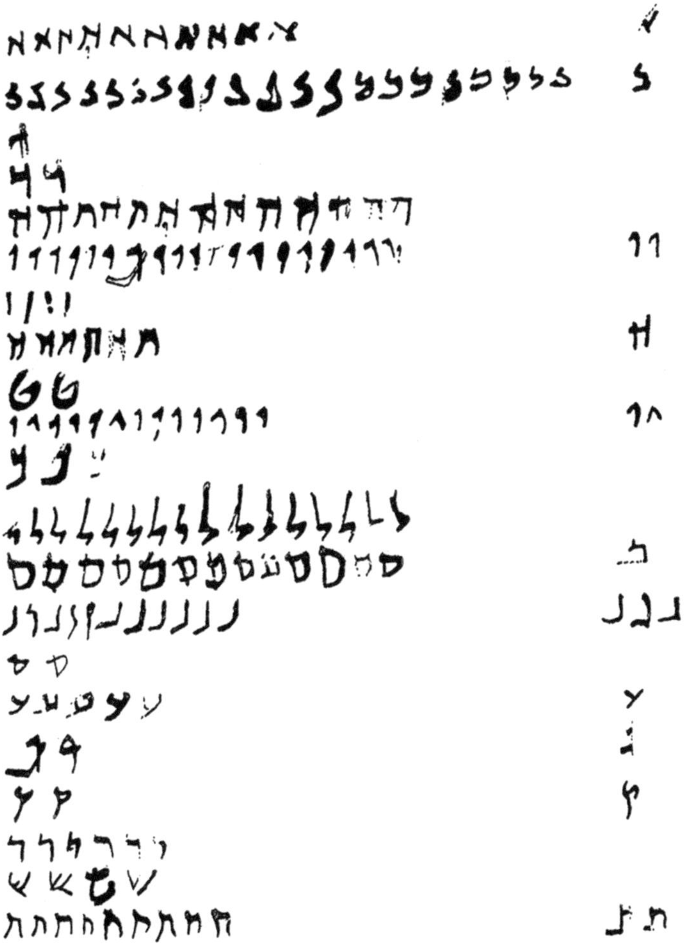

Figure 3. Tableau comparatif de l'écriture des ostraca KhQ 1996/1–2

THE NATURE AND AIMS OF THE SECT KNOWN FROM THE DEAD SEA SCROLLS

John J. Collins

The Dead Sea Scrolls have shed important light on many aspects of ancient Judaism. Perhaps the most central issue, however, concerns the information they provide about a sectarian movement, which is generally assumed to have occupied the site of Qumran and to have been responsible for hiding the scrolls. The initial press release by the American School of Oriental Research, published in the *Times* of London on April 12, 1948, identified one of the scrolls as "a manual of discipline of some comparatively little-known sect or monastic order, possibly the Essenes."[1] The nature and history of this group remains controversial, nearly sixty years later, and the publication of the fragments from Qumran Cave 4, mainly over the last fifteen years, has complicated rather than clarified the issues. The Scrolls are notoriously reticent about historical information, which is given only obliquely and in code.[2] But even more ostensibly straightforward matters, such as the organization of the sect and its *raison d'être*, on which a consensus existed at one time, have again become controversial in recent years.

The main source of confusion in this regard is that the Scrolls include not just one "Manual of Discipline" or Community Rule, but also another rulebook, the so-called Damascus Document, or CD, and it now appears that both Rules existed in different recensions. The Damascus Document had been found in the Cairo Geniza at the end of the 19th century and published in 1910,[3] but its relationship to the scrolls from Qumran was immediately evident.[4] Perhaps the most obvious point of

---

[1] See J.C. VanderKam, *The Dead Sea Scrolls Today* (Grand Rapids: Eerdmans, 1994), 6. The release was written by Millar Burrows.

[2] See my assessment of the state of the debate on this issue in "The Time of the Teacher: An Old Debate Renewed," in *Studies in the Hebrew Bible, Qumran, and the Septuagint: Essays Presented to Eugene Ulrich* (ed. P.W. Flint et al.; VTSup 101; Leiden: Brill, 2006), 212–29.

[3] S. Schechter, *Documents of Jewish Sectaries. 1. Fragments of a Zadokite Work* (Cambridge: Cambridge University Press, 1910; repr., New York: Ktav, 1970).

[4] See especially H.H. Rowley, *The Zadokite Fragments and the Dead Sea Scrolls* (Oxford: Blackwell, 1952).

connection lay in the references in the Pesharim to the "Teacher of
Righteousness" and "spouter of lies," designations previously known
only from the Damascus Document. Several other analogies in religious
and organizational terminology were noted. For example, the expressions מורה היחיד and אנשי היחיד in CD XX 1, 32 (MS B) are usually
and plausibly emended to מורה היחד and אנשי היחד, thereby referring
to the יחד, the term used for the sectarian community, the Community
Rule, or *Serek ha-Yaḥad*. The discovery of eight copies of the Damascus
Rule in Qumran Cave 4, as well as small fragments in Caves 5 and 6,
established beyond doubt that it was part of the corpus of the Dead Sea
Scrolls.[5] The Cave 4 fragments of the Damascus Rule include a section
of a penal code that is clearly based on the same text as the one in
1QS VII, whether the two shared a common source or one depended
on the other.[6] The relationship between the rule books was further
complicated by the discovery of the so-called 4QSerek Damascus, or
4QMiscellaneous Rules (4Q265), whose contents are closely related
to the legal part of the Damascus Document, the central part of the
Community Rule (1QS VI–VIII and parallels), and *Jub.* 3.[7]

   But while there is certainly some relationship between the Damascus
Rule and the Serek texts, scholars have been increasingly impressed by
the differences between them.[8] Most famously, CD allows for women
and children in the "new covenant," while they are not acknowledged
at all in the Community Rule. עדה, rather than יחד, is the preferred
term for the community. CD lacks the multi-stage admission procedures
that are spelled out in the Serek. There are significant differences in

---

   [5] For the Cave 4 texts see J.M. Baumgarten, *DJD* 18.
   [6] 4Q266 10 ii; 4Q270 7 i. On this passage see C. Hempel, "The Penal Code Reconsidered," in *Legal Texts and Legal Issues: Proceedings of the Second Meeting of the International
Organization for Qumran Studies, Cambridge, 1995, Published in Honour of Joseph M. Baumgarten*
(ed. M.J. Bernstein et al.; STDJ 23; Leiden: Brill, 1997), 337–48. See also S. Metso,
"Constitutional Rules at Qumran," in *The Dead Sea Scrolls after Fifty Years: A Comprehensive
Assessment* (ed. P.W. Flint and J.C. VanderKam; Leiden: Brill, 1998), 202.
   [7] J.M. Baumgarten, "265: 4QMiscellaneous Rules," *DJD* 35:57–78. C. Hempel,
The Damascus Texts (Sheffield: Sheffield Academic Texts, 2000), 89–104. Hempel
argues that 4Q265 pre-dates the extant forms of the Community Rule and Damascus
Document. J.M. Baumgarten ("Scripture and Law in 4Q265," in *Biblical Perspectives:
Early Use and Interpretation of the Bible in Light of the Dead Sea Scrolls* [ed. M.E. Stone and
E.G. Chazon; STDJ 28; Leiden: Brill, 1998], 17–26) regards it rather as dependent
on the rulebooks.
   [8] C. Hempel, "Community Structures in the Dead Sea Scrolls: Admission, Organiza-
tion, Disciplinary Procedures," in *The Dead Sea Scrolls after Fifty Years*, 67–92; E. Regev,
"The Yahad and the Damascus Covenant: Structure, Organization and Relationship,"
RevQ 21/82 (2003): 233–62.

the attitude towards the temple in the two rules.[9] Other differences in terminology have been noted. The משכיל is only mentioned twice in CD, in passages that deal with the regulations for the camps (CD XII 21; XIII 22).[10] In contrast, the מבקר, who has a central role in CD, appears rarely in 1QS (VI 12, 20).[11]

These differences have been accounted for in different ways. The most widely accepted theory holds that the Damascus Rule was a rule for "the marrying Essenes," while the Serek was the rule for a celibate community that lived at Qumran.[12] Thus stated, this explanation is certainly too simple. The Serek clearly provides for several small communities, with a quorum of ten, and cannot be regarded as the rule for a single community at Qumran.[13] The Damascus Rule, too, envisions more than one form of community, since it contrasts "the men of perfect holiness" with "those who live in camps according to the order of the land and marry and have children," although it seems to be primarily concerned with the latter.[14] The issue, then, is more complicated than a simple contrast between celibate and marrying Essenes would suggest, although it remains true that the Damascus Rule is primarily concerned with married people, while the Serek does not acknowledge them at all.

Even if both rules were in use contemporaneously, as the paleography of the manuscripts would suggest, it is plausible that one originated before the other. At various times, scholars have proposed a diachronic explanation of the relationship between the two rule books. Milik argued for the priority of the Community Rule and thought that

---

[9] H. Evans Kapfer, "The Relationship between the Damascus Document and the Community Rule: Attitudes toward the Temple as a Test Case," *DSD* 14 (2007): 152–77.

[10] A further reference is restored in 4Q266 5 i 17 (*DJD* 18:48).

[11] See S. Metso, "Qumran Community Structure and Terminology as Theological Statement," *RevQ* 20/79 (2002): 438–40. Regev ("The Yahad and the Damascus Covenant") draws further contrasts between the two rules with respect to the structure of authority.

[12] See especially G. Vermes, *The Complete Dead Sea Scrolls in English* (Allen Lane: Penguin, 1997), 26–48.

[13] See my essays, "Forms of Community in the Dead Sea Scrolls," in *Emanuel: Studies in Hebrew Bible, Septuagint, and Dead Sea Scrolls, in honor of Emanuel Tov* (ed. S.M. Paul et al.; VTSup 94; Leiden: Brill, 2003), 97–111 and "The Yahad and 'The Qumran Community,'" in *Biblical Traditions in Transmission: Essays in Honour of Michael A. Knibb* (ed. C. Hempel and J.M. Lieu; JSJSup 111; Leiden: Brill, 2005), 81–96.

[14] CD VII 5–8. See J.M. Baumgarten, "The Qumran-Essene Restraints on Marriage," in *Archaeology and History in the Dead Sea Scrolls* (ed. L.H. Schiffman; Sheffield: JSOT, 1990), 13–24.

the Damascus Rule reflected Pharisaic influences.[15] This position has
been taken most recently by Eyal Regev, who further argues that the
Damascus Rule belongs to "an entirely different movement" from the
יחד.[16] The priority of the Damascus Rule has enjoyed greater support
in recent years. Philip Davies has argued that the יחד represented by
the Community Rule was an offshoot that broke away from the parent community, which is reflected in CD, although that document is
further complicated by an alleged "Qumran recension."[17] The idea
that "the Qumran community" was the result of a split in the broader
Essene movement has been taken up in the Groningen hypothesis of
García Martínez and Van der Woude[18] and in the theory of Gabriele
Boccaccini, which equates the early Essenes with "Enochic Judaism."[19]
This theory of a split within the Essenes seems to me to have little or
no foundation in the texts. The Damascus Document claims that some
people refused to accept the Teacher and turned back with the Man
of the Lie, but I am aware of no reason to say that these people were
Essenes.[20] The Damascus Document, as we have it, is clearly a product
of people who revered the Teacher, and the Teacher is associated with
the יחד in the Pesharim. The account of the community that we get in
the Damascus Rule (and equally in the other documents) is, of course,
ideological and may be distorted,[21] but it posits continuity between
the so-called "parent community" and the followers of the Teacher

---

[15] J.T. Milik, *Ten Years of Discovery in the Wilderness of Judea* (London: SCM, 1963),
83–93. F.M. Cross (*The Ancient Library of Qumran* [Sheffield: Sheffield Academic Press,
1995], 71, n. 2) also seems to assume the priority of the Serek, since he argues that
in the development of Essenism the term "camp" replaced יחד for all but the desert
settlement. Cross assumed that יחד refers to the settlement at Qumran.

[16] Regev, "The Yahad and the Damascus Covenant," 233–62 (262).

[17] P.R. Davies, *The Damascus Covenant: An Interpretation of the 'Damascus Document'*
(Sheffield: JSOT, 1983). He finds the "Qumranic recension" especially in CD XIX
33b–XX 34 (173–97).

[18] F. García Martínez and A.S. van der Woude, "A Groningen Hypothesis of
Qumran Origins and Early History," *RevQ* 14/56 (1990): 522–42 (537); repr. in
F. García Martínez, *Qumranica Minora I: Qumran Origins and Apocalypticism* (STDJ 63;
Leiden: Brill, 2007).

[19] G. Boccaccini, *Beyond the Essene Hypothesis: The Parting of the Ways between Qumran
and Enochic Judaism* (Grand Rapids: Eerdmans, 1998).

[20] See my comments in "Enoch, the Dead Sea Scrolls and the Essenes," in *Enoch
and Qumran Origins* (ed. G. Boccaccini; Grand Rapids: Eerdmans, 2005), 345–50 and
already in "The Origins of the Qumran Community," in *Seers, Sibyls and Sages in
Hellenistic-Roman Judaism* (JSJSup 54; Leiden: Brill, 1997), 239–60.

[21] On the perils of reconstructing history from the Damascus Document see M.L.
Grossman, *Reading for History in the Damascus Document: A Methodological Study* (STDJ 45;
Leiden: Brill, 2002).

(who are apparently identified with the יחד). The existence of 4Q265, which is related to both rules, and the presence of multiple copies of the Damascus Rule at Qumran also argue against the view that the differences between the two rules were due to a schism. Diachronic considerations may still be relevant to the differences between the two rules, but the theory of a split in the Essene sect is unfounded and should be abandoned.

I do not propose to address here all the issues raised by the relationship between the Serek and the Damascus rules, but to give some thought to one major aspect of the problem: the *raison d'être* and goals of the movement as described in each of the textual traditions. As many scholars have realized, the Serek reflects a sharper break with the wider Jewish community than does the Damascus covenant. It seems to me that a good case can be made for development from the D texts to the Serek, although this development is complicated by the fact that both sets of texts continued to be copied and modified over a period of time.

The Damascus Rule

The designation "Damascus Document" is an *ad hoc* label, derived from the mention of Damascus a couple of times in the text. Steven Fraade has suggested that the work might more appropriately be called "The Elaboration of the Laws" (פרוש המשפטים), the phrase used in the conclusion of the work, attested in 4Q266 11 17 (paralleled in 4Q470 7 ii 12): "this is the elaboration of the laws to be followed by them during the entire period [of visitation]."[22] It also appears near the end of the Geniza document, MS A, in CD XIV 18, just before a reference to the messiahs of Aaron and Israel (so, perhaps, referring to the interpretation of the laws to be followed until the coming of the messiahs). Joseph Baumgarten, in the DJD edition, reconstructs the same phrase in the opening line of 4Q266 1 as a virtual title, but we do not in fact know whether these were the opening words.[23]

---

[22] S.D. Fraade, "Law, History, and Narrative in the Damascus Document" (a paper presented to the Qumran section of the Society of Biblical Literature in Philadelphia, 20 November 2005), in *Meghillot 5–6* (Dimant Festschrift, forthcoming 2007).

[23] Baumgarten, *DJD* 18:31–32.

פרוש המשפטים may refer more narrowly to the legal exposition and penal code at the end of the work.[24]

Most scholars of CD have distinguished between the Admonition, in the first part of the work, and the Laws, in the latter part. Fraade rightly points out that "important statements of law and legal scriptural interpretation are central to the Admonition itself" and that the importance of instruction in "the deeds of God" is recognized in the Laws, in the role assigned to the מבקר in CD XIII 7–8. The blend of exhortation and law, in any case, is typical of Deuteronomy, often thought to be the prototype for CD and more generally of covenantal texts. The word ברית, covenant, occurs some 40 times in CD, including notable references to "the new covenant" (VI 19; XIX 33; XX 12) or "the new covenant in the land of Damascus" (VIII 21; cf. XX 12), of which the addressees of the text are members. The text addresses the motivation for making and keeping this covenant and also provides the stipulations that it entails. In this respect, it is not primarily a rulebook, or "manual of discipline" for a specific community. Most of the laws cited are applicable in principle to all Israel. The text includes more specific regulations for the assembly of the camps (CD XII 22–23; XIII 20) and for the assembly of all the camps (CD XIV 3). The new covenant entails some rules that have no biblical precedent, such as the contribution of two days' salary each month (CD XIV 12–13). The penal code found in the D fragments from Qumran increase the rule-like element in this text, but on the whole it is concerned with the interpretation, or reinterpretation, of the Law of Moses more than with regulations for community life. This covenantal character of the D rule is not significantly changed by the opening paragraph. The framework of the discussion is in any case supplied by the Law of Moses and the distinctive interpretation thereof to which this text subscribes.

The Damascus Rule is concerned with the Law of Moses as it should apply to all Israel, but it is also concerned with an elite group within

---

[24] The beginning of the text is preserved in very fragmentary form in 4Q266, with parallels in 4Q267 and 268. It appears that the opening section in the medieval manuscript was preceded by a passage that exhorts "the sons of light" to keep apart from the way[s of wickedness] and which refers to "the voice of Moses" and to "slander against the commandments of God." The designation "sons of light" is not otherwise used in the D manuscripts, and this raises the possibility that this particular recension of the D Rule may be influenced by the Serek. Compare Davies' "Qumranic recension" in CD XX, but the יחד should not be simply identified with Qumran. Note however the reference to "the lot of light" in CD XIII 12 and to the Prince of Lights in V 18.

Israel, who recognize that the Law is not being properly observed. God, we are told, caused this group to sprout from Israel and Judah in the age of wrath 390 years after he had given Israel into the hand of Nebuchadnezzar (CD I 6–7). This group is often described by modern scholars as "a penitential movement." David Lambert has objected to this designation, noting that the initiative is said to come from God, whose salvific intervention is prior to any action on their part.[25] They then realized their iniquity and knew that they were guilty. Their appropriate conduct at this point leads to another divine intervention—the sending of the Teacher of Righteousness. Throughout this text there is a dialectic of divine and human initiative. The wicked are such because "God did not choose them at the beginning of the world, and before they were established he knew their deeds" (II 7). "Those he hates, he causes to stray" (II 13). Nonetheless, they are guilty and are punished for the choices they make. Similarly, those who remain faithful to the covenant are beneficiaries of divine providence, but they will also be rewarded, first by further revelations and ultimately by eternal life (III 20).

The group that sprouts from Aaron and Israel is distinguished from the rest of Israel, even while it claims to be the true Israel.[26] They are the remnant that remained to Israel (CD I 3–5), the שבי ישראל (IV 2; VI 5; VIII 16) or שבי פשע (XX 17), or elect of Israel (IV 2–4). God reveals to them "the hidden matters in which all Israel had gone astray" (III 13), including calendrical matters and other laws. The text proceeds to give several examples of Israel's errors, such as the three nets of Belial, fornication, wealth, and defilement of the temple. It is apparent from the discussion that the rest of Israel was not necessarily repudiating these laws entirely, but that they did not understand them properly by sectarian standards. So, for example, taking two wives within one's lifetime is considered fornication, although polygamy is never prohibited and often condoned in the Hebrew Bible. The goal of this group, then, is the correct interpretation and fulfillment of the

---

[25] D. Lambert, "Beyond Repentance: Divine over Human Agency in Second Temple Judaism," (*CBQ*, forthcoming).

[26] Compare P.R. Davies, "The 'Damascus' Sect and Judaism," in *Pursuing the Text: Studies in Honor of Ben Zion Wacholder on the Occasion of his Seventieth Birthday* (ed. J.C. Reeves and J. Kampen; Sheffield: Sheffield Academic Press, 1994), 70–84 (77–78); J.J. Collins, "The Construction of Israel in the Sectarian Rule Books," in *The Judaism of Qumran: A Systemic Reading of the Dead Sea Scrolls* (vol. 3 part 5 of *Judaism in Late Antiquity*; ed. A.J. Avery-Peck et al.; Leiden: Brill, 2001), 25–42 (26–30).

laws, in accordance with their own teachings. While it is understood
that this can only happen by divine initiative, something is also required
of the elect. They must enter into a new covenant, as envisioned by
Jer 31:31. This is still the covenant based on the Law of Moses, but
those who are Israelites by birth do not automatically qualify. This
covenant is potentially for all Israel (XV 5), even proselytes.[27] The
individual "must impose upon himself to return to the law of Moses
with all his heart and soul" (XV 12). He must also impose the oath of
the covenant on his son when he reaches the age of enrollment (XV
5–6). Those who then reject the rulings of the sect, or do not abide
by them, are subject to expulsion, as is made clear in the conclusion
of the text in 4Q266 11 5–8:

> And any one who rejects these regulations, (which are) in accordance with
> all the statutes found in the law of Moses, shall not be reckoned among
> all the sons of his truth; for his soul has despised righteous instruction.
> Being in rebellion, let him be expelled from the presence of the Many.

The new covenant, in effect, creates a new community.

The group described in the Damascus Document was not the first
movement in Second Temple Judaism to call for a "return" to a strict
interpretation of the Law of Moses. Something analogous is found in
the books of Ezra and Nehemiah. In Neh 10:29 certain people "enter
into a curse and an oath to walk in God's law, which was given by
Moses the servant of God, and to observe and do all the commandments of the Lord our God and his ordinances and his statutes."[28] As
in CD, these people agree to abide by a particular interpretation of the
law, one that prohibits them from intermarriage with foreign peoples.
They also undertake to support the temple with various contributions
and offerings. In Ezra 10:8 we find that people who did not comply
with Ezra's directives could be banned from "the congregation of the
exiles." The situation of Ezra and Nehemiah differs from that of the
Damascus Document, insofar as both have the backing of the Persian

---

[27] CD XIV 4, 6. Davies ("The 'Damascus Sect' and Judaism," 75) claims that the
reference is to "a proselyte to the sect, and thus one in the process of initiation into
it," but there is no parallel for such usage. See Hempel, "Community Structures in
the Dead Sea Scrolls," 77.

[28] The analogy with the Dead Sea Scrolls was already noted by M. Smith, "The
Dead Sea Sect in Relation to Judaism," *NTS* 7 (1961): 347–60. See also A. Sivertsev,
"Sects and Households: Social Structure of the Proto-Sectarian Movement of Nehemiah 10 and the Dead Sea Sect," *CBQ* 67 (2005): 59–78; idem, *Households, Sects, and
the Origins of Rabbinic Judaism* (JSJSup 102; Leiden: Brill, 2005), 94–118.

government and have control of the temple. The movement described in the Damascus Document has power to enforce internal discipline and to expel members who fail to conform, but it does not have power over the society at large, and so it relies on the threat of divine punishment. It also offers the prospect of reward in the afterlife, an idea that is not attested in Ezra and Nehemiah.

The "congregation of the exiles" in Ezra and Nehemiah was made up of families, who separated themselves from the people of the land in the sense that they did not mingle with them. Did the Damascus Document require any greater degree of separation? CD IV 2 says that "the priests are the converts of Israel who left the land of Judah," but the passage is notoriously ambiguous and the language may be entirely symbolic. Again, we do not know whether the references to the new covenant in the land of Damascus have any geographical value. We are told that some members of the movement "reside in camps in accordance with the rule of the land and marry and have children" (VII 6–7). These people are evidently not members of a quasi-monastic community, such as has been imagined in the case of Qumran. These appear to be distinguished from the "people of perfect holiness" who are assured that they will live for a thousand generations, presumably because they will not marry and have children. But we are given no other indication that there is a spiritual elite within the covenant, or how or where any members who were not married might live. The regulations at the end of the document include provision for marriage and divorce (CD XIII 16–17) and for the instruction of children (4Q266 9 iii 6) and even regulate sexual relations between married people (4Q267 9 vi 4–5; 4Q270 7 i 12–13). The document includes a rule for the assembly of the camps (XII 22–XIII 22) and a rule for the assembly of all the camps (XIV 3), a kind of general assembly of scattered communities. We are told that members were to contribute the salary of two days a month at least. There does not seem here to be any withdrawal to the wilderness, physically or symbolically. There is, nonetheless, far-reaching community discipline. Members were not even free to marry or divorce without informing the מבקר (XIII 16–17). We are given a hint that some members pursue an ideal of perfect holiness, but the document does not describe their way of life or make clear whether it is any different from that of those who live in camps.

There is also a personal reward in the Damascus Rule, beyond the fulfillment of the covenant: those who walk in perfect holiness are assured that they shall live a thousand generations (VII 5) or that they will acquire eternal life and all the glory of Adam (III 20). The hope for reward in the afterlife brings an apocalyptic dimension to the Torah-centered piety of the Damascus Rule, but it is not developed. The emphasis in this text is on the fulfillment of the law rather than on the hope for the afterlife.

THE SEREK

The situation is rather different in the Community Rule. We now have a clearer picture of the evolution of this document than we have in the case of the Damascus Document.[29] The form of the Rule preserved in 1QS and 4QS^b is the most elaborate. 4QS^d evidently lacked the opening covenantal ceremony and the Instruction on the Two Spirits. 4QS^e concluded with the calendrical text 4QOtot (4Q319) instead of the hymnic material found in 1QS X–XI. Each of these manuscripts, however, attests some form of the rules in 1QS V–IX, which form the core of the Serek. Whether, or in what sense, the Serek should be described as a rule book is also debated. While a greater proportion of the text consists of community rules than is the case in CD, it also includes extensive instructional and motivational material. Philip Alexander suggests that "it is best taken as a manual of instruction to guide the Maskil in his duties towards the community."[30]

The rules in the Serek have some features in common with the Damascus Rule. Here, as in CD, the person joining the community must "swear a binding oath to return to the law of Moses, according to all that he commanded, with his whole heart and whole soul" (1QS

---

[29] See especially S. Metso, *The Textual Development of the Qumran Community Rule* (STDJ 21; Leiden: Brill, 1997). Metso argues that the manuscripts 4QS^b (4Q256), 4QS^d (4Q258), and 4QS^e (4Q259), while paleographically later than 1QS, preserve an older (and shorter) form of the text. See also her essay, "In Search of the Sitz im Leben of the Qumran Community Rule," in *The Provo International Conference on the Dead Sea Scrolls* (ed. D.W. Parry and E.C. Ulrich; STDJ 30; Leiden: Brill, 1999), 306–15. P.S. Alexander, in contrast, has argued that the paleographic dating reflects the more probable order of composition in "The Redaction-History of Serekh Ha-Yahad: A Proposal," *RevQ* 17/65–68 (1996): 437–56. For the 4Q fragments see P.S. Alexander and G. Vermes, *DJD* 26.

[30] Alexander, "The Redaction-History of Serekh ha-Yahad," 439. So also, Vermes, *The Complete Dead Sea Scrolls*, 97; C. Newsom, *The Self as Symbolic Space: Constructing Identity and Community at Qumran* (STDJ 54; Leiden: Brill, 2004), 102.

V 8–9).[31] As in CD XIII, the association is organized in communities with a minimum number of ten members (1QS VI 3,4). Both have strict disciplinary codes. Nonetheless, it becomes apparent that a different kind of community is envisioned in the Serek. There is no mention of women or children, and there is a greater degree of communal activity.[32] The members are said to eat, bless, and take counsel together. They also relieve each other interpreting the Torah, night and day, and keep watch together for one third of each night. Members apparently are required to turn over all their possessions to the inspector, although they are still credited to their accounts (VI 19–20). This greater cohesiveness and tighter community structure is reflected in the designation for the community (יחד).[33]

Charlotte Hempel has noted that the simple process of admission by swearing an oath in 1QS V contrasts with the elaborate, multi-stage process of admission described in 1QS VI 13b–23, and suggests that it is "a case of an earlier piece of communal legislation having been preserved in 1QS alongside the later and more elaborate procedure," and that the legislation in question derives from the "parent" community described in CD XV.[34] This may be, but it should be noted that the older requirement for admission, swearing an oath, is not contravened by the more elaborate procedure, but is rather supplemented. The Damascus Rule already required that the מבקר examine admittees with regard to character, intelligence, and wealth (CD XIII 11). We may suppose that the יחד initially had a similar, simple procedure and later devised a more elaborate one. The more exacting process of admission reflects a higher standard for the community, although it has the same basis in the law of Moses as the Damascus Rule.

Hempel has also argued that the passage in 1QS VI 1c–8a, which refers to multiple gatherings with a quorum of ten, "is of a heterogeneous character and contains some rather early and organizationally

---

[31] Compare 4Q256 5 6–7; 4Q258 1 i 6. The differences between the manuscripts with regard to the "Sons of Zadok" do not concern us here.

[32] See Sivertsev, *Households, Sects, and the Origins of Rabbinic Judaism*, 130–40.

[33] The analogies between the Serek and Hellenistic voluntary associations were noted especially by M. Weinfeld, *The Organizational Pattern and Penal Code of the Qumran Sect: A Comparison with Guilds and Religious Associations of the Hellenistic-Roman World* (Fribourg: Editions Universitaires, 1986).

[34] Hempel, "Community Structures," 72.

primitive material alongside some apparently later additions."[35] Sarianna Metso has argued similarly that the reference to communities with a quorum of ten is likewise a relic of older legislation.[36] The organization in groups of at least ten is also found in CD XII 22–XIII 7, where the units in question are called camps, and if we accept the thesis that the Damascus Rule reflects an older form of sectarian organization than the יחד, then it is reasonable to infer that the reference to groups of at least ten in the Serek was derived from the older Rule. The question that concerns us here, however, is not so much the source of this passage as its function within the Serek. On one view, which I hold,[37] יחד was an umbrella term for several communities of variable size. On the alternative view, the term rather referred to a single large community (usually called "the Qumran community"), and the passage in 1QS VI is included as "an earlier, time-honored set of directives" that is anachronistic in the context of the Serek.[38] The "Rule for the assembly of the many" that begins in 1QS VI 8b seems to envision a large community with multiple priests. But this is not incompatible with the continued existence of multiple smaller communities. The assembly may be conceived in the same way as "the assembly of all the camps" in CD, or, alternatively, it may be the rule for any assembly of יחד members, on the assumption that large communities were the norm. The provision that members could meet in small groups with a quorum of ten is never contravened in the Serek, and I see no reason to regard it as anachronistic.

1QS VI 3 refers to "every place where there shall be ten men *from* the council of the community" (מעצת היחד). Metso takes the preposition "from" in a locative sense and spins out a scenario of "traveling Essenes":

> members of the *yaḥad* (i.e. members *from* the council of the community, מעצת היחד) while they were visiting areas outside large Essene settlements such as the one at Qumran, and would have been in contact with Essenes

---

[35] C. Hempel, "Interpretative Authority in the Community Rule Tradition," *DSD* 10 (2003): 59–80 (63).

[36] S. Metso, "Whom Does the Term Yaḥad Identify?" in *Biblical Traditions in Transmission: Essays in Honour of Michael A. Knibb* (ed. C. Hempel and J.M. Lieu; JSJSup 111; Leiden: Brill, 2005), 213–35.

[37] Collins, "Forms of Community in the Dead Sea Scrolls," 104; idem, "The Yaḥad and 'the Qumran Community.'"

[38] So Metso, "Whom does the Term Yaḥad Identify?" 227. The passage is found in 4QSᵈ, which Metso takes to reflect the oldest form of the Serek.

living in towns and villages and lodging in settlements small enough that gathering the quorum of ten would have been an issue.

She refers here to Josephus (*J.W.* 2.124): "They have no one city, but many settle in each city; and when any of the sectarians come from elsewhere, all things they have lie available to them." But Josephus clearly assumes that Essenes, apparently of the same order, live in many cities, so the parallel lends no support to the view that only the visitors were members of the יחד. Neither does the Serek say anything to indicate that the passage refers to situations where members are traveling, and I do not think that the word מגוריהם, their places of sojourning (usually translated "their places of residence"), can be taken to imply travel out of community.[39] It is surely easier to accept that the preposition "from" is partitive and that members living in villages and towns, in smaller communities, were just as much members of the יחד as those in a larger community such as the one commonly supposed to have lived at Qumran.[40] This assumption also frees us from the need to suppose that the passage in 1QS VI 1c–8a is only a fossil of an earlier time and not reflective of the community described in the rest of the Serek.

If the יחד is conceived as an umbrella term, like the "congregation" of the Damascus Rule, this strengthens the continuity between the communities envisioned in the two Rules, insofar as both are broad movements embracing several communities. Nonetheless, differences remain, as we have already noted, in the lack of any reference to family and the more extensive demands on the members in the Serek.

The renewed covenant of the Damascus Rule required purity and to some degree the pursuit of holiness. The members were charged, among other things, "to keep apart from the sons of the pit... to separate clean from unclean and separate the holy from the common" (CD VI 14–18). We have noted that the Damascus Rule also refers to "those who walk in perfect holiness" (VII 5; cf. XX 2, 5, 7), although it does not specify their way of life as distinct.

---

[39] *Pace* Metso. The statement "in this way shall they behave in all their places of sojourning" relates immediately to the practice of reproof in the preceding verses, and it would make little sense to suppose that this law only applied to travelers.

[40] Regev, "The Yahad and the Damascus Covenant," 236, recognizes that the Serek provides for a number of smaller communities, but his argument that the phrase "council of the community" refers to a local community, rather than to the association as a whole, is untenable.

The ideal of holiness is even more prominent in the Serek. The members of the יחד are to make atonement for all who offer themselves willingly for holiness in Aaron and for the house of truth in Israel" (1QS V 6). In 1QS V we read of "the purity of the men of holiness" (V 13) and of "the congregation of holiness" (V 20). The person who swears to return to the law of Moses also swears to be segregated from all the men of injustice (V 10).

The ideal of the יחד is set out most fully in 1QS VIII. The opening section (VIII 1–4a) announces that there shall be "in the council of the community twelve men and three priests, perfect in everything that has been revealed from all the law" (VIII 1). This section is followed by three paragraphs, each of which begins with the phrase, "when these are in Israel."

The first of these (VIII 4b) reads: "when these are in Israel, the council of the community shall be established on truth, as an everlasting plantation, a holy house for Israel and a council of supreme holiness for Aaron, true witnesses for the judgment and elect of good will to atone for the land and to render the wicked their retribution." The function of atoning, which was traditionally exercised by the temple cult, is here claimed for the יחד.[41] This is a notable development over against the Damascus Rule, where the temple cult was criticized, even rejected, but the theme of the community as a replacement for the cult was not developed.[42] There is a further temporal clause in VIII 10b–11: "when these have been established in the foundation of the community for two full years in perfection of way they will be separated as holy in the midst of the council of the men of the community, and every matter

---

[41] See Newsom, *The Self as Symbolic Space*, 157–60 and the older treatments of B. Gärtner, *The Temple and the Community in Qumran and the New Testament* (Cambridge: Cambridge University Press, 1965) and G. Klinzing, *Die Umdeutung des Kultus in der Qumrangemeinde und im Neuen Testament* (SUNT 7; Göttingen: Vandenhoeck & Ruprecht, 1971). See also L.H. Schiffman, "Community Without Temple: The Qumran Community's Withdrawal from the Jerusalem Temple," in *Gemeinde ohne Tempel. Community without Temple: Zur Substituierung und Transformation des Jerusalemer Tempels und seines Kults im Alten Testament, antiken Judentum und frühen Christentum* (ed. B. Ego et al.; WUNT 118; Tübingen: Mohr Siebeck, 1999), 267–84.

[42] See CD IV 17–18; V 6–7; VI 13–14 (4Q266 3 ii 17–19). 4Q266 11 1–5, par. 4Q270 7 i 15–19, seems to prescribe repentance, instead of temple offerings, for inadvertent sin, but does not speak of the life of the community as a means of atonement. See Evans, "The Relationship between the Damascus Document and the Community Rule."

hidden from Israel but which as been found out by the Interpreter, he should not keep hidden from them for fear of a spirit of defection."

The second paragraph begins in VIII 12b: "when these are a community in Israel[43]... they shall be separated from the midst of the dwelling of the men of iniquity, to go to the wilderness to prepare there the way of Him, as it is written, 'in the wilderness prepare the way of ****.' This is the study of the law, which he commanded by the hand of Moses."

The third paragraph, beginning in IX 3, reads "when these are in Israel in accordance with these rules in order to establish the spirit of holiness in truth eternal." This passage is not found in 4QS[e], which lacks VIII 15–IX 11. The paragraph beginning in IX 3 seems to duplicate VIII 4b–10.

The twelve men and three priests have been variously understood as an inner council[44] or as the founding members of the Qumran community.[45] According to VIII 10–11, however, they are a sub-group who are set apart as holy within the council of the men of the community after they have been established in its principles for two years. They receive full instruction from the Interpreter and then retreat to the wilderness to prepare the way of the Lord. By so doing, they bring the יחד to completion.[46]

Sarianna Metso has objected to this reading on the basis of 1QS IX 5–6, which she translates as follows: "At that time the men of the community shall separate themselves as a holy house of Aaron, that they may be united as a holy of holies, and as a house of community for Israel, as those who walk in perfection." She argues, rightly, that "the men of the community" are the entire יחד and that walking in perfection is required of the entire יחד elsewhere in the Serek.[47] But on my own reading of column 8, it is also the whole יחד that constitutes the holy house, not just the elite group that constitutes its pinnacle, and so

---

[43] בהיות אלה ליחד בישראל; ליחד is inserted above the line and appears to be missing in 4QS[d]. See DJD 26:107.

[44] Milik, Ten Years, 100.

[45] E.F. Sutcliffe, S.J., "The First Fifteen Members of the Qumran Community," JSS 4 (1959): 134–38; J. Murphy-O'Connor, "La Genèse Littéraire de la Règle de la Communauté," RB 66 (1969): 528–49.

[46] See further Collins, "Forms of Community," 105–7; idem, "The Yahad and 'The Qumran Community,'" 88–90.

[47] Metso, "Whom Does the Yahad Signify?" 230. Cf. 1QS I 8; II 2; III 9, etc.

there is no necessary contradiction with this passage.[48] But in any case, 1QS VIII 10–11 says quite clearly that certain people who have been established in the community for two years will be set apart as holy in its midst. In the extant text, the antecedent is the group of twelve men and three priests. Metso claims that this passage is "more naturally understood as a reference to the period of two years of probation that is required of all new community members."[49] But this would require that the statement in question is out of context and that this section of the Serek is a collection of statements that are only loosely related. Such a view of the Serek may be possible. 4Q265, which contains a parallel to 1QS VIII 1,[50] does in fact seem to be a random collection of laws and statements. But a reading that posits coherence in the passage should be preferred. It seems to me, then, that 1QS VIII does indeed posit the existence of an elite group within the יחד, which is said to consist of twelve men and three priests. Unfortunately, we do not know what part this group played in the history of the movement. It is possible that the retreat of this pioneering group to the wilderness marked the beginning of "the Qumran community," as has often been claimed. If so, it should be noted that it did not arise from a schism in a parent group and did not by itself constitute the יחד but was part of a larger whole. It would also, of course, have to have grown in size. The numbers have symbolic significance, referring to the twelve tribes and three priestly families,[51] and we cannot be sure that this group ever came to be. But it is presented as an ideal, which would bring the community to completion.

It is true, as Metso has argued, that the aims of this group can hardly be distinguished from those of the broader יחד. All were supposed to walk in perfection of the way; all were supposed to pursue a life of holiness. But to say that the entire יחד was consecrated to a life of holiness is not to deny that different degrees of holiness were possible. The great concern for holiness in the Serek is evidently related to the fact that it envisions the יחד as a substitute for the temple cult.

---

[48] It should also be noted that this passage is not found in 4QS^e and, on Metso's reconstruction of the Serek, is part of a secondary addition. She also notes that in 4QS^d the words "men of the community" are lacking in this passage.

[49] Cf. M.A. Knibb, *The Qumran Community* (CCJW 2; Cambridge: Cambridge University Press, 1987), 133.

[50] "When there are in the community council fifte[en men]...the community coun[cil] will be firmly established."

[51] Milik, *Ten Years*, 100.

Traditionally, the whole temple was holy, but there was still an area marked off as "the holy of holies." Even if all Jerusalem was regarded as holy, the temple was still especially holy. According to the editors' reconstruction of 4QMMT, Israel is holy, but the priests are most holy and should not intermarry with those who are merely holy.[52] The holiness of the whole body is enhanced by the existence of a part that is especially holy. As Carol Newsom has observed, with reference to this passage, "As a description of the most dedicated and highest form of community life, it serves not merely as yet one more account of community procedure but rather as an expression of its highest potential and its telos."[53]

In the case of this elite group, the intensification of holiness is reflected in the retreat to the desert. In part, this is simply obedience to a dictum of Scripture: in the wilderness prepare the way of the Lord.[54] In part, it is a return to the situation of Israel in the wilderness at the time of the original Sinai revelation. It dramatizes the separation of the יחד from the people of iniquity. Hindy Najman has suggested an analogy with the thought of Philo, who explained the remote location of the Sinai revelation by arguing that "he who is about to receive the holy laws must first cleanse his soul and purge away the deep-set stains which it has contracted through contact with the motley promiscuous horde of men in cities. And to this he cannot attain except by dwelling apart, nor that at once, but only long afterwards" (*Decal.* 10–11).[55] Philo's philosophical presuppositions were, of course, quite different from anything found in the Dead Sea Scrolls. For him, the goal was the separation of the soul from the corporeal world for a life of contemplation. The Serek shows no familiarity with the Platonic idea of the soul. Nonetheless, contemplation also had its place in the life of the יחד. The analogy with Philo is useful as it reminds us that the goal of the יחד was not only the reformation of Israel by proper observance of the Torah, but also the spiritual transformation of its members.

---

[52] 4QMMT composite text, B 17–82. See *DJD* 10:172–73.

[53] Newsom, *The Self as Symbolic Space*, 153.

[54] G.J. Brooke, "Isaiah 40:3 and the Wilderness Community," in *New Qumran Texts and Studies* (ed. idem and F. García Martínez; STDJ 15; Leiden: Brill, 1994), 117–32. Symbolism does not preclude literal enactment.

[55] H. Najman, "Revelation in the Desert: The Therapeutae and the Essenes" (paper presented at the SBL meeting in Philadelphia, 21 November 2005).

INDIVIDUAL TRANSFORMATION

Carol Newsom has astutely observed that the Serek ha-Yahad is roughly shaped to recapitulate the stages of life as a sectarian: from motivation, to admission, instruction, life together and leadership.[56] This is true of all extant forms of the Serek, but is more elaborate in the longer recension found in 1QS. Both the shorter recension (approximately 1QS V–IX) and the longer one represented by 1QS begin with a motivational paragraph, followed by a ritual of entry (the covenant ceremony in 1QS I–II, the oath in 1QS V) and rules for the common life. Both recensions include instructions for the Maskil at or near the end of the composition.[57] Newsom argues that this organization of the material encourages one "to see in the character of the Maskil the telos of the disciplines and teaching that the Serek ha-Yahad has described."[58] The inclusion of the first-person hymn in 1QS XI gives the Maskil a vivid voice and presence, even though it is formulaic in its sentiments and expression. In Newsom's view, "the self-presentation of the Maskil provides a model of the ideal sectarian self. If one is properly shaped by the teachings and disciplines of the community, as they have been described in the Serek ha-Yahad, then this is the kind of voice with which one will speak."[59]

This voice is in part self-deprecating, reflecting what Newsom calls "the masochistic sublime" ("I belong to evil humankind, to the assembly of unfaithful flesh," 1QS XI 9).[60] But in part it is also mystical:

> For from the source of his knowledge he has disclosed his light, and my eyes have beheld his wonders, and the light of my heart the mystery that is to be...My eyes have observed that which is forever, wisdom that has been hidden from humankind, knowledge and prudent understanding (hidden) from the sons of man...To those whom God has selected he has given them as everlasting possession; and he has given them an inheritance in the lot of the holy ones. He unites their assembly to the sons of heaven for a council of community (עצת יחד) and a foundation

---

[56] Newsom, *The Self as Symbolic Space*, 107.

[57] 4QS^d includes text parallel to 1QS XI 7–8, 14–15. 4QS^e, which has a form of 4QOtot instead of the final hymn, has a parallel to 1 QS IX 21–24, the beginning of the rules for the Maskil.

[58] Newsom, *The Self as Symbolic Space*, 107.

[59] Ibid., 167.

[60] Ibid., 220.

of the building of holiness to be an everlasting plantation throughout all future ages (1QS XI 3–8).

The theme of fellowship with the angels is familiar from the Hodayot.[61] In the context of the Community Rule, it represents the culmination of the life of holiness: the angels are the "holy ones" par excellence.[62] The association with the heavenly "holy ones" explains some aspects of the lifestyle of the יחד. As is well known, the eschatological rule, 1QSa, specifies that no one defiled by any of the impurities of man, or by any physical blemish, shall enter the council of the community in the last days, "for angels of holiness are among their congregation."[63] The company of angels is probably also the reason for the absence of women and children in Serek ha-Yahad. The logic of celibacy in an angelic context is most explicitly set forth in the Book of the Watchers in *1 En.* 15. Enoch is told to chide the Watchers for having lain with women, and defiled themselves with the daughters of men, and taken for themselves wives, and done as the sons of earth. God had given women to human beings so that they might beget children and not vanish from the earth. But God did not give women to those who existed as spirits, living forever, and not dying for all the generations of eternity. Sex has no place in the angelic or heavenly life (compare the saying of Jesus in Mark 12:25: "when they rise from the dead, they neither marry nor are given in marriage but are like angels in heaven"). While neither the Damascus Rule nor the Serek ever explicitly requires celibacy, this same logic most probably underlies the guarantee in CD VII 5–6 that those who walk in perfect holiness shall live a thousand generations (this is followed immediately by the statement "And if they live in camps in accordance with the rule of the land, and take women and beget children…"). When the community is regarded as a

---

[61] See especially H.W. Kuhn, *Enderwartung und gegenwärtiges Heil* (SUNT 4; Göttingen: Vandenhoeck & Ruprecht, 1966); G.W.E. Nickelsburg, *Resurrection, Immortality and Eternal Life in Intertestamental Judaism and Early Christianity* (HTS 56; expanded ed.; Cambridge, Mass.: Harvard, 2006), 181–93; D. Dimant, "Men as Angels: the Self-Image of the Qumran Community," in *Religion and Politics in the Ancient Near East* (ed. A. Berlin; Bethesda, Md.: University Press of Maryland, 1996), 93–103; J.J. Collins, *Apocalypticism in the Dead Sea Scrolls* (London: Routledge, 1997), 117–23.

[62] See Dimant, "Men as Angels." She emphasizes the communion with the angels in the praise of God, as illustrated in the Songs of the Sabbath Sacrifice.

[63] 1QSa II 3–9; J.A. Fitzmyer, "A Feature of Qumran Angelology and the Angels of 1 Cor 11:10," in *Paul and the Dead Sea Scrolls* (ed. J. Murphy-O'Connor and J.H. Charlesworth; New York: Crossroad, 1990), 31–47.

metaphorical temple, as is the case in the Serek, requirements of purity create an additional obstacle to sexual relations.

The ideal of personal transformation, as expressed in the hymn of the Maskil, must be seen in the context of the community ideal expressed in columns 8 and 9. The holiness of the individual members is required by the view of the community as temple, whose role is to atone for the land. If any of the members were sinful, or otherwise defiled, the community/temple would be polluted and unable to carry out its function.[64] The ultimate goal of the יחד is the redemption of Israel and the restoration of right order on earth. This goal, of course, is eschatological, something that would only be accomplished when the messiahs of Aaron and Israel came. But in the meantime, the pursuit of the life of holiness was a goal in itself, one that paradoxically led to increasing withdrawal from society at large, a withdrawal symbolized by the call to go to the wilderness in 1QS VIII.

CONCLUSION

There is much that is unclear about the relation between the Damascus Rule and the Community Rule, or Serek ha-Yahad. There obviously is a relationship between them. Arguments that they reflect two different sects are unpersuasive both because of parallels in terminology and organization and because fragments of both are found in Qumran Cave 4. I agree with those who find the more primitive form of community organization reflected in the Damascus Rule, although the issue is clouded by the fact that that Rule seems to have undergone some revision in light of the Serek. The popular theory that the Damascus Rule represents an order that practiced marriage, while the Serek was the rule for celibates requires some qualification, but is still substantially correct. The Damascus Rule is primarily concerned with households. It allows for some other members who walk in perfect holiness, but says little about their way of life. The Serek, in contrast, is primarily concerned with those who walk in perfect holiness. While it allows for multiple communities with a quorum of ten members, in the manner of the "camps" of the D rule, it makes no mention of women or

---

[64] Newsom, *The Self as Symbolic Space*, 159. There is no distinction between moral and ritual purity in the Dead Sea Scrolls. See J. Klawans, *Impurity and Sin in Ancient Judaism* (New York: Oxford University Press, 2000), 67–91.

children. It reflects a more intense preoccupation with holiness and provides for an elite group that pursues it to a higher degree in the wilderness. The heightened quest for holiness arises in large part from the view that the community life is a substitute for the temple cult in atoning for the land. This view is not yet found in the Damascus Rule and reflects a more complete break with the temple cult. The pursuit of holiness also offered a goal of individual transformation, insofar as the members of the יחד aspired to fellowship with the angelic host. I see no reason to attribute the differences between the two rules to a schism. Since both rules continued to be copied, it would seem that the kind of family-based movement envisioned in the Damascus Rule was not simply superseded, but continued to exist in tandem with the more intensive communities of the יחד.

The widely assumed identification of the sect known from the scrolls with the Essenes has played no part in my description of the movement. It is obviously compatible with it in several respects. The Essenes also had multiple communities. According to Josephus, "they are not in one town only, but in every town several of them form a colony" (*J.W.* 2.184). Philo says that they lived in a number of towns and also in villages and in large groups.[65] Pliny and Josephus indicate that the Essenes practiced celibacy, but Josephus also tells us of another order of Essenes who, "although in agreement with the others on the way of life, usages and customs, are separated from them on the subject of marriage" (*J.W.* 2.160). It remains true that many of the beliefs and concerns reflected in the Hebrew Rules are not reflected in the classical accounts. Steve Mason has argued vehemently that Josephus would not have idealized an apocalyptic sect, such as is described in the Scrolls.[66] But Mason himself has shown exhaustively that Josephus's account of the Essenes conforms to the stereotypes of idealizing ethnography in the Hellenistic world. It remains unclear how much Josephus actually

---

[65] Philo, *Hypothetica*, apud Eusebius, *Praep. ev.* 8.6–7. G. Vermes and M. Goodman, *The Essenes According to the Classical Sources* (Sheffield: Sheffield Academic Press, 1989), 26–27.

[66] S. Mason, "Essenes and Lurking Spartans in Josephus' *Judean War*: From Story to History," in *Making History: Josephus and Historical Method* (ed. Z. Rodgers; JSJSup 110; Leiden: Brill, 2007), 219–61. See also idem, "What Josephus Says about the Essenes in his *Judean War*." http://orion.mscc.huji.ac.il/orion/programs/Mason00-1.shtml Part of this essay (roughly, the latter half) appeared under the same title in S.G. Wilson and M. Desjardins, eds., *Text and Artifact in the Religions of Mediterranean Antiquity: Essays in Honour of Peter Richardson* (Waterloo: Wilfrid Laurier University Press, 2000), 434–67.

knew about this sect. Despite his claim that he made trial of all three
major Jewish sects before he was nineteen, he could not have gone
through the multi-year process of initiation described in the Serek.[67]
He must have been dependent on either a written source or an oral
informant for the details of his account, and we know that the יחד
was highly secretive.[68] Josephus did not necessarily have a complete or
accurate picture of the beliefs of the sect, and his account is tailored to
reflect positively on Judaism. It seems to me unlikely that there existed
another previously unknown sect that resembled the Essenes so closely
in organization. But if the sect known from the Hebrew sources was
indeed the Essenes, then the classical sources are not very reliable or
adequate. Ultimately, the question of the identification is of secondary
importance. It is to the Scrolls themselves that we must look in order
to understand this strange and fascinating movement, which was largely
lost to history for nearly two thousand years.

---

[67] Josephus, *Life*, 10–11. See S. Mason, *Life of Josephus: Translation and Commentary*
(Leiden: Brill, 2001), 21.
    [68] See further my essay "Josephus on the Essenes: The Sources of his Information,"
to appear in the Festschrift for Sean Freyne.

FLAVIO GIUSEPPE E LA FILOSOFIA DEGLI ESSENI

Alessandro Catastini

Nel mondo classico si tese talora a interpretare la religione ebraica alla stregua di una filosofia;[1] ne testimoniano Teofrasto,[2] Megastene,[3] Clearco di Soli.[4] Per il primo gli Ebrei erano "filosofi per stirpe: conversano fra di loro sulla divinità e di notte osservano il moto degli astri". Per il secondo "tutte le opinioni espresse dagli antichi in merito alla natura si trovano anche fra i filosofi al di fuori della Grecia: alcune fra i Bramani indiani, altre in Siria fra i cosiddetti Giudei". Il terzo riferisce le parole di Aristotele in merito a un Ebreo di Celesiria—e questi Ebrei sarebbero stati chiamati "Calani" in India—il quale "aveva l'animo di un Greco e parlava greco; inoltre, conduceva vita austera e sobria".

Questa prospettiva si sviluppò anche in senso inverso. La profonda influenza esercitata dalla cultura ellenistica sul giudaismo della madrepatria e della diaspora condusse una cospicua componente dell'*élite* intellettuale ebraica ad accogliere le speculazioni delle scuole filosofiche greche,[5] nonché a ricercare in esse forti punti di contatto con i principî della religione ebraica, al punto di affermare che le prime dipendevano dalla seconda: il filosofo ebreo Aristobulo giunse a dire che la legislazione mosaica sarebbe stata determinante nientemeno che per il pensiero di Pitagora, Socrate e Platone.[6] Si pensi poi alla tesi squisitamente filosofica che animò l'autore del *IV Maccabei*, ossia che la ragione può prevalere sulla forza delle passioni.[7] Secondo Clemente Alessandrino, inoltre, non solo Aristobulo e Filone Alessandrino, ma anche "«molti altri»... interpretarono la filosofia greca come la risultante naturale di quella delle scritture ebraiche".[8]

---

[1] Cfr. Troiani 1997, 19.
[2] *De Pietate*, in Porfirio, *De Abstinentia* 2.26: cfr. Stern 1974, n° 4.
[3] *Indica*, in Clemente Alessandrino, *Stromata*, 1.15.72.5: cfr. Stern 1974 n° 14.
[4] *De Somno*, in Flavio Giuseppe, *Ap* 1.176–83: cfr. Stern 1974, n° 15. Sulle notizie di tutti e tre gli autori, cfr. Gabba 1989, 618–24.
[5] Cfr., ancora valido, quanto esposto nel capitolo II di Hengel 1974.
[6] Troiani 1997, 132–33.
[7] Troiani 1997, 221.
[8] Troiani 1997, 51.

La prospettiva "filosofica" fu accolta con favore da Flavio Giuseppe, almeno per quel che si può vedere nel *Bellum*[9] e nelle *Antiquitates*.[10] Giuseppe mostra di condividere i principî della dottrina stoica, alla quale egli riconduceva la setta dei Farisei (*Vita* 12). Ponendo se stesso e buona parte dell'*élite* giudaica in siffatta classificazione, lo storico si incanalava nella corrente più tranquillizzante per l'ideologia del Principato romano: lo Stoico, fidando nella Provvidenza che opportunamente interveniva in un contesto comunque disegnato dalla divinità, finiva per proporsi come modello di persona che non avrebbe procurato problemi all'autorità. Diversamente, il meccanicismo dell'Epicureo destava preoccupazioni per l'ordine costituito.[11]

Riprendendo una polemica che dovette essere interna al giudaismo, Giuseppe non mancò comunque di accostare all'epicureismo un'altra componente dell'*élite* del suo popolo, i Sadducei. L'accostamento non fu tuttavia esplicito: venne effettuato in *Ant* 10.266–281, in un contesto ove da un lato veniva espressa, sempre in termini allusivi, l'equazione Stoici = Farisei, mentre dall'altro l'equazione Epicurei = Sadducei vi veniva contrapposta secondo argomentazioni che a un Ebreo colto dovevano rendere immediato un messaggio che, a seguito di un'attenta analisi, neanche a noi può sfuggire.[12] Questo si rendeva necessario poiché parlare di epicureismo poteva essere pericoloso per Giuseppe; o meglio, poteva esserlo l'avvicinare all'epicureismo anche solo una parte del popolo ebraico. A scanso di equivoci, Giuseppe pensò bene di esprimersi in termini esplicitamente contrari a tale dottrina sempre in *Ant* 10.277–281, così da non incorrere nel pericolo di confermare certe accuse delle quali gli Ebrei erano fatti oggetto: insocievolezza, irreligiosità, ateismo.[13]

---

[9] Cfr. ad esempio Mason 1991.

[10] Cfr. Catastini 1997, 496–502.

[11] Non è questo il luogo per trattare tali fondamentali e dibattute questioni; per un primo accostamento, resta fondamentale Pohlenz 1970.

[12] Cfr. Catastini 1997, 508–14.

[13] Per questo, Giuseppe scrisse il *Contra Apionem*, ove l'interpretazione in chiave filosofica del giudaismo veniva messa da parte per privilegiare il buon lignaggio della tradizione e gli aspetti positivi che le concezioni della religione ebraica comportavano anche per chi non fosse Ebreo. Giuseppe aveva capito che era meglio non inglobare più il giudaismo nel genere filosofico in un periodo in cui Plutarco tuonava contro gli Epicurei e Apione contro gli Ebrei. Meglio proporre una visione irenica e prospettare i buoni insegnamenti che una religione impartisce. Questo fu dunque un cambiamento di rotta, uno dei vari che il nostro storico sapeva bene quando fosse il caso di operare: cfr. Catastini 1997, 510–11.

L'essenismo fu a sua volta descritto da Giuseppe come una filosofia:[14] nelle *Antiquitates* egli ne traccia le coordinate generali affermando che gli Esseni si distinguevano per il perseguire un comportamento "che presso i Greci fu insegnato da Pitagora" (*Ant* 15.371).[15] Nella lunga descrizione degli Esseni fatta in *Bell* 2.119–161,[16] il modo di vita degli Esseni richiama in effetti e assai marcatamente i precetti che ispirarono le comunità pitagoriche. Le comunanze pertinentemente apprezzabili in proposito sono state da tempo messe in luce: si pronunciò inizialmente in tal senso E. Zeller,[17] mentre I. Lévy[18] trattò l'argomento nella maniera più ampia, documentando i numerosi elementi si somiglianza: l'ambiente ove condurre l'esistenza, i modi di cooptazione, il noviziato, il giuramento iniziatico, l'espulsione e la reintegrazione, la comunione dei beni e la vita in comune, l'amministrazione, Dio e la Provvidenza, la venerazione del sole, la preghiera prima del pranzo, la preghiera in genere, il divieto di prestare giuramento e di pronunciare il nome di Dio, i sacrifici, la figura del legislatore, i libri sacri, la divinazione, l'etica e le osservanze, il triplo canone (φιλόθεον, φιλάρετον, φιλάνθρωπον), i comandamenti, i bagni, le concezioni di purità, l'abbigliamento, la dieta alimentare, il celibato, il matrimonio, l'ascetismo, la concezione dell'anima.[19] Lévy mise in parallelo queste peculiarità partendo dal dato che già le fonti giudaiche avevano da un lato richiamato l'influenza che Pitagora avrebbe avuto a seguito di contatti con l'Oriente e con gli Ebrei, dall'altro avevano dipinto Mosè con colori fortemente pitagorici: in particolare, il ritratto fattone da Filone alessandrino avrebbe moltissimi aspetti in comune con le biografie di Pitagora. L'accostamento fra almeno una delle sette giudaiche e il pitagorismo parve quindi più che giustificata e la conclusione fu analoga a quella che già Zeller aveva avanzato: gli Esseni avevano tratto dal neopitagorismo quelle peculiarità che li distinguevano all'interno del giudaismo.[20] Negli studi posteriori

---

[14] Cfr. Bilde 1998, 62.

[15] γένος δὲ τοῦτ᾽ ἔστιν διαίτη χρώμενον τῇ παρ᾽ Ἕλλησιν ὑπὸ Πυθαγόρου καταδεδειγμένῃ.

[16] Per alcune rassegne sulla descrizione di Flavio Giuseppe, cfr. Bergmeier 1993, Mason 2002.

[17] Zeller 1868, 275–92; l'opinione di Zeller fu contestata da Bousset 1926, 458–59; Bauer 1903, 427; di recente, Bergmeier 1993, 94–104, ha negato il carattere "pitagorico" degli Esseni di Qumran.

[18] Lévy 1927.

[19] Lévy 1927, 270–88.

[20] Zeller 1868, 285; Lévy 1927, 288–89; questa opinione ebbe numerosi oppositori: cfr. le esposizioni in Lévy 1927, 269 e Lévy 1965, 62–63.

che hanno variamente interpretato la descrizione degli Esseni nel *Bellum*, si possono isolare tre linee di interpretazione:

1. gli Esseni avrebbero di fatto subìto l'influenza del pitagorismo;[21]
2. Esseni e Pitagorici condivisero indipendentemente gli uni dagli altri delle peculiarità che furono comunque comuni ad altre organizzazioni comunitarie;[22]
3. Flavio Giuseppe ci tramanda una interpretazione volutamente "colorata" in termini pitagorici.[23]

Prescindendo per il momento da una soluzione definitiva, pure non si può negare che Giuseppe abbia voluto descrivere gli Esseni, almeno in massima parte, secondo le peculiarità di quella dottrina pitagorica che lo storico del resto aveva puntualmente evocato nelle *Antiquitates* come termine di raffronto.[24] Sono eloquenti le comunanze di motivi con le descrizioni delle comunità pitagoriche fatte da autori, pur posteriori a Giuseppe ma portatori di tradizioni più antiche, come Porfirio nella *Vita Pythagorae* e Giamblico nel *De vita Pythagorica*:[25] si pensi alla vita in comune, ai beni gestiti insieme, agli indumenti e così via. Perfino l'attenzione che gli Esseni rivolgono al sole è elemento di non poco conto: la questione dell'affinità con l'adorazione solare dei Pitagorici è stata oggetto di discussione fra gli studiosi,[26] ma un richiamo pare evidente.

È inoltre possibile evidenziare caratteristiche ulteriori che collegano gli Esseni ai Pitagorici, almeno secondo la visuale che Giuseppe intese

---

[21] Cfr. Zeller 1868, 275–92; Cumont 1930, 100; Dupont-Sommer 1955, 86–91; Wagner 1960, 156–65.

[22] Cfr. Leaney 1966, 62; Beall 1988, 132; da segnalare la particolare opinione di Mendels 1979: questi mette a paragone la pratica di vita essena descritta da Giuseppe e Filone con l'utopia idealizzata da Giambulo (III/II sec. a.C.: epitome in Diodoro Siculo 2.55–60) sottolineandone le analogie (Mendels 1979, 210–18) concludendo che gli Esseni sarebbero più vicini agli ideali delle utopie ellenistiche che non ai Pitagorici.

[23] Hengel 1974, 245–46, Bilde 1998, 49, 63.

[24] Un collegamento particolare tra Pitagora e l'ebraismo si volle riconoscere sia dagli autori giudeo-ellenisti quanto da quelli greco-romani: per i primi, cfr. Lévy 1927, 137–38); per i secondi, Stern 1974, nn° 25, 26, 40, 250 (e quanto detto a 94), Stern 1980, n° 456a.

[25] Per le fonti di Porfirio, cfr. Des Places 1982, 13–16; per Giamblico, cfr. Rohde 1901; Giangiulio 1991, 46–80; Brisson e Segonds 1996, LXI–LXX; Staab 2002, 217–37.

[26] Si sono dichiarati favorevoli all'affinità: Lévy 1927, 277; Dupont-Sommer 1953, 155; Dupont-Sommer 1955, 87. Hanno espresso parere contrario: Hengel 1974, 245; Beall 1988, 132.

offrire al lettore. Di fatto, lo storico descrive altri aspetti che costituirono parte del pitagorismo tardo ch'egli dovette conoscere, come si evince dall'affermazione secondo la quale gli Esseni "per la cura delle malattie... studiano le radici medicamentose e le proprietà delle pietre" (*Bell* 2.136).[27] In particolare la prima arte, cioè la rizotomia, fu disciplina della quale le fonti greche ci offrono numerose testimonianze, in speciale connessione con la medicina:[28] a questo riguardo, l'interesse di Pitagora per lo studio delle proprietà delle piante ci è testimoniato da più fonti classiche.[29]

Un altro elemento da mettere in rilievo, di valore fondamentale, è costituito dalle procedure per l'ammissione di un nuovo membro nella comunità, così descritte in *Bell* 2.137–138:

> 137. A chi desidera far parte della loro setta non viene concesso di entrare immediatamente, ma lasciandolo fuori per un anno gli fanno seguire la stessa norma di vita, dandogli una piccola scure e la predetta fascia per i fianchi e una veste bianca. 138. Dopo che in questo periodo di tempo egli abbia dato prova della sua temperanza (ἐγκράτεια), viene ammesso a un più completo esercizio della regola e ottiene acque più pure per la purificazione, ma non ancora è introdotto nella comunità. Infatti dopo aver dimostrato la sua fermezza (καρτερία) per altri due anni, viene sottoposto a un esame del carattere (τὸ ἦθος δοκιμάζεται) e solo allora, se appare degno, viene ascritto alla comunità.[30]

Questa tradizione permette di mettere in rilievo un ulteriore punto in comune con il pitagorismo: l'esame fisiognomico.

Nel mondo antico si è ampiamente fatto uso della fisiognomica quale modalità specifica per condurre l'esame psicologico degli uomini. Partendo dal presupposto che il carattere umano avesse una stretta connessione con le caratteristiche fisiche e comportamentali di un individuo, questa tecnica doveva permettere di comprendere le prime esaminando

---

[27] ἔνθεν αὐτοῖς πρὸς θεραπείαν παθῶν ῥίζαι τε ἀλεξητήριον καὶ λίθων ἰδιότητες ἀνερευνῶνται. Le traduzioni italiane dei brani del *Bellum* corrispondono a Vitucci 1974. Per la terminologia relativa agli erboristi, cfr. Delatte 1961, 23. Nel *Libro dei Giubilei* (10:12) la comprensione delle proprietà delle piante è attribuito a Noè.

[28] Si vedano in proposito: Lloyd 1983, Scarborough 1991.

[29] Cfr. Festugière 1938, 117; Festugière 1939, 58, 63, 71.

[30] 137 Τοῖς δὲ ζηλοῦσιν τὴν αἵρεσιν αὐτῶν οὐκ εὐθὺς ἡ πάροδος ἀλλ᾽ ἐπὶ ἐνιαυτὸν ἔξω μένοντι τὴν αὐτὴν ὑποτίθενται δίαιταν ἀξινάριόν τε καὶ τὸ προειρημένον περίζωμα καὶ λευκὴν ἐσθῆτα δόντες. 138 ἐπειδὰν δὲ τούτῳ τῷ χρόνῳ πεῖραν ἐγκρατείας δῷ πρόσεισιν μὲν ἔγγιον τῇ διαίτῃ καὶ καθαρωτέρων τῶν πρὸς ἁγνείαν ὑδάτων μεταλαμβάνει, παραλαμβάνεται δὲ εἰς τὰς συμβιώσεις οὐδέπω. μετὰ γὰρ τὴν τῆς καρτερίας ἐπίδειξιν δυσὶν ἄλλοις ἔτεσιν τὸ ἦθος δοκιμάζεται καὶ φανεὶς ἄξιος οὕτως εἰς τὸν ὅμιλον ἐγκρίνεται.

le seconde. La fisiognomica ha lasciato le sue prime tracce nella cultura mesopotamica,[31] per poi venire coltivata nel mondo classico.[32] I *Physiognomonica* dello Pseudo-Aristotele[33] costituiscono la più antica esposizione metodica a noi giunta delle regole di indagine psicologica sulle caratteristiche fisiche dell'individuo umano, mentre altri estensori di analoghi trattati furono Losso e Polemone: del primo non ci è rimasta l'opera, ma solo citazioni,[34] mentre i *Physiognomonica* di Polemone sono stati trasmessi essenzialmente in traduzione araba.[35] Al di là dei trattati sistematici, l'interesse per lo studio dei caratteri fisici onde discernere quelli morali è testimoniato in opere varie: nei testi ippocratici, nei *Memorabilia* di Senofonte, nei testi platonici e in quelli aristotelici.[36] Di Aristotele, oltre ai *loci physiognomonici* occasionalmente presenti nelle opere, si ha notizia di un Φυσιογνωμωνικόν andato perduto di cui è memoria in Diogene Laerzio 5.25; i Φυσιογνωμωνικά summenzionati appartengono nondimeno alla stessa scuola aristotelica.[37]

D'altro lato la fisiognomica costituì uno dei criteri, fra i più importanti, per l'ammissione alle comunità pitagoriche. Suggestiva, in tal senso, la testimonianza di Aulo Gellio, *Noctes Atticae* 1.9.1–2:

> Ordo atque ratio Pythagorae ac deinceps familiae <et> successionis eius recipiendi instituendique discipulos huiuscemodi fuisse traditur: Iam a principio adulescentes, qui sese ad discendum obtulerant, ἐφυσιογνωμόνει.[38] Id verbum significat mores naturasque hominum coniectatione quadam de oris et vultus ingenio deque totius corporis filo atque habitu sciscitari.

La notizia verrà riportata sino in epoca tarda attraverso Porfirio,[39] Proclo di Costantinopoli[40] e Ippolito Romano,[41] ma è Giamblico a offrire in merito testimonianze alquanto significative. Questi riferisce dell'esame fisiognomico che Pitagora praticava ai suoi discepoli in *De vita Pythagorica* 1.17.71–74; si tratta di un passo di tradizione antica: i paragrafi 71–73

---

[31] Cfr. Bottéro 1974, 107–9; Pettinato 1998, 49–52.
[32] Cfr. la bibliografia in Campanile 1999, 287, n. 57.
[33] Cfr. Evans 1969, 7–10; Raina 1994, 24–35.
[34] Cfr. Evans 1969, 10–11.
[35] Cfr. Evans 1969, 11–15; Campanile 1999, 286–89, con bibliografia alla n. 53.
[36] Cfr. Raina 1994, 13–19.
[37] Evans 1969, 7.
[38] De Vogel 1966, 218, ha sostenuto che il termine φυσιογνωμωνῆσαι per indicare lo studio dei tratti del volto quale σημεῖον del carattere risale con ogni probabilità allo stesso Pitagora.
[39] *Vita Pythagorae* 13.54.
[40] *In Platonis Alcibiadem comm.* 103 B 9–15.
[41] *Refutatio omnium haeresium* 1.2, 5.

risalgono con probabilità a Timeo di Tauromenio (IV–III sec. a.C.), come dimostra la presenza nel testo della ripresa di una testimonianza di quest'ultimo,[42] mentre il 74 è da ricondurre a Nicomaco di Gerasa (seconda metà del I sec. d.C.).[43] In particolare, viene detto ai paragrafi 71–72 che il filosofo prescriveva di esaminare τὸ ἦθος del neofita prima di ammetterlo alla comunità. Proprio sul termine ἦθος, menzionato anche da Flavio Giuseppe in *Bell* 2.138, e sul testo di Giamblico vale la pena di soffermarsi.

Nel *De vita Pythagorica* sono distinte tre fasi di esame dei candidati alla comunità di Pitagora. Venivano esaminati dapprima il comportamento, l'aspetto (τὸ εἶδος), l'andatura e i movimenti (τὴν ὅλην τοῦ σώματος κίνησιν) in maniera che "analizzandone la fisiognomica, per mezzo dei tratti fisici [Pitagora] rendeva visibili quelle caratteristiche (che sono) invisibili nell'anima". Dopo aver così esaminato (δοκιμάσειεν), Pitagora passava alla successiva valutazione (δοκιμάζων), che prevedeva un periodo di tre anni durante il quale occorreva dar prova di fermezza (πῶς ἔχει βεβαιότητος). Infine, un ulteriore periodo di tre anni serviva a giudicare l'autocontrollo (ἐγκράτεια) del candidato. È a questo punto particolarmente istruttivo osservare il singolare impiego stilistico del sostantivo ἦθος al paragrafo 71, all'interno della frase che è stata poco sopra direttamente tradotta e riportata tra virgolette: τοῖς τὲ τῆς φύσεως γνωρίσμασι φυσιογνωμονῶν αὐτοὺς σημεῖα τὰ φανερὰ ἐποιεῖτο τῶν ἀφανῶν ἠθῶν ἐν τῇ ψυχῇ. Ora, gli ἤθη dell'anima sono invisibili (ἀφανῆ) ed è per mezzo dell'opposizione a questa caratteristica che sono messi in relazione con τὰ σημεῖα τῆς φύσεως, i quali sono invece visibili (φανερά): in questa osservazione viene definita esemplarmente la funzione della fisiognomica attraverso la stretta corrispondenza terminologica tra σημεῖον ed ἦθος. Nei Φυσιογνωμωνικά dello Pseudo-Aristotele il termine ἦθος sarà largamente impiegato e assumerà un senso metonimicamente traslato: a partire da 805a, 29, indica direttamente le caratteristiche esteriori dalle quali desumere la tipologia dell'animo,[44] mettendo in atto la corrispondenza tra σημεῖον ed ἦθος presente in Giamblico.

Dal canto suo Flavio Giuseppe, in *Bell* 2.137–138, parla di tre fasi esaminatorie: la verifica della ἐγκράτεια per la durata di un anno e della

[42] Cfr. Giangiulio 1991, 203; Brisson e Segonds 1996, 170; Staab 2002, 306–7.
[43] Cfr. Giangiulio 1991, 203; Brisson e Segonds 1996, 171.
[44] Cfr. quanto osservato da Raina 1994, 60, n. 10.

καρτερία per altri due anni,[45] per poi passare all'esame dello ἦθος. In effetti non si può dire che negli altri luoghi dell'opera di Giuseppe ove ricorre,[46] questo termine rivesta il significato di "caratteristica fisica": il senso è "disposizione d'animo, carattere" e questo escluderebbe l'ipotesi di un'interpretazione in chiave fisiognomica. V'è tuttavia un elemento distintivo nella descrizione delle verifiche esposte in *Bell* 2.137–138. Le prime due sono esposte definendo le loro modalità: in sostanza, la sopportazione di due stili di vita dei quali il secondo appare più severo (πρόσεισιν μὲν ἔγγιον τῇ διαίτῃ) rispetto al primo. Ma c'è di più: il fatto che si precisi la durata per l'una e per l'altra implica da parte del candidato la manifestazione di doti delle quali occorre dar prova nel corso di un determinato periodo poiché si tratta di virtù che richiedono una costanza che occorre esaminare nel tempo. La mancanza di una precisazione temporale per la terza verifica ne denuncia la diversità dalle altre due in merito alla modalità poiché l'esame dello ἦθος viene condotto a prescindere da una partecipazione attiva del candidato, dal momento che non viene condotto sulla campionatura di un periodo. Piuttosto, è da supporre l'intervento di uno specifico esaminatore—il cui compito è da vedere descritto nell'uso del verbo δοκιμάζειν—che opera in un tempo relativamente breve per interpretare quei tratti fisiognomici che anche qui sono indicati per metonimia nel termine ἦθος.[47]

Si può osservare ulteriormente che le tre fasi esaminatorie mostrano analogie con quelle riferite da Giamblico: la medesima suddivisione in tre momenti, nonché l'utilizzo di termini specifici come δοκιμάζειν, ἐγκράτεια e lo stesso ἦθος. La corrispondenza strutturale diverge tuttavia in due punti principali: la durata dei periodi in cui si valutano gli aspetti morali del candidato e la diversa collocazione dell'analisi dello ἦθος nella successione degli esami. Nondimeno, è proprio quest'ultimo aspetto che ci conferma in Flavio Giuseppe l'identificazione tra ἦθος ed esame fisiognomico, già peraltro esplicitata nello Pseudo-Aristotele.

Flavio Giuseppe ci trasmette quindi una descrizione di ambiente pitagorico ove lo ἦθος non mantiene il significato che gli è proprio in

---

[45] Che l'espressione δυσὶν ἄλλοις ἔτεσιν sia da riferirsi alla verifica della καρτερία è determinato dal fatto che questo termine—come in definitiva l'altro, ἐγκράτεια—denoti una capacità di resistenza.

[46] *Bell* 1.124, 468, 564; 2.76, 166; 4.85; 6.190, 356; *Ant* 6.45; 9.25; 14.308; 19.329; *Vita* 430.

[47] La questione può essere ulteriormente collegata all'esame dei testi fisiognomici di Qumran: di questo argomento tratterò tuttavia in un contributo a parte.

altri luoghi della sua opera:[48] in *Bell* 2.138 egli riecheggia il parallelismo con σημεῖον della fonte riportata da Giamblico.

BIBLIOGRAFIA

Bauer, W. 1903. "Essener". *RE* Suppl. 4:386–430.

Beall, T.S. 1988. *Josephus' Description of the Essenes Illustrated by the Dead Sea Scrolls*. Cambridge: Cambridge University Press.

Bergmeier, R. 1993. *Die Essener-Berichte des Flavius Josephus. Quellenstudien zu den Essenertexten im Werk des jüdischen Historiographen*. Kampen: Kok Pharos.

Bilde, P. 1998. "The Essenes in Philo and Josephus". Pagine 32–68 in *Qumran Between the Old and New Testament*. A cura di F.H. Cryer e T.L. Thompson. Sheffield: Sheffield Academic Press.

Bottéro, J. 1974. "Symptômes, signes, écritures en Mésopotamie ancienne". Pagine 70–197 in *Divination et rationalité*. A cura di J.P. Vernant et al. Paris: Seuil.

Bousset, W. 1926. 3 ed. *Die Religion des Judentums im späthellenistischen Zeitalter*. A cura di H. Gressmann. Tübingen: Mohr.

Brisson, L., e A.Ph. Segonds. 1996. *Jamblique: Vie de Pythagore*. Introduction, traduction et notes par L. Brisson et A. Ph. Segonds. Paris: Les Belles Lettres.

Campanile, M.D. 1999. "La costruzione del sofista. Note sul βίος di Polemone". Pagine 269–315 in *Studi ellenistici XII*. A cura di B. Virgilio. Pisa: Giardini.

Catastini, A. 1997. "Stoici ed Epicurei in Flavio Giuseppe, *Ant* X, 266–281". *Studi Classici e Orientali* 46 [1999]:495–514.

Cumont, F. 1930. "Esséniens et Pythagoriciens d'après un passage de Josèphe". CRAI, 99–112.

Dupont-Sommer, A. 1953. *Nouveaux Aperçus sur les manuscrits de la mer Morte*, Paris: Maisonneuve.

———. 1955. "Le problème des influences étrangères sur la secte juive de Qoumrân". *RHPR* 35:75–79.

———. 1960. "Exorcismes et guérisons dans les écrits de Qoumrân". Pagine 246–61 in *Congress Volume Oxford 1959*. VTSup 7. Leiden: Brill.

Evans, E.C. 1969. *Physiognomics in the Ancient World*. Philadelphia: American Philosophical Society.

Festugière, A.-J. 1938. 2 ed. *La révélation d'Hermès Trismégiste Vol. 1: L'astrologie et les sciences occultes*, Paris.

———. 1939. "L'expérience religieuse du médecin Thessalos". *RB* 48:42–77.

Gabba, E. 1989. "The Growth of Anti-Judaism or the Greek Attitude Towards the Jews". Pagine 614–56 in *The Cambridge History of Judaism. Volume Two: The Hellenistic Age*. A cura di W.D. Davies e L. Finkelstein. Cambridge: Cambridge University Press.

Giangiulio, M. 1991. "Un neoplatonico sulla soglia del tardo-antico e la tradizione del pitagorismo. Appunti su Giamblico e la «Vita pitagorica»". Pagine 5–81 in Giamblico, *La vita pitagorica*, introduzione, traduzione e note. A cura di Maurizio Giangiulio. Milano: Rizzoli.

Hengel, M. 1974. *Judaism and Hellenism. Studies of their Encounter in Palestine During the Early Hellenistic Period*. Philadelphia: Fortress.

Leaney, A.R.C. 1966. *The Rule of Qumran and Its Meaning*. London. SCM Press.

---

[48] Alla luce delle suddette considerazioni, ritengo inadeguata l'interpretazione di Vermes e Goodman 1989, 150, e Rajak 1994, 150, che vedono nello ἦθος il riferimento alle virtù ("courage and wisdom") secondo l'etica platonico-aristotelica.

Lévy, I. 1927. *La légende de Pythagore de Grèce en Palestine*. Paris: Honoré Champion.
———. 1965. *Recherches esséniennes et pythagoriciennes*. Paris: Minard.
Lloyd, G.E.R. 1983. "Theophrastus, the Hippocratics and the Root-Cutters". Pagine 119–35 in *Science, Folklore and Ideology: Studies in the Life Sciences in Ancient Greece*. Cambridge: Cambridge University Press.
Mason, S. 1991. *Flavius Josephus on the Pharisees. A Composition-Critical Study*. Leiden: Brill.
———. 2002. "What Josephus Says about the Essenes in his *Judean War*", http://orion.mscc.huji.ac.il/orion/programs/Mason00-1.shtml (part 1), pagine 1–15 (secondo il "print preview" del browser); http://orion.mscc.huji.ac.il/orion/programs/Mason00-2.shtml (part 2), pagine 1–19 (secondo il "print preview" del browser); il sito è stato da me visionato il 13/11/06.
Mendels, D. 1979. "Hellenistic Utopia and the Essenes". *HTR* 72:207–22.
Pettinato, G. 1998. *La scrittura celeste. La nascita dell'astrologia in Mesopotamia*. Milano: Mondadori.
Places, É. des. 1982. "Notice". Pagine 9–27 in Porphyre, *Vie de Pythagore. Lettre à Marcella*. Texte établi et traduit par É. des Places avec un appendice d'A.-Ph. Segonds. Paris: Les Belles Lettres.
Pohlenz, M. 1970. 4 ed. *Die Stoa. Geschichte einer geistigen Bewegung*. Bd. I–II. Göttingen: Vandenhoeck & Ruprecht.
Raina, G. 1994. 2 ed. "Introduzione". Pagine 7–49 in Pseudo Aristotele, *Fisiognomica*—Anonimo Latino, *Il trattato di fisiognomica* (introduzione, traduzione e note di G. Raina). Milano: Rizzoli.
Rajak, T. 1994. "Ciò che Flavio Giuseppe vide: Josephus and the Essenes". Pagine 141–60 in *Josephus and the History of the Greco-Roman Period. Essays in Memory of Morton Smith*. A cura di F. Parente e J. Sievers. Leiden: Brill.
Rohde, E. 1901. "Die Quellen des Iamblichus in seiner Biographie des Pythagoras". Pagine 102–71 in *Kleine Schriften*, II. Tübingen: Mohr. = *RheinMus* 26 (1871): 554–76; 27 (1872): 23–61.
Scarborough, J. 1991. "The Pharmacology of Sacred Plants, Herbs and Roots". Pagine 138–74 in *Magika Hiera. Ancient Greek Magic and Religion*. A cura di C.A. Faraone e D. Obbink. New York: Oxford University Press.
Staab, G. 2002. *Pythagoras in der Spätantike. Studien zu dem* De Vita Pythagorica *des Iamblichos von Chalkis*, München: Saur.
Stern, M. 1974. *Greek and Latin Authors on Jews and Judaism. Edited with Introductions, Translations and Commentary. Vol. I. From Herodotus to Plutarch*. Jerusalem: Israel Academy of Sciences and Humanities.
———. 1980. *Greek and Latin Authors on Jews and Judaism. Edited with Introductions, Translations and Commentary. Vol. II: From Tacitus to Simplicius*. Jerusalem: Israel Academy of Sciences and Humanities.
Troiani, L. 1997 (a cura di). *Letteratura giudaica di lingua greca*. Vol. V degli *Apocrifi dell'Antico Testamento*. Sotto la direzione di P. Sacchi. Brescia: Paideia.
Vermes, G., e M.D. Goodman. 1989. *The Essenes According to the Classical Sources*, Sheffield: JSOT.
Vitucci, G. 1974. Flavio Giuseppe, *La guerra giudaica*. A cura di G. Vitucci. 2 voll. Milano: Mondadori.
Vogel, C.J. de. 1966. *Pythagoras and Early Pythagoreanism. An Interpretation of Neglected Evidence on the Philosopher Pythagoras*, Assen: Van Gorcum.
Wagner, S. 1960. *Die Essener in der wissenschaftlichen Diskussion vom Ausgang des 18. bis zum Beginn des 20. Jahrhunderts. Eine wissenschaftsgeschichtliche Studie*. BZAW 79. Berlin: Töpelmann.
Zeller, E. 1868. 2 ed. *Die Philosophie der Griechen in ihrer geschichtlichen Entwicklung*, III.2. Leipzig: Reisland.

ASIDAIOI AND ESSENES*

Étienne Nodet

This paper aims at challenging a widely admitted opinion that the Essenes are the heirs of the *asidaioi* referred to in 1–2 Maccabees. It proceeds in four steps:

(1) A survey of the problems at hand: first, the origin of the very name *essaios-essenos* is still unclear; Josephus, who introduces a notice on the three schools (Pharisees, Sadducees, Essenes) within his paraphrase of 1 Maccabees, refrains from making any connection. Second, the Teacher of Righteousness may have been a Zadokite priest, but the very notion of a Zadokite dynasty of high priests is unwarranted, not to speak of any connection with the Sadducees, supposed to be the most ancient "philosophy."

(2) A literary analysis of Josephus' evidence on the Essenes, with some consequences on the relative dating of the schools: the Pharisees are the most ancient, and the two others (Sadducees and Essenes) form a kind of twin phenomenon.

(3) A study of the occurrences of *asidaioi* in 1–2 Maccabees: they are used as a literary device to establish the credentials of Mattathias and Judas from different points of view.

(4) On the Essenes: they do include some Hellenizing features in their tenets and lifestyle, and, unlike the other schools, they were known in Egypt. Their wisdom allowed them to see beyond the appearances, hence healings and prophecies, so that the best explanation of their name is to be found in an Aramaic root which means "healers," quite close to "Therapeutae," a school praised by Philo of Alexandria.

1. Unresolved problems

It is often taken for granted that the Essenes were the successors of the *asidaioi* mentioned with Mattathias (1 Macc 2:42) and with Judas

* I thank Gregory Tatum for his useful comments and his corrections of the English.

Maccabee (2 Macc 14:10). The reasons adduced concern the very word "Essene" and historical considerations.

1.1. *On the Name "Essene"*

There can be little doubt that the Greek form *asidaioi* comes from the Hebrew *ḥasīdīm*, either by addition of a Greek adjective suffix *-aios* or by transcription of an aramaized plural form *ḥasīdayā*. In Hebrew, *ḥesed* means "faithfulness, loyalty, love."[1] As for the *essaioi*, "Essenes," Philo connects their name with *hosioi*, "pious,"[2] which is the normal translation of *ḥasīdīm* in the LXX, but his philology is always driven by symbolism and often by similarity of sound, so that we cannot know whether he gives a comment or an explanation.

In Biblical Syriac, i.e., Christian Aramaic, *ḥasīdīm* is translated *ḥasen* or *ḥasayā* (emphatic). Both forms are tolerably close to the names given indifferently by Josephus, *essaioi* and *essenoi*, the latter being ignored by Philo. In Jewish Aramaic, however, the rare root *ḥsy* conveys the ideas of "scrap, sneer," which is quite unsatisfactory, but it is attested once in the Dead Sea scrolls with the meaning "righteous."[3]

Two further facts can be added. First, one of Josephus' notices on the three schools is inserted in Jonathan's story (*Ant.* 13.371–373) at the time of the Maccabean crisis. He does not connect the Essenes with the *asidaioi*, although he had two opportunities to do so in previous sections. When he paraphrases Mattathias' story and the decision to permit defensive war on the Sabbath (*Ant.* 12.277), he mentions the Jews who joined him and appointed him their leader and says that Mattathias taught them to defend themselves, without mentioning any recent decision to this effect, whereas in 1 Macc 2:42 the *asidaioi* join Mattathias after the decision has been taken. When the high priest Alcimus arrived with the Syrian general Bacchides (1 Macc 7:13), the *asidaioi* welcomed his proposal of peace, but Josephus speaks only of "some of the people." This may have been on purpose, but since there

---

[1] N. Glueck, *Ḥesed in the Bible* (Cincinnati: HUC Press, 1967). L. Gulkowitsch, "Die Entwicklung des Begriffes *ḥsd* im Alten Testament," *Acta et commentationes Universitatis tartuensis Dorpatensis* 32 (1934): 5–38, had shown that *ḥasid* always has a moral meaning and never hints at any statutory membership. In the Dead Sea scrolls, the word occurs in some texts, where it depends on biblical phraseology and does not characterize a specific group.

[2] The most explicit definition is somewhat casual (*Quod omnis probus* 91) τὸν λεχθέντα τῶν Ἐσσαίων (or Ἐσα-) ἢ ὁσίων ὅμιλον "the group called of the Essenes or of the Pious." Eusebius, *Praep. ev.* 8.11.1, follows this explanation.

[3] See *DJD* 22:35 (4Q213a 1 6).

are good reasons to believe that he used a Hebrew form of 1 Maccabees,[4] it is easier to suppose that he read *ḥasīdīm* or *ḥasīdayā* and plainly
understood "pious," which fits in the context. We cannot surmise that
he was not fluent in Hebrew and Aramaic.

The second fact is that the translator of 1 Macc 7:13–17 has not
stressed the relationship between the murdered *asidaioi* and the biblical
verse quoted in the sequel: "The flesh of your saints *(hosiôn)* and their
blood they shed all around Jerusalem and they did not have a grave-
digger." This is a quotation of Ps 79:2–3, where the "saints," *ḥasīdīm*
in the MT, are normally rendered *hosioi* in the LXX. The translation,
however, is not identical with the LXX. So the conclusion should be
either that the Greek form of the Psalm was peculiar or that the translator of 1 Maccabees himself rendered the verse into Greek. In both cases,
he did not connect the two words. Thus, if he did read them in his
Hebrew source, they were different, so we should conclude that *asidaioi*
is a transcription of the Aramaized form *ḥasīdayā*, viewed as a proper
name by the translator, but not by Josephus. But such an explanation
may beg the question, without solving it, and we shall see that there are
text-critical questions about the *asidaioi*. The form appears regularly in
the targums. It points at a kind of nickname given by Aramaic speaking people in Judea or elsewhere for these pious people. Incidentally,
we may note that all the Jewish events are recorded according to the
Babylonian calendar.

1.2. *Historical Issues*

The identification of the Essenes with the *asidaioi* and the common
view that during the persecution they fled to the desert and founded
the school or sect at Qumran[5] involve three historical considerations
which entail some problems.

The first point is to identify the *asidaioi*, who join Mattathias after
the decision about the war on the Sabbath, with the people "concerned
with righteousness and law" who withdrew to the wilderness and
endured persecutions there (1 Macc 2:29–38). The decision followed

---

[4] See É. Nodet, *La crise maccabéenne: Historiographie juive et traditions bibliques* (Paris: Le
Cerf, 2005), 407–31.

[5] F.M. Cross, *The Ancient Library of Qumran* (3d ed.; Sheffield: Academic Press, 1995).
J.M. Baumgarten, "The Heavenly Tribunal and the Personification of Zedeq in Jewish
Apocalyptic," *ANRW* 2/19.1: 219–39. C. Hempel, *The Damascus Texts* (CQS 1; Shef-
field: Academic Press, 2000), 60–65.

the persecution, but there is no hint of any connection between the *asidaioi* and the wilderness.

The second is related to the site of Qumran, supposed to be the very foundation place of the Essenes around the time of the Maccabean crisis. But a reassessment of the excavations indicates that for the Hellenistic period no finding can be dated before 100 B.C.E. The most ancient structures seem to belong to a patrician *villa* from the time of Alexander Jannaeus, which was later squatted by a group of Essenes who refined the water system.[6]

The third concerns the Teacher of Righteousness. According to CD I 7–10, he was chosen by God to become the guide of the "sons of Zadok" after a wrath of 390 years. If one reckons from the fall of Jerusalem in 587 or 586 B.C.E. (CD I 5–8, quoting Ezek 44:15), that is around 175 B.C.E. This dating is close to Antiochus IV's crowning, after which Jason usurped the high priesthood of his brother Onias and introduced offensive Hellenistic practices into Jerusalem (2 Macc 4:7–10). He was succeeded by one Menelaus (171–163), followed by Alcimus (162–159), the last Aaronide high priest mentioned in the sources (1 Macc 7:14). After the latter's death, there was a seven-year gap in the high-priesthood, which Josephus mentions in his summary of the high priests since Aaron until Jonathan son of Mattathias received it from the Syrian king (1 Macc 10:17–21). This was the beginning of rule of the Hasmonean dynasty, which may have been of Aaronide stock (1 Macc 2:1). But it is difficult to admit that the whole Temple cult was interrupted for seven years,[7] without any comment on such a situation. Thus, the sources must hide something: A common hypothesis is that after Alcimus, the Teacher of Righteousness was indeed the high priest during that time span till he was expelled by Jonathan, and his memory was eventually banned from the official accounts. The Zadokite movement he founded was a kind of legitimist party, striving to restore the true Zadokite priesthood which had fallen apart after Onias, with Jason, Menelaus, and Alcimus. Some scholars conclude he was actually Onias' son.[8] Stating this implies that Onias was the last good Zadokite

---

[6] See J.-B. Humbert, "Espaces sacrés à Qumrân," *RB* 101 (1994): 161–214; idem, "Qumrân, esséniens et architecture," in *Antikes Judentum und frühes Christentum: Festschrift H. Stegemann* (ed. B. Kollmann et al., BZNW 97; Berlin: de Gruyter, 1999), 183–96.

[7] King Ahaz boldly thought otherwise: he locked the Temple gate (2 Chr 28:24), then replaced the cultic furniture, in order to change the worshipping system (2 Kgs 15:17–18).

[8] See É. Puech, "Le grand prêtre Simon (III) fils d'Onias III, le Maître de Justice?" in *Antikes Judentum und Frühes Christentum*, 137–58, who conjectures that this son, a

high priest before the crisis (see 2 Macc 3:1–3). However, the very existence of such a Zadokite dynasty is not warranted by the sources (see below). As for the unexplained gap in the Jerusalem high priest-hood, it certainly requires some conjecture, but from the account of Josephus we can extract a better explanation, namely, that the so-called Onias temple in Egypt became for some time the reference shrine, as shown elsewhere.[9]

Indeed, the fourth problem concerns the succession of the high priests since Aaron or Zadok.[10] The data available can be summarized in two tables.

The chart below summarizes the data for the biblical period.

Here, Josephus uses non biblical sources, maybe from the Temple archives (see *C. Ap.* 1:31), but no mention is made of the high priest Yehoyada, who rescued the Davidic dynasty and lived 130 years (2 Chr 24:15), unless we identify him with Josephus' Udea, but he spells the name differently (Ἰώδας, *Ant.* 9.141). In fact, there are very few clues between the high priests and the kings of Judah. The point to be stressed here is that Zadok is nothing more than a name in the lists. Moreover, in the books of Samuel and Kings, his descent is never specified. In 1 Chr 24, he is somewhat connected with the priestly courses of Eleazar's descent, but not really included. It has been taken for granted that Ezekiel mentions the "sons of Zadok" as high priests, but the verse runs (Ezek 44:15): "and the priests the levites sons of Zadok who maintained the service of my temple when the sons of Israel strayed far away from me." The phrase "sons of Zadok" means either a moral quality of some priests and levites or a third category of faithful Israelites.[11] The latter meaning is supported by CD III 21–IV 3, which reads "the priests *and* the levites *and* the sons of Zadok." At any

---

grandson of Simon the Righteous, had received by papponymy the same name Simon. This hypothesis was first aired by P.A. Rainbow, "The Last Oniad and the Teacher of Righteousness," *JJS* 48 (1997): 30–52; for him, this Simon (a Zadokite) was the Teacher of Righteousness.

[9] See Nodet, *La crise maccabéenne*, 272–88.

[10] For a fuller statement, see É. Nodet, "Benei Zadoq, Sadducees, Priests," in *Proceedings of the 10th Orion Colloquium, Jerusalem 2005* (forthcoming).

[11] According to Ezek 48:11, the future Temple will be given "to the priests sanctified among the sons of Zadok who have kept my charge, who did not go astray when the sons of Israel went astray as the levites went astray." The verse is difficult if we look for a priestly Zadokite genealogy, but very clear if "sons of Zadok" is just the quality of the sons of Israel who did not go astray, so that the priests are chosen among them. To put it otherwise, the tribe of Levi is removed (including the priestly branches) and the future priests will be chosen ("sanctified") among the righteous Israelites.

Chart 1. Genealogies of high priests, from Aaron through Ezra.

1 Chr 5:30–41 (cf. 6:35–36)	Josephus, *Jewish Antiquities*		Ezra 7:1–5
Aaron	Aaron (5:361; 20:228)		Aaron
Eleazar	Eleazar	Itamar	Eleazar
Pinhas	Pinhas		Pinhas
Abishua	Abiezer (Joseph, cf. 8:12)		*Abishua*
Buqqi	Buqqi		Buqqi
Uzzi	Uzzi		Uzzi
Zerahya		Eli of Silo (5:318)	Zerahya
Merayot		Ahiya (6:107)	Merayot
Amarya			*Azarya*
Ahitub		Ahitub (6:122)	Ahitub
		Ahimelek (6:242)	
Zadok (1 Chr 24:3)	**Zadok**	Ebyatar (7:110)	**Zadok**
Ahimaaz	Ahimaaz (10:152–153)		
Azarya	Azarya		
Yohanan	Yoram		
	Isos (?)		
Azarya	Axioram (Ahiyoram ?)		
Yohanan	Phideas (Pidiyyah ?)		
Azarya	Soudeas (?)		
	Yoël		
Amarya	Yotam		
Ahitub	Urya		
Zadok	Nerya		
	Udea (Hodayyah, Yehoyada 9:141)		
Shallum	Shallum		Shallum
Hilqiyya	Hilqiyya		Hilqiyya
Azarya	(Azarya ?)		Azarya
Seraya	Seraya		Seraya
Yehozadaq	Yehozadaq		**Ezra** *(under Artaxerxes!)*
	Joshua, under Cyrus, see Neh 12:10–11		

(In the 1 Chronicles column, the vertical bars indicate the repetition of the same names, a feature ignored by Josephus, who gives different names. In the Josephus column, the vertical bar separates the two lines of Aaronide high priests as he presents them.)

rate, it is impossible to infer from only this verse the very existence of a Zadokite dynasty of high priests.[12]

---

[12] Such is the conclusion of the well-documented study of M. Brutti, *The Development of the High Priesthood during the pre-Hasmonean Period: History, Ideology, Theology* (JSJSup 108; Leiden: Brill, 2006), 76–115.

Chart 2. The succession of the high priests in later periods.

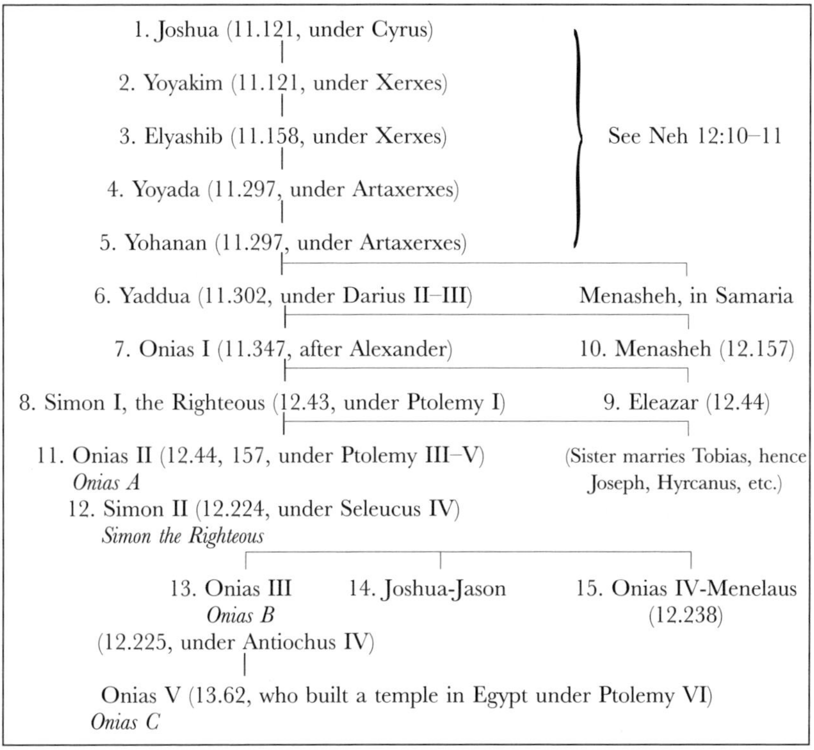

```
1. Joshua (11.121, under Cyrus)
       |
2. Yoyakim (11.121, under Xerxes)
       |
3. Elyashib (11.158, under Xerxes)              }  See Neh 12:10–11
       |
4. Yoyada (11.297, under Artaxerxes)
       |
5. Yohanan (11.297, under Artaxerxes)
       |
6. Yaddua (11.302, under Darius II–III)         Menasheh, in Samaria
       |
7. Onias I (11.347, after Alexander)            10. Menasheh (12.157)
       |
8. Simon I, the Righteous (12.43, under Ptolemy I)    9. Eleazar (12.44)
       |
11. Onias II (12.44, 157, under Ptolemy III–V)   (Sister marries Tobias, hence
    Onias A                                       Joseph, Hyrcanus, etc.)
12. Simon II (12.224, under Seleucus IV)
    Simon the Righteous
       |
13. Onias III      14. Joshua-Jason          15. Onias IV-Menelaus
    Onias B                                       (12.238)
(12.225, under Antiochus IV)
       |
Onias V (13.62, who built a temple in Egypt under Ptolemy VI)
Onias C
```

(The figures before the names indicate the order of succession; see the sequence 8, 9, 10, 11. The labels *Onias A, B, C* indicate a new proposal.)

The genealogy of the high priests in the Persian and Hellenistic period is no better, as shown in the second chart above, which depends entirely on the *Antiquities*.

It is now admitted that Simon the Righteous is the father of the Onias who was superseded by his brother Jason under Antiochus IV (175 B.C.E.). Thus, the succession of the high priests before him is actually hard to assess: first, nothing is reported of the reigns of Onias I and Simon I, and one may suspect that they have been introduced with "papponymic" names to fill up the gap between Alexander's time and the later Simon and Onias. Second, Josephus had to locate under Ptolemy II (282–246) the high priest Eleazar, responsible for the Septuagint translation of the Pentateuch according to the *Letter of Aristeas*. This results into a very complicated system of succession. But it is now recognized that the translation has been done much later; this is even

unwillingly stressed by some recent attempts to prove its dating under
Ptolemy II.[13] Again, the notion of a Zadokite dynasty is shaky.

2. Josephus on the Essenes

As a preliminary step, we have to examine Josephus' testimony, in order
to understand why he does not connect the Essenes with the *asidaioi*.

He gives several descriptions of the Pharisees, Sadducees, and Essenes.
According to one of them, they were already well defined parties or
schools by the time of the Maccabean crisis (*Ant.* 13.171–173). But it
has been pointed out that this short notice is quite strange for at least
three reasons. (1) It is inserted in the paraphrase of 1 Maccabees after
Jonathan's letter to the Spartans at the exact place of the ancient letter of King Areus referred to by Jonathan (1 Macc 12:20–23), but
without regard to the context. (2) In a subsequent passage on the tax
exemption that Herod granted the Pharisees and Essenes (*Ant.* 15.371),
Josephus explains that he will define these parties later, which he does
in 18.11–22, after Herod's death (as he had done for the notices given
in *B.J.* 2.119–166); thus, we may ask why in *Ant.* 15 he does not refer
the reader to the previous account. (3) However, in the story of Hyrcanus' banquet (*Ant.* 13.288–298), he adds important details about the
Pharisees and Sadducees (their attitude vis-à-vis Scripture) and clearly
refers to the notices given earlier, after Jonathan's letter.

One could invoke Josephus' well known sloppiness to explain away
these features, but there is a better hypothesis, which involves some
editing of the *Antiquities* by the author, a problem dealt with by many
scholars, since the work has two conclusions and may have included
the *Vita* at some early stage.

Let us first examine John Hyrcanus' famous banquet, or more
accurately, its insertion in the narrative of the *Antiquities*, for it is not
mentioned in the *War* (table below). One may note that the story in
War, albeit poorly documented, is consistent: a sedition is defeated. But
in the *Antiquities*, the context of the banquet is not consistent, for the
hostility of the Pharisees does not amount to the sedition eventually

---

[13] See N.L. Collins, *The Library in Alexandria and the Bible in Greek* (VTSup 82; Leiden:
Brill, 2000). E.J. Bickerman, "Zur Datierung des Pseudo-Aristeas," in *Studies in Jewish
and Christian History. Part 1* (AGJU 9.1; Leiden: Brill, 1976), 109–36 concludes from the
diplomatic formulae and the political geography that it has been done in the second
half of the 2nd century B.C.E.

quieted, for the objection of the Pharisees lasted for a long time after
Hyrcanus' death till Queen Alexandra. Something is missing, as if the
insertion of the banquet has disturbed the flow of the narrative.

Chart 3. The story of Hyrcanus' banquet in its context (parallel
portions in italics).

B.J. 1	*Ant.* 13
(67) *Because of the prosperous fortunes of John and his sons, the envy (φθόνος) of his countrymen provoked a sedition (στάσιν).* Large numbers of them held meetings to oppose them and continued to agitate, until the smoldering flames burst out in open war,	(288) *As for Hyrcanus, the envy (φθόνον) of the Jews was aroused against him by his own successes and those of his sons.* Particularly hostile to him were the Pharisees, who are one of the Jewish schools, as we have related before (171). ((Summary of 289–298: A banquet is offered by Hyrcanus to the Pharisees, who urge him to give up the high priesthood and be content with governing the people; Hyrcanus eventually deserts the Pharisees, joins the Sadducees and abrogates the traditional regulations, rejected by the Sadducees as non scriptural, hence the hatred of the people)).
and the rebels were defeated.	(299) *Hyrcanus quieted the sedition (στάσιν)*
(68) *For the rest of his days John lived in prosperity.*	*and lived happily thereafter.*

As for the story of the banquet itself, it has awkward features. Above
all, the accusation of being unfit for high priesthood because his
mother was a captive is identical to the claim of the people against
King Alexander Jannaeus (*Ant.* 13.272). Strangely enough, the charge
is voiced toward the end of Hyrcanus' eventful reign (135–104 B.C.E.).
Moreover, Alexander on the verge of dying advised his wife Alexandra
to reconcile with the Pharisees, something he could not do, because they
were behind the people who did not accept him; this suggests that he
was the one who rejected the Pharisaic traditions. Such a conclusion is
supported by another source: *b. Qidd.* 66a relates a banquet story with
the same features as in Josephus, but the ruler is Alexander Jannaeus,

who eventually shifts to the Sadducees and bans the oral traditions of the Pharisees. This version makes much more sense.[14]

Indeed there is a gap between John Hyrcanus the high priest and King Alexander. Hyrcanus' succession was somewhat confused, and his son Aristobulus emerged for a short period (104–103) with the title of king, as can be seen on his coins. Alexander was Aristobulus' brother, and the title shift suggests that there may have been a problem for high-priesthood. When he presents his own credentials, Josephus stresses this gap, maybe unwillingly, for he states (*Vita* 2): "Not only were my ancestors priests, but they belonged to the first of the twenty-four courses, and to the most eminent of its constituent clans; moreover, on my mother's side I am of royal blood, for the posterity of Hasamoneus, from whom she sprang, for a very considerable period were high priests and kings."

The first course was Yoyarib's (1 Chr 24:7), to which Mattathias and his son John Hyrcanus belonged, too (1 Macc 2:1); this should be "the most eminent clan." For his mother's side, Josephus mentions "royal blood" and not "high-priestly blood," which could match the Judean rulers from Alexander Janneus onward, who can be termed the true Hasmoneans.

To sum up, we can conclude that Josephus came to know of the banquet story after he had already written large portions of the subsequent books of the *Antiquities*. Besides possible ideological reasons, Josephus' insertion of this isolated piece of information in the wrong reign can be simply explained by a confusion of names, for Yannay (Jannaeus) can be a nickname for either Yohanan (John Hyrcanus) or Jonathan (Alexander).[15]

Incidentally, some remarks about stichometry suggest an explanation of the narrative distortions. In *Ant.* 20.267 Josephus says that the whole work contains sixty thousand lines; by chance, the Loeb edition has roughly the same number of lines. Now, it happens that in the biblical paraphrase a few details are given at the wrong place, but some thirty lines before or after the right position, as if a correction written between

---

[14] This is the conclusion of E. Main, "Les Sadducéens selon Josèphe," *RB* 97 (1990): 161–206; so G. Stemberger, *Pharisäer, Sadduzäer, Essener* (SBS 144; Stuttgart: Kathol. Bibelwerk, 1991), 100–102. J. Le Moyne, *Les Sadducéens* (EB; Paris: Gabalda, 1972), 59, already leant toward the same conclusion.

[15] J. Derenbourg, *Essai sur l'histoire et la géographie de la Palestine* (Paris: Imprimerie impériale, 1866), 1:80.

two columns had been subsequently inserted into the wrong one by a copyist. Thus, the whole work would contain two thousand columns of thirty lines, each book or scroll having an average of one hundred columns. Now, the banquet story contains sixty-four lines or two columns and several lines. So, if it has been inserted as an afterthought, this may explain why the context has been unduly compressed, by Josephus himself or by a careless assistant, for the insertion overlapped a portion of a third column.

The hypothesis of a later editing is aptly defended by J. Sievers.[16] He first notes that the banquet story and the first notice on the schools (under Jonathan) are connected, since the former refers to the later; both are the product of the same revision. For the narrative to make sense, since it mentions the Pharisees and the Sadducees, it was necessary to introduce the schools before Hyrcanus' reign, and even before that of his father Simon. In fact, Simon's reign is briefly narrated by Josephus, while Jonathan's is lengthy. Now, Sievers observes that the notice has the same size as Areus' letter, which was reported earlier, and concludes that the space left in "formatted" columns was the right place to insert the notice.

The conclusion of this discussion is that the denominations of Sadducees and Pharisees are not attested before Alexander Jannaeus' reign; the schools may, however, have existed earlier, with or without these denominations. As for the relationship between these two schools, Josephus never says in his notices that the Sadducees fought against the Pharisees to prevent their *adding* non-scriptural regulations, but that they fought against the widespread Pharisean customs. This indicates that they emerged after them, as we see in the banquet story. Their insistence on *sola scriptura* should be related to a renewed authority of Scripture and especially of *Jewish* Scriptures after the Pentateuch, but this is beyond the scope of this paper.

An objection to this conclusion is that Josephus always says that the Essenes were the most recent school, but in *B.J.* 1.78 (and again in *Ant.* 13.311), by Aristobulus' time (around 104) he mentions the predictions of an elderly Essene, who had many disciples in Jerusalem. This indicates that the school had already some maturity, but we shall see

---

[16] J. Sievers, "Josephus, First Maccabees, Sparta, The Three *Haireseis*—and Cicero," *JSJ* 32 (2001): 241–51.

that Josephus' definition of the Essenes, which may have been valid in his own time, is very restrictive.

As for the *asidaioi*, we can conclude first that the notices on the schools in Jonathan's time do not provide us with any view upon the Jewish parties at that time and second that Josephus, when he related the Maccabean crisis, did not see any connection between the *asidaioi* and what he already knew about the Essenes.

3. THE *ASIDAIOI*

The *asidaioi* are mentioned three times only, but in very different contexts.

(1) In 1 Macc 2:42, they join Mattathias and his friends after the decision on the armed defense on the Sabbath, but it is not stated whether they actually used this permission, for no further specific event is reported till Mattathias' death (2:49). Later, his son Jonathan violates the Sabbath in self-defense and wins, but no reference is made to any previous formal decision (1 Macc 9:43–49).

(2) In 1 Macc 7:13, the *asidaioi* welcome Alcimus, the new high priest, for he is of Aaronide descent, but many of them are eventually murdered. Alcimus has come to Jerusalem with a Syrian general, Bacchides, who leads an important army. Seeing it, Judas Maccabee refuses the latter's peace proposal. Thus, there seems to be a difference of view between the *asidaioi* and Judas, though he has been appointed Mattathias' heir (1 Macc 2:66).

(3) In 2 Macc 14:6, the same Alcimus denounces to the Syrian king the *asidaioi*, whose leader is Judas Maccabee, as warmongers. Later on, Nikanor, another Syrian general, learns that Judas is in the countryside on a Sabbath and decides to launch a hazardless attack on that day (2 Macc 15:1–5): this indicates that he is not to face any defense. There is no hint at Mattathias' decision. In a previous episode, a Syrian general managed to prevent the closure of the Jerusalem gates on the Sabbath and so could kill the defenseless Jews (2 Macc 5:24–26).

It is difficult to extract a consistent picture of the *asidaioi* from these pieces of narratives, if we take them as plain information. Thus, a closer literary analysis is appropriate.

3.1. *Did the Asidaioi Join Mattathias?*

The story of Mattathias seems to begin at Jerusalem, for it is stated that during the persecutions he "left Jerusalem and settled at Modein" (1 Macc 2:1). But his actual Jerusalem tenure is unclear for several reasons. First, this does not match his character, for when he sees the impieties perpetrated in Jerusalem, he grieves and then rebels out of zeal as did Pinhas (see Num 25:14). Second, Modein, the town of his ancestors with the family grave (1 Macc 13:25–27), belongs to the districts of Samaria annexed some twenty years later to Judea (1 Macc 11:34). Third, the real activities of Mattathias remained outside Judea and apparently within the Samaria mountains.[17]

Mattathias' only specific action reported is his rebellion at Modein. He calls together "all who are zealous for the sake of the Law" and flees with his sons "to the mountains, leaving behind all their possessions in the town" (1 Macc 2:27–28).

Then is reported the story of the people "who went down to dwell in the desert, seeking justice and right, they and their children and their wives and their cattle, hard pressed by the persecutions." Eventually, they were slain on the Sabbath (1 Macc 2:29–38). This episode is unconnected to Mattathias' flight. The place is different and the religious vocabulary is different: for Mattathias "Law and covenant" terms are frequently used in 1–2 Maccabees, but for the desert refugees "justice and right," a phrase which never occurs elsewhere in these books, but hints at the wisdom literature (Job 29:14; 34:5; Prov 1:3; 2:9) and the Psalms (37:6; 72:2; 89:15; 94:15; 97:2; 119:75). Thus, the episode, which is briefly mentioned in 2 Macc 6:11, has been taken from a written source, maybe a collection of martyr stories like the ones found in 2 Maccabees. In his paraphrase, Josephus wanted to stress that Mattathias was one of the dead of these pious Jews; he felt the discrepancy and stated that Mattathias fled in the desert (*Ant.* 12.271). Thus, he was close to them.

But in the following passage, the news reaches Mattathias and his friends, and they decide to fight against any attacker on the Sabbath. Then a company of *asidaioi* joined them (1 Macc 2:39–42). In view of the position displayed in 2 Maccabees, it is remarkable that there is no discussion on the topic. No representative of the refugees is mentioned,

---

[17] J. Schwartz and J. Spanier, "On Mattathias and the Desert of Samaria," *RB* 98 (1991): 252–71.

and we cannot be sure of their approval, for nothing is said of the extent
of the authority of Mattathias and his friends. Again, Josephus felt the
looseness of the story and said boldly that the refugees who escaped
joined Mattathias and appointed him their leader; then "he instructed
them to fight even on the Sabbath" and gathered around him a large
force (*Ant.* 12.275–277). The *asidaioi* are not mentioned.

Then Mattathias and his friends "smote the sinners in their anger
and the lawless men in their wrath, so that the survivors fled to the
Gentiles for their lives" (1 Macc 2:44–48). No details are given, but
the meaning is that they fought apostasy, without meeting any opposition from Syrian authority. This action matches neither the Modein
incident nor the massacre in the desert, when Judaism was officially
prohibited and the observant Jews persecuted by the Syrians. A much
better context is given earlier, when "lawless men arose in Israel and
seduced many with their plea: Come, let us make a covenant with the
Gentiles around us" (1 Macc 1:11–15). In other words, the summary
of Mattathias' activity is a reaction against apostasy freely accepted by
Jews, that is, against the very beginning of hellenization, when Jason
usurped the high priesthood around 175 B.C.E., close to the beginning of Antiochus IV's reign (2 Macc 4:7–10). The chronological data
support this view, for Mattathias died in 166 B.C.E., one year after
the prohibition of Judaism and the building of the Abomination of
Desolation upon the altar (1 Macc 1:54). Or maybe the same year, if
we follow the chronological system of 2 Macc 5:27–6:1, where Judas
Maccabee, Mattathias' son and successor, withdraws to the mountains
to organize a resistance *before* the prohibition of Judaism and the desecration of the Temple.

The conclusion of this discussion is twofold. First, the attribution
of the permission of fighting on the Sabbath to Mattathias and his
friends is a literary device, meant to justify what Jonathan did several
years later. Second, we can accept at face value[18] that the *asidaioi* have
joined Mattathias in his fight against apostasy, but this tells us nothing

---

[18] However, there is a slight discrepancy between v. 44 (the big force kills or casts
away the apostates) and v. 45 ("Mattathias and his friends" destroy the pagan altars
and circumcise the babies). This suggests that the big force, including the *asidaioi*, may
have grown up independently of Mattathias himself and that his being their leader is
a redactional effect. See N. Martola, *Capture and Liberation: A Study in the Composition of
the First Book of Maccabees* (Åbo: Academic Press, 1984), 157–59.

about their acceptance of the armed defense on the Sabbath—which is indeed unlikely. In any case, these *asidaioi* give credit to Mattathias' activity, at least in the narrative, for they are "mighty warriors of Israel," a phrase frequently used in the Bible, which has an overtone of religious righteousness[19] (e.g., Boaz in Ruth 2:1; the priests in Neh 11:14); Saul and Goliath are not given this qualification.

3.2. *The Asidaioi and the High Priest Alcimus*

In 162 B.C.E., Demetrius I had Antiochus V slain and became king of Syria. Then Alcimus, who wanted to be high priest, came before him with a party of "wicked men of Israel," i.e., who accepted to some extant the hellenization. They complain that Judas Maccabee has driven them out from their land after having killed their friends (1 Macc 7:1–7). Incidentally, the wording of the charge is identical to the activity of Mattathias' party.

Then the king sends Alcimus, confirmed in the high priesthood, with a large force led by Bacchides, a high-ranking general. Seeing the large force, Judas Maccabee refuses any peace proposal. However, a group of scribes accepts a meeting with Alcimus and Bacchides. At this point, the *asidaioi* get involved, but the account of the events is not clear. Here is the text (1 Macc 7:12–17).

(12) καὶ ἐπισυνήχθησαν πρὸς Ἄλκιμον καὶ Βακχίδην συναγωγὴ γραμματέων ἐκζητῆσαι δίκαια.	And an assembly of scribes gathered before Alcimus and Bacchides to seek justice.
(13) καὶ πρῶτοι οἱ Ασιδαῖοι ἦσαν ἐν υἱοῖς Ισραηλ καὶ ἐπεζήτουν παρ' αὐτῶν εἰρήνην.	And the *asidaioi* were the first among the sons of Israel, and "they" sought peace at their hands.
(14) εἶπον γάρ Ἄνθρωπος ἱερεὺς ἐκ σπέρματος Ααρων ἦλθεν ἐν ταῖς δυνάμεσιν καὶ οὐκ ἀδικήσει ἡμᾶς.	For they said: "A man who is priest from Aaron's stock has come with the forces, and he will not wrong us."

---

[19] As well as in CD II 17; III 9 and in the *Temple Scroll* (57:9; 58), see Y. Thorion, "Zur Bedeutung von נבורי חיל למלחמה in 11QT LVII:9," *RevQ* 10/40 (1981): 597–98. The phrase נבור (ה)חיל has two main renderings in the LXX, which are symmetrical: δυνατὸς (sometimes + ἐν or τῇ) ἰσχύι, which occurs more frequently, and ἰσχυρὸς δυνάμει, given here and in 1 Macc 2:66 for Judas. For a woman, the equivalent is אשת חיל, rendered with γυνὴ ἀνδρεία in Prov 12:4 and 31:10, and γυνὴ δυνάμεως in Ruth 3:11.

(15) καὶ ἐλάλησεν μετ᾽ αὐτῶν λόγους εἰρηνικοὺς καὶ ὤμοσεν αὐτοῖς λέγων Οὐκ ἐκζητήσομεν ὑμῖν κακὸν καὶ τοῖς φίλοις ὑμῶν.
(16) καὶ ἐνεπίστευσαν αὐτῷ.
καὶ συνέλαβεν ἐξ αὐτῶν ἑξήκοντα ἄνδρας καὶ ἀπέκτεινεν αὐτοὺς ἐν ἡμέρᾳ μιᾷ κατὰ τὸν λόγον ὃν ἔγραψεν αὐτόν·
(17) Κρέας[20] ὁσίων σου καὶ αἷμα αὐτῶν ἐξέχεαν κύκλῳ Ιερουσαλημ καὶ οὐκ ἦν αὐτοῖς ὁ θάπτων.

And he spoke with them in peaceful terms and swore to them, saying: "We shall not seek to harm you and your friends."
And they trusted him.
And he took sixty men from them and killed them in one day, in accordance with the verse which the prophet wrote (see Ps 79:2–3):
"The flesh of your saints and their blood they have shed around Jerusalem, and they did not have a grave-digger."

Two difficulties are apparent: first, v. 13 introducing the *asidaioi* is awkward, and removing it would smooth the passage; second, in the sequel it is unclear who is the one who leads the discussion and eventually slays the sixty men. The latter point can be cleared away if we admit that the speaker is Bacchides, who leads the force and later operates in Judea (v. 19–20) and in his anger kills many Jews who were on his side. Thus, the presence of Alcimus is meant to give credit to Bacchides' word. Josephus understood the sentence in this way (*Ant.* 12.395–396).

Bacchides' speech is consistent with the peace proposal sent to Judas, and the wording of his oath matches the request of the scribes. Many commentators identify the scribes with the *asidaioi*, but if so, the "scribes of the people" who follow Judas (1 Macc 5:42) are another entity with the same name, which is confusing.[21] But above all, the verse does not suggest this identification. Its plain meaning is a general statement on the *asidaioi* (imperfect tense): they are noteworthy people whom "they" approach to seek peace. The plural "they" can hardly refer to Bacchides and Alcimus, as if they were coming before the *asidaioi*. In the text as it stands, one could understand, with an aorist meaning, that the scribes take the advice of the *asidaioi*—or even have consulted them before the meeting, so that the statement on Alcimus' trustworthiness is theirs. This is possible, but somewhat artificial.

---

[20] Some MSS add σάρκας, a harmonisation after Ps 79[78]: 2 LXX (MT בשׂר).
[21] See J. Kampen, *The Hasideans and the Origins of Pharisaism: A Study in 1 and 2 Maccabees* (SBLSCS 24; Atlanta: Scholars Press, 1989), 117. The word γραμματεύς may render either סופר "scribe" or שׁוטר "officer."

Now the psalm verse quoted matches the murder, whatever the victims' identity can be, the scribes and/or the *asidaioi*. It is not a quotation from the LXX, but a direct translation from the Hebrew verse.[22] It misses, however, the obvious connection with the *asidaioi*, since the "saints" are the *ḥasīdīm*. This indicates that it was not so obvious for the translator.

If we combine this observation with the fact that the verse on the *asidaioi* disturbs the narrative flow, a very simple hypothesis can be ventured: the translator did not read the verse, which was added later *in the Greek* without altering the context. The addition was prompted by the verse as well as the importance of the *asidaioi* in the story of Mattathias. In fact, ancient writers saw the whole psalm as a prophecy fulfilled during the Maccabean crisis,[23] the "saints" being all the martyrs of the persecution, including the scribes. Now, we can consider that it was written after the events, but before the composition of the Hebrew original of 1 Maccabees. Incidentally, Josephus, who used a Hebrew version, mentions the Jews attending the meeting as "some of the citizens" without further specification of holiness, which suggests that he did not connect them specifically with the "saints" of the verse, in other words, that he did not read the verse on the *asidaioi*. At any rate, his silence at this point on the Essenes or the *asidaioi* means nothing.

3.3. *Judas Maccabee Head of the Asidaioi?*

According to 2 Macc 14:6, Judas Maccabee is the leader of the *asidaioi*, a Jewish faction or party. This is the only mention of them in the book.

The context is the same as in the preceding section or more accurately one step before: at the very beginning of Demetrius' reign, Alcimus, who cannot be high priest any more because of some religious unfitness, approaches him to denounce Judas and his *asidaioi* as rebels and enemies of peace; they have brought upon the whole nation a big

---

[22] Ps 79[78]:2–3 LXX is longer: τὰς σάρκας τῶν ὁσίων σου τοῖς θηρίοις τῆς γῆς· ἐξέχεαν τὸ αἷμα αὐτῶν ὡς ὕδωρ κύκλῳ Ιερουσαλημ καὶ οὐκ ἦν ὁ θάπτων.

[23] E.g., Eusebius, *Dem. ev.* 10.1.12. The common modern view, that it refers to the fall of Jerusalem in 587, is summarized by M.E. Tate, *Psalms 51–100* (WBC 20; Dallas: Word Books, 1990), 299. C.A. Briggs, *The Book of Psalms* (ICC; Edinburgh: T&T Clark, 1907), 2:197, felt this was not satisfactory, and conjectured that some glosses (vv. 3, 9, 10, 12) were added after the Maccabean crisis.

misfortune. Then the king sends Nikanor—and not Bacchides—with a force as governor of Judea, with the mission to do away with Judas and restore Alcimus as high priest. Nikanor is eventually killed, and the book ends with the institution of a commemoration of his defeat (Adar 13th). This is not the place to disentangle the confusion of the various campaigns of Nikanor and Bacchides.

In 1 Macc 7:13, the *asidaioi* are put on the side of the scribes who accept to meet Bacchides, while Judas did not trust his peace proposal. But in view of the preceding section, this is not a serious problem if we admit that the verse has been introduced out of a literary concern. On the contrary, the position of the *asidaioi* on the rebellious side fits what was said of them about Mattathias in 1 Macc 2:42. Judas was Mattathias' heir, and if we leave aside the decision about defensive war on the Sabbath as well as the personal prominence and authority of Mattathias, the common feature is that the *asidaioi* are intransigent religious Jews who cannot accept any bit of hellenization within Judea or at least within Jerusalem. This was indeed in keeping with tradition, at least since Antiochus III's statute given to Jerusalem around 200 B.C.E. (*Ant.* 12.145–146). Thus, the *asidaioi* are truly the "mighty warriors of Israel" on religious grounds. The starting point of their gathering around Judas may well be when he first withdrew to the mountains during the persecutions and managed to keep clear of any defilement (2 Macc 5:27).

But the verse discussed in the previous section presents the *asidaioi* as peace-seekers. Now, we may observe that Alcimus' speech to Demetrius is the only discourse we have of a Jewish opponent to Judas. The very word *asidaioi* cannot have a precise meaning for the Syrian ruler, but it is clear for the reader, who is supposed to be on the side of Judas. This way we can discern what Alcimus had to conceal: his ambition to recover the high priesthood in spite of some defilement did lead to sizeable disturbances. It is not easy to locate precisely his previous tenure, which should have been after the removal of Menelaus (2 Macc 13:3–8), but here the point made is clear for the reader: Judas and the *asidaioi* want both peace and religious faithfulness. In the sequel, a strange passage expounds an unexpected friendship between Nikanor and Judas Maccabee (2 Macc 14:20–25). Seeing this, Alcimus runs to the king to denounce Nikanor's betrayal, so that the war starts again till Nikanor's death and Judas' victory.

3.4. *Conclusion: The* Asidaioi *are Babylonian Jews*

Whatever may be the historical accuracy of the stories, the picture of the *asidaioi* which emerges takes some shape: they are adamant on the exclusively Jewish identity of Jerusalem. They admittedly seek peace, but not at any cost. We may admit that facing persecution some of them accept martyrdom; others prefer to fly to remote places; others take weapons and resist. Thus, we see some consistency in the three mentions of the *asidaioi*, who cannot be considered as an organized party: the refugees in the wilderness, the martyrs, Judas, and his friends, all of them can be qualified *asidaioi*, the "warriors" of the Torah. This is indeed the general meaning of the *ḥasūdīm* of Ps 79:3; so the use of the very word *asidaioi*, with an Aramaic flavor, may have been a literary device only. One may add that not everyone agreed with the armed resistance. The sketch of the Maccabean crisis given in Dan 11:33–35 suggests that for the author this attitude was not the best one.

As for the main tenets of the *asidaioi*, there is above all the separatedness from the nations as well as a strict observance of the Sabbath. About their origin, two facts are to be considered. First, they act according to the statute granted by Antiochus III one generation before the crisis; so they are not newcomers, while the Hellenizers strive for some novelties. Second, 2 Macc 2:13–14 indicates that Judas was a follower of Nehemiah, the Babylonian layman who rebuilt the Jerusalem walls and eventually enforced a complete separatedness of the Jews, especially for the Sabbath, which indeed necessitates the protection of a city wall. Josephus reports the story of the brother Anilaius and Asilaius, two Babylonian Jews who brought havoc upon their nation because one of them led a war on a Sabbath and married a foreign woman (*Ant.* 18.310–379), so violating the typical Nehemiah regulations. Incidentally, the problem of security on the Sabbath, which can be easily solved by a wall for a small group, emerged with the Hasmonean state. The necessary decision to allow the armed defense has been covered by the (literary) authority of Mattathias.

The Nehemiah rules match the very name "Pharisees," a transcription of *perīšīn* or *perīšayā*, another Aramaic word which means "separated." We may add that the "oral traditions" which characterize the Pharisees appear with Nehemiah: he has the Book of Moses read in Jerusalem before the returnees from exile, something which seems to be new for them (Neh 8:13–18). Later, another portion of the book is

discovered, but it gives credit to an action which does not correspond
to its plain meaning (Neh 13:1–3).

To sum up, the *asidaioi* can be called proto-Pharisees, which is
generally recognized, but with two precisions: first, they must be connected with the Babylonian Jewish culture, a feature which runs till
the publication of the Mishnah several centuries later. Second, they do
not have any identifiable relationship with the Essenes.

4. Essenes and Sadducees

The first observation to be made is that the terminology around the
schools is confusing. The Essenes are certainly very pious people, and
Philo qualifies them with the word which renders *ḥasīdīm* in the LXX,
as stated above. The members are called "sons of Zadok" in the DSS
documents, a phrase which could hint at the Sadducees. Incidentally,
the word *perušīm* "separated" qualifies the people of 4QMMT C 9 in
a positive way ("We are separated from most of the people"); on the
contrary, in *t. Ber.* 3:25, the same word is used negatively for sectarians
(*mīnīm*). This suggests that the names of the schools were first nicknames
given from outside.

In order to compare the Essenes and the Sadducees, which look quite
different, this section will look for a common denominator.

4.1. *The Sadducees as reformers*

To clear up the ground, some preliminary remarks are appropriate. First,
the Sadducees cannot be defined as the heirs of an ancient legitimist
Zadokite party, which never existed. Second, Josephus presents the Sadducees as rejecting the oral traditions of the Pharisees and demanding
that all the Jewish way of life be founded upon Scripture only, but he
never says that the Pharisees have added anything to the Sadducean
doctrines. Third, Josephus dislikes the Sadducees and suggests that they
were Epicurians (*Ant.* 10.218; 13.173); later rabbinic tradition holds
the same biased approach and states that they are apostates, hence the
common misleading view that they were a kind of hellenized party.[24]

---

[24] But the Qaraites, a reform movement demanding a return back to Scripture and
aware of rabbinic sources, understood themselves as following the Sadducees, a purely
Jewish school, see Le Moyne, *Les Sadducéens*, 137–38.

Fourth, the mention of the Sadducees as the party close to the high priest in Acts 5:17 is misleading,[25] too, for the high priest named here in the Western text and in the context as the head of a very strange court (Acts 4:5–6) is Annas or Ananos. Now, Josephus tells us that the only high priest who belonged to the school of the Sadducees was Ananos II (*Ant.* 20:199–200), son of Ananos I who was removed after Augustus' death (*Ant.* 18.34). A literary analysis of chs. 4–7 indicates that something of the Ananos II story, a prominent Sadducee who convened a Sanhedrin to have James stoned, has been introduced in the book of Acts to stress the official Jewish refusal of the preaching of the disciples.[26]

The Sadducees are first mentioned, at least under this name, during the reign of King Alexander Jannaeus, when he was rejected as high priest, if we take into account the reassessment of John Hyrcanus' banquet discussed above. Their name involves one Zadok, for which we have two clues which may be the same one. First, it may depend on the very verse Ezek 44:15 used by the Essenes to define the faithful Israelites. Second, a parallel can be drawn between King Solomon and Jannaeus, for Solomon acted as high priest (1 Kgs 8:62–66), although he was not of Aaronide stock, and the then high priest Zadok, who was devoid of any clear Aaronide pedigree, did not object. The parallelism was felt, for Josephus reports, on one hand, that Jannaeus placed a wooden barrier around the altar to prevent the access of the people who did not accept him as high priest (*Ant.* 13.373). On the other hand, Josephus has added to his paraphrase of the first Temple building the non-biblical detail that Solomon surrounded the precinct with a parapet "called *geision* in the native tongue and *thrinkos* by the Greeks," in order to keep the multitude from entering (*Ant.* 8.95). The Aramaic and Greek words point to a much later device. In other words, there was a tradition stating that Jannaeus' barrier was just the restoration of an ancient feature of the Temple.

As for the Sadduccees' requirement that everything should depend on Scripture (*Ant.* 13.297), Josephus says that they "reckon as a virtue to dispute with the teachers of the path of wisdom that they pursue" (*Ant.* 18.16). This can be understood very simply if this "virtue" is to

---

[25] J. Jeremias, *Jerusalem in the Time of Jesus: An Investigation into Economic and Social Conditions during the New Testament Period* (London: SCM Press, 1969), 309–11.

[26] See J. Taylor, *Les Actes des deux apôtres* (EB, NS 41; Paris: Gabalda, 2000), 4:151–52.

check that every teaching is clearly connected with a verse and to sift accordingly. This attitude was later sported by R. Aqiba, the main character of the early rabbinic tradition, who was afraid to have "two Torahs," one written and one oral, and strove to keep both in connection with the help of hermeneutic rules (see *b. Zebaḥ.* 13a).

The Sadducees' major interest for Scripture can be put in a particular context, for there were signs of a renewal of its authority during the last two centuries B.C.E. Here are some significant literary facts. According to 2 Macc 5:21–22, Antiochus IV appointed officials "to maltreat our race: Philip at Jerusalem... and Andronicus at Mount Gerizim"; and later he sent other people to defile the two Temples (6:2). If indeed Jews and Samaritans are viewed as one nation, these remarkable statements, found in a book of Babylonian flavor which mentions the feast of Purim (2 Macc 15:36) and is quite uninterested in a Jewish state, elicit two questions. What was for the author the authority of Deuteronomy, which requires only one shrine? If the final split between the Jews and Samaritans occurred after the Maccabean crisis (under John Hyrcanus, who destroyed the Gerizim Temple), how can we explain the reduced Samaritan Bible, which includes only the Pentateuch and a shorter form of Joshua?

To deal with these issues would lead far beyond the scope of this paper, but we may add another set of questions. Nehemiah is known by Sir 49:13 and Josephus (*Ant.* 11.159–183) as the indefatigable builder of the Jerusalem walls. Both ignore the passages cited above on the discovery of Scripture in Jerusalem by the returnees from exile. Thus, we may wonder what is the origin of these chapters, which pose insuperable chronological problems. Incidentally, we may note that Philo ignores entirely the historical books, from Joshua through 2 Chronicles. We cannot conclude that they were not extant in his time, for he uses the Psalms, which depend largely on them. For him, these books were simply devoid of any authority.

To sum up, it makes sense to consider that the authority of Scripture grew in Judea by the time of the Hasmonean state and that a school took shape around it.

4.2. *About the Essenes*

Josephus describes the Essenes as a network of communities of co-opted members sharing everything. Besides their beliefs and their Pythagorean likeness (*Ant.* 15.371), which may or may not be accurate,[27] these features have nothing to do with biblical tradition, which always speaks of a people or of tribes with a clear genealogical definition, but do have something in common with various Greek or Hellenistic structured groups of volunteers. The connection of the Essenes with the site of Qumran, among other places, is provided by a short description of Pliny the Elder (*Nat.* 5.15.73), who speaks of a large crowd of *Esseni.* This may refer to pilgrimage congregations, for otherwise they are much involved in the farming of the land of Israel and to the religious duties attached to its produce.

Josephus' description may be inaccurate or biased, for some of the Qumran documents recognize a kind of private property (1QS) or do not imply strict community life (CD). But by all account we cannot underestimate the centrality of Scripture for them and especially of Deuteronomy. Josephus says that for them the blasphemy of God and the blasphemy of Moses (i.e., the Law) are at the same level (*B.J.* 2.145). They deserve the title of "sons of Zadok" by their righteousness and purity.

The fact that Philo knew and appreciated them, while he never mentions the other schools, is instructive in many respects. He knows that they live in "Syria-Palestina" and that agriculture is their chief occupation (*Quod omnis probus* 75). He defines them as excellent worshippers of God, using the word *therapeutai*. In another treatise (*De vita contemplativa*),[28] Philo describes other groups called *therapeutai*, who live in the desert, especially around Alexandria, but also elsewhere in the world. He was unsure about the etymology of their name, which he explained as meaning either physicians of souls or servants of God, which means that by his time the origins of the Therapeutae were already lost in the past.

There are striking similarities between them and the Essenes, together with dissimilarities. Two of the latter are of special interest here. First, the Therapeutae are contemplative, while the Essenes lead an active life; this should be connected with agriculture, which has a religious meaning in the land of Israel only, as stated in Deut 26:1–11. Second, the Therapeutae abstain from meat and wine, unlike the Essenes. Besides

---

[27] See J.J. Taylor, *Pythagoreans and Essenes: Structural Parallels* (Leuven: Peeters, 2004).
[28] See Schürer, *The History of the Jewish People*, 2:593–97.

ascetism in a Greek way, this may have a Jewish or biblical meaning
quite close to the difference between both schools about agriculture.

According to Josh 5:2–12, the Israelites, upon entering the Promised
Land, renewed the Covenant (circumcision), celebrated Passover as
prescribed in Exod 13:5, and began to eat the produce of the land.
The most typical items of this produce, in connection with several
Pentecosts that both the Essenes and the Therapeutae had, are bread,
wine, and oil. Thus, the abstinence of flesh and wine indicates that
the Therapeutae did not eat the paschal lamb and saw themselves
outside the Land of Israel. Incidentally, we may note that according
to the Slavonic version of Josephus' *War*, a wild man named John the
Baptist in the Gospels was staying beyond the Jordan river, close to the
Promised Land but a little outside, and accordingly would not celebrate
Passover and would not eat bread nor drink wine, i.e., abstained from
the produce of the Land.[29]

Now, since it is admitted that Essenes and Therapeutae share a
common origin,[30] we may venture a simple hypothesis based on the
fact the Therapeutae are older (Philo) and the Essenes quite recent
(Josephus). It is convenient to isolate three steps.

First, around the time of the Maccabean crisis, Josephus tells us that
one Onias fled to Egypt. Then he built a little Jerusalem—with the
famous Onias temple—in order to bring some unity among a multitude
of Jewish shrines, for there were disagreements about the cult (*Ant.*
13.65–66). We can imagine that some Therapeutae, with some Greek
features, were among this multiplicity.

Second, some of these Therapeutae reached the Promised Land,
or more accurately the Hasmonean state. If they followed the path of
the biblical sons of Israel, as Theudas wanted to do much later (*Ant.*
20.97–99), they crossed the Jordan around Jericho. Now we can imagine
that they found in Qumran a convenient place to celebrate Joshua's
Passover, hence later pilgrimages in the same area. This would provide
a chronological clue, somewhere in the first century B.C.E.

Third, a junction existed with the Sadducees, the local sons of Zadok,
who did not lose some relationship with Babylonian Jewry. As a result,

---

[29] See H. and K. Leeming, *Josephus'* Jewish War *and Its Slavonic Version: A Synoptic
Comparison* (Leiden: Brill, 2003), 259 (after *B.J.* 2.168).
[30] See M. Simon, *Les sectes juives au temps de Jésus* (Mythes et religions 40; Paris: PUF,
1960), 105–13; F. Daumas and P. Miquel, *De vita contemplativa* (Œuvres de Philon 20;
Paris: Le Cerf, 1963), 57.

their way of life underwent some changes (agriculture, language), but they kept some Greek community features. And they became Essenes, the most recent school according to Josephus. Incidentally, no Qumran sectarian manuscript can be dated before the 1st century B.C.E.

This way, the best explanation of the very name "Essenes" should be an aramaization of "Therapeutai." Indeed, there is an Aramaic root which fits perfectly, *'asé* "physician, wonderworker."[31] The two plural forms *'asén* and *'asayā* reasonably match the two Greek forms *essenos* and *essaios*.

As for the Essene seer who made a prophecy about King Aristobulus' brother (*B.J.* 1.78–80), somewhat before the appearance of the Sadducees, it suffices to consider that he was a Therapeutes, for whom Josephus used spontaneously the Aramaic equivalent.

In conclusion, the difference between Essenes and *asidaioi* is the same as between Alexandria and Babylonia.

---

[31] This was the suggestion G. Vermes, "The Etymology of 'Essenes,'" *RevQ* 2/7 (1960): 427–43.

MEMORIA COLECTIVA E IDENTIDAD DE GRUPO EN QUMRÁN

Jaime Vázquez Allegue

Memoria social, memoria colectiva, memorial cultural

El estudio de las ciencias sociales aplicado a la investigación bíblica y extrabíblica está dando lugar a una nueva lectura en interpretación de la literatura antigua. Los diferentes acercamientos y métodos de análisis aportan luz a los documentos desde distintas ópticas y categorías.[1] Uno de ellos, relacionado con la antropología cultural y la sociología del momento histórico concreto es el que podíamos llamar acercamiento metodológico de la "memorial social".[2]

La memoria individual recuerda los acontecimientos personales del pasado. La suma de muchas memorias individuales de una misma colectividad suele dar lugar a una de las visiones más objetivas de la historia que se puede realizar como alternativa a la recreación particular y subjetiva que suelen hacer los historiadores a título personal. Sacar a la luz la memoria equivale a recordar el pasado o un momento determinado de lo que sucedió. Los psicólogos trabajan con la memoria como una de las formas más profundas de conocer la personalidad de un sujeto o de una comunidad. En la memoria encontramos los principios y las razones que justifican una forma de actuar o una forma de ser. Pero recurrir a la memoria no es algo nuevo ni pertenece al mundo de la psicología moderna. Ya en la antigüedad, griegos y romanos utilizaban la memoria como un observatorio para comprender el presente. Además, el uso de la memoria permite aprender y recordar fórmulas, frases o fórmulas literarias como discursos, poesía o cualquier otro recurso de expresión pública. La memoria era el instrumento principal de la retórica clásica. Los filósofos también utilizaban la memoria como causa objetiva de reflexión sobre el pasado y explicación del

---

[1] Cf. D.C. Duling, "Social Memory and Biblical Studies: Theory, Method, and Application", *BTB* 36 (2006): 1–4.

[2] Cf. J.J. Climo y M.G. Cattell, *Social Memory and History: Anthropological Perspectives* (Walnut Creek, Calif.: AltaMira Press, 2002).

presente. La memoria tiene su epicentro en el cerebro humano. Ahí es en donde ejerce toda su dimensión de recreación y desarrolla si misión. Lo contrario a la memoria lo encontramos en la amnesia, el olvido y la demencia como tres elementos vinculados al complejo desarrollo cerebral. En la actualidad, la memoria es uno de los principales elementos relacionados con las terapias de recuperación emocional. Los estudios más recientes han puesto de manifiesto que el acto de recordar a través de la memoria es un ejercicio de interpretación de acontecimientos del pasado que vuelven al cerebro para ser revisados desde perspectivas diferentes. La memoria nunca recuerda un acontecimiento de la misma manera sino que cada vez que el cerebro trae a la memoria un hecho lo hace desde una perspectiva o motivación diferente. Es como ver la contemplación de un cuadro desde ángulos diferentes cada uno de los cuales ofrece una perspectiva distinta sobre la misma obra. En este sentido, la recuperación es un ejercicio que se hace sobre el pasado para proyectarlo en el presente.

La suma de memorias personales o individuales sobre un mismo acontecimiento permite ver el pasado desde los más variados planos y puntos de vista. La suma de estas visiones permite al analista establecer una reconstrucción de los acontecimientos memorizados con mucho mayor rigor y objetividad, la objetividad que resulta de la suma de visiones subjetivas de un hecho. A esta suma de memorias individuales es a la que llamamos "memoria colectiva" o "memoria social" y que es aplicada a grupos y colectivos con elementos comunes o características similares. La memoria colectiva o social desarrolla un elemento que crea conciencia de grupo que es lo que los sociólogos llaman "memorial cultural". La memorial colectiva afecta a grupos más reducidos con elementos comunes. La memoria cultural proviene de colectividades más grandes o numerosas. En un grupo como el de los hombres de Qumrán, la memoria colectiva es en algún sentido también memorial cultural, pero es, sobre todo, memorial colectiva, resultado de la expresión sobre el pasado manifestada a través de los escritos que el grupo hace sobre si mismo.

Memoria colectiva en Qumrán

La fórmula metodológica de la antropología cultural y las ciencias no sociales llega a los manuscritos del Mar Muerto de una forma particular. Aunque tenemos que reconocer que el acercamiento metodológico tiene su origen en el estudio de la literatura cristiana primitiva y el Nuevo Testamento, no podemos negar que en los manuscritos de Qumrán adquiere una razón de ser mucho más evidente y definitiva. Si hay una literatura antigua que tiene como referente principal la memoria esa es la que surge en la biblioteca de Qumrán. Por esa razón, una buena parte de las más recientes publicaciones sobre los manuscritos del Mar Muerto recurren al acercamiento metodológico como válido para emitir novedades sobre lo que los textos dicen sobre sí mismos y sus autores.[3]

En Qumrán, como en la tradición bíblica, la memoria se convirtió en un baluarte para mantener viva la tradición a través de la transmisión oral de la propia identidad.[4] Los autores de los textos de Qumrán recurren a la memoria para recrear tradiciones de la Biblia hebrea y, al mismo tiempo, interpretarla. La memoria colectiva es, en este sentido, un instrumento de interpretación que nace en el exilio babilónico y encuentra en la redacción de los últimos libros de la Biblia hebrea su mayor esplendor.[5] Qumrán no sólo no es ajeno a este proceso sino que lo convierte en método de trabajo. La memoria colectiva en Qumrán es el recuerdo del pasado que tiene su punto de partida en las tradiciones bíblicas más antiguas y su último eslabón en los últimos acontecimientos vividos por el judaísmo en la época del Segundo Templo, primero en el momento en el que el movimiento esenio decide separarse del judaísmo mayoritario y segundo en el instante en el que surge el grupo de Qumrán como una escisión del movimiento esenio. Desde este punto de vista, la figura del Maestro de Justicia es, para los hombres de Qumrán, el representante de esa memoria colectiva como el garante autorizado de la visión del pasado.[6]

---

[3] Veánse los resúmenes y futura publicación del *Tenth Annual International Orion Symposium. New Perspectives on Old Texts. January 9–11, 2005.* De manera especial las siguientes aportaciones: D. Mendels, "Societies of Memory in Antiquity"; L.T. Stuckenbruck, "The Legacy of the Teacher of Righteousness and the Dead Sea Scrolls"; L. Schiffman, "Memory and Manuscript: Books, Scrolls and the Tradition of the Dead Sea Scrolls"; Y.Z. Eliav, "Rabbis Remembering their Past: The Case of the Temple Mount".

[4] Cf. J.D. Crossan, "Memory and Orality", en *The Birth of Christianity. Discovering What Happened in the Years Immediately after the Execution of Jesus* (San Francisco: Harper San Francisco, 1998), 2:45–89.

[5] Cf. M.I. Aguilar, "Rethinking the Judean Past: Questions of History and a Social Archaeology of Memory in the First Book of the Maccabees", *BTB* 30 (2000): 58–67. Del mismo autor: "The Archaeology of Memory and the Issue of Colonialism: Mimesis and the Controversial Tribute to Caesar in Mark 12:13–17", *BTB* 35 (2005): 60–66.

[6] "However, the way of remembering and characterising people and events shows that this inheritance was claimed by them in a new way. In their recollection of the

Para los hombres de Qumrán, la memoria colectiva comienza con la mirada a sus propias tradiciones desde la nueva situación de desierto en la que se encuentran. La opción por retirarse al desierto obligó a los miembros de la comunidad a hacer una nueva lectura de momentos destacados de la historia de Israel relacionados con el desierto, el exilio y el contacto directo con Dios. La imagen del Éxodo y el pacto de la alianza con Dios se mantiene en la memoria de los textos de Qumrán reflejando la mentalidad de los que componían el grupo. La comunidad estaba convencida de ser el nuevo pueblo elegido por Dios. Ellos se sentían llamados a renovar la alianza de Moisés de ahí que considerasen que su grupo era el pueblo de la nueva alianza o de la alianza renovada. El pacto o la alianza está dirigida directamente a Dios ya que es con Dios con quien se realiza el pacto. Así, en el *Documento de Damasco* leemos: *Pero Dios recordó la alianza de los primeros y suscitó de Aarón hombres de conocimiento, y de Israel hombres sabios, y les hizo escuchar* (CD-A VI 2–3a).[7] Aquí es en donde la memoria colectiva entra en juego para imaginar lo que pudo ser el pasado y proyectarlo sobre el presente y sobre la situación en la que se encuentran.

La memoria de las fiestas (el calendario)

Con toda seguridad, una de las motivaciones que llevaron a los hombres de Qumrán a retirarse al desierto fue el problema del calendario y, en consecuencia, la celebración de las fiestas de la tradición bíblica. Esta situación llevó a los autores de los textos a insistir en el recuerdo a las celebraciones establecidas como obligación y cumplimiento en fidelidad a Dios.[8] Así, por ejemplo, en la colección de ordenanzas leemos: *[...] en el día del sábado... [...] sin contar los sábados [...] [...] para celebrar el*

---

past they applied two strategies, which resulted in a redefinition of the Israelite collective memory. On the one hand, they selected people and events, ignoring an important part of the memory (especially that associated with Jerusalem: priests, kings, etc.). And on the other hand, they re-defined figures and events of the past giving prominence to the some aspects (Abraham in the heavenly banquet; the persecuted prophets; Abel as a prophet)". S. Guijarro, "Social Memory and Group Identity in Q", *International Meeting of the Context Group "Early Christian Writings in Context", June 28–July 2* (Salamanca: Universidad Pontificia de Salamanca, 2006, en prensa).

[7] Para la versión española de los textos de Qumrán, seguimos la traducción de F. García Martínez, *Textos de Qumrán* (Madrid: Trotta, 1992).

[8] Para los hombres de Qumrán el texto de Deuteronomio no ofrece duda: *Guárdate de olvidar a Yahveh tu Dios descuidando los mandamientos, normas y preceptos que yo te prescribo hoy* (Dt 8,11).

recuerdo de [...] el error de la ceguera (4Q513 3 4). En el documento legal de la *Regla de la Comunidad* se establece la normativa de cumplimiento de las tradiciones relativas a la celebración de las fiestas y el calendario a través de la memoria colectiva o memoria de la comunidad para conservar la fidelidad a Dios. El prólogo del *Serek* utiliza en distintas ocasiones, una serie de expresiones que aluden a un problema que se convirtió en una de las razones que llevaron a la ruptura de los hombres de Qumrán con el judaísmo oficial de Jerusalén y, probablemente, con el mismo movimiento esenio: *Las cosas reveladas sobre los tiempos fijados de sus testimonios* (1QS I 9); *No se apartarán de ninguno de todos los mandatos de Dios sobre sus tiempos* (1QS I 13–14); *No adelantarán sus tiempos ni retrasarán ninguna de sus fiestas* (1QS I 14–15). El problema del cambio de las fiestas sagradas y la modificación del calendario se convirtió, para aquellos hombres, en un tema vital y trascendente que nosotros, a estas alturas y a la luz de lo dicho anteriormente sobre la cuestión, consideramos un tema teológico de primera fila.[9]

El calendario y el cumplimiento de la fiestas es una garantía visible del cumplimiento de los preceptos normativos de la legislación mosaica. Los hombres de Qumrán mantienen su fidelidad a Dios cumpliendo la Ley a través de la realización de sus preceptos, con el cumplimiento de las normas de tipo cultual y litúrgico (celebración de las fiestas, calendario sagrado...) y por medio de la pureza (ritos y fórmulas de purificación). Todo ello como manifestación de la memoria colectiva, como representación del recuerdo de las tradiciones y su puesta en práctica. En la mentalidad de los hombres de Qumrán, las fiestas y el calendario son fijados por Dios porque Él es el señor del tiempo y de la historia. Por esa razón su cumplimiento y realización sólo se puede realizar haciendo un ejercicio de memorial colectiva que ayude a la comunidad a ofrecer una respuesta fiel a los mandamientos divinos. El calendario fijado por los hombres de Qumrán pretendía ser el estable-cido por la legislación bíblica.[10] "La gran ventaja de este calendario es

---

[9] El calendario de los hombres de Qumrán, de origen sacerdotal, se oponía al calendario lunar aceptado por el judaísmo mayoritario de Jerusalén, y hacía que todas las fiestas se celebrasen un día fijo de la semana manteniendo absoluta fidelidad a las dataciones festivas establecidas en la tradición bíblica. la memorial colectiva, en este sentido, trataba de recuperar el recuerdo de las celebraciones en las fechas señaladas y no en otras.

[10] Recuperar la memoria colectiva era recuperar el calendario. Ese intento no era exclusivo de los hombres de Qumrán. La memoria en favor del calendario la encon-tramos en textos como *Jub* 6,29–33; *1Henoc* 74,11–12; 82,11–18. Sin embargo, son

su regularidad y precisión, que hace de él un útil ideal para el empleo litúrgico: cada estación y cada año comienzan de nuevo en el mismo día de la semana (en miércoles, el día de la creación de las lumbreras celestes), cada sábado cae siempre en la misma fecha y cada fiesta tiene una fecha fija dentro del año, que además no puede coincidir nunca con un sábado".[11]

La memoria colectiva con respecto al calendario para los hombres de Qumrán consiste en celebrar las fiestas siguiendo el orden bíblico y de la tradición. De esta forma, la memoria se convierte en un aliado de la ley en favor de la fidelidad del grupo a las tradiciones más antiguas.[12] Algo parecido sucede con otros aspectos ajenos al problema del calendario y la celebración de las fiestas. Cuestiones relativas a la visión del pasado desde la perspectiva de la memoria y el recuerdo de la comunidad. En realidad, la memoria colectiva de la comunidad además de acercarse a la visión más objetiva de la tradición permite descubrir los elementos subjetivos que configuran la propia historia de un grupo.[13]

EL RECUERDO DEL TEMPLO

Para los hombres de Qumrán, la ruptura con el Templo de Jerusalén y con las instituciones judías tuvo que ser un paso difícil de dar. Los textos de Qumrán ponen de manifiesto de forma reiterada la imagen del Templo a la que otorgan una nueva categoría. En cierto sentido, los hombres de Qumrán se adelantan a los acontecimientos históricos creando una comunidad sin Templo cuando todavía el Templo como lugar sagrado tiene su escenario en Jerusalén, como la que el judaísmo tendrá que asumir tras la destrucción del edificio por parte de los

---

estos hombres retirados al desierto los que sabemos con seguridad que lo pusieron en práctica. El calendario y el debate sobre los días de las fiestas mantenían un trasfondo apocalíptico en el que confluía el recuerdo del elemento puramente celebrativo y festivo de una fecha señalada con ese sentimiento apocalíptico de esperanza mesiánica y del final de los tiempos en el que el calendario jugaba el papel más destacado. La memoria colectiva es, en este caso, una mirada al pasado que se vive en el presente apuntando hacia el futuro.

[11] F. García Martínez, "Calendarios en Qumrán (I)", *EstBíb* 54 (1996): 331.

[12] Para una mirada al pasado en forma de recuerdo o memorial véase el trabajo de J. Blenkinsopp, "Memory, Tradition and the Constructions of the Past in Ancient Israel", *BTB* 27 (1997): 76–82.

[13] Cf. F. García Martínez, "La memoria inventada: el «otro» en los manuscritos de Qumrán", en *Congreso Internacional "Biblia, Memoria Histórica y Encrucijada de Culturas"* (ed. J. Campos y V. Pastor; Zamora: Asociación Bíblica Española, 2004), 49–71.

romanos. Digamos que el grupo de Qumrán no sólo se adelanta a la vivencia de un judaísmo sin Templo, sino que se convierte en referente para el judaísmo que sobrevive a la destrucción del lugar sagrado.

La memoria colectiva de los hombres de Qumrán establece un criterio definitivo sobre el Templo bajo una nueva perspectiva. La ausencia del recinto convierte en obsesión a los hombres de Qumrán, la existencia permanente de un nuevo Templo que proyectan en la propia comunidad. La memoria colectiva es, de esta forma, un baluarte incuestionable para traducir la sacralidad del espacio físico al nuevo espacio comunitario. El resultado de esta doble vertiente deriva en una convulsión comunitaria obsesionada con la ritualidad, la pureza, los gestos litúrgicos y la compleja jerarquía de la comunidad.

Esta situación de obsesión compulsiva en los hombres de Qumrán es mitigada por la propia memorial colectiva, la memoria de la historia pasada, el refugio de las tradiciones y el recuerdo de la propia identidad. De esta forma, los hombres de Qumrán recrean dos situaciones históricas que perfilan como modelo de conducta y recuerdo del pasado. La primera es la que se remonta a la historia de presencia de Israel en el desierto. Las tradiciones del éxodo son para los hombres de Qumrán un reflejo en el pasado, una forma de salvaguardar la situación en la que se encuentran en donde por un lado carecen de Templo, como en el éxodo y, por otro, se encuentran en el desierto de Judá, escenario que convierten paralelo al del éxodo por el desierto del Sinaí. La segunda tiene que ver con el exilio de Babilonia, en donde los hombres de Qumrán vuelven a verse reflejados como en un espejo en el que la ausencia de Templo como recinto sagrado vuelve a ser una característica destacada. Con estos dos razonamientos históricos, los hombres de Qumrán demuestran que el judaísmo no tiene porqué estar vinculado irremediablemente a un lugar específico ni a un edificio concreto. En cierto sentido podemos decir que los hombres de Qumrán son unos reformadores de la causa judía con alegaciones propias a la identidad de la propia tradición. En las experiencias de un judaísmo sin Templo, la sensación de transitoriedad se convierte en uno de los ideales que configuran el pensamiento y la propia memoria colectiva como grupo. A la luz de los relatos del Éxodo, los israelitas caminan hacia la tierra prometida convencidos de la temporalidad o transitoriedad de su situación. Para los israelitas que viven el exilio de Babilonia, su situación es pasajera y temporal, a la espera de una pronta liberación y regreso a la ciudad santa. Para los hombres de Qumrán, la transitoriedad se vuelve escatológica con la esperanza de la llegada del final de los tiempos y la recepción de un nuevo Templo situado en una categoría distinta y a la vez distante. Para los hombres de Qumrán, la memoria entresacada de la tradición y de la propia historia sirve como disculpa para convertir una ausencia, la del Templo, en una presencia permanente que ve en la comunidad una dimensión nueva del escenario sagrado.

Resimbolización en Qumrán

Hemos visto dos ejemplos que determinan la forma de actuar de los hombres de Qumrán. Por un lado el problema del calendario visto desde la perspectiva de la memoria colectiva que lleva a la comunidad a rechazar el calendario oficial de las autoridades religiosas de Jerusalén. Por otro lado, ya en el desierto, el recuerdo en forma de memorial del Templo de la capital convertido ahora en una consagración sin lugar sagrado ya que su nueva concepción de vida ve en la memoria colectiva, en la memoria de la comunidad, la experiencia de Dios desde su concepción de pueblo elegido aún cuando no había Templo, cuando vivía como pueblo itinerante por el desierto. Estos dos ejemplos ponen de manifiesto cómo la memoria colectiva se convierte en determinante de la forma de proceder de todo el grupo. La revisión del pasado desde la perspectiva del presente que afronta la comunidad tiene una consecuencia ineludible, la resimbolización de los elementos que en pasado constituyeron la esencia del culto y los ritos sagrados.

La resimbolización que hacen los hombres de Qumrán consiste, sobre todo, en otorgar a la simbología tradicional una nueva clave de interpretación. Como tales, los símbolos tenían que ser interpretados para dar sentido a su existencia. La nueva situación en la que se encuentra la comunidad hace que los símbolos de antes sean ahora vistos de otra manera y, por tanto, revisados. El ejemplo más claro de la resimbolización realizada en Qumrán la encontramos en el sentido de los sacrificios y en la ausencia del Templo. La comunidad de Qumrán está convencida de vivir en los últimos del fin, en los *últimos días*, en el último período de la historia, en esos últimos tiempos que ya han comenzado pero cuya consumación aún se espera. Esta aguda conciencia apocalíptica permitió a la comunidad realizar las innovaciones teológicas más sorprendentes desde la memoria colectiva del pasado. La memoria colectiva permite a los miembros de la comunidad sustituir el culto sacrificial del Templo profanado, en la espera de la restauración definitiva, por "la ofrenda de los labios", reemplazando con la oración los sacrificios sangrientos. En la misma memoria colectiva de la comunidad encontramos la comunión con la liturgia angélica. También en la memorial colectiva descubrimos que los ángeles se hallan presentes en su medio, y de exigir por consiguiente a todos sus miembros un nivel de pureza angélica.

La memoria colectiva bien podría ser interpretada a través de la idea de la purificación de los conocimientos (1QS I 12).[14] Una purificación que ha de realizarse a la luz del recuerdo y cumplimiento de los preceptos de Dios. De esa manera, la liturgia manifestada a través de los ritos de purificación, los calendarios y la celebración de las fiestas sagradas nos pone ante el talante ritual y celebrativo del grupo como comunidad orante. La comunidad necesita un proceso de purificación y eso exige un tiempo de adaptación, de conversión, de vivencia y de sacrificio en lo que los textos definen como período de prueba (4Q 177).

La resimbolización en Qumrán es una estrategia de supervivencia. Una revisión del pasado a través de la memoria que convierte a elementos vitales para la tradición como el Templo, los sacrificios, ritos, fórmulas litúrgicas, en símbolos que adquieren un nuevo significado. La resimbolización efectuada en Qumrán es progresiva, las diferentes etapas redaccionales de algunos textos, sobre los de carácter legal y normativo confirman una evolución que va configurando este proceso de cambio de sentido y significado de signos y símbolos que recuperan su dimensión original y originaria. La resimbolización como proceso realizado en el grupo de Qumrán afecta a los rituales y el capital heredado y transmitido a través de la memoria colectiva que se posiciona frente a condiciones propias de una nueva existencia. La resimbolización no rechaza una nueva simbología sino que sobre la existente trata de recuperar su condición originaria purificandola de las influencias que a lo largo del tiempo han ido desvirtuando el verdadero significado de los símbolos. Este proceso de resimbolización en Qumrán puede ser contemplado como una deconstrucción de la propia historia. Así, por ejemplo, el desierto en donde se establecen los hombres de Qumrán vuelve a ser el escenario privilegiado para la resimbolización de la renovación de aquella alianza y ellos, sintiéndose grupo nuevamente elegido y llamado por Dios, se presentan ante la sociedad como el pueblo

---

[14] Cf. 1QS V 7.

capaz de volver a establecer el verdadero culto en sustitución del culto pervertido del Templo de Jerusalén en su nueva simbolización.[15]

Lo mismo sucede con las imágenes simbólicas leídas desde la nueva perspectiva de la resimbolización realizada desde la memoria colectiva que llevan a los hombres de Qumrán a hablar de una nueva Jerusalén o, de un nuevo Templo, desde una perspectiva escatológica. Así como otros muchos símbolos que cobran una nueva dimensión y ofrecen al miembro del grupo de Qumrán una visión diferente de la realidad, como la impureza en la que ha caído el Templo, las influencias helenistas en la organización del culto, la pérdida del valor de la clase sacerdotal, la celebración de las fiestas y el calendario, la supresión de los sacrificios, las esperanzas mesiánicas, la importancia de la pureza y de los baños rituales, razones todas ellas que determinaron la separación y ruptura del grupo con el judaísmo oficial de Jerusalén.

Como vemos, en la resimbolización que hacen los hombres de Qumrán sobre sus tradiciones se introducen elementos nuevos pero también se enfatizan otros. Por ejemplo, la literatura legal pone de manifiesto la fuerte insistencia en el ejercicio de la oración y de la piedad por parte de los componentes de la comunidad (1QS VIII 1–4). El hecho constitutivo de que la comunidad fuese un grupo religioso estaba en el gesto simbólico de la oración y la fidelidad a la Ley por encima de cualquier cosa y su resimbolización. Con este proceso, la oración en Qumrán adquiere un sentido más profundo y especial al ser ésta la que suple los sacrificios que se realizaban en el Templo.

Todo este proceso de resimbolización tiene en la memoria colectiva su referencia evidente. De esta forma, el cúmulo de memorias individuales permiten establecer el denominador común de la memoria colectiva. Así, la resimbolización debería ser un proceso objetivo. Sin embargo, al tratarse de elementos muy antiguos, propios de una tradición que ha ido modificando y adaptándolos a las diferentes circunstancias de la historia, la resimbolización que hacen los hombres de Qumrán, corre el riesgo de realizarse desde una única perspectiva y, por tanto, no ser tan objetiva.

---

[15] Cf. W. Kelber, "The Generative Force of Memory", *BTB* 36 (2006): 15–22.

MEMORIA LITERARIA EN LOS MANUSCRITOS

Con razón sostiene el profesor García Martínez, que "todo texto literario que se ha desarrollado durante un largo período de tiempo, muestra inevitablemente en las palabras que utiliza las huellas de los cambios ideológicos, sociológicos o de cualquier otro tipo, operados durante su desarrollo. Una de las maneras de percibir estos cambios es la de prestar la debida atención a las palabras que los textos utilizan y a aquellas que no emplean".[16] Estas palabras, aplicadas a vocablos que contienen un gran calado simbólico como puede ser el término "Israel" viven un proceso de desarrollo que llamamos evolución y que evidencian la historia literaria de su significado. Algo así como lo que entenderíamos hoy como memorial literaria del grupo de que la utiliza en sus escritos.

Los manuscritos del Mar Muerto son un buen testimonio de la evolución histórica de los símbolos que se recrean a través de la memoria colectiva de la comunidad. Las fiestas del calendario, el Templo (ejemplos que ya hemos visto), Israel con toda la carga de intenciones que encierra el vocablo, son algunos de los muchos aspectos literarios que cambian, se modifican o derivan en nuevas concepciones a la luz de la visión retrospectiva del pasado. Lo que en teoría decíamos de la resimbolización lo encontramos ahora en el momento en el que el grupo de Qumrán recupera términos antiguos de su propia historia que determinan su identidad pero que ahora la comunidad reinterpreta resimbolizándolos. En la comunidad de Qumrán, una buena parte de los vocablos, además de los significados que ya tenían, adquieren otros significados totalmente nuevos que sirven para definir y precisar la identidad del grupo. Esta característica es el resultado de la integración del vocablo en la identidad de la comunidad entrando a formar parte del lenguaje propio o especializado de su vocabulario. Así, en Qumrán, hablar del Templo ya no equivale a hacer una referencia al edificio con unas características determinadas situado en un lugar específico de la geografía de Jerusalén. El carácter novedoso que adquiere el término en el seno de la comunidad resulta de su visión del pasado y de su novedosa proyección hacia el futuro. El templo de Qumrán tiene una dimensión apocalíptica y escatológica a la vez que resulta de la combinación y adaptación de la memoria de la comunidad y

---

[16] García Martínez, "La memoria inventada", 50.

del nuevo lenguaje que se ha establecido como moda en la literatura apocalíptica del momento.

La memoria literaria que el grupo de Qumrán ejerce sobre su propio pasado refleja los momentos más críticos en donde el judaísmo vivió situaciones de opresión, deformación o cualquier otro tipo de depresión. La memoria literaria como la memoria colectiva o la memoria histórica lo que pretende es hacer una revisión—terminológica en este caso—para recuperar el sentido y significado original y primario de las ideas y conceptos literarios auténticos. Siempre, en todo proceso de liberación o recuperación de los derechos, los colectivos responden con un proceso de reivindicación de su propia memoria silenciada o manipulada durante un tiempo. En la mayoría de las ocasiones este tiempo es considerado perdido por lo que el grupo lo que pretende es retrotraerse en el pasado hasta alcanzar el momento de la desconexión para de esta forma recuperar la unión con el pasado original.[17]

MEMORIA DEL PASADO, PERSPECTIVA DE FUTURO

La memoria colectiva manifestada en la literatura de Qumrán no sólo refleja la importancia que tenía en la comunidad el recuerdo del pasado como una actividad personal y comunitaria, también era una garantía de fidelidad a las tradiciones y a Dios. Para los hombres de Qumrán, recuperar la memoria del pasado era asegurarse el futuro. Los textos reflejan el temor de la comunidad a desviarse de la tradición lo que justificaría la obsesión por el cumplimiento de los preceptos y mandatos divinos de forma escrupulosa. Sólo de esta forma los miembros del grupo podían vivir con la conciencia tranquila, sumergidos en la seguridad externa que produce el control de la vida a través de las normas, leyes y requisitos exigidos por las autoridades de la comunidad. Desde un punto de vista objetivo, la comunidad de Qumrán estaba formada por un grupo de hombres que hacían un compromiso en forma de opción de vida para someterse al dictamen de unas leyes y normas que garantizaban la buena regulación de la vida presente y aseguraban la participación en otra vida futura más allá de la muerte. La escatología de

---

[17] Sirva como ejemplo el trabajo de J. Assmann, "Cultural Memory: Script, Recollection, and Political Identity in Early Civilizations", *Historiography East and West* 1 (2003): 154–77. Del mismo autor véase: *Moses the Egyptian. The Memory of Egypt in Western Monotheism* (London: Harvard University Press, 1997).

Qumrán desarrolla nuevas perspectivas sobre la dimensión trascendental de una vida más allá de la terrena. La visión esperanzadora sobre el más allá une el carácter mesiánico, apocalíptico y escatológico de una buena parte de los grupos y movimientos del judaísmo de la época. Sin embargo y a diferencia de otros muchos grupos de corte escatológico como el mismo cristianismo naciente, el grupo de Qumrán mira hacia el futuro con los dos pies sobre el pasado. Aquí es en donde la memoria colectiva adquiere su razón de ser.

La memoria como recurso que garantiza la fidelidad a las tradiciones sirve, a la vez, como salvoconducto para lograr ese futuro metahistórico. A través de la memoria colectiva, cada miembro de la comunidad se siente protegido y seguro en todos sus actos. No necesita pensar o tomar decisiones para mantenerse fiel a Dios y a su propia identidad, lo único que necesita es cumplir las normas y preceptos que la memoria colectivo ha recuperado. Por otro lado, esta seguridad personal garantiza a quien cumple con la legalidad establecida el futuro anunciado desde la perspectiva escatológica de la comunidad. La memoria colectiva es el eslabón que une la literatura de los textos manuscritos con el pensamiento y la teología del grupo. De lo que se trata es de mirar al pasado desde el presente para asegurar el futuro. Esto es lo que hacen los miembros de la comunidad en el momento que asumen su compromiso de formar parte del grupo a través de los ritos y fórmulas de ingreso, lo que reafirman cada vez que se reúnen como grupo, lo que analizan los sectores con autoridad cuando juzgan a sus correligionarios. La memoria colectiva sirve como medio para obtener unos fines determinados que garantizan una estabilidad y aseguran el futuro.

El judaísmo de la época del segundo Templo vivía una situación de fragmentación muy definida. Una buena parte de las divisiones y enfrentamientos tenían su razón de ser en las expectativas de futuro que se cernían sobre cada grupo. La literatura apocalíptica surge ante la necesidad de proyectar sobre el futuro un signo de esperanza y, al mismo tiempo, orientar un presente lleno de dificultades, dudas e incertidumbre. El cristianismo fue uno de esos grupos de marcado contenido escatológico que orientaron toda su doctrina hacia el anuncio del Reino de los Cielos, el más allá, la resurrección, la vida eterna. Otros grupos, como los fariseos y los saduceos discrepaban sobre la existencia de otra vida después de la terrena. La apocalíptica literaria se volvió reflexión escatológica en la mayoría de las ocasiones. El cristianismo primitivo fue una confirmación de esta dimensión. Los manuscritos del Mar Muerto fueron otra visión escatológica de la vida que fundamentó su reflexión en la mirada al pasado a través de la memoria colectiva.

Hemos ido viendo algunos documentos representativos que ponen de manifiesto la importancia de la memoria colectiva en el grupo de Qumrán y en el movimiento esenio en un momento determinado de la historia en el que la memoria se convierte en un aliado de identidad y la fidelidad a las tradiciones heredadas de los antepasados. En este momento hacemos un recorrido por algunos de los textos en los que de manera explícita queda reflejada la necesidad de los hombres de Qumrán de recordar el pasado para vivir el presente y proyectarse en el futuro.[18]

(a) 4Q252 IV 2: "Tú serás la memoria de Amaleq". En una serie identificada como *Bendiciones Patriarcales* (4Q252)[19] o, también, como un comentario al Génesis,[20] que nos remiten a la literatura legal de la Biblia hebrea encontramos una referencia a la colección de prescripciones legales (Dt 21–25). En el texto de Qumrán leemos: "*Vacat* Y él dijo a Moisés: En los últimos días tú serás el memorial de Amaleq bajo los cielos. *Vacat*" (4Q252 IV 2). Un texto que recrea la lectura de Dt 25,19: "Así pues, cuando el Señor tu Dios te haga descansar de todos tus enemigos de alrededor, en el país que el Señor tu Dios te dará en herencia, serás bajo el cielo la memoria de Amaleq, no lo olvides". Este texto en la literatura de Qumrán, además de ser un recurso tomado de la literatura bíblica es, al mismo tiempo, una fórmula tipológica en la que se anuncia el precepto divino de ser la memoria, el recuerdo y el guardián de las tradiciones relacionadas de forma simbólica con Amaleq.[21]

(b) 4Q219 II 27: "Y tu nombre y tu memoria". En uno de los apócrifos más populares nos encontramos con la referencia en tono

---

[18] Véanse textos de la literatura de Qumrán en donde la forma verbal "recordar" es utilizada como recurso para mantener viva la memoria: CD I 4; 1QS VI 27; 1QM X 7.

[19] Así en García Martínez, *Textos de Qumrán*, 265.

[20] Así en F. García Martínez y E.J.C. Tigchelaar, *The Dead Sea Scrolls Study Edition* (Leiden: Brill, 1997), 1:500–505. Véase la edición oficial G. Brooke, *DJD* 22:185–207.

[21] Cf. Ex 17,8–16 y Núm 24,20.

amenazante del *Libro de los Jubileos* a los riesgos de la infidelidad y el alejamiento del cumplimiento de los preceptos divinos. El texto de Qumrán afirma: "Y tu nombre y tu memoria desaparecerán de toda la tierra" (4Q219 II 27).

(c) 4Q88 VII 14–15: "Que tu memoria sea bendecida por siempre". También la literatura poética en su colección de *Salmos Apócrifos* encontramos referencias a la memoria como el mejor elemento para mantener vivas las tradiciones y su cumplimiento. "[*Vacat.* Yo te re]cuerdo, [Sión,] para la bendición; te he amado [con todas mis fuerzas.] [¡Que tu recuerdo sea bendecido por siempre!]" (4Q88 VII 14–15; 11Q5 XXII 1–3),[22] en medio de los restos de un salmo de Sión, el autor alude a la memoria como la mejor fórmula para mantener vivos los momentos de mayor esplendor de la vida del Templo de Jerusalén.

(d) 1QM XIII 8: "En todos los decretos de tu gloria ha habido un recuerdo [de tu gracia]". En donde encontramos el término hebreo como sustantivo sinónimo del vocablo "memoria". En el texto del *Libro de la Guerra* encontramos una clara alusión a la memoria eterna como garantía de fidelidad a la alianza (1QM XIII 8).

De las muchas ocasiones en las que encontramos referencias a la "memoria" como recurso formal para mantener la fidelidad y para recuperar las tradiciones perdidas podemos concluir que el uso se convierte en abuso que pone de manifiesto el carácter obsesivo del grupo de Qumrán por interpretar el presente a la luz del pasado a través del ejercicio de la memoria colectiva.[23]

Conclusión

El estudio de los manuscritos del Mar Muerto ha estado relacionado con el mundo de la filología y exégesis bíblica desde su recuperación a lo largo de la segunda mitad del siglo XX. La interdisiplinariedad de los estudios de los textos de Qumrán ha sido una de las características más destacadas de los últimos cincuenta años. Durante este tiempo y a medida que avanzaba la identificación de los documentos la exégesis bíblica se iba acercando a los escritos para analizarlos desde distintas

---

[22] Así en F. García Martínez, *Textos de Qumrán* (Madrid: Trotta, 1992), 341.

[23] Cf. otros textos en donde la "memoria" como sustantivo contiene referencias colectivas al pasado como referente para el presente: CD XX 19; 1QS X 5; 1QM III 7; VII 13; XVI 4; XVIII 4; 1QHª IX 26.

perspectivas metodológicas y acercamientos más diversos. Hoy los estudios bíblicos abordan la literatura sagrada desde muchas y muy variadas perspectivas. La antropología cultural, uno de los acercamientos metodológicos ha desarrollado una variante formal que permite descubrir lo que dicen los textos de sí mismos y de su propio pasado. Así surgió la memoria colectiva como una mirada al pasado de la literatura misma. Esta aplicación a la literatura sagrada ha provocado múltiples descubrimientos y aportado novedades a la lectura clásica de los textos.[24]

La literatura de los manuscritos del Mar Muerto no puede quedar ajena a este proceso de revisión de la propia historia. Consideramos que los autores de los manuscritos de Qumrán habían desarrollado una sensibilidad especial a la hora de mirar al pasado y definir lo que hoy llamamos memoria colectiva o comunitaria. Por esta razón hemos querido asomarnos al grupo de hombres que redactó los manuscritos y a sus escritos para intentar descubrir la importancia que la memoria colectiva tenía en el contexto de la comunidad. Si los presupuestos iniciales eran obvios, los resultados se me antojan evidentes. El grupo de Qumrán tenía en la memoria el último y más importante bastión en su defensa de la propia identidad. Aquellos hombres convirtieron la mirada retrospectiva puesta en el pasado más lejano en la mejor disculpa para justificar su opción de vida y las razones que les llevaron a romper con el judaísmo. El recurso de la memoria no sólo justificaba sus actitudes sino que llevó en un momento determinado a provocar una obsesión sobre los miembros de la comunidad sobre todo lo que afectaba al mantenimiento de la fidelidad y el cumplimiento de los preceptos y mandatos de las tradiciones más antiguas. La lectura de los textos evidenciaba la mentalidad obsesiva de sus autores pero la interpretación de los textos a la luz de la memoria colectiva justifica esta obsesión como un recurso imprescindible, necesario y único para que la opción de vida tuviera sentido a lo largo de la vida de quienes pertenecieron al grupo.

---

[24] Estudios recientes sobre la memoria colectiva en los textos del Nuevo Testamento y en los primeros escritos cristianos: Aguilar, "The Archaeology of Memory"; P.F. Esler, "Paul's Contestation of Israel's (Ethnic) Memory of Abraham in Galatians 3", *BTB* 36 (2006): 23–34; A. Kirk y T. Thatcher, eds., *Memory, Tradition, and Text. Uses of the Past in Early Christianity* (Atlanta: Society of Biblical Literature, 2005); J.K. Olick, "Products, Processes, and Practices: a Non-Reificatory Approach to Collective Memory", *BTB* 36 (2006): 5–14.

"NOBODY DARED TO ADD TO THEM, TO TAKE FROM THEM, OR TO MAKE CHANGES" (JOSEPHUS, *AG. AP.* 1.42) THE TEXTUAL STANDARDIZATION OF JEWISH SCRIPTURES IN LIGHT OF THE DEAD SEA SCROLLS

Armin Lange

To contribute to a Festschrift for Florentino García Martínez is a special privilege as Florentino is not only a friend but also one of the most erudite scholars among the Dead Sea Scrolls specialists. In his extensive œuvre, Florentino worked not only on the non-biblical manuscripts from the Judean Desert but edited and studied also various biblical manuscripts.[1] Hence, an essay on the textual standardization of the Hebrew Bible is a fitting contribution to a Festschrift for Florentino García Martínez.[2]

In the early second century C.E., Josephus Flavius claims in his defense of Judaism *Against Apion*:

> [38] With us are not myriads of books which are at variance and contradict each other, but only twenty-two books, which contain the record of all times—being trusted rightly so... [42] for during so many ages as have already passed, nobody dared to add to them, to take from them, or to make changes. (Josephus, *Ag. Ap.* 1.38, 42)[3]

---

[1] See e.g., F. García Martínez, "Les manuscrits du désert de Juda et le Deutéronome," in *Studies in Deuteronomy in Honour of C.J. Labuschagne on the Occasion of His 65th Birthday* (ed. idem et al.; VTSup 53; Leiden: Brill, 1994), 63–82; idem and E.J.C. Tigchelaar, "Psalms Manuscripts from Qumran Cave 11: A Preliminary Edition," *RevQ* 17/65–68 (1996): 73–107; idem, E.J.C. Tigchelaar, and A.S. van der Woude, *DJD* 23:1–14, 29–205.

[2] Due to space restriction, the discussion of scholarly literature cannot be extensive. A history of research can be found in I. Young, "The Stabilization of the Biblical Text in Light of Qumran and Masada: A Challenge for Conventional Qumran Chronology?" *DSD* 9 (2002): 364–90 (365–70). A more extensive version of this article will be published in *From Qumran to Aleppo* (ed. J. Zsengellér et al.; FRLANT; Göttingen: Vandenhoeck & Ruprecht, forthcoming).

[3] Translation by Armin Lange.

When discussing the canonical history of the Hebrew Bible, scholars often refer to this text as a key reference.[4] What is mostly ignored is that Josephus emphasizes not only that the Jews have twenty-two holy books but also that their text was never changed. In *Ag. Ap.* 1.42, Josephus is making this claim of an unchangeable text of the Jewish scriptures by alluding to the so-called "canonical" formula of Deut 4:2 (cf. e.g. Deut 13:1; Eccl 3:14; Sir 18:6; 42:21) "You must neither add anything to what I command you nor take away anything from it, but keep the commandments of the Lord your God with which I am charging you" (NRSV).

The original intention of this phrase does not agree with its reading by Josephus. Far from emphasizing the canonicity of Deuteronomy, Deut 4:2 employs a phrase which is widespread in the ancient Near East and is also attested in ancient Greek treatises. By threatening divine retribution, these formulae try to achieve an unaltered textual transmission.[5] That texts like Deut 4:2 need to use formulations against textual alterations shows such alterations were the rule and not the exception in the ancient Near Eastern and ancient Greek societies. For Josephus, Deut 4:2 gains a new meaning. It applies not only to the law code of Deuteronomy but to the text of all twenty-two holy books of Judaism. And for Josephus, the formula of Deut 4:2 does not try to counteract textual alteration but claims unchanged textual character as a fact. It is the text of all twenty-two holy books that remained unchanged since they were written, i.e., Josephus argues that the Jewish holy books exist only in one standard text form from their very beginnings.

How does Josephus' claim of textual stringency relate to the textual transmission of the individual biblical books as attested by the Dead Sea Scrolls and other ancient manuscripts? The manuscript evidence from the Qumran library seems to argue not for one standard text but for textual plurality.[6] The three main medieval textual traditions

---

[4] See e.g., S. Mason, "Josephus on Canon and Scripture," in *From the Beginnings to the Middle Ages (Until 1300), Part 1: Antiquity* (vol. 1 of *Hebrew Bible/Old Testament: The History of Its Interpretation*; ed. M. Sæbø; Göttingen: Vandenhoeck & Ruprecht, 1996), 217–35 (with R. Kraft); P.R. Davies, *Scribes and Schools: The Canonization of Hebrew Scriptures* (Library of Ancient Israel; Louisville, Ky.: Westminster John Knox Press, 1998), 107–8, 178–79.

[5] Cf. e.g. M. Weinfeld, *Deuteronomy and the Deuteronomic School* (Oxford: Clarendon Press, 1972; repr. Winona Lake, Ind.: Eisenbrauns, 1992), 261–62; and A.C. Hagedorn, *Between Moses and Plato: Individual and Society in Deuteronomy and Ancient Greek Law* (FRLANT 204; Göttingen: Vandenhoeck & Ruprecht, 2004), 76–77.

[6] The system of categorizing the biblical manuscripts among the DSS which I use in this article was developed by Emanuel Tov, see e.g. "The Biblical Texts from the

of the Hebrew and Greek bibles have forerunners among the biblical manuscripts of the Qumran library.

1. THE BIBLICAL DEAD SEA SCROLLS[7]

Of the Greek biblical manuscripts from the Qumran library (7QpapLXXExod, 4QLXXLev[a, b], 4QLXXNum, 4QLXXDeut), 4QLXXLev[a, b] attest to the Old Greek translation of the Pentateuch, while 4QLXXNum represents an early recension of this text (see below).[8] The Hebrew *Vorlage* of the Old Greek is attested in 4QJer[b]. Furthermore, the supralinear correction in 4QGen[j] and 5QDeut correct their base texts towards the Hebrew *Vorlage* of the Old Greek. Other manuscripts show resemblance with the *Vorlage* of the Old Greek but need to be classified as non-aligned (4QExod[b], 4QLev[b], 11QLev[b], 4QSam[a, b]) or are almost equally close to the *Vorlage* of the Old Greek and the Samaritan Pentateuch (4QLev[d]). Of these, 4QSam[a, b] are the most interesting as their non-aligned texts seem to have developed out of the Hebrew *Vorlage* of the Old Greek of 1–2 Samuel.

In the case of the Pentateuch, two manuscripts attest to a text which lacks the ideological variants of the Samaritan Pentateuch but shares all other readings with it (4QpaleoExod[m], 4QNum[b]). They are therefore classified as pre-Samaritan. Of 4QGen[c], 4QGen[e], 4QGen[f], 4QGen[g], 4QGen[j], 4QLev[c], 4QLev[e], 4QDeut[d], 4QDeut[f], 4QDeut[i], 4QDeut[o], and

---

Judaean Desert: An Overview and Analysis of the Published Texts," in *The Bible as Book: The Hebrew Bible and the Judaean Desert Discoveries* (ed. E.D. Herbert and E. Tov; London: The British Library, 2002), 139–66; "The Biblical Texts in Ancient Synagogues in Light of Judean Desert Finds," *Meghillot* 1 (2003): 185–201, VIII–IX [Hebrew]; "The Text of the Hebrew/Aramaic and Greek Bible Used in the Ancient Synagogues," in *The Ancient Synagogue From Its Origins until 200 C.E.: Papers Presented at an International Conference at Lund University, October 14–17, 2001* (ed. B. Olsson and M. Zetterholm; ConBNT 39; Stockholm: Almqvist & Wiksell International, 2003), 237–59. To avoid any suggestion of group specific texts in ancient Judaism, I will use the terms semi-Masoretic and proto-Masoretic texts as opposed to Tov's proto-Rabbinic I and proto-Rabbinic II. Semi-Masoretic texts are defined as textual witnesses which deviate more than two percent from the consonantal text of the MT, while proto-Masoretic texts are those textual witnesses which deviate less than 2 percent from the consonantal text of the MT.

[7] For details concerning textual character and paleographic date of individual manuscripts as well as the numbers and statistics presented in this article, see my forthcoming *Die biblischen Handschriften* (vol. 1 of *Handbuch zu den Textfunden vom Toten Meer*; Tübingen: Mohr Siebeck, in preparation).

[8] 7QpapLXXExod and 4QLXXDeut are too damaged for textual classification. Below, only those biblical Dead Sea Scrolls are listed, of which enough text is preserved for textual classification.

5QDeut, the passages containing the typical long texts of the SP are not preserved. Otherwise they are equally close to SP and MT.

In case of the Masoretic text, only very few biblical manuscripts found at Qumran differ less than 2 percent from the consonantal text of the MT (4QDeut^g, 1QIsa^b, 4QJer^a, 4QEzek^a, 2QRuth^a). These manuscripts can be classified as proto-Masoretic. A large group of manuscripts is close to the consonantal text of the MT but differs nevertheless more than 2 percent from it (4QGen-Exod^a, 4QpaleoGen-Exod^l, 4QDeut^c, 4QDeut^e, 4QDeut^i, 4QJosh^b, 1QSam, 4QKgs, 4QIsa^{a,} $^{b, d-g}$, 2QJer, 4QJer^c, 4QEzek$^{a, b}$, 11QEzek, 4QXII$^{b, e, g}$, 4QPs^c, 11QPs^c, 4QRuth^a, 1QDan^b, 4QDan^d). These manuscripts can be classified as semi-Masoretic.

In addition to forerunners of the Hebrew Bible's medieval text traditions, a significant number of biblical manuscripts from Qumran attest to texts which align with none of the medieval versions (4QRP^b, 4QRP^c, 4QRP^d, 4QRP^e,[9] 4QExod^b, 4QExod^c, 4QExod-Lev^f, 4QLev-Num^a, 11QpaleoLev, 1QDeut$^{a, b}$, 4QDeut$^{b, j, k1, k2, m, n}$, 4QpaleoDeut^r, 4QJosh^a, 4Qpaleo paraJosh, 1QJudg, 4QJudg$^{a, b}$, 4QSam$^{a, b, c}$, 6Kgs, 1QIsa^a, 4QIsa^c, 4QJer^d, 4QXII$^{a, c}$, 4QPs$^{a, b, e, f, k, n, q}$, 11QPs$^{a, b}$, 4QJob^a, 4QRuth^b, 4QCant$^{a, b}$, 6QCant, 4QQoh^a, 4QDan$^{a, b}$). They are therefore categorized as non-aligned texts. This group might very well combine several different texts and text types. Examples are the different non-Masoretic Psalms collections attested in the Qumran manuscripts: 11QPs$^{a, b}$, 4QPs^e, (+ 4QPs^n?) on the one hand and 4QPs^f on the other hand.

A non-aligned text seems also to be attested by the only more extensively preserved Aramaic translation of a biblical book from the Qumran library, i.e. 11QtgJob.[10]

In ancient Jewish literature, textual plurality is not restricted to the Qumran library. It is also reflected in the quotations of and allusions to biblical books in Jewish literature from Hellenistic times. Good examples are the quotations of and allusions to the book of Jeremiah in the 3rd, 2nd, and 1st c. B.C.E.[11]

---

[9] For 4QRP^b, 4QRP^c, 4QRP^d, 4QRP^e as biblical manuscripts, see e.g. M. Segal, "Biblical Exegesis in 4Q158: Techniques and Genre," *Textus* 19 (1998): 45–62; idem, "4QReworked Pentateuch or 4QPentateuch?" in *The Dead Sea Scrolls Fifty Years after Their Discovery: Proceedings of the Jerusalem Congress, July 20–25, 1997* (ed. L.H. Schiffman et al.; Jerusalem: Israel Exploration Society, 2000), 391–99.

[10] 4QtgLev and 4QtgJob are too damaged for textual classification. In what is preserved both manuscripts are close to the consonantal text of MT.

[11] The quotations of and allusions to the other biblical books in Jewish literature from Hellenistic time confirm the evidence of the Jeremiah quotations and allusions but

	MT	LXX	non-aligned
Jer 1:10	Sir 49:7		
Jer 1:18	Sir 36:24		
Jer 4:31	1QHᵃ XI 8		
Jer 6:19	4QDibHamᵃ 6 2		
Jer 7:34		Bar 2:23	
Jer 10:12–13			11QPsᵃ XXVI 13–15
Jer 10:13		11QPsᵃ XXVI 15	
Jer 18:23		Neh 3:37	
Jer 20:9	1QHᵃ XVI 31		
Jer 25:11	Dan 9:2		
	Sib. Or. 3.280		
Jer 27:12–14		Bar 2:21	
Jer 27:12	Sir 51:26		
Jer 29:13–14		*Jub.* 1:15	
		4QWorks of God 1 6	
Jer 30:8		4QOrdᵃ 2–4 2	

The situation changes radically when the manuscript finds move closer to the time when Josephus wrote his apology *Against Apion*. During the first Jewish war, the rebels against the Roman Empire who occupied Masada took manuscripts of biblical books and other texts with them. The textual character of six of the biblical manuscripts can still be identified (MasLevᵃ, ᵇ, MasDeut, MasEzek, MasPsᵃ, ᵇ). All deviate less than 2 percent from the consonantal text of the MT and can thus be described as proto-Masoretic in character.

During the second Jewish war, caves in the Naḥalim at the Dead Sea served both as rebel bases and refugee camps. In these caves, manuscripts of biblical books were found, too. The textual character of seven of these biblical manuscripts can still be identified. MurGen-Ex.Numᵃ,[12] MurXII, XḤev/SeNumᵇ, 5/6ḤevPs, SdeirGen, and 4QGenᵇ[13] deviate

---

cannot be discussed here for reasons of space. For the quotations of and allusions to the other biblical books, see my *Die biblischen Handschriften*. For a more detailed discussion of the textual plurality of Jewish scriptures in Hellenistic times, see A. Lange, "From Literature to Scripture: The Unity and Plurality of the Hebrew Scriptures in Light of the Qumran Library," in *One Scripture or Many? Canon from Biblical, Theological, and Philosophical Perspectives* (ed. C. Helmer and C. Landmesser; Oxford: Oxford University Press, 2004), 51–107 (77–81, 98–100).

[12] For MurGen-Ex.Numᵃ (Mur1) as one manuscript, see J.T. Milik, "Genèse, Exode, Nombres," *DJD* 2:75–78 (75).

[13] For 4QGenᵇ as coming from one of the Dead Sea refugee caves of the second Jewish war, see J.R. Davila, "4QGenᵇ," *DJD* 12:31–38 (31).

less than 2 percent from the consonantal text of MT and are thus
proto-Masoretic in character. 8HevXII gr attests to a recension of the
Old Greek translation of the Minor Prophets towards the consonantal
text of MT (see below).

The manuscript evidence from the non-Qumranic sites at the Dead
Sea seems thus to suggest a proto-Masoretic standard text during
the time of the first and the second Jewish wars. In this context, it is
important to see that the paleographic dates of all biblical manuscripts
from Masada predate the first Jewish war.[14] The rebels who occupied
Masada during the first Jewish war must have acquired their manuscripts
before they went to Masada. Does this mean that textual standardization started well before the first Jewish war and that the destruction of
the Herodian temple was not its cause?[15]

2. THE EARLY RECENSIONS AND OTHER EVIDENCE OF TEXTUAL STANDARDIZATION

The early recensions of the Old Greek text of several biblical books
as well as supralinear corrections in two biblical Qumran manuscripts
provide a positive answer to this question.

2.1. *8HevXII gr and the Kaige/Theodotion Recension*

The Dead Sea Scrolls contribute in several ways to the understanding
of early recensions of the Old Greek translations of biblical books.
The most important manuscript is the Greek Minor Prophets scroll
from Naḥal Ḥever (8HevXII gr).[16] The handwriting of both scribes
involved in copying this manuscript dates to the later part of the 1st

---

[14] MasLev^a (30–1 B.C.E.), MasLev^b (ca. 0), MasDtn (30–1 B.C.E.), MasEz (50–1 B.C.E.), MasPs^a (30–1 B.C.E.), MasPs^b (50–1 B.C.E.).

[15] A position still argued for by B. Albrektson, "Reflections on the Emergence of a Standard Text of the Hebrew Bible," in *Congress Volume: Göttingen 1977* (VTSup 29; Leiden: Brill, 1978), 49–65; and D. Barthélemy, *Ézéchiel, Daniel et les 12 Prophètes* (vol. 3 of *Critique textuelle de l'Ancien Testament: Rapport final du Comité pour l'Analyse Textuelle de l'Ancien Testament Hébreu institué par l'Alliance Biblique Universelle*; OBO 50.3; Freiburg, Schweiz: Universitätsverlag, 1992), cxiii.

[16] For 8HevXII gr, see D. Barthélemy, *Les devanciers d'Aquila: première publication intégrale du texte des fragments du Dodécaprophéton trouvés dans le désert de Juda, précédée d'une étude sur les traductions et recensions grecques de la Bible réalisées au premier siècle de notre ère sous l'influence du rabbinat palestinien* (VTSup 10; Leiden: Brill, 1963); E. Tov, *The Greek Minor Prophets Scroll from Naḥal Ḥever (8HevXII gr)* (DJD 8).

c. B.C.E.[17] 8HevXII gr attests to a Greek text which reworks the Old Greek translation towards the consonantal text of MT.[18] In this way, a rather verbal translation is achieved. One of the characteristics of the 8HevXII gr-recension is that it translates Hebrew וגם with Greek καί γε. Hence, the text attested by 8HevXII gr as well as the whole recension group have been dubbed *Kaige*. A good example for its recensional characteristic is to be found in Jonah 3:3.

> OG: καθὼς ἐλάλησε κύριος ("as the Lord spoke")
> 8HevXII gr: κατ]α το ρημα ‏ﭏ[יﭏﭏ‎ ("according to the word of the Lord")
> MT: ‏כדבר יהוה‎ ("accord]ing to the word of the L[ord")

Barthélemy[19] has shown that 8HevXII gr is not an isolated example but that the characteristics of its recension are also attested in the so-called Theodotion recension (sixth column of Origen's Hexapla), in the fifth column of Origen's Hexapla, in Codex Washingtonensis, in the Septuagint versions of Ruth, Ecclesiastes, Lamentations, and Daniel, in several parts of Codex Vaticanus (Judges, 2 Sam 11:1–1 Kgs 2:11, 1 Kgs 22:1–2 Kgs 25:30), and in the biblical quotations of the writings of Justin Martyr. More recent studies understand these similarities not as attesting to one overall recension of Old Greek translations of biblical books but as a group of recensions.[20] It remains uncertain if all recensions date as early as the one attested by 8HevXII gr. It is undisputable though that Theodotion is not the author of the Kaige recensions and that at least parts of this recension group go back to pre-Christian times, i.e. the reworking of the Old Greek towards the consonantal text of the MT is not a Jewish response to its appropriation by early Christianity but started earlier and has other causes.

---

[17] See P.J. Parsons, "The Scripts and Their Date," *DJD* 8:19–26.
[18] Cf. e.g. Barthélemy, *Les devanciers*, 179–272; Tov, *Greek Minor Prophets Scroll*, 145–58; K.H. Jobes and M. Silva, *Invitation to the Septuagint* (Grand Rapids: Baker Academic, 2000), 171–73.
[19] See Barthélemy, *Les devanciers*, 203–65.
[20] See e.g. G. Howard, "The Quinta of the Minor Prophets," *Bib* 55 (1974): 15–22; A. van der Kooij, *Die alten Textzeugen des Jesajabuches: Ein Beitrag zur Textgeschichte des Alten Testaments* (OBO 35; Freiburg, Schweiz: Universitätsverlag, 1981), 127–50; Jobes and Silva, *Invitation*, 171–73, 284–87; N. Fernández Marcos, *The Septuagint in Context: Introduction to the Greek Version of the Bible* (Leiden: Brill, 2001), 142–54.

2.2. *4QLXXNum*

4QLXXNum is another Qumran manuscript which is regarded as attesting to an early recension of an Old Greek translation towards the consonantal text of MT. The manuscript dates to the late 1st c. B.C.E. or the early 1st c. C.E.[21] Originally Skehan considered 4QLXXNum as an even earlier translation of Numbers than the one attested by the major LXX manuscripts.[22] But a careful analysis by Skehan and Wevers identified the Greek text of 4QLXXNum as a pre-Christian recension which resembles *Kaige*: "it is instead a considerable reworking of the original LXX to make it conform both in quantity and in diction to a Hebrew consonantal text nearly indistinguishable... from that of MT."[23] Good examples for recensional activity can be found in Num 3:40 and 4:6, 8, 11, 12.

Num 3:40
OG: ἐπίσκεψαι ("examine")
4QLXXNum: αριθμησο[ν ("coun[t")
MT: פקד ("count")

Num 4:6, 8, 11
OG: ἀναφορεῖς ("[carrying]-poles")
4QLXXNum: αρτηρας ("carrying-poles")
MT: בדים ("carrying-poles")

Num 4:12
OG: καὶ ἐμβαλοῦσιν ("and they shall lay")
4QLXXNum: και θησουσιν ("and they shall put")
MT: ונתנו ("and they shall put")

---

[21] P.J. Parsons, "The Paleography and Date of the Greek Manuscripts," *DJD* 9:7–13 (11).

[22] P.W. Skehan, "The Qumran Manuscripts and Textual Criticism," in *Volume du congrès: Strasbourg 1956* (VTSup 4; Leiden: Brill, 1957), 148–60 (156–57); idem, "The Biblical Scrolls from Qumran and the Text of the Old Testament," *BA* 28 (1965): 87–100 (92); E. Ulrich, "The Septuagint Manuscripts from Qumran: A Reappraisal of their Value," in *Septuagint, Scrolls and Cognate Writings: Papers Presented to the International Symposium on the Septuagint and Its Relation to the Dead Sea Scrolls and Other Writings (Manchester, 1990)* (ed. G.J. Brooke and B. Lindars; SBLSCS 33; Atlanta, Ga.: Scholars Press, 1992), 49–80 (70–74, 76); *DJD* 9:187–94 (188–89).

[23] P.W. Skehan, "4QLXXNum: A Pre-Christian Reworking of the Septuagint," *HTR* 70 (1977): 39–50, (39; cf. 39–40); cf. also J.W. Wevers, "An Early Revision of the Septuagint of Numbers," *ErIsr* 16 (1982): 235*–39*.

2.3. *Papyrus Fouad Inv. 266b and 266c*

The label Papyrus Fouad Inv. 266 designates four papyrus manuscripts[24] from Egypt which might have been found in the Fayoum.[25] Papyrus Fouad Inv. 266 a (Rahlfs #942), 266b (Rahlfs #948), and 266c (Rahlfs #947) attests to different parts of Gen (266a) and Deut (266b–c). Papyrus Fouad Inv. 266b–c are of interest for the question of early recensions of the Old Greek text of Deuteronomy.

Papyrus Fouad Inv. 266b dates paleographically to the middle of the 1st c. B.C.E.[26] Its text of Deuteronomy runs close to the Old Greek but is characterized "durch Korrekturen nach der masoretisch überlieferten Textform." Papyrus Fouad Inv. 266b attests thus an early recension of the Old Greek text of Deuteronomy towards the consonantal text of the MT.[27] A good example is Deut 22:9:

> OG: μετὰ τοῦ γενήματος τοῦ ἀμπελῶνός σου ("with the yield of your vineyard")
>
> Pap. Fouad. Inv. 266b: και το γενη[μα του αμπελωνος σου ("and the yie[ld of your vineyard")
>
> MT: ותבואת הכרם ("and the yield of your vineyard")

Papyrus Fouad Inv. 266c dates paleographically to the second half of the 1st c. B.C.E. or the early 1st c. C.E.[28] Though more damaged than Papyrus Fouad Inv. 266b, Papyrus Fouad Inv. 266c might also preserve traces of a recension of the Old Greek translation of Deuteronomy towards the consonantal text of MT.[29] An example is Koenen's reconstruction of VII 16 (Deut 33:19) which shows that the reconstructed

---

[24] Cf. L. Koenen, "Introduction," in *Three Rolls of the Early Septuagint: Genesis and Deuteronomy: A Photographic Edition Prepared with the International Photographic Archive of the Association Internationale de Papyrologues* (ed. Z. Aly; PTA 27; Bonn: Habelt, 1980), 1–23 (1–10, 21).

[25] F. Dunand, *Papyrus grecs bibliques (Papyrus F. Inv. 266): Volumina de la Genèse et du Deutéronome: introduction* (RAPH 27; Cairo: Institut Français d'Archéologie Orientale, 1966), 1.

[26] For the paleographic date of Papyrus Fouad Inv. 266b, see Dunand, *Papyrus grecs bibliques*, 12.

[27] See R. Hanhart, "Die Söhne Israels, die Söhne Gottes und die Engel in der Masora, in Qumran und in der Septuaginta: Ein letztes Kapitel aus Israel in hellenistischer Zeit," in *Vergegenwärtigung des Alten Testaments: Beiträge zur biblischen Hermeneutik, FS R. Smend* (ed. C. Bultmann et al.; Göttingen: Vandenhoeck & Ruprecht, 2002), 170–78 (171); idem, review of F. Dunand, *Papyrus grecs bibliques*, *OLZ* 73 (1978): 39–45 (42–45); Koenen, "Introduction," 1–2, 9.

[28] See Koenen, "Introduction," 6 n. 28.

[29] See Koenen, "Introduction," 9, 18–20.

text provides enough space for a Greek rendering of the MT text but not for the Old Greek:[30]

OG: ἔθνη ἐξολεθρεύσουσιν καὶ ἐπικαλέσεσθε ("They shall utterly destroy nations, and you shall call")

Papyrus Fouad Inv. 266c: \εθν[η επι]/κ[αλ]εσο[νται εις το ορος ("they sh]all ca[ll] peopl[es to the mountain")

MT: עמים הר יקראו ("they shall call peoples to the mountain")

The evidence of Papyrus Fouad Inv. 266b and 266c is all the more interesting as the manuscripts attest to recensions towards the consonantal texts of MT from ancient Egypt. This asks for caution in assigning ancient versions to different geographical locations, like Palestine, Egypt, and Mesopotamia.[31] Furthermore it shows that the early recensional work on the Old Greek translations was not restricted to Judah itself but happened in the Diaspora, too.

2.4. *Recensions and Supralinear Corrections Towards other Texts than MT*

Early recensional efforts are not restricted to reworking Old Greek translations towards a semi- or proto-Masoretic text. Recensional efforts are also attested towards other Hebrew texts. As these are of less interest for the question of how proto-MT became the Jewish standard text of the 1st c. C.E., I will briefly summarize the evidence.

2.4.1. *The Proto-Lucianic Recension*

Supposedly, Lucian of Antioch (ca. 250–312 C.E.) undertook a revision of both the Greek Old Testament and the New Testament, which was primarily stylistic in character. It remains uncertain though if Lucian was responsible for this recension or not. Therefore, it is also called the Antiochene text. This Lucianic recension comprises some historical books (esp. 1–2 Samuel, 1–2 Kings, and 1–2 Chronicles) but also the prophets and psalms. The most important witnesses to the so-called Lucianic recension are the manuscripts boc₂e₂ (Rahlfs #19 108 82 127 93). Readings attested by these manuscripts also occur in Old Testa-

---

[30] See Koenen, "Introduction," 16, 18.

[31] See most prominently the "local text theory" as developed by W.F. Albright ("New Light on Early Recensions of the Hebrew Bible," *BASOR* 140 [1955]: 27–33) and F.M. Cross ("The Evolution of a Theory of Local Texts," in *Qumran and the History of the Biblical Text* [ed. idem and S. Talmon; Cambridge, Mass.: Harvard University Press, 1975], 306–20).

ment quotations by some pre-Lucianic church fathers (Justin, Cyprian, and Tertullian), in the Old Latin Translation (Vetus Latina), in the writings of Josephus Flavius, and even in Old Testament quotations in the New Testament. Hence, Lucian must have based his work on an earlier recension of pre-Christian origin. For lack of a better term, this Jewish recension is called proto-Lucianic.[32] In the case of 1–2 Samuel, the Hebrew text towards which the proto-Lucianic recension reworked the Old Greek translation is preserved in a somewhat more developed stage in the Qumran manuscript 4QSam[a].[33]

2.4.2. *5QDeut and 4QGen[j]*

Two Hebrew manuscripts from the Qumran library, i.e. 4QGen[j] and 5QDeut, are of particular interest when it comes to recensional reworkings. 5QDeut was copied in the first half of the 2nd c. B.C.E.[34] In Deut 7:15; 8:2, 19; 9:2, supralinear corrections were added to 5QDeut in an early Herodian bookhand (30–1 B.C.E.). As far as the manuscript is preserved, the main text of 5QDeut reads against the Old Greek in every variant. But the four supralinear additions correct the main text of 5QDeut every time towards the Hebrew *Vorlage* of the Old Greek.[35] Therefore, the supralinear corrections of 5QDeut can be viewed as a recension of a Hebrew text towards the Hebrew *Vorlage* of the Old Greek.

The evidence of 4QGen[j] is less definite. The manuscript was copied in the last quarter of the 1st c. B.C.E.[36] Only two supralinear corrections are preserved in Gen 41:16, 24. Both read with the Old Greek translation against MT.[37] Not enough text is preserved to arrive at a paleographic date of the supralinear corrections.

---

[32] For the Lucianic and proto-Lucianic recensions, see e.g. B.M. Metzger, *Chapters in the History of New Testament Textual Criticism* (NTTS 4; Leiden: Brill, 1963), 1–41; Fernández Marcos, *Septuagint in Context*, 223–38.

[33] See e.g. F.M. Cross, "The History of the Biblical Text in the Light of the Discoveries in the Judaean Desert," in idem and Talmon, *Qumran and the History of the Biblical Text*, 177–95 (188–93); E.C. Ulrich, *The Qumran Text of Samuel and Josephus* (Missoula, Mont.: Scholars Press, 1978).

[34] See J.T. Milik, "1. Deutéronome," *DJD* 3:169–71 (169).

[35] See Milik, "Deutéronome," *DJD* 3:170–71.

[36] See J.R. Davila, "9. 4QGen[j]," *DJD* 12:65–73 (65).

[37] See Davila, "4QGen[j]," 66.

2.5. *The Process of Textual Standardization in the 1st c. C.E.*

An idea how in Judah of the 1st c. C.E. textual standardization towards
proto-MT was achieved might be preserved in a baraita of the Talmud
Yerushalmi, tractate *Taʿanit* (4:68a).[38]

> Three scrolls did they find in the Temple courtyard. These were the *Maon*
> scroll ["Dwelling"], the *Zaatuti* scroll ["Little ones"], and the *He* scroll. In
> one of these scrolls they found it written "The eternal God is your dwell-
> ing place (*maon*)" (Deut. 33:27: "The eternal God is your dwelling place,
> and underneath are the everlasting arms. And he thrust out the enemy
> before you, and said, 'Destroy'"). And in two of the scrolls it was written,
> "The eternal God is your dwelling place (*meonah*)." They confirmed the
> reading found in the two and abrogated the other. In one of them they
> found written "They sent the little ones of the people of Israel" (Exod
> 24:5: "And he sent young men of the people of Israel, who offered burnt
> offerings and sacrificed peace offerings of oxen to the Lord."). And in
> the two it was written, "They sent young men..." They confirmed the
> two and abrogated the other. In one of them they found written, "He
> [he written in the feminine spelling] nine times, and in two, they found
> it written that way eleven times." They confirmed the reading found in
> the two and abrogated the other.[39]

That *y. Taʿan.* 4:68a describes a 1st c. C.E. procedure is advised by the
fact that only since the 1st c. C.E. the biblical Dead Sea Scrolls from
the non-Qumran sites attest to such a standard text. But *y. Taʿan.* 4:68a
describes not only how such a standard text was reached, i.e. how
proto-MT was created, but also where and by whom it was created,
i.e. by priests in the Jerusalem temple.[40] That in Judah priests at the
Jerusalem temple were responsible for the textual standardization of
the Mosaic law and other Jewish scriptures could also be corroborated

---

[38] Cf. also *Sipre Deut.* 356; *y. Seqal.* 4,3,48a; *b. Ketub.* 19b, 106a; *b. Pesaḥ.* 112a. For
the historicity of this tradition, see G. Stemberger in *Hermeneutik der Jüdischen Bibel und
des Alten Testaments* (idem and C. Dohmen; Studienbücher Theologie 1.2; Stuttgart:
Kohlhammer, 1996), 76. For further study, see S. Talmon, "The Three Scrolls of the
Law That Were Found in the Temple Court," *Textus* 2 (1962): 14–27; E. Tov, *Textual
Criticism of the Hebrew Bible* (2d rev. ed.; Minneapolis, Minn.: Fortress Press, 2001), 28,
32–33; idem, "The History and Significance of a Standard Text of the Hebrew Bible,"
in *From the Beginnings to the Middle Ages (Until 1300)*, 49–66.

[39] Translation according to J. Neusner, *The Talmud of the Land of Israel: A Preliminary
Translation and Explanation* (CSHJ; Chicago: The University of Chicago Press, 1987),
18.253–54.

[40] For the idea of a standardized biblical text cf. also *b. Ned.* 37b. For further details
how the proto-MT standard text was created, see F.M. Cross, "The Fixation of the
Text of the Hebrew Bible," in idem, *From Epic to Canon: History and Literature in Ancient
Israel* (Baltimore: Johns Hopkins University Press, 1998), 205–18 (213–16).

by various remarks in the writings of Josephus. In *Ant.* 3.38, 5.61, and 10.57, Josephus mentions that books or the holy books of Moses were laid up in the Jerusalem temple. In *Ant.* 4.303–304, Josephus even claims that Moses would have given autographs of his writings to the priests for safekeeping. Especially when read in light of *Ag. Ap.* 1.38–42, for the 1st c. C.E., these remarks could refer to master copies of Jewish scriptures in the Jerusalem temple.[41] Although 2 Macc 2:13–15 mentions a temple library already with regard to the time of Nehemiah, it does not mention special copies of any book. Considering the overwhelming evidence for textual plurality and the lack of any evidence for textual standardization in Judah up to the 2nd half of the 1st c. B.C.E., it seems highly unlikely that in the Jerusalem temple master copies of any text existed significantly earlier than the 1st c. C.E. Josephus' claims to master copies or even autographs of Mosaic books and other Jewish scriptures are thus projections of circumstances of his own time onto past history. Furthermore, the remark about Moses depositing the autographs of his writings with the priests (*Ant.* 4.303–304) reminds of similar stories about Spartan master copies of Homeric texts (see below 119–20). Josephus might have shed a particularly Hellenistic light on the master copies of the Jerusalem temple to propagandize the non-Jewish part of his audience.

2.6. *First Conclusions*

In Judah, the biblical Dead Sea Scrolls as well as quotations of and allusions to Jewish scriptures attest to textual plurality up to the 1st c. C.E. But 8ḤevXII gr and 4QLXXNum are witnesses to pre-Christian recensions of Old Greek translations towards a semi- or proto-Masoretic text. The proto-Lucianic recension as well as supralinear corrections in 4QGenʲ and 5QDeut demonstrate that these recensional efforts were not directed towards semi- or proto-Masoretic texts only. The evidence shows that in Judah efforts towards textual standardizations started some time in the second half of the 1st c. B.C.E., i.e. after the conquest of Syro-Palestine by Pompey in 63 B.C.E. The biblical manuscripts among the non-Qumranic Dead Sea Scrolls show that the 1st c. C.E. knew a dominant standard text. Rabbinic evidence as well as remarks by

---

[41] For master copies of Jewish scriptures in the Jerusalem temple, see Tov, "The Text of the Hebrew/Aramaic and Greek Bible Used in the Ancient Synagogues," 243–49.

Josephus Flavius suggest that this standard text was created by priests in the Jerusalem temple based on the principle of majority readings.

For Egyptian Judaism, Papyrus Fouad Inv 266b (cf. Papyrus Fouad Inv. 266c) attests to recensional efforts towards a semi- or proto-Masoretic text already before the middle of the 1st c. B.C.E., i.e., in ancient Egypt, textual standardization of Jewish scriptures began before it was conquered by Augustus in 31 B.C.E.

As all these recensions predate the destruction of the Jerusalem temple in 70 C.E., its destruction could thus not have been the cause of textual standardization. The early recensions described above predate Christianity, too. Revising the Old Greek texts was not a response to the Christian appropriation, as was claimed time and again. Hence, the initial impulse towards textual standardization cannot be a Jewish response to early Christianity either.

Most of the early efforts towards textual standardization are found in revising the Old Greek translation. This could point to a Greek influence. Is the textual standardization of Jewish scriptures thus due to Greek influence? This suspicion could be confirmed by Josephus' apology *Against Apion*. Josephus clearly implies that Judaism is far better than Hellenism in not having changed its holy scriptures. And it is the basic rhetoric strategy of an apology to claim that your own culture realizes the cultural values of the opponent culture much better than the opponent culture itself.

To answer these questions, I will give a sketch of textual standardization in the Graeco-Roman world. Afterwards, I will ask how Egyptian Judaism developed the idea of textual standardization and what caused textual standardization in Judah itself.

3. Textual Standardization in the Graeco-Roman World[42]

Early efforts towards textual standardization can already be found in Peisistratid Athens in the first half of the 6th c. B.C.E. Herodotus reports how the tyrant Hipparchus is involved in the editing of the oracle collection of Musaeus (*Hist.* 7.6). This fits well with the remarks

---

[42] For textual standardization in classical and pre-classical Greece as well as in Roman culture, see H. Cancik, "Standardization and Ranking of Texts in Greek and Roman Institutions," in *Homer, the Bible, and Beyond: Literary and Religious Canons in the Ancient World* (ed. M. Finkelberg and G.G. Stroumsa; JSRC 2; Leiden: Brill, 2003), 117–30.

of Plato (*Hipparch.* 228b–c) that Hipparchus forced the rhapsodes to perform the Homeric poems in a fixed sequence—something that Diogenes Laertius (1.57) also claimed for Solon the Lawgiver. Although a standardized text is not mentioned in either context, the sequencing of Homeric poems or the exclusion of insertions into oracle collections hints to an effort towards textual integrity. For epic texts like Homer or the famous tragedies of Aeschylus, Sophocles, and Euripides, textual standardization seems to have been necessitated by performances during different Athenian festivals. Groups of actors needed to have identical texts to perform them.[43]

For the collection of the tragedies of Aeschylus, Sophocles, and Euripides, such efforts towards textual integrity developed in the 4th c. B.C.E. into the idea of a standardized text. This standard text of the works by the three tragedians was ensured and secured by way of a master copy which was kept in Athens. Pseudo-Plutarch claims in his *Lives of the Ten Orators* that Lycurgus legislated these master copies.

> He also introduced laws...; the law that bronze statues of the poets Aeschylus, Sophocles, and Euripides be erected, that their tragedies be written out and kept in a public depository, and that the clerk of the State read them to the actors who were to perform their plays for comparison of the texts and that it be unlawful to depart from the authorized text in acting. (*Mor.* 841F)[44]

Pseudo-Plutarch is confirmed by Galen when the latter remarks that Ptolemy III Euergetes borrowed the Athenian master copies to have them copied for the library of Alexandria.[45]

In classical Greece, the idea of textual standardization was not restricted to Athens. The Spartans, e.g., created a legend of how Lycurgus—the reformer who created Sparta's military society—secured for Sparta a copy of Homer's works that was very close to the original autograph.

> From Crete, Lycurgus sailed to Asia, with the desire, as we are told, of comparing with the Cretan civilizations, which was simple and severe, that

---

[43] See e.g. G. Nagy, *Poetry as Performance: Homer and Beyond* (Cambridge: Cambridge University Press, 1996), 105–206.

[44] Translation according to H.N. Fowler, *Plutarch's Moralia: With an English Translation* (17 vols.; LCL; Cambridge, Mass.: Harvard University Press, 1949), 10.399, 401.

[45] *In Hippocratis Epidemiarum librum 3.1 Commentarius* 2.4. For the Greek text, see E. Wenkebach, *Galeni in Hippocratis Epidemiarum librum 3* (CMG 5.10.2.1; Leipzig: Teubner, 1936), 79.

of the Ionians, which was extravagant and luxurious, just as a physician compares with healthy bodies those which are unsound and sickly; he could then study the difference in their modes of life and forms of government. There too, as it would appear, he made his first acquaintance with the poems of Homer, which were preserved among the posterity of Creophylus; and when he saw that the political and disciplinary lessons contained in them were worthy of no less serious attention than the incentives to pleasure and license which they supplied, he eagerly copied and compiled them in order to take them home with him. For these epics already had a certain faint reputation among the Greeks, and a few were in possession of certain portions of them, as the poems were carried here and there by chance; but Lycurgus was the very first to make them really known. (Plutarch, *Lyc.* 4.4)[46]

Beginning in the 3rd c. B.C.E., the scholars of the library of Alexandria started to compile canonical lists of distinct Greek authors which were structured according to the genres of ancient Greek literature. These literary heroes were designated ἐγκριθέντες ("selected ones"). However, the efforts of the Alexandrian scholars were not restricted to compiling lists of authorities. They also prepared critical editions of their works. The most outstanding example is the editorial work of Aristarchus of Samothrake on the Homeric epics. These critical editions had become necessary as the works of Homer and others were attested in multiple textforms. As with ancient Jewish scriptures, textual plurality was the rule and not the exception.[47]

In the 1st c. C.E., Quintilian's description of the work of the Alexandrian scholars shows that the Alexandrian texts and canons gained respect and popularity in the Roman world and became part of the overall Graeco-Roman cultural continuum.

The old school of teachers indeed carried their criticism so far that they were not content with obelising lines or rejecting books whose titles they regarded as spurious, as though they were expelling a supposititious child

---

[46] Translation according to B. Perrin, *Plutarch's Lives: With an English Translation* (11 vols.; LCL; Cambridge, Mass.: Harvard University Press, 1959), 1.215.

[47] For the library of Alexandria, its canons, and its editions, see R. Pfeiffer, *Geschichte der klassischen Philologie: Von den Anfängen bis zum Hellenismus* (Reinbeck bei Hamburg: Rowohlt Taschenbuch Verlag, 1970), 114–285; E.A. Parsons, *The Alexandrian Library: Glory of the Hellenic World: Its Rise, Antiquities, and Destructions* (London: Elsevier Press, 1952); M. El-Abbadi, *Life and Fate of the Ancient Library of Alexandria* (2d rev. ed.; Paris: UNESCO/UNDP, 1992); *The Library of Alexandria: Center of Learning in the Ancient World* (ed. R. MacLeod; London: Tauris, 2000).

from the family circle, but also drew up a canon of authors, from which some were omitted altogether. (Quintilian, *Inst.* 1.4.3)[48]

This brief sketch of textual standardization in the Graeco-Roman world shows, before there is any hint towards textual standardization in Jewish culture, Greek culture developed standardized texts. The pinnacle of the Greek editorial efforts towards standardized texts are the critical editions of the Alexandrian library, which in turn left its mark on the Roman empire.

4. THE ORIGINS OF TEXTUAL STANDARDIZATION IN EGYPTIAN JUDAISM

The paleographic date of papyrus Fouad Inv. 266b in the middle of the 1st c. B.C.E. shows that recensions of the Old Greek translation towards the consonantal text of MT started in Egypt before its conquest by the Roman Empire in 31 B.C.E. At this time, Alexandria itself was one of the cultural foci of ancient Judaism. As attested by a wealth of Greek Jewish literature, the academic elite of Alexandrian Judaism strove for Greek education. Greek Jewish legend has it that even the Old Greek translation of the Pentateuch, i.e. the very beginning of Greek Jewish literature, was instigated by the search for books for the Alexandrian library (see e.g., *Let. Aris.* 10–11). In reporting this legend, the *Letter of Aristeas*—written in the late 2nd c. B.C.E.[49]—relates the translation of the Pentateuch into Greek with an effort of textual standardization. It laments that the low quality and textual plurality of the Pentateuch manuscripts available in Egypt would be due to lacking royal patronage and that an "accurate version" (διηκριβωμένα; 31) should be acquired from the Jerusalem temple. At its end the *Letter of Aristeas* describes how such a master copy arrived in Egypt.

> To the great king from Demetrius. Your command, O King, concerned the collection of missing volumes needed to complete the library, and of items which accidentally fell short of requisite condition. I gave highest priority and attention to these matters, and now make the following further report: 30 Scrolls of the Law of the Jews, together with a few others,

---

[48] Translation according to H.E. Butler, *The Institutio Oratoria of Quintilian: With an English Translation* (4 vols.; LCL; Cambridge, Mass.: Harvard University Press, 1996), 1.63.

[49] For the dating of the *Letter of Aristeas* in the late 2nd c. B.C.E., see E.J. Bickerman, "Zur Datierung des Pseudo-Aristeas," in *Studies in Jewish and Christian History. Part 1* (AGJU 9.1; Leiden: Brill, 1976), 123–36.

are missing (from the library), for these (works) are written in Hebrew characters and language. But they have been transcribed somewhat carelessly and not as they should be, according to the report of the experts, because they have not received royal patronage. 31 These (books) must also be in your library in an accurate version, because this legislation, as could be expected from its divine nature, is very philosophical and genuine. (*Let. Aris.* 29–31)

So they arrived with gifts which had been sent at their hands and with the fine skins on which the Law had been written in letters of gold in Jewish characters; the parchment had been excellently worked, and the joining together of the letters was imperceptible. (*Let. Aris.* 176)[50]

On the one hand, the phrase "accurate version" (διηκριβωμένα; 31) reflects knowledge about the standards of the Alexandrian critical editions.[51] On the other hand, the phrase indicates that the Egyptian Jews themselves started to distinguish between accurate and inaccurate copies of their scriptures, i.e. they started to apply the Alexandrian idea of an accurate standard text versus a multitude of inaccurate textual traditions to their own scriptures. This means, in Egyptian Judaism revising the Old Greek translations and working towards a standard text was instigated and motivated by the role model of the editorial work in the Alexandrian library.

5. The Origins of Textual Standardization in Judah

Was textual standardization in Judah thus initiated by contacts with Egyptian or Alexandrian Jews? And if yes, for which reason did these ideas fall on favorable ground in Judah only in the second half of the 1st c. B.C.E., while textual standardization seems to have started earlier in Egyptian Judaism?

To answer these questions, a brief sketch of the cultural politics of the Roman Empire in its provinces and vassal states is needed.[52] In the time of the emperors only very few Roman officials were needed outside

---

[50] Translations according to R.J.H. Shutt, "Letter of Aristeas (Third Century B.C.–First Century A.D.): A New Translation and Introduction," in *OTP* 2:7–34 (14–15, 24).

[51] For the influence of Alexandrian scholarship on the *Letter of Aristeas*, see S. Honigman, *The Septuagint and Homeric Scholarship in Alexandria: A Study in the Narrative of the Letter of Aristeas* (London: Routledge, 2003).

[52] For more detailed information, see C. Freeman, *Egypt, Greece, and Rome: Civilizations of the Ancient Mediterranean* (Oxford: Oxford University Press, 1996), 422–39.

of Rome to administer and govern Rome's provinces and vassal states. In the provinces, most of the positions in provincial government were filled by local elites who were thoroughly Romanized and were Roman citizens. To create these Romanized local elites, the Roman Empire followed a cultural policy of active Romanization. In the eastern part of the empire, this meant that the Roman and Greek cultures were imprinted more intensely on the educated local elites than even in the time of the Hellenistic kingdoms. A description of how this policy was applied to the natives of Britain can be found in Tacitus's biographical notes on his father in law, Agricola, who was responsible for much of the Roman conquest of Britain.

> In order that a population scattered and uncivilized, and proportionately ready for war, might be habituated by comfort to peace and quiet, he would exhort individuals, assist communities, to erect temples, market-places, houses: he praised the energetic, rebuked the indolent, and the rivalry for his compliments took the place of coercion. Moreover, he began to train the sons of the chieftains in a liberal education, and to give a preference to the native talents of the Briton as against the trained abilities of the Gaul. As a result, the nation which used to reject the Latin language began to aspire to rhetoric: further, the wearing of our dress became a distinction, and the toga came into fashion, and little by little the Britons went astray into alluring vices: to the promenade, the bath, the well-appointed dinner table. (Tacitus, *Agr.* 21)[53]

In this context, it needs to be remembered that the earliest evidence for textual standardization in Judah postdates the conquest of Syro-Palestine by Pompey in 63 B.C.E. This means: in Judah, textual standardization started most likely after the Roman conquest. Is textual standardization in Judah thus part of the Romanization of the local elites? This could be all the more likely as the first efforts towards standardization can be observed in the Greek versions of Jewish scriptures, i.e. their revision towards semi- or proto-Masoretic texts. Revisional work on Greek manuscripts requires extraordinary Greek language skills and a thorough education in Hellenistic culture. How much the translators and revisers of the Old Greek were immersed in Hellenistic culture and education is illustrated by the description of the LXX translators in *Let. Aris.* 121: "Eleazar selected men of the highest merit and of

---

[53] Translation according to M. Hutton and E.H. Warmington, *Tacitus: Agricola, Germania, Dialogus* (5 vols.; LCL; Cambridge, Mass.: Harvard University Press, 2000) 67.

excellent education... they had not only mastered the Jewish literature, but had made a serious study of that of the Greeks as well."[54] But was the Romanization of the local elites as effective in Judah as elsewhere in the Roman Empire? Were the Jews of Judah thus open to the Alexandrian idea of a standard text due to their Romanization? After its conquest by Pompey, is there evidence for increased Hellenistic and Roman influence in Judah?

The example of the Jewish quarter excavations in Jerusalem gives a positive answer to these questions. In early Roman times, this area of Jerusalem was inhabited by the wealthy and educated Jewish (priestly) elites. Nahman Avigad summarizes their Graeco-Roman lifestyle as documented by the material culture of their mansions as follows.

> However, the Jewish quarter excavations uncovered another Jerusalem—a secular, everyday Jerusalem with a residential quarter whose splendor outshone everything previously known about the city. This was a wealthy quarter, with large mansions embellished with frescoes and colorful mosaics, complex bathing installations, luxury goods and artistic objects—all "status symbols" of the times. These were well-cultivated homes lavishing under the influence of a style common throughout the Hellenistic-Roman world.[55]

Examples for this Graeco-Roman lifestyle are Roman tables, terra sigillata ceramics, marble trays, a Greek glass pitcher from Sidon, columns with Corinthian capitals, frescoes, and mosaics.[56]

6. CONCLUSIONS

In ancient Judaism, the earliest evidence for textual standardization is Papyrus Fouad Inv. 266b (paleographic date ca. 50 B.C.E.; cf. Papyrus Fouad Inv. 266c) and the *Letter of Aristeas* (written in the late 2nd c. B.C.E.). This locates the beginnings of the textual standardization of Jewish scriptures in Egyptian if not Alexandrian Judaism. The *Letter of Aristeas* connects Jewish textual standardization closely with the role

---

[54] Translation according to Shutt, "Letter of Aristeas," in *OTP* 2:21.

[55] N. Avigad, *Discovering Jerusalem* (Oxford: Blackwell, 1984), 260.

[56] For an instructive survey of the material culture of early Roman Jerusalem as documented by the Jewish quarter excavations, see Avigad, *Discovering Jerusalem*. For a more detailed excavation report, see *Jewish Quarter Excavations in the Old City of Jerusalem: Conducted by Nahman Avigad, 1969–1982* (ed. H. Geva; 3 vols.; Jerusalem: Israel Exploration Society, 2000–2006).

model of the library of Alexandria and its critical text editions. Hence, it seems feasible that the beginnings of Jewish textual standardization go back to Greek influence. In Egyptian Judaism, both Papyrus Fouad Inv. 266b and the *Letter of Aristeas* link textual standardization with the Old Greek translation of the Pentateuch and its recensions.

The biblical Dead Sea Scrolls show that in Judah the origins of textual standardization are also linked with early recensions of Old Greek translations of Jewish scriptures (see e.g., 8ḤevXII gr and 4QLXXNum). Responsible for the first Judean efforts towards a standard text of Jewish scriptures were Jewish (priestly) elites which were highly educated both in Jewish and Graeco-Roman culture. But textual standardization starts significantly later in Judah than in Egyptian Judaism. That Judean Judaism remained reluctant to accept the Alexandrian idea of a Jewish standard text might be due to the rejection of Hellenized Hasmonean royalty by the majority of Judah's religious elites.[57] The skeptic attitude towards Greek ideas among Judean educated elites changed after Judah's conquest by Pompey in 63 B.C.E. The archeological evidence of the Jerusalem Jewish Quarter excavations shows that the Roman policy of Romanization and—in the case of the empire's eastern territories—Hellenization changed the cultural alignment of the Judean religious elites. Hence, Greek educated Jews were more open towards the idea of standardizing the texts of Jewish scriptures after Judah became a Roman client state.

Rabbinic literature and the Dead Sea Scrolls attest to a variety of editorial signs which were used by the scribes of the late Second Temple period. Already Lieberman has shown that some of these scribal signs were also employed by the Alexandrian grammarians as editorial signs in their critical text editions.[58] But a detailed analysis of the complete evidence by Tov argues against a significant Alexandrian influence in the editorial praxis of late Second Temple Judaism.[59] "The majority of Alexandrian critical signs used in the editions of earlier literary

---

[57] See most prominently the conflicts between Pharisees and Hasmoneans during the rule of Alexander Jannai (cf. Josephus, *Ant.* 13.372–383, 398–404; *J.W.* 1.88–98).

[58] S. Lieberman, *Hellenism in Jewish Palestine: Studies in the Literary Transmission Beliefs and Manners of Palestine in the I Century B.C.E.–IV Century C.E.* (2d rev. ed.; New York, N.Y.: The Jewish Theological Seminary of America, 1962), 28–46.

[59] Contra M. Greenberg, "The Stabilization of the Text of the Hebrew Bible, Reviewed in the Light of the Biblical Materials from the Judean Desert," in *The Canon and Masorah of the Hebrew Bible: An Introductory Reader* (ed. S.Z. Leiman; Library of Biblical Studies; New York, N.Y.: Ktav, 1974), 298–326.

texts have not been used in the Judean Desert texts: *asteriskos, obelos, diple..., diple obelismene..., keraunion, ancora.*"[60] Although the Greek ideas of standard text and master copy influenced late Second Temple Judaism, the Alexandrian editorial praxis did not leave a significant mark.

Whether proto-MT was developed by the Pharisees by the early 1st c. C.E. due to the influence of Hillel and became regnant as a Jewish standard text after the destruction of the Herodian temple in 70 C.E.—as F.M. Cross[61] thinks—remains doubtful. The multiplicity of texts of Jewish scriptures used by Josephus in his *Antiquities* even after 70 C.E. asks for caution.[62] It seems also doubtful if the Zealots occupying the Masada during the 1st Jewish war were all members of the Pharisaic party. Nevertheless, only proto-Masoretic manuscripts were discovered on the Masada (see above 109).

Consciousness for the Greek character of the idea of standardizing Jewish scriptures is still perceptible in Josephus' apology *Against Apion*. When he emphasizes, "with us are not myriads of books which are at variance and contradict each other" (*Ag. Ap.* 1.38) and when he stresses "for during so many ages as have already passed, nobody has dared either to add to them, to take from them, or to make changes" (*Ag. Ap.* 1.42), Josephus employs the typical argumentative strategy of an apology. He claims that his own culture fulfills a cultural value of the opponent culture better.

In the time of Josephus, the consonantal text of MT evolved as the standard text of Jewish scriptures, as demonstrated by the biblical manuscripts from Masada, Wadi Murabba'at, and Naḥal Ḥever. But in its beginnings, Jewish textual standardization was not yet aimed at the consonantal text of MT exclusively. The proto-Lucianic recension as well as the supralinear corrections of 5QDeut demonstrate that originally other texttypes were also favored as standard texts.

---

[60] E. Tov, *Scribal Practices and Approaches Reflected in the Texts Found in the Judean Desert* (STDJ 54; Leiden: Brill, 2004), 274, cf. also 188, 200–201, 214, 273–74.

[61] Cross, "Fixation," 216–18.

[62] For Josephus' use of "non-Masoretic" textforms, see e.g. E.C. Ulrich, *The Qumran Text of Samuel and Josephus* (HSM 19; Missoula, Mont.: Scholars Press, 1978), 165–259; L.H. Feldman, *Josephus' Interpretation of the Bible* (Hellenistic Culture and Society 27; Berkeley, Calif.: University of California Press, 1998), 23–36, 63–64.

LES TITRES DES LIVRES BIBLIQUES : LE TÉMOIGNAGE DE LA BIBLIOTHÈQUE DE QUMRÂN*

Katell Berthelot

Les spécialistes des manuscrits de la mer Morte se sont beaucoup intéressés aux citations bibliques et aux formules d'introduction de ces citations dans des textes comme les *pesharim* ou l'*Écrit de Damas*,[1] ainsi qu'à la lumière que pouvaient projeter les textes de la bibliothèque de Qumrân sur la question de la constitution du canon des Écritures.[2]

---

* C'est un honneur et un plaisir de dédier cet article à Florentino García Martinez, et de saluer à cette occasion le travail immense qu'il a accompli dans le domaine des études qumrâniennes, ainsi que sa façon généreuse de partager son savoir avec les autres, en particulier les jeunes chercheurs.

[1] Cf., entre autres, J.A. Fitzmyer, "The Use of Explicit Old Testament Quotations in Qumran Literature and the New Testament," *NTS* 7 (1960–61): 297–333; G. Vermes, "Biblical Proof-Texts in Qumran Literature," *JJS* 34 (1989): 493–508; M.J. Bernstein, "Introductory Formulas for Citation and Re-citation of Biblical Verses in the Qumran Pesharim: Observations on a Pesher Technique," *DSD* 1 (1994): 30–70; J.C. Vander-Kam, "Authoritative Literature in the Dead Sea Scrolls," *DSD* 5 (1998): 382–402; T.H. Lim, "Biblical Quotations in the Pesharim and the Text of the Bible—Methodological Considerations," *The Bible as Book. The Hebrew Bible and the Judaean Desert Discoveries* (ed. E.D. Herbert and E. Tov; London: The British Library, 2002), 71–79 (et, dans le même livre, les contributions de S. Metso, E. Tigchelaar et J. Høgenhaven).

[2] Voir, en particulier, les travaux d'E. Ulrich, *The Dead Sea Scrolls and the Origins of the Bible* (Grand Rapids: Eerdmans; 1999); idem, "Canon," *The Encyclopedia of the Dead Sea Scrolls* (ed. L.H. Schiffman and J.C. VanderKam; New York: Oxford University Press, 2000), 1:117–20; idem, "Qumran and the Canon of the Old Testament," *The Biblical Canons* (ed. J.-M. Auwers and H.J. de Jonge; Leuven: Leuven University Press, 2003), 57–80; idem, "The Non-Attestation of a Tripartite Canon in 4QMMT," *CBQ* 65 (2003): 202–14. Voir également F.M. Cross, *From Epic to Canon: History and Literature in Ancient Israel* (Baltimore: Johns Hopkins University Press, 1998), 203–29; A. van der Kooij, "The Canonization of Ancient Books Kept in the Temple of Jerusalem," *Canonization and Decanonization* (ed. idem and K. van der Toorn; Leiden: Brill, 1998), 17–40; J. Lust, "Quotation Formulae and Canon in Qumran," ibid., 67–77; J.A. Sanders, "The Scrolls and the Canonical Process," *The Dead Sea Scrolls after Fifty Years: A Comprehensive Assessment* (ed. P.W. Flint and J.C. VanderKam; 2 vols.; Leiden: Brill, 1999), 2: 1–23; J.G. Campbell, "4QMMT^d and the Tripartite Canon," *JJS* 51 (2000): 181–90; G. Xeravits, "Considerations on Canon and the Dead Sea Scrolls," *The Qumran Chronicle* 9 (2000): 165–78; C.A. Evans, "The Dead Sea Scrolls and the Canon of Scripture in the Time of Jesus," *The Bible at Qumran. Text, Shape and Interpretation* (ed. P.W. Flint; Grand Rapids: Eerdmans, 2001), 67–79; J.C. VanderKam, "Questions of Canon Viewed Through the Dead Sea Scrolls," *The Canon Debate* (ed. L.M. McDonald and J.A. Sanders; Peabody: Hendrickson, 2002), 91–109; S. Talmon, "The Crystallization of the 'Canon of Hebrew Scriptures' in Light of Biblical Scrolls from Qumran," *The*

Mais, à ma connaissance, aucun livre ou article n'a été consacré au problème des *titres* des livres bibliques dans les manuscrits de la mer Morte. Cette question entretient pourtant des liens étroits avec (1) celle des citations bibliques et (2) celle de la constitution du canon, comme on va tenter de le montrer à partir de quelques exemples.

1. CITATIONS BIBLIQUES ET TITRES

Les textes de Qumrân présupposent pour la plupart l'existence des livres qui formeront par la suite le canon massorétique, sous une forme ou sous une autre. La nature des relations qu'ils entretiennent avec eux est très variée : réécriture, paraphrase, citation, référence ponctuelle aux personnages bibliques, etc. Dans les cas de citations ou de références explicites, comment les auteurs des textes de Qumrân nommaient-ils les livres bibliques qu'ils utilisaient ? En d'autres termes, quel *titre* utilisaient-ils pour tel ou tel livre biblique, quand ils citaient un livre en particulier ? Le désignaient-ils par le nom de l' "auteur" présumé ? Peut-on dégager une tendance quelconque ?

Il faut avant tout rappeler un fait peu familier aux lecteurs modernes : dans l'Antiquité, un livre n'était pas toujours doté d'un titre. Comme l'écrit Philippe Hoffman, «Au début de l'âge grec le titre n'existe pas nécessairement. Ni Héraclite, ni Aristote, ni Hérodote ni Thucydide n'ont ressenti le besoin d'un titre pour désigner leurs écrits».[3] Il est probable que certains livres bibliques ont d'abord circulé sans titre défini, et l'histoire des titres des livres du Pentateuque, pour ne mentionner qu'eux, est loin d'être claire.

Mais même dans les cas où le titre d'un ouvrage est *a priori* connu, les références à cet ouvrage ne sont pas forcément explicites, et ne nomment pas toujours le titre. La formule qui introduit la citation peut faire référence à l'auteur présumé, mais pas au livre en tant que tel,

---

Bible as Book, 5–20 ; A. Lange, "The Status of the Biblical Texts in the Qumran Corpus and the Canonical Process," ibid., 21–30 ; idem, "The Parabiblical Literature of the Qumran Library and the Canonical History of the Hebrew Bible," *Emanuel* (ed. S.M. Paul et al. ; Leiden : Brill, 2003), 305–21 ; idem, "From Literature to Scripture. The Unity and Plurality of the Hebrew Scriptures in Light of the Qumran Library," *One Scripture or Many? Canon from Biblical, Theological and Philosophical Perspectives* (ed. C. Helmer and C. Landmesser ; Oxford : Oxford University Press, 2004), 51–107.

[3] "Titrologie et paratextualité," *Titres et articulations du texte dans les œuvres antiques. Actes du Colloque International de Chantilly 13–15 décembre 1994* (dir. J.-Cl. Fredouille et al. ; Paris : Institut d'Etudes Augustiniennes, 1997), 582.

comme dans la formule : « X a dit que... ». Dans 11QMelchisédeq, par exemple, l'auteur commente le verset d'*Isaïe* « Qu'ils sont beaux, sur les montagnes, les pieds de celui qui annonce une bonne nouvelle » (52,7) en citant Dn 9,25 : « Et celui qui annonce, c'e[st (celui qui est)] oint par l'esp[rit], selon ce qu'a dit Dan[iel à son propos : "Jusqu'à un chef ayant reçu l'onction, il y a sept semaines" » (11Q13 II 18).[4] La formule introductive (כאשר אמר) renvoie à la personne plutôt qu'au livre. Parfois, lorsqu'un texte se réfère à une parole plutôt qu'au livre biblique dans lequel elle est mise par écrit, celle-ci est attribuée à Dieu.[5] Ainsi, dans CD XIX 11–12, on lit : « comme (cela) eut lieu durant la période de la première visite, dont il a dit [12] par l'intermédiaire d'Ezéchiel : "marquer la marque sur le front de ceux qui soupirent et qui gémissent" (Ez 9,4) ». Le scribe avait commencé par écrire : « dont Ezéchiel a dit », puis a rectifié en rajoutant ביד, « par l'intermédiaire de ».[6]

Inversement, la citation peut être introduite par une formule qui souligne qu'il s'agit d'un texte écrit, mais sans que l' "auteur" ou la source du texte soit identifié(e). C'est le cas par exemple dans 1QS V 15, qui affirme : « qu'on s'éloigne de lui (l'impie) en toute chose, car il est ainsi écrit (כיא כן כתוב) : "De toute chose frauduleuse tu t'éloigneras" (Ex 23,7) ». Il semble que, pour les lecteurs ou auditeurs de 1QS, l'indication de la source ait été superflue.

Enfin, certaines citations ne sont absolument pas introduites. Ainsi, en CD VI 3–4, on observe un enchaînement assez abrupt : « et Il (Dieu) leur a fait entendre (sa voix), et ils ont foré le puits : "Le puits (que) des princes ont foré, que les nobles du peuple ont creusé avec un sceptre" (Nb 21,18). Le puits, c'est la Loi ». La citation des *Nombres* est insérée dans le texte sans formule introductive (à la manière d'une apposition, en quelque sorte), puis commentée. On notera que tel n'est pas le cas dans 4Q266 et 4Q267, qui présentent un texte différent et introduisent

---

[4] C'est en effet la reconstitution la plus plausible. Cf. F. García Martínez et al., *DJD* 23 : 225 et 232 :

והמבשר הו[אה]מ[שיח הרו[ח] כ֯אשר אמר דנ[י]אל עליו עד משיח נגיד שבועים שבעה...

[5] Cf. VanderKam, "Authoritative Literature," 391.

[6] Voir également CD III 21 (« par l'intermédiaire d'Ezéchiel le prophète ») ou CD IV 13 (« par l'intermédiaire d'Isaïe le prophète »), sans rature cette fois. Pour d'autres exemples de citations précédées d'une formule du type « Dieu a dit », cf. 1QM XI 5–7 et 11–12 ; 4Q252 IV 2–3.

la citation des *Nombres* en ces termes : « [Ils ont] foré [l]e puits, au sujet duquel Moïse a dit : "Le puits..." ».[7]

Une pluralité d'usages cohabitent parfois au sein d'un même texte. Prenons l'exemple des citations du *Deutéronome* dans l'*Écrit de Damas*. Pour ce seul cas de figure, on rencontre d'ores et déjà presque toutes les formules d'introduction possibles. En CD VIII 9, la citation de Dt 32,33 est introduite par les mots « dont Dieu à dit, à leur propos » (אשר אמר אל עליהם). Immédiatement après, en CD VIII 14–15, deux autres versets du *Deutéronome* (9,5 et 7,8) sont cités partiellement et introduits par la formule « Et (ce) que Moïse a dit » (ואשר אמר משה). En CD XIX 1, à l'inverse, la citation de Dt 7,9 est précédée de la formule « comme il est écrit » (כאשר כתוב), sans plus de précision. En CD V 1, on trouve une formule légèrement différente, « à propos du prince, il est écrit » (על הנשיא כתוב), suivie de Dt 17,17 (« Il ne multipliera pas pour lui-même les femmes »). Enfin, à la ligne suivante (CD V 2), le texte poursuit en expliquant : « Mais David n'avait pas lu le livre scellé de la Loi (החתום בספר התורה) qui se trouvait [3] dans l'arche ». On peut s'interroger sur ce que désigne l'expression « le livre scellé de la Loi » : s'agit-il du *Deutéronome* ou du Pentateuque dans son ensemble, de la *Torah* ? Nous reviendrons sur ce point dans la seconde partie de cet article. Pour l'instant, bornons-nous à constater que l'on recense pas moins de cinq manières différentes de citer ou de se référer au *Deutéronome* dans le seul *Écrit de Damas*, et que l'une d'elle seulement fait intervenir un titre (dont la signification exacte reste ambiguë).

Examinons à présent les citations d'*Isaïe* dans ce même texte. En CD IV 13–14, une citation d'Is 24,17 est introduite par la formule « ainsi que Dieu (l') a dit par l'intermédiaire d'Isaïe le prophète, fils d'Amoç, en disant » (כאשר דבר אל ביד ישעיה הנביא בן אמוץ לאמר). En CD VI 7–8, un passage qui poursuit le commentaire de Nb 21,18 évoqué plus haut, un extrait d'Is 54,16 est cité et introduit par la formule « à propos duquel Isaïe a dit » (אשר אמר ישעיה). Enfin, en CD VII 10–11, on rencontre la combinaison de deux formules dans la phrase « quand s'accomplira la parole qui est écrite dans les paroles d'Isaïe fils d'Amoç, le prophète, [11] qui a dit » (בבוא הדבר אשר כתוב בדברי ישעיה בן אמוץ הנביא אשר).

---

[7] Cf. 4Q267 2 8–10, dans *DJD* 18 : 97 :

8 (...) וֹיֹחֹפֹּ[ן]וֹ[רֹ]וֹ[ן]

9 [א]ֹת הֹבאֹרֹ אֹשֹר אמֹר מושה באֹר חֹפֹּ[ר]וה שרים כֹּרוה

10 נֹדיֹבֹי [העם] במחוקק

De même, en 4Q266 3 ii 10, on lit : אשר אמר מוֹשֹה.

אמר), suivie d'une citation d'Is 7,17. L'expression «les paroles d'Isaïe fils d'Amoç, le prophète» équivaut à un titre. Dans la Bible, l'emploi du mot דברי comme élément d'un titre est bien attesté, qu'il soit suivi d'un nom propre (souvent celui d'un prophète)[8] ou d'un nom commun (comme dans דברי הימים).[9] Cette fois encore, on observe qu'il existe dans CD plusieurs manières de citer ou de se référer à *Isaïe*. Tantôt Dieu dit quelque chose par l'intermédiaire d'Isaïe, tantôt le propos est attribué au prophète lui-même (ce qui ne signifie pas que la source de ses paroles n'est pas Dieu), ou encore on fait référence au livre d'*Isaïe* en le désignant par un titre.

La coexistence de ces modes de citation au sein d'une même œuvre montre que le fait d'écrire «Dieu a dit» plutôt que «Moïse a dit» (opposition Dieu/messager), ou de privilégier la formule «ainsi qu'il est écrit dans le livre d'Isaïe le prophète» plutôt qu'«Isaïe a dit» (opposition écrit/parole), n'a pas forcément d'implications théologiques ou idéologiques. Néanmoins, la comparaison entre CD A et les manuscrits de l'*Écrit de Damas* issus de la grotte 4 montre que, par endroits, le copiste de CD A a évité la formule «Moïse a dit», comme soucieux d'attribuer le contenu de la révélation à Dieu lui-même et de ne pas insister sur l'intermédiaire humain. Les manuscrits de CD étant d'époque médiévale, toute la question est de déterminer à quel moment cette évolution a eu lieu. En outre, on trouve malgré tout dans CD A des exemples de versets introduits par la formule «X a dit», si bien que l'on ne peut parler d'une tendance systématique à éviter l'attribution d'un passage biblique à un auteur humain.[10]

On peut conclure de l'étude conjointe des citations bibliques et des titres dans les textes de Qumrân que l'usage du titre pour introduire une citation n'est pas la règle. Il est toutefois un peu plus fréquent dans le cas des livres attribués aux prophètes Isaïe, Jérémie, Ezéchiel, Daniel et Zacharie.[11] C'est peut-être un hasard si l'on n'a pas retrouvé d'exemples de ce genre pour *Amos, Osée, Michée* ou *Malachie*, dont des ver-

---

[8] Voir par exemple 1 Ch 29,29; 2 Ch 9,29; 12,15, etc. דברי suivi d'un nom propre est également utilisé dans des *incipit* en forme de titres: Jr 1,1; Am 1,1; Qo 1,1; Ne 1,1.

[9] Voir entre autres 1 R 14,19; Ne 12,23; 1 Ch 27,24.

[10] Cf. les deux exemples mentionnés *supra*, CD VIII 14–15 et VI 7–8.

[11] Cf. T.H. Lim, "The Alleged Reference to the Tripartite Division of the Hebrew Bible," *RevQ* 20/77 (2001): 32–33.

sets sont cités dans certains textes de Qumrân, ou encore pour *Habacuc*
et *Nahum*, qui sont commentés dans des *pesharim*. De manière générale,
on rencontre un peu plus de titres liés aux personnes (ou de citations
introduites par une formule faisant intervenir le nom d'une personne)
que de titres relatifs au contenu ou représentant l'*incipit* du livre.

Prenons l'exemple du livre des *Psaumes*, que la tradition massorétique
nomme ספר תהלים. Dans les textes bibliques eux-mêmes, le mot תהלים
n'est pas attesté, ni *a fortiori* utilisé comme titre. La première attestation
du titre ספר התהלים se rencontre à Qumrân, dans 4Q491 17 4 (*Règle
de la Guerre*ᵃ), où il désigne vraisemblablement les *Psaumes*, bien que
l'absence de contexte ne permette pas d'en être certain.[12] En 11QPsᵃ
XXVII 5 est attribuée à David la composition de 3600 תהלים, mais dans
ce contexte il s'agit d'un nom commun, non d'un titre. À l'inverse, dans
11QMelchisédeq II 9–10, une citation du Ps 82,1 est introduite par
les mots «comme il est écrit à son sujet dans les Cantiques de David,
qui a dit» (כאשר כתוב עליו בשירי דויד אשר אמר). La combinaison de
כאשר כתוב et אשר אמר rappelle CD VII 10–11. Le titre donné ici au
livre des *Psaumes* n'est autre que *Les Cantiques de David*. Dans 4Q177
12–13 i 2,[13] la citation du Ps 6,2–3 est introduite par la formule «au
sujet duquel David a dit» (אשר אמר דויד). Dans un autre passage de
4Q177 (5–6 7),[14] le Ps 11,1 est cité mais apparemment sans introduction,
hormis l'*incipit* du psaume lui-même, למנצח] לדויד. Enfin, aux lignes
11–12 des mêmes fragments 5–6 de 4Q177, les mots «c]omme il est
écrit à leur sujet dans le livre[»] (כ]אשר כתוב עליהם בספר]) semblent
bien introduire le Ps 12,1. La lacune est ici particulièrement regrettable,
car, complète, cette ligne aurait permis de déterminer si le titre donné
aux *Psaumes* dans 4Q177 était le *Livre de David* ou le *Livre des Psaumes*,
ou un autre titre dont le souvenir s'est perdu. Enfin, si l'on accepte
l'analyse que j'ai proposée de 4QMMT C 10,[15] il faut considérer le nom
«David» à la fin de cette ligne comme une référence aux *Psaumes*, tout
comme le nom «Jérémie» est utilisé pour se référer au *Livre de Jérémie*

---

[12] Cf. M. Baillet, *DJD* 7: 40–41.

[13] Col. XI 7 selon la reconstruction d'A. Steudel, *Der Midrasch zur Eschatologie aus der Qumrangemeinde (4QMidrEschat*ᵃˑᵇ*)* (STDJ 13; Leiden: Brill, 1994), 74.

[14] Col. VIII 7 selon A. Steudel, ibid., 71.

[15] Dans "4QMMT et la question du canon de la Bible hébraïque," *From 4QMMT to Resurrection: Mélanges qumraniens en hommage à Émile Puech* (ed. F. García Martínez et al.; STDJ 61; Leiden: Brill, 2006), 1–14. Pour E. Ulrich, la lecture ובדוי]ד est toutefois sujette à caution; cf. "The Non-Attestation of a Tripartite Canon in 4QMMT," 211.

dans 4Q163 1 4. Malgré quelques incertitudes, on peut conclure que dans leurs références aux *Psaumes*, les textes de Qumrân font davantage intervenir le nom de David qu'un titre comme תהלים.

2. Titres et processus de canonisation

Considérations générales

Il faut noter d'emblée que la plupart des discussions autour du canon et de ses différentes parties («Torah», «Prophètes» et «Écrits») ne prennent pas en compte le fait que ces mots sont également des *titres* de sections. L'histoire de l'émergence du canon de la Bible hébraïque recoupe dans une large mesure l'histoire des titres de ses sections. De même, le processus de canonisation n'est pas sans rapport avec l'apparition d'un terme générique désignant l'ensemble des écrits considérés comme canoniques, que ce terme soit «Écritures saintes», «Bible», «Tanakh» ou un autre.[16] Il n'y a donc pas de canon sans titres, qu'il s'agisse du titre global donné au corpus ainsi constitué, des titres de ses parties (lorsqu'il est subdivisé en différentes parties) ou des titres des livres qui le composent.

Le chercheur intéressé par l'histoire de la constitution du canon dans ses différentes parties doit néanmoins conserver présente à l'esprit une vérité d'évidence : le terme תורה, «loi», ne représente pas nécessairement un titre. Dans la majorité des cas, que ce soit dans la Bible ou dans les textes de Qumrân, il désigne plutôt la Loi de Dieu, c'est-à-dire l'ensemble des commandements donnés par Dieu. Si l'on prend l'exemple des livres bibliques les plus tardifs, rédigés à l'époque perse ou au début de l'époque hellénistique,[17] on constate que le terme תורה y désigne encore souvent la loi, et non un ensemble littéraire appelé *Torah*. Ainsi, en 2 Ch 14,3, Asa dit à Juda «de mettre en pratique la loi et le commandement (לעשׂות התורה והמצוה)». Ou encore, en Ne 10,30, le peuple s'engage à suivre la loi de Dieu, littéralement à «marcher dans la loi de Dieu» (ללכת בתורת האלהים). Il ne peut s'agir du

---

[16] Philon utilise des expressions comme ἱεραὶ βίβλοι, ἱεραὶ γραφαί, ἱεροὶ νόμοι, ἱερὸς λόγος, ὁ νόμος, νομοθεσία, mais ils désignent dans la plupart des cas le seul Pentateuque. Cf. N.G. Cohen, "The Names of the Separate Books of the Pentateuch in Philo's Writings," *SPhilo* 9 (1997): 54–78.

[17] Comme les *Chroniques*. Cf. S. Japhet, *I & II Chronicles. A Commentary* (London: SCM Press Ltd, 1993), 23–28; G.N. Knoppers, *I Chronicles 1–9. A New Translation with Introduction and Commentary* (New York: Doubleday, 2003), 116.

Pentateuque. En Dn 9,10, la même expression est utilisée, mais le terme תורה est cette fois au pluriel. Daniel prie et reconnaît que le peuple n'a pas écouté Dieu, «pour suivre ses lois (ללכת בתורתיו) qu'il avait mises devant nous par l'intermédiaire de ses serviteurs, les prophètes». De même, une attestation de תורה au pluriel a été préservée dans un texte de Qumrân, 4QPsaumes non canoniques B (4Q381), dont Eileen Schuller date la composition de la fin de l'époque perse ou du début de l'époque hellénistique. Sur le frag. 69 5, on lit: «[...Il a donné des dé]crets, des lois et des commandements par l'alliance (qu')il a établie par l'intermédiaire de[Moïse]».[18] Dans ce contexte, le mot תורה est bien sûr un nom commun.

De même, le terme נביאים, «prophètes», désigne avant tout les êtres humains considérés comme des prophètes, et ne renvoie pas nécessairement à des livres, ni—a fortiori—à une section du canon.[19] Il n'est donc pas surprenant que les textes de Qumrân utilisent des expressions comme «le livre d'Isaïe le prophète» (par exemple dans 4Q174 1–2 i 15, 4Q265 1 3 ou 4Q177 5–6 5) ou «les livres des prophètes» (cf. CD VII 17 et le parallèle en 4Q266 3 iii 18), dans lesquelles la présence du mot ספר lève toute ambiguïté.

Même dans le cas où l'on rencontre les expressions «livres de la Loi» et «livres des prophètes» (CD VII 15 et 17), une question demeure. Ces livres sont-ils désignés ainsi parce qu'ils constituent ensemble une partie d'un canon, ou parce qu'ils appartiennent à une même catégorie d'ouvrages? Ne confondons-nous pas canonisation et taxinomie? Une erreur semblable a été commise par F.H. Colson à propos d'un terme employé par Philon, οἱ προτρεπτικοί (λόγοι), qu'il considérait comme une autre appellation du *Deutéronome*, alors qu'il s'agit en réalité

---

[18] Cf. E. Schuller, *DJD* 11: 149–52 («Non-Canonical Psalms B»):

°°° [משה] נתן ח[ו]קים תורות ומצות בברית העמיד ביד[...]

Elle souligne qu'il existe de nombreux points communs entre ce texte et *Néhémie* 9 (et, dans une moindre mesure, *Esdras* 9).

[19] Dans Sir 49,10, les mots «les douze prophètes» désignent clairement des personnes. Mais cette expression laisse aussi entendre que les livres associés à ces prophètes étaient déjà regroupés. On notera que le *Siracide* ne fait jamais référence aux livres bibliques en tant que tels, mais qu'il évoque plusieurs figures de l'histoire d'Israël, juges, rois, prophètes ou prêtres. Sur les références bibliques dans le *Siracide*, cf. entre autres P.C. Beentjes, "Canon and Scripture in the Book of Ben Sira," *Hebrew Bible/Old Testament. The History of Its Interpretation. Vol. I From the Beginnings to the Middle Ages (Until 1300)* (ed. M. Saebø; Göttingen: Vandenhoeck & Ruprecht, 2000), 591–605.

de discours d'exhortation, c'est-à-dire d'une *catégorie* de discours.[20] Il confondait titre et classement.

Or, les livres du Pentateuque ont probablement été rassemblés parce qu'ils étaient attribués à un même "auteur," Moïse. De même, les livres prophétiques ont en commun d'être attribués à des prophètes (qui, à la différence de Moïse, ne sont pas des législateurs). Le canon n'a-t-il pas pour origine un classement des livres en fonction du type d'auteur qui leur était attribué ? L'expression «livres des prophètes» renvoie peut-être d'abord à un critère d'attribution et non à un statut (l'appartenance à la seconde section du canon). On notera que les *Psaumes*, attribués à David, font généralement l'objet d'une référence séparée, et qu'ils n'ont pas été intégrés à la section des livres prophétiques, en dépit de l'inspiration prophétique reconnue de David. Cela s'expliquerait très bien si les sections du canon s'étaient développées en lien avec une classification des livres fondée—au moins en partie—sur les fonctions attribuées à leurs auteurs présumés. En effet, l'inspiration de David ne fait pas pour autant de lui un prophète au sens où Samuel, Nathan ou Isaïe ont été des prophètes. David demeure avant tout un roi, le modèle même du roi idéal d'Israël. Si l'appartenance à la section canonique «Prophètes» dépendait de l'inspiration attribuée à l'auteur ou de son don prophétique, tous les livres bibliques devraient y prendre place, y compris ceux de la *Torah*, attribués au plus grand des prophètes, Moïse. Mais si l'on tient compte du fait que Moïse fut davantage qu'un prophète, à savoir l'intermédiaire par lequel la Loi fut donnée à Israël au Sinaï, et que David fut avant tout un roi, alors la répartition Torah/ Prophètes/Psaumes fait sens. Son principe est la distinction faite entre des types d' "auteurs."[21]

---

[20] Cf. Cohen, "The Names of the Separate Books," 66–70.

[21] En ce qui concerne les livres dits «historiques» (les prophètes antérieurs), leur attribution à des prophètes est certes moins nette que dans le cas des livres prophétiques postérieurs, mais le témoignage des *Chroniques* la rend très vraisemblable. En effet, les *Chroniques* se réfèrent à plusieurs reprises à des documents du type «*Les paroles de Nathan le prophète*» (2 Ch 9,29) à propos des règnes des différents rois. Il pourrait s'agir de sources utilisées par les rédacteurs des *Chroniques*, mais aussi—dans certains cas—de titres attribués à des parties de l'ensemble *1–2 Samuel + 1–2 Rois*, dont l'usage se serait perdu par la suite.

L'autre principe classificateur présidant de toute évidence à la répartition des livres entre «Torah» et «Prophètes», puis—dans le canon massorétique—entre «Prophètes antérieurs» et «Prophètes postérieurs», n'est autre que l'ordre chronologique.

La Torah: loi, livre(s), section du canon

Dans la Bible, le mot תורה, nous l'avons dit, renvoie le plus souvent à la loi (ou Loi, comme ensemble de commandements émanant de Dieu, par opposition à *Torah*, ensemble de cinq livres). Il peut aussi remplir la fonction de titre, mais c'est plus clair quand il est accompagné du mot ספר, comme par exemple dans *Néhémie* 8–9, où l'on relève plusieurs occurrences de תורה accompagnées de ספר. Ne 8,1 parle de la lecture du ספר תורת משה, du matin jusqu'au milieu du jour; Ne 8,3 poursuit en utilisant l'expression ספר תורה; en Ne 8,8, il est question de lire «dans le livre, dans la Loi de Dieu (בספר בתורת אלהים)» (ici «Loi» est un élément du titre); Ne 8,18 évoque la lecture du «livre de la Loi de Dieu» (ספר תורת אלהים); enfin, Ne 9,3 se réfère au «livre de la Loi de YHWH» (ספר תורת יהוה). Il est permis de penser que, dans ces chapitres, c'est l'ensemble du Pentateuque qui est visé (bien qu'en théorie, l'expression pourrait ne pas inclure la *Genèse*, par exemple). En effet, le livre de la loi est lu devant l'assemblée non seulement toute la matinée du premier jour, mais pendant sept jours (Ne 8,18). De plus, d'après Ne 8,14–15, ils découvrent dans le livre l'obligation de célébrer la fête des Huttes avec des feuillages, précision qui ne figure que dans le *Lévitique*.[22] Cet exemple nous montre qu'au sein d'un même texte, dont l'unité est indéniable, co-existent plusieurs façons de désigner la *Torah*. On notera au passage qu'elle est désignée tantôt comme «livre de la Loi de Moïse» et tantôt comme «livre de la Loi de Dieu/de YHWH», sans qu'une connotation idéologique particulière soit attachée à ces appellations.

De même, à Qumrân, le mot תורה, qu'il soit associé à Moïse ou à Dieu, désigne généralement l'ensemble des commandements qu'il faut mettre en pratique.[23] Mais l'on rencontre aussi les expressions «livre de Moïse», «livre de la Loi», «livres de la Loi», etc., appliquées à la *Torah* ou à l'un des livres qui la composent. Dans certains cas, l'expression «livre de Moïse» ou «livre de la Loi» semble en effet renvoyer au seul *Deutéronome*, à moins qu'elle ne renvoie à un passage du *Deutéronome*

---

[22] Sur la fête des Huttes, cf. Lv 23,34–43 et Dt 16,13–15. En organisant la lecture publique de la Loi, le prêtre Esdras obéit en outre à l'injonction prononcée en Dt 31,10–12.

[23] Cf. CD XV 9 et 12; XVI 2 et 5; 1QS V 8; VIII 15 et 22; 4Q162 2 7; 4Q382 15 7; etc. Certains passages sont ambigus. Ainsi, CD VI 14 affirme: «Ils prendront soin d'agir selon l'interprétation exacte de la Loi (כפרוש התורה) au temps de l'impiété». Le mot פרוש indique-t-il que la תורה est un livre? Pas forcément, car les lois aussi ont besoin d'être interprétées …

au sein de l'ensemble qu'est la *Torah*.[24] Ainsi, dans 4QMMT C, il est fait référence au «livre de Moïse» (lignes 10 et 21) dans un contexte où c'est le *Deutéronome* qui est cité ou paraphrasé.[25] De même, en CD V 2, après une citation de Dt 17,17aα (un passage qui interdit au roi de multiplier ses femmes), la polygamie de David est excusée par le fait qu'il «n'avait pas lu le livre scellé de la Loi qui se trouvait dans l'arche» (ודויד לא קרא בספר התורה החתום אשר היה בארון). Le commandement de Dt 17,17 ne se trouvant dans aucun autre livre de la *Torah*, on en déduit que David n'avait pas lu le *Deutéronome*, qui devrait donc logiquement être identifié au «livre scellé de la Loi». Mais il n'est pas exclu que cette expression désigne toute la *Torah*, dont le *Deutéronome* ne serait qu'une section.[26]

La reprise de *Deutéronome* 17 dans le *Rouleau du Temple* contient elle aussi une occurrence de l'expression «livre de la Loi», la seule attestée dans les manuscrits relatifs à cette œuvre. En s'inspirant de Dt 17,10–11, l'auteur du passage écrit: «Tu agiras conformément à la loi que (les prêtres) te diront et conformément à la parole qu'ils prononceront pour toi d'après le livre de la Loi» (11Q19 LVI 3–4).[27] Le parallèle entre la «loi» (תורה) dite et la «parole» (דבר) prononcée montre que la

---

[24] Dans la Bible, l'expression «livre de Moïse» est utilisée en lien avec une citation du *Deutéronome* dans Ne 13,1 et 2 Ch 25,4. À l'inverse, dans Esd 6,18 et 2 Ch 35,12 (les deux autres occurrences de ספר מושה), il n'y a pas de lien avec le *Deutéronome*. Quant à l'expression «livre de la Loi» (ספר התורה), il s'agit dans la Bible d'une expression deutéronomique, désignant à l'origine le *Deutéronome* lui-même (cf. Dt 28,61 ; 29,20 ; 30,10 ; 31,26 ; Jos 8,34 ; 24,26 ; etc.).

[25] Sur ce point, cf. M.J. Bernstein, "The Employment and Interpretation of Scripture in 4QMMT: Preliminary Observations," *Reading 4QMMT: New Perspectives on Qumran Law and History* (ed. J. Kampen and M.J. Bernstein ; SBLSS 2 ; Atlanta : Scholars Press, 1996), 29–51 (46–50) ; M. Kister, "Studies in 4QMiqṣat Maʿaśe ha-Torah and Related Texts: Law, Theology, Language and Calendar," *Tarbiz* 68 (1999): 317–71 (349) ; S.D. Fraade, "Rhetoric and Hermeneutics in Miqṣat Maʿaśe ha-Torah (4QMMT): The Case of the Blessings and Curses," *DSD* 10 (2003): 150–161 ; Berthelot, "4QMMT et la question du canon," 6–10.

[26] Par ailleurs, dans 4Q177 1–4 14 (X 14 selon la reconstruction de Steudel dans *Der Midrasch zur Eschatologie*, 73), l'expression ספר התורה שנית, «le livre de la seconde Loi», pourrait renvoyer au *Deutéronome*. Steudel choisit toutefois de comprendre le mot שנית comme un adverbe, et traduit : «das] ist wiederum das Buch der Thora» (79).

[27] Texte hébreu (cf. *The Temple Scroll* [ed. E. Qimron ; Jerusalem : IES, 1996], 81):

3 ועשיתה על פי התורה אשר ינידו לכה ועל פי הדבר
4 אשר יואמרו לכה   מספר התורה וינידו לכה באמת
5 מן המקום אשר אבחר לשכין שמי עליו ושמרתה לעשות
6 ככול אשר יורוכה ועל פי המשפט אשר יואמרו לכה
7 תעשה לוא תסור מן התורה אשר ינידו לכה ימין
8 ושמאול (...)

première occurrence de תורה est à traduire par «loi» et non par *Torah*. La comparaison avec Dt 17,10–11[28] montre en outre que le mot דבר, utilisé à deux reprises dans Dt 17,10–11, a été remplacé dans 11Q19 par le mot תורה. Enfin, les mots ועל פי הדבר אשר יואמרו לכה מספר התורה ויגידו לכה באמת (11Q19 LVI 3–4) ne figurent pas dans Dt 17,10–11. Les mots «d'après le livre de la Loi» (מספר התורה) sont donc une précision introduite par l'auteur de ce passage du *Rouleau du Temple* pour indiquer quelle est la source des enseignements sacerdotaux. Or, il est peu probable que ces derniers soient tirés du seul *Deutéronome*.[29] Par conséquent, l'expression ספר התורה dans 11Q19 LVI 4 désigne vraisemblablement la *Torah*.

Dans d'autres manuscrits de Qumrân, l'expression «livre de la Loi» pourrait également renvoyer à la *Torah*, mais l'absence de contexte ou son imprécision ne permettent pas de trancher de manière catégorique. Ainsi, d'après 4Q273 2 1 (papD[h]) recoupé avec 4Q267 5 iii 4–5, parmi les personnes à la vision ou à l'élocution défectueuse, «[...aucune d'entre elles] ne lira dans le livre de la Lo[i...]».[30] Ou encore, dans 6Q9 21 3 («Un apocryphe de Samuel-Rois»), on lit sur un fragment très abîmé: «[...écrits dans le li]vre de la Lo[i...]».[31] D'après M. Baillet, le vocabulaire de ce passage est de type deutéronomique, mais cela signifie-t-il que le «livre de la Loi» est à identifier avec le *Deutéronome*? Certes, dans l'historiographie deutéronomiste, l'expression «livre de la Loi» désigne généralement le *Deutéronome*.[32] Dans le cas de 6Q9, le texte est cependant trop fragmentaire pour qu'une conclusion définitive puisse être tirée. L'exemple de 4Q249 montre par ailleurs que l'expression «livre de Moïse», souvent associée à des citations ou des paraphrases du *Deutéronome*,[33] peut désigner un ensemble plus vaste, peut-être même toute la *Torah*. Au verso de 4Q249, on lit en effet un titre, *Interprétation*

---

[28] Dt 17,10–11 TM:

ועשית על־פי הדבר אשר יגידו לך מן־המקום ההוא אשר יבחר יהוה ושמרת לעשות ככל אשר יורוך: על־פי התורה אשר יורוך ועל־המשפט אשר־יאמרו לך תעשה לא תסור מן־הדבר אשר־יגידו לך ימין ושמאל

[29] En matière pénale, voir par exemple Ex 21,12–22,16.

[30] Cf. J.M. Baumgarten, *DJD* 18: 195: איש מאלה [לֹא <י>קרא בספר התו]רה (pour 4Q267, cf. 102).

[31] Cf. Baillet, *DJD* 3: 120: הכתובים בס[פֵר התור]ה

[32] Cf. Jos 8,34 (après Jos 8,31 qui cite le *Deutéronome*); 2 R 22,8 et 11; 23,24; et le récit parallèle en 2 Ch 34,15.

[33] Cf. *supra*, n. 24. Voir également le cas de 4QMMT C, mentionné *supra*. Dans 2Q25 1 3 (*DJD* 3: 90), l'expression כתוב בספר מוש]ה est dénuée de contexte, et il est donc impossible d'identifier à quel passage biblique cela renvoie.

du livre de Moïse (מדרש ספר מושה),[34] tandis qu'au recto, rédigé en écriture cryptique, il semble que le texte traite des lois concernant la maison "lépreuse" (*Lévitique* 14).[35] Il est probable que, dans ce cas, le «livre de Moïse» ait correspondu à la *Torah*. Enfin, un dernier cas de figure se présente dans 4Q434 2 12–13 (4QBarkhi Nafshi[a]), où nous lisons: «[12] [...]pour la Loi tu as établi [13] [...] le livre de tes statuts».[36] Le «livre de tes statuts» désigne peut-être la *Torah*, et le terme «Loi» à la ligne 12 pourrait lui-même renvoyer non à la Loi comme ensemble de commandements, mais bel et bien à la *Torah*. Cependant, une fois de plus, le caractère fragmentaire du texte ne permet pas de conclusion définitive.

Le meilleur exemple de l'emploi du mot «Loi» (תורה) en lien avec un ensemble de livres (et pas seulement un ensemble de lois) reste sans doute CD VII 15, qui évoque «*les livres* de la Loi», ספרי התורה. Bien sûr, le pluriel ne prouve pas qu'il s'agissait des cinq livres qui constituent actuellement la *Torah*, mais c'est malgré tout l'hypothèse la plus probable. On trouve en outre dans 1Q30 1 4, dans un passage malheureusement très abîmé et dépourvu de contexte, l'expression «cinq livres» (ס]פרים חומשים °[), qui renvoie certainement au Pentateuque.[37]

Le témoignage combiné de ces deux derniers textes[38] amène à conclure que la *Torah* comme ensemble de cinq livres est bel et bien attestée dans la bibliothèque de Qumrân, même si les titres individuels de chacun des cinq rouleaux, eux, ne le sont pas, à l'exception de ברשית dans 4QGen[h] (4Q8c). Elle semble avoir été désignée tantôt comme

---

[34] Cette façon d'indiquer le titre au verso du manuscrit est attestée sur d'autres manuscrits de Qumrân (comme 4Q504 ou 1Q28), ainsi que sur des manuscrits grecs (plus tardifs); cf. L. Holtz, "Titre et incipit," *Titres et articulations du texte dans les œuvres antiques*, 472. En ce qui concerne les titres de livres bibliques, à Qumrân on relève une seule occurrence d'un titre au verso; il s'agit du mot ברשית (sans א) dans 4QGen[h] (4Q8c). Cf. J.R. Davila, *DJD* 12: 63; E. Tov, *Scribal Practices and Approaches Reflected in the Texts from the Judean Desert* (STDJ 54; Leiden: Brill, 2004), 118 et 120–21. Comme le souligne très justement Tov, ce ברשית représente la première attestation manuscrite de la formation d'un titre de livre biblique à partir du (ou des) premier(s) mot(s) du livre.

[35] Cf. S. Pfann, *DJD* 35: 18–24.

[36] Cf. M. Weinfeld and D. Seely, *DJD* 29: 279:

12 [...]לתורה הכינותה
13 [...]ך ספר חוקיך

[37] Plutôt qu'aux *Psaumes*, qui sont certes divisés en cinq parties, mais ne sont pas désignés par le titre de «cinq livres». Cf. J.T. Milik, *DJD* 1: 133.

[38] Auquel il faudrait ajouter l'examen des manuscrits bibliques (sur un même manuscrit peuvent figurer la fin d'un livre du Pentateuque et le début du livre suivant) et le témoignage du *Reworked Pentateuch*. Mais cela dépasse le propos de cet article.

le «Livre de Moïse», tantôt comme le «Livre de la Loi», voire «les Livres de la Loi».

Si les citations et paraphrases des livres attribués à des prophètes ne sont pas nécessairement accompagnées de références au titre du livre, cela est donc encore plus vrai des cinq livres qui constituent la *Torah*, dont les titres—qu'il s'agisse de ceux attestés dans la Septante ou de ceux de la tradition massorétique—ne figurent dans aucun manuscrit de Qumrân. Cette absence s'explique en partie par l'usage fréquent de formules imprécises du type «comme il est écrit» (sans indication de source), «X a dit» ou «Dieu a dit», que l'on rencontre aussi dans le cas de citations de livres au titre bien attesté par ailleurs (comme *Isaïe*), mais elle demeure curieuse. Elle est parfois compensée par l'usage d'un titre plus général, comme «le *Livre de Moïse*», «le *Livre de la Loi*» ou «les *Livres de la Loi*», qui préfigure l'appellation «*Torah*» donnée par la suite à l'ensemble *Genèse*—*Deutéronome*. Enfin, il est possible que ces deux titres aient, à l'origine, désigné le seul *Deutéronome*, et n'aient servi à nommer l'ensemble des cinq livres attribués à Moïse que dans un deuxième temps, par synecdoque. En tout cas, le témoignage des textes de Qumrân tend à montrer que les titres donnés aux livres de la *Torah* dans la tradition rabbinique émergèrent tardivement.[39] Ce constat n'est pas incompatible avec l'autorité attribuée à ces livres. En effet, que le titre d'un livre soit indéterminé ne signifie pas que ce livre ne fait pas autorité. Inversement, qu'un livre soit doté d'un titre ne préjuge en rien de sa popularité ou de son degré d'inspiration.

---

[39] La différence, sur ce point, entre livres de la *Torah* et livres prophétiques, s'explique très bien si l'on accepte l'idée que les livres furent d'abord nommés d'après leurs "auteurs" présumés. Moïse étant considéré comme l'auteur des cinq livres constituant la *Torah*, le système d'appellation traditionnel ne permettait pas de distinguer entre les différents livres de Moïse.

QUMRAN READINGS IN AGREEMENT WITH THE SEPTUAGINT AGAINST THE MASORETIC TEXT PART TWO: JOSHUA–JUDGES

Corrado Martone

As a follow-up to my previous contribution devoted to the Pentateuch,[1] the present study aims to provide scholars with a tool that will allow for easy consultation of the few verses of the books of Joshua and Judges in agreement with the Septuagint against the Masoretic text attested in the manuscripts from Qumran. As already noted,[2] the list will hopefully cover the entire Bible in the near future.

As in the previous one,[3] at the end of this contribution the reader will find the bibliographic reference of the *editio princeps* of all of the quoted manuscripts as well as a brief palaeographical description. On the other hand, the reader will need to refer to the article in *Henoch* for more detailed bibliographic information[4] as well as for the methodological assumptions underlying this project.[5]

All in all, it is a privilege and a pleasure to offer this brief step forward in my research to Florentino García Martínez in modest gratitude for all that he has taught me and an entire generation of scholars.

* * *

Josh 3:15

4QJosh[b] 2–3 1–2 (*DJD* 14:155)

‫1 15 נשאי הארון נטבלו בקצ]ה המי[ם וה]...[2 בימי קציר חטים‬
‫16 ויעמדו המים הירדים מל]...[‬

---

[1] C. Martone, "Qumran Readings in Agreement with the Septuagint against the Masoretic Text: Part One: The Pentateuch," *Henoch* 27 (2005): 53–113.

[2] Martone, "Qumran Readings," 54.

[3] Martone, "Qumran Readings," 108–13.

[4] As an *addendum*, it is worth noting that a *Biblia Qumranica* series has been launched by Brill. The volume devoted to the Minor Prophets has appeared so far: B. Ego et al., *Minor Prophets* (Biblia Qumranica 3; Leiden: Brill, 2005).

[5] It should be remembered, however, that in the *Textual Notes* are registered *only* the variant readings regarding the LXX: other variant readings, if any, though at the reader's disposal, are not indicated in the *Notes*.

ὡς δὲ εἰσεπορεύοντο οἱ ἱερεῖς οἱ αἴροντες τὴν κιβωτὸν τῆς διαθήκης ἐπὶ
τὸν Ιορδάνην καὶ οἱ πόδες τῶν ἱερέων τῶν αἰρόντων τὴν κιβωτὸν τῆς
διαθήκης κυρίου ἐβάφησαν εἰς μέρος τοῦ ὕδατος τοῦ Ιορδάνου—ὁ δὲ
Ιορδάνης ἐπλήρου καθ᾽ ὅλην τὴν κρηπῖδα αὐτοῦ ὡσεὶ ἡμέραι θερισμοῦ
πυρῶν—

וּכְבוֹא נֹשְׂאֵי הָאָרוֹן עַד־הַיַּרְדֵּן וְרַגְלֵי הַכֹּהֲנִים נֹשְׂאֵי הָאָרוֹן נִטְבְּלוּ בִּקְצֵה
הַמָּיִם וְהַיַּרְדֵּן מָלֵא עַל־כָּל־גְּדוֹתָיו כֹּל יְמֵי קָצִיר:

Textual Notes
חטים || πυρῶν]] > 𝔐

Josh 4:3
4QJosh[b] 2–3 8 (DJD 14:155)

[...]וַיְצַו אוֹתָם לֵאמֹר שְׂאוּ] לָכֶם מִתּוֹךְ הַ]יַּרְדֵּן 8 [...³]

σύνταξον αὐτοῖς λέγων Ἀνέλεσθε ἐκ μέσου τοῦ Ιορδάνου ἑτοίμους δώδεκα
λίθους καὶ τούτους διακομίσαντες ἅμα ὑμῖν αὐτοῖς θέτε αὐτοὺς ἐν τῇ
στρατοπεδείᾳ ὑμῶν, οὗ ἐὰν παρεμβάλητε ἐκεῖ τὴν νύκτα.

וְצַוּוּ אוֹתָם לֵאמֹר שְׂאוּ־לָכֶם מִזֶּה מִתּוֹךְ הַיַּרְדֵּן מִמַּצַּב רַגְלֵי הַכֹּהֲנִים
הָכֵן שְׁתֵּים־עֶשְׂרֵה אֲבָנִים וְהַעֲבַרְתֶּם אוֹתָם עִמָּכֶם וְהִנַּחְתֶּם אוֹתָם בַּמָּלוֹן
אֲשֶׁר־תָּלִינוּ בוֹ הַלָּיְלָה:

Textual Notes
שְׂאוּ] לָכֶם מִתּוֹךְ הַ]יַּרְדֵּן || Ἀνέλεσθε ἐκ μέσου τοῦ Ιορδάνου]] 𝔐
שְׂאוּ־לָכֶם מִזֶּה מִתּוֹךְ הַיַּרְדֵּן

Josh 5:6
4QJosh[a] I 9–10 (DJD 14:147)

9 [בני ישראל במדבר עד תם כל הגוי] אנשי המלח[ן]מה היצאים
ממצרים אשר לא שמעו] 10 [בקול יהוה אשר נשבע יהוה להם לב]לתי
ראות את ה]ארץ אשר נשבע יהוה לאבותם]

τεσσαράκοντα γὰρ καὶ δύο ἔτη ἀνέστραπται Ισραηλ ἐν τῇ ἐρήμῳ τῇ
Μαδβαρίτιδι, διὸ ἀπερίτμητοι ἦσαν οἱ πλεῖστοι αὐτῶν τῶν μαχίμων τῶν
ἐξεληλυθότων ἐκ γῆς Αἰγύπτου οἱ ἀπειθήσαντες τῶν ἐντολῶν τοῦ θεοῦ, οἷς
καὶ διώρισεν μὴ ἰδεῖν αὐτοὺς τὴν γῆν, ἣν ὤμοσεν κύριος τοῖς πατράσιν
αὐτῶν δοῦναι ἡμῖν, γῆν ῥέουσαν γάλα καὶ μέλι.

כִּי ׀ אַרְבָּעִים שָׁנָה הָלְכוּ בְנֵי־יִשְׂרָאֵל בַּמִּדְבָּר עַד־תֹּם כָּל־הַגּוֹי אַנְשֵׁי
הַמִּלְחָמָה הַיֹּצְאִים מִמִּצְרַיִם אֲשֶׁר לֹא־שָׁמְעוּ בְּקוֹל יְהוָה אֲשֶׁר נִשְׁבַּע יְהוָה
לָהֶם לְבִלְתִּי הַרְאוֹתָם אֶת־הָאָרֶץ אֲשֶׁר נִשְׁבַּע יְהוָה לַאֲבוֹתָם לָתֶת לָנוּ
אֶרֶץ זָבַת חָלָב וּדְבָשׁ:

Textual Notes
ראות || ἰδεῖν αὐτοὺς]] 𝔐 הַרְאוֹתָם

Josh 6:5

4QJoshᵃ II 1 (*DJD* 14:148)

1 ⁵ נדולה ונפלה חמת [...] ועלה העם [א]יש [נ]נדו [...]

καὶ ἔσται ὡς ἂν σαλπίσητε τῇ σάλπιγγι, ἀνακραγέτω πᾶς ὁ λαὸς ἅμα, καὶ ἀνακραγόντων αὐτῶν πεσεῖται αὐτόματα τὰ τείχη τῆς πόλεως, καὶ εἰσελεύσεται πᾶς ὁ λαὸς ὁρμήσας ἕκαστος κατὰ πρόσωπον εἰς τὴν πόλιν

וְהָיָה בִּמְשֹׁךְ ׀ בְּקֶרֶן הַיּוֹבֵל בשמעכם⁶ אֶת־קוֹל הַשּׁוֹפָר יָרִיעוּ כָל־הָעָם תְּרוּעָה נְדוֹלָה וְנָפְלָה חוֹמַת הָעִיר תַּחְתֶּיהָ וְעָלוּ הָעָם אִישׁ נֶנְדּוֹ:

Textual Notes

וְעָלוּ ׀ ועלה ‖ καὶ εἰσελεύσεται ‖ 𝔐

Josh 7:13

4QJoshᵃ IV 2–4 (*DJD* 14:149)

2 [...] לא תשמידו החדם מקרבבם ¹³קם קדש את העם ואמתר

3 [התקדשן] למחר כי כה אמר יהוה אלהי ישראל חרם בקרבכם

4 [ישראל ל]א תוכל לקום לפני אויכים עד הסירכם החרם מקרבכם

ἀναστὰς ἁγίασον τὸν λαὸν καὶ εἰπὸν ἁγιασθῆναι εἰς αὔριον· τάδε λέγει κύριος ὁ θεὸς Ισραηλ Τὸ ἀνάθεμα ἐν ὑμῖν ἐστιν, οὐ δυνήσεσθε ἀντιστῆναι ἀπέναντι τῶν ἐχθρῶν ὑμῶν, ἕως ἂν ἐξάρητε τὸ ἀνάθεμα ἐξ ὑμῶν.

קֻם קַדֵּשׁ אֶת־הָעָם וְאָמַרְתָּ הִתְקַדְּשׁוּ לְמָחָר כִּי כֹה אָמַר יְהוָה אֱלֹהֵי יִשְׂרָאֵל חֵרֶם בְּקִרְבְּךָ יִשְׂרָאֵל לֹא תוּכַל לָקוּם לִפְנֵי אֹיְבֶיךָ עַד־הֲסִירְכֶם הַחֵרֶם מִקִּרְבְּכֶם:

Textual Notes

בקרבכם ‖ ἐν ὑμῖν ‖ 𝔐 בְּקִרְבְּךָ; אוייבים ‖ τῶν ἐχθρῶν ὑμῶν ‖ Med אֹיְבֶיךָ ‖ 𝔐

Josh 8:10

4QJoshᵃ V 10 (*DJD* 14:150)

10 ¹⁰] ...ויעל הוא ו[הזקנים 11 [...]

καὶ ὀρθρίσας Ἰησοῦς τὸ πρωὶ ἐπεσκέψατο τὸν λαόν· καὶ ἀνέβησαν αὐτὸς καὶ οἱ πρεσβύτεροι κατὰ πρόσωπον τοῦ λαοῦ ἐπὶ Γαι

וַיַּשְׁכֵּם יְהוֹשֻׁעַ בַּבֹּקֶר וַיִּפְקֹד אֶת־הָעָם וַיַּעַל הוּא וְזִקְנֵי יִשְׂרָאֵל לִפְנֵי הָעָם הָעָי:

---

⁶ Kethib. Qere: כִּשְׁמַעֲכֶם.

Textual Notes

וְזִקְנֵי יִשְׂרָאֵל [וְ]הַזְקֵנִים || καὶ οἱ πρεσβύτεροι ‖ 𝔐

Josh 8:14

4QJosh^a V 12–13 (*DJD* 14:150)

12 [... ¹⁴וַיְהִי] כַּרְאוֹת 13 [מֶלֶךְ הָעַי] יְמַהֵר[וּ .. לִק]רָאתָם

καὶ ἐγένετο ὡς εἶδεν βασιλεὺς Γαι, ἔσπευσεν καὶ ἐξῆλθεν εἰς συνάντησιν
αὐτοῖς ἐπ’ εὐθείας εἰς τὸν πόλεμον, αὐτὸς καὶ πᾶς ὁ λαὸς ὁ μετ’ αὐτοῦ,
καὶ αὐτὸς οὐκ ᾔδει ὅτι ἔνεδρα αὐτῷ ἐστιν ὀπίσω τῆς πόλεως.

וַיְהִ֞י כִּרְא֣וֹת מֶֽלֶךְ־הָעַ֗י וַֽיְמַהֲר֡וּ וַיַּשְׁכִּ֡ימוּ וַיֵּצְא֣וּ אַנְשֵֽׁי־הָעִ֣יר
לִקְרַאת־יִשְׂרָאֵ֨ל לַמִּלְחָמָ֜ה ה֧וּא וְכָל־עַמּ֛וֹ לַמּוֹעֵ֖ד לִפְנֵ֣י הָֽעֲרָבָ֑ה וְה֣וּא לֹ֣א
יָדַ֔ע כִּֽי־אֹרֵ֥ב ל֖וֹ מֵאַחֲרֵ֥י הָעִֽיר׃

Textual Notes

לִקְרַאת־יִשְׂרָאֵל [לִק]רָאתָם || εἰς συνάντησιν αὐτοῖς ‖ 𝔐

Josh 8:35

4QJosh^a I 1–2 (*DJD* 14:147)

1 [...] הַתּוֹרָה ³⁵לֹא הָיָה דָבָר מִכָּל צִוָּה מֹשֶׁה [אֶת יְהוֹ]שֻׁעַ אֲשֶׁר לֹא קָרָא
יְהוֹשֻׁעַ נֶגֶד כָּל 2 [קְהַל יִשְׂרָאֵל ...] אֶת הַיַּרְדֵּ[ן] וְהַנָּשִׁים וְהַטַּף וְהַגֵּ[ר]
הַהוֹלֵךְ בְּקִרְבָּם אַחַר אַחַר אֲשֶׁר נָתְקוּ [...]

LXX 9:2 οὐκ ἦν ῥῆμα ἀπὸ πάντων, ὧν ἐνετείλατο Μωϋσῆς τῷ Ἰησοῖ,
ὃ οὐκ ἀνέγνω Ἰησοῦς εἰς τὰ ὦτα πάσης ἐκκλησίας υἱῶν Ισραηλ, τοῖς
ἀνδράσιν καὶ ταῖς γυναιξὶν καὶ τοῖς παιδίοις καὶ τοῖς προσηλύτοις τοῖς
προσπορευομένοις τῷ Ισραηλ.

לֹֽא־הָיָ֣ה דָבָ֗ר מִכֹּ֤ל אֲשֶׁר־צִוָּ֣ה מֹשֶׁ֔ה אֲשֶׁ֛ר לֹֽא־קָרָ֥א יְהוֹשֻׁ֖עַ נֶ֣גֶד כָּל־קְהַ֣ל
יִשְׂרָאֵ֑ל וְהַנָּשִׁ֣ים וְהַטַּ֔ף וְהַגֵּ֖ר הַהֹלֵ֥ךְ בְּקִרְבָּֽם׃

Textual Notes

[אֶת יְהוֹ]שֻׁעַ || τῷ Ἰησοῖ ‖ > 𝔐

Judg 6:11

4QJudg^a 1 6 (*DJD* 14:162)

6 [¹¹ בְּעָפְרָה] אֲשֶׁר לְיוֹאָשׁ הָאֲבִיעֶזְרִי וְגִ[דְעוֹן בְּנוֹ חֹבֵט חִטִּים בַּת
לְהָנִיס מִפְּנֵי מִדְיָ[ן]

LXX A Καὶ ἦλθεν ἄγγελος κυρίου καὶ ἐκάθισεν ὑπὸ τὴν δρῦν τὴν
οὖσαν ἐν Εφραθα τὴν τοῦ Ιωας πατρὸς Αβιεζρι, καὶ Γεδεων ὁ υἱὸς αὐτοῦ
ἐρράβδιζεν πυροὺς ἐν ληνῷ τοῦ ἐκφυγεῖν ἐκ προσώπου Μαδιαμ.
LXX B Καὶ ἦλθεν ἄγγελος κυρίου καὶ ἐκάθισεν ὑπὸ τὴν τερέμινθον τὴν
ἐν Εφραθα τὴν Ιωας πατρὸς τοῦ Εσδρι, καὶ Γεδεων υἱὸς αὐτοῦ ῥαβδίζων
σῖτον ἐν ληνῷ εἰς ἐκφυγεῖν ἀπὸ προσώπου τοῦ Μαδιαμ.

וַיָּבֹ֞א מַלְאַ֣ךְ יְהֹוָ֗ה וַיֵּ֙שֶׁב֙ תַּ֣חַת הָֽאֵלָ֔ה אֲשֶׁ֣ר בְּעָפְרָ֔ה אֲשֶׁ֥ר לְיוֹאָ֖שׁ אֲבִ֣י
הָֽעֶזְרִ֑י וְגִדְע֣וֹן בְּנ֗וֹ חֹבֵ֤ט חִטִּים֙ בַּגַּ֔ת לְהָנִ֖יס מִפְּנֵ֥י מִדְיָֽן׃

Textual Notes

הָאֲבִיעֶזְרִי || LXX A: Αβιεζρι ‖ 𝔐 אֲבִי הָעֶזְרִי || LXX B: πατρὸς τοῦ Εσδρι

Judges 9:42
1QJudg 7 3 (*DJD* 1:63)

3 [...]ה[שדה וינד

καὶ ἐγενήθη τῇ ἐπαύριον καὶ ἐξῆλθεν ὁ λαὸς εἰς τὸ πεδίον, καὶ ἀπηγγέλη τῷ Αβιμελεχ

וַיְהִי מִמָּחֳרָת וַיֵּצֵא הָעָם הַשָּׂדֶה וַיַּגִּדוּ לַאֲבִימֶלֶךְ :

Textual Notes
וינד || καὶ ἀπηγγέλη ‖ 𝔐 וַיַּגִּדוּ

REFERENCE LIST

Joshua
4QJosh^a   [4Q47]: E. Ulrich. Pages 143–52, pls. XXXII–XXXIV in E. Ulrich et al. *Qumran Cave 4.IX: Deuteronomy to Kings.* DJD 14. Oxford: Clarendon Press, 1995. Palaeography: Hasmonean script (second-first c. B.C.E.).

4QJosh^b   [4Q48]: E. Tov. Pages 153–60, pl. XXXV in E. Ulrich et al., *Qumran Cave 4.IX: Deuteronomy to Kings.* DJD 14. Oxford: Clarendon Press, 1995. Palaeography: Late Hasmonean script (middle first c. B.C.E.).

Judges
1QJudg   [1Q6]: D. Barthélemy. Pages 62–64, pl. XI in D. Barthélemy and J.T. Milik, *Qumran Cave 1.* DJD 1. Oxford: Clarendon Press, 1955. Palaeography: Herodian formal script (ca. 30–1 B.C.E.).

4QJudg^a   [4Q49]: J. Trebolle. Pages 161–64, pl. XXVI in E. Ulrich et al., *Qumran Cave 4.IX: Deuteronomy to Kings.* DJD 14. Oxford: Clarendon Press, 1995. Palaeography: Hasmonean (or early Herodian) formal script (ca. 50–25 B.C.E.).

A QUALITATIVE ASSESSMENT OF THE TEXTUAL PROFILE OF 4QSAM^A

Eugene Ulrich

It is a pleasure to offer *flores* to Professor Florentino García Martínez. Not only did he have the vision to establish the International Organization for Qumran Studies and work tirelessly to publish a profuse panoply of scholarship essential to Qumran studies, he has also been a warm personal friend for almost twenty-five years, beginning in the glorious Plaza Mayor in Salamanca at the Septuagint conference in the summer of 1983. In his honor I present this analysis of a major Qumran scroll.

Frank Moore Cross and Richard Saley recently published an article analyzing the textual character of the large Samuel scroll from Cave 4 Qumran.[1] It was primarily a quantitative, statistical study, and as a companion to it, I would like to present a qualitative analysis of the textual character of that important and richly instructive manuscript. How do we situate 4QSam^a in the history of the text of Samuel? How do we describe the type of text it displays in relation to other texts of Samuel?

I will first outline the approach I have gradually formed for understanding and mapping the history of the biblical text in general, and then present a number of significant readings in 4QSam^a that will illumine the textual character of the manuscript. The goal will be to articulate the relationship between 4QSam^a and our other texts of Samuel according to that approach to the history of the text.

---

[1] F.M. Cross and R.J. Saley, "A Statistical Analysis of the Textual Character of 4QSamuel^a (4Q51)," *DSD* 13 (2006): 46–54. Their analysis is derived from the recent publication of 4QSam^a in F.M. Cross et al., *DJD* 17.

I. The History of the Biblical Text

The picture I have formed of the history of the biblical text can be labeled a theory of "successive editions" of biblical books or passages.[2] The text of each book developed organically from its earliest, usually oral, beginnings until it was abruptly frozen around the time of the "Great Divide,"[3] that is, sometime around the Jewish revolts against Rome (roughly the beginning of the second c. C.E.). The main lines illustrating that developmental composition for each book are mapped by tracing how the core of each book underwent a repeated succession of new and expanded editions of the traditional materials. These new and expanded editions were formed by the deliberate activity of a series of creative scribes who set about producing the new literary editions of a particular book.

A. *Theories About the History of the Text*

It will be instructive to review briefly some dominant views attempting to discern the history of the biblical text in light of the biblical scrolls from Qumran and other related sites. There are still good reasons to study the works of pre-1947 scholars regarding this history, but they were limited to evidence from the second period only.[4] They wrote with only the light shed by the MT, the SP, and the LXX, and with minor flickers provided by the versions, Josephus, Philo, and quotes in the NT and Talmud.[5]

---

[2] See Ulrich, "Pluriformity in the Biblical Text, Text Groups, and Questions of Canon," originally published in *Proceedings of the International Congress on the Dead Sea Scrolls—Madrid, 18–21 March 1991* (ed. J. Trebolle Barrera and L. Vegas Montaner; STDJ 11/1; Leiden: Brill, 1992), 23–41; repr. with related studies in *The Dead Sea Scrolls and the Origins of the Bible* (SDSS; Grand Rapids: Eerdmans, 1999).

[3] For the term see S. Talmon, "The Crystallization of the 'Canon of Hebrew Scriptures' in the Light of Biblical Scrolls from Qumran," in *The Bible as Book: The Hebrew Bible and the Judaean Desert Discoveries* (ed. E.D. Herbert and E. Tov; London: The British Library and Oak Knoll Press, 2002), 5–20 (14).

[4] The biblical scrolls have illumined the early period in the history of the biblical text, the period of developmental composition of the books. Before the discovery of those pluriform texts our data were predominantly only from the "second period," i.e., after the "Great Divide," the period of the uniform MT.

[5] For a discussion of pre-Qumran scholarship see S. Talmon, "The Old Testament Text," in *The Cambridge History of the Bible. 1. From the Beginnings to Jerome* (ed. P.R. Ackroyd and C.F. Evans; Cambridge: Cambridge University Press, 1970), 159–99 [repr. in F.M. Cross and S. Talmon (eds.), *Qumran and the History of the Biblical Text* (Cambridge, Mass.: Harvard University Press, 1975), 1–41].

The scene changes in 1947 with the availability of the ca. 230 biblical scrolls from Qumran and other sites. Shortly after these discoveries, Frank Cross and Patrick Skehan, the two Americans chosen for the original editorial team, found illuminating discoveries. Cross demonstrated the textual similarities of the Cave 4 Samuel scrolls with the LXX, and Skehan demonstrated the textual similarities of 4QpaleoExod^m (4Q22) with the SP. This brought those two formerly somewhat dubious textual witnesses into the center stage of textual significance as faithful witnesses to alternate Hebrew texts.

William Foxwell Albright, noting those textual affiliations, saw an analogy with NT textual criticism and suggested a theory of three-fold local texts. Cross developed that theory extensively and put the fattened flesh of evidence on the theoretical bones, by providing numerous examples from significant readings in the scrolls. It was his creative and insightful, empirically based contribution which sparked and laid the foundations for the whole modern discussion of the history of the biblical text. In an over-simplified sentence: he sought to explain how a single Urtext developed into the three known textual forms (the MT, the SP, and the LXX) through independent development in three isolated localities: Palestine, Egypt, and a third, presumably Babylon.

Shemaryahu Talmon approached the topic from a different angle: his observation was that "the further back the textual tradition of the Old Testament is followed, i.e. the older the biblical manuscripts perused…, the wider is the over-all range of textual divergence between them."[6] Thus, in his view, the pattern to explain was—not the one Urtext to three textforms pattern—but how the many textual forms that had earlier circulated were eventually reduced to *only* three (the opposite from Cross). Through a socioreligious lens he saw that only three Jewish groups—the Rabbis, the Samaritans, and the Christians—had survived the revolts against the Romans, and each preserved its own text form: the MT, the SP, and the LXX, respectively.

I have still not worked out whether those two approaches of Cross and Talmon are compatible or mutually exclusive. But a limitation of each that I see is that the local text theory does not explain how specifically the different localities were responsible for the different versions, and that Talmon's socioreligious theory does not explain why the three different religious groups chose their specific variant text forms, especially

---

[6] Talmon, "The Old Testament Text," 162 [repr. p. 4].

since a comparative examination of the variants shows that no group changed their text in light of their religious differences (except for the Samaritans' emphasis on Mount Gerizim, and the MT "Mount Ebal" at Deut 27:4 and Josh 8:30).[7]

As time went by and more manuscripts were published, Emanuel Tov saw that three "text types" were inadequate to explain the multiplex variation that Cross and Talmon had observed. He correctly saw that much of the variety was not due to text types and saw more than three groupings. Thus he somewhat discounts text-types as a full explanation, and in his *Textual Criticism of the Hebrew Bible* he lists five categories into which he thinks the Qumran biblical scrolls fall: (1) Texts Written in the Qumran Practice, (2) Proto-Masoretic (or: Proto-Rabbinic) Texts, (3) Pre-Samaritan (or: Harmonizing) Texts, (4) Texts Close to the Presumed Hebrew source of 𝔊, and (5) Non-Aligned Texts.[8] This has the distinct advantage, especially for students or non-specialists, of helping the textual situation of the new scrolls be quickly seen and filed in our minds. But it is a first, pedagogical step, not a final stage.

I have proposed, in contrast, categories that I think are more suited to the first centuries B.C.E. and C.E. Jews would not have had available, or used, textual categories such as "Masoretic or Proto-Masoretic Text, or even Proto-Rabbinic"; they are anachronistic terms. Moreover, in my view "Non-Aligned texts" cannot be viewed as an operative category in the ancient world. In the Second Temple period there was no "standard text" according to which a manuscript could be "aligned" or "non-aligned."[9] Rather, it seems increasingly clear that the text of each book developed through successive revised literary editions, whereby an earlier form of the book was intentionally revised to produce a newer revised edition. For an extended period of time, the earlier edition would have co-existed alongside the newer edition.

---

[7] See Ulrich, "The Absence of 'Sectarian Variants' in the Jewish Scriptural Scrolls Found at Qumran," in *The Bible as Book*, 179–95, and "47. 4QJoshª," *DJD* 14:145–48. Talmon ("The Old Testament Text," 184 [26]) agrees: "There is nothing specifically sectarian in the external appearance of the Qumrân Scrolls, in the scribal customs to which their copyists adhered, or in the majority of the deviant readings found in them…Genetically the biblical texts from Qumrân are 'Jewish.'"

[8] E. Tov, *Textual Criticism of the Hebrew Bible* (2d. ed.; Minneapolis: Fortress, 2001), 114–17.

[9] The textual character of the MT differs from book to book, just as we know that the textual character of the Septuagint differs from book to book, and the textual character of each Qumran scroll differs from book to book. So one cannot use "MT" as a category of text type unless one specifies which book is being discussed.

Accordingly, since the texts were pluriform and developing through-out the Second Temple period, I propose that "successive editions" of biblical books is a more accurately descriptive term to clarify how the texts developed. Literary and historical critics since the Enlightenment, when analyzing the biblical books, have theorized that the books which we receive usually began in small oral units and gradually evolved through incorporation into larger complexes, to form the composite books known and transmitted in our Bible since the "Great Divide." That organic process continued throughout the Second Temple period and apparently showed no sign of termination.[10] Thus the successive literary editions visible at Qumran provide manuscript documentation of the theories of biblical development hypothesized by scholars since the Enlightenment; together they confirm that the Scriptures were pluriform and organically developing from their very beginnings and throughout their history up to the "Great Divide." The text of each book developed organically from its earliest beginnings until it was abruptly frozen around the time of the Jewish revolts against Rome, due to the threats of the Romans to their political identity and of the Christians to their religious identity.[11]

Thus the main lines tracing that developmental composition for each book are mapped by tracing how the core or Urtext of that book underwent a repeated succession of new and expanded editions of the traditional materials. Each new and expanded edition was formed by the deliberate activity of a creative scribe who produced the new literary edition of a given book. That new edition in turn formed a new Urtext, and those two Urtexte would have lived parallel lives for some period of time.

B. *Orthography, Individual Variants, and Variant Editions*

To set the stage for mapping the textual history, let me start with the process by which the text critic begins encountering the various witnesses

---

[10] As the rich biblical and parabiblical Jewish literature unearthed at Qumran testifies, there were still creative scribes developing the biblical texts, just as there were creative authors producing Scripture-related compositions, such as the pesharim, *Jubilees*, the *Temple Scroll*, etc.

[11] Talmon ("The Old Testament Text," 198 [40]) concurs: "Contradictory as it may sound, one is almost inclined to say that the question to be answered with regard to the history of the Old Testament text does not arise from the extant 'plurality of text-types' but rather from the disappearance of other and more numerous textual traditions."

to a text, then moves through some of the steps in the process, in the hopes of finally being able to explain the character of each particular witness and chart the text history of that book. I see three distinct principal layers: orthography, individual textual variants, and variant literary editions.

For example, comparison of a manuscript such as the Great Isaiah Scroll from Cave 1 with a text like the MT produces what first appears as chaos in the types of variants observed.[12] To help dispel that sense of chaos, I suggest the distinction between the different levels and types of variation: orthographic differences, individual textual variants, and variant literary editions. It has been shown that these three levels are independent of each other; the three different categories of variation arise at different moments or different stages in the history of the text, due to different causes.[13]

So first, it is helpful to sift out the orthographic differences between texts, because they are usually relatively insignificant and have little or nothing to do with the specifically textual character of manuscripts. One usually meets the phenomenon of different spelling practices—not a "system" but simply different approaches toward spelling, though there are almost always counter-examples, where the same word is spelled one way in one verse and a different way somewhere else in the text. For example, *DJD* 17 lists seven whole pages of orthographic differences between 4QSam[a] and the MT. "Of the 233 total orthographic differences between 4QSam[a] and 𝔐..., 𝔐 has 19 readings that are fuller than 4QSam[a], 4QSam[a] has fuller readings than 𝔐 in 210 examples. In four instances, the orthography is different, but neither tradition is fuller than the other."[14] But the point to stress in a discussion of the history of the text is that purely orthographic differences do not entail a difference in meaning, and normally the orthographic profile of a manuscript has little or nothing to do with the textual character of the witness; the two are caused by different factors and operate on independent levels.

---

[12] This apparent chaos is a factor in Emanuel Tov's categorization of the biblical scrolls as "Written in the Qumran Practice" and "Non-Aligned" as well as the MT, SP, and LXX categories.

[13] See Ulrich, "The Palaeo-Hebrew Biblical Manuscripts from Qumran Cave 4," and "Orthography and Text in 4QDan[a] and 4QDan[b] and in the Received Masoretic Text," in *Scrolls and Origins*, 121–47, and 148–62.

[14] *DJD* 17:9–15.

Secondly, once the level of orthographic differences is peeled off and distraction by them is removed, the critic isolates the individual textual variants that populate every text: the pluses, minuses, alternate renderings, transpositions, and errors. Then each individual variant is explored to discover the various possible reasons that might explain it, and each is ascribed a preliminary judgment regarding how it arose. One does this for every variant in the entire text. Often that is as far as the textual variants can take us, because we have fairly narrow window on major textual forms from antiquity, since our earliest extant witnesses date only from the late third century B.C.E., and any further significant textual development is cut off after approximately the second Jewish Revolt in 132–135 C.E.

But a third and qualitatively higher level can now be identified by the extant witnesses for many biblical books: that of variant literary editions of the book. Many of the individual variants may sporadically point in different, random directions, since they invaded the ongoing text through unrelated errors or impulses at different times; but sometimes a large and significant group of variants displays the same intentional schema. Once all the individual variants have been studied, one sifts through them to determine whether large-scale patterns emerge: was someone intentionally producing a significant set of variants for discernible motives? Synthetic, comprehensive examination of the full list of individual textual variants sometimes illumines a large-scale intentional pattern exhibited by a significantly large number of the variants. If one can demonstrate that a reasonably large number of similar textual variants indicate consistent motivation by a single purposeful scribe, then a variant literary edition has been isolated.[15] A creative religious leader or scribe has taken the existing form of the book and intentionally, systematically, repeatedly inserted new, interrelated material at numerous points in the old text.

Examples of such new and expanded editions would be 4QpaleoExodᵐ (or the Samaritan Exodus) compared to the earlier edition in the MT of Exodus; or the MT of Jeremiah compared to the earlier edition in 4QJerᵇ,ᵈ and the Septuagint of Jeremiah; or the Septuagint of Daniel

---

[15] One clear and well-known example of this practice with respect to the text of Samuel would be the Greek *Kaige* recension. The early Jewish community took the Old Greek translation of Samuel and systematically revised it in order to conform more literally to the vocabulary and syntax of a Hebrew text of the type from which the Masoretic Samuel descended.

compared to the earlier edition in the MT of Daniel and 1QDan[b] and 4QDan[d].[16]

Thus the major patterns of variation between texts are due primarily to the intentional new literary editions of a previous form of that book. The Qumran scrolls, and the MT, the SP, and the LXX display variant literary editions of many of the biblical books, and in each case it can be shown that one of the literary editions developed from another in successive linear form. So one can envision the process as a series of developing Urtexte. There is one major form of the text for a period of time. Then a creative religious leader produces a new edition of the book due to some religious, social, or historical factors. For some length of time both the older and the newer editions are circulating, but eventually the older form gradually disappears from use.

C. *Mapping the Relationships between Texts*

Once all the types of variation have been examined and understood, one can chart the history of the text. (1) The major lines in the history of the text for each biblical book are formed by the successive new and expanded literary editions of the book from its beginnings until the text is frozen around the time of the First or the Second Jewish Revolt. There can be only one, or there can be two, three, or even (in the case of Exodus) four such major lines depicting variant editions circulating simultaneously. Each major edition will have numerous exemplars, each of which will eventually develop individual textual variants.

(2) The secondary lines between manuscript witnesses of a given book are formed by the individual textual variants. These show text affiliation in differing degrees. If two or more MSS show only a relatively few minor variants but many agreements, especially in errors and secondary readings, that would indicate MSS within the same "text family" (or close-knit group of MSS). If they show a moderate number of variants but some notable agreements, that would indicate "text groups" (if viewed synchronically or horizontally) or "text traditions" (if viewed diachronically or vertically). If there are many, major variants with no discernible intentional pattern, that would identify distant exemplars of the same edition.

---

[16] See Ulrich, *Scrolls and Origins*, 39–41, 64–65, 96–98.

(3) Orthographic differences are basically irrelevant to the history of the text of a particular book, except within the same close-knit "text family" to indicate sequence. That is, if two manuscripts exhibiting close family affiliation differ in orthographic approach, usually the fuller or more developed *plene* orthography indicates that the manuscript with the fuller orthography is subsequent to the one with the shorter[17] orthography, since the tendency in the late Second Temple period was toward fuller, and thus clearer, orthography.

II. The Textual Profile of 4QSam^A

A. *Additions in 4QSam^a*

1 Sam 1:11 (*DJD* 17:29–30; *Qumran*, 39–40)[18]

𝔔 ≈ 𝕮	ויין ושכר לוא ישתה ו[מורה לא יעבור עֹל ראשו]	ונתתיהו ל[פניך נזיר עד יום מותו
𝔐	ומורה לא יעלה על ראשו	כל ימי חייו ונתתיו ליהוה

I will set him before you as a nazirite until the day of his death. He shall drink neither wine nor intoxicants....

This reading should be analyzed in tandem with the following reading. The reconstruction of "nazir" is based on the Greek word δοτόν (and probably Josephus, *Ant.* 5.344) here and the occurrence of "nazir" in v 22, and it appears to be a secondary addition. The reconstruction of the longer reading is based on the requirements of space and the longer Greek text.

1 Sam 1:22 (*DJD* 17:30–37; *Qumran*, 165–66)

𝔔 ≈ Josephus	ונת[תיהו נזיר עד עולם כול ימי [חייו
𝔐	>

I will offer him as a nazirite for all time.

---

[17] The English term "defective" is an unfortunate term and should perhaps be abandoned. The identical Latin form *defective*, parallel to *plene*, is understandable, since it simply means "lacking," but the English "defective" connotes failure. The shorter spelling of a word is not "defective," but simply shorter. Both the shorter and the longer forms are legitimate, permissible ways of spelling the word, just as, e.g., "honor" and "honour."

[18] The readings are taken from *DJD* 17 and *BHS*; for fuller discussion see *DJD* 17 and Ulrich, *The Qumran Text of Samuel and Josephus* (HSM 19; Missoula: Scholars Press, 1978). The latter owes a significant debt to Frank Cross's unpublished notes.

This reading is a secondary addition. It is attested by Josephus (*Ant.* 5.347) who uses "prophet" in view of his Greco-Roman audience, just as he does for the nazir Samson (*Ant.* 5.285). In light of these first two readings, one could suspect an intentional pattern of variants; but the pattern is seen nowhere else in the book.

1 Sam 1:24 (*DJD* 17:30–37; *Qumran*, 40–41)

𝔔 ≈ 𝕮   וי[שחט]²⁵   והנער [עמם ויביאוהו לפני יהוה וישחט אביהו את]הזבח [כ]אשר
[יעשה מימים ימימה ליהוה

𝔐   וישחטו²⁵   נער   והנער

and the boy with them. They brought him before the LORD,
and his father slaughtered the sacrifice, as he customarily did each year to the LORD.

This appears to be a simple inadvertent loss of text by 𝔐; see 1 Sam 11:9 below as well as the clear case of homoioteleuton in 𝔐 at 14:41.

1 Sam 2:22 (*DJD* 17:39–47; *Qumran*, 133)

𝔔   ²²ועלי זקן מאד בן תשעים שנה [ושמונה שנים] וישמע
𝔐   ²²ועלי זקן מאד   ושמע

Eli was very old, ninety-eight years old,

The explicit mention of Eli's age is quite probably a secondary addition in line with all witnesses at 4:15 (note also 1 Sam 2:22 under "B. Additions in 𝔐" below).

1 Sam 2:24 (*DJD* 17:39–47; *Qumran*, 41–42)

𝔔   הש[מ]ועה אשר אנכ̇י שֹמ̇[ע אל תעשון כן כי לו]א טוב[ות השמועות]אשר אני שומע
𝔐   שמע   השמעה אשר אנכי

(not a good) report that I hear. Do not act thus, for they are not good reports that I hear

This longer reading appears to be simply a double rendering in the scroll.

1 Sam 10:27–11:1 (*DJD* 17:65–67; *Qumran*, 69–70, 166–70)

𝔔 = Josephus   ונ[ח]ש מלך בני עמון הוא לחץ...(+3 1/2 lines)... ויהי כמו חדש
ויעל נחש העמוני ויחן¹¹:¹
𝔐   ויעל נחש העמוני ויחן¹¹:¹   ויהי כמחריש:

Now Nahash, king of the Ammonites, had been grievously oppressing...

This paragraph, attested also by Josephus (*Ant.* 6.67–69), appears to be an original reading accidentally lost from 𝔐 and other traditions;

cf. 2 Sam 24:16 below. If it were judged to be a secondary intentional addition, one does not find similarly motivated additions.

1 Sam 11:9 (*DJD* 17:67–69; *Qumran*, 133)

𝔔	\ [ואמר]ו אנש[י] יביש ⁱ⁰	\ ...לכם פתחו הש[ער]	\מיהוה התש[ו]עה...
𝔐	¹⁰ויאמרו אנשי יביש	>	תהיה לכם תשועה...

for you. Open the gate(?)

The scroll has three lines of text (marked by \ ) in contrast to two lines in 𝔐; thus, as seen in 1 Sam 1:24 above, it has an entire line not in 𝔐. It is impossible to determine whether the extra text is an addition in the scroll or a loss by 𝔐, but either way it is a major variant.

2 Sam 6:2 (*DJD* 17:123–29; *Qumran*, 194)

𝔔	בעלה היא קר[י]ת יערים אשר] ליהו[ד]ה
𝔐	מבעלי יהודה

to Baal(ah), that is Kiriath-jearim of Judah,

The scroll adds a secondary ("footnote") identification of the place; cf. Josh 15:9.

2 Sam 6:7 (*DJD* 17:123–29; *Qumran*, 195)

𝔔 (> 𝕰)	האלוהי[ם על] אש[ר] שלח ידו] על [ה]ארון
𝔐	האלהים על השל

because (Uzzah) reached out his hand to the ark

This appears to be a simple corruption in 𝔐.

2 Sam 8:7 (*DJD* 17:132–34; *Qumran*, 45–48)

𝔔 ≈ 𝕰	ירוש[ל]י[ם]גם[ ]אותם ל[קח אחר שושק מלך מצרים ב[ע]לותו אל יר[ו]שלים]
	בימי רחבעם בן שלו[מה
𝔐	ירושלם:

These, moreover, Shishak king of Egypt later took, when he came to Jerusalem in the time of Rehoboam.

This reading is a secondary intentional addition, incorporating a later, related historical detail; cf. 1 Kgs 14:25–26.

2 Sam 10:6 (*DJD* 17:136–38; *Qumran*, 152–56)

𝔔 ≈ J	עמון]אלף ככר כסף...צוב]ה רכב ופרשים [...]שנים שלושי[ם אלף רכב
	[ואת מלך ...] עמון נאספו מן

𝔐   >   ...   >   ...צובא   >   עמון
             >   ...[ואת מלך

The scroll has a longer list of differing details about the Ammonites' military allies.

2 Sam 13:21 (*DJD* 17:147–52; *Qumran*, 84–85)

Q   ויחר לו מאד ולוא עצב את רוח אמנון בנו כי אה]בו כי בכור]ו הוא
𝔐   ויחר לו מאד

he became very angry, but he would not punish his son Amnon, because he loved him, for he was his firstborn.

The scroll inserts a secondary addition about David's emotions, attested by 𝕲 and Josephus (*Ant.* 7.173).

2 Sam 13:27 (*DJD* 17:147–52; *Qumran*, 85)

Q   כו]ל בני המלך [ויעש אבשלום משתה כמשתה ה]מ]ל]ך]
𝔐   כל בני המלך:

Absalom made a feast like a king's feast.

The scroll inserts a secondary addition about Absalom's feast, attested by 𝕲 and Josephus (*Ant.* 7.174).

2 Sam 24:16 (*DJD* 17:192–95; *Qumran*, 156–57)

Q   אר]נא הי]ב]וסי ו]שא [דו]יד...וירא את מלאך] ע]ל [פנ]יהם   (+2 lines)...
          מתכ]סים ב]שקים ו]י]אמר דויד¹⁷
𝔐   ¹⁷ויאמר דוד   האורנה היבסי:

and David looked up and saw the messenger of the Lord…on their faces, covered with sackcloth.

Again, 𝔐 seems to have lost two lines of text, attested by 1 Chr 21:16 and Josephus (*Ant.* 7.327), through parablepsis דוד ויאמר⌐דוד וישא; cf. 1 Sam 10:27–11:1 above.

2 Sam 24:20 (*DJD* 17:192–95; *Qumran*, 157–59)

Q   בשקים וארנא דש ח]טים]. ... עברים אליו מתכ]סים בשקים בא]ים אליו ויצא
𝔐   ויצא   עברים עליו   >

with sackcloth. Arna was threshing wheat…coming to him, covered with sackcloth, coming to him and he went out

The scroll has lengthy narrative details, again attested by 1 Chr 21:20 and Josephus (*Ant.* 7.330), but lost through parablepsis in 𝔐.

B. *Additions in 𝔐*

1 Sam 2:22 (*DJD* 17:39–47; *Qumran*, 57–58)

𝔔   [וַ]יֹּאמֶר²³   לבני ישראל

𝔐   וַיֹּאמֶר²³ לכל ישראל ואת אשר ישכבון את הנשים הצבאות פתח אהל מועד

and how they lay with the women who served at the entrance to the tent of meeting.

Whereas 4QSam^a inserted one addition, Eli's age, at the beginning of this verse (see 1 Sam 2:22 under "Additions in 4QSam^a" above), 𝔐 inserts another addition, the sin of Eli's sons, at the end of the verse.

1 Sam 2:31–32 (*DJD* 17:39–47; *Qumran*, 58–59)

𝔔   יהיה [וְלוֹא]³²   [... בית אביך

𝔐   בית אביך מהיות זקן בביתך ³²והבטת צר מעון בכל אשר ייטיב את ישראל ולא יהיה

your ancestor's family, so that no one in your family will live to old age. [32]*Then in distress you*
will look with greedy eye on all the prosperity that shall be bestowed upon Israel; and no one

𝔐 appears to be expanded with doublets here.

2 Sam 5:4–5 (*DJD* 17:118–23; *Qumran*, 60–62)

𝔔   (4QSam^a does not have the two verses)

𝔐   *David was 33 years old and reigned 40 years: at Hebron 7½ years, and at*
Jerusalem 33 years.

𝔐 adds a secondary notation of the chronological details about David's reign, possibly taken from 1 Kgs 2:11.

C. *Conclusions for 4QSam^a*

Once we view these larger instances of pluses and minuses in 4QSam^a and the MT, and also think of the hundreds of other textual variants between these two texts, the question rises: do these two Hebrew text traditions display simply a large number of individual textual variants, or rather two variant editions of the book of Samuel?

I think that a survey of these examples—and the same would hold true for the bulk of the remaining variants—indicates not an intentional new edition in either the scroll or the MT, but rather two exemplars of the same general edition, simply distantly related due to separate transmission, where each has gained numerous innocent and predictable additions, and each has suffered either losses or double renderings or corruption. But they do not represent intentionally produced variant literary editions. No significant intentional pattern of similarly motivated variants emerges to indicate a new edition.

The most promising passages that might suggest two variant literary editions would be the David-Goliath episode in 1 Sam 17–18, the Hannah-Elkanah narrative of the birth of Samuel in 1 Sam 1–2, and the Nahash passage as an introduction to 1 Sam 11.

But the Nahash passage appears to be simply a single, inadvertent loss of this paragraph in the MT—thus no intentional new edition. If the paragraph were in fact shown to be a deliberate addition in 4QSam^a, that would still not constitute a variant edition of the Book Samuel, because it is an isolated, unrepeated phenomenon. Either way it simply points to two noticeably different text traditions, only distantly related.

Regarding the Hannah episode, I agree with Stanley Walters[19] and Emanuel Tov[20] that there is a significant cluster of variants between the various texts. But I am so far not persuaded that one version is an intentional new edition of the passage by a single editor, since the variants do not seem to form a fully intentional pattern of variants.

Finally, the David–Goliath episode is, I think, a variant literary edition of that passage in 1 Sam 17–18. The Old Greek version has the short original text, whereas the MT displays an intentional double version. The MT tradition has inserted a "romantic tale" into the earlier "heroic tale" seen in the Old Greek;[21] the details of the "romantic tale" have been interspersed into the "heroic tale" the same way the Priestly flood story was interspersed into the Yahwistic flood story in Gen 6–8. But no parallel phenomena with similar motivations are visible anywhere else in the book of Samuel. Thus chs. 17–18 are an example of a variant literary edition of a single short passage, but 4QSam^a and MT–Samuel

---

[19] S.D. Walters, "Hannah and Anna: The Greek and Hebrew Texts of 1 Samuel 1," *JBL* 107 (1988): 385–412.

[20] E. Tov, "Different Editions of the Song of Hannah and of Its Narrative Framework," in idem, *The Greek and Hebrew Bible: Collected Essays on the Septuagint* (VTSup 72; Leiden: Brill, 1999), 433–55.

[21] For detailed discussions of the two editions, see D. Barthélemy, D.W. Gooding, J. Lust, and E. Tov, *The Story of David and Goliath: Textual and Literary Criticism: Papers of a Joint Research Venture* (OBO 73; Fribourg, Suisse: Éditions Universitaires, 1986). I agree with the position of Tov and Lust and disagree with that of Barthélemy and Gooding. The terms "heroic tale" and "romantic tale" are Lust's (p. 14).

are not examples of variant literary editions of the full book. 4QSam^a and the Old Greek are close members of one text tradition of Samuel, a tradition that was used by the Chronicler and by Josephus; and they are quite removed from text tradition used by the MT and by the *Kaige* and Hexaplaric Greek texts. Thus 4QSam^a and the MT are distant representatives of the same general edition of the book of Samuel. This conclusion coincides perfectly with the conclusions reached by Cross and Saley in their statistical analysis.[22]

---

[22] Cross and Saley, "A Statistical Analysis," 46–47, 53–54.

THE TEXTUAL CHARACTER OF THE
UNIQUE READINGS OF 4QSAM[A] (4Q51)

Donald W. Parry

The introduction of *DJD* 17 provides details regarding 4QSam[a]'s provenance, physical condition, contents, orthography, widths of columns and margins, paragraphing, paleography, and textual character. With regard to its textual character, we the authors of *DJD* 17 conclude that

> the study of the full manuscript has reinforced our early conclusions that 4QSam[a] stands in the same general tradition as the Hebrew text upon which the Old Greek translation was based...A proper emphasis on the fidelity of MT and on the wisdom and accuracy of its transmitters must not compromise our estimates of the fidelity of many Old Greek translators, and especially that of the Old Greek translator of Samuel. The fragments of 4QSam[a] underline the seriousness with which the Old Greek translator dealt with the Hebrew text, and confirm most emphatically the usefulness of the Old Greek for the establishment of a more nearly original Hebrew text.[1]

Despite our presentation of these various elements in the introduction of *DJD* 17 we do not provide facts and data regarding the textual character of variant readings that are unique to 4QSam[a], yet these unique readings comprise approximately 28.67 of the total of extant variant readings in this Qumran manuscript.

A recent statistical count of the textual variants of 4QSam[a], as compared with the Masoretic Text (MT) and Septuagint (LXX), reveals that there are 1,117 variants. Of these variants, 429 are extant (they exist on the leather fragments) and about 688 are reconstructed (based on the evidence of space requirements and/or support from other ancient versions).[2] Further statistical counts disclose 241 unique or nonaligned

---

[1] F.M. Cross, D.W. Parry, R.J. Saley, E. Ulrich, *Qumran Cave 4: XII: 1–2 Samuel* (DJD XVII; Oxford: Clarendon Press, 2005), 25, 27. See the full quotation on the textual character of 4QSam[a] in light of the Old Greek translators on pp. 25–27.

[2] These statistical counts, derived from the variants and reconstructed variants of *DJD* 17 were prepared by F.M. Cross and R.J. Saley, "A Statistical Analysis of

readings in 4QSam^a.[3] Of 4QSam^a's unique readings, 123 are attested and 118 are reconstructed.[4]

This paper will examine the textual character of the unique readings of 4QSam^a. Only extant variants readings will be examined. Reconstructed readings, although significant to the study and understanding of the scroll, will not be examined. By definition, a unique reading[5] is where 4QSam^a ≠ MT/LXX^B/LXX^L/LXX^{BL}. Readings where 4QSam^a = Chronicles or Josephus (versus MT/LXX^B/LXX^L/LXX^{BL}) are also considered to be unique readings.[6] The unique readings may be divided into four categories: (1) accidental errors that have occurred during transmission of the text, (2) intentional changes of the text on the part of the scribes and copyists of either MT or 4QSam^a, (3) synonymous readings, and (4) scribes' stylistic approaches and conventions to the text. Not all unique readings, of course, fit neatly into one of these four categories; some readings are indeterminate.

(1) Accidental Errors

Various handbooks that reveal the nature of textual criticism refer to mishaps that occur during the transmission of texts.[7] These include

---

the Textual Character of 4QSamuel^a (4Q51)," *DSD* 13 (2006): 47–51; see especially Tables 1 and 2.

[3] According to E. Tov, *Textual Criticism of the Hebrew Bible* (Minneapolis: Fortress, 1992), 116, the Qumran "texts which are most manifestly non-aligned, and actually independent, are texts which contain readings that diverge significantly from the other texts, such as 4QDeut^{j,n}, 4QJosh^a, 4QJudg^a, and 5QDeut. 4QSam^a holds a special position in this regard, since it is closely related to the Vorlage of G, while reflecting independent features as well." See also idem, "Hebrew Biblical Manuscripts from the Judaean Desert," *JJS* 34 (1988): 32.

[4] Cross and Saley, "A Statistical Analysis," 47–51; see especially Tables 1 and 2.

[5] Scholars have used many terms to describe non-aligned readings, including *individualistic, exclusive, unique, independent,* and *nonaffiliated.*

[6] For this definition of unique readings, see Cross and Saley, "A Statistical Analysis," 50. Furthermore, readings from Chronicles or Josephus that support 4QSam^a are also classified as unique readings, as per Cross and Saley, 50 n. 6.

[7] The most complete and up-to-date study of biblical Hebrew textual criticism is Tov's *Textual Criticism of the Hebrew Bible.* See also C.D. Ginsburg, *Introduction to the Massoretico-Critical Edition of the Hebrew Bible* (London: Trinitarian Bible Society, 1897; repr. with prolegomenon by H.M. Orlinsky; New York: Ktav, 1966); J. Weingreen, *Introduction to the Critical Study of the Text of the Hebrew Bible* (Oxford: Oxford University Press, 1982). Compare also the more brief treatments of the subject by J. Trebolle Barrera, *The Jewish Bible and the Christian Bible* (Leiden: Brill, 1998), 367–421, and E. Würthwein, *The Text of the Old Testament* (Grand Rapids: Eerdmans, 1995), 107–22.

pluses (e.g., dittography, conflate readings), minuses (e.g., haplography, *homoioteleuton*,[8] *homoioarcton*), changes (e.g., misdivision of letters or words, ligatures, graphic similarity), and differences in sequence (interchange of letters or metathesis and transposition of words). All of these major categories of accidental errors are present in both of the Hebrew witnesses to Samuel. The accidental errors cause a variety of configurations of variant readings among the versions, such as 4QSam^a = MT ≠ LXX, 4QSam^a = LXX ≠ MT, and 4QSam^a ≠ MT = LXX. Here we are interested in the later configuration, where 4QSam^a exhibits non-alignments with regard to either MT or LXX. It should be understood that examples of 4QSam^a's unique readings do not exist solely because of the scribal activity of that scroll or its ancestors but because of the scribal activity of all of the major witnesses. Most of these scribal errors may easily be categorized according to the rules of textual criticism. A single type of reading does not dominate the deviations between 4QSam^a and other witnesses where 4QSam^a is unique. The following examples serve to illustrate the variety of such variant readings listed above.

Pluses

During the process of textual transmission, "there are certain small, common words which were easily inserted in the text, such as לאמר, שם, אשר, עתה, אחד, כל, ו."[9] These function words account for many of the unique readings that form the text of 4QSam^a, for example, the *waw* plus in 4QSam^a 1 Sam 6:5 or the addition of כול in 4QSam^a 1 Sam 10:18 and 2 Sam 3:34.

A possible dittography, which has no support from the other witnesses, exists in 4QSam^a 1 Sam 2:16: ה[בשר יקח את מזלג שלוש השנים] כבשלת[ן ביד]ו והכה] בסיר או בפרור[כו]ל[אשר יעלה המזלג יקח. This long reading likely has its basis in MT 1 Sam 2:13–14: כבשל הבשר והמזלג שלש השנים בידו והכה בכיור או בדוד או בקלחת או בפרור כל אשר יעלה המזלג יקח. Twelve words are identical in 4QSam^a 1 Sam 2:16 and MT 1 Sam 2:13–14; additionally, two words are nearly identical (כבשלת versus כבשל and והמזלג versus מזלג). The primary differences in the two readings are

---

[8] Ginsburg, *Introduction to the Massoretico-Critical Edition*, 171–82, features a methodical examination of minuses caused by *homoioteleuton*.

[9] J. Wellhausen, *Der Text der Bücher Samuelis* (Göttingen: Vandenhoeck & Ruprecht, 1871), 26.

the additional verb and direct object marker in 4QSam^a (את יקח) and
the reading of four cooking vessels in MT versus the two vessels of
4QSam^a.[10] If the long plus of 4QSam^a represents a dittography, then
the reading has subsequently experienced changes. It is always possible,
of course, that this long plus was lost to the proto-Masoretic tradition
through a haplographic accident.

Some deviate readings between the witnesses, where 4QSam^a has
a unique reading, are conflated readings. Although conflated readings
are not always clear-cut, one or more textual critics have identified a
conflated element in the deviations. Four examples adequately portray
this phenomenon: 2 Sam 15:2, where "the variants to the Qumran
reading arise from a conflation of two older readings,"[11] and 1 Sam
2:16 and 2 Sam 3:34 and 6:7 where LXX is conflate. Compare also
the category of Exegetical Plus, found below.

Minuses

Unique readings in the Qumran text of Samuel originated, on occasion,
when either MT or 4QSam^a experienced the loss of words or phrases
through haplography or omission by *homoioteleuton* or *homoioarcton*. For
instances of minuses in 4QSam^a, see 2 Sam 12:15 (the omission of
ויאנש, which is found in other versions as well as Josephus, *Ant.* 7.154);
2 Sam 13:27 (where 4QSam^a lacks אתו in the phrase וישלח אתו את; and
2 Sam 4:12 (a haplographic error which came about when the scribe
failed to add the *waw* suffix on לקח because his eye skipped to the next
character which was also a *waw*, e.g., לקח ויקבר, cf. MT ויקבר (לקחו.
Another unique reading in Qumran exists (see 1 Sam 11:9, לכם פתחו
(הש[ער]) because of a *parablepsis* in MT (also found in LXX and other
versions). Compare also 4QSam^a 2 Sam 11:5, אנוכי הרה [הנ]ה, with MT,
LXX^L, אנכי הרה and LXX^BO אנוכי הרה. At 24:16 there is a long passage
in 4QSam^a וי̇שא [דו]י̇ד] את עיניו וירא את מלאך יהוה עומד בין] הארץ ובין]
ה̇ש[מ]י̇ם וחר[ב]ו̇ שלופה בידו נטוא̇[ה על ירושלים ויפלו הזקנים ע[ל [פנ]יהם
מתכ[ו]סים בש[ק]ים (cf. 1 Chr 21:16; Josephus, *Ant.* 7.327) that is not found
in MT or LXX, a loss because of *parablepsis*.

---

[10] With regard to the variant readings of the list of cooking vessels between MT
and 4QSam^a, see D.W. Parry, "How Many Vessels? A Examination of MT 1 Sam
2:14//4QSam^a 1 Sam 2:16," in *Studies in the Hebrew Bible, Qumran, and the Septuagint:
Presented to Eugene Ulrich* (P.W. Flint et al.; VTSup 101; Leiden: Brill, 2006), 84–95.

[11] *DJD* 17:155; see also P. Kyle McCarter, Jr., *II Samuel: A New Translation with Introduction, Notes and Commentary* (AB 9; Garden City, N.Y.: Doubleday, 1984), 354.

Graphic Similarity[12]

Graphically similar readings account for a small number of the unique readings of 4QSam^a, where either the copyists of MT or the Qumran scroll incorrectly copied the text by using graphically similar characters. An example is located in 2 Sam 5:6, where 4QSam^a reads [הסית[ור versus הסירך of MT. *Resh* and *tav* are graphically similar, or the original reading may have included either the comparable רו or ת.

A more complex example of graphically similar readings is located in David's Song of Praise (2 Sam 22 = Ps 18) where three Hebrew witnesses (4QSam^a, MT 2 Sam 22:43 = MT Ps 18:43) attest to variants that are graphically similar. Each of the three variants has an *alef*, *resh* or *dalet* (*resh* and *dalet* are commonly confused), *qof*, and final *mem*. 4QSam^a reads אדקעם; MT 2 Sam 22:43 conflates two readings (אדקם אדקעם), the first of which is strikingly akin to אדקעם; and the reading of MT Ps 18:43 (אריקם), too, is graphically comparable to אדקעם. Of the three words—אדקם, אריקם, and אדקעם—the latter serves best as the parallel for ואשחקם which appears in the first half of this couplet.[13] The Greek words of LXX are difficult to equate to the Hebrew and can only be approximated.[14]

Four additional examples of graphically similar words occur in 1 Sam 2:9 and 2 Sam 3:29, 35, and 12:14.

Misdivision of Words

Two examples of misdivided words[15] are associated with 4Q's unique readings. (1) In 4QSam^a 2 Sam 3:35 the copyist joined two words together (כל and או) to create a single word (אוכל), an inadvertent error. MT, followed by LXX, correctly reads או כל. (2) 4QSam^a 1 Sam 1:24 reads משלש בקר [בן בפר], versus MT בפרים שלשה. A copyist misplaced the initial *mem* of משלש which ultimately (with the addition of a *yod*)

---

[12] See Weingreen, *Introduction to the Critical Study*, 38–45, for examples of graphically similar letters together with examples of variants in the HB.

[13] אדקעם is apparently from the root רקע. See L. Koehler and W. Baumgartner, *HALOT*, 3:1292.

[14] See E.C. Ulrich, *The Qumran Text of Samuel and Josephus* (HSM 19; Missoula, Mont.: Scholars Press, 1978), 104.

[15] For a discussion of word division and a list of misdivided words, consult E. Tov, *The Text-Critical Use of the Septuagint in Biblical Research* (JBS 4; Jerusalem: Simor, 1981), 174–77; Ginsburg, *Introduction to the Massoretico-Critical Edition*, 158–62; Weingreen, *Introduction to the Critical Study*, 48–53.

resulted in the pluralization of "bulls." The primary reading is believed to be בפר משלש.[16] Textual critics believe MT's reading to be suspect, in part because the following verse announces that Samuel's family slaughtered a single, rather than three bullocks. The reading of בן בקר in 4QSam[a] may be a harmonization based on Pentateuchal readings, such as Exod 29:1 and Lev 4:3.

Interchange of Letters or Metathesis[17]

Three examples of unique readings in 4QSam[a] occurred because of metathesis or the interchange of letters. These are 4QSam[a] 2 Sam 12:14 יומח versus MT, LXX ימח; 4QSam[a] 2 Sam 3:29 יואב versus MT, LXX אביו; and 4QSam[a] 1 Sam 2:18 חונר versus MT חנור. Similarly, there are two examples of transposition of texts, both based on partial reconstructions: 4QSam[a] 2 Sam 3:10 [ויהודה [על ישראל and MT על ישראל ועל יהודה; 4QSam[a] 2 Sam 13:6 [תמר [אחותי and MT אחתי תמר.

Changes to Proper Names

There are more than thirty variants in 4QSam[a] and MT that pertain to proper names (e.g., 1 Sam 5:10; 11:1; 12:11; 15:31; 25:5; 27:10, 12; 30:29; 2 Sam 3:4; 17:25; 24:16, etc.). Of these variants, four readings are unique to 4QSam[a] versus MT and LXX:

(1) 1 Sam 14:49—4QSam[a] וא[ש] בעל, MT וישוי. MT is followed by all of the versions.
(2) 1 Sam 15:32—4QSam[a] [אנ[ון], MT אגג. The reading of the Qumran witness is less certain because of its fragmented nature.
(3) 2 Sam 6:6—4QSam[a] נודן, MT נכון; cf. 1 Chr 13:9 כידן. The final *nun* is the only common element in the three variants, the *kaf* is common to two witnesses, and the initial *nun* is also common to two witnesses.
(4) 2 Sam 13:3—4QSam[a] שמעיה, MT שמעה; cf. 1 Chr 20:7 שמעא. The shorter theophoric names became increasingly more popular after the exile.

---

[16] O. Thenius, *Die Bücher Samuels erklärt* (2d ed.; Leipzig: n.p., 1864), 8. See especially E.A. Speiser, "The Nuzi Tablets Solve a Puzzle in the Book of Samuel," *BASOR* 72 (1938): 15–17.
[17] For additional examples of metathesis in the Hebrew Bible, see H. Junker, "Konsonantenumstellung als Fehlerquelle und textkritisches Hilfsmittel im AT," in *Werden und Wesen des Alten Testaments* (ed. P. Volz et al.; BZAW 66; Berlin: Töpelmann, 1936): 162–74.

(2) Intentional Changes

The unique readings of 4QSam^a exist because of intentional changes of the text on the part of the scribes and copyists of either MT or 4QSam^a. These changes include exegetical pluses or late editorial additions, harmonizations, morphological smoothing, morphological updating, updating the vocabulary, euphemistic changes, orthographic variants, and phonetic differences. These changes may also include the creation of nomistic readings (by the scribes of 4QSam^a) or, more likely, the omission of nomistic readings by scribes belonging to the proto-Masoretic tradition.

Exegetical Plus

4QSam^a 2 Sam 6:2 is an example of an exegetical plus (בעלה היא קר[ית] יערים אשר] ליהו[ה ["to Baal, that is Kiriath Jearim which belongs to Judah"]; cf. 1 Chr 13:6, בעלתה אל קרית יערים אשר ליהודה ["to Baalah, to Kiriath Jearim which belongs to Judah"]). The plus is introduced with the feminine pronoun היא, a feature that belongs to such exegetical additions (compare the pronouns היא or הוא in other examples of exegetical pluses that pertain to proper names of places—Gen 14:3; 36:1; Josh 15:18; 18:13). The reading of 4QSam^a 2 Sam 6:2 is based on tradition or possibly Josh 15:9–11 and 18:14 (קרית בעל היא קרית יערים עיר בני יהודה ["Kiriath Baal, that is, Kiriath Jearim, a town of the people of Judah"]). MT lacks the plus with its reading of מבעלי יהודה ("from Baale of Judah"). The city's original name (based on Josh 18:14) was likely בעל or possibly בעל יהודה.[18] An additional challenge (perhaps unsolvable) remains with the text. Were David and his forces traveling "to Baal" (= 4QSam^a בעלה) or "from Baal" (= MT מבעלי)? Additional possible examples of exegetical pluses, where 4QSam^a stands unaligned with MT or LXX, are found in 4QSam^a 1 Sam 2:16 (+ הכוהן כיום); MT 1 Sam 9:7 (+ לנערו); MT 2 Sam 11:4 (+ מטמאתה).

Harmonizations

A handful of readings where 4QSam^a is unique versus MT or LXX signal the existence of harmonizations within the framework of 4QSam^a, MT, or LXX. A harmonization occurs when a scribe blends one reading

---

[18] See S.R. Driver, *Notes on the Hebrew Text and the Topography of the Books of Samuel* (Oxford: Clarendon Press, 1913), 265–66.

with a second reading that is located in the immediate or greater context, or with a parallel text. Harmonizations may be intentional efforts on the part of a scribe or they may be unintentional. According to Emanuel Tov, "harmonizations on the textual level... belong to the scribal transmission of compositions after their literary shape had been finalized. Harmonizations, that is, secondary approximations of details, may take place within one text—in one sentence or chapter—or between two remote texts."[19]

It is often difficult to properly classify harmonizations, because they sometimes may be better understood as inadvertent scribal errors (the result of haplography or dittography) or explicating pluses. The following examples illustrate possible harmonizations in either 4QSam^a or MT, where 4QSam^a displays unique readings.

(1) 4QSam^a 1 Sam 1:22 [יהוה] וישב לפני (lacking in MT) harmonizes with לפני יהוה in v. 11.

(2) 4QSam^a 1 Sam 1:22 [חייו] כול ימי (lacking in MT) also harmonizes with MT כול ימי חייו in v. 11.

(3) 4QSam^a 1 Sam 2:16 וענה האיש וא[מ]ֿר אל נער הכוהן (cf. MT ויאמר אליו האיש). Here 4QSam^a is reminiscent of a similar expression in v. 15.

(4) 4QSam^a 1 Sam 11:9 [ועה] לכם [מיהוה התש]ו (cf. MT תהיה לכם תשועה; cf. also 𝕲^B לכם תשועה). In this passage 4QSam^a corresponds to תשועה יהוה in v. 13.

(5) MT 2 Sam 6:7 עם ארון האלהים (cf. 4QSam^a [והים]ל[א]ל[פני הא]ֿל; 1 Chr 13:10 לפני אלהים). MT apparently harmonizes the reading to agree with אל ארון האלהים of v. 6 and עם ארון האלהים of v. 4.

Morphological Smoothing

Smoothing, together with archaizing and modernizing, are "three related skewing processes which are involved in text production and

---

[19] E. Tov, "The Nature and Background of Harmonizations in Biblical Manuscripts," *JSOT* 31 (1985): 3. See also examples of harmonizations in the Samaritan Pentateuch versus MT in B.K. Waltke, "The Samaritan Pentateuch and the Text of the Old Testament," in *New Perspectives on the Old Testament* (ed. J.B. Payne; Waco, Tex.: Word Books, 1970), 221–22. For examples of possible harmonizations in parallel biblical texts see throughout A. Bendavid, *Parallels in the Bible* (Jerusalem: Carta, 1972) [Hebrew].

preservation."[20] Morphological smoothing is a scribal activity that seeks to remove textual unevenness or inconsistencies through leveling out the text. Such inconsistencies may pertain to morphological, phonological, or syntactical structures. A possible example of morphological smoothing in 4QSamᵃ appears in 2 Sam 12:31, where the scribe of the Qumran scroll (or its ancestor) crafted singular nouns when he listed the three tools—saw, pick, and axe, [במגרה ובח]רץ [הברזל ובמגזרה]. Or, it is equally possible that the scribe of MT leveled out the text by using plurals—iron picks and axes, ובחרצי הברזל ובמגזרת הברזל.

Morphological Updating

Moran's study of the infinitive absolute in Amarna and Ugaritic texts provides ample evidence of the antiquity of this form. In time, however, this form in biblical Hebrew texts was often replaced with finite forms.[21] Evidence of this is found in variants that exist between MT and the Samaritan Pentateuch[22] as well as variants in parallel texts of Samuel and Chronicles; for example, where the infinitive absolute is used as an imperative in Samuel, the synoptic reading in Chronicles usually employs a finite verb.[23] There is an example of an infinitive absolute in 4QSamᵃ (see 2 Sam 3:34)[24] where the reading of MT is a finite verb (הנשו). 4QSamᵃ presents the older reading.

Another example of updating morphological forms pertains to the replacement of a *waw*-consecutive verb with a verb that is preceded with the non-converting *waw* conjunction. Waltke's comparison of MT Pentateuch with the Samaritan Pentateuch addresses examples of such forms.[25] Two examples of variants of this type are extant in 2 Sam 4:4 (4QSamᵃ ויהי; MT היה) and 2 Sam 6:13 (4QSamᵃ [והי֯ה֯; MT ויהי).

---

[20] B.K. Waltke and M. O'Connor, *An Introduction to Biblical Hebrew Syntax* (Winona Lake, Ind.: Eisenbrauns, 1990), 11. For examples of smoothing from the Samaritan Pentateuch, see 13.

[21] W.L. Moran, "The Hebrew Language in its Northwest Semitic Background," in *The Bible and the Ancient Near East* (ed. G.E. Wright; Garden City, N.Y.: Doubleday, 1961), 64–65.

[22] Waltke, "The Samaritan Pentateuch," 215–16.

[23] G. Gerleman, "Synoptic Studies in the Old Testament," *LUÅ* (N.F. Avd. 1) 44 (1948): 18.

[24] Although the reading of 4QSamᵃ (הנ{ש}) is somewhat indeterminate because of the erasure of a character (possibly a *yod*), we conclude that it read an infinitive absolute; see *DJD* 17:115.

[25] Waltke, "The Samaritan Pentateuch," 215.

Evidence indicates that the locative *he* began to fall out of usage in later periods of biblical Hebrew.[26] Two nonaligned readings of 4QSam^a illustrate variants of the locative *he*; in the first example, 4QSam^a lacks the *he locale* (4QSam^a 2 Sam 8:2 אַרְצָה]; MT אַרְצָה), and in the second, 4QSam^a provides it (4QSam^a 2 Sam 15:29 יְרוּשָׁלֵימָה]; MT יְרוּשָׁלַם).

Updating the Vocabulary

Occasionally scribes from both Hebrew witnesses of Samuel have updated the vocabulary, replacing archaic and outdated words with contemporary usage. An example exists in the literary unit comprising six verses that details Eli's sons' practice of seizing sacrificial meats through unconventional means (1 Sam 2:12–17). According to the text, Eli's sons would strike a three-pronged fork into a cooking pot while searching for the finest portions of the sacrificial meat. The text's author likely recorded a single cooking pot in the primitive version of the narrative, not two or four, as recorded in the Hebrew witnesses: MT (v. 14) בַּסִּיר; 4QSam^a (v. 16) בכיור או בדוד או בקלחת או בפרור או בפרור. MT 1 Sam 2:14 and 4QSam^a 1 Sam 2:16 feature five different words to represent the vessels: כיור, דוד, קלחת, פרור, and סיר. Three words are unique to MT (קלחת, דוד, כיור), one to 4QSam^a (סיר), and the fifth (פרור) is found in both lists.[27]

The best candidate for the original narrative is סיר ("large pot"),[28] in part because it fits the physical description of a cooking pot large enough to hold sacrificial meats of larger animals. The largeness of the pot is put forward by LXX with its adjective "large." Vessels lists are very uncommon in the HB, and only two exist, the Shiloh list and 2 Chr 35:13. The later speaks of three vessels (בסירות ובדודים ובצלחות) used at the time of Josiah in Jerusalem. There is evidence that the list of

---

[26] According to Waltke ("The Samaritan Pentateuch," 217), "the presence of the *he locale* afformative in Ugaritic indicates that its absence in the [Samaritan Pentateuch] is best understood as a later modernization of the text of the [Samaritan Pentateuch]."

[27] LXX, too, presents a variety of readings. All LXX readings list three vessels, except for the conflated reading of LXXc₂, which lists four. The Lucianic manuscripts (boc₂e₂) order the final two vessels differently, בפרור או בקלחת versus בקלחת או בפרור. The modifier of סיר (i.e., בסיר הגדולה), unknown to the Hebrew witnesses, is added to LXX perhaps in an attempt to describe the size of this vessel relative to the other vessels in the list. It appears that קלחת was not translated by the Greek translators, but simply transliterated.

[28] See my argument in "How Many Vessels? A Close Examination of MT 1 Sam 2:14," 84–95.

vessels in Chronicles was influenced by the Samuel list. The other three
vessels (minus כיור or "wash-basin")[29]—דוד, קלחת, and פרור[30]—were
added to the narrative during the transmission of the Samuel text to
modernize the vocabulary for contemporary readers.

Euphemistic Changes

Biblical scholars provide examples of indelicate words or anthropomorphisms that have been removed from the HB and replaced with
euphemisms[31] or dysphemisms. Yeivin, for example, cites *b. Meg.* 25b,
"Wherever the text is written indelicately, we read it delicately" and
posits that "in 16 cases in the Bible, the *qere* form presents a euphemism."[32] Ginsburg maintains that the practice of removing indelicate
words and anthropomorphisms was practiced by many "authoritative
redactors of the Sacred Scriptures."[33]

2 Sam 12:14 displays a euphemism in both Hebrew traditions,
where 4QSam^a has a unique reading.[34] David's role in the narrative of
Bathsheba and Uriah (2 Sam 11:1–27) prompted Nathan's accusation
of the king (2 Sam 12:1–14). Nathan first presented a parable to David
and then, following David's response, delivered a lengthy accusation.
The final verse of the pericope in MT reads: אפס כי נאץ נאצת את איבי
יהוה בדבר הזה גם הבן הילוד לך מות יומת, "Yet because you have certainly

---

[29] סיר was once part of the textual history of MT (1 Sam 2:14) until a copyist misread
this word and wrote כיר. A subsequent copyist saw and added the *waw* to read כיור
or "wash-basin," consequently סיר > כיר > כיור. There is no doubt that כיור figured
prominently in the temple cult, but as a "wash-basin," not a cooking pot.

[30] דוד, in terms of the frequency of its usage in the HB, is primarily a basket and
only secondarily a cooking pot; more significantly, it was a vessel whose form and
mouth were too small to hold large cuts of meat. קלחת is never mentioned in connection with the temple cult, other than with regard to the questionable Shiloh list. פרור
is a common, inexpensive pot, not what one would expect to be used in a formalized
temple system where elaborate vessels were employed.

[31] On euphemisms in the Bible, see the study of A. Geiger, *Urschrift und Übersetzungen
der Bibel in ihrer Abhängigkeit von der innern Entwicklung des Judenthums* (Breslau: Hainauer,
1857; repr., Frankfurt: Madda, 1928), 267–68.

[32] I. Yeivin, *Introduction to the Tiberian Masorah* (trans. E.J. Revell; Missoula, Mont:
Scholars Press, 1980), 56.

[33] Ginsburg, *Introduction to the Massoretico-Critical Edition*, 346–47; see also 347–404.

[34] For a study of this euphemism, see D.W. Parry, "The 'Word' or the 'Enemies'
of the Lord? Revisiting the Euphemism in 2 Sam 12:14," in *Emanuel: Studies in Hebrew
Bible, Septuagint, and Dead Sea Scrolls in Honor of Emanuel Tov* (ed. S.M. Paul et al.; VTSup
94; Leiden: Brill, 2003), 367–78.

spurned[35] the enemies of the Lord in this matter, the son that is born to you will surely die" (2 Sam 12:14). With regard to the phrase "enemies of the Lord," the majority of the Greek witnesses, the Vulgate, the Targum, and the Syriac share the same reading as MT.

Textual critics have held that *enemies* in this passage is a secondary insertion because its inclusion makes little sense contextually. The story's setting presents no clue as to whom the Lord's enemies are.[36] Nathan's accusation against David pertains to the king's role in the Uriah and Bathsheba story and does not relate directly to either David's or the Lord's enemies. *Enemies* is supplied as a euphemism elsewhere in Samuel (1 Sam 20:16, Jonathan's self-curse;[37] 1 Sam 25:22, David's self-curse).[38] Unfortunately, none of the three Qumran Samuel witnesses attest either of these passages. Because *enemies* is featured regularly as a euphemistic expression in the rabbinic writings,[39] it is possible that these writings supplied the inspiration for the euphemistic reading in MT 1 Sam 20:16 and 25:22 and 2 Sam 12:14.

4QSam[a] has a variant to MT's reading of נאץ נאצת את איבי יהוה (2 Sam 12:14). The Qumran witness reads: נ[א]ץ נאצ[ת] א֗ת דבר יהוה ("you have certainly spurned the word of the Lord").[40] The Coptic version (*verbum*

---

[35] Elsewhere נאץ may have triggered a change in 1 Sam 2:17, where it was evidently directly coupled with the Divine Name before the insertion of the secondary, euphemistic האנשים. See the discussion in D. Barthélemy, "La qualité du Texte Massorétique de Samuel," in *The Hebrew and Greek Texts of Samuel: Proceedings of the Congress of the International Organization for Septuagint and Cognate Studies (Vienna 1980)* (ed. E. Tov; Septuagint and Cognate Studies; Jerusalem: Academon, 1980), 5. Psalm 10:3 may be included in this same discussion, because the expression "spurned" (נאץ) was apparently changed to "blessed" (ברך). Correspondingly, there are instances where scribal changes reflect ברך rather than קלל (see 1 Kgs 21:10, 13; Job 1:5, 11; 2:5, 9).

[36] As Mulder reminds us, David's enemies could not have known about David's sin, because it was committed in secret (בסתר, see 2 Sam 12:12). M.J. Mulder, "Un euphémisme dans 2 Sam. XII 14?" *VT* 9 (1968): 111.

[37] "What is expected is not that Yahweh should require it from the hand of David's enemies, but from the hand of David himself, in case he should fail to fulfill the conditions of the covenant," writes Driver, *Notes on the Hebrew Text*, 165–66; see also McCarter, *I Samuel*, 337.

[38] McCarter, *II Samuel*, 296, calls this reading in MT a "euphemistic expansion" that is "unquestionably late and scribal."

[39] See for example, the following sources: *b. Ta'an.* 7a, see I.W. Slotki, *Hebrew-English Edition of the Babylonian Talmud, Ta'anith* (London: Soncino, 1984); *b. Suk.* 29a, see Slotki, *Hebrew-English Edition*; G. Dalman, *Grammatik des jüdisch-palästinischen Aramäisch* (Darmstadt: Wissenschaftliche Buchgesellschaft, 1960), 109; *b. Soṭah* 11a, see I.L. Rabinowitz, "Euphemism and Dysphemism: In the Talmud," in *EncJud* 6:962; *Lev. Rab.* 25:1, see *Midrash Rabbah: Leviticus* (trans. by J.J. Slotki; London: Soncino, 1939), chapters XX–XXXVII; *Mekilta of Rabbi Ishmael* uses *enemies* euphemistically on a regular basis.

[40] The apparatus of *BHS* errs with its reading of the Qumran text (ל[ד]בר).

Domini), presented in the Brook, McLean, and Thackeray apparatus,[41] supports the reading of 4QSam^a for this verse. The probable source for דבר in 4QSam^a is found in the same pericope under discussion. In 2 Sam 12:9, Nathan asks David, מדוע בזית את דבר יהוה לעשות הרע בעיניו; ("why have you despised the word of the Lord, to do evil in his sight?)" (2 Sam 12:9). Vv. 9 and 14 have a number of corresponding points. In both verses, Nathan is the speaker and David is the addressee. Both sentences include an accusation in which the prophet accuses the king—in v. 9 Nathan pronounces, בזית את דבר יהוה and in v. 14 he declares, נאצת את דבר יהוה. One notes the similarity between these two phrases: they are syntactically identical—second masculine singular perfect verb, object marker, noun in construct, and Divine Name. Most significantly, דבר יהוה is found in both passages (of 4QSam^a). It appears that a scribe belonging to the 4QSam^a tradition was influenced by v. 9[42] when he copied v. 14. Whether דבר was an intentional or unintentional plus is difficult to determine.

Yet another variant to *enemies* and *word* in 2 Sam 12:14 is found in "c," a Greek cursive that is part of the Lucianic Manuscripts.[43] This cursive, with no support from other witnesses, has נאץ נאצת את יהוה, lacking both איבי and דבר. Most scholars hold that this Greek cursive presents the primitive reading—"you have certainly spurned the Lord."[44] Both of the terms *enemies* and *word*, then, are secondary readings or scribal expansions that serve as euphemisms that changed an offensive reading to an inoffensive reading.

---

[41] A.E. Brooke, N. McLean, and H. St. John Thackeray, *The Old Testament in Greek according to the text of Codex Vaticanus, supplemented from other uncial manuscripts, with a critical apparatus containing the variants of the chief ancient authorities for the text of the Septuagint* (Vol. 2 of *The Later Historical Books: Part I: I and II Samuel*; London: Cambridge University Press, 1927), 142.

[42] Verse 9 also has a variant reading where דבר appears. Although MT reads דבר together with the majority of Greek witnesses (as well as the Syriac and the Targum), both the Lucian group and Theodotion lack דבר. Based on these last two mentioned witnesses, it is probable that דבר is secondary in verse 9, as it is in verse 14. Unfortunately, only a small fragment of 4QSam^a exists where 2 Sam 12:9 is found, and it is unknown whether the Qumran witness attested or lacked דבר.

[43] The Larger Cambridge LXX uses the sigla boc₂e₂ to represent the Lucianic Manuscripts. The Göttingen edition uses the numbers 19+108, 82, 127, and 93 for the same.

[44] A. Geiger, *Urschrift und Uebersetzungen der Bibel*, 267; Driver, *Notes on the Hebrew Text*, 292; Ulrich, *The Qumran Text of Samuel and Josephus*, 138.

Orthographic Variants

Discoveries in the Judaean Desert 17:5–16 presents a section that treats the orthographic practices of 4QSam^a and includes a seven-page table (Table 2) that lists approximately 234 orthographic variants that exist between 4QSam^a and MT. A small number of the orthographic variants are both unique to 4QSam^a and feature an archaic orthography: (a) MT 2 Sam 13:25 portrays a reading where the orthography is archaic (נכבד), versus the reading of 4QSam^a (נכביד); (b) 4QSam^a 2 Sam 14:19 has a reading where the orthography is archaic (ולהשמאל; cf. 4QSam^c [ל]אולהשמא), versus the reading of MT (ולהשמיל; but compare two manuscripts that read ולהשמאיל and two manuscripts that read ולהשמיאל);[45] and (c) one or more of 4QSam^a's unique variants originated because of the confusion of certain letters by copyists of either MT or 4QSam^a in early Hebrew. The proper name *Nachon* (2 Sam 6:6) has three variants in the Hebrew texts (MT נכון; 4QSam^a נודן; 1 Chr 13:9 כידן) and additional variants in the other versions and Josephus, *Ant.* 7.81.[46] Inasmuch as the initial and final *nun* are common to all three and the *dalet* belongs to two of the Hebrew texts, it is believed that "all the variant forms probably go back to נדן in early orthography. Perhaps vocalize *nôdān* < *nôdôn* from a root *nwd*."[47]

Phonetic Differences

Archaic versus late pronunciation of letters and words account for one (or more) unique readings in 4QSam^a. The syncopation in 4QSam^a לעלות (1 Sam 10:8) versus MT להעלות indicates a late articulation. Additionally, MT ופלשתים (versus 4QSam^a ופלשתיים; see 2 Sam 5:18) designates a contracted form, brought about as a result of a later pronunciation.

Nomistic Readings

In contrast to other versions, 4QSam^a sometimes features unique readings that correspond to or have an affinity with Pentateuchal legal texts' phraseology. While many such readings are unique to this Qumran witness, others have support of LXX. Alexander Rofé, under the title

---

[45] See *DJD* 17:153.
[46] See *DJD* 17:127.
[47] See *DJD* 17:127.

"The Nomistic Correction in Biblical Manuscripts and Its Occurrence in 4QSam^a" claims that "the copyists of biblical books breathe in a nomistic atmosphere and this necessarily affects the product of their work. In the course of their copying, they sometimes consciously correct the biblical text; in other instances they inadvertently alter it. The distinction between conscious and unconscious interventions is not always clear cut."[48] Accordingly, Rofé offers that copyists of biblical texts,[49] principally during the Persian and Hellenistic periods, corrected their texts to include nomistic readings. While these corrections are manifest in MT, Samaritan Pentateuch, and LXX, there are a number of examples in 4QSam^a. "Indeed, 4QSam^a offers such daring nomistic readings, that sometimes they are better defined as revisions rather than corrections."[50]

Notwithstanding Rofé's claims regarding nomistic corrections in 4QSam^a, it is not always clear which of the versions presents the original readings—the text with the nomistic readings or the one that lacks them. It is possible that copyists belonging to the proto-Masoretic textual tradition of Samuel made errors or alterations from an original text that contained nomistic readings so that MT now lacks many of the legalistic readings that are part of 4QSam^a.

1 Sam 1:11 relates, as part of the Nazarite's vow, the phrase regarding a razor coming upon Samuel's head. MT (also LXX, Syr., Vulg.) attests ומורה לא יעלה על ראשו; 4QSam^a uses a different verb, ומורה לא יעבור על[ראשו]. This verb coincides with the reading of Numbers 6:5, a text concerning the law of the Nazarites: תער לא יעבור על with יעבור ראשו. Judges 13:5 is the probable source for MT 1 Sam 1:11, where it is stated regarding Samson the Nazarite, "ומורה לא יעלה על ראשו."

1 Sam 1:22 offers a second example of a legalistic, unique reading in 4QSam^a with its attestation of ונת[תיהו נזיר עד עולם]. This reading is supported by Josephus (*Ant.* 5.347) against all other witnesses.[51] It is believed that ונתתיהו לפניך נזיר has been lost from MT because of a

---

[48] A. Rofé, "The Nomistic Correction in Biblical Manuscripts and Its Occurrence in 4QSam^a," *RevQ* 14/54 (1989): 248–49.

[49] "Nomistic corrections are attested in different degrees and at distinct points in the different textual witnesses." Rofé, "The Nomistic Correction in Biblical Manuscripts," 250.

[50] Rofé, "The Nomistic Correction in Biblical Manuscripts," 252.

[51] On the agreement of 4QSam^a with Josephus, see Ulrich, *The Qumran Text of Samuel and Josephus*, 165–66.

"haplography caused by *homoioteleuton*: עד עולם ונתתיהו נזיר עד עולם."[52]
Compare also the partially reconstructed reading of [ונתתיהו ל[פניך נזיר
in 4QSamᵃ 1 Sam 1:11, supported by LXX. נזיר is not found in MT
narrative of 1 Sam 1, although an implicit reference to the law of
a Nazarite appears in 1:11 with mention of the cutting of the hair.
In the context of the Nazarite law, one may also compare another
unique reading in 4QSamᵃ 1 Sam 2:16 that pertains to the law of the
Nazarite. The expression מזֹ[זה התנופה ושו[ק הימין, which is lacking in
all other witnesses, "is based on the old law of the Nazarite vow in
Num 6:19–20 (cf. also Exod 29:26–28; Num 18:18; Lev 7:31–32; 9:21;
1 Sam 9:24)."[53]

An additional example of a nomistic, unique reading is located in
4QSamᵃ 1 Sam 1:24, where the text has [בפר בן] בקר משלש, versus MT
בן בקר בפרים שלשה, attested in the Pentateuch (e.g., see Exod 29:1; Lev
4:3), appears to be a nomistic reading in the Qumran witness.

The 4QSamᵃ reading of [יקטר הכוהן כיום הֹ[חלב] (1 Sam 2:16) includes
"the priest" in accord with the Pentateuchal והקטיר הכהן את החלב (Lev
7:31) against MT קטר יקטירון כיום החלב (1 Sam 2:16). 4QSamᵃ "the
priest" may be a nomistic reading or it may signify an explicating
plus.

(3) Synonymous Readings[54]

Textual variants, where 4QSamᵃ has a nonaligned reading, include
synonymous readings. According to Talmon, synonymous readings are
characterized as follows:

> a) They result from the substitution of words and phrases by others which
> are used interchangeably and synonymously with them in the literature
> of the OT. b) They do not affect adversely the structure of the verse,
> nor do they disturb either its meaning or its rhythm. Hence they cannot
> be explained as scribal errors. c) No sign of systematic or tendentious
> emendation can be discovered in them. They are to be taken at face

---

[52] *DJD* 17:33.

[53] *DJD* 17:45.

[54] See S. Talmon, "Synonymous Readings in the Textual Traditions of the Old
Testament," *ScrHier* 8 (1961): 335–83. See also Tov, *Textual Criticism of the Hebrew Bible*,
260–61 and F. Díaz Esteban, *Sefer Okhlah we-Okhlah* (Madrid: Consejo Superior de
Investigaciones Científicas, 1975), 193–94 on the interchange of synonymous expressions "and he spoke" versus "and he said" in the manuscripts.

value…If, as far as we can tell, they are not the product of different chronologically or geographically distinct linguistic strata.[55]

אמה and שפחה are examples of synonymous readings in the Hebrew Bible. The two terms are synonymous variants in MT versus Samaritan Pentateuch in Gen 31:33, and they are used interchangeably in MT of Hannah's encounter with Eli (1 Sam 1:15–18), the David and Abigail narrative (1 Sam 25:23–31), and David's meeting with the Tekoah woman (2 Sam 14:4–17). Twice, אמה and שפחה are variants in Samuel, where 4QSam^a uses אמה in a nonalignment pattern with other versions: 1 Sam 8:16 (4QSam^a אמתיכם; MT שפחותיכם) and 2 Sam 14:19 (4QSam^a אמתך; MT שפחתך). In early usage שפחה and אמה have distinctive meanings and indicate dissimilar social positions. Although both are bound by service, "שפחה is a girl who is not free but is as yet untouched, whose duty was primarily to serve the woman of the house…אמה is a woman who is not free, and who could be a man's secondary wife, as well as the wife of man who like her is bound in service."[56]

Beyond אמה and שפחה, unique readings in 4QSam^a account for other synonymous readings.[57] Two variant imperatival readings are attested in 2 Sam 11:6 (4QSam^a שלחה; MT שלח), and variants of the impersonal verbs occur in 2 Sam 18:5 (4QSam^a שמעים; MT שמעו) and 2 Sam 19:15 (4QSam^a וישלח; MT וישלחו). It is often difficult to determine the Hebrew *Vorlage* of LXX when dealing with synonymous readings in the Hebrew.

(4) Stylistic Readings

The stylistic choices, conventions, or idiosyncrasies of copyists or scribes account for a number of variant readings that exist in the Hebrew witnesses of Samuel. Examples of scribal stylistic preferences, where 4QSam^a presents a unique reading, include the following.

---

[55] Talmon, "Synonymous Readings," 336. Sanderson defines synonymous readings as "those variants for which no preferable reading can be determined even with probability. They are different legitimate ways of expressing the same idea." J.E. Sanderson, *An Exodus Scroll from Qumran* (Atlanta: Scholars Press, 1986), 41; see also 109–10.

[56] *HALOT*, 4:1621. Compare also the discussion of the two social roles of אמה and שפחה in Talmon, "Synonymous Readings," 365.

[57] Some of the examples may be linguistic-stylistic readings (see Tov, *Textual Criticism of the Hebrew Bible*, 259), while others may be synonymous terms.

4QSamᵃ's scribe prefers using the nonattached preposition מן when it precedes the article, while MT attaches the preposition to the article (see 4QSamᵃ 1 Sam 28:23 מן [הא]רץ; MT מהארץ; 4QSamᵃ 2 Sam 2:27 מן [הבקר; MT מהבקר; 4QSamᵃ 2 Sam 13:15 מן האהב]ה; MT מאהבה). In 2 Sam 3:24, MT reads הנה; 4QSamᵃ attests הן, a rarer form. Similarly, in 2 Sam 12:18, MT has איך where 4QSamᵃ reads ואי[כ]ה, also a rarer form. Other variant readings may be from scribal preference, including the usage of the negative particles לוֹא versus אל (2 Sam 3:29) or the common interchange of the prepositions אל and על (see 1 Sam 2:34, 14:32, 27:10, 31:3; 2 Sam 3:33, 20:10, 23:1).

Compare also the following variants: prepositions, 2 Sam 2:6 (4QSamᵃ אתכם; MT עמכם),1 Sam 6:2 (4QSamᵃ אל מקומו; MT למקומו), 1 Sam 14:32 (4QSamᵃ על; MT אל), 2 Sam 11:8 (4QSamᵃ אל[אוריה; MT לאוריה); interjections, 2 Sam 3:24 (4QSamᵃ הן; MT הנה), 2 Sam 12:18 (4QSamᵃ ואי[כ]ה; MT ואיך); *nota accusativi*, 1 Sam 24:19 (4QSamᵃ אשר; MT את אשר), 2 Sam 3:32 (4QSamᵃ קולו; MT את קולו), 2 Sam 6:2 (4QSamᵃ את; MT and 1 Chr 13:6 omit); particles of negation, 2 Sam 3:29 (4QSamᵃ ולוֹא; MT ואל), 2 Sam 14:14 (4QSamᵃ בל]תי; MT לבלתי); adjectives, 2 Sam 8:8 (4QSamᵃ רבה; MT הרבה); and nouns, 1 Sam 2:16 (4QSamᵃ בחזק; MT בחזקה).

CONCLUSIONS

The unique readings are scattered throughout 1 and 2 Samuel. The readings belong to various prosaic and poetic-type sections such as historical narrative (e.g., 1 Sam 5:8, 11; 6:2, 5; 10:8, 14, 17; 11:9), song (e.g., Royal Song of Thanksgiving, 2 Sam 22:37, 40, 43, 46, 48), lament (e.g., 2 Sam 3:34), prayer (Prayer of Hannah, see 1 Sam 2: 9–10; Prayer of David, 2 Sam 7:25, 28), prophecy (e.g., Prophecy against Eli's House, 1 Sam 2:29, 34; 2 Sam 12:14), genealogical list (1 Sam 14:49), dialogue (1 Sam 24:19), oath formula (1 Sam 26:22; 2 Sam 2:27; 4:10), benediction (2 Sam 2:6), and curse (2 Sam 3:29–30). Generally, the readings do not indicate a particular struggle on the part of a scribe(s) to understand vocabulary that is specific to a type of literature or to comprehend archaic words and forms, possible Aramaisms, or loan words.

Although the unique readings are dispersed throughout Samuel in various prosaic and poetic sections, clusters of readings exist. For example, six are located in the pericope detailing the birth and conse-

cration of Samuel (1 Sam 1:22–23, 28), two in the latter part of the
Song of Hannah (1 Sam 2:9, 10), eight in the section describing the
sins of the sons of Eli (1 Sam 2:16, 22, 23, 25), twelve in the Murder of
Abner pericope (2 Sam 3:22–39),[58] four within seven verses describing
the Second Ammonite Campaign (2 Sam 11:1–27), three in two verses
in the section on the death of Bathsheba's child (2 Sam 12:17–18), and
seven in the Royal Song of Thanksgiving (2 Sam 22:36–37, 40, 43, 46,
48). These numbers, of course, may present a skewed picture of unique
readings in 4QSam^a because of the fragmented nature of the scroll.

What does a profile of the unique readings of 4QSam^a look like? Or
what is the textual character of the scroll's unique readings? There is
no single characterization that typifies 4QSam^a because of the many
complexities that are involved. One can, however, order the various
components into four main groupings.

(1) The textual character of the unique readings of 4QSam^a consists of accidental errors of transmission. These include haplography
(*homoioarcton, homoioteleuton*), dittography, graphic similarity, misdivision of
words, interchange of letters, transposition of texts, and so forth. These
errors of transmission, typical among many texts during the process of
transmission, belong to both Hebrew witnesses—4QSam^a and MT. At
times the unique reading of 4QSam^a originated from a copyist error
in that scroll or its forebears; on other occasions the unique reading of
4QSam^a was the result of an error in the transmission of MT.

(2) The unique readings of 4QSam^a may be characterized by intentional changes of the text on the part of scribes of either MT or 4QSam^a.
These changes include exegetical pluses or late editorial additions,
harmonizations, morphological smoothing, morphological updating,
updating the vocabulary, euphemistic changes, orthographic variants,
and phonetic differences. These changes may also include the creation
of nomistic readings on the part of 4QSam^a or their omission (through a
series of errors) by scribes belonging to the proto-Masoretic tradition.

(3) 4QSam^a's unique readings may be characterized by its synonymous readings, as contrasted with the readings of MT or LXX. אמרה
and שפחה serve as examples of such readings.

(4) A range of scribes' stylistic methods and conventions among the
various versions reveal the textual character of the unique readings

---

[58] For a discussion of such readings, see D.W. Parry, "The Aftermath of Abner's
Murder," *Textus* 20 (2000): 83–96.

182   DONALD W. PARRY

of 4QSamª. Examples include the use of הנה versus הן or איך versus
איכה.

When did 4QSamª's unique readings become part of that scroll's
textual character? Many of its unique readings probably predate LXX,
including those superior readings[59] that formed part of the earliest form
of the books of Samuel. These superior readings include, especially,
unique readings where 4QSamª = Chronicles or Josephus, versus MT/
LXX^B/LXX^L/LXX^{BL}.[60] Other pre-Septuagint unique readings of
4QSamª may consist of synonymous readings, stylistic preferences, and
scribal conventions, that is, words that belong to the socio-religious fabric
of this Qumran scroll. For examples of such words, see the subheadings
III. Synonymous Readings and IV. Stylistic Readings. Unfortunately,
textual critics cannot easily determine which, if any, of the unique
readings of 4QSamª actually predate the translation of the Greek.

The remaining nonaligned readings belong to the period of time
(about two centuries) between the translational work of LXX and 50
B.C.E., the date of 4QSamª.[61] During this period of time, when 4QSamª
was both socially and geographically remote from other versions of
Samuel, many copyists' errors, together with modernizations of terms,
late editorial additions, harmonizations, morphological smoothing and
updating, euphemistic changes, and so forth became part of the text.

The nonaligned readings of 4QSamª are significant, because they
reveal the practices and exegetical work of the scribe or scribes who
transmitted this copy of Samuel and its forebears. They reveal details
about the socio-religious background of the proto-Masoretic text,
4QSamª, and LXX. These unique readings are not isolated items, nor
are they rare. Rather, there are 123 attested nonaligned variant readings in 4QSamª, representing about 29 percent of all textual variants
that belong to 4QSamª.

---

[59] Cross and Saley's statistical study provides data regarding those unique readings
in 4QSamª that are superior in contrast to those that are inferior. Cross and Saley,
"A Statistical Analysis," 50. "Sixty (33 reconstructed) superior, 56 (28 reconstructed)
inferior" (50).
[60] "Many of the superior unique readings represent the preservation of lost readings
of text—words and sentences—lost by *parablepsis*—with the majority of these being
corroborated by Chronicles or Josephus, or both. The inferior readings are idiographic
marks of 4QSamª or its immediate manuscript forebears," ibid., 53.
[61] A paleographic study of the Qumran scroll under discussion reveals that its script
is Late Hasmonean to Early Herodian, which dates it to 50–25 B.C.E. *DJD* 17:4–5.

FIVE SURPRISES IN THE QUMRAN PSALMS SCROLLS*

Peter W. Flint

Since the early 1990s I have devoted much time and energy investigating all the Psalms scrolls from Qumran, with fullest documentation in my book *The Dead Sea Psalms Scrolls and the Book of Psalms* (1997),[1] in a long article in *Vetus Testamentum* (1998),[2] and in the first volume of the Princeton Symposium on the Dead Sea Scrolls (2006).[3] This research has yielded or recognized five notable features, or five "surprises,"[4] surrounding the Psalms scrolls from Qumran, culminating with the publication of 11QPs[b], 11QPs[c], 11QPs[d], and 11QPs[e] in *DJD* 23 in 1998.[5]

The underlying quest of the present essay is to identify another copy of the Psalter represented by the Great Psalms Scroll, which I term the "11QPs[a]-Psalter." The discussion will bring some focus on a somewhat neglected manuscript, 11QPs[b] (11Q6), and its unique contribution towards research on the book of Psalms in the Dead Sea Scrolls.

THE FIRST SURPRISE:
THE GREAT PSALMS SCROLL AND THE "11QPs[A]-PSALTER"

The first Psalms scrolls to be discovered were published in 1955 (Cave 1)[6] and in 1962 (Caves 2, 3, 5, 6, 8).[7] These did not arouse great excitement

---

[1] P.W. Flint, *The Dead Sea Psalms Scrolls and The Book of Psalms* (STDJ 17; Leiden: Brill, 1997).

[2] P.W. Flint, "The Book of Psalms in the Light of the Dead Sea Scrolls," *VT* 48 (1998): 453–72.

[3] P.W. Flint, "Psalms and Psalters in the Dead Sea Scrolls," in *Scripture and the Scrolls* (ed. J.H. Charlesworth; *The Bible and the Dead Sea Scrolls 1*; Waco, Tex.: Baylor University Press, 2006), 233–72.

[4] This term, as well as the essay title, echoes back to a seminal article by J.A. Sanders, "Cave 11 Surprises and the Question of Canon," *McCQ* 21 (1968): 1–15; repr. in *New Directions in Biblical Archaeology* (ed. D.N. Freedman and J.C. Greenfield; Garden City, N.Y.: Doubleday, 1969), 101–16; repr. in *The Canon and Masorah of the Hebrew Bible: An Introductory Reader* (ed. S.Z. Leiman; New York: KTAV, 1974), 37–51.

[5] F. García Martínez et al., *DJD* 23:37–78 and plates III–VIII.

[6] 1QPs[a], 1QPs[b], and 1QPs[c] in *DJD* 1:69–72 and plate XIII.

[7] 2QPs, 3QPs, 5QPs, pap6QPs, and 8QPs in *DJD* 3.1:69–71, 94, 112, 148–49, 174; *DJD* 3.2. Plates XIII, XVIII, XXIII, XXXI, XXXVII.

among scholars, since they were very fragmentary and seemed similar to the Masoretic Psalter.

However, with James Sanders' edition of 11QPsᵃ (11Q5) as the fourth volume in the DJD series (1965),[8] the situation changed decisively. The Great Psalms Scroll proved to be a major surprise, for three reasons: (a) 11QPsᵃ is by far the best-preserved of all the Psalms scrolls, thus for the first time facilitating scholarly discussion based on a substantial physical text rather than theoretical constructs; (b) this scroll diverges from the MT-150 Psalter in its ordering of contents; and (c) 11QPsᵃ also diverges radically from the MT-150 Psalter by including several additional compositions.

It would seem appropriate at this point to list the overall contents of 11QPsᵃ, but this can only be done after the second "surprise" ("A Missing Portion of 11QPsᵃ") has been discussed below.

Four Conclusions on the Psalms Scrolls

Viewed now with the hindsight of time, the previous work of James Sanders can only be described as pioneering, visionary, and brilliant. Building on his quintessential contribution—but critically assessing it—, my own research on 11QPsᵃ has solidified around four conclusions:

(1) 11QPsᵃ bears witness to a Psalter that was stabilized over time in two distinct stages: first Ps 1–89 and then Ps 90 (or 93?) onwards (the precise cutoff point is unclear, since Ps 93 is the earliest Psalm in 11QPsᵃ [XXII 16–17] according to the Masoretic sequence).[9]

(2) The Psalms scrolls attest to at least two editions of the book of Psalms: the "11QPsᵃ-Psalter" and the "MT-150 Psalter" (the latter unambiguously attested only at Masada).[10]

(3) 11QPsᵃ represents the latter part of a Psalter that was viewed and used as Scripture at Qumran, and is not a secondary collection dependent upon Ps 1–150 as found in the Masoretic Text.[11]

---

[8] J.A. Sanders, *DJD* 4.

[9] Flint, *Dead Sea Psalms Scrolls*, 135–49; idem, "Book of Psalms," 459–61; idem, "Psalms and Psalters," 240–42.

[10] Flint, *Dead Sea Psalms Scrolls*, 150–71; idem, "Book of Psalms," 459, 461–64; idem, "Psalms and Psalters," 242–45.

[11] Flint, *Dead Sea Psalms Scrolls*, 202–27; idem, "Book of Psalms," 459, 464–69; idem, "Psalms and Psalters," 245–49.

(4) Although 11QPs^a may have been *copied* at Qumran, there is no evidence that the 11QPs^a-Psalter as a collection *originated* there; it was more likely compiled among wider circles that embraced the 364-day solar calendar.[12]

A Decade of Heated Debate

In the decade following the publication of 11QPs^a, a heated debate ensued between a formidable band of scholars such as Shemaryahu Talmon,[13] M.H. Goshen-Gottstein,[14] and Patrick Skehan,[15] on the one hand, and James Sanders, who stood virtually alone. Whereas they all viewed the Psalms Scroll as a liturgical collection that is secondary to, or dependent upon, the Masoretic Text, Sanders steadfastly defended and refined his view that 11QPs^a contains the latter part of an authentic edition of the book of Psalms.[16]

The debate between Sanders and these seasoned opponents con-stitutes the first phase of the Psalms debate (up to ca. 1980), since it featured almost exclusively on a single manuscript.[17] Further evalua-tion of the relation of 11QPs^a and other Psalms scrolls to the book of Psalms could only properly take place with recourse to additional data. In particular, was there further evidence for the 11QPs^a-Psalter in any scrolls other than the Great Psalms Scroll itself?

The quest is actually threefold: (a) Are there any other Psalms scrolls that preserve the *distinctive arrangement* (sequence of Psalms) found in

---

[12] Flint, *Dead Sea Psalms Scrolls*, 198–201; idem, "Book of Psalms," 459, 469–71; idem, "Psalms and Psalters," 249–51.

[13] S. Talmon, "Pisqah Be'emsa' Pasuq and 11QPs^a," *Textus* 5 (1966): 11–21; idem, review of J.A. Sanders, *The Psalms Scroll From Qumran*, *Tarbiz* 37 (1967): 99–104 (100–101).

[14] M.H. Goshen-Gottstein, "The Psalms Scroll (11QPs^a): A Problem of Canon and Text," *Textus* 5 (1966): 22–33.

[15] P.W. Skehan, "A Liturgical Complex in 11QPs^a," *CBQ* 34 (1973): 195–205; idem, "Qumran and Old Testament Criticism," in *Qumrân: Sa piété, sa théologie et son milieu* (ed. Mathias Delcor; BETL 46; Paris: Duculot, 1978), 163–82; idem, "The Divine Name at Qumran, in the Masada Scroll, and in the Septuagint," *BIOSCS* 13 (1980): 14–44, (42).

[16] See, for example, J.A. Sanders, "Variorum in the Psalms Scroll (11QPs^a)," *HTR* 59 (1966): 83–94; idem, "Cave 11 Surprises and the Question of Canon," 1–15; idem, "The Qumran Psalms Scroll (11QPs^a) Reviewed," in *On Language, Culture, and Religion: In Honor of Eugene A. Nida* (ed. M. Black and W.A. Smalley; The Hague: Mouton, 1974), 79–99.

[17] As George Brooke observes, this phase largely resulted in an impasse (G.J. Brooke, "Psalms 105 and 106 at Qumran," *RevQ* 14/54 [1989]: 267–92 [269]).

11QPs^a? (b) Do any other Psalms scrolls contain the *distinctive contents* (compositions absent from the MT-150 Psalter)[18] found in 11QPs^a? (c) If 11QPs^a indeed contains the latter part of an authentic edition of the book of Psalms, are there any Psalms scrolls that preserve *earlier sections* of this Psalter? Evidence was to come forward in the Psalms scrolls from Cave Four, and—most notably—in one scroll from Cave Eleven (11QPs^b).

THE SECOND SURPRISE:
A MISSING PORTION OF THE "11QPs^A-PSALTER"

A significant piece of 11QPs^a was not available to James Sanders as he prepared his critical edition, which was published in 1965.[19] Two years later he produced a companion volume, often termed the "Cornell Edition," with a more general audience in view.[20]

Sanders reports that—after the DJD edition had appeared and when the more popular edition was already in the publisher's hands—a telegram from the Israeli scholar Yigael Yadin arrived in December 1965, announcing that he had gained possession of a missing section of 11QPs^a.[21] Designating this piece as "Fragment E," Yadin was to publish a preliminary edition soon afterwards (1966).[22] Although it was now too late to incorporate this important new material in the body of the Cornell volume, Sanders was fortunately able to append a *Postscriptum*, which includes a photograph, transcription, and English translation of the new fragment.[23]

Could this missing fragment, this second "surprise," contain Psalms from the earlier part of the Psalter, thus proving that 11QPs^a as published in *DJD* 4 was actually the latter part of a larger Psalms scroll?

---

[18] I.e. (in the order of 11QPs^a): the Catena, Ps 154, the Plea for Deliverance, Sir 51, the Apostrophe to Zion, the Hymn to the Creator, David's Last Words, David's Compositions, Ps 151A, and Ps 151B.

[19] Sanders, *The Psalms Scroll of Qumrân Cave 11 [11QPs^a]*.

[20] Sanders, *The Dead Sea Psalms Scroll* (Ithaca, N.Y.: Cornell University Press, 1967).

[21] The large fragment contains parts of Ps 118, 104, 147, and 105 in that order, joining frg. D and col. I of the larger manuscript.

[22] Y. Yadin, "Another Fragment (E) of the Psalms Scroll from Qumran Cave 11 (11QPs^a)," *Textus* 5 (1966): 1–10 + pls. I–V. The fragment is quite substantial, containing parts of three columns.

[23] Sanders, *Dead Sea Psalms Scroll*, 155–65.

Unfortunately, this large fragment does not contain material from the earlier part of the Psalter, but Ps 118, 104, 147, and 105 in that order. However, it constitutes a vital missing link, joining frg. D and col. I of the larger manuscript published in the DJD edition.

With the data from frg. E in hand, we now focus on the contents of 11QPsᵃ. Copied in ca. 50 C.E., the Great Psalms Scroll preserves forty-nine compositions—with at least one more (Ps 120) now missing but originally present. The order of contents is generally assured, since from col. I onwards the various compositions are physically joined on one continuous scroll.

THE CONTENTS OF 11QPsᴬ BY COMPOSITION*

Frgs. a–e	Psalm 101	Col. XVI	→Catena
	→102	Cols. XVI–XVII	→145
	→103	Cols. XVII–XVIII	[+ subscript]
	109		→154
	118	Cols. XVIII–XIX	+ Plea for Deliverance
	→104	Cols. XIX–XX	→139
	→147	Cols. XX–XXI	→137
Frg. e–Col. I	→105		→138
Cols. I–II	→146	Cols. XXI–XXII	→Sirach 51
	→148		→Apostrophe to Zion
	[+ 120]		→Psalm 93
Col. III	→121	Cols. XXII–XXIII	→141
	→122		→133
	→123	Cols. XXIII–XXIV	→144
Cols. III–IV	→124		→155
	→125	Cols. XXIV–XXV	→142
	→126		→143
	→127	Cols. XXV–XXVI	→149
Cols. IV–V	→128		→150
	→129		→Hymn to the Creator
	→130	Cols. XXVI–XXVII	→David's Last Words
Cols. V–VI	→131		→David's Compositions
	→132		→Psalm 140
Cols. VI –XIV	→119	Cols. XXVII–XXVIII	→134
Cols. XIV–XV	→135		→151A
Cols. XV–XVI	→136		→151B [end of scroll]

* An arrow → indicates that a passage is continuous with the one listed before it. The plus sign + indicates that a passage follows the one before it, even though some text is no longer extant.

THE THIRD SURPRISE:
SUPPORT FOR THE SEQUENCE OF THE 11QPsᴬ-PSALTER IN 4QPsᴱ (?)

A new phase of discussion was introduced by a series of articles and a Yale dissertation by G.H. Wilson,[†] which appeared from 1983 to 1985.[24] Wilson had the decided advantage of access to the Cave Four Psalms scrolls, since Patrick Skehan (editor of the Cave Four biblical scrolls) had given him copies of his own notes and transcriptions. Thus Wilson was able to take into consideration not only 11QPsᵃ, but almost all of the twenty-three Cave Four scrolls as well,[25] which empowered him to expand the Psalms debate in a significant way. His conclusions support key elements of Sanders' earlier proposals, especially that the Psalms scrolls provide evidence for stabilization of the Psalter over time and the status of 11QPsᵃ as a true scriptural Psalter as opposed to a secondary collection.

But is there a true exemplar of the 11QPsᵃ-Psalter among the Cave Four scrolls? With respect to *distinctive arrangement*, seven of the Cave Four Psalms diverge from the MT-150 Psalter in the ordering of contents: 4QPsᵃ, 4QPsᵇ, 4QPsᵈ, 4QPsᵉ, 4QPsᵏ, 4QPsⁿ, and 4QPsᵠ.[26] With respect to *distinctive contents*, only one (4QPsᶠ) contains apocryphal compositions.

A survey of these eight manuscripts shows that, with one possible exception, none can be a copy or exemplar of the 11QPsᵃ-Psalter. 4QPsᶠ, for example, contains fragmentary text from the Apostrophe to Zion (vv 4–6, 24–28) which is also found in 11QPsᵃ. In the Cave Four scroll, however, the Apostrophe directly follows Ps 109, whereas in the Cave Eleven scroll it directly follows text from Sir 51. Moreover, 4QPsᶠ contains two compositions (or one) that are lacking in 11QPsᵃ: the Eschatological Hymn and the Apostrophe to Judah[27] (H. Eshel and

---

[†] The untimely passing of this fine and collegial Psalms scholar on November 11, 2005 is hereby noted.

[24] G.H. Wilson, "The Qumran Psalms Manuscripts and the Consecutive Arrangement of Psalms in the Hebrew Psalter," *CBQ* 45 (1983): 377–88; idem, "The Qumran Psalms Scroll Reconsidered: Analysis of the Debate," *CBQ* 47 (1985): 624–42; idem, *The Editing of the Hebrew Psalter* (Chico, Calif.: Scholars Press, 1985).

[25] I.e., 4QPsᵃ (4Q83) to 4QPsᵠ (4Q98), plus 4QPsʳ (4Q98a) to 4QPsʷ (4Q98f) and 4QPs 89 (4Q236). For the edition, see *DJD* 16:7–160, 163–68 and pls. I–XX.

[26] For example, Ps 31→33 in 4QPsᵃ and 4QPsᵠ (the siglum → indicates that the second composition in a sequence directly follows the first).

[27] For the complete contents of 4QPsᶠ, see *DJD* 16:85–106 and pls. XII–XIV, and Flint, *Dead Sea Psalms Scrolls*, 259.

J. Strugnell have proposed, perhaps convincingly, that these two pieces form a single composition).[28]

In similar vein, 4QPs[a] and 4QPs[q] preserve material only from the first two books of the Psalter[29] and thus cannot be viewed as an exemplar of the 11QPs[a]-Psalter (although they could admittedly be from the earlier part of that Psalter). 4QPs[b] does preserve text in common with 11QPs[a], but with differing sequences—for example, in 4QPs[b], Ps 93 is almost definitely preceded by Ps 92, while in 11QPs[a] it follows the Apostrophe to Zion. Moreover, in 4QPs[b], Ps 103 is followed directly by Ps 112, while in the Cave 11 scroll it is most likely followed by Ps 109.

Like 11QPs[a], 4QPs[d] contains Ps 104 and 147 as directly adjacent Psalms—but in the opposite order.[30] Two additional scrolls that differ from the MT-150 Psalter in the ordering of contents are also at variance with 11QPs[a]. The first is 4QPs[k], where Ps 135 appears to be followed by another Psalm, which in turn is directly followed by Ps 99 (cf. Ps 135→136→Catena→145 in 11QPs[a]).[31] The second is 4QPs[n], where Ps 135:6–8, 11–12 is directly followed by Ps 136:22–24 (cf. Ps 135:1–6, X, 7 [+8] 9 [+10–16] 17–21→Ps 136:1–7, X, 8–16 [+17–25] 26 in 11QPs[a]).[32]

My research has shown that the Cave 4 Psalms scrolls represent several different collections of Psalms, and that some of these are only small liturgical collections. For example, 4QPs[g], 4QPs[h], and 5QPs probably contained only Ps 119, and 4QPs[b] may have ended with Ps 118.[33]

There is only one Cave Four scroll that *may* qualify as an exemplar of the 11QPs[a]-Psalter: 4QPs[e], which preserves text beginning with Ps 76:10

---

[28] H. Eshel and J. Strugnell, "Alphabetical Acrostics in Pre-Tannaitic Hebrew," *CBQ* 62 (2000): 441–58, esp. 446–49.

[29] The text preserved in 4QPs[a] ranges from Ps 5:9 to Ps 69:1–19, while 4QPs[q] contains Ps 31:24–25→Ps 3:1–7, X, 8–14 [+ 15] 16–18 [+19–22]; Ps 35:[1–3+] 4–5 [+6–7] 8 [+9] 10 [+11] 12 [+13] 14–15 [+16] 17 [+18] 19–20 (in this listing, the siglum X denotes a verse not found in the Masoretic version of the Psalm). For the complete contents of 4QPs[a], see *DJD* 16:7–22 and pls. I–II; Flint, *Dead Sea Psalms Scrolls*, 257.

[30] Compare 4QPs[d] (Ps 147:1–4 [+5–12] 13–17 [+18–19] 20 → Ps 104:1–5 [+6–7] 8–11 [+12–13] 14–15 [+16–21] 22–25 [+ 26–32] 33–35) with 11QPs[a] (Ps 104:1–6 [+7–20] 21–35 → Ps 147:1–2, 3(?) [+4–17] 18–20); cf. *DJD* 16:63–71 and pl. X; Flint, *Dead Sea Psalms Scrolls*, 258.

[31] For the complete contents of 4QPs[k], see *DJD* 16:123–25 and pl. XVII; Flint, *Dead Sea Psalms Scrolls*, 259.

[32] In this sequence, the siglum X denotes an additional verse or text. For the complete contents of 4QPs[n], see *DJD* 16:135–37 and pl. XVIII; Flint, *Dead Sea Psalms Scrolls*, 260.

[33] See Flint, *Dead Sea Psalms Scrolls*, 32, 34–35; idem, "Psalms and Psalters," 244–45; cf. idem, "Book of Psalms," 463.

and ending with Ps 130:6. Although the document is very fragmentary, 4QPs^e seems to have originally contained a *distinctive arrangement* found in the 11QPs^a-Psalter: the sequence of Ps (?)118→104→[147]→105(?) →146. Here are the relevant transcriptions (14–18 ii 20–24) from the DJD edition:[34]

Frg. 14 Ps 118:29 + 104:1–3

1	[ליהוה כי]טוֹב כי לע[ולם חסדו] *vacat* [
2	[לדויד בר]כִֿי נפשי את יהוה יה]וה אלוהינו גדלתה מאוד הוד והדר לבשתה$^{104:1}$	
	[עוטה^2	
3	[אור כשלמ]הֿ נוטה שמים כי]ריעה ^{3}המקרה במים עליותיו השם עבים רכובו]
4	[המהלך על]כנפי רוח] ^{4}עושה מלאכיו רוחות משרתיו אש לוהטֿ^{5} [

Frgs. 15–16 Ps 104:20–22

top margin

1	[מבואו ^{20}תשת חושך ויהי ליל]ה בו תרמוש כול חית]וֹ יער]
2	[^{21}הכפירים שואנים לטרף]ולבקש מא]כִֿל]אֹכֿל]ם ^{22}תזרח]
3	[השמש ויאספון ואל מעונותי]הֿם יר]בצון]^{23}

Frgs. 17–18 i Ps 105:1–3

3	[$^{105:0}$הודו ליהוה כי טוב כי לעולם חסדו ^{1}הודו ליהוה]
4	[קראו ב]שמו הוד]יֿעו בעמים עלילותיו ^{2}שירו לו זמרו ל]וֹ]
5	[שיחו בכול נפלאו]תיו ^{3}התה]ללו בשם קדשו ישמח]לב]

Frg. 19 Ps 105:23–25

1	ויבוא ישראל]מצרים י]עקוב]
2	ויעצמהו]מצריו ^{25}ה]פך]

Frgs. 18 ii 20–24 Ps 105:36–45 + 146:1(?)

top margin

1	[^{36}ויך כול בכור בארצ]מֿ ראשית לכו]ל אונם ^{37}ויוצֿא עמ]ו בכסף וזהב]
2	[ואי]ן בשבטי]וֿ] כושל ^{38}שמחו מ]צרי]מֿ בצאתם כי נפֿל פחֿ]דם עליהם]
3	[^{39}פרש]ענֿ]ן למסך ואש להאיֿרֿ]לי]לה ^{40}שֿאֿל ו]בֿא שליו ולחם]
4	[ש]מים י]שֿביעם ^{41}פתח צור ויזובו]מים הלכו בציות נ]הר ^{42}כי]זכר את]
5	[דבר קוד]שו]אתֿ] אברהם עבדו ^{43}ויוצֿא ע]מֿו בש]שון ברנה]
6	[את בחיר]יו ^{44}יתן להם א]רצות נ]וים ועמל לואמים יירשו ^{45}בעבור]
7	[ישמרֿ]וֿ חוקיו ותורותיו י]נצוֿרוֿ]וֿ הללו יה]
8	[הללויה]$^{146:1}$

---

[34] See *DJD* 16:81–82 and pl. XI.

If this sequence is correct—which is open to debate—, 4QPs^e may be regarded as the only exemplar of the 11QPs^a-Psalter from Cave Four. Since 4QPs^e also contains material from the earlier part of this Psalter (Ps 76–89),[35] it suggests that 11QPs^a contains the latter part of a larger Psalter that was being stabilized in two stages: first Ps 1–89 and then Ps 90 onwards (the precise cutoff point not being clear).

This identification is admittedly tentative. For one thing, it lacks any of the *distinctive contents* (compositions lacking in the MT-150 Psalter) found in the 11QPs^a-Psalter. Moreover, Ulrich Dahmen has more recently challenged my proposal that 4QPs^e preserves the *distinctive arrangement* found in 11QPs^a.[36] It is beyond the scope of the present article to address his critique, which I will do on another occasion. Suffice it to say (for now) that stronger evidence than 4QPs^e is required to affirm the existence of more than one copy of the 11QPs^a-Psalter.

THE FOURTH SURPRISE:
SUPPORT FOR THE SEQUENCE AND CONTENTS OF THE
11QPs^A-PSALTER IN 11QPs^B

Somewhat analogous to the Hebrew University Isaiah Scroll (1QIsa^b) being almost completely overshadowed by the Great Isaiah Scroll (1QIsa^a), 11QPs^b has often been lost in discussion of the Psalms scrolls, because so much attention has been paid to 11QPs^a. Nevertheless, it has been known to Dead Sea Scrolls scholars for some time that 11QPs^b is an exemplar of the 11QPs^a-Psalter.

This scroll contains not one, but two, surprises, owing to a crucial difference between the preliminary edition of 1967[37] and the critical DJD edition some twenty years later.[38] The first surprise, already observed by Van der Ploeg in 1967, is that 11QPs^b preserves part of the distinctive arrangement and some of the distinctive contents of the 11QPs^a-Psalter.

---

[35] I.e., Ps 76:10–12 [+13]; 77:1; 78:6–7 [+8–30] 31–33; 81:2–3; 86:10–11; 88:1–5; 89:44–48, 50–53.

[36] U. Dahmen, *Psalmen- und Psalter-Rezeption im Frühjudentum. Rekonstruktion, Textbestand, Struktur und Pragmatik der Psalmenrolle 11QPs^a aus Qumran* (STDJ 49; Leiden: Brill, 2003), 52–59.

[37] J.P.M. van der Ploeg, "Fragments d'un manuscrit de Psaumes de Qumran (11QPs^b)," *RB* 74 (1967): 408–12 and pl. XVIII.

[38] *DJD* 23:37–47 and pl. III.

Frg. 7 preserves the *distinctive arrangement* of Ps 141→133→144 found in 11QPs^a. In the following transcription of frg. 7a–e, material that overlaps with 11QPs^a XXIII 6–13 is underlined.[39]

Frgs. 7a–e Ps 141:10; 133; 144:1–2

[	*vacat*	[רשעים יחד אנוכי עד]אעבור[	1
	שיר$^{133:1}$*vac*]המעל[ות לדויד הנה מה ט]וב ומה נעים שבת אחים[	2
	נם יחד ^{2}כשמן] הטוב על הרואש] יורד על הזקן זקן אהרון[	3
	שיורד על פי מדיו ^{3}כטל חרמון שיורד[ר על הר ציון כי שמה צוה]	4
[	*vacat*	י]ה[וה את הברכה] עד עו]לם שלום על]ן ישראל	5
	vac[*at*	]$^{144:1}$ברוך יהוה צו]רי המלמ]ד ידי לקרב ואצבעותי[	6
	למלחמה]^{2}חסדי ומצודתי משנ]בי ומפל[ט לי מנני ובו חסיתי הרודד[	7
	עמ]ים ^{3}תחתי אלוהים מה אדם ותדעהו בן אנוש ותחושבהו[	8
	]o	9

11QPs^b also preserves *distinctive contents* that are characteristic of 11QPs^a, namely parts of three "extra-biblical" compositions: the Catena with its order of Ps 118:1→15→16 in frg. 3 (cf. 11QPs^a XVI 1–2);[40] verses 1–15 of the Plea for Deliverance (cf. 11QPs^a XIX 1–15);[41] and two words of the Apostrophe to Zion (cf. 11QPs^a XXII 4–5).[42]

The Fifth Surprise:
Evidence for an Earlier Section of the 11QPs^A-Psalter in 11QPs^B

There has been much confusion as to the precise contents of this manuscript, which only became clear with the publication of the DJD edition in 1998,[43] when most discussion around the Psalms scrolls had abated. It is in this edition that our final surprise emerges—that 11QPs^b preserves material from the earlier part of the 11QPs^a-Psalter.

There are nine fragments altogether, of which the seven largest belong to six (or less likely seven) columns. The editors (F. García Martínez, E. Tigchelaar, and A.S. van der Woude) date the scroll on paleographical

---

[39] *DJD* 23:45; cf. Van der Ploeg, "Fragments d'un manuscrit," 411.
[40] *DJD* 23:42; cf. Van der Ploeg, "Fragments d'un manuscrit," 412.
[41] *DJD* 23:42–43; cf. Van der Ploeg, "Fragments d'un manuscrit," 409–10.
[42] *DJD* 23:44.
[43] *DJD* 23:37–47 and pl. III.

grounds to the Herodian period (30 B.C.E.–70 C.E.).[44] The contents are as follows:

> Psalm 77:18–21
> →78:1[45]
> 109:3–4(?)[46]
> 119:163–165
> 118:1→15→16 *[Catena]*
> Plea for Deliverance 1–15
> Apostrophe to Zion 4–5
> 141:10
> →133:1–3, X[47]
> →144:1–2
> (plus fragment)

The inclusion of Ps 77:18–79:1 in 11QPs[b] resolves the important issue of whether the 11QPs[a]-Psalter contained material prior to Ps 93. Patrick Skehan had argued that 11QPs[a] is almost fully extant and originally began with Ps 101 in the first preserved part of the scroll (frg. A). This bolstered his view that 11QPs[a] never contained text from Ps 1–89 (or Ps 1–92, seeing that Ps 93 is earliest Psalm in 11QPs[a] according to the order of the Masoretic Psalter).[48] Since reconstruction of 11QPs[a] indicates that frg. A began at the top of a column, Skehan may well be correct in asserting that the scroll began with Ps 101—which casts strong doubt on whether the 11QPs[a]-Psalter originally contained material prior to Ps 93.

With respect to their inclusion of Ps 77:18–78:1 as frg. 1 of 11QPs[b], the editors write: "Van der Ploeg included this fragment with 11QPs[c] on the basis of a superficial similarity between it and 11QPs[c] 8. However, the scribal hand of frg. 1 bears a marked affinity with that of 11QPs[b] and is dissimilar to that of 11QPs[c]… In addition, the line length of frg. 1

---

[44] *DJD* 23:38.

[45] For the siglum → see note 20 above

[46] In the critical edition (*DJD* 23:46), the editors list this piece near the end as frg. 8, since it preserves material from either Ps 109:3–4 (תנ ם תחח[ן), or Ps 154:16 (שובי[ם) תחמֹ[ל) as in XVII 14 of 11QPs[a]. In this essay, the fragment is placed before Ps 119, in accordance with the order of 11QPs[a] and on the assumption that it contains Ps 109:3–4.

[47] The siglum X denotes a verse not found in the Masoretic version of the Psalm.

[48] In Skehan's view, for 11QPs[a] to begin with Ps 101 would be appropriate since this is the first Psalm in Book IV beginning with לדו(י)ד, thus serving as the starting-point for an expanded Davidic collection ("Qumran and Old Testament Criticism," 163–82, esp. 170).

matches that of 11QPs^b and not that of 11QPs^c."[49] The transcription
of this piece is as follows:

Frg. 1 Ps 77:18–78:1[50]

top margin

[אף הצציכה יתה]לכו ^{19}קול רעמכה בנלנל האירו בר̇ק[ים]	1
[תבל רנזה ותרעש האר̇ץ ^{20}בים דרככה וש]ביליכה במים ר[בים]	2
[ועקבותיכה לוא נודעו ^{21}נ]חית כצאן עמכה בי[ד מושה ואה̇[רון]	3
[<i>vacat</i> <i>vacat</i>]	4
[מ̇שכיל לאסף̇ האוינה עמי תורתי]ה̇טו אוזנכמה לא[מרי] $^{78:1}$ <i>vac.?</i>]	5

Here is a scroll that is undisputedly a copy of the 11QPs^a-Psalter that
contains text prior to Ps 93 (the earliest Psalm in 11QPs^a according
to the Masoretic sequence). 11QPs^b provides clear proof that—even
if 11QPs^a itself began with Ps 101—the full 11QPs^a-Psalter contained
Psalms prior to those that are preserved in 11QPs^a.

Conclusion

The underlying quest of this essay has been to identify another copy
of the Psalter represented by the Great Psalms Scroll, which I term
the "11QPs^a-Psalter." The contents have been organized around five
"surprises" presented by the Psalms scrolls from Qumran.

The Great Psalms Scroll (11QPs^a) itself was the first major surprise,
since it diverges radically from the MT-150 Psalter in its ordering of
contents and by including several additional compositions. The second
surprise was a missing section ("Fragment E") of 11QPs^a, preserving
material from Ps 118, 104, 147, and 105 in that order. The third surprise
was 4QPs^e, which seems to have originally contained a *distinctive arrangement* found in the 11QPs^a-Psalter: Ps (?)118→104→[147]→105(?)→146.
However, this identification is tentative.

The fourth surprise was found in 11QPs^b, which is undisputedly a
copy of the 11QPs^a-Psalter since it preserves the *distinctive arrangement*
of Ps 141→133→144 found in 11QPs^a, as well as *distinctive contents*
characteristic of 11QPs^a, namely the Catena (Ps 118:1→15→16), verses

---

[49] *DJD* 23:40; cf. J.P.M. van der Ploeg, "Fragments de Psaumes de Qumrân," *Intertestamental Essays in Honour of Józef Tadeusz Milik* (ed. Z.J. Kapera; Qumranica Mogilanensia
6; Kraków: Enigma Press, 1992), 233–37 and pl. II (234).

[50] For the transcription, see *DJD* 23:40.

1–15 of the Plea for Deliverance, and two words of the Apostrophe to Zion.

The final surprise emerged in the critical edition of 11QPs^b (*DJD* 23 in 1998), by the inclusion Ps 77:18–78:1 as frg. 1. The fact that this scroll contains text prior to Ps 93 (the earliest Psalm in 11QPs^a according to the Masoretic sequence) provides clear proof that—even if 11QPs^a itself began with Ps 101—the full 11QPs^a-Psalter contained earlier material from the Psalter.

THE QUMRAN ARAMAIC TEXTS AND THE
QUMRAN COMMUNITY

Devorah Dimant

The documents known as the Dead Sea Scrolls, or more accurately those discovered at Qumran, have had a curious fate. They turned up quite by chance in ten caves near the Dead Sea more than fifty years ago, and it took five decades to complete their publication. This long and often tortuous process finally brought to light the remains of some nine hundred manuscripts originally placed in the caves.[1] But the delay in publication of many scrolls from cave 4 had a negative effect on the course and general orientation of the research in several important respects. Because the full content of the Qumran library was unknown and inaccessible to the scientific community for many years, Qumran works were often discussed without being related to the library as a whole. The diversity and range of scrolls, recently coming to light, and the fast growing research on them have reinforced this tendency rather than encourage more comprehensive surveys.

For particular reasons such has been the case of the Aramaic texts found among the scrolls. Since only recently the complete set of those texts has become available for study, for a long time attention was paid mainly to specific texts such as *1 Enoch* or the *Aramaic Levi Document*.[2] This was because both were known in translations long before the discovery of the scrolls and had a solid scholarly tradition behind them. They were partly published relatively early in the history of the Qumran research, and students of the scrolls could have easily fitted

---

[1] The precise number of the Qumran texts stands now on the remains of 942 scrolls. This figure includes 128 manuscripts initially assigned to existing scrolls but now are recognized as separate. However, dealing as it does with literary texts from the Qumran library the present survey does not apply to 48 non-literary documents found at Qumran and therefore they are omitted here from the overall number of the Qumran manuscripts. These non-literary documents include 21 phylacteries, 6 *mezuzoth*, 3 writing exercises and 18 other documentary texts.

[2] See J.T. Milik, "Le Testament de Lévi en araméen: Fragment de la grotte 4 de Qumrân," *RB* 62 (1955): 398–406; idem, *The Books of Enoch: Aramaic Fragments of Qumrân* (Oxford: Clarendon Press, 1976).

them into an already familiar picture.[3] Therefore these writings have been usually discussed in the context of the non-Qumranic corpus of Jewish Pseudepigrapha. Such, for instance, is the perspective of three recent surveys of "Pseudepigrapha" at Qumran by Michael Stone, Moshe Bernstein, and Peter Flint.[4] In such surveys no distinction is made between works written in Hebrew and in Aramaic. Nor has any attempt been made to examine *1 Enoch* and the *Aramaic Levi Document*, or other Aramaic texts, in the particular context of the Aramaic corpus from Qumran.[5]

This is not to say that the overall perspective has been ignored completely. Over the years several comprehensive collections of Aramaic texts have been published. Such is one collection edited by Joseph Fitzmyer and Daniel Harrington in English and one published by Klaus Beyer in German.[6] However, motivated by the desire to provide first editions, and interested mainly in the linguistic character of Palestinian Aramaic, the editors in both cases offer texts of various literary types and provenance without attempting any classification or literary analysis. As a result the particular character of the Qumran Aramaic texts is quite lost in these collections.

That the Aramaic texts should be considered a distinct group within the Qumran library is suggested by their particular language, style, and content. Furthermore, the Aramaic texts contain nothing of the specifi-

---

[3] Milik's *The Books of Enoch* is a typical example of this attitude. It is an erudite reconstruction of Enochic fragments in context of what has been known before Qumran. However, besides supplying much of the missing lines in the various manuscripts Milik also reconstructed a dubious historical context for *1 Enoch*. These features have diminished the usefulness of his volume. For a revised edition of the Enochic copies by L.T. Stuckenbruck and E. Cook, see *Parabiblical Texts* (*DSSR 3*), 454–561. But by printing the literary units which constitute *1 Enoch* in separate grouping rather than in the way they are assembled in the Ethiopic version and in the Qumran manuscripts, this new edition misrepresents *1 Enoch* in the shape we know it.

[4] Cf. M.E. Stone, "The Dead Sea Scrolls and the Pseudepigrapha," *DSD* 3 (1996): 270–95; M.J. Bernstein, "Pseudepigraphy in the Qumran Scrolls: Categories and Functions," in *Pseudepigraphic Perspectives: The Apocrypha and Pseudepigrapha in Light of the Dead Sea Scrolls* (ed. E.G. Chazon and M.E. Stone; STDJ 31; Leiden: Brill, 1999), 1–26; P.W. Flint, "'Apocrypha,' Other Previously-Known Writings, and 'Pseudepigrapha' in the Dead Sea Scrolls," in *The Dead Sea Scrolls After Fifty Years* (ed. idem and J.C. VanderKam; 2 vols.; Leiden: Brill, 1999), 2:1–66.

[5] Cf. however, the short comments made by J.C. Greenfield, M.E. Stone, and E. Eshel, *The Aramaic Levi Document. Edition, Translation, Commentary* (SVTP 19; Leiden: Brill, 2004), 11–44.

[6] Cf. J.A. Fitzmyer and D.J. Harrington, *A Manual of Palestinian Aramaic Texts* (BibOr 34; Rome: Biblical Institute Press, 1978); K. Beyer, *Die aramäischen Texte vom Toten Meer* (2 vols.; Göttingen: Vandenhoeck & Ruprecht, 1984 and 2004).

cally sectarian terminology or ideology and therefore do not belong with the sectarian literature.[7] Even the mention of the Sons of Light and the Sons of Darkness (בני נהורא ובני חשוכא) in the so-called *Visions of Amram*, and the peculiar demonology introduced by this work, do not make it a sectarian composition. Rather than pointing to a sectarian origin, they attest to the wide dissemination of the dualistic thought.[8]

As a distinct entity within the Qumran library then, the Aramaic texts should be examined separately. Only in this way do individual Aramaic compositions acquire their proper significance, and their origin and background may be investigated.

A systematic description of the Aramaic Qumran texts as such is still lacking. By way of introduction I would like to outline here the main themes and literary characteristics of the Aramaic corpus and note some of their implications.[9]

Let me begin with a few fundamental data.[10] Remains of one hundred and twenty-one Aramaic texts were found at Qumran, slightly more than 13 percent of the total nine hundred manuscripts retrieved from the caves. However, thirty-two of these documents are too fragmentary for significant assessment. Another five manuscripts, some of which were given the impressive names "apocryphon" and "apocalypse" (4Q488, 4Q489,[11] 6Q14, 6Q19, 6Q23), have preserved so little that not much can be said about their content and character. They are significant only as pointers to the number of Aramaic texts originally housed in the library. Thus fragments of only eighty-four Aramaic manuscripts, or some 9 percent of the entire Qumran collection, have preserved enough text to be considered in a meaningful way. Yet the original library may have contained more Aramaic texts that have perished

---

[7] As noted already in my classification. Cf. D. Dimant, "The Qumran Manuscripts: Contents and Significance," in *Time to Prepare the Way in the Wilderness* (ed. eadem and L.H. Schiffman; STDJ 16: Leiden: Brill, 1995), 32.

[8] Cf. the comments of J. Frey, "Different Patterns of Dualistic Thought in the Qumran Library," in *Legal Texts and Legal Issues* (ed. M.J. Bernstein et al.; STDJ 23; Leiden: Brill, 1997), 275–335; R. Bauckham, "Qumran and the Fourth Gospel: Is there a Connection?" in *The Scrolls and the Scriptures: Qumran Fifty Years After* (ed. S.E. Porter and C.A. Evans; JSPSup 26; Sheffield: Academic Press, 1997), 267–79.

[9] I have discussed some of the material reviewed here from a different perspective in D. Dimant, "Old Testament Pseudepigrapha at Qumran," in *The Bible and the Dead Sea Scrolls: The Dead Sea Scrolls and the Qumran Community* (vol. 2; ed. J.H. Charlesworth; Waco, Tex.: Baylor University Press, 2006), 447–67.

[10] The data are culled from *DJD* 39:221–25.

[11] Published by M. Baillet, *DJD* 7:10–11. The only word that may serve the title "vision" is the verb "and I saw it" (וחזיתה—4Q489 1 2), but this is not much to go on.

altogether. Even the surviving texts have not endured in their entirety. Of some manuscripts only tiny fragments were preserved, of others more substantial pieces.

Nevertheless, what we possess today is of immense value, as it recuperates segments of an unknown Jewish Aramaic literature from Second Temple times. For the remains of those eighty-four scrolls come from twenty-nine different works, only three of which were known prior the discovery of the scrolls. They are *Tobit; 1 En.* 1–36, 72–106; and the *Aramaic Levi Document*, probably a source of the Greek *Testament of Levi*. Also of note is the fact that twelve of the twenty-nine works are extant in more than one exemplar.[12]

From the thematic perspective the Aramaic texts may be divided into six rubrics:

I.   **Works about the Period of the Flood**: *1 Enoch* (4Q201–202, 4Q204–207, 4Q212); the *Astronomical Work* (4Q208–211); the *Book of Giants* (1Q23–24, 2Q26, 4Q203, 4Q206 2–3[?], 4Q530–532, 4Q533[?], 6Q8[13]). The first part of the *Genesis Apocryphon* (1Q20) also is to be considered under this rubric.

II. **Works dealing with the History of the Patriarchs**: the *Aramaic Levi Document* (1Q21, 4Q213, 4Q213a, 4Q213b, 4Q214, 4Q214a, 4Q214b); the *Visions of Amram* (4Q543–548, 4Q549[?]); the *Testament of Qahat* (4Q542); the *Testament of Joseph* (4Q539); the *Words of Benjamin* (4Q538); the *Testament of Jacob*(?) (4Q537); as well as the later part of the *Genesis Apocryphon* (1Q20).

III. **Visionary Compositions**: The *New Jerusalem* (1Q32[?], 2Q24, 4Q554, 4Q554a, 4Q555, 5Q15, 11Q18);[14] the *Four Kingdoms*

---

[12] These are the following: *1 Enoch*, the *Book of Giants*, the *Aramaic Levi Document*, the *Apocryphon of Levi*, the *Visions of Amram*, *Pseudo-Daniel*, the *New Jerusalem*, the *Four Kingdoms*, the *Birth of Noah*, *Tobit*, the so-called *Apocalypse* (4Q556–558), and *Proto-Esther*. J.T. Milik, "Les modèles araméens du livre d'Esther dans la Grotte 4 de Qumrân," *RevQ* 15/59 (1992): 321–406, distinguished between six *Proto-Esther* manuscripts. Cf. also E. Cook, *DSSR* 6:6–13.

[13] The various copies of this work were published in several volumes of the DJD series. All are conveniently assembled in *DSSR* 6:39–74. Cf. also Beyer, *Die aramäischen Texte vom Toten Meer*, 2:129–38.

[14] For this list see É. Puech, "À propos de la Jérusalem Nouvelle d'après les manuscrits de la mer Morte," *Sem* 43–44 (1992): 87–102 (87–88). Puech follows Milik's suggestion that 4Q232 may come from a Hebrew version of the Aramaic work. Cf. ibid., 88 n. 3, citing Milik, *The Books of Enoch*, 59.

(4Q552–553); the so-called *Apocryphon of Daniel* (4Q246);[15] the *Words of Michael* (4Q529); the so-called *Birth of Noah* (4Q534–536);[16] the so-called *Apocryphon of Levi*(?) (4Q540–541, 5Q15[?]);[17] *Pseudo-Daniel* (4Q243–245).

IV. **Legendary Narratives and Court-Tales**: *Tobit* (4Q196–199); The *Prayer of Nabonidus* (4Q242); *Proto-Esther* (4Q550, 4Q550a, 4Q550b, 4Q550c, 4Q550d, 4Q550e); *Daniel-Suzanna* (4Q551).

V. **Astronomy and Magic**: Zodiology and brontology (4Q318); Exorcism (4Q560); Physiognomy/ Horoscope (4Q561).

VI. **Varia**: Bible Targums: of Leviticus (4Q156); of Job (4Q157, 11Q10). There are small remains of three other works: List of False Prophets (4Q339), Apocalypse (4Q556–558);[18] Biblical Chronology (4Q559); and Aramaic proverbs (4Q569).

A salient feature emerging from the list is the predominance of two clusters of themes, one related to the Flood, the other to the Patriarchal history. Twenty-one Aramaic manuscripts deal with events connected with the Flood; eighteen scrolls are devoted to the lives of the Patriarchs.

---

[15] 4Q246 was connected by most scholars with the biblical book of Daniel on basis of similarity of themes and vocabulary. Cf. É. Puech, "246: 4QApocryphe de Daniel ar," *DJD* 22:165–84 and his summary of research on 178–84. However, the name of Daniel does not occur in the surviving fragment, nor do the details correspond to specific details of the book of Daniel. Moreover, the center of this single fragment is a messianic figure not found in the biblical Daniel. The single mention of a messianic figure in Dan 7:13–14 may have inspired this description, but the Qumran text does not go beyond a certain literary development of this theme with a few stylistic links to the description of Daniel.

[16] The name the *Birth of Noah* for these fragments was suggested by Joseph Fitzmyer some forty years ago on basis of various arguments, and it has been generally accepted. Cf. idem, "The Aramaic 'Elect of God' Text from Qumran Cave IV," *CBQ* 27 (1965): 348–72. It is also adopted by É. Puech in his recent re-edition of the text. Cf. idem, *DJD* 31:117–70. However, the name of Noah is never mentioned in the text, nor do all the features of the personage described therein fit him. Further arguments suggest that the initial name, given by J. Starcky (in *Mémorial du cinquantenaire 1914–1964: École des langues orientales anciennes de l'Institut Catholique de Paris* [Paris, 1964], 51–66), namely "the Elect of God," is better suited for the content of the work. Cf. my comments in the review of Puech's volume in *DSD* 10 (2003): 292–304.

[17] The label "Apocryphon of Levi" is another problematic title, assuming more than may be substantiated by the texts. See my comments in my review of Puech's publication, 300–302.

[18] The fourteen fragments were edited by E. Cook, "4Q556 (4QVision^a ar)," in *DSSR* 6:136–40. Two other manuscripts are identified as copies of the same work, 4Q557 (4QVision^c ar) and 4Q558 (4QVision^b ar), also edited by Cook in the same volume. The manuscripts are too fragmentary for a precise assessment of their literary character and their relation to each other. The names "Apocalypse" or "Vision" imply more than the fragments actually say.

The *Genesis Apocryphon* covers both subjects, bringing the total number of manuscripts dealing with those themes to forty. Thus scrolls concerned with the Flood and the Patriarchs' history account for nearly half of the eighty-three readable Aramaic texts, coming as they do from nine compositions, or twelve, if we consider separate the Enochic works assembled in the anthology of *1 Enoch*. Remarkably, the works concerning the figures and events surrounding the Flood are the best represented among the Aramaic texts: nine copies of the Enochic anthology of *1 Enoch* and ten copies of the *Book of Giants*. However, also well represented are writings related to the Patriarchs. The *Aramaic Levi Document* and the so-called *Visions of Amram* are extant in seven copies each.

Let us pause for a moment to reflect on the thematic configuration revealed by these two rubrics of the list. First, note that both Flood themes and Patriarchal history are also treated by Hebrew Qumranic texts. Still, these subjects are treated mostly by non-sectarian parabiblical or rewritten Bible works. In the sectarian literature such themes are dealt with systematically only in pesher-type works, such as 4Q180, the so-called *Pesher on the Ages*,[19] or in admonitory context such as that of the *Damascus Document* II 17–21.[20] Thus, the systematic reworking of narratives dealing with pre-Sinaitic times is shared only by the Qumran Aramaic corpus and the parabiblical non-sectarian texts. However, their respective approaches to these materials widely diverge. While the Hebrew parabiblical texts rework more or less closely the biblical Hebrew text and elaborate or comment on it, the Aramaic writings treat biblical materials more freely. For the Aramaic texts the biblical version is just a peg on which large chunks of aggadic non-biblical expansions are hung. This freedom in reworking biblical themes is expressed in particular literary forms, chiefly pseudepigraphic testaments and discourses, framed in aggadic narratives. None of these literary forms is employed by the Hebrew parabiblical texts.

There are, however, two exceptions to these general characteristics, namely, the Aramaic *Genesis Apocryphon* and the Hebrew book of *Jubilees*. Written in Aramaic as it is, the *Genesis Apocryphon* shares with the Aramaic

---

[19] Cf. D. Dimant, "The 'Pesher on the Periods' (4Q180) and 4Q181," *IOS* 9 (1979): 77–102.

[20] The theme of the flood is set in an admonitory context also in 4Q370 i. However, no sectarian elements may be detected in it, so it cannot be considered part of the typical sectarian literature. Cf. C. Newsom, "4Q370: 4QAdmonition on the Flood," *DJD* 19:85–110.

corpus the subjects of its discourse: ancient and Patriarchal history. However, by following closely the biblical story it treats these materials in a manner similar to the Hebrew parabiblical texts. The book of *Jubilees* represents the reverse case. Written in Hebrew, it shares with parabiblical Hebrew text the technique of reworking the biblical Hebrew version, but the topics it covers are the ones dealt with by the Aramaic corpus. These peculiarities stress the special character of the two writings, and further study is needed to clarify them. However, these being exceptions, they confirm the general rule typifying the Aramaic works of these groups.

One may further observe that while the Aramaic texts share with the Hebrew parabiblical ones the preoccupation with the Flood and the Patriarchs, nothing in the Aramaic corpus parallels the intense interest of the Hebrew texts in later Israelite history. No Aramaic work deals systematically and in detail with Moses and Joshua, the period of the Judges, or the kingdoms of Judah and Israel. For that matter, nothing in Aramaic is related to the biblical Prophets. Obviously, in the understanding of the authors of these texts, Hebrew belonged to the sphere of Israelite history proper, whereas Aramaic is relegated to earlier generations. Indeed, such a view is expressed by *Jubilees* (12:25–26) and perhaps by the Qumranic 4Q464 3 i 9[21] and may underlie the clear thematic division between the Aramaic and the Hebrew works.

As a concluding remark about this type of Aramaic texts groups, it should be noted that, seen in their perspective, *1 Enoch* or the *Aramaic Levi Document* are not unique or isolated cases. They belong to a well-defined literary genre and traditions and should be studied in their context.

Equally important at Qumran was a complex of Aramaic visionary apocalyptic tales, represented in the third group on the list. Twenty manuscripts, coming from seven different works, belong here. Unfortunately, most of them are quite fragmentary and therefore provide an incomplete picture of the original writings. These texts describe visionary scenes, often dealing with figures and events of the eschaton. A good example of this type of writing is offered by the work entitled the *New Jerusalem*, apparently popular at Qumran, since it is extant in seven copies. In this

---

[21] Cf. M.E. Stone and E. Eshel, "An Exposition on the Patriarchs (4Q464) and two other Documents (4Q464ᵃ and 4Q464ᵇ)," *Le Muséon* 105 (1992): 243–63. The text is published by Eshel and Stone, "Exposition on the Patriarchs," *DJD* 19:215–30.

work an angelic being shows a seer the enormous size and buildings of the future Jerusalem and Temple. The text builds on Ezek 40–48, but the name of the seer has not been preserved, and the work cannot be considered a rewritten Ezekiel or an Apocryphon of Ezekiel.[22]

Another interesting feature of this group is the fact that at least some of the works are set in a Diaspora context. This may have been the literary stage of the *New Jerusalem* writings and the *Apocryphon of Daniel*. Aramaic was apparently selected as the language of composition precisely because of such a setting, as it was for Dan 2. It certainly reflects the reality during the Persian period.

The fourth group on the list is smaller, but most significant for understanding the nature of the corpus. It includes edifying tales not situated in or explicitly attached to biblical contexts and themes. The book of *Tobit* is a typical example of this genre. Many of these texts share with the visionary compositions the setting of the royal court of great Gentile monarch. This well-known form of court-tale was widely disseminated in antiquity, in both Jewish and non-Jewish literature, such as Daniel, *Tobit*, and the Aramaic *Story of Achikar*. The Qumran library has added an important number of previously unknown specimens of this genre.

In light of such new additions to the Aramaic Jewish literature, *Tobit* and the Aramaic chapters of Daniel now appear as survivors of a large Aramaic literature that flourished during Second Temple times. The place of the book of Daniel is particularly intriguing, for a number of texts from this group build upon or are influenced by it. They are the *Prayer of Nabonidus, Pseudo-Daniel, Proto-Esther*, the *Four Kingdoms*, and the so-called *Apocryphon of Daniel*. Some of them clearly depend on Daniel, such as *Pseudo-Daniel*. But others seem to be contemporaries of Daniel, sharing the same milieu and literary conventions. Mapping the precise relationship of those texts should have important implications for the understanding the origins and background of the Jewish apocalyptic literature.

Finally a word must be said of the date and possible background of the Aramaic corpus discussed here. It is most striking that Babylonian elements are clustered in writings related to the Flood on the one

---

[22] Cf. recently L. DiTommaso, *The Dead Sea New Jerusalem Text* (TSAJ 110; Tübingen: Mohr Siebeck, 2005), and my review in *Henoch* 29 (2007): 156–58.

hand,[23] and both Babylonian and Iranian elements are found in non-biblical court-tales and visionary narratives on the other hand.[24] That the theme of the Flood attracts Babylonian traditions is understandable, since Babylon is the initial source of this motif for biblical as well as later developments. But the prominence of the Iranian elements in the visionary court-tales comes as a surprise. Although this is still uncharted terrain, enough is known to suggest that manifold Babylonian and Iranian traditions have found their way into the Aramaic texts from Qumran. The few magical and astrological Aramaic texts found there, listed in group five, reinforce this conclusion.[25] Indirectly it is also corroborated by the non-sectarian character of the Aramaic texts and by the early dates of several copies. For instance, one copy of the Enochic *Astronomical Work*, 4Q208 (= 4QEnastr^a), is dated to the end of the third century B.C.E.[26] Three copies of the *Visions of Amram*, 4Q543, 4Q544, and 4Q547, date to the middle of the second century B.C.E. But even when Aramaic texts were copied in later times, mostly the first century B.C.E, the presence of several exemplars of many works points to older originals.[27] Thus, both date and background betray an early time and external sources for the Qumran Aramaic texts.

Why the particular themes developed by the Aramaic texts so fascinated the Qumranites is a subject for another paper. But the data already at hand demonstrates the need to consider these texts as a specific group, which requires further detailed investigations along these lines.

---

[23] Cf. for instance the references to Gilgamesh as one of the giants in the *Book of Giants* (4Q530 2 ii 2; 4Q531 22 12).

[24] Cf. e.g. the *Prayer of Nabonidus* (4Q242), edited by J.J. Collins, *DJD* 22:83–93, and the Persian background portrayed by 4Q550 (4QPrEsther^a) 5–7, edited by E. Cook in *DSSR* 6:6.

[25] On the astrology in 4Q318 see J.C. Greenfield and M. Sokoloff, "An Astrological Text from Qumran (4Q318) and Reflection on Some Zodiacal Names," *RevQ* 16/64 (1995): 507–25. On the physiognomic text 4Q561 see M. Popović, "Physiognomic Knowledge in Qumran and Babylonia: Form, Interdisciplinarity, and Secrecy," *DSD* 13 (2006): 150–76.

[26] For this date see Milik, *The Books of Enoch*, 273. His dating is substantially accepted. See the subsequent edition by E.J.C. Tigchelaar and F. García Martínez, "208: 4QAstronomical Enoch ar^a," *DJD* 36:104–31 (106).

[27] According to Greenfield, Stone, and Eshel, for instance, the composition of *Aramaic Levi Document* should go back to the third century B.C.E. at the latest. Cf. Greenfield, Stone, and Eshel, *The Aramaic Levi Document*, 22.

THE SONS OF AARON IN THE DEAD SEA SCROLLS*

Charlotte Hempel

The evidence of the Dead Sea Scrolls on the priestly designations "sons of Aaron" and "sons of Zadok" is one of the areas where the more recently published texts have provided scholars with a significant amount of additional evidence. One thinks here, for instance, of the important textual variants between 1QS V and 4QS^d I and 4QS^b IX.[1] The topic of the priesthood as depicted in the non-biblical scrolls has been one that has been the subject of a number of studies since the earliest decades after the discovery and has been lavished with even more attention in the last two decades.[2] In what follows I would like to look particularly at the evidence of the scrolls on the sons of Aaron.

---

* It is a great privilege to publish these thoughts in a *Festschrift* for Florentino García Martínez. Ever since I first read his work as a senior undergraduate, I was profoundly impressed and influenced by his scholarship. I first met Florentino at the Meeting of the International Organization of Qumran Studies in Cambridge in 1995. Ever since, I have benefited tremendously from Florentino's boundless generosity, energy, and efficiency. He has done a tremendous amount for the discipline, and his hard and selfless labour has paved a much smoother path for my own generation of scholars. I should also like to thank Menaham Kister. I benefited greatly from an informal discussion while writing this paper.

[1] See, e.g., G. Vermes, "Preliminary Remarks on Unpublished Fragments of the Community Rule from Qumran Cave 4," *JJS* 42 (1991): 250–55; P.S. Alexander, "The Redaction-History of *Serek ha-Yahad*: A Proposal," *RevQ* 17/65–68 (1996): 437–53; A.I. Baumgarten, "The Zadokite Priests at Qumran: A Reconsideration," *DSD* 4 (1997): 137–56; M. Bockmuehl, "Redaction and Ideology in the Rule of the Community (1QS/4QS)," *RevQ* 18/72 (1998): 541–60; J.H. Charlesworth and B.A. Strawn, "Reflections on the Text of *Serek ha-Yahad* Found in Cave IV," *RevQ* 17/65–68 (1996): 403–35; P. Garnet, "Cave 4 MS Parallels to 1QS 5:1–7: Towards a *Serek* Text History," *JSP* 15 (1997): 67–78; C. Hempel, "Comments on the Translation of 4QSd I,1," *JJS* 44 (1993): 127–28; M.A. Knibb, "Rule of the Community," in *Encyclopedia of the Dead Sea Scrolls* (ed. L.H. Schiffman and J.C. VanderKam; New York: Oxford University Press, 2000), 2:793–97; and S. Metso, *The Textual Development of the Qumran Community Rule* (STDJ 21; Leiden: Brill, 1997).

[2] For an excellent concise overview with ample bibliography, see R.A. Kugler, "Priests," in *Encyclopedia of the Dead Sea Scrolls*, 2:688–93. See also idem, "Priesthood at Qumran," in *The Dead Sea Scrolls After Fifty Years: A Comprehensive Assessment* (ed. P.W. Flint and J.C. VanderKam; Leiden: Brill, 1999), 2:93–116. See also G. Vermes, "The Leadership of the Qumran Community: Sons of Zadok, Priests, Congregation," in *Geschichte-Tradition-Reflexion: Festschrift für Martin Hengel zum 70. Geburtstag* (ed. H. Cancik et al.; Tübingen: Mohr Siebeck, 1996), 1:375–84.

My impression is that, both in some of the primary sources as well as in the secondary literature, the sons of Aaron have suffered under the dominant place allotted to the sons of Zadok in a number of places.[3] This situation is recognized also by G. Vermes, when he regretfully observes the way in which

> the terminological clash between sons of Zadok and sons of Aaron largely remained untouched for some four decades of Qumran research during which period most scholars... happily and simply maintained, without any proviso, that the sect was governed by the sons of Zadok the priests.[4]

I have always been puzzled by the awkward coexistence of both designations in the Rule texts.[5] I was inspired to reflect more closely on the picture that emerges about the somewhat elusive Aaronides by the excellent recent article by H.-J. Fabry, "Zadokiden und Aaroniden in Qumran."[6] There, Fabry offers an overview over and analysis of the complex evidence on the priesthood as it emerges from various strands in the Hebrew Bible such as the Deuteronomistic History, the Priestly work, the book of Ezekiel, the Chronicler to the Greek Bible, Ben Sira, and Qumran. With reference to the scrolls, he rightly emphasizes the way in which references to the sons of Aaron the priests vastly outnumber references to the sons of Zadok the priests.[7] I agree with a great deal of what he has to say but wish to add some further nuances to this ongoing debate. In particular, this article is intended respectfully to contradict his conviction that "Die Regelliteratur lässt uns keine inhaltlichen und konzeptionellen Unterschiede [with respect to

---

[3] See, e.g., the seminal article by J. Liver, "The 'Sons of Zadok the Priests' in the Dead Sea Sect," *RevQ* 6/21 (1967): 3–30. For a different point of view see P.R. Davies, *Behind the Essenes: History and Ideology in the Dead Sea Scrolls* (BJS 94; Atlanta: Scholars Press, 1987), 51–72, where he concludes "Scholars of Qumran simply must stop talking Zadokite" (71); and already G. Klinzing, *Die Umdeutung des Kultus in der Qumrangemeinde und im Neuen Testament* (SUNT 7; Göttingen: Vandenhoeck & Ruprecht, 1971), 136.

[4] Vermes, "Leadership of the Qumran Community," 379.

[5] See, e.g., C. Hempel, "The Earthly Essene Nucleus of 1QSa," *DSD* 3 (1996): 253–69; eadem, "Interpretative Authority in the Community Rule Tradition," *DSD* 10 (2003): 59–80, and most recently eadem, "The Literary Development of the S-Tradition: A New Paradigm," *RevQ* 22/87 (2006): 389–401 (395–97). See already Liver, "Sons of Zadok the Priests," 13 where he notes, "The selfsame texts in the Rule Scroll, wherein mention is made of 'the sons of Zadok the priests,' contain parallel references to 'the sons of Aaron the priests' or to the priests in general."

[6] H.-J. Fabry, "Zadokiden und Aaroniden in Qumran," in *Das Manna fällt auch heute noch: Beiträge zur Geschichte und Theologie des Alten, Ersten Testaments: FS E. Zenger* (ed. F.L. Hossfeld and L. Schwienhorst-Schönberger; Freiburg: Herder, 2004), 201–17.

[7] Fabry, "Zadokiden und Aaroniden," 209.

Aaronides and Zadokites] mehr wahrnehmen."[8] In what follows I will argue that despite the fact that both traditions co-exist in some sources, we are in a position to trace a trajectory of development in the rule texts and beyond. The topic of this investigation seems a fitting one in a *Festschrift* for Florentino García Martínez, who has written on the ways in which the priests in the Qumran community continued to undertake priestly functions in a community that did not participate in the temple cult.[9]

In order to form as full a picture as possible, I have considered all the references to the sons of Aaron and the sons of Zadok in the scrolls. Before looking at the evidence, it is worth noting that I have left out of consideration the references to a priest or priests that do not supply a reference to their genealogical descent. I have argued elsewhere recently that a number of passages that speak of incipient communal life in a small-scale context lack concern for the genealogical descent of the priest(s), i.e. 1QS VI 2–4 and 1QS VIII 1.[10] Both of these passages share with some of the material discussed below an emphasis on priestly authority in the community without any expressed concerns for the kind of priest required.

Finally, a number of scholars have argued—frequently in the days before the complex evidence of the 4QS manuscripts had become available—that there is no issue to debate since "sons of Zadok" and "sons of Aaron" are simply synonyms for one and the same entity.[11] This view seems unlikely to me. As we will see, the full range of passages also indicates that there are contexts in which only one of the two sets

---

[8] Fabry, "Zadokiden und Aaroniden," 213. He continues by granting that such differences "müssen aber bestanden haben" on the basis of the terminology in messianic contexts.

[9] F. García Martínez, "Priestly Functions in a Community Without Temple," in *Gemeinde ohne Tempel. Community without Temple: Zur Substituierung und Transformation des Jerusalemer Tempels und seines Kults im Alten Testament, antiken Judentum und frühen Christentum* (ed. B. Ego et al.; WUNT 118; Tübingen: Mohr Siebeck, 1999), 303–19.

[10] "Diversity and Identity in the S Tradition," in *Defining Identities: We, You, and the Others in the Dead Sea Scrolls* (ed. F. García Martínez and M. Popović; Leiden: Brill, forthcoming).

[11] See, e.g., G.A. Anderson, "Aaron," in *Encyclopedia of the Dead Sea Scrolls*, 1:1–2; Klinzing, *Umdeutung des Kultus*, 135f.; M.A. Knibb, *The Qumran Community* (CCJW 2; Cambridge: Cambridge University Press, 1987), 105; A.R.C. Leaney, *The Rule of Qumran and Its Meaning* (NTL; London: SCM, 1996), 177, who comments with reference to 1QS 5:22, "Sons of Aaron is no more than a variant for sons of Zadok here." Further, G. Vermes in E. Schürer, *The History of the Jewish People in the Age of Jesus Christ (175 B.C.–A.D. 135)* (rev. and ed. G. Vermes et al.; 3 vols.; Edinburgh: T&T Clark, 1973–1987), 2:252–53, n. 56.

of terms are employed, which points towards a subtle difference in the use of the terminology.[12] In what follows I hope to draw up a profile of the occurrences of both sets of terms.

The Damascus Document

The Admonition of this text never refers to the sons of Aaron. Noteworthy, however, are repeated references to the people as a whole in terms of "Aaron and Israel," both in contexts describing communal origins (cf. CD I 7 // 4Q266 2 i 11 // 4Q268 1 14; CD VI 2 // 4Q267 2 8) as well as in eschatological contexts that refer to a Messiah of Aaron and Israel (cf. CD XIX 11; XX 1).

References to the expectation of a Messiah of Aaron and Israel are also interspersed in the legal part of the *Damascus Document*, cf. CD XII 23; CD XIV 19 // 4Q266 10 i 12 // 4Q269 11 i 2. However, unlike the Admonition the legal part of the *Damascus Document* contains six references to the sons of Aaron, including one in the catalogue of transgressions. Of these, four references are preserved in the material dealing with the disqualification of certain categories of priests.

a. 4Q266 5 ii 5 // 4Q267 5 iii 8

"[one] of the sons of Aaron who is taken captive by the nations"
b. 4Q266 5 ii 8

"one of the sons of Aaron who departs to ser[ve the nations"
c. 4Q266 5 ii 9–10

"[one of the sons of] Aaron who causes his name to fall from the truth (corrected to: whose name was thrown from the peoples)"[13]
d. 4Q266 5 ii 12

"from Israel, the counsel[14] of the sons of Aaron"

---

[12] Note also the point made by Fabry, namely, that we would expect a more evenly distributed number of references to each designation if their employment was more or less random in the scrolls, see "Zadokiden und Aaroniden," 209.

[13] The text appears to be corrected from "fallen from the truth" to "was thrown from the peoples," cf. J.M. Baumgarten, *DJD* 18:51. The latter would correspond more closely with the interest of this passage in Gentiles. By contrast, the reference to someone who has diverted from the truth has a more restricted ring to it and is reminiscent of the penal code as noted by Baumgarten, ibid.

[14] The term counsel/council is interesting, since it is a key term in the *Community Rule*, where it describes one of the central elements of fellowship of community members. However, the reference to "Israel" immediately before the reference to the sons of Aaron seems to indicate that we are still in a national context of Israel and the nations

Two further references to the sons of Aaron occur in the Laws. One spells out the responsibility of the sons of Aaron to diagnose skin disease, cf. 4Q266 6 i 13 // 4Q272 1 ii 2.[15] Finally, the catalogue of transgressions lists someone who fails to "[give to] the sons of Aaron [the fourth (year)] planting," cf. 4Q270 2 ii 6. Although part of this statement is reconstructed, the preserved text in the lines that follow leaves little doubt that this part of the catalogue deals with priestly dues.[16]

In sum, the Laws of the *Damascus Document* frequently refer to the sons of Aaron in contexts that are not community specific. The national context (Israel and the nations) is repeatedly in focus in the material on priestly disqualifications. Moreover, the catalogue of transgressions and the skin disease material both employ sons of Aaron terminology to refer to traditional priestly duties and privileges, rather than as figures of authority in a particular community.

The sons of Aaron play no role in the Admonition, as we saw. However, the *Damascus Document* does contain a reference to "the so]ns of Zadok the priests" (4Q266 5 i 16) in an intriguing passage that includes material reminiscent both of the Admonition and the Laws (4Q266 5 i // 4Q267 5 ii).[17] By combining references to the "returnees/penitents of Israel" with references to "the sons of Zadok," the former passage is reminiscent of CD III 20c–IV 4a, which comprises a quotation and interpretation of Ezek 44:15, applying it to three phases in the reform movement's development. In the latter well-known passage, the sons of Zadok are identified as the elect of Israel at the end of days. It is the "sons of Zadok" terminology found here in the Admonition that gave rise to the document's earlier title *Fragments of a Zadokite Work*.[18] In any

---

as in a number of earlier references. On this issue see also García Martínez, "Priestly Functions," 314–15. In contrast to the emphasis placed here, García Martínez examines these laws against a community-internal rather than national backdrop.

[15] We may compare this to CD XIII 4–7a, which clarifies that it is a priestly duty to diagnose skin disease, even if the priest is a simpleton and needs help and advice from the overseer.

[16] See Baumgarten, *DJD* 18:142–46, and C. Hempel, *The Damascus Texts* (CQS 1; Sheffield: Sheffield Academic Press, 2000), 33–34, 42–43, 87–88 and further literature referred to there.

[17] See Baumgarten, *DJD* 18:4–5; 47–49; C. Hempel, *The Laws of the Damascus Document: Sources, Traditions and Redaction* (STDJ 29; Leiden: Brill, 1998), 171–74; eadem, *Damascus Texts*, 34.

[18] S. Schechter, *Documents of Jewish Sectaries: I. Fragments of a Zadokite Work* (Cambridge: Cambridge University Press, 1910). The earlier title is favourably recalled by Baumgarten, *DJD* 18:1. For a more recent treatment see M.L. Grossman, *Reading for History in the Damascus Document: A Methodological Study* (STDJ 45; Leiden: Brill, 2002), 185–209.

case, it seems clear that, both in the "mixed passage" in 4Q266 5 i and in the Admonition, "sons of Zadok" is the preferred terminology. Noteworthy, moreover, is the community-specific background of both references. In the "mixed passage," the references to the overseer and the *maśkīl* in nearby lines make this clear. In CD III–IV "sons of Zadok" refers not to the priests, in particular, but apparently to the community as a whole.[19] In short, it seems to me quite clear that we may observe a distinctive use of the terminology "sons of Aaron" in the *Damascus Document*, namely in non-community-specific contexts with reference to traditional priestly duties and rights.

THE COMMUNITY RULE

Before turning to references to the sons of Aaron, it is worth noting that not unlike the *Damascus Document*, the *Community Rule* also refers to the make-up of the community in the present and the future in terms of Aaron and Israel, cf. 1QS V 6 // 4QS^b IX 5–6 // 4QS^d I 5; 1QS VIII 6 // 4QS^e (4Q259) II 14; 1QS VIII 8–9 // 4QS^d VI 2–3 // 4QS^e II 17–18 and 1QS IX 5–6 // 4QS^d VII 6–7. Again very reminiscent of the picture painted in the *Damascus Document*, 1QS IX 11—but not 4QS^e—includes a reference to the expectation of "a prophet and messiahs of Aaron and Israel." Of particular interest for the present enquiry are two places in the *Community Rule* manuscripts where the sons of Aaron are assigned the role of leading authority figures in the community.

The first passage is found in 1QS V 21 // 4QS^d (4Q258) II 1–2

1QS	4QS^d
"according to the authority of the sons of Aaron...*and*[20] the authority of the multitude of Israel."	"according to the authority of the sons of Aaron...the authority of the multitude of Israel."

The common ground between 1QS and 4QS^d in this particular passage is extremely interesting, since it contrasts sharply with the much more widely discussed instance in 1QS V // 4QS^d, where both manuscripts

---

[19] Cf. Liver, "Sons of Zadok the Priests," 10.

[20] The absence of the conjunction in 4QS^d may be significant, cf. Hempel, "Interpretative Authority," 76–79.

differ sharply in their authority structure. I have recently drawn attention to the immense significance of the shared tradition in 1QS V 21 // 4QS^d II 1–2 and elsewhere in the S manuscripts.[21] It seems to me that the earliest elements in the growth of the S tradition are to be found in the common ground between the manuscripts, allowing us glimpses of the state of affairs before the manuscripts went their separate ways, so to speak. What is significant for the current enquiry is the presence in the S tradition—and if I am correct in the earliest strands of the S tradition—of an endorsement of the sons of Aaron's leading role in the community. This tradition differs from the strong endorsement of the sons of Zadok in other parts of S, esp. 1QS V.

A similar picture emerges from the second passage I wish to focus on, namely 1QS IX 7 // 4QS^d (4Q258) VII 7, which contains a further endorsement of the authoritative role of the sons of Aaron in both 1QS and 4QS^d.

1QS IX 7 // 4QS^d (4Q258) VII 7[22]

1QS	4QS^d
"Only the sons of Aaron shall rule with regard to judgment and property *and on their authority decisions shall be taken concerning any rule of the people of the community.*"	"Only the sons of Aa]ron [shall ru]l[e with regard to] judgment and property. *Vacat.*"

The emphatically placed adverb "only" seems to imply that there was scope for disagreement in some circles.

In sum, the *Community Rule*, which in parts of its textual history is well-known for promoting the authority of the sons of Zadok over and against "the many" (esp. the early parts of 1QS V),[23] also contains two important passages where several manuscripts (1QS V 21 // 4QS^d II 1–2 and 1QS IX 7 // 4QS^d VII 7) favour the sons of Aaron as authority figures in the community.[24] This is exceedingly interesting in itself and contains, as I tried to argue elsewhere, important clues to the textual

---

[21] "The Literary Development of the S-Tradition."

[22] This passage forms part of the section lacking in 4QS^e, cf. P.S. Alexander and G. Vermes, *DJD* 26:11, 144–49, and Metso, *Textual Development*, 69–74.

[23] See note 1 above.

[24] Cf. in this context the emphatic statement by Fabry, "*Man kommt um die Feststellung nicht herum, dass die ältere Stufe der Gemeinderegel nicht von den Zadokiden spricht!*" [italics his] ("Zadokiden und Aaroniden," 212).

development of the S tradition.[25] It is instructive, moreover, to reflect
on the significant differences in the employment of the terminology
"sons of Aaron" in the *Community Rule* and the *Damascus Document*. In
the *Community Rule* the group is clearly priestly, but their role falls fairly
and squarely within the community rather than within a national frame
of reference, as was the case in the *Damascus Document*. It seems likely,
therefore, that we can observe a certain trajectory in the references to
priestly authority in the scrolls beginning with the sons of Aaron in a
national/non-community-specific context (D), via the sons of Aaron as
priestly authorities within the community (S), to the sons of *Zadok* as
priestly authorities within the community in a different literary stage
of S.

4Q286 BERAKHOT[A26]

A reference to the sons of Aaron in 4QBerakhot[a] may appropriately be
discussed at this juncture because of its notable resemblance to 1QS
IX 7. Thus, 4Q286 17b 1–2 seems to refer to the sons of Aaron as
figures of authority in matters of judgment and wealth (משפט ובהון).
This is an exceedingly interesting and curious piece of evidence
because of the obvious terminological overlap with 1QS IX 7 which
equally singled out "only the sons of Aaron" as in charge of judgment
and wealth (במשפט ובהון). The overlap is noted by Bilhah Nitzan, the
editor of 4QBerakhot.[27] Nitzan relates this statement to "the cultic
arrangements of the community for atonement of sins."[28] However,
since the language used ("wealth and judgment") occurs frequently in
the *Community Rule* to outline key areas of communal life and fellowship without necessarily implying a cultic context (e.g. 1QS V 2–3; V
16; VI 9), this may also be the case in 4Q286. It is just as likely that
fragment 17b, like fragments 20a, b, 13 and 14, deals with matters of
communal organization such as reproof and authority.[29] The impor-

---

[25] See Hempel, "Literary Development of the S Tradition." Fabry also recognizes,
"Die fortlaufende Redaktionsgeschichte der S-Literatur zeigt einen Kompetenzgewinn
der Zadokiden" ("Zadokiden und Aaroniden," 212).
[26] B. Nitzan, "4QBerakhot," *DJD* 11:1–74 (38–39).
[27] Ibid.
[28] Ibid., 39.
[29] On 4Q286 and 4Q288 fragments dealing with reproof, see Nitzan, *DJD*
11:40ff.

tant point to notice here is the presence of a reference to the sons of Aaron's authority within the community in a text which never mentions the sons of Zadok. There is no need, therefore, to spell out "*only* the sons of Aaron" as in 1QS IX 7. In contrast to this passage, we may point to 1QS V 2–3 (where the sons of Zadok and the multitude of the people of their covenant oversee wealth and judgment) and the corresponding material in 4QS^b and 4QS^d (where the many are in charge of wealth and torah). It appears, therefore, that 4Q286 supports the picture painted by 1QS/4QS, namely, that an earlier "sons of Aaron" strand was challenged by a "sons of Zadok" strand in the development of these texts and possibly also in the communal realities they claim to report. In any case, this passage provides further clear evidence of the authority of the sons of Aaron in the community.

4Q279 (4QFour Lots; olim 4QTohorot D)

This text was published in *DJD* 26 as a "Related Text" to S and may therefore be suitably discussed at this point.[30] It contains a reference to the sons of Aaron in 4Q279 5 4. With reference to this fragment the editors comment

> Frg. 5 seems to be eschatological in content, and to refer to the assignment of rewards ("lots") to the priests, the Levites, the Israelites and the proselytes in the messianic age...If this is the case, then we would very tentatively suggest that 4Q279 is the remains of a Messianic Rule.[31]

The fragment begins with a reference to a written hierarchical membership record ("his [f]ellow written down after [him]") familiar from S (1QS V 23; VI 22) and D (cf. CD XIII 12; XIV 4; 4Q270 7 i 10). The presence of proselytes would bring this scenario closer to D than S, cf. esp. CD XIV 4.6, where we also have a fourfold community structure: priests, levites, Israelites, and proselytes.[32] The first and fourth component correspond in the present text and D, with the noteworthy difference that 4QFour Lots explicitly uses "sons of Aaron" rather than more generally "the priests" as in D. This reference to the sons of Aaron clearly falls within the community-specific realm (note especially the

---

[30] See Alexander and Vermes, *DJD* 26:217–23.

[31] Alexander and Vermes, *DJD* 26:218.

[32] See ibid., 223: "If our interpretation is correct...then the mention of a reward for proselytes in the messianic age is noteworthy."

reference to a written record of the hierarchical make-up of the community). However, rather than employing this language to refer to the role of the sons of Aaron as figures of authority, the present passage is concerned with the make-up of the community in real or ideological terms. Since they are the first of the four groups referred to here, their preeminent place in the community is nevertheless evident.

4Q265 MISCELLANEOUS RULES OLIM SEREKH DAMASCUS[33]

4Q265 7 3 prohibits priests, who are referred to as belonging to the seed[34] of Aaron, from sprinkling purifying waters on the Sabbath. Apart from the emphasis on the Sabbath, the passage explicitly stresses the priestly prerogative of the sprinkling.[35] As pointed out by Baumgarten, 4Q274 (4QTohorot A) 2 i 2 attests a further such prohibition in the Qumran corpus.[36] Moreover, 4Q277 (4QTohorot B^b) 1 ii 5–7 restricts sprinkling anyone defiled with corpse impurity to priests and further prohibits a child from sprinkling the impure.[37] Baumgarten takes the latter to refer to the level of maturity of the priest.[38]

One of the noteworthy characteristics of 4Q265 is that it contains a mixture of general halakhic topics alongside clearly community-internal legislation, such as the make-up of the council of the community or the penal code. In certain respects, such a broad range of material is reminiscent of the Laws of the *Damascus Document*. In my view the material devoted to the Sabbath, both in 4Q265 and in the *Damascus Document*, lacks an explicit basis in the life of the community.[39] These rules were clearly handed on and cherished in the community,

---

[33] For text, translation, and commentary, see J.M. Baumgarten, *DJD* 35:69–71. See also Hempel, *Damascus Texts*, 89–104, and L. Doering, *Schabbat* (TSAJ 78; Tübingen: Mohr Siebeck, 1999), 242–46. For general discussion of the sprinkling ritual see Baumgarten, *DJD* 35:83–87, and idem, "The Red Cow Purification Rites in Qumran Texts," *JJS* 46 (1995): 112–19.

[34] On this terminology see García Martínez, "Priestly Functions," 303.

[35] See e.g. Baumgarten, "Red Cow Purification Rites," 118.

[36] Baumgarten, *DJD* 35:103–5. For a general discussion of issues of purity see ibid. 79–96, and H.K. Harrington, *The Purity Texts* (CQS 5; London: T&T Clark, 2004).

[37] See Baumgarten, *DJD* 35:116–18. A possible further attestation of such a prohibition is found in 4QD, although the crucial word "sprinkle" is restored in both manuscripts (4Q269 8 ii 6 // 4Q271 2 13), see Baumgarten, *DJD* 18:130–32, 173–75, and idem, *DJD* 35:118.

[38] *DJD* 18:82–83 and idem, "Red Cow Purification Rites," 118.

[39] See Hempel, *Laws*, 15–72, and eadem, *Damascus Texts*, 96–98, 103–4.

but the context lacks references to sectarian organizational structures. Moreover, the reference to the Temple (4Q265 7 6) points to a wider context. This reference to the priestly rite of sprinkling (or rather *not* sprinkling on the Sabbath) belongs, then, closer to the priestly duties in the non-community-specific realm, which we witnessed in the Laws of the *Damascus Document*.

THE RULE OF THE CONGREGATION[40]

Much more within the realm of community-internal affairs are two references to the sons of Aaron as figures of authority in 1QSa I 15–16 // 4Q249c (4Qpap cryptA Serekh ha-Edah[c])[41] 5 and 1QSa I 23–24. I have argued elsewhere that the large central section of this text is reminiscent of the communal rules contained in the *Damascus Document* and was only secondarily associated with the messianic age.[42] Moreover, an interesting crux in this text, as in the S tradition, is the, in my view, awkward endorsement of the sons of Zadok as authority figures alongside the sons of Aaron often in the same context, cf. 1QSa I 2, 24; II 3. Finally, the messianic assembly in the latter part of this text also speaks of the [sons of] Aaron the priests.[43] It is in any case fairly clear that 1QSa stands much closer to the end of the spectrum that envisages the sons of Aaron as communal leaders—be it in this age or the age to come—, rather than speaking of what one may call their traditional cultic roles in a national context. In sum, the role allocated to the sons of Aaron in 1QSa is reminiscent of the way in which the terminology is used in the *Community Rule*. This resemblance emerges first from their role as community leaders rather than cultic officials. Secondly, 1QSa and S both speak of sons of Aaron *and* sons of Zadok with both groups vying (literarily in any case) in effect for the same job.

---

[40] On the priestly designations in this text see, e.g., Fabry, "Zadokiden und Aaroniden"; Hempel, "Earthly Essene Nucleus"; L.H. Schiffman, *The Eschatological Community of the Dead Sea Scrolls* (SBLMS 38; Atlanta: Scholars Press, 1989); H. Stegemann, "Some Remarks to 1QSa, to 1QSb and to Qumran Messianism," *RevQ* 17/65–68 (1996): 479–505; and Vermes, "Leadership of the Qumran Community."

[41] For the edition of the cryptic manuscripts of the Rule of the Congregation, see S. Pfann, *DJD* 36:513–74 (551).

[42] "Earthly Essene Nucleus."

[43] Most scholars take 1QS II 11–21a to describe a messianic event. An exception is Stegemann, "Some Remarks."

The War Scroll[44]

Three kinds of references to Aaron occur in the M tradition.

a. Akin to the *Damascus Document*, esp. the Admonition, the *War Scroll* contains a number of references to the people of God as comprising the traditional elements "Israel" and "Aaron," cf. 1QM III 12–14 // 4QM[f45] 10 4 (the make-up of the people to be written on a banner). A further inscription, including the name of the prince of the congregation that refers to "Israel," "Levi," "Aaron," and the names of the twelve tribes, is prescribed in 1QM V 1.[46]

b. 1QM XVII 2 contains a historical reference to Aaron's sons Nadab, Abihu, Eleazar, and Ithamar (cf. Num 3).

c. Finally, the scroll allocates a crucial role to the sons of Aaron alongside the Levites in guiding the battle, cf. 1QM VII 9–IX 9.[47] A comparable scenario emerges from 4Q493 (4QM[c]) 1–2, part of a manuscript containing a different recension of the *War Scroll* from 1QM.[48] Both in 1QM and in 4QM[c], the priests play a leading role in the battle and are identified in the first instance as "sons of Aaron."

It is interesting that this text refers to the priests genealogically explicitly as the sons of Aaron, while never employing sons of Zadok language.[49] This feature aligns the *War Scroll* with a sizeable group of texts such as MMT, the legal part of D, and curiously also 4QS.

---

[44] For a recent edition of the text of M, see M.G. Abegg in *Texts Concerned with Religious Law* (*DSSR* 1), 208–43. See also Y. Yadin, *The Scroll of the War of the Sons of Light Against the Sons of Darkness* (Oxford University Press, 1962), and J. Duhaime, *The War Texts: 1QM and Related Manuscripts* (CQS 6; London: T&T Clark, 2004).

[45] The 4QM[f] recension of the *War Scroll* is similar to 1QM, though allotting in fragment 10 a more prominent role to the prince of the congregation than is the case in 1QM in the form of two superlinear additions. Cf., e.g., Duhaime, *War Texts*, 22–23. See also M. Baillet, *DJD* 7:56–68.

[46] According to Yadin, *Scroll of the War*, 278–79, this inscription was to be made on a shield.

[47] For discussion and analysis see Yadin, *Scroll of the War*, 208–28.

[48] Cf. Baillet, *DJD* 7:49–53, esp. 50, where he identifies this manuscript as evidence of a "recension différente." See also Duhaime, *War Texts*, 30, 41.

[49] Cf. also Davies, *Behind the Essenes*, 57; Fabry, "Zadokiden und Aaroniden," 210; and Vermes, "Leadership of the Qumran Community," 379.

4QMMT[50]

4QMMT speaks of the sons of Aaron in two passages, while never referring to the sons of Zadok at all.[51]

a. 4QMMT B17 (4Q394 3–7 i 19–ii 1 // 4Q395 1 10–11)

At the end of a section dealing with the red cow ritual, the sons of Aaron are admonished to ensure the proper conduct in cultic matters ("the sons of Aaron are to take care of"). A similar phrase occurs at other junctures, but only here does the text employ the genealogically explicit terminology "the sons of Aaron" for the priests, cf. B11–12 and B25–27. The priests' role is to ensure proper conduct in cultic matters.

b. B79 (4Q396 1 2 iv 8)

A second reference to the sons of Aaron occurs in a passage that forbids unsuitable marital unions. Scholars differ as to whether this passage concerns the condemnation of marriages between priests and laity (so Qimron and Himmelfarb)[52] or Israelites and foreigners (so Baumgarten, Hayes, and Sharpe).[53]

What is of interest for our purposes is the occurrence of sons of Aaron to refer to the priestly component of the people. In short, in MMT akin to the Laws of the *Damascus Document*, the sons of Aaron occur in passages relating to their priestly role in society at large, rather than their authoritative status within a community.

---

[50] For the text, introduction, and analysis of its various aspects, see E. Qimron and J. Strugnell, *DJD* 10.

[51] So also Fabry, "Zadokiden und Aaroniden," 209–10.

[52] Qimron and Strugnell, *DJD* 10:171–75; and M. Himmelfarb, "Levi, Phinehas, and the Problem of Intermarriage at the Time of the Maccabean Revolt," *JSQ* 6 (1999): 1–24.

[53] Qimron and Strugnell, *DJD* 10:171, n. 178a; C. Hayes, *Gentile Impurities and Jewish Identities: Intermarriage and Conversion from the Bible to the Talmud* (Oxford: Oxford University Press, 2002), 82–91; and C.J. Sharpe, "Phinean Zeal and Rhetorical Strategy in 4QMMT," *RevQ* 18/70 (1997): 207–22.

TEMPLE SCROLL

The picture is rather similar when we turn to the *Temple Scroll*. Like MMT this text never refers to the sons of Zadok,[54] and references to the sons of Aaron occur in contexts referring to the cultic role of the priests.

a. 11Q19 XXII 4–5[55] // 11Q20 V 25[56] notes the role of the sons of Aaron to sprinkle the sacrificial blood on the altar after the sons of Levi have done the slaughtering. This passage forms part of the "Festival Calendar," a part of the scrolls that is widely believed to be an originally independent piece inserted after the description of the altar.[57] The prominent role of the Levites in the *Temple Scroll* has often been noted.[58] What is of interest for our present purposes is the cultic and non-community-specific part played by the sons of Aaron in this passage.

b. 11Q19 XXXIV 13–14[59] refers to the sons of Aaron's role of burning the sacrifices upon the altar and forms part of the description of the inner court of the Temple, especially the slaughter house.[60]

c. A third reference to the sons of Aaron occurs in the context of the allocation of storerooms in 11Q19 XLIV 5.[61]

In sum, the *Temple Scroll* falls clearly within the large group of texts that employ sons of Aaron terminology in a non-community-specific sense emphasizing their traditional cultic duties. Again, this text never employs sons of Zadok language.

---

[54] So already Davies, *Behind the Essenes*, 57 and Fabry, "Zadokiden und Aaroniden," 209–10.

[55] Cf. Y. Yadin, *The Temple Scroll: II. Text and Commentary* (Jerusalem: IES, 1983) and E. Qimron, *The Temple Scroll: A Critical Edition with Extensive Reconstructions* (Beer-Sheva/Jerusalem: Ben-Gurion University of the Negev/IES, 1996).

[56] Cf. F. García Martínez et al., *DJD* 23:357–409. The word "the priests" is added superlinearly in 11Q20, cf. ibid. 378.

[57] Cf. S. White Crawford, *The Temple Scroll and Related Text* (CQS 2; Sheffield: Sheffield Academic Press, 2000), 49–57, and earlier literature cited there. Further, F. García Martínez, "Temple Scroll," in *Encyclopedia of the Dead Sea Scrolls*, 2:927–33.

[58] Cf. White Crawford, *Temple Scroll*, 56. See also M. Stone, "Levi," in *Encyclopedia of the Dead Sea Scrolls*, 1:485–86, and further literature cited there. Fabry eloquently speaks of the "Archivierung umfangreicher Materialien aus der Levi-Tradition in Qumran" and asks whether this interest might have been stimulated by a search for the common roots of the two rival priestly traditions ("Zadokiden und Aaroniden," 213).

[59] Cf. Yadin, *Temple Scroll*, 2:147.

[60] See White Crawford, *Temple Scroll*, 36–38.

[61] Cf. Yadin, *Temple Scroll*, 2:185f.

4Q174 Florilegium[62]

4Q174 5 2[63] contains a reference to Israel and Aaron in a fragmentary context. Brooke suggests that we have here the remains of a reference to the expected messiah of Israel and Aaron.[64] This interpretation has been questioned by Steudel, who thinks of a phrase "Israel and Aaron" to describe the make-up of the community as attested, e.g., also in CD I.[65] Also reminiscent of D and S is the reference to the sons of *Zadok* in 4Q174 1–2 i 17[66] in a passage interpreting Ezek 37:23.[67] We saw above that Ezek 44 was interpreted in the *Damascus Document* (cf. CD III 20–IV 4) with reference to various phases in the community's emergence. 4QFlorilegium is thus closely aligned with those texts that speak of the make-up of the community both in terms of "Israel and Aaron" and in terms of the sons of Zadok, the latter inspired by Ezekiel, in particular the Admonition of the *Damascus Document*.

4Q390 Apocryphon of Jeremiah C[e]

4Q390 is one of six manuscripts of 4QApocryphon Jeremiah C published by Devorah Dimant.[68] One of the characteristic features identified by Dimant is that the composition seems to speak of events known from the scriptures in the past tense, whereas non-scriptural Second Temple period events and the eschatological period are referred to in the future tense, as is the case in the passage to be considered below. Dimant proposes a revelation received by Jeremiah as the most likely "narrative context" of the composition[69] and suggests that the composition is best understood as "an apocalypse."[70] As far as the provenance

---

[62] Cf. J.M. Allegro, *DJD* 5:53–57. See also J. Strugnell, "Notes en marge du volume V des 'Discoveries in the Judaean Desert of Jordan,'" *RevQ* 7/26 (1970): 163–276 (220–25).

[63] Reconstructed by Steudel to occur at 4Q174 4 7, see *Der Midrasch zur Eschatologie aus der Qumrangemeinde (4QMidrEschat^{a.b})* (STDJ 13; Leiden: Brill, 1994), 26, 32.

[64] G.J. Brooke, *Exegesis at Qumran: 4QFlorilegium in its Jewish Context* (JSOTSup 29; Sheffield: Sheffield Academic Press, 1985), 160f.

[65] See Steudel, *Midrasch zur Eschatologie*, 49.

[66] Reconstructed by Steudel to occur at 4Q174 3 17, see *Midrasch zur Eschatologie*, 25, 31–32.

[67] Cf. e.g. Knibb, *Qumran Community*, 261 and Steudel, *Midrasch zur Eschatologie*, 32.

[68] See D. Dimant, *DJD* 30.

[69] Cf. *DJD* 30: 97–98, 100, 243.

[70] Ibid., 100.

of the work is concerned, Dimant proposes to consider the Apocryphon as "a type of intermediate category, related, but not identical, to the sectarian literature" and comparable to *Jubilees* and the *Temple Scroll* in this regard.[71]

The fragmentary passage that is of immediate relevance for our present enquiry occurs in 4Q390 1 2–3 and forms part of an historical overview of the Second Temple period.[72] The period is presented in Deuteronomistic style as a cycle of wrongdoing and punishment referring to a seventy-year period of priestly rule.[73] The present passage belongs with those parts of the scriptures and the scrolls that speak of the sons of Aaron as the legitimate, God-given priesthood. Moreover, the preserved text clearly refers to their leading role over Israel. The present passage is fragmentary, and it is somewhat ambiguous whether or not the sons of Aaron or the Israelites are here the subject of polemic.[74] A critical attitude towards the priests is a feature that characterizes other parts of this composition.[75] Whatever the case may be, this text clearly offers a further attestation of the sons of Aaron in what appears to be a national (non-community-specific) context.

4Q513 ORDINANCES[B][76]

4Q513 10 ii 8 mentions the sons of Aaron in a fragmentary context. The preceding lines speak of the sanctuary and purity, the issue of mixing, and the children of Israel. The context in this particular fragment and in the text as a whole is clearly national and cultic.

The remaining references to Aaron in the scrolls occur in historical, scriptural, and exegetical contexts and will not need to be considered here.[77]

---

[71] Ibid., 112.
[72] Ibid., 237–44.
[73] Ibid., 97, 237–38.
[74] Ibid., 239.
[75] Ibid., 112, 116.
[76] See Baillet, *DJD* 7:287–95 (291) and Pl. LXXII.
[77] Nor will the remaining isolated reference to the sons of Aaron in a text classified as "non-caractérisé" (i.e. 5Q20 1 2) shed much light, see J.T. Milik, *DJD* 3:193–97.

CONCLUSION

In sum, I hope to have shown that the priestly terminology in the scrolls, especially the terms sons of Aaron and sons of Zadok, do not appear to be employed entirely randomly and synonymously. Rather, a line of development appears to have left its mark on the literature.

a. We have a sizeable group of texts that speak of the sons of Aaron in a non-community-specific, national context. These texts usually emphasize the cultic duties of the sons of Aaron[78] and do not refer to the sons of Zadok at all.

b. A second group of texts speak of the sons of Aaron with reference to the make-up of the community, in particular its priestly (versus lay) component. "Sons of Aaron" is never used to refer to the community as a whole as is the case with the sons of Zadok in CD III–IV.[79]

c. A third group of texts refers to Aaron to describe the priestly messiah, who is expected alongside a lay or royal messiah.

d. Finally, the sons of Aaron appear as authority figures alongside the sons of Zadok in a number of community-specific texts, esp. the *Community Rule* and 1QSa. In this context we emphasized the important witness of one element of the tradition that employs sons of Aaron terminology in a community-specific context to the exclusion of the sons of Zadok in several manuscripts, see esp. 1QS V 21 // 4QS^d II 1–2 and 1QS IX 7 // 4QS^d VII 7. This shared element of common ground between 1QS and 4QS seems to me to come from an early period in the growth of the S tradition.

The view that the Zadokites played a key role at the very beginning of the community's existence and that matters of priestly descent were crucial in the events that led to the parting of the ways has gradually

---

[78] Fabry already pointed in a similar direction when he observes the exclusively liturgical functions and actions of the sons of Aaron in the Temple Scroll, MMT and M. See "Zadokiden und Aaroniden," 211. Earlier still Liver had rightly highlighted the way in which the sons of Zadok are allocated "primarily not cultic but didactic functions" and "the lack of allusion to any ritual function of the sons of Zadok the priests in these prefatory phrases is ample evidence that their unique place among the priesthood as a whole, lay not in the cultic sphere." "Sons of Zadok the Priests," 6, see also 28–30.

[79] Pace Anderson, "Aaron," 2, who claims "Aaron and Zadok function as ciphers for the sect as a whole."

been losing ground.[80] The results of the above survey and the profile that can be derived from it also speak rather in favour of the sons of Aaron as the earlier strand in the scrolls even in community-specific contexts.[81] Moreover, we noted that a number of passages dealing with the earliest forms of communal life lack interest in the genealogical background of the priestly leadership altogether (cf. 1QS VI 2–4 and 1QS VIII 1).[82]

There has been a considerable amount of scholarly interest in the equally complex portrayal of the sons of Aaron in the Hebrew Bible.[83] I am particularly intrigued by the way in which the evidence of the scrolls, which goes back to a later period, seems to mirror the complexity of the Hebrew Bible. The impression one gets is that the developments that left their mark on the Bible are coming around in further waves in writings of a later time.[84] I hope to have shown that, despite the complexity of the evidence, a certain trajectory can be traced based on the use of sons of Aaron terminology across a varied spectrum of non-biblical texts from the corpus of the scrolls.

---

[80] See, e.g., Kugler, "Priesthood at Qumran," 97–100 and J.J. Collins, "The Origin of the Qumran Community: A Review of the Evidence," in *To Touch the Text: Biblical and Related Studies in Honor of Joseph A. Fitzmyer, S.J.* (ed. M. P. Horgan and P.J. Kobelski; New York: Crossroad, 1989), 159–78.

[81] Here my own conclusions differ significantly from those reached by Kugler, "Priesthood at Qumran," 101.

[82] Cf. Hempel, "Diversity and Identity in the S-Tradition."

[83] See, e.g., J. Blenkinsopp, "The Judaean Priesthood during the Neo-Babylonian and Achaemenid Periods: A Hypothetical Reconstruction," *CBQ* 60 (1998): 25–43; idem, "Bethel in the Neo-Babylonian Period" and G.N. Knoppers, "The Relationship of the Priestly Genealogies to the History of the High Priesthood in Jerusalem," in *Judah and the Judeans in the Neo-Babylonian Period* (ed. O. Lipschits and J. Blenkinsopp; Winona Lake: Eisenbrauns, 2003), 93–107 and 109–33, and further literature cited there. Further, G. Nickelsburg, "Aaron," in *RAC* (Supplement-Band I; Stuttgart: Hiersemann, 2001), cols. 1–11.

[84] In Fabry's view the post-exilic rivalries simply continued up to a much later period, "Die Konflikte in der nachexilischen Priesterschaft blieben bestehen und wirkten sich offensichtlich bis ins 1.Jh. v.Chr., möglicherweise sogar bis in neutestamentliche Zeit hinein aus." See "Zadokiden und Aaroniden," 215.

DAMASCUS DOCUMENT IV 10–12

Johannes Tromp

In this article I should like to propose a new interpretation of the *Damascus Document* IV 10–12.[1] These lines consist mainly of allusions to biblical passages, but their meaning within the context of the *Damascus Document* is not easy to establish. This is partly due, as I shall suggest, to a mistaken view on the specific textual unit to which these lines belong: whereas most scholars regard the allusions in IV 10–12 as the conclusion of the preceding section, it is here suggested that they be read as the opening lines of a new section. In IV 12–21 the relevance of the allusions to the circumstances of the author and his audience is clarified.

1. Outline of CD III 12–IV 10

In the part of the *Damascus Document* commonly designated as the "Admonition," the author seeks to establish the historical position of the community to which he belongs, in particular as compared to the rest of the people of Israel. He presents his community as a section of the people as a whole, a minority that has remained faithful to God's commandments, especially according to the authoritative interpretation of the commandments provided by one of the past leaders of the community. The group which is reflected in the Admonition considers itself as the holy community of the "real" members of God's covenant with Israel.[2]

This point is repeatedly made in the *Damascus Document*; on page IV of the Cairo Genizah manuscript, it is the essence of an interpretation of Ezek 44:15.[3] It is related in CD III 12–20 that, after the divine

---

[1] I thank my colleagues Matthijs J. de Jong and Wido T. van Peursen for their critical reading of an earlier draft of this article.

[2] See, e.g., C.A. Evans, "Covenant in the Qumran Literature," in *The Concept of the Covenant in the Second Temple Period* (ed. S.E. Porter and J.C.R. de Roo; JSJSup 71; Leiden: Brill, 2003), 55–80.

[3] D.R. Schwartz, "To Join Onself to the House of Judah (Damascus Document IV, 11)," *RevQ* 10/39 (1981): 435–46.

punishment for the general apostasy from the original covenant, God has established another, renewed covenant and is ready to pardon the sins of those who remain faithful to this covenant (as opposed to "all Israel" who have gone astray). It is to this group of faithful covenanters that Ezek 44:15 (quoted in CD III 21–IV 1) is applied in CD IV. In Ezekiel, mention is made of priests, levites, and Zadokites who are to serve in God's temple when the children of Israel have strayed far away. The author of the *Damascus Document* explains this as references to three divisions within his community: the converts of Israel who left the land of Judah (cf. CD VI 5), those who joined them, and the chosen of Israel who will serve in the temple in the end of days (CD IV 2–4).[4]

The author then announces a list of names, complete with the individuals' relations, the time in which they served and suffered, the years of their living abroad, and a list of their deeds (CD IV 4–6). However, in the text as it survives there follows no list, possibly because it was left out by a copyist for whom the list had lost its relevance,[5] or because of physical damage to the model from which the Cairo manuscript was copied, for instance the loss of a page. The latter possibility would explain the fact that the text of the Cairo manuscript continues with an incomplete sentence: if the omission had been made on purpose, one would expect the responsible copyist to have started a new sentence at the point where he resumed his work. The incomplete sentence reads: הקודש שונים אשר כפר אל בעדם (CD IV 6–7). A generally accepted conjectural emendation makes the second word read הרשונים הם, so that the phrase can be taken as part of a sentence that originally went something like: "This concludes the list of the first holy men for whom God made atonement" (a reference to the atonement mentioned in III 18).

Next, a number of statements is made about these holy men: their ideas about right and wrong, based on a particular interpretation of the law, are correct and without compromise; therefore, as much as God has been prepared to atone for them, he will also atone for those

---

[4] For a useful discussion of these lines, see P.R. Davies, *The Damascus Covenant: An Interpretation of the "Damascus Document"* (JSOTSup 25; Sheffield: JSOT Press, 1982), 91–95.

[5] So J.M. Baumgarten and D.R. Schwartz, "Damascus Document (CD)," in *Damascus Document, War Scroll and Related Documents* (vol. 2 of *The Dead Sea Scrolls: Hebrew, Aramaic, and Greek Texts with English Translations*; ed. J.H. Charlesworth; Tübingen: Mohr [Siebeck], 1995), 4–57 (19).

who have subsequently joined them (the author's community) (CD IV 6–10).

2. Reading CD IV 10–12 as the Conclusion of the Preceding Section

The following statements are usually considered as a conclusion to what precedes:[6] when the number of years is complete, it is no longer possible to join the community, "but rather each one standing up on his watch tower. The wall is built, the boundary far away" (CD IV 10–12). When it is stated in the next sentence that during all these years, Belial will be set loose against Israel, this is commonly regarded as the beginning of a new section. In that case, the exposé about the holy men and the faithful community of the covenant for whom God makes atonement is concluded with a number of clauses that are difficult to understand: to stand upon a watch tower, a wall that is built, and a boundary that is far away. These are unexpected concepts, which seem to fit in poorly with their immediate contexts. It is unclear how these clauses add to what has been said in the preceding lines, or what conclusion they might draw from them.[7]

Part of the solution to this problem is the insight that these phrases are passages, or allusions to passages, in the Hebrew Bible: Hab 2:1 and Mic 7:11.

(a) In CD IV 11 it is said that "there will no longer be any joining with the house of Judah," meaning that once the number of predetermined years is fulfilled, one can no longer join the community of the covenant. Instead, one can only "stand upon one's watch tower." The opposition in meaning between both phrases is underlined by a

---

[6] See e.g., G. Vermès, *Les manuscrits du désert de Juda* (2d ed.; Tournai: Desclée, 1954), 162–63; cf. idem, *The Complete Dead Sea Scrolls in English* (London: Penguin, 1997), 129–30; C. Rabin, *The Zadokite Documents* (2d ed.; Oxford: Clarendon Press, 1958), 14; É. Cothenet, "Le Document de Damas," in *Les Textes de Qumrân II* (ed. J. Carmignac, et al.; Paris: Letouzey et Ané, 1961), 129–204: 160; O.J.R. Schwarz, *Der erste Teil der Damaskusschrift und das Alte Testament* (Diest: Lichtland, 1965), 19–20; Davies, *The Damascus Covenant*, 76–78; Schwartz, "To Join Oneself," 437; Baumgarten and Schwartz, "Damascus Document (CD)," 5. J. Murphy-O'Connor, "An Essene Missionary Document? CD II, 14–VI, 1," *RB* 77 (1970): 201–29 (216–19) argues for CD IV 9b–12a as a separate unit (within the larger passage of II 14–VI 1), but recognizes that line 12b provides "a close and natural link with the preceding section."

[7] Contrast Davies, *The Damascus Covenant*, 78.

construction that ties them close together syntactically: אין עוד with the
lamed-infinitive להשתפח, contrasted with כי אם with the *lamed*-infinitive
לעמוד.[8] The author's wish to make his point in this form accounts for
the deviation of the quotation in CD IV 11–12 from its source, Hab
2:1. A comparison of both lines, however, strongly suggests that the
reference to the biblical text is intentional:

(כי אים) לעמוד איש על מצודו CD IV 11–12
על משמרתי אעמדה ואתיצבה אל מצורי Hab 2:1

CD IV 11–12 can be read as a reference to the parallel verse-lines
in Habakkuk in a compressed form: the words עמד and על are taken
from the first *stichos*, whereas מצודו reflects מצורי in the second half of
Hab 2:1. At this point, we need not be detained by the fact that מצוד
and מצור are different words: they are paleographically nearly identical,
and both words are very similar to each other in meaning too.[9] I shall
return to this question in section 3c. below.

(b) Next, reference is made to Mic 7:11:

נבנתה הגדר רחק החוק החוק CD IV 12
יום לבנות נדריך יום ההוא ירחק חק Mic 7:11

There can be little doubt that this allusion is also intentional. The
agreement between the *Damascus Document* and Micah in this instance
becomes even clearer if it is remembered that the building of the wall
takes place, according to the *Damascus Document*, at the fulfilment of a
certain period of time; this corresponds to Micah's יום ההוא, that may
have been understood as "this will be the day."

The fact that CD IV 10–12 consists mainly of the quotation of
biblical passages contributes to our understanding of these lines in CD
IV 10–12. The author of the *Damascus Document* may have assumed
that his readers were familiar with the lines he quoted and also with
a particular interpretation of those lines, on account of which they
would have made sense in the context of the *Damascus Document*. The

---

[8] See P. Joüon, *Grammaire de l'hébreu biblique* (Rome: Institut biblique pontifical, 1923),
§ 160j.

[9] Segal, as reported by Rabin (*The Zadokite Documents*, 15), proposed to emend מצדו
into מצורו. So also E. Qimron in *The Damascus Document Reconsidered* (ed. Magen Broshi;
Jerusalem: Israel Exploration Society, 1992), 17, referring to 4Q177 10 ii 6: איש על מצודו;
Habakkuk's reading is supported by 1QpHab VI 13. Variance between מצדתה and
מצרתה occurs in Isa 29:7 MT and 1QIsaᵃ, respectively; I thank Wido T. van Peursen
for this reference.

recognition that CD IV 11–12 consists of allusions to other texts may explain the unexpected presence of these phrases. It still does not explain, however, what these phrases mean.

The first phrase, "each man standing on his watch tower," is the most difficult to understand. Several proposals have been made, but in my opinion none satisfactorily explains the presence of this phrase. Lohse translated "jeder soll stehen auf seiner Warte," noted the allusion to Hab 2:1, and commented: "The watch-tower designates the community of the covenant, in which people take refuge in the end of time."[10] In that case, the house of Judah, to which the watch-tower is set in contrast, must indicate something valued negatively by the author. However, this understanding of CD IV 10 has definitively been refuted by Schwartz, who has shown that the "house of Judah" designates the holy community.[11]

Murphy-O'Connor has proposed to understand the allusion to Habakkuk in the light of 1QpHab VII 1: "God told Habakkuk to write down the things that will come to pass in the last generation, but the consummation of time he did not make known to him." Murphy-O'Connor interprets this as "an exhortation to perpetual vigilance."[12] However, Murphy-O'Connor too easily passes over the fact that the interpretation in 1QpHab concerns Hab 2:2, not Hab 2:1. Moreover, one does wonder whether it is good methodology to make the interpretation of a biblical verse in one text automatically valid for another.

Knibb has suggested it should be taken to mean that everybody should be standing on his watch-tower "to receive God's decision at the judgement as to his fate." This interpretation understands the allusion to include the second half of Hab 2:1, where it says: "I will watch to learn what he will say through (or 'to') me, and what I shall reply when I am challenged."[13] However, that the speaker in Hab 2:1 plans to take a stand on his watch-tower in order to receive information concerning God's decisions does not imply the same meaning for CD IV 11–12,

---

[10] E. Lohse, *Die Texte aus Qumran* (2d ed.; München: Kösel, 1971), 73, with annotation on 284: "Gemeint ist die Warte, die die Gemeinde des Bundes ist und zu der man seine Zuflucht in der letzten Zeit nimmt." Cf. J. Maier, *Die Qumran-Essener: Die Texte vom Toten Meer I* (München: Reinhardt, 1995), 13.

[11] Schwartz, "To Join Onself"; see already Murphy-O'Connor, "An Essene Missionary Document?" 217.

[12] Murphy-O'Connor, "An Essene Missionary Document?" 217–18.

[13] M.A. Knibb, *The Qumran Community* (CCJW 2; Cambridge: Cambridge University Press, 1987), 38.

where the allusion is made to the first half of the verse only. It is far from certain that the author of the *Damascus Document* was interested in the original context of the passages he quotes. Therefore, we should not be projecting that original context upon his quotations and allusions, but should try to understand these within their new context in the *Damascus Document*.

3. Reading CD IV 10–12 as the Introduction of the Section that Follows

Interestingly, Schechter, the first translator of the *Damascus Document*, did not recognize or acknowledge the allusion to Hab 2:1. Consequently, he does not import meanings or contexts from Habakkuk into the *Damascus Document*, but simply attempts a translation in which the lines under discussion make sense in their proper context. Schechter's translation reads "every man shall stand up against his net." In a footnote, he explains: "that is to watch over the net lest he be caught."[14] The common translation of מצוד, "watch-tower," derives from the root מצד. However, if one takes the derivation of it from the root צוד, as Schechter does, the meaning of the word is "net." In CD IV 15 the word is again used (albeit in a feminine form, מצודות),[15] and there its meaning is undoubtedly "net," referring to the three "nets" with which Belial ensnares sinners and from which there is no escape. According to Schechter then, the meaning of CD IV 10–12 is that everybody should take care not to step into the devil's trap.

The great importance of Schechter's suggestion is that it does not take CD IV 10–12 as the conclusion to the preceding section.[16] Instead, these lines are taken as the introduction to what follows. Read in this way, there soon appears to be more intimate connections between CD IV 10–12 and their sequel: not only does the concept of a "net" return, but there is also further development of the motif of building a wall.

---

[14] S. Schechter, *Documents of Jewish Sectaries. 1. Fragments of a Zadokite Work* (Cambridge: Cambridge University Press, 1910; repr., New York: Ktav, 1970), XXV (67). Schechter was followed by R.H. Charles, "Fragments of a Zadokite Work," *APOT* 2:785–824 (809), but Charles does not comment on the meaning of the phrase "to stand up against one's net."

[15] Both the feminine and the masculine forms are attested in the Hebrew Bible.

[16] He took them as part of the section IV 3–19; Schechter, *Fragments*, XXXV–XXXVI (67–68).

Moreover, the contents of both CD IV 10–12 and the lines immediately following are set in the period of the fulfilment of time, with CD IV 12–13 explicitly referring back to CD IV 10. In contrast to CD III 12–IV 10, which looks back upon the community's history leading up to the present, the section beginning in CD IV 10–12 describes the present as part of the final stage of history and looks forward to the end of time. I shall now describe the connections between CD IV 10–12 and what follows in more detail, beginning with the eschatological positioning and continuing with the motifs of the net and the wall.

a. *The Fulfilment of Time*

CD IV 10 begins with an adjunct of time, ובשלום הקץ למספר השנים האלה, that is, "when the period corresponding to the number of these years is complete," or "at the completion of the end according to its number of years," as in *As. Mos.* 1:18: *in consummatione exitus dierum*.[17] This expression implies that there is only a limited number of years in history (their number being predetermined by God) and that at some point that number is reached, so that history ends. This is of course a well-known concept in eschatological writings; see e.g., Dan 7:25; 12:7, 11–12; 1QpHab VII 6–10; also Tob 14:5.[18]

Often, an author wishes to convince his audience that they are living in the days immediately preceding the end of time; such an author may then write that "the end is near" (e.g., 1 Pet 4:7; Rev 1:3; 22:10) or even "is fulfilled" (e.g., Mark 1:15). With this expression, the author impresses upon his audience that there is an urgent need to choose the right path: soon, God will visit his creation, and then there will no longer be an opportunity to repent or convert.[19] This is clearly also the intention of CD IV 10–11: when the time at which history comes to a close is reached, "there will no longer be any joining with the house of Judah," that is, it will no longer be possible to join the community of the holy ones for whose sins God will make atonement. The adjunct

---

[17] A. Schalit, *Untersuchungen zur Assumptio Mosis* (ALGHJ 17; Leiden: Brill, 1989), 206–8.

[18] J.J. Collins, "The Expectation of the End in the Dead Sea Scrolls," in *Eschatology, Messianism, and the Dead Sea Scrolls* (ed. C.A. Evans and P.W. Flint; SDSS; Grand Rapids: Eerdmans, 1997), 74–90.

[19] E. Meyer, *Die Gemeinde des neuen Bundes im Lande Damaskus: Eine jüdische Schrift aus der Seleukidenzeit* (Abhandlungen der preussischen Akademie der Wissenschaften, Jahrgang 1919, philosophisch-historische Klasse, Nr. 9; Berlin: Verlag der Akademie der Wissenschaften, 1919), 33.

of time, then, with which CD IV 10–12 begins, lends great urgency to the warning it contains and implies that the author sees himself and his community as living in the final phase of history.[20]

CD IV 12–13 continues with another adjunct of time: בכל השנים האלה, "during all these years." It is not immediately clear which years are intended by "all these years." However, the following clauses strongly suggest that this expression also indicates the final phase of history.[21] It is said that during all these years יהיה בליעל משלח בישראל, "Belial will be set loose against Israel." If "these years" refers to the final stage of history, in which the author and his intended readers are supposed to be living, this remark about Belial's enmity towards Israel does make sense. Connected to the warning that there is no time to lose, these lines warn that evil, too, knows that its hour glass is running out and that it has therefore begun its final assault, its ultimate attempt to prevent the Israelites from escaping perdition. The motif that the final age is a time of ever greater and all-surpassing hardships is again very common in eschatological writings.[22] A particularly interesting parallel is found in 2 Tim 3:1, where the author warns that there will be "hard times in the final age"; he does so immediately after having expressed the hope that there may still be some people who can escape from the devil's trap of sinfulness (2 Tim 2:26; see further below, section b.). For the view that the devil intensifies his attacks on humankind the more the end is approaching, see also 1 Pet 5:8.

The eschatological positioning of both CD IV 10–12 and CD IV 12–13 strongly suggests that these lines should be read in connection with each other and that they belong to the same textual unit, of which CD IV 10–12 is then the introduction. These lines announce that the following section will be about the final phase of history, preparing the audience for a description of the sinfulness that is generally regarded as characteristic of that final stage.

---

[20] Cf. Murphy-O'Connor, "An Essene Missionary Document?" 217.

[21] H. Kosmala, "The Three Nets of Belial: A Study in the Terminology of Qumran and the New Testament," *ASTI* 4 (1965): 91–113: 92; A. Dupont-Sommer, "Écrit de Damas," in *La Bible: Écrits intertestamentaires* (ed. A. Caquot and M. Philonenko; Bible de la Pléiade; Paris: Gallimard, 1987), 133–83; 150, commentary on "En toutes ces années-là": "durant les années qui précèdent la consommation du temps, c'est-à-dire au regard de l'auteur, durant la période présente."

[22] P. Volz, *Die Eschatologie der jüdischen Gemeinde im neutestamentlichen Zeitalter* (Tübingen: Mohr, 1934), 153–55; K. Berger, *Die griechische Daniel-Diegese: Eine altkirchliche Apokalypse* (StPB 27; Leiden: Brill, 1976), 70–75.

b. *Belial's nets*

A net, in which birds, fish, or game are caught for consumption, or as royal entertainment, is a common metaphor for the highly perilous situation in which somebody may find himself because of the evil schemes of his enemies.[23] Technically, the nets in which birds, fish, or gazelles are caught differ from each other, and there are several Hebrew terms for net, probably reflecting those various types. However, as metaphors, all these terms appear to be interchangeable. The commonest word is פח, usually translated in the Septuagint as παγίς;[24] מצוד or מצודה is another, for which the Septuagint offers various translations (if it is not taken to mean something altogether different as in Job 19:6; Qoh 7:26; Ezek 13:21; 19:9), including δίκτυον (Ezek 12:13) and ἀμφίβληστρον (Prov 9:12). Outside the biblical literature, מצוד or מצודה occurs with this meaning in 1QHᵃ XI 27: "When all the traps of the pit (פחי שחת) are open, all the snares of wickedness (מצודות רשעה) are spread"; XII 12 "so they may act like fools in their feasts so they will be caught in their nets (במצדותם)."

In CD IV 15, the one who sets these traps is Belial, the personification of evil. That evil contrives its plans using traps, snares, and pits was a well developed image, to which witness is borne by 4Q171 1–2 ii 9–10; 1QHᵃ X 23, 31 (Suk. II 21, 29); as well as 1 Tim 3:7 and 2 Tim 2:26 (τοῦ διαβόλου παγίς).[25] It is this image that underlies the interpretation of Isa 24:17, quoted in CD IV 14: פחד ופחת ופח עליך יושב הארץ, that is, "fear, and pit, and a net over you who lives in the land." The author explains that this refers to the "three nets of Belial" (שלושת מצודות בליעל), with which evil captures Israel: fornication, wealth, and defilement of the sanctuary.[26] According to the author, his audience should know of these nets from a speech of Jacob's son

---

[23] J. Schneider, "παγίς, παγιδεύω," *TWNT* 5:593–96. For the quasi universal validity of this metaphor (which can be applied in many more ways than referred to here), cf. I. Scheftelowitz, *Das Schlingen- und Netzmotiv im Glauben und Brauch der Völker* (Religionsgeschichtliche Versuche und Vorarbeiten XII, 2; Gießen: Töpelmann, 1912).

[24] D. Kellermann, "פח," *ThWAT* 6:547–52 (549, 551–52), asserts that this instrument indicated by the Hebrew word is specifically used for catching birds; the same cannot be said of the Greek rendering.

[25] Cf. J.D. Quinn and W.C. Wacker, *The First and Second Letters to Timothy* (Grand Rapids: Eerdmans, 2000), 266–67.

[26] Cf. Kosmala, "The Three Nets of Belial"; M. Pesthy, "The Three Nets of Belial from Qumran to the *Opus imperfectum in Matthaeum*," in *Jerusalem, Alexandria, Rome: Studies in Ancient Cultural Interaction in Honour of A. Hilhorst* (ed. F. García Martínez and G.P. Luttikhuizen; JSJSup 82; Leiden: Brill, 2003), 243–53.

Levi. It has been argued that the reference is to *ALD* 6:3,[27] although there is no mention of nets on that occasion. It is in any case obvious that the author of the *Damascus Document* was familiar with the concept of Belial's snares before he applied it to the quotation from Isaiah (or *ALD*, for that matter).

If CD IV 10–12 is to be read in direct connection with what follows, it becomes likely that the quotation from Hab 2:1 has a meaning in its new context that differs strongly from the meaning in its original context. In the book of Habakkuk, the phrase may mean something along the lines set out by Knibb, quoted above in section 2. But in the new context of CD IV 10–19, מצוד in line 12 was probably understood in the sense of מצודה in line 15, that is, "net." In that case, the contrast in CD IV 10–12 can be paraphrased as follows: in the final phase of history, one can no longer join the holy community, but everybody is stuck in his net, i.e., one of Belial's nets from which there is no escape ("he who escapes from this is caught by that...").[28]

It is true that the phrase עמד על מצוד is not naturally translated as "to get caught in a net." However, the wording can be explained as determined by Hab 2:1, to which it alludes and which the author of the *Damascus Document* apparently associated with Belial's nets. That the ancient hermeneutics of biblical writings sometimes followed surprising trajectories is well attested by 1QpHab or other exegetical procedures in the *Damascus Document* itself. Also, the related meanings "to stay with," or "to insist on," are lexicographically possible for עמד על,[29] and the immobility expressed by עמד neatly contrasts with השתפח, the *verbum movendi* to which it stands in opposition. Finally, this suggestion not only explains the meaning which the quoted phrase may have in the context of CD IV 10–19, but it also explains why the author, being preoccupied with the subject of Belial's nets, misread Habakkuk's מצור as מצוד.

To conclude: reading CD IV 10–12 in connection with what follows provides a context within which the allusion to Hab 2:1 can be meaningfully understood. The subject broached in this section is that of the snares set up by the powers of evil, a concept well-known from

---

[27] J.C. Greenfield, M.E. Stone, and E. Eshel, *The Aramaic Levi Document: Edition, Translation, Commentary* (SVTP 19; Leiden: Brill, 2004), 5; cf. H. Drawnel, *An Aramaic Wisdom Text from Qumran: A New Interpretation of the Levi Document* (JSJSup 86; Leiden: Brill, 2004), 266–67.

[28] Baumgarten and Schwartz, "Damascus Document," 19, felicitously compare Luke 16:26.

[29] See the current dictionaries of biblical Hebrew.

contemporary Jewish literature and perfectly at home in a context depicting the moral decay brought about by diabolical forces during the final stage of history.

c. *The Wall*

The allusion to Hab 2:1 is immediately followed by the quotation from Mic 7:11: "the wall is built, the boundary far away" (CD IV 12). As already mentioned above, the image of the wall returns in the following lines: in CD IV 19–21 (immediately after the author's explanation of Isa 24:17 as referring to Belial's nets, from which there is no escape), the author sets out that some people are even caught in the net of fornication twice. These people he calls "the builders of the wall who go after Zaw," בוני חיץ אשר הלכו אחרי צו (CD IV 19).

With the expression "the builders of the wall," the author returns in line 19 to what he said in line 12. There he stated that "the wall is built," and now he is elaborating upon the sins of those who have built it. It is likely that the author expected his audience to be familiar with the image, since it is used again in CD VIII 12; XIX 24–25. There, the author gives his commentary on Deut 32:33 and adds that these matters are not understood by "the builders of the wall, who whitewash it." The phrase is a clear reference to Ezek 13:10, a section on prophets who cause the ruin of Jerusalem, because of the false comfort they give to the people against God's will. Their behaviour is described as merely "whitewashing the wall," as opposed to building a solid wall around Jerusalem and repairing its breaches (Ezek 13:5, 10–12).[30] God hates these builders of the wall, as is said in CD VIII 18, and his wrath has been kindled against them—concepts that can also be read against the background of Ezek 13:13, 15.

The people who have built the wall are characterized as going after צו. The question of the meaning of "Zaw" is debatable;[31] with regard to Hos 5:11, where the expression "go after Zaw" also occurs, opinions vary from a vulgar term for human excrement (cf. the Vulgate's rendering *sordes*) to a word for foolishness, esp. as applied to idols (in the Septuagint's rendering of Hos 5:11 μάταια). I am inclined to think

---

[30] Lohse, *Die Texte*, 288; Davies, *The Damascus Covenant*, 112–13.
[31] See, e.g., Schechter, *Fragments*, XXXVI (68): "the commanding one"; Charles, "Fragments," 810: "law"; Davies, *The Damascus Covenant*, 112: "(false) commandment"; Dupont-Sommer, 151: "sorte d'onomatopée, désigne ici le grand prêtre persécuteur."

that the latter is in the main correct and may perhaps suggest that Zaw in CD IV 12 can designate what other Hebrew authors prefer to call "Shaw" (שׁוא), a common Hebrew word for falsehood and lying. Again, this term is repeatedly used in Ezek 13:1–16 (Ezek 13:6, 8, 9).

It seems, then, that the theme and motifs discussed in Ezek 13:1–16 were in some way or other so familiar to the author of the *Damascus Document* that he could use terms such as "whitewashers" and "builders of the wall" as common invectives, without having to explain their identity or refer to a biblical passage. As other examples of this way of designating people one could cite "the Spouter of Lies," "the Impious Priest," but also "the Teacher of Righteousness." The author and his audience called certain people "whitewashers," those who did not take the eschatological import of the biblical message seriously and were unwilling or unable to acknowledge and accept the proper explanation of God's commandments.[32]

This, finally, explains the remaining words of CD IV 10–12: after the author, alluding to Mic 7:11, has stated that the wall has been built, he adds, still referring to the same prophetic passage: "the statute is far away." In the book of Micah, the phrase probably says something about the future expansion of the land's boundaries, but in the context of the *Damascus Document* it means that, for the builders of the wall (with their erroneous understanding of God's will), the proper interpretation of the divine commandments is far beyond reach.

To conclude, it can be noted that the reading together of CD IV 10–12 with lines 12–19 and 19–21 reveals a meaningful structure of the text. After having stated that he will now be speaking of the ultimate stage of history, the author introduces the images of a net and a wall and then continues by explaining first the net, then the wall. The net represents Belial's snares; the wall evokes the poor qualities of false prophets and teachers. The author drives a single conclusion home: in the last days, a life according to God's commandments is impossible for those outside the holy community, who let themselves be guided by false informants.

---

[32] Cf. H. Stegemann, *Die Entstehung der Qumrangemeinde* (Bonn: private publication, 1971), 168–69. A negative assessment of building walls is probably also expressed in *As. Mos.* 4:7; cf. N.J. Hofmann, *Die Assumptio Mosis: Studien zur Rezeption massgültiger Überlieferung* (JSJSup 67; Leiden: Brill, 2000), 58.

CONCLUSION

In this article, I have argued that CD IV 10–12 are the introduction to a new textual unit. They first announce that the author will be speaking about the final phase of history and set out summarily, with the help of allusions to biblical prophecies, that during this final stage (which the author believes to be impending or already in process) the entrance into the holy community of God's renewed covenant will become impossible because of the forces of evil (personified by Belial) that are constantly working to catch people in their snares of sinfulness.

A paraphrase of CD IV 10–12 might run as follows: "When the time of the end, according to its number of years, is reached, one can no longer join the holy community. Everybody will be caught in a net; they have built their wall, and the commandment is out of their reach."

SOME ASPECTS OF *NEW JERUSALEM*

Hugo Antonissen

The Aramaic text of *New Jerusalem* (Editiones principes: 1Q32: Milik 1955; 2Q24: Baillet 1955, 1962; 4Q554, 4Q554a, and 4Q555: DiTommaso 2005; 5Q15: Milik 1962; 11Q18: García Martínez et al. 1998) belongs to the literary genre of apocalypse (Collins 1979, 9; 1992, 58–62; García Martínez 2003, 102) and is conceived as a kind of "tour," in which the author is led by a guide through the city and the temple. In the latter they witness the performance of rituals. One column contains eschatological references (4Q554 2 iii). The earliest studies relating to the mentioned text appeared in 1955 with the publication of the editio princeps of manuscript 1Q32 by Milik and of manuscript 2Q24 by Baillet. Inspired by Florentino García Martínez, I started a dissertation on the subject in 2003.[1] Even though a lot of work was done in the meantime, further improvement and additional progress is conceivable. In this article, four different aspects of the text in view are dealt with: (1) Ground plan: square or rectangle? (2) Writing numbers by figures: "24" or "25" and "17" or "18"? (3) Different ways of reproducing the concept "same dimension," and (4) The shape of 5Q15 1.

1. Ground Plan: Square or Rectangle?

The ground plan of the new Jerusalem has the form of a square in Ezek 48:30–35, measuring 4500 × 4500 cubits. In the Aramaic *New Jerusalem*, the ground plan is a rectangle, measuring 100 × 140 stadia.[2]

---

[1] *Nieuw Jeruzalem: Tekststudie van een architectuurbeschrijvende Aramese apocalyps*. KUL = Katholieke universiteit Leuven, Faculteit letteren, Taal- en regiostudies, Nabije oosten studies. Promotor: Professor dr. Florentino García Martínez (KUL, Faculteit Theologie), and co-promotors: Professor dr. Pierre Vanhecke (KUL, Faculteit letteren, Taal- en regiostudies, Nabije oosten studies), and Prof. dr. Angelika Berlejung (Universität Leipzig; Theologische Fakultät).

[2] In 4Q554 1 i 12–1 ii 11 the following figures are attested or should be reconstructed: 35 + [35] + 35 + [35] + [25] + 25 + [25] + [25] + [35] + [35] + [35] + [35] + [25] + [2]5 + [2]5 + 25 stadia (figures between brackets are reconstructed).

In the Apocalypse of John (21:16), the whole city appears like a cube, measuring 12000 × 12000 × 12000 stadia. Milik was the first one to observe that the author of the Aramaic text changed the ground plan from a square into a rectangle (1962, 185). According to García Martínez, the author of the Aramaic text completed the *Torah of Ezekiel* (Ezek 40–48) by specifying the plan of the city. The author did not only specify the plan but also transformed it consciously into a rectangle, thus re-thematizing the original concept (1988, 449–50). Frey wonders why the *New Jerusalem* text differs from the traditio-historical line running from Ezekiel down to the Apocalypse of John and why it did not retain the square from Ezekiel's vision (2000, 813–14).

In a particular passage, somewhat hidden in his book on the *New Jerusalem* Scroll, while discussing the proportions of numbers, Chyutin (1997, 142) draws our attention to the proportions reproduced by the large rectangular enclosure of the city: 140:100 = 7:5, which represents the relation between the side and the diagonal of a square:

> These oblong dimensions are surprising, because according to the tradition of ideal planning in the Jewish sources, we would have expected a square enclosure containing a square city. However, in the description of the land of contribution in Ezekiel, the square city is also located within an oblong enclosure. The oblong design is not coincidental but deliberate, for the proportions of the dimensions of the enclosure present a solution to the second geometrical problem of the ancient world, the problem of the diagonal of the square. The ratio 7:5…is the value accepted in the ancient world, in Plato (*Republic*, 546) and in the Talmud, for the relation between lengths of the diagonal and the side of the square.

The observation by Chyutin allows us to draw the following conclusion: as the proportions mentioned were known by Plato and appear frequently in the Talmud, they may have been known to the author of the Aramaic text and incorporated by him in the form and the measurements of the perimeter of the city. The concept of the square is still present but not reproduced as such. It is represented in an indirect way by its proportions, so proving that the author of Aramaic *New Jerusalem* had not lost the original square design out of sight.

Milik acknowledges that the perimeter of the city measures 140 × 100 stadia and that the city area is crossed by six boulevards, three of them running east-west, the other south-north. The opposite gates are all of them connected by a boulevard. In this manner the city is divided into four parallel horizontal strokes, measuring each 35 × 100 stadia. The temple is located in the middle of the city at the cross road of the two largest boulevards. From here on, Milik tries to harmonize the text of *New Jerusalem* with the division of the holy territory in Ezekiel. The temple was in the centre of the territory that was assigned to the priests. The northern stroke was inhabited by the Levites. The strip south of the territory of the priests was a kind of buffer zone between the latter and the city inhabited by the lay people. The southern strip, as a matter of course rectangular, was assigned to the workers originating from all the tribes of Israel. It was completely filled with blocks. In Ezekiel only a part of the southern strip is built on (1962, 185–86). Inspired by Milik, two groups of scholars attempted in their turn to harmonize the square design of Ezekiel's ground plan with the rectangular enclosure of the city in the Aramaic text. Common to the view of both groups is the location of the temple outside of the residential city. The difference between both views depends on the form of the latter city. According to Licht and Broshi, the rectangular shape as described in the Aramaic text includes a square residential city and at its exterior, the temple. According to Chyutin, VanderKam, and Flint, the rectangular shape is reserved to the residential city while the square includes both the city and the temple. In Licht's view (1979, 50), the author of the Aramaic text adhered quite meticulously to Ezekiel's specifications. The result of his calculations seems to confirm the dimensions of the residential city as given by Ezekiel: 5000 × 5000 (1979, 50–52). Licht (48) accepts that the temple is on the left/north of the main east-west boulevard. In his view the main east-west boulevard was a kind of plaza or place of assembly adjoining the temple and situated at the southern perimeter of the street network. The heart of Licht's view was by adopted by Broshi (1992, 15). In Chyutin's view the residential city is rectangular indeed. The rectangle measures 22 × 14 *rēs* (1997, 84–85). The ground plan of the global city though is a square of 22 × 22 *rēs*, as the temple is not located within the lay city (85–86). According to Lee, the rebuilding of the temple with the sacrificial system in it suggests that the city is divided into a residential area and a temple area. The general dimension of the whole city is a square (Lee 2001, 126). VanderKam and Flint adopted Chyutin's point of view (2002, 369, 371). DiTommaso does not combine the rectangular ground plan with the location of the Temple, which stands outside the residential blocks (2005, 105). By locating the Temple, which, according to him, is not a freely accessible structure, in another place than the centre of the residential area and by segregating it by walls and courts, *New Jerusalem* reflects the influence of Ezek 40–48 (2005, 107).

García Martínez (1992, 187–88) and Puech (2003, 390–91) demonstrated that the ground plan as described in 2Q24, 4Q554, and 5Q15
shows clearly the form of a rectangular grid. The two main boulevards,
one running from east to west, one running from south to north, cut
across in the heart of the city. The temple is north of the main east-west
boulevard (Licht 1979, 48; García Martínez 1999, 456; Puech 2003,
383).[3] Two remarks have to be made concerning the latter view. The
word שמאל (north) means also "left."[4] The main south-north boulevard
is explicitly located in the middle of three parallel boulevards (4Q554
1 ii 21 // 5Q15 1 i 5). The location of the largest boulevard of all is
only specified by its position with regard to the Temple but not with
regard to the other two east-west boulevards (4Q554 1 ii 18 // 5Q15
1 i 4). In the view of the author, the location of the boulevard with
regard to the temple was probably obvious enough: the central location of the temple must have been self-evident and consequently the
location of the largest boulevard also.

The traditio-historical line concerning the ground plan, running
down from Ezekiel to the Apocalypse of John, was not broken by the
author of *New Jerusalem*. The square, appearing in Ezekiel in its plain
two-dimensional form and in the Apocalypse in his three-dimensional
form, is represented by the author of the Aramaic text in a more
subtle and indirect way: it is represented by its internal proportions.
The temple in Ezekiel is explicitly located outside the residential city;
in *New Jerusalem*, on the contrary, it is right in the middle of it. In the
Apocalypse there is no temple at all, but the concept of the presence
of God in the city is maintained in a very clear way: God and his
lamb are the Temple.

---

[3] Some scholars introduced the Roman terminology *decumanus maximus* and *cardo maximus*, which were used to divide a terrain destined to a military camp or any other form of new human settlement into four *regiones*, which in turn were divided in still smaller parts by parallel marks (Chantraine 1969).

[4] Translation by "north": Milik 1962, 185, 190, 191; Beyer 1984, 217; García Martínez 1992, 194; García Martínez and Van der Woude 1995, 151; *DSSU* 1992, 44; Cook 1996, 182; VanderKam and Flint 2002, 370; translation by "left": *MPAT* 1978, 55; Licht 1979, 49; García Martínez 1987, 219; 1994, 131; Maier 1995, 301 (5Q15); *DSSSE* 1998, 1108, 1109 (4Q554), 1138–1139 (5Q15); DiTommaso 2005, 33 (4Q554); *DSSR* 2005, 18 (4Q554), 53 (5Q15); translation by "left" = "north": Maier 1997, 322 (4Q554).

2. Writing Numbers by Figures: "24" or "25" and "17" or "18"?

Where other authors read "25," Maier (1995, 733; 1997, 321) and DiTommaso (2005, 30) read "24." Cook (1996, 181) translates by "twenty four." The readings refer to the figures in 4Q554 1 ii 7, 11. The former author reproaches others their lack of explanation: "and without comment." Regarding the reading in 4Q554 1 ii 7, one must note that

- because of the structure of the content of the text, the same number is expected as in 4Q554 1 i 18, 19, 21, 22; ii 8, 9, 11.
- the figure is completely preserved in 4Q554 1 ii 11 and almost entirely in 4Q554 1 i 19. In 4Q554 1 i 9, the figure "20" is nearly completely maintained. If the unit "5," only the upper part of a down stroke is preserved, which may belong to the ligature on the first two of the mentioned lines. In 4Q554 1 ii 7, two strokes are partially preserved. Eventually they belong to the ligature of the figure "5." In 4Q554 1 i 18, 21, 22, and ii 8, the figure is lost entirely.
  Some authors read/translate the figure "25": Chyutin (1997, 25); (*DSSSE* 1998, 1106); Abegg (2003, 955); Beyer (1994, 96–97; 2004, 130); and *DSSR* (2005, 46). *DSSU* (1992, 41, 44) reads mostly "24" and once "25" (line 18), but translates by "twenty-five res." Others integrate the dimension "25" in the perimeter of the city wall: Milik (1962, 185); Broshi (1995, 12–13); and Puech (1995, 98–99; 2003, 382). García Martínez (1992, 194) only mentions the 35 *res* of the north and south sides of the wall. Aune (1999, 632) integrates the number "25" implicitly in the dimensions of the enclosure of the city.

According to DiTommaso, three arguments may be in favour of an error by the scribe, who wrote 24 where 25 was meant:

- the scribe of 4Q554 stroked out signs and committed a number of errors. The manuscript shows many traces of sloppiness. In 4Q554 1 ii 18, the word אמין was written incorrectly, which consequently had to be stroked out.
- a planned orthogonal city demands a large amount of regularity regarding the relationship between the wall segments, the gates, and internal structures, such as streets and buildings. The required regularity is only possible by manipulation of the dimensions of the city and its structures. A wall measuring 100 (25 × 4) × 140 (35 ×

4) stadia has a more regular shape than a city with a perimeter of 96 (24 × 4) × 140 (35 × 4) stadia.

– according to most editions, 1432 (4Q554 2 ii 15–16) towers were constructed on the city walls. This number seems to fit a city perimeter of 100 × 140 stadia.

In the view of DiTommaso the aforementioned arguments are questionable for three different reasons:

– the dimension of 24 stadia occurs also on 4Q554 1 ii 10–11. The example on 4Q554 1 ii 6–7 is ambiguous, as only the three latter subsigns are preserved. It is not very plausible that the scribe repeatedly committed the same error while reproducing the same number.

– although it is true that 100 (25 × 4) × 140 (35 × 4) stadia correlate more conveniently with a planned city than 96 (24 × 4) × 140 (35 × 4) stadia, the former point of view is not supported by the actual dimensions of the internal elements of *New Jerusalem*. Many of the preserved or reconstructed numbers are either multiples of the number seven (no divisor of 96 or 100) or often odd dimensions: 126 (4Q554 1 ii 18), 67 (4Q554 1 ii 21), 13 (4Q554 1 ii 22), 13 (4Q554 1 iii 15), and 19 (4Q554a ii 7) have hardly any or no affinity at all with the external dimensions of the city.

– the number of towers was probably not 1432.

Consistent with his point of view, DiTommaso reads on 4Q554 1 ii 18 the figure "17" in stead of "18" (2005, 32). It is imperative to point out that in 5Q15 1 i 4, a parallel passage, the number concerned is reproduced by words: תמנית עשר[ה‎ (eighteen). According to DiTommaso, the figure "18" represents an error, and most certainly the figure "17" was meant (2005, 41). In my opinion a more reasonable explanation can be offered by reading the last signs as ligatures. Two kinds of such ligatures can be discerned: (1) a simple ypsilon formed ligature, representing the number "two," and (2) a simple ypsilon formed ligature, extended by a foot, representing the number "three" as the number "3." DiTommaso correctly reads the figure "7" on 4Q554 1 ii 14 (2005, 32). This reading does not fit into his own logic, according to which the ligature of the figure "18" on 4Q554 1 ii 18 has to be read as "1 + 1 = 2." Because of the 51 reeds at the beginning of line 4Q554 1 ii 13, the figure at the beginning of line 4Q554 1 ii 14 can only be read as "7": 51 × 7 = 357 cubits. The manner in which the figure "9" is reproduced by nine vertical strokes at the end of line 4Q554 1 ii 20 is a remarkable phenomenon indeed.

The following table demonstrates that figures, representing units, are reproduced in three different ways:

		1. exclusively separate strokes; each stroke represents "one"
2	4Q554 1 ii 18	two curved strokes reclining to the left
9	4Q554 1 ii 20	nine short vertical strokes
12	4Q554a ii 7	vertical strokes reclining to the right
[1]3	4Q554 1 iii 14	visible: remains of two vertical strokes
21	4Q554 1 ii 15	one vertical stroke
21	4Q554a ii 4	stroke reclining to the right
51	4Q554 1 ii 13 (2 x)	twice one vertical stroke, reclining to the left
92	4Q554 1 ii 22	two vertical strokes, reclining to the left
126	4Q554 1 ii 19	preserved: two short vertical strokes
		2. separate strokes + *in fine* a simple ypsilon formed ligature which represents "two"
4	4Q554 1 ii 21	two vertical strokes + simple ligature
7	4Q554 1 ii 14; iii 17	five vertical strokes, the latter two reclining to the right + simple ligature
14	4Q554 1 iii 14, 19 (2 x); 4Q554a ii 5	two vertical strokes, reclining to the right + simple ligature
		3. separate strokes + *in fine* a simple ypsilon formed ligature, extended by a foot; the extended ligature represents "three"
18	4Q554 1 ii 19	five vertical strokes, two of them reclining to the left + extended ligature
25	4Q554 1 i 19	two vertical strokes + extended ligature
	4Q554 1 ii 11	
[2]5	4Q554 1 ii 7	visible: vertical stroke and foot of the extended ligature

The difference in the reclining of the vertical strokes either to the right or to the left allows one to distinguish two different handwritings in the manuscripts 4Q554 (to the left) and 4Q554a (to the right). The numeric value of the ligatures is confirmed either by the double mention of dimensions or by parallel passage, where numbers are produced by figures on one manuscript and in words on the other:

4		9 reeds (= 63 cubits) + 4 cubits = 67 cubits
	4Q554 1 ii 21	67 לשׁוק חד לאמי[ן] 4 ואמין 9 קנין
	// 5Q15 1 i 5	קנין ת[שׁעה] ואמין א[ר]⁵ע לשׁוק חד אמי[ן] שׁתין ושׁבע
14	4Q554 1 iii 19 (2 x); 5Q15 1 ii 1	14 (...) קנין תרין א<>מין 14 קנין תרין א[מין] קנין תרין אמין א[ר]בע עשׂרה (...) קנין תרין אמין ארבע ע[שׂרה]ותרע
14	4Q554a ii 5	14 קנין תרין אמין
	// 5Q15 1 ii 8	קנין ת[ר]ין א[מי]ן ארבע [עשׂרה
357	4Q554 1 ii 14 // 5Q15 1 i 1	51 reeds × 51 = 357 350 7 אמין 51 ב 51 תלת מאה ו[חמשׁין ושׁבע
18	4Q554 1 ii 19 // 5Q15 1 i 4	18 reeds 18 קנין {אמין} קנין תמנית עשׂ[ר

The data concerning the way units are produced by figures on the manuscripts from cave 4 lead to the following conclusions:

- no consistent logic is applied.
- two kinds of ligature are used: a simple one, representing the numeric value of "two," and an extended one, representing the numeric value of "three." The simple ligature can be seen as the join between two strokes, the extended one as the join between three.
- the figures "18" on 4Q554 1 ii 19 and "25" on 4Q554 1 i 25; ii 7, 11 have been read positively in this way.

The reading "25" allows us to calculate a clearly regular city wall of 100×140 stadia, representing the exact proportion of: 5:7. As shown above this is the proportion of the side of a square to its diagonal. A less regular proportion of a perimeter measuring 96×140 stadia, as suggested by DiTommaso, represents $4\frac{8}{10}{:}7$.

In the appendix DiTommaso acknowledges explicitly the three different forms (2005, 77–78). As already explained above, in his view both the extended ligatures have the numeric value "2" and not "3."

3. Different Ways of *Formulating* the Concept "Same Dimension"

The term משחה (dimension) is used explicitly to refer to objects with the same length and width. Three different set phrases serve this purpose: כמשחת, במשחה, and משחה חדה.

כמשחת (just like the dimension):

- And a gate <was> opposite the/a <northern> gate, opened towards the interior of the block, with the same dimension as (= just like the dimension of) the exterior gate (4Q554 1 iii 19–20 // 5Q15 1 ii 1–2).
- And he led me into interior of the entry hall and see, <there was> another entry hall a gate alongside the interior wall, which <was> on the right side just like the dimen[si]on of the exterior gate: its width <was> cubits four, and its height cubits 7 and two gatelids (4Q554 1 iii 16–17 // 5Q15 1 i 18).

במשחה (with a dimension):

- And the g[ates opposite the <other> gates] the <other> gates with <the same> dimension. 4Q554 1 iii 21–22 // 5Q15 1 ii 3–4.

משחה חדה (one dimension):

- [...and] its [wid]th <had> one (= the same) measurement [...] (2Q24 5 2)
- (...) and on the left its length <had> one (= the same) dimension: two reeds by two, fourteen cubits (4Q554 1 iii 21 and 22 // 5Q15 1 ii 3).
- And their width <measured> one (= the same) dimension (4Q554 2 ii 16).

Before considering the different readings, it is interesting to note that the difference between the first and the second set phrase not only relates to the preposition but also to syntactical construction. The first set phrase contains the following elements: preposition כ + noun משחה in *construct state* + noun תרע + adjective ברי in *determined state*. The second set phrase only consists of the preposition + noun משחה in *absolute state*.

This set phrase differs qua form from the abovementioned first one and has undoubtedly the same meaning as the set phrase משחה חדה. This is confirmed by the following translations: Milik (1962, 191): "les mêmes dimensions"; Bernhardt (1970, 62): "dasselbe Maß"; *DSSU* (1992, 45): "each with dimensions corresponding"; García Martínez and Van der Woude (1995, 154): "heeft dezelfde afmetingen"; *DSSSE* (1998, 1109, 1141): "the same size"; *MPAT* (1978, 59): "with its measurement"; DiTommaso (2005, 44): "the same measurement"; and *DSSR* (2005, 49): "a like measurement."

The first set phrase has been read in the same way by Milik (1962, 190), Bernhardt (1970, 55), *MPAT* (1978, 59), Abegg (2003, 880), and *DSSR* (2005, 54). Despite the fact that the first sign is clearly a *kap*, because its roof and base have the same dimensions and the back is quite long, the set phrase is read differently by *DSSSE* (1998, 1108) and DiTommaso (2005, 43): במשחת. The second set phrase has been read במשחה by Beyer (2004, 131) and by DiTommaso (2005, 43). Notwithstanding the first sign being clearly a *bet* with a short back and a base that projects to the left beyond the roof, a number of scholars propose a different reading: *DSSU* (1992, 42): כמש{ח}ת, on the one hand, and Bernhardt (1970, 55), *DSSU* (1992, 42), *DSSSE* (1998, 1108), Abegg (2003, 880), and *DSSR* (2005, 48): כמשחת, on the other hand. The set phrase referred to is not constructed with any other element.

The corresponding phrases in Ezekiel are כמדת // כמשחת (Ezek 40:21, 22, 24, 28, 29, 32, 33, 35) and מדת חדה // משחה חדה (Ezek 40:10, 46: 22).

The use of three different set phrases on three consecutive lines to reproduce the same concept offers only one example of the style variation of the author of *New Jerusalem*. Other examples can be found in the different formulas reproducing the survey of the city wall and the mention of length and width of architectural parts.

4. The Shape of 5Q15 I

The manuscript 5Q15 preserves 80 fragments. 60 of them were grouped in two columns of fragment 1 by the editor, Milik (1962, XL–XLI). The join thus presented is supported by the combination of three criteria: (1) the reconstruction based on parallel passages in 2Q24 (not mentioned by Milik) and 4Q554; (2) the material form of the fragments concerned; and (3) the coherence as regards content. Concerning the lines 5Q15 i

1–7 (right half), the combined criteria aforementioned can be applied as shown hereafter[5] and confirm the reading by Milik (1962, 189):

(1) [סחור א]מין [תלת מאה ו]חמשין ושבע >ו<לכל [רו]ח ושבק סוחר סחור לפרזֹתא
ברית שוק [קנין תלתא א]מין עשרין

(2) [וחדא] וכדן [אחזיאני מ]שחת פר[זיא כלהן בין פרזא לפרזא שוק] פתה קנין
שת[א] אמין ארבעין ותרתין

(3) [ושקי]א רברביא [די] נפקין[ן] מן מדנח[א למערבא [קנין עשרא פות]י שקא אמי[ן]
שב[עין תרי]ן מנהון ותליתיא

(4) [די על שמא]ל מק[דשא משח] קנין תמנית עש[ר] פותי אמין מ[אה עשרי]ן [ו]שת
ופו[חתי שקיא] די בפקין מן דרומ[א]

(5) [לצפונא תר]ין מ[נהון] קנין ת[שעה] ואמין א[ר]ᵖע לשוק חד אמי[ן] שתין ושבע
[ו]מצ[יעא די במצ]יעת קרית

(6) [משח פותין]ה קנ[ין תל]תת עשר ואמה חדה לאמין תשע[ין] ותר[תין] וכל [שוקא
[וקריתא ר]צֹיפין באבן חור

(7) [ ] [ ]..[ ] .רנ[א]א ואן

(1) [around three hundred and] fifty-seven cubits. <And> on each side {and} a peristyle/open space <was> around the block. <This was> the portico/outer side of the street: [three ro]ds, twenty[-one] cubits. (2) And he also [showed me the mea]surement/mea]surements of the blo[cks of all of them.[6] Between one block and <another> block <there was> the street.] Her width <was> si[x] rods, forty-two cubits. (3) [And] the main streets, [which <were> runnin[g] from eas[t to west:] the widt[h of the street] [of tw]o of them is ten rods, seve[nty cubits.] And the third, (4) [which <was> on the lef]t/nort]h of the tem[ple: he measured]: eighteen rods width, one hundred and twenty six cubits. And the widt[h of the streets,] which <were> run[ning] from south (5) [to north: tw]o o[f them] <were> ni[ne] rods and fo[u]r cubits each one, sixty-seven cubits [and] the one in the mid[dle, which <was> in the center of the city: (6) [he measured] its [width]: [thi]rteen rod[s and a cubit, nine[ty]-two cubits. And every street and the whole city <were> pa]ved with white stone (7) [...]...[...]...[ ]...[...]...[ ]

Milik himself has certain reservations concerning three smaller fragments: the one with מין in the beginning of line 1, the one with שב and וֹפ at the end of the lines 3 and 4, and the one with קני at the beginning of line 5 (1962, 184–85; Bernhardt 1970, 18).

---

[5] Underlined: parallel passages (= //) in 4Q554 and/or in 2Q24: line 1 // 4Q554 1 ii 13–15 and 2Q24 1 2; line 2 // 4Q554 1 ii 15–16 and 2Q24 1 3–4 (2Q24 has apparently a slightly different wording in the use of כול); line 3 // 4Q554 1 ii 16–18; line 4 // 4Q554 1 ii 18–20; line 5 // 4Q554 1 ii 20–22; line 6 // 4Q554 1 ii 22–23.

[6] Reading according to 4Q554 1 ii 15. 2Q24 1 3: "And he showed me all the measurements (...)."

The reconstruction of the next lines, i.e. 5Q15 1 i 7 (left)–14, as proposed by Milik, is not supported by any parallel text. As reconstructed by Milik, these lines seem to refer to a coherent architectural description related to precious construction materials (5Q15 1 i 7), the number, the measurements and the doors of the posterns (5Q15 1 i 8–9), the measurements and the description of the main gates (5Q15 1 i 10–11), and the towers of these gates (5Q15 1 i 12–14). The contents of 5Q15 1 i 1–6/7 are: the exterior dimensions of the blocks (5Q15 1 i 1–2), the dimensions of the streets surrounding each one of the blocks (5Q15 1 i 1–2), the orientation and the dimensions of the six boulevards (5Q15 1 i 3–6), the location of the Temple with regard to the boulevards (5Q15 1 i 4), and finally construction materials, i.e. white stone, of the streets and the city (5Q15 1 i 6).

On the photographs none of the fragments containing the remains of the lines 7 (left half) and 8 are joined directly to the fragments containing the remains of the lines 6 and 7 (right half). PAM 42 320 does not show any of the fragments containing the lines 7 (left half)–14 at all. PAM 41.034 and PAM 42.323 do show some of the fragments concerned but all of them in an isolated position. Consequently, the entirety of fragments forming the lines 7 (left half)–14 according to Milik do not necessarily belong to column I due to of the lack of material grounds. The only reason to locate the fragments in question immediately following the lines 6 and 7 could be based on content. The laconic mention of two precious materials, albaster and onyx, is hard to locate. Does it refer to the preceding passage concerning construction materials which were used (white stone), or does it belong to the following description?

With regard to the location of 5Q15 1 i 7 (left half)–14, the following question has to be formulated: "Is a logical sequence respected by returning to the outer parts of the city wall, i.e. not only to the posterns but also to the main gates and their towers, after the tour was explicitly directed into the city itself?" In 4Q554 1 ii 12, it is stated clearly that the visitor was led into the city. What follows is the description of the general form of the blocks and the indirect representation of the grid-formed street pattern. There is no explicit mention that the tour is continued from the outside of the city. If the guide and the visitor inspect the posterns and the gates, is it logical they do so from the city centre onward?

The question with regards to content can only be solved either by external evidence or by deducing a form of logic from the text itself. External evidence can be produced by texts describing similar subjects.

Two other texts contain a systematic description of gates within a larger architectural scope: *The Temple Scroll* and Ezekiel. In both texts a temple complex embracing more than one court is described and not a city plan. Both have their own logic concerning the direction of the description. The first text gives a consistent description of the complex from the interior to its exterior. In Ezekiel the description evolves essentially in the opposite direction. The first gate described is the east gate of the outer court (Ezek 40:6–16). Its description is detailed and comprehensive. The two remaining gates of the outer court are described by referring to the shape and measurements of the east gate (Ezek 40:19–20). The orientation of the outer court as well as its general interior form and its measurements can be deduced from the location of its gates in the absolute spatial sense, on the one hand, and their location in relation to the gates of the inner court, on the other. The distance between the gates of the outer court and those of the inner point to the square form of the plan of the complex (Ezek 40:23). This is confirmed later in the text by the measurements of the exterior walls of the complex (Ezek 42:15–20). The first gate of the inner court described is the south one while entering the court from the outer court onward. If one accepts that the author of the Aramaic *New Jerusalem* text follows Ezekiel's model consistently and if one also accepts that the prophet's description of the temple complex can be applied to the city, the description of the city pattern has to be preceded by the description of its gates. Moreover, locating the description of the gate by which the guide and the visitor enter the city before they explicitly do so is in accordance with the logic of the tour in the Aramaic text. As shown elsewhere, the author of the latter text does not hesitate, however, to deviate from his model or to modify it. The logic presented by the Aramaic text itself is not contradicted by the immediate continuation of the description of the grid-pattern by means of the description of the gates and the posterns from the interior onward. The pattern concerned is formed by the six main arteries on a larger scale and the streets surrounding each block on a smaller scale. At least the twelve main gates themselves are directly connected two by two to the six main arteries. The direct spatial relationship of the posterns with the more refined aspects of the grid pattern is less evident and is still open to discussion.[7]

---

[7] Spatial relationship between the posterns and the number of blocks based on mathematical grounds was calculated by Starcky (1977,39): 480 × 3 (= 1440−8) = 1432 or 358 × 4. The numbers 480 and 1432 are partially restored. The first concerns the

As other fragments, which cannot be inserted in 5Q15 1 i, discuss structures in the walls (4Q554 2 ii), one must seriously consider not to necessarily integrate 1 i 7 (left half)–14 in the reconstruction of 4Q554 1 iii 1–11, as performed by DiTommaso (2005:43) but to consider the entirety of the joined fragments temporarily as a separate fragment by assigning it number 22. Discarding the entirety of fragments forming the lines 7 (left half)–14 according to Milik from col. i is possible as none of the fragments concerned are joined in the material way to fragments of the above line, as the photographs show.

The relation between 5Q15 1 i 14 and the fragments on the lower part of the column is even more difficult to establish. No material join nor any parallel passage, nor is any direct coherence with respect to content at hand. Because of the bottom margin preserved on one of the fragments containing the lines 15–19,[8] the fragments concerned have to be maintained at the bottom of the first column of 5Q15. Their mutual location in particular as well as their location regarding the general course of the text are both supported by parallel passages of manuscript 4Q554 1 iii 16–18, on the one hand, and the continuation of the text in 5Q15 ii, on the other. The continuation mentioned is sustained by parallel passages of 4Q554 1 iii 18–22 and 4Q554a ii 12.

Conclusion

As only a very small part of the Aramaic *New Jerusalem* text has been preserved, it raises a large number of problems. In the present article four problematical aspects have been discussed. The following conclusions have been drawn:

posterns, the second the towers on the city wall minus two towers on each of the four corners. Starcky's calculation was supported by García Martínez (1992,199) and Puech (1995,91–92). Recently it was rejected by DiTommaso (2005,60–61).

[8] According to the counting by Milik (1962,185): "De plus, la longueur d'une colonne du manuscrit 4Q n'est pas en faveur d'une colonne de 5Q15 qui dépasserait 19 lignes, autrement dit, qui exigerait l'addition d'une ou plusieurs lignes entre i 14 et 15." Bernhardt (1970,18): "Infolge der unterschiedlichen Längen der Kolumnen von 4Q und 5Q macht es sich nötig, zwischen Zeile 14 und 15 der ersten Kolumne noch eine oder mehrere, nicht näher erhaltene Zeilen an zu nehmen."

- The form of the eschatological city is undoubtedly rectangular. The temple is in its centre at the intersection of the two main arteries. The original square of Ezekiel survives in the relation between the length and the width of the rectangular city wall, i.e. 7:5.
- The readings 25 and 35 instead of the readings 24 and 34 as proposed by some authors are sustained by the way the numbers concerned are written in words, on the one hand, and the parallel figure signs in their three different shapes, on the other.
- The concept "of same size" can be produced by three different phrases: משחה חדה, כמשחת, and the unique במשחה.
- The material form of the fragments concerned and the coherence with respect to content do not point convincingly to the location of the passage 5Q15 i 7 (left half)–14 in the first column of fragment 1.

BIBLIOGRAPHY

Abegg, M.G., Jr. et al. 2003. Pages 773–946, 943–56 passim in *The Non-Biblical Texts from Qumran: Parts One and Two*. Vol. 1 of *The Dead Sea Scrolls Concordance*. Leiden: Brill.

Aune, D.E. 1999. Qumran and the Book of Revelation. Pages 622–48 in *The Dead Sea Scrolls after Fifty Years: A Comprehensive Assessment*. Edited by P.W. Flint and J.C. VanderKam. Leiden: Brill.

Baillet, M. 1955. Fragments araméens de Qumrân 2: Description de la Jérusalem Nouvelle. *Revue Biblique* 62:222–45, pls. ii–iii.

———. 1962. 24: Description de la Jérusalem Nouvelle. Pages 84–89, pl. XVI in *DJD* 3. Oxford: Clarendon Press.

Bernhardt, W. 1970. *Die kultur- und religionsgeschichtliche Bedeutung des Qumranfragments 5Q15*. Dissertation Jena.

Beyer, K. 1984. *Die aramäischen Texte vom Toten Meer*. Göttingen: Vandenhoeck & Ruprecht.

———. 1994. *Die aramäischen Texte vom Toten Meer: Ergänzungsband*. Göttingen: Vandenhoeck & Ruprecht.

———. 2004. *Die aramäischen Texte vom Toten Meer: Band 2*. Göttingen: Vandenhoeck & Ruprecht.

Broshi, M. 1995. Visionary Architecture and Town Planning in the Dead Sea Scrolls. Pages 9–22 in *Time to Prepare the Way in the Wilderness: Papers on the Qumran Scrolls*. Edited by D. Dimant and L.H. Schiffman. Studies on the Texts of the Desert of Judah 16. Leiden: Brill.

Chantraine, H. 1969. Limitation. *KlPauly* 3:666–67.

Chyutin, M. 1997. *The New Jerusalem Scroll from Qumran: A Comprehensive Reconstruction*. Journal for the Study of the Pseudepigrapha Supplement Series 25. Sheffield: Sheffield Academic Press.

Collins, J.J. 1979. *Apocalypse: The Morphology of a Genre*. Semeia 14. Chico, California: Society of Biblical Literature.

———. 1992. *Apocalypticism in the Dead Sea Scrolls*. London: Routledge.

Cook, E. 1996. The Vision of New Jerusalem. Pages 181–84 in *The Dead Sea Scrolls: A Translation*. Edited by M.O. Wise et al. San Francisco: HarperSanFrancisco.

DiTommaso, L. 2005. *The Dead Sea New Jerusalem Text: Contents and Contexts*. Texts and Studies in Ancient Judaism 110. Tübingen: Mohr Siebeck.

DJD: Discoveries in the Judaean Desert. Oxford: Clarendon Press.
DSSR: Parry, D.W. and E. Tov, with the assistance of N. Gordon. 2005. *The Dead Sea Scrolls Reader: Part 6: Additional Genres and Unclassified Texts.* Leiden: Brill.
DSSSE: García Martínez, F. and E.J.C. Tigchelaar. 1998. *The Dead Sea Scrolls Study Edition.* Leiden: Brill.
DSSU: Eisenman, R. and M. Wise. 1992. The New Jerusalem (4Q554). Pages 39–46 in *The Dead Sea Scrolls Uncovered.* Shaftesbury, Dorset: Penguin.
Frey, J. 2000. The *New Jerusalem Text* in Its Historical and Traditio-Historical Context. Pages 800–16 in *The Dead Sea Scrolls Fifty Years after their Discovery: Proceedings of the Jerusalem Congress, July 1997.* Edited by L.H. Schiffman, E. Tov, and J.C. VanderKam. Jerusalem: Israel Exploration Society in cooperation with the Shrine of the Book, Israel Museum.
García Martínez, F. 1987. Les Traditions Apocalyptiques à Qumrân. Pages 201–35 in *Apocalypses et voyages dans l'au-delà.* Edited by C. Kappler. Paris: Le Cerf.
———. 1988. L'interprétation de la Torah d'Ézéchiel dans les MSS. de Qumrân. *Revue de Qumran* 13/49–52:441–52.
———. 1992. The "New Jerusalem" and the Future Temple of the Manuscripts from Qumran. Pages 180–213 in *Qumran and Apocalyptic: Studies on the Aramaic Texts from Qumran.* Studies on the Texts from the Desert of Judah 9. Leiden: Brill.
———. 1994. *The Dead Sea Scrolls Translated: The Qumran Texts in English.* Leiden: Brill.
———. 1999. The Temple Scroll and the New Jerusalem. Pages 431–60 in *The Dead Sea Scrolls after Fifty Years: A Comprehensive Assessment.* Edited by P.W. Flint and J.C. VanderKam. Leiden: Brill.
———. 2003. Apocalypticism in the Dead Sea Scrolls. Pages 89–111 in *The Continuum of Apocalypticism.* Edited by B. McGinn et al. New York: Continuum International Publishing Group.
García Martínez, F. and A.S. van der Woude. 1995. *De rollen van de Dode Zee: Ingeleid en in het Nederlands vertaald.* Kampen: Kok.
García Martínez, F. et al. 1998. 18: 11QNew Jerusalem ar. Pages 305–55, pls. XXXV–XL and LIII in *DJD* 23. Oxford: Clarendon Press.
Lee, P. 2001. *The New Jerusalem in the Book of Revelation: A Study of Revelation 21–22 in the Light of its Background in Jewish Tradition.* Wissenschaftliche Untersuchungen zum Neuen Testament 2. Tübingen: Mohr Siebeck.
Licht, J. 1979. An Ideal Town Plan from Qumran:The Description of the New Jerusalem. *Israel Exploration Journal* 29:45–59.
Maier, J. 1995. *Die Qumran-Essener: Die Texte vom Toten Meer: Band I: Die Texte der Höhlen 1–3 und 5–11.* UTB 1862. München: Ernst Reinhardt.
———. 1997. *Die Tempelrolle vom Toten Meer und das »Neue Jerusalem«: 11Q19 und 11Q20; 1Q32, 2Q24, 4Q554–555, 5Q15 und 11Q18: Übersetzung und Erläuterung: Mit Grundrissen der Tempelhofanlage und Skizzen zur Stadtplanung.* UTB 829. München: Ernst Reinhardt.
Milik, J.T. 1955. Description de la Jérusalem Nouvelle (?). Pages 134–35, pl. XXXI in *DJD* 1. Oxford: Clarendon Press.
———. 1962. 15: Description de la Jérusalem Nouvelle. Pages 184–93, pls. XL–XLI in *DJD* 3. Oxford: Clarendon Press.
MPAT: Fitzmyer, J.A. and D.J. Harrington. 1978. *A Manual of Palestinian Aramaic Texts (Second Century B.C.–Second Century A.D.).* Biblica et Orientalia 34. Rome: Biblical Institute Press.
Puech, É. 1995. À propos de la Jérusalem Nouvelle d'après les manuscrits de la mer Morte. *Semitica* 43–44:87–102.
———. 2003. The Names of the Gates of the *New Jerusalem* (4Q554). Pages 379–92 in *Emanuel: Studies in Hebrew Bible, Septuagint and Dead Sea Scrolls in Honor of Emanuel Tov.* Edited by S.M. Paul, R.A. Kraft, L.H. Schiffman, and W.W. Fields. Supplements to Vetus Testamentum 94. Leiden: Brill.

Starcky, J. 1977. Jérusalem et les manuscrits de la Mer Morte. *Le Monde de la Bible* 1:38–40.
VanderKam, J.C. and P.W. Flint. 2002. *The Meaning of the Dead Sea Scrolls: Their Significance for Understanding the Bible, Judaism, Jesus, and Christianity.* San Francisco: HarperCollins.

THE IMAGINAL CONTEXT AND THE VISIONARY OF THE ARAMAIC *NEW JERUSALEM**

Eibert Tigchelaar

The preserved fragments of the Aramaic *New Jerusalem* (*NJ*) show that it was written in accordance with the model of Ezek 40–48, in which a visionary reports of a guided tour through a city and its temple; the text gives architectural details, including the measurements of walls, gates, houses and even rooms and windows; the seer reports of the rituals he witnessed in the temple, and of the words the guide spoke to him. In view of the correspondences with Ezek 40–48 and other texts adhering to this model, the guide may be identified as an angel, and the city as a New Jerusalem. The identity of the seer, however, remains unclear, especially since the beginning of the text, which may have identified him, has not been preserved.

No scholar has published so much on *NJ* as Florentino García Martínez. The publication of the Cave 11 *NJ* fragments (11Q18) was entrusted to him,[1] and he has provided several critical surveys of scholarship of *NJ*, that remain, up to the present day, the most thorough

---

* This essay is an elaboration of one part of a lecture I gave in March 2007 at the joint Nijmegen-Louvain conference on the otherworld, which was co-organized by Florentino García Martínez. More essays on *NJ* and the Qumran Aramaic texts are planned. This contribution is in honour of Florentino who has introduced me, both academically and socially, into the field of Dead Sea Scrolls studies, and whose collegiality and friendship have surrounded me the past twelve years. I want to thank Matthew Goff and Hindy Najman for their very valuable suggestions with regard to this paper.

[1] Initially, the KNAW, which had acquired the rights of most of the Cave 11 fragments, entrusted the publication of the Cave 11 texts to A.S. van der Woude (Groningen) and J.P.M. van der Ploeg (Nijmegen). One fragment, overlapping with 2Q24 frag. 4, was published by B. Jongeling, "Publication provisoire d'un fragment provenant de la grotte 11 de Qumrân (11Q Jér Nouv ar)," *JSJ* 1 (1970): 58–64 (with an additional note ibid., 185–86). Eventually, publication of the fragments was entrusted to Florentino who published two preliminary editions of fragments, "The Last Surviving Columns of *11QNJ*," in *The Scriptures and the Scrolls: Studies in Honour of A.S. van der Woude on the Occasion of his 65th Birthday* (ed. F. García Martínez et al.; VTSup 49; Leiden: Brill, 1992), 178–92, Pls. 3–9; and "More Fragments of 11QNJ," in *The Provo International Conference on the Dead Sea Scrolls: New Texts, Reformulated Issues, and Technological Innovations* (ed. D.W. Parry and E. Ulrich; STDJ 30; Leiden: Brill, 1999), 186–98. The official edition was published in *DJD* 23:305–55, Pls. 35–45.

and comprehensive introductions to the text.[2] Yet, in all his research on *NJ* he has not dealt with the question of the identity of its seer, an aspect that most scholars seem to consider inconsequential to the understanding of the text. One may argue that since the preserved text does not clearly divulge the identity of the seer, any speculation would in the end be inconclusive, and never reach beyond degrees of possibility or plausibility. In this contribution in honor of Florentino, I would nonetheless like to initiate this search, for two different reasons. The first is to assess all the textual and contextual clues that might shed light on the identity of the seer. Secondly, however, there lies a more important issue behind this query, namely whether the identity of the seer in a visionary or apocalyptic text is tangential, or essential to the imaginal world of the author(s) of the text. In this paper, therefore, different enterprises are intertwined. Florentino's caution in not pursuing the essentially literary-historical, and ultimately unanswerable, question about the identity of the implied author (the seer) of *NJ*, should be regarded as correct. Instead, however, I suggest to transform that question, and to examine the interpretive context for the seer in *NJ*. To what extent can we re-imagine the imaginal world lying behind the text?[3]

---

[2] Seminal was "La 'nueva Jerusalén' y el Templo futuro en los MSS de Qumrán," in *Salvación en la Palabra: Targum—Derash—Berith: en memoria del profesor Alejandro Díez Macho* (ed. D. Muñoz León; Madrid: Cristiandad, 1986), 563–90, a critical survey of existing scholarship with new solutions for major problems; this survey was revised as "The «New Jerusalem» and the Future Temple of the Manuscripts from Qumran," in *Qumran and Apocalyptic: Studies on the Aramaic Texts from Qumran* (STDJ 9; Leiden: Brill, 1992), 180–213. His contributions to the two major comprehensive works of Dead Sea Scrolls scholarship could also incorporate all the Cave 4 and Cave 11 *NJ* materials: "The Temple Scroll and the New Jerusalem," in *The Dead Sea Scrolls after Fifty Years: A Comprehensive Assessment* (ed. P.W. Flint and J.C. VanderKam; 2 vols.; Leiden: Brill, 1999), 2:431–60 (445–60); and "New Jerusalem," in *Encyclopedia of the Dead Sea Scrolls* (ed. L.H. Schiffman and J.C. VanderKam; New York: Oxford University Press: 2000), 2:606–10. Some other publications by Florentino discussing the *New Jerusalem* are "L'interprétation de la Torah d'Ézéchiel dans les MSS. de Qumrân," *RevQ* 13/49–52 (1988): 441–52, translated as "The Interpretation of the Torah of Ezekiel in the Texts from Qumran," in *Qumranica Minora II: Thematic Studies on the Dead Sea Scrolls* (STDJ 64; Leiden: Brill, 2007), 1–12; "Il Rotolo del Tempio e la Nuova Gerusalemme: quanti esemplari possediamo?," *Henoch* 21 (1999): 253–83 (279–83).

[3] I am using the term "imaginal world" inspired by Henry Corbin, but not in the full technical sense as developed in his *Creative Imagination in the Sūfism of Ibn 'Arabi* (Princeton; Princeton University Press, 1969), translated from the 1958 French edition.

1. Suggestions for the Identity of the Seer

From the very beginning the correspondences between *NJ* and Ezek 40–48 were clear, but Maurice Baillet pointed out that formulas such as חזי הוית עד די, "and while I was watching," also linked the text to the literary tradition attested by Dan 7.[4] It is mainly on the basis of the correspondences of both form and content, and in view of the many rewritings of biblical books, that some scholars have nevertheless, more or less tentatively, considered the possibility that the seer of this text was Ezekiel. A different kind of possible textual clue became known in 1993 when Émile Puech published 4Q554 3 iii.[5] The contents of this column had already been briefly described by Jean Starcky, who stated that it mentioned the final war in which the Kittim and Babel were involved, but also Edom, Moab and the Ammonites.[6] The publication of the text, however, showed that the column mentions the war as part of an angelic speech to the seer. The clause ויבאשון זרעך, which Puech translated without further comments as "et ils feront mal à ta race," is important for the identification of the seer. Klaus Beyer explicitly took זרעך to refer literally to the descendants of the seer, implying that the seer would be an ancestor of either entire Israel or of the priests.[7] In yet another publication, Puech referred to a different kind of literary evidence, namely later traditions as referred to in *2 Bar.* 4:5–6 (God showed the New Jerusalem to Moses on Mount Sinai), and asked whether *NJ* might attest to the antiquity of that tradition.[8] Jörg Frey followed Beyer's lead, but considered an ancestor of entire Israel more likely than an ancestor of the priests only.[9]

---

[4] M. Baillet, "Fragments araméens de Qumrân 2: Description de la Jérusalem Nouvelle," *RB* 62 (1955): 222–45, pls. ii–iii (244).

[5] É. Puech, *La croyance des Esséniens en la vie future: Immortalité, résurrection, vie éternelle? II: Les données qumrâniennes at classiques* (EB 22; Paris: Gabalda, 1993), 593–95.

[6] J. Starcky, "Jérusalem et les manuscrits de la Mer Morte," *Le Monde de la Bible* 1 (1977): 38–40 (39)

[7] K. Beyer, *Die aramäischen Texte vom Toten Meer: Ergänzungsband* (Göttingen: Vandenhoeck & Ruprecht, 1994), 95; idem, *Die aramäischen Texte vom Toten Meer: Band 2* (Göttingen: Vandenhoeck & Ruprecht, 2004), 129.

[8] É. Puech, "À propos de la Jérusalem Nouvelle d'après les manuscrits de la mer Morte," *Semitica* 43–44 (1995): 87–102 (92 n. 15). Cf., however, H. Jacobson, *A Commentary on Pseudo-Philo's* Liber Antiquitatum Biblicarum *with Latin Text and English Translation* (2 vols.; AGJU 31; Leiden: Brill, 1996), 1:480: "2Baruch 4.5 is not helpful, since the latter passage says nothing more than what the Bible tells us."

[9] J. Frey, "The New Jerusalem Text in Its Historical and Traditio-Historical Context," in *The Dead Sea Scrolls Fifty Years after their Discovery* (ed. L.H. Schiffman et al.; Jerusalem: IES, 2000), 800–16 (804).

In sum, whereas most scholars, including Florentino, have refrained from an identification, the following four suggestions have been made with different degrees of hesitation: (1) "probably the prophet Ezekiel himself,"[10] (2) "Jacob? Levi? Qahat? Amram?"[11] (3) "probably one of the ancestors of Israel,"[12] (4) perhaps Moses?[13] The issue is not whether any of these suggestions would be unlikely or plausible on a literary-historical plane, but whether the query concerning the identity of the seer may help us to explore the imaginal world of the authors.

We may start off with the basic observation that even though the name of the visionary has not been preserved, it is virtually certain that he was indeed associated with a "biblical" figure. Visions, dreams, and apocalyptic revelations in literary garb are typically attributed to founding figures of the past, such as Enoch, Noah, Moses, Jeremiah, Ezra, etc.[14] In view of the other literature from the period, it is less likely that the seer would have been an anonymous figure, or someone from the present.[15]

The phrase ויבאשון זרעך, "and they will do evil to your seed," is found after a series of lines mentioning kingdoms, Kittim, Edom, Moab and Ammon, and the land of Babylon, and before two lines that refer to "(all) nations." Two things are of interest: the text does not refer to "Israel," or "your people," but by using the term "your seed" refers in all likelihood to descendants of the addressee. For that reason, it is unlikely that the seer is either Ezekiel, or even Moses. Second, as mentioned by Frey, the contrast with the nations suggests that "your

---

[10] A. Lange, *DJD* 39:126 n. 9. Similarly, D. Dimant, "Apocalyptic Texts at Qumran," in *The Community of the Renewed Covenant: The Notre Dame Symposium on the Dead Sea Scrolls* (ed. E. Ulrich and J.C. VanderKam; CJAS 10; Notre Dame, Ind: University of Notre Dame Press, 1994), 175–91 (183) "Ezekiel himself or someone going through a similar experience." For more references and brief discussion see L. DiTommaso, *The Dead Sea New Jerusalem Text: Contents and Contexts* (TSAJ 110; Tübingen: Mohr Siebeck, 2005), 112.

[11] Beyer, *Ergänzungsband*, 98; *Band 2*, 132.

[12] Frey, "Traditio-Historical Context," 804.

[13] Puech, "À propos de la Jérusalem Nouvelle," 92 n 15.

[14] For the idea of Second Temple discourses linked to founders, cf. H. Najman, *Seconding Sinai. The Development of Mosaic Discourse in Second Temple Judaism* (JSJSup 77; Leiden: Brill, 2003), 12–19.

[15] A problematic case are the canonical and non-canonical texts attributed to Daniel. Even though there is evidence that Daniel (*Dn'il*) was a legendary figure, known from Ugaritic literature, and alluded to in Ezekiel, it remains unclear why he became the protagonist of the Daniel literature. And then, early Christian apocalypses and visions testify to the phenomenon that new figures (e.g. Peter) can turn into founding figures.

seed' is here also the nation, not a specific part of Israel, such as the priesthood.[16] That would make it less likely that for example Levi, Qahat or Amram was the seer.

A consideration that has—to the best of my knowledge—hitherto not been voiced explicitly, is that the Aramaic texts from Qumran only comprise special categories. The vast majority of the Aramaic narrative texts found amongst the Dead Sea Scrolls belong to two main categories, namely (1) texts related or ascribed to pre-Mosaic figures (Enoch, Noah?, Abraham, Jacob, Judah?, Levi, Qahat, Amram), or (2) narratives that have an Eastern Diaspora setting (Tobit, proto-Esther, Nabonidus, Daniel).[17] Only a few Aramaic narrative texts do not fit neatly in either of those two categories, but it is remarkable that none of the biblical figures from Moses onwards, through David, and up to the prophets, is connected with Aramaic literature. The exception is Daniel, who is associated with the Eastern diaspora. If we take this feature of Aramaic texts seriously, we should regard it highly unlikely that the seer would have been either Moses or Ezekiel. The statistics, however, show that if a text has a first person narrative of a pre-Mosaic figure, the language would in all likelihood have been Aramaic, and not Hebrew.[18] In short, on the basis of these considerations, it would be most likely if one of the forefathers of Israel, such as Abraham, Isaac, or Jacob would have been the seer of the text. Further considerations should be based on possible clues in (1) *NJ*, (2) other Aramaic texts found at Qumran, (3) the Qumran library at large, as well as (4) other Second Temple and Jewish texts.

(1) *NJ* itself does not give any clear evidence in favour of any of those forefathers. One might argue that the names of the gates,[19] named after

---

[16] Both in Isaac's blessing of Levi (*Jub.* 31:15–17) and in his blessing of Judah (*Jub.* 31:18–20) there is an opposition between their descendants and the nations, but there the references to the nations are quite general.

[17] For a somewhat different categorization, cf. D. Dimant, "The Qumran Aramaic Texts and the Qumran Community," in this volume.

[18] *4QTestament of Naphtali* (4Q215) is the one exception of a first person narrative of a pre-Mosaic figure written in Hebrew. A. Lange's classification of Parabiblical texts related to biblical figures and books in *DJD* 39:121–29 confirms this tendency. 1Q19 (1QNoah), written in Hebrew, does not seem to be a first person narrative. The two texts referred to as *Testament of Judah* are extremely fragmentary, but preserve names of sons of Jacob (in 3Q7 only Levi is certain; in 4Q484 we find Issachar). It is not certain that these reflect a *Testament of Judah*, nor that they are first person texts, and it is even unclear in which language 4Q484 was written.

[19] On the names of the gates, cf. É. Puech, "The Names of the Gates of the *New Jerusalem* (4Q554)," in *Emanuel: Studies in Hebrew Bible, Septuagint and Dead Sea Scrolls in*

the twelve sons of Jacob, would fit nicely if the seer were Jacob, but then, Ezek 48:30–35 and the Temple Scroll (11QTᵃ XXXIX 11–XLI 11; cf. also 4Q365 2 ii 1–4), as well as Rev 21:12 (twelve tribes), show that this was a tradition that was not as such dependent on the identity of the seer. Likewise, one may argue that if Edom (in the enumeration "Edom, Moab, and the Ammonites") is contrasted to "your seed," it would be more likely that Jacob were the ancestor, since Edom (as descendants of Esau) would—strictly speaking—belong to the seed of Abraham and Isaac. However, Edom is only one of several items of a list, and it may stretch the evidence too far to argue that the author wanted to contrast Edom to "your seed."

(2) The other Aramaic texts found at Qumran exhibit little interest for the temple as such, let alone a New Jerusalem. An exception is Tob 13:9–18, which in part has been preserved in 4Q196 17 ii and 18. The *Aramaic Levi Document* (*ALD*) displays a large concern with priesthood and ritual, but not at all with a future city or temple.[20] In *ALD* the teachings of the priesthood are preceded by a vision (*ALD* 4), but there again there is no interest in city or temple. The same also goes for the *Testament of Levi*, in its present form a Christian work based on the *ALD*, which recounts two visions, in *T. Levi* 5 and 7. The first vision recounts that Levi saw the holy temple and the Most High upon a throne of glory (*T. Levi* 5:1), but the aim of the vision, which is clearly reworked, is to commission Levi, not to show him the Temple. In *T. Levi* 7 seven angels install Levi as a priest. In short: the Levi traditions, as preserved in *ALD* and in the *Testament of Levi*, have interest in priesthood and ritual, but not in city or Temple.[21] Likewise, visions of the city or the temple, or even concern with the temple, are not attested in the preserved fragments of the *Testament of Qahat* (4Q542) or the *Visions of 'Amram* (4Q543–549). This may of course be due to the fragmentary

---

Honor of Emanuel Tov (ed. S.M. Paul et al.; VTSup 94; Leiden: Brill, 2003), 379–92 who argues that *New Jerusalem* has the same provenance as Aramaic compositions such as the *Testament of Levi*, the *Testament of Qahat*, the *Visions of 'Amram*, etc. (391–92).

[20] Cf. *ALD* 5–10, according to the chapter division in the edition of J.C. Greenfield, M.E. Stone, and E. Eshel, *The Aramaic Levi Document. Edition, Translation, Commentary* (SVTP 19; Leiden: Brill, 2004).

[21] For an explanation of the function of the two visions, cf. J.L. Kugel, *The Ladder of Jacob: Ancient Interpretations of the Biblical Story of Jacob and His Children* (Princeton: Princeton University Press, 2006), 141–50. Though there are few cases where Kugel's book has directly and concretely influenced this paper, his subtle work of re-creating the imaginal world behind the Jacob and Levi traditions on the basis of Second Temple and rabbinic literature has been a source of inspiration.

state of those compositions, especially of the *Testament of Qahat*, but the topics of the sections that we do know (choosing between good and evil; keeping purity in the priestly line) do not make it very likely that there would have been references to such visions.

In the other Aramaic manuscripts ascribed to the patriarchs, there is only one fragment that may be pertinent to the inquiry as to whether one of the patriarchs had visions of the temple, namely 4Q537 12. This fragment, which was first referred to by Milik,[22] reads

> [1] [...] and how [its] construction[23] should be [...and how] their [priests] would be dressed and [their hands] purified [2] [and how they were] to offer sacrifices on the altar and ho[w each da]y [in] the [ent]ire [la]nd they would eat some of their sacrifices, [3] [and how they would drink(?) the water] that would exit the city and from underneath its walls, and where [much water] would be [shed] [4] [...] *Blank* [5] [...] before me a land of two quarters(?) and a l[and.

The fragment is part of a manuscript (4Q537) of which only a few fragments are of any substance, and the interpretation of both the text of the fragments and of the composition as a whole, is not entirely certain. Milik observed that 4Q537 1 + 2 + 3 corresponds closely to *Jub.* 32:21–22, therefore concluded that the first person in this text was Jacob, and called the text *Visions of Jacob*. Puech concurs with the assignment of the text to Jacob, but characterizes the composition as a testament, including both visions, and parenetical and eschatological materials.

This fragment refers to future priestly sacrifices in a city, but it is not clear from the preserved text whether Jacob saw this in a vision, read this on the tablets that were given to him (according to 4Q537 1 + 2 + 3 and *Jub.* 32:21–22), or was told by an angel. However, it may be of interest that virtually all the preserved elements in this fragments are found in *NJ*. The בנין or "construction" in line 1 is probably a building or wall in the temple complex,[24] as in 11Q18 9 4–5; the

---

[22] J.T. Milik, "Écrits préesséniens de Qumrân: d'Hénoch à Amram," in *Qumrân: Sa piété, sa théologie et son milieu* (ed. M. Delcor; BETL 46; Leuven: University Press, 1978), 91–106 (104). Published first by É. Puech, "Fragments d'un apocryphe de Lévi et le personnage eschatologique 4QTestLévi^c–d^(?) et 4QAJa," in *The Madrid Qumran Congress: Proceedings of the International Congress on the Dead Sea Scrolls—Madrid, 18–21 March 1991* (ed. J. Trebolle Barrera and L. Vegas Montaner; STDJ 11/2; Leiden: Brill, 1992), 449–501 (495–96); official publication, differing in some details, É. Puech, *DJD* 31:181–82. For easy access to the text and an English translation, cf. *DSSR* 3:404–5.

[23] Or, in stead of "[its] construction," perhaps "[the] building."

[24] A בנין could be any kind of building, but in the Hebrew Bible it is only used in relation to constructions on the temple compound (Ezek 40:5; 41:12, 15; 42:1, 5, 10;

preserved parts of *NJ* do not describe ordinary priestly attire, but that
of the high-priest (11Q18 14 ii; 16 i); 11Q18 deals extensively with
the bringing of sacrifices to the altar (11Q18 13) and with the eating
of the flesh of sacrifices and drinking (11Q18 25); finally the water of
4Q537 12 3 ("water" is reconstructed!) may be found in 11Q18 10 i,
though it is impossible to say whether this is the same water.[25] These
correspondences do not indicate that *NJ* and 4Q537 are dependent,
since different texts describing rituals in the Temple would plausibly use
the same vocabulary. Yet, those are the only two Aramaic compositions
from Qumran that describe rituals and sacrifices in relation to specific
architectural features of the temple, and 4Q537 12 shows that there
existed a tradition that details of the temple and its ritual had been
revealed in some way to Jacob.

(3) According to *Jub.* 32, Jacob had a vision at night when he went
back to Bethel (cf. Gen 35). First the Lord appeared to him, and later
an angel descended from heaven with seven tablets in his hands.[26]

> And he [the angel] gave them to Jacob and he read and knew what was
> written in them and what would happen to him and his sons in all ages.
> [22] And he showed him what was written in the tablets, and he said to him:
> [23] Do not build this place and do not make it an eternal sanctuary, and
> do not dwell in this place, because this will not be the place... [24] ...do
> not fear; because whatever you have seen and read, thus will all things
> written altogether come to pass.

The section from *Jubilees* is dense, and may combine several traditions.
First, we may note that there are two appearances, the first by God
in the night (*Jub.* 32:17–20; cf. Gen 35:9–13), then, apparently immediately following, in a vision in the same night, by the angel with the
seven tablets. In the first appearance, in terms that are on the whole
identical in Gen 35:9–13 and *Jub.* 32:17–20, God announces that

---

Ezra 5:4). The term could also refer to the temple-complex as a whole (cf. *2 Bar.* 4:3
benyānā). In his commentary in *DJD* 31:182, Puech does not dwell on the building, apart
from referring to the "sanctuaire central de Jérusalem." However, in his comments on
4Q540 1 5 (*DJD* 31:221–22) he refers to 4Q537 12 1 as an example of a text dealing
with the reconstruction of the *destroyed temple*.

[25] One might continue listing idiomatic correspondences. For example, both "city"
and "wall" are also found in the *NJ* texts.

[26] On the heavenly tablets in *Jubilees*, cf. F. García Martínez, "The Heavenly Tablets
in the Book of Jubilees," in *Studies in the Book of Jubilees* (ed. M. Albani et al.; TSAJ 65;
Tübingen: Mohr Siebeck, 1997), 243–60. Though the seven tablets could also be considered to be heavenly tablets (p. 250), they are not called heavenly here, and their function
in the narrative is different from the references to heavenly tablets in *Jubilees*.

Jacob will be called Israel, will multiply, kings shall come forth from him, who will rule over the nations, and his seed will inherit al the land/earth. The second vision with the angels and the tablets seems to elaborate on the history: Jacob reads everything that would happen to him and his sons during all ages (*Jub.* 32:21). However, the text returns to a motif that was mentioned in *Jub.* 32:16 ("Jacob planned to build up that place and to build a wall around the court, and to sanctify it, and to make it eternally holy for himself and his sons after him"). In *Jub.* 32:22 the angel with the tablets shows Jacob what was written on the tablets and tells him not to build that place, and not to turn it into a sanctuary, because it is not the place. First one may note that the text refers repeatedly to Jacob reading the tablets, but also to the angel showing him what was written on the tablets.[27] Second, the explicit mention of reading the tablets is related to future history,[28] but the vision which the angel shows him is followed by the prohibition to build the sanctuary. Even though *Jubilees* emphasizes that he saw what was written, perhaps implying that the visions strengthen the written revelation, it would seem to me plausible that we have here two different traditions: Jacob reading Israel's history throughout all ages, and Jacob's vision of a temple, apparently underlying the commandment not to build a sanctuary at Bethel.

But which temple could Jacob have seen, and how does that relate to the history of Israel, and the commandment not to build at Bethel? In the light of the end of *Jubilees* (chs. 49–50) the contrast would be that Jacob would know from the history of Israel that the sanctuary would be built not at "this place" (Bethel), but at a different place (Jerusalem).[29] Within the broader context of the Qumran library, it may mean still something else, namely that Jacob should not build a sanctuary at Bethel, since he had seen the eschatological temple.

Mention of an eschatological temple is found in several texts, including the so-called *Eschatological Midrash* (4Q174 + 4Q177), but of most interest here is the much discussed section of the *Temple Scroll*, 11QT^a XXIX 8–10.

---

[27] *Jub.* 32:21 (the angel gives tablets, which Jacob *reads*), 22 (the angel *shows* Jacob what was written on the tablets), 24 ("as you have *seen* and *read*"), 25 ("seen and read"; "read and saw"), 26 ("read and seen"; "read and seen").

[28] *Jub.* 32:21 "what would happen to him and his sons during all ages."

[29] There is an explicit reference to the sanctuary in Jerusalem in *Jub.* 1:28–29, but note that the reference is not to the first or second temple, but to the eschatological temple in the time after the renewal of the earth.

> And I will dwell [8] with them for ever and ever, and I will sanctify my sanctuary with my glory, which I will cause to dwell [9] upon it, until the day of the blessing/creation when I shall create my sanctuary [10] to establish it forever for me, according to the covenant which I made with Jacob at Bethel

Florentino has referred to this passage repeatedly in his publications, discussing the reading of the uncertain word (יום הבריה or יום הברכה), the identity of the eschatological temple, and the motif of a second creation.[30] Other scholars have wondered what the covenant with Jacob at Bethel has to do with this new temple.[31] Yadin already referred to a correspondence with *Jub.* 32,[32] but the exact relation has remained unclear. Admittedly, all our texts are fragmentary, but on the basis of a connection of 4Q537, *Jub.* 32, 11QT^a XXIX 8–10 and the *NJ*, one might make a case for a renewal of the covenant with Jacob at Bethel, followed by the reading of the tablets and plausibly a vision of the eschatological temple.[33]

(4) Other Second Temple or rabbinic texts do not hail Jacob as the visionary of the eschatological Temple. Most of the traditions of Jacob as a visionary are based on Gen 28, and elaborate on the ladder and on the angels going up and down.[34] Some later midrashic explanations interpreted the angels as guardian angels of other nations, and the ladder, as Kugel calls it, the "staircase of history." Jacob sees his descendants' future according to different stages of history. Two things may be noted here: the contents of the non-biblical second vision with the tablets of *Jub.* 32 have been ascribed in later literature to the first (biblical) dream vision at Bethel of Gen 28. Second, the eschatological description of history, as described in 4Q554 3 iii, neatly fits those later

---

[30] For example in Florentino García Martínez, *Qumranica Minora II. Thematic Studies on the Dead Sea Scrolls* (STDJ 64; Leiden: Brill), 11, 61, 234–35.

[31] M.O. Wise, "The Covenant of the Temple Scroll XXIX, 3–10," *RevQ* 14/53 (1989): 49–61 denies a specific connection between Jacob and a future temple. He suggests that the text continued on the next column with references to covenants made with Isaac and Abraham, and argues that the covenant was not per se related to a temple, but concerned God's presence. For this argumentation, Wise underemphasizes the terminology that refers explicitly to a sanctuary.

[32] Y. Yadin, *The Temple Scroll: II. Text and Commentary* (Jerusalem: IES, 1983), 129.

[33] Perhaps the composition *4QNarrative and Poetic Composition* (4Q371–373 and 4Q373a) should be taken with those other texts. 4Q372 3 9 refers to [a covenant] "which he cut with Jacob to be with him for ever and ever." The immediate context would suggest that the implication is deliverance from enemies.

[34] Cf. Kugel, *The Ladder of Jacob*, ch. 2 ("The Ladder of Jacob").

descriptions of Jacob's visions.[35] In other words, the later midrashic narratives about Jacob's vision are in part the result of exegesis of the biblical text,[36] and in part the transformations of earlier traditions.

An earlier, intriguing passage is Wis 10:10 which tells that Wisdom showed Jacob (the reference is to the righteous man who fled from his brother's wrath, and like the other figures in Wis 10 his name is not mentioned) the kingdom of God (βασιλείαν θεοῦ) and knowledge of holy things (γνῶσιν ἁγίων). It is not certain, however, whether the "kingdom" of God is meant here to refer to the heavenly realm (in which case an ascent may be implied), to the eschatological kingdom (suggesting a revelatory vision), or as a metaphor for God's law given to Israel.[37] Likewise, the "holy things" (or "holy ones"!) could be interpreted differently. In view of the correspondence with Agur's oracle in Prov 30:1–4 (vs. 3 LXX θεὸς δεδίδαχέν με σοφίαν καὶ γνῶσιν ἁγίων ἔγνωκα)[38] one might argue that knowledge of holy things is related to heavenly ascent (LXX vs. 4 τίς ἀνέβη εἰς τὸν οὐρανὸν καὶ κατέβη), in which case Wis 10:10 may refer to Jacob's visions of the New Jerusalem and New Temple with its rituals.[39]

Explicit references to Jacob as a visionary of the eschatological city or temple are scarce, however. VanderKam, in a discussion of 11QTᵃ XXIX 9–10, refers to *Gen. Rab.* 69.7 which discusses Gen 28:17, and tells that Jacob had seen the sanctuary built, destroyed and rebuilt, the

---

[35] DiTommaso, *The Dead Sea* New Jerusalem *Text*, 170–76, suggests that 4Q554 3 iii (in his numbering 2 iii) contains a four-kingdom schema. This is problematic, but it would go well with similar periodizations being part of Jacob's vision in later literature.

[36] Cf. especially Kugel, *The Ladder of Jacob*, who argues that the motifs in these narratives were created on the basis of details of the biblical text.

[37] For Second Temple references describing God giving his laws to Jacob = Israel, cf. Kugel, *The Ladder of Jacob*, ch. 7.

[38] A. Rofé, "Revealed Wisdom from the Bible to Qumran," in *Sapiential Perspectives: Wisdom Literature in Light of the Dead Sea Scrolls* (ed. J.J. Collins et al.; STDJ 51; Leiden: Brill, 2004), 1–11 argues that the LXX "God taught me wisdom," is preferable over the Hebrew of the Masoretic text "I have not learned wisdom" (11).

[39] W.A. Meeks, "The Man from Heaven in Johannine Sectarianism," *JBL* 91 (1972): 44–72 is over-confident in stating that Wis 10:10 "proves that, at this significantly early date, Jacob's vision at Bethel was understood as a vision of the *merkābāh*" (52 n. 33). P.W. Skehan, *Studies in Israelite Poetry and Wisdom* (CBQMS 1; Washington D.C.: The Catholic Biblical Association of America, 1971), 42–43 even identified Agur with Jacob. For a forthcoming discussion of Wis 10:10 interpreted in the light of later Jewish mystical texts, cf. S. Schorch's contribution to the Fourth International Conference on the Deuterocanonical Books, Pápa, Hungary, May 2007 (reference to Schorch's lecture by M. Goff).

latter in the age to come.[40] The same explanation of Gen 28:17 is also found in *Sifre Devarim* (Finkelstein, 410) on Deut 33:12, which, however, relates that not only Jacob, but also Abraham and Isaac, saw the temple built, destroyed and rebuilt, thereby effectively denying a special role of Jacob. Like *Sifre Devarim*, other texts also claim that the eschatological temple or the eternal city has been seen by biblical figures. Thus, *2 Bar.* 4 states that the city addressed in Isa 49:16 ("In the palms of my hands I have engraved you") "is not the building (*benyānā*) that is in your midst now," but the eternal one that was already prepared when God decided to create paradise and which he showed to Adam before he sinned, to Abraham in the night between the portions of the victims, and to Moses on Mount Sinai. This shows that in later traditions the viewing of the temple was not regarded as related to any specific figure.

In short, whereas later traditions interpret Jacob's first dream at Bethel as referring to the future history of his descendants, *Jubilees* and the Qumran evidence suggests that he saw at his return to Bethel both future history *and* the future temple. None of this proves in a formal sense that Jacob was the visionary of *NJ*. Yet, the discussed texts form an interpretive context, which attest to an imaginal world in which Jacob was granted visions of the future and the temple. At the same time, the preserved contemporary texts do not envision other figures seeing a new temple or Jerusalem. Hence I will call the identification of the visionary as Jacob probable.

2. Does it Matter?

The probable identification of Jacob as the visionary of the *NJ* gives another perspective to 11QT[a] XXIX 8–10 and 4Q537 12, even though the identification in its turn is supported by those texts. All those texts portray a relation between Jacob and the new Temple. The identification also invites us to reconsider *Jub.* 32 and the traditions lying behind the text. The different modes and contents of revelation in *Jub.* 32 suggest that the author is combining different traditions. Above I noted the differences between reading and seeing, between the fate of the descendants and the issue of the temple. The correspondences and differences between the seven tablets in *Jub.* 32 and the heavenly tablets

---

[40] J.C. VanderKam, "The Theology of the Temple Scroll: A Response to Lawrence H. Schiffman," *JQR* 85 (1994): 129–35 (134).

elsewhere in *Jubilees*, also suggest a separate tradition relating Jacob to tablets from heaven.[41] The date of *Jubilees* in relation to that of the Aramaic texts found at Qumran is disputed, but there is no indication that a text like 4Q537 was dependent on *Jubilees*.

Against the background of this identification, the position of Jacob in *Jubilees* may also be reviewed. The omission of Jacob from the line of priestly instruction (Isaac instructs Levi) may be due to the fact that he is focused on the future temple and its priesthood. We may also review 4Q537 12: rather than being part of instruction of Levi (in which case one may have expected second person forms), it may have been a summary of the description of the eschatological temple.

A different matter altogether is why an author would choose Jacob to be the visionary of the new city and temple, and implied author of *NJ*. The choice of Jacob as visionary, is, I suggest, in part determined by the topic of the text. Jacob stands for all of Israel, including both priests and non-priests, and separating Israel from the other nations. This makes sense in a text that deals with city *and* temple, with Israelites[42] bringing offerings and priests performing rituals and eating from them. It also makes sense in a text that refers to the nations in some kind of eschatological conflict. One may wonder to what extent the names of the nations mentioned in 4Q554 3 iii are of relevance.[43] The section is too fragmentary as to be sure about the subject of "and they will do evil to your seed." Are these all the aforementioned nations, or only some of them? The enumeration in 4Q554 3 iii 18 "with them Edom and Moab, the Ammonites,"[44] draws one's attention to 1QM I 1–2, referring to the first attack of the eschatological war, involving

---

[41] As noted by García Martínez (The Heavenly Tablets," 250), neither the Ethiopic nor the Latin text use here the term "heavenly," but the *Prayer of Joseph* (Frag. B; cf. *OTP* 2:714) refers to the *Jubilees* episode and says: "I have read in the tablets of heaven all that shall happen to you and your children." In spite of this later identification, the fact remains that the tablets are called differently in *Jubilees*, and that this is the only occasion where tablets are actually read in the narrative of *Jubilees*.

[42] Cf. the mentioning of Israel in three fragments dealing with the bringing of sacrifices in 11Q18 23 ii 7; 25 1; 27 1.

[43] The section was first published and briefly discussed by É. Puech, *La croyance des Esséniens en la vie future: Immortalité, résurrection, vie éternelle? II: Les données qumraniennes et classiques* (EB 22; Paris: Gabalda, 1993), 593–95. The treatment of DiTommaso, *The Dead Sea* New Jerusalem *Text*, 62–65, and 170–76, is problematic in many respects, including the mistaken join with a fragment that has been identified as 4QDan^a 6. Cf. my forthcoming review in *DSD* 14.3 (2007).

[44] The line breaks off after the Ammonites, and we cannot exclude that the lost text also included other nations, such as e.g. the Philistines.

on the one side the troops of Edom, Moab, the Ammonites, the…,
Philistia and the troops of the Kittim of Assyria, on the other side the
sons of Levi, the sons of Judah, and the sons of Benjamin. Yet, at the
same time, one should not forget the battles fought by Jacob and his
sons against in part these same nations (Moab, Ammon, Philistines,
Edomites, Hurrians) in *Jub.* 38:4–9.[45] In that sense, Jacob may be seen
as the personification of Israel, indicating that the scope and purport
of *NJ* transcend specific Levitical or other interests.

It is generally argued that the interest for the eschatological Jerusalem and temple implies at least some kind of criticism of the actual
Jerusalem and its temple, or even of the ritual taking place in the temple.
This may plausibly also be the case in *NJ*, in which case the choice
for Jacob might have yet another meaning for scribes at Qumran. The
fact that Jacob (according to *Jubilees*) did not build a sanctuary, did not
dwell in the holy place, and did not bring sacrifices, may have served as
an example for those who did neither serve in the temple nor dwell at
Jerusalem, but awaited an eschatological temple and new Jerusalem.

In sum, in spite of our fragmentary evidence, we may recreate the
traditions and imaginal world of the author(s) of Second Temple texts.
After Jacob's return from exile, during his second visit to Bethel, God
cuts a covenant with Jacob at Bethel. He allows Jacob to read the
future of Israel on some kind of heavenly tablets, and Jacob receives
a vision that the Holy One will build his sanctuary in the eschaton,
on the day of blessing/(re-)creation, presumably after a final conflict
between his sons and the nations. In this imaginal world, the focus is
on the future city and temple, as opposed to a historically existing one
at Jerusalem. We may surmise that this imaginal world was also that
of the author of *NJ*.

---

[45] The distribution of Jacob's sons (Enoch, Reuben's son, replaces Joseph) over four
sides of the tower, on each side three, may be related to the idea of the twelve gates
named after Jacob's sons.

READING THE HUMAN BODY AND WRITING IN CODE: PHYSIOGNOMIC DIVINATION AND ASTROLOGY IN THE DEAD SEA SCROLLS*

Mladen Popović

INTRODUCTION

In Shakespeare's tragedy *Macbeth*, Duncan, ignorant of his impending doom, says "there's no art to find the mind's construction in the face." Lady Macbeth, however, proves him wrong and accurately tells her husband, when he is brooding, that his face "is as a book, where men may read strange matters."[1]

Physiognomics is the art of discerning people's characters, dispositions, or destinies not just from their faces, but also from the shape, appearance, and movement of their entire bodies. The human body is understood to be a signifier; it is full of signs that show the knowledgeable reader certain things (the signified) he might be looking for to know about another person.[2]

---

* This article was read as a paper at the CNRS colloquium *Divination et écriture: écriture de la divination* organized by Jean-Jacques Glassner, Paris, December 9, 2005. That paper is available online at the CNRS website. This is a revised version. I thank Ian Werrett for checking the English. The ideas expressed here, for which I bear sole responsibility, are the result of my PhD research, which Florentino García Martínez, together with Eibert Tigchelaar, supervised. It seems therefore fitting to dedicate it to Florentino as a small token of my great appreciation for the inspiring example he sets as a scholar and as a person. Živeli i *ad multos annos*!

[1] William Shakespeare, *Macbeth* 1.4.11–12; 1.5.62–63. Cf. A.G. Clarke, "Metoposcopy: An Art to Find the Mind's Construction in the Forehead," in *Astrology, Science, and Society: Historical Essays* (ed. P. Curry; Woodbridge, Suffolk: Boydell, 1987), 171–95.

[2] For more general treatments of physiognomics, see e.g. J. Caro Baroja, *Historia de la Fisiognómica: El rostro y el carácter* (Madrid: Ediciones Istmo, 1988); M. Blankenburg, "Physiognomik, Physiognomie," in *Historisches Wörterbuch der Philosophie* (vol. 7; ed. J. Ritter and K. Gründer; Basel: Schwabe, 1989), 955–63; R. Campe and M. Schneider, eds., *Geschichten der Physiognomik: Text, Bild, Wissen* (Freiburg im Bresgau: Rombach, 1996); L. Rodler, *Il corpo specchio dell'anima: Teoria e storia della fisiognomica* (Milan: Mondadori, 2000).

Etymologically, "physiognomonics" (from the Greek φυσιογνωμονία) would be the more correct word, but I use "physiognomics," because it is more familiar in English. Cf. T.S. Barton, *Power and Knowledge: Astrology, Physiognomics, and Medicine under the Roman Empire* (Ann Arbor: University of Michigan Press, 1994), 95 n. 1.

As far as our sources are concerned, physiognomics appears as a form
of divination for the first time in Jewish culture during the Hellenistic-
Early Roman period. The most important evidence comes from the
Dead Sea Scrolls: the Hebrew text 4Q186 (*4QZodiacal Physiognomy*) and
the Aramaic text 4Q561 (*4QPhysiognomy ar*).[3] These copies are dated on
paleographic grounds to ca. 50 B.C.E.–20 C.E. The two texts represent
technical lists or catalogues. They are structured according to a number
of descriptions of the human body. Their style is terse and succinct.
Here, I shall concentrate on the Hebrew text *4QZodiacal Physiognomy*.[4]

In his article "Magic in the Dead Sea Scrolls," Florentino argues that
sectarian and nonsectarian texts show in what way forbidden forms of
magic were adapted to the needs of the Qumran community. In light
of the biblical interdiction against all magic in Deut 18:10–12, also
known to the community in the form of God's own words in 11QT^a
LX 16–19, and the use of the Watchers' story in *1 Enoch* to explain
the origin of evil, the forms of magic in the Dead Sea Scrolls could be
qualified as forbidden magic. Such a qualification, however, did not deter
people from the community from having knowledge and making use of
exorcism and divination. The reason for this appropriation lies in the
deterministic and dualistic world-view of the Qumran community.[5]

One of the magical texts that Florentino discusses is *4QZodiacal
Physiognomy*. In his characteristic style, Florentino lucidly explains the
interest of this text in the division between light and darkness against
the background of the deterministic and dualistic world-view of
Qumran, as reflected in the *Two Spirits Treatise* in 1QS III 13–IV 26,
and of the importance of the casting of lots at the time of admitting
new members (1QS VI 13–23).

---

[3] In the course of time, 4Q186 received the name *4QHoroscope*, but this name gives
the wrong impression that the text represents a horoscope or a collection of horoscopes,
which it does not. The text is rather a physiognomic catalogue concerned with zodiacal
astrology; it is a physiognomic-astrological list. Therefore, I have renamed it *4QZodiacal
Physiognomy*. 4Q561 was named *4QPhysiognomy/Horoscope ar*, but the textual
remains have
nothing to do with horoscopes, so *4QPhysiognomy ar* seems appropriate.

[4] See further, M. Popović, *Reading the Human Body: Physiognomics and Astrology in the Dead
Sea Scrolls and Hellenistic-Early Roman Period Judaism* (STDJ 67; Leiden: Brill, 2007).

[5] F. García Martínez, "Magic in the Dead Sea Scrolls," in *Qumranica Minora II:
Thematic Studies on the Dead Sea Scrolls* (STDJ 64; Leiden: Brill, 2007), 109–30. Published
previously in *The Metamorphosis of Magic from Late Antiquity to the Early Modern Period* (ed.
J.N. Bremmer and J.R. Veenstra; GSCC 1; Leuven: Peeters, 2002), 13–33.

Members of the Qumran community may well have used this physio-gnomic-astrological text in divinatory practices. However, limiting our appreciation of *4QZodiacal Physiognomy* within the context of Qumran, we are in danger of ignoring problematic features of this text and its interpretation. It is therefore important to study it also in comparison with other physiognomic and astrological writings from antiquity. This results in a new understanding of *4QZodiacal Physiognomy* and its function both inside and outside the community of Qumran.

The manuscript of *4QZodiacal Physiognomy* immediately catches the reader's attention due to the way it is written. Contrary to the regular direction of writing in Hebrew, the text is written from left to right. Also, characters from different scripts have been used. In addition to the regular, so-called square script, the writer or copyist used ancient, or paleo, Hebrew, Greek, and cryptic letters. These two features—inverted and mixed writing—make this text exceptional. There are no other known examples of Jewish texts written entirely in reversed order as well as in mixed scripts.

Even more puzzling than the writing of this manuscript is its content. The fragmentary remains belong to a physiognomic catalogue that reveals certain astrological matters to its intended reader. The text contains different physical descriptions of individual types of people. Following the physical descriptions, each entry says that the type of person described has a spirit that is divided, apparently on a nine-point scale, between the "house of light" and the "house of darkness," for example: "There is a spirit for him in the house of light (of) six (parts), and three (parts) in the house of darkness" (4Q186 1 ii 7–8). It is not immediately clear what this terminology means or what kind of concept is involved. The next data given in an entry has to do with the horoscope at the date of birth, for example: "And this is the horoscope under which he was born: in the foot of *Taurus* [...] And this is his animal: *Taurus*" (4Q186 1 ii 8–9). Again, it is not directly clear what is referred to by the words "in the foot of *Taurus*," nor whether, and if so, how, this information has anything to do with the previous data concerning the division of a spirit between the "house of light" and the "house of darkness."

Why was this text of physiognomic divination written in the way that it is, namely, in reversed order and with mixed scripts? Moreover, is the writing of *4QZodiacal Physiognomy* related to its content as a physio-gnomic-astrological list?

THE TEXT OF *4QZodiacal Physiognomy*

As is true of most manuscripts from the Dead Sea Scrolls, the manuscript of *4QZodiacal Physiognomy* is in a very fragmentary state, and what remains, two large and four smaller fragments,[6] is only a small portion of a much larger text. The first larger fragment has the remains of four columns, but not one is preserved in its entirety. As an example of the text of *4QZodiacal Physiognomy*, here are the second and third columns of the first fragment:

4Q186 1 ii:
1. [   ] ... unclean
2. [   ] a granite stone
3. [   ] a bli[nd (?)] man
4. [(and) lo]ng, ... [...] ... sec[re]t parts (?)
5. and his thighs are long and slender, and his toes are
6. slender and long. And he is from the second column.
7. There is a spirit for him in the house of light (of) six (parts), and three (parts) in the house of
8. darkness. And this is the horoscope under which he was born:
9. in the foot of *Taurus*. He will be humble, and this is his animal: *Taurus*.

4Q186 1 iii:
4. and ... [   ]
5. and his head [   ] ... [   ]
6. terrifying [   ] and his teeth are protruding. And the fingers of
7. his hands are <th>ick, and his thighs are thick and each one is hairy.
8. His toes are thick and short. And there is a spirit for him in the house of
9. [darkness (of) ei]ght (parts), and one (part) from the house of light. And ...

From the extant text we can infer that there were different entries for different types of people that consisted of the following elements: (1) physiognomic descriptions of types of individuals; (2) the person

---

[6] See M. Popović, "A Note on the Reading of שמונה and עמוד השני in *4Q186 2 i 7*," *RevQ* 21/84 (2004): 635–41; idem, *Reading the Human Body*, 17–67.

described is said to be "from the second column";[7] (3) a division of numbers with regard to the person's רוח ("spirit") in the "house of light" and the "house of darkness"; (4) certain zodiacal information concerning the moment of birth of the individual described; (5) predictions concerning the type's character ("he will be humble"); (6) stones, probably in relation to a person's physiognomic traits and zodiacal sign.

It is noteworthy that the text combines physiognomic and astrological learning. In addition to character, disposition, or fate, this ancient Jewish text attests to the belief that certain astrological data can be discerned through physiognomic inquiry.

THE INVERTED AND MIXED WRITING OF *4QZodiacal Physiognomy*

Why was *4QZodiacal Physiognomy* written or copied in the manner that it was? There are several perspectives on this issue.

The manner of writing may demonstrate some sort of scribal pride, displaying the level of acquired skills. The writing is executed with a fine hand; it seems hardly the work of a beginning scribe. Together with the use of characters from various scripts, the inverted writing of the entire manuscript can be considered a distinguishing mark, indicating scribal craftsmanship and perhaps scholarly pride.

There may also be more to it than a mere display of scribal skills. For example, in Jewish magical texts and Greek curse tablets, the names of illnesses, demons, and gods were sometimes intentionally corrupted, as well as letters or words in incantation texts, which was believed to enhance its magical effects.[8] The magical power of using different scripts is also demonstrated in later Arabic magic.[9] The difference, however, is that in the case of *4QZodiacal Physiognomy* the entire text is written

---

[7] However, only in 4Q186 1 ii 6 is the position of this phrase clearly set between the physiognomic description and the part concerning the "house of light" and the "house of darkness." This is certainly not the case in 4Q186 1 iii and 4Q186 2 i, where the words ורוח לו ("And there is a spirit for him"), introducing the part concerning the "house of light" and the "house of darkness," follow immediately upon the physiognomic sections. This suggests that it was maybe not a fixed element in the entries.

[8] See J. Naveh, "Lamp Inscriptions and Inverted Writing," *IEJ* 38 (1988): 36–43; idem, "Fragments of an Aramaic Magic Book from Qumran," *IEJ* 48 (1998): 252–61.

[9] Cf. D. De Smet, "L'alphabet secret des Ismaéliens ou la force magique de l'écriture," in *Charmes et sortilèges: Magie et magiciens* (ed. R. Gyselen; Bures-sur-Yvette: Groupe pour l'Étude de la Civilisation du Moyen-Orient, 2002), 51–60.

in an inverted manner and words that are written with mixed scripts
also appear in normal, square characters. These considerations make it
unlikely that these two scribal features were intended for magical effect.
Yet, it may suggest that the regular order of writing represented some
form of magical power. Only two words in the manuscript appear in
normal writing from right to left, namely אבן צונם, a granite stone mentioned in 4Q186 1 ii 2. Perhaps this granite stone represents a magical
stone, and maybe it was thought that the normal direction of writing
enhanced magical power in this otherwise inverted written text. Both
Babylonian and Greco-Roman astrology were familiar with various
connections between the zodiacal signs and particular stones, as well
as other elements. It is possible that *4QZodiacal Physiognomy* associated
certain stones with different physiognomic types and zodiacal signs.[10]

In addition to the possibility of an intended magical effect, the
inverted and mixed writing possibly represents a scribal strategy of
secrecy, limiting the availability of and accessibility to the physiognomic-
astrological learning in the text. The manner of writing prevents people
from easily reading the text and quickly obtaining knowledge of its
subject matter. The use of inverted and mixed writing "show that the
contents of the text were not intended for everybody, and that uttermost
care was taken to keep them accessible only to a very few experts."[11]
The composition of *4QZodiacal Physiognomy* is non-sectarian, which
means it was composed outside the Qumran group, but it is possible
that this copy was made within the community. One letter appears in
the manuscript, the *yod* in בבית ("in the house [of light]") in 4Q186 1
ii 7, which resembles the so-called Cryptic A script that seems to have
been a sectarian script. This may suggest that the coding of this document was done within the Qumran community, but we do not know
that for certain.[12]

If the coded writing was used in order to obscure the content of
the manuscript, because this was not intended for everybody to read,
the question, of course, is why the content of *4QZodiacal Physiognomy*
had to be restricted. It has been argued that this was done because of
its controversial nature. Astrology would have been valued negatively
within the Qumran community: this is indicated by the use of various

---

[10] Popović, *Reading the Human Body*, 35–54, 213–15, 235–37.
[11] García Martínez, "Magic in the Dead Sea Scrolls," 127.
[12] Popović, *Reading the Human Body*, 8–11.

scripts, which would have given the impression of impurity to Jewish readers.[13] However, both assumptions fail to convince. The latter assumption is contradicted by epigraphic evidence from Masada where ostraca with characters of the paleo-Hebrew script in combination with Greek letters and ostraca with specific names that combine characters from square, paleo-Hebrew, and Greek scripts were found.[14] Also, from Gamla comes a coin from the First Revolt in which paleo-Hebrew and square script characters are used to write "For the redemption of Jerusalem the H(oly)."[15]

These epigraphic examples show that the use of various scripts did not signal a notion of impurity to Jews in antiquity. As to the first assumption, there is no need to presuppose a negative view of astrology on the part of the Qumran community. With the publication of all the Dead Sea Scrolls and particularly wisdom texts such as *Instruction* and *Mysteries*, scholars have drawn attention to various references to times of birth, the position of stars, and horoscopes. These references are couched in general terms, but they may demonstrate the acceptance of particular astrological notions.[16] Also, as Florentino has argued, the interest in so-called forbidden magic did not preclude the appropriation of this magic within the context of the deterministic and dualistic world-view of the Qumran community.

Instead of the possibly controversial character of the learning contained in *4QZodiacal Physiognomy*, it may rather have been the high status accredited to the kind of knowledge transmitted by the text that was the reason for the manner in which it was written. Submitted to writing in technical lists, the arts of physiognomics and astrology unmistakably represented higher forms of learning handled by educated

---

[13] M. Albani, "Horoscopes in the Qumran Scrolls," in *The Dead Sea Scrolls After Fifty Years: A Comprehensive Assessment* (ed. P.W. Flint and J.C. VanderKam; 2 vols.; Leiden: Brill, 1999), 2:279–330.

[14] Y. Yadin and J. Naveh, *The Aramaic and Hebrew Ostraca and Jar Inscriptions* (vol. 1 of *Masada: The Yigael Yadin Excavations 1963–1965: Final Reports*; Jerusalem: IES, 1989).

[15] See D. Syon, "Gamla: City of Refuge," in *The First Jewish Revolt: Archaeology, History, and Ideology* (ed. A.M. Berlin and J.A. Overman; London: Routledge, 2002), 134–53 (146–49).

[16] See, e.g., E. Tigchelaar, "Your Wisdom and Your Folly: The Case of 1–4QMysteries," in *Wisdom and Apocalypticism in the Dead Sea Scrolls and in the Biblical Tradition* (ed. F. García Martínez; BETL 168; Leuven: Peeters, 2003), 67–88; F. Schmidt, "'Recherche son thème de géniture dans le Mystère de ce qui doit être:' Astrologie et prédestination à Qoumrân," in *Qumrân et le judaïsme du tournant de notre ère* (ed. A. Lemaire and S.C. Mimouni; Collection de la Revue des études juives 40; Leuven: Peeters, 2006), 51–62.

people. *4QZodiacal Physiognomy* demanded a certain level of knowledge of those who were suitable to handle its learning, analogous to the demands expressed in the Babylonian *Esagil-kīn-apli Catalogue* about the physiognomic series *šumma alamdimmû* ("If the form") or the prohibitions in Greco-Roman astrological treatises not to transmit knowledge to the uninitiated,[17] which in turn affected the way the manuscript was written. Literacy at Qumran may have been widespread, but must not be exaggerated.[18] The inverted and mixed writing was effective enough to discourage insufficiently skilled and knowledgeable members of the community from taking account of its contents.

Bearing in mind Pierre Bourdieu's notion of cultural capital, the learning of *4QZodiacal Physiognomy* may be appreciated as a prized piece of knowledge signaling and confirming the status of those having access to and possessing it.[19] It perhaps objectified the speculative, scientific interests of some elite members of Hellenistic-Early Roman period Jewish society or of the Qumran community. The pursuit and possession of that knowledge may have confirmed that elite status. One can, therefore, perhaps say that the written form of *4QZodiacal Physiognomy* signified the cultural capital that the text's learning represented and that possession of the manuscript bestowed symbolic capital on the people in possession of it. The knowledge in the physiognomic-astrological list may have been valued in itself as a piece of speculative, scientific learning about man and certain cosmic elements. In order to understand the high status of this learning, it is necessary to observe its contents more closely.

---

[17] See Popović, *Reading the Human Body*, 81–83, 100.

[18] P.S. Alexander, "Literacy among Jews in Second Temple Palestine: Reflections on the Evidence from Qumran," in *Hamlet on a Hill: Semitic and Greek Studies Presented to Professor T. Muraoka on the Occasion of his Sixty-Fifth Birthday* (ed. M.F.J. Baasten and W.T. van Peursen; OLA 118; Leuven: Peeters, 2003), 3–24.

[19] See e.g. P. Bourdieu, *Distinction: A Social Critique of the Judgement of Taste* (trans. R. Nice; London: Routledge & Kegan Paul, 1984); idem, "The Forms of Capital," in *Handbook of Theory and Research for the Sociology of Education* (New York: Greenwood, 1986), 241–58. Cf. N. Veldhuis, "Elementary Education at Nippur: The Lists of Trees and Wooden Objects" (Ph.D. Diss., University of Groningen, 1997), 137–46, for the use of Bourdieu's concept of cultural capital to explain the social uses of the science of writing in Old Babylonian education.

PHYSIOGNOMICS, ASTROLOGY, AND UNDERSTANDING THE NATURE OF
PEOPLE'S ZODIACAL SPIRITS

The combination of astrology and physiognomics in *4QZodiacal
Physiognomy* demonstrates the belief that the zodiacal signs have an
effect on the appearance of the human body. In Babylonian as well
as in Greco-Roman astrological traditions, people believed that the
configuration of zodiacal signs and planets at the moment of birth
influenced the shape and appearance of the human body.[20]

When presenting the opinion of those who defend the Babylonian
horoscopic predictions, Cicero says they argue that there is a certain
force in the zodiac influencing everything both in heaven and on earth,
and "so also children at their birth are influenced in soul and body and
by this force their minds, manners, disposition, physical condition, career
in life and destinies are determined."[21] Cicero was not wrong about
the Chaldeans. Recently, a Late Babylonian astrological text has been
discussed, which is, among other things, concerned with determining
the physical characteristics of those born under a certain zodiacal sign.[22]
In the second century C.E., Ptolemy of Alexandria accepts this aspect
of the Babylonian tradition, devoting a whole chapter in his book on
astrology to explain the influence of each planet and zodiacal sign on
the form and mixture of the human body.[23] The Greek astrological
lists called *zodiologia* are another example. These are arranged according to the order of the signs of the zodiac. Under each zodiacal sign
are listed various character traits and bodily features ascribed to those
born under that sign.[24]

The difference between *4QZodiacal Physiognomy* and these other texts
is that it is structured according to physiognomic, not astrological,
criteria: the entries in the list seem to begin with descriptions of the
human body, not signs of the zodiac. Following the physical descriptions,

---

[20] For more details on the astrological aspects of *4QZodiacal Physiognomy*, see Popović,
Reading the Human Body, 119–71.

[21] Cicero, *Div.* 2.89. Trans. from W.A. Falconer, *Cicero: On Old Age, On Friendship, On
Divination* (LCL 154; Cambridge, Mass.: Harvard University Press, 2001).

[22] E. Reiner, "Early Zodiologia and Related Matters," in *Wisdom, Gods and Literature:
Studies in Assyriology in Honour of W.G. Lambert* (ed. A.R. George and I.L. Finkel; Winona
Lake, Ind.: Eisenbrauns, 2000), 421–27.

[23] Ptolemy, *Tetrab.* 3.12.

[24] See W. Gundel, "Individualschicksal, Menschentypen und Berufe in der antiken
Astrologie," *Jahrbuch der Charakterologie* 4 (1927): 135–93.

the text mentions the division between light and darkness and the zodiacal moment of birth. The human body signifies astrological matters; through physiognomic inquiry, people were able to determine a person's zodiacal sign. There is an intriguing remark by the astrologer Hephaestion of Thebes (fourth century C.E.), which provides important evidence for the belief that astrological matters could be learned through physiognomic inquiry. If one cannot ascertain which of two zodiacal signs above the horizon represents the horoscope sign (= the ascendant) of a certain individual, it is possible, says Hephaestion, to determine it by looking at the shape of the person's body and see which of the two zodiacal signs he resembles more.[25] *4QZodiacal Physiognomy* is a text structured according to this line of reasoning. It thus provides fascinating evidence for the history of physiognomics and astrology in antiquity in general. This Jewish text testifies to the existence of the belief that the human body could signify astrological matters, whereas in practically every other ancient example of technical lists that combine astrology and physiognomics the signifying relationship is reversed.

The key to understanding the astrological framework lies in the words "in the foot of *Taurus*" in 4Q186 1 ii 9.[26] These words presuppose a division of the zodiacal sign *Taurus* and are a reference to a specific ecliptical part of the sign.[27] There are various astrological lists from antiquity that give divisions of the zodiacal signs. In one tradition the different subsections are understood as body parts of the zodiacal signs.[28] One example from this tradition is the so-called Rhetorius-Teucer text.[29] Regarding the zodiacal sign *Taurus*, this text reads: "From 1° to 3° the head rises, from 4° to 7° the horns, from 8° to 10° the neck, from 11° to 13° the breast, from 14° to 18° the loins, from 19° to 21° the hip joints, from 22° to 24° the feet, from 25° to 27° the tail, from 28° to 30° the hoofs."[30]

---

[25] Hephaestion, *Astr.* 2.2.27.

[26] Here I follow Albani, "Horoscopes in the Qumran Scrolls." For another interpretation, see F. Schmidt, "Astrologie juive ancienne: Essai d'interprétation de *4QCryptique (4Q186)*," *RevQ* 18/69 (1997): 125–41.

[27] The zodiacal signs are schematic 30° sections of the ecliptic, the line that the course of the sun follows through the sky. In ancient astrology the zodiacal signs were subdivided in smaller sections, such as 10°, 2;30°, or even smaller sections.

[28] O. Neugebauer, "Melothesia and Dodecatemoria," in *Studia biblica et orientalia. Vol. III: Oriens Antiquus* (AnBib 12; Rome: Pontificio Istituto Biblico, 1959), 270–75.

[29] See *Catalogus codicum astrologorum Graecorum* 7 (Brussels: Henri Lamertin, 1908), 192–213.

[30] In the case of *Taurus*, the sign is divided into nine parts, but this is not so for all zodiacal signs in this text, indicating that nine is not a set number.

This tradition is helpful to explain the astrological framework in *4QZodiacal Physiognomy*. The assumption is that the position "in the foot of *Taurus*" results in the division of the zodiacal sign *Taurus* between "the house of light" and the "house of darkness." These latter phrases must be understood as references to cosmological areas above and below the earth. The image is one of rising zodiacal signs at the eastern horizon. It takes a certain amount of time before the entire 30° section has risen entirely above the horizon, approximately two hours. This means that during the time of ascension an ever-greater part appears above the horizon, leaving an ever-smaller part below the horizon. One could, in theory, count which parts of the sign have risen above the horizon and which parts still remain below the horizon. If the section "foot of *Taurus*" represents the ascendant part of the zodiacal sign at the time of which a person was born, one could count which parts have already risen and which parts of the sign still have to rise. Thus, according to this interpretation of 4Q186 1 ii 7–9, at the moment of birth six parts of *Taurus* were above the horizon, "in the house of light," whereas three parts were still below the horizon, "in the house of darkness."

The position of the ascendant "in the foot of *Taurus*" determines the number of parts of the sign above and below the horizon, understood here in terms of "house of light" and "house of darkness." The ancient users need not have been aware that this division was a result of the zodiacal position. Or maybe they did know that, but they need not have known exactly about the complicated methods for calculating zodiacal rising times. They were content to know the division of the zodiacal sign. That was enough. They need not have been interested to understand how this came about. The text listed what they wanted to know. Thus, in the original text of *4QZodiacal Physiognomy*, each physiognomic type would have been related to different divisions of each zodiacal sign. The entire manuscript would have been an elaborate text listing physiognomic typologies that would lead the intended reader to the various subdivisions between light and darkness of the twelve signs of the zodiac.

What is the relevance and function of knowing someone's zodiacal sign and its position and division at birth? In order to understand this, one more element figuring prominently in the text must be addressed. The text explicitly connects the numbers in the "house of light" and the "house of darkness" with the spirit there is said to be for the person described. If the allocation of numbers between the "house of light" and the "house of darkness" is astrologically the result of the ascendant zodiacal sign that is divided between the areas above and below the horizon, what then is the meaning of רוח ("spirit")? Against the background of the *Two Spirits Treatise* in the *Rule of the Community*, scholars have usually understood this to be the human spirit, which is divided between light and darkness. Like Philip Alexander, Florentino assumes that the "link with the Zodiac makes it likely that only twelve human types were described."[31] Within the astrological framework of the text, however, this is unlikely. Considering how many different combinations between parts of light and darkness can be made for a human spirit that is thought of as having nine parts, there are only eight such arrangements possible.[32] I suggest instead that the word רוח ("spirit") is used in *4QZodiacal Physiognomy* to refer to spirits that are related to the zodiacal signs—zodiacal spirits.[33] That the concept of zodiacal spirits was known in antiquity is clear from the *Testament of Solomon*.[34] This text, especially chapter 18, provides important evidence that spirits and demons were thought to inhabit or to be identical with zodiacal signs and decans.

4QZodiacal Physiognomy augmented the importance of the zodiacal sign for people's fates by the notion of the zodiacal spirit. Like the zodiacal signs, these zodiacal spirits have a close relationship with human beings. There are twelve zodiacal spirits, one for each zodiacal sign. Due to the position of the ascendant at the moment of birth, the division of the zodiacal spirit differed between different types of people, although they shared the same zodiacal sign. *4QZodiacal Physiognomy* not only mentions the division between light and darkness, but also states what zodiacal sign is the birth sign of the types of people (4Q186 1 ii 9: "And this is his animal: *Taurus*"). The text identifies people's zodiacal birth sign and provides information with regard to the nature of the zodiacal spirit at the time of birth, thus differentiating between the two. Although the division between the "house of light" and the "house of darkness" is astrologically the result of the ascendant zodiacal sign's

---

[31] García Martínez, "Magic in the Dead Sea Scrolls," 129. Cf. P.S. Alexander, "Physiognonomy [sic!], Initiation, and Rank in the Qumran Community," in *Geschichte, Tradition, Reflexion: Festschrift für Martin Hengel zum 70. Geburtstag, Band I Judentum* (ed. H. Cancik et al.; Tübingen: Mohr [Siebeck], 1996), 385–94 (389).

[32] Popović, *Reading the Human Body*, 191–92.

[33] Popović, *Reading the Human Body*, 172–208.

[34] The composition of the *Testament of Solomon* dates to sometime between the fourth–sixth centuries C.E., but the text contains older traditions that may date back to the first century B.C.E. or first century C.E., such as chapter 18 on the decans.

position vis-à-vis the eastern horizon, in *4QZodiacal Physiognomy* this was understood in terms of the zodiacal spirit being divided between light and darkness.

The division between light and darkness served as an indication for the nature of the zodiacal spirits. It was important to know what the nature was of the zodiacal spirit that attended someone, because it could be a potentially dangerous and harmful being. The *Testament of Solomon* speaks of the thirty-six decanal spirits as "the thirty-six demons that plague humanity."[35] Zodiacal spirits could attack people, causing illnesses or other calamities and inconveniences during life. The number of parts within the "house of light" and the "house of darkness" served to reveal the more or less beneficent or maleficent nature of people's zodiacal spirits. More parts of light would have been indicative of a beneficial character, while more parts of darkness of a maleficent one. To ancient readers of *4QZodiacal Physiognomy*, the division of light and darkness may have indicated the degree to which zodiacal spirits were potentially harmful, whether a spirit could be really harmful or not very. The more light, the less harmful, the more darkness, the more harmful an attack by a zodiacal spirit would have been. This knowledge may have been used as a diagnostic tool in different practical contexts, both inside and outside of the sectarian Qumran community.[36]

4QZodiacal Physiognomy can be seen as an attempt to draw connections between different types of people and the natures of their zodiacal spirits. It structures and classifies these relationships in a list that connects the shape and appearance of the human body with the subdivisions of the signs and their spirits in the "house of light" and the "house of darkness." In this way, the text demonstrates an interest in knowledge of cosmic matters and relationships between heavenly elements and human beings. To have knowledge of these matters was to understand the power and influence of the signs and spirits upon people.

The interpretation of *4QZodiacal Physiognomy* put forward here is compatible with what we know about the deterministic and dualistic world-view of the Qumran community. The zodiacal spirits can be seen as another sort of spirit or demon inhabiting the world and possibly causing trouble for members of the Qumran community. The

---

[35] *T. Sol.* 18:42.
[36] See Popović, *Reading the Human Body*, 209–39.

knowledge in *4QZodiacal Physiognomy* may have been used in the Qumran community as it wished to guard itself against demonic attacks from Belial, his spirits, and the Sons of Darkness.

In both Babylonian and Greco-Roman traditions, the physiognomic and astrological arts or sciences were the domain of intellectual elites: the *āšipu* ("magician-exorcist"), philosopher, doctor, or astrologer. It is unlikely that specialized, technical texts such as the Babylonian physiognomic omen series *Alamdimmû* or the pseudo-Aristotelian *Physiognomonica* circulated widely across many levels of society. Interest in and access to these texts would have been very limited. It is not possible to determine who exactly was familiar with learned knowledge of physiognomic and astrological arts in Hellenistic-Early Roman period Judaism. Presumably, scholarly scribes and teachers would have been the sort of people to have access to a technical list such as *4QZodiacal Physiognomy*, being interested in the knowledge they contained and perhaps also responsible for copying them. In the Qumran community, expert and learned members may have been responsible for the coded writing of the manuscript. Written in code, the contents of the manuscript were protected against those members of the community not initiated in the learned knowledge contained in it.

REWRITTEN BIBLE AS A BORDERLINE
PHENOMENON—GENRE, TEXTUAL STRATEGY,
OR CANONICAL ANACHRONISM?

Anders Klostergaard Petersen

1. From "Rewritten Bible" towards "Rewritten Scripture"

It is a delight to celebrate and honour Florentino García Martínez, who
by the quality and number of his works on the Dead Sea Scrolls has
placed himself as one of the most outstanding scholars on the subject.
In addition, his amicable nature, his straightforwardness, and his open-
mindedness to new ideas is exemplary of an academic *habitus*. Let me
also express my gratitude to Professor García Martínez for his interest
in my work and for his friendship during the past years.

The subject of this paper has also attracted the scholarly attention
of García Martínez: the phenomenon that he—among others—has
aptly designated the problem of borderlines.[1] I shall focus on one distinct aspect of this discussion that recently has become a controversial
subject of scholarly debate, the understanding of the category of
rewritten Bible. The subject of the debate has been about whether the
concept—originally coined by Geza Vermes in 1961—is most adequately
conceived of in terms of a genre or in terms of a textual strategy.[2]

---

[1] See F. García Martínez, "Biblical Borderlines," in *The People of the Dead Sea Scrolls: Their Writings, Beliefs and Practices* (ed. idem and J. Trebolle Barrera; transl. by W.G.E. Watson; Leiden: Brill, 1995), 123–38. This essay was originally published in Spanish ("Las fronteras de «lo bíblico»") in *Scripta Theologica* 23 (1991): 759–84. The discussion of the problem of borderline texts with regard to the Qumran writings was at the focus of the debate at the Madrid Qumran Congress of March 1991. The proceedings of the conference are available in J. Trebolle Barrera and L. Vegas Montaner, ed., *The Madrid Qumran Congress: Proceedings of the International Congress on the Dead Sea Scrolls, Madrid 18–21 March 1991* (STDJ 11; Leiden: Brill 1992).

[2] See most recently the contributions by G.J. Brooke, "Rewritten Bible," in *Encyclopedia of the Dead Sea Scrolls* (ed. L.H. Schiffman and J.C. VanderKam; New York: Oxford University Press, 2000), 2:777–81; S. Docherty, "*Joseph and Aseneth*: Rewritten Bible or Narrative Expansion?" *JSJ* 35 (2004): 27–48; M.J. Bernstein, "'Rewritten Bible': A Generic Category Which Has Outlived its Usefulness?" *Textus* 22 (2005): 169–96; and M. Segal, "Between Bible and Rewritten Bible," in *Biblical Interpretation at Qumran* (ed. M. Henze; SDSS; Grand Rapids: Eerdmans, 2005), 10–29; J.G. Campbell, "'Rewrit- ten Bible' and 'Parabiblical Texts': A Terminological and Ideological Critique," in *New*

Both perceptions have some basis in Vermes' own understanding, since it is not altogether clear in what sense he speaks of rewritten Bible as a genre. Whereas most scholars have understood him to see rewritten Bible as a distinct genre, he actually seems to oscillate between the two approaches—genre or textual strategy—that have constituted the bone of contention in contemporary discussions. My essay is part of a larger project aimed at a determination of the analytical relationship between the generic categorisations that have been used with regard to the intertextual influences exerted by authoritative scriptural antecedents on subsequent compositions of the later Second Temple Period. At this stage of the project, I shall restrict myself to the discussion of the category in terms of a genre or a textual strategy as a predominantly theoretical problem.

First, I shall raise the supplementary question to what extent the category itself is a slightly distorting misnomer. If an increasing number of scholars—not least on the basis of the entire corpus of Dead Sea Scroll manuscripts—acknowledge that the borders between alleged biblical writings and non-biblical texts were conspicuously more fluid than acknowledged at the time when Geza Vermes coined the concept, should that not call the continued use of the term into question? To push my point to the extreme, if one acknowledges the anachronistic nature of the category biblical with regard to the historical situation during which the majority of the writings relevant for the discussion of rewritten Bible were composed, it is reasonable to abandon the term.[3] Such abandonment, however, does not necessarily entail that the idea underlying the concept should be given up. It would, on the contrary, be futile to renounce the heuristic value which the term has had during almost half a century of scholarship. On the other hand, I find it problematic that scholars today have to initiate their employment of the label by first distancing themselves from the anachronistic and canonical

---

Directions in Qumran Studies: Proceedings of the Bristol Colloquium on the Dead Sea Scrolls, 8–10 September 2003 (ed. idem et al.; LSTS 52; London: T&T Clark, 2005), 43–68.

[3] B. Chiesa, "Biblical and Parabiblical Texts from Qumran," *Henoch* 20 (1998): 131–51, emphasises the anachronistic nature of terms like rewritten Bible and parabiblical texts. See also S. White Crawford, "The Rewritten Bible at Qumran," in *The Bible and the Dead Sea Scrolls. Volume One. The Hebrew Bible and Qumran* (ed. J.H. Charlesworth; N. Richland Hills, Tex.: Bibal Press, 2000), 173–95 (176–77). Similarly Campbell, "'Rewritten Bible,'" 48–53, underlines the anachronistic nature of the terms and argues in favour of their abandonment by pleading for a new terminology.

implications entailed by the term.[4] From my perspective, the best solution is to maintain the basic idea underlying Vermes' concept, but to replace rewritten Bible by another term that is not anachronistically misleading: rewritten Scripture.[5]

In English, Scripture can, of course, denote the Bible, but in that case it is commonly used in the plural as Scriptures, or attributed the predicate Holy. As a singular noun Scripture, however, can designate any writing or book that is attributed a particular authoritative status—especially in the context of writings of a sacred or religious nature. It is in this latter sense that I propose to replace Bible with Scripture in the phrase *rewritten Scripture*. By Scripture I do not mean a canonically homogeneous collection of writings that have been completely demarcated or formally closed. Nor do I think of texts the wording of which has been ultimately laid down. The idea is to capture the essence of Vermes' concept while making it more fluid, so that the plurality of different text forms as well as the dynamic processes that eventually lead to the formation of various canons is taken into account. In this essay Scripture simply means any Jewish composition to which a particular group of people imputed a particular authority.

By replacing Bible with Scripture the notion of authoritative writings that are intertextually decisive for the formation of new forms of texts is maintained. Contrary to Bible, however, Scripture does not entail the idea of a closed and—even in wording—fixed collection of writings. By use of the term rewritten Scripture, the way is paved for an acknowledgement of the reciprocal relationship that exists between authoritative texts and the writings they occasion. In a simultaneous process authoritative writings are used as matrices for the creation of authoritatively derivative texts that by virtue of being rewritings contribute to the authoritative elevation of their literary antecedents.[6]

---

[4] See, for instance, White Crawford, "The Rewritten Bible at Qumran," 176–77; Segal, "Between Bible and Rewritten Bible," 11, n. 2; Bernstein, "A Generic Category," 172, n. 3.

[5] I understand from Campbell that James VanderKam has similarly endorsed the view that rewritten Bible should be replaced with the improved term: rewritten Scripture. See J.C. VanderKam, "The Wording of Scriptural Citations in Some Rewritten Scriptural Works," in *The Bible as Book: The Hebrew Bible and the Judean Desert Discoveries* (ed. E.D. Herbert and E. Tov; London: British Library, 2002), 41–56. Unfortunately, this book has not been available to me in the process of writing this contribution. I, therefore, cite it according to Campbell, "'Rewritten Bible,'" 49, n. 32.

[6] This reciprocal relationship by which new writings as rewritings of literary antecedents sun themselves in the authoritative light of their predecessors, while simultaneously

Scripture has the additional advantage compared to Bible that it allows us to include writings like Deuteronomy and the books of Chronicles to the category without having to make an artificial distinction between inner-biblical and extra-biblical forms of rewritten Bible. And it allows us to take early Christian writings into account in which we can observe a comparable literary strategy at work. Is it, for instance, completely inappropriate to think of Matthew's rewriting of Mark in terms of a form of rewritten Scripture? And does the Johannine rewriting of the Synoptic tradition not represent an example of rewritten Scripture? Finally, by employing the term Scripture we do not have to exclude texts from the category, which have been composed in other languages than Hebrew,[7] nor do we—by virtue of the name—have to rule out that even "secondary" writings like the *Temple Scroll*, the *Book of Jubilees*, the Enochic literature, etc. could be imputed an authoritative status if not surpassing, then at least equalling that of their literary antecedents.[8]

---

adding authority to them, has been poignantly described by G.J. Brooke, "Between Authority and Canon: The Significance of Reworking the Bible for Understanding the Canonical Process," in *Reworking the Bible: Apocryphal and Related Texts at Qumran* (ed. E.G. Chazon et al.; STDJ 58; Leiden: Brill, 2005), 85–104 (96).

[7] Segal, "Between Bible and Rewritten Bible," 17, for one, emphasises among the criteria he lists for identifying a text as belonging to the genre of rewritten Bible that "on the simplest level, one can posit that any composition which presumes to present a copy of its source will be composed in the same language as its *Vorlage*." It is not entirely clear to what extent this criterion entails not only that texts like *Antiquitates*, *Liber Antiquitatum Biblicarum* (hereafter *LAB*), and the *Genesis Apocryphon* are left out of the discussion, but also that they—due to their language of composition—are understood to be incompatible with the genre designation. To the extent that they are perceived to be generically incongruent with the inclusion into rewritten Bible texts, I find the criterion rather odd, not only because it leaves out of discussion compositions traditionally conceived to be paradigmatic exemplars of the alleged genre, but also because it does not pay satisfactory heed to the fact that many Jews were fluent in more than one language. Similarly E. Tov, "Biblical Texts as Reworked in Some Qumran Manuscripts with Special Attention to 4QRP and 4QParaGen-Exod," in *The Community of the Renewed Covenant: The Notre Dame Symposium on the Dead Sea Scrolls* (ed. E. Ulrich and J.C. VanderKam; Notre Dame: Notre Dame University Press, 1994), 111–34 (113), excludes the *Genesis Apocryphon* from rewritten Bible texts, since its language of composition is Aramaic.

[8] Brooke, "Between Authority and Canon," 89–90: "In other words, the reworking of earlier tradition may have been viewed by some Jews in the latter half of the Second Temple period as a standard way through which any composition might lay some claim to authority. In the case of the books of Chronicles this eventually led to them acquiring canonical status; and the same happened to the *Book of Jubilees* in some religious communities. Over against modern views of rewritings as self-evidently secondary and plagiaristic, in early Judaism such imitation with its own form of exegetical innovation was entirely justifiable as a claim to authoritative voice of the tradition."

Recently, Jonathan Campbell has voiced a critique against the use of rewritten Bible which on many points is comparable to my criticism of the nomenclature. Additionally, however, he criticises the replacement of rewritten Bible with rewritten Scripture. His main contention against this classification is that the defining "rewritten" in the expression is incurably ambiguous, since it does not clarify the scriptural status of the work in question.[9] His examples are *Jubilees* and Sir 44–46. Whereas the first by virtue of its authorial claim arrogates to itself an authoritative status on a par with Gen 1—Exod 25, the latter does not plead scriptural status. The *Ben Sira* passage represents an "exegetical entity distinct from scripture." That may well be, but Campbell does not differentiate between analytical levels. He is, of course, right that rewritten Bible is a problematic and not particularly illuminating term when it comes to the understanding of the authoritative status attributed by readers in antiquity to the works under examination. If, however, rewritten Scripture is an analytical category that pertains to the generic and intertextual relationship between different writings (mainly) of the Second Temple Period, Campbell's objection is unimportant. How different people understood the different writings is another important question, but it belongs to a different analytical level. In order to advance the discussion and to clarify the level of analysis at which the nomenclature has a bearing, we shall proceed by raising the question of the generic status of the term. It is obvious to initiate the examination by discussing Vermes' own understanding of the category.[10]

2. Ambiguities Pertaining to Vermes' Understanding of Rewritten Bible

The ambiguities that pertain to Vermes' understanding as well as to the subsequent discussion of the concept may stem from the fact that neither Vermes nor anybody else has provided an analytical definition of the term. The closest one comes to a definition are the nine criteria advanced by Philip Alexander in an important article in which

---

[9] Campbell, "'Rewritten Bible,'" 50. Contrary to Campbell, Tov, "Biblical Texts as Reworked," 114, 134, endorses the view that rewritten Bible texts were merely literary exercises that did not enjoy the status of authoritative writings.

[10] When referring to the history of scholarship on the term, I shall use "rewritten Bible," whereas I shall use "rewritten Scripture" as an improved nomenclature to designate the phenomenon traditionally referred to by the former term.

he discusses the inclusion of particular writings under the rubric of rewritten Bible.[11] Although helpful and significant, Alexander's nine principal characteristics constitute a description of the phenomenon that embraces a variety of different aspects rather than a genuine analytical definition.[12] This does not subtract from the merits of Vermes' and Alexander's works on rewritten Bible. If one takes a look at the *Wirkungsgeschichte* of Vermes' neologism and the recent discussion— strongly influenced by Alexander's pioneer work—, one is impressed by the influence of the term in subsequent scholarship. Nevertheless, some of the ambiguities of the current debate originate in the uncertainty pertaining to Vermes' own understanding of the category.

In 1961 he spoke of rewritten Bible as an "exegetical process" by which a midrashist "in order to anticipate questions, and to solve problems in advance" inserted "haggadic development into the biblical narrative."[13] He examined a late medieval text, *Sefer ha-Yashar*, which in his understanding both preserved and developed traditions that emanated in the pre-Tannaitic period. The manner in which *Sefer ha-Yashar* related to biblical literary antecedents, Vermes said, illustratively exemplified an exegetical technique also embodied by writings like the Palestinian *Targumim*, Josephus' *Antiquitates*, *LAB*, and the *Genesis Apocryphon* (hereafter *GA*).[14] The same perception lies behind the sec-

---

[11] P.S. Alexander, "Retelling the Old Testament," in *It is Written: Scripture Citing Scripture: Essays in Honour of Barnabas Lindars* (ed. D.A. Carson and H.G.M. Williamson; Cambridge: Cambridge University Press, 1988), 99–121 (116–18).

[12] To pay justice to Alexander, he nowhere claims to provide an analytic definition of the term. What he aspires to do is to advance a definition of the category by the establishment of criteria for admission to, or exclusion from the genre. The last section of his article is, in fact, entitled "The 'Rewritten Bible': Towards the Definition of the Genre." The qualities of Alexander's article notwithstanding, it suffers from the fact that he takes his point of departure in *Jubilees*, the *Genesis Apocryphon*, *LAB*, and *Antiquitates*, and makes these writings the standard for his definition of the term. Thus, there is a certain circularity pertaining to his argument, since his choice of texts is decisive for his subsequent definition of the genre. Additionally, he does not discuss to what extent his understanding of genre is determined by the particular perspective through which he filters the writings he is examining, that is that his perception of genre is correlative with his analytical perspective.

[13] G. Vermes, *Scripture and Tradition in Judaism: Haggadic Studies* (StPB 4; Leiden: Brill, 1961), 95.

[14] The inclusion of the Palestinian *Targumim* (*Neofiti*, *Fragment Targum*, *Geniza* fragments, and *Ps.Jonathan*) into the category of rewritten Bible has hardly been followed by other scholars. It is also noticeable that Vermes himself does not discuss the Targumim in the context of rewritten Bible in his later works on the subject. The only exception—to my knowledge—is Brooke, "Rewritten Bible," 780, who mentions the two Qumran Targums on Job (4QtgJob, 11QtgJob) in the context of rewritten Bible and concludes his entry

tion on biblical midrash in the New Schürer, for which Vermes was responsible. He writes that:

> the regular reading of Scripture and the constant meditation on it with a view to interpreting, expounding and supplementing its stories and resolving its textual, contextual and doctrinal difficulties, resulted in a pre-rabbinic haggadah which, once introduced into the scriptural narrative itself, produced a "rewritten" Bible, a fuller, smoother and doctrinally more advanced form of the sacred narrative.[15]

At the same time, however, he also speaks of rewritten Bible as a distinct and definite genre perceived to include the following writings: *Antiquitates, Jubilees, GA, LAB*, the *Book of Noah* (1Q19 and 19bis), the *Testament of Kohath* (4QTQahat), the *Testament of Amram* (4QAmram^(a–e)), a *Samuel Apocryphon* (4Q160), and the *Martyrdom of Isaiah*. In the context of rewritten Bible he also mentions the *Testaments of the Twelve Patriarchs* and the *Life of the Prophets*, but they are relegated to another chapter since they have been subjected to Christian adaptations. The books of Chronicles, which most scholars today include under the heading of rewritten Bible, are treated in the New Schürer under the rubric of haggadic midrash or historical midrash, but it is simultaneously said to embody the same exegetical technique as that found in later writings like *Jubilees* and the *GA*.[16] Be that as it may, the ambiguity in Vermes' perception reflecting an oscillation between a conception of the category in terms of a distinct genre and an understanding in terms of a textual strategy can also be found in a brief article, which he wrote on Qumran and Bible interpretation. On the one hand, he speaks of rewritten Bible as a literary genre, which "seeks to incorporate various explanatory devices into the biblical narrative with a view to clarifying, embellishing, completing or updating it;"[17] on the other hand, he writes of the category as a type of exegesis.

---

on rewritten Bible by arguing that: "Once both the form and content of the biblical books were fixed in Hebrew, Rewritten Bible continued only in the Targums."

[15] G. Vermes, "Bibical Midrash," in *The History of the Jewish People in the Age of Jesus Christ* (ed. idem et al.; rev. ed. of E. Schürer; 3 vols.; Edinburgh: T&T Clark, 1986), 3:308–41 (3:308).

[16] *The History of the Jewish People in the Age of Jesus Christ*, 2:346.

[17] G. Vermes, "Bible Interpretation at Qumran," *Eretz Israel* 20 (1989): 185*–88* (187*). Vermes distinguishes in the article between three different grades of biblical interpretation: (1) implicit exegesis of an editorial type best represented by the *Temple Scroll*; (2) exegesis of individual books of the Bible exemplified by *GA* and the various *Pesharim*; and (3) exegesis of excerpts from various writings assembled according to common themes. The differentiation is interesting for several reasons. Apart from the

3. REWRITTEN BIBLE AS A TEXTUAL STRATEGY

One group of scholars—most noticeably represented by George Nickelsburg and Daniel Harrington—understand rewritten Bible in terms of a
textual strategy by which biblical texts were expanded and paraphrased,
and thus, implicitly commented upon. Nickelsburg emphasises that
rewritten Bible texts:

> employ a variety of genres: running paraphrases of longer and shorter
> parts of the Bible, often with lengthy expansions (*Jubilees*, Genesis Apocry-
> phon, *Biblical Antiquities*); narrative blocks in a non-narrative genre (stories
> about the flood in the apocalypse or testament known as *1 Enoch*); a nar-
> rative roughly shaped by a non-narrative genre (the quasi-testamentary
> *Apocalypse of Moses*); poetic presentations of biblical stories in epic and
> dramatic form (Philo the Elder, Theodotus, Ezekiel the Tragedian.[18]

In addition to Vermes' list of rewritten Bible texts, Nickelsburg adds the
following writings to the category: *1 En* 6–11; 12–16; 65–67; 83–83;
106–107; the *Book of Giants* (4QEnGiants[a–f]); the *Apocalypse of Moses*;
the *Life of Adam and Eve*; Philo the Epic Poet; Theodotus the Epic Poet;
Ezekiel the Tragedian; *1 Esdras* 3–4; additions to the book of Esther;
the catalogue of Davidic compositions in *11QPs[a]* 27:2–11; *Baruch*; the
Epistle of Jeremiah; and the *Prayer of Azariah* and the *Song of the three
Young Men*.[19]

Daniel Harrington, similarly, emphasises the plurality of genres
traditionally subsumed under the heading of rewritten Bible. He even

---

fact that Vermes by his distinctions paves the way for a preliminary and very crucial
typology of different gradations of intertextuality with regard to "biblical" exegesis, he
clearly places the *Temple Scroll* in another group than those writings subsumed under
the category of rewritten Bible texts. Scholars like Bernstein who argues in favour of a
very narrow definition of rewritten Bible—allegedly—in accordance with Vermes' initial
understanding overlooks the fact that Vermes not only ignores, but, in fact, discards
the *Temple Scroll* from the category of rewritten Bible in the only work—that is to my
knowledge—in which he discusses the composition in connection with the subject of
rewritten Bible. See Bernstein, "A Generic Category," 193–95.

[18] G.W.E. Nickelsburg, "The Bible Rewritten and Expanded," in *Jewish Writings
of the Second Temple Period* (ed. M.E. Stone; CRINT 2,2; Assen: Van Gorcum, 1984),
89–156 (89–90).

[19] Contrary to Vermes and all other scholars who have worked on rewritten Bible,
Nickelsburg leaves out—without explanation—Josephus' *Antiquitates* from his list of
works subsumed under the heading. It may have to do with the fact that Josephus is
treated in a separate chapter authored by H.W. Attridge in the same volume, but it
is nevertheless conspicuous that Nickelsburg does not even mention *Antiquitates* in the
context of rewritten Bible.

increases the number by suggesting the inclusion of additional writings into the category. He adds to Vermes' initial list—with the exception of the Palestinian *Targumim*—the *Assumption* (or *Testament*) *of Moses* and a little surprisingly the *Temple Scroll*. Surprising, since he nowhere discusses the inclusion of a legal text type into the category.[20] In the periphery of these writings, mention is also made of the *Paralipomena of Jeremiah*, the *Life of Adam and Eve*, and the *Ascension of Isaiah*, which—although they do not have the same close, structural intertextual relationship to the biblical narrative—are nevertheless said to have a close connection to the previously mentioned works. The category is further expanded by Harrington's proposal that: "the restriction to Palestinian writings taking the flow of the biblical narrative as their structural principle is admittedly artificial, since there is a good deal of possible biblical interpretation in *1 Enoch*, the other Qumran writings, 4 Ezra, *2 Baruch*, etc."[21]

In the same vein he suggests that some works of Philo could possibly be subsumed under the rubric in spite of the fact that Philo's "literary form of exposition and his allegorical method set him apart from" the remaining writings.[22] Not surprisingly—taking the wide spectrum of different text types into account—Harrington argues in favour of a comprehensive understanding seeing rewritten Bible as a kind of activity or process rather than a distinct genre: "In conclusion, it is

---

[20] D.J. Harrington, "The Bible Rewritten (Narratives)," in *Early Judaism and Its Modern Interpreters* (ed. R.A. Kraft and G.W.E. Nickelsburg; Atlanta: Scholars Press, 1986), 239–47. There has been a substantial discussion during recent years whether one should, in fact, also include halakhic texts into the category of rewritten Bible. A majority of scholars now seem inclined to expand the category to also encompass legal texts. See, for instance, D.D. Swanson, *The Temple Scroll and the Bible: The Methodology of 11QT* (STDJ 14; Leiden: Brill, 1995), 227; D. Dimant, "The Scrolls and the Study of Early Judaism," in *The Dead Sea Scrolls at Fifty: Proceedings of the 1997 Society of Biblical Literature Qumran Section Meetings* (ed. R.A. Kugler and E.M. Schuller; SBLEJL15; Atlanta: Scholars Press 1999), 43–59 (50); Brooke, "Rewritten Bible," 779; Bernstein, "A Generic Category," 193–95. The expansion of the category to include legal material as well is in my view an additional argument in favour of a more comprehensive understanding of the phenomenon rather than a perception of it in terms of a narrow genre.
[21] Harrington, "The Bible Rewritten (Narratives)," 239.
[22] Harrington, "The Bible Rewritten (Narratives)," 239. The inclusion of some of Philo's works into the category has also been suggested by Peder Borgen, who proposes to categorise the *Life of Moses* and the *Exposition of the Laws* (*De opificio mundi; De Abraham; De Iosepho; De decalogo; De specialibus legibus; De virtutibus; De praemiis et poenis*; and the two lost tractates *De Isaac* and *De Iacobo*) as rewritten Bible texts. See P. Borgen, "Philo of Alexandria," in *Jewish Writings of the Second Temple Period*, 233–82 (234). The understanding is further developed in idem, "Rewritten Bible?" in *Philo of Alexandria: An Exegete for His Time* (NovTSup 86; Leiden: Brill, 1997), 63–79.

tempting to place all these books, as well as others, under the broad literary genre of "rewritten Bible," but unfortunately the diversity and complexity of the materials will not allow it."[23]

4. REWRITTEN BIBLE AS A GENRE

Contrary to this line of scholarship, another group of scholars has taken its point of departure in Vermes' designation of rewritten Bible as a distinct genre. Before presenting his nine criteria for inclusion into, or exclusion from the genre, Alexander rhetorically raises the question, if, in fact, *Jubilees*, the *GA*, *Antiquitates*, and the *LAB* represent a definite and distinct literary genre. He answers affirmatively by arguing that the similarities shared by these four writings far surpass the differences that pertain to their language, audience, style, and individual emphasis.[24]

Similarly to Alexander, Moshe Bernstein has recently and (quite vigorously) argued in favour of a narrow understanding of the category to designate a distinct genre only. In his view a comprehensive understanding of the category entails a broadening of the classification that renders the notion an excessively vague all-encompassing term.[25] His main concern is to preserve the category as a valuable classificatory device. He, therefore, endorses the view that the term should be employed in a disciplined and constrained fashion only. He grants the line of scholarship represented by Nickelsburg and Harrington among others that almost the entire Jewish literature of the last part of the Second Temple Period in one way or another can be said to rely on "biblical" literary antecedents and, thus, to exemplify a kind of rewritten Bible. But in order to distinguish between this more general understanding and a narrow definition of the term, Bernstein proposes to differentiate between *rewritten Bible* as a designation for a specific genre and *rewriting the Bible* as a description of the process that encompassed almost the whole literary production of Second Temple Judaism.[26]

---

[23] Harrington, "The Bible Rewritten (Narratives)," 243; cf. Brooke, "Rewritten Bible," 780.

[24] Alexander, "Retelling the Old Testament," 116.

[25] Bernstein, "A Generic Category," 187.

[26] Bernstein, "A Generic Category," 195. Cf. C.A. Newsom, *The Self as Symbolic Space: Constructing Identity and Community at Qumran* (STDJ 52; Leiden: Brill, 2004), 6: "Echoes of the biblical text haunt virtually all of the new literary compositions of this period. It is the 'super adequacy' of the biblical idiom that authors of this period have to confront, a traditional language that facilitates and authorizes their speech but at the

He keenly recognises that in order to maintain a narrow definition it is crucial to fence it off on two fronts, which both challenge its distinctiveness. On the one hand, it is essential to distinguish rewritten Bible texts from writings that either represent alternate versions of Bible texts or revised editions.[27] On the other hand, it is correspondingly important to distinguish rewritten Bible texts from writings that have a much looser relationship to their biblical *Vorlage*, that is, writings that use a particular biblical motif, a specific biblical passage, or a certain narrative character, etc., as a springboard for developing an entirely new composition. Since all the compositions that come under discussion to different degrees take their point of departure in biblical literary antecedents, Bernstein is concerned to delimit rewritten Bible texts from writings "which are more loosely parabiblical and whose relationship with the Bible is much more tenuous."[28] Compositions like the *Life of Adam and Eve*, *1 Enoch*, the Qumran *Apocryphon of Jeremiah*, and *pseudo-Ezekiel* are hence classified as parabiblical literature rather than rewritten Bible, since they have a much freer relationship to the

---

same time dominates it. This is not to say that the literary production of the Second Temple Judaism was not creative but to note that authors were always glancing over their shoulders at the speech of scripture."

[27] In the previously mentioned article by Segal, "Between Bible and Rewritten Bible," he attempts to establish such a criteriology that would enable scholarship to distinguish between compositions, which represent alternate or revised versions of biblical texts and rewritten Bible texts. The main difference between the two categories is that the latter group of writings embodies a rewriting on a much grander scale in comparison to the former group of texts. Bernstein concurs with Segal's argument on most points; see Bernstein, "A Generic Category," 193.

[28] Bernstein, "A Generic Category," 193. Bernstein owes the distinction between rewritten Bible and parabiblical literature to White Crawford, "The Rewritten Bible at Qumran," 174, who defines parabiblical literature as texts that, although tied to some person, event, or pericope in the present canonical text, "do not actually reuse extensively the biblical texts." Rewritten Bible, conversely, designates writings that have "a close narrative attachment to some book contained in the present Jewish canon of scripture, and some type of reworking, whether through rearrangement, conflation, omission, or supplementation of the present canonical biblical text" (173f.). See also the attempt by Tov, "Biblical Texts as Reworked," 111, to differentiate between a reworking or rewriting of the Bible and a rephrasing of it: "In our terminology, a distinction is made between reworking/rewriting which involved a limited intervention in the biblical text, and rephrasing involving a major intervention, often in such a way that the underlying biblical text is hardly recognizable. Adding exegetical comments to the biblical text is a form of rewriting." Parabiblical is a term used in several of the DJD volumes, in which it is defined by the chief editor Emanuel Tov as "closely related to texts or themes of the Hebrew Bible." See E. Tov, "Foreword," in *DJD* 13: ix–x (ix). Needless to say, such a definition only increases the fuzzy nature of the category, since it overlaps with the traditional definition of works belonging to rewritten Bible.

biblical texts. Apart from the *Temple Scroll*, some of the manuscripts of
4QReworked Pentateuch,[29] and the *Apocryphon of Joshua*, Bernstein confines
rewritten Bible to include the non-targumic writings of Vermes' initial
classification only. Although he does not provide an analytical definition of the genre proper, he promulgates a narrow use of the term that
demands a "comprehensive or broad scope rewriting of narrative and/
or legal material with commentary woven into the fabric implicitly, but
perhaps *not* merely a biblical text with some superimposed exegesis."[30]
In this manner, he presupposes a textual continuum consisting of three
classes digitally divided by two caesuras. One pole of the textual axis
is constituted by revised or alternate versions of biblical texts, whereas
the other pole is represented by parabiblical writings. Hence, rewritten
Bible texts are situated between these two groups of writings.

Needless to say in light of the previous discussion, I find Bernstein's
typology skewed by its anachronistic biblical categories. Although he
is keenly aware of the problems pertaining to an anachronistic use of
language with regard to works of Second Temple Judaism,[31] he nevertheless uses categories like rewritten Bible and parabiblical literature.
If, however, no canon existed prior to, say, the late 1st century C.E.,
the appellation "biblical" appears rather odd and misleading. The
ambiguity pertaining to Bernstein's understanding is evident from his
argument that "(1) *biblical* texts (however we shall define them; I assert,
if it *is* [or was intended to be] a biblical text, then it is not rewritten
Bible, and (2) biblical translations. In the case of biblical texts, of course,
matters of canon and audience may play a role. One group's rewritten

---

[29] Bernstein, "A Generic Category," 195–96, is of the opinion that not all of the
manuscripts traditionally attributed to *4QRP* represent a single text. Since 4Q158 seems
to include non-biblical material to such an extent that it cannot be categorised as revised
Bible, Bernstein tends to classify it under the heading of rewritten Bible. One cannot
help asking, however, whether it is the underlying distinction between allegedly revised
forms of the Bible text and rewritten forms of the Bible text that ultimately leads
Bernstein to drive in a wedge between the different manuscripts belonging to *4QRP*.
If it is acknowledged that the differentiation between various gradations of intertextual
dependence on authoritative literary antecedents represents our ways of conceiving
a particular issue of interest to the contemporary scholarly community, that is the
subject of scriptural intertextuality, rather than something "in the texts themselves,"
Bernstein's argument looses its force. For another understanding of the relationship
between 4Q158 and *4QRP*, see Tov, "Biblical Texts as Reworked," 125–26.

[30] Bernstein, "A Generic Category," 195.

[31] Bernstein, "A Generic Category," 172 n. 3.

Bible could very well be another's biblical text!"[32] On the basis of this understanding, I think Bernstein should categorise a work like *Jubilees* as Bible rather than rewritten Bible, and that perhaps demonstrates the ambiguities of his categorisation.

5. Challenges to the Current Debate

If the choice of approach to rewritten Scripture, however, is not only a matter of the individual scholar's predilection for a comprehensive understanding or a more narrow definition, we shall raise the question which of the two approaches provides us with the most adequate understanding of the category? To what extent does it make sense to speak of rewritten Scripture as a particular and distinct genre, and in what sense is it helpful to conceive of it as a more general textual phenomenon or strategy common to a variety of works belonging to different genres? Do the two approaches exclude each other or are they at some point compatible?

I concur with Bernstein that in order to serve as a valuable classificatory device it is important to use scholarly categories in a disciplined and constrained fashion. If rewritten Scripture is conceived of in a manner that has turned the notion into an excessively vague category that encompasses a wide generic spectrum of different texts produced throughout the Second Temple Period, it may be close to useless—from the perspective of a generic understanding. If, on the other hand, the idea underlying the notion is to designate a textual strategy shared by a multiplicity of works mirroring different genres, then a comprehensive use of the term does not in itself constitute a problem.

Bernstein so adamantly emphasises the necessity for clear definitions that he seems to turn a blind eye to the problems that have caused George Nickelsburg, Daniel Harrington, and others to give up the idea of rewritten Bible as a distinct genre. If the main argument for upholding rewritten Bible as a designation of a distinct genre confined to a few texts only is the need for a scholarly disciplined terminology, that argument is seriously challenged if the term can be maintained only at the cost of ignoring important parts of the empirical data. Even if we exclude the writings attributed to rewritten Bible by, for instance,

---

[32] Bernstein, "A Generic Category," 175.

Nickelsburg and Harrington, and confine ourselves to the compositions originally proposed by Vermes to be the paradigmatic exemplars of the genre, do these works, in fact, belong to a distinct and common genre? And if so, what exactly is meant by genre? From what analytical perspective is it meaningful to speak of rewritten Scripture?

If one examines the history of research of the category, it seems to be taken for granted by almost all scholars that rewritten Bible can only be conceived in terms of an ancient literary genre. But is that a valid assumption? Even scholars who prefer to think of rewritten Bible in terms of a literary strategy seem to perceive genre from an *emic* perspective only. This is also characteristic of Jonathan Campbell who has most fervently spoken in favour of abandoning the term altogether:

> In the context of late Second Temple Judaism, therefore, "Rewritten Scripture(s)" and "Rewritten Bible" are unsatisfactory terms. Both fail to take account of the fact that scribes could produce material in their own name or pseudepigraphically and readers could receive books as recent literature or antique scripture. These complexities mean that, from a late Second Temple perspective, there was no genre incorporating all the works regularly denoted "Rewritten Bible" or, more recently, "Rewritten Scripture" by scholars.[33]

Campbell and others, however, do not raise the question whether it would be tenable to acknowledge rewritten Scripture as a generic term, if we accept that only an *etic* perspective makes it meaningful and heuristically valuable to operate with such a category.

It follows that there is more involved in the current discussion of rewritten Bible than any individual scholar's preference for narrow definitions compared to more comprehensive ones and vice-versa. The debate about rewritten Bible is indicative of the manner in which we conceive of the relationship between "biblical" and "parabiblical" texts. The focus on the question how different writings intertextually relate to biblical literary antecedents is a problem of interest to a scholarly community situated in a social and cultural context in which the Bible—in whatever precise canonical form—plays a decisive role. We should, however, acknowledge that our particular concerns do not necessarily reflect the interests of the ancient authors of these compositions. It may be a trivial point, but it needs to be underlined that the ancient writers did not compose their texts with our intertextual interests in mind. Authoritative scriptures were intertextually decisive as matrices

---

[33] Campbell, "'Rewritten Bible,'" 50.

for the formation of new compositions in the latter part of the Second Temple Period, but this literary relationship cannot account for the creation of the new writings themselves. They were composed with others aims in mind.

Before we reach a conclusion with regard to the main question of this essay, whether we should think of rewritten Scripture as a distinct genre or as a more comprehensive textual strategy, let us return to the subject of borderline writings. This issue has come even more to the fore of the discussion following the complete publication of the "biblical" and "parabiblical" material from Qumran.[34] The debate about rewritten Bible, therefore, has been considerably advanced with the publication of this textual data, since we now have a more extensive and thorough knowledge of the diversity of forms of biblical exegetical techniques than was available at the time when Geza Vermes and Philip Alexander wrote their pioneer studies on rewritten Bible.

6. Borderline Texts

In the previously mentioned study on borderline texts, Florentino García Martínez elucidates the notion by arguing that the term designates the two-fold problem of, how, on the one hand, a clear-cut differentiation can be made between the "biblical" text and "biblical" texts, and, on the other hand, how a precise distinction can be drawn between "biblical" and "non-biblical" writings.[35] The question has an obvious affinity with the classificatory problems that prompted Moshe Bernstein to develop a tripartite typology of revised Bible texts, rewritten Bible texts, and parabiblical literature. In 1991 García Martínez emphasised the importance of this debate and foretold that: "without any doubt at all, (it) will determine the discussions of the next few years and will make itself heard in many publications."[36]

The truth of García Martínez' prediction has been proved by the rapid development within the field of early biblical interpretation in

---

[34] See the extensive discussion of the subject by M.J. Bernstein, "The Contribution of the Qumran Discoveries to the History of Early Biblical Interpretation," in *The Idea of Biblical Interpretation: Essays in Honor of James L. Kugel* (ed. H. Najman and J.H. Newman; JSJSup 83; Leiden: Brill, 2004), 215–38 (216).

[35] García Martínez, "Biblical Borderlines," 123.

[36] García Martínez, "Biblical Borderlines," 123 (the original "Las fronteras de «lo bíblico»" is from 1991).

general and Qumran scholarship in particular. Numerous works have recently been published that focus on either one of the two poles that constitute the textual spectrum of early Scriptures and exegesis. The relationship between the two entities has obviously a fuzzy character, since the transitions between them are fluid by nature, and the category Scripture itself embodies works that are exegetically exploiting scriptural antecedents. Deuteronomy, for instance, may be seen as a rewritten Scripture of law material originating in Exodus, Leviticus, and Numbers. At the same time, however, Deuteronomy itself functions as Scripture, that is—as the Latinised Greek name suggests—a second collection of laws, that on its own has caused new instances of rewritten Scripture.

If, for a moment, we disregard the blurriness of the categories and decide for analytical purposes to make a clear-cut distinction between them, we are confronted with two different types of questions. First, and at the one end of the spectrum, there is the important discussion about distinctions between different versions of Scriptures or "bible" texts. This debate is concerned with the criteriological question how and when to decide whether a particular writing represents a revision of a "biblical" text or an alternate version of it. This question has especially come to the fore with the acknowledgement of a number of Qumran "biblical" writings that on different points deviate from the known textual witnesses, but simultaneously preserve versions that are remarkably similar to already known textual types.[37] In the previously mentioned study on the differences between Bible and rewritten Bible, Michael Segal has formulated this problem with regard to *4QReworked Pentateuch* very concisely. He raises the question: "How should one classify texts that exhibit such similarity to the known versions of the Torah, yet simultaneously attest to hitherto unknown readings and passages?"[38] At the same time, this discussion raises the correlated question how to demarcate the point beyond which Scripture or—conventionally expressed—"biblical" writing gradually slides into an interpretation of a scriptural text. In other words, when does a scriptural text cease to be a scriptural writing and becomes an interpretation of a scriptural composition? Despite the fuzzy nature of the transitions between the

---

[37] See particularly the important collection of essays by E. Ulrich, *The Dead Sea Scrolls and the Origins of the Bible* (SDSS; Grand Rapids: Eerdmans, 1999); and Tov, "Biblical Texts as Reworked."

[38] Segal, "Between Bible and Rewritten Bible," 15.

two categories—clearly exemplified by Deuteronomy—and the problems involved in providing definite answers, it is urgent to be able to
differentiate between deviations from Scripture that originate in exegesis
on the part of the author(s)/editor(s) and writings that simply reflect
alternate versions.

Secondly, and at the opposite end of the spectrum, the discussion is
concerned with the question how to differentiate between writings that
by their grades of paraphrasing, rephrasing, reworking, and rewriting of
Scripture differ from each other.[39] It is crucial to delineate those points
that determine the relationship between different modes of writings all
presupposing the existence of a scriptural *Vorlage*, which to a greater
or lesser extent they develop in different manners. During recent years
we have witnessed a variety of different concepts like *rewritten Bible, texte
continué, retold Bible, reworked Bible, paraphrased Bible, biblical midrash,* and
parabiblical literature, etc., that all point to the existence of different literary
modes that each develop scriptural antecedents in different ways. At the
same time, however, the existence of the different notions also document a lack of conceptual clarity when it comes to the understanding
of the precise relationship between each of these different categories—a
fact exemplified by the frequent synonymous use of some of these
terms in the works of single scholars. Additionally, one may also point
to the rich nomenclature that pertains to the designation of various
Qumran texts like *4QPseudo-Moses, 4QApocryphon of Moses, 4QReworked
Pentateuch, 4QCommentary on Genesis, 4QParaphrase of Genesis and Exodus,*
etc. This pluriformity of designations underlines the ambiguities that
pertain to a clear generic understanding of the writings. In lieu of this
situation, it is urgent that we begin our examination of the borderline
phenomenon by acknowledging the fuzzy nature of the problem with
regard to both poles of the textual spectrum. In an essay on the Bible
and biblical interpretation in Qumran by Julio Trebolle Barrera, he
poignantly states that:

> Now this borderline has become much more vague and the transition
> from biblical to para-biblical forms seems to be more fluid. The para-
> biblical forms can go back to ancient lost texts, which never succeeded
> in becoming part of the authorised or canonical biblical text, or they can
> represent developments on the margin of the text which was authorised

---

[39] Cf. Bernstein, "A Generic Category," 193.

later. These textual forms could still be part of biblical manuscripts which
were in circulation until the start of the Christian era.[40]

In addition to Trebolle's acute observation, we may add that the problem is even more complex due to the fact that some writings are of a
Protean nature. Dependent on the analytical perspective, we find texts
like Deuteronomy and the books of Chronicles that simultaneously
fit into the category Scripture and into the rubric of rewritten Scripture.
Both are rewritings of scriptural antecedents. Whereas Deuteronomy
rewrote parts of Exodus, Leviticus, and Numbers, the books of
Chronicles were dependent on Samuel and Kings as a literary matrix
for the formation of a new composition. At the same time, both writings gave rise to the creation of new compositions. Whereas 1 Esdras
is partly a rewritten Scripture of Chronicles, a number of works rewriting either the Pentateuch or parts of it were strongly influenced by
Deuteronomy.

7. The Location of the Generic Question

Contrary to scholars of Graeco-Roman literature, we are not in the
fortunate position that an ancient meta-theoretical literature of genres
and textual forms existed with regard to the ancient Hebrew and
Aramaic literature. Whereas it is possible to classify a number of Jewish
Hellenistic works composed in Greek according to the narrative patterns, the rhetorical genres, the different topoi and motifs discussed in
the rhetorical and epistolary handbooks of the Graeco-Roman world,
this is more difficult with regard to the majority of Hebrew compositions that during the past decade have come to the forefront of the
scholarly debate. The lack of an ancient meta-theoretical literature
on different scriptural and exegetical genres, however, does not release
scholarship from the attempt to develop the theoretical framework for
such a discussion.

Since no ancient categories or concepts comparable to our abstract
designations *rewritten Bible, parabiblical literature, reworked Bible, rewritten
Scripture*, etc. existed, the discussion primarily belongs to an *etic* level of
analysis. It is the interest of the contemporary scholarly community that

---

[40] J. Trebolle Barrera, "The Bible and Biblical Interpretation in Qumran," in *The
People of the Dead Sea Scrolls*, 99–121 (104).

determines the need for such designations. Despite the *etic* nature of the debate, however, the classificatory attempt does also have a certain *emic* foundation to the extent that the *etic* categories relate to different modes of scriptural and rewritten scriptural literature that simply were not acknowledged as such by particular genre designations of the ancient world.[41] The ancient author(s) or editor(s) did not conceive of their works in terms of our particular analytical focus on how their textual creations intertextually relate to scriptural writings proper. This problem is seldom acknowledged in the scholarly literature, but it does have a bearing on the discussion of rewritten Scripture.

From an *etic* level, it may be quite reasonable to classify, for instance, the first eleven books of Josephus' *Antiquitates* (*Ant.* 1–11.296) as exemplifying rewritten Scripture. Despite the problem involved in a genre designation that encompasses a part of the work only, it should be recognised that this was not the way Josephus understood his work. On the contrary, he describes it—in line with a Graeco-Roman historiographical tradition—as an attempt to "embrace our entire ancient history and political constitution, translated from the Hebrew records" to the Greek-speaking world as a whole (*Ant.* 1.5).[42]

A comparable problem may be seen with regard to *Jubilees*, where there also seems to be a discrepancy between the modern genre designation and the manner in which the work presents itself. Similar to the Josephus example, it is—as most scholars do nowadays—from an *etic* perspective appropriate to classify *Jubilees* as a piece of rewritten Bible,[43] but it is far from evident that this was the way the author(s)/redactor(s) perceived their work. On the contrary, *Jubilees* introduces itself as on a par with God's revelation on Mount Sinai and, thus, invokes a claim to scriptural authority. *Jubilees* explicitly states that the content of the book had been given to Moses by the angel of the presence acting on God's behalf during the forty days Moses was on Mount Sinai to receive the law. In this manner, *Jubilees* arrogates to itself a claim to Mosaic authority that is not secondary to the scriptural writings proper. *Jubilees* presents itself as a revelatory discourse, which from an *emic* perspective

---

[41] Cf. A. Fowler, "The Formation of Genres in the Renaissance and After," *New Literary History* 34/2 (2003): 185–200 (188): "The absence of a genre label is of course no argument against the genre's existence; after all, the architectural orders themselves went unnamed for more than 1500 years."

[42] Translation by H.St.J. Thackeray in the LCL-edition.

[43] See most recently M. Segal, *The Book of Jubilees: Rewritten Bible, Redaction, Ideology and Theology* (JSJSup 117; Leiden: Brill, 2007), esp. 4–5.

makes it more appropriate to categorise the composition in connection with other apocalyptic writings—in spite of the fact that apocalyptic is obviously also an *etic* category.

Be that as it may, it may well be that no ancient meta-theoretical discourse of different genres of scriptural and rewritten scriptural works existed. But that, of course, does not entail that the individual writings did not comply with particular literary standards with regard to both content and form. Even if the genres were not acknowledged to the extent that they were made the object of a meta-theoretical discourse, authors composed their writings functionally dependent on already existing system of genres, which they to a greater or lesser extent of artistic skill developed and transformed in different ways.[44] Texts are neither with regard to content nor form created *de novo*. They are woven together by different threads and are part of a larger cultural and social tapestry, since they presuppose the existence of other writings and textual forms, which they simultaneously challenge, develop, and are strongly influenced by.[45] On the basis of such an understanding, it is reasonable to define genre in terms of the number of properties pertaining to both content and form that a certain group of writings—to a greater or lesser extent—share and by which they differ from other types of texts. Such an approach simultaneously enables us to take the continuous generic modulations seriously and to acknowledge the relative stability of a given genre.

Karlyn Campbell and Kathleen Jamieson, in fact, have made the recurrence of certain properties the basis of their definition of genre. They write that "if the recurrence of similar forms establishes a genre, then genres are groups of discourses which share substantive, stylistic and situational characteristics." Some of these properties may, of course, also be found in other text types, but the point made by Campbell and Jamieson is that "a genre is a group of acts unified by a constellation of forms that recurs in each of its members. These forms, *in isolation*, appear in other discourses. What is distinctive about the acts in a genre is the recurrence of the forms *together* in constellation."[46] Given such

---

[44] Cf. T. Todorov, "The Origin of Genres," *New Literary History* 8 (1976): 159–70 (161).

[45] Cf. A. Fowler, *Kinds of Literature: An Introduction to the Theory of Genres and Modes* (Oxford: Clarendon Press, 1982), 23, who rightly emphasises the liquid nature of genres.

[46] K.K. Campbell and K.H. Jamieson, "Form and Genre in Rhetorical Criticism: An Introduction," in *Form and Genre: Shaping Rhetorical Action* (ed. K.K. Campbell and

an understanding of genre, it is fairly easy to dismantle the idea of rewritten Scripture as a genre from an *emic* perspective. Bruce Fisk has forcefully made the argument that:

> On closer inspection, however, these allegedly similar works prove to be remarkably diverse; they all share a narrative framework and depend heavily upon antecedent Scripture, but they differ widely in apparent purpose, modes of embellishment, and in the demands they place on their readers. As a generic category, "rewritten Bible" implies neither a particular method of borrowing nor the extent of literary dependence.[47]

Contrary to Jonathan Campbell, however, I think there is good reason to maintain the category—although with a slightly different name—even if it is abandoned at the *emic* level. We shall just have to acknowledge that rewritten Scripture is not situated at the *emic*, but at the *etic* level. The taxonomic focus on the intertextuality between scriptural works and subsequent compositions that rewrite their scriptural antecedents is a legitimate concern that cannot simply be relegated to the realm of later canonical interests. It is not only entirely appropriate but also crucial to raise the typological question, how different types of scriptural and rewritten scriptural literature—belonging to the same textual spectrum—differ from each other with regard to discursive properties.

8. A Brief Conclusion

Returning to our initial question, whether we should conceive of rewritten Scripture in terms of a distinct genre or more comprehensively in terms of a textual strategy, we have reached a paradoxical conclusion. On the one hand, we have to side with those scholars who have emphasised the generic pluriformity of the writings traditionally classified as rewritten Bible over advocates of a narrow generic understanding. From an *emic* perspective, it is not meaningful to think of rewritten Bible as a distinct literary genre. For that purpose, the compositions under examination are too different to be meaningfully classified under the same generic rubric. On the other hand, however, it is legitimate to perceive rewritten Scripture in terms of genre, if we acknowledge that

---

K.H. Jamieson; Falls Church, Va.: Speech Communication Association, 1978), 9–32 (20–21). Cf. Todorov, "The Origin of Genres," 162.

[47] B.N. Fisk, *Do you not Remember? Scripture, Story and Exegesis in the Rewritten Bible of Pseudo-Philo* (JSPSup 37; Sheffield: Sheffield Academic Press, 2001), 14.

the generic categorisation is located at the *etic* level and that the generic essence of this category is constituted by the taxonomic interest in scriptural intertextuality. Hence, we are confronted with the challenge—at the *etic* level—to develop a typology of scriptural intertextuality that enables us to differentiate not only between different species on a common textual continuum, but also to expound a criteriology by which the criteria for classifying different compositions into particular types or groups become lucid.[48] It is urgent that such a typology is dynamic and fluid to the extent that different writings—dependent on the analytical perspective—may take up different positions on the textual axis.

Previous scholarly debates on the differences between biblical, apocryphal, and pseudepigraphal writings did, obviously, also embody an awareness of the problem of borderline texts. The acknowledgement, however, of the extent to which this problem is intrinsic to the manner we perceive the biblical writings has not and (presumably) could not be recognised prior to the publication of the "biblical" material of the Dead Sea Scrolls.[49] Florentino García Martínez, for one, has been a pioneer in pointing to the importance of the Dead Sea Scrolls for a renewed and refined understanding of the borderline problem.

---

[48] In spite of my disagreements at some points with Bernstein, "A Generic Category," and Segal, "Between Bible and Rewritten Bible," I value their endeavour to develop the framework for such a typology.

[49] Trebolle Barrera, "The Bible and Biblical Interpretation in Qumran," 102.

ANNOTAZIONI SU ALCUNI TEMI ENOCHICI A QUMRAN

Giovanni Ibba

In questo contributo vorrei riportare alcune mie annotazioni riguardanti l'influenza di temi enochici su alcune opere trovate nelle grotte qumraniche. Sono: l'origine del male nel mondo; la lista di quattro angeli; la visione angelica.

LA CADUTA ANGELICA E I GIGANTI

Nel capitolo 6 libro del libro della Genesi e, soprattutto, nel *Libro dei Vigilanti* (1 Enoc 6–7),[1] c'è una spiegazione diversa dell'origine del male nel mondo rispetto a quella che si vede nel capitolo 3 del primo libro della Bibbia: si legge di angeli che si unirono a delle donne, le quali concepirono "Giganti" (si vedano Gen 6,2 e *Libro dei Vigilanti*: 1 Enoc 6,2–7,2), esseri che portarono un tale grado di disordine e di contaminazione in tutta l'umanità (1 Enoc 7,3–6) che Dio si vide costretto a cancellare la maggior parte degli uomini con il diluvio (Gen 6,17; 1 Enoc 10,2) e ad abbreviare la vita dell'uomo a cento venti anni (Gen 6,3).

I frammenti del *Libro dei Vigilanti* trovati a Qumran con questo episodio sono andati persi, mentre rimane la versione etiopica del testo (in 1 Enoc) che probabilmente contiene aggiunte redazionali. In ogni caso tale racconto viene riportato per esempio in modo metaforico dal *Libro dei Sogni*.

Di questi Giganti se ne parla anche in alcuni manoscritti qumranici scritti in aramaico databili tra la prima e la seconda metà del I sec. a.C. che, per quello che si riesce a capire vista la loro frammentarietà, contengono in parte anche un riassunto del *Libro dei Vigilanti*. Tali

---

[1] R.H. Charles, *The Book of Enoch or 1 Enoch* (Oxford: Clarendon Press, 1912); L. Fusella, "Libro dei Vigilanti", in *Apocrifi dell'Antico Testamento, I* (a cura di P. Sacchi; 2. ed.; Torino: UTET, 1989), 413–667; G.W.E. Nickelsburg, *1 Enoch 1: A Commentary on the Book of 1 Enoch, Chapters 1–36; 81–108* (Hermeneia; Minneapolis: Fortress Press, 2001), soprattutto 165–87; G.W.E. Nickelsburg e J.C. VanderKam, *1 Enoch* (Minneapolis: Fortress, 2004), 19–49.

manoscritti hanno la seguente sigla di catalogazione: 1QGiganti^{a-b}, 2QGiganti, 4QGiganti^{a-e} e 6QGiganti.[2]

Nel frammento 8, righe 3–14, di 4QGiganti^a (4Q203)[3] si legge:

פרשגן לוחא תנ[י]נא די אי[גרתא...] 3
בכ[ת]ב יד חגוך ספר פרשא [...] 4
וקדישא לשמיחזה ולכול ח[נברוהי 5
ידיע להוא לכון ד[י כו]ל[ל...][4] 6
ועובדכון ודי נשיכון[...] 7
אנון [ו]בני[הון ונ[שׁיא ד[י בניהון [...] 8
בזנותכון בארעא והות[ן ע]ליכ[ון ...] 9
וקבלה עליכון [וע]ל עובד בניכון[...] 10
חבלא די חבלתון בה vacat[...] 11
עד רפאל מטה ארו אבד[נא...] 12
ודי במדבריא וד[י] בימיא 13

3 Copia della sec[on]da tavola della le[ttera...]
4 in uno sc[ri]tto della mano di Enoc, scriba dell'interpretazione[5][...]
5 e santo, a Shemihaza e a tutti i [suoi] com[pagni...]
6 gli fa sapere ch[e ogn]i [...]
7 le vostre opere e le vostre mogli [...]
8 esse [e] i [lo]ro figli e le [mo]gli de[i loro figli...]
9 con la vostra prostituzione nella terra. Sarà[con]tro di vo[i...]
10 Riceveranno contro di voi e [con]tro le opere dei vostri figli[...]
11 il male che avete fatto *vacat* [...]
12 fino a quando non sarà giunto Raffaele. Ecco (ci sarà) distru[zione...]
13 nei deserti e nei mari.

Evidente è l'episodio che si collega con quanto scritto nel *Libro dei Vigilanti* (1 Enoc 15,1–5), quando Dio spiega a Enoc cosa dovrà riferire agli angeli peccatori. Presente anche il tema della conoscenza della

---

[2] 1Q23–24: J.T. Milik, *DJD* 1:97–99, tavole XIX–XX; 2Q26: M. Baillet, *DJD* 3:334, tavola XVII; 4Q203: Milik, *The Books of Enoch. Aramaic Fragments of Qumran Cave 4* (Oxford: Clarendon Press, 1976), 310–17, tavole XXX–XXXII; 4Q530–533: É. Puech, *DJD* 31:19–115, tavole I–VI; 6Q8: Baillet, *DJD* 3:116–19, tavole XXIV e XXIX; Puech, "Les fragments 1 à 3 du *Livre des Géants* de la Grotte 6 (pap6Q8)", *RevQ* 19/74 (1999): 227–38 (232–38).

[3] 4Q203: Milik, *The Books of Enoch*, 310–17. Cf. F. García Martínez, *Qumran and Apocalyptic. Studies on the Aramaic Texts from Qumran* (STDJ 9; Leiden: Brill, 1992), 97–115; L.T. Stuckenbruck, *The Book of Giants from Qumran* (TSAJ 63; Tübingen: Mohr, 1997), 66–100.

[4] Alla fine della riga 6, seguendo un suggerimento datomi cortesemente da É. Puech, leggo sulla tavola [...]ל[כו]ל[ד[י e non [...]ל[ל[י]ד[come in L.T. Stuckenbruck, *DJD* 36:28.

[5] Riguardo alla radice פרשׁ si veda Puech, *DJD* 31:35.

storia tramite lettura di una tavola celeste; quello degli angeli, di cui qui si nomina Shemihaza; quello del loro peccato nel riferimento alle "loro mogli" (degli angeli), e dei "giganti" (cioè i "loro figli").

Si parla anche del fatto che un giorno verrà Raffaele, che si collega a quanto si legge nel *Libro dei Vigilanti* quando Dio comanda a Raffaele di legare Azazel mani e piedi e di porlo nella tenebra (1 Enoc 10,4).

In seguito, durante il diluvio, secondo quanto si legge in un altro manoscritto qumranico databile paleograficamente alla seconda metà del I sec. a.C. e denominato come *Ammonizione basata sul Diluvio*,[6] si apprende che tali giganti perirono tutti I 2–6:

2   ...והני הם אז עשו הרע בעיני אמר יהוה ויאמרו אל במ[עלי]ליהם

3   וישפטם יהוה כ[כ]ל דרכיהם וכמחשבות יצר לבם ה[רע]וירעם עליהם בכח[ו וי]נעו כל

4   מוסדי אר[ץ ומ]ים נבקעו מתהמות כל ארבות השמים נפתחו ופצו כל תהמו[ת מ]ים אדרים

5   וארבות השמים ה[רי]קו מטר[ו]אבדם במבול [...]ים כלם כיעבר [...]ה[...]

6   עלכן נ[מחו] כלאש[ר ב]חרבה וי[מ]ת האדם וה[בהמה וכל]צפר כל כנף והנ[בור] ים לוא נמלטו

...ed è qua che essi un tempo hanno fatto ciò che è male ai miei occhi, dice JHWH. Si ribellarono contro Dio con le loro az[io]ni. 3 JHWH li giudicò secondo [og]ni loro comportamento e secondo i propositi dell'inclinazione ca[ttiva] del loro cuore. Tuonò contro di loro con [sua] forza [e va]cillarono tutte 4 le fondamenta della te[rra e le acq]ue irruppero dagli abissi; tutte le cateratte del cielo si aprirono e spalancarono tutti gli abis[si delle ac]que grandiose. 5 Le cateratte del cielo ver[sa]rono piogge [e] li fece perire col diluvio [...]—sterminò essi. Così attraverserà (?) [—]. 6 Così s[parì] tutto quel[lo che c'era nella] terraferma: m[or]ì l'uomo e il [suo bestiame e ogni]uccello, ogni alato, e i Gi[gan]ti non scamparono.

Il testo si collega alla narrazione che si ha nel *Libro dei Vigilanti* (1 Enoc 10,2) riguardo al diluvio che Dio manda dopo il peccato distruggendo tutto. 4Q370 aggiunge, rispetto al *Libro dei Vigilanti*, la spiegazione che perirono anche i Giganti.

---

[6] 4Q370: C. Newsom, *DJD* 19:85–97, tavola XII.

I Vigilanti e gli uomini

La storia della caduta angelica del *Libro dei Vigilanti* (1 Enoc 6–7) si trova in una parte del *Documento di Damasco*[7] che, come accade per molti altri scritti, è un'opera sviluppatasi in un arco di tempo abbastanza lungo, presentando stratificazioni redazionali evidenti. La parte che riguarda i Vigilanti potrebbe essere considerata come appartenente a uno degli strati più antichi dell'opera. Anche qui gli angeli, i "Vigilanti", sono visti come coloro che hanno contaminato l'umanità, dunque facendo il male, unendosi con donne e generando i giganti, provocando la punizione di Dio col diluvio. Si legge (II 17–III 1):

17 II   בלכתם בשרירות ...
18   לבם נפלו עירי השמים בה נאחזו אשר לא שמרו מצות אל
19   ובניהם אשר כרום ארזים נבהם וכהרים נויותיהם כי נפלו
20   כל בשר אשר היה בחרבה כי נוע ויהיו כלא היו בעשותם את
21   רצונם ולא שמרו את מצות עשיהם עד אשר חרה אפו בם
1 III   *vacat* בה תעי (תעו) בני נח ומשפחותיהם

II 17...A causa del loro procedere nella durezza 18 del loro cuore i Vigilanti dei cieli sono caduti. In essa sono stati presi, poiché non hanno osservato i comandi di Dio. 19 I loro figli—come l'altitudine dei cedri la loro statura, come montagne i loro corpi—caddero. 20 Ogni carne che si trovava sull'asciutto spirò, e fu come se non fossero esistiti, per aver fatto 21 il loro volere e non aver osservato i comandi del loro Artefice, fino a che non si accese la sua ira contro di loro. III 1 *vacat* Per essa errarono i figli di Noè e le loro famiglie.

In aggiunta a quanto si legge nel *Libro dei Vigilanti* nel *Documento di Damasco* (= CD) si dice che esiste una tendenza a commettere il male oltre che negli angeli anche nell'uomo, e che quindi non è solo il peccato angelico a corrompere. Tale causa a fare il male viene indicata come "durezza del loro cuore" (cf. CD II 17–18: שרירות לבם), durezza attribuita agli angeli, ma anche ai figli di Noè (CD III 1: "per essa errarono i figli di Noè e le loro famiglie"). Da collegare a questa "durezza di cuore" c'è quanto scritto poco dopo, quando si parla di "desiderio dello spirito"

---

[7] S. Schechter, *Documents of Jewish Sectaries, I. Fragments of a Zadokite Work* (Cambridge: Cambridge University Press, 1910); S. Zeitlin, *The Zadokite Fragments. Facsimile of the Manuscripts in the Cairo Genizah Collection in the Possession of the University Library, Cambridge, England* (Philadelphia: Dropsie College, 1952); 4Q266–273: J.M. Baumgarten, *DJD* 18:23–198, tavole I–XLII; 6Q15: Baillet, *DJD* 3:127–28, tavola XXVI; cf. F. García Martínez, "Testi di Qumran", in *Letteratura giudaica intertestamentaria* (a cura di G. Ananda Pérez et al.; Brescia: Paideia, 1998, 42; orig: *Literatura judía intertestamentaria* (Estella: Editorial Verbo Divino, 1996).

(CD III 3: רצון רוח) dell'uomo, che Abramo decise di non seguire per mettere i pratica i precetti di Dio. Nel *Libro dei Vigilanti* infatti si parla solo della durezza di cuore degli angeli (1 Enoc 16,3).[8]

La narrazione della caduta angelica è ripresa nel *Libro dei Giubilei*,[9] in cui si afferma con maggior forza sia la cattiveria congenita dell'uomo nella preghiera di Mastema a Dio (10,8: "grande è la cattiveria dei figli degli uomini"), sia la corresponsabilità degli angeli ribelli a fare il male.

GLI "SPIRITI DEI BASTARDI"

In un frammento, indicato con 4Q510 e chiamato *4QCantici del Saggio*,[10] viene evidenziata la credenza del ruolo del diavolo, indicato in vari modi, nel comportamento iniquo dell'uomo, anche per coloro che cercano di aderire alla volontà di Dio. Nel brano pervenutoci, che molto probabilmente aveva una funzione apotropaica, si legge di "spiriti dei bastardi" (ורוחות ממזרים), che è un'espressione che ricorda molto quella che si trova nel *Libro dei Vigilanti* (1 Enoc 10,9) quando si parla dei Giganti nati dall'unione degli angeli con le donne.[11] L'episodio aveva come contesto il comando di Dio a Gabriele di andare contro i "bastardi", chiamati così perché figli di una unione illegittima.

Nei *Cantici del Saggio* si legge (4Q510 1 4–6):

4   [...ואני משכיל משמיע הוד תפארתו לפחד ולב]הל[
5   כול רוחי מלאכי חבל ורוחות ממזרים שדאים לילית אחים ו]...[
6   והפונעים פתע פתאום לתעות רוח בינה ולהשם לבבם

E io, Saggio, annuncio la magnificenza del suo splendore
per spaventare e terrorizza[re]
5 tutti gli spiriti degli angeli distruttori:

---

[8] Si veda Nickelsburg e VanderKam, *1 Enoch*, 38: "hardness of heart".

[9] R.H. Charles, *The Ethiopic Version of the Hebrew Book of Jubilees* (Oxford: Clarendon Press, 1895); idem, *The Book of Jubilees or the Little Genesis* (London: Black, 1902; repr. 1972); L. Fusella, "Libro dei Giubilei", in *Apocrifi dell'Antico Testamento*, I, 213–411. Riguardo alla bibliografia sui frammenti qumranici del *Libro dei Giubilei* 1Q17–18; 2Q19–20; 3Q5; 4Q176; 4Q218–4Q222; 11Q12, si veda García Martínez, "Testi di Qumran", 112–13.

[10] Baillet, *DJD* 7:215–19, tavola LV. Cf. B. Nitzan, "Hymns from Qumran— 4Q510–4Q511", in *The Dead Sea Scrolls; Forty Years of Research* (a cura di D. Dimant e U. Rappaport; STDJ 10; Brill: Leiden, 1992), 53–63.

[11] Il termine etiopico è tradotto così ("the bastards") anche nella recente edizione a cura di Nickelsburg e VanderKam, *1 Enoch*, 29.

spiriti dei bastardi, *shēdi'm*,
Lilit, *'eḥim* e[...]
6 e tutti coloro che colpiscono improvvisamente
per sviare lo spirito d'intelligenza
e per rendere attonito il loro cuore.

"Spiriti dei bastardi" (רוחות ממזרים) è una sequenza che si può collegare con quanto si legge nel *Libro dei Vigilanti* (1 Enoc 15,4–12), dove si spiega come dal corpo dei Giganti siano usciti gli spiriti malvagi che stanno sulla terra. Così anche nel *Libro dei Giubilei*, dove si vede che ciò che rimane dei Giganti (che si possono identificare coi "bastardi" del *Libro dei Vigilanti*) dopo il castigo è lo spirito. Vengono per questo denominati, per esempio nella preghiera di Noè, come "spiriti malvagi" (*Libro dei Giubilei* 10,3). Essi, sempre secondo il *Libro dei Giubilei* (cf. 10,8: la preghiera di Mastema), sono fatti per corrompere, funzione attribuita nel *Rotolo della Guerra*[12] a Belial (13,10–11: "Tu hai fatto Belial per corrompere, egli è l'angelo dell'inimicizia"), se si accetta un determinato modo di tradurre un suo passo.[13] Tale concezione nel *Libro dei Vigilanti* non compare, per cui può essere vista come un elemento aggiuntivo rispetto al pensiero teologico del primo enochismo. Mastema e i suoi spiriti hanno dunque, nel *Libro dei Giubilei*, il compito di provare l'uomo, in quanto esso è intrinsecamente cattivo e Dio ha forse bisogno di sapere come si comporta se tentato. Nel frammento di 4Q510 gli "spiriti dei bastardi" sono posti assieme ad altri demòni probabilmente perché tali spiriti hanno ormai acquisito, per chi l'ha composto, una funzione sicuramente equiparabile a quella delle presenze maligne originatesi dalla morte dei Giganti. In 4Q510 si cerca di tenere lontani tali spiriti.

4QLA DONNA DEMONIACA

Credo che si possa identificare con lo spirito "bastardo" dei *Cantici del Saggio* e con lo "spirito del male" o "impuro" del *Libro dei Giubilei*, come anche con Belial del *Rotolo della Guerra* (XIII 10–11), il personaggio descritto nel manoscritto 4Q184,[14] soprattutto per quello che provoca

---

[12] E.L. Sukenik, *'Oṣar ha-megillot ha-genuzot* (Jerusalem: Bialik, 1955).

[13] Molti interpreti traducono infatti לשחת "per la fossa", anziché leggere un infinito costrutto del verbo שחת. Quindi: "Tu hai fatto Belial per la fossa".

[14] J.M. Allegro, *DJD* 5:82–85, tavola XXVIII; J. Strugnell, "Notes en marge du volume V des 'Discoveries in the Judaean Desert of Jordan'", *RevQ* 7/26 (1970): 163–276 (263–68).

nell'essere umano. Nello scritto, databile agli inizi del I secolo d.C., si legge:

1 [...]ה תוציא הבל וב[...]א תועות תשחר תמיד[ל]שן דברי[ה...]

2 וקלס תחלן[י]ק ולהליץ יחד בש[פתי] עול לבה יכין פחתן וכליותיה מק[שות
עיניה]¹⁵

3 בעול נגעלי הוה תמכו שוח רגליה להרשיע ירדו וללכת באשמות[...]¹⁶

4 מוסדי חושך רוב פשעים בכנפיה [...] ה תועפות לילה ומלבשיה [...]¹⁷

5 מכסיה אפלות נשף ועדיה ננוע שחת ערשיה {יצועיה} יצועי שחת[...]

6 מעמקי בור מלונותיה משכבי חושך ובאישני ליל[ה]אשלותיה ממוסדי אפלות

7 תאהל שבת ותשכון באהלי דומה בתוך מוקדי עולם ואין נחלתה בתוך כול

8 מאירי {.} נונה והיאה ראשית כול דרכי עול הוי לכול נוחליה ושדדה
לכ[ול]¹⁸

9 תומכי בה כיא דרכיה דרכי מות ואורחותיה שבילי חטאת מעגלותיה משגות

10 עול ונתיבו[תי]ה אשמות פשע שעריה שערי מות בפתח ביתה תצעד שאו[ל]

11 כ[ו]ל[ן]באיה בל[ ]ישובון וכול נוחליה ירדו שחת והי[ן]א במסתרים תארוב [...]

12 כול[...]ברחובות עיר תתעלף ובשערי קריות תתיצב ואין להרגן[יע]ה [

13 מה[זנו]ת תמיד עיניה הנה והנה ישכילו ועפעפיה בפחז תרים לראו[ת ל]אי[ש]¹⁹

14 צדיק ותשיגנהו ואיש[ע]צום ותכשילהו ישרים להטות דרך ולבחורי צדק

15 מנצור מצוה סמוכי [הלב]להביל לדהביל בפחז והולכי ישר להשנות חו[ן]ק להפשיע

16 ענוים מאל ולהטות פעמיהם מדרכי צדק להביא צדק זד[ו]ן ב[לב]במה בל ידרוכו²⁰

17 במעגלי יושר להשנות אנוש בדרכי שוחה ולפתות בחלקות[ן כול]²¹ בני איש

1 [...]—emette vanità
e in[...]—
Ricerca perpetuamente insanie
[per] affilare le paro[le della sua bocca...].
2 Si fa beffe, insulta,
per schernire la comunità con lab[bra] perverse.
Il suo cuore prepara fosse,
i suoi fianchi re[ti.
I suoi occhi] 3 sono insozzati dal male,
le sue mani hanno afferrato la corruzione,
i suoi piedi sono scesi per fare il male
e per procedere coi delitti[...].

---

¹⁵ Leggo עול [בש]פתי (Strugnell, "Notes", 264) al posto di עול [בש]וא (Allegro, *DJD* 5:82). Riguardo פחתן, al posto di פחו (Allegro, ibid.), seguo un cortese suggerimento di É. Puech.

¹⁶ Leggo ידיה (Strugnell, ibid.) al posto di הוה (Allegro, ibid.).

¹⁷ Leggo ורוב (Strugnell, "Notes", 265) al posto di רוב (Allegro, ibid.).

¹⁸ Leggo מאירי (Strugnell, ibid.) al posto di מאזרי (Allegro, ibid.).

¹⁹ Leggo תמיד in luogo dei segni di lettura incerta messi da Allegro, ibid., secondo le indicazioni di Strugnell, ibid..

²⁰ Leggo ידרוכו (Strugnell, "Notes", 266) al posto di ערוכי[ם] (Allegro, ibid.).

²¹ Grazie a un gentile suggerimento di É. Puech dopo בחלקות colmo lo spazio non segnalato da Allegro, ibid., con [כול], come fa Strugnell, ibid.

4 Fondamenta di tenebra
e moltitudine di misfatti fra le sue ali
I suoi[…] tenebre notturne,
i suoi vestiti […]
5 I suoi veli oscurità crepuscolari,
mentre i suoi ornamenti macchie di corruzione.
I suoi letti {i suoi giacigli}, letti di corruzione[…]
6 dalle profondità della fossa.
I suoi alberghi sono giacigli di tenebra,
in mezzo alla not[te]le sue tende.
Nelle fondamenta delle tenebre
7 pone la sua abitazione,
e ha preso dimora nelle tende del silenzio,
in mezzo al fuoco eterno.
Non c'è (per lei) eredità
fra 8 coloro che splendono {.} chiarore.
Lei è principio di tutte le vie della perversione.
Guai! È disgrazia per tutti coloro che l'ereditano,
devastazione per tut[ti] 9 coloro che la tengono;
poiché le sue vie sono vie di morte,
i suoi sentieri, sentieri di peccato,
le sue tracce, sbagli 10 di perversione,
le sue strad[e], colpe di crimini,
le sue porte, porte di morte,
e all'ingresso della sua casa avanza lo Sceo[l].
11 Tu[tt]i [coloro (che vanno) da lei non]torneranno
e tutti coloro che l'erediteranno scenderanno nella fossa.
L[e]i è in agguato in nascondigli—[…]
12 tu[tti…]nelle piazze della città si vela,
e alle porte delle città si presenta;
non c'è nessuno che può fermar[la]
13 dalle for[nica]zioni continue.
I suoi occhi questo e quello osservano,
le sue palpebre con sfrontatezza solleva
per vede[re] l'uo[mo] 14 giusto per farlo deviare,
e l'uomo[fo]rte per farlo inciampare,
ai retti far deviare la via,
agli eletti giusti 15 dal custodire il precetto;
coloro che adagiano il [cuore] fa cadere con sfrontatezza,
mentre a quelli che vanno rettamente fa cambiare il pre[ce]tto
per fare ribellare 16 gli umili contro Dio
e deviare i loro passi dalle giuste vie;
per far entrare l'insol[en]za nel loro [cuo]re:
non potranno camminare 17 sulle tracce rette;
per far perdere l'uomo nelle vie della fossa,
e sedurre con lusinghe[tutti] i figli dell'uomo.

Anche se leggendo il testo non è immediatamente chiaro chi sia l'essere femminile di cui si parla, tuttavia vedendo le funzioni attribuitegli non è da considerarsi come la donna in genere, che per sua natura sarebbe dunque capace di portare alla perdizione il maschio.[22] È molto più verosimile che indichi metaforicamente lo stesso Belial o qualche suo "spirito". Forse può essere indicativo che la parola "spirito" in ebraico è al femminile[23] e che, per tale motivo, chi ha scritto il testo potrebbe averlo paragonato, pensando a quello del male, a una donna. È da rilevare che questo personaggio spinge infatti il fedele ad allontanarsi dalla luce e a cadere nella tenebra e nella fossa. Quello che prepara la Donna Demoniaca è una vera e propria trappola, dalla quale bisogna stare lontani. Si trovano espressioni per descrivere, ad esempio, il suo abbigliamento, quali "i suoi veli (sono) oscurità crepuscolari" (riga 5), oppure "i suoi alberghi sono giacigli di tenebra, in mezzo alla not[te]le sue tende" (riga 6). Lo scritto afferma che la dimora di questa donna si trova nelle fondamenta dell'oscurità, che essa non ha la sua eredità fra coloro che "splendono" (riga 8). Lei è il principio di tutte le vie della perversione (riga 8). Questa donna è sicuramente ciò che provoca, a differenza di Dio che invece illumina, l'oscuramento dell'esistenza umana: allontana dalla verità e dalla vita. Il personaggio che ha le sembianze del male, chiunque sia, è oscuro. Il pericolo era sentito presso i gruppi di persone che vivevano nei pressi di Qumran (la "comunità", יחד, r. 2), e ciò spiega il ritrovamento di questa composizione, che doveva quindi avere una funzione apotropaica all'interno del gruppo, composta cioè per allontanare questo spirito del male dai fedeli. Nella comunità il pericolo di questo personaggio era evidente: nel testo si legge che è capace di far deviare il giusto (r. 14).

---

[22] Così anche la donna straniera in Pr 7, a cui forse l'autore si è ispirato. Si vedano le varie interpretazioni su questo personaggio in: J.M. Allegro, "Wiles of the Wicked Woman: A Sapiential Work from Qumran's Fourth Cave", *PEQ* 96 (1964): 53–55; J. Carmignac, "Poème allégorique sur la secte rivale", *RevQ* 5/19 (1965): 361–74; A.M. Gazov-Ginzberg, "Double-Meaning in a Qumran Work: The Wiles of the Wicked Woman", *RevQ* 6/22 (1967): 279–85; H. Burgmann, "The Wicked Woman: Der Makkabäer Simon?" *RevQ* 8/31 (1974): 323–59; R.D. Moore, "Personification of the Seduction of Evil: 'The Wiles of the Wicked Woman'", *RevQ* 10/40 (1981): 505–19; J.M. Baumgarten, "On the Nature of the Seductress in 4Q184", *RevQ* 15/57–58 (1991): 133–43; Y. Zur, "Parallels between Acts of Thomas 6–7 and 4Q184", *RevQ* 16/61 (1993): 103–7.

[23] In qualche rara eccezione la parola רוח può essere al maschile, ma non è questo il caso: si veda *HALOT* 3:1197.

L'Angelo della Tenebra, i due cuori e i due spiriti

Dopo aver spiegato la natura dei due spiriti nell'uomo (III 18–19), la *Regola della Comunità* (= 1QS)[24] chiarisce che in modo speculare ci sono due personaggi che governano gli uomini: il "Principe della Luce" e "l'Angelo della Tenebra" (1QS III 20–21). Quest'ultimo ha esattamente lo stesso compito descritto per la Donna Demoniaca, ossia di far perdere i figli della Giustizia (1QS III 21–22). L'Angelo della Tenebra è responsabile dei peccati, delle colpe e delle empietà degli uomini. Anche delle sventure dei figli della Luce. Si legge che gli spiriti di questo angelo cercano di far cadere i figli della Luce (1QS III 24–25). La *Regola della Comunità* elenca gli effetti dell'azione dello "spirito cattivo" nell'uomo (1QS IV 9–11):

9　ולרוח עולה רחוב נפש ושפול ידים בעבודת צדק רשע ושקר גוה ורום לבב כחש
ורמיה אכזרי

10　ורוב חנף קצור אפים ורוב אולת וקנאת זדון מעשי תועבה ברוח זנות ודרכי נדה
בעבודת טמאה

11　ולשון נדופים עורון עינים וכבוד אוזן קושי עורף וכיבוד לב ללכת בכול דרכי
חושך וערמת רוע

allo spirito cattivo (sono da imputare):
avarizia e lentezza delle mani nel servizio della giustizia;
empietà e inganno;
orgoglio e alterigia di cuore;
calunnia e lassismo;[25]
crudeltà 10 e grande empietà;
impazienza e grande stoltezza e zelo superbo;
azioni abominevoli (fatte) nello spirito della fornicazione
e comportamenti[26] impuri al servizio dell'impurità;
11 e lingua blasfema;
cecità degli occhi e sordità delle orecchie;
durezza di cervice e pesantezza di cuore,
per procedere in tutte le vie della tenebra e dell'astuzia del male.

Si legge dunque che tale "spirito cattivo" provoca empietà, orgoglio, falsità e lassismo, crudeltà e grande empietà, impazienza, grande stoltezza e zelo arrogante, impudicizie, impurità, blasfemia, cecità e sordità,

---

[24] M. Burrows, *The Dead Sea Scrolls of St. Mark's Monastery, Volume 2. Fascicle 2: Plates and Transcription of the Manual of Discipline* (New Haven: The American Schools of Oriental Research, 1951).

[25] Qui ho seguito la traduzione di P. Sacchi, *La Regola della Comunità* (Brescia: Paideia, 2006), 108.

[26] Anche qui accetto l'interpretazione di Sacchi, ibid.

durezza di cervice e pesantezza di cuore. Come si vede, ci sono cose in comune con quanto si legge in 4Q184. Belial ha dunque la funzione di tentare gli uomini, siano essi appartenenti ai "figli della luce", siano essi appartenenti al resto dell'umanità. Per i primi, comunque, è prevista la salvezza, nonostante gli attacchi del male. Colui che sta nella comunità degli eletti farà di tutto affinché nel cuore non risieda Belial (1QS X 21).

Abbinato allo sviluppo della concezione dello spirito del male che causerebbe il comportamento iniquo nel mondo—concezione che trae la sua origine dal primo enochismo con la narrazione della caduta dei Vigilanti e la conseguente comparsa degli spiriti malvagi—c'è quella della tendenza insita nell'uomo a fare il male, concezione che trae probabilmente a sua volta origine dalla letteratura biblica (si vedano Gen 8,21 e Gb 4,17–18). Si è già visto che nel *Documento di Damasco* si attribuisce la "durezza di cuore" sia agli angeli Vigilanti (II 17–18) sia agli uomini (II 1). Dalla concezione che lo spirito del male genera l'iniquità nell'uomo tentandolo, si è prodotta l'idea che doveva esserci nell'essere umano qualcosa che avesse una natura simile a questo spirito del male e che potesse accogliere le sue sollecitazioni. In alcuni testi tale parte nell'uomo viene indicata sempre con "spirito".[27]

I QUATTRO ANGELI

D'aiuto agli uomini contro gli attacchi di Belial e dei suoi spiriti Dio ha posto degli angeli. Nel *Rotolo della Guerra* è sottesa probabilmente questa credenza,[28] per il fatto che è rimasto un elenco di quattro angeli scritti,

---

[27] Si veda anche quanto scritto sopra sul desiderio dello "spirito" in CD III 3. Secondo il *Testamento di Ruben* nella natura umana ci sarebbe principalmente uno spirito capace di rendere l'uomo indifeso davanti al potere di Beliar: lo spirito di *pornéia* (*Testamento di Ruben* 4,10). Secondo il testo esso è posseduto anche dai Vigilanti, al punto che per colpa sua si sono lasciati abbagliare dalla bellezza femminile e hanno peccato con le donne (*Testamento di Ruben* 5,6–7). Nel *Testamento di Ruben* la donna è capace, stimolando tale spirito, di far cadere il maschio nella perdizione. Cf. R.H. Charles, *The Testaments of The Twelve Patriarchs*, in *APOT*, 2:296–360; M. de Jonge, *The Testaments of the Twelve Patriarchs. A Critical Edition of the Greek Texts* (Leiden: Brill, 1978); P. Sacchi, *Testamento di Ruben*, in *Apocrifi dell'Antico Testamento*, I, 767–78.

[28] Chiara è la funzione solo di Michele (XVII 6–7), ma va subito detto che tale funzione gli è stata attribuita con molta probabilità successivamente alla composizione della lista dei quattro angeli della colonna IX, che dovrebbe appartenere, secondo un mio recente studio, allo strato redazionale più antico di 1QM (cf. G. Ibba, *Le ideologie*

non a caso, su degli scudi che servono da protezione ai combattenti. Nel *Rotolo della Guerra* (colonna IX 14–16) si legge:

14   ... ועל כול מגני המגדלות

15   יכתובו על הראישון מי[כא]ל[ן] על השני נבריאל על השלישין] שריאל על הרביעי רפאל

16   מיכאל ונבריאל לי[מין ושריאל ורפאל לשמאול

Su tutti gli scudi delle torri 15 scriveranno (secondo questo ordine): sul primo Mi[che]le, [sul secondo Gabriele, sul terzo] Sariele, sul quarto Raffaele. 16 Michele e Gabriele a d[estra, Sariele e Raffaele a sinistra.

I nomi dei quattro angeli compaiono in due dei testimoni aramaici del *Libro dei Vigilanti* trovati nella grotta 4. Si tratta di 4QEn[a] e 4QEn[b] (4Q201 e 4Q202)[29] in cui c'è la stessa lista con l'ordine dei nomi leggermente diverso ("Michele, Sariele, Raffaele e Gabriele").

4QEn[a] (4Q201) 1 iv 6:

6   מיכאל [ושריאל ו]רפאל ונברי[אל]

4QEn[b] (4Q202) 1 iii 7:

7   [מיכאל ושריא]ל ורפאל ונ]ברי[אל]

Nella versione *ge῾ez* (1 Enoc 9,1) del *Libro dei Vigilanti* compare la medesima sequenza, anche se contiene un probabile errore di lettura del nome di Sariele.[30] Vorrei far notare un'altra lista,[31] dove la funzione di ciascun angelo è ben esplicata. Si trova nel *Libro delle Parabole di Enoc* (1 Enoc 40),[32] in cui si legge di Michele, di Raffaele, di Gabriele e di Fanuele. Sariele viene sostituito da un altro nome: Fanuele. In ogni modo, anche se l'opera è certamente più tarda della parte del *Rotolo della Guerra* con l'elenco dei quattro angeli, e certamente molto di più riguardo a quella del *Libro dei Vigilanti*, qui è importante sottolineare che la loro funzione è quella di aiutare l'uomo in vari modi, ciascuno con un compito precipuo. Questo potrebbe suggerire che anche in

---

del Rotolo della Guerra [1QM]. Studio sulla genesi e la datazione dell'opera [Firenze: Giuntina, 2005]).

[29] Milik, *The Books of Enoch*, 139–78 e 340–46, tavole I–IX.

[30] In 1 Enoc è *sure῾ēl*, probabilmente derivato da cattiva lettura del testimone greco che ha "Uriele". Cf. Nickelsburg, *1 Enoch 1*, 202–5.

[31] Un altro elenco, però è incompleto, si trova in 1Q19bis (*Libro di Noè*) 2 4 (cf. *DJD* 1:84–86, tavola XVI): "[...Raf]faele e Gabriele [...],] רפ[א]ל ונבריאל.

[32] R.H. Charles, *The Ethiopic Version of the Book of Enoch* (Oxford, Clarendon Press, 1906); L. Fusella, "Libro delle Parabole", in *Apocrifi dell'Antico Testamento*, I, 513–72; S. Chialà, *Libro delle parabole di Enoc* (Brescia: Paideia, 1997).

precedenza si credesse che i quattro angeli avessero questo ruolo, cosa che dovrebbe essere confermata col *Rotolo della Guerra* nel momento in cui riporta i loro nomi su degli scudi.

LA VISIONE ANGELICA NEL CANTO DEL SACRIFICIO SABBATICO E NEL LIBRO DEI VIGILANTI

L'illuminazione in molti manoscritti qumranici corrisponde, oltre alla conoscenza che Dio dà ai suoi fedeli (*Inni* XI 4)[33] e al ministero che devono compiere i figli della luce (*Rotolo della Guerra* I 8), alla straordinaria dinamica che intercorre tra Dio e i suoi angeli. Come si legge nei *Canti del Sacrificio Sabbatico* essi risplendono la sua luce con varie tonalità di colori, essendo essi di natura particolare e pura.

La rappresentazione della corte celeste che si trova nella visione di Enoc, dopo il suo accesso nell'edificio di fuoco (1 Enoc 14), ha forse punti di contatto con la visione degli angeli-sacerdoti dei *Canti del Sacrificio Sabbatico*. Il testo, contenuto in alcuni manoscritti trovati a Qumran[34] e a Masada,[35] deve essere stato considerato importante. Il gran numero di copie di quest'opera testimonia la seria attenzione ai temi che tratta da parte dei fedeli che hanno vissuto in quelle zone. La copia più antica è materialmente databile alla metà del I sec. a.C. e la più recente, quella trovata a Masada, alla metà del I sec. d.C. L'opera è composta da tredici canti (*shirim*), da recitare ciascuno in un sabato, ognuno dei quali ha una formula fissa, a parte il settimo canto. I protagonisti di questi canti sono gli angeli. Si parla di sacerdozio angelico, e si menziona anche, fra questi angeli-sacerdoti, Melchisedek. Pertanto chi ha scritto questi canti attribuisce agli angeli funzioni sacerdotali che devono essere espletate periodicamente secondo un calendario liturgico. Tali angeli-sacerdoti compiono una grande liturgia, che è congiunta con quella degli uomini-sacerdoti, come si evince nel canto per il secondo sabato. Nel canto settimo, invece, c'è una elaborata esortazione alla lode, a cui seguono le lodi che vengono fatte dalle parti costitutive

---

[33] *Hodayot*: 1QH^a: *'Oṣar ha-megillot ha-genuzot*, tavole XXXV–LVIII; 1QH^b o 1Q35: Milik, *DJD* 1:136–38; 4Q427–432: E. Schuller, *DJD* 29:77–232, tavole IV–XIV e XXVIII. La numerazione delle colonne segue la ricostruzione più recente: si veda É. Puech, "Quelques aspects de la restauration du Rouleau des Hymnes (1QH)", *JJS* 39 (1988): 38–55.

[34] 4Q400–407: C. Newsom, *DJD* 11:173–401, tavole XVI–XVIII; XX–XXXI; 11Q17: F. García Martínez et al., *DJD* 23:257–304, tavole XXX–XXXIV.

[35] Masada ShirShabb: Newsom, *DJD* 11:239–52, tavola XIX.

del tempio celeste. Le parti del tempio sono gli stessi angeli, per cui il tempio è vivo, come sono vive appunto le sue parti.

In ciò che rimane del tredicesimo canto (manoscritto 4Q405, frammento 23, colonna II), in cui si tratta del sommo sacerdozio angelico e di chi collabora con esso, viene descritto il vestito di colori e di luce di costoro (II 7–10):

7   ... במעמד פלאיהם רוחות רוקמה כמעשי אורג פתוחי צורות הדר
8   בתוך כבוד מראי שני צבעי אור רוח קודש קדשים מחזקות מעמד קודשם לפני[   ]
9   [מ]לך רוחי צבעי[טוהר]בתוך מראי חור ודמות רוח כבוד כמעשי אופירים
     [   ]מאירי[
10   ]אֹו[ר

... Nella loro meravigliosa postazione ci sono spiriti con veste variopinta, simile all'opera (prodotta da) tessitore, (fatta) di incisioni; di decorazioni di madreperla. 8 Nel mezzo della gloriosa apparizione scarlatta (i) colori della luce dello spirito del santo dei santi si fissano nella loro santa posizione di fronte 9 al [r]e. Sono spiriti di [puri]colori nel mezzo dell'apparizione di bianco soffuso. Immagine dello spirito glorioso è come il prodotto di opere d'oro di Ofir, che diffonde 10 [lu]ce].

Questa descrizione, che probabilmente proviene da una visione avuta da chi ha scritto il testo, parla di entità angeliche, indicate come "spiriti con veste variopinta", poste nel tempio celeste e ognuna collocata in un suo sacro e preciso spazio ("meravigliosa postazione"). Insieme formano un'immagine meravigliosa, simile a un tessuto ricamato riccamente. La funzione di ciascun angelo è autonoma e insieme indispensabile a tutto il tempio celeste. Ognuno di essi è parte dell'unico tempio e dell'unica liturgia. Già negli *Inni* (XII 6) la lode a Dio, il ringraziamento, è consequenziale alla illuminazione. Questo processo si evidenzia anche negli angeli: c'è un angelo ("spirito del santo dei santi") che ha funzione di sommo sacerdote, il quale irradia una luce che si fissa, in ciascuno degli angeli a lui sottoposti nel servizio del tempio celeste, in un colore particolare, pur mantenendo anche una parte della totalità cromatica racchiusa nel bianco, il quale continua a irradiarsi con meno forza da questi angeli. La visione viene detta scarlatta, forse perché il colore dominante è il rosso, ma si parla anche di luce in senso generale. Inoltre si dice che il colore prevalente dello spirito del santo dei santi, che dovrebbe essere quello del sommo sacerdote, è d'oro puro ("oro di Ofir": si veda Gb 22,24). Seguendo questa dinamica, si può dire che la luce viene da Dio, la quale viene riflessa dall'angelo che sta nel santuario ("santo dei santi") con colore oro: la luce poi si riflette sugli altri spiriti, e ognuno risplende di luce con colore diverso, a seconda della funzione che ha. La luce, dunque, anche nel contesto del tempio celeste, è la manifestazione dell'amore di Dio, che tutto vivifica e ordina. Gli angeli riflettono, più di quello che potrebbero gli uomini, la luce in tutto il suo spettro, così da mostrare l'ordine esatto della liturgia e delle funzioni sacerdotali, viste come indispensabili alla salvezza dell'uomo.

In una delle visioni di Enoc (1 Enoc 14,8–23) dopo le nuvole, la nebbia, le stelle e i fulmini, compare un muro di cristallo con lingue di fuoco attorno. All'interno del fuoco c'è una casa anch'essa di cristallo, ma stavolta di un cristallo composto come un mosaico con riflessi di vario colore. Il soffitto dell'edificio è il cielo stellato contenente anche i fulmini; in mezzo ad essi cherubini di fuoco. Attorno alle pareti ancora fuoco. Enoc entra nella casa, che è allo stesso tempo calda e fredda, e nota che non vi è vita. Per ciò è preso da spavento e si prostra col viso a terra. Ha un'altra visione, dove vede un'altra casa come la prima, ma molto più grande, fatta di fuoco e con le porte aperte. Il posto è magnifico e grandioso. Il pavimento, che probabilmente corrisponde al tetto della casa vista prima, è fatto di stelle, fulmini e fuoco. Enoc guarda all'interno e vede un "alto trono" di cristallo, circolare e splendente come il sole, e ode la voce dei Cherubini. Da sotto il trono fuoriescono fiumi di fuoco. Sopra al trono sta la "Grande Gloria" vestita con una tunica più splendente del sole e bianchissima. Gli angeli non possono avvicinarsi: nessuno può guardare il volto del Glorioso. Attorno, ma distanti da lui, si trovano fuoco e migliaia di angeli. Perennemente vicini alla Grande Gloria stanno invece degli angeli che vengono indicati come Santi.

Nei *Canti del Sacrificio Sabbatico* si legge dello "spirito glorioso", che potrebbe avere un significato simile a ciò che veniva indicato nella visione di Enoc, quando parla della "Grande Gloria". La visione del tredicesimo Canto viene detta "scarlatta", forse perché il colore dominante è il rosso: nella visione di Enoc il fuoco è un elemento importante. Nel testo qumranico si legge della presenza di "spiriti di [puri] colori" che si trovano "nel mezzo dell'apparizione di bianco soffuso"; nella descrizione della visione di Enoc si legge che la Grande Gloria è vestita di una "tunica bianca" e che è posta in mezzo agli angeli. Nella descrizione della veste degli angeli dei *Canti* si dice che ha vari colori e che è prodotta da un abile tessitore; nella visione di Enoc si dice che dappertutto c'è molta magnificenza, preziosità e grandezza.

Nella visione del Cantico è evidente un gioco di riflessi di luci, come avviene nel *Libro dei Vigilanti* in quanto tutto è di cristallo e di fuoco.

CONCLUSIONI

Come si è visto i temi enochici presi in esame fin qui sono l'origine del male con il mito della caduta dei Vigilanti e della nascita dei Giganti; la genesi degli spiriti del male dai Giganti morti; gli angeli difensori e il tempio cosmico. Da rilevare è sicuramente la presenza di questi argomenti in vari testi scoperti a Qumran: si può parlare di nuclei archetipali che si presentano costantemente con elementi che possono variare da un'opera a un'altra. Certamente, il mito della caduta dei Vigilanti e della nascita dei Giganti, che spiega l'origine del male nel mondo, ha prodotto elementi di riflessione in alcune correnti di pensiero del giudaismo, soprattutto in quelle che, legando la tradizione mosaica con quella enochica, hanno formato i gruppi di fedeli che si sono poi stanziati nei pressi di Qumran. La fama dei Giganti doveva essere grande presso le persone che hanno composto molte delle opere rinvenute nelle grotte, soprattutto vedendo il gran numero di frammenti di un'opera dedicata esclusivamente a questi personaggi. Secondo diverse testimonianze, dopo la loro distruzione rimase lo spirito, la cui presenza sulla terra generò molte complicazioni. Gli uomini sono stati visti come facile preda di questi spiriti in quanto avrebbero una parte della loro natura che li accomuna in qualche modo ad essi. Lo spirito maligno agisce nell'uomo grazie a questa parte. Pertanto, secondo quel poco che rimane di alcuni scritti, Dio ha preposto angeli che hanno il compito di difendere gli uomini dagli attacchi dello spirito del male. Gli angeli, inoltre, hanno la funzione di lodare Dio, cosa che è già evidente, oltre che nella letteratura biblica, nel primo enochismo, a partire soprattutto dal *Libro dei Vigilanti*.

Considerando i *Canti del Sacrificio Sabbatico*, dove gli angeli sono sacerdoti di un tempio cosmico, si nota che anche la casa di fuoco e di cristallo descritta nella visione di Enoc ha l'aspetto, anche se non viene detto esplicitamente, di un vero e proprio tempio cosmico, simile per certi aspetti a quello descritto nel testo qumranico. Il sacerdozio angelico di cui parla i *Canti del Sacrificio Sabbatico* esprime inoltre una indubbia esaltazione della funzione sacerdotale con un probabile uso di un contesto proveniente dalla tradizione enochica. Infine, da aggiungere a queste annotazioni, è la constatazione che la conoscenza data a Enoc avviene tramite visione che, data la natura dell'argomento che tratta, dovrebbe essere avvenuta anche per chi ha scritto i *Canti*.

Come si vede, sono tutti temi indipendenti rispetto alla tradizione mosaica (a parte alcuni casi come il racconto sintetico di Gen 6), ma sono stati a volte usati assieme ad essa in determinati contesti. Ciò che emerge in modo evidente è che questi elementi teologici provenienti dalla tradizione enochica sono serviti a completare in certi casi la dottrina emergente dalla tradizione mosaica e rappresentata dal *corpus* di testi che chiamiamo biblico. Si è visto, per esempio, la questione del male originario nella caduta angelica e degli spiriti da essi originatisi (enochismo) e della tendenza a seguire il male nella natura umana (mosaismo). Pertanto questi nuclei provengono da una letteratura in qualche modo già nettamente separata da quella che oggi indichiamo come biblica e attribuita alla tradizione mosaica.

SOBRE LA SINTAXIS VERBAL EN EL HEBREO DE QUMRAN[1]

Luis Vegas Montaner

La sintaxis verbal es uno de los temas principales del análisis gramatical de los textos hebreos en general, y de Qumran en particular, que puede llegar a ser clave para ilustrar la evolución de la lengua hebrea a través de sus períodos sucesivos. Sin embargo, en comparación con los estudios léxicos o morfológicos, hasta fechas recientes no han sido muchos los trabajos sintácticos publicados sobre el valor en los textos de Qumran de las conjugaciones preformativa (*yiqṭol*) y aformativa (*qaṭal*), precedidas o no por *waw* (*wayyiqṭol, weqaṭal*).

El primer tratamiento general de algunos fenómenos sintácticos de los manuscritos del Mar Muerto fue el de Goshen-Gottstein,[2] quien abordaba el uso de los tiempos, el *waw* consecutivo, el "pseudo-cohortativo", infinitivos, etc.

Al año siguiente Kutscher[3] marcó un punto de inflexión en la historia del estudio del hebreo de Qumran, y algunas de sus conclusiones de sintaxis verbal resultaron muy influyentes. Estudios recientes basados también sobre variantes de las formas verbales entre los manuscritos bíblicos han actualizado sus apreciaciones.[4]

---

[1] Supone para mí una enorme satisfacción y expresión de amistad colaborar en este volumen de homenaje al Prof. Florentino García Martínez, merecido reconocimiento de su trayectoria científica en el estudio de los manuscritos del Mar Muerto. El presente trabajo se inserta dentro del proyecto de investigación HUM2005–05747, financiado por el Ministerio de Educación y Ciencia.
[2] M.H. Goshen-Gottstein, "Linguistic Structure and Tradition in the Qumran Documents", *ScrHier* 4 (1958): 101–37, cf. especialmente 124–25, 128–30.
[3] E.Y. Kutscher, *The Language and Linguistic Background of the Isaiah Scroll (1QIsaᵃ)* (STDJ 6; Leiden: Brill, 1974) (Traducción inglesa del original hebreo de Jerusalem: Magnes, 1959). Cf. también sus anotaciones en *EncJud* 16:1587–88 y *A History of the Hebrew Language* (ed. R. Kutscher; Jerusalem: Magnes, 1982), 99–100. Cf. A. Rubinstein, "Singularities in Consecutive-Tense Constructions in the Isaiah Scroll", *VT* 5 (1955): 180–88.
[4] Véanse, en T. Muraoka y J.E. Elwolde, eds., *Diggers at the Well. Proceedings of a Third International Symposium on the Hebrew of the Dead Sea Scrolls and Ben Sira* (STDJ 36; Leiden: Brill, 2000), los trabajos de S.E. Fassberg, "The Syntax of the Biblical Documents from the Judean Desert as Reflected in a Comparison of Multiple Copies of Biblical

El estudio clásico de Qimron se concentra más en el aspecto morfológico de las conjugaciones (preferentemente la preformativa), con sólo
aisladas, aunque relevantes, alusiones a características estrictamente
sintácticas, por otra parte extensamente desarrolladas para los usos
del infinitivo.[5]

Ciertamente, para el estudio de las conjugaciones y el grado de
conservación de los llamados tiempos consecutivos la identificación
morfológica de los mismos es tarea importante. Por ejemplo, una
característica bien conocida del hebreo de Qumran es la distribución
divergente entre la 1ª y la 2ª/3ª personas de las formas *yiqṭol* con *waw*,
que coinciden así con las formas de cohortativo y yusivo respectivamente. Este fenómeno, que comenzó en el período preexílico,[6] se
extendió en época postexílica, y en el hebreo de los manuscritos del
Mar Muerto el *waw* exigía la forma אקטלה en 1ª persona también.[7]
Qimron ha defendido que ya en el hebreo bíblico lo que condiciona
la forma breve en 2ª/3ª persona es la presencia de *waw*, sea este *waw*
consecutivo o conjuntivo.[8]

Tales consideraciones tienen su importancia cuando tratamos con
los materiales de Qumran, carentes de vocalización y, por tanto, de
una distinción morfológica, como en la tradición masorética, entre
waw consecutivo y conjuntivo con *yiqṭol*. Pero si Qimron está en lo
cierto cuando afirma que la distribución de formas larga y breve en
yiqṭol afecta por igual a ambos tipos de *waw*, consecutivo y conjuntivo,
y expresa dudas sobre su diferencia real en el hebreo de Qumran,[9]

Texts", 94–109, y T. Muraoka, "An Approach to the Morphosyntax and Syntax of
Qumran Hebrew", 193–214.

[5] E. Qimron, *The Hebrew of the Dead Sea Scrolls* (HSS 29: Atlanta, Ga.; Scholars Press,
1986), 44–85. Téngase en cuenta también la aproximación morfológica al verbo por
parte de S. Morag, "Qumran Hebrew: Some Typological Observations", *VT* 38 (1988):
148–64.

[6] Cf. G. Bergsträsser, *Hebräische Grammatik* (Leipzig: Vogel, 1918–1929), II §5d, en
referencia al imperfecto consecutivo; Qimron, *Hebrew DSS*, 44–46.

[7] E. Qimron, "Consecutive and Conjunctive Imperfect: the Form of the Imperfect
with *Waw* in Biblical Hebrew", *JQR* 77 (1986/87): 149–61. Cf. también E.J. Revell, "First
Person Imperfect Forms with *Waw* Consecutive", *VT* 38 (1988): 419–26.

[8] Qimron, "Consecutive and Conjunctive Imperfect", 158.

[9] Qimron, *Hebrew DSS*, 45 n. 7: "it is unclear whether DSS Hebrew has a distinct
form for consecutive *waw*, as the short imperfect is used even in cases where the *waw*
does not convert the tense"; *Consecutive*, 150: "without becoming embroiled in the question
of whether the Scrolls distinguished between *waw* consecutive and *waw* conjunctive, as
in the MT". Cf. también T. Thorion-Vardi, "The Use of the Tenses in the Zadokite
Documents", *RevQ* 12/45 (1985): 65–88: "It may be methodically incorrect to call those
verbs which denote past WAYIQTOL and those which denote future WEYIQTOL, but
for the sake of clarity, this is the best approach that I can find" (74).

debemos superar esta aparente falta de distinción morfológica por medio de análisis sintácticos que permitan detectar en el hebreo de Qumran otros posibles criterios de discriminación. Similares dudas sobre la distinción formal entre imperfecto conjuntivo y consecutivo manifestamos en nuestro análisis de las *Hodayot*.[10]

Si tenemos en cuenta, además, que los tiempos verbales de la propia Biblia reciben diversas interpretaciones (temporales o aspectuales, por ejemplo) y que para algunos autores las diferentes vocalizaciones del *waw* no implican necesariamente un sentido opuesto,[11] vemos que es preciso seguir investigando para una mayor clarificación.

Hay ya algunos trabajos sintácticos sobre la prosa de Qumran, como los de Revell,[12] DeVries,[13] Kesterson,[14] Thorion-Vardi[15] y Smith.[16] Sobre textos poéticos pueden citarse DeVries[17] y Vegas Montaner.[18]

---

[10] L. Vegas Montaner, "Some Features of the Hebrew Verbal Syntax in the Qumran *Hodayot*", en *The Madrid Qumran Congress* (ed. J. Trebolle Barrera y L. Vegas Montaner; STDJ 11; Leiden: Brill, 1992), 1:273–86. En la tradición oral del Pentateuco Samaritano y en la Hexapla no hay diferencia entre el *waw* consecutivo y el *waw* conjuntivo, véase Z. Ben Hayyim, *A Grammar of Samaritan Hebrew Based on the Recitation of the Law in Comparison with the Tiberian and Other Jewish Traditions* (Jerusalem: Magnes, 2000; traducción de la edición hebrea de 1977), 102. Sobre la ambigüedad del material en la 2ª columna de la Hexapla puede verse G. Janssens, *Studies in Hebrew Historical Linguistics based on Origen's Secunda* (Leuven: Peeters, 1982).

[11] Cf., por ejemplo, las opiniones de H. Rosen, אסקטים בעברית המקראית, *Sepher Biram* (Jerusalem, 1956), 205–18 (213–14), y D. Michel, *Tempora und Satzstellung in den Psalmen* (Bonn: Bouvier, 1960), 51, que se apartan del consenso general y no perciben una diferencia esencial en el valor del imperfecto cuando va precedido de *waw* conjuntivo o consecutivo.

[12] E.J. Revell, "The Order of the Elements in the Verbal Statement Clause in 1Q Serek", *RevQ* 3/12 (1962): 559–69; "Clause Structure in the Prose Documents of Qumran Cave I", *RevQ* 5/17 (1964): 3–22.

[13] S.J. DeVries, "Consecutive Constructions in the 1Q Sectarian Scrolls", *Doron. Hebraic Studies in Honor of Abraham I. Katsh* (ed. I.T. Naamani and D. Rudavsky; New York: National Association of Professors of Hebrew, 1965), 75–87.

[14] J.C. Kesterson, "Cohortative and Short Imperfect Forms in *Serakim* and *Dam. Doc.*", *RevQ* 12/47 (1986): 369–82; "A Grammatical Analysis of 1QS V, 8–17", *RevQ* 12/48 (1987): 571–73.

[15] T. Thorion-Vardi, "The Use of the Tenses in the Zadokite Documents", *RevQ* 12/45 (1985): 65–88. Vid. 66–67 sobre las dificultades metodológicas a la hora de abordar las formas verbales en los textos de Qumran.

[16] M.S. Smith, "Converted and Unconverted Perfect and Imperfect Forms in the Literature of Qumran", *BASOR* 284 (1991): 1–16; *The Origins and Development of the Waw-Consecutive. Northwest Semitic Evidence from Ugarit to Qumran* (HSS 39; Atlanta, Ga.: Scholars Press, 1991), cap. 3; "The *Waw*-Consecutive at Qumran", *ZAH* 4 (1988): 161–64.

[17] S.J. DeVries, "The Syntax of Tenses and Interpretation in the Hodayot", *RevQ* 5/19 (1965): 375–414.

[18] Vegas Montaner, "Verbal Syntax in the Qumran *Hodayot*"; idem, "Quelques structures syntactiques des *Hodayot*: parfait et imparfait non initiaux", en *New Qumran Texts and Studies* (ed. G.J. Brooke; STDJ 15; Leiden: Brill, 1994), 287–304.

La teoría predominante en los estudios gramaticales de Qumran es el valor temporal de las formas verbales. Por ejemplo, DeVries, al tratar de las diferencias entre imperfecto consecutivo y conjuntivo, tiende a trabajar con esta distinción (que él postula sin reticencias) sobre una base exclusivamente temporal. Aunque utiliza también otros criterios,[19] la diferencia morfológica afecta a una minoría de ejemplos y la dependencia respecto al verbo gobernante, aunque *a priori* válida y puramente sintáctica, se aplica con un automatismo y rigidez que no hace justicia a la realidad de las *Hodayot*. El criterio principal, sin embargo, es el temporal. Y aquí el razonamiento de DeVries resulta circular: tras haber discriminado entre imperfecto consecutivo/conjuntivo de conformidad con dicho criterio, proponiendo leer un consecutivo cuando la forma verbal tiene sentido pasado, concluye que el imperfecto consecutivo aparece exclusivamente en tiempo pasado[20] (lo que hay que esperar necesariamente al ser éste el criterio previo de selección).

En su estudio de las formas *qaṭal* y *yiqṭol* con *waw* prefijado en algunas de las principales obras en prosa de la literatura de Qumran, Smith[21] menciona algunos parámetros para la identificación de las formas convertidas y no convertidas, que pueden distinguirse claramente por marcadores contextuales. Así, si a la forma con *waw* le precede o le sigue un perfecto simple, que indica tiempo pasado, *wyqṭl* es convertido, mientras que *wqṭl* no. A la inversa, una forma de imperfecto anterior o posterior indica un perfecto convertido, pero un imperfecto no convertido.

Cualquier palabra o frase adverbial anterior o posterior referida al ámbito temporal de los verbos con *waw* indica a menudo el tiempo de esas formas verbales; lo más frecuente es que sean de tiempo futuro, indicando perfectos convertidos e imperfectos no convertidos.

Considera, al igual que lo hiciera Thorion-Vardi, que las formas con *waw* prefijado que pertenezcan a cadenas de mandatos son futuras, por lo que *wqṭl* será convertido y *wyqṭl* no convertido. Sigue a dicha autora en la omisión de formas verbales en posición inicial en las prótasis y apódosis de las oraciones condicionales. Quedan igualmente excluidas

---

[19] DeVries, "The Syntax of Tenses", 378: "One must determine his identification of what is an imperfect consecutive upon the following criteria: (1) final root letter missing in hiphils of 'lamed-he' verbs; (2) time relationship; (3) syntactical dependence on governing 'opposite' verb (a perfect or equivalent); (4) poetic parallelism".

[20] DeVries, "The Syntax of Tenses", 412. "There are, however, fifty-five certain or very probable imperfect consecutives, every one of which refers to the past".

[21] Smith, "Converted and Unconverted Perfect and Imperfect Forms, 2–3.

las formas con *waw* prefijado en posición inicial en oraciones finales y consecutivas.

Vemos, por tanto, que la preocupación básica de los estudios de los textos de Qumran ha sido identificar los tiempos consecutivos, frente a los conjuntivos, sobre la base de una teoría temporal del verbo hebreo. Pero, conforme a las nuevas tendencias de la sintaxis hebrea, será conveniente tener en cuenta no sólo el posible valor temporal de cada forma verbal individual, sino la coherencia en la inserción de tales formas verbales en un contexto más amplio que la propia oración.

Convendrá, pues, tener en cuenta la lingüística textual y su distinción básica entre textos discursivos y narrativos, para lo que resultan imprescindibles los estudios pioneros de Talstra.[22] Este autor, siguiendo la Gramática textual de Schneider,[23] establece que la diferencia entre perfecto simple y perfecto consecutivo en textos discursivos (únicos en los que resulta normal el empleo del perfecto consecutivo) radica en que el perfecto simple ofrece una información referida a lo que ya es existente antes del momento de la comunicación (razones, presupuestos, posibilidades, hechos), es decir, un tiempo de perspectiva pasada; mientras que el perfecto consecutivo se refiere a lo que es consecuente a la situación de comunicación, es decir, un tiempo de perspectiva futura.

Ahora bien, estas conclusiones están basadas en el análisis de textos en prosa y es preciso introducir alguna matización en el valor del perfecto consecutivo en textos poéticos, al menos para Salmos. En nuestro trabajo sobre este libro[24] concluíamos que el valor de *weqaṭal* depende no tanto de la forma verbal precedente (*qaṭal* o *yiqṭol*) como de la

---

[22] Cf., por ejemplo, E. Talstra, "Text Grammar and Hebrew Bible. I: Elements of a Theory", *BiOr* 35 (1978): 169–74; "Text Grammar and Hebrew Bible. II: Syntax and Semantics", *BiOr* 39 (1982): 26–38.

[23] W. Schneider, *Grammatik des biblischen Hebräisch* (München: Claudius, 1974; 5ª ed. 1982), cf. §48.3. En esta misma línea teórica podemos destacar el estudio de A. Niccacci, *Sintaxis del hebreo bíblico* (trad. G. Seijas; Estella: Verbo Divino, 2002; edición actualizada del original *Sintassi del verbo ebraico nella prosa biblica classica* [Jerusalem: Franciscan Printing Press, 1986]) y las visiones panorámicas de C. van der Merwe, "Discourse Linguistics and Biblical Hebrew Grammar", en *Biblical Hebrew and Discourse Linguistics* (ed. R.D. Bergen; Dallas: SIL, 1994), 13–49; F.J. del Barco, *Profecía y Sintaxis. El uso de las formas verbales en los Profetas Menores preexílicos* (Madrid: CSIC, 2003), 1–31. Cf. asimismo las obras de conjunto de W.R. Bodine, ed., *Linguistics and Biblical Hebrew* (Winona Lake, Ind.; Eisenbrauns, 1992); E. Talstra, ed., *Narrative and Comment: Contributions to Discourse Grammar of Biblical Hebrew presented to Wolfgang Schneider* (Amsterdam: Societas Hebraica Amstelodamensis, 1995).

[24] L. Vegas Montaner, "Sobre *weqaṭal* en los Salmos", en *IV Simposio Bíblico Español (I Ibero-Americano)* (editado por J.R. Ayaso et al.; Valencia: Fundación Bíblica Española, 1993), 121–32.

mayor o menor autonomía de *weqaṭal* respecto a dicha forma, es decir, del contexto prosódico reflejado en la acentuación masorética.[25] Así, *weqaṭal*[26] indica normalmente secuencialidad cuando va precedido de acento conjuntivo (lo cual se da exclusivamente tras *qaṭal*); en tales casos las formas *qaṭal* coordinadas en rápida secuencia están al mismo nivel textual (= indicativo) y *weqaṭal* es conjuntivo. Por el contrario, cuando está separado del verbo anterior (tanto *qaṭal* como *yiqṭol*) mediante acento disyuntivo, *weqaṭal* se sitúa normalmente a distinto nivel textual, indicando posterioridad (finalidad o consecuencia) o, más frecuentemente, simultaneidad. A diferencia de la prosa bíblica, por tanto, tras *qaṭal* y, sobre todo, tras *yiqṭol* es muy frecuente en Salmos el uso de *weqaṭal* en simultaneidad y sin que esté presente la idea de consecuencia (lógica o temporal) derivada de la oración anterior.

Como hemos visto, los estudios existentes utilizan en general un criterio temporal para considerar si un tiempo es consecutivo o no. Por una parte, *weqaṭal* será conjuntivo (y alternativa de *wayyiqṭol*) si indica tiempo pasado. Ahora bien, no debe insistirse demasiado en la escasez de uso de *weqaṭal* no convertido como ejemplo de pérdida de esta construcción en el hebreo de Qumran, pues *weqaṭal* en pasado es una forma de por sí muy escasa en hebreo bíblico. En los Salmos solamente se dan 9 *weqaṭal* en la esfera temporal de pasado, siempre tras *qaṭal* en rápida secuencia, como acabamos de indicar. Son también muy escasos en los textos proféticos[27] y en la prosa bíblica.[28]

Por otra parte, se afirma que *weqaṭal* será consecutivo si hay un *yiqṭol* futuro en el contexto inmediato.[29] A este respecto, la frecuente

---

[25] Y debería, en mi opinión, prestarse una atención mayor que la habitual al carácter del acento que precede a *weqaṭal*, y no exclusivamente al del propio *weqaṭal*. Es una pena que suela pasarse por alto cómo reflejaron los masoretas una determinada interpretación sintáctica del texto bíblico.

[26] Que en Salmos aparece siempre de forma individual, no en cadena (Ps 89,23ss es el único caso de una cadena de *weqaṭal* extendida a lo largo de varios versículos).

[27] Cf. del Barco, *Profecía*, 144; E. Tov, *The Greek Minor Prophets Scroll from Naḥal Ḥever (8ḤevXIIgr)* (DJD 8; Oxford: Clarendon Press), 121–26 detecta solamente un *weqaṭal* no convertido.

[28] Sobre la distribución de *weqaṭal* en la Biblia, véanse las estadísticas de L. McFall, *The Enigma of the Hebrew Verbal System: Solutions from Ewald to the Present Day* (Sheffield: Almond, 1982), apéndice 2. Sobre la escasez de ejemplos en la narrativa tardía, véase M. Eskhult, "Verbal Syntax in Late Biblical Hebrew", en Muraoka y Elwolde, *Diggers at the Well*, 84–93 (84–85).

[29] Pero téngase presente que, al menos en los Salmos bíblicos, no es el *yiqṭol* o *qaṭal* precedente lo que discrimina una forma como consecutiva o no (y, por tanto, el tiempo

sustitución de *weqaṭal* por *yiqṭol* en los textos bíblicos de Qumran parece prueba de la desintegración de las construcciones consecutivas y de un uso ya no vivo de *weqaṭal* consecutivo.[30] De todo ello podría deducirse que *weqaṭal* y *yiqṭol* carecen de diferencias esenciales. Sin embargo, la selección entre ambas formas no es arbitraria por parte del autor, pues no son sin más intercambiables. La elección de una u otra no dependerá, obviamente, de criterios temporales (ambas formas coinciden en tiempo futuro), sino textuales, de estrategia comunicativa. Y es aquí donde podemos analizar si el uso de las formas es fluido y natural o, por el contrario, da muestras de una rigidez poco natural que puede llevarnos a la conclusión de un uso sintáctico artificial y, por ende, arcaizante.

Uno de los casos aducidos, por ejemplo, sobre el uso aparentemente indiscriminado de *yiqṭol* y *weqaṭal* en futuro se encuentra en la col. VI de *1QMilhama*, donde el verbo עמד aparece en futuro como *weqaṭal* ועמדו (lin. 1 y 4) y como *yiqṭol* יעמודו (lin. 8 y 10).[31]

1QM VI 1–10

...שבע פעמים ושבו למעמדם¹	
ואחריהם יצאו שלושה דגלי בינים	*w*-x-*yiqṭol*
ועמדו בין המערכות	*weqaṭal*
הדגל הראישון ישליך אל ² מערכת האויב שבעה זרקות מלחמה	0-x-*yiqṭol*
ועל לוהב הזרק יכתובו ברקת חנית לנבורת אל	*w*-x-*yiqṭol*
ועל השלט השני יכתובי ³ זיקי דם להפיל חללים באף אל	*w*-x-*yiqṭol*
ועל הזרק השלישי יכתובו שלהובת חרב אוכלת חללי און במשפט	
אל	*w*-x-*yiqṭol*
כול אלה יטילו שבע פעמים ⁴	0-x-*yiqṭol*

futuro, presente o pasado de la acción), sino la estructura prosódica del contexto, cf. *supra*.

[30] Cf. los trabajos citados en notas 3 y 4. Aunque hay que reconocer, con Goshen-Gottstein, que 1QIsᵃ es un manuscrito peculiar dentro de la literatura qumránica y no puede tomarse sin más como representativo del hebreo de Qumran, las variantes aportadas por Fassberg y Muraoka entre los propios textos bíblicos de Qumran, con fluctuación *weqaṭal/weyiqṭol*, parecen confirmar dicha tendencia. Para comprender adecuadamente los ejemplos que presento en este trabajo conviene tener en cuenta que analizo la alternativa *weqaṭal/w*-x-*yiqṭol* (*weyiqṭol* indicativo en la prosa de 1QM se da solamente en VI 11; en textos poéticos, cf. un caso en XVII 6 y los dos yusivos de XIII 13).

[31] En los ejemplos que siguen el texto hebreo de *1QMilhama* (ed. J. Duhaime) está tomado de E. Tov, ed., *The Dead Sea Scrolls Electronic Library* (rev. ed.; Leiden: Brill, 2006). La traducción española es de F. García Martínez, *Textos de Qumrán* (5ª ed.; Madrid: Trotta, 2000).

ושבו למעמדם	*weqaṭal*
ואחריהם יצאו שני דגלי בינים	w-x-*yiqṭol*
ועמדו בין שתי המערכות	*weqaṭal*
הדגל 5 הראישון מחזיק חנית ומגן	0-x-Ptc
והדגל השני מחזיקי מגן וכידן	w-x-Ptc
להפיל חללים במשפט אל	0-p-Inf
ולהכניע מ⸢ל⸣כת 6 אויב בגבורת אל	w-p-Inf
לשלם גמול רעתם לכול גוי הבל	0-p-Inf
והיתה לאל ישראל המלוכה	*weqaṭal*
ובקדושי עמו יעשה חיל	w-x-*yiqṭol*
vacat 7	
8 ושבעה סדרי פרשים יעמודו גם המה לימין המערכה ולשמאולה	w-x-*yiqṭol*
מזה ומזה יעמודו סדריהם	0-x-*yiqṭol*
שבע מאות 9 פרשים לעבר האחד ושבע מאות לעבר השני	SN
מאתים פרשים יצאו עם אלף מערכת אנשי הבנים	0-x-*yiqṭol*
וכן 10 יעמודר לכול ע[ב]ר⸣י המחנה...	w-p-*yiqṭol*

[1] siete veces y volverán a sus posiciones. Después de ellos saldrán tres batallones de infantería y tomarán posición entre las líneas. El primer batallón arrojará contra [2] la línea del enemigo siete jabalinas de guerra. En la punta de la jabalina escribirán: «Brillo de la lanza por el poder de Dios». En el segundo dardo escribirán: [3] «Flecha de sangre para hacer caer muertos por la cólera de Dios». Y sobre la tercera jabalina escribirán: «Llama de la espada devoradora de los muertos inicuos por el juicio de Dios». [4] Todos éstos arrojarán siete veces y retornarán a sus posiciones. Y después de ellos saldrán dos batallones de infantería y tomarán posición entre las dos líneas. El batallón [5] primero estará armado con una lanza y un escudo, y el segundo batallón estará armado con un escudo y una espada para hacer caer muertos por el juicio de Dios y para humillar la línea del [6] enemigo por el poder de Dios, para pagar la recompensa de su maldad a todas las naciones de vanidad. Pues la realeza pertenece al Dios de Israel y por los santos de su pueblo obrará proezas. [7] *Vacat.* [8] Y siete formaciones de caballería tomarán posición también ellas a la derecha y a la izquierda de la línea. Sus formaciones tomarán posición a un lado y a otro, setecientos [9] caballeros a un flanco y setecientos en el segundo flanco. Doscientos caballeros saldrán con los mil soldados de infantería de una línea. Y así [10] tomarán posición en todos los flancos del campamento.

En ll. 1 y 4 se trata de *weqaṭal* individuales con el mismo sujeto que el *yiqṭol* precedente. No describen cómo se sitúan en sus posiciones (ועמדו) o vuelven (ושבו), sino que, en estrecha vinculación con la acción anterior y como desarrollo de la misma, indican finalidad ("para situarse") o simple sucesión cronológica ("y retornarán").

En l. 8, por el contrario, comienza un nuevo segmento textual (cf. *vacat* en l. 7), con introducción del nuevo sujeto en posición inicial, adoptando así el mismo esquema sintáctico que en los comienzos de los segmentos precedentes: w-x-*yiqṭol*. El mismo verbo se repite después, también en *yiqtol*, pero esta vez asindético (0-x-*yiqtol*), indicando así que no se produce una progresión textual, sino que se retoma la acción anterior para explicar cómo se dispondrán los batallones. Y a diferencia de ll. 1 y 4 (ועמדו...יצאו), en l. 10 se opta por la forma *yiqtol* (יצאו...וכן יעמודו), plenamente justificada porque aquí no se trata de la acción particular del grupo recién mencionado, sino de una recapitulación de todos los flancos.

En este texto aparece otra forma *weqatal* (והיתה, l. 6) que, a diferencia de las demás, no está precedida por *yiqtol* en la oración anterior, sino que muestra un alto grado de independencia, retomando el hilo principal del discurso tras una serie de infinitivos constructos.[32] La oración siguiente tiene el esquema sintáctico *w-x-yiqtol*, alternancia muy común en los textos de tipo discursivo de la Biblia para expresar tanto el paralelismo con *weqatal* precedente como también la conclusión de las cadenas de *weqatal*.[33]

Que la opción por *yiqtol* o *weqatal* no es indiscriminada se puede observar también en la col. I, donde, tras un primer verbo con forma de Infinitivo constructo y valor injuntivo (להחל, l. 1), la descripción de las acciones de los hijos de la luz tiene lugar con formas *yiqtol*: ילחמו (l. 2), יעלו (l. 3). Prosigue la descripción con un *yiqtol* (יצא, l. 4) y dos infinitivos con valor de verbos finitos (להשמיד ולהכרית, l. 4). El texto sigue así en las ll. 5–7:

1QM I 5–7

ON	אה עת ישועה לעם אל וקץ ממשל לכול אנשי גורלו [ ]ס ⁵
	וכלת עולמים לכול גורל בליעל

weqatal	והיתה מהומה ⁶ ג[דולה]בני יפת
weqatal	ונפל אשור ואין עוזר לו
weqatal	וסרה ממשלת כתיים להכניע̇ רשעה לאין שארית
w-x-yiqtol *vacat*	ופלטה לוא תהיה ⁷ ל[בנ]י חושך

---

[32] Nótese que el último infinitivo (לשלם, l. 6) es asindético porque, mientras que los dos infinitivos anteriores, unidos entre sí por *waw*, indican acciones paralelas, éste no presenta otra acción sucesiva a las anteriores, sino que actúa como resumen de las mismas.

[33] Cf. del Barco, *Profecía*, 71, 190; Niccacci, *Sintaxis*, 81; F.J. del Barco y G. Seijas, "The syntax of parallelism in Isaiah and the Minor Prophets: a comparative study", *JNSL* 32 (2006): 113–30.

⁵ […Se]guirá un tiempo de salvación para el pueblo de Dios y un período de dominio para todos los hombres de su lote, y de destrucción eterna para todo el lote de Belial. Habrá pánico ⁶ g[rande entre] los hijos de Jafet, y caerá Asur, y no habrá socorro para él; el dominio de los Kittim se acabará, siendo abatida la impiedad sin que quede un resto, y no habrá escape ⁷ [para los hi]jos de las tinieblas. *Vacat.*

Tras una oración nominal múltiple con varios elementos coordinados,[34] en la que se menciona la destrucción del bando de Belial, se especifica dicha destrucción mediante una cadena de *weqaṭal*,[35] en la que se trata individualizadamente a cada una de las potencias enemigas. No son aquí acciones sucesivas, sino un mismo hecho global desglosado en tres partes simultáneas.[36] El bloque textual se cierra con una oración en paralelismo,[37] que constituye un resumen de la desgracia global de los hijos de las tinieblas, mediante el ya mencionado esquema de conclusión *w-x-yiqṭol*.

La descripción de la guerra en el resto de la columna se articula mediante verbos *yiqṭol*, lo mismo que en la col. II, donde se usa exclusivamente la forma *yiqṭol*.

En las columnas siguientes, la reiterativa descripción de las trompetas y estandartes militares (III 1–V 2) se efectúa sistemáticamente mediante la forma *yiqṭol*,[38] que además es siempre del mismo verbo: 32 veces יכתובו en posición no inicial: (*w*)-x-*yiqṭol*. Evidentemente, no tendría sentido repetir tantas veces וכתבו y centrar así el interés en una serie de acciones sucesivas (que, además, serían siempre la misma); lo que el autor destaca aquí es el elemento nominal, es decir, cada uno de los estandartes sobre los que se ha de escribir una leyenda.

Un ejemplo interesante de la opción contraria, es decir, la articulación del texto mediante cadenas de *weqaṭal*, lo encontramos en la col. VIII.

---

[34] La palabra fragmentaria inicial es seguramente והיא, cf. al final de I 11.

[35] El texto paralelo de 4Q496 fr. 3 atestigua esta misma secuencia.

[36] Lo cual resulta excepcional en 1QM. Cf. XVIII 2, donde mediante paralelismo se logra el mismo efecto de las tres acciones: Inf. (Asur)—*weqaṭal* (Jafet)—*w-x-yiqṭol* (Kittim).

[37] De todo el conjunto anterior, y esto es precisamente lo que busca el autor al optar por una cadena de *weqaṭal* que constituya un bloque textual diferenciado de las formas *yiqṭol* del entorno.

[38] En todo este pasaje sólo hay tres formas de *qaṭal* inicial (III 9–10; IV 3), que no forman parte del hilo discursivo, sino de las palabras escritas en las trompetas y estandartes.

1QM VIII 1–13

0-*yiqtol*	¹ החצוצרות תהיינה מריעות לנצח אנשי הקלע עד כלותם להשליך שבע ² פעמים
w-x-*yiqtol*	ואחר יתקעו להם הכוהנים בחצוצרות המשוב
weqatal	ובאו ליד המערכה ³ הראישונה להתיצב על מעמדם
weqatal	ותקעו הכוהנים בחצוצרות המקרא
weqatal	ויצאו ⁴ שלושה דגלי בינים מן השערים
weqatal	ועמדו בין המערכות ולידם אנשי הרכב ⁵ מימין ומשמאול
weqatal	ותקעו הכוהנים בחצוצרות קול מרודד ידי סדר מלחמה
w-x-*yiqtol*	⁶ והראשים יהיו נפשטים לסדריהם איש למעמדו
w-p-Inf.	ובעומדם שלושה סדרים
weqatal	⁷ ותקעו להם הכוהנים תרועה שנית קול נוח וסמוך ידי מפשע
0-p-Inf.	עד קורבם ⁸ למערכת האויב
weqatal	ונטו ידם בכלי המלחמה
w-x-*yiqtol*	והכוהנים יריעו בשש הצוצרות ⁹ החללים קול חד טרוד לנצח מלחמה
w-x-*yiqtol*	והלויים וכול עם השופרות יריעו ¹⁰ קול אחד תרועת מלחמה נדולה להמס לב אויב
w-x-*yiqtol*	ועם קול התרועה יצאו ¹¹ זרקות המלחמה להפיל חללים
0-*yiqtol*	קול השופרות יחישו
w-x-*yiqtol*	יהיו ¹² הכוהנים מריעים קול חד טרוד ידי מלחמה עד השליכם למערכת *vacat* ¹³ האויב שבע פעמים ובח[צון]צרות

¹ Las trompetas seguirán sonando para dirigir a los honderos hasta que hayan acabado de arrojar siete ² veces. Después los sacerdotes harán sonar para ellos las trompetas de regreso y ellos volverán al flanco de la línea ³ primera para mantenerse en sus posiciones. Y los sacerdotes harán sonar las trompetas de llamada y saldrán ⁴ tres batallones de infantería de las puertas y tomarán posición entre las líneas; a su lado, hombres de caballería, ⁵ a derecha y a izquierda. Los sacerdotes harán sonar las trompetas con un toque continuo, la señal del orden de batalla. ⁶ Y las columnas se desplegarán en sus formaciones, cada uno en su posición. Cuando estén en tres formaciones, ⁷ los sacerdotes harán sonar para ellos un segundo toque, bajo y sostenido, la señal de marcha, hasta que se acerquen ⁸ a la línea del enemigo y echen mano de sus armas de guerra. Los sacerdotes harán sonar las seis trompetas ⁹ de matanza con un toque agudo y entrecortado para guiar la batalla. Y los levitas y toda la turba con cuernos de carnero harán sonar ¹⁰ un toque único, una alarma de guerra ensordecedora, para derretir el corazón del enemigo. Y con el toque de alarma volarán ¹¹ las jabalinas de guerra para hacer caer muertos. Cesará el toque de los cuernos de carnero, pero en las trompetas, ¹² los sacerdotes continuarán haciendo sonar un toque agudo y entrecortado para guiar las manos guerreras hasta que hayan arrojado contra la línea ¹³ del enemigo siete veces.

El autor opta por una cadena de *weqatal* exclusivamente (VIII 2–5), aunque por la variación de sujetos y temas podría haber intercalado oraciones de esquema *w*-x-*yiqtol*. Pero hay un motivo para su elección.

Por una parte, el sujeto de las tres oraciones del verbo תקע en este pasaje es el mismo (los sacerdotes), lo que hace innecesario anteponer הכוהנים las tres veces. Por otra parte, el autor quiere presentar todas las acciones correspondientes al primer tañido de los sacerdotes como un todo (tanto el repliegue de los honderos como la salida de la infantería), por lo que renuncia a especificar cada acción mediante el esquema *w-x-yiqtol*, que sí utiliza a continuación (l. 6) con su función de cierre de la cadena, como anteriormente vimos.

El esquema diferente de dos oraciones aparentemente similares, ambas con el mismo sujeto, en l. 7 (ותקעו להם הכוהנים, *waw* de apódosis) y l. 8 (והכוהנים יריעו), no es caprichoso y se explica por motivos de estructura textual. Esta última oración da inicio a un segmento textual de tres oraciones *w-x-yiqtol* con sujetos diferentes: (1) sacerdotes; (2) levitas y toda la turba; y (3) jabalinas.[39] La asíndesis de la oración siguiente marca una tenue separación e introduce un pequeño bloque (0-x-*yiqtol* / *w-x-yiqtol*) de contenido antitético: cese / continuación del tañido (cf. igualmente 1QM IX 1; XVII 14–15).

La combinación de dos pasajes de la col. XVI (ll. 3–6 y 11–15) puede resultar muy ilustrativa para ver las diferencias de uso de las formas verbales, sobre todo del verbo תקע, que aparece en las formas tanto *weqatal* (ll. 4 y 5) como *yiqtol* (ll. 3, 12 y 13). Evidentemente todas las acciones son de tiempo futuro, y lo que debemos analizar es si se elige *weqatal* o *yiqtol* indiscriminadamente o hay algún motivo especial para ello, que no podrá ser temporal, sino contextual.

1QM XVI 3–6; 11–15

	vacat ²
0-x-*yiqtol*	³את כול הסרך הזה יעשו] ה[הואה
p-Inf.	על עומדם נגד מחני כתיים
w-x-yiqtol	ואחר יתקעו להמה הכוהנים בחצוצרות ⁴ הזכרון
weqatal	ופתחו שערי המ]לחמה
weqatal	וי]צאו אנשי הבינים
weqatal	ועמדו ראשים בין המערכות
weqatal	ותקעו להם הכוהנים ⁵ תרועה סדר
w-x-[Part.]	והראשים] ו[ם לקול החצוצרות
p-Inf.	עד התיצבם איש על מעמדו
weqatal	ותקעו להם ⁶ הכוהנים תרועה שני]ת[התק]רב

---

[39] Véase 1QM XVII 10ss para un caso similar.

²*Vacat.* ³ Obrarán de acuerdo con toda esta regla en este [día], cuando estén situados frente al campamento de los Kittim. Después el sacerdote hará sonar para ellos las trompetas ⁴ de recuerdo, y las puertas de la batalla se abrirán. Los hombres de infantería saldrán y tomarán posiciones en columnas entre las líneas. Los sacerdotes harán sonar para ellos ⁵ la llamada de formación, y las columnas [se desplegarán] al son de las trompetas hasta que cada hombre se halle estacionado en su posición. Los sacerdotes harán sonar para ellos ⁶ una segunda llamada [...para el asa]lto.

	vacat ¹⁰
w-p-Inf.	¹¹ [ ] לעזרת בני חושך וּבהתאזֹר
w-x-*yiqtol* + p-Inf.	וחללי הבינים יחלו לנפול ברזי אל
w-p-Inf.	ולבחון בם כול חרוצי המלחמה
w-x-*yiqtol*	¹²וֹהכ[ון]הנים יתק[עו] בחצ[ו]ן צלֹרות המקרא
p-Inf.	לצאת מערכה אחרת חליפה למלחמה
weqatal	ועמדו בין המערכות
w-x-*yiqtol*	¹³וֹלמתקרבֹי[ם במ]לחֹמֹה יתקעו לשוב
weqatal	וננש כוהן הרואש
weqatal	ועמד לפני המערכה
weqatal	וֹחזק את ¹⁴ לבבם ב[ן] *vacat* א[ל] וֹאֹת ידֹיהם במלחמתו
weqatal	¹⁵וענה
weqatal	ואמרֹ]

¹⁰ *Vacat.* ¹¹ Cuando [Belial] se ciña para ayudar a los hijos de las tinieblas y comiencen a caer los muertos de la infantería según los misterios Dios, y todos los designados para la batalla sean probados por ellos, ¹² harán sonar los sacerdotes las trompetas de llamada para hacer salir otra línea de reserva al combate y tomarán posición entre las líneas. ¹³ Y para los enzarzados en el combate harán sonar la retirada. El Sumo Sacerdote se acercará y tomará posición ante la línea, y fortalecerá ¹⁴ sus corazones [con el poder de Di]os y sus manos en su combate. *Vacat.* ¹⁵ Y tomando la palabra dirá:

Tras el *yiqtol* יתקעו de la l. 3,⁴⁰ el texto se articula mediante una cadena de *weqatal*, incluso en las acciones de los sacerdotes con el doble tañido de sus trompetas (ll. 4 y 5–6).

Por el contrario, el doble tañido de los sacerdotes en ll. 12 y 13 se expresa mediante *yiqtol*. El motivo es de índole textual y tiene que ver con la compleja sintaxis de este pasaje. En primer lugar, la estructura

---

⁴⁰ A primera vista podría pensarse que pudiera haberse dado ya aquí *weqatal*, comenzando la cadena tras el *yiqtol* יעשו de la oración precedente, pero ésta no es inicial del texto siguiente, sino que funciona como resumen de la disposición bélica anterior (XV 1–7) y el himno a recitar en ese momento (XV 7–XVI 1). Ahora empieza un nuevo segmento textual, con el tañido de las trompetas (cf. cols. VIII–IX). Cf. XVII 10.

w-x-*yiqṭol* en l. 11 tras el infinitivo inicial se debe a la disposición en quiasmo de la oración, que incluye además dos infinitivos constructos: otro infinitivo en coordinación con el anterior (en lugar de esta oración con *yiqṭol*) habría hecho inviable un texto inteligible. Resulta llamativa la apódosis *w*-x-*yiqṭol* en l. 12, en lugar de la frecuente apódosis con *weqaṭal*, que aquí no se da.[41] El motivo de יתקעו והכוהנים en lugar de הכוהנים ותקעו radica en la opción del autor por dar preeminencia al elemento nominal de cada una de las oraciones implicadas. Así, presenta tres oraciones con el esquema *w*-x-*yiqṭol* para tres temas diferentes: heridos—sacerdotes (toque de llamada)—enzarzados en combate (toque de retirada). Es precisamente la oposición entre los toques de llamada y retirada lo que quiere resaltar el autor; no son presentados como dos hechos sucesivos, sino formando parte de la misma situación: llamada a las tropas de refresco y retirada de los que están cayendo en combate. Una vez producida la retirada, y ya dentro de este tema, el autor pasa a la presentación de una serie de acciones sucesivas del sumo sacerdote para con los retirados mediante el uso de una cadena de *weqaṭal*.

El esquema de este pasaje sería, pues, el siguiente:

1)   Infinitivo (Belial)
2)   *w*-x-*yiqṭol* (heridos); quiasmo
3)   *w*-x-*yiqṭol* (sacerdotes); toque de llamada
3b)   *weqaṭal* (sacerdotes)
4)   *w*-x-*yiqṭol* (enzarzados en combate); toque de retirada
4b)   *weqaṭal*...*weqaṭal*...etc. (sumo sacerdote)

La oposición queda reforzada por el uso del mismo verbo (יתקעו) en 3) y 4).

Si tomamos en consideración todas las cadenas de *weqaṭal* atestiguadas en 1QM, podemos ver que, salvo en I 6 (3 *weqaṭal*) (cf. *supra*), XIII 1–2 (4) y XVIII 6 (3), donde los *weqaṭal* en cadena indican acciones simultáneas, en el resto de los casos la cadena indica una serie de acciones sucesivas: VIII 2–5 (5);[42] X 2 (2); X 6–8 (3), cita bíblica; XIV 2–4 (6);

---

[41] Que comience aquí la apódosis o ya con el *yiqṭol* anterior es irrelevante para el análisis que proponemos. En ambos casos tendríamos el mismo esquema oracional en la apódosis y la triple utilización de la misma estructura *w*-x-*yiqṭol*.

[42] En el comentario de este pasaje hemos indicado cómo, aunque las acciones individuales son sucesivas, el efecto logrado mediante el uso de la cadena de *weqaṭal* es un todo conjunto.

XV 4–7 (7); XVI 4–5 (5); XVI 13–15 (5); XVII 1 (2), en himno; XVIII 4 (2); XIX 11–13 (2?). Por ejemplo,

XIV 2–4   ...יכבסו בגדיהם... ורחצו...ושבו...וברכו...ורוממו...וענו ואמרו

> Por la mañana lavarán sus vestidos y se lavarán ³ de la sangre de los cadáveres culpables. Volverán al lugar de sus posiciones, donde organizaron sus líneas antes de que cayesen los muertos del enemigo. Y allí bendecirán ⁴ todos al Dios de Israel y exaltarán su nombre en un gozoso unísono. Tomarán la palabra y dirán:

Ante la casi exclusiva preocupación en los estudios qumránicos por establecer el tiempo de *weqaṭal*, se suele pasar por alto que esta forma aparece de dos maneras diferentes (individual y en cadena), con diferencias entre sí a nivel textual:

- *weqaṭal* individual no llega a constituir un subtexto y se muestra en estrecha dependencia del verbo precedente, al que está en cierta medida subordinado a distinto nivel textual, frecuentemente con valor final/consecutivo de la acción anterior;
- *weqaṭal* en cadena sí configura un subtexto, pues la cadena adquiere un mayor grado de autonomía respecto al verbo precedente, constituyendo un segmento textual al mismo nivel, en el hilo principal de las acciones del texto (de tipo predictivo o normativo). No es, por tanto, que el *yiqṭol* anterior "transfiera" su valor a *weqaṭal*, que resultaría así equivalente, sino que, dentro de un tipo de texto discursivo con *yiqṭol* se puede desarrollar una cadena de *weqaṭal*, que mantiene la coherencia textual discursiva.

Los pasajes de 1QM analizados demuestran que la alternancia *weqaṭal*/*yiqṭol* no es indiscriminada, por lo que existe todavía conciencia de un valor diferente de ambas formas.[43] Ahora bien, la significativa disminución de los tiempos consecutivos en el hebreo bíblico tardío, y el uso de *yiqṭol* en lugar de *weqaṭal* en numerosas variantes entre los manuscritos bíblicos de Qumran, confirman una acusada tendencia a la eliminación de *weqaṭal* consecutivo.

Podría decirse que en el hebreo literario (clásico) de la Biblia existe un sistema de comunicación basado en cadenas de tiempos consecutivos

---

[43] Aunque el uso de *weqaṭal* en 1QM carece de la variedad atestiguada en la Biblia, cf. *infra*.

(*wayyiqṭol* en la narración, normalmente en pasado; *weqaṭal* en el discurso, normalmente en futuro), mientras que con el paso del tiempo tiende a abandonarse el uso de tales cadenas. Este cambio de estrategia comunicativa puede deberse al influjo de la lengua hablada, pues en la expresión oral prima la sucesión de oraciones individuales y, a lo sumo, una relación entre oraciones próximas, más que el diseño global de un texto amplio. Por eso en el estadio lingüístico posterior se va percibiendo progresivamente como artificial y arcaizante el recurso a los consecutivos, tan vital en el estilo de composición literaria precedente.

Esta atomización textual queda confirmada por la tendencia al cambio en el orden de palabras. En hebreo clásico el lugar preferente del verbo como hilo principal de la comunicación es la posición inicial en la oración. En el hebreo de Qumran se produce una tendencia clara a desplazar el verbo finito de la primera posición de su oración, lo que por sí mismo constituye una técnica de interrupción textual.[44]

En sentido inverso, y como ha sido notado por muchos autores, se da en los textos de Qumran una mayor profusión de oraciones sindéticas, con uso exhaustivo de *waw* iniciando las oraciones. La ligazón textual que en hebreo clásico se producía por las formas verbales en primera posición se asegura ahora mediante el recurso a la conjunción.

Estas consideraciones sintácticas nos sitúan ante el debatido problema del carácter oral o literario del hebreo de Qumran.

Frente a la opinión de Qimron,[45] para quien la mayoría de los manuscritos del Mar Muerto reflejan la lengua hablada de sus escribas (que además identifica con el dialecto de Jerusalem), Blau[46] afirma que el hebreo de Qumran refleja básicamente el último estadio de la lengua bíblica (literaria), expuesta a la influencia de las lenguas vernáculas habladas, es decir, el arameo y algún tipo de hebreo medio que más tarde cristalizó como hebreo misnaico. Más que inventar un dialecto

---

[44] Sobre las dificultades a la hora de aplicar las teorías actuales de lingüística textual a pasajes amplios de *Milhama* con *yiqṭol* en posición no inicial, véase S. Holst, *Verbs and War Scroll: Studies in the Hebrew Verbal System and the Qumran War Scroll* (København: Det Teologiske Fakultet, Københavns Universitet, 2004).

[45] E. Qimron, "The Nature of DSS Hebrew and Its Relation to BH and MH", en Muraoka y Elwolde, *Diggers at the Well*, 232–44. Cf. S. Morag, "Qumran Hebrew: Some Typological Observations", *VT* 38 (1988): 148–64, quien aduce 11 características que en su opinión atestiguan la lengua hablada de los autores de los manuscritos.

[46] J. Blau, "A Conservative View of the Language of the Dead Sea Scrolls", en Muraoka y Elwolde, *Diggers at the Well*, 20–25.

inexistente, considera más simple y convincente atribuir la mayoría
de rasgos lingüísticos ausentes del hebreo bíblico y atestiguados en el
hebreo de Qumran a cambios que surgieron en la lengua literaria de
los manuscritos del Mar Muerto debido a escuelas de escribas, modas,
inclinaciones personales, géneros, etc. Adoptando una posición interme-
dia, Hurvitz[47] concluye que el hebreo de Qumran es una lengua com-
puesta de elementos literarios y no literarios. Sin duda presenta huellas
de una lengua hablada que se aparta en algunos aspectos importantes
de la tradición aceptada del hebreo bíblico, pero cualquier intento de
clasificar al hebreo de Qumran como "hablado" es incompatible con
la naturaleza lingüística general de los manuscritos. En este mismo
sentido, ya Morag[48] indicaba que no es la lengua hablada de Qumran
lo que emerge de la literatura de los manuscritos, aunque pueden
reconocerse en los textos características de esta lengua; los textos mismos son literarios, y es a través de la diversificada expresión literaria
como resulta discernible la subestructura de una lengua hablada de los
miembros de la secta.

Es importante considerar hasta qué punto los estudios sintácticos
pueden aportar luz en este debate, máxime cuando los argumentos
principales suelen hasta ahora centrarse, como en el caso de Blau y
Qimron, en la morfología.

Como conclusión del presente estudio, pasamos a resumir las principales
características sintácticas de 1QM que hemos analizado.

Weqaṭal consecutivo[49] es todavía un elemento vivo en la lengua del
autor de Milhama, pues la opción entre *yiqṭol* y *weqaṭal* no es caprichosa
e indiscriminada, sino que sirve para articular los diferentes segmentos
textuales.

Se reproduce la secuencia sintáctica del hebreo bíblico (*w*)-x-*yiqṭol*—
weqaṭal, con un valor secuencial a distinto nivel textual (final, consecutivo)
en el caso de *weqaṭal* individual.

Por el contrario, cuando hay cadenas de *weqaṭal*, éstas constituyen
una secuencia de acciones en el nivel principal del texto, con valor
indicativo, no modal. Éste es también un uso bíblico frecuente, pero

---

[47] A. Hurvitz, "Was QH a 'Spoken' Language? On Some Recent Views and Positions: Comments", en Muraoka y Elwolde, *Diggers at the Well*, 110–14.

[48] S. Morag, מחקרים בלשון המקרא‎ (Studies on Biblical Hebrew) (Jerusalem: Magnes, 1995), 114–15.

[49] Que aparece exclusivamente en los pasajes en prosa, salvo el doble caso de XVII 1.

se aprecia una diferencia textual importante. En la Biblia se pueden articular textos amplios mediante *weqaṭal* como hilo conductor del discurso, mientras que en 1QM las cadenas de *weqaṭal* configuran segmentos textuales reducidos. En la Biblia se pueden dar (y se dan frecuentemente) cadenas de *weqaṭal* discontinuos (con *w-x-yiqṭol* u otros sintagmas intercalados), de suerte que determinados *weqaṭal* que retoman el hilo principal de la comunicación se encuentran distantes del verbo introductorio (normalmente *yiqṭol*) del segmento textual, con apariencia a veces de independencia. En 1QM, por el contrario, las cadenas de *weqaṭal* son continuas y limitadas a un ámbito textual reducido.

Una excepción a este uso se encuentra en 1QM VI 6,[50] donde והיתה se comporta como un marcador macrosintáctico al estilo bíblico.

Por otra parte, en 1QM se encuentran varios casos de *weqaṭal* de apódosis, fenómeno frecuente en la Biblia.[51]

Respecto a *yiqṭol*, si sólo nos fijamos en su tiempo habitual, el futuro, no debe extrañarnos su frecuente utilización en un texto de tipo normativo/predictivo como *Milhama*. Pero si prestamos atención al uso textual de *yiqṭol*, no podemos pasar por alto el hecho de que nunca aparece en posición inicial.[52] El esquema *w-x-yiqṭol* es preponderante y debe hacernos reflexionar en el hecho de que el discurso no se articula sobre las acciones verbales, sino sobre los elementos nominales que las preceden (lo que implica, por su propia naturaleza sintáctica, constantes interrupciones del flujo de acciones, subsanadas por el masivo uso de *waw*). En otras palabras, se ha producido respecto al hebreo clásico un significativo cambio en la estrategia comunicativa, con una atomización en segmentos textuales pequeños, frente al diseño de textos más amplios característico de la Biblia.

Un análisis del hebreo de Qumran que tenga en cuenta estos datos podrá arrojar luz al debatido tema de la influencia del hebreo hablado por los escritores de Qumran en el hebreo literario de sus escritos. El

---

[50] Cf. también 1QM XV 4, con ועמד tras un *vacat* de media línea. *Weqaṭal* inicial en XI 11 es una cita bíblica.

[51] Cf. VIII 7.8; IX 2; X 2 (2), 7–8 (3); XVIII 2. Predominan los *weqaṭal* individuales, a diferencia de otros textos de Qumran, como el Rollo del Templo, donde tras el *waw* de apódosis pueden desarrollarse cadenas de *weqaṭal* más amplias, cf. por ejemplo 11Q19 LXIII 12–13; LXIV 3–6; LXV 9–15.

[52] En contados casos *yiqṭol* inicia la apódosis de un esquema sintáctico prótasis-apódosis.

cambio en el orden de palabras, con anteposición del elemento nominal, se considera por parte de algunos autores[53] como rasgo distintivo del hebreo oral, y la fragmentación textual que comporta parece confirmarlo.

---

[53] Cf. J. McDonald, "Some Distinctive Characteristics of Israelite Spoken Hebrew", *BiOr* 32 (1975): 162–75 (174).

3 KINGDOMS COMPARED WITH SIMILAR
REWRITTEN COMPOSITIONS

Emanuel Tov

3 Kingdoms (1 Kings)[1] poses a greater challenge for the researcher
than the other three books of the Greek Kingdoms (1–2, 4 Kingdoms).
The many problems discussed over the past half-century relating to the
kaige-Theodotion revision in 2 and 4 Kingdoms and the evaluation of
the Hebrew text of 1–2 Samuel in the wake of the Qumran discoveries
are very complex. However, they are less complicated than the evaluation of the Greek text of 1 Kings. From the many studies published
in the past half century it has become clear that there is no consensus
concerning the evaluation of that version.

The discrepancies between the Hebrew and Greek texts resulted from
changes made in either MT or the LXX and cannot be described easily
in neutral terms. The 2005 monograph by P.S.F. van Keulen, which
includes an excellent summary of the previous research and of the issues
themselves, describes the features of 3 Kingdoms as follows:[2]

> The student of 3 Regum is not only struck by the high rate but also by
> the diversity of differences vis-à-vis 1 Kings that are contained in the
> book. Pluses and minuses are frequent, as well as word differences. Some
> of the pluses in 3 Regum consist of duplicate renderings of passages
> appearing elsewhere in the translation. One plus even involves a rival
> version of events already recounted in the preceding narrative (i.e., 3 Reg
> 12: 24a–z). Furthermore, corresponding sections may appear at different
> positions in 3 Regum and 1 Kings, thus causing a different arrangement
> of narrative materials. Most of these sequence differences occur in the
> first half of the book. Another peculiar deviation from MT, typical of
> the second half of 3 Regum, pertains to the chronological data for kings
> following Solomon.

---

[1] Modern research distinguishes between:
  (1) Kingdoms α (1 Samuel).
  (2) Kingdoms ββ (2 Sam 1:1–11:1).
  (3) Kingdoms βγ (2 Sam 11:2–1 Kgs 2:11).
  (4) Kingdoms γγ (1 Kgs 2:12–21:15) to be referred to below as "3 Kingdoms."
  (5) Kingdoms γδ (1 Kgs 22:1–2 Kgs 24:15).
[2] P.S.F. van Keulen, *Two Versions of the Solomon Narrative: An Inquiry into the Relationship
between MT 1 Kgs. 2–11 and LXX 3 Reg. 2–11* (VTSup 104; Leiden: Brill, 2005), 1.

Van Keulen focused on the first half of the book in which these features are evident, but they also occur in the second half, albeit less frequently. Among other things, in the second half there are no parallels to the Summaries of chapter 2 or the alternative version in chapter 12.

1. Background of the Discrepancies between 1 Kings and 3 Kingdoms

In evaluating the extensive differences between the two versions, scholars consider that the LXX reflects either a Hebrew text like MT[3] or forms a faithful translation of a Hebrew book very different from 1 Kings. In the latter case, we are confronted with two different compositions rather than scribal developments.

Several studies, some of them book-length, have focused on individual chapters in 1 Kings, especially chapter 2, while others are devoted to the book as a whole. The latter studies have the advantage of offering an overall view; the former are more detailed, but are limited with regard to the validity of their conclusions. Thus, one of the problematic aspects of the studies, including my own,[4] of the Summaries ("Additions") in 1 Kgs 2 (see below, paragraph 4) is that they refer to a very small unit without linking the analysis to the major features of the other Solomonic chapters or the book as a whole.

Gooding was the first scholar to submit the problems of the Greek translation to a thorough discussion. In a long series of studies (1964–

---

[3] In this case, the major differences between the Hebrew and Greek were created either by a Greek reviser (see below) or by a free translator. The latter option was embraced by J.W. Wevers: "Exegetical Principles Underlying the Septuagint Text of 1 Kings ii 12–xxi 43," in *Oudtestamentische Studiën* (ed. P.A.H. de Boer; OTS 8; Leiden: Brill, 1950): 300–322. Wevers identified various tendencies in relatively small details in the LXX, but he did not suggest often that a different Hebrew text lay at the base of the LXX. Nor did he realize that the LXX reflects a completely different composition.

[4] J.A. Montgomery, "The Supplement at End [*sic*] of 3 Kingdoms 2 (I Reg. 2)," *ZAW* 50 (1932): 124–29; G. Krautwurst, *Studien zu den Septuagintazusätzen in 1 (3.) Könige 2 und ihren Paralleltexten* (Ph.D. diss., Mainz, 1977); E. Tov, "The LXX Additions (Miscellanies) in 1 Kings 2," *Textus* 11 (1984): 89–118; repr. in *The Greek and Hebrew Bible: Collected Essays on the Septuagint* (VTSup 72; Leiden: Brill, 1999), 549–70. For Gooding's monograph on this chapter, see n. 6.

1969),[5] including a monograph on chapter 2[6] and a summary article in 1969,[7] he presented the deviations in the LXX as reflections of Midrashic exegesis (as he did in other LXX books as well).[8] Gooding's argumentation is innovative, clear, and appealing, but has weaknesses. Like most theories explaining a multitude of details, Gooding's reasoning is flawed by one-sidedness. The LXX indeed rewrites the MT, but probably only in some cases[9] do these revisions reflect rabbinic exegesis. Gooding demonstrated that the changes in the LXX are not isolated phenomena, but are part of a deliberate scheme of re-ordering and re-interpreting. His summarizing article discusses the question of at which level the changes entered the LXX. He concludes that the majority of the changes were probably inserted by an inner-Greek reviser of the LXX: "This revision was probably based, at least in part, on written Hebrew (or Aramaic) traditions of one kind or another."[10] These traditions may be pinpointed in some cases in rabbinic sources,

---

[5] D.W. Gooding, "Ahab According to the Septuagint," *ZAW* 76 (1964): 269–80; idem, "Pedantic Timetabling in the 3rd Book of Reigns," *VT* 15 (1965): 153–66; idem, "The Septuagint's Version of Solomon's Misconduct," *VT* 15 (1965): 325–35; idem, "An Impossible Shrine," *VT* 15 (1965): 405–20; idem, "Temple Specifications: A Dispute in Logical Arrangement between the MT and the LXX," *VT* 17 (1967): 143–72; idem, "The Septuagint's Rival Version of Jeroboam's Rise to Power," *VT* 17 (1967): 173–89; idem, "The Shimei Duplicate and Its Satellite Miscellanies in 3 Reigns II," *JSS* 13 (1968): 76–92; idem, "Text-Sequence and Translation-Revision in 3 Reigns IX 10–X 33," *VT* 19 (1969): 448–63.

[6] D.W. Gooding, *Relics of Ancient Exegesis: A Study of the Miscellanies in 3 Reigns 2* (SOTSMS 4; Cambridge: Cambridge University Press, 1976).

[7] D.W. Gooding, "Problems of Text and Midrash in the Third Book of Reigns," *Textus* 7 (1969): 1–29.

[8] For an analysis along the lines of Gooding's, see R.P. Gordon, "The Second Septuagint Account of Jeroboam: History or Midrash," *VT* 25 (1975): 368–93; idem, "Source Study in 1 Kings XII 24a–n," *TGUOS* 25 (1973–1974 [1976]): 59–70; M. Aberbach and L. Smolar, "Jeroboam's Rise to Power," *JBL* 88 (1969): 69–72.

[9] Note, for example, the Greek version of 1 Kgs 15:5: "For David had done what was pleasing to the Lord and never turned throughout his life from all that he had commanded him, *except in the matter of Uriah the Hittite*." The omission of the italicized words in the LXX may well represent an attempt to "whitewash" Solomon (Gooding's explanation in "Text and Midrash," 21 was preceded by H.St.J. Thackeray, *The Septuagint and Jewish Worship: A Study in Origins* [The Schweich Lectures, The British Academy, 1920; London: the British Academy, 1923], 18, who used exactly the same term without referring to rabbinic exegesis). Gooding's special contribution is the reference to rabbinic literature, where in Gooding's words "there is a similar attempt to whitewash king David": "Rab said: When you examine [the life of] David, you find nought but 'save only in the matter of Uriah the Hittite.' Abaye the Elder pointed out a contradiction in Rab['s dicta]: Did Rab say thus? Surely Rab said: David paid heed to slander? The difficulty remains" (*b. Šabb.* 56a).

[10] Gooding, "Text and Midrash," 2.

and Gooding provisionally calls them "haggadic midrash." Gooding's many studies speak of inner-Greek Midrashic revision, usually without referring to a Hebrew base, and only in his summarizing study does he systematically invoke the possibility of this Greek revision being based on a Hebrew source of some sort. Throughout his studies, Gooding explains the LXX as being revised on the basis of (proto-)rabbinic traditions by an inner-Greek reviser, and not a translator.[11] This complicated construction of inner-Greek activity probably involves an unnecessary stage. However, we are very much in debt to Gooding who, with his developed literary feeling, identified tendencies in the LXX, which help us to achieve a better understanding of its background.

Like Gooding, Talshir describes the LXX as a Midrashic edition elaborating on MT.[12] Although her conclusions pertain to all of 3 Kingdoms, she bases herself mainly on two chapters analyzed at earlier occasions, 1 Kgs 11[13] and 12.[14] Talshir describes the Midrashic edition as having been created in Hebrew and translated faithfully by the LXX.[15] Like Gooding,[16] Talshir recognizes several parallels between this early Greek revision of 1 Kings and the work of the Chronicler in Hebrew.[17]

Polak likewise describes the LXX as representing a Greek version of an earlier Hebrew edition of 1 Kings.[18] Differing from other scholars who posit a Hebrew version behind the LXX, Polak reconstructs

[11] Although the possible involvement of a translator was mentioned (e.g. "Text and Midrash," 17), ultimately Gooding does not accept this option. Such a possibility would be defensible in light of parallels in Greek Scripture, mainly Job, were it not that the *Vorlage* of the LXX of 3 Kingdoms often differed from MT. See below, paragraph 2.

[12] Z. Talshir, "The Image of the Septuagint Edition of the Book of Kings," *Tarbiz* 59 (1990): 249–302 (302) [Heb. with English abstract]. See also Talshir's study, "The Contribution of Diverging Traditions Preserved in the Septuagint to Literary Criticism of the Bible," in *VIII Congress of the International Organization for Septuagint and Cognate Studies, Paris 1992* (ed. L. Greenspoon and O. Munnich; SBLSCS 41; Atlanta: Scholars Press, 1995), 21–41.

[13] Z. Talshir, "1 Kings and 3 Kingdoms: Origin and Revision, Case Study: The Sins of Solomon (1 Kgs 11)," *Textus* 21 (2002): 71–105.

[14] Z. Talshir, *The Alternative Story of the Division of the Kingdom 3 Kingdoms 12:24a–z* (Jerusalem Biblical Studies 6; Jerusalem: Simor, 1993).

[15] Talshir, "The Alternative Story," 256.

[16] Gooding, "Text and Midrash," 27.

[17] Z. Talshir, "The Reign of Solomon in the Making: Pseudo-Connections between 3 Kingdoms and Chronicles," *VT* 50 (2000): 233–49.

[18] F.H. Polak, "The Septuagint Account of Solomon's Reign: Revision and Ancient Recension," in *X Congress of the International Organization for Septuagint and Cognate Studies, Oslo, 1998* (ed. B.A. Taylor; SBLSCS 51; Atlanta: Scholars Press, 2001), 139–64.

a complex transmission history of the Hebrew book. Both the LXX and MT reflect recensions of an earlier text, the LXX being a late one ("RecL") and MT an earlier one, or the main one ("RecM").[19]

Trebolle Barrera and Schenker followed a similar line to that of Talshir and Polak in assuming that 3 Kingdoms is based on a Hebrew composition that differs from MT. However, they describe that composition as being anterior rather than subsequent to MT and superior to it. MT is a later text in which various editorial developments have taken place since the time of the LXX translation. Credit is due to Trebolle Barrera for being the first to develop this line of thinking, which he named "historia de la recension."[20] In a detailed study,[21] Schenker continues this approach, but gives it more content. Schenker, more so than Trebolle Barrera, identifies the tendencies of "the late text" of MT in some verses dating to 250–130 B.C.E., probably closer to the

---

[19] In Polak's words, "I thus propose the hypothesis that MT and the Hebrew text reflected by LXX both contain a secondary recension of the ancient Solomon account. This account served as a literary source text for the recension embodied by MT (the main recension, recM) and the recension reflected by the LXX (the late recension, RecL)" ("Septuagint Account," 149).

[20] J.C. Trebolle Barrera, "Testamento y muerte de David," *RB* 87 (1980): 87–103 (102). See especially his monograph *Salomón y Jeroboán: Historia de la recensión y redacción de 1 Reyes, 2–12; 14* (Institución San Jerónimo 10; Bibliotheca Salmanticensis, Dissertationes 3; Salamanca: Universidad Pontificia, 1980), esp. 278, 321; idem, "Redaction, Recension, and Midrash in the Books of Kings," *BIOSCS* 15 (1982): 12–35; idem, "The Text-critical Use of the Septuagint in the Books of Kings," in *VII Congress of the International Organization for Septuagint and Cognate Studies, Leuven 1989* (ed. C.E. Cox; SBLSCS 31; Atlanta: Scholars Press, 1991), 285–99.

[21] A. Schenker, *Septante et texte Massorétique dans l'histoire la plus ancienne du texte de 1 Rois 2–14* (CahRB 48; Paris: Gabalda, 2000). Among other things, Schenker's view is based on the Greek version of 1 Kgs 2:35. According to the MT of this verse, Solomon appointed "Zadok the priest" instead of Ebiatar, while according to the LXX, Zadok was appointed as "the first priest." Schenker considers the LXX to be the earlier version, reflecting the appointment of the high priests by the kings, while MT reflects a later situation, which was initiated with Simon Maccabee in 140 B.C.E. when kings could no longer make such appointments. According to Schenker, MT repressed the earlier formulation in this case as well as in one other. The singular בית הבמות of MT 1 Kgs 12:31 and 2 Kgs 17:29, 32 replaced the earlier plural reading of οἴκους ἐφ' ὑψηλῶν (et sim.) in the LXX. According to Schenker (144–46), the plural of the LXX reflected the earlier reality of more than one sanctuary in Shechem, which was changed by MT to reflect the building of a single Samaritan sanctuary. Therefore, this correction (also reflected in the Old Greek version, reconstructed from the Vetus Latina, in Deut 27:4) may be dated to the period of the existence of a temple on Mt. Gerizim between 300 and 128 B.C.E. Equally old elements are found in the LXX version of 1 Kgs 20:10–20 that mentions groups of dancing men as well as King David's dances, elements that were removed from MT, according to Schenker, probably in the second c. B.C.E.

later end of this spectrum. Both Trebolle Barrera and Schenker provide a number of text examples, sometimes referring to minute details. In a recent study, P. Hugo continues this line of research.[22]

Van Keulen's[23] main conclusions regarding the Greek translation of 1 Kgs 2–11 are close to those of Gooding. In a detailed and refined analysis, he shows that the LXX reworked MT, but unlike Gooding he does not define this reworking as Midrashic. He describes in detail the differences between the structure of MT and the LXX, the latter revising the former. The LXX reflects a rewritten and reorganized composition, into which the Summaries have been added (p. 274). Although Van Keulen occasionally recognizes Hebrew words behind elements of the LXX that deviate from MT, he concludes that the revisional activity took place at the Greek level.[24]

In sum, scholars who offered an overall explanation of the features of the LXX described the LXX as reflecting either: (1) an inner-Greek revision of an earlier Greek translation (Gooding, Van Keulen) or (2) a faithful Greek translation of a rewritten Hebrew text. That rewritten composition was either (2a) anterior (Trebolle Barrera, Schenker, Hugo) or (2b) subsequent (Talshir, Polak) to MT. Also Gooding and Van Keulen (1) admit that the inner-Greek revision was ultimately based on a Hebrew source.[25] This range of possibilities is usual within LXX scholarship.[26] Theory 1 is intrinsically less likely than theories 2a and

---

[22] P. Hugo, *Les deux visages d'Élie-Texte massorétique et Septante dans l'histoire la plus ancienne du texte de 1 Rois 17–18* (OBO 217; Fribourg: Academic Press, 2006).

[23] Van Keulen, *Two Versions*.

[24] Van Keulen, *Two Versions*, 302.

[25] Gooding, "Text and Midrash," passim (e.g. 29); Van Keulen, *Two Versions*, 302.

[26] With such diverse solutions given, how is it possible, asks Van Keulen (*Two Versions*, 19), that scholars came up with such differing theories? They probably turned to different types of reference material: "Gooding and Talshir refer to early Jewish exegesis and to biblical and para-biblical rewriting tendencies in order to demonstrate the Midrashic character of 3 Regum. Schenker, on the other hand, draws attention to historical, religious and geographical data which may suggest that the version attested by the LXX is anterior to the MT-version" (19). This observation is probably correct, but we should also realize that some scholars lean more towards MT, while others favor the LXX. Diametrically opposed suggestions have been proposed for all discrepancies between the MT and LXX. For example, the translations of Esther and Daniel are viewed by some as preceding MT and by others as rewriting those books. For references, see my study, "The Nature of the Large-Scale Differences between the LXX and MT S T V: Compared with Similar Evidence in Other Sources," in *The Earliest Text of the Hebrew Bible: The Relationship between the Masoretic Text and the Hebrew Base of the Septuaginta Reconsidered* (ed. A. Schenker; SBLSCS 52; Atlanta: Scholars Press, 2003), 121–44 (129–30). Likewise, the LXX of Job is explained by some as having been shortened by the translator, while others consider it as reflecting a short Hebrew

2b because of the lack of parallels for inner-Greek content revisions in the LXX. The only parallels of this type appear in Gooding's own writings, who surmised similar inner-LXX revision in Exod 35–40[27] and Josh 5,[28] but in both cases internal Greek activity is very unlikely. Parallels for rewriting Scripture in Hebrew (2b) abound within Hebrew Scripture itself (especially Chronicles), at Qumran and elsewhere (see below, paragraphs 6, 7). This view is followed here.[29]

2. The Discrepancies between 1 Kings and 3 Kingdoms Originated in Hebrew

Since it is difficult to decide between the two opposing explanations regarding the nature of 3 Kingdoms, the decision as to whether the deviations were created at either the Hebrew or Greek level would limit the options.

The following types of arguments could support the suggestion that the discrepancies were created at the Greek level: (1) indication of original Greek, (2) lack of Hebraisms, and (3) differences between the translations of parallel passages.[30] The following arguments could support the suggestion that the discrepancies were created at the Hebrew

---

text. Therefore, the differences between the views expressed regarding 3 Kingdoms should not surprise us.

[27] D.W. Gooding, *The Account of the Tabernacle* (TS NS 6; Cambridge: Cambridge University Press, 1959). The discrepancies between the LXX and MT in these chapters probably constitute the greatest challenge for LXX scholarship. The problems may not be more vexing than those in 1 Kings, Esther, and Daniel, but the difficult subject matter complicates the analysis. For a brief summary, see my study, *The Text-Critical Use of the Septuagint in Biblical Research* (2d ed.; Jerusalem Biblical Studies 8; Jerusalem: Simor, 1997), 256. A. Aejmelaeus (*On the Trail of Septuagint Translators* [Kampen: Kok Pharos, 1993], 116–30 [125]) probably indicated the correct direction for a solution by pinpointing variant readings in the translator's Hebrew *Vorlage* and by studying his translation technique.

[28] D.W. Gooding, "Traditions of Interpretation of the Circumcision at Gilgal," in *Proceedings of the Sixth World Congress of Jewish Studies* (Jerusalem: World Union of Jewish Studies, 1977), 149–64. In this paper, the background of the LXX of Josh 5:4–5 is described as rabbinic (cf. *Šir Haššîrîm Rabba* I, 12, 2). However, in my view, the deviating translation of this section resulted from syntactical-exegetical difficulties presented by some rather awkward Hebrew sentences.

[29] My earlier research (Tov, "LXX Additions") referred to the Summaries only. The suggestion expressed there concerning the lack of a coherent plan in these Summaries is now abandoned.

[30] See, however, notes 34–35.

level: (1) presence of Hebraisms,[31] (2) reflection of Hebrew readings in the LXX differing from MT, and (3) recognition of faithful translation technique.[32]

Turning to some or all of these criteria does not necessarily guarantee objective results, since every type of result may be interpreted in different ways. In my view no compelling arguments have been presented in favor of the assumption of revision at the Greek level, neither by Gooding nor by Van Keulen. The Greek renderings of parallel passages differ occasionally,[33] but such inconsistency also occurs in translations produced by a single translator.[34] Besides, the various translations, even when differing slightly, share several unique renderings.[35] On the other hand, there are compelling arguments in favor of a Hebrew source at the base of 3 Kingdoms: Tov[36] records Hebraisms in the Summaries,[37] described in greater detail by Polak[38] and Schenker (relating to all of 1 Kings),[39] and Tov[40] and Schenker[41] list variants reflected in the LXX. Even Gooding accepts the view that 3 Kingdoms has a Hebrew base. The Hebrew *Vorlage* of the duplicate version of the Jeroboam story (1 Kgs 12:24a–z) has been reconstructed by Debus[42] and Talshir,[43] while that of the Summaries in chapter 2 has been reconstructed in my own

---

[31] For the background, see Tov, *Text-Critical Use*, 83–85.

[32] Analysis of the level of freedom and literalness in the translators' approaches forms a key element in our understanding of them and their use as an ancient document in the study of Hebrew Scripture. In short, the argument runs as follows. If a translator represented his Hebrew text faithfully in small details, we would not expect him to insert major changes in the translation. Therefore, when we find major differences between the LXX and MT in relatively faithful translation units, they must reflect different Hebrew texts. These differing Hebrew texts are of central importance to our understanding of Hebrew Scripture. On the other hand, if a translator was not faithful to his parent text in small details, he also could have inserted major changes in the translation.

[33] See Gooding, "Text and Midrash," 18; idem, *Relics*, 111; Van Keulen, *Two Versions*, 274, 302.

[34] See, for example, T. Muraoka, "The Greek Texts of Samuel-Kings: Incomplete Translation or Recensional Activity?" *Abr-Nahrain* 21 (1982–83): 28–49 (30–31).

[35] For some examples relating to chapter 2, see Tov, "LXX Additions," 568.

[36] Tov, "LXX Additions," 568.

[37] 35g, k, l.

[38] Polak, "Septuagint Account," 143–48.

[39] Schenker, *Septante*, e.g. 54 (relating to 10:23–25), 130–39 (chapters 6–8), 149.

[40] Tov, "LXX Additions," 551–62.

[41] Schenker, *Septante*, 5–9.

[42] J. Debus, *Die Sünde Jerobeams* (FRLANT 93; Göttingen: Vandenhoeck & Ruprecht, 1967), 55–65.

[43] Talshir, *The Alternative Story*, 38–153.

study.[44] Wevers[45] and Talshir[46] indicate that the translator of 1 Kings rendered his source faithfully.

As a result, there is sufficient support for the assumption that 3 Kingdoms was based on a Hebrew source. This text could have been anterior or subsequent to MT. Since the tendencies of the Greek 3 Kingdoms are easily recognized (see below), and since no overall reverse theory has been suggested for corresponding tendencies in MT,[47] we accept Talshir's view[48] that the *Vorlage* of 3 Kingdoms reworked a text resembling MT. Polak expressed a similar view.[49] Ultimately, this view is close to Gooding's theory, except that he believes that the rewriting activity was carried out in Greek by a reviser and not in the Hebrew text consulted by the translator.

3. Characteristic Features of 3 Kingdoms

The following features not only characterize the Greek 3 Kingdoms but are in most cases unique to it:

i. Addition in chapter 2 of two theme *summaries*[50] (previously named Additions or Miscellanies) focusing on Solomon's wisdom. These summaries repeat various sections occurring elsewhere in the book (see further below).[51] To the best of my knowledge, this device is not used elsewhere in MT or the Greek Bible.[52] The closest parallel is the added

---

[44] Tov, "LXX Additions."

[45] Wevers, "Exegetical Principles," 300.

[46] Talshir, "Image," 256.

[47] Schenker (*Septante*, 151) mentions some elements of supposed revision in MT, but they do not cover the large differences between the two versions.

[48] Talshir, "Image."

[49] Polak, "Septuagint Account."

[50] To the best of my knowledge, this term has been used only by J. Gray, *1 & 2 Kings: A Commentary* (OTL; London: SCM, 1964), 45.

[51] See below, paragraph 4. The location of these summaries is inappropriate since Solomon is not yet a central person in this chapter. Possibly the location was determined by the scope of the ancient scrolls. Summary 1, after 1 Kgs 2:35, occurred at the end of a scroll containing the second half of 2 Samuel (Kingdoms βγ), while Summary 2, after 2 Kgs 2:46, occurred at the beginning of the scroll of 3 Kingdoms (Kingdoms γγ).

[52] Schenker (*Septante*, 9) compares the theme summaries with Josh 10:40–42; 12:1–8; 13:2–7; Judg 2:11–3:6, even Judg 1–2:5, but these texts are of a different nature. Most of them indeed include an element of summary of previous stories or data (Judg 1 does not!), but they rephrase the earlier narratives, while most of the summaries in 3 Kgdms 2 simply repeat complete verses occurring elsewhere. MT contains many additional summaries (for example, summarizing historical accounts like Josh 24 or

summary before the LXX of Dan 5 (see below), although that summary is not a theme summary.

ii. *Duplication* of sections based on the rewriting tendencies. Beyond the passages mentioned in section i, referring to summaries that constituted new literary compositions, the rewritten text of 3 Kingdoms repeated 1 Kgs 22:41–51 (description of Jehoshaphat's activities) in 3 Kgdms 16:28a–h and 1 Kgs 9:24 in v. 9a of the same chapter in 3 Kingdoms. To the best of my knowledge, the device of repeating sections is not used elsewhere in the Greek Bible or MT.[53]

iii. Inclusion of an *alternative version*. An alternative history of Jeroboam extant only in the LXX (3 Kgdms 12:24a–z) presents a rival story juxtaposed with the original one found in all textual sources including the LXX (1 Kgs 11, 12, 14). The technique of juxtaposing two versions of the same story was used from ancient times onwards in the composition of Hebrew Scripture. For example, different accounts of the creation and the flood were juxtaposed and partially intertwined in Genesis. In all these cases, the two versions are now included in all textual witnesses. However, with one exception (1 Sam 16–18),[54] there is no parallel for the juxtaposition of two alternative versions appearing in one textual witness but not in the others.

iv. The transposition of verses to other environments in accord with the reviser's tendencies. For example, 1 Kgs 3:1 and 9:16–17 are repositioned as 3 Kgdms 5:14a;[55] 1 Kgs 5:7–8 is repositioned as 3 Kgdms 5:1 (see paragraph 4); 1 Kgs 5:31–32 and 6:37–38 are moved to 3 Kgdms 6:1a–d; 1 Kgs 8:11–12 is placed in 3 Kgdms 8:53a;[56] verses from

---

historical Psalms like Ps 106), but none of them creates a mosaic of verses like the theme summaries in 3 Kgdms 2.

[53] The case of the duplicated verses in the MT of Joshua-Judges, especially in Josh 24 and Judg 1–2 is a different one, as these duplications resulted from complications in the creation of these books. Among other things, possibly an initially combined book Joshua-Judges was separated into two different ones.

[54] In these chapters the originally short story of the encounter of David and Goliath as narrated in the LXX was joined by an alternative story in MT. See my analysis in "The Composition of 1 Samuel 17–18 in the Light of the Evidence of the Septuagint Version," in *Empirical Models for Biblical Criticism* (ed. J.H. Tigay; Philadelphia: University of Pennsylvania Press, 1985), 97–130; repr. in *The Greek and Hebrew Bible: Collected Essays on the Septuagint* (VTSup 72; Leiden: Brill, 1999), 333–60; D. Barthélemy et al., *The Story of David and Goliath: Textual and Literary Criticism: Papers of a Joint Research Venture* (OBO 73; Fribourg: Éditions Universitaires, 1986).

[55] See the sample from 1 Kgs 3 below.

[56] According to Gooding ("Text and Midrash," 22–25) the transposition of these verses to v. 53a created a new text sequence in the beginning of the Greek chapter

9:15–22 are placed in 10:22a–c;[57] etc. This technique is also evidenced elsewhere in the LXX and MT.[58]

4. 3 KINGDOMS AS A REWRITTEN VERSION OF 1 KINGS

Having established that 3 Kingdoms is based on a Hebrew source, and having described some special techniques used in that composition, we now focus on its nature. The techniques described in the previous paragraph leave no doubt regarding the direction of the changes. The content summaries in chapter 2 are very inappropriate in their context (see n. 51). They would not have belonged to an initial stage of writing. By the same token, repetition of verses and the juxtaposition of an alternative account are secondary features. Further, the tendencies of this rewritten composition are clearly visible (see below). We therefore believe that, in the main, MT represents an earlier layer in the composition of 1 Kings and that 3 Kingdoms reflects later rewriting.

The reshaping in 3 Kingdoms involves the addition, repetition, omission, reordering, and changing of large sections as well as small details. These techniques are similar to those used in other compositions in the biblical realm, both within and beyond Greek and Hebrew Scripture. In the past, the techniques of 3 Kingdoms have been compared to those of the Midrash,[59] not only because the rewriting in 1 Kings sometimes resembles Midrash techniques, but also because Gooding located specific parallels with rabbinic literature in subject matter (above, note 9). This is not the place to analyze these parallels, not all of which are equally relevant, but it would perhaps be more appropriate to describe the

---

8 in which Solomon is now portrayed in a more pious way. After the glory entered the Temple, the king immediately turned his face away. See also Van Keulen, *Two Versions*, 164–80.

[57] The transposition possibly shows that Solomon's measures against the Canaanites are now presented as another token of his wisdom (thus Van Keulen, *Two Versions*, 191–201).

[58] Cf. several transpositions elsewhere in the LXX, for which see my paper, "Some Sequence Differences between the MT and LXX and Their Ramifications for the Literary Criticism of the Bible," *JNSL* 13 (1987): 151–60; repr. in *The Greek and Hebrew Bible: Collected Essays on the Septuagint* (VTSup 72; Leiden: Brill, 1999), 411–18.

[59] Thus especially Gooding (note the name of his summarizing study, "Text and Midrash"); see also Talshir, "Image," 302; V. Peterca, "Ein midraschartiges Auslegungs-beispiel zugunsten Salomos: 1 Kön 8, 12–13–3 Re 8,53a," *BZ* 31 (1987): 270–75.

technique as rewriting Scripture.[60] The Hebrew composition behind
3 Kingdoms rewrote a book resembling the composition contained in
MT. The comparison with rewritten Bible compositions at Qumran
and elsewhere is illuminating, but it also opens up a Pandora's box of
problems, as pointed out by Bernstein in another context.[61]

The reshaped compositions, both within and beyond the Greek and
Hebrew Scripture canons, were not intended to create new entities. The
revisers wanted their new creations to be as close as possible to the old
ones, thus ensuring that they would be accepted as authentic. The
rewriting sometimes merely involved contextual exegesis, but at other
times it included tendentious changes.

Some of the tendencies of the Greek version of 3 Kingdoms, already
recognized by Thackeray,[62] were described well by Gooding and Van
Keulen. Gooding presents the simplest analysis by describing the first
ten chapters as being rewritten around Solomon's wisdom, including the
whitewashing of his sins, chapters 11–14 as presenting a more favorable account of Jeroboam and chapters 16–22 as whitewashing Ahab.[63]
For Gooding, 3 Kingdoms takes the form of a Greek commentary on
1 Kings.[64] Likewise, for Van Keulen (p. 300), one of the main features
of the first part of this rewritten composition was the presentation
of a more favorable picture of Solomon and a rearrangement of the
sequence of events (named "pedantic timetabling" by Gooding[65]).

The rewriting techniques of 1 Kings are illustrated by three text
samples:

---

[60] Talshir, "Image," uses similar terms. The group of rewritten Bible compositions
forms a category in its own right described as follows by D.J. Harrington, S.J., "Palestinian Adaptations of Biblical Narratives and Prophecies," in *Early Judaism and its
Modern Interpretations* (ed. R.A. Kraft and G.W.E. Nickelsburg; Atlanta: Scholars Press,
1986), 242–47: "Because they paraphrase the biblical text, they have been called targumic. Because these books interpret biblical texts, they have been seen as midrashic.
But careful literary analysis has demonstrated that they are neither Targums nor
midrashim" (242).

[61] M.J. Bernstein, "'Rewritten Bible': A Generic Category Which Has Outlived its
Usefulness?" *Textus* 22 (2005): 169–96 (181: "One person's reworked Bible is another's
Bible").

[62] Thackeray, *The Septuagint and Jewish Worship*, 18. See also by the same author:
"The Greek Translators of the Four Books of Kings," *JTS* 8 (1907): 262–78; idem,
A Grammar of the Old Testament in Greek according to the Septuagint (Cambridge: University
Press, 1909), 9–10.

[63] Gooding, "Text and Midrash," *passim*.

[64] Gooding, "Text and Midrash," 28.

[65] Gooding, "Pedantic Timetabling."

1. The MT of 1 Kgs 2 covers the end of David's reign and Solomon's accession to the throne (vv. 1–12), the tragic end of Adonijah (vv. 13–35), and the death of Shimei (vv. 36–46). The parallel text of the LXX covers the same events, but in the middle and end of the chapter, it adds two long "theme summaries" relating to Solomon's wisdom. The summaries were intended to stress the God-given (cf. v. 35a) wisdom of Solomon, just as 1–2 Chronicles and 11QPs^a XXVII stress David's wisdom. The first one, Summary 1, inserted after v. 35, contains fourteen verses denoted 35a–o. Summary 2, inserted after v. 46, contains eleven verses denoted 46a–l. Summary 1 is not connected to the context, while Summary 2 is. These summaries repeat verses occurring elsewhere in 1 Kgs 3–11. They are out of chronological order, since the Solomonic history only starts with chapter 3. The clearest indication of the assumed rewriting process is probably the reworking of the story of Pharaoh's daughter. While several episodes of this story occur in different chapters in MT and the corresponding passages in the LXX, it is only in the added Summary 1 that they have been combined into one organic unit. Solomon's building activities (vv. d–g), placed between the two parts of the story, form an integral part of the narrative.

2. Several of the elements in chapter 5 of MT are included in the LXX in a different sequence, while others are newly added or are lacking. The sequence in the LXX is the provisions brought to Solomon (v. 1 = vv. 7–8 MT), his daily consumption of food (vv. 2–3), the extent of his realm (v. 4), his wisdom (vv. 9–14), Solomon's marriage to Pharaoh's daughter (v. 14a = MT 3:1; 14b = MT 9:16–17), his negotiations with Hiram (vv. 15–26), and the forced labor (vv. 27–32). Several verses of MT that are lacking in the LXX translation of this chapter are found in Summary 2 after 2:46: vv. 4:20–5:1 (the extent of Solomon's realm and its internal prosperity) appear in 2:46a–b and vv. 5–6 (internal prosperity, provisions) in 2:46g, i. These verses did not fit the topic of the rewritten and abbreviated form of chapter 5 in the LXX. More so than MT, the LXX forms a literary unity, which was probably generated after the creation of the disharmonious text of MT in which diverse material is often juxtaposed.

3. The content of the first eight verses of chapter 11 of MT differs from that of the LXX. Both versions depict the sins of King Solomon in marrying foreign wives and being involved in idolatry, but the LXX makes the latter sin more acceptable to the reader. The fact that he was married to foreign women in his old age made him an easy prey for

them, since they induced him to venerate non-Israelite gods. In MT,
on the other hand, Solomon himself initiated idolatrous acts.[66]

5. WHY ONLY 3 KINGDOMS OR WHY ONLY 1 KINGS?

Before turning to a comparison of the rewriting techniques in the
Greek 3 Kingdoms with Qumran compositions, we turn to the question
regarding why only the Old Greek of 3 Kingdoms or MT of 1 Kings
was rewritten within 1–4 Kingdoms.[67] To the best of my knowledge,
this issue has not been addressed in the literature.[68] The question can
be posed in two different ways referring to either the Greek or Hebrew
book.

i. Did the rewriting contained in the *Greek* 3 Kingdoms cover once
also 1–2, and 4 Kingdoms? Since we do not know why 3 Kingdoms
would have been singled out for content rewriting, it is possible that
all four books of Samuel-Kings (or just the two books of Kings) were
rewritten in Hebrew and that the rewritten versions were rendered into
Greek. The issue is complex, since we have no access to the Old Greek
translation of all of 1–4 Kingdoms any more. However, we do have
the Old Greek translations of 1 Samuel (Kingdoms α) and of the first
half of 2 Samuel (Kingdoms ββ), and they do *not* reflect any rewriting
such as in 3 Kingdoms. If these two segments were translated by the

---

[66] The description of the sins in 1 Kgs 11 was problematic also for the Chronicler
who simply omitted the chapter in his account of Solomon.

[67] Greek Scripture contains an amalgam of old and new, namely the Old Greek
versions of Kingdoms α and ββ and γγ (see n. 1) and the *kaige*-Th revision of Kingdoms βγ and γδ.

[68] A related question has been posed, namely why does 3 Kingdoms start at its present place in 1 Kgs 2:12, but no fully acceptable reply has been offered to that question.
Thackeray (*The Septuagint and Jewish Worship*, 18) merely distinguished between the Old
Greek and revised sections (see previous note), but he did not realize that the Old
Greek sections differ much among themselves. According to Thackeray, the sections
that now contain the *kaige*-Theodotion revision "were omitted as unedifying by the early
translators" (p. 18; similarly: "Greek Translators," 263). Another related question was
answered by D. Barthélemy (*Les devanciers d'Aquila: Première publication intégrale du texte des
fragments du Dodécaprophéton trouvés dans le désert de Juda* [VTSup 10; Leiden: Brill, 1963],
140–41): why was section βγ (2 Sam 11:2–1 Kgs 2:11) revised by *kaige*-Th.? Barthélemy
suggested that the translator wished to correct the chapters relating to the "failures and
calamities of the house of David." These chapters were not covered well in the Old
Greek, and because there existed no Greek version of these chapters in Chronicles,
their correction was an urgent task for the reviser.

person who rendered 3 Kingdoms, as is likely,[69] we do not know why 3 Kingdoms differs so drastically from 1–2 and 4 Kingdoms.[70] We therefore conclude that it is unlikely that a *Greek* rewritten text of all of 1–4 or 1–2 Kingdoms ever existed.

ii. Did a *Hebrew* version of 1–2 Samuel and 2 Kings that rewrote MT in a similar way to the Hebrew source of 3 Kingdoms once exist? This option is very well possible. The Hebrew 1 Kings was probably contained in one of the two scrolls of Kings. We suggest that the Old Greek translator mistakenly used a mixed set of Hebrew scrolls for his translation, one scroll of the rewritten type (1 Kings) and three unrevised scrolls.[71] This theory cannot be verified, since the Old Greek translations of Kingdoms βγ and γδ have been lost. Crucial to this scenario is the assumption of the use of scrolls of different types, which would have been understandable due to the scarcity of scrolls. Equally crucial is the assumption that at least the two Hebrew books of Kings were included in two separate scrolls. Support for this suggestion comes from the realm of the LXX, where a shift in translation character in some books has been ascribed to the use of different scrolls in the archetype of Greek Scripture.[72] There is no direct support from Qumran for the writing of the Hebrew book of Kings in two separate scrolls. The only (negative)

---

[69] Thackeray, "The Greek Translators," produces some evidence for the distinction between the translations of 1 Samuel and 1 Kings, but the evidence is not convincing (274–76). Muraoka, "The Greek Texts," assumes the unity of the Old Greek of Kingdoms α, ββ, γγ (45), while focusing on the relation between these sections and the "Lucianic" manuscripts in Kingdoms βγ, γδ. D. Barthélemy describes the Old Greek as "composite," but he only refers to the internal problems of 3 Kingdoms: "Prise de Position sur les Communications du Colloque de Los Angeles," in *Etudes d'Histoire du Texte de l'Ancien Testament* (OBO 21; Fribourg: Éditions Universitaires, 1978), 255–88 (258).

[70] It cannot be countered that the content of these two books differed from 3 Kingdoms, since also 1 Kingdoms and the first part of 2 Kingdoms provide sufficient occasion for rewriting, especially in the stories about Saul and David.

[71] The circulation of four different scrolls, although of different sizes and of a different nature, was also assumed by Barthélemy, "Prise de position," 257.

[72] For the bisection of 2 Samuel, Jeremiah, and Ezekiel in the LXX scrolls, see E. Tov, *The Septuagint Translation of Jeremiah and Baruch: A Discussion of an Early Revision of Jeremiah 29–52 and Baruch 1:1–3:8* (HSM 8; Missoula, Mont.: Scholars Press, 1976), 161–65. Likewise, in the classical world large compositions were subdivided into independent units (scrolls), often regardless of their content. See T. Birt, *Das antike Buchwesen in seinem Verhältniss zur Litteratur* (Berlin: Hertz, 1882; repr. Aalen: Scientia-Verlag, 1974), 131–40; H.Y. Gamble, *Books and Readers in the Early Church: A History of Early Christian Texts* (New Haven, Conn.: Yale University Press, 1995), 42–66 with references to earlier literature.

evidence relates to the books 1–2 Samuel that are joined in 4QSamᵃ.[73] On the other hand, the great majority of the other Scripture books, including the books of the Torah and the Five Scrolls, are contained in separate scrolls.[74] This evidence does support the assumption that 1–2 Kings would have been contained in two different scrolls.

6. Comparison with Rewritten Bible Compositions in Hebrew

The technique used by the Hebrew source of 3 Kingdoms is that of rewriting an earlier source. Within the LXX the closest parallels for this assumed technique are the translation of Esther whose major deviations reflect a Hebrew composition freely translated into Greek. Another parallel within Greek Scripture is Dan 4–6.[75]

We now expand our observations to other rewritten Hebrew Bible compositions as found among the Qumran scrolls and in the Samaritan Pentateuch.

The Samaritan version of the Torah rewrote a composition like MT. The rewriting is partial, as all rewriting, but it is manifest. In the main, the rewriting in the SP does not bear a Samaritan character, since earlier non-sectarian texts from Qumran (named pre-Samaritan)[76] carry the exact same content as the SP. However, the SP contains a small number of Samaritan sectarian readings. Together these texts are named the "SP group."

Some of the Qumran compositions likewise resemble the rewriting in the LXX books, even more so than the SP group. The best preserved rewritten Bible texts[77] from Qumran are 11QTᵃ LI–LXVI, 4QRP

[73] However, the division of scrolls for Samuel was not necessarily identical to the one in Kings.

[74] A few Torah scrolls contained two books. For details, see my book, *Scribal Practices and Approaches Reflected in the Texts Found in the Judean Desert* (STDJ 54; Leiden: Brill, 2004), 74–79.

[75] The parallels between these three texts have been pointed out in my forthcoming studies, "Three Strange Books of the LXX: 1 Kings, Esther, and Daniel Compared with Similar Rewritten Compositions from Qumran and Elsewhere"—*volume Wuppertal Septuaginta Deutsch*; idem, "The LXX Translation of Esther: A Paraphrastic Translation or a Free Translation of a Rewritten Version of MT?" *FS Pieter van der Horst.*

[76] Especially 4QpaleoExodᵐ and 4QNumᵇ; see E. Tov, "Rewritten Bible Compositions and Biblical Manuscripts, with Special Attention to the Samaritan Pentateuch," *DSD* 5 (1998): 334–54.

[77] For the evidence and an analysis, see G.J. Brooke, "Rewritten Bible," in *Encyclopedia of the Dead Sea Scrolls* (ed. L.H. Schiffman and J.C. VanderKam; New York: Oxford

(4Q158, 4Q364–367), the *Genesis Apocryphon* (1Q20), and *Jubilees*.[78] These parallels strengthen our aforementioned assertions relating to the rewriting in some LXX books and reversely the LXX helps us in clarifying the canonical status of the Qumran compositions.

The main feature these compositions have in common with the reconstructed sources of the LXX translations relates to the interaction between the presumably original Scripture text and exegetical additions. All the Qumran compositions present long stretches of Scripture text, interspersed with short or long exegetical additions, especially 4QRP (4QReworked Pentateuch). Among the Qumran rewritten Bible compositions, this text exhibits the longest stretches of uninterrupted text that may be classified as Scripture as found in either MT or the pre-Samaritan text.[79] As far as we can tell, it has a relatively small number of extensive additions. The exegetical character of this composition is especially evident from several pluses comprising 1–2 lines and in some cases more than 8 lines.[80] This composition also rearranges some Torah pericopes.[81] 11QT[a] LI–LXVI (constituting a paraphrase of the legal chapters of Deuteronomy)[82] changes the text sequence more frequently

University Press, 2000), 2:777–81; E. Tov, "Biblical Texts as Reworked in Some Qumran Manuscripts with Special Attention to 4QRP and 4QParaGen–Exod," in *The Community of the Renewed Covenant: The Notre Dame Symposium on the Dead Sea Scrolls* (ed. E. Ulrich and J.C. VanderKam; CJAS 10; Notre Dame, Ind.: University of Notre Dame Press, 1994), 111–34; M. Segal, "Between Bible and Rewritten Bible," in *Biblical Interpretation at Qumran* (ed. M. Henze; SDSS; Grand Rapids: Eerdmans, 2005), 10–29; Harrington, "Palestinian Adaptations."

[78] Pseudo-Philo's *Biblical Antiquities* and Josephus' *Jewish Antiquities* also provide valuable parallels, but they are less relevant since they make no claim to sacred status.

[79] The underlying text of 4Q158 and 4Q364 is clearly pre-Samaritan, that of 4Q365 possibly so (see *DJD* 13:192–96). See n. 89.

[80] The most clear-cut examples of this technique are the expanded "Song of Miriam" in 4Q365 (4QRP[c]) 6a ii and 6c counting at least 7 lines. By the same token, the added text in 4Q158 (4QRP[a]) 14 counts at least 9 lines. 4Q365 (4QRP[c]) 23 contains at least ten lines of added text devoted to festival offerings, including the Festival of the New Oil and the Wood Festival. Further, if 4Q365a (published as "4QTemple?") is nevertheless part of 4Q365 (4QRP), that copy of 4QRP would have contained even more nonbiblical material (festivals, structure of the Temple) than was previously thought.

[81] In one instance, a fragment juxtaposing a section from Numbers and Deuteronomy (4Q364 23a–b i: Num 20:17–18; Deut 2:8–14) probably derives from the rewritten text of Deuteronomy, since a similar sequence is found in SP. In the case of juxtaposed laws on a common topic (*Sukkot*) in 4Q366 4 i (Num 29:32–30:1; Deut 16:13–14), one does not know where in 4QRP this fragment would have been positioned in Numbers, as the fragment is presented in *DJD* 13, or in Deuteronomy.

[82] The close relation between that scroll and Hebrew Scripture is reflected in the name given to the scroll by B.Z. Wacholder and M.G. Abegg, "The Fragmentary Remains of 11QTorah (Temple Scroll)," *HUCA* 62 (1991): 1–116.

than 4QRP and also adds several completely new sections (for example, cols. LVII 1–LIX 21, providing the statutes of the king).[83] The SP group likewise inserts a number of extensive additions.[84]

The recognition of a group of rewritten Bible compositions at Qumran and elsewhere is accepted among scholars, even though they disagree with regard to the characterization of specific compositions[85] and the terminology used for the group as a whole.[86]

In the past, the LXX translations were not associated with the Qumran rewritten Bible texts. When making this link, we recognize the similarity in the rewriting style of Scripture books. More specifically, the LXX translations meet some of the characterizing criteria that Segal set for rewritten Bible compositions: new narrative frame, expansion together with abridgement, and a tendentious editorial layer.[87] In all these matters, 3 Kingdoms (as well as the LXX of Esther and Daniel) resembles several rewritten Bible texts from Qumran and elsewhere, including the SP. We will now review the similarities in techniques.

Two of the central techniques used in 3 Kingdoms, not known from MT or Greek Scripture, were used in the SP group, viz., the duplication of various sections in 3 Kingdoms and the insertion of theme summaries.

a. *Duplication.* Central to the literary principles of the SP group is the wish to rewrite Hebrew Scripture based on its editorial principles without adding new text pericopes. The addition of new passages would have harmed the authenticity of the rewritten Bible compositions, and therefore the SP group limited itself to copying passages. For this purpose they duplicated all the segments of Moses' first speech in Deut 1–3 in Exodus and Numbers as foreshadowers of Deuteronomy.[88] In both texts, the duplications have a certain purpose. In 3 Kingdoms, they serve an exegetical or chronological purpose, while in the SP group the

---

[83] For additional material supplementary to the Pentateuchal laws, see the list in Y. Yadin, *The Temple Scroll* (3 vols.; Jerusalem: Israel Exploration Society, Institute of Archaeology of the Hebrew University, Shrine of the Book, 1983), 1:46–70.

[84] For a detailed analysis, see Tov, "Rewritten Bible Compositions."

[85] See n. 103 below with regard to 4QRP.

[86] See Bernstein, "Rewritten Bible."

[87] Segal, "Between Bible and Rewritten Bible," 20–26.

[88] For a detailed analysis, see Tov, "Rewritten Bible Compositions."

duplication of segments from Deuteronomy in Exodus and Numbers is meant to make Deut 1–3 comply with the earlier books.[89]

b. *Theme summaries.* The two collections of verses in 3 Kgdms 2 summarize in the beginning of the Greek book verses relating to the central theme of the first ten chapters, Solomon's wisdom. By the same token, the added tenth commandment of SP (not found in the pre-Samaritan texts) is a theme summary of verses describing the sanctity of Mt. Gerizim. The added[90] tenth commandment of SP in both versions of the Decalogue describing and prescribing the sanctity of Mount Gerizim is made up of verses occurring elsewhere in Deuteronomy.[91]

In its major features 3 Kingdoms thus shares significant features with several rewritten Bible texts from Qumran and elsewhere. The same pertains to Esther and Daniel.[92]

7. TEXT AND CANON

The recognition that the Greek versions of 1 Kings, Esther, and Daniel represent rewritten versions of MT has important implications for our understanding of the canonical status of these books and of canonical issues in general. All three Greek books were considered to be authoritative by ancient Judaism and Christianity alike. In due course, they were rejected within Judaism, but for Christianity they remained authoritative in different ways.

It is no coincidence that two of the three books (Esther, Daniel) suffered a similar fate within the Christian canon, since they have much in common. They share large expansions that were considered disturbing, and therefore were ultimately removed from the running text in the case of Esther. The large expansions of Esth-LXX now have a deutero-canonical status in the Catholic Church even though they never

---

[89] A similar duplication is found in 4QDeut[n] V 5–7 where the motive clause for the Sabbath commandment in Exod 20:11 has been added after the motive clause in the Qumran scroll immediately after the motive clause of Deuteronomy. See J.H. Tigay, "Conflation as a Redactional Technique," in *Empirical Models for Biblical Criticism* (ed. idem; Philadelphia: University of Pennsylvania Press, 1985), 53–96 (55–7).

[90] The Samaritans consider the first commandment of the Jewish tradition as a preamble to the Decalogue, so that in their tradition there is room for an additional commandment.

[91] Deut 11:29a, 27:2b–3a, 27:4a, 27:5–7, 11:30—in that sequence.

[92] See Tov, "Three Strange Books."

existed separately. At the same time, the medium-sized expansions were left in the text. The medium-sized expansions of Daniel were likewise left in the text (4:14a [17a], 33a–b, 37a–c). However, two book-sized appendixes were placed at the beginning or end of the book (Susanna, Bel and the Serpent), while the large Expansion named the "Prayer of Azariah and the Song of the Three Young Men"[93] was left in the text between 3:23 and 3:24 but given deutero-canonical status. 3 Kingdoms could have undergone the same fate, but all the expansions including the large ones in chapters 2 and 12 were left in the text.

When the LXX translation was produced, the Hebrew source of 3 Kingdoms was considered to be as authoritative as 1 Kings, at least in some circles. Otherwise it would not have been rendered into Greek. This pertains also to the assumed Hebrew (Aramaic?) sources of Esther and Daniel.[94] The Greek translators and the Alexandrian Jewish community considered the original Hebrew and Aramaic versions, as well as their Greek translations, as authoritative as Baruch[95] or any other book included in those collections.

Several scholars assume that the canonical conceptions behind the "Alexandrian canon" reflect the views of the mother community in Palestine.[96] The link with Palestine is even closer for Esther, as there is strong evidence that this book was translated in that country.[97]

---

[93] Although placed in the text itself, this added text is usually believed to have enjoyed a separate existence. This Addition is composed of three or four separate compositions: the Prayer of Azariah (vv. 1–22), the prose narrative (vv. 23–28), the Ode (vv. 29–34), and the Psalm (vv. 35–68). See C.A. Moore, *Daniel, Esther, and Jeremiah. The Additions* (AB 44; Garden City, N.Y.: Doubleday, 1977), 40–76.

[94] See J.J. Collins, *Daniel: a Commentary on the Book of Daniel* (Hermeneia; Minneapolis, Minn.: Fortress, 1993), 195–207, 405–39.

[95] The book was translated by the same translator who rendered Jeremiah into Greek and was revised by the same reviser who revised at least the second part of the LXX of Jeremiah. See my study, *The Septuagint Translation of Jeremiah and Baruch*.

[96] Especially A.C. Sundberg, *The Old Testament of the Early Church* (HTS 20; Cambridge: Harvard University Press, 1964), 60–65.

[97] The main manuscripts of the LXX contain a note at the end of the book, the only such note in the LXX, translated by E.J. Bickerman, "The Colophon of the Greek Book of Esther," in *Studies in Jewish and Christian History: Part 1* (AGJU 9.1; Leiden: Brill, 1976), 225–45 (245) as follows: "In the fourth year of the reign of Ptolemy and Cleopatra <78–77 B.C.E.>, Dositheus—who said he was a priest—and Levitas, and Ptolemy his son deposited the preceding Letter of Purim, which they said really exists and had been translated by Lysimachus (son of) Ptolemy, (a member) of the Jerusalem community." The implication of this note is that the Greek version of Esther was produced in Jerusalem and deposited (*eisfero*) in the year 78–77 B.C.E. in an archive in Egypt.

The Greek canon includes 3 Kingdoms, Esther, and Daniel, constituting rewritten versions of earlier books such as now included in MT.
The rewritten books were considered authoritative in their Semitic as
well as Greek forms, although by different communities. The SP, likewise
a rewritten version of MT, as well as its pre-Samaritan forerunners,
enjoyed similar authority. Rewritten versions, as well as the earlier
versions on which they were based (for example, the MT of 1 Kings,
Esther, and Daniel), were considered equally authoritative, by different
communities and in different periods.

This brings us back to the rewritten Bible compositions found at
Qumran. We do not know to what extent these compositions were
accepted at Qumran or elsewhere, if at all, but probably at least some
of the "non-canonical" books were accepted as authoritative by that
community.[98] *Jubilees*, represented by 15–16 copies at Qumran, may have
had such a status.[99] The same may be said about 4Q–11QTemple, but
several types of evidence need to be taken into consideration.[100]

The decision is very difficult since no group has survived like Judaism,
Christianity, or the Samaritans that endorsed some of these compositions. Because of the lack of convincing evidence, we turn to the one
composition which from the point of view of its contents is so close
to Hebrew Scripture and to the rewritten works within Greek Scripture that it probably enjoyed the same authoritative status as Greek
Scripture. We refer to 4QReworked Pentateuch.[101] This composition,
published as a non-biblical composition, now has to be reclassified as
a Bible text similar in character to some of the rewritten LXX books

---

[98] For an analysis, see Brooke, "Rewritten Bible."

[99] *Jubilees* is quoted expressly in CD XVI 2–3: "As for the exact determination of
their times to which Israel turns a blind eye, behold it is strictly defined in the *Book of
the Divisions of the Times into their Jubilees and Weeks*." The book is written as authoritative
Scripture, with God announcing Israel's future to Moses on Sinai. For an analysis, see
J.C. VanderKam, "Jubilees," in *Encyclopedia of the Dead Sea Scrolls*, 1:437.

[100] In this composition Israel's laws are rewritten, especially in cols. LI–LXVI that
follow the sequence of Deuteronomy, albeit with many differences. God is mentioned
in the first person. This composition is known from five Qumran manuscripts (three
from cave 11 and two from cave 4), a number that is probably large enough to assume
its popularity at Qumran. It is less clear whether this composition is quoted in the
Qumran writings.

[101] E. Tov and S.A. White, "4QReworked Pentateuch[b–e]" and "4QTemple?" *DJD*
13:187–351, 459–63 and plates XIII–XXXXVI.

like 3 Kingdoms.[102] For a more detailed analysis of the issues involved, see my study elsewhere.[103]

In conclusion, our analysis of 3 Kingdoms suggested that this Greek translation rendered a Hebrew composition that reworked 1 Kings. The reworking was rather penetrating involving the addition of long summaries and an alternative story as well as the duplication of passages. The revision involved tendentious changes regarding Solomon, Jeroboam, and Ahab. As a result, the composition included in the LXX reflects a stage subsequent to that in MT. We believe that the Greek translations of Esther and Dan 4–6 attest to similar stages. All three books were based on Semitic texts, and their underlying texts rewrote compositions resembling MT. We found several characteristic features in these three compositions that are shared with rewritten Bible compositions from Qumran, especially 4QRP. These findings have implications for the LXX translations, the Qumran scrolls, and canonical conceptions.

---

[102] S. White Crawford, who published 4QRP together with me, recognizes the possibility that this text possibly was an authoritative Bible text, but decides against it because of lack of positive evidence: "The Rewritten Bible at Qumran," in *The Hebrew Bible at Qumran* (ed. J.H. Charlesworth; N. Richland Hills, Tex: Bibal, 2000), 173–95; eadem, *Rewriting Scripture in Second Temple Times*, forthcoming.

[103] "The Many Forms of Scripture: Reflections in Light of the LXX and 4QReworked Pentateuch," forthcoming. M. Segal and E. Ulrich were ahead of us when claiming in 2000 that this text is Scripture: M. Segal, "4QReworked Pentateuch or 4QPentateuch?" in *The Dead Sea Scrolls, Fifty Years After Their Discovery: Proceedings of the Jerusalem Congress, July 20–25, 1997* (ed. L.H. Schiffman et al.; Jerusalem: Israel Exploration Society, The Shrine of the Book, Israel Museum, 2000), 391–99; E. Ulrich, "The Qumran Biblical Scrolls: The Scriptures of Late Second Temple Judaism," in *The Dead Sea Scrolls in their Historical Context* (ed. T.H. Lim et al.; Edinburgh: T&T Clark, 2000), 76.

JÉRÉMIE LE PROPHÈTE DANS LE TM ET LES LXX
DE SON LIVRE

Francolino J. Gonçalves

INTRODUCTION

Jérémie est, de loin, le livre biblique qui emploie le plus souvent le groupe lexical נבא, avec 134 de ses 445 occurrences bibliques. Il dépasse tous les autres livres prophétiques pris ensemble, où ce vocabulaire se lit 109x. De dimensions comparables à celles de *Jérémie*, le livre d'Isaïe ne l'emploie que 8x. *Jérémie* est encore remarquable en raison de l'écart entre la fréquence du groupe lexical נבא dans le TM et celle de son correspondant προφήτης dans les LXX: 134x contre 97.

Le livre de Jérémie grouille de prophètes, et abonde en activités prophétiques. On y rencontre apparemment plusieurs classes de prophètes anonymes. Deux d'entre elles sont contemporaines, et, sauf quelques exceptions,[1] elles sont disqualifiées et vouées à la disparition. L'une forme souvent une paire avec les prêtres,[2] et est aussi associée à d'autres classes dirigeantes.[3] L'autre appartient au monde des devins.[4] À l'opposé, deux autres classes appartiennent au passé, et elles sont les modèles prophétiques: les prophètes qui, depuis toujours, ont prophétisé la guerre à des nations nombreuses et à de grands royaumes (Jr 28,8); les «serviteurs du Seigneur les prophètes» qui ont exhorté—en vain—Israël à la conversion.[5]

Jérémie met en scène plusieurs personnes qui prophétisent, sans pour autant les appeler prophètes. À l'exception de Uryahu fils de Shemayahu

---

[1] Jr 18,18; 29,1. En l'absence d'indications contraires, par commodité, les références au livre de Jérémie au-delà du chapitre 25 renvoient au TM. Les références aux LXX suivront la numérotation de l'édition critique de J. Ziegler, *Ieremias—Baruch—Threni—Epistula Ieremiae* (Septuaginta. Vetus Testamentum Graecum Auctoritate Societatis Litterarum Gottingensis editum 15; Göttingen: Vandenhoeck & Ruprecht, 1957).

[2] Jr 2,8; 5,31; 6,13; 8,10 (propre au TM); 14,18; 23,11.33–34; 26,7.8.11.16.

[3] Jr 2,26; 4,9; 8,1; 13,13; 18,18; 29,1; 32,32. Les prophètes de ce type se trouvent seuls en Jr 2,30; 5,13; 23,13–15.16–22*.25–32; 27,12–18; 29,15; 37,19.

[4] Jr 14,13–16; 27,9–10; 29,8–9.

[5] Jr 7,25–26; 25,4–7; 26,3–6; 29,16–20 (propre au TM); 35,15.17; 44,2–6. Cf. 11,7–8.

(Jr 26,20–23), elles sont d'ailleurs disqualifiées : le prêtre Pashehur (Jr 20,1–6), Ahab fils de Qolaya, Sédécias fils de Maaséya (Jr 29,21–23) et Shemaya le Néhélamite (Jr 29,30–32). Jérémie et son antithèse, Hananyah (Jr 28), sont les seuls individus que le livre appelle prophète.

Notre propos est très limité : essayer de dégager le caractère prophétique de Jérémie dans les deux formes de son livre représentées par le TM et les LXX, en nous fondant sur l'usage des groupes lexicaux נבא et προφήτης.[6] L'hébreu emploie נבא 42x en rapport direct avec Jérémie : 10 sous forme verbale (9x נבא et 1x התנבא) et 32 sous forme nominale (נביא). Dans les LXX, le groupe lexical προφήτης se réfère à Jérémie seulement 15x : 10 sous forme verbale et 5 sous forme nominale. D'où l'écart qui existe entre le nombre d'emplois du vocabulaire prophétique dans les deux formes du livre. Nous nous rangeons à l'hypothèse de ceux qui voient dans les LXX le témoin d'une édition du livre antérieure à celle qui est représentée par le TM.[7] Notre étude lui apportera une confirmation.

Nous commencerons par les 10 emplois du verbe « prophétiser » ayant Jérémie pour sujet. Nous examinerons ensuite le récit de son institution comme prophète des nations (1,4–10). Enfin, nous passerons en revue les textes qui lui donnent le titre de prophète, d'abord les 4 communs aux deux formes du livre, et ensuite les 27 propres au TM.[8]

ACTIVITÉ PROPHÉTIQUE DE JÉRÉMIE

Au fil du texte, Jérémie est sujet du verbe « prophétiser » la première fois en Jr 11,21. Jérémie cite les gens d'Anatot qui lui disent : « Ne prophétise pas au nom de Yahvé et tu ne mourras pas de notre main. » Le texte ne motive pas explicitement l'interdiction. Les concitoyens de Jérémie lui dénient-ils le droit de prophétiser au nom du Seigneur parce qu'ils ne le reconnaissent pas comme prophète ? Le contexte conseille plutôt d'y voir la dramatisation du refus que le peuple oppose aux appels de

---

[6] J. Hill, "The Book of Jeremiah MT and Early Second Temple Conflicts about Prophets and Prophecy," *ABR* 50 (2002) : 28–42 et L.J. de Regt, "The Prophecy in the Old and New Edition of Jeremiah," *The New Things: Eschatology in Old Testament Prophecy. Festschrift for Henk Leene* (ed. F. Postma et al. ; Amsterdamse Cahiers. Suppl. Series 3 ; Maastricht : Shaker, 2002), 167–74, ont un propos plus large.

[7] P.-M. Bogaert, "Le livre de Jérémie en perspective : Les deux rédactions antiques selon les travaux en cours," *RB* 101 (1994) : 363–406.

[8] C'est avec la plus grande joie que je m'associe à l'hommage rendu au Prof. Florentino García Martínez. Vieilles de décennies, son amitié ainsi que celle d'Annie, son épouse, me sont très chères.

Jérémie à écouter les paroles de l'alliance (vv. 1–17). En restreignant l'accusation aux gens d'Anatot, Jr 11,21 illustre l'opposition des siens dont Jérémie est l'objet (Jr 12,6).

L'action prophétique de Jérémie réapparaît en Jr 19,14–20,1. En Jr 19,14, on lit: «Jérémie revint du Tophèt où Yahvé l'avait envoyé prophétiser (…)». Jérémie y avait annoncé le malheur de Juda et de Jérusalem, en le préfigurant par le bris d'une cruche (Jr 19,1–13). La raison du malheur est le culte qu'ils rendent à des dieux autres que Yahvé. Le v. 15 réitère l'annonce du malheur de Jérusalem, et Jr 20,1–3a rapporte la réponse: «Or le prêtre Pashehur, fils d'Immer, qui était le chef de la police dans le Temple du Seigneur, entendit Jérémie prophétisant ces choses/paroles» (v. 1), le frappa et le mit au carcan (v. 2). Après sa libération (vv. 3b–6), Jérémie répète de nouveau l'annonce, en ajoutant que le malheur atteindra tout Juda, et que Pashehur sera amené captif à Babylone, où il mourra, lui et tous ses amis, à qui il a prophétisé faussement (בשקר ... נבאת/ἐπροφήτευσας ... ψευδῆ). Le texte s'achève ainsi sur l'opposition entre Pashehur et Jérémie sur le terrain de l'activité prophétique. Prophétisant sans mandat du Seigneur, Pashehur est disqualifié.

En JrLXX 25,14, le verbe «prophétiser» se trouve dans un titre. D'après la leçon courante τὰ Αιλαμ, le texte se rapporte à l'Élam («les peuples d'Élam») ou, plus probablement, à l'ensemble des nations visées en JrLXX 25,15–31,44, considérées comme des vassales d'Élam. D'après une forme ancienne du texte, qui n'a pas l'article avant Élam, JrLXX 25,14 pourrait juxtaposer deux titres : le titre général des oracles sur les nations «Ce qu'a prophétisé Jérémie sur les nations» et le titre particulier «Élam», la première des nations visées (JrLXX 25,15–26,1).[9] La partie générale du titre est devenue en JrTM 25,13bβ un élément du titre de l'oracle de la coupe (JrTM 25,15–29).[10] En JrTM 25,30/JrLXX 32,16, Dieu ordonne à Jérémie de prophétiser à toutes les nations qu'Il va les juger.

Le verbe «prophétiser» revient à trois reprises dans la seconde version de l'oracle contre le temple (JrTM 26,1–16/JrLXX 33,1–16). Par

---

[9] P.-M. Bogaert, "Le livre de Jérémie en perspective," 378–80; "La datation par souscription dans les rédactions courte (LXX) et longue (TM) du livre de Jérémie," *L'apport de la Septante aux études sur l'Antiquité* (ed. J. Joosten et P. Le Moigne; LD 203; Paris: Le Cerf, 2005), 140.

[10] Bogaert, "La datation par souscription," 141. Ce titre est repris par une partie de la tradition grecque dans l'oracle de la coupe. Il est retenu dans l'édition de Rahlfs des LXX (32,13), mais non dans l'édition critique de Ziegler.

l'entremise de Jérémie, le Seigneur s'adresse aux Judéens en vue de les amener à se détourner chacun de sa mauvaise conduite, de sorte à éviter le malheur dont Il entend les frapper. S'ils ne suivent pas la loi du Seigneur, en écoutant les paroles de ses serviteurs les prophètes, le Seigneur traitera le temple comme Il a traité Silo, et fera de Jérusalem une malédiction pour toutes les nations. En entendant cela, les prêtres et les prophètes se saisissent de Jérémie et lui déclarent qu'il va être mis à mort parce qu'il a prophétisé la ruine du temple et de Jérusalem. Finalement, les princes (שרים/ἄρχοντες) et tout le peuple, devant qui les prêtres et les prophètes accusent Jérémie, reconnaissent le bien-fondé de la prétention qu'il a de parler au nom du Seigneur. Ils lui épargnent ainsi la peine de mort que les prêtres et les prophètes brandissaient contre lui.

Dans ce récit, l'action de Jérémie et son résultat sont exprimés généralement par le radical דבר, qui est rendu par λαλέω-λόγος, sauf au v. 2, où il est traduit 2x par χρηματίζω, et 1x par ῥῆμα. En 13 de leurs 16 emplois, ces termes ont Jérémie pour sujet : sous la plume du narrateur (vv. 7.8.10), sur les lèvres du Seigneur (v. 2), de Jérémie lui-même (vv. 12.15) et des personnages qui lui sont favorables (v. 15). Dans les trois emplois restants, ces termes ont pour sujet le Seigneur lui-même (vv. 1.13) ainsi que ses serviteurs les prophètes (v. 5). En revanche, les prêtres et les prophètes, dans leur accusation de Jérémie, expriment son action au moyen de נבא/προφητεύω (vv. 9 et 11). Prophétiser doit donc avoir une portée polémique. Jérémie relève le défi, puisqu'il reprend ce verbe dans sa défense (v. 12).

Le récit résulte sans doute d'un processus rédactionnel, et a plus d'un but. Il légitime l'action prophétique de Jérémie qui reçoit la caution des princes. Du même coup, il explique aussi comment Jérémie a échappé à ceux qui voulaient le mettre à mort à cause du message de malheur qu'il annonçait au nom du Seigneur. JrTM 36,19/JrLXX 43,19 attribue également aux princes un rôle semblable, en conseillant à Baruch de se cacher, lui et Jérémie (v. 19). Un autre but de JrTM 26,1–16/JrLXX 33,1–16 est de montrer que Jérémie se conforme au modèle des «serviteurs du Seigneur les prophètes» (v. 5), et se place donc dans leur lignée. En effet, le récit prête à Jérémie les trois traits caractéristiques de ces personnages : l'envoi divin (שלח/ἀποστέλλω/ἐξαποστέλλω)[11] et

---

[11] Dit, avec beaucoup d'insistance, des «serviteurs du Seigneur les prophètes» (JrTM 26,5/Jr LXX 33,5; ailleurs dans le livre, Jr 7,25; 25,4; JrTM 29,19; JrTM

l'exhortation adressée au peuple à écouter (שמע/ἀκούω/εἰσακούω),[12] et
à se convertir (שוב/ἀποστρέφω) chacun de sa mauvaise conduite.[13] Cela
dit, le récit n'accorde jamais le titre de prophète à Jérémie. Le narrateur
l'appelle par son nom propre (vv. 7.8.9.12); les prêtres, les prophètes et
les princes le désignent par l'expression «cet homme».

Jérémie prophétise de nouveau en JrTM 29,27/JrLXX 36,27. JrTM
29,24–32 est une annonce de malheur motivée. Adressés par Yahvé à
Shemaya le Néhélamite (vv. 24–25a), les vv. 25b–28 sont essentielle-
ment une citation de celui-ci (vv. 26–28), laquelle incorpore une citation de Jérémie l'Anatotite (v. 28). Shemaya proteste auprès du prêtre
Sophonie. En raison de sa charge de surveillant du temple, Sophonie
aurait dû arrêter Jérémie, parce qu'il y prophétise (v. 27).[14] Les vv.
26–27 semblent supposer que Shemaya ne reconnaît pas à Jérémie
la compétence pour prophétiser. Cela dit, au v. 28, Shemaya vise certainement la teneur de la lettre que Jérémie a adressée aux déportés.
Contredisant le consensus des prophètes, Jérémie y annonce que l'exil
sera long (JrTM 29,4–7/JrLXX 36,4–7). Voilà ce que Shemaya conteste. Si Jérémie avait annoncé le retour imminent, il n'aurait rien à
lui reprocher. Au contraire!

Au v. 29, le narrateur rapporte, sans commentaire, que le prêtre
Sophonie lit à Jérémie la lettre de Shemaya à son sujet. Cette notice fait
la transition avec les vv. 30–32, qui contiennent un oracle de malheur
contre Shemaya le Néhélamite. La cause de son malheur est le fait
qu'il prophétise parmi les exilés, alors que Yahvé ne l'a pas envoyé, les
faisant donc se confier dans le mensonge (בטח על־שקר), c'est-à-dire dans
l'imminence du retour des exilés (Jr 27,16; 28,3–4.15). Le message de
Shemaya est donc aux antipodes de celui de Jérémie (v. 28). L'oracle
se termine par le châtiment que Yahvé va appliquer à Shemaya parce
qu'il a prophétisé sans son mandat (v. 31).

35,15/JrLXX 42,15; JrTM 44,4/JrLXX 51,4); dit par Jérémie de lui-même (JrTM
26,12.15/JrLXX 33,12.15).
    [12] En rapport avec les «serviteurs du Seigneur les prophètes» (JrTM 26,5/JrLXX
33,5; ailleurs dans le livre, Jr 7,26; 25,7; JrTM 29,19; JrTM 35,15/JrLXX 42,15;
JrTM 44,5/JrLXX 51,5); dit par Jérémie (JrTM 26,3.4.13/JrLXX 33,3.4.13).
    [13] En rapport avec les «serviteurs du Seigneur les prophètes» (Jr 25,5; JrTM
35,15/JrLXX 42,15; JrTM 44,5/JrLXX 51,5); dit par Jérémie (JrTM 26,3/JrLXX
33,3). Cf. F.J. Gonçalves, "Concepção deuteronomista dos profetas e sua posteridade,"
Didaskalia 33 (2003): 82–92.
    [14] Seul texte où Jérémie est le sujet de התנבא. Il reprend cette forme verbale du verset
précédent, qui met en parallèle le participe מתנבא et le syntagme איש משגע (homme
fou); cf. 2R 9,11 et Os 9,7.

JrTM 29,24–32 est parallèle à Jr 20,1–6. Les deux textes mettent en scène le prêtre chargé de la surveillance du temple. L'enjeu est dans les deux cas l'opposition entre Jérémie, qui prophétise avec le mandat de Yahvé, et une personne qui prophétise sans le mandat de Yahvé : Shemaya en JrTM 29,24–32 et Pashehur en Jr 20,1–6 ; ce dernier cumule la surveillance du temple et la fausse activité prophétique. Les opposants de Jérémie sont l'objet d'un oracle de malheur chacun (Jr 20,3b–6 et JrTM 29,31–32).

JrLXX 36,24–32 diffère beaucoup de son correspondant en JrTM 29,24–32, surtout aux vv. 25–28, dont l'enchaînement logique n'est pas toujours clair.[15] Je signalerai ses principales particularités pertinentes pour l'image prophétique de Jérémie. Aux vv. 24–28, le Seigneur s'adresse, par l'entremise de Jérémie, d'abord à « Samaia l'Élamite » (v. 24), et lui déclare : « Je ne t'ai pas envoyé en mon nom » (v. 25a). Samaia est donc disqualifié d'entrée de jeu. Le Seigneur lui-même s'adresse ensuite à Sophonie fils de Maassaia, le prêtre, pour lui rappeler la charge qu'il a de surveiller les activités prophétiques qui ont lieu dans le temple (vv. 25b–26). Finalement, le Seigneur demande à la fois à Samaia et à Sophonie, unis dans le même reproche : « Eh bien, pourquoi avez-vous calomnié Jérémie d'Anatot qui vous avait prophétisé ? » (v. 27).[16] Le Seigneur lui-même reproche non seulement à Samaia mais aussi à Sophonie leur comportement à l'égard de Jérémie, dont Il légitime ainsi l'activité prophétique.

La dernière attestation du verbe « prophétiser » ayant Jérémie pour sujet se trouve en JrTM 32,3/JrLXX 39,3. Jérémie est en prison dans Jérusalem assiégée. Sous la forme d'une question, Sédécias donne la raison pour laquelle il l'a fait emprisonner : « 3 ... Pourquoi toi, prophétises-tu, disant : Ainsi dit Yahvé : "Voici que je donne cette ville dans la main du roi de Babel, et il la prendra ? 4 Et Sédécias, roi de Juda[17] n'échappera pas à la main des Chaldéens, car vraiment il sera livré dans la main du roi de Babel, et sa bouche parlera à sa bouche, et ses yeux verront ses yeux. 5 Et à Babel il emmènera Sédécias, et là il sera..."».[18] Ce que le roi condamne, c'est la teneur du message de Jérémie.

---

[15] Y. Goldman, *Prophétie et royauté au retour de l'exil. Les origines littéraires de la forme massorétique du livre de Jérémie* (OBO 118; Göttingen: Vandenhoeck & Ruprecht, 1992), 106–22.
[16] Goldman, *Prophétie et royauté*, 108–9.
[17] Le titre « roi de Juda » est propre au TM.
[18] Dans les LXX, le v. 5 se lit: « Et Sédécias ira à Babylone, et là il résidera ».

Jérémie Prophète des Nations (Jr 1,4–10)

«4 La parole de Yahvé me[19] fut adressée, disant: 5 "Avant de te former au ventre maternel, je t'ai connu; avant que tu ne sortes du sein, je t'ai consacré; prophète pour les nations,[20] je t'ai institué." 6 Et je dis: Ah! Seigneur Yahvé, voici, je ne sais pas parler, car je suis un enfant! 7 Mais Yahvé me dit: "Ne dis pas: 'je suis un enfant'! car vers tous ceux à qui je t'enverrai, tu iras, et tout ce que je t'ordonnerai, tu le diras. 8 Ne les crains pas, car je suis avec toi pour te délivrer, oracle de Yahvé." 9 Yahvé étendit sa main, et toucha ma bouche; et Yahvé me dit: "Voici, je mets mes paroles dans ta bouche. 10 Vois! je t'établis, ce jour, sur les nations et sur les royaumes, pour arracher et abattre, pour ruiner et démolir, pour bâtir et planter."»[21]

On s'accorde pour voir en Jr 1,4–10 un tissu de références et allusions à de nombreux textes de *Jérémie* ainsi que d'autres livres bibliques. Je relèverai celles qui me semblent plus pertinentes pour le portrait prophétique de Jérémie. Le v. 5 applique à Jérémie ce que plusieurs textes de Is 40–66 disent de l'élection du Serviteur/Israël (Is 44,1–2; 49,1.5; cf. 46,3); il situe le début du rapport de Yahvé avec Jérémie avant même sa conception. Comme le fait remarquer Bovati, l'association de la connaissance de quelqu'un à sa conception suggère l'idée de paternité (Is 63,16).[22] Or, la filiation et l'élection divines sont deux attributs à la

---

[19] Les mss BS, 239 et 410 ont προς αυτον («lui»), leçon retenue par Ziegler.

[20] Les mss 62 et 130 ont le singulier εθνος, sans doute une leçon facilitante; cf. W. McKane, *Jeremiah*, 1. *Introduction and Commentary on Jeremiah I–XXV* (ICC; Edinburgh: T&T Clark, 1986), 6–7.

[21] Dans les LXX, la description de l'action de Jérémie comporte seulement cinq verbes, הרס ou נתץ n'y ayant pas d'équivalent; J.G. Janzen, *Studies in the Text of Jeremiah* (HSM 6; Cambridge, Mass.: Harvard University Press, 1973), 35; W.L. Holladay, *Jeremiah 1* (Hermeneia; Minneapolis: Fortress Press, 1986), 391. La citation de ce verset dans le texte grec de Ben Sira (49,7) a également cinq verbes, κακοῦν y prenant la place de κατασκάπτειν et οἰκοδομεῖν celle de ἀνοικοδομεῖν. En revanche, dans le Ms B du texte hébreu de Ben Sira, on lit après les six verbes du TM le début d'un septième verbe; cf. P.C. Beentjes, *The Book of Ben Sira in Hebrew: A Text Edition of All Extant Hebrew Manuscripts and a Synopsis of All Parallel Hebrew Ben Sira Texts* (VTSup 68; Leiden: Brill, 1997), 88.

[22] P. Bovati, "'Je ne sais pas parler' (Jr 1,6): Réflexions sur la vocation prophétique," *Ouvrir les Écritures. Mélanges offerts à Paul Beauchamp* (ed. P. Bovati et R. Meynet; LD 162; Paris: Le Cerf, 1995), 42–44.

fois du roi[23] et du peuple.[24] Par ailleurs, la consécration assimile Jérémie aux lévites (Nb 3,12–13) et à l'ensemble du peuple (Ex 19,6; Dt 7,6, 14,1–2).[25] La dynastie davidique, les lévites et le peuple se retrouvent associés en JrTM 33,14–26, un passage propre au TM. En Jr 1,5a, Jérémie apparaît ainsi d'emblée comme une personnification d'Israël, avec des traits royaux et, peut-être aussi, lévitiques.

Le v. 5b rappelle JrTM 28,8/JrLXX 35,8. D'après ce passage, les prophètes que Jérémie prend pour modèles ont prophétisé à de nombreux pays et à de grands royaumes. La déclaration du v. 5b rappelle aussi celle que le Seigneur fait au Serviteur, en Is 49,6 («je t'institue lumière des nations»).[26] La qualification de Jérémie comme «prophète pour les nations», qui intrigue tant les exégètes, a probablement partie liée avec son assimilation au Serviteur/Israël, présenté sous des traits royaux. Le roi davidique et son héritier, Israël, ont une mission auprès des nations.[27]

L'incapacité de parler (v. 6bα) renvoie à Moïse (Ex 4,10; 6,12.30). Le jeune âge (v. 6bβ) rappelle Samuel (1S 2,11; 3,1.8), et peut-être aussi Salomon (1R 3,7).

Le Seigneur envoie (שלח) et Jérémie va (הלך) (v. 7bα). Cette paire de verbes se lit plusieurs fois dans les récits de l'envoi de Moïse (Ex 3,10–15; 4,12–13), et une fois dans l'envoi de Gédéon (Jg 6,14). Elle se trouve aussi dans le contexte de l'envoi d'Ézéchiel (Ez 2,3–5; 3,4–6). Elle structure le récit de l'envoi d'Isaïe (Is 6,8–9), qui l'emploie deux fois. Le conseil divin (royal), auquel Isaïe assiste en vision, cherche un volontaire pour une mission. Le Seigneur demande: «Qui enverrai-je? Qui ira pour nous?» Isaïe répond: «Me voici, envoie-moi». À son tour, le Seigneur répond: «Va...». Is 6,8–9 est le texte le plus proche de Jr 1,7bα, tant du point de vue de la formulation que du contexte. Le verbe «envoyer» exprime souvent le rapport entre le Seigneur et

---

[23] Filiation Ps 2,7; 89,27–28; 110,3 (LXX); 2S 7,14; 1Chr 17,13; élection Dt 17,15; 2S 6,21; 1R 8,16; 11,34; Ps 78,70; 89,4; cf. 1S 10,24; 16,8–10; 2S 16,18.

[24] Filiation Os 11,1–4; Ex 4,22–23; élection Dt 7,6; 14,2; 1R 3,8; Is 14,1; 41,8–9; 42,1; 43,10; 44,1–2; 45,4; 49,6–7; Ps 33,12; 135,4.

[25] P. Bovati, "Je ne sais pas parler," 44–46.

[26] Cf. aussi Is 42,1.6.

[27] F.J. Gonçalves, "Yahvé, su pueblo y los demás pueblos en el Antiguo Testamento," *Radicalidad evangélica y fundamentalismos religiosos* (ed. G. Tejerina Arias; Bibliotheca Salmanticensis, Estudios 256; Salamanca: Publicaciones Universidad Pontificia, 2003), 150–53.

les prophètes.[28] Il est particulièrement fréquent en Jérémie, où il est un terme-clé. Le prophète s'y définit par l'envoi du Seigneur. Celui qui a été envoyé par le Seigneur est authentique;[29] celui que ne l'a pas été est faux.[30] On remarquera en passant que, au lieu de désigner l'action divine qui déclenche l'activité prophétique par l'expression «vocation prophétique», comme on le fait habituellement, il serait plus adéquat de l'appeler «envoi prophétique», sauf dans le cas de Samuel, en 1S 3, où le verbe קרא joue un rôle-clé.

Avec de menues variantes, la phrase «... et tout ce que je t'ordonnerai, tu le diras» (v. 7bβ) revient, également en rapport avec Jérémie, au v. 17a et en JrTM 26,2.8/JrLXX 33,2.8. Elle se lit aussi dans le *Deutéronome*, en rapport avec le prophète que le Seigneur va susciter en Israël (Dt 18,18bβ), et avec tout prophète (Dt 18,20aα).[31]

L'exhortation à ne pas craindre (ירא) devant eux (v. 8a) est à rapprocher de l'exhortation à ne pas être effrayés (חתת) devant eux (v. 17b).[32] L'objet de la crainte est cependant différent: les nations auxquelles Jérémie est envoyé (v. 8a); les Judéens (v. 17b). La motivation de l'ordre, en Jr 1,8b, est identique à celle de Jr 1,19b. La phrase revient encore en Jr 15,20b. En JrTM 46,27–28/JrLXX 26,27–28 et en JrTM 30,10–11 (propre au TM), le Seigneur adresse l'exhortation à ne pas craindre et à ne pas être effrayé à son Serviteur Jacob/Israël. Ces versets sont apparentés à plusieurs textes d'*Isaïe* 40–55, surtout 41,8–10.13–14; 43,1.5 et 44,1–2. De même que Jr 1,4–10 (vv. 5 et 8), Is 44,1–2 associe la conception et l'encouragement. La formule d'encouragement est originaire de l'oracle royal, une forme littéraire commune à l'ancien monde sémitique.[33] Dans l'Ancien Testament elle ne s'est jamais détachée entièrement de son origine.

---

[28] Élie 2R 2,2.4.6; Ml 3,23; Aggée 1,12; Zacharie 2,12.13.15; 4,9; 6,15; cf. aussi Dt 34,11; Is 61,1; 66,19; Mi 6,4; Za 1,10; 7,12; Ml 3,1.

[29] Jérémie 1,7; 19,14; 25,15.17; 26,12.15; 42,5.21; 43,2; 49,14; les «serviteurs du Seigneur les prophètes» Jr 7,25; 25,4; 26,5; 29,19 (TM); 35,15; 44,4; cf. 2R 17,13; 2Ch 36,15; prophète en général Jr 28,9.

[30] Jr 14,14.15; 23,21.32; 27,15; 28,15; 29,9.31; cf. aussi Ez 13,6 et Ne 6,12.

[31] En Ex 7,2, la phrase est employée en rapport avec Moïse et Aaron son prophète.

[32] Au v. 17b, les LXX mettent en parallélisme φοβέομαι et πτοέομαι, qui traduisent ירא (v. 8a) et חתת (v. 17b).

[33] M. Weippert, "Assyrische Prophetien der Zeit Asarhaddons und Assurbanipals," *Assyrian Royal Inscriptions: New Horizons in Literary, Ideological, and Historical Analysis* (ed. F. M. Fales; Orientis Antiqui Collectio 17; Rome: Istituto per l'Oriente, 1981), 71–115; M. Nissinen, "Fear Not: A Study on an Ancient Near Eastern Phrase," *The Changing Face of Form Criticism for the Twenty-First Century* (ed. M.A. Sweeney and E. Ben Zvi; Grand Rapids: Eerdmans, 2003), 122–61.

García López a attiré l'attention sur les affinités qui existent entre Jr 1,7ab–8a d'une part, et Dt 7,17–21 et 18,21–22 d'autre part.[34] Les ressemblances formelles entre ces textes sont indéniables. Ils ont aussi en commun le thème du rapport avec les nations. Cela dit, ni les nations ni la nature des rapports avec elles ne sont les mêmes dans les deux cas. Alors que le *Deutéronome* se réfère aux peuples de Canaan, Jr 1,5.10 doit se rapporter aux peuples qui figurent dans le recueil des oracles contre les nations, dont les peuples de Canaan ne font pas partie. La nature du rapport entre Israël ou Jérémie d'une part, et les nations d'autre part, est elle aussi différente. Dans le *Deutéronome*, le Seigneur ordonne à Israël d'exterminer les peuples du pays où Il va le faire entrer pour en prendre possession (Dt 7,1–6). Rien de tel en Jr 1,10. La tâche que le Seigneur y confie à Jérémie est certes ambivalente. Ses aspects négatifs prédominent, mais elle comprend aussi des aspects positifs. Jr 1,5.10 fait sans doute de Jérémie une personnification d'Israël. L'Israël en question n'est cependant pas celui du *Deutéronome*, mais celui de plusieurs passages d'*Isaïe* 40–55, figure royale chargée d'une mission auprès, et en définitive, en faveur des nations.[35]

Exprimé dans les mêmes termes, le geste de toucher la bouche (v. 9) figure également dans le récit de l'envoi d'Isaïe. L'un des séraphins purifie la bouche d'Isaïe en la touchant avec une braise (Is 6,7). En Jr 1,9, c'est le Seigneur lui-même qui touche, de sa main, la bouche de Jérémie pour y mettre ses paroles. Exprimée dans les mêmes termes, la mise des paroles du Seigneur dans la bouche d'un prophète se retrouve en Dt 18,18bα. Il s'agit alors du prophète comme Moïse que le Seigneur suscitera.

Attesté 29x dans la Bible, dont 10 en *Jérémie*, הפקד ne se retrouve pas ailleurs dans le contexte de l'envoi prophétique. Jr 1,10 est aussi le seul passage du livre, et l'un des quatre de la Bible, où il a le Seigneur pour sujet,[36] habituellement un roi, le plus souvent dans le contexte de la nomination de ses fonctionnaires.[37] En Jr 37,21, le seul autre passage où il a Jérémie pour complément d'objet direct, le verbe exprime l'action du roi Sédécias confinant Jérémie dans la cour de garde.[38] En *Jérémie*,

---

[34] F. García López, "Élection-vocation d'Israël et de Jérémie : Deutéronome VII et Jérémie I," *VT* 35 (1985): 1–12.

[35] Cf. supra n. 27.

[36] Lv 26,16 ; Is 62,6 et Ps 109,6.

[37] Gn 39,4.5 ; 41,34 ; 1S 29,4 ; 1R 11,28 ; 2R 7,17 ; 1Ch 26,32 ; Est 2,3.

[38] En Jr 36,20, il désigne l'action des hauts fonctionnaires judéens qui déposent le rouleau dans la salle du secrétaire Elishama.

il a surtout Nabuchodonosor pour sujet et Godolias pour complément d'objet direct: Nabuchodonosor institue/nomme Godolias dans le pays (Jr 40,5.7; 41,2.18) ou sur ceux qu'il a laissés en Juda (40,11; 2R 25,22).[39] Les textes ne précisent pas quels étaient le titre et le statut de Godolias. On s'accorde pour dire qu'il était gouverneur provincial, mais certains indices suggèrent qu'il pouvait être roi.[40] En bref, l'emploi de הפקד, en Jr 1,10, attire l'attention sur le caractère royal de Yahvé, et peut-être aussi, de Jérémie. Le roi des nations et des royaumes, fait de Jérémie son représentant auprès de ses sujets.

En Jr 1,10, le Seigneur ordonne à Jérémie non pas de transmettre un message aux nations, comme aux vv. 6–7 et 9, mais de réaliser des actions portant sur elles. De façon semblable, le récit de l'envoi d'Isaïe juxtapose deux ordres: transmettre au peuple un discours du Seigneur (Is 6,9); réaliser des actions qui ont le peuple pour objet (Is 6,10). JrTM 1,10 évoque la tâche de Jérémie au moyen de six verbes d'action: les quatre premiers expriment l'idée de destruction;[41] les deux derniers, celle de construction. Comportant entre six et trois membres, cette série de verbes apparaît 7x dans le livre de Jérémie, dont elle est caractéristique. Jr 1,10 est le seul passage où Jérémie est le sujet des verbes. Dans tous les autres, le sujet est le Seigneur. Jr 1,10 est aussi le seul passage où toutes les actions, destructrices et constructrices, sont reliées par la conjonction copulative, et se trouvent donc sur le même plan. En Jr 18,7–10, une série de cinq de ces verbes fait partie d'un texte qui montre comment le sort accordé par le Seigneur à chaque nation dépend de sa conversion. Tel est peut-être aussi le sens de Jr 12,14–17. Le plus souvent ces séries de verbes se rapportent à Israël, Juda ou Jérusalem pour annoncer leur destruction (Jr 45,4), mais, surtout, leur restauration de façon inconditionnelle (Jr 24,6; 31,28.38–40) ou conditionnelle (Jr 42,10).

---

[39] 2R 25,23. En Jr 41,10, le verbe exprime l'action d'un fonctionnaire babylonien qui confie tout le peuple et les filles du roi (de Juda) à Godolias.

[40] F. J. Gonçalves, "Exílio babilónico de 'Israel'. Realidade histórica e propaganda," *Cadmo* 10 (2000): 178.

[41] Les LXX n'ont que cinq verbes, dont trois expriment la destruction; cf. supra n. 21.

JÉRÉMIE LE PROPHÈTE

1. *Les quatre passages communs aux LXX et au TM*

Dans les LXX, la première attribution du titre de prophète à Jérémie se trouve dans l'introduction du récit de l'action symbolique qui conclut les oracles contre Babylone, en JrLXX 28,59 : « La parole que *le Seigneur* a ordonné à Jérémie, le prophète, *de dire* à Saraia fils de Neria... ». Ce verset a son correspondant en JrTM 51,59 : « L'ordre que Jérémie, le prophète, donna (צוה) à Seraya fils de Néryya... ». Contrairement à la tendance habituelle, le texte des LXX est plus long que le TM, le substantif κύριος et le verbe εἰπεῖν n'ayant pas d'équivalent dans l'hébreu. Alors que les LXX rapportent un ordre que le Seigneur donne à Jérémie pour que celui-ci le transmette à Saraia, le TM rapporte un ordre que Jérémie lui-même donne à Seraya. Le Seigneur est l'auteur de l'annonce de la ruine de Babylone dans les deux formes du livre (v. 62), mais l'initiative de la dramatiser, en jetant à l'Euphrate le livre qui la contient, revient au Seigneur dans les LXX, à Jérémie dans le TM. Celui-ci attribue donc à Jérémie une autorité plus grande que les LXX. Ces textes ne sont pas les seuls témoins d'une évaluation différente de l'autorité de Jérémie dans les LXX et le TM. L'image de Jérémie que donne JrTM 51,59 est, en réalité, celle qui encadre le TM. On la retrouve immédiatement après le récit de JrTM 51,59–64a, dans l'*explicit* du livre, qui est propre au TM : « Jusqu'ici les paroles de Jérémie » (v. 64b). Or, comme P.-M. Bogaert l'a fait remarquer, l'*explicit* correspond au titre : « Les paroles de Jérémie... » (JrTM 1,1).[42] De façon semblable, l'image de Jérémie qui ressort de JrLXX 28,59 est celle qui figure dans le titre de cette forme du livre : « La parole de Dieu qui advint à Jérémie... » (JrLXX 1,1). Étant plus modeste, l'image de Jérémie que donnent les LXX est probablement la plus ancienne, car on comprend mieux son agrandissement que sa réduction.

Deux autres attestations du titre prophétique de Jérémie communes se trouvent dans le récit de la fuite en Égypte (JrTM 42,2 ; 43,6/JrLXX 49,2 ; 50,6). Le récit donne deux images fort différentes de Jérémie le prophète. D'après l'une de ces images, celle qui occupe la plus grande place, Jérémie est la personne à laquelle les Judéens restés dans le pays

---

[42] P.-M. Bogaert, "De Baruch à Jérémie. Les deux rédactions conservées du livre de Jérémie," *Le Livre de Jérémie. Le prophète et son milieu. Les oracles et leur transmission* (ed. P.-M. Bogaert ; BETL 54 ; Leuven : University Press, 1981), 169–70.

recourent, en le suppliant d'intercéder en leur faveur auprès du Seigneur, son Dieu. La faveur qu'ils demandent au Seigneur consiste dans la réponse à la question de savoir ce qu'ils doivent faire. Jérémie jouit d'un rapport spécial avec Dieu. À ce titre, il joue un rôle d'intermédiaire. Il communique à Dieu la question du peuple, et au peuple la réponse de Dieu. Jérémie n'est cependant pas un simple messager. Il peut influencer la décision de Dieu, en l'amenant à donner les instructions que les Judéens lui demandent par son entremise.

Au début du récit, les chefs et tout le peuple partagent cette image de Jérémie. Mais à peine eut-il transmis le message du Seigneur que les chefs l'ont rejeté, et ils ont changé d'avis au sujet de Jérémie : « 43,2 Azarya, fils de Hoshaya, Yohanân, fils de Qaréah, et tous ces hommes insolents[43] dirent à Jérémie : "C'est un mensonge, ce que tu dis. Le Seigneur notre Dieu ne t'a pas envoyé (nous) dire : 'N'allez pas en Égypte pour y séjourner.'" 3 Mais c'est Baruch, fils de Nériyya, qui t'excite contre nous, afin de nous livrer aux mains des Chaldéens, pour qu'ils nous mettent à mort ou nous exilent à Babylone. » Les chefs retournent contre Jérémie l'accusation de mensonge qu'il porte lui-même contre ses adversaires, surtout contre ses concurrents directs, les prophètes et autres personnes qui prophétisent au nom de Dieu.[44] La différence la plus remarquable réside dans l'origine des mensonges. D'après Jérémie, les prophètes mettent dans la bouche du Seigneur leurs propres fantaisies ; d'après les chefs, Jérémie prête au Seigneur les plans de Baruch, faisant ainsi de Jérémie un imposteur manipulé par Baruch.

Le narrateur laisse bien entendre que le tableau brossé par les chefs est aux antipodes de la réalité. Jérémie ne ment pas. Le Seigneur lui a vraiment parlé (JrTM 42,7/JrLXX 49,7), et Il l'a envoyé au peuple (JrTM 43,2/JrLXX 50,2 ; cf. JrTM 42,5/JrLXX 49,5). Les menteurs sont, au contraire, les chefs qui accusent Jérémie de mensonge. JrTM 43,2 souligne le caractère négatif du jugement porté sur les chefs en les traitant de זדים, terme sans équivalent dans les LXX.[45] En qualifiant d'insolents les détracteurs de Jérémie, le TM les discrédite d'emblée, révélant la raison du refus qu'ils opposent à la fois au message du Seigneur et à Jérémie qui le leur transmet. L'autre image que le récit

---

[43] Le qualificatif הזדים (« insolents, arrogants ») est propre au TM.

[44] Jr 14,14 ; 20,6 ; 23,25.26.32 ; JrTM 28,15/Jr LXX 35,15 ; 29,21/Jr LXX 36,21.

[45] Il y a d'autres différences entre les LXX et le TM, celui-ci étant, comme d'habitude plus long ; J. Cook, "The difference in the order of the books of the Hebrew and Greek versions of Jeremiah—Jeremiah 43 (50) : a case study," *OTE* 7 (1994) : 175–92.

donne de Jérémie le prophète est celle d'un homme privé de liberté, à la merci des chefs, qui l'entraînent en Égypte (JrTM 43,5–6/JrLXX 50,5–6).

Selon l'ordre des LXX, la dernière attribution du titre prophétique à Jérémie se trouve dans l'en-tête de l'oracle que le Seigneur adresse à Baruch lui annonçant qu'il aura la vie sauve alors que les autres Judéens réfugiés en Égypte seront exterminés (JrLXX 51,31/JrTM 45,1).

2. Attributions du titre de prophète à Jérémie propres au TM

Des 27 attributions du titre de prophète à Jérémie propres au TM, 25 se trouvent sous la plume du narrateur : 21 dans des récits biographiques ; 5 dans l'introduction d'autant d'oracles contre les nations ; 1 dans l'introduction d'un oracle contre Juda. Les 2 autres sont mises dans la bouche du kushite Ebed-Melek et du roi Sédécias (Jr 38,9–10). La première se lit en Jr 20,2, dans un texte qui emploie 2x le verbe « prophétiser » ayant Jérémie pour sujet. Le titre se retrouve en 25,2, dans l'introduction d'un oracle qui annonce la ruine de Juda parce qu'il a refusé obstinément les appels à la conversion que Jérémie et, avant lui, « les serviteurs de Yahvé les prophètes », lui ont adressés (Jr 25,1–13a).

Jérémie reçoit le titre de prophète de façon exceptionnellement fréquente dans le récit de sa dispute avec Hananya. La comparaison entre les deux formes de ce texte est particulièrement intéressante pour notre propos. En JrLXX 35, seul Hananya reçoit un titre, ὁ ψευδοπροφήτης (le faux prophète), et une seule fois, dans sa présentation (v. 1). Hananya est en outre le sujet du verbe προφητεύειν, qui a son correspondant dans le TM (v. 6). JrTM 28, en revanche, dans une sorte de symétrie, accorde le titre נביא 6x à chacun des adversaires : la dispute est entre Hananya le prophète (vv. 1.5.10.12.15.17), et Jérémie le prophète (vv. 5.6.10.11.12.15).[46] Le plus simple est de penser que le traducteur a rendu un texte hébraïque qui ne donnait aucun titre à Jérémie.[47] En revanche, il donnait à Hananya le titre de נביא, rendu

---

[46] Le nom de Hananya n'est pas suivi de titre 3x (vv. 11.13.15) ; celui de Jérémie 1x (v. 12).

[47] L'étude de J. Reiling, "The Use of ψευδοπροφήτης in the Septuagint, Philo and Josephus," *NovT* 13 (1971): 147–56, est antérieure au changement qui est intervenu dans l'étude des rapports entre JrLXX et JrTM, en grande partie, à cause des manuscrits qumraniens de ce livre. Elle repose encore sur le présupposé selon lequel la *Vorlage* des LXX de Jérémie était identique au texte hébreu reçu (TM). Or cela paraît peu vraisemblable dans le cas précis de JrLXX 35/JrTM 28.

par ὁ ψευδοπροφήτης, et en exprimait l'action au moyen du verbe נבא.
La traduction de נבִיא par ψευδοπροφήτης, qui implique un jugement
de valeur, est caractéristique du livre de Jérémie, où elle revient à 8
autres reprises: au singulier (Jr 6,13) et, surtout, au pluriel (JrLXX
33,7.8.11.16; 34,7; 36,1.8).[48] En bref, les LXX témoignent d'une version de la dispute qui ne considérait pas Jérémie comme un prophète;
en revanche, Hananya l'était. Et pourtant, Hananya, le prophète
patenté, ne conteste pas à Jérémie, l'intrus, le droit de prophétiser; ce
qu'il récuse, c'est son message, et il lui en oppose un autre de signe
contraire. Alors que, au nom du Seigneur, Jérémie exige la soumission
au roi de Babylone et annonce que l'exil de ceux qui ont été déportés
à Babylone en 597 sera long (JrTM 29,4–7/JrLXX 36,4–7), Hananya
prophétise, également au nom du Seigneur, que celui-ci a brisé le joug
du roi de Babylone et que, dans deux ans, Il ramènera à Jérusalem les
ustensiles du temple et les exilés (JrTM 28,2–4/JrLXX 35,2–4).

Certes c'est Hananya qui prend l'initiative de la confrontation, mais
Jérémie en fixe les règles. Il fait de la teneur de la prophétie le critère
fondamental permettant de savoir si elle vient ou non de Dieu. Les
prophètes qui les ont précédés, lui-même et Hananya, dit Jérémie,
«depuis toujours, ont prophétisé pour beaucoup de nations et pour de
grands royaumes la guerre» (Jr 28,8).[49] Son annonce place Jérémie
dans la lignée de ces prophètes; il est donc l'un d'eux. Au contraire, la
prophétie de paix est une innovation qui doit être mise à l'épreuve. Le
prophète qui prophétise la paix, c'est quand s'accomplit sa parole que
l'on saura que Dieu l'a envoyé véritablement (v. 9). Ce texte restreint
au prophète de bonheur le critère de l'authenticité que Dt 18,21–22
applique au prophète en général, indépendamment de la teneur de sa
prophétie. Hananya ne réussit pas l'épreuve. Bien au contraire, il devient
le paradigme du faux prophète. Hananya est lui-même l'objet d'un
oracle de malheur. Le Seigneur s'adresse à lui. Il ne le fait cependant pas
directement—et pour cause, le Seigneur ne lui ayant jamais parlé!—,
mais par l'entremise de Jérémie. Le Seigneur contredit le message que
Hananya prétendait avoir reçu de Lui, lui déclare formellement qu'Il
ne l'a pas envoyé et, en conséquence, lui annonce qu'il mourra dans
l'année. Ce qui arriva le septième mois (vv. 12–17).

---

[48] Cf. aussi Za 13,2.
[49] Dans le TM, on lit après «la guerre», «le malheur et la peste».

Pour ce qui est du rapport entre JrTM 28 et JrLXX 35, l'hypothèse de l'antériorité du TM me paraît exclue. En effet, il faudrait admettre qu'un éditeur de la *Vorlage* des LXX ou son traducteur grec a supprimé toutes les mentions du titre prophétique de Jérémie, et il en a laissé une en rapport avec Hananya, alors qu'il le tient pour un faux prophète. En revanche, on comprend que l'éditeur du TM ait créé une symétrie formelle entre Jérémie et Hananya pour faire ressortir le contraste entre eux : l'un vrai prophète et l'autre faux.

Jr 29,1 donne le titre de prophète à Jérémie dans l'introduction de la lettre qu'il envoie à ceux qui ont été déportés en 597. Jr 29,29 et 32,2 font partie de récits qui attribuent à Jérémie l'action de prophétiser. Le contexte de Jr 29,29 est très proche de celui de Jr 20,2. Jr 34,6 rapporte que Jérémie le prophète a communiqué à Sédécias le message que le Seigneur l'avait chargé de lui transmettre : le Seigneur, lui-même, va livrer Jérusalem aux mains de Nabuchodonosor ; Sédécias ira en captivité à Babylone. Jr 36 accorde deux fois le titre de prophète à Jérémie (vv. 8.26), et celui de scribe à Baruch (vv. 26.32). Ni l'un ni l'autre de ces titres ne se trouvent en JrLXX 43. Le v. 8 rapporte l'exécution de l'ordre que Jérémie le prophète a donné à Baruch de lire le livre dans le temple. Le v. 26 rapporte l'ordre du roi Joiaqim d'arrêter Baruch le scribe et Jérémie le prophète. Cet ordre est resté sans effet car les intéressés étaient cachés. D'après JrLXX 43,26, ils s'étaient cachés eux-mêmes (καὶ κατεκρύβησαν), en conformité avec le conseil que les hauts fonctionnaires avaient donné à Baruch (v. 19). D'après JrTM 36,26, c'est Yahvé lui-même qui les a cachés (ויסתרם יהוה), insistant ainsi sur la protection que Yahvé accorde à Baruch et à Jérémie.

Dans l'introduction du règne de Sédécias (JrTM 37,2), le narrateur déclare que ni le roi ni le peuple n'ont écouté les paroles que le Seigneur leur a adressées par l'entremise de Jérémie le prophète. Et, pourtant, au verset suivant, il rapporte que Sédécias a demandé à Jérémie le prophète d'intercéder pour le peuple auprès de Yahvé (v. 3). Le narrateur accorde de nouveau le titre de prophète à Jérémie, au v. 6, dans l'introduction d'un oracle. Les Chaldéens, qui avaient levé le siège, reviendront, s'empareront de Jérusalem et y mettront le feu. Un peu plus loin (v.13), Jérémie le prophète est arrêté pour trahison. Au chapitre suivant, on le retrouve donc au fond d'une citerne, où on l'avait jeté, et où il risquait de mourir de faim. À la suite d'une démarche du kushite Ebed-Melek, le roi Sédécias ordonne de faire remonter Jérémie le prophète de la citerne (Jr 38,9–10). D'après Jr 38,14–15, Sédécias fait venir Jérémie le prophète et lui dit : « "J'ai une chose à te demander, ne me cache rien !" Jérémie répondit à Sédécias : "Si je te la dis, ne

me feras-tu pas mourir? Et si je te conseille, tu ne m'écouteras pas."»
Jérémie met alors Sédécias devant le choix suivant: s'il se rend aux
officiers du roi de Babylone, il aura la vie sauve, ainsi que sa famille, et
Jérusalem ne sera pas incendiée: au contraire, s'il résiste, la ville sera
incendiée (vv. 17–18). Je signale finalement Jr 42,4a, qui introduit la
réponse de Jérémie à la demande d'intercession des chefs du peuple.
Alors que JrTM 42,2 et JrLXX 49,2 accordent à Jérémie le titre de
prophète dans l'introduction de la demande, seul JrTM 42,4a reprend
ce titre dans l'introduction de la réponse.

Jérémie reçoit le titre de prophète dans l'introduction de cinq oracles
contre les nations: en général (Jr 46,1), l'Égypte (Jr 46,13), les Philistins (Jr 47,1), l'Élam (Jr 49,34) et Babylone (Jr 50,1). P.-M. Bogaert
a montré que JrTM 25,13b; 46,1 et 49,34 «...sont la diffraction d'un
seul et même titre en *ʾašèr* qui introduisait la section des oracles contre
les nations et que nous lisons de fait en LXX 25, 14, en tête des oracles
contre les nations...».[50] La diffraction relève du processus de déplacement des oracles contre les nations à la fin du livre et de leur réorganisation. Ce fut alors que Jérémie a reçu le titre de prophète en Jr 46,1 et
49,34. Dans l'en-tête de l'oracle contre les Philistins (Jr 47,1), le nom et
le titre de Jérémie sont également le fruit d'une réélaboration du texte
plus court qui se lit en JrLXX 29,1 (ἐπὶ τοὺς ἀλλοφύλους).[51] Le titre de
Jérémie ne fut pas non plus le seul apport à l'intitulé du second oracle
contre l'Égypte (Jr 46,13). De même, dans l'oracle contre Babylone
(Jr 50,1), le nom et le titre de Jérémie font partie d'un développement
plus vaste du texte court représenté par JrLXX 27,1.[52]

CONCLUSIONS

La teneur de la polémique contre les נביאים de son temps, que les deux
formes du livre mettent dans la bouche de Jérémie, exclut l'idée qu'il

---

[50] Bogaert, "Le livre de Jérémie en perspective," 379.

[51] P.-M. Bogaert, "Relecture et déplacement de l'oracle contre les Philistins. Pour
une datation de la rédaction longue (TM) du livre de Jérémie," *La vie de la Parole. De
l'Ancien au Nouveau Testament. Études d'exégèse et d'herméneutique bibliques offertes à Pierre Grelot*
(Paris: Desclée, 1987), 139–50.

[52] Janzen, *Studies in the Text of Jeremiah*, 60, 112–14; W.L. Holladay, *Jeremiah 2*
(Hermeneia; Minneapolis: Fortress Press, 1989), 391; H.-J. Stipp, *Das masoretische und
alexandrinische Sondergut des Jeremiabuches. Textgeschichtlicher Rang, Eigenarten, Triebkräfte* (OBO
136; Göttingen: Vandenhoeck & Ruprecht, 1994), 75.

ait été l'un d'eux. Et pourtant la tradition en a fait un prophète.[53] Au terme de l'examen des emplois des groupes lexicaux נבא/προφήτης en rapport direct avec Jérémie, essayons d'esquisser le processus de sa «nebiisation».

1. La première étape a consisté sans doute dans l'attribution à Jérémie de l'action de prophétiser. Jérémie est sujet du verbe «prophétiser» 10x, dans sept passages situés dans les chapitres 11–32 du TM et 11–39 des LXX. Parmi les dix emplois, huit ont pour cadre cinq récits biographiques ou autobiographiques qui rapportent plusieurs épisodes d'une campagne menée contre Jérémie à cause de son activité prophétique. À cinq reprises prophétiser y fait l'objet d'une accusation que portent contre lui ses ennemis, surtout d'autres personnes qui prophétisent, et aussi les gens d'Anatot, les prophètes, les prêtres, le roi. En JrTM 26,12/JrLXX 33,12, le verbe est dans la bouche de Jérémie lui-même, mais celui-ci reprend, dans sa défense, le terme qu'employaient ses accusateurs (vv. 9 et 11). Dans le récit de Jr 19,1–20,6, le verbe se trouve sous la plume du narrateur. Celui-ci rapporte d'abord que le Seigneur a envoyé Jérémie prophétiser (Jr 19,14), et ensuite que, l'ayant entendu prophétiser le malheur de Jérusalem, Pashehur a pris des mesures contre lui (Jr 20,1–2). Dans les deux emplois restants, le verbe fait partie de l'introduction d'un oracle (JrLXX 25,14/JrTM 25,13b), et exprime un ordre divin dans un autre (JrLXX 32,16/JrTM 25,30).

Jérémie prophétise la ruine de Jérusalem, du Temple et de Juda, ainsi que l'exil et sa longue durée. Rejetant absolument cette annonce, les ennemis de Jérémie cherchent à le réduire au silence par tous les moyens, ne reculant pas devant l'idée de le faire mourir. Ce que Jérémie prophétisait ne tarda pas à arriver lors de la conquête babylonienne. Selon le critère de l'accomplissement (Dt 18,21–22), on devait conclure que le Seigneur était véritablement l'auteur des annonces de malheur faites par Jérémie, et que celui-ci était son porte-parole authentique. Les annonces de signe contraire ayant été vite démenties par les faits, on devait conclure que leurs auteurs parlaient faussement au nom du Seigneur, qui ne les avait pas envoyés. Les événements ont donc donné raison à Jérémie sur toute la ligne.

---

[53] Jérémie ne fut pas le seul qui a eu ce sort. Cf. F.J. Gonçalves, "Les 'Prophètes Écrivains' étaient-ils des נביאים?," *The World of the Aramaeans I: Biblical Studies in Honour of Paul-Eugène Dion* (ed. P.M.M. Daviau et al.; JSOTSS 324; Sheffield: Sheffield Academic Press, 2001), 144–85.

Prophétiser en vérité devint ainsi synonyme d'annoncer le malheur. Contrairement à ce que croyaient les ennemis de Jérémie, l'annonce de malheur n'était donc pas un crime passible de la peine de mort, mais plutôt la marque de la véritable prophétie. En fait, tous les emplois du verbe «prophétiser» ayant Jérémie pour sujet se réfèrent à des annonces de malheur. Jérémie se conforme ainsi entièrement au modèle prophétique auquel il propose de se mesurer, lui et Hananya (JrTM 28,8/JrLXX 35,8). En réalité, ce texte pose comme étalon prophétique le portrait de Jérémie que brossent les passages que nous avons examinés.

On remarquera le rôle joué par JrTM 26,1–16/JrLXX 33,1–16 dans la création du personnage prophétique de Jérémie. Les princes y reconnaissent qu'il parle au nom du Seigneur (v. 16). Le rôle attribué aux princes révèle sans doute l'origine du récit. Par ailleurs, grâce aux vv. 3–5.13, le récit assimile Jérémie aux «serviteurs du Seigneur les prophètes». Et pourtant ni ce récit ni les autres qui attribuent à Jérémie l'action de prophétiser, du moins dans les LXX, ne l'appellent prophète ou lui donnent ce titre. Am 7,10–17 témoigne de la même dissociation entre l'action de prophétiser et l'appellation prophétique. En effet, Amos nie être prophète ou «fils de prophète» (v. 14) mais, en même temps, il déclare que le Seigneur lui a ordonné d'aller prophétiser (נבא) à Israël (v. 15). Auld a sans doute raison lorsqu'il suggère qu'il a été plus aisé d'attribuer aux éponymes des livres prophétiques l'action de prophétiser—à défaut d'un terme propre—que de les reconnaître comme prophètes et de leur donner ce titre.[54]

2. Des quatre attributions du titre de prophète à Jérémie communes aux LXX et au TM, trois se trouvent dans la même section, dans des passages presque contigus : le récit de la fuite en Égypte (JrTM 42–43/ JrLXX 49–50) et l'oracle de Baruch (JrTM 45/JrLXX 51,31–35). Ces textes ont en commun le personnage de Baruch : le premier le met en scène de deux façons différentes, le second s'adresse à lui. La quatrième attestation a pour cadre l'introduction de JrTM 51,59–64a/JrLXX 28,59–64a, un récit qui prête à Seraya un rôle comparable à celui que son frère Baruch joue en JrTM 36/JrLXX 43. Cela suggère que Jérémie doit son titre de prophète à un cercle auquel la famille de Baruch et de Seraya appartenait.

---

[54] A.G. Auld, "Prophets through the Looking Glass: Between Writings and Moses," *JSOT* 27 (1983) : 5–7.

Pourquoi a-t-on donné à Jérémie le titre de prophète, précisément, dans le contexte de ces récits ? Serait-ce à cause de son livre dont JrTM 32–45/JrLXX 39,1–51,35 rapporte l'écriture et la préservation ?[55] Il est aussi question d'un livre de Jérémie dans le contexte de l'autre attribution du titre de prophète à Jérémie commune aux LXX et au TM. Serait-ce parce que JrTM 42–43/JrLXX 49–50 prête à Jérémie un rôle et un sort identiques à ceux des « serviteurs du Seigneur les prophètes » ?

Le titre prophétique de Jérémie est pratiquement 8x plus fréquent dans le TM que dans les LXX. Il apparaît pour la première fois en JrTM 20,2, dans un passage où Jérémie prophétise dans les deux formes du livre. Même le TM, le plus souvent, laisse Jérémie sans titre. La fréquence plus grande du titre prophétique de Jérémie dans le TM n'est pas un fait isolé. En effet, le TM nomme les personnages et donne à chacun son titre beaucoup plus souvent que les LXX.[56] Le Seigneur lui-même reçoit l'épithète צבאות 82x, et son équivalente (παντοκράτωρ) seulement 14. L'hypothèse de la multiplication du titre prophétique dans le TM est, a priori, plus probable que celle de sa soustraction dans les LXX. Pourquoi un éditeur ou le traducteur grec aurait-il gommé le titre de Jérémie ? Sa multiplication fait sans doute partie du processus d'agrandissement de l'image de Jérémie dont témoignent plusieurs passages du TM.[57] Dans le cas de JrTM 28, où l'on trouve la plus grande concentration du titre prophétique de Jérémie, l'hypothèse de l'antériorité du TM serait peu vraisemblable.

De même, les cinq attestations du titre prophétique de Jérémie que l'on trouve dans autant d'oracles contre les nations (JrTM 46–51) font partie d'une réécriture de l'en-tête des oracles respectifs. Dans deux cas au moins, la réécriture a été une conséquence du déplacement des oracles contre les nations du milieu (LXX) à la fin du livre, ainsi que de leur réorganisation (TM).

3. Sans différences appréciables entre les deux éditions du livre, le récit de l'institution de Jérémie comme prophète—une composition anthologique—en fait finalement le prophète des nations, et du même coup une personnification d'Israël ayant des traits royaux.

---

[55] F.J. Gonçalves, "Baruc e Jeremias nas duas edições mais antigas do livro de Jeremias conhecidas," *Didaskalia* 35 (2005): 85–115.

[56] Janzen, *Studies in the Text of Jeremiah*, 139–55. Par exemple, Baruch reçoit 2x le titre de scribe dans le TM (36,26.32), et aucune dans les LXX.

[57] JrTM 1,1; 36,26; 51,59.64b (propre au TM) comparés à JrLXX 1,1; 43,26 et 28,59, pour ne rappeler que les textes examinés.

JOSHUA AND COPERNICUS: JOSH 10:12–15
AND THE HISTORY OF RECEPTION[1]

Ed Noort

The city of Groningen lies in a magnificent Northern landscape. The low horizon and gigantic sky, the threatening clouds and wind are the backdrop for the grey, brown and blue of the day and the flaming red between light and darkness. This is a primeval land filled with wind, water and clouds situated on the edge of the sea. That is the stuff of which stories are made. Even before the brothers Grimm started collecting their tales, the wondrous world of evil spirits and princesses, devils and giants was recounted and recorded in Groningen.[2] In one of these tales, a boy who wanted to carry off a princess and her treasure flees. He is pursued by villains. When all is nearly lost, we hear him say, "Then I said to my day and night carrier: 'Hurl the night behind us and the day before us!' He did that, and we were able to escape unseen. Behind us it was night and before us it was day." The fleeing thief will probably have been unaware that he had an illustrious precursor who also commanded the sun and moon, day and night to stand still. Joshua's commanding shout "Sun stand still at Gibeon and Moon in the valley of Aijalon!" (Josh 10:12b) during the campaign against the Amorite kings and framed by the conquest narratives in the Hebrew Bible has caused a good deal more controversy than the little rascal from Groningen.

The biblical narrative begins pleasantly. A treaty is agreed between Israel and Gibeon. Subsequently the partner Gibeon comes under military threat. The city risks being taken by a coalition of hostile forces, but after receiving a call for help, Joshua marches through the night to rescue it. The enemy is overwhelmed, panics and flees. Joshua 10:1–10

---

[1] Revised and enlarged version of the opening address to the SBL International Meeting at the University of Groningen (25–7–2004) and presented as a guest lecture at the Catholic University of Leuven (12–5–2005) at the invitation of Florentino García Martínez.

[2] E. J. Huizenga-Onnekes, *Het boek van Trijntje Soldaats* (Groningen: Noordhoff, 1928), re-edited by C. Dieters and C. Rombouts (Bedum: Profiel, 2003). The stories in *Trijntje Soldaats* were told to an eleven-year-old boy who recorded them in 1804.

tells the story of a rescue in a case of dire need. The story presupposes a mutual assistance treaty between Gibeon and Israel.[3] But there is no evidence that the deuteronomistic rejection of such a treaty, as reflected in Josh 9 and in the final version of Deut 20,[4] plays a role here.

From a narrative perspective, Joshua's campaign has just begun. The rescue of Joshua's allies is only the immediate cause of the story. What is highlighted is the confrontation with the enemy with the aim of destruction. The use of the technical term חרם starts only in v. 28, the intended totality of the חרם, however, is already present. It is not a matter of conquering land but of destroying the enemy completely. Their flight is prevented by the God of Israel who throws huge stones, אבנים גדלות, from heaven to kill the fleeing enemy. And in the final version, even this participation of the Divine Warrior is not the climax of the narrative. That is reached when Joshua calls down the aid of the cosmic powers. Sun and moon as time markers must stand still to allow him more time to execute the last of the enemy. Sun and moon obey and the commenting narrator remarks that never before had a human voice been heard as Joshua's voice was heard that day (10:14)!

And what about the אבנים גדלות flung from heaven with divine force? On the one hand, they are literally naturalized, an explanatory remark turns them into hailstones (10:11).[5] On the other, they are recycled in the narrative. The cave to which the five kings flee is sealed with huge stones (v. 18). The אבנים גדלות play an important role. They connect the narrative of the battling divine warrior with the escape of the kings and their execution. The stones kill the soldiers, the kings think they are

---

[3] E. Noort, "Zwischen Mythos und Realität: Das Kriegshandeln YHWHs in Jos 10,1–11," in H.H. Schmid, ed., *Zwischen Mythos und Rationalität* (Gütersloh: Gütersloher Verlag, 1988), 149–61.

[4] The action of the Gibeonites is based on the distinction made between towns far away and nearby, the basic assumption of the final version of Deut 20, especially vv. 15–18. Cf. C. Schäfer-Lichtenberger, "Das gibeonitische Bündnis im Licht deuteronomischer Kriegsgebote. Zum Verhältnis von Tradition und Interpretation in Jos 9," *BN* 34 (1986): 58–81; E. Noort, "Das Kapitulationsangebot im Kriegsgesetz Dtn 20:10ff. und in den Kriegserzählungen," in *Studies in Deuteronomy: In Honour of C.J. Labuschagne on the Occasion of His 65th Birthday* (ed. F. García Martínez et al.; VTSup 53; Leiden: Brill, 1994), 197–222.

[5] Verse 11 connects אבנים גדלות with שלך Hiphil and the divine subject. The construction is unique. אבן ברד or אבני הברד appear in Isa 30:30; Josh 10:11; Sir 43:15. The sending of ברד is expressed by זרם, נתן, מטר. The return of the אבנים גדלות in Josh 10:18, 27 favours the explanation that real boulders are meant. Cf. Sam Chronicles II HS 2 28b 10–13. Instead of the אבנים גדלות G reads already in the first part of v. 11 κύριος ἐπέρριψεν αὐτοῖς λίθους χαλάζης.

safe in a cave, but this safe place will be their grave with the help of
these selfsame stones. Finally, the stones are given a leading etiological
role. The stones marking the grave of the executed kings (v. 27) serve
as a visual bridge between then and now, between narrator and reader.
It is a story with rapidly changing roles: First there is Gibeon against
an Amorite coalition (v. 5). Then comes the real enemy: Joshua and
all Israel (v. 7) against *all* Amorite kings. And finally, YHWH appears
in the arena (v. 10). He decides the battle and kills the enemies with
boulders from heaven (v. 11). And with divine approval (v. 14), Joshua
even commands the cosmic powers: the sun and moon are on his side
(v. 13). The comment of v. 14 makes the event unique. This climax of
the narrative, however, is not without problems. M^6 reads:

12aa	Then Joshua spoke to YHWH
12ab	on the day YHWH[a] gave the Amorites
12ac	into the power of the sons[b] of Israel[f-f]
12ba	and he said[c] [d]before the eyes of [e]Israel[d]:
12bb	—O Sun, stand still[g] at Gibeon!
12bc	and Moon, at the valley of Aijalon!
13aa	And the sun stood still[e] and the moon stayed
13ab	until a nation[d] took vengeance[f] on its[a] enemies—.
13ac	[b]Is it not written in[e] the Book of Yashar[b]?
13ba	And the sun stayed in the midst of heaven
13bb	and did not hasten to go down for a whole day.
14aa	There has been no day like it before or since
14ab	when YHWH[a] obeyed a human voice[b],
14b	for YHWH fought[e] for Israel.
15aa	[a]Then Joshua returned, and all Israel with him,
15ab	to the camp at Gilgal[a]

12 **a** *G* ὁ θεός; **b** >*GS*; **c** *G* εἶπεν Ἰησοῦς; **d-d** >*G* לעיני ישראל; **e** *S*+ בני; **f-f** >*M*
"when he smashed them in Gabaōn and they were smashed the sons of Israel":
ἡνίκα συνέτριψεν αὐτοὺς ἐν Γαβαων καὶ συνετρίβησαν ἀπὸ προσώπου υἱῶν
Ισραηλ; **g** *M* דמם "to be still" both in opposition to speech (Lev 10:3 [Aaron]; Ezek
24:17 [Ezekiel]; Amos 5:13 [the prudent] as well as α' and σ') and motion (1 Sam
14:9 [Jonathan]; Isa 30:18 conjec uncertain, cf. H. Wildberger, *Jesaja* [BKAT

---

[6] Sigla according to *BHQ.*

X/3; Neukirchen-Vluyn: Neukirchener Verlag, 1982], 1190, 1193; Jer 47:6
[sword]). There is no real proof for a priority of the negation of speech or
noise over the negation of motion. In *M*, however, more references are related
to the first possibility, cf. Exod 15:16; Jer 48:2; Ps 62:6. *G* reads στήτω for דום
and chooses the second possibility, the stopping of a motion, as does a broad
majority of the modern Bible translations (NBG, NBV, RSV, NRS, JPS, TNK,
LUT). The interpretation is sustained by the use of עמד in v. 13aα and in the
report of the narrator v. 13bα. The same is the case for *G* in v. 13 "sun and
moon stayed in stationariness."[7]

13 **a** *GT* τοὺς ἐχθροὺς <u>αὐτῶν</u>; **b-b** >*G* הלא־היא כתובה על־ספר הישר—
MG ספר הישר 2 Sam 1:18; *G* 1 Kgs 8:53 >*M*: "written in the book of the
Song"; **c** *SV* בספר instead of על־ספר; **d** *G* ὁ θεὸς instead of גוי; **e** see 12 **g**; **f** *G*
"till (the) God repelled (ἠμύνατο) their enemies." Normally נקם is rendered by
ἐκδικεῖν (e.g. Lev 26:25; Num 31:2), and twice by ἐκδικάζειν (Lev 19:18; Deut
32:43). The remarkable verb sustains the reading of ὁ θεὸς (not a corruption
of ἔθνος) and underlines the active role of the deity during the battle.

14 **a** θεὸν instead of YHWH;[8] **b** >*G* קול; **c** *G* "fought with"
συνεπολέμησεν.

15 **a-a** >*G* as in 10:43.

Qumran is not much help here. The differences in between 4Q47
(4QJosh[a]), *M* and *G* concerning Josh 10:4, 9, 11 are not so significant
that 4Q47 clearly aligns with *M* or *G* or presents a recognizable own
textual tradition. With the edition of the Schøyen papyri, however, a
new player appeared on the stage, supporting the view that *G** indeed
does not refer to a return to Gilgal in 10:15, 43.[9]

---

[7] A.G. Auld, *Joshua: Jesus Son of Nauē in Codex Vaticanus* (SCS; Leiden: Brill, 2005),
33.

[8] A.G. Auld, "Judges 1 and History: a Reconsideration," *VT* 25 (1975): 261–85;
idem, "Joshua: The Hebrew and the Greek Texts" (VTSup 30; Leiden: Brill, 1979),
1–14 (13).

[9] For the textual evidence: K. De Troyer, "LXX, Joshua IX 33–XI 3 (MS 2648),"
in *Papyri Graecae Schøyen (PSchøyen I)* (ed. R. Pintaudi; Papyrologica Florentina 35; Flor-
ence: Gonnelli, 2005), 81–145; eadem, "Did Joshua Have a Crystal Ball? The Old
Greek and the MT of Joshua 10:15, 17 and 23," in *Emanuel: Studies in Hebrew Bible,
Septuagint and Dead Sea Scrolls in Honor of Emanuel Tov* (ed. S.M. Paul et al.; VTSup 94;
Leiden: Brill, 2003), 571–89; eadem, "Reconstructing the OG of Joshua," in *Septuagint
Research: Issues and Challenges in the Study of the Greek Jewish Scriptures* (ed. W. Kraus and
R.G. Wooden; SBLSCS 53; Atlanta: SBL, 2006), 105–18.

Without that return the narratives of 10:1–11 and 16–27 are directly connected, as already suggested above by the references to the אבנים נדלות in *M*. Due to the influence of Martin Noth, who focused on the etiological character of vv. 16–27,[10] the two narratives were separated in nearly all commentaries. The natural boundary between the two narratives was the return to Gilgal in v. 15. Both the content of *M* and of *G** demonstrate that such a separation is not necessary. The two versions, however, each tell their own story. In v. 11, *G* refers to λίθους χαλάζης, "hailstones," whereas M reads אבנים נדלות. Possibly *M* introduced the אבנים נדלות of v. 11a as a link to the stones of the vv. 18, 27. Assuming that *G* reflects an older pre-*M Vorlage* in this passage, the mentioning of the hailstones does not mean that the focus on the divine action is lessened. By not knowing a return to Gilgal in v. 43, *G* ends his narrative with "YHWH, the God of Israel, fought on the side of Israel" (10:42). In v. 12: "When he smashed them in Gibeon and they were smashed in face of the sons of Israel," the subject of συνέτριψεν must be "the god" as explicitly stated in v. 13: "till the god repelled their enemies." *G* doubles the reference—the action of the deity and the results concerning the enemies—before Joshua's unique command is quoted. With the same verb as in v. 42, the active role of the divine warrior in v. 14 is stressed (συνεπολέμησεν). The camp of Israel at Makkedah (v. 21) has a natural place in the narrative without a previous return to Gilgal. Without the reference to the Book of Yashar in *G*, Joshua's command to the sun and the report of the fulfilment are smoothly interwoven.

The active role of YHWH is stressed in *M* too. With his boulders from heaven YHWH kills the enemies. The return to Gilgal is not in line with the story itself (v. 21), but instead reflects the role of Gilgal in the whole book of Joshua with its concentration on the camp at Gilgal (Josh 4:19, 20; 5:9, 10; 9:6; 10:6, 7, 9; 12:23; 14:6; 15:7?). *M* did notice that Joshua's command does not fit into the context. The valley of Aijalon is nowhere mentioned in the narrative. Though 13aa explicitly mentions that "the moon stayed," everything in 13ac–13bb is focused on the sun. The moon has literally disappeared. Moreover, 12aa states that Joshua speaks to YHWH, but he addresses the sun and moon. The overall picture of the narrative is the active, battling deity. In these lines, however, Joshua himself is at centre stage. He

---

[10] M. Noth, *Das Buch Josua* (HAT I/7; Tübingen: Mohr/Siebeck, 1953), 61.

commands, sun and moon obey. The framing statements of v. 12aa and v. 14a ensure the theological correctness, but the spotlight is on Joshua. Therefore the reference to the obscure "Book of Yashar" and the suggestion of a quote make sense.

Both versions stress in their various stages the centrality of the poetic lines of 12bb–13ab.[11] The sun and the moon as cosmic powers take part in the battle in the same way as in the song of Deborah in Judg 5:21. Verse 13b, however, explains the participation of sun and moon as a real standstill. It is this explanation, not the supposed original meaning of the poetic fragment,[12] that I want to focus on. For this combination, the applauded Joshua (v. 14) and the standing still of the sun (v. 13b) are the starting points for a highly remarkable history of reception.

I have discussed the problem of the legitimacy of religion-inspired violence elsewhere, so now I will concentrate on the second item in the history of the reception of Josh 10: the collision between heliocentric and geocentric cosmological worldviews.

As a narrative, Josh 10 is nothing special. Throughout history all embattled parties have begged for, told about and sung hymns recounting victories through divine help. In the Odyssey Athena lets the sun rise for Ulysses.[13] And to save the threatened Greeks, it sets prematurely in the Iliad.[14] How did people regard Joshua and his sun miracle? Within

---

[11] In most commentaries (Noth, *Josua*, 56; M.A. Beek, *Jozua* [POT; Nijkerk: Callenbach, 1981], 117; T.C. Butler, *Joshua* [WBC 7; Waco: Word Books, 1983], 107; V. Fritz, *Das Buch Josua* [HAT I/7; Tübingen: Mohr (Paul Siebeck), 1994] 108; R.D. Nelson, *Joshua* [OTL; Louisville: Westminster John Knox Press, 1997], 135; J.L. Sicre, *Josué* [Nueva Biblia Española; Estella: Editorial Verbo Divino, 2002], 265–69) the poetic lines start with the command to the sun and end with the remark on the quote (v. 14), leaving vv. 12bb–13ab for the poem itself. An exception is Boling, who starts the poem in v. 12ba "he said in the sight of Israel" on syntactical grounds (R.G. Boling, *Joshua* [AB; New York: Doubleday, 1982], 282–84). More important is the careful analysis of the later cardinal Bernardus Alfrink. He defends an original poem starting with v. 12aa and ending with v. 13bb. The vv. 12–13 are a poetic version of the prose text of vv. 8–11 with one difference. Verses 8–11 leave the initiative to YHWH, vv. 12–15 to Joshua. Originally, vv. 12–15 were placed behind v. 42. An editorial hand moved them to their present place. Alfrink understood the "standing still" of sun and moon as an atmospheric darkness (Hab 3:11) and related it to meteorological phenomena (Exod 14:24; Ps 77:17–19; 1 Sam 7:10; thunderstorm; Judg 4:15 rain) of vv. 10–11 (B. Alfrink, "Het 'stil staan' van zon en maan in Jos 10,12–15," *Studia Catholica* 24 [1949]: 238–68; idem, *Josue* [BOT; Roermond: Romen, 1952], 61–68).

[12] Overviews may be found in Alfrink, "Het 'stil staan,'"; Nelson, *Joshua*, 142–45; Sicre, *Josué*, 266–69.

[13] Homer, *Od.* 23.241ff.

[14] Homer, *Il.* 18.239ff.

the Hebrew Bible, the "Fortschreibung" already changes the name of Joshua's burial place of תמנת־סרח (Josh 24:30) to תמנת־חרס (Judg 2:9). חרס with the meaning "sun" refers to his most famous deed.[15] In the topographical search for traditions about Joshua's grave, we find nine burial places from the land of Samaria to Syria and Libanon.[16] But one of the most impressive ones, the necropolis southwest of *Kafr Ḥāris* on the West Bank, is in its Hellenistic form decorated with a sun.[17] In the Hellenistic book of Sirach, Joshua is remembered as the man who stopped the sun and lengthened the day till the enemies were defeated and executed: οὐχὶ ἐν χειρὶ αὐτοῦ ἐνεποδίσθη ὁ ἥλιος καὶ μία ἡμέρα ἐγενήθη πρὸς δύο (Sir 46:4).

And the great exegete Origen (ca. 185–ca. 253) states in his sermon on Josh 10 that Moses, in contrast to Joshua, never commanded the sun to stand still. Here Joshua is greater than Moses[18] and that is saying something in a tradition in which Joshua is nearly always in the shadow of the "Übervater" Moses. And the famous mosaic map of Madaba connects the name of Joshua with the miracle of the sun and moon: "Ailamon where stood the moon in the time of Joshua, son of Nun, one day."[19] This is remarkable because space on the map in this area is very limited. If it had been the conquest of Jericho that had to be remembered, then the mosaicist would have used the available space for that. However, he focused on the sun and moon miracle, rather than on the conquest of Jericho.

So for large portions of the reception history, including iconography, Joshua is the man of the sun miracle. Stopping the sun is highlighted as the exceptional nature of Joshua's action, it demonstrates in the eyes of later generations his confidence in YHWH, and stresses the

---

[15] E. Noort, "Josua 24,28–31, Richter 2,6–9 und das Josuagrab. Gedanken zu einem Straßenschild," in *Biblische Welten: Festschrift für Martin Metzger zu seinem 65. Geburtstag* (ed. W. Zwickel; OBO 123; Freiburg: Universitätsverlag, 1993), 109–30.

[16] I. Goldziher, "Muhammedanische Traditionen über den Grabesort des Josua," *ZDPV* 2 (1879): 13–17.

[17] C.R. Conder and H.H. Kitchener, *The Survey of Western Palestine, Vol II Samaria* (London 1882, reprint Jerusalem: Kedem, 1970), 374–78.

[18] Origène, *Homélies sur Josué* (ed. A. Jaubert; SC 71: Paris: Le Cerf, 1960), 106ff: Moyses non dixit: Stet sol nec maximis imperavit elementis, sicut Iesus fecit. Stet, inquit, sol super Gabaon et luna super vallem Aelom et praeterea addit Scriptura et dicit quia: Numquam sic audivit Deus hominem (I 5).

[19] ΑΙΛΑΜΩΝ on the map. ΑΙΛΩΜ/ΑΙΑΛΟΝ: Eusebius, *Das Onomastikon der biblischen Ortsnamen* (ed. E. Klostermann; Leipzig: J.C. Hinrichs, 1904) 18,14 "at a distance of three milestones east of Baithel."

positive reaction of YHWH. For just one moment, he is allowed to be greater than Moses.

Cosmological debates, so crucial for later times, are not raised in any way in the reception history of the first centuries. From Late Antiquity on, however, cosmological problems played a role in the theological and philosophical discussions. Hooykaas demonstrated that a reconciliation between worldview and the biblical texts was practised in three ways.[20] First, literalistic concepts of biblical exegesis were combined in an artificial way with the spherical shape of the earth. Second, exegesis dealt with an allegorical model in which "Scripture had a second hidden meaning which referred to concrete cosmological truths."[21] And last but not least, the dogmatic concept of accommodation helped to explain the rift between the text and the newly observed reality. The Holy Spirit accommodated itself to the common people of those times. In the 16th century, when the conflict about cosmology really broke out, when the "founding myth of conflict between science and religion"[22] was shaped, new solutions were needed. We will see, however, that the old solutions had a very long life. In the conflict concerning the heliocentric system, Josh 10 served as the keystone[23] to the whole intellectual battle between Copernican and Ptolemaic, between heliocentric and geocentric worldviews.

The publication of Nicholas Copernicus's main work, *De Revolutionibus*, reveals the quarter in which the problems arose. Sometime between 1508 and 1514, Copernicus (1473–1543) had already explained his system in his handwritten *Commentariolus*, which was never printed.[24] The *editio princeps* of the *De Revolutionibus*[25] appeared in 1543, but the title was

---

[20] R. Hooykaas, *G.J. Rheticus' Treatise on Holy Scripture and the Motion of the Earth* (Verhandelingen der Koninklijke Nederlandse Akademie der Wetenschappen, Afd. Letterkunde NR 124; Amsterdam: KNAW, 1984), 28–35.

[21] Hooykaas, *Rheticus*, 31.

[22] W.B. Drees, *Religion, Science and Naturalism* (Cambridge: Cambridge University Press, 1996), 55.

[23] Other texts used in the debate: 2 Kgs 20:11; Ps 19:6–7; 104:5; Qoh 1:4–5; Matt 5:45. The focus, however, was on Josh 10:12–14.

[24] Excerpts are found in Georg Joachim Rheticus, *Narratio prima* (Danzig, 1540 [published anonymously]), reprinted as an appendix in the second edition of *De Revolutionibus*, Basel 1566.

[25] Nicholas Copernicus, *De Revolutionibus [Orbium Coelestium]* (Nuremberg; Iohannes Petreius, 1543; 2d ed.: Basel: Ex officina Henric Petrina, 1566).

modified to include *orbium coelestium*, and Copernicus's own preface was replaced by that of the Protestant Osiander. This point is particularly striking. Given Luther's[26] and Melanchthon's[27] disapproval, Osiander's unsigned preface presents the book as a mere hypothesis. He may be criticized for his unauthorized action. His preface, however, enabled Copernicus to be discussed widely in Protestant ecclesiastical circles.

Much information on the relationship between the Bible and the new worldview can be gleaned from a thesis by Copernicus's most devoted student, Rheticus.[28] Rheticus presumed not only that the Copernican model and the Bible were consistent, but also that Scripture shows that Copernicus was correct. He finds evidence in Psalms speaking about heaven as the dwelling place of God.[29] Heavens will not be moved, so the earth must be moveable! Job 9:6 "Who moves the earth from its place, and its pillars are shaken?" demonstrates that the earth can be moved.[30] Passages in Scripture that speak about the mobility of the sun are explained as accommodation. What happened in Josh 10:12–14? Rheticus argues that our *ratio* knows that the sun is unmoveable, our eyes, however, see differently.[31] We speak about sun*rise* and sun*set*.[32] God's power permitted the earth to stand still, but this is veiled in accommodating language[33] so that the non-astronomer Joshua can command the sun and moon, and not the earth, to halt. In this way, accommodation was still a strong point, not only for Rheticus, but in the entire field of the new

---

[26] Weimarer Ausgabe: *Tischreden* nr. 4638.

[27] Philippus Melanchthon, *Initia doctrinae physicae, dictata in Academia Vuitebergensi* (Wittenberg: Hans Lufft, 1549).

[28] The study by Rheticus, *Epistola de Terrae Motu,* has a remarkable history. According to Hooykaas, *Rheticus,* 18–19, the study was written between 1532 and 1541. It was published, however, only in 1651 in Utrecht. During the century between authorship and publication, arguments had already been exchanged, refused or accepted. Nevertheless, it is one of the best compendia focusing on the debate of that time. Hooykaas supposes that the original title was *De Terrae Motu et Scriptura Sacra* (41).

[29] Ps 2:4; 11:4; 14:2; 19:7; 20:7; 33:13; 53:3; 76:9; 80:15; 102:20; 115:3; 123:1; 139:8.

[30] I follow the edition of Hooykaas, *Rheticus,* here 15.

[31] Hooykaas, *Rheticus,* 58: Ita cum recta ratio concludat, solem esse immobilem, oculi vero eum moveri judicent.

[32] Hooykaas, *Rheticus,* 58: Solem oriri, occidere, suo motu diem et annum conficere, etiamsi teneamus haec de apparenti motu esse vera.

[33] Nevertheless, Rheticus tried to demonstrate his view by quoting Ps 76:9 "From the heavens you uttered judgement, the earth feared and *was still* (terra tremuit et quievit), when God rose up to establish judgement." This "being still of the earth" is only possible if it was moving before. It stopped at the moment of the divine judgement. Something like that must have happened in Josh 10:12–14 too!

science that tried to justify itself before the forum of the well-known and
well-established religious systems. Johannes Kepler (1571–1630), however,
refused to explain Josh 10:12–14 in any way at all. Joshua only wanted
the day to be lengthened and how that happened is secondary.[34] On the
other hand, Galileo (1564–1642) saw "The sun *stood still* in the midst of
heaven" as the ultimate proof of his theory that the sun revolves only
around its own axis. In doing that, the sun causes the movement of the
earth and the planets. When the sun stops, the earth cannot move either
and extends in this way the length of the day.[35]

Even after the heliocentric system was more or less accepted, the attempts
to reconcile biblical text and mathematical reality continued. As an
example I refer to two voices from the Netherlands. In his *Annotationes*,
written in 1644, Hugo Grotius (1583–1645) opined that Joshua's call was
a poetical expression, a *phrasis poetica*. Nevertheless, he, too, tried to give it
a "natural" explanation. In his view, the sun set normally, but the sunlight
was reflected by a cloud above the horizon. This extended the daylight.
The urge to explain miracle stories rationally continues unabated. In
1670, Baruch Spinoza goes a step further. He assumes a refraction of
the light from the sun that had set; this light was then reflected from
the falling hailstones. In this way he links together the sun miracle and
the hailstones. But by now we have reached the second half of the 17th
century. The situation was more complex in the early days.

The excellent study by Rienk Vermij[36] demonstrates how the young Dutch
Republic, born out of the war with Spain, founded new universities and
these universities flourished as humanistic centres of learning. Their most
important role came partly from the absence here of earls, princes or
royal courts, which elsewhere became or were the centres of culture.[37]
I will focus on the University of Groningen, founded in 1614. In this
early period, preceding Galileo's condemnation, the Copernican system
caused a big commotion. The historian Ubbo Emmius (1547–1625), the
later founding rector, saw in 1608 the whole system of religious doctrine

---

[34] Johannes Kepler, *Astronomia Nova* (Prague 1609), in *Gesammelte Werke Band III* (ed.
M. Caspar; Munich: C.H. Beck, 1937), 31.
[35] Hooykaas, *Rheticus*, 175.
[36] R. Vermij, *The Calvinist Copernicans: The Reception of the New Astronomy in the Dutch
Republic, 1575–1750* (History of Science and Scholarship in the Netherlands 1; Amsterdam: Edita KNAW, 2002).
[37] Vermij, *Calvinist Copernicans*, 13.

collapsing and argued that if Copernicus was correct Moses was a liar: *Deus bone, quo abit impietas! Quid magis facere potest ad evertendam universam doctrinam et religionem nostram! Fundamenta enim convellunt. Nam haec si vera sunt, ut vehementer autorem contendere intelligo, Moses est falsus, falsae totae sacrae literae.*[38] (*italics* E.N.)

His colleague Nicolaus Mulerius (1564–1630), the astronomer, and the Groningen professor of medicine and mathematics, was much more cautious and, after weighing the question for twenty-five years, decided to stay with the main part of the Ptolemaic system. He accepted Venus and Mercury within a heliocentric system. But, for him, the centre was and remained the earth. After all, even an earth that rotated on its own axis could still be stable. What he did not want to accept was the annual movement of the earth, or a complete heliocentric system, and this for religious reasons.[39] His mother had been buried alive by the Inquisition; he became a strict Calvinist, and that meant that the literal text of the Bible was very important for him. So he argued in his *Tabulae Frisicae* that it is understandable that some should give preference to Pythagoras, but the authority of Holy Scripture contradicts this.[40] The tone of the debate is remarkable. However many major interests of scientific theory may have been at stake, heretics' hoods were not passed out: "This dispute is learned and sharp, but without hatred."[41]

Not always, however, was an irenic style maintained. With the appointment of Samuel Maresius (1599–1673), widely known for his conflicts with Voetius (1589–1676), and in 1643 successor to Franciscus Gomarus (1563–1641), a militant polemist entered the arena.[42] Copernicanism was not at the centre of his disputations; for him it was clear that it contradicted Scripture. As there is no other source in theology, it can be discussed as a mathematical hypothesis. Maresius published a clear rejection of Copernicanism three years before his death in 1673.[43]

---

[38] Ubbo Emmius to Sibrandus Lubbertus September 19, 1608 (H. Edema van der Tunk, *Johannes Bogerman* [Groningen: Wolters, 1886], 317).

[39] Vermij, *Calvinist Copernicans*, 45–52.

[40] Nicolaus Mulerius, *Tabulae Frisicae Lunae-Solares quadruplices, e fontibus Cl. Ptolemaei, Regis Alfonsi, Nic. Copernici, & Tychonis Brahe, recens constructae* (Alkmaar: Jacobus de Meester, 1611), 318.

[41] Nicolaus Mulerius, *Institutionum astronomicarum libri duo* (Groningen: Hans Sas, 1616), Praefatio: erudita et acris sed sine odio contentio haec est!; Vermij, *Calvinist Copernicans*, 540.

[42] The standard work is still the monumental biography by D. Nauta, *Samuel Maresius* (Amsterdam: H.J. Paris, 1935).

[43] Samuel Maresius, *De abusu philosophiae Cartesianae* (Groningen, 1670).

But the time for total rejection was past. Already in 1648, the Groningen philosopher Martinus Schoock (1614–1669) presided over a disputatio with questions concerning the moveability of the heavens *or* the earth and the possibility of taking the sun as the centre of the universe. "Both questions were answered 'ut lubet' ('as it pleases'); that is, the defendant was ready to argue either side of the argument."[44] Alumni like Balthasar Bekker (1634–1698) and Christophorus Wittichius (1625–1687) embraced Cartesianism, which proved to be a suitable vehicle to promote Copernicanism successfully. As time passed new viewpoints concerning Josh 10 became rarer and rarer. The positions are now fixed. The new worldview is becoming increasingly accepted. And when a Groningen minister defended the old truth, claiming "that those who teach that the earth moves around the sun, call God a liar to his face" he was rebuked by Nicolaus Engelhard (1696–1765), the Groningen professor of philosophy. In his reply the words "ignorance" and "old hat" aimed at the discussion play a role.[45] By now, we are already in 1737. In 1779 there is certainty that Josh 10:12–14 teaches that the sun stood still and the earth moved![46]

When reviewing the different stages of the conflict, it can be seen that openings were sought from the very beginning. If an astronomical approach could only produce mere hypotheses, the question of truth was not at issue. Or, it is even possible that observations and experiments only clarified the true meaning of Scripture. In the opposite camp, astronomy formulated truth and Scripture contained only a *phrasis poetica*. And as a theological argument, there was always the accommodation theory. Joshua was not an astronomer. God had to adapt his truth to normal people. After initial timidity and difficulty with the texts, Josh 10:12–14 became entwined in systems. Joshua and his enthusiastic command became a pawn in the game of systems, until the system tottered and modifications, and even reversals, slowly became visible. The result? As stated above, the Bible says that the earth moves and the sun stands still.

---

[44] Vermij, *Calvinist Copernicans*, 179; *Disputatio historico-physica tertia expendens naturalis historiae certitudinem quam . . . sub praesidio . . . Martini Schoockij . . . publicè defendam suscipit Daniel à Sanden* (Groningen: Samuel Pieman, 1648).

[45] Vermij, *Calvinist Copernicans*, 367.

[46] Rutgerus Ouwens, *Redenvoering, betogende, dat de stelling van Ptolemaeus, aangaande het lopen der sonne strydig is tegen de H. Schrift, of dat men het lopen der sonne, na de stelling van Ptolemaeus, verkeerdelijk poogd te bewyzen uit Josua X:v.12.13* (The Hague: Munnikhuizen & Plaat, 1779).

But there is more at stake here than the erratic paths of exegesis. Here worldviews, the real world and scientific observations were being laid on the line. It slowly became evident that there was a broad gap between worldview and the real world. And this disrupted the entire tradition and philosophy. Among the first opponents of the Copernican system were Luther and Melanchthon. Scripture, their weapon against Rome, was at stake. Conversely, Rome was warned. The Reformation had already shown plainly the kind of power that Scripture and its explanation set loose. Europe was small, contact between scholars was intense. That applied not only to allies but also to arguments fought out in pamphlets, broadsheets and debates. In The Netherlands the country's universities served as the arena. There was no well-defined border between theologians, philosophers, orientalists, mathematicians and astronomers. The sciences battled one another for the one truth. This debate, which took place four hundred years ago, is an example of how science sharpened its instruments on religion and its sources: sometimes cautiously, sometimes haltingly, sometimes filled with the enthusiasm of new knowledge and new abilities. The reception shows clearly that the different systems continued to wrestle throughout a long period. Scientists lived with a foot in each camp. The doggedness of the Copernican model was one of long endurance, of trial and error, of power and knowledge, and of a slowly growing certainty that this was the best possible explanation for the phenomena observed. Joshua 10 is a model for what could happen to texts. And the mechanisms that became visible in the reception history of the aspect of violence and in the debate on cosmology have a surprisingly topical value. They can serve as a reminder and warning when reflecting on religion's role as a cohesive or divisive element in modern society. That is why I shall add some brief comments on this Bible text's journey through time in view of the academic task of biblical exegesis.

For what is the intention and achievement of such a story where an originally local conflict grows mythically into a cosmic drama? The objective of these narratives is not the conquest as such, nor the adulation of divine or human military power. It is ultimately a matter of *receiving* the land, and that last as a *tabula rasa*.[47] But even this *tabula*

---

[47] E. Noort, "Zwischen Mythos und Realität," 149–61. The recapitulation of the conquest narratives in Josh 11:16–23; 21:43–45 are the conclusion of concepts presented by Deut 7:1–6; 20:15–18, etc.

rasa is not an objective but merely an element. Behind all the din of arms there is a conception of the land as the spatial dimension of the Torah within a strictly conditioned view of the covenant. The land becomes the space where one may live the Torah. And in this view, that land must be a *tabula rasa*, so that the responsibility remains fully with Israel.[48] Land becomes the collateral for faithfulness to the Torah. The means with which this ideological purpose must be reached—in modern terms genocide—are literally life-threatening. As long as these texts and their environment rested under the dust of past history, an academic approach had little to do beyond interpreting these texts philologically and historically, to place them as accurately as possible in their environment. They were just memories from the history of culture, nothing more.

But matters change when these texts have a claim to validity in the present, when they are part of the classic sources of present-day faith and community life. These pretensions to validity have in the course of history offered opportunities to claim religion-based ideological support. These texts played a role from the time of the conquests of the Byzantine rulers, in the call for the first crusade in 1095, the conquest of South America and the treatment of indigenous peoples during the colonization of the New World, Africa and the Far East. Moreover, as we have seen, they played a very important role in the debate on cosmology in the 16th and 17th centuries.

What meaning does this have for the *academic* explanation of religious texts, including the Bible? Since these texts are distinguished from Egyptian, Mesopotamian or Hittite texts by the pretension that they can be related to present-day belief systems, they all have a long, effective, reception history. This means our philological and historical explanation aiming at the original meaning of the text no longer suffices, a *critical, ethical* judgement is requested, also in academia. Hermeneutically, the reception history will have to become a part of the way we ask questions. The intellectual efforts we have spent during the last centuries of historical-critical exegesis on the explanation of the growth of a biblical text should be balanced by the same efforts in reception history, at least for texts so crucial to cultural history as Josh 10:12–14. When reception history is linked in this way to ethical judgements, it can make evident where and why religion turns criminal and where and why it adds to social coherence. This is a situation

---

[48] As demonstrated by the reworking of Josh 21:43–45 in 23:1–16.

that goes beyond the standard role of exegesis, beyond confessional approaches or so-called neutral ones, because of the specific character and setting of the texts and their history of interpretation. This is why the ambivalent history of Joshua is more than just a cultural memory. For religion did not disappear from our multicultural society as our knowledge grew. And the clash of religiously motivated worldviews and religiously inspired violence is nowadays more actual than ever. Therefore, this case study of the history of interpretation can be a model for the treatment, the use and the abuse of classic religious texts in a time when the search for identity plays a role in determining the relationship between "we" and "others." This fits both aspects of the history of reception of Josh 10: religiously inspired violence and the clash on cosmology. In his Presidential Address to SBL at Toronto in 2002, John Collins remembered biblical exegetes of their own burden in the blazing debates on Islam after the events of 9/11.[49] He saw the main problem in the presupposed divine authority of the texts, "for the Bible has contributed to violence in the world precisely because it has been taken to confer a degree of certitude that transcends human discussion and argumentation."[50] The task of biblical criticism should be to destroy that certitude.

With regard to the questions discussed in this paper, I prefer to go one step further. The problems that arose in the 16th century led directly to the Enlightenment. And the central problem of the Enlightenment is that of tolerance, not tolerance as a kind of diluted *laissez-faire*, but as part of one's own stance. To explore the possibilities and boundaries of this tolerance is part of the task of academic biblical exegesis.

This paper started and will end with a view on the city and the University of Groningen. It is dedicated to Florentino García Martínez, a great scholar and friend, who spent many years of his academic life at the Qumran Institute of our Faculty. Such a combination of scholarship and friendship is a precious gift. *Ad multos annos!*

---

[49] J.J. Collins, "The Zeal of Phineas: The Bible and the Legitimation of Violence," *JBL* 122 (2003): 3–21.
[50] Collins, "Zeal," 21.

EZEKIEL'S UTOPIAN EXPECTATIONS

Johan Lust

Florentino García Martínez's interesting contribution on the apocalyptic interpretation of Ezekiel in the Dead Sea Scrolls[1] invited me to reconsider my views on Ezekiel's prophecies about Israel's future. What are the expectations described in that prophetic book, and what are the differences between the shorter version and the longer one in these matters? In a search for answers to these questions,[2] the well-documented dissertation of P. Schwagmeier is to be taken into account, as well as the most recent PhD thesis of A.S. Crane and S. Scatolini's essay on Ezek 36–39.[3]

INTRODUCTORY REMARKS

It should be clear that, when Ezekiel is referred to here, the reference is not to the historical prophet, but to the book carrying his name. That book is known in a shorter and in a longer version. The former is no longer preserved in Hebrew, but still accessible in the Old Greek. Old Greek here means the earliest Greek translation known to us. Papyrus 967 is its main witness.[4] The longer version can be found in the

---

[1] F. García Martínez, "The Apocalyptic Interpretation of Ezekiel in the Dead Sea Scrolls," in *Interpreting Translation: Studies on the LXX and Ezekiel in Honour of Johan Lust* (ed. idem and M. Vervenne; BETL 192; Leuven: Peeters, 2005), 163–76.

[2] The search for answers will unavoidably imply some repetitions of my earlier contributions on related topics, such as "Messianism in LXX-Ezekiel: Towards a Synthesis," in *The Septuagint and Messianism* (ed. M.A. Knibb; BETL 195; Leuven: Peeters, 2006), 417–30.

[3] P. Schwagmeier, *Untersuchungen zur Textgeschichte und Entstehung des Ezechielbuches in masoretischer und griechischer Überlieferung* (Inauguraldissertation; Zürich, 2004); A.S. Crane, *The Restoration of Israel in Ezekiel 36–39 in Early Jewish Interpretation: A Textual-Comparative Study of the Oldest Extant Hebrew and Greek Manuscripts* (Ph.D. diss.; Murdoch Univ., 2006); idem, *Ezekiel 36–39 in P967 and the Rest: Theology makes the Difference* (paper presented at the SBL sessions on "Theological Perspectives on the Book of Ezekiel," 2006); S.S. Scatolini, "Ezek 36, 37, 38 and 39 in Papyrus 967 as Pre-text for Re-reading Ezekiel," in *Interpreting Translation: Studies on the LXX and Ezekiel*, 331–57.

[4] The *Vetus Latina Codex Wirceburgensis* is another witness, see especially P.-M. Bogaert, "Le témoignage de la Vetus Latina dans l'étude de la tradition des Septante: Ézéchiel et Daniel dans le Papyrus 967," *Bib* 59 (1978): 384–95.

Masoretic Text and in its early translations, including the Septuagint as printed in its critical editions. In earlier contributions, we suggested that the short form of the text is not the result of an abbreviation, but an earlier form of the book.[5] The longer form is based upon it. The recently discovered Ezekiel fragments from Massada prove that it already existed in the first or even second century B.C.E. This, however, does not imply that the shorter version no longer circulated at that time. Both versions may have been used alongside each other for quite some time.

We will first turn to the shorter version in the Old Greek and to its presumed Hebrew *Vorlage* and compare it with the longer version in the Masoretic text. Then we will gradually try to elucidate the motivations behind these differences.

THE SHORT VERSION: STRUCTURE

The section of the book with most of the oracles and visions relevant to our investigation is to be found in Ezek 34–39, a section which D. Block calls "The Gospel according to Ezekiel: Proclaiming the Good News."[6] In the Old Greek, the order of the chapters is as follows: 34–36, 38–39, 37. The central composition consists of two panels: the Edom section in Ezek 35–36 and the Gog section in Ezek 38–39 to which 37:1–14 forms a conclusion. The composition as a whole is framed by two David sections: Ezek 34 and 37:15–28.

34:1–39 Israel Dispersed. The Bad Shepherds and David the Good Shepherd
34:23 David, the Other Shepherd
34:25 A Covenant of Peace with David

35–36	Edom-Seir. Name Profanation and Sanctification	38–39	Gog-Magog. Name Profanation and Sanctification
35:1–9	Edom: Accusation and Punishment. "Son of man, fix your face towards Mount Seir"	37:1–14 38:1–9	Gog and his army called upon. "Son of man, fix your face towards Gog"

---

[5] Both Schwagmeier and Crane accept this view: see respectively *Untersuchungen*, 366–68 and *Ezekiel 36–39*, 4–7. Scatolini seems to remain undecided ("Ezek 36, 37, 38 and 39," 353–54).

[6] D.I. Block, *The Book of Ezekiel: Chapters 25–48* (NICOT; Grand Rapids: Eerdmans, 1998), 268, 273.

35:10–15	Edom's motivation	38:10–23	Gog's coming and wrong motivation
36:1–7	Destruction of Edom	39:1–8	Destruction of Gog
36:8–12	Repopulation of Israel	39:9–16	Burial of Gog
36:13–15	No more (sacrificial) eating of men	39:17–20	Sacrificial meal
36:16–23	Name sanctification	39:21–29	Name sanctification
(36:8–12	Repopulation of Israel)	37:1–14	Revitalisation of Israel

37:15–28 Gathered Israel. David Unifies
37:24 David, the One Shepherd
37:26 A Lasting Covenant of Peace with the Israelites

The framework in Ezek 34 and 37:15–28 announces the replacement of the former bad shepherds by the Lord's servant David. According to 34:23, he will be "another" (ἕτερον) shepherd, that is to say: unlike the former ones he will not be corrupt. Also, he will be the one and only shepherd (37:24) of the unified people. The Lord grants him (34:25) and his people (37:26) an everlasting promise of peace. The Lord's dwelling place will be with them.

Within that frame, two sets of oracles are closely linked with each other: The Edomite sayings in Ezek 35–36 and the oracles against Gog in Ezek 38–39, 37:1–14 are two panels of a diptych. After the word-event formula, both sections continue with the same introductory command: "Son of man, set your face against…" In both collections Israel's enemy is given more or less mythological features. Edom and Gog are not well defined historical nations, but typological representations of "the enemy": Edom, the brother and arch-enemy of Israel, and Gog, representing the enemy from abroad.[7]

The Edom oracles end up in a promise leading to the Gog section: The Lord will sanctify his name and act so that the nations will know that he is the Lord (36:22–23, 39:28). He will not do this by an intervention in favour of or against Israel, but rather through his action against Gog (Ezek 38–39; esp. 38:16,23; 39:6–7). In this light, one has to understand the utterance at the end of chapter 36 in LXX: "It is not for your sake, house of Israel, that I am about to act, but because of

---

[7] Compare J. Lust, "Edom—Adam in Ezekiel, in MT and LXX," in *Studies in the Hebrew Bible, Qumran, and the Septuagint: Presented to Eugene Ulrich* (ed. P.W. Flint et al.; VTSup 101; Leiden: Brill, 2006), 387–401 (397–400).

my holy name, which you have profaned among the nations" (36:22).
In an eschatological war, Gog and his hordes will be defeated, but also
the Israelites will all fall by the sword (39:23). The description of these
events leads to the vision of the revival of the dry bones in 37:1–10.
Whereas the corpses of the enemies will be gathered and buried
(39:11–16), the dry bones of the people of Israel will be brought back
to life (37:1–14). The result will be that Israel will no longer carry the
reproach of the nations (נשא כלמה 34:29), they will carry their own
guilt (נשא כלמה 39:26).[8]

THE LONG VERSION. STRUCTURE

The insert of Ezek 36:23bβ–38, combined with the transposition of
Ezek 37 and some other minor changes, results in a different structure.
The oracles against Gog (38–39) are disjoined from the Edom composition (35–36) and from the revitalisation section (37:1–14). The latter is
now connected to the newly inserted conclusion of the Edom diptych
(36:23bβ–38). The sign-act symbolizing the unification of Israel under
shepherd-king David, in chapter 37:15–28, forms an inclusion with the
oracles about Israel's shepherd-kings in chapter 34.

The new structure, and its main linking phrases, can be schematised
as follows:[9]

34–37   *Restoration and Unification under David*
34   *Israel's Bad Shepherds, and David the Good Shepherd*
34:23   David, the *one* shepherd
34:25   A promise of Peace
    34:31   *"you my flock* (צאן)*...you are human"* (אדם)
    35 against Edom (אדום)
    36–37:14 Restoration of Israel (אדם)*, insert of 36:23bβ–38*
    transition to 37:1–14
    36:37–38   *"human flock"* (צאן אדם)
37   *Restoration and Unification of Israel under King David*
37:24   David, the one shepherd
37:26   A promise of Peace

38–39   *Final Battle against Gog*

---

[8] Here the presumed *Vorlage*, identical with MT, is to be quoted, because the translator did not use the same Greek equivalents in both instances.

[9] Differences with LXX or/and p967 are italicised.

The allusions to a flock of men (אדם) in Ezek 34:31 and 36:37–38, missing in LXX, form a strong inclusion surrounding the oracles against Edom (אדום), oracles that find their climax in the promise that Israel will again be populated by אדם, replacing אדום (36:10–12). The announcement of the coming of David and of an eternal promise of peace surrounds the Adam-Edom block. The oracles against Gog are no longer part of it, but constitute an independent composition.[10]

Whereas in the short version the sanctification of the Lord's name, profaned among the nations, is restored by means of the Lord's action through the nations (38–39), in the long version the vindication of his holiness is realized by means of a re-creation of the Israelites. This recreation is announced in the insert at the end of chapter 36 (vv. 23b–38) and further described in the vision of the dry bones (37:1–11). It is an answer to the plea of the Israelites in 36:37: "This also I will let the house of Israel ask me to do for them: to increase their men like a flock." The dry bones in the field are "the whole house of Israel" (37:11). According to Schwagmeier, "the whole house of Israel" here means all the Israelites, from the beginning of the nation's history up to now. In his view, this implies a "realistic" interpretation of the resurrection of the dry bones, similar to the one given in 4Q385 (4QPseudo-Ezekiel^a) 2, where a physical resurrection is granted to the "just" as a reward for their loyalty (חסד) (line 3).[11] We will have to come back to this assertion.

Many phrases of the insert Ezek 36:23b–38 are taken from other sections in Ezekiel and are slightly reformulated, so as to prepare for the transposed chapter 37. The motif of the gathering in v. 24, for example, echoes 20:34, 41; 37:21; 39:27. In 36:26–27, one finds an almost literal correspondence with 11:19–21. In both passages God promises to give his people a new heart and a new spirit. Here in 36:27, however, the editor adds that God will give them *his* spirit. Through this intervention, the redactor introduces the line of thought found in 37:14, where the Lord effectively gives *his* spirit to the revitalised nation. Rephrasing 36:22, the insert also repeats that the Lord will not intervene for the sake of his people, but for the sanctification of his holy name (36:23bβ, 32).[12]

---

[10] Compare Lust, "Edom—Adam," 387–95.

[11] Schwagmeier, *Untersuchungen*, 280–84, 303; see also the following section in the present essay.

[12] The new life is not given because of the merits of the just, as in 4QPseudo-Ezekiel.

A comparison with the short text shows that the insert gives the announced intervention of the Lord a completely new interpretation. Instead of an action in relation to the foreign nations, represented by Gog, it becomes an action in relation to Israel. It will comprise a number of feats: (1) A gathering of the Israelites and their entry in their land (36:24), a theme well known in Ezekiel and in Jeremiah; (2) a cleansing of the nation (36:25, 33), recalling priestly rituals as in Num 19:13, 20; (3) a recreation, including a new heart and a new spirit (36:26–28), the result of which will be that the people will walk in the Lord's statutes, which recalls Jer 31:31–33; (4) a restoration of the ideal surroundings and life-sphere of Eden (26:29–30, 33–38). This final theme takes up the thoughts developed in 34:25–31 and forms an inclusion, especially around the phrase צאן אדם "flock of men" (34:31,36:37–38).

The Gog oracles in 38–39 are a separate unit, confronting another type of foreign nations. In 25–32 the Lord dealt with Israel's neighbours (28:26 סביבות); in 34–37 he turned to Edom, Israel's brother-enemy, the anti-Adam; and in 38–39 he now finally convokes Gog and the remotest nations from the extreme north, the eschatological enemy.[13]

"Resurrection" and the identity of Ezekiel's David

We already noted that, according to Schwagmeier, the revitalisation of the dry bones in MT-Ezek 7:1–11 implies a material resurrection, absent from the Old Greek. This has implications for the identification of David: In MT he is the historical David, risen from the tomb.[14]

The opposite view is defended by Crane. Like Schwagmeier, he is of the opinion that the two different chapter orders, in MT and the Old Greek, reveal two different eschatological viewpoints. Unlike Schwagmeier, he holds that the physical resurrection is required by the order in the Old Greek. There the dry bones are the dead, fallen in the battle against Gog. These real dead need a real resurrection, rather than a metaphorical revival. In the re-ordering of MT "the resurrection of the dry bones is primarily a metaphor of the people, uniting under a military Davidic leader," ready for a battle against Gog.[15] A material

---

[13] Compare Schwagmeier, *Untersuchungen*, 285.

[14] *Ibid.*, 284. In the short text his identity remains more vague: see 279–80, 294, 310.

[15] Crane, *Restoration*, 326–27.

resurrection is not needed, since the people of Israel are not physically
dead. The battle is still to come.

Why does Schwagmeier postulate a physical resurrection in MT
and not in the Old Greek? The main reason given is that the reader
of MT reaches the programmatic saying of 37:11 "These bones are
the whole (כל) house of Israel," after having read the people's prayer
in 36:37–38 (absent from LXX): "This I will let the people of Israel
ask me to do for them: to increase for them their men like a flock."
According to Schwagmeier, a physical resurrection is required to bring
back "all (כל)" the Israelites who belonged to the house of Israel in the
course of its long history."[16] That way, the promise given in 36:11 will
be fulfilled: "I will restore you as in former times (כקדמותיכם), and do
more good to you than ever before." Obviously, the editor envisages a
comeback to life of all those who ever belonged to the house of Israel,
including David.[17] Schwagmeier finds further support for his views in
24:1–14, where the bones of the flock (צאן), representing Israel, are
"filling (מלא)" (24:4) the pot and being "burnt up" (24:10), symbolizing
a harsh punishment of Israel. Recalling that passage, 36:38 announces
that, in the coming future, Israel will be filled (מלא) with flocks (צאן) of
men. Read after this introduction, the scene of the dry bones in 37:1–10
evokes the death of the Israelites and the need of a physical revitalisation. The situation is different in the Old Greek. There the scene of the
valley of the dry bones is introduced by the promise in 39:25–29. The
Greek has no counterpart for כל in 39:25 and thus reads "I will have
mercy on the house of Israel (ἐλεήσω τὸν οἶκον Ισραηλ)." Moreover,
it did not find in its *Vorlage* the last part of 39:28, nor the particle עוד
of 39:29. The implication is that the Old Greek does not witness to
any of the expressions of finality and totality found here in MT. The
Old Greek does not seem to imply a total and physical restoration
of "all of Israel." Schwagmeier adds some more minutiae which we
cannot all repeat here. His observations are valuable and demonstrate
that the text of MT is a harmonious composition full of inter-textual
links. They show how MT underlines the final and total character of
the promised restoration and harmonious unification of "all of Israel"
before the eschatological war against Gog, but they hardly seem to
necessitate a physical resurrection.

---

[16] Schwagmeier, *Untersuchungen*, 280.
[17] Ibid., 280.

Something similar applies to Crane's reasoning. The core of his argumentation runs as follows: In the chapter order of the Old Greek, the slaughter in 38–39 included Israel, which required a physical resurrection of the people (37:1–14), allowing them to unite under the leadership of David (37:15–28) and then to build the new temple (40–48). In the order of the received text, however, the slaughter in 38–39 is of Gog and his hordes, not of Israel. This re-ordering, as well as the spiritual renewal announced in the insert of 36:23bβ–38, evoke a spiritual revival of Israel, rather than a physical resurrection.[18]

It is slightly amazing that Crane seeks to underpin his argumentation in favour of the idea of physical resurrection in the Old Greek with a reference to הרוגים האלה, "these slain" in 37:9. "These slain" identify the dry bones of chapter 37 with the Israelites fallen in battle. According to Crane, the order of the Old Greek makes it clear that the battle in question is the war against Gog described in 38–39. He seems to overlook, however, that the equivalent of הרוגים האלה in the Old Greek is τοὺς νεκροὺς τούτους, "these dead," which does not imply any direct reference to a battle.

All in all, neither of the two chapter orders appears to postulate a physical resurrection. It is tempting to read it into the text, in order to obtain an easier identification of David. In that scenario, Ezekiel's David would be the resurrected David of old. It is much more likely, however, that both the shorter and the longer texts herald a view of Israel's history according to which the installation of the real David,[19] as well as the entry into the promised land, had not happened yet.

The Role of David. Minor Differences in the Long and Short Texts

At first glance, the description of the role of David is pretty much the same in MT and in the *Vorlage* of OG. Some minor differences may be due to the translator or to errors of copyists of the Hebrew text.

According to Ziegler's critical edition of 34:23, supported by p967, the Lord promises to raise up David as *another* (ἕτερον) shepherd, whereas in MT he will install him as the *one* shepherd. The difference

---

[18] Crane, *Restoration*, 113.

[19] Note that הקים על in 34:23 does not refer to a resurrection, but rather to an installation of a king: compare Deut 28:36.

here is probably caused by a confusion of ך and ד in the Hebrew. MT אֶחָד, "one" may be a corruption of an original אַחֵר, "other," which fits the context better: the former bad shepherds are replaced by another shepherd, a good one this time. The misreading may have been influenced by the parallel verse 37:34 where the topic is the unification of the nation and where "one" אֶחָד leader is called for.

In 34:25, the promise of peace is "with David" in the Greek text, whereas MT has "with them"; here the replacement of "them" by "David" may be due to the translator who connected the verse with the foregoing verses where David is at centre stage.

In 34:29 the φυτὸν εἰρήνης, "a plant of peace," probably translates מַטַּע שָׁלוֹם which is a misreading of מַטַּע לְשֵׁם, "a planting of renown." Although Schwagmeier holds a different view,[20] the difference between MT and OG does not have any implications for the role of David. A comparison with Isa 60:21 shows that a "plant of renown" does not have more Davidic connotations than "a plant of peace."[21]

Some other differences may be due to the editor of MT. The title ἄρχων, "prince" given to David in 34:24 as well as in 37:22, 24, 25 fits the general policy of Ezekiel in the Old Greek where the monarch of Israel is never given the title "king" מֶלֶךְ by the Lord, since the Lord "reigns" himself over Israel (20:32). MT on the other hand seems to hesitate when David is concerned. In 34:24 and 37:25 he receives the title נָשִׂיא corresponding to ἄρχων, but in 37:22, 24 he is said to be מֶלֶךְ, "king." The editor of MT may have no longer felt the need to reserve the title "king" of Israel to the Lord.[22] But there may be more to it. Ezekiel is a priestly writing, using priestly vocabulary and style and reflecting priestly thinking. According to A. van der Kooij, the use of ἄρχων in LXX-Ezekiel suggests that the translator associated David with an ideology of the high-priesthood.[23] The original Hebrew text did not do so. Van der Kooij finds a first trace of this ideology in the Greek text of 28:11–19, where the king of Tyre is called ἄρχων and is described as a high-priest. He overlooks that the Greek text most likely reflects a

---

[20] Schwagmeier, *Untersuchungen*, 309–10.
[21] See M. Greenberg, *Ezekiel* (AB 22A; Garden City, N.Y.: Doubleday, 1983), 703.
[22] For further bibliography and information about the title נָשִׂיא and its Greek equivalents, see Lust, "Messianism in LXX-Ezekiel," 422.
[23] A. van der Kooij, "The Septuagint of Ezekiel and Hasmonaean Leadership," in *The Septuagint and Messianism* (ed. M.A. Knibb; BETL 195; Leuven: Peeters, 2006), 437–46.

more original Hebrew text, which definitely referred to the rejection of
Israel's leader in Jerusalem and the final destruction of Israel. The later
editor of MT could not accept the harsh character of this oracle against
Jerusalem and its king-high-priest and therefore applied it to the king
of Tyre and his people.[24] Van der Kooij further finds evidence of an
association of David with the high-priesthood in the Greek text of Sir
45:24–25. It must be admitted, though, that both the Hebrew and the
Greek texts are open to different interpretations. Returning to Ezekiel,
we suggest that its original text, composed in priestly circles towards the
end of the exile and in the first stages of the return, favoured a priestly
leadership in Israel. Later on, the Hasmonaeans slightly adapted the
text, suiting their needs. Since they claimed royal authority and had
Davidic ambitions, they may have replaced נשיא by the royal title מלך
in the announcement of the coming of David in Ezek 37:22, 24.

MT-Ezek 37:25 has a longer plus: (המה) ובניהם ובני בניהם עד־עולם
"(they) and their children and their children's children for ever." We
will have to return to it.

The importance of these differences may become clearer when taken
together with the changed order of the chapters and the inserts of
36:23b–38 and 12:26–28. These combined factors reveal a remarkable
shift in the view of Israel's history.

EZEKIEL'S VIEW OF ISRAEL'S FUTURE IN LXX AND IN MT

What are the characteristic features of that history? In Ezekiel's opinion,
Israel's past was particularly dark and gloomy. Already from its earliest beginnings the people betrayed the Lord (20:5–8; see also 16:2–3).
As the prophet sees it, they have not reached the promised land yet.
He repeatedly assures that, after the exile and dispersion all over the
nations, the Lord still has to "bring" (בוא *hiphil*) them there. Influenced
by their reading of Jeremiah, who in similar contexts always uses the
verb "to bring back" (שוב *hiphil*) and by their preconceived comprehension of Israel's history, translators and commentators tend to find the
notion of a return also in Ezekiel, when in fact he most often, if not

---

[24] P.-M. Bogaert, "Montagne Sainte: jardin d'Éden et sanctuaire (hiérosolymitain)
dans un oracle d'Ézéchiel contre le prince de Tyr (Éz 28,11–19)," in *Le Mythe: Son
langage et son message: Actes du colloque de Liège et Louvain-la-Neuve 1981* (ed. H. Limet and
J. Ries; Homo religiosus 9; Louvain-la-Neuve: Centre d'Histoire des Religions, 1983),
131–53.

always,[25] refers to the entry into the promised land and not to its return. Of course, Ezekiel knew that, before the exile, his people had been living in Israel. But, in his opinion, at that time Israel was not yet the promised land. Of course, he was aware of the fact that some of his people remained in Jerusalem during the exile. But those inhabitants of Jerusalem, who claimed the land as their inheritance, were not the real elected people. They were not fully Israel, or as he calls it, they did not belong to "the whole of Israel, all of it" (כל בית ישראל כלה 11:15, 20:40, 36:10). They were rather to be assimilated with Edom.

It is impossible to give here a fully developed exposition of the views sketched in the above.[26] We will conclude this section with a more detailed reading of Ezek 37:25 in the two versions. This passage seems to contradict our presentation of Ezekiel's views concerning Israel's history. The wordings of MT clearly assume Israel's presence in the promised land before the exile. The Old Greek, however, may offer a different picture.

The unaccented text of the Old Greek, preserved in p967, reads as follows:

και κατοικησουσιν επι της γης αυτων ην εδωκα τω δουλω μου Ιακωβ· ου κατωκησαν εκει οι πατερες αυτων· και κατοικησουσιν επ αυτης αυτοι και Δαυιδ ο δουλος μου αρχων αυτων εις τον αιωνα

The reader, when not influenced by MT, normally translates this text as follows:

They shall live in *their* land that I gave to my servant Jacob; *their* fathers did *not* live there; but they [   ] shall live upon it, and David, my servant, their *ruler* forever.[27]

Why did Ezekiel associate the promise of the land with Jacob rather than Abraham? Why not prefer Abraham to whom the promise was originally given and to whom its eternality was more accentuated (see Gen 13:15–17, 17:1–8; contrast Gen 28:13–15, 35:9–15)? The reason is that the reference to Jacob evokes the antagonism between him and his brother Esau, between Israel and Edom. For Ezekiel, Jacob-Israel

---

[25] An exception can be found in Ezek 20:27–29, a late insert in the text already attested in the Old Greek.

[26] For a more expanded exposé, see J. Lust, "'Gathering and Return' in Jeremiah and Ezekiel," in *Le livre de Jérémie* (ed. P.-M. Bogaert; 2d ed.; BETL 54; Leuven: Peeters, 1997), 119–42 and 428–30.

[27] Differences with MT are in italics; minuses are signalled by square brackets.

and his descendants represent real Israel, whereas Esau-Edom and his descendants represent the brother and arch-enemy Edom. Ezekiel wishes to emphasize that the land was given to Jacob and the Israelites and not to Esau and the Edomites.

"Their fathers did not live on it." Who are these "fathers"? They are not the patriarchs Abraham, Isaac, and Jacob. In Ezekiel the notion "their/your fathers" always refers to the generations of Israelites who were taken out of Egypt and brought into the desert where they offended the Lord again and again, so that they had to be punished.[28] They never reached the land. But their descendants will be brought into it, they and David their ruler.

Let us now turn to the differences in MT. Where the Old Greek reads ου κατωκησαν εκει "their fathers did not live there," MT has אֲבוֹתֵיכֶם בָּה יָשְׁבוּ אֲשֶׁר "where your fathers lived." It is not excluded that the translator had before him a *Vorlage* identical with MT. If so, he used the particle ου as an adverb rendering אֲשֶׁר "where" and not as a negation. In Ezekiel, similar constructions, where ου is to be read as an adverb, can be found rather frequently.[29] In all these parallels, however, the antecedent of οὗ immediately precedes the adverb: see, for example, 37:21: ἐκ τῶν ἐθνῶν οὗ εἰσήλθοσαν ἐκεῖ, "from among the nations where they have gone." Moreover, in almost all of the parallels, οὗ...ἐκεῖ renders אֲשֶׁר...שָׁם and not אֲשֶׁר...בְּ as here in 37:21. In a literal translation such as LXX-Ezekiel one expects οὗ...ἐν in this context, see, for example, Ezek 11:17. Finally, one must agree with Zimmerli that the second אֲשֶׁר clause in MT-Ezek 37:25 is inelegantly connected with the first.[30]

This leads to the suggestion that in Ezek 37:25 the Old Greek may have read in its *Vorlage* לֹא יָשְׁבוּ שָׁם אֲבוֹתֵיכֶם.[31] The editor of MT could not accept this statement and changed it in agreement with 36:28 "and you shall dwell in (בּ יְשַׁבְתֶּם) the land which (אֲשֶׁר) I gave to your fathers," a verse belonging to his long addition 36:23b–38 which has no counterpart in the Old Greek. The second person address in the second relative clause in 37:21 ("your fathers") amidst third person forms may have preserved a trail betraying its provenience. The editor

---

[28] See 2:3; 20:4, 18, 24, 27, 30, 36, 42.
[29] 6:9, 13; 11:16; 12:16; 28:25; 29:13; 34:12; 36:20, 21, 22; 37:21, 25.
[30] W. Zimmerli, *Ezechiel* (BKAT 13; Neukirchen: Neukirchen-Vluyn, 1969), 906.
[31] It must be admitted that, to my knowledge, no early translations or commentaries can be adduced in support of this reading.

further added the phrase "(they) and their children, and their children's children" where the Old Greek and its presumed Hebrew *Vorlage* simply read αὐτοί. The Greek pronoun expresses an emphasis: they, not their ancestors, shall live there. Inserting a plus, the editor of MT changed the emphasis, insisting that the people of Israel would live in their land forever. It must, however, be admitted that this suggestion remains very hypothetical and tentative.

David's Role in Israel's History in LXX and in MT

In the past Israel had been ruled by several kings, including David. But, in Ezekiel's view, the David of the past had not been the real messianic David. This David was still to come, once the entry in the promised land was realized. When Ezekiel says: the Lord will "set up over them another shepherd, my servant David" (34:23 LXX), he does neither refer to a resurrection of the historical David, nor to a new king like David, belonging to the Davidic line. He means that the real David is still to come.

When and how will that happen? According to LXX-Ezekiel, first the land of brother-enemy Edom is to be made desolate (35–36:7, esp. 35:15); then, "after many days,"[32] in the "latter days,"[33] in a final battle, the Lord will sanctify his holy name by his actions against Gog and the nations from the farthest north (38–39). Then he will revitalise the Israelites who suffered terribly in these final events (37:1–14). He will give them his spirit and recreate them. He will bring them into the Land and unify them under one leader David (37:15–28). Then the land will be organised and find its vital centre in the temple, the abode of the Lord (40–48). The rather vague indication of the times in which these events will happen seems to imply that they are scheduled for a remote future. In a period of growing apocalyptic tendencies these views may have aroused much interest and may even have been at the origin of these tendencies.

To many Israelites this may have given the impression that Ezekiel's prophecies were without any value, because their outcome was too vague and uncontrollable. They even seem to have accused their prophet of false prophecy. The editors of MT wished to make it clear that Ezekiel

---

[32] מימים רבים 38:8.
[33] באחרית הימים 38:8, באחרית השנים 38:16.

was not a false prophet and that the future he was talking about was not far off. They phrased the objection of false prophecy explicitly and formulated an answer. They inserted it in 12:26–28, in Ezekiel's composition against false prophets and prophetesses (12:21–13:23). The form and wordings of this insert are inspired by the immediately foregoing verses 12:21–25. It is formulated as a dispute: "The word of the Lord came to me: Son of man, the house of Israel is saying, 'The vision that he sees is for many years ahead; he prophesies for distant times.' Therefore say to them, Thus says the Lord God: None of my words will be delayed any longer, but the word that I speak will be fulfilled, says the Lord God." These verses are not yet attested in the shorter text preserved in p967.

The editors of MT also slightly changed the order of the chapters of the book, transposing the vision of the dry bones, together with the oracle about the opening of the graves and the prophecy about the unification of Israel under David, the one shepherd, right behind Ezek 36. In order to prepare for this transposition, they added a new composition and appended it to the end of Ezek 36 in the original text (36:23bα). In doing so, they disconnected the revitalisation of Israel from the end of Ezek 38–39 and their description of the final battle against Gog and moved it to the times of the humiliation of Edom, "who gave my land to themselves as a possession" (36:5) and the announcement of the imminent coming of the Lord's people to its land (36:8).

Why and when were these changes and new features inserted into the book? Before trying to give a tentative answer to these questions, it may be appropriate to repeat earlier warnings, reformulated by Scatolini. Although there is little, or perhaps nothing at all, preventing several plausible and meaningful synchronic readings of Ezekiel, it cannot be denied that "it shows signs of having been the result of a compilation of pericopes that have grown over time."[34] It would be slightly foolish to seek to detect in the short text a perfect systematic composition, later reworked into a longer equally systematic composition, expressing a different view of Israel's history. Nevertheless, it might be worthwhile to try to identify a common denominator behind the changes in the long text.

In an earlier contribution, I suggested that the transformations might have been brought about by the religious factions responsible for the

---

[34] "Ezek 36, 37, 38 and 39," 355.

masoretic canon because of their aversion of apocalyptic tendencies. While this may remain a possible explanation, it may not be the only one. Crane's thesis may perhaps provide us with a complementary motivation. In his view, the shorter original Ezekiel text, preserved in p967 (and La^w) reflects the situation and theology of a writer living in exile. He announces that the Lord is about to sanctify his name through his interventions in favour of his people (Ezek 36:20–23bα). He will defeat the arch-enemy Edom (Ezek 35–36), and in an eschatological battle he will defeat the mythological enemy Gog (Ezek 38–39). After this final battle he will revive his people, recreating it (37:1–14). He will unify them under the prince-priestly leader David (37:24–25). He will finally bring them into the promised land and set his sanctuary among them (37:26–28, 40–48). There they will live peacefully for ever, in and around the holy city carrying the name "The Lord is there," living signs of the Lord's sanctity (48:35).[35]

To those living in the land, in the times of the Seleucids, this picture may have seemed too utopic and its promises of a final peace too unrealistic. They found their identity threatened by the Seleucids who profaned all things holy in the eyes of the religious authorities and the righteous Jews. They needed a leader and a call to arms rallying the nation against the present enemy. A new reading of Ezekiel suited that purpose. Reordering the verses in Ezek 7:1–10 and introducing the notion of the צפירה (7:7, 10), referring to Antiochus IV, they strongly suggested that Ezekiel's oracles and visions about the final day dealt with the threat of the Seleucid king. Against those who rejected Ezekiel's book as useless and false because of its utopian apocalyptic features, they inserted a rejoinder attached to Ezekiel's disputation speech about false prophecy in 12:26–28. In his answer to the objections, the Lord assures that none of his words will be delayed any longer. They are not dealing with some vague idealistic future times; they are concerned with the present events. In this situation, Ezekiel's oracles about a revival of the people and about the coming of a Davidic leader reuniting the people sounded promising. A reordering of the final chapters obtained an even better adapted text. Transferring Ezek 37 from its original location after Ezek 39 to its actual position after Ezek 36, and inserting

---

[35] The *Vorlage* of the translator must have been identical with MT here; the differences between LXX and MT are due to the interpretation of the adverb שמה, "there" (MT), as a suffixed noun שמ/ה, "its name" (LXX), and to a double rendition of the proper noun יהוה, read as a form of the verb היה: γένηται and ἔσται.

36:23bβ as a transition, they interpreted Ezekiel's announcement of a reunification under the one leader David as a call to arms, preparing for the final war against Gog, representing the Seleucid threat.[36]

Simultaneously with the de-apocalypticizing process preserved in MT, other re-interpretations of Ezekiel developed the apocalyptic views expressed in LXX-Ezekiel. F. García Martínez demonstrated that 4QPseudo-Ezekiel bears witness to such a tendency in the Judaism of the second century B.C.E. The Qumran manuscript, however, significantly modifies Ezekiel's expectations. He reads his vision of the dry bones as an answer to the question of individual righteousness and retribution and no longer as a promise of national restoration and entry into the promised land.

Summarizing Conclusions

(1) The text of Ezekiel has been preserved in a shorter and a longer version. In the longer version, the insert of Ezek 36:23bβ–38, combined with the transposition of Ezek 37 and some other minor changes, results in a different structure.

(2) None of the two chapter orders postulates a physical resurrection of the Israelite people and of David.

(3) According to the prophet, the Lord's people have not yet reached the promised land. He repeatedly assures that, after the exile and dispersion all over the nations, the Lord still has to "bring" them there. This implies that the real David is still to come.

(4) Of course, Ezekiel was aware of the fact that some of his people remained in Jerusalem during the exile. But those inhabitants of Jerusalem, who claimed the land as their inheritance, were not the real elected people. They were rather to be assimilated with Esau-Edom, the enemy-brother.

(5) Ezekiel's reference to Jacob as the patriarch to whom the land was given (37:25) evokes the antagonism between him and his brother Esau, between Israel and Edom. For Ezekiel, Jacob-Israel and his descendants represent real Israel, whereas Esau-Edom and his descendants represent the brother and arch-enemy Edom. Ezekiel

---

[36] Crane, *Ezekiel 36–39*, 12–15.

emphasizes that the land was given to Jacob and the Israelites and not to Esau and the Edomites.

(6) How and when will the Lord bring his people into the land? According to LXX-Ezekiel, first the land of brother-enemy Edom is to be made desolate (35:15). Then, "after many days," in the "latter days," in a final battle, the Lord will sanctify his holy name by his actions against Gog and the nations from the farthest north. Finally, he will gather his people and bring them to the land. His servant David will unify the nation. The rather vague indication of the times in which these events will happen seems to imply that they are scheduled for a remote future.

(7) MT re-interpreted Ezekiel's future expectations. In the received text, the announcement of a reunification under the one leader David follows upon the revitalisation of Israel after the battle against Edom. The rally around David seems to be interpreted as a call to arms, preparing for the final war against Gog, representing the Seleucid threat.

(8) In contradistinction with MT-Ezekiel, 4Q*Pseudo-Ezekiel* develops the apocalyptic tendencies of LXX-Ezekiel. F. García Martínez rightly notes, however, that the author of the scroll completely modified the text of Ezekiel. For him, the vision is no longer a promise of national restoration, but a prophecy of individual resurrection as a reward for individual justice.[37]

---

[37] "The Apocalyptic Interpretation," 170.

LA CONSTRUCTION D'HAMAN DANS LE LIVRE D'ESTHER

Jesús Asurmendi

Le livre d'Esther est un vrai bijou, tant du point de vue littéraire que théologique. Il suscite de plus en plus d'intérêt.[1] Bien que la question de la construction des personnages ait été amplement travaillée par les narratologues[2] et qu'il y existe un ouvrage de très grande qualité sur le livre d'Esther traitant en partie la question,[3] il m'est apparu utile de focaliser l'attention, dans ces quelques pages, sur la construction de l'un des personnages clé du livre d'Esther : Haman. A première vue en effet, c'est le personnage d'Esther qui domine l'horizon. Le nom par lequel on désigne le livre le montre clairement. Ce n'est pas forcément faux mais, d'un certain point de vue, on pourrait considérer ce personnage comme faisant partie du duo Mardochée-Esther, l'intrigue et le ressort du texte se concentrant sur le duel Haman-Mardochée. Quoi qu'il en

---

[1] Quelques éléments bibliographiques donnent déjà une bonne base documentaire : C.A. Moore, *Daniel, Esther, and Jeremiah. The Additions* (AB 44 ; Garden City, N.Y. : Doubleday, 1977) ; S.B. Berg, *The Book of Esther: Motifs, Themes and Structure* (SBLDS 44 ; Missoula, Mont. : Scholars Press, 1979) ; eadem, "After the Exile: God and History in the Books of Chronicles and Esther," *The Divine Helmsman: Studies of God's Control of Human Events* (éd. J.L. Crenshaw et S. Sandmel ; New York : KTAV, 1980), 107–27 ; W. Dommershausen, *Ester* (NEB.AT 2 ; Würzburg : Echter Verlag, 1980) ; M.V. Fox, "The Structure of the Book of Esther," *I.L. Seeligmann Memorial Volume* (éd. A. Rofé ; Jérusalem : Rubenstein, 1983), 291–303 ; A. Meinhold, "Zu Aufbau und Mitte des Esterbuchs," *VT* 33 (1983) : 435–45 ; D.J.A. Clines, *The Esther Scroll. The Story of the Story* (JSOTSup 30 ; Sheffield : JSOT, 1984) ; M.V. Fox, *Character and Ideology in the Book of Esther* (2e éd. ; Grand Rapids : Eerdmans, 1991) ; L. Day, *Three Faces of a Queen* (JSOTSup 186 ; Sheffield : Sheffield Academic Press, 1995). A. Schmitt, *Wende des Lebens. Untersuchungen zu einem Situations-Motiv der Bibel* (BZAW 237 ; Berlin : de Gruyter, 1996). J. Vílchez, *Rut y Ester* (Estella : Verbo Divino, 1998).

[2] La bibliographie est immense. Pour ce qui est du monde biblique on peut renvoyer au colloque du RRENAB (Réseau de Recherche en Narrativité Biblique) : *Analyse narrative et Bible. Deuxième colloque international du RRENAB, Louvain-la-Neuve, avril 2004* (éd. C. Focant et A. Wénin ; BETL 191 ; Leuven : Peeters, 2005), dont les conférences majeures et un certain nombre de séminaires furent consacrés aux personnages du récit et, en partie, à leur caractérisation. Dans sa contribution, J.N. Aletti y présente une «fiche technique» de la caractérisation qui résume fort à propos beaucoup d'éléments de cette dimension de l'analyse narrative.

[3] Fox, *Character and Ideology*. Voir également A. Lacocque, "Haman in the Book of Esther," *HAR* 11 (1987) : 207–22 qui concentre son attention sur la condition Agaguite (Esth 3,1) du personnage.

soit de cette dernière observation, il est indéniable qu'Haman joue un rôle clé dans le récit du livre d'Esther. Certes, dans son état actuel la pointe du livre apparaît claire : donner une justification à la fête de Pourim (9,20–32). Mais quoi qu'il en soit de la solidité de l'enracinement factuel de cette fête dans le livre, Haman joue un rôle majeur dans le récit qui lui sert de justification.

Bien que l'article de Burnett[4] concentre son attention sur les récits évangéliques, et plus particulièrement sur Pierre dans l'évangile de Matthieu, bon nombre de ses observations sont fort pertinentes dans le terrain de la caractérisation des personnages. On ne peut qu'être d'accord avec lui et bien d'autres sur le fait que la caractérisation est le produit des éléments textuels du récit et du processus de lecture ou, comme dit Todorov cité par Burnett, «le personnage est un effet (/pro-duit) de la lecture».[5] «Un personnage est donc construit par le lecteur à partir des indices, des éléments («indicator» en anglais) disséminés tout au long du continuum textuel. Les traits (du personnage) sont induits par le lecteur en partant des indices».[6] En fait, la caractérisation des personnages est l'un des outils essentiels du narrateur, de l'auteur implicite, pour matérialiser la voix narrative, et celle-ci a pour but de proposer un monde et un horizon au lecteur. De ce point de vue il est vrai aussi que le narrateur d'Esther, maître d'œuvre du récit, construit son personnage Haman, pas à pas mais sûrement, de manière univo-que, comme un véritable continuum.[7] Mais ce personnage a un nom, et quel nom comme on le verra, ce qui renforce encore son statut de «personnage» car «un personnage est certes un paradigme bâti avec un certain nombre de traits que le lecteur colle sur un nom».[8]

La *construction*[9] du personnage d'Haman est *restreinte* car, en fait, il n'y a qu'un trait mis en avant : la soif démesurée de gloire et de reconnais-sance. C'est le moteur et le ressort de tout le récit le concernant. Mais néanmoins, ce n'est pas ce que la voix narrative fait passer ; en effet, pour elle, telle qu'elle se manifeste en 3,4 et 6,13, il s'agit d'affirmer que le

---

[4] F.W. Burnett, "Characterization and Reader Construction of Characters in the Gospel," *Semeia* 11 (1993): 3–28.

[5] *Ibid.*, 3 et 5.

[6] *Ibid.*, 5.

[7] *Ibid.*, 15.

[8] S.B. Chatman, *Story and Discourse: Narrative Structure in Fiction and Film* (Ithaca: Cornell University Press, 1978), 137, cité par Burnett, "Characterization," 17.

[9] Les termes «construction» et «caractérisation» des personnages sont utilisés équi-valemment tout au long de ces pages.

salut du peuple juif est assuré et garanti malgré toutes les vicissitudes et les dangers qu'il encourt. Il est clair que ce ressort ne peut fonctionner si, «en face», il n'y a pas un autre personnage pour mettre des bâtons dans les roues de sa soif de gloire, de reconnaissance et de pouvoir. Ceci permet de souligner encore et toujours ce trait caractéristique.

A côté de ce trait, il y en un autre, celui de l'astuce qui apparaît quand le vizir présente son plan. Ce trait du personnage est manifesté uniquement par le discours d'Haman lui-même, par la façon de le structurer. Son discours, en effet, est fait de vérités arrangées, de demi-mensonges et de purs mensonges.[10] On peut aussi ajouter que la «modération» d'Haman dont le narrateur fait état à la sortie du premier dîner d'Esther, quand il voit qu'une fois de plus, Mardochée ne se plie pas à sa volonté de puissance et de gloire, fait partie de sa capacité, non seulement de penser son plan mais de le mener à terme. Cet autocontrôle est d'ailleurs tout relatif car même en se maîtrisant, Haman va brusquer les choses par sa précipitation à suivre les conseils de sa femme et des amis/sages.

Cependant, on peut malgré tout parler d'une certaine dose de *caractérisation diversifiée* car tous les traits ne vont pas dans le même sens. En effet, à côté des traits qui dépeignent l'orgueil et la soif de gloire du personnage, qui sont le fait du narrateur et des discours du personnage même, voire de ceux des amis et de sa femme dans un premier temps, on a les traits mis en avant par le discours d'Esther lors du deuxième banquet. Là, effectivement, on voit le personnage sous l'angle négatif : «L'oppresseur et l'ennemi, c'est Haman, ce pervers». Ceci était déjà vrai dans certaines prises de parole du narrateur quand il traite Haman d'«oppresseur des Juifs» 3,10 ; 8,1 ; 9,10.24 comme le fait Esther dans son discours, laquelle tout en n'utilisant pas l'expression «oppresseur des juifs», emploie la même racine צרר 7,4.6. Cette dernière devient une sorte de titre, son identité propre, une sorte de synonyme sémantique d'«Agaguite».

Ces qualificatifs «oppresseur, pervers, ennemi» relèvent, particulièrement les deux premiers, d'un niveau que l'on pourrait qualifier d'éthique. Ils demandent à être déployés logiquement dans des actions dont Haman est le sujet,[11] en 3,6 au niveau du projet d'abord : «Haman

---

[10] Fox, *Character and Ideology*, 47–51.

[11] Il semble que dans la littérature ancienne en général le «character» de quelqu'un est révélé par ses actions, ce qui constitue une méthode indirecte de construction du personnage (Burnett, "Characterization," 11).

chercha à exterminer le peuple de Mardochée dans tout le royaume de Xerxés». Projet qu'il ne peut par lui-même mener à terme mais qui nécessite l'aide du roi, d'où son discours au souverain où il lui présente de manière insidieuse son projet tout en cachant certains de ses éléments essentiels 3,8–9.

Une fois le feu vert acquis, il se met à l'œuvre en «donnant des ordres» 3,12. L'action et le déploiement de l'«oppression» culminent en 3,13 avec l'écrit royal cacheté par son sceau selon lequel on devait «exterminer, tuer et anéantir tous les Juifs le 13 du douzième mois». Une variante et sorte d'anticipation du sort final de tous les juifs apparaît, bien sûr, dans la pendaison de Mardochée projetée par Haman, à la fin de 5,14: «La chose plut à Haman, et il fit faire le gibet». Lancé dans l'action, «Haman était venu dans la cour extérieure du palais dire au roi de pendre Mardochée au gibet qu'il avait fait préparer pour lui» 6,4.

A ces traits du personnage et comme en écho complémentaire de sa description, on doit ajouter quelques touches de ses réactions qui, par la bouche du rédacteur, complètent le portrait du personnage. On ne peut pas nier que le personnage est «réactif». En effet, en 3,5 et 5,9, «il fut rempli de fureur». Cet état psychologique contraste avec la bonne humeur et la joie qu'il manifeste par ailleurs; en 5,9 par exemple dans une succession plus que rapide de réactions, il sort très fier et content de chez Esther après le premier banquet, car il est flatté dans son orgueil, et dans la seconde qui suit, il est rempli de fureur car Mardochée lui tient tête; le narrateur joue encore, de ce point de vue, avec les contrastes et les «renversements». Mais comme déjà souligné, Haman arrive à contrôler ses états d'âme 3,6 et 5,10, tout juste pour donner un peu plus de suspense à l'intrigue en 5,10, ou pour situer le conflit dans toute son ampleur en 3,6. Un dernier trait psychologique doit être signalé en 6,12 où il est dit qu'«il rentra à sa maison abattu et la tête basse», prélude de sa déchéance finale. Les trois phases d'une courbe qui épouse celle de l'intrigue, apparaissent dans la construction psychologique du personnage: fureur-joie-abattement.

Le point de départ de la caractérisation du personnage n'est autre que l'élévation aux plus hautes fonctions du royaume: «Après ces événements, le roi Xerxès donna une haute situation à Haman, le fils de Hammedata, un Agaguite; il l'éleva et le fit siéger au-dessus de tous les ministres qui étaient avec lui» (3,1). Il faut noter que cette première touche dans la caractérisation d'Haman apparaît impromptue et n'est pas justifiée. Et si les deux facettes (orgueil/gloire et oppresseur) de la caractérisation du personnage sont ses deux paramètres principaux, on peut également dire que sa construction suit une courbe qui correspond aux deux moments de l'intrigue : ascension et chute. Ceci est largement reconnu par les commentateurs comme le ressort narratif essentiel du livre : le retournement des situations.

On a souvent discuté sur le « tournant » de l'intrigue dans le livre d'Esther. Ainsi Berg pense que le tournant se trouve en 4,13–17.[12] A juste titre, Fox considère que ces versets constituent le tournant décisif du personnage d'Esther mais pas de l'intrigue du livre en tant que tel.[13] En revanche, la construction des chapitres 3 à 8 sous forme de « thèse/antithèse » est facilement reconnaissable, et le tournant narratif apparaît alors en 6,10 où la parole du roi condamne Haman à reporter sur Mardochée la gloire qu'il pensait lui être destinée : « La série de thèses précède 6,9 où commence celle des antithèses. Le tournant narratif en 6,10 est encadré par les deux banquets d'Esther : le premier gonfle l'orgueil d'Haman, le second l'écrase. Haman lui-même désigne, ironiquement, sa propre chute en brossant la récompense de Mardochée et ainsi, par ses propres mots, il commence la série d'antithèses qui contiennent sa destruction. La femme et les amis d'Haman reconnaissent qu'il s'agit du tournant, le *commencement* de sa chute (6,13) ».[14]

Cette manifestation d'Haman est comme approfondie par une focalisation interne du narrateur omniscient lequel, utilisant une expression hébraïque classique pour ce type de focalisation, « il se dit dans son cœur », montre ainsi une fois de plus la mégalomanie du personnage renforçant son portrait. On aboutit ainsi au *point d'arrivée* de la caractérisation du personnage qui est, évidemment, aux antipodes du départ. Si celui-ci avait été l'exaltation d'Haman, son parallèle en négatif caractérisera sa chute. C'est ainsi que celle-ci commence par sa pendaison 7,10, celle de ses enfants 9,14 et la perte de ses biens 8,1. Le tout est symbolisé par la remise de l'anneau royal à Mardochée : « Enlevant son anneau qu'il avait retiré à Haman, le roi le donna à Mardochée » 8,2.

Un point très important de la construction du personnage d'Haman réside dans la manière dont *le narrateur*, et lui seul, *qualifie le personnage*. En effet, בן המדתא האגגי est la désignation du personnage par le narrateur en

---

[12] Berg, "After the Exile," 110.
[13] Fox, *Character and Ideology*, 66, 162.
[14] *Ibid.*, 162.

3,1.10; 8,5 et 9,24. En 8,3 on trouve seulement הָאֲגָגִי comme apposition au nom propre Haman. Explicitement l'appellatif «un Agaguite» ne joue aucun rôle ni dans l'intrigue ni à aucun autre niveau du récit. Mais au niveau implicite, voire dans le registre de l'intertextualité, de l'avis d'un grand nombre de commentateurs, les choses semblent différentes. Selon *1 Samuel* 15, Saül se bat contre Amaleq mais ne respecte pas la consigne donnée par Samuel concernant l'anathème à tel point que ce dernier élimine Agag, le roi des Amalécites qui avait été épargné par Saül. Cette désobéissance, d'après le texte, aurait coûté à Saül la couronne et l'appui de la divinité. Par ailleurs en Ex 17,8–16 et Dt 25,17–18 Amaleq apparaît comme l'adversaire irréconciliable à jamais d'Israël. Le qualificatif «Agaguite» devient ainsi une désignation stéréotypée de l'ennemi d'Israël, du peuple juif. Ceci expliquerait le point de départ du récit: l'animosité non justifiée de Mardochée par rapport à Haman. Mardochée le Juif ne pouvait admettre la soumission et la reconnaissance de supériorité que supposait la prosternation devant Haman. Car il est vrai que l'attitude de Mardochée ne se justifie ni ne se comprend historiquement, ni culturellement, ni bibliquement.[15] En qualifiant Haman d'Agaguite, le narrateur fait résonner chez le lecteur la corde qui le classe comme l'ennemi type d'Israël. Grâce à l'utilisation de ce trait, le récit peut se bâtir, de manière logique et compréhensible, sur l'opposition entre deux personnages types en vue de mettre en évidence la thèse du narrateur: malgré les déboires de toute sorte le peuple juif recevra toujours secours et salut. Le renversement des rôles et des situations le montre par l'ensemble de l'intrigue.

Cette «dénomination/appellation» ainsi que les émotions et les états d'âme mentionnés plus haut permettent au lecteur la construction du personnage et peuvent également lui donner l'illusion d'avoir à faire à quelque chose d'indépendant du texte, à une sorte de référent *historique*. Comme dit Sternberg: «Si, pour un agent biblique, entrer en scène sans nom [an-onyme] équivaut à le déclarer sans visage, alors porter un nom équivaut à assumer une identité: devenir un être singulier, avoir une place dans l'*history* et un avenir dans la story.»[16] Dans ce cadre se pose aussi une des questions qui agitent depuis longtemps le monde de l'analyse du récit. S'agit-il d'un «agent», d'un «type» ou d'un véritable

---

[15] Vílchez, *Rut y Ester*, 264.
[16] M. Sternberg, *The Poetics of Biblical Narrative: Ideological Literature and the Drama of Reading* (Bloomington, Ind.: Indiana University Press, 1985), 331.

«personnage»? Si ce dernier est présenté avec un nombre de traits qui dépassent les besoins du récit et de son intrigue, on aurait à faire, d'après Berlin, à un véritable personnage.[17] Si, en revanche, les traits sont quelque peu «stéréotypés» et limités en nombre et qu'ils représentent une sorte de «classe» de gens, on aurait à faire à un «type». Cette distinction fort pertinente permet, semble-t-il, de comprendre la figure d'Haman dans le livre d'Esther plutôt comme un «type» que comme un véritable personnage. En effet, tout ce qui est dit de lui contribue uniquement au profil de son rôle dans l'intrigue.

Dans ce sens les *autres personnages* du récit collaborent puissamment et directement à la construction du personnage d'Haman. Ainsi en est-il du roi, sans l'action duquel rien n'aurait été possible, et cela dans les différentes phases du récit: tout d'abord dans l'exaltation de l'Agaguite 3,1, ensuite dans le fait d'entrer dans le jeu et dans le plan que son vizir a monté en vue de faire disparaître le peuple juif, une fois que celui-ci a exposé au roi de manière astucieuse et assez subtile son plan, le souverain va aller dans son sens: «Alors le roi enleva son anneau de son doigt et le donna à Haman, le fils de Hammedata, l'Agaguite, oppresseur des Juifs. Puis le roi dit à Haman: «L'argent, on te l'abandonne, et aussi le peuple pour lui faire ce qu'il te plaira» (3,10–11). Il l'honore également en acceptant de bon coeur que son vizir soit de la partie dans les deux banquets que la reine leur offre, et encore avec une certaine ironie, fruit de son ignorance, en posant la question à Haman concernant les honneurs qu'il faut attribuer à celui que le roi veut honorer et en le chargeant de les mettre en œuvre 6,6.10. Le roi contribue aussi à la construction du personnage dans sa chute et sa mort 7,5–6.8–9. Fait aussi partie de cette chute le transfert des biens d'Haman à Esther 8,1–2 ainsi que la pendaison de ses dix enfants 9,10.12; enfin comme dernier corollaire de la contribution du roi à la construction du personnage d'Haman, l'ordre donné de rédiger de nouvelles lettres pour sauver les juifs, en totale contradiction avec celles qu'Haman a fait écrire.

Esther aussi collabore à la construction du personnage d'Haman car, par la stratégie qu'elle met en œuvre, les deux facettes du vizir vont être soulignées. En effet, le premier banquet va contribuer puissamment à cultiver l'orgueil d'Haman qui prend l'invitation de la reine comme un privilège et un honneur, ce qu'à première vue l'initiative d'Esther

---

[17] A. Berlin, *Poetics and Interpretation of Biblical Narrative* (Sheffield: Almond, 1983), 32.

semble dire. C'est ce qu'il exprime en rentrant chez lui et en exposant sa gloire à sa femme et à ses amis: le dîner chez la reine est l'un des éléments importants de sa gloire. En même temps cette scène est contrebalancée par sa «sortie» au cours de laquelle il rencontre Mardochée qui, par son attitude, lui laisse voir que sa gloire a une ombre 5,9–10. Le deuxième banquet d'Esther va précipiter et concrétiser la chute d'Haman quand la reine le dénonce avec des mots sans équivoque: «l'oppresseur et l'ennemi, c'est Haman, ce pervers!» 7,6.

Mais plus qu'Esther encore et autant que le roi, Mardochée contribue vigoureusement à profiler le personnage d'Haman. Tout d'abord son attitude vis-à-vis du vizir déclenche le conflit: «Mais Mardochée ne s'agenouillait pas et ne se prosternait pas» 3,2. S'obstinant dans son attitude, il fait en sorte que cela arrive aux oreilles d'Haman et la guerre peut commencer. Car c'est bien dans l'affrontement des deux hommes qu'est le cœur de l'intrigue et du livre: «Voyant que Mardochée ne s'agenouillait pas et ne se prosternait pas devant lui, Haman fut rempli de fureur» 3,5. A la suite de quoi il va mettre en œuvre son plan. Ce qui surprend d'abord c'est que ce plan déborde Mardochée comme le précisent 3,4.6 qui en donnent la clé: «Il leur (les serviteurs du roi) avait révélé qu'il était Juif…Mais il dédaigna de porter la main sur Mardochée, car on lui avait révélé quel était le peuple de Mardochée. Haman chercha alors à exterminer son peuple, à savoir tous les Juifs présents dans tout le royaume de Xerxès.» De manière explicite et directe Mardochée ne contribue plus à la construction du personnage d'Haman, sauf dans l'épisode de la sortie du premier banquet chez la reine 5,9–10. Sans doute est-il en première ligne dans cet affrontement qui l'oppose à Haman l'exécutant: la parade triomphale en pleine capitale pour honorer Haman au nom du roi signe, en même temps, le commencement de sa chute 6,1–11. Ce renversement de situation qui constitue le fil rouge du livre et met Mardochée à la place d'Haman en contribuant ainsi à profiler ce dernier, apparaît de manière exemplaire et presque caricaturale dans la remise de l'anneau royal qui passe du doigt d'Haman à celui de Mardochée. Le transfert des biens d'Haman à Mardochée via Esther et les autres corollaires ne sont que les conséquences de cette substitution d'Haman par Mardochée comme détenteur du sceau royal. A la substitution d'Haman par Mardochée comme détenteur du sceau royal, correspond celle de Mardochée par Haman sur le gibet.

Quelques personnages secondaires occupent également une place importante dans la construction du personnage d'Haman. Un rôle clé jouent sans doute les serviteurs du roi. Certes, le récit doit trouver un moyen pour qu'Haman soit mis au courant de la situation «a-normale» qui va déclencher le conflit de l'intrigue. Ce seront donc les serviteurs qui se chargeront de cette mission: «Alors ils informèrent Haman pour voir si les affirmations de Mardochée tiendraient: en effet, il leur avait révélé qu'il était Juif». Insensiblement l'information prend une couleur particulière, car non seulement les faits sont transmis mais aussi une autre réalité qui, sans le dire, apparaît comme la motivation de l'attitude de Mardochée et le déclencheur de la colère d'Haman ainsi que du projet meurtrier qu'il va monter.

La femme d'Haman et ses amis vont collaborer aussi à façonner son profil narratif dans les deux facettes du personnage. Tout d'abord dans la scène de 5,10–14, après qu'Haman se soit vanté de ses richesses, du pouvoir que le roi lui a confié et de l'honneur que la reine lui a fait au-dessus de tous les autres princes et nobles du royaume; femme et amis creusent le sillon de l'honneur orgueilleux d'Haman blessé par Mardochée, en lui proposant de monter le gibet pour y pendre son ennemi. Dans la deuxième scène, 6,12–14, ils annoncent la chute du vizir en donnant une curieuse raison: «si Mardochée est de la race des Juifs, tu ne pourras rien contre lui, mais tu vas sûrement continuer de déchoir devant lui». Cette explication «consonne» avec celle donnée par les serviteurs du roi en 3,3–6. Ainsi en qualifiant de «juive» l'opposition à Haman l'Agaguite, 6,13 contribue fortement à présenter le conflit du livre comme ayant une dimension foncièrement ethnique.

Plus généralement au sujet de la caractérisation des personnages, on peut se poser la question de savoir quels sont les effets de la caractérisation d'Haman sur le lecteur. Les différents éléments du portrait du vizir s'articulent autour d'un trait récurrent: son orgueil démesuré. Mais la manière de décliner ce trait a une influence certaine sur la perception que le lecteur en a. En effet, toutes les touches que le récit introduit dans la construction du personnage contribuent à forger chez le lecteur une antipathie manifeste dont la composante affective est loin d'être absente. Rien dans la narration permet de rendre, ne fut-ce qu'un instant, Haman *sympathique* aux yeux du lecteur. Quel lecteur, en effet, pourrait s'identifier avec un tel personnage? Même le lecteur fervent des Protocoles des Sages de Sion aura beaucoup de mal à s'identifier à Haman tant son projet et son destin prennent une tournure catastrophique et, en plus, ceux-ci sont présentés comme paradigmatiques pour tous ceux qui prétendent s'affronter «aux Juifs», comme l'affirment de manière lapidaire la femme et les amis-sages d'Haman: «Si Mardochée devant qui tu as commencé à déchoir, est de la race des Juifs, tu ne pourras rien contre lui» (6,13).

Pour enfoncer le clou, il n'est pas inutile de rappeler également la dimension burlesque de la peinture du personnage. Le côté «fanfaron» apparaît d'emblée et tout au long du récit mais cette dimension caricaturale du portrait du vizir atteint son sommet, c'est le cas de le dire, dans l'affaire du gibet. En effet, Haman est pendu au gibet que lui-même avait ordonné de dresser pour y pendre son ennemi, le Juif Mardochée. De cette dimension fait aussi partie le passage des biens d'Haman aux mains d'Esther et de Mardochée. En ceci le personnage s'intègre parfaitement dans l'intrigue et en dépend. Comme cela a déjà été reconnu par tous les commentateurs, le ressort essentiel de ce récit n'est autre que le «renversement» des situations, illustrant de manière caricaturale la catégorie de «péripétie» d'Aristote.[18] Ce que le récit explicite de manière cristalline en 9,1 : «Le douzième mois, c'est-à-dire 'Adar', le 13, jour où l'on devait exécuter l'ordonnance du roi et son décret, où les ennemis des Juifs espéraient dominer sur eux, il y eut un renversement de situation». La dimension burlesque fait donc partie de la caractérisation du personnage servant de repoussoir au lecteur et elle est au service de l'intrigue dont le ressort n'est autre que le renversement des situations.

CONCLUSION

La construction du personnage d'Haman dans le mal nommé «Livre d'Esther» est linéaire et univoque, voire restreinte, car la représentation et le portrait que le lecteur s'en fait ne contiennent ni nuances ni subtilités, hormis quelques touches soulignant les deux traits essentiels du vizir: l'orgueil et la démesure d'une part et la haine des Juifs de l'autre. Les autres personnages du récit et le narrateur collaborent dans la construction de ce personnage qui devient le prototype d'un conflit entre deux groupes: les Juifs et les autres. Mais le fil conducteur du récit étant le renversement des situations et la manifestation du salut des juifs, garanti envers et contre tous, Haman incarne lui-même le

---

[18] «La péripétie est, comme on l'a dit, le changement en leur contraire des actions accomplies et ce, d'après notre formule, selon la vraisemblance ou le nécessaire; ainsi dans *Œdipe*, le messager qui est arrivé en pensant réjouir Œdipe et le délivrer de ses craintes au sujet de sa mère, en lui révélant son identité, produit le contraire». Aristote, *Poétique* (Paris: Les Belles Lettres, 2001), 1452a 22–27.

mécanisme du renversement, passant du sommet de la gloire à l'abîme du déshonneur et de la mort. Le récit et ses personnages ne sont qu'une expression de ce conflit entre groupes et de l'issue de l'affrontement sans que la narration n'explicite le ressort qui permet un tel renversement ni son agent. Les personnages ont l'air de marionnettes dirigées par une «main invisible» que le texte ne désigne pas. Ils sont au service exclusif de l'intrigue assez sophistiquée et subtile. La peinture et le profil d'Haman le sont moins.

1 ENOCH 73:5–8 AND THE SYNCHRONISTIC CALENDAR

James C. VanderKam

1 Enoch 73:5–8 is the first section in the Book of the Luminaries (*1 En.* 72–82) which gives specific information about the changing illumination of the moon. The initial verse in the chapter identifies *1 En.* 73 as "a second law for the smaller luminary whose name is the moon" to distinguish it from the first law, the one for the sun, which can be read in *1 En.* 72 (see v. 2).[1] In vv. 2–3, the writer supplies information about the moon, including the statement: "Each month its emergence and setting change, and its days are like the days of the sun. When its light is evenly distributed (over its surface), it is one-seventh the light of the sun."[2] The system with which the writer works involves dividing the half of the moon facing the earth into fourteen parts, with one-fourteenth part of light added each day the moon waxes and one subtracted each day the moon wanes. One would expect, therefore, a simple listing of these fractions for a month or set of months; instead, the reader finds details about what appear to be only two consecutive days (more on this below) and a more complicated set of statements which have proved to be an exegetical challenge.

This essay has two parts. The first surveys the history of scholarship on these verses, while the second offers a critical text and interpretation influenced by information from the synchronistic calendar found in 4Q208–209 (4QEnastr^{a-b})[3] and related data from Mesopotamian astronomical texts.

---

[1] Quotations of *1 Enoch*, unless otherwise indicated, are from G.W.E. Nickelsburg and J.C. VanderKam, *I Enoch: A New Translation* (Minneapolis: Fortress, 2004).

[2] The ratio of 7:1 derives from Isa 30:26, a passage which played an important role in Enochic astronomy. See J.C. VanderKam, "Scripture in the Astronomical Book of Enoch," in *Things Revealed: Studies in Early Jewish and Christian Literature in Honor of Michael E. Stone* (ed. E.G. Chazon et al.; JSJSup 89; Leiden: Brill, 2004), 89–103.

[3] E.J.C. Tigchelaar and F. García Martínez, "4QAstronomical Enoch^{a-b} ar," *DJD* 36:95–171 with pls. III–VII.

I. History of Scholarship

The most important of the early commentaries on 1 Enoch was written by A. Dillmann, and his interpretation of *1 En.* 73:5–8 in it has had a lasting influence on the field. Dillmann argued on the basis of v. 5 that the writer was speaking about one-half of the moon. He rendered the first four Ethiopic words in the verse as "Und die eine Hälfte davon ragt um ein Siebentheil hervor." The reference to "one-fourteenth part of its light" at the end of the verse meant that the moon "ragt vor um 1/7 nämlich der halben, d.i. um 1/14 der ganzen Scheibe."[4] From this he drew the conclusion that wherever the text mentioned sevenths, it was speaking about half of the moon; when it referred to fourteenths, it intended the whole moon, though he thought the writer expressed this in a clumsy way.[5] From v. 6, Dillmann inferred another and perhaps unexpected fraction. Verse 5, he believed, dealt with a day in a month that had fifteen days until full moon, but v. 6 presented details about a day in a month with only fourteen days from conjunction until full moon (a hollow month). As he understood it, v. 6 meant: "und wann er ein Siebentheil und die Hälfte (eines Siebentheils) von seinem Lichte, also 1 1/2 Siebentheile (aber nach dem halben Mond berechnet) Licht annimmt, so beträgt ein Licht (nach dem ganzen Mond berechnet) 1/7 + 7 und die Hälfte davon, d.i. ein 1/14 und 1/28 = 3/28."[6]

The idea that sevenths have to do with half the moon, fourteenths with all of the moon, and that the writer even divided the lunar surface into twenty-eighths became the standard way in which to read the text. In his commentary on *1 Enoch*, R.H. Charles lent his considerable authority to Dillmann's exegesis. In connection with v. 5, he wrote: "In this verse and the next the *fractions are fractions of half the moon.* Thus, 1/7th of it, i.e. of the half moon = 1/14th of whole moon, and 1/14th of half moon = 1/28th of whole moon."[7] He translated the first part of v. 5 as "And the one half of her goes forth by a seventh part"; the end of the verse he emended slightly by placing a conjunction between the two fractions: "with the exception of one-seventh part of it, (and)

---

[4] A. Dillmann, *Das Buch Henoch* (Leipzig: Vogel, 1853), 228.

[5] *Ibid.* By half the moon he presumably meant the half visible from the earth.

[6] *Ibid.* The relevant part of this verse reads in Dillmann's edition: *wa-ba-ʿelata yenaśśeʾ sābeʿāyu ʾeda wa-manfaqa berhānu* (*Liber Henoch Aethiopice ad quinque codicum fidem editus* [Leipzig: Vogel, 1851], 49 [it is *1 En.* 74:6 in his edition]).

[7] R.H. Charles, *The Book of Enoch or 1 Enoch* (Oxford: Clarendon Press, 1912), 157.

the fourteenth part of her light." He supported his emendation by arguing that *'em-* (from) read by some manuscripts is a corruption of *wa-* (and).[8]

Once the idea that the writer worked with twenty-eighths arose, it became necessary to sort out how he incorporated such small fractions into his system. For this purpose, the notion that 73:5–8 deals with a day in both a hollow and a full month proved helpful. Dillmann found in 73:4 a reference to a hollow month: "it [the moon] emerges on the thirtieth day, and on that day it is visible. It becomes for you the beginning of the month on the thirtieth day with the sun in the gate where the sun emerges." The thirtieth day here is, he believed, the thirtieth day of a solar month. If the new moon is visible already in the evening of this day in a solar month, it shows that the previous lunar month was hollow, that is, one that lasted only twenty-nine days.[9] Dillmann inferred, as a result, that the writer of ch. 73 shared the view expressed in chs. 74 and 78:15–16, 79:4–5 (and implied in 74:10–11, 14–16) that lunar months alternate between twenty-nine and thirty days. When there is a month of thirty days (with fifteen days until full moon), the author posits "ein überschüssiges halbes Vierzehntel."[10]

Charles, who surmised that vv. 5–6 described a day in a month with twenty-nine days, found the extra 1/28 in v. 5: "thus 3/28ths of the whole moon are lighted on the first day of the new moon, when there are but 14 days to the full moon." About v. 6, he commented that the text did not say the moon received 1/14 + 1/28 of its light on the first day of the month; it mentions only fourteenths, not parts of them. "...it seems, therefore, that the moon is supposed to have this 1/28th to begin with. It is different in the case of the 15 days' period. On the first day of such a period the moon receives 1/28th part of light."[11] Charles thought vv. 7–8 treated the first day in a thirty-day month with fifteen days from conjunction to full moon. "On the first day the moon receives 1/28th part of light, and has advanced to some slight degree out of conjunction, but still practically sets with the sun, and

---

[8] *Ibid.* He did not explain how the corruption might have arisen, nor is the point mentioned in his edition of Ethiopic Enoch (*The Ethiopic Version of the Book of Enoch* [Anecdota Oxoniensia; Oxford: Clarendon Press, 1906]; p. 138 n. 14 would have been the place to note it).

[9] Dillmann, *Das Buch Henoch*, 227.

[10] *Ibid.*, 228.

[11] Charles, *The Book of Enoch*, 157. In this too he followed Dillmann (*Das Buch Henoch*, 228–29).

may be said to be invisible. On the second day she receives 1/14th part of light, and becomes visible to that extent. Thus the 1/28th part is ignored as being practically invisible. During the remaining 13 days the moon receives daily 1/14th part of light."[12]

In other words, when a month has fifteen days until full moon, on day one the moon has 1/28 of its light, and on each of the next fourteen days receives a 1/14 of its light. When a month has fourteen days until full moon, on day one the moon already has 3/28 of its light and receives an extra 1/14 each of the next thirteen days.[13]

O. Neugebauer, whose introduction to, translation of, and commentary on the Astronomical chapters of Enoch is only thirty-four pages long, made a disproportionate contribution to understanding the text and the kind of astronomical information found in it. Yet, while his contribution was large indeed, he offered a unique reading of some numbers in ch. 73 that seems unlikely to be correct. He maintained that there were two scales present in the text for expressing the increasing illumination of the moon: "first, in absolute terms for 1^p to 14^p (hence proportional to the illuminated area), and, secondly, in terms of solar brightness, hence increasing from $1/14 \cdot 1/7 = 1/98$ on the first day to 1/7 at full moon (cf. 73,3)."[14] He translated the last words in 73:5 as: "And its whole disc is empty (i.e.) without light, excepting its seventh part of a fourteenth part (i.e. 1/98) of the light (of the sun)." He

---

[12] Charles, *The Book of Enoch*, 158.

[13] Although Charles claimed that the 1/28th was ignored, his theory entails that at full moon the smaller luminary somehow has 29/28 of its light. One can find the approach to the fractions and months in ch. 73 taken by Dillmann and Charles repeated in more recent works. M.A. Knibb, for example, reiterates the claim about sevenths, fourteenths, and twenty-eighths and also thinks that 73:4–8 deal with months of twenty-nine and thirty days (*The Ethiopic Book of Enoch: A New Edition in the Light of the Aramaic Dead Sea Fragments* [2 vols.; Oxford: Clarendon Press, 1978], 2:171–72). D. Olson (*Enoch: A New Translation* [N. Richland Hills, TX: BIBAL, 2004], 150) also mentions months of twenty-nine and thirty days and adds: "Our author, however, is enormously fond of the number seven and prefers to speak of halfmoons (the texts merely say, 'halves') so that he may refer to each of the 14 sections as a 'seventh' (i.e., each section is a seventh of a halfmoon—a fourteenth, of course, of the whole moon)."

[14] O. Neugebauer, *The 'Astronomical' Chapters of the Ethiopic Book of Enoch* (72–82) (Det Kongelige Danske Videnskabernes Selskab Matematisk-fysiske Meddelelser 40:10; København: Munksgaard, 1981), 14 (73:3 is the verse with the statement that the light of the moon is one-seventh that of the sun). After appearing separately, Neugebauer's commentary was incorporated into M. Black, *The Book of Enoch or I Enoch: A New English Edition* (SVTP 7; Leiden: Brill, 1985) as Appendix A (pp. 386–414). For proof that fractions as precise as ninety-eighths were used, Neugebauer was able to point to Ethiopic computus texts.

continues this line of interpretation for v. 6: "And on (this) day (the moon) takes on a seventh part of one half (i.e. 1/14) of its light, and (thus) its light is the seventh of the seventh part and one half of it (i.e. 1/98 of the light of the sun)."[15]

He agreed with other commentators that v. 4 identified the previous month as hollow, but he was the first expositor to recognize that *rexuq* in v. 5 ("is distant") is not a mistake, as others had regularly claimed.[16] Rather it is a technical term: "the elongation of the moon from the sun at the evening of the first visibility is 1/14 of the total elongation (reached at full moon). The use of *reḥeqa* in the technical sense of 'elongation' is well attested in computus treatises."[17]

II. TEXT AND COMMENTARY

All of these scholars have, of course, made decisions about which readings were the preferred ones among those offered by the manuscripts. With our present evidence, I believe the following is the best Geʿez text that can be attained for 73:5–8, the one that is the basis for the translation given below. If it is the superior text, it excludes some of the readings proposed by the scholars whose views have been surveyed and

---

[15] His translation is based on some readings that differ significantly from those that underlie the translation given below. See the next section for a discussion of the preferred readings. E. Isaac has also found reference to ninety-eighths in his rendering of 73:5–8 (see v. 5: "one-seventh part of the fourteenth part of the light [of the sun]") ("1 [Ethiopic Apocalypse of] Enoch," in *OTP* 1:53).

[16] J. Flemming and L. Radermacher (*Das Buch Henoch* [GCS; Leipzig: Hinrichs, 1901], 95 n. 17; cf. Flemming, *Das Buch Henoch: Äthiopischer Text mit Einleitung und Commentar* [TUGAL 7; Leipzig: Hinrichs, 1902], 95 note to line 16; F. Martin, *Le Livre d'Hénoch* [Paris: Letouzey et Ané, 1906], 170 note to v. 5) explained *rexuq*, which they considered meaningless, as the result of a mistake followed by a faulty correction: the translator into Geʿez found the word ορατος (= seen, visible) in the base text and rendered it with a little used (or otherwise unused) form *reʾuy* (= seen, visible); a copyist misread this rare term as the more familiar *rexuq* of the present text. Charles's (*The Book of Enoch*, 157 note to v. 5; the same explanation appears in *The Ethiopic Version of the Book of Enoch*, 138 n. 7) translation reads "And the one half of her goes forth by a seventh part." He explains that *rexuq* = ἐξέχων, "which is used of the rising or appearing of the sun. ἐξέχων might in turn be a rendering of ܢܨ, which is used of the rising of the sun and stars." Knibb (*The Ethiopic Book of Enoch*, 2:172 note to v. 5) suggests, after calling *rexuq* "quite unintelligible," that the two Ethiopic roots *rehqa* and *šaraqa* (to rise) have been confused. Dillmann (*Das Buch Henoch*, 228) did not think the word needed to be changed; for him it meant that one-seventh of half the lunar disc or one-fourteenth of the whole is distant, that is, projects.

[17] Neugebauer, *The 'Astronomical' Chapters*, 15.

calls into question a number of their inferences regarding the teachings about the moon in *1 En.* 73.

5 ወመንፈቁ፡ ርኁቅ፡ ሰብዐተ፡ እደ፡ አሐደ፡ ወኵሉ፡ ክበቡ፡ ዚአሁ፡ በ኎፡ ዘአልቦ፡ ብርሃነ፡ ዘእንበለ፡ ሰብዐተ፡ እዴሁ፡ ዐሥርተ፡ ራብዐተ፡ እደ፡ ብርሃኑ፡ **6** ወበዕለተ፡ ይነሥእ፡ ሰብዓተ፡ እደ፡ መንፈቀ፡ ብርሃኑ፡ ወይከውን፡ ብርሃኑ፡ ሰብዐተ፡ እደ፡ አሐቲ፡ ወመንፈቃ። **7** ወየዐርብ፡ ምስለ፡ ፀሐይ፡ ወሶበ፡ ይሠርቅ፡ ፀሐይ፡ ይሠርቅ፡ ምስሌሁ፡ ወይነሥእ፡ መንፈቀ፡ እደ፡ ብርሃነ። ወበይእቲ፡ ሌሊት፡ በርእሰ፡ ጽባሕ፡ ዚአሁ፡ በቅድመ፡ ዕለቱ፡ ለወርን፡ የዐርብ፡ ወርን፡ ምስለ፡ ፀሐይ፡ ወይጸልም፡ በይእቲ፡ ሌሊት፡ ፮ሰብዐተ፡ እደ፡ ወንፍቃ። **8** ወይሠርቅ፡ በይእቲ፡ ዕለት፡ ሰብዐተ፡ እደ፡ ጥንቁቀ፡ ወይወፅእ፡ ወይዐዝን፡ እምሥራቅ፡ ፀሐይ፡ ወይበርሁ፡ በትራፈ፡ ዕለቱ፡ ስድስተ፡ ሰብዐተ፡ እደ፡

5 Its half is distant one-seventh part (from the sun?), and all its disc is empty, with no light except its seventh part, one-fourteenth part of its light. **6** During the day it takes on a seventh part of half its light (i.e., one-fourteenth) and its illuminated section is a half of a seventh part. **7** It sets with the sun, and when the sun rises it rises with it and receives a half part of light. During that night, at the beginning of its day, at the beginning of the moon's day, the moon sets with the sun and is dark that night six seventh parts and a[18] half. **8** It rises during that day (with) a seventh part exactly. It emerges and recedes from the rising of the sun and is bright in the rest of its day six seventh parts.

Notes on selected readings:
73:5 The statement at the end of the verse has been important in the accepted theory about fractions of the lunar surface: "its seventh part, one-fourteenth part of its light." The key question is the relation between the two phrases. In the text above, there is no explicit connection between them; they are simply juxtaposed. Commentators have assumed that in the first, half the moon is under consideration; in the second, all of it is. A number of MSS (m, t; β)[19] read the preposition *'em-* (from) before "one-fourteenth," yielding literally: its seventh part

---

[18] In Nickelsburg and VanderKam, *1 Enoch*, "its" appears here rather than "a."

[19] For the sigla, see G.W.E. Nickelsburg, *1 Enoch 1: A Commentary on the Book of 1 Enoch, Chapters 1–36, 81–108* (Hermeneia; Minneapolis: Fortress, 2001), 17. The first two listed here (m, t) belong to the group α which generally preserves an older form of the text, while the siglum β includes many MSS which often give a later text form.

from one-fourteenth part of its light. This reading is the basis for Dillmann's "bis auf einen Siebentheil von seinen vierzehn Lichttheilen" and seems to underlie Neugebauer's rendering ("its seventh part of a fourteenth part"). It will be recalled that Charles accepted this reading but emended it to *wa-* (and), translating the phrases as "one-seventh part of it, (and) the fourteenth part of her light." Given the absence of *'em-* from the oldest MSS (T⁹, g, q, u), one should consider it an addition made to solve the perceived problem of the connection between the two phrases. The manuscript evidence indicates they should be read without a connecting word. For a proposal regarding the meaning, see below.

73:6 The β group and m, t, u from the α group prefix a conjunction to *manfaqa* ("half of [its light]"); it is the reading in the editions of Dillmann, J. Flemming,[20] and Knibb;[21] but Charles properly recognized that the better supported text lacks *wa-*. The preferred reading yields a reasonably clear statement that the moon receives the equivalent of one-fourteenth of its light (one-seventh of half its light) on the first day of the lunar month.

At the end of the verse, a more problematic passage occurs. For "a seventh part," t and almost all β MSS read a compound number, with most having *7(-wa-)7* (= 7 [and] 7), a few *7(-wa-)6*. The compounds are clearly incorrect readings, as Charles recognized;[22] they represent an attempt to make the text deal with fourteenths. They have, nevertheless, found their way into several translations (Dillmann [necessarily], Knibb, Neugebauer, Uhlig)[23] and have been used as evidence that the text refers to twenty-eighths (or ninety-eighths for Neugebauer). For the last word in the verse, one could easily argue that a better reading is to place a conjunction before *manfaqā*, because it is supported not only by the β MSS but also by most MSS in the α category. Only T⁹, q, i omit it, and in p (Knibb's MS) the conjunction is written supralinearly.

---

[20] Flemming, *Das Buch Henoch*, 96. For his edition Dillmann had access only to MSS which are now classified as belonging to the β group.

[21] Since Knibb's edition is a photographic reproduction of one MS from the β family, he had no choice in the reading. But he also does not emend it in his translation where he at times introduces corrections of his one MS.

[22] Charles, *The Ethiopic Version of the Book of Enoch*, 138 n. 20. He wondered whether the compound reading was drawn from v. 8.

[23] S. Uhlig, *Das Äthiopische Henochbuch* (JSHRZ 5.6; Gütersloh: Gütersloher Verlagshaus, 1984).

Understandably, then, the translators have read the conjunction: one-seventh part *and* its half. For a justification of the translation "a half of a seventh part," see below.

73:7 At the end of the verse ("six seventh parts and a half"), one could make a case that the better supported reading is "seven seven parts and a half." Although many MSS attest that reading (including g, u) and it appears in Charles's translation ("the fourteen parts"; cf. Uhlig), it represents a misunderstanding of the text. The reading "six seventh [parts]" enjoys the support of m, q, t, and T⁹, along with a couple of the later copies. The better reading indicates that the text is speaking about 13/14 of the lunar surface.

73:8 The word rendered "is bright" (*yebarreh*) is the reading with the greatest manuscript support, but it makes no sense in this verse. At this point in the text, where the second day of the lunar month is being described, we expect to read that the moon was illuminated over one-seventh (= 2/14) of its surface and thus was bright in one-seventh part, not in six-sevenths. Unless this note is a stray remnant from a more complete list that included days at the end of a month and is thus out of sequence here where the second day of the month is under discussion, a verb with the meaning "is dark" would be expected. See below for a suggestion regarding how the Geʿez text arose.

These textual notes are meant to prepare the way for a solution to the meaning of the passage. The following paragraphs offer evidence that two widely accepted conclusions about the pericope are unsupported by it. First, there is no indication in *1 En.* 73:5–8 that some verses deal with the first day in a month of twenty-nine and others with the first day in a month of thirty days. Information about months with these varying lengths is explicit in 78:15–16, 79:4–5 (cf. 74:10–11, 14–16) but not in 73:5–8. A straightforward reading of 73:5–8 shows that two consecutive days at the beginning of one month are the subject, not days taken from two months of different lengths.[24] *1 Enoch* 73:5–7

---

[24] Although the commentators regularly claim that days from months of two different lengths figure in these few verses, they do not agree which verses attest a hollow and which a full month. Dillmann (*Das Buch Henoch*, 228–29): v. 5 = thirty-day month, vv. 6–7 = twenty-nine-day month; Martin (*Le Livre d'Hénoch*, 170): vv. 5–6 = twenty-nine-day month, vv. 7–8 = thirty-day month; Flemming-Radermacher (*Das Buch Henoch*, 95–96): only twenty-nine-day months perhaps, but v. 5 deals with a case of conjunction in the evening, v. 6 with conjunction in the morning (they thought this

provide data for day 1; v. 8 begins to supply them for day 2. Second, the notion that the writer mentions twenty-eighths of the lunar surface is a product of misreading.

In the next paragraphs, comments are made on each of the verses in 73:5–8 in order to document the claims made in the previous paragraph and to explain the meaning of the passage.

But first it is necessary to comment on v. 4 which introduces the section under discussion: "In this way it [= the moon] rises with its beginning toward the east; it emerges on the thirtieth day, and on that day it is visible. It becomes for you the beginning of the month on the thirtieth day with the sun in the gate where the sun emerges." The passage begins with the time of first lunar visibility which occurs the night of what is termed day thirty. This day thirty has been understood since Dillmann as the thirtieth day in a solar month.[25] By writing that the crescent first becomes visible on the thirtieth of the solar month, the author would be indicating that his calendar is synchronistic; experts have also concluded from this line that the previous lunar month was hollow, that is, it lasted twenty-nine days. It was an easy inference from the text so understood that here, as elsewhere, the writer knows about hollow months and therefore also about full months. If this is the case, the system would differ from the ideal astronomical year of 360 days with twelve thirty-day months (solar and lunar) found in a series of cuneiform texts (MUL.APIN, *Enuma Anu Enlil* XIV, etc.) with which the Book of the Luminaries otherwise shows such close parallels.[26] However, J. Ben-Dov, who has studied the Mesopotamian evidence in comparison with the Enochic astronomy and that of the Qumran calendrical texts, maintains that the thirtieth day refers to the previous lunar month

---

interpretation avoided the problematic result that in months with fifteen days until full moon the moon acquired 29/28 of its light); Charles (*The Book of Enoch*, 157): vv. 5–6 = twenty-nine-day month, vv. 7–8 = thirty-day month; Knibb (*The Ethiopic Book of Enoch*, 2.171–72): vv. 4–5 = twenty-nine-day month, vv. 7–8 = thirty-day month (v. 6 is obscure). Neugebauer finds no such division here, nor apparently does Uhlig. E. Rau also takes the position that the text deals with two days from a single period ("Kosmologie, Eschatologie und die Lehrautorität Henochs: Traditions- und formgeschichtliche Untersuchungen zum äth: Henochbuch and zu verwandten Schriften" [Ph.D. dissertation, University of Hamburg, 1974], 198–99).

[25] *Das Buch Henoch*, 227–28.

[26] The fullest published study of this topic to date is M. Albani, *Astronomie and Schöpfungsglaube: Untersuchungen zum Astronomischen Henochbuch* (WMANT 68; Neukirchen: Neukirchener Verlag, 1994).

and cites parallels in cuneiform texts for this practice.[27] What should be remembered for our purposes is that, even if v. 4 implies that the author of this law was aware of hollow and full months, it does not follow that the tabulation in vv. 5–8 illustrates both types.

73:5 The position of the moon relative to the sun and the amount of the moon's surface that is illuminated on the first day of its month are the subjects of v. 5. Neugebauer considered the first clause ("Its half is distant one-seventh part") the end of the preceding verse.[28] It would then be another preliminary statement before the scheme of fractions of light begins in the remainder of v. 5. Wherever it belongs, an important term is the word *rexuq* ("is distant"; no cognate is preserved in the Aramaic fragments). As we have seen, Neugebauer recognized the word as referring to the elongation of the moon from the sun. "At the beginning of the new month the moon has obtained enough (easterly) elongation from the sun to be visible at sunset. At conjunction, however, the moon is still nearer to the sun and thus rises and sets (invisibly) in the same gate as the sun."[29] So the meaning is that on the night when the moon is first visible it is one-fourteenth the elongation from the sun that it will achieve at full moon. Neugebauer translated: "(but) at a distance (from the sun) of half of a seventh part." That is, he takes *manfaqu*, the first word in the sentence, to belong together with the words "one-seventh part."[30] Neugebauer's explanation best accounts for the text and has been accepted by Uhlig and Albani.[31] Consequently the first part of

---

[27] J. Ben-Dov, "Astronomy and Calendars at Qumran: Sources and Trends" (Ph.D. dissertation, Jerusalem: Hebrew University of Jerusalem, 2005), 73 [Hebrew]. From the words "its days are like the days of the sun" in 73:3, he concluded that the model here works only with a schematic calendar in which, as in the traditional Mesopotamian calendar, there were always thirty days in a month, whether a solar or a lunar month (72). M. Albani had wondered whether this was the case but thought Neugebauer's view—that the clause means a lunar and solar day have the same length—was more likely to be correct (*Astronomie and Schöpfungsglaube*, 82 n. 125).

[28] Neugebauer, *The 'Astronomical' Chapters*, 15.

[29] Neugebauer, *The 'Astronomical' Chapters*, 15. He adds a parenthetical comment that matters are so simple only "in the schematic lunar calendar which ignores, of necessity, all complexities of the actual lunar motion."

[30] The ways in which some other commentators read the first sentence of v. 5 were catalogued above.

[31] Uhlig, *Das Äthiopische Henochbuch*, 645 n. 5a; Albani, *Astronomie and Schöpfungsglaube*, 197 n. 151. At an earlier time, Rau had underlined the fact that, while in ch. 72 the course of the sun is described without reference to that of the moon, here the path of the moon is depicted in relation to that of the sun ("Kosmologie," 199–202).

the verse quantifies the distance the moon is from the sun, a distance or elongation that allows the crescent to be seen.

Having specified the distance of the moon from the sun on the first lunar day, the author next reports that, regarding illumination, the lunar disc is devoid of light apart from "its seventh part, one-fourteenth part of its light." As we have seen, earlier expositors inferred that the former phrase referred to half the moon, the latter to the entire moon. The Aramaic copies of the synchronistic calendar from Qumran cave 4 prove helpful for exploring this issue.[32] In them, the fractions used for the light/dark parts of the moon are sevenths and halves of sevenths, that is, fourteenths, but in them fourteenths are only implied, not explicit. In 1 Enoch 73:5 the words "its seventh part," which can hardly mean "one-fourteenth part," may be the result of a mistake which is explainable from the wording of the Aramaic fragments. In them one-half of a seventh is expressed as שביע פלג (e.g. 4Q208 10a 6; 209 2 ii 5, 7; 6 8) or פלג שביע (see 4Q208 10a 8; 209 11 1). If the latter expression appeared in the original text of 73:5, it could have been translated as if פלג meant "part" rather than "half." The original meaning of the statement would, then, have been "one half of (its) seventh," with the words "one-fourteenth part" serving to gloss the same fraction in different terms.[33] With this suggestion, a meaningful text results. On the first day of the lunar month, a half of a seventh, that is, 1/14 of the moon's surface is covered with light.

73:6 Continuing the description for day one in a lunar month, the text says that the moon receives or takes a certain fraction of its light.[34] Again there are many variants in the MSS as copyists attempted to make sense of the tabulation. Here, too, it is helpful to consult the wording of fractions in the Aramaic fragments of the synchronistic

---

[32] No claim is made here that a small part of the synchronistic calendar known now from 4Q208–209 is the original text (via a Greek translation) behind *1 En.* 73:5–8. The items listed in the two texts show too many differences to allow such a conclusion. Rather, the claim is that *1 En.* 73:5–8 exhibits the pattern for the increasing illumination of the moon present in the Qumran copies.

[33] Since fourteenths are never expressed in the surviving fragments of 4Q208–209, a phrase such as "one-fourteenth part of its light" in the *Book of the Luminaries* would have to be considered a later explanation of the implied fraction.

[34] Since the word *berhānu* ("its light") follows the verb, it is unlikely that Tigchelaar and García Martínez are correct in claiming that *yenaśśe'* (or *tenaśśe'*) here is "a misinterpretation of the (Greek) translator of the verb קבל which signifies here 'to be dark', or 'to darken (itself)'" (*DJD* 36:98).

calendar, because they provide a plausible explanation for the strange wording in the Ethiopic copies. Since the writer has said that the moon has no light of its own but receives it from the sun, he employs a verb meaning *to take or receive (naś'a)*, and after it he expresses the fraction of its light, that is, the illuminated part of the lunar surface, on this first day. The expression in the first clause is verbose but does mean "a seventh part of half its light."

The second expression is more problematic (literally: its light becomes one seventh part [and?] its half). There are two principal difficulties here. First, the words *sab'ata 'eda* have accusative endings after the verb *yekawwen*, as is normal. The word *'eda*, which is treated as feminine in this instance, serves in expressions indicating the part of a whole or fractional numbers, as Dillmann calls them.[35] The number *'aḥatti* should modify *'eda*, but the form is not accusative as one would expect (a couple of MSS do supply an accusative ending, but their reading is not likely to be original). In this context, the word probably is the equivalent of an indefinite article. Second, the word *manfaq* is the equivalent of פלג in the Aramaic fragments. Throughout those fragments, there is repeated use of חד and the two words that express the fractions (seventh[s], half of a seven). The Aramaic equivalent of the Ethiopic would be (if *wa-* is prefixed to *manfaqā*) שביע חד ופלג (see 4Q209 7 ii 10). Another expression is פלג שביע חד (see 4Q209 6 8). The first means one-seventh and one-half; the second means one-half seventh.

I propose that the form *(wa-)manfaqā* represents a mistaken attempt at some point in the transmission history of the text to make sense of it. If we suppose that the original was שביע פלג, as in v. 5, then the first fraction repeats the information from the preceding verse: the moon receives one-half of a seventh part of its total light so that its illuminated portion is one-fourteenth of its surface facing the earth. The Ethiopic MSS betray some confusion regarding the meaning of the word for "half" when positioned after the word for "seventh." As a result "a seventh part of half its light" is the curious way in which they express "one-fourteenth of its light." Insertion of "and" before "half" marks a further attempt to reinterpret the text as though it referred to one-seventh plus one-half of the seventh. Or, if a word for "one" is retained (a form of it is present in all the Ethiopic copies), one could posit that

---

[35] A. Dillmann and C. Bezold, *Ethiopic Grammar* (2d ed.; London: Williams & Norgate, 1907), 159 2 (f) (p. 373).

an original פלג שביע חד was reinterpreted as if the word פלג referred to an additional half of a seventh; to make this meaning clear, פלג was moved to final position in the expression, set off with a conjunction, and reinforced with a suffix. For use of the number "one" (*'aḥatti*) with "seventh," see חד in 4Q208 7 3; 209 2 ii 10; 6 8; 7 ii 8, 10, 11, 13.

73:7 The verse completes the treatment of day one in a lunar month. It adds information beyond the previous verses by noting that the sun and moon, since the time is so close to their conjunction (and thus the invisibility of the moon), still rise and set at (nearly) the same time. The half part of light the moon receives is the 1/14 that has been mentioned several times. If 1/14 of the lunar surface was lighted by the sun, then on that first day 13/14 of it remained dark. The literal wording for the latter fraction is "six seventh parts and a half" which comports with the way this fraction would have been expressed in the Aramaic fragments (less the suffix; see 4Q209 2 ii 8).

73:8 The last verse of the chapter takes up the second day of a lunar month but, after it furnishes more limited information about it than the previous verses gave about day one, it breaks off and the tabulation is not resumed. When the moon rises on this second day, exactly one-seventh of its surface is illuminated. This illustrates the expected pattern, evident in the Aramaic fragments, that each day of the waxing period an additional 1/14 of the moon's surface receives light from the sun.

The remainder of the verse raises several questions that have exercised the commentators and led to various attempts at calculating the fractions with which the author was working. The first part of this section ("It emerges and recedes from the rising of the sun") deals with the moon's elongation from the sun. The same phenomenon was listed regarding day one in the lunar cycle (73:5). The text reads literally "from the east of the sun," "but one should expect a motion 'away from the sun toward east' (as in verse 4) instead of a 'receding from the rising sun.' Perhaps this is simply a scribal error."[36] It may be, however, that *'em-mešrāqa ḍaḥay* means "on the east side of the sun" (see 74:6), not "from the east side of the sun." Isaac translates: "and recedes toward the east (away) from where the sun rises." A parallel is Gen 2:8, where

---

[36] Neugebauer, *The 'Astronomical' Chapters*, 15–16.

the garden is said to be מקדם, which the Septuagint renders as κατα ανατολας. Or, one could translate *mešrāqa* as *rising* rather than *east*. The moon, then, is pictured correctly as appearing farther away from the sun than on the first day.

The last clause of the verse ("and is bright in the rest of its day six seventh parts") says the opposite of what one would expect. The pattern, if it is correctly understood, calls for a statement that the moon is illuminated during the remainder of day two on 1/7 of its surface facing the earth and that 6/7 of the surface remains dark. But the text says that 6/7 (some MSS read 7/7) of the surface is lighted. There are no variants of any importance for solving this interpretive problem, so scholars have turned to other kinds of solutions. Dillmann translated "und macht an seinen übrigen Tagen die sieben und sieben Theile leuchten." That is, he understood the words to be addressing the remaining *days* of the moon's waxing, during which the other parts of it would receive light from the sun, until all fourteen parts of it were illuminated.[37] For Dillmann, the subject of the sentence is not just day two but days two through fourteen of a month. Flemming, Martin, Charles, and Knibb adopted the same solution (though they correctly preferred the reading 6 and 7 = thirteen parts).[38] A problem with this solution is that the word *'elatu* is singular, not plural and that therefore the text is not speaking about the rest of its days (of waxing) but about the remainder of *day* two. If the writer intended *days*, he would have used *māwa'el* as he does in 74:2, 6, 7, 8, when addressing the same subject.[39] Neugebauer properly translated "during the remaining (part) of its day."[40]

A text-critical proposal may solve the problem. First, because the entry for lunar day two is truncated, the final clause may be the result

---

[37] *Das Buch Henoch*, 228–29.

[38] Flemming, *Das Buch Henoch*, 95–96; Martin, *Le Livre d'Hénoch*, 171; Charles, *The Book of Enoch*, 158; Knibb, *The Ethiopic Book of Enoch*, 2.173.

[39] In 78:6, the writer shows how he expresses the idea that Dillmann and the others have thought is present in 73:8: "on the fourteenth it completes its light" (cf. 78:11).

[40] *The 'Astronomical' Chapters*, 14 (Uhlig translates as Neugebauer did: "während des übrigen [Teiles?] seines Tages" [*Das Äthiopische Henochbuch*, 646]), although Neugebauer adds: "Why the 'remaining part of the day' is mentioned in the present context I do not know." The fragments of 4Q208–209 show that "in the rest of this day" occurs as part of the pattern in the synchronistic calendar, both for the first and the second part of a month, although the Aramaic does not speak of the moon's shining in the rest of the day but in the rest of the night. It does use the expression "it is covered the rest of this day" but for the second half of the month (*DJD* 36:97–99).

of combining two (or more) separate items in what would once have been a full listing of data for each day. The entry for day one ends with an indication of how large a fraction of the moon remains dark (v. 7) after statements about how much was illuminated. When the section for day two was abbreviated, the verb of one clause (shines) may have accidentally been combined with the fraction from another sentence, thus producing the current text. Where it should have said something like "it shines one-seventh part in the rest of its day and is dark six-seventh parts," it now says "it shines six-seventh parts." Such a confusion could have been encouraged by the similarity in the wording of the fractions which caused parablepsis to occur. Or, if the text is correct as attested by the Ethiopic copies, this clause would have come from an entry for the third to the last day of the month, when the moon has 1/7 of its light remaining and two lunar days in which to lose it. This seems less plausible than the first solution.

To conclude, 1 Enoch 73:5–8 supplies full details for the first day in a lunar month and begins to do so for the second day in that same month before the text breaks off. The original formulae, which used only the terms sevenths and halves of sevenths, have been modified so that the Ethiopic texts speak of both sevenths and fourteenths. Neither the Aramaic nor the Ethiopic text evidences fractions so small as twenty-eighths or ninety-eighths. In the pattern underlying these verses, in each day of a schematic month the moon, as it recedes from the sun, receives light over 1/14 of its surface during the waxing period; the reverse presumably happened in the second part of the month (as it does in the synchronistic calendar of 4Q208–209). Confusion was caused in the transmission of the text by the expression שביע פלג which, as the Aramaic fragments show, means "one-half of a seventh," that is, a fourteenth. When it was taken to mean "a seventh, a half," it took on the sense of a seventh and its half and thus altered the text and produced the confusing statements found especially in vv. 5–7. These confusing statements in turn led to modern claims that the text deals at times with half, at times with all of the moon. 1 Enoch 73:8 may be a remnant from a later entry in a full list of the days in a lunar month, or more likely, the wrong verb has found its way into the text from a parallel line regarding the amount of the moon's surface that remained dark.

EVIDENCE OF *1 ENOCH* 10:4 IN MATTHEW 22:13?

Joseph Verheyden

As is well known, some Christian authors at least were familiar with certain themes and motifs from the Enochic tradition and probably even from Enochic literature itself and this from very early on. There are not only the allusions and citations in Clement of Alexandria or Origen, but also some New Testament authors prove to have had access to this literature or the traditions reflected in it. The most famous instance is of course the explicit reference to *1 Enoch* (1:9) in Jude 14–15. In the margins of NA[27], one finds several other possible parallels and allusions.[1] In the following, I propose to have a new look at a passage in the Gospel of Matthew that does not figure in this list, but that has been linked to *1 Enoch* by a few commentators and in a couple of specific studies.

I

Matthew's version of the Parable of the Marriage Feast (22:1–10), which most probably stems from Q (Q 14:16–24), not only contains a very harsh and provocative verse that is not attested in the parallel in Luke (v. 7), but also continues beyond the original parable to include the story of the confrontation between the king-host and the guest with no wedding garment (22:11–14).[2] At the order of the king, the man

---

[1] See the list on pp. 804–805 (Appendix IV). Cf. also R.H. Charles, *The Book of Enoch* (Oxford: Clarendon Press, 1893), 41–49.

[2] The Q origin of the parable is not undisputed, and neither is the origin of the extra verse 7 and of the expansion at the end. See the discussion by R. Hoppe, "Das Gastmahlgleichnis Jesu (Mt 22,1–10/Lk 14,16–24) und seine vorevangelische Traditionsgeschichte," in *Von Jesus zum Christus: Christologische Studien: Festgabe für Paul Hoffmann zum 65. Geburtstag* (ed. idem and U. Busse; BZNW 93; Berlin: de Gruyter, 1998), 277–93; H.T. Fleddermann, *Q: A Reconstruction and Commentary* (BiTS 1; Leuven: Peeters, 2005), 722–39. On the parable, cf. U. Luz, *Das Evangelium nach Matthäus (Mt 18–25)* (EKK I/3; Zürich: Benziger, 1997), 229–51; W.D. Davies and D.C. Allison, *The Gospel According to Matthew* (vol. 3; ICC; Edinburgh: T&T Clark, 1997), 193–209.

is bound hand and foot and cast into the outer darkness (13 δήσαντες αὐτοῦ πόδας καὶ χεῖρας ἐκβάλετε αὐτὸν εἰς τὸ σκότος τὸ ἐξώτερον).[3]

In the *Book of the Watchers* (*1 En.* 10:4a), it is told that Raphael, as second of the archangels, receives an identical command by the Lord to bind Asael by his hands and his feet and throw him out into the darkness.[4] The various versions of 10:4a run as follows (for A see below):

> Gp Καὶ τῷ 'Ραφαὴλ εἶπεν Δῆσον τὸν Ἀζαὴλ ποσὶν καὶ χερσίν, καὶ βάλε αὐτὸν εἰς τὸ σκότος
>
> Gs Καὶ τῷ 'Ραφαὴλ εἶπε Πορεύου, 'Ραφαήλ, καὶ δῆσον τὸν Ἀζαήλ· χερσὶ καὶ ποσὶ συμπόδισον αὐτόν, καὶ ἔμβαλε αὐτὸν εἰς τὸ σκότος
>
> E "And secondly the Lord said to Raphael, 'Bind Azaz'el hand and foot (and) throw him into the darkness!'"

The description of the judgement that Raphael has to execute goes on in 10:4b–6 and is followed in 10:7–8 by a positive counterpart on

---

[3] The variant reading ἄρατε αὐτὸν κτλ. (D it sy) is retained by H. von Soden in his edition (*Die Schriften des Neuen Testaments* [Berlin: Duncker, 1902–1913]), and of course by F. Blass, *Evangelium secundum Matthaeum* (Leipzig: Teubner, 1901), 79, and by A. Merx, *Das Evangelium Matthaeus* (Berlin: Reimer, 1902), who calls it "die vernünftige Anordnung, wenn man Jemand hinauswerfen will" (299), which as a matter of fact explains why it is most probably the secondary reading. See also J. Wellhausen, *Das Evangelium Matthaei* (2d ed.; Berlin: Reimer, 1914), 107.

[4] On the structure and composition of the *Book of the Watchers* (*1 En.* 6–11), see most recently G.W.E. Nickelsburg, *1 Enoch 1: A Commentary on the Book of 1 Enoch, Chapters 1–36, 81–108* (Hermeneia; Minneapolis: Fortress, 2001), 165–72; S. Bhayro, *The Shemihazah and Asael Narrative of 1 Enoch 6–11. Introduction, Text, Translation and Commentary with Reference to Ancient Near Eastern and Biblical Antecedents* (AOAT 322; Münster: Ugarit-Verlag, 2005), 11–20. Bhayro is critical of Nickelsburg's suggestion to look for Hellenistic parallels (the Prometheus myth) for the narrative about Asael helping humankind and rather sides with P.D. Hanson, "Rebellion in Heaven, Azazel, and Euhemeristic Heroes in I Enoch 6–11," *JBL* 96 (1977): 195–233, in turning to Near Eastern parallels. *1 Enoch* 10:4 is preserved in the Ethiopic version (E) and in a double version in Greek, in the codex Panopolitanus (Gp) and in the *Chronography* of George Syncellus (Gs). There also exists a scrap of the Aramaic (A), which will be dealt with below. The issue of which text of *1 Enoch* to cite is a notoriously difficult question as the Aramaic is mostly too fragmentary, and none of the versions can claim to represent the original all throughout. I will cite both Gp and Gs when available and Isaac's translation of E, which renders the text of the oldest known manuscript, but while also noting relevant variants. See E. Isaac, "1 (Ethiopic Apocalypse of) Enoch," in *OTP* 1:5–89. The Greek is cited according to the edition of M. Black, *Apocalypsis Henochi graece* (PVTG 3; Leiden: Brill, 1970). The whole dossier of texts is now collected again by Bhayro, *Asael Narrative*, 55–115 (94). Bhayro edits E according to the seventeenth-century manuscript EMML 6686 that resembles the one used by M.A. Knibb for his edition (see the comments on 45–49 [47]).

the restoration of the earth.[5] The resemblance of the commission in 10:4 with Matt 22:13 seems to have gone unnoticed in Enochic studies for quite some time. A.G. Hoffmann and A. Dillmann compared the motif of the temporary punishment of the fallen angel with Jude 6 and 2 Pet 2:4, a line of interpretation that can be traced back to Grotius and Scaliger.[6] Hoffmann contrasts the way the concept of darkness is used in *1 Enoch* to that in Matt 8:12; 22:13; 25:30. For the evangelist, it had a metaphorical meaning ("des höchsten Glückes beraubt und dem grössesten Elende Preis gegeben seyn"), whereas in *1 Enoch* it would refer to the equally biblically well-attested "Vorstellung des dunkeln Kerkers" (e.g., Ps 107:10, 14).[7] Older commentators have mostly focused on the identification of the mysterious Duda'el with the "wilderness" of Lev 16:10, 22. First suggested by E.E. Geiger, this interpretation was emphatically defended by R.H. Charles: "This is clearly the Dudael mentioned in the verse, and it is thus a definite locality in the neighbourhood of Jerusalem."[8] F. Martin was more reserved: "Dudaël serait identique à Bethkhaduda."[9] More critical still was A. Lods, who wondered where the initial *he* has gone and why the word is transformed in *1 Enoch* by adding *-el*.[10] Lods seems to have been the

---

[5] Cf. the text of 10:4b–6 according to:

Gp καὶ ἄνοιξον τὴν ἔρημον τὴν οὖσαν ἐν τῷ Δαδουὴλ κἀκεῖ βάλε αὐτόν, 5 καὶ ὑπόθες αὐτῷ λίθους τραχεῖς καὶ ὀξεῖς καὶ ἐπικάλυψον αὐτῷ τὸ σκότος. καὶ οἰκησάτω ἐκεῖ εἰς τοὺς αἰῶνας, καὶ τὴν ὄψιν αὐτοῦ πώμασον καὶ φῶς μὴ θεωρείτω· 6 καὶ ἐν τῇ ἡμέρᾳ τῆς μεγάλης τῆς κρίσεως ἀπαχθήσεται εἰς τὸν ἐνπυρισμόν.

Gs καὶ ἄνοιξον τὴν ἔρημον τὴν οὖσαν ἐν τῇ ἐρήμῳ Δουδαήλ, καὶ ἐκεῖ πορευθεὶς βάλε αὐτόν 5 καὶ ὑπόθες αὐτῷ λίθους ὀξεῖς καὶ λίθους τραχεῖς καὶ ἐπικάλυψον αὐτῷ σκότος. καὶ οἰκησάτω ἐκεῖ εἰς τὸν αἰῶνα καὶ τὴν ὄψιν αὐτοῦ πώμασον καὶ φῶς μὴ θεωρείτω· 6 καὶ ἐν τῇ ἡμέρᾳ τῆς κρίσεως ἀπαχθήσεται εἰς τὸν ἐμπυρισμὸν τοῦ πυρός.

E "And he made a hole in the desert which was in Duda'el and cast him there; 5 he threw on top of him rugged and sharp rocks. And he covered his face in order that he may not see light; 6 and in order that he may be sent into the fire on the great day of judgment." Bhayro reads imperatives all through vv. 4 and 5 and inserts "and let him dwell there forever" in the midst of v. 5.

[6] See A.G. Hoffmann, *Das Buch Henoch* (Die Apokalyptiker der ältern Zeit unter Juden und Christen; Jena, 1833), 135. A. Dillmann, *Das Buch Henoch übersetzt und erklärt* (Leipzig: Vogel, 1853), 100: "Aus dem N.T. ist über diese vorläufige Strafhaft der gefallenen Engel zu vergleichen Judae V. 6., 2 Petr. 2,4."

[7] Hoffmann, *Henoch*, 136.

[8] Charles, *Enoch*, 22–23. Cf. E.E. Geiger, "Einige Worte über das Buch Henoch," *Jüdische Zeitschrift für Wissenschaft und Leben* 3 (1864–1865): 196–204 (200).

[9] *Le Livre d'Hénoch traduit sur le texte éthiopien* (Documents pour l'étude de la Bible: Les apocryphes de l'Ancien Testament; Paris: Letouzey et Ané, 1906), 23.

[10] *Le Livre d'Hénoch: Fragments grecs découverts à Akhmîm (Haute-Égypte): Publiés avec les variantes du texte éthiopien* (Paris: Leroux, 1892), 117: "Le rapprochement est séduisant; seulement que serait devenu le ה et pourquoi aurait-on ajouté -ηλ?"

first to refer to Matt 22:13 for the expression "hand and foot," but only to point out the inversion in the latter, not to suggest that there might be a link between the two passages.[11] Martin cites Matt 22:14 (not 13), together with 20:16 and 24:31 (and Mark 13:19; Luke 21:23; Rev 17:14) in connexion with *1 En.* 1:1 as variant ways of referring to "the day of affliction."[12] J.T. Milik saw no need to mention the parallel in Matt 22:13.[13] And neither did Knibb, who appears to be charmed by S. Aalen's rather more gratuitous suggestion that Gp's "together" (E reads "instantly") in *1 En.* 99:9 might be compared to another verse from the same parable (Luke 14:18 ἀπὸ μιᾶς).[14] M. Black dwells on the motif of the darkness, which he refuses to connect with cosmological thoughts (contra Milik) or to associate with death and hell (as was done before by Hoffmann, see above n. 5) and definitely not with Matthew: "it seems unlikely that...Mt. 8:12 had ever crossed the original writer's mind in this verse."[15] G.W.E. Nickelsburg cites several instances of the fettering of a person (Acts 12:7; 16:24–27; Josephus, *Ant.* 19.295) or even of a demon (Raphael binding Asmodeus in Tob 8:3) and calls it "a quasi-technical term for the neutralising of a demon," with reference to *T. Levi* 18.12; Mark 3:27 par.; 5:3–4; Rev 20:2.[16] He continues to note, "The language of v 4b as a whole becomes traditional and is reflected in Matt 22:13 and possibly in *Ahikar* 7.27 (Arab.),"[17] but apparently that is as far as he wants to go with regard to the parallel in Matthew.

A.H. M'Neile has been credited with having introduced the parallel in Matthean studies when concluding his commentary on 22:13, which in its current form he ascribed to the evangelist, by observing that the verse "may be influenced by [1] Enoch x.4."[18] His suggestion

---

[11] *Ibid.*: "Azaël doit être lié pieds et mains (AS χερσὶ κ. ποσὶ, ordre plus ordinaire 88,1. 3; cf. pourtant Mt. 22,13)."

[12] Martin, *Le Livre d'Hénoch*, 1.

[13] J.T. Milik, *The Books of Enoch: Aramaic Fragments of Qumrân Cave 4* (Oxford: Clarendon Press, 1976).

[14] M.A. Knibb, *The Ethiopic Book of Enoch: A New Edition in the Light of the Aramaic Dead Sea Scrolls* (Oxford: Clarendon Press, 1978), 2:233.

[15] *The Book of Enoch or I Enoch: A New English Edition with Commentary and Textual Notes* (SVTP 7; Leiden: Brill, 1985), 134.

[16] *1 Enoch 1*, 221 and n. 11.

[17] *Ibid.*

[18] *The Gospel according to St. Matthew* (London: MacMillan, 1915; repr. New York: St. Martin's Press, 1965), 317. The reference to M'Neile is from Rubinkiewicz (see below). A quick search in a number of nineteenth-century commentaries seems to confirm that he may have been the first to have suggested such an influence.

went largely unnoticed, as D.C. Sim has pointed out, adding only the name of R.H. Gundry as the one other commentator who offers a comparably general comment.[19] A few years earlier, R. Rubinkiewicz had argued that there must be a literary relationship between the two passages on the pre-Matthean level.[20] Rubinkiewicz indeed regards the parable of 22:11–14 as a pre-Matthean composition, which the evangelist largely left unaltered when copying it into his gospel. He bases his conclusion about the connexion on the correct observation that Matt 22:13 is almost identical in structure and wording with *1 En.* 10:4a, both in E and in Gp/Gs. The few differences there are between Matt 22:13 and these three versions are easily explainable as either immaterial, as variant or possibly secondary readings, or as due to the difference in context. For obvious reasons, Matthew leaves out the name of Asael. E's Azazel (for original Asael) is an attempt to strengthen the allusion to Lev 16:10, 21–22. E and Gs read "hands and feet," while Gp agrees with Matthew in inverting the order. The accusative in Matthew (πόδας καὶ χεῖρας) instead of the dative does not argue against dependence and neither does Matthew's compound ἐκβάλλω (Gp βάλε, Gs ἔμβαλε) or τὸ ἐξώτερον, which most probably stems from his pen.[21] Rubinkiewicz could have mentioned the possibility that ειπε in Gs can be read as an aorist (εἶπε; so E and Gp) or as an imperative εἰπέ, though the latter is rather implausible as Black has pointed out.[22] He also seems to have missed the fact that in Gs it is possible to take the phrase "hands and feet" with συμπόδισον instead

---

[19] *Matthew: A Commentary on His Literary and Theological Art* (Grand Rapids: Eerdmans, 1982), 440: a mere "Cf. *1 Enoch* 10:4." Cf. D.C. Sim, "Matthew 22.13a and 1 Enoch 10.4a," *JSNT* 47 (1992): 3–19 (3). One can now add the names of Davies and Allison who "deem literary influence likely" (*Matthew*, 3:206). D.A. Hagner, *Matthew 14–28* (WBC 33B; Dallas, Tex.: Word Books, 1995), 631, speaks of "possible dependence" but leaves it open. Luz, on the other hand, is not convinced: "Trotz der sprachlichen Nähe von V 13 zu gr Hen 10,4…, glaube ich nicht, das jener Text Mt 22,11–13 beeinflusst hat" (*Matthäus*, 3:245 n. 71). Both the binding and the casting out are said to be "geläufige Wendungen" (with reference to Josephus, *Ant.* 19.294 for the first one; see also John 11:44 and Acts 21:11), but it is not noted that the combination of the two is not commonly attested.

[20] *Die Eschatologie von Henoch 9–11 und das Neue Testament* (ÖBS 6; Klosterneuburg: Österreichisches Katholisches Bibelwerk, 1984), 97–113. The work originally appeared in Polish (Lublin, 1980).

[21] *Ibid.*, 97–100.

[22] *I Enoch*, 133: "it seems hardly likely that one archangel would convey the instructions of the Holy One to other archangels." The same form, as an aorist, also in Gs 10:1.

of δῆσον.[23] But such differences, which are probably secondary (see below), do not substantially change the meaning of the text. Rubinkiewicz therefore confidently concludes, "Aus dieser Analyse kann man den begründeten Schluss ziehen, dass wir es im Falle von Mt 22,13a mit einem Zitat von Hen 10,4 zu tun haben."[24] At least, we would have here a somewhat free translation of the original.[25]

D.C. Sim is one of the very few Matthean scholars who have supported this conclusion.[26] However, he takes issue with the hypothesis of a pre-Matthean origin of the Parable of the Wedding Garment. Sim strongly argues that the parable is Matthew's own creation, which has always remained a minority position.[27] The tensions or inconsistencies between 22:1–10 and 11–14 that Rubinkiewicz (and others) have singled out do not argue against such a conclusion. Rubinkiewicz lists five:[28] The son of v. 2 is no longer mentioned later on and disappears completely in favour of the father-king. The town is destroyed in v. 7, yet the wedding goes on as if no such thing has happened. No condition for admission to the wedding is mentioned in vv. 1–10, but one guest is nevertheless kicked out for not being properly dressed. The conclusion in v. 14 would not match what is said in v. 9 about the king (desperately) extending his invitation to whomsoever is found on the crossroads. And finally, the servants (δοῦλοι) of 22:1–10 (see vv. 3, 4, 6, 8) have now become διάκονοι in v. 13. The first two of these tensions are not directly related to the question of the origin of the parable of vv. 11–14. The focus of the parable in vv. 1–10 never was on the son, but solely on the father-king and on his many initiatives to have people invited, and so the former quite understandably fades away immediately after

---

[23] See the punctuation in the edition of Black as cited above. It is less plausible that the phrase should be cut up, reading "hands" with the first and "feet" with the second imperative.

[24] *Eschatologie*, 100.

[25] *Ibid.*, "Die geringfügigen Unterschiede in der Wortwahl lassen höchstens vermuten, dass Mt eine dem Gleichnis vom Gewand angepasste freie Übersetzung des aramäischen Originals sein kann." For a survey of instances where E goes with Gp or with Gs against the other Greek version in *1 En.* 6–11, see now Bhayro, *Asael Narrative*, 221–23.

[26] "We are left…with little option but to concur with Rubinkiewicz that Mt. 22.13a is directly dependent upon *1 En.* 10.4a" ("Matthew 22.13a," 6). A.-M. Denis, *Introduction à la littérature religieuse judéo-hellénistique* (vol. 1; Turnhout: Brepols, 2000), refers to Sim, but clearly is rather more reserved: "peut-être inspiré de *Hen.*" (119).

[27] Cf. "Matthew 22.13a," 8 n. 13. For the details of his argumentation, see 7–9. His list of those who support this position is limited to Gundry, G. Barth, and F.W. Beare (see 8 n. 13).

[28] *Eschatologie*, 103–5.

he was mentioned in v. 2 to evoke the setting of a wedding.[29] The text does not give any clue on how to reconcile v. 7 with vv. 11–14, and one can only speculate on how to imagine the situation. Palace and town obviously are not identical. The former—perhaps located on the acropolis—was apparently not affected by the fire that destroyed the city. Matthew in any case does not seem to have been utterly concerned about stressing the king's excessively brutal reaction in v. 7.[30] The three remaining objections are taken together by Sim when arguing, "even granting that such a tension exists between the two parables (and this in itself is a very subjective judgment), then the 'source and heavy redaction hypothesis' [= Rubinkiewicz's position] provides no better explanation for it than does the alternative 'composition hypothesis' [Sim's qualification for his own position]. On either view Matthew has allowed the tension to stand."[31] Of course, such argument in itself does not settle the issue of the origin of the parable, as Sim recognises: "this argument does not prove that there is no pre-Matthaean core to Mt. 22.11–13, but it does substantially reduce the necessity to put one."[32] Sim differs from Rubinkiewicz on one other point. The latter does not further specify which version of *1 Enoch* was used in the parable. For Sim, the triple agreement between Matt 22:13 and Gp on εἶπεν ("least significant"), on the absence of the longer introduction of Gs and of συμπόδισον αὐτὸν ("of far greater significance"), and on the order of "feet and hands," would offer proof that Matthew was familiar with the text of *1 En.* 10:4a as preserved in the codex Panopolitanus or a text very much like it.[33] Such a conclusion might be too strong since

---

[29] Luke, who is probably true to Q here, speaks only about a "great supper" (δεῖπνον μέγα). Cf. the reconstruction by J.M. Robinson et al., *The Critical Edition of Q* (Leuven: Peeters, 2000). Fleddermann (*Q*, 724) regards the adjective as redactional. There is no reason for assuming with Gundry (*Matthew*, 433–34) that Matthew would have made the change to "wedding" to compensate for omitting the parable of Luke 14:7–14.

[30] Commentators have been puzzled by it, but have traditionally interpreted the verse in the light of Matthew's interest in having Jesus polemicise with the Jewish authorities. See, as an example, the comments by B. Weiss, *Das Matthäusevangelium und seine Lucas-Parallelen* (Halle: Buchhandlung des Waisenhauses, 1876), 470: "Damit ist aber das schon 21,41 den Hierarchen gedrohte Verderben ebenso näher bestimmt, wie ihre Schuld in v. 6, und zwar als Untergang durch Feindeshand…Und nun erhellt erst ganz, weshalb der Gastgeber ein König sein musste, der seine Heeresmacht wider die Frevler aufbieten konnte." Similar overly harsh verdicts are not exceptional in the gospels: see Matt 24:51 par. Luke, and Luke 19:27, which Harnack once connected with the one of Matt 22:7.

[31] "Matthew 22.13a," 8.

[32] *Ibid.*

[33] *Ibid.*, 10.

JOSEPH VERHEYDEN

all three versions have been affected by "secondary features," as Sim acknowledges.[34]

II

There is a double problem with this "dependence" or "citation hypothesis," however appealing it may look and regardless of whether or not Matthew himself is made responsible for introducing the allusion to *1 Enoch*. The first problem has to do with the interpretation of Matt 22:13. One could argue that Matthew was alluding to *1 En.* 10:4, because he liked the power and the vividness of the image. But that is not how Rubinkiewicz and Sim see it. For them Matthew was citing *1 Enoch* because of what it says about Asael. The incident in v. 13 has variously been interpreted as a conflict on social rules and policy or as a metaphor for dealing with a theological issue. On the former hypothesis, it is a matter of not being dressed for the occasion. Matthew does not expand on the how and why this happened—by neglect, or because the man, who was gathered from the streets, did not possess the right dress—; he simply notes the fact, its consequences, and the rather rude measures that are taken against the poor guest. On the other hypothesis, the wedding garment stands for meeting the criteria, whatever these might be, for being allowed to enter and stay in the Kingdom/Church. Rubinkiewicz proposes to interpret the garment, which he thinks on the pre-Matthean level was not yet a wedding dress, from the Asael/Azazel tradition as found in *Apoc. Ab.* 13:12–14. There, it is said that the angel who acts as guide and discussion partner of Abraham explains to him that Azazel stands for ungodliness (13:10) and goes on contrasting his fate to that of Azazel. Azazel is told that the garment that once was his property in heaven has been taken from him. Instead, as the scapegoat with whom he is identified, he will be clothed with the sins of Abraham. Their fates will be reversed, "for Abraham's portion is in heaven, and yours is on earth (13:7)."[35] Rubinkiewicz argues that the man without the garment represents all those who have distanced

---

[34] *Ibid.*, 9 n. 15.
[35] Cited after R. Rubinkiewicz, "Apocalypse of Abraham," in *OTP* 1:695.

themselves from God.[36] He further suggests, by way of conclusion, that on the pre-Matthean level it is the Jewish leaders who are targeted for not having recognised the signs of the coming of the Kingdom and for having declined Jesus. Matthew then turned this into a critique and warning of fellow Christians who fail to stay true to their commitment to God.[37] Sim basically follows this line of reasoning, except of course that he makes Matthew responsible for the allusion to *1 Enoch* (and to *Apocalypse of Abraham*).[38]

This interpretation of Matt 22:13 is open to discussion for several reasons. First and foremost, it is assumed that Matthew and his audience were familiar with two motifs featuring Asael/Azazel, one (the "binding"), for which he would be citing from another document, and one (the "garment"), for which he would have borrowed from tradition and not from *Apocalypse of Abraham* itself,[39] that do not elsewhere occur together in this constellation and most probably represent independent strands of traditions, as Sim rightly notes.[40]

Second, Matthew's is a very indirect and most incomplete, indeed one should say, incorrect, allusion to and use of the motif in *Apocalypse of Abraham*. In the latter, Abraham's sin is transferred to Azazel, but as Sim again rightly observes, "The expiatory role of Asael clearly plays no role in the Gospel of Matthew."[41] But Matthew would not just have missed the point of the garment motif as found in *Apocalypse of Abraham*; he would have modified it considerably. Matthew 22:13 is not about a reversal of fortune in favour of somebody else. It is not said that the man who was entitled to the garment and a place in heaven lost or forfeited these to others who could not bring forward such a claim.[42]

---

[36] *Eschatologie*, 101–2 and 111: "Er repräsentiert einen jeden, der die wichtigste Teilnahmebedingung des messianischen Mahles nicht erfüllt. Aus ApAbr 13,15 [14] erfahren wir, dass das 'Gewand' den Zustand der Nähe Gottes bedeutet, an welcher auch der Satan vor seinem Fall teilhatte."

[37] *Ibid.*, 112.

[38] "Matthew 22.13a," 13–17.

[39] *Ibid.*, 15: "he seems to have had access to the same oral tradition as those available to its [*Apoc. Abr.*] author." Why could this not also apply for the parallel with *1 Enoch*?

[40] *Ibid.*, 14. On Asael and Azazel in Jewish tradition, see C. Molenberg, "A Study of the Roles of Shemihaza and Asael in Enoch 6–11," *JSS* 35 (1984): 136–46 (on the "contest" between the two and how the latter gradually overshadowed the other); R.T. Helm, "Azazel in Early Jewish Tradition," *AUSS* 32 (1994): 217–26 (217–22).

[41] Sim, "Matthew 22.13a," 14 n. 22.

[42] Sim (*ibid.*, 15) does not seem to be aware of this problem when writing, "Just as Asael forfeited to the righteous Abraham..., so too will the wicked."

A wicked person he certainly is—he is one of the πονηρούς Matthew mentions in v. 10, hereby changing the Q version of the parable[43]—, but his "curriculum" is very different from that of Asael. The man had never been in heaven before, and he can hardly be identified with the fallen angel.[44] As a matter of fact, it is not even clear from Matthew what precisely may have been his mistake.[45] This makes it also difficult, and hazardous, to speculate about his identity.[46]

Finally, it is puzzling, to say the least, that Matthew in 22:11–14 does not refer or allude in any way to the punishment by fire that is so emphatically mentioned in *1 En.* 10:4–6 and in most of the parallels in *1 Enoch* that speak of binding the wicked as part of the judgement that is brought upon them (see below). Yet, this particular motif is well known also to Matthew (3:10–12; 7:19; 13:40, 42, 49; 18:8–9; 25:41; also 5:22). Instead, he concludes the parable with two stock phrases (22:13b, 14). The first one is characteristic of his gospel and shows the binding to be part of an even harsher treatment. It does not end with merely being kicked out.[47] The "gnashing and weeping" is combined with the fire motif in 13:42, 50. In 22:13b the latter is lacking, as is also the case in 8:12; 24:51; and 25:30. One could of course argue with Sim that "since the fire motif is not found in 22:11–13, this notion must be inferred from the Gospel as a whole."[48] But why would Matthew in the first place have omitted it when it figures in his source?

All this makes it highly implausible that Matthew (or his source) was citing this one phrase of *1 En.* 10:4a when composing 22:13a. Moreover, in the next section it will be argued that there is good reason to

---

[43] See Fleddermann, *Q*, 734 n. 171: "The addition of πονηρούς τε καὶ ἀγαθούς prepares for Matthew's further addition of the Man without a Wedding Garment."

[44] See Luz, *Matthäus*, 3:245 n. 71: "Dem mt Skopus, der auf die einzelnen Gemeindeglieder zielt, würde eine satanologische Deutung des Gastes gerade nicht entsprechen." Cf. also Davies and Allison (*Matthew*, 3:206: "Certainly we cannot equate the il-prepared man with Azazel"), who then go on paraphrasing Sim as cited here above in n. 42.

[45] Note the uncertainty in Rubinkiewicz in defining the meaning of the garment, which for him variously stands for the state of innocence and friendship with God or of being close to God (*Eschatologie*, 111), but which he then describes on the next page as symbolising those who were called but refused to reconcile themselves with God (112), a motif that is in no way reflected or alluded to in the parable.

[46] The Jewish leaders for Rubinkiewicz (see *Eschatologie*, 112); "a composite figure who represents all the wicked, both Jewish and Christian" for Sim ("Matthew 22.13a," 15 n. 23).

[47] Cf. Gundry, *Matthew*, 440.

[48] "Matthew 22.13a," 15.

doubt whether the latter is even an allusion to *1 Enoch* at all and that
the parallel may have to be explained in quite a different way.

III

The binding "hands and feet" and the casting of Asael in the dark is
told in a strikingly similar way in Gp, Gs, and E. A slightly variant form
of the same motif (said of the stars) occurs in the Ethiopic version of
1 En. 88:1, 3 (the Greek is lacking here). The second of these passages
is partially attested in one of the Aramaic fragments from Qumran
that have been edited by J.T. Milik in 1976.[49] Milik also claimed to
have discovered traces of the Aramaic version of *1 En.* 10:3–4 in three
small scraps of text, which he labeled *l*, *m*, *n*, and catalogued as 1En[a]
1 v (= 4Q201 v).

(1) I begin with the remnants of 10:3–4. They contain the following
text (as read or suggested by Milik): frag. *l* line 3]לנצ [; line 4 *vacat* ה[
]מ[; and line 5]ל יתה[; frag. *m* line 1]שט[; and line 2]מנה[; and frag.
n line 1] עד [; and line 2]א ד[.

Milik assumed that the Aramaic was closest to Gs and brilliantly,
and daringly, reconstructed the passage accordingly:[50]

```
[    ]o[ˡ                                                              ]   1
[                                                                      ]   2
אלף ᵐק[שט]ה מה יעבד ובן למך לנפשה לחיין לנצ[לה]             ]   3
vacat ולמפלט[ᵑ עד [עלמה ו[מנה] תתנצב נצבה ותתקים כל דרי על[מ]י[ה]  4
ולדרפאל אמ[ן]ר א[ז]ל נא רפאל ואסר לעסאל ידין ורנלין ורמא [יתה ל[חשוכה]  5
```

[... [10] 3 Instruct] the righteous (man) [what he is to do, and the son of
Lamech (how)] to preserve [his soul unto life], [and to escape] for[ever.
And from him [will be planted a plant and it will be established (for)
all the generations] of worlds.

[[4] And to Raphael (the Lord) said: "Do go, [Raphael, and bind
'Asaʾel hand and foot and cast] him into [the darkness...]"

The display Milik suggested for the three fragments has been taken
over by F. García Martínez and E.J.C. Tigchelaar and by J. Maier,

---

[49] For recent surveys of research on the Aramaic fragments of *1 Enoch*, see Denis, *Introduction*, 100–103; Nickelsburg, *1 Enoch*, 9–11; M. Langlois, "Les manuscrits araméens d'Hénoch: Nouvelle documentation et nouvelle approche," in *Qoumrân et le judaïsme du tournant de notre ère* (ed. A. Lemaire and S.C. Mimouni; Paris: Peeters, 2006), 111–21.
[50] *Books of Enoch*, 161–62 (reconstruction), 343 (diplomatic transcription), and Plate V.

though the former do not attempt to fill out all of the lacunas in the Aramaic as is the case in 4Q201 1 iv (but they do so for the translation), while the latter opts for a minimal solution.[51]

One should well realise that much in Milik's reconstruction remains very shaky indeed. In each of the three fragments, one or more letters are only partially preserved. As a matter of fact, only a few letters are undisputed. It is all but certain that the second line of fragment *n* is to be read as]א רֹ[. More importantly, Milik reads לְ[חשׂוכה] at the end of line 5, but the *lamed* is not clearly attested. It is difficult to take the vertical stroke on the third line of fragment *l* as the top of this *lamed*, because it would then be raised high above the line (cf. line 1 of the same fragment). Moreover, it seems that the stroke is interrupted, and if it would be the remains of a *lamed*, this letter would apparently have overlapped with the ה that Milik proposes to read after ית.

Further, we cannot be absolutely sure that the three fragments do indeed belong together. The second line of fragment *n* could maybe also be read as רי. The fragment would then also fit in 4QEnª (4Q201) 1 ii (2:1–5:6), where Milik reconstructs lines 6 and 7 (*1 En.* 3:1; 4:1) as:

6   [ולא מחדתין עליהן עד] דתרתין ותלת שנין [יעברן] חזו לכן לדנלי
7   [קיטה דשמשה בהן כוי]ה ושלקה ואנתן טלֹלֹ וֹמֹסֹתרין בעין מן קדמיה

6 (3:1) [and they do not renew their foliage until] two or three years [pass]. Observe ye the signs

7 [of summer, that the sun burns] and glows; and ye seek shade and shelter before it[52]

On this hypothesis, 4QEnª 1 v would contain no trace whatsoever of the beginning of *1 En.* 10:4.

It also remains possible that the three fragments represent a version of *1 Enoch* that differs from the ones that are preserved in E and Gp/s, as is probably the case with the other fragments that Milik had assigned

---

[51] Cf. F. García Martínez and E.J.C. Tigchelaar, *The Dead Sea Scrolls Study Edition* (Leiden: Brill, 1997–1998), 2:402–3. J. Maier, *Die Texte der Höhle 4* (vol. 2 of *Die Qumran-Essener: Die Texte vom Toten Meer*; UTB 1863; München: Reinhardt, 1995), 141:

(1) [   ]. [-] (2) [--] (3) [...Wa]hrhe[it...] zu ret[ten]

(4) [und zu erretten] auf [ewig, und] darau[s...aller Ew]igke[it]en [(leer)] (5) [Und zu Rafael sag]te Er: G[eh doch hin...Und wirf] ihn in die [Finsternis]

Bhayro, *Asael Narrative*, 52–53 and especially 225–26, on the other hand is highly critical of Milik's reconstruction and does not even reproduce the Aramaic of 10:3–4 (cf. 94).

[52] *Books of Enoch* 146–47. The same passage occurs in 4QEnᶜ 1 i (1.9–5.1) but in a disposition that does not match with *n* (see text in *Books of Enoch*, 185).

to 4QEnᵃ (2–8) and were recently published by L.T. Stuckenbruck.[53]

So, maybe the single most important comment that is to be made is the one Milik himself added after his reconstruction: "Only the identification of *l* is relatively certain."[54] And even that may be too strong an assertion. The few letters on lines 2 and 3 of *l* offer very little to go on. Milik reconstructs 10:3a in line with Gs, which reads καὶ τὴν ψυχὴν αὐτοῦ εἰς ζωὴν συντηρήσει (diff. Gp E, see below). The last word would render לנצ]לה (if that is the correct reading). The same Greek word occurs (as a noun) at *1 En.* 1:8 καὶ ἐπὶ τοὺς ἐκλεκτοὺς ἔσται συντήρησις καὶ εἰρήνη (section missing in A).[55]

Hence, one has to conclude that 4QEnᵃ 1 v does not offer any positive and solid evidence for the text of E/G 10:4a.

Part of the phrase is attested in the Aramaic version of *1 En.* 88:3 in 4QEnᶜ 4 i (88:3–89:6). Line 12 clearly reads [כלהון ידין ורגלין ורמא, which Milik rightly completes on the basis of E and renders as "he bound] all of them hand and foot and cast [them into the depths of the earth]."[56] It has generally been recognised that *1 En.* 83–90 has been influenced by certain sections from the *Book of the Watchers*, particularly, though not exclusively, from chs. 6–11.[57] For Sim, the parallel in 88:3 "shows the direct dependence of the *Animal Apocalypse* on the *Book of the Watchers*."[58] There certainly is similarity of content with comparable passages from the *Book of the Watchers*. But 88:3 does not as such prove that the phrase also must have stood in 10:4. The parallel is not only and indeed not primarily with 10:3–4, but with 10:11–12,[59] or rather with 18:14–16 and even more with 21:2–6, which

---

[53] *DJD* 36:3–7. Note his comment on p. 3: "None of the fragments corresponds to anything among the extant recensions of *1 Enoch* traditions. If they relate to the same work as the other 4Q201 fragments (i.e. to the *Book of Watchers*), then the original content of this writing diverged from what is preserved among the Greek recensions and Ethiopic versions."

[54] *Books of Enoch*, 162.

[55] E reads, "He will preserve the elect, and kindness shall be upon them."

[56] *Books of Enoch*, 238. Cf. E, "then he bound all of them hand and foot, and cast them into the pits of the earth."

[57] See, e.g., P.A. Tiller, *A Commentary on the Animal Apocalypse of 1 Enoch* (SBLEJL 4; Atlanta: Scholars Press, 1993), 83–96; Nickelsburg, *1 Enoch*, 359–60; Bhayro, *Asael Narrative*, 255.

[58] "Matthew 22.13a," 6 n. 9.

[59] So Nickelsburg, *1 Enoch*, 374, for the motif of binding the enemy "in the valleys of the earth." One should also note that E 88:3 is not completely identical with A and contains one element (throwing rocks from heaven; see also the earthquake in 2) that does not stem from *1 En.* 10.

both describe the defeat of the stars (not of Asael or any of the other angels) that will be bound and, according to 21:3, also cast in a place of burning fire.[60] Furthermore, it cannot a priori be excluded that the motif was introduced in E/G 10:4a from 88:1, 3. The influence must not only have gone in one direction. Thus, the evidence of *1 En.* 88:3 does not really change the conclusion that was reached above: there is no positive proof that A 10:4a read the phrase about binding and casting Asael in the dark.

(2) All this does not mean of course that the reading of E/G 10:4a is certainly not original, but here too there may be some reason for being cautious. The fact that E and G represent versions of *1 Enoch* that have been transmitted by Christians and may even have originated in Christian circles, hardly needs to be documented. Its consequences should duly be taken into account when it comes to reconstruct the original, i.e. non-Christian, text of *1 Enoch*.

Likewise, there is little need to demonstrate that very often E and Gp/s differ amongst each other in such a way that it is not always easy to decide which version is (closest to) the original one. Even in a verse such as 10:4, in which the three are very much parallel to each other, they are not completely identical. Gp's "feet and hands," if not original, might reflect secondary influence from Matthew. If Gs's συμπόδισον αὐτόν was part of the text, it may have dropped out by oversight (see the double ποσί / -ποδισ- and the double αὐτόν) or because it was felt to be redundant. But it is equally and probably even more likely that the phrase was added by Gs (or its model), as it is one of several such "redundancies" in the same verse (see πορευθείς and Πορεύου, Ῥαφαήλ). While the absence of the latter of these two in Gp E could arguably be explained from oversight (Raphael is mentioned twice), the opposite explanation becomes the more plausible one when taking into account the two comparable instances in 10:9, 11. In Gs the command of the Lord is formulated in a perfectly identical way in all three verses:

10:4 καὶ τῷ Ῥαφαὴλ εἶπε Πορεύου, Ῥαφαήλ,...
10:9 καὶ τῷ Γαβριὴλ εἶπε Πορεύου, Γαβριήλ,...
10:11 καὶ τῷ Μιχαὴλ εἶπε Πορεύου, Μιχαήλ,...

---

[60] Cf. Gp¹ καὶ ἐκεῖ τεθέαμαι ἑπτὰ τῶν ἀστέρων (Gs² has ἀστέρας) τοῦ οὐρανοῦ δεδεμένους καὶ ἐρριμμένους ἐν αὐτῷ (Gs² + ὁμοῦ) ὁμοίους ὄρεσιν μεγάλοις καὶ ἐν πυρὶ καιομένους. E "And there I saw seven stars of heaven bound togther in it, like great mountains, and burning with fire."

Gp (and E), on the other hand, reads:

> 10:4 καὶ τῷ Ῥαφαὴλ εἶπεν (E adds "the Lord")
> 10:9 καὶ τῷ Γαβριὴλ εἶπεν ὁ κύριος· Πορεύου (= E)
> 10:11 καὶ εἶπεν Μιχαήλ· Πορεύου (E "And to Michael God said, Make known (*v.l.* Go)...").[61]

Obviously, the differences in Gp and E cannot all be explained by oversight, for it would mean that they were systematically overseeing various elements of the same clause. It must have been Gs that was harmonising the variants.

Gs offers a different and longer version of 10:3 than the one that is found in Gp E.[62] The shorter reading cannot be explained by mere oversight. At best, this could go for the omission of δίκαιον after δίδαξον that looks somewhat similar. But Gp E did not just jump from δι᾽ αἰῶνος to τοῦ αἰῶνος, for the content of 10:3b Gs about the plant that will be kept, as well as part of the wording (the ending), is also voiced and found in Gp E (καὶ μενεῖ τὸ σπέρμα—"his seed will be preserved"). There is no reason why Gp E would have reduced the more elaborate and vivid expression of Gs into a mere ὅπως ἐκφύγῃ, καὶ μενεῖ τὸ σπέρμα αὐτοῦ. The reading of Gs has the better chance then of being secondary.[63] Gs has been expanding upon a shorter version. It does so partly by repeating from 10:1 a "redundant" explicitation (τὸν υἱὸν Λάμεχ of 10:1 Gp/s E occurs again in Gp 10:3), partly by anticipating a motif that occurs later on in 10:16, 18–19 (Gp and E; Gs is lacking here) and partly by introducing more vivid and stronger images and phrases which, moreover, carry a biblical, and more specifically, a Matthean ring. The phrase καὶ τὴν ψυχὴν αὐτοῦ εἰς ζωὴν

---

[61] Cf. also *1 En.* 13:1 Ὁ δὲ Ἐνὼχ τῷ Ἀζαὴλ εἶπεν· Πορεύου· οὐκ ἔσται σοι εἰρήνη and E "As for Enoch, he proceeded and said to Azaz'el, 'There will not be peace unto you'" (Gs lacking). On the secondary character of E's "the Lord" and of Gs, see Bhayro, *Asael Narrative*, 183 and 197–98.

[62] Gs δίδαξον τὸν δίκαιον τί ποιήσει, τὸν υἱὸν Λάμεχ, καὶ τὴν ψυχὴν αὐτοῦ εἰς ζωὴν συντηρήσει, καὶ ἐκφεύξεται δι᾽ αἰῶνος, καὶ ἐξ αὐτοῦ φυτευθήσεται φύτευμα καὶ σταθήσεται πάσας τὰς γενεὰς τοῦ αἰῶνος.

Gp καὶ δίδαξον αὐτὸν ὅπως ἐκφύγῃ, καὶ μενεῖ τὸ σπέρμα αὐτοῦ εἰς πάσας τὰς γενεὰς τοῦ αἰῶνος.

E "And now instruct him in order that he may flee, and his seed will be preserved for all generations."

E and Gp are nearly but not completely identical.

[63] So also emphatically, Bhayro, *Asael Narrative*, 93–94 ("embellishments") and 223–24; cf. also his comments (33–37) on the source of Gs here and on the plant motif in general.

συντηρήσει is not found as such in any of the gospels. But the motif of "saving/loosing one's life" occurs in all three of the synoptic gospels. Matthew even brings it twice, once expressing the contrast with εὑρίσκω—ἀπόλλυμι (10:39) and once with σῴζω/εὑρίσκω—ἀπόλλυμι (16:25). Did the twofold occurrence of the latter verb in 10:2 inspire Gs to come up with the "Matthean" motif in 10:3? Matthew also particularly likes the phrase εἰς ζωήν (with a verb of going),[64] while τί ποιήσει recalls the rich man's request in 19:16 (par. Mark). The combination of συντηρέω and δίκαιος (see Gs 10:3) reminds one of Mark's description of Herod's treatment of John the Baptist in 6:20. But the same verb is not unknown to Matthew either (9:17, here in combination with ἀπόλλυνται, cf. *1 En.* 10:2), who further also once writes that "the righteous (will go) into eternal life" (25:46 οἱ δίκαιοι εἰς ζωὴν αἰώνιον).[65]

All the above shows that the text of *1 En.* 10:3–4 has been reworked, and also that some of the (most probably) additional material in Gs resembles words and phrases that occur in the Gospel of Matthew and possibly somehow may have been influenced by it.

The motif of "the binding of the wicked one" shows up repeatedly in the *Book of the Watchers*, from 10:4 on and all through to ch. 22.[66] Apart from 10:4, it is also found in 10:11–14 (Michael binding Shemihazah);[67]

---

[64] See 19:17 diff. Mark and 25:46; and especially also 7:14 and 18:8–9 par. Mark, the first of which offers another instance of a contrast between ἀπωλεία and εὑρίσκω, while the second contains a variant on the "hand and foot" motif and speaks of "throwing away," βάλε ἀπὸ σοῦ, and of "the eternal fire" and "the hell of fire," a motif that is crucial also in the description of the fate of the wicked all throughout the *Book of the Watchers*.

[65] On this last phrase and a possible connexion with 4Q548, see J. Verheyden, "The Fate of the Righteous and the Cursed at Qumran and in the Gospel of Matthew," in *Wisdom and Apocalypticism in the Dead Sea Scrolls and in the Biblical Tradition* (ed. F. García Martínez; BETL 168; Leuven: Peeters, 2003), 427–52.

[66] It is of course not limited to this section only. See, e.g., *1 En.* 54:3–6; 56:1–3; 67:4; 69:28; 88:1, 3; 90:23–24.

[67] A Gp and E agree in reading "tell," "inform," δήλωσον in 10:11, against Gs which has δῆσον. The latter verb is attested also in G E 10:12 (A lacking) and has probably been anticipated in 10:11 by Gs from 10:12. Gs's κατακρίθη in 10:14 against Gp E κατακαυθῇ—"will burn") is likewise a secondary reading, as is most probably also the case for the variant δεηθήσεται in 10:14 (so Gs Paris. gr. 1171, against Gp δεθήσονται and E "will be bound"). Note also the reference to the prison (E and Gp/s δεσμωτήριον) in 10:13, the repeated use of a form of ἀπόλλυμι in 10:12 (noun; E Gp/s) and in 10:15–16 (verb; Gs is lacking here), and the verb ἀπαχθήσεται (Gp/s, E "will lead them") as a synonym for βάλλω (see already 10:6).

13:1–2 (Enoch foretelling Asael's and the other angels' binding);[68] 14:5–6 (Enoch repeating his threat against Asael);[69] 18:14–16 (the angel binding the stars and the powers of heaven);[70] 21:2–6 (once more on the binding of the stars and partly overlapping in wording with the previous passage);[71] 22:11 (binding of the souls of the wicked);[72] and 9:4.[73]

Two comments are to be made. First, while all these passages are roughly comparable in the way they describe the judgment and punishment of the wicked angels/stars/souls, *1 En.* 10:4–6, the first in the

---

[68] A "grave judgment" (Gp κρίμα μέγα; Gs lacking) is announced, but the focus is solely on the binding.

[69] The passage resembles in part 13:1 (Gp reads in 14:5 ἐν τοῖς δεσμοῖς τῆς γῆς ἐρρέθη δῆσαι ὑμᾶς), a feature that is still more emphasised by a variant reading of E ("and you will not have peace"), considered to be secondary by Knibb (*Enoch*, 2:96: "It is not entirely clear whether or not anything corresponding to this clause did stand in Aramᶜ 1 v 14, but it seems unlikely"), but the text also echoes verbs and phrases from 10:11–14 (on the destruction of the beloved ones).

[70] Note again the mention of δεσμωτήριον in 18:14 (see before in 10:13) and the qualification ὀργίσθη for the angel in 18:16 (comp. the king's reaction in Matt 22:7). The different ending in Gp and E is probably due to a mistake: cf. Charles, *Enoch*, 51; Knibb, *Enoch*, 2:106: "a corrupt Greek *Vorlage*" behind E.

[71] The binding is mentioned thrice, both in E and in Gp, which has the whole passage copied twice. In Gp 21:3 and 4, the verb is connected with a verb of throwing (ῥίπτω), but the first instance is lacking in E. Knibb (*Enoch*, 2:107), who regards it as "a gloss introduced under the influence of v. 4." The place of punishment is called "an empty place" in E (21:2; cf. 10:4), which Gp renders as τόπον ἀκατασκεύαστον καὶ φοβερόν. *1 Enoch* 21:2–4 is also preserved very fragmentarily in A (4QEnᵉ 1 xxi). Milik offers an attempt at a reconstruction, while at the same time observing that Gp and E "differ widely from what may be read and supplied in our fragment" (*Books of Enoch*, 228), which is not without importance when identifying and reconstructing similar fragmentary pieces. Maier does not reconstruct and García Martínez and Tigchelaar omit the passage.

[72] Torment, destruction, curse, and even vengeance are mentioned here, but not the punishment by fire, as in the other instances. The binding ("forever") occurs emphatically at the end of the verse.

[73] Gs stands alone in offering a longer version of 9:4 that combines binding with throwing into the abyss, but that has all the appearance of being a kind of summary by Syncellus. After εἰς πάντας τοὺς αἰῶνας (Gp/s, also E), Gs goes on with καὶ τὰ ἑξῆς. τότε ὁ ὕψιστος ἐκέλευσε τοῖς ἁγίοις ἀρχαγγέλοις, καὶ ἔδησαν τοὺς ἐξάρχους αὐτῶν καὶ ἔβαλον (Paris. gr. 1711 ἔβαλλον) αὐτοὺς εἰς τὴν ἄβυσσον, ἕως τῆς κρίσεως, καὶ τὰ ἑξῆς. καὶ ταῦτα μὲν ὁ Ἐνὼχ μαρτυρεῖ. Finally, a very different meaning is giving to the act of "binding" in 6:4–6 when Shemihazah calls upon his fellow angels to stay together in their wicked plans and urges them to seal this with an oath and a curse (Gp ὁμόσωμεν ὅρκῳ πάντες καὶ ἀναθεματίσωμεν πάντες ἀλλήλους…; likewise in Gs, with a slight difference in word order; E reads "Let us all swear an oath and bind everyone among us by a curse…" The motif of "staying together" is taken up again in 21:3, but now to describe their "unity" in their fate: E "bound together"; Gp² δεδεμένους καὶ ἐρριμμένους ἐν αὐτῷ ὁμοῦ (probably dropped out by mistake in Gp¹ due to the word ὁμοίους that follows right after it); Milik reconstructs it also for A.

series, stands out among the others in several respects. It is the only one in the list that mentions "the hands and feet." In the other passages, the way of binding is not further specified. The combination of "binding" with some form of "throwing/casting" is found only once more, in 21:3–4 (and 9:4 Gs), but the verb differs (ῥίπτω).[74] 10:4 is also the only passage to mention "the darkness" in this connexion. The word is found elsewhere in *1 Enoch* (see, e.g., 17:6; and also 102:7; 103:8; 104:8), but not in combination with "throwing/casting." Finally, and most importantly, the phrase in 10:4a is quite general—there is no explicit mention of the judgmental aspect yet, as in 10:6 and in the other passages—and rather redundant in combination with the long description of the execution of the verdict that follows in 10:4b–6. The other passages listed above do not have this kind of "introductory" verse, and immediately proceed to the details of the verdict using more "concrete" language (abyss, fire).

Second, taking into account the singular character of 10:4a and the fact that there is evidence of glosses in 10:3–4 and similar passages,[75] there may be also some reason to be suspicious about the authenticity of the phrase ποσὶν καὶ χερσίν, καὶ βάλε αὐτὸν εἰς τὸ σκότος. As for its origin, one possible source might be *1 En.* 88:1, 3, where E and A (for 88:3) offer a closely similar phrase, except that instead of "the darkness," the victims (not Asael but the stars, as in 21:3–6) are thrown into "an abyss" (88:1 E; cf. 9:4+ Gs; 17:7, 8; 21:7) and into "the pits of the earth" (88:3 E; cf. χαός in 10:13; 20:5). Alternatively, Matt 22:13 offers an even closer, indeed formally identical, parallel. *1 Enoch* 10:4a would then be proof of the influence of Matthew's gospel on the textual tradition of *1 Enoch* as it was transmitted and preserved in a Christian milieu.

---

[74] In 10:5 Gp/s have ὑπόθες for which Lods (*Livre d'Hénoch*, xxxvi) proposed ἐπίθες, but see Black's defense of the former (*I Enoch*, 134). E renders "he threw on top of him..."

[75] See above on 10:3 and 21:3. Note also the repetition of ἐν τῇ ἐρήμῳ in Gs 10:4b.

BETWEEN JACOB'S DEATH AND MOSES' BIRTH: THE INTERTEXTUAL RELATIONSHIP BETWEEN GENESIS 50:15–EXODUS 1:14 AND *JUBILEES* 46:1–16

Jacques van Ruiten

This paper deals with the rewriting of Gen 50:15–Exod 1:14 in the *Book of Jubilees* 46:1–16. The events of *Jub.* 46 take place after Jacob's death and burial (*Jub.* 45:13–16; cf. Gen 47:28–50:14), and before the return of Amram, which precedes Moses' birth in a situation of distress in which all male first-born children are threatened with death (*Jub.* 47:1–9; cf. Exod 1:15–2:10). During this period, the story changes from one about Jacob's sons to a story of the people of Israel. Central points in this transitional period are Joseph's death and the occurrence of a new king in Egypt. Before these events Israel was prosperous and honored by the Egyptians; thereafter it was put into slavery and detested. It has been suggested that the reduction in Joseph's significance and the elevation of Levi and his line are the chief interests driving the exegesis in *Jub.* 46.[1] This is debatable, however. I hope to show that, with his transformations of Genesis and Exodus, the writer is addressing problems in the biblical text, and not the diminution of Joseph.

The overall structure of *Jub.* 45:13–47:9 is as follows:

45:13–16	Jacob's death
46:1–2	Prosperity of Israel
46:3–11	Death of Joseph and his brothers and new king in Egypt
46:12–16	Slavery of Israel
47:1–9	Moses' birth in situation of distress

1. GEN 50:15–26 AND EXOD 1:1–14

The story from Jacob's death until Moses' birth crosses the boundaries of the biblical books Genesis and Exodus. The final passage of the book of Genesis (Gen 50:15–26), after Jacob's deathbed and subsequent

---

[1] See B. Halpern-Amaru, "Burying the Fathers: Exegetical Strategies and Source Traditions in *Jubilees* 46," in *Reworking the Bible: Apocryphal and Related Texts at Qumran* (ed. E.G. Chazon et al.; STDJ 58; Leiden: Brill, 2005), 135–52 (152).

death and burial (Gen 47:28–50:14), consists of two parts.[2] First, it
tells the story of Joseph and his brothers (Gen 50:15–21), in which the
relationship between Joseph and his brothers is put under discussion.
After their father's death, the brothers again doubt the kindness and
forgiveness Joseph has shown before. But Joseph reassures and comforts
his brothers. Gen 50:15–26 is not rendered in *Jub.* 46.

Then the report of Joseph's death is mentioned (Gen 50:22–26). The
structure of this passage has some similarities with Jacob's death report
(Gen 47:28–50:14), although it is much shorter. The exposition (Gen
50:22) contains a summary of Joseph's life (cf. Gen 47:28). After this,
the text tells of Joseph's relationship with the grandchildren of Ephraim
and Manasseh (Gen 50:23; cf. Gen 48:3–12).[3] The farewell speech to
the brothers (Gen 50:24) starts with the announcement of the coming
death, and contains a promise for the exodus and the possession of the
land (cf. Gen 48:21). The burial instructions (Gen 50:25) in the form
of an oath (cf. Gen 47:31) do not contain a detailed description of a
burial place as in Gen 49:29–32. The passage ends (Gen 50:26) with
the explicit mention of Joseph's death, the reference to the total age,
and the execution of the burial instructions. The last will of Joseph
has not yet been executed (cf. Exod 13:19; Josh 24:32).

Exodus 1 can be divided into two parts.[4] In the first part (1:1–7), the
story of the development of the children of Jacob into the people of
Israel is told. It begins with a list of names of the sons of Israel who
had come to Egypt as free men, seventy people (including Joseph) who
became much more numerous. The second part (1:8–22) tells about
the measures of oppression undertaken by the new king. First, Israel

---

[2] For Gen 50:15–21, cf. H. Gunkel, *Genesis: Übersetzt und erklärt* (9th ed.; HKAT
1.1; Göttingen: Vandenhoeck & Ruprecht, 1977), 490–91; G.W. Coats, *Genesis with an
Introduction to Narrative Literature* (FOTL 1; Grand Rapids: Eerdmans, 1983), 311–15;
G.J. Wenham, *Genesis 16–50* (WBC 2; Waco, Tex.: Word Books, 1994), 489–91;
C. Westermann, *Genesis 37–50* (3d ed.; BKAT 1.3; Neukirchen-Vluyn: Neukirchener
Verlag, 2004), 230–38.

[3] Cf. Gen 48:12 for the expression "born on Joseph's knees" in Gen 50:23b.

[4] For the composition of Exod 1, see, e.g., C. Houtman, *Exodus I* (COT; Kampen:
Kok, 1986), 212–17; J.I. Durham, *Exodus* (WBC 3; Waco, Tex.: Word Books, 1987), 2–3,
6–7; W.H. Schmidt, *Exodus 1: Exodus 1–6* (BKAT 2.1; Neukirchen-Vluyn: Neukirchener
Verlag, 1988), 9–16; P. Weimar, "Exodus 1,1–2,10 als 'Eröffunungskomposition des
Exodusbuches,'" in *Studies in the Book of Exodus* (ed. M. Vervenne; BETL 126; Leuven:
Peeters, 1996), 179–208 (188–97); J. Siebert-Hommes, *Let the Daughters Live! The Literary
Architecture of Exodus 1–2 as a Key for Interpretation* (BIS 37; Leiden: Brill, 1998), 82–83;
W.H.C. Propp, *Exodus 1–18* (AB 2; New York: Doubleday, 1999), 119–36.

is oppressed and enslaved (Exod 1:8–14), and then the lives of all first-born males are put under threat (1:15–22).

The opening passage of Exodus (Exod 1:1–7) functions as a transitional unit between the story of the patriarchs and that of the exodus. In a summarizing way, it refers back to the final part of the preceding Genesis.[5] Using few words, the author recalls the entrance of Jacob and his family to Egypt, where Joseph already was.[6] The list of names of Jacob's sons (Exod 1:1–5) occurs four times in Genesis.[7] With regard to the name order, Exod 1:1–5 resembles Gen 35:23–26. The framework, however, has verbal similarities to Gen 46:8–27. Compare Exod 1:1 with Gen 46:8 and Exod 1:5 with Gen 46:27. After the list, Joseph's death is restated briefly (Exod 1:6; Gen 50:26), with the author adding that the entire generation of those who went to Egypt died. With regard to the adventures of the new generation it is said that they were numerous indeed (Exod 1:7). The use of the verb refers back to the promises to the patriarchs.[8]

The second passage (Exod 1:8–14) describes the oppressive measures taken by the new king. After an introduction (1:8–9a), the new king gives a speech to his people, proposing to diminish the people of Israel (1:9b–10). The subsequent narrative (1:11–14) formulates the execution of this plan. First, they make Israel suffer heavy burdens, that is, they make them build cities (1:11). The plan does not have the desired effect; on the contrary, the people increase in number (1:12). Thereupon, they enslave Israel by force using new measures (1:13–14).[9] Exodus 1:13–14 presents a somewhat intensified version of the forced labor of Exod 1:11, taking it to a more severe level. It seems as if the measures taken in 1:15–22 are more suitable than forced labor for achieving the king's goal, the diminishing of Israel.

---

[5] See the repetition of "And Joseph died" of Gen 50:26 in Exod 1:6 and the mention of "in Egypt" in Gen 50:26 and Exod 1:5. Cf. M. Fishbane, *Text and Texture: Close Readings of Selected Biblical Texts* (New York: Schocken Books, 1979), 63; Siebert-Hommes, *Let the Daughters Live*, 82–83; Weimar, "Exodus 1,1–2,10," 197–200. Cf. Houtman, *Exodus*, 212; Durham, *Exodus*, 2–3.

[6] See Gen 37–49; compare especially Exod 1:1, 5 with Gen 46:8a, 27b.

[7] See Gen 29:32–30:24; 35:23–26; 46:8–24; 49:3–27.

[8] Cf. Gen 17:20; 28:3; 35:11; 47:27; 48:4; see also: Gen 1:22, 28; 8:17; 9:1, 7.

[9] Note that in the Masoretic text of Exod 1:9–12, singular pronouns and verbs are used (referring to "people" in 1:9b), whereas in 1:13–14, plural forms are used.

2. An Overall Comparison between Gen 50:15–Exod 1:14 and *Jub.* 46:1–16

The following outline facilitates comparison between Gen 50:15–Exod 1:14 and *Jub.* 46:1–14.

Gen 50		*Jub. 46*	
15–21	Joseph and his brothers		
22–26	Joseph's death with instruction for burial		
Exod 1			
1–5	Jacob's sons to Egypt		
		1–2	Prosperity of Israel
6	Joseph's death and death of his brothers	3–4	Joseph's death and death of his brothers
7	Prosperity of Israel		
		5–6c	Joseph's instruction for burial
8	New king	6d–7	New king and war story
		8ab	Joseph's death and burial
		8c–11	Death brothers, their burial and war story
9–14	Oppression and slavery of Israel	12–16	Oppression and slavery of Israel
15–22	Threatening first-born sons		

The overview shows that the rewriting in *Jub.* 46 starts after Jacob's death with a description of the events in Exod 1:6–7 stated in reverse order. First, the prosperity of the children of Israel in Egypt during Joseph's lifetime is described, followed by Joseph's death. The passages Gen 50:15–21 ("Joseph and his brothers") and Exod 1:1–5 ("Jacob's sons to Egypt") are omitted in *Jub.* 46. Joseph's death report (Gen 50:22–26) is combined with the death report in Exod 1:6 and integrated in a completely new story in which, however, both texts are distinctly recognizable. Examples include the occurrence of Gen 50:24–25 in *Jub.* 46:5–6c; of Gen 50:26 in *Jub.* 46:3a, 8ab; and Exod 1:6 in *Jub.* 46:4, 8c. Because of the reversal of Exod 1:6 and 1:7, the events of Exod 1:6 (death and burial of Joseph and his brothers) and 1:8 (the rise of a new king) are strongly related and reworked and integrated into a war story (*Jub.* 46:3–11). The passage about Israel's oppression (Exod 1:9–14) is rewritten quite closely in *Jub.* 46:12–16, whereas Exod 1:15–22 is integrated in the rewriting of the story of Moses' birth (*Jub.* 47:1–9).

3. An Analysis of the Rewriting of Gen 50:15–Exod 1:14 in *Jub*. 46:1–16[10]

The Omission of Gen 50:15–21

It has been suggested that the family story of Jacob's children has been omitted intentionally by the author of *Jubilees* and replaced by the national story of Israel in *Jub*. 46:1–2, in which there is a harmonious relationship among fellow Israelites and between the Israelites and the Egyptians. The substitution avoids a problematic scene. The elevation of Joseph takes place in the public domain and not in the context of the family, and the author of *Jubilees* is interested in downplaying Joseph's role in the family.[11]

In my opinion, the non-elevation of Joseph in the context of his family cannot be based on the omission of Gen 50:15–21. The passage of the prosperity of Israel (*Jub*. 46:1–2) does not replace Gen 50:15–21 but is based on a reworking of Exod 1:7. Moreover, other passages in *Jubilees* stress family harmony and the sincerity of Joseph's reconciliation. For the author of *Jubilees*, there seems to be no contradiction whatsoever between his public and private appearances.

One could interpret the scene in Gen 50:15–21 as if previously there had never been a genuine reconciliation between Joseph and his brothers. In this interpretation, the text is in contradiction with Gen 45:1–15; 46:28–47:12, 27, in which the reconciliation of Joseph with his family is described extensively. The author of *Jubilees* summarizes this in *Jub*. 43:14–20; 45:1–7, in which the emotional and familial character of the events is stressed. The unity and harmony of all of Jacob's sons seems to be a central issue for the author of *Jubilees*.

The fear of Joseph's brothers and their submission (Gen 50:18–21) is partly based on Joseph's dreams (Gen 37:5–11). These dreams are not taken over by *Jubilees*, and therefore the passage Gen 50:18–21 misses a contextual reference. In *Jub*. 46:1–2, the author stresses the mutual

---

[10] The narrative of the story of the children of Israel after Jacob's death until the arrival at Mount Sinai (Gen 47:28–50:26 and Exod 1:1–19:1) is rendered very summarily in *Jubilees* (*Jub*. 45:13–50:13). Moreover, in this abbreviated rendering, much attention is paid to the description of the Pesach in *Jub*. 49 (using Exod 12:1–50) and the description of the sabbath in *Jub*. 50:6–13. In addition, the abbreviated rendering of the biblical text is interwoven with the use of other traditions. Because of this heavily abbreviated rewritten story, one should be very cautious of drawing far-reaching conclusions, especially with regard to the omissions.

[11] Halpern-Amaru, "Burying the Fathers," 137, 139.

love of the children of Israel (46:1c–e: "All of them were of the same mind so that each one loved the other and each one helped the other") that continued after Jacob's death (46:2a: "There was no Satan or any evil throughout all of Joseph's lifetime after his father Jacob").

In conclusion, the omission of Gen 50:15–21 is not motivated by the non-elevation of Joseph in the context of his family. *Jubilees* stresses the harmony of the family. It is more plausible that the author of *Jubilees* considered Gen 50:15–21 as somewhat redundant and containing elements contradicting other biblical passages.

The Omission of Exod 1:1–5

Exodus 1:1–5 has no parallel in *Jub.* 46. This omission seems not to be due to the strategy of the author of *Jubilees* to put the transition of a family into a people during Joseph's life.[12] This reversal of the order of the events (the prosperity of Israel before Joseph's death) offers hardly any clues for the omission of Exod 1:1–5. The author could have combined the rewriting of Exod 1:7 with Exod 1:1–5 and put it before the description of Joseph's death. The reason for the omission of this opening passage therefore seems to be a different one, namely the fact that no new information is given. The first pericope of the book of Exodus (Exod 1:1–7) has a clear transitional purpose and functions as the opening of a new book. It refers back to the final part of Genesis and serves as a prelude to the subsequent exodus. For the author of *Jubilees*, Exodus is not a separate book; it contains the continuation of the story begun in Genesis. In this respect, the references to Genesis are redundant. The list of names of Jacob's sons occurs several times in Genesis.[13] One of these lists (Gen 46:8–27) is rewritten quite closely in *Jub.* 44:11–34. Apart from the sons' names (cf. Exod 1:2–4), I refer especially to the rewriting of Gen 46:8a (cf. Exod 1:1) in *Jub.* 44:11 ("These are the names of Jacob's children who went to Egypt with their father Jacob") and of Gen 46:27b (cf. Exod 1:5) in *Jub.* 44:33 ("All the persons of Jacob who entered Egypt were 70 persons"). The insertion of Exod 1:1–5 seems therefore unnecessary.

---

[12] According to Halpern-Amaru, the chronological order of Exodus (a family went to Egypt, Joseph's death, growth of the family into a people) is changed in *Jubilees* (a family went to Egypt and became a people; Joseph's death)." Cf. Halpern-Amaru, "Burying the Fathers," 136.

[13] Cf. above, n. 7.

Jub. 46:1–2 and Exod 1:7

Jubilees 46:1–2 can be considered an addition with regard to the text of Gen 50:15–26 and Exod 1:1–14. At the same time, however, it is clear that the theme of the multiplication of the children of Israel is taken from Exod 1:7.[14]

Exod 1:7	Jub. 46:1–2	
	1a	AFTER THE DEATH OF JACOB, the children of Israel became numerous
7a The children of Israel became numerous		
b *and brought forth abundantly*;		
c *they multiplied*		IN the land OF EGYPT.
d *and grew exceedingly strong;*	b	*They became a populous nation,*
e SO THAT the land WAS FILLED WITH THEM	c	AND ALL OF THEM WERE OF THE SAME MIND
	d	SO THAT EACH ONE LOVED THE OTHER
	e	AND EACH ONE HELPED THE OTHER.
	f	*They became numerous*
	g	*and increased very much*—EVEN FOR TEN WEEKS OF YEARS (= 70 YEARS) FOR ALL OF JOSEPH'S LIFETIME.
	2a	THERE WAS NO SATAN OR ANY EVIL ONE THROUGHOUT ALL OF JOSEPH'S LIFETIME THAT HE LIVED AFTER HIS FATHER JACOB
	b	BECAUSE ALL THE EGYPTIANS WERE HONORING THE CHILDREN OF ISRAEL FOR ALL OF JOSEPH'S LIFETIME.

---

[14] Quotations from the biblical text follow the Revised Standard Version, with slight modifications, whereas quotations from *Jubilees* are according to J.C. VanderKam, *The Book of Jubilees: II* (CSCO 511; Scriptores Aethiopici 88; Leuven: Peeters, 1989). *Jub.* 46:1–16 is partly preserved in Latin (*Jub.* 46:1, 12–16). Both the Latin and Ethiopic translations go back to a Greek translation of the Hebrew original. Cf. VanderKam, *Book of Jubilees: II*, vi–xxxi; K. Berger, *Das Buch der Jubiläen* (JSHRZ 2.3; Gütersloh: Mohn, 1981), 285–94. The edition of the Latin text of *Jub.* 16:1–9 can be found in J.C. VanderKam, *The Book of Jubilees: I* (CSCO 510; Scriptores Aethiopici 87; Leuven: Peeters, 1989), 298. The text-critical value of the Latin text of *Jub.* 46:1, 12–16 is discussed in the notes to the translation of the Ethiopic text in VanderKam, *Book of Jubilees: II*, 300, 302–4. The text of *Jub.* 46:1–3 is partly preserved in 2Q20. Cf. J.C. VanderKam, *Textual and Historical Studies in the Book of Jubilees* (HSM 14; Missoula, Mont.: Scholars Press for Harvard Semitic Museum, 1977), 88–91.

Exod 1:7 is taken up in *Jub.* 46:1a, b, f, g.[15] Whereas Exod 1:7 uses four different verbs to describe the growing of the children of Israel (פרה, שרץ, רבה, עצם), *Jub.* 46:1–2 uses only two different verbs: *bazḥa* ("be numerous"; "increase") occurs three times in *Jub.* 46:1, f, g and *fadfada* ("increase"; "multiply") once in *Jub.* 46:1g. Whereas the biblical text states that the children of Israel became numerous "so that the land was filled with them," the text of *Jubilees* merely states that they became numerous "in the land." The passage in *Jubilees* describes the ideal conditions for Jacob's descendants during the days of Joseph's life.[16] Israel not only multiplied greatly and lived in mutual love (*Jub.* 46:1c–e), but also "all the Egyptians were honoring the children of Israel" (*Jub.* 46:2).

The author puts the multiplication of the children of Israel (Exod 1:7) *before* Joseph's death (Exod 1:6). In this sense, one can speak of a rearrangement of Exod 1:7. The author of *Jubilees* stresses that Israel's growth into a nation took place during Joseph's lifetime (cf. *Jub.* 46:1g, 2a, 2b: "for all of Joseph's lifetime"). The rearrangement of Exod 1:7 does not necessarily mean that the author of *Jubilees* changes the chronology of the biblical story. The multiplication of the people of Israel in Egypt is already mentioned in Gen 47:27 ("Thus *Israel* dwelt *in the land of Egypt*, in the land of Goshen; and they gained possessions in it, and *were fruitful and multiplied exceedingly*"). Interestingly, Gen 47:27 is put immediately before Jacob's deathbed (Gen 48:1–49:33). Although the author of *Jubilees* does refer to Gen 47:13–26 in *Jub.* 45:8–12 and to Gen 47:28 in *Jub.* 45:13, he does not refer there to Gen 47:27. It is true that in the rewriting of *Jubilees* the growth of the children of Israel is put after Jacob's death.[17] The importance of this notion is even stressed in *Jub.* 46:2a ("all of Joseph's lifetime *that he lived after his father Jacob*"). For the author of *Jubilees*, Jacob's death seems to be of importance for the growth of a family into a nation. However, one should not overlook the mention of "ten weeks of years" that Israel increased (*Jub.* 46:1g). This refers not to the period after Jacob's death, but to the period from the entrance of Jacob and his family into Egypt

---

[15] Cf. also Exod 1:9, 12, 20.

[16] Cf. J.C. VanderKam, *The Book of Jubilees* (Guides to Apocrypha and Pseudepigrapha; Sheffield: Sheffield Academic Press, 2001), 81.

[17] So Halpern-Amaru, "Burying the Fathers," 136–37.

until Joseph's death.[18] It seems therefore somewhat exaggerated to stress the fact that Jacob's death replaces Joseph's death with regard to the periodization of Israel's history.[19] The author of *Jubilees* emphasizes that before Joseph's death Israel was prospering and growing, whereas after his death, Israel was threatened.

Jub. 46:3–11 and Exod 1:6, 8

Jubilees 46:3–11 can be considered the rewriting of Exod 1:6, 8, making use of Gen 50:24–26 and extensively of non-biblical traditions. In the following synopsis, I put Exod 1:6–8 and *Jub.* 46:3–11 side by side:[20]

Exod 1:6–8		*Jubilees 46:3–8*
[cf. Gen 50:26]	3a	Joseph died when he was a hundred and ten years old.
	b	HE HAD LIVED FOR 17 YEARS IN THE LAND OF CANAAN;
	c	FOR TEN YEARS HE REMAINED ENSLAVED;
	d	HE WAS IN PRISON FOR THREE YEARS;
	e	AND FOR 80 YEARS HE WAS RULING THE ENTIRE LAND OF EGYPT UNDER THE PHARAOH.
[ ]		
6a *Joseph* died and all his brothers and all of that generation.	4a	*He* died and all his brothers and all of that generation.
7a The children of Israel became numerous		[cf. *Jub.* 46:1–2]

---

[18] R.H. Charles, *The Book of Jubilees or the Little Genesis* (London: Black, 1902), 244–45.

[19] See Halpern-Amaru, "Burying the Fathers," 136. She writes that for the author of *Jubilees*, "the death of Joseph is neither a turning point in the narrative nor of major significance in Israelite history...The author of *Jubilees* retains the biblical notice of the growth of the Israelite population as the primary marker for the shift to a new epoch, but detaches that notice from its association with the deaths of Joseph, his brothers, and the emigrant generation in Exodus 1 and moves it to immediately after the death of Jacob."

[20] In the synoptic overviews, I have tried to present a classification of the similarities and dissimilarities between Exodus and *Jubilees*. I have used small caps and square brackets to highlight those elements of Exodus which do not occur in *Jubilees*, and vice versa, i.e., the omissions and additions. Small caps in one text correspond to square brackets in the other. I have used normal script for the corresponding elements between both texts, i.e., the verbatim quotations of one or more words from the source text in *Jubilees*. I have used italics to indicate the variations between Exodus and *Jubilees*, other than additions or omissions. Sometimes there is a rearrangement of words and sentences. I have underlined those elements.

Table *(cont.)*

Exod 1:6–8	Jubilees 46:3–8

b *and brought forth abundantly*;
c *they multiplied*
d AND GREW EXCEEDINGLY STRONG;
e SO THAT THE LAND WAS fiLLED
WITH THEM.

[cf. *Gen 50:24–25*]	5a BEFORE HE DIED
	b *he ordered the children of Israel to take his bones along at the time when they would leave the land of Egypt.*
	6a *He made them swear about his bones*
[ ]	b BECAUSE HE KNEW THAT THE EGYPTIANS WOULD NOT AGAIN BRING HIM OUT
	c AND BURY HIM ON THE DAY IN THE LAND OF CANAAN,
	d SINCE MAKAMARON, THE KING OF CANAAN—WHILE HE WAS LIVING IN THE LAND OF ASUR—FOUGHT IN THE VALLEY WITH THE KING OF EGYPT
	e AND KILLED HIM THERE.
	f HE PURSUED THE EGYPTIANS AS FAR AS THE GATES OF ERMON.
	7a HE WAS UNABLE TO ENTER
8a [ ] A new king ruled Egypt, WHO DID NOT KNOW JOSEPH.	b BECAUSE ANOTHER new king ruled Egypt [ ].
[ ]	c HE WAS STRONGER THAN HE,
	d SO HE RETURNED TO THE LAND OF CANAAN
	e AND THE GATES OF EGYPT WERE CLOSED WITH NO ONE LEAVING OR ENTERING EGYPT
[*cf. Gen 50:26a*]	8a *Joseph died in the forty-sixth jubilee, in the sixth week, during its second year (2242).*
[*cf. Gen 50:26b*]	b *He was buried in the land of Egypt,*
[*cf. Exod 1:6*]	c *and all his brothers died* AFTER HIM.

Table *(cont.)*

	Jubilees 46:9–11 (No Parallel in Exodus)
9a	THEN THE KING OF EGYPT WENT OUT TO FIGHT WITH THE KING OF CANAAN IN THE FORTY-SEVENTH JUBILEE, IN THE SECOND WEEK, DURING ITS SECOND YEAR (2263).
b	THE CHILDREN OF ISRAEL BROUGHT OUT ALL THE BONES OF JACOB'S SONS EXCEPT JOSEPH'S BONES.
c	THEY BURIED THEM IN THE FIELD, IN THE DOUBLE CAVE IN THE MOUNTAIN.
10a	MANY RETURNED TO EGYPT
b	BUT A FEW OF THEM REMAINED ON THE MOUNTAIN OF HEBRON.
c	YOUR FATHER AMRAM REMAINED WITH THEM.
11a	THE KING OF CANAAN CONQUERED THE KING OF EGYPT
b	AND CLOSED THE GATES OF EGYPT.

Jubilees 46:3–11 can be divided into two units. The first part deals with Joseph's death and burial (*Jub.* 46:3–8), the second part with the transfer of the bones of Joseph's brothers to Canaan (*Jub.* 46:9–11). Both parts are interrelated by the mention of Joseph's brothers (cf. *Jub.* 46:4a, 8c, 9bc) and by the mention of a war between the king of Egypt and the king of Canaan (cf. *Jub.* 46:6d–7, 9a, 11).

The specific way in which Exod 1:6, 8 is rewritten in *Jub.* 46:3–11 is in my opinion at least partly caused by some problems in the biblical text, such as the fact that Joseph is not buried in Canaan immediately after his death (Gen 50:24–26), the unmotivated mentions of a new king (Exod 1:8) and a war (Exod 1:10), the unexplained change in the attitude of the Egyptians with regard to the children of Israel (Exod 1:9–12), and finally the somewhat odd formulation of the journey of Moses' father before his birth (Exod 2:1: "A man from the house of Levi *went*"). The author of *Jubilees* tries to solve these problems, and probably makes use of non-biblical traditions to achieve his aim.

It is striking that the author of *Jubilees* mentions three times that Joseph died (*Jub.* 46:3a, 4a, 8ab), because he has considerably abbreviated the text of Gen 45–Exod 19. Moreover, he usually avoids repetitions.

This shows that Joseph's death was an important issue for him.[21] The first mention (*Jub.* 46:3a) is a quotation of the death report of Gen 50:26a, in which his age is given. The second mention (*Jub.* 46:4) is a quotation of Exod 1:6, in which additional information is given in that "all his brothers and all of that generation" also died. Finally, the formulation of the death report in *Jub.* 46:8 combines Gen 50:26 and Exod 1:6. Here, Joseph's total age (Gen 50:26a) is formulated according to the absolute chronology of the book (*Jub.* 46:8a). The statement that he is buried "in the land of Egypt" (*Jub.* 46:8b) refers to Gen 50:26bc ("and they embalmed him and he was put in a coffin in Egypt"), although it does not mention that they embalmed him and put him in a coffin. Again it mentions that "all his brothers" died, but new information is also given. They died "after him" (*Jub.* 46:8c).

It is clear that *Jub.* 46:5–6a refers to Gen 50:24–25 with variations. The biblical text is clearly structured in two speeches of Joseph to his brothers (the children of Israel):

A	24a	And Joseph said to *his brothers*:
	b	"I am about to die;
B	c	but God will visit you,
C	d	and bring you up from this land
		to the land which he swore to Abraham, to Isaac, and to Jacob."

A'	25a	And Joseph made *the children of Israel* swear, saying:
B'	b	"God will visit you,
C'	c	and you will bring up my bones from here."

In the first speech, Joseph announces that he is about to die, but he reassures his brothers by saying that God will take care of them; he will lead them out of Egypt and bring them to the promised land. In the second speech, Joseph makes the children of Israel swear an oath that they will carry his bones with them when they leave Egypt. The phrasing of both speeches is quite parallel, especially the phrasing of 50:24d ("He will bring you up from this land") and 50:25c ("You will bring up my bones from here").

The author of *Jubilees* refers to this passage in *Jub.* 46:5–6a.

5a	Before he died
b	he ordered the children of Israel to take his bones along at the time when they would leave the land of Egypt.
6a	He made them swear about his bones

---

[21] Cf. above, n. 19.

The direct speech of Gen 50:24–25 is not taken over. Moreover, the author of *Jubilees* concentrates mainly on the second speech, the oath to carry his bones, which he even mentions twice. From the first speech, he takes over the reference to the exodus in *Jub.* 46:5b ("at the time when they would leave the land of Egypt"). The active part of God in the exodus ("God will visit you"; "God will bring you up") seems to be of no relevance in this part of the rewriting. The author integrates Gen 50:24–25 in his rewriting to solve a problem. The biblical text does not make clear why Joseph did not ask for his bones to be taken to Canaan right away, as was the case with the bones of Jacob (Gen 49:29–33; 50:1–14).[22] The author of *Jubilees* suggests an answer to this question. A war had caused the border between Egypt and Canaan to be closed. That is why his bones could not be transported immediately to Canaan. Therefore, Joseph asked his brothers to make sure that he would be buried in Canaan. Gen 50:24–25 refers forward to the exodus out of Egypt. In the biblical text, Joseph's request is executed by Moses during the exodus from Egypt (Exod 13:19; cf. Josh 24:32). In his rewriting, the author of *Jubilees* explains that Joseph knew what would happen in the near future ("Because *he knew* that the Egyptians would not bring him out again and bury him on the day in the land of Canaan").[23] The impossibility of transferring Joseph's bones is not attributed to a change in the attitude of the Egyptians with regard to the children of Israel. This is in accordance with the description of the positive relationship between Egypt and Israel (*Jub.* 46:1–2). The reversal takes place at a later stage, after Joseph's death (*Jub.* 46:12–16; Exod 1:9–14).

The insertion of a war story offers an opportunity to explain the postponement of Joseph's funeral in Canaan. He also uses this war story to examine the rise of a new king. The text of Exod 1:8 looks straightforward.[24] However, the failure of the writer to mention the death of the previous king and his subsequent succession led the author of *Jubilees* to

---

[22] See also the burial of Sarah (Gen 23:1–20), Abraham (Gen 25:1–11), and Isaac (Gen 35:27–29) in Hebron.

[23] The author of *Jubilees* speaks about a Joseph who *knew* what the Egyptians would do in the near future, whereas in the biblical text it is said that the new king did *not know* Joseph. *Jubilees* omits this qualification of the new ruler.

[24] According to A. Salvesen, *Symmachus in the Pentateuch* (JSM 15; Manchester: University of Manchester, 1991), 63, the mention of a "different" (אחר) king would have been more obvious.

introduce a story in which the old king died in the war between Egypt and Canaan and in which a new king was appointed.[25]

The second part of the addition deals with the burial of the bones of all of Jacob's sons, except those of Joseph, in Hebron (*Jub.* 46:9–11). The transfer of these bones is linked to the mention of their death (*Jub.* 46:4; Exod 1:6). The author of *Jubilees* specifies that they died after Joseph (*Jub.* 46:8c). This is not said explicitly in the biblical text, although it can be inferred from Gen 50:24–25. The burial of the bones is made possible by yet another battle between the king of Egypt and the king of Canaan. The burial of the bones was executed by the children of Israel (*Jub.* 46:9b), who are not specified, but are meant to be the children and grandchildren of the patriarchs. After the burial of the patriarchs, most of the Israelites returned to Egypt. A few, however, remained on the mountain of Hebron, among whom was Moses' father Amram, the grandson of Levi (cf. Exod 6:16–20; Num 26:58–59).

The mention of Amram is justified by Exod 2:1 ("And a man from the house of Levi went"). The author of *Jubilees* interprets this phrase as "your father came from the land of Canaan" (*Jub.* 47:1). The location of Amram on the mountain of Hebron is motivated by the activities that have taken place, that is, the burial of the bones of Joseph's brothers at Hebron.[26]

The reason why Amram and the others stayed in Canaan is not made clear. Possibly, it may have been because after a while the king of Canaan prevailed over Egypt: "The king of Canaan conquered the king of Egypt and closed the gates of Egypt" (*Jub.* 46:11). It is not said for how long the gates of Egypt remained closed. In any case, Amram stayed 40 years in Canaan. He arrived in Canaan in the second year

---

[25] In rabbinic literature, there are arguments as to whether this king was really a different king or merely the same one implementing different policies with respect to the children of Israel. Cf. *Exod. Rab.* 1:8. Some of the ancient versions of the biblical text seem to reflect the same problem: LXX reads ετερος ("other"), Aquila αλλος ("other"), and Symmachus δευτερος ("second"). Josephus mentions that the king passed to another dynasty (*Ant.* 2.202). See Salvesen, *Symmachus*, 63. *Jubilees* reads "*another* new king."

[26] According to Halpern-Amaru, Amram was placed on the mountain because the author of *Jubilees* wished to put Amram on one line with Abraham, Isaac, and Jacob. By placing Amram on the mountain of Hebron, the author of *Jubilees* assigns to Amram the role that he has taken away from the biblical Joseph. *Jubilees* consistently deconstructs the biblical characterization of Joseph. See Halpern-Amaru, "Burying the Fathers," 144–45. I am not convinced that a deconstruction of Joseph and an elevation of Levi at the expense of Joseph has influenced the rewriting here.

of the second year-week of the 47th jubilee, which is *a.m.* 2263 (cf. *Jub.* 46:9), and he arrived back in Egypt in the seventh year of the seventh year-week of the 47th jubilee, which is *a.m.* 2303 (cf. *Jub.* 47:1a).

Nowhere in the biblical literature does it state that the brothers of Joseph were also to be buried in Canaan. According to the author of *Jubilees*, this must have been quite natural. Not only the patriarchs and Joseph were to be buried in Canaan, but also his brothers. This seems to be in line with the family harmony mentioned earlier. Both Joseph and his brothers are treated equally, but that is not the same as a diminution of Joseph. Moreover, it is important for the author of *Jubilees* that all the children of Israel were liberated from Egypt and that all could enter Canaan.[27]

The second part of the war story possibly also tries to explain the change in the mind of the Egyptians with regard to the children of Israel. Until that moment the children of Israel were prospering in Egypt. They were honored greatly by the Egyptians. When, for example, Jacob was buried at Canaan, all the servants of Pharaoh went with him, and the inhabitants of Canaan said: "This is a grievous mourning to the Egyptians" (Gen 50:11). The biblical text does not work out the reasons for this change in attitude of the Egyptians after Joseph's death and after the rise of a new king. According to the author of *Jubilees*, the king of Egypt went out to fight with the king of Canaan in a second stage of the war, twenty-one years after Joseph's death. This enabled the Israelites to transport the bones of the sons of Jacob outside Egypt in order to bury them in Canaan (*Jub.* 46:9–10). The king of Egypt was afraid of the Israelites because of the fact that they went to Canaan to bury their forefathers. This showed that "their minds and faces look toward the land of Canaan" (*Jub.* 46:13). The king was not only afraid that Israel would fight against Egypt and unite with the enemy, that is, the king of Canaan, but also that they would leave the land. The motivation for this statement could have been that some of them remained in Canaan. Therefore, he conceived an evil plan against Israel (cf. *Jub.* 46:12). Thus the longing of the children of Israel for Canaan, which finds concrete expression in their crossing the border to bury their fathers, is the motivation for this fear.

I have tried to show that the particular way Exod 1:6–7 is rewritten in *Jub.* 46:3–11 seems to serve several goals. It explains why Joseph was

---

[27] *Jub.* 44:33–34 mentions that five of the grandsons of Jacob died in Egypt and were buried there.

not buried in Canaan immediately after his death, and it contextualizes
the rise of a new king and the changed attitude of Egypt with regard
to the children of Israel. It also makes clear why the bones of Joseph's
brothers could have been transferred to Canaan at a later stage. Finally,
it makes explicit that Amram, Moses' father, had to make a journey
before impregnating Jochebed.

The fact that the author of *Jubilees* opted for a war story could reflect
a historical situation, according to some exegetes. The kings of Canaan
and Egypt might reflect the conflicts between the Seleucides who controlled Palestine and the Ptolemies in Egypt.[28] It might, however, be
legendary. It is possibly motivated by the text of Exodus, which speaks
about a war (Exod 1:10: "if *war* comes").[29] The biblical text states that
the new king of Egypt is afraid that Israel will unite with the enemy
and fight against Egypt, but the war is not elaborated as such.

The author of *Jubilees* could himself have invented the legend about
a war between Egypt and Canaan in relation with the postponement of
Joseph's burial and the transport of the bones of Joseph's brothers from
Egypt to Canaan. However, it is also possible that he used an already
existing tradition not found in the Bible that connects the transport
of the bones with a war between Egypt and Canaan. Although the
rewriting of *Jubilees* answers several questions concerning the biblical
text, it opens up some new questions, which remain unanswered. Why
was it possible to transport the bones during a war between Egypt and
Canaan? Who was involved in the funeral? Why did many return to
Egypt but not all? Why did Amram and some unnamed others remain
in Hebron?

Halpern-Amaru rightly states that this war legend acquired the status
of a tradition with its own literary history.[30] The story about the transport of the bones of Joseph's brothers, sometimes in relation to a war,
can be found in several other texts, for example *4Q543–548* (*4QVisions
of Amram*), the *Testaments of the Twelve Patriarchs*, Flavius Josephus, and
the New Testament.

In the case of *4QVisions of Amram*, we are dealing with a fragmentary
and reconstructed text. There are several copies of the same composi-

---

[28] Berger, *Buch der Jubiläen*, 537–38; VanderKam, *Book of Jubilees*, 81–82. Charles, *Book of Jubilees*, 245–46, points to an earlier period in history.
[29] So also Berger, *Buch der Jubiläen*, 537.
[30] Halpern-Amaru, "Burying the Fathers," 145.

tion, sometimes with additional information. Here is the translation of one of the copies (4Q544 1).[31]

1 Qahat there to stay and to dwell and to bui[ld the tombs of our fathers…many from the sons of my uncle together …]
2 a man, and about our work it was very much un[til the dead were buried…rumor of war, frightening those returning from here to the land of Egypt …]
3 quickly, and they did not build the tombs of their fathers. [And my father Qahat let me go…and to build and to obtain from them…from the land of Canaan …]
4 until we build. *Blank* And war broke out between [Philistea and Egypt and was winning…]
5 And they closed the b[ord]er of Egypt and it was not possible to […]
6 forty-one years, and we could not […]
7 between Egypt and Canaan and Philistea. *Blank* […] And [during al]l th[is…]
8 she was not. *Blank* I, myself, [did not take] ano[ther] woman […]
9 all: that I will return to Egypt in peace and I will see the face of my wife […]
10 in my vision, the vision of the dream.

In this fragmentarily preserved text, we can read that Amram went together with his father Qahat from Egypt to Canaan "to stay and to dwell and to build" the tombs for the burial of their fathers. The reconstructed part of line 1 adds that Amram also went together with the sons of his uncle (cf. 4Q545 1a–b ii 14). This work was interrupted by a rumor of war (thus the reconstructed part of line 2; cf. 4Q545 1a–b ii 16: "rumor of war"). It is possible that Amram went back to Egypt together with the others after these rumors (4Q544 1 3: "quickly, and they did not build the tombs of their fathers"), but this is not completely certain. It is also possible that he did not go back to Egypt with the others. After a while, Amram received permission from his father to remain or to go back to Canaan (the reconstructed text of line 3 "And my father Qahat let me go" is taken from 4Q546 2 3) to finish the work ("until we build"). When he was there, war broke out between Philistea, Canaan, and Egypt, and because of this war the borders were closed (line 5) for forty-one years (line 6), during which

---

[31] The translation is taken from F. García Martínez and E.J.C. Tigchelaar, *The Dead Sea Scrolls Study Edition* (Leiden: Brill, 1998), 2:1086–89. Most reconstructions are taken from the other manuscripts. The official publication of the manuscripts is by É. Puech. Cf. *DJD* 31:322–24.

he did not take another woman (line 8). Line 9 seems to contain a reference to his wife. Apparently she did not go with him to Canaan, and during his stay there he did not see her.

The similarities with the second part of the additions in *Jub.* 47 (v. 8–11) are clear. Both have to do with a burial in Canaan; in both cases this burial is associated with a war between Canaan and Egypt. In both cases Amram is participating, and in both cases the border (or gates) between Egypt and Canaan is closed. There are however also some differences. In *4QVisions of Amram*, Amram's father and his wife are explicitly mentioned. In *4QVisions of Amram*, it is not clear if there are two wars, as is the case in *Jubilees*. The text speaks first about the "rumor" of war (4Q544 1 2; 4Q545 1a–b ii 16) and later about the outbreak of the war (4Q544 1 4; cf. 4Q543 4 3; 4Q545 1a–b ii 19). With regard to the rumor of war, the fear of the people and their returning is mentioned (4Q544 1 2; 4Q545 1a–b ii 16). The border of Egypt is closed only after the war (4Q544 1 4). A closing of the gates is not mentioned in relation to the rumor of war. Finally, Amram remains forty-one years in Canaan according to *4QVisions of Amram*, whereas according to *Jubilees* he remains forty years (*Jub.* 46:9 and 47:1).

Based on the similarities and dissimilarities between *Jub.* 46:5–11 and *4QVisions of Amram*, one can suggest that the author of *Jubilees* probably knew of a comparable tradition, as found in *4QVisions of Amram*, that he integrated into his rewriting of the Exodus story. At the same time, he seems to have adapted this tradition in that he created two wars, each time with a closing of the gates. The first war is antedated and put in relation to Joseph's death. In *4QVisions of Amram* the rumor of war is mentioned in relation to building the tombs in Canaan, which causes the return to Egypt. In *Jubilees*, a second war takes place twenty-one years later. *4QVisions of Amram* does not disclose the distance in time between the rumor and the outbreak of the war. *Jubilees* suggests that the second war opened up the possibility for the burial in Canaan. This cannot be found in *4QVisions of Amram*.

Elements of this tradition can also be found in the *Testaments of the Twelve Patriarchs*. There, too, it is said that the bones of all the patriarchs were buried in Hebron.[32] In the case of Simeon and Benjamin, a war between Egypt and Canaan is also mentioned (*T. Sim.* 8:2; *T. Benj.* 12:3). It is not clear whether, according to the *Testaments of the Twelve*

---

[32] Cf. *T. Reu.* 7:1–2; *T. Sim.* 8:1–2; *T. Levi* 19:5; *T. Jud.* 26:4; *T. Zeb.* 10:6; *T. Dan* 7:2; *T. Naph.* 9:1–2; *T. Gad* 8:3–4; *T. Ash.* 8:1; *T. Benj.* 12:1–4.

Patriarchs, the bones of all the patriarchs, with the exception of Joseph, were transported at the same time to Hebron, as *Jubilees* puts it, or at different times. Whereas with regard to Simeon and Benjamin the text speaks about a war, with regard to Gad the text speaks about a period of five years after his death before his bones were transported (*T. Gad* 8:4), and in the case of Levi, Zebulon, and Dan it is said that they were transported "later" (cf. *T. Levi* 19:5; *T. Zeb.* 10:6; *T. Dan* 7:2).[33]

The tradition that the bones of Joseph's brothers were brought from Egypt to Canaan before the bones of Joseph is also found in Flavius Josephus, although no war is mentioned: "His brothers also died in Egypt, after a rich and prosperous life. Their bodies were taken later by their descendants and buried in Hebron. The bones of Joseph were carried away to Canaan much later, when the Hebrews moved away from Egypt" (*Ant.* 2.199–200).

Acts also speaks about the transport of the bones, but does not mention a war: "And Jacob went down into Egypt. And he died, himself and our fathers, and they were carried back to Shechem and laid in the tomb that Abraham had bought for a sum of silver from the sons of Hamor in Shechem" (Acts 7:15–16).[34]

Jub. 46:12–16 and Exod 1:9–14

The author of *Jubilees* connects the rise of a new king (Exod 1:8) strongly with rewriting the death and burial of Joseph and his brothers (*Jub.* 46:3–11), whereas he integrates Exod 1:15–22 in the rewriting of the story of Moses' birth (*Jub.* 47:1–9). Therefore, we will confine ourselves here to the rewriting of Exod 1:9–14 in the last section of *Jub.* 46. As can be seen in the following synopsis, *Jub.* 46:12–16 follows the text of Exodus quite closely.[35]

---

[33] Cf. Charles, *Book of Jubilees*, 245.

[34] Likewise, in rabbinic literature it is said that the bones not only of Joseph but also of his brothers were eventually taken for burial to Hebron. Cf. *Mek. R. Ishmael, Beshallah*, Introduction; *Mek. R. Shimon bar Yohai* 14; *Gen. Rab.* 100:11.

[35] It seems as if the author of *Jubilees* was not aware of the ambiguity of the reference to "he" in *Jub.* 46:12 when he returned to the biblical text after the digression of the war story. In Exod 1:9a, it is quite clear that the subject is the new king who ruled Egypt (Exod 1:8), but in *Jub.* 46:12 it could refer either to the "king of Egypt" or to the "king of Canaan" of the preceding sentence (*Jub.* 46:11). The Latin text of *Jub.* 46:12 reads *rex chanaam* which is accepted by Berger. See Berger, *Buch der Jubiläen*, 537, 539. *Jub.* 46:13i ("they leave our land because their minds and faces look toward the land of Canaan") makes clear, however, that the king of Egypt is speaking here. So does VanderKam, *Book of Jubilees: II*, 302.

Exod 1:9–14		Jub. 46:12–16	
		12a	HE CONCEIVED AN EVIL PLAN AGAINST THE CHILDREN OF ISRAEL TO MAKE THEM SUFFER.
[ ]			
9a	He said to *his people*:	b	He said to *the Egyptians*:
b	"Behold, the people of the children of Israel *are too many* [ ]	13a	"Behold, the people of the children of Israel *has now grown* AND INCREASED MORE THAN WE.
	AND TOO MIGHTY FOR US.		[ ]
10a	Come on,	b	Come on,
b	let us act wisely with *it*,	c	let us act wisely with *them*
c	*lest it* increases.	d	*before they* increase.
	[ ]	e	LET US MAKE THEM SUFFER IN SLAVERY
d	*If* war comes [ ],	f	*before* war comes TO US
e	and *it*, too, <u>will unite with</u> *our enemies*	g	and *they*, too, <u>fight against us.</u>
f	<u>and *it* fights against us</u>	h	OTHERWISE *they* <u>will unite with the enemy</u>
g	and *goes up from the* land [ ]."	i	and *leave our* land BECAUSE THEIR MIND(S) AND FACE(S LOOK) TOWARD THE LAND OF CANAAN."
1a	*They* appointed taskmasters over *it* to make *it* suffer *with their burdens*.	14a	*He* appointed taskmasters over *them* to make *them* suffer *in slavery*.
b	*It* built *store* cities for the pharaoh, Pithom and Ramses. [ ]	b	*They* built *fortified* cities for the pharaoh—Pithom and Ramses.
		c	THEY BUILT EVERY WALL AND ALL THE FORTIFICATIONS WHICH HAD FALLEN DOWN IN THE CITIES OF EGYPT.
	[cf. Exod 1:13a]	15a	*They* <u>were enslaving *them* by force,</u>
12a	But *the more* they make *it* suffer,	b	but *however much* they make *them* suffer
b	the more *it* would multiply	c	the more *they* would multiply
c	and the more *it* would increase.	d	and the more *they* would increase.
d	*They were in dread of* the children of Israel.	16a	*The Egyptians considered* the children of Israel *detestable*.
13a	<u>*The Egyptians* were enslaving *the children of Israel* by force,</u>		[cf. *Jub.* 46:15a]
14a	AND MADE THEIR LIVES BITTER WITH HARD SLAVERY, IN MORTAR AND BRICK, AND IN ALL KINDS OF WORK IN THE FIELD;		[ ]
b	IN ALL THEIR WORK THEY WERE ENSLAVING THEM BY FORCE.		

The author of *Jubilees* makes some small but interesting alterations with regard to the biblical text. In the first place, the rewriting of *Jubilees* characterizes right from the beginning the plan of the new king as "an evil plan" and specifies its goal (*Jub.* 46:12a: "in order to make them suffer"). The description of the goal is also mentioned within the direct speech of the king (*Jub.* 46:13e: "Let us make them suffer in slavery") and in the execution (*Jub.* 46:14a, 15ab). The formulation of this plan differs from the formulation in Exodus. It is not so much the "birth control" (Exod 1:10c), but the suffering of Israel in slavery.[36] In the second place, the unmotivated fear of the king for an Israel that would fight with the enemy and leave the country (Exod 1:10e–g) is motivated in *Jubilees*: "because their minds and faces look toward the land of Canaan" (*Jub.* 46:13i). In the preceding passage, the king of Canaan is presented as the principal enemy of the king of Egypt (*Jub.* 43:3–11). In the third place, the addition in *Jub.* 46:14c is related to the "*fortified* cities" (*Jub.* 46:14b) and may be motivated by Exod 1:14a ("mortar and brick"), but it is probably also influenced by the preceding war stories. In the fourth place, one can point to the fact that first in Exod 1:11–12 ענה Piel ("to afflict") is used and then in Exod 1:13–14 עבד Hiphil ("to cause to serve; enslave"). In the Ethiopic version of *Jubilees*, both *ḥamama* ("to suffer") and *qanaya* ("cause to serve") are put together (*Jub.* 46:13e, 14a, 15ab).[37] Finally, whereas in Exodus the plot of the story develops from plan (Exod 1:9b–10) to execution (Exod 1:11) to failure (Exod 1:12) followed by a new, more severe execution (Exod 1:13–14), in *Jubilees* it develops from plan (*Jub.* 46:12–13) to execution (*Jub.* 46:15b) to failure (*Jub.* 46:15c–16).

Many small deviations in *Jub.* 46:12–16 with regard to the Masoretic text of Exod 1:9–14 are due to the fact that the author of *Jubilees* uses a biblical text different from the Masoretic one. In these cases, deviations in *Jubilees* vis-à-vis the Masoretic text can also be found in the biblical texts of, for example, the Septuagint or the Samaritan Pentateuch. In these cases, we cannot consider this deviation as a variation of the bibli-

---

[36] Related to this, one can point to the difference of "*lest* it increases" (Exod 1:10c; MT, SP, LXX) and "*before* they increase" (*Jub.* 46:13d). However, the Peshitta of Exod 1:10 also has the reading in *Jubilees*. We cannot be sure, therefore, that the author of *Jubilees* changed his biblical *Vorlage*.

[37] See, however, the Latin version of *Jubilees*, which reads in *Jub.* 46:13e: *humiliemus eos in operibus ipsorum* ("let us humble them through their works") and in *Jub.* 46:14a: *ut adfligant eos in operibus ipsorum* ("to make them suffer through their works"). Cf. VanderKam, *Book of Jubilees: II*, 303.

cal text. VanderKam suggests that in Palestine there was a biblical text of Genesis-Exodus that agreed more often with the LXX and SP than with the MT but that was an independent witness.[38] Mostly, it concerns small variations. In *Jub.* 46:12–16, there are plural forms, whereas the MT reads in the singular. In all cases, the plural is attested to in one of the versions: *Jub.* 46:13b–d, 13g–i, 14a–b, 15cd.[39] The versions, however, do not consistently use either plural or singular. The diversity within the textual tradition is probably due to the expression "the people of the children of Israel" (Exod 1:9), to which one can refer with a singular ("the people"), but also with a plural ("the children of Israel"). From Exod 1:12d–13a onwards (where the phrase "the children of Israel" is used twice), the MT also uses the plural (Exod 1:14). In one case *Jubilees* uses a singular (*Jub.* 46:14a). The MT, the SP and the Peshitta have a plural (Exod 1:11), but the singular is attested in the LXX, Old Latin, and the Ethiopic. *Jubilees* 46:13f has the small addition "to us," which is also found in the SP, the LXX, the Peshitta, and the Ethiopic. In *Jub.* 46:13a, two items are mentioned ("grown"/ "increased"), which reflects the double reading of the LXX of Exod 1:9b, where the MT has only one item ("many"). The second adjective of the MT (עצום), which is presented as the third element in the LXX, is not taken over by Jubilees. *Jubilees* 46:14b reads "fortified cities," where the MT of Exod 1:11b has "store cities," but where the Septuagint reads: πόλεις ὀχυράς.

CONCLUSIONS

The comparison between *Jub.* 46:1–16 and Gen 50:15–Exod 1:14 shows that the author of *Jubilees* reorganized the sequence of events. He omits passages that can be considered redundant (e.g., Exod 1:1–5) or contradictory to other scriptural passages (e.g., Gen 50:15–21). He rearranges material with regard to Israel's prosperity to the period before Joseph's death (*Jub.* 46:1–2), and this relocation is in line with records in the book of Genesis. At the same time, he stresses the importance of Joseph's death by taking the references to his death in Genesis and

---

[38] See, e.g., J.C. VanderKam, "Jubilees and the Hebrew Texts of Genesis-Exodus," *Textus* 14 (1988): 71–85; repr. in *From Revelation to Canon: Studies in the Hebrew Bible and Second Temple Literature* (JSJSup 62; Leiden: Brill, 2000), 448–61 (460).

[39] Cf. VanderKam, *Book of Jubilees: II*, 302–4.

Exodus together while reworking it into a new story, integrating it with non-scriptural material (*Jub.* 46:3–11). I have tried to show that this reworking was motivated by problems in the biblical text, such as the fact that Joseph is not buried in Canaan immediately after his death, the unmotivated mentions of a new king and a war, the unexplained change in the attitude of the Egyptians with regard to the children of Israel, and finally the somewhat odd formulation of a journey of Moses' father before Moses' birth. The effect of the reorganization is, in the first place, to provide a smooth transition from Genesis to Exodus. There is no break between the two biblical books. In the second place, there is a highly organized sequence of events, from Israel's prosperity to Joseph's death and the rise of a new king and Israel's enslavement.

The special treatment of Levi at Jacob's deathbed, which is heavily abbreviated in *Jubilees* (*Jub.* 45:13–16), immediately preceding *Jub.* 46, and the equal treatment of all Jacob's sons with regard to their burials does not mean a reduction of Joseph's significance in the context of his family. The author of *Jubilees* stresses the harmony of the family of which Joseph is also a full member. Thanks to the efforts of Joseph described in the preceding chapter, the family is able to survive in Egypt and even to prosper. It is only after his death that the misery for Israel begins.

MOSES' FATHER SPEAKS OUT

Pieter W. van der Horst

In the Bible, Moses' father Amram does not speak. He is mentioned as a second-generation Levite, the son of Kohat, and father of Moses, but otherwise he is just "a biblical figure without a narrative."[1] He appears mainly in late genealogical lists (Exod 6:14–25; Num 26:58–59; 1 Chr 5:24–29), but is not even mentioned by name in the story of Moses' birth, where he is only referred to in passing as "a man from the tribe of Levi" (Exod 2:1). However, this unsatisfactory situation is remedied dramatically in post-biblical Jewish literature. There we see Amram gradually coming out of the shadows and becoming a personality, and a strong personality at that. What we witness is no less than the making of a hero.

The first evidence of Amram's rise to importance is found in the book of *Jubilees* (ca. mid-second century B.C.E.) and the Dead Sea Scrolls. In *Jub.* 47:9 it says that Amram taught Moses how to write. This may at first sight look like a current *topos* in ancient biography. However, it shows that, in contrast to the contemporary view that Moses was "educated in all the wisdom of the Egyptians" (Acts 7:22; cf. Philo, *Mos.* 1:23–24; Ezek. Trag., *Exag.* 36–38), there was also another tradition according to which Moses in fact did not learn from Egyptian teachers but from his Hebrew father. Learning to write, of course, here implies learning to read, that is, to get access to the contents of the writings of the great patriarchs and of the heavenly tablets which play such an important role in *Jubilees* (e.g., 8:2–3).[2] In other words, Amram here enables his son to imbue himself in the ancient traditions of his own people.[3]

---

[1] J.W. Wright, "Amram," *ABD* 1:217.

[2] See K. Berger, *Das Buch der Jubiläen* (JSHRZ 2.3; Gütersloh: Mohn, 1981), 539–40 note a.

[3] It is interesting to compare here the Preface of the much later (3rd–4th c. C.E.) *Sefer ha-Razim* which mentions Amram in a chain of tradents of knowledge of mysteries contained in a book revealed to Noah. Amram passes on this secret knowledge to Moses, Moses to Joshua, etc.; see M.A. Morgan, *Sefer ha-Razim: The Book of Mysteries* (Chico: Scholars Press, 1983), 19.

There are several Dead Sea Scrolls that mention Moses' father.[4] No less than six copies of an Aramaic document with the title *The Book of the Words of the Visions of Amram* were found in Cave 4 (4Q543–548), showing "that the work must have had some importance for the Qumran covenanters."[5] The text dates from somewhere in the second century B.C.E., possibly slightly later than *Jubilees*. It relates the words Amram spoke to his children on his deathbed. One would expect a document with a deathbed setting, which is typical for the Testament genre, to be entitled *Testament of Amram*, but it seems that the author wanted to emphasize the importance of Amram's visions, as Josephus does later as well (see below). Unfortunately, great parts of the text are irretrievable because of the fragmentary state of the manuscripts. In what has survived, we can decipher the following:[6]

Because of a war between Egypt, Canaan, and the Philistines, so Amram tells us, he was in Canaan while his wife Jochebed was far away in the land of Egypt, but although she was not with him for a very long time (forty-one years), he did not take another wife (4Q543 4; also in 4Q544 1, 4Q545 1a–b), so he is a person of great faithfulness and righteousness. In the next fragments we are told that in a vision Amram sees two angels who have the authority to rule over humankind. They ask him which of them he would choose to be ruled by. One has a dark serpent-like face and is wearing multi-coloured clothes; the other has a laughing (or happy) face, but the text describing the colour of his clothes is lost (4Q543 5–9; 4Q544 1). It seems that these two angels argue about Amram (see also 4Q547 1–2 iii 10–11). Amram asks the latter, the more cheerful one, his name, and the angel answers that he has three names (4Q543 14). Unfortunately, we do not find out what these names are, because the text is missing, although one of them may be Melchizedek, since the first angel, who is the ruler of darkness, is

---

[4] For a survey see M.E. Stone, "Amram," in *Encyclopedia of the Dead Sea Scrolls* (2 vols.; ed. L.H. Schiffman and J.C. VanderKam; New York: Oxford University Press, 2000), 1:23–24.

[5] Stone, "Amram," 23. For the *editio princeps* see J.T. Milik, "4Q Visions de 'Amram et une citation d'Origène,'" *RB* 79 (1972): 77–97, but now rather É. Puech's edition in *DJD* 31 is to be consulted. I also consulted the edition in K. Beyer, *Die aramäischen Texte vom Toten Meer: Ergänzungsband* (Göttingen: Vandenhoeck & Ruprecht, 1994), 85–92.

[6] I use here *Parabiblical Texts* (DSSR 3; Leiden: Brill, 2005), 412–43. Note that the *Visions of Amram* are here categorized as belonging to the Testaments section.

called Melchiresha (4Q544 2).[7] This dualism of light and darkness is of course also well-known from other Dead Sea Scrolls, but it is not confined to the sectarian documents among them.[8] Furthermore, in several of the fragments we find a marked emphasis on the importance of the Levitical priesthood of Aaron, Amram's second son (4Q545 4; 4Q546 11; 4Q547 6, 9), an element that links the document to two other Qumran documents, *Aramaic Levi* and the *Testament of Qahat*, writings that were composed "in order to legitimate the priestly line and its teaching."[9] Finally, some fragments of text survive in which Amram addresses his children with warnings about the eschatological fate of the sons of light and the sons of darkness: the former are destined for light, goodness, and safety, the latter for destruction (4Q548 1-2). Thereupon "he departed to his eternal home" (4Q549 2, 6). The difference with the silent Amram in the Bible is striking: here he has become a character in his own right.

The next document of relevance to our theme is the Pseudo-Philonic *Liber Antiquitatum Biblicarum* from the first century C.E. In chapter 9 of that work,[10] the author retells the story of Exod 1-2, but with some major additions. After the king of Egypt had decreed that all sons born to the Hebrews must be thrown into the river, the Jewish people gathered together and decided to remain celibate so as not to have anymore children. Amram, however, protests vigorously. He says that the universe will be destroyed sooner than the people of Israel, that the covenant of God with Abraham will be fulfilled, and that for that reason he will have children with his wife, no matter what the others decide, for God will not forget his people forever. He exhorts others to do the same and not to throw their sons, the fruits of their wombs, into the river. "Who knows if God will act zealously on account of this to free us from our humiliation" (9.6). God is very pleased by Amram's words and responds as follows, through an interior monologue:

---

[7] See P.J. Kobelski, *Melchizedek and Melchireša'* (Washington: Catholic Biblical Association of America, 1981). F. García Martínez, "4QAmram B I, 14: 'Melki-reša' ou Melki-ṣedeq?" *RevQ* 12/45 (1985): 111-14.

[8] Stone, "Amram," 24.

[9] Stone, "Amram," 24. See also A. Caquot, "Les testaments qoumrâniens des pères du sacerdoce," *RHPR* 78 (1998): 3-26.

[10] For an elaborate commentary on this chapter, see H. Jacobson, *A Commentary on Pseudo-Philo's* Liber Antiquitatum Biblicarum (AGJU 31; Leiden: Brill, 1996), 400-430. Pages 104-6 contain Jacobson's English translation, which I use when quoting from the text.

> Because Amram's plan has pleased me, and he has not put aside the
> covenant between me and his fathers, behold therefore (*ideo*) now, he
> who will be born from him will serve me forever and I will do wonders
> through the house of Jacob through him and I will perform through him
> signs and wonders for my people that I have not done for anyone else.
> And I will place my glory among them and proclaim to them my ways.
> And I, God, will kindle on his behalf my lamp to reside in him, and I
> will show him my house that no one has seen. I will reveal to him my
> majesty and statutes and judgments, and I will kindle an eternal light
> for him, because I thought of him in the days of old, when I said, "My
> spirit will not be a mediator among man forever, because he is flesh and
> his days will be 120 years." (*LAB* 9.7–8)

The story then goes on to tell how Amram and Jochebed had two
children, Aaron and Miriam, and how Miriam had a vision in which
she saw an angel who predicted that her mother would give birth to the
future leader of the Jewish people. When Moses was born, his parents
laid him in a basket and floated it on the river, whereupon the elders of
the people quarreled with Amram, saying that it is exactly for this reason
that they had said that it would be better to die without children than
to cast the fruit of their wombs into the water. But this time Amram
did not respond to that, or he did not listen to them (9.12–14).[11]

This is a highly significant passage for a number of reasons. Firstly,
as we will see later, in rabbinic midrash, Amram is always presented
as *taking part* in the celibacy plan proposed by the elders of the people;
it is only in *LAB* that he *opposes* it. He does so "by virtue of his absolute, unyielding and uncompromising confidence in God."[12] Secondly,
the text explains why Moses is chosen for such an exalted role in the
future history of Israel, a question that is never answered in the Bible.
Because Amram had been very faithful and trusting, God rewards
him by choosing his son to be the saviour of the Jewish people.[13]
As Howard Jacobson reminds us, "Amram's speech here against the
decision to become celibate is paralleled in other midrashic texts by
Miriam's speech against such a resolution. While the substance of the
two speeches differs greatly, the rhetoric and the effect are quite similar
(see e.g. *Sotah* 12a)."[14] Thirdly and finally, the emphasis on the fact that

---

[11] On the translation problem here see Jacobson, *Commentary*, 426.
[12] Jacobson, *Commentary*, 404.
[13] Jacobson, *Commentary*, 404.
[14] Jacobson, *Commentary*, 404.

Amram's attitude and behaviour please God puts him on a par with the great patriarchs.

Josephus also devotes more attention to Amram than the biblical text does. In *Ant.* 2.210–217, he introduces Amram as one of the high-born among the Hebrews, a man who feared that the cruel measures of the Pharaoh would result in the extinction of the entire Jewish people. As his wife was pregnant at the time in that dangerous situation, he prayed to God desperately, imploring him to deliver his people from the prospect of destruction. Out of compassion God appeared to Amram in a dream and urged him not to despair, because he would keep to the promises he had made to his ancestors. God reminds him of everything he had done for Abraham, Isaac, Ishmael, and Jacob who arrived in Egypt together with only seventy souls while they now counted more than six hundred thousand. "And now be it known to you that that I am looking after the common welfare of you all and your own fame" (2.215). He then announces that his soon-to-be-born son will deliver the Hebrews from their bondage and be remembered so long as the universe endures, even among foreigners. That is the favour, God says, that will be bestowed upon Amram, and he finally adds that his other son will be so blessed that he and his descendants will hold the priesthood forever.[15]

This passage shows similarities to several elements we have already seen in earlier sources and will see again in later sources. First, there is the element of a heavenly vision or dream granted to Amram. This is strikingly reminiscent of what we saw in the Qumran document mentioned earlier.[16] Again this element underscores the great divine favour Amram receives. Other favours that God bestows upon Amram are that one of his sons will be the one who liberates his people from bondage, while the other and his offspring will be priests forever. Secondly, the fact that Josephus introduces Amram as one of the high-born among the Hebrews is paralleled in both Philo (*Mos.* 1.7: "His mother and father were among the noblest of people") and rabbinic literature, where he is called the leading man of his generation or even the head of the

---

[15] For an elaborate commentary on this passage, see L.H. Feldman, *The Judaean Antiquities 1–4* (FJTC 3; Leiden: Brill, 2000), 190–93.

[16] In rabbinic literature Moses' birth is predicted not in a vision or through a dream but through a prophecy of Miriam; see *b. Sotah* 12b–13a. But in *LAB* 9.10, Miriam does have a predictive dream about Moses' birth. Cf. Matt 1:20–23.

Sanhedrin (*Exod. Rabba* 1.13, 1.19; *b. Sotah* 12a).[17] The fact that Amram is said to have prayed to God prior to fathering another child makes clear that Moses' birth actually had been ordered by God. Whereas in Pseudo-Philo's *LAB* 9.4 it is Amram himself who admonishes the elders of his people not to despair of the future, in Josephus it is God who does so to Amram.

We finally turn briefly to the role of Amram in rabbinic literature. Targumic material about Amram is scarce, but what little there is certainly deserves our attention. In it we discover the motif of (and motive for) Amram's divorce from Jochebed. In Targum Pseudo-Jonathan on Exod 2:1, the biblical verse where Amram is introduced as a man from the tribe of Levi but not mentioned by name, we find the following rendition: "Amram, a man from the tribe of Levi, went and sat under the bridal canopy and in the wedding chamber with Jochebed, his wife, whom he had divorced because of Pharaoh's decree. Now, she was a hundred and thirty years old when he took her back. But a miracle was performed for her and her youth was restored just as she was when she was young." The same Targum again refers to this tradition in Num 11:26, where after mentioning the two men who had remained behind in the camp, the prophets Eldad and Medad, the meturgeman adds that these were the sons of Elisaphan bar Parnak: "Jochebed, daughter of Levi, gave birth to them for him at the time when Amram her husband divorced her and to whom she was married before she gave birth to Moses."

These curious passages deserve some discussion. As James Kugel has shown, it is the biblical text of Exod 2:1 itself that gave rise to the motif of Amram's divorce.[18] When the text says, "A man went out from the house of Levi, and he took a daughter of Levi," the question that arises is naturally: Why say first that he went *out of* the house of Levi and then add that he took a daughter from that very same house?[19]

---

[17] Cf. *Qoh. Rab.* 9.17.1. In *Gen. Rab.* 19.7, Amram is reckoned among "the seven righteous men": Abraham, Isaac, Jacob, Levi, Kohath, Amram, Moses. Cf. also *Lev. Rab.* 1.2, *Num. Rab.* 13.2, and in quite another sense *Num. Rab.* 3.6, *Song of Songs Rab.* 5.1.1, *Pesiq. Rab Kah.* 1.1.

[18] J.L. Kugel, *Traditions of the Bible: A Guide to the Bible as It Was at the Start of the Common Era* (Cambridge, Mass.: Harvard University Press, 1998), 524–26.

[19] Most of the current translations render וילך איש מבית לוי by "a man from the tribe of Levi went," but the rabbis try to make sense of the somewhat cumbersome wording of the whole phrase by reading the text in a different way, as sketched in the following part of the main text.

Amram's going out from the house of Levi and only then marrying someone who is from the same house of Levi seems to imply that after his going out he *returned* and then married her. Moreover, since the story is set in a time that the house of Levi had not yet developed into a tribe (Levi was Amram's grandfather, so only at a remove of two generations), "house" (could be taken to mean Levi's immediate family or) בית maybe even the actual house in which this family lived. In addition to that, since the immediately preceding verse mentions Pharaoh's decree that every son that is born should be cast into the Nile (Exod 1:22), going out to get married would not seem to make much sense since their offspring, if male, would be drowned. Yet the next verses (2:2–3) state not only that the mother did conceive and bear a son, Moses, but also that the boy had an older sister, Miriam, who then must have been born out of a previous marriage.

> Out of all these considerations developed a tradition to the effect that Amram had changed his mind about married life. At first he was married to Jochebed, Levi's daughter (and it was then that his son Aaron and his daughter Miriam were born). Later, however, when Pharaoh decreed that the newborn boys should be killed, Amram separated from his wife Jochebed lest they have a son who might fall victim to the decree. It was then that he "went out of the house of Levi," leaving his divorced wife behind. Still later, he thought better of his action, and returned "and took [back] the daughter of Levi [his former wife]."[20]

It is this exegetical tradition that we find reflected in several rabbinic documents. The Bavli records it in *Sotah* 12a–b, which says, commenting upon Exod 2:1, that Amram, having heard the decree of the Pharaoh, thought that begetting children would be pointless, so he divorced his wife. But then his daughter Miriam criticized him saying that he was even more severe than Pharaoh, because the King's decree involved only boys, but Amram's decree involved boys *and* girls! She put forward further arguments, which so convinced Amram that he took back his wife. This anecdote about Miriam's criticism of her father is one of the nice and unexpected elements of this haggadic tradition. This tradition is also hinted at in *b. B. Bat.* 120a as well as in the long exegetical passage found in *Num. Rab.* 13.20. In *Pesiq. Rab.* 43.4, we read that as soon as Amram heard the decree of the Pharaoh, he ordered the Israelites

---

[20] Kugel, *Traditions*, 525. How this remarriage is to be reconciled with the biblical prohibition of marrying the same woman twice is still unclear to me (see Deut 24:1–4).

to divorce their wives. But when his six-year-old daughter Miriam reproached him saying, "Father, Pharaoh is kinder to Israel than you are," he brought her before the Sanhedrin (of which he himself was the head) where she repeated these words. After a debate between the members of the Sanhedrin and Amram, he relented and took Jochebed back (the description of the scene is much more detailed than in this brief summary).

In conclusion, we can say that the Jewish exegetical tradition of the post-biblical period gradually clothed Amram with the status he deserved, that of a heroic figure and a worthy father of his son, Moses.[21]

---

[21] In spite of his rise to fame in the early post-biblical period, we do not find the name Amram used very often among Jews in that period. T. Ilan lists only three instances in her *Lexicon of Jewish Names in Late Antiquity. Part 1: Palestine 330 B.C.E.–200 C.E.* (TSAJ 91; Tübingen: Mohr Siebeck, 2002), 203. Likewise, the name Moses is also used very sparingly among Jews in later antiquity.

I owe thanks to Mrs. Petry Kievit-Tyson (NIAS) for the correction of my English and to the Netherlands Institute for Advanced Study for the opportunity to finish this article in a stimulating ambience.

SOME REMARKS ON THE FIGURE OF ELIJAH IN
LIVES OF THE PROPHETS 21:1–3

Géza G. Xeravits

The prophet Elijah is one of those figures of the Hebrew Bible who has continuously attracted the attention of ancient Jewish and Christian thought. This seems to be entirely natural, for we find already in the biblical presentation of Elijah a couple of remarkable characteristics, which could inspire the thinking of later theologians and mystics. The end of his earthly career—just like Enoch's—closes in an uncustomary way: his death is not reported; the Deuteronomist closes the description of his life with the astonishing event of his ascension (2 Kgs 2:9–13). Furthermore, even the proto- and deuterocanonical Old Testament assumes his activity after his earthly life, relating him as having important tasks during the eschatological events (Mal 3:23–24 and Sir 48:10).[1]

In this short paper I focus on a relative rarely studied early Jewish work, the *Lives of the Prophets*, which transmits some remarkable details concerning the birth of Elijah. I dedicate these pages with pleasure to Professor Florentino García Martínez, with whom I had the privilege to work on my doctoral thesis, and who—with his vast knowledge and critical eye—actively contributed to its birth.

Narratives of miraculous births are recurring both in the Bible and in the extrabiblical Jewish literature. The Hebrew Bible often relates extraordinary circumstances when speaking about the birth of the patriarchs: we find here and there the presence of angels, or direct divine revelation, or other miraculous events (cp. e.g. Gen 16:7–15; 18:9–15; 25:22–26), and we can find the same in the case of some later important biblical figures (Judg 13; 1 Sam 1). In later Jewish literature this interest becomes intensified, relating the miraculous birth of such figures, where the Bible remains silent concerning this important stage of life. We can mention among these not only Elijah but also,

---

[1] We treated some aspects of the early Jewish reflection on the eschatological activity of Elijah (*redivivus*) in: "Some Data Pertaining the Early Jewish Presentation of Elijah *Redivivus*," *Athanasiana* 14 (2002): 133–42 [Hungarian], and *King, Priest, Prophet: Positive Eschatological Protagonists of the Qumran Library* (STDJ 47; Leiden: Brill, 2003), 184–91.

for example, Noah, Melchizedek, and Elisha. We will investigate some
traditions connected to these figures together with the narrative about
Elijah in the *Lives of the Prophets*.

The literary heritage of ancient Christianity transmitted to us in
many languages and in multiple forms an early Jewish writing, which
is—according to its title—about the prophets: Ὀνόματα προφητῶν καὶ
πόθεν εἰσὶ καὶ ποῦ ἀπέθανον καὶ πῶς καὶ ποῦ κεῖνται ("The names
of the prophets, and where they are from, and where they died and
how, and where they lie").[2]

The *Lives of the Prophets* was originally written in Palestine, somewhere
in the 1st c. C.E. Despite the fact that it was preserved among Christian
writings, it is a Jewish work—the undeniably Christian passages seem
to be later additions.[3]

As for its contents, the *Lives of the Prophets* treats a number of figures in
a series of nearly equally shaped units. These figures consist of sixteen
Old Testament prophetic writers (including Daniel!), some other prophets (Elijah, Elisha, Nathan, Achijah, Jehoad, Azarijah), and, in several
versions, personalities known from Christian writings (Zechariah and
Shimeon from Luke 1–2, and John the Baptist). The units of the work
deal with the origin, death, and burial of the prophet—as indicated by
the title. Furthermore, several passages mention certain events of the

---

[2] We know the main types of the Greek text of the *Lives of the Prophets*. The most
ancient witness is the so-called *codex Marchalianus* (Vat.gr. 2125) from the sixth c. C.E.
(*An1*); scholars agree that every other text-type of the work originates from this version. Two versions are preserved among the writings of Epiphanios of Salamis (*Ep1*
and *Ep2*), one MS from the 13th c. C.E. and one from the 10th century. Another
witness is preserved among the writings of Dorotheos of Antioch (*Dor*) in a Ms from
the 13th century. The recension which is closest to the *codex Marchalianus* text is called
"recensio anonyma" (*An2*), which comes from the 10th century. Finally, another type
of the work can be reconstructed from various passages of the church fathers (*Schol*,
i.e. "recensio scholiis adiecta"). Besides the Greek versions, we know various other
translations of the *Lives of the Prophets* in Latin, Syriac, Armenian, Ethiopic, Georgian,
Arabic, Church Slavonic, and Old Irish, which shows that the ancient Church read this
work with predilection. On the main scholarly discussion of the *Lives of the Prophets* see
A.M. Schwemer, *Studien zu den frühjüdischen Prophetenlegenden Vitae Prophetarum* (2 vols.;
TSAJ 49–50; Tübingen: Mohr Siebeck, 1995–96), 1:12–90; D.R.A. Hare, "The Lives
of the Prophets," in *OTP* 2:379–84 (in this paper we quote the *Lives* according to this
translation). See furthermore A.M. Denis et al., *Introduction à la littérature religieuse judéo-
hellénistique* (2 vols., Turnhout: Brepols, 2000), 577–607.

[3] On an interpretation of the *Lives* as a Christian document, see: D. Satran, *Biblical Prophets in Byzantine Palestine: Reassessing the* Lives of the Prophets (SVTP 11; Leiden: Brill, 1995).

prophet's life. These small parabiblical passages testify interestingly to the hagiographical views of contemporary Judaism.

Chapter 21 of the *Lives of the Prophets* is devoted to the figure of Elijah. First, his origin and the circumstances of his birth are reported (21:1–3). Then, after the introductory words τὰ δὲ σημεῖα ἃ ἐποίησεν, εἰσὶ ταῦτα ("and the signs which he did are these"), a summary of his wondrous acts is given with some expansions compared to the biblical data (21:4–14).[4] Unlike the other units of the work, the death of Elijah is obviously missing—the pericope closes with the words τὸ τελευταῖον ἀνελήμφθη ἅρματι πυρός ("finally, he was taken up in a chariot of fire," 21:15). The middle part of the unit contains only a handful of additions to the biblical story of the prophet's deeds. Yet, the first part contains surprising details, testifying to the interest of early Judaism in the miraculous figure of Elijah.[5]

1.[6] Ἠλίας[7] Θεσβίτης ἐκ γῆς Ἀράβων, φυλῆς Ἀαρών, οἰκῶν ἐν Γαλαάδ, ὅτι ἡ Θεσβεὶ δόμα ἦν τοῖς ἱερεῦσι.	Elijah, a Thesbite from the land of the Arabs, of Aaron's tribe, was living in Gilead, for Thesbe was given to the priests.
2. ὅτε εἶχε τεχθῆναι,[8] ἴδεν Σοβαχὰ ὁ πατὴρ αὐτοῦ,[9] ὅτι ἄνδρες[10] λευκοφανεῖς αὐτὸν προσηγόρευον, καὶ ὅτι ἐν πυρὶ αὐτὸν ἐσπαργάνουν καὶ φλόγα πυρὸς ἐδίδουν αὐτῷ φαγεῖν.	When he was to be born, his father Sobacha saw that men of shining white appearance were greeting him, and wrapping him in fire, and they gave him flames of fire to eat.

---

[4] The text mentions eight wonders: rain, the jar and the son of the widow of Zareptah, the affair with the priests of Baal at Mt. Carmel, the death of King Ahaziah, the death of the king's two captains, the ravens, and the division of the Jordan.

[5] The following text is from recension *An1*, see T. Schermann, "De prophetarum vita et obitu (recensio anonyma)," in *Prophetarum vitae fabulosae indices apostolorum discipulorumque Domini Dorotheo, Epiphanio, Hippolyto aliisque vindicata* (Leipzig: Teubner, 1907), 93 and Schwemer, *Studien*, 2:224, 62*–64*.

[6] Before verse 1, *Dor* contains a longer introduction, with the Christian interpretation of the figure of Elijah.

[7] *Ep1*: *add.* ὁ προφήτης.

[8] *Ep1*: ἔτεκεν ἡ μήτηρ αὐτοῦ; *Dor*: ἔμελλε τεχθῆναι; *An2*: ἤμελλε τεχθῆναι; *Ep2*: ἔμελλε τίκτεσθαι.

[9] *Ep1*: *add.* ὀπτασίαν.

[10] *Dor*: ἄγγελοι.

3. καὶ ἐλθὼν ἀνήγγειλεν ἐν   And he went and reported in Jerusa-
   Ἰερουσαλήμ,[11]   lem, and the oracle told him:
   καὶ εἶπεν αὐτῷ ὁ χρησμός· μὴ   "Do not be afraid, for his dwelling will
   δειλιάσης·[12]   be light, and his word judgment, and
   ἔσται γὰρ ἡ οἴκησις αὐτοῦ[13] φῶς he will judge Israel."
   καὶ ὁ λόγος αὐτοῦ ἀπόφασις,[14]
   καὶ κρινεῖ τὸν Ἰσραήλ.[15]

Although the text contains a lot of interesting features, in what follows, we would like to highlight only those that are connected with the birth of the child.

The appearance of Men

The birth of the child is followed immediately by a visual experience of his father. Most textual variants of the unit are not unambiguous concerning the nature of this experience. Although *Ep1* explicitly says "vision" (ὀπτασίαν), the other variants report a concrete appearance of figures. Similarly, only one of the actual variants defines these figures: *Dor* mentions "angels" (ἄγγελοι) instead of the "men" (ἄνδρες) of the other versions. Yet, the angelic nature of these figures is implicit in every variant: the color white might indicate cultic matters in the Hebrew Bible and in early Jewish thought, but, on the other hand, it denotes the transcendent sphere (as is evident by such passages as Dan 7:9 both in the Old Greek and in Theodotion; New Testament passages also suggest such a notion as reflected in the transfiguration of Jesus [Matt 17:2 and par], the appearance of the angel at the tomb [Matt 28:3 and par], and all the occurrences of the word λευκός in Revelation).

These "men of white appearance" have no business with the father—their only tasks are greeting the child and supplying him with provisions. As for the first, the Greek uses the verb προσαγορεύω, which has a double meaning: "to greet" and "to name." The Septuagint uses both (on the one hand Wis 14:22 and 1 Macc 14:40; on the other 2 Macc 1:36; 4:7; 14:37), the New Testament uses the latter

---

[11] *Ep1: add.* τοῖς ἱερεῦσι.
[12] *Ep2:* θάρσει.
[13] *Ep1:* τοῦ παιδός σου.
[14] *An2: add.* καὶ ἡ ζωὴ αὐτοῦ μετὰ τῶν πετηνῶν καὶ ὁ ζῆλος αὐτοῦ ἄρεστος ἐνώπιον κυρίου.
[15] *Ep1, Ep2, Dor, An2: add.* ἐν ῥομφαίᾳ καὶ ἐν πυρί.

(Heb 5:10). In the present case, the verb clearly means "to greet," for the latter part of the unit does not contain any further references to a name or to naming.

Anna Maria Schwemer is certainly right when she interprets the presence of the angels at this birth as an act that frames the entire life of Elijah. According to the Bible, the transcendent sphere breaks into the earthly realm (the chariot of fire) at the end of Elijah's earthly activity. The transcendent figures who assist at his birth form an obvious parallel to this.[16]

LIGHT

The angels that appear in this story are "shining white," but even the child is connected with the realm of light/fire/shining. The angels are wrapping him in fire, he eats flames, and the oracle given to his father asserts that the child's dwelling will be light.

It is worth mentioning in this regard the early Jewish tradition about the birth of Noah. Its fullest version is found in chapter 106 of the *Ethiopic Book of Enoch*, but fragmentary versions of the tradition are preserved also in manuscripts from Qumran. We can quote here the testimony of a Hebrew text from the Qumran Library that seems to deal explicitly with the figure of Noah (1Q19),[17] and we find similar traditions in columns II–V of the Aramaic *Genesis Apocryphon* from Qumran Cave 1.[18] According to this tradition, when Noah was born, his father, Lamech, had serious doubts regarding his paternity and suspected that the child was from the angels ("I have begotten a strange son: he is not like an ordinary human being, but he looks like the children of the angels of heaven to me...It does not seem to me that he is of me, but of angels," *1 En.* 106:5–6).[19] Lamech thought this because the child emanated white light ("And his body was white

---

[16] Cf. Schwemer, *Studien*, 2:235.

[17] Edition: J.T. Milik, "19: Livre de Noé," in *DJD* 1:84–86; cf. F. García Martínez, "4QMess Ar and the *Book of Noah*," in *Qumran and Apocalyptic: Studies on the Aramaic Texts from Qumran* (STDJ 9, Leiden: Brill, 1992), 1–44. Transl. of "4Q Mes. Aram. y el libro de Noé," *Salmanticensis* 28 (1981): 195–232.

[18] See *inter alia* J.A. Fitzmyer, *The Genesis Apocryphon of Qumran Cave 1: A Commentary* (BibOr 18; Rome: Pontifical Biblical Institute, 1966).

[19] The translation of *1 Enoch* is from E. Isaac, "1 (Ethiopic Apocalypse of) Enoch," in *OTP* 1:5–89.

as snow…and as for his eyes, when he opened them the whole house glowed like the sun," *1 En.* 106:2).

Part of the description of the shining appearance of the child was preserved also in a fragment of 1Q19: "the fir]st-born is born, but the glorious ones […] his father, and when Lamech saw […] the chambers of the house like the beams of the sun (כחדודי השמש) […] to frighten the […]" (1Q19 3 3–6).[20]

Similarly, the version of the legend preserved in the *Genesis Apocryphon* also emphasizes the curious, shining appearance of the newborn baby: "his face has lifted to me and his eyes shine like [the] s[un (ורנחא עינוהי כשמשא)…] of this boy is a flame (נור) and he […]" (1QapGen V 12–13).[21]

The idea of light that comes out from a person, or one's abode in light, is connected to the angels or to *angelification* in Jewish thought. It is perhaps enough to refer to two Qumranic descriptions of the angelification of Moses, which is related in 4Q374 and 4Q377.[22] Both passages emphasize the shining face of Moses when he descends from the Mount. When doing this, these passages do not simply repeat what we find in Exod 34:29–35. In the Exodus story, the face of Moses is shining when he comes down from the Mount, while in 4Q374 his face begins to shine in order to strengthen the frightened people of Israel. We can refer further to the beginning of the *Slavonic Book of Enoch*, where the angels are described as follows: "Their faces were like the shining sun; their eyes were like burning lamps; from their mouths fire was coming forth" (*2 En.* 1:5).[23] This image is present also in the New Testament, when at the beginning of the book of Revelation it relates the coming Christ (Rev 1:12–16; cp. Dan 7:9–10).

---

[20] The translation is taken from F. García Martínez and E.J.C. Tigchelaar, *The Dead Sea Scrolls Study Edition* (2 vols.; Leiden: Brill, 1997–98), 1:27.

[21] The translation is taken from García Martínez and Tigchelaar, *Study Edition*, 1:31.

[22] Cf. Xeravits, *King, Priest, Prophet*, 121–27; and two studies of C.H.T. Fletcher-Louis, "4Q374: A Discourse on the Sinai Tradition: The Deification of Moses and Early Christology," *DSD* 3 (1996): 236–52; and "Some Reflections on Angelomorphic Humanity Texts among the Dead Sea Scrolls," *DSD* 7 (2000): 292–312.

[23] Edition of the Slavonic text is A. Vaillant, *Le Livre des secrets d'Hénoch: Texte slave et traduction française* (Paris: Institut d'études slaves, 1952). Translation is taken from F.I. Andersen, "2 (Slavonic Apocalypse of) Enoch," in *OTP* 1:91–221.

FOOD

The men who appeared gave to the newborn Elijah flames of fire to eat. The figure of the fire-eating prophet has undeniable connections with the biblical account of the commissioning of Isaiah, where the fire makes the prophet's lips clean, and so he becomes able to manage his prophetic task. From this perspective, by the act of fire-eating, Elijah has been made capable to be a prophet since the very moment of his birth.

The symbolic or programmatic nature of the food is a recurrent topic in the Jewish and Christian tradition. One can, of course, think about the strict dietary customs of Daniel and his fellows in the court of the Babylonian king. But from the present perspective perhaps even more telling is the way that John the Baptist (Elijah *redivivus* [!]) eats according to the Gospels—for his food itself witnesses to his eschatological role. Furthermore, in the *Slavonic Book of Enoch*, we find a passage where a child, after his birth, obtains such food that evokes his future role: this is at the end of *2 Enoch*, a long and complicated story about the birth of Melchizedek (chapter 71).

This story has a number of parallel characteristics with the tradition of Noah's birth testified in *1 Enoch* and the *Genesis Apocryphon*. The mother of Melchizedek (Sophanim or Sotonim [Софоним]) is infertile; yet, before her death she becomes pregnant—without having sexual intercourse with her husband—and hides herself (*2 En.* 71:1–3). When the husband is informed about the matter, he sends the woman away. When she is not successful in explaining the situation (she tries to refer to her age), she dies (71:4–9). Nir, the husband, asks God for forgiveness, and, according to the shorter recension of the text, the angel Gabriel appears to him (*angelus interpres*). Gabriel comforts Nir and explains that, on the one hand, it was not he who caused the death of his wife and, on the other hand, that the newborn child is a gift from God (71:10–11). Nir hurries to his brother Noah to relate the events to him. The latter runs back to Nir's chamber, where the dead woman begins to give birth to a child. The two brothers decide to bury the corpse of Sophanim in secret, but when they arrive back after the preparations for burial, they find the newborn baby on the bed of the dead mother. Nir and Noah are frightened for the child is fully developed physically (according to the longer recension he is like three-years old, ꙗко трилѣтень) and is praising God (71:12–19).

The child bears a priestly sign (**печать свѧтителства**). Seeing these, Noah and Nir bless God for renewing the priestly blood; they wash the child, dress him as a priest, give him food, and name him Melchizedek (71:20–21). Up to this point, the story of the birth of Melchizedek in *2 Enoch* shows numerous parallels with the story of Noah's birth in *1 Enoch* and the *Genesis Apocryphon*. Yet, *2 Enoch* has a detail which is missing in these two writings, but appears in the Elijah story of the *Lives of the Prophets*. Noah and Nir, after clothing the child (cp. ἐν πυρὶ αὐτὸν ἐσπαργάνουν in the *Lives*), give him extraordinary food. In the *Lives*, this food consists of the prophetic flames of fire (φλόγα πυρὸς), while in *2 Enoch* it is the holy bread (**ризы свѧтителства**, *2 En.* 71:21). So the child—a pre-eminent priest—eats the food of the priests of the temple (cp. Matt 12:4).

Oracle and Judgment

We can find two more motifs in the "infancy narrative" of Elijah, which are important and interesting. The first one is his father's visit in Jerusalem; the other is the announcement of Elijah's future role.

Some of the early Jewish writings cited above relate that the father, frightened by the miraculous birth, asks for someone's help in interpreting the event. Noah's father, Lamech, first asks his own father Methushelah, who, being unable to handle the event, runs to his own father, Enoch (*1 En.* 106:4–9; 1*QapGen* IV 19–23). Both *1 Enoch* and the *Genesis Apocryphon* emphasize that the case is so important that Methushelah takes a considerably long visit, to the ends of the earth and to the far region of Parwain, to consult Enoch (*1 En.* 106,8 and 1*QapGen* IV 23). In both narratives, Enoch gives the interpretation of the curious events. As for Melchizedek's birth in *2 Enoch*, we read something similar. On the one hand, Nir, the father, goes to ask his brother Noah; however, on the other hand, Noah is less successful than Enoch, for his competence extends only to manage a horrific funeral.

All in all, the request for advice is common in all of these narratives. The only difference is that in the case of Elijah, it is not one of the relatives of the father, but the "oracle" (χρησμός) in Jerusalem that is being asked. That the "oracle" is no other than the high priest of the temple of Jerusalem is shown by two characteristics. On the one hand, formally, the answer given starts with a familiar element of a typical priestly genre of the Hebrew Bible (the so-called *priesterliche Heilsorakel*):

the "fear-not" formula.[24] On the other hand, the next chapter of the *Lives of the Prophets* relates the followings concerning the birth of the prophet Elisha:

2b. ἡνίκα ἐτέχθη ἐν Γαλγάλοις   When he was born in Gilgal,
    ἡ δάμαλις ἡ χρυσῆ ὀξὺν ἐβόησεν,   the golden calf bellowed shrilly,
    ὥστε ἀκουσθῆναι εἰς   so that it was heard in Jerusalem;
    Ἰερουσαλήμ·

3. καὶ εἶπεν ὁ ἱερεὺς διὰ τῶν δήλων,   and the priest declared through the
    ὅτι προφήτης ἐτέχθη Ἰσραήλ.   Urim that a prophet had been born
                                    to Israel.

Here the birth of the child is also connected with Jerusalem; the identi-fication of the newborn person is made by "the priest" (ὁ ἱερεύς). The δῆλοι of the passage are the priestly Urim and Thummim.[25]

Finally, the priest of Jerusalem characterizes the figure of Elijah by referring to "judgment." With this term, the passage nicely closes the thematic development that begins with the appearance of the angels. The judgment is in parallel with the tradition witnessed to the prophet Malachi, the book of Ben Sira, the Qumranic texts 4Q521 and 4Q558, and the New Testament. These writings and corpora testify to the belief of the coming Elijah as precursor of the end times and the final judgment of God. These parallels permit the originality of the shorter variant of the recension An1 of the *Lives of the Prophets* to be maintained in this instance. The amplification of the other versions of the *Lives* (ἐν ῥομφαίᾳ καὶ ἐν πυρί) focuses on two historical activities of Elijah (the priests of Baal and the fire from the sky) instead of his pre-eminent role as *redivivus*. In doing this, this amplified text disturbs the theological line of the "infancy narrative" of Elijah.

The prophet Elijah was undeniably one of the most important figures of the Hebrew Bible—both for early Judaism and nascent Christianity. We cannot deny that his figure intensively inspired the thinking of the authors of the period. The reinterpretation of Elijah's figure regularly

---

[24] See among others J. Begrich, "Das priesterliche Heilsorakel" (originally 1934); repr. in *Gesammelte Studien zum Alten Testament* (ThB.AT 21; München: Chr. Kaiser, 1964), 217–31; and E.W. Conrad, "Second Isaiah and the Priestly Oracle of Salva-tion," *ZAW* 93 (1981): 234–46; idem, "The 'Fear Not' Oracles in Second Isaiah," *VT* 34 (1984): 129–52.

[25] On this, see Schwemer, *Studien*, 2:317–20.

concerns his eschatological role in the judgment of God. This short passage in the *Lives of the Prophets*—although strictly speaking it addresses his birth—hails him as the forerunner of this judgment. Nevertheless, when relating the extraordinary and miraculous elements of his birth and early childhood, it equally stresses the glory and power of God and the authority of Elijah himself. The Judaism of the turn of the era strongly needed such exemplary figures who were fitting to direct their attention towards the providence of God within the hard situation of its contemporary history. Thus, this passage undoubtedly served well in the reinforcement of the perseverance and faith of its readers.

TEMPLE AND CULT IN THE APOCRYPHA AND
PSEUDEPIGRAPHA: FUTURE PERSPECTIVES

Michael A. Knibb

This short study is intended as a sequel to an earlier study entitled "Temple and Cult in Apocryphal and Pseudepigraphical Writings from before the Common Era."[1] The latter, which was published in the context of a volume of essays entitled *Temple and Worship in Biblical Israel*, was concerned with the way in which the temple is presented—whether as an institution from Israel's past, a contemporary reality, or an object of future expectation—in non-canonical writings from the second and first c. B.C.E., particularly Sirach, *1 Enoch*, and writings that reflect the impact of the desecration of the temple by Antiochus IV and the events that followed (1 and 2 Maccabees, Judith, and 3 Maccabees). The aim of the present study is to carry forward that earlier study by examining the way in which the temple is presented in the *Psalms of Solomon*, the *Assumption of Moses*, and the Baruch literature. The Baruch writings are all set at the time of the Babylonian exile and reflect the idea that Israel was still in a state of exile. With the exception of Baruch, to a considerable extent they represent a reaction to the fall of Jerusalem and the destruction of the temple in 70 C.E., and they offer very different responses to these events. However, before considering these writings I wish to examine the references to the temple in the *Psalms of Solomon* and the *Assumption of Moses*, which both also reflect the impact of specific historical events.

I

The majority of the eighteen psalms that together make up the *Psalms of Solomon* are concerned with individual piety and contrast the behaviour and ultimate destiny of the righteous and the wicked. A much smaller

---

[1] M.A. Knibb, "Temple and Cult in Apocryphal and Pseudepigraphical Writings from before the Common Era," in *Temple and Worship in Biblical Israel* (ed. J. Day; London: T&T Clark, 2005), 401–16.

number contain veiled historical allusions and describe a situation of
distress in which Jerusalem has been attacked, part of the population
slaughtered, the sons and daughters of the leaders led away captive, and
the temple desecrated by the enemy (cf. 2:1–2, 5–7; 8:14–21; 17:11–14;
concern that the temple is in imminent danger of being desecrated
by Gentiles is reflected in 7:1–3). It has long been recognized that the
historical background to these psalms is the struggle for power between
Aristobulus and Hyrcanus and the intervention of Pompey in affairs
in Jerusalem (cf. Josephus, *Ant.* 13.405–14.79), and that the *Psalms of
Solomon* as a collection dates from not long after the death of Pompey
in 48 B.C.E. The attack on Jerusalem is seen to have been instigated by
God (8:14–15; 2:1–8, 16–18, 22), and to be the fully justified response
for the sin of the people, particularly the pollution of the temple.

The fullest description in the *Psalms of Solomon* of the sins that were the
cause of God bringing Pompey against Jerusalem occurs in 8:8–13:

8 God exposed their sins in the full light of day; the whole earth
   knew the righteous judgments of God.
9 In secret places underground was their lawbreaking, provoking
   (him), son involved with mother and father with daughter;
10 Everyone committed adultery with his neighbour's wife; they made
   agreements with them with an oath about these things.
11 They stole from the sanctuary of God as if there were no redeeming heir.
12 They walked on the altar of the Lord, (coming) from all kinds of
   uncleanness; and with menstrual blood they defiled the sacrifices
   as if they were common meat.
13 There was no sin they left undone in which they did not surpass
   the gentiles.[2]

The sins listed include incest, adultery, theft from the temple, and pollution of the temple (cf. v. 22), and the passage may be compared with
the somewhat older CD IV 12b–V 15a, VI 15b–17a. The reference in
Pss. Sol. 8:12 to defilement of the sacrifices through menstrual blood
provides a striking parallel to CD V 6b–7a ("Also they make the sanctuary unclean inasmuch as they do not keep separate in accordance with
the law, but lie with a woman who see the blood of her discharge";

---

[2] Adapted from the translation by R.B. Wright, in *OTP* 2:659.

cf. 4Q266 6 ii 1–2), and underlying both passages would appear to be disputes concerning the proper interpretation of the laws relating to the ritual uncleanness of a woman after menstruation (cf. Lev 15:19–24, 31). The passage may also be compared with the strong criticism of the sons of Levi in *T. Levi* 14:5–8; 16:1–2.

Those accused of defiling the sacrifices in *Pss. Sol.* 8:12 are fairly obviously the priests, and it is also very likely that it is priests who are accused of robbing the temple (v. 11). Atkinson, on the basis of a comparison between *Pss. Sol.* 8 and a number of passages in the Hebrew Bible, the Scrolls, and the Mishnah relating to purity, has gone further than this and has interpreted vv. 8–13 as a whole as being concerned with priestly transgressions.[3] However, it is not necessary to assume that the accusations of incest and adultery were also directed specifically at priests, and they may well have been intended to have a wider application.

The pollution of the temple of the Lord is also mentioned in *Pss. Sol.* 1:8 and 2:3. In the latter passage the pollution of the temple is attributed to "the sons of Jerusalem," who are said to have been "profaning the offerings of God with lawless acts," and is regarded as the cause of the desecration of the altar by the Gentiles (vv. 1–2). Here "the sons of Jerusalem" may well be the priests, but in vv. 11–13, where "the sons of Jerusalem" and "the daughters of Jerusalem" are accused of sexual sins, the reference would appear to be to the inhabitants of Jerusalem in general.[4]

Psalms of Solomon 1 serves as an introduction to the collection of psalms as a whole and may have been composed for this purpose. In the psalm Jerusalem, personified as a mother, is alarmed by the threat of war, but comes to acknowledge that, despite seeming righteousness, she cannot be assured of divine protection because of the sin of her children. The psalm ends with the statement that they (the inhabitants) had "completely profaned the temple of the Lord," and this serves as

---

[3] K. Atkinson, *I Cried to the Lord: A Study of the Psalms of Solomon's Historical Background and Social Setting* (JSJSup 84; Leiden: Brill, 2004), 64–80. While some of the comparisons drawn by Atkinson are illuminating, they are not all plausible. For example, he interprets the reference to sins committed "in secret places underground" (v. 9) in relation to a purification ritual for priests performed in a chamber under the temple, which is described in *m. Tamid* 1:1. However, it seems much more likely that the phrase "in secret places underground" is poetic metaphor and that the reference in v. 9 is to sexual sins committed in secret (cf. 4:5; 1:7).

[4] Cf. S. Holm-Nielsen, *Die Psalmen Salomos* (JSHRZ 4.2; Gütersloh: Mohn, 1977), 63.

a transition to the references to the desecration and pollution of the temple at the beginning of *Pss. Sol.* 2.[5]

In view of the critical attitude towards the temple cult and the priests that is reflected in *Pss. Sol.* 2 and 8, it is perhaps surprising that in *Pss. Sol.* 17, the third of the three most important psalms to contain veiled historical allusions, the Hasmonaeans—the most likely group intended by the reference to "sinners" in v. 3—are condemned for having arrogantly usurped the throne of David, not for the way they discharged their high priestly duties (vv. 3–5; contrast Josephus, *Ant.* 13.288–292, 372–373). There is also no reference to the temple or cult in the condemnation of the sin of the population at large in *Pss. Sol.* 17:20. However, it does appear that the description of the messianic kingdom that the psalmist appeals to God to establish (17:21–46) includes, at least implicitly, the expectation of a purified temple (vv. 30–31):

30 And he will have gentile nations serve him under his yoke, and he will glorify the Lord in (a place) prominent (above) the whole earth.

And he will purge Jerusalem (and make it) holy as it was even from the beginning,

31 (for) nations to come from the end of the earth to see his glory, to bring as gifts her children who were exhausted, and to see the glory of the Lord with which God has glorified her.[6]

The passage draws on a number of Old Testament texts, particularly Isa 2:2–4; 55:5; 60:8–10; 66:18–21, that depict the Gentiles streaming to Jerusalem to worship Yahweh and bringing the exiles back with them. The text is awkward and the meaning not entirely clear,[7] but although the phrase "the glory of the Lord" could refer to the Davidic messiah, to whom the nations come to render homage (cf. Ps 72:9–11), it seems more likely that the word "glory" refers to the purified temple (cf. Isa 60:7; 64:10).

The condemnation of the sacrificial cult that appears in *Pss. Sol.* 1, 2 and 8 represents a continuation of the attitude reflected in a num-

---

[5] Cf. G.W.E. Nickelsburg, *Jewish Literature between the Bible and the Mishnah: A Historical and Literary Introduction* (2d ed.; Minneapolis: Fortress Press, 2005), 238.

[6] Adapted from the translation by Wright, in *OTP* 2:667.

[7] On the problems of the text, see Holm-Nielsen, *Die Psalmen Salomos*, 103.

ber of texts, for example Mal 1:6–2:9; *1 En.* 89:73; *Jub.* 1:14;[8] *As. Mos.* 4:8; 6:1, in which the post-exilic cult is presented as being unclean and illegitimate, but in this case it is directed quite specifically at the contemporary situation. It seems clear that the *Psalms of Solomon* as a whole stems from dissident circles that were highly critical of the priests and the conduct of the cult in their own day, but the extent of their alienation from the temple cult remains uncertain. Atkinson draws attention to the importance attached to prayer in the *Psalms of Solomon* (cf. 3:3; 5:1; 6:1–2; 7:6–7; 15:1) and notes that fasting is said to make atonement for sins of ignorance (3:8). He also observes in respect of several psalms (6, 9, 3, 10) that the author does not mention the temple cult, and he argues that the *Psalms of Solomon* stem from a sectarian community that had withdrawn from the temple, met for worship in their own synagogues, and stressed the importance of prayer and fasting as a substitute for the temple cult.[9] Further, he takes the mention of the συναγωγαὶ ὁσίων (17:16; cf. 10:7) to be "a reference to the physical structure where the psalmist's community chose to gather for worship in place of the Temple."[10] But while Atkinson is right to stress the importance of prayer and of individual piety in the *Psalms of Solomon*, and while the circles behind them were clearly dissatisfied with the conduct of the temple cult, there is insufficient evidence in the *Psalms of Solomon* for us to know what the dissatisfaction would have meant in practice and whether it would have led the circles behind the *Psalms* to go so far as to withdraw from the temple. The attitude reflected in *Pss. Sol.* 7:1–2 would suggest otherwise.

II

Israel's attitude towards the temple and cult forms a major concern of the "prophecy" of Israel's history, from the occupation of the land to her exaltation to heaven, that is spoken by Moses to Joshua and takes up the major part of the *Assumption of Moses*. The "prophecy" represents a new application, a reworking of the Song of Moses (Deut 32:1–43); it uses the Deuteronomic historical scheme and divides the

---

[8] Cf. M.A. Knibb, *Jubilees and the Origins of the Qumran Community* (an Inaugural Lecture delivered at King's College London on Tuesday 17 January 1989, London, 1989), 11.

[9] Atkinson, *I Cried to the Lord*, 211–20, cf. 176, 182, 191, 195–97, 201.

[10] Atkinson, *I Cried to the Lord*, 213, cf. 201.

history into two cycles (chs. 2–4 and 5–10), namely sin (2; 5:1–6:1), punishment (3:1–4; 6:2–8:5), turning point (3:5–4:4; 9), and salvation (4:5–9; 10). The author is less concerned to provide an accurate chronological account than to provide a theological interpretation of events, and his account is abbreviated and in some respects does not correspond with the biblical narrative. The *Assumption* dates from the early part of the first c. C.E. and reflects the impact of direct Roman control of Judaea and the threat, to the Jewish nation and the Jewish faith, that this represented; the last identifiable events mentioned, in 6:9, are the burning of the temple porticoes by Sabinus and the intervention by Varus, the governor of Syria, in 4 B.C.E. (Josephus, *Ant.* 17.250–298, *B.J.* 2.39–79).[11] However, it has been argued that chs. 6–7, which clearly refer to the Hasmonaeans and to Herod and his sons, are an interpolation, and that the original work dates from during the persecution by Antiochus Epiphanes. Thus Nickelsburg, who has been a leading proponent of this view, has argued that the second historical cycle should be analyzed as follows: sin (5:1–6:1), punishment (6:2–9), sin (7), punishment (8), turning point (9), and salvation (10). He maintains that the sin of the hellenizers, which he believes to be depicted in 5:1–6:1, has no specific punishment, but that the problem is solved if chs. 6–7 are an interpolation; ch. 8 then provides a description of the punishment of the hellenizers by Antiochus.[12] Nickelsburg also maintains that ch. 8 is a quite unique and specific account of the persecution by Antiochus and is best understood as an eyewitness account,[13] and he believes that the author of ch. 9 (Taxo's exhortation to his seven sons to die rather than transgress the commandments) may have witnessed innocent deaths of the kind prefigured in the chapter.[14]

While, however, the possibility of interpolation cannot be ruled out in principle, the analysis of the literary structure of the *Assumption of Moses* by Hofmann would suggest very strongly that the text is a unity.[15]

---

[11] This identification, which is generally accepted, still seems to me correct. But note the cautious qualifications of this view expressed by J. Tromp, *The Assumption of Moses: A Critical Edition with Commentary* (SVTP 10; Leiden: E.J. Brill, 1993), 116–17, 204–5.

[12] G.W.E. Nickelsburg, "An Antiochan Date for the Testament of Moses," in *Studies on the Testament of Moses* (ed. idem; SBLSCS 4; Cambridge, Mass.: Society of Biblical Literature, 1973), 33–37; idem, *Jewish Literature*, 74–76, 247–48.

[13] Nickelsburg, "An Antiochan Date," 34.

[14] Nickelsburg, *Jewish Literature*, 76.

[15] N.J. Hofmann, *Die Assumptio Mosis: Studien zur Rezeption massgültiger Überlieferung* (JSJSup 67; Leiden: Brill, 2000), 45–80, cf. 62, 69–70, 329; cf. Tromp, *Assumption of Moses*, 120–23.

The author of the *Assumption* does not attempt to describe everything that happened in the post-exilic period, and in 5:1–6:1 he gives only a broad-brush description of the period that he believes prefigures the end and characterizes as marked by apostasy and injustice; 6:1 clearly refers to the Hasmonaeans, and ch. 5 may well refer to the hellenizers, but the details are left vague. In view of the overall character of the account of Israel's history in *As. Mos.* 2:1–10:10, we should not be surprised that there is no reference to the persecution of Antiochus in 5:1–6:1, even though we might expect it. The description of the period of sin begins in 5:1 with the following statement: "And when the times of judgment will approach, revenge will come through kings who participate in crime and who will punish them."[16] It makes most sense to see 6:2–8:5 as a whole as a description of the period of punishment at the hands of "kings who participate in crime," first Herod (the *rex petulans* of 6:2) and his sons (6:2–7), then Varus (*occidentes rex potens*; 6:8–9), and finally the *rex regum terrae* (8:1), the king of the last days sent by God to punish Israel, the account of whose reign draws on—and exaggerates—motifs from the accounts of the persecution of Antiochus (ch. 8). On this view ch. 7 can be seen to provide a description of the age in which the author was living,[17] the rule of the "pestilent and impious men" that lay just before the final period of woe. At the beginning of ch. 8, the author then turns to the future, but it seems more likely that his description of the persecution to be unleashed by the king of the kings of the earth has been written in the light of the accounts of the persecution by Antiochus in 1 and 2 Maccabees than that it is an eyewitness report of the persecution by Antiochus itself. Similarly, it would seem likely that the account of Taxo's exhortation to his seven sons is a reworking of the story of the martyrdom of the mother and her seven sons (2 Macc 7).

As already indicated, Israel's attitude towards the temple and cult is seen as a key factor in determining the outcome of the events "foretold" by Moses. Thus, in the first cycle, which covers the period from the occupation of the land to the early post-exilic era (*As. Mos.* 2–4), it is the abandonment of the covenant with God by the two southern tribes and their worship of foreign gods that is presented as the cause of the

---

[16] Tromp, *Assumption of Moses*, 187.
[17] Cf. M.A. Knibb, "The Exile in the Literature of the Intertestamental Period," *HeyJ* 17 (1976): 261, n. 33 and 34.

exile: "They will also abandon the covenant of the Lord...they will sacrifice their children to foreign gods, and erect idols in the tabernacle and serve them, and they will act disgracefully in the house of the Lord, and sculpt many idols of all kinds of animals" (2:7b–9).[18] The capture of Jerusalem, the burning of the city and temple, the carrying off of the temple vessels, and the taking of the entire people into exile (3:1–3) are all the consequence of the abandonment of the covenant manifested in the worship of foreign gods.

The return from exile (4:5–7) follows repentance (3:5–14) and a prayer on the people's behalf by an unnamed intercessor (4:1–4). The rebuilding of the temple is not specifically mentioned, but the comment that is made on the post-exilic cult raises some problems: "But the two tribes will hold on to the allegiance that was ordained for them, mourning and weeping, because they will not be able to bring offerings to the Lord of their fathers" (4:8).[19] Moses's "prophecy" contradicts historical reality inasmuch as sacrifices were offered in the post-exilic period, but the passage indicates that it was faithful Jews, those who "h(e)ld on to the allegiance that was ordained for them," who were unable to offer sacrifice, not the majority of the population.[20] The passage thus represents a further reflection of the view that the post-exilic cult was unclean and illegitimate. Israel had returned to the land, and the cult had been re-established, but the restored cult is seen to have been invalid.[21]

The "prophecy" of events in the post-exilic period continues in ch. 5, but a new beginning is marked in v. 1 by the temporal clause, "And when the times of judgment approach." The author believed that he was living in the period just before the end of the present age, and the second part of the "prophecy" covers the period preceding the eschatological era (*As. Mos.* 5–7) and the eschatological events that would lead to the establishment of the reign of God (*As. Mos.* 8–10). This second cycle follows the pattern of the first and represents an intensification of it. The period preceding the author's own age is characterized by the pollution of the temple and the worship of foreign gods (5:2–4) and by crime and injustice in society (5:5–6). As noted, this passage may well

---

[18] Tromp, *Assumption of Moses*, 159.

[19] Tromp, *Assumption of Moses*, 181.

[20] See the detailed discussion of this passage by Tromp, *Assumption of Moses*, 181–83.

[21] Cf. Knibb, "Exile," 261.

refer to the hellenizers, but in any case it is clear that 6:1 refers to the Hasmonaeans, and they also are accused of polluting the temple ("they will act most impiously against the Holy of Holies"). For the author, the post-exilic cult had continued to be impure and illegitimate. There follow allusions to the reign of Herod and his sons (6:2–7) and to the intervention of the Romans under Varus (6:8–9), and, as has been suggested, these events are to be seen as the beginning of the time of judgment on the sin depicted in 5:1–6:1.

It is then "foretold" that Israel will be ruled by "pestilent and impious men" who will commit every kind of sin and iniquity (*As. Mos.* 7)—but at this point the author has reached his own age. Such was the sinfulness of this age that he expected God would shortly bring "the king of the kings of the earth" to carry out God's final judgment on his people. The account of the persecution that this king would unleash (*As. Mos.* 8) is based, as already noted, on the accounts of the persecution of Antiochus Epiphanes, and what is depicted is the attempt to compel the Jews under threat of crucifixion and torture to abandon their faith and to adopt paganism—to deny circumcision, publicly to carry idols of pagan gods, and to blaspheme the word of God. In this situation it would only be the sinlessness of Taxo and his family and his willingness to "die rather than transgress the commandments of the Lord of lords, the God of our fathers" (9:4–7) that would precipitate the intervention of God to punish the nations, to destroy their idols, and to exalt Israel to heaven (10:1–10). The salvation that is envisaged for Israel in this case is not in a restored land with a restored temple, but an angelic existence "in the heaven of the stars" (11:9–10).

We know very little about the author of the *Assumption*, but the concern with the temple and cult that runs throughout the work raises the possibility, as Nickelsburg observes, that he was a priest.[22] If so, he was clearly a dissident figure who believed that the temple cult was polluted, and who, on the evidence of ch. 7, was radically opposed to the ruling authorities of his day. He also appears to have been concerned at the continuing threat posed to the proper observance of the Jewish faith by the attractions of the worship of pagan gods. He wrote at a time when Judaea had recently come under the direct control of the Romans, and when it must have appeared that the survival of the Jewish state and the Jewish faith was under threat. In this situation one of

---

[22] Nickelsburg, *Jewish Literature,* 76–77.

his main concerns was to urge the strict observance of the commandments of God, which alone offered the hope of salvation (cf. 3:11–12;
9:4–7; 12:10–11).

III

The book of Baruch is a composite work whose individual parts have
been linked together to form a literary unity: public reading of the book
written by Baruch (1:1–15aα) is followed by confession that the exile
was the fully-merited consequence of the sin of the people (1:15aβ–3:8),
an appeal to follow the commandments of God, the way of wisdom
(3:9–4:4), and then the promise of salvation, of return from exile (4:5–
5:9).[23] The book purports to have been written by Baruch in Babylon
five years after Jerusalem was taken and burnt by the Babylonian forces
in 587 (1:2), and the viewpoint of the entire work is summed up in the
final words of the prayer of confession: "See, we are today in our exile
where you have scattered us, to be reproached and cursed and punished for all the iniquities of our ancestors, who forsook the Lord our
God" (3:8 NRSV). However, the error in the historical introduction of
making Belshazzar the son of Nebuchadnezzar (1:11, cf. Dan 5:2, 11,
18, 22), and the parallels between 1:15aβ–3:8 and the prayer in Dan
9:4–19 and between 4:36–5:9 and *Pss. Sol.* 11, point to a much later
date for the composition of the work.[24] The positive attitude towards the
Babylonians reflected in the command, which is based on Jer 29:7, to
pray for the life of Nebuchadnezzar and Belshazzar (1:11–12) suggests
that Baruch dates from a time when the contemporary ruling power
was friendly disposed towards the Jews, and there is some plausibility in
the view that Baruch dates from the early part of the second c. B.C.E.,
from before about 175;[25] but, it has to be recognized that the lack of
evidence makes a precise dating impossible.[26] In any event the book
reflects the view that Israel had remained in a state of exile.

---

[23] For the literary unity of Baruch, cf. A. Kabasele Mukenge, *L'unité littéraire du Livre
de Baruch* (EBib, NS 38; Paris: Gabalda, 1998).

[24] Cf. C.A. Moore, *Daniel, Esther and Jeremiah: The Additions* (AB 44; Garden City,
N.Y.: Doubleday, 1977), 256.

[25] Cf. Moore, *Daniel, Esther and Jeremiah: The Additions*, 260.

[26] A number of scholars have suggested that Nebuchadnezzar and Belshazzar are
"stand-ins" for Antiochus IV and Antiochus V and that behind Jehoiakim (1:7) we are
perhaps meant to see Alcimus (1 Macc 7:5–25, 9:54–57). On this view Baruch dates
from the time of Antiochus V and was intended to gain support for the view that sub-

For present purposes, it is the references to the temple and cult in the prayer of repentance and in the historical introduction that are of interest. The prayer includes the words: "And the house that is called by your name you have made as it is today, because of the wickedness of the house of Israel and the house of Judah" (2:26 NRSV). In the supposed context of the immediate aftermath of the capture and burning of Jerusalem in 587, it is natural to take these words to refer to the destruction of the temple, and the Lucianic recension, by the addition of the gloss "a ruin," did interpret the passage in this way. But the passage, which may be intended as an allusion to Jer 7:14, is couched in ambiguous language and may mean no more than that the temple was in a run-down condition at the time at which the prayer was composed.[27]

The account of the reading of the book written by Baruch before Jehoiachin and all the people, which was intended as a positive contrast to the account of the reading of the scroll before Jehoiakim (Jer 36), is dominated by references to cultic matters: the collection of money and the sending of this to the otherwise unknown (high) priest Jehoiakim (1:5–7); the return of the silver temple vessels that had supposedly been made by Zedekiah after Jehoiachin had been taken to Babylon (1:8–9); the instruction that the collection was to be used to pay for sacrifices "on the altar of the Lord our God," which were to be accompanied by prayers on behalf of Nebuchadnezzar and Belshazzar (1:10–12); and the instruction that those in Jerusalem were to read Baruch's book and to make confession "in the house of the Lord" on feast days (1:14). None of this—apart from the indication in Jer 41:5 that sacrifice did continue in some form on the site of the temple after 587—has any historical basis in the accounts of the exilic period in the Old Testament, and it represents rather an idealized account of what is supposed to have happened already at the beginning of the exilic period. What is surprising is that the re-established cult is presented in an entirely

---

mission to the Seleucids (cf. 1:11–12) was at that stage the right policy; it was perhaps also intended as propaganda on behalf of Alcimus. Cf. Nickelsburg, *Jewish Literature*, 97; O.H. Steck, "Das Buch Baruch," in *Das Buch Baruch, Der Brief des Jeremia, Zusätze zu Ester und Daniel* (ed. idem et al.; ATD, Apokryphen 5; Göttingen: Vandenhoeck & Ruprecht, 1998), 22–23, 31–32; J.A. Goldstein, "The Apocryphal Book of 1 Baruch," *PAAJR* 46–47 (1979–80): 179–99. However, it seems to me difficult to believe that Nebuchadnezzar and Belshazzar are meant to represent Antiochus IV and Antiochus V and that the book's readers were being urged to offer prayers on their behalf.

[27] Cf. Moore, *Daniel, Esther and Jeremiah: The Additions*, 289.

positive light, and this stands in sharp contrast to the attitude towards the post-exilic cult in other contemporary writings. The actions of Jehoiachin and the exiles in providing for the sacrificial cult are seen to be exemplary, and the narrative, like the book as a whole, provides a model of the appropriate response for Jews in a later age still living in a condition of exile. The account of the collection and the return of the temple vessels anticipates what is described in Ezra 1:6–11; 5:14–15; 6:5; 7:15–19; 8:26–30, and the return of the temple vessels may have been intended as a partial fulfilment of Jer 27:22: "They (sc. the temple vessels) shall be carried to Babylon, and there they shall stay, until the day I give attention to them, says the LORD. Then I will bring them up and restore them to this place" (NRSV).[28] The effect of the account of the return of the vessels is to present the cult re-established at the very beginning of the exilic period as the legitimate continuation of the pre-exilic cult.[29]

IV

Three other writings associated with Baruch, namely *2 Baruch, 3 Baruch*, and *4 Baruch (Paralipomena Jeremiae)*, are also set at the time of the fall of Jerusalem in 587, but in reality were written in reaction to the fall of Jerusalem in 70 C.E., for which the events of 587 provided a thinly disguised cover.[30] All three can be dated to the late first or early second c. C.E., but they differ considerably from one another in their response to the loss of Jerusalem and the temple.

Distress at the loss forms a leitmotif in *2 Baruch*.[31] The theme is summed up in the lament in ch. 35, which significantly Baruch utters "amid the ruins" of the temple (v. 1, cf. 10:5):

---

[28] Steck, "Das Buch Baruch," 31.

[29] For the theme of continuity in relation to the temple vessels, see P.R. Ackroyd, "The Temple Vessels: A Continuity Theme," in *Studies in the Religion of Ancient Israel* (VTSup 23; Leiden: Brill, 1972), 166–81; repr. in *Studies in the Religious Tradition of the Old Testament* (London: SCM Press Ltd., 1987), 46–60, 261–63.

[30] Limitations of space prevent the consideration of *4 Ezra*, which otherwise would also deserve consideration here. But see H. Lichtenberger, "Zion and the Destruction of the Temple in 4 Ezra 9–10," in *Gemeinde ohne Tempel. Community without Temple: Zur Substituierung und Transformation des Jerusalemer Tempels und seines Kults im Alten Testament, antiken Judentum und frühen Christentum* (ed. B. Ego et al.; WUNT 118; Tübingen: Mohr Siebeck, 1999), 239–49.

[31] For the theme of the temple in *2 Baruch*, see F.J. Murphy, "The Temple in the Syriac Apocalypse of Baruch," *JBL* 106 (1987): 671–83. Murphy rightly points out that

Would that my eyes were springs *of water*,
And mine eyelids a fountain of tears;
For how shall I lament for Zion,
And how shall I mourn for Jerusalem?
Because in the very place where I now lie prostrate.
The high priest of old offered holy sacrifices,
And burned incense of fragrant odours.
But now our pride has turned to dust,
And our hearts' desire to ashes. (*2 Bar.* 35:2–5)[32]

But it is reflected also in such passages as 3:1; 5:1, 6–7; 6:2; 9:2; 10:6–11:7; 13:3; 31:4.

Part of the author's response to this situation is to make clear that the destruction of Jerusalem was the consequence of the people's sin (1:2–3; 13:9; 77:8–10; 79:1–2) and that it was brought about by God (1:4), who used the enemies of the nation as his agent (5:2–3) in order to chasten his people (1:5; 4:1; 13:10). Furthermore, the author has Baruch witness the hiding of the temple vessels in the earth, the burning of the temple, and the pulling down of the walls of the city by the angels before the enemy entered, in order to prevent the enemy boasting that they had "thrown down the wall of Zion" and "burnt the place of the mighty God" (6:1–8:2; 80:1–3).

The author's response to the destruction of Jerusalem and the temple also includes the expectation of a new Jerusalem and a new temple,[33] but apparently with some differences of view between the relevant passages.[34] On the one hand, the description of the hiding of the temple furnishings and vessels in the earth by the angel is accompanied by the command to the earth to keep them safe "until the last times" so that,

---

Jerusalem and the temple are inextricably interlinked in *2 Baruch* and that "the significance of the loss of Jerusalem is that the temple no longer exists." The same point could be made in relation to *4 Baruch*, while in *3 Baruch* the temple is not separately mentioned, but is subsumed in the references to Jerusalem.

[32] All quotations from *2 Baruch* are taken from the translation of R.H. Charles revised by L.H. Brockington, *AOT*, 841–95.

[33] Quite distinct from the references to a new temple at the end of this age is the mention of the building of the Second Temple that occurs in 68:5–7 in the context of the interpretation of the Vision of the Black and the Bright Waters. Here, as we have seen elsewhere, a negative judgement is passed on the post-exilic cultus: "And then, after a short interval, Zion will be rebuilt, and its offerings will be restored again, and the priests will return to their ministry, and the Gentiles also will come and acclaim it. However, things will not be as they were in former times. And after this disaster will strike many nations."

[34] Cf. P.-M. Bogaert, *L'Apocalypse syriaque de Baruch* (2 vols.; SC 144–145; Paris: Le Cerf, 1969), 1:422–24.

when the earth is ordered, they can be restored (6:8, cf. Jer. 27:22). The passage continues: "For the time has come when Jerusalem also will be delivered for a time, until it is said that it shall be restored again for ever (6:9)." Here the expectation would appear to be of the manifestation in the last times of an ideal version of the earthly Jerusalem and temple,[35] and the vessels serve as a guarantee of continuity with the temple as it existed before the exile.

On the other hand, 4:1–7 clearly expresses the idea of the existence of a heavenly Jerusalem and temple, of which the earthly Jerusalem and temple are copies. In 32:2–4, reference to the building and the destruction of the second temple (vv. 2–3) is again linked with the expectation of a new temple (v. 4): "For after a little while the building of Zion will be shaken so that it may be built again. But that building will not endure, but will after a time be razed to the ground, and it will remain desolate until the *appointed* time. And afterwards it must be renewed in glory and be made perfect for evermore."[36] Here it is the manifestation in the new age of the heavenly temple to which v. 4 refers.[37] However, although the expectation of a heavenly temple is clearly present in *2 Baruch* as part of the author's response to the destruction of Jerusalem and the temple, the theme, as Murphy rightly points out, is not further developed.[38] In particular, the theme of the heavenly temple plays no part in the description in 51:7–13 of the heavenly existence of the resurrected righteous, who will be made like the angels.

V

2 Baruch and *4 Baruch* differ considerably from one another in their literary form—the former an apocalypse, the latter best described by the broad term "haggadah"[39]—and their theological views, but the numer-

---

[35] Murphy, "The Temple in the *Syriac Apocalypse of Baruch*," 679, argues that this passage "must refer to the building of the Second Temple and not a third." But the fact that the vessels are to be kept "until the last times" and that the new temple is to last "for ever" suggests that this is not the case.

[36] On the interpretation of this passage, see Knibb, "Exile," 270–71, n. 69.

[37] Cf. D.C. Harlow, *The Greek* Apocalypse of Baruch (3 Baruch) *in Hellenistic Judaism and Early Christianity* (SVTP 12; Leiden: E.J. Brill, 1996), 72–73, n. 125; Bogaert, *L'Apocalypse syriaque de Baruch*, 1:422–24.

[38] Murphy, "The Temple in the *Syriac Apocalypse of Baruch*," 676.

[39] Cf. J. Herzer, *Die Paralipomena Jeremiae: Studien zu Tradition und Redaktion einer Haggada des frühen Judentums* (TSAJ 43; Tübingen: Mohr, 1994), 37.

ous parallels between them, particularly in their narrative framework (cf. *2 Bar.* 1:1–10:19; 77:12–26; *4 Bar.* 1:1–4:9; 6:8–7:12), make it clear that there is a relationship between them. This has been explained on the assumption that *4 Baruch* is dependent on *2 Baruch*,[40] but is perhaps better explained on the assumption that they are separately dependent on a common source, a cycle of Jeremiah legends, as Schaller amongst others has recently argued.[41]

The problem that *4 Baruch* is concerned to address is the destruction of Jerusalem (and the temple) and the taking of the people into captivity in Babylon; the theme is summed up in Baruch's lament in 4:6–9 and in Jeremiah's words to Baruch in 2:7, and the distress caused by the destruction is underlined by the references to the lamentation undertaken by Jeremiah and Baruch (2:1–2, 5–6, 8–10; 4:5, 10; cf. 3:3). It is made clear that the delivery of the city into the hands of the Babylonians was the consequence of the sin of the people (1:1, 7; 4:6–7; 6:21), and in response to Jeremiah's fear that the king would boast he had "prevailed against the holy city of God" (1:5–6), it is further made clear that the Babylonians were only able to enter the city, because God first opened the gates and destroyed the city (1:8–10; 4:1).

The above is all similar to what occurs in *2 Baruch*. However, in *4 Baruch*'s version of the destruction of the city by the angels (3:1–14), Jeremiah takes the initiative in asking what should be done with the temple vessels and is told to consign them to the earth and to say: "Listen, O earth, to the voice of him who created you in the abundance of the waters, who sealed you with seven seals in seven periods of time, and who will afterwards receive your beauty: guard the vessels of the service till the coming of the beloved" (3:8).[42] The passage may be compared with *2 Bar.* 6:8, in which the earth is commanded by the angel to guard the temple vessels "until the last times" so that, when ordered to do so, it might restore them. In *4 Bar.* 3:8, "the beloved" is probably Israel, and the earth is to preserve the vessels until the gathering of the nation in the last days.[43] Again, while in *2 Bar.* 10:18

---

[40] Cf. e.g. Herzer, *Die Paralipomena Jeremiae*, 33–77.

[41] B. Schaller, *Paralipomena Jeremiou* (JSHRZ 1.8; Gütersloh: Gütersloher Verlagshaus, 1998), 670–75.

[42] All quotations from *4 Baruch* are taken from the translation by R. Thornhill, *AOT*, 821–33. But see also the next footnote.

[43] Thornhill (*AOT*, 823) translates the final phrase of this passage as "till the coming of the Beloved One," as if the reference were to a messianic figure, but it is more likely that the reference is to the return of Israel, and it is possible that λαοῦ dropped

Baruch commands the priests to throw the keys of the sanctuary up
to heaven, and to give them to the Lord and say "Guard thy house
thyself, for we have been found false stewards," in *4 Bar.* 4:3 Jeremiah
himself throws the keys up in the face of the sun and instructs the
sun to guard them "until the day when the Lord tells you what to do
with them; because we have proved unworthy guardians of them and
faithless stewards." But notwithstanding the references in *4 Bar.* 3:8;
4:3 to the possibility that there would be a new temple, the temple as
such, as Herzer points out, plays no further part in the development
of the author's thought.[44]

It is true that, after he has led the exiles back to Jerusalem, Jeremiah
is said to offer sacrifice on an altar on the day of atonement, and that
he acts as high priest (9:1–2; cf. his role in relation to the temple vessels
and the temple keys, 3:8; 4:3), and behind this might lie the expectation of an eschatological high priest and a restored eschatological
temple. But if this is so, as Schaller observes, the idea is only hinted
at.[45] Instead of this, the author's expectations of salvation are focused
on the belief in the bodily resurrection of the dead, of which the figs
that remained fresh throughout the exilic period are symbols (6:2–7;
cf. 7:17), and the gathering of the people ("the beloved") in the last
times in the heavenly Jerusalem.

The clearest expression of the latter belief occurs in 5:34, in which
Abimelech gives some of the figs to the old man and assures him:
"God will light your way to the city of Jerusalem which is above." It
is reflected also in Jeremiah's words to the people in Babylon: "Do
everything you have been told to do in the letter, and God will bring
us to our city" (7:22) and in his command to the Samaritans: "Repent,
for the angel of righteousness is coming and will lead you to your place
on high" (8:9; cf. 9:5). The repeated assurances that God would bring
the people back from exile in Babylon conditional upon their obedience
(3:10; 4:8; 6:13, 22; 7:28), and the account of the return from Babylon
under the leadership of Jeremiah at the end of the exilic period (ch.
8), point forward to this expectation of the gathering of the people in
the heavenly Jerusalem in the last times.

---

out of the text by homoioteleuton after τοῦ ἠγαπημένου; see Schaller, *Paralipomena
Jeremiou*, 718.

[44] Herzer, *Die Paralipomena Jeremiae*, 50, 144, 146, 147, 184, 194.

[45] Schaller, *Paralipomena Jeremiou*, 685.

VI

If *4 Baruch* at best only hints at the possibility of the restoration of the temple as part of its eschatological expectations, the *Greek Apocalypse of Baruch* (*3 Baruch*) has no place at all for such a restoration. This latter work, although Christian in its present form, is generally recognized to be Jewish in origin. It has the literary form of the account of an otherworldly journey, and it describes the ascent of Baruch, accompanied by an angel, to the fifth heaven. It has sometimes been thought that the work is incomplete, and that it originally described Baruch's further ascent to a sixth and seventh heaven, but Daniel Harlow has convincingly argued that although the work does presuppose the existence of further heavens, probably a sixth and a seventh heaven, it deliberately aborts Baruch's ascent in the fifth heaven (11:1–16:4).[46] In the fifth heaven he sees Michael ascend to the highest heaven to present the virtues of humans before God and to bring back their respective rewards and punishments (15:1–16:4).

3 Baruch, like *2 Baruch* and *4 Baruch*, was written in response to the fall of Jerusalem in 70 C.E. and begins, in a similar way to these writings, with Baruch lamenting the loss of the city: Why had God permitted Nebuchadnezzar to lay waste Jerusalem and not requited them with another punishment (1:1–2).[47] An angel appears to Baruch and, somewhat surprisingly, tells Baruch not to concern himself so much over the salvation of Jerusalem (1:3), that is, over its restoration.[48] This message is reinforced by the command from the angel: "Cease irritating God, and I will disclose to you other mysteries greater than these" (1:6); in response to this Baruch promises not to speak further (1:7), and he does not thereafter mention the fall of Jerusalem. He is then led by the angel through the five heavens and is shown a series of mysteries concerning the punishment of the wicked and the reward of the righteous (2:1–16:4), which are presented as being greater than

---

[46] Harlow, *The Greek Apocalypse of Baruch (3 Baruch)*, 34–76.

[47] According to the Greek title, v. 2, Baruch was weeping over the captivity of Jerusalem "by the beautiful gates where the Holy of Holies stood," and this may be compared with *2 Bar.* 34:1; 35:1. On the relationship between the Greek and the Slavonic version of *3 Baruch*, see Harlow, *The Greek Apocalypse of Baruch (3 Baruch)*, 5–10. All quotations from *3 Baruch* are taken from the translation by H.E. Gaylord, Jr., in *OTP* 1:653–79.

[48] Cf. Harlow, *The Greek Apocalypse of Baruch (3 Baruch)*, 89.

the mystery concerning the salvation of Jerusalem. He is then abruptly brought back to earth (17:1–4).

The implication of the command not to be concerned over the salvation of Jerusalem is that the rebuilding of Jerusalem and the reconstruction of the temple play no part in the author's eschatology. Jerusalem and the temple have become dispensable. Instead the author's hopes for salvation are focused on the individual. Humans are held to be responsible for their own actions (cf. 4:16), and their reward or punishment depend on whether they have good works that can be presented by Michael before God (11:3–16:4). Those who have many, or at least some, good works are assured that they will be rewarded by God (15:1–4) and—according to the Greek version—are offered the prospect that their souls will dwell in the heavenly realm (ch. 10). Those who have no works to offer are condemned to punishment in this life (16:1–3) and are destined—according to the Greek—to dwell in Hades (4:3–5) and to be burnt in eternal fire (4:16).[49] The description of the fifth heaven,[50] and the action of Michael in presenting the works of humans before God, forms the climax of *4 Baruch*, and although there is evidence of Christian editing in chs. 15–16, there is no reason to doubt the Jewish basis of the account.

VII

To summarize, in conclusion, the results of this study. On the one hand, the *Psalms of Solomon* and the *Assumption of Moses* provide evidence for the continuation down into the first c. C.E. of the view, which can be found already in Mal 1:6–2:9 and *1 En.* 89:73, that the post-exilic temple and cult were unclean and illegitimate. This view stands in sharp contrast to the attitude reflected in Baruch, which serves to present the cult re-established at the very beginning of the post-exilic period as the legitimate continuation of the pre-exilic cult.

On the other hand, the Baruch writings that date from after 70 C.E. reflect a changed perspective in which the main concern is to respond to the distress and anguish caused by the fall of Jerusalem and the loss of

---

[49] See the detailed discussion by Harlow, *The Greek* Apocalypse of Baruch (3 Baruch), 109–62 (156).

[50] The author, as Harlow points out (*The Greek* Apocalypse of Baruch [3 Baruch], 34–36) uses temple imagery in describing the fifth heaven, but does not make it part of the celestial temple.

the temple. What is remarkable in these writings is that, notwithstanding the expression of distress at the loss of the temple, expectations of the restoration of the earthly temple recede further and further into the background, and the focus is rather on participation in the life of the heavenly realm, on the gathering of the people in the Jerusalem which is above.

HOW SHOULD WE CONTEXTUALIZE PSEUDEPIGRAPHA? IMITATION AND EMULATION IN *4 EZRA*[1]

Hindy Najman

> The fact is that every writer *creates* his own precursors.
> His work modifies our conception of the past, as it
> will modify the future.
> —Jorge Borges, "Kafka and his Precursors"

We would all readily admit that contextualization is an essential part of historical study. If we can identify the context in which a text was produced, then we can use the context to draw conclusions about the text, and we can use the text to draw conclusions about the context. However, it is often difficult to locate the context in which a text was written and the author by whom it was composed. Indeed, even if we can identify an author or a collaborative group that was responsible for producing a text, it can sometimes still be quite a challenge to determine the text's historical value. But for those of us who work on pseudepigraphical texts, the job is particularly challenging. First these texts deliberately efface their relations to their contexts of composition, because they present themselves as written by another author, often from another time. Second, scholars have often contextualized these texts within modern practices of authorship and composition—hence as forgery, clerical deception or plagiarism.

The problems facing those of us who work on pseudepigrapha may seem insuperable. However, we should not assume that political contextualization or religious affiliation is the only way of doing history, or the most important. I want to suggest that *intellectual, cultural and spiritual practices* also constitute contexts within which texts can be rendered intelligible. Instead of constituting an obstacle, authorial self-effacement should be an object of study. By considering the practices of authorial effacement and pseudepigraphic attribution, we can come to

---

[1] This essay is dedicated to Florentino García Martínez. His scholarship, dedication to the field, and collegiality are exemplary, which makes this paper particularly appropriate. *Neiro ya'ir*: May the light of Professor García Martínez continue to shine ever more brightly for many years to come.

understand much about the way the unknown and unknowable authors related to their own present.

In this paper, I will focus on *4 Ezra*, a post-70 C.E. text that pseudepigraphically attributes itself to Ezra, who is said to have just experienced the destruction of the First Temple. This essay seeks to explain the pseudepigraphic claims of *4 Ezra* by situating it within the context of practices of the emulation and imitation of the sage and the struggle to overcome destruction by recovering a perfect, holy and idealized past.[2]

* * *

"Ezra" in *4 Ezra* is associated with a renewed presentation of the law to the returnees from Babylon, and is also linked to the re-establishment of temple worship.[3] However, that is not the only relationship with the temple that is preserved in Ezra-Nehemiah along with other traditions from the Second Temple period. *4 Ezra* participates in the ambivalence with which the newly formed Second Temple Judeans greeted the establishment of the new Temple as is found in Ezra 3:10–12.[4] In addition, much like the "Ezra" of Neh 8:1–8, "Ezra" surely needed to present the new law (vision seven of *4 Ezra*), but first he would have to be trained as a leader who participates in the mourning of Zion (vision 4 of *4 Ezra*).[5] The impossibility of singing again after the first exile (e.g.,

---

[2] For general background see M.E. Stone and T.A. Bergren, eds., *Biblical Figures Outside the Bible* (Harrisburg, Pa.: Trinity Press International, 1998); J.J. Collins and G.W.E. Nickelsburg, eds., *Ideal Figures in Ancient Judaism* (SBLSCS 12; Chico, Calif.: Scholars Press, 1980). On the matter of exemplarity and perfection see S. Cavell, *Cities of Words: Pedagogical Letters on a Register of the Moral Life* (Cambridge, Mass.: Belknap, 2004); and P. Hadot, *Qu'est-ce que la philosophie antique?* (Paris: Gallimard, 1995) and *Exercices spirituels et philosophie antique* (CEA/SA 88; Paris: Études augustiniennes, 1981); translated as *What is Ancient Philosophy?* (trans. M. Chase; Cambridge, Mass.: Belknap, 2002) and *Philosophy as a Way of Life: Spiritual Exercises from Socrates to Foucault* (trans. M. Chase; Oxford: Blackwell, 1995). See also A. Davidson's introduction to this English edition, "Introduction: Pierre Hadot and the Spiritual Phenomenon of Ancient Philosophy," 1–45.

[3] E.g. Neh 8:1–8.

[4] See M.A. Knibb, "Exile in the Damascus Document," *JSOT* 25 (1983): 99–117 and "The Exile in the Literature of the Intertestamental Period," *HeyJ* 17 (1976): 253–72.

[5] In Ezra 3:12–13 the re-established Temple is received with simultaneous shouts of joy and of weeping:

> (12) Many of the Priests and Levites and the chiefs of the clans, the old men who had seen the first house, wept loudly at the sight of the founding of this house. Many others shouted joyously at the top of their voices. (13) The people could

Ps 137) and overcoming the destruction compromised the holiness and perfection of a prior Judean self-presentation (e.g. Lamentations). Thus, the loss of a utopian past continued to haunt the priestly, liturgical and historical traditions—both scriptural and para-scriptural.[6]

Faced with destruction and an insurmountable exile, was it possible for Judeans in forced or self-imposed exile to recover that which was lost to Judaism in a post-destruction environment? Here I intend to think about what the aspiration is to overcome that exile and to recover an idealized perfection of the past or of the future. What is it to be perfect: is it to be god-like, live in a pure or holy way, or to live in accordance with Mosaic Law? What happens to the aspiration to perfection within a community that undergoes the destruction of its political and religious institutions, and that is exiled from its homeland?

The term "Perfection" signifies an end-state of moral progress, beyond which further progress is neither necessary nor possible. There are at least two conceptions of perfection, all making use of the above notion.

The first conception: *Human beings are perfectible, i.e., perfection is attainable and good.*

On the second conception: *Human beings are not perfectible, i.e., perfection is unattainable, but it can still serve as an ideal guiding moral progress.* This is essentially the view presented by Pierre Hadot in his well-known and extensive work on ancient Greek philosophy: there may be no living sages, but the idea of the sage is of central importance. What would such an ideal do for an individual? Hadot would respond by emphasizing the ongoing formation of the soul in an ever-increasing

---

not distinguish the shouts of joy from the people's weeping, for the people raised a great shout, the sound of which could be heard from afar.
Such bittersweet reception reflected the impossibility of overcoming the first exile in a way that it lingered throughout the Second Temple period. So, when *4 Ezra* or later rabbinic midrash and qinnot mourn the Second Temple as it if were the first (or read texts about the first destruction as though it already anticipates the second), we should consider the texts from the Second Temple period to reflect a destruction that was never fully overcome.
   [6] See R. Kraft's "Para-Mania: Beside, Before, and Beyond Bible Studies" (forthcoming in *JBL* 2007; available at http://ccat.sas.upenn.edu/rs/rak/publics/new2/sblpres2006-all.html), where he discusses defining the term "para-scriptural" to signify those texts that are beside and beyond the corpus which will later be designated "Bible." Also see W. Adler, "The Pseudepigrapha in Early Christianity," in *The Canon Debate* (ed. L.M. McDonald and J.A. Sanders; Peabody, Mass.: Hendrickson, 2002), 211–28.

approximation which can never reach its goal but which nevertheless constitutes moral progress.[7]

How can one pursue perfection within a community that experiences the loss of its institutions, and that is exiled from its native land? Is perfection, or progress towards perfection, to be thought of only in terms of restoration and return from exile? Or are there ways in which perfection, or progress towards perfection, are possible even in the midst of suffering—perhaps even *by means* of suffering?

What would such an ideal do for an individual or for a community? I want to suggest that the practice of pseudonymous attribution of new texts to past exemplars provides one answer: it is an attempt to recover an idealized or utopian past. Or, perhaps, an attempt to work out the impossibility of recovering that past by grounding the present now in an idealized past that, in the minds of the later writers, was full of divine access, prophecy and political independence. By extending a discourse attached to a founder of an earlier period, writers in the late Second Temple period and even after the destruction of the Second Temple are able to authorize and link their new texts to old and established traditions and founders.

"Ezra" in *4 Ezra* speaks after 70 C.E. as though it is just after the first destruction:

> In the thirtieth year of the destruction of our country, I, Shealtiel, who is Ezra, was in Babylon. And I lay on my bed, I was upset and thoughts welled up in my heart because I saw the destruction of Zion. (*4 Ezra* 3:1)

"Ezra" writes as if the Second Temple has not yet been built, as if it is still to be hoped for. Since the text was in fact written after 70 C.E., this may be seen as a mode of consolation for the destruction: what has not yet been built cannot have been destroyed. What distinguishes such consolation from delusion is the long-standing sense that the Second Temple never was the restoration of the First.

Only after the fourth vision, when he learns how to lament over the loss of temple and Zion, is "Ezra" is transformed from a figure who is paralyzed by destruction into a figure who is worthy of receiving vision.[8]

> 10:19 So I spoke again to her, and said, 20 "Do not do that thing, but let yourself be persuaded because of the troubles of Zion, and be consoled

---

[7] See above, n. 2.

[8] See M.E. Stone's discussion of this already in his *Fourth Ezra: a Commentary on the Book of Fourth Ezra* (Hermeneia; Minneapolis: Fortress Press, 1990), 318–21, 326–27.

because of the sorrow of Jerusalem. 21 For you see that our sanctuary has been laid waste, our altar thrown down, our temple destroyed; 22 our harp has been laid low, our song has been silenced, and our rejoicing has been ended; the light of our lampstand has been put out, the ark of our covenant has been plundered, our holy things have been polluted, and the name by which we are called has been profaned; our free men have suffered abuse, our priests have been burned to death, our Levites have gone into captivity; our virgins have been defiled, and our wives have been ravished; our righteous men have been carried off, our little ones have been cast out, our young men have been enslaved and our strong men made powerless. 23 And, what is more than all, the seal of Zion—for she has now lost the seal of her glory, and has been given over into the hands of those that hate us. 24 Therefore shake off your great sadness and lay aside your many sorrows, so that the Mighty One may be merciful to you, and the Most High may give you rest from your troubles." (*4 Ezra* 10:19–24)

"Ezra"'s transformation is described through an intricate invocation of multiple traditions. However, in the process of incorporating older and contemporaneous traditions, a figure emerges who differs from the Ezra of Ezra-Nehemiah. He is characterized not only as a scribe, but also as a Mosaic lawgiver, as a Daniel-like dreamer, and as a Jeremianic prophet.[9] The emergence is accomplished by a series of transformations that may be called *exemplary*: they offer *a model for emulation and imitation* to the reader who strives for perfection in the face of destruction.[10]

* * *

"Ezra" is not, then, reducible to the earlier Ezra. Yet it is nevertheless essential that "Ezra" is identified with Ezra. How does this identification work?

Let us first draw the distinction, common in perfectionist ethics, between emulation and imitation. If I am supposed to imitate an exemplar, then I ought to become *like* him or her. Sometimes, however, imitation is said to be insufficient, inauthentic or, at any rate, second best: I am supposed to *emulate* the exemplar, to become *identical* to him or her. As we have seen, "Ezra" is portrayed as imitating various exemplars, such as Moses, Jeremiah, and Daniel. But, insofar as he is identified as Ezra, he also emulates the earlier founder of this discourse, namely

---

[9] In *4 Ezra* 12:42 a plea is made to "Ezra" that he is the only prophet who has not abandoned his people.

[10] See below in this essay where I discuss the difference between emulation and imitation.

Ezra himself who represents the Torah in Neh 8:1–8, the paradigmatic exemplar in *4 Ezra*.

What is the difference between imitation and emulation—or, here, between comparing the protagonist to earlier figures and identifying him as one? Here it is helpful to appeal to the distinction between *metaphor* and *simile*. When Romeo says, "Juliet is the sun," he is employing a metaphor. Had he said, "Juliet is like the sun," he would have been using a simile. On one account, the difference is as follows. The metaphorical assertion "Juliet is the sun" is indeterminate and pregnant with possibility: she is radiant, warm, generous, light, remote or untouchable, *and so on.*[11] In contrast, the simile is determinate: Juliet is like the sun in some determinate respect. Whereas a simile deals in analogies, we might say that a metaphor effects an *identification*. Just as there are indefinitely many things to say about the sun, so are there indefinitely many things to say about what is identified with it.

Similarly, we may say, the analogies between the protagonist of *4 Ezra* and various figures are similes with determinate implications. In contrast, the pseudepigraphic attribution to Ezra acts as a metaphorical identification, pregnant with indeterminate implications. While the text presents "Ezra" imitating several exemplary figures, only one exemplar is held out as a model for emulation, i.e., Ezra of the Second Temple period.

Thus, "Ezra" *imitates* Daniel insofar as he receives apocalyptic visions:

> He said to me, "This is the interpretation of the vision which you have seen: *The eagle which you saw coming up from the sea is the fourth kingdom which appeared in a vision to your brother Daniel. But it was not explained to him as I now explain it to you.* Behold, the days are coming when a kingdom shall arise on earth, and it shall be more terrifying than all the kingdoms that have been before it." (*4 Ezra* 12:10–12)

Then, in the seventh vision, "Ezra's" vision is implicitly *likened* to that of Moses insofar as he is told that God will lead the people from bondage to law:[12]

---

[11] See S. Cavell, *Must We Mean What We Say?* (Cambridge: Cambridge University Press, 1969), 78–79. Also see later discussions in D. Hills, "Aptness and Truth in Verbal Metaphor," *Philosophical Topics* 25 (1997): 117–53.

[12] See also Stone's discussion of Mosaic comparison in *4 Ezra* 14, *Fourth Ezra*, 410–12 and 415–18.

Then he (God) said to me, "I revealed myself in a bush and spoke to Moses when my people were in bondage in Egypt; and I sent him and led my people out of Egypt; and I led him up to Mount Sinai. And I kept him with me many days; and I told him many wondrous thinking, and showed him the secrets of the times and declared to him the end of the times. Then I commanded him, saying: 'These words you shall publish openly, and these you shall keep secret.' And now I say to you; Lay up in your heart the signs that I have shown you, the dreams that you have seen and the interpretation that you have heard; for you shall be taken up from among men, and henceforth you shall be with my servant and with those who are like you, until the times are ended." (*4 Ezra* 14:3)

These are examples of imitation, but not emulation. "Ezra" is not asked to become Moses. He is not asked to efface himself entirely, but he is repeatedly likened to Moses and is asked to imitate him.

Of course, "Ezra" is a stand-in for the actual, unknown author of *4 Ezra*. We cannot reconstruct the original audience for *4 Ezra* or identify the author of the seven visions. So, how are we to make sense of pseudonymous attribution without simply calling the work a forgery? My suggestion is that *pseudonymous attribution should be seen as a metaphorical device, operating at the level of the text as a whole, whereby the actual author emulates and self-identifies as an exemplar.*[13] Accordingly, the practice of pseudonymous attribution should be seen as a spiritual discipline, an asceticism of self-effacement.

* * *

In addition to the figure of "Ezra," the text of *4 Ezra* may also be considered a metaphor, since it is identified as an Ezra-produced text. So are the esoteric and exoteric books of the seventh vision.

Earlier, I noted that, through the identification with Ezra of "Ezra," who has additional attributes, Ezra himself is transformed. Similarly, through the identification of the text of *4 Ezra* and the texts mentioned in *4 Ezra* with Ezra-produced texts, earlier texts are transformed insofar as later readers will read the figure of Ezra in Ezra-Nehemiah through the prism of the later "Ezra" as he develops and expands the traditions associated with him. The earlier and later traditions associated with the

---

[13] See D.S. Russell's thesis about "corporate personality" in *Between the Testaments* (London: SCM Press, 1960), 116–18 and *The Method and Message of Jewish Apocalyptic, 200 B.C.–A.D. 100* (OTL; London: SCM Press, 1964), 132–39. See also G.W.H. Lampe, "The Reasonableness of Typology," in *Essays on Typology* (ed. G.W.H. Lampe and K.J. Woollcombe; SBT 22; Naperville, Ill.: Allenson, Inc., 1957), 9–38.

founding figure of Ezra are now members of a corpus of texts that retrospectively transform the reputation and the achievement of the founding figure of the past.[14] Prophecy persists after the destruction of the Second Temple, not only in the transformation of exemplary figures of the past and in the creation of new texts, but also in the erasure of the difference between present and past.

Pseudepigraphic texts such as *Jubilees*, *1 Enoch* and *4 Ezra*, efface their own compositional contexts when they attach their new traditions to a founding figure from the past. In so doing, however, they situate themselves within another context: a perfectionist practice of effacing oneself in order to emulate an exemplary figure.[15] This practice provides a context for overcoming the present period of destruction by expanding the legacy of founders from the past.

---

[14] Compare, for example, the transformation of the reputation of Moses in later, post-deuteronomic, traditions.

[15] I am indebted to John Collins, Paul Franks, Robert Kraft, Judith Newman, George Nickelsburg, Andrei Orlov, Annette Yoshiko Reed, Michael Stone, Eibert Tigchelaar, Benjamin G. Wright III and Robin Darling Young for their incisive responses to earlier versions of this paper. Many thanks also to my student, Eva Mroczek, for her helpful suggestions.

THE ENVY OF GOD IN THE PARADISE STORY ACCORDING TO THE GREEK *LIFE OF ADAM AND EVE*

Lautaro Roig Lanzillotta

Anyone acquainted with the factors and actors of envy, and who has been forced by circumstances to reflect on its origin, character, and development, sooner or later unavoidably realises or intuits that this passion has a deeper dimension and significance that escapes a first analysis. The apparent triangular structure of envy, comprising the envied spiritual or material goods, the envious person, and the person who is the target of the envy, is simply not enough to explain the complex set of feelings and relations triggered by this emotion. This is obvious in the fact that envy may arise not only in the individual who does not possess a given good and desires to have it, but also in him who possesses it and attempts by all means to prevent others from having it.

It thus seems that there are other less visible factors that are likely to explain its appearance in human relations. At any rate, there are certain necessary conditions that must concur in order for envy to appear. These are, for example, the existence of a comparative frame in which two individuals may establish themselves as terms of a comparison[1] in their quest for goods, a value scale that determines an individual's higher or lower value according to his ability to acquire status tokens, and, of course, the symbolic value of objects insofar as they provide the individual with an idea of his personal value.[2]

In this homage to Professor Florentino García Martínez, I would like to approach this complex conceptual world through the motif of

---

[1] The comparative attitude of individuals as well as the comparative frame in which they are involved has always been envisaged as triggering envy. According to Spinoza, *Ethica* III, prop. XXXII, the former is inherent to humans beings (*ex eadem naturae humanae proprietate*). Also for D. Hume, *A Treatise of Human Nature* II, part. II, sect. VII, the value we give to reality depends more on comparison than on the intrinsic value of things. See furthermore I. Kant, *Metaphysik der Sitten* II, 2, 1, 36 and L. Festinger, "A Theory of Social Comparison Process," *Human Relations* (1954): 114–40.

[2] For the importance of the symbolic value of goods, see W. McDougal *apud* H. Sullivan, *Clinical Studies of Psychiatry* (New York: Norton, 1954), 128–29; P. Salovey and A.J. Rothman, "Envy and Jealousy: Self and Society," in *The Psychology of Jealousy and Envy* (ed. P. Salovey; New York: Guilford, 1991), 271–86 (284).

the envy of God developed in chapters XV to XVIII of the Greek *Life of Adam and Eve (LAE).*[3] In order to do so, I shall first focus on this *passus.* I shall then proceed to compare it with the model the author is paraphrasing (Gen 2:16–17 and 3:1–7) in order to see whether the Bible story *mutatis mutandis* might have provided him with the elements of his interpretation or whether one should surmise the influence of external factors, such as the existence of discussions or commentaries that intended to cast some light upon divine motivation. I shall finally compare it with the gnostic appropriation and reinterpretation of a motif that suited their *Weltanschauung* very well.

1. THE ENVY OF GOD IN THE GREEK LIFE OF ADAM AND EVE

In chapter 15 of *LAE*, Adam and Eve decide to call their children together in order to tell them about the transgression they committed in the past. Once they have all arrived, Eve narrates how the Enemy deceived them (110–112). She begins by relating that God had placed them in paradise, allotting each of them the surveillance of a different part of the Garden (113–118). But the devil enrols the serpent with a view to getting the first couple thrown out of Paradise (118–127). By means of the serpent, the devil manages to get into conversation with Eve (133ff.) in order to surreptitiously instil in her an interpretation of God's motivation and an attitude toward His commandments (142–151) that will result in the first couple's exile from the Garden of Eden (154–226).

It will be clear from the beginning that in this dialogue, which is a clear amplification and a paraphrase of Gen 2:16–17 and 3:1–7, there are no elements alien to the Old Testament story (below). God's prohibition to eat from the tree in the middle of Paradise is the same, the devil's temptation in order that Eve may obviate the prohibition is the same, and the results of the transgression are also the same. The serpent/devil slightly alters the interpersonal parameters of the Genesis story, and the resulting new evaluative frame allows a complete transformation of the relationship between the human and divine spheres.

At any rate, the devil begins the conversation by asking Eve what she is doing in Paradise and she naively answers that God put them

---

[3] For the Greek text I use the edition by J. Tromp, *The Life of Adam and Eve in Greek: A Critical Edition* (PVTG 6; Leiden: Brill, 2005).

there to watch over it and to eat from it (132–136). The devil asks then if they may eat from *every* tree in the Garden, and Eve answers that they may eat from *all* the trees *except* from the one in the middle of Paradise (139–141): κἀγὼ εἶπον· ναί, ἀπὸ πάντων ἐσθίομεν, παρὲξ ἑνὸς μόνου ὅ ἐστιν μέσον τοῦ παραδείσου, περὶ οὗ ἐνετείλατο ἡμῖν ὁ θεὸς μὴ ἐσθίειν ἐξ αὐτοῦ, ἐπεὶ θανάτῳ ἀποθανεῖσθε.

It is interesting to note that God's menace (θανάτῳ ἀποθανεῖσθε) implies that the first couple already possessed one of the divine attributes, i.e. not being liable to death.[4] The snake, however, obviates this important issue, and instead of focusing on what they do have, namely immortality, it focuses on what they do not. By making her conscious of what she lacks, the snake automatically introduces Eve to the fictitious evaluative frame that will result in her and her man's exile from Paradise (142–151):

> τότε λέγει μοι ὁ ὄφις· ζῇ ὁ θεός, ὅτι λυποῦμαι περὶ ὑμῶν. οὐ γὰρ θέλω ὑμᾶς ἀγνοεῖν. δεῦρο οὖν καὶ φάγε καὶ νόησον τὴν τιμὴν τοῦ ξύλου. [2] ἐγὼ εἶπον αὐτῷ· φοβοῦμαι μήποτε ὀργισθῇ μοι ὁ θεὸς καθὼς εἶπεν ἡμῖν. [3] καὶ λέγει μοι· μὴ φοβοῦ. ἅμα γὰρ φάγῃς, ἀνοιχθήσονταί σου οἱ ὀφθαλμοί, καὶ ἔσεσθε ὡς θεοὶ γινώσκοντες τί ἀγαθὸν καὶ τί πονηρόν. τοῦτο δὲ γινώσκων ὁ θεὸς ὅτι ἔσεσθε ὅμοιοι αὐτοῦ, ἐφθόνησεν ὑμῖν καὶ εἶπεν· οὐ φάγεσθε ἐξ αὐτοῦ. [5] σὺ δὲ πρόσχες τῷ φυτῷ καὶ ὄψει δόξαν μεγάλην.

There are many interesting aspects in this text, but we shall focus on the most relevant for our present purpose. One of them is the already mentioned omission of any reference to the impending death of the first couple should they transgress the prohibition. By obviating this, the snake is able to depict knowledge as the most relevant aspect of the divine. The section abounds in implicit and explicit references to an all-embracing kind of knowledge (142–143: οὐ...ἀγνοεῖν; 143: νόησον; 147–148: ἀνοιχθήσονταί σου οἱ ὀφθαλμοί; 148: γινώσκοντες; 149: γινώσκων). It should be noted, however, that this knowledge, if deprived of eternity, amounts to nothing or, at any rate, not to the kind of knowledge Eve strives for. Her deception lies precisely in the fact that Eve, by acquiring knowledge, will be deprived of eternal life, as a result of which the acquired knowledge—insofar as it is no increase in insight in what was, what is, and will be—will just be a pale reflection of divine knowledge. Incidentally, passing though it might be, this reference in *LAE* already indicates that we are no longer dealing with the Old

---

[4] Cf., however, Gen 3:22; but see *Ps.-Clem. Homil.* 16.6.3–4.

Testament conception of divinity mainly focused on "divine identity,"
as R. Bauckham suggested,[5] but with an idea of God that denotes the
influence of Greek philosophical thought on the issue, which was more
interested in the description of His divine attributes.

The most important issue in the section, however, is the stratagem by
means of which the serpent convinces Eve to eat from the tree in the
middle of Paradise. After making Eve aware of what she lacks, the devil
completes the circle of his argument by pointing to God not only as the
possessor of her desired good, but also as responsible for her lacking it:
it is an intentional grudge by the divinity that determines Eve's lack.
In the devil's words, God's envy is the reason behind the prohibition
to eat from the tree, insofar as he intended to prevent Adam and Eve
from acquiring the status token that would make them gods.

The scenario of envy is now complete. In the first place we have Eve's
envy: after realising what she lacks, Eve peremptorily needs to achieve
what she might have but has not. This need is increased after she hears
that her lack is due to an intentional grudge by one who has it, i.e. God.
Eve's envy can then be described as *ascendant envy*. On the other hand,
we have God's envy. The devil affirms that God's prohibition is based on
his own interest, namely that by begrudging the first couple the knowledge, he actually intends to preserve for himself that which determines
his superiority. God's envy can be described as *descendant envy*.[6]

In order for this complex evaluative universe to appear, however,
there are also certain factors required. I shall now mention just two
of them. In the first place, one needs the existence of a comparative
frame in which God and the first couple may represent the two terms
of a value comparison. In Eve's case, however fictitious her impression
might be, she must in one way or another believe that she has *almost* the
same status as God, since it is only knowledge that seems to separate
her from God's loftiness. The same applies to God's envy, since in the

---

[5] R. Bauckham, *God Crucified: Monotheism and Christology in the New Testament* (The
Didsbury Lectures, 1996. Carlisle: Paternoster, 1998), 8–9.

[6] I cannot therefore agree with the interpretation of the *passus* by W.C. van Unnik,
"Der Neid in der Paradiesgeschichte nach einigen gnostischen Texten," in *Essays on the
Nag Hammadi Texts in Honour of Alexander Böhlig* (ed. M. Krause; NHS 3; Leiden: Brill,
1972), 120–32. The author classes it among the examples of descendant envy, namely,
as an example, exclusively, of God's envy towards man. But our analysis reveals that
the passage is much more complex than Van Unnik is ready to admit, since placing
God and Eve in the same comparative frame includes both directions of envy. On the
second variety, see next note.

serpent's opinion it is a grudge on the part of the divinity that caused the prohibition, and this kind of descendant envy intends to prevent those who are inferior but rather close to the superior individual from reducing the distance that separates them.[7]

Secondly, we need the development of the status tokens that represent the focus of both envious attitudes. In our text these are both eternity and knowledge, insofar as they determine, as already stated, divine status.

Consequently, we may suggest that, however disturbing the devil's accusation against God might be, the focus of our passage is not so much on God's envy as on Eve's envy. The devil's stratagem is intended to seduce or deceive Eve, and he achieves this by fictitiously transposing her into an evaluative frame in which she has a *right* to have what God has. By pointing to what she lacks and by mentioning God's envy, the serpent actually triggers Eve's own envy. The blind quest for what she apparently lacks prevents Eve from realising that, like the dog in Aesop's fable, if she goes after what she does not have, she will even lose what she has.[8]

The end of the story is well known: Eve yields to her desire for knowledge and eats from the tree, then gives it to her husband as well, and, as a result, both of them are expelled from the Garden of Eden. From now on they will be subject to the chains of mundane existence.

2. The Alleged External Influences of this Interpretation of Gen 2:16–17 and 3:4–5

In a rather confusing article on the motif of envy in the Paradise story, W.C. van Unnik dealt with our section of *LAE* together with other examples from the Nag Hammadi texts.[9] Following with hesitation

---

[7] See H. Schoeck, *Der Neid und die Gesellschaft* (Freiburg: Herder, 1971).

[8] See Babrius, "canis per fluvium carnem ferens."

[9] Van Unnik, "Der Neid," 120–32. I refer to the article as confusing, because the author not only mixes rather different texts with one another and the different types of envy included in them, but also does not attempt a systematic analysis of the quoted passages in order to achieve a consistent explanation. He first deals with the envy of the archons towards men in the *Titellose Schrift* 166–167 [*OrigWorld* (NHC II,5) 118.25–119.6] and in the *Hypostasis of the Archons* 137–138 [89.31–90.19], then proceeds to describe two general sorts of envy, i.e. ascendant and descendant, in order to jump afterwards to rather different envy examples (in this case Jaldabaoth's envy against Sabaoth in *Titellose Schrift* 154 [*OrigWorld* (NHC II,5) 106.19–30] and *Hypostasis of the Archons* 144

R.M. Grant,[10] who in turn followed A. von Harnack,[11] Van Unnik surmised that the origin of this paraphrase might be a Marcionite attribution of envy to the God of the Old Testament.[12] As support for this suggestion, he quotes texts from Theophilus and Irenaeus, who mention disapprovingly the opinion of "some" to the effect that God acted from envy. These people, Van Unnik feels, might be Marcionites.[13] As we shall see, however, there are some problems with this explanation.

To begin with, as already proposed, if we exclude the motif of envy, the passage in *LAE* does not add relevant new elements to its biblical model. An important argument to disprove the alleged Marcionite origin of the motif is the absolute lack of a divine dichotomy, either between the righteous and the good God, or between the highest God and the creator.

Besides, it is not in a general argument by the writer that the text presses charges of envy against God. Rather, it is the devil—a clear antagonist whom the text depicts as a deceiver acting out of malice and hatred against God and the first couple—who issues the accusation. This argument seems to be supported by the fact that, differently than in gnostic texts that rewrite the Paradise story,[14] the serpent is clearly said to "deceive" Eve (*LAE* 111–112; 124–123).

Last but not least, the transgression does not report any good for the first couple, as is the case in the gnostic texts that endorse the theory of divine envy as a background for the prohibition. As in the biblical story, Eve not only does not achieve what she strives for, but she is also expelled together with Adam from Paradise, as a punishment for her disobedience.

[96.3–15]. He then brings in Aristotle's *Rhetorica* in order to affirm afterwards that the previous examples are in fact diverse. The most important problem, however, is that the passage from *LAE* is confusingly included as if the reference to God's envy were a general argument by the writer. Rather, on the contrary, the charges of envy are issued by the devil in the form of the serpent in a way that closely resembles the biblical story.

[10] R.M. Grant, *Theophilus of Antioch Ad Autolycum* (Oxford: Clarendon Press, 1970), 67.

[11] A. von Harnack, *Marcion: das Evangelium vom fremden Gott* (Leipzig: Hinrichs, 1924), 414–15, who refers to Ambrosius, *De Paradiso* 6.30.

[12] Van Unnik, "Der Neid," 125–26.

[13] Theophilus, *Ad Autolycum* 2.25, διὸ οὐχ ὡς φθονῶν αὐτῷ ὁ θεός, ὡς οἴονταί τινες, ἐκέλευσεν μὴ ἐσθίειν ἀπὸ τῆς γνώσεως; Irenaeus, *Haer.* 3.23.6, *Quapropter et eiecit eum de Paradiso et a ligno vitae longe transtulit, non invidens ei lignum vitae, quemadmodum audent quidam dicere, sed miserans eius.*

[14] G.P. Luttikhuizen, *Gnostic Revisions of Genesis Stories and Early Jesus Traditions* (NHMS 58; Leiden: Brill, 2005), 76 points out that a significant difference between the biblical story and its gnostic revisions lies in the fact that the latter do not affirm, as the former does, that the serpent deluded or seduced Eve.

It seems obvious, consequently, that the author does not endorse this view. On the contrary, he puts the accusation in the mouth of the serpent, as a paraphrasing and amplifying version of the Genesis story that makes explicit what a reader of the Hellenistic period might interpret as implicit in the text. After all, according to Wisdom, the devil was held responsible for introducing envy to the world.[15]

This becomes clear by closely comparing *LAE* to its biblical model. The Genesis story is well known, but I include it in order to facilitate the comparison of both passages. The first relevant section is Gen 2:16–17, in which God commands Adam not to eat from the tree of knowledge of good and evil:

> καὶ ἐνετείλατο κύριος ὁ θεὸς τῷ Αδαμ λέγων Ἀπὸ παντὸς ξύλου τοῦ ἐν τῷ παραδείσῳ βρώσει φάγῃ,[17] ἀπὸ δὲ τοῦ ξύλου τοῦ γινώσκειν καλὸν καὶ πονηρὸν οὐ φάγεσθε ἀπ' αὐτοῦ· ᾗ δ' ἂν ἡμέρᾳ φάγητε ἀπ' αὐτοῦ θανάτῳ ἀποθανεῖσθε.

The other passage is Gen 3:2–7, in which the actual conversation between the snake and Eve takes place:

> καὶ εἶπεν ἡ γυνὴ τῷ ὄφει Ἀπὸ καρποῦ ξύλου τοῦ παραδείσου φαγόμεθα,[3] ἀπὸ δὲ καρποῦ τοῦ ξύλου ὅ ἐστιν ἐν μέσῳ τοῦ παραδείσου εἶπεν ὁ θεὸς Οὐ φάγεσθε ἀπ' αὐτοῦ οὐδὲ μὴ ἅψησθε αὐτοῦ ἵνα μὴ ἀποθάνητε.[4] καὶ εἶπεν ὁ ὄφις τῇ γυναικί Οὐ θανάτῳ ἀποθανεῖσθε·[5] ᾔδει γὰρ ὁ θεὸς ὅτι ἐν ᾗ ἂν ἡμέρᾳ φάγητε ἀπ' αὐτοῦ διανοιχθήσονται ὑμῶν οἱ ὀφθαλμοί, καὶ ἔσεσθε ὡς θεοὶ γινώσκοντες καλὸν καὶ πονηρόν.

It is not difficult to see that *LAE* actually conflates both sections of Genesis, since Eve declares that they might not eat from the "tree in the middle of Paradise," as in Gen 3:3, and, should they do so, the result will be that "they will surely die," as in Gen 2:17 (θανάτῳ ἀποθανεῖσθε). However, *LAE* nevertheless preserves all the important details without changing the basic story.

As a matter of fact, one might, at the most, accuse *LAE*'s devil of overinterpreting the Genesis sentence: ᾔδει γὰρ ὁ θεὸς ὅτι ἐν ᾗ ἂν ἡμέρᾳ φάγητε ἀπ' αὐτοῦ διανοιχθήσονται ὑμῶν οἱ ὀφθαλμοί, καὶ ἔσεσθε ὡς θεοὶ γινώσκοντες καλὸν καὶ πονηρόν. But how should this sentence actually be explained? How should we understand the devil's assertion in the biblical passage that the prohibition not to eat of the tree of knowledge of good and evil is due to the fact that "God knows that

---

[15] Wis 2:24, φθόνῳ δὲ διαβόλου θάνατος εἰσῆλθεν εἰς τὸν κόσμον.

on the day you eat of it your eyes will be opened, and you will be like
gods, knowing good and evil."

The first possible explanation could be that the serpent of the Genesis
story simply intended to underline the inherent limits of the human
condition, by establishing a clear-cut difference between the divine and
human spheres—Adam and Eve possess eternal life but not unlimited
knowledge. In doing so, the serpent's intention would be simply tempting Eve by establishing, first, the difference between the human and
divine spheres in order to point immediately afterwards to that which
apparently could blur these borders. From this perspective the theme of
the Genesis story would be Eve's *hybris*, an arrogant attitude on her side
that would lead her to transgress the prohibition in order to achieve
divine status. This explanation implies a culture in which the world of
the gods and that of human beings is unbridgeable, an archaic religious conscience, of which Greek mythology also provides numerous
examples and according to which any human attempt to trespass the
inherent limits results in his ruin.[16]

However, that the serpent of the biblical passage had God's envy
in mind as a reason for the prohibition of course remains a possibility.
The biblical passage is ambiguous enough not to allow such a clear-cut
distinction between the divine and human spheres, at least not at the
moment that the whole Paradise story takes place: Adam and Eve are
the first humans, but they live in Paradise and possess eternal life. Even
though they are creatures of God, and therefore inferior to him, in one
possible interpretation, they nonetheless possess certain divine attributes
that bring them close to God. It is from this perspective that envy as a
background for God's motivation becomes a possible interpretation.

I think it is precisely in this context that we have to place *LAE*'s version
of the serpent's words, since it deliberately blurs the borders between
the divine and human spheres and, by placing God and men side by
side, introduces them in a comparative frame. The key of the devil's

---

[16] See, for example, the famous cases of Tantalus and Bellerophontes, which perfectly
exemplify the loss of human measure (κόρος), the arrogant attitude that follows it (the
ὕβρις ἀτάσθαλος), and the punishment of the gods it necessarily attracts, a sort of
blindness (ἄτη), which results in their ruin. Both mythological heroes were favoured
by the gods with a steady well-being (the former shared the table with them and the
latter was supported in all his affairs), as a result of which they thought they were as
infallible as the gods. In the case of Bellerophontes, his attempt to blur the borders
between the divine and human spheres is properly punished in a way that clearly reaf-
firms them: angry with him when he tried to reach the Olympus on his winged horse
Pegasus, Zeus simply sent an insignificant mosquito to face him.

interpretation lies in the meaning he gives to the section: ἔσεσθε ὡς θεοί. While the biblical passage depicts divine *status*, to which eternity and knowledge belong, namely "you will become gods," in *LAE* the serpent interprets the expression as "to be *like* God is." With this in mind, the devil introduces an explicit explanation (149–150): τοῦτο δὲ γινώσκων ὁ θεὸς ὅτι ἔσεσθε ὅμοιοι αὐτοῦ, ἐφθόνησεν ὑμῖν κτλ. ("As God knew that you would become like him, he envied you, etc."). By referring to God's envious grudge and thus implying the possibility of Eve's existential promotion, the serpent triggers her envy.

LAE's amplification and epexegetic sentence clearly introduces an interpretation of the biblical passage, but do we need to suppose an external source to explain this paraphrase? In point of fact, *LAE*'s paraphrase looks more like a gloss on the text, as a commentary that intended to clarify the expression ὡς θεοί, rather than a radical interpretation of the biblical passage.

In a last analysis, the devil's intention in Genesis is as denigratory as in *LAE*. Independently of the explanation one gives to the serpent's assertion, either as an authoritative denial or as an envious grudge, the fact remains that it seduces Eve who, the victim of *hybris* or of envy, yields to her desire to achieve that which might make her a god or like the gods.

The passages by Theophilus and Irenaeus may or may not reflect the "Meinung bestimmter Lehrer,"[17] as Van Unnik affirms, but in my view, what they do not necessarily echo is a gnostic or pre-gnostic appropriation and reinterpretation of the Paradise story. They might simply testify to explanatory attempts concerning what the serpent was actually asserting in the Genesis account.

3. The Envy of the Demiurge according to some Gnostic Texts

In the gnostic retelling of the Genesis story one finds a wholly different conceptual world. For the first time one can speak of a *revision* in the strict sense of the word, since the story is included in a completely new narrative frame. The scene becomes an essential episode both in the history of human devaluation—from the heights of transcendence to the lowest abode of the sublunar world—and in the process of the

---

[17] Van Unnik, "Der Neid," 125–26.

recovery of the primal condition. Consequently, gnostic texts including a rewriting of the story completely alter the setting, the actors, their identities, interpersonal relations, and the reasons that determine human and divine motivation.[18]

To begin with, all the Nag Hammadi texts dealing with the passage endorse the second of the possible interpretations (above) of God's prohibition, namely, they recognise the background of a grudging envious attitude towards the first humans. An obvious corollary of this interpretation is that, according to the gnostics, the Paradise story could not be describing the actions of the *real* God.[19] Behind this view we may have the influence of Plato's assertion that God is free of envy in *Phaedrus* and *Timaeus*,[20] or, even more importantly, Plato's conception of (descendant) envy as the most serious obstacle to the development and transmission of virtue, which can be found in the *Laws* and several other places.[21] However, an interesting passage from the first book of Aristotle's *Metaphysics* might provide an even more suitable parallel for the theme we are dealing with. In discussing the question whether or not knowledge about greater matters is beyond human power—namely knowledge about the phenomena of the moon, the sun, and the stars, and about the genesis of the universe—the Philosopher categorically denies the possibility of an envious divinity who withholds knowledge from humans:

---

[18] As Luttikhuizen, *Gnostic Revisions*, 75, has pointed out, the *Testimony of Truth*, for example, "does not entirely reject the biblical Paradise story. In fact, the actual events are not doubted. The controversy concerns the identity of the actors appearing in the story (the creator, the serpent and the first human beings) and the real meaning of what was said and what was done."

[19] See, for example, the conclusion to *Testim. Truth*'s retelling of the Paradise Story (NHC IX,3; 48.1–4): "What sort of God is this? First [he] was envious of Adam that he should eat from the tree of knowledge. And secondly he said, 'Adam where are you?' So, God did not have foreknowledge?…What sort of God is this? Indeed, great is the blindness of those who read (this) and have not recognized him!"

[20] Plato, *Phdr.* 247 A 7, φθόνος γὰρ ἔξω θείου χοροῦ ἵσταται; *Tim.* 29E 1–2, ἀγαθὸς ἦν, ἀγαθῷ δὲ οὐδεὶς περὶ οὐδενὸς οὐδέποτε ἐγγίγνεται φθόνος.

[21] Plato, *Laws* 730E–731A 2 generally deals with those cases in which descendant envy is an obstacle for a good functioning of the polis: the first place in honour corresponds to him who having achieved *sophrosyne* and *phronesis* does not impede others from achieving it, but rather actively helps them to do so. In the lowest place of social esteem, we find the envious individual who has the spiritual goods and intentionally prevents others from reaching them; see also *Prot.* 327A 4–327B 6, where the unenvious transmission of *arete* and justice is also the basis of a well-functioning polis. In *Menex.* 93C 6–9, envy is an obstacle to the transmission of *arete* from parents to children (cf. *Hipp. Maj.* 283E 6 and Pseudo-Plato, *De virtute*). See L. Roig Lanzillotta, *La envidia en el pensamiento griego: Desde la época arcaica al helenismo* (Diss., Univ. Complutense, 1997), 419–24.

If, then, there is something in what the poets say, and jealousy is natural to the divine power, it would probably occur in this case above all, and all who excelled in this knowledge would be unfortunate. But the divine power cannot be jealous (nay, according to the proverb, "bards tell a lie"), nor should any other science be thought more honourable than one of this sort.[22]

According to the gnostic view, consequently, the Paradise story depicts the attempts by the lower Demiurge (on occasion, by the rulers of the material world)[23] to prevent humans from coming to know themselves and their real nature.[24] There are several texts that include a revision of the Genesis story.[25] Obviating now the particular differences, we may generally sketch the rewriting as follows.

After the Demiurge (or the rulers) has involuntarily insufflated the Mother's light power in Adam, the first man is cast down by the creator to the lowest regions of matter, lest he come to know his true superior nature.

As could be expected, however, the good and higher God intervenes in order that humans may come to know their true belonging and may begin their way back to their original abode. With this in mind, he sends a helper to assist them,[26] which is normally the serpent[27] but, on occasion, can also be Christ himself[28] or even an eagle sitting on the tree—which is actually Epinoia, the Light Reflection.[29]

---

[22] Aristotle, *Metaph.* 982 B 32–983 A 5. In this trend, see *Gos. Truth* (NHC I,3) 18.34–19.10; *Tri. Trac.* (NHC I,5) 62.20–33; *Interpr. Know.* (NHC XI,1) 15.18–21.

[23] *Ap. John* (NHC II,1) 22.3–7; BG 57.8–18.

[24] See *Testim. Truth* (NHC IX,3) 47.28–30; 48.8–13; *Hyp. Arch.* (NHC II,4) 90.6–10; *Orig. World* (NHC II,5) 119.5

[25] So, for example, *Ap. John* (NHC II,1) 21.16–22.15; *Testim. Truth* (NHC IX,3) 47.14–48.13; *Hyp. Arch.* (NHC II,4) 89.31–90.19; *Orig. World* (NHC II,5) 118.16–119.18; cf. *Gos. Truth.* (NHC I,3) 18.24–29.

[26] *Ap. John* (NHC II) 20.9–19 (BG 52.17–53.10), "The Blessed Father had mercy on the power of the Mother which had been drawn out of the first ruler...And through his beneficent Spirit and his great mercy, he sent a helper to Adam."

[27] *Hyp. Arch.* (NHC II,4) 90.6, 31. In this text, however, the instructor is actually the female spiritual principle that comes in the snake and teaches them (see 89.31–32); *Orig. World* (NHC II,5) 119.25–27.

[28] *Ap. John* (NHC II,1) 22.9. See also *Gos. Truth* (NHC I,3) 18.24–29, which, in an allusion to Gen 3:3, says that Christ was nailed on the cross and "became the fruit of knowledge of the Father. It did not, however, cause destruction because it was eaten, but to those who ate it, it gave (cause) to become glad in the discovery."

[29] *Ap. John* (BG 60.19–61.7). On the motif of the eagle, see I. Czachesz, "The Eagle on the Tree: A Homeric Motif in Jewish and Christian Literature," in *Jerusalem, Alexandria, Rome: Studies in Ancient Cultural Interaction in Honour of A. Hilhorst* (ed. F. García Martínez and G.P. Luttikhuizen; JSJSup 82; Leiden: Brill, 2003), 87–106.

It is in this context that the Paradise scene is framed. Adam and Eve have received the commandment not to eat from the tree of knowledge not from God but from the Demiurge, and this with a view to keeping them ignorant of their superior condition. Here we find the first relevant transformation: the actors of the story have been changed. It is not the higher God who is envious, but the lower one. Aware of the latter's stratagem, the higher divinity intervenes to frustrate his intentions, since he is in fact willing humans to achieve knowledge. As the *Gospel of Truth* asserts, God does not withhold knowledge from humans, but temporarily retains their perfection "granting it to them as a return to him and a perfect and unitary knowledge."[30]

As an emissary of the supreme God, the serpent is the "instructor" who will inform Eve about the real reason of the prohibition and encourage her to eat from the tree of knowledge so that her eyes might be opened. Its role, consequently, is also reversed: from being the seducer (in Genesis) or, as a means for the devil, the introducer of envy to the world (*LAE*), it becomes now the benefactor of humanity. In accordance with its positive role in the story, its description acquires a more favourable character. As G.P. Luttikhuizen has pointed out, the *Testimony of Truth* notably upgrades the serpent, which no longer belongs to the earth but to Paradise and is described as an "animal" instead of as a "beast."[31]

The same transformation applies, of course, to the results of the transgression committed by the first humans. Once they eat from the tree, the first thing Adam and Eve become aware of is their imperfection, due to their lack of *gnosis*. The transgression is, consequently, no longer the beginning of the fall, but rather the beginning of the recovery of their lost condition, insofar as awareness of one's own imperfection is a precondition for reaching perfection.[32] It is this knowledge that will start the gradual process of self-knowledge that in its turn will allow the ascent and recovery of their primal condition.

As an example of the previous generalising sketch of the gnostic rewriting of the Paradise story, it will suffice now to present one of the versions. It is perhaps the *Hypostasis of the Archons* that includes the most compact account of the story:

---

[30] See *Gos. Truth* (NHC I,3) 18.34–19.10.
[31] See Luttikhuizen, *Gnostic Revisions*, 76–77.
[32] See *Gos. Truth* (NHC I,3) 21.14–25.

> Then the female spiritual principle came in the snake, the instructor, and it taught them, saying, "What did he say to you? Was it, 'From every tree in the garden shall you eat; yet—from the tree of recognizing evil and good do not eat'?"
>
> The carnal woman said, "Not only did he say 'Do not eat,' but even 'Do not touch it; for the day you eat from it, with death you are going to die.'"[33]

The introductory section already reveals important differences: to begin with, the snake remains an implement of a higher instance, but in this case is not, as in *LAE*, the devil that speaks through it, but the female spiritual principle. The revaluation of the snake is clear not only in its description as "the instructor," but also in the fact that it is acquainted with the words the Demiurge issued to Eve. The divergences increase as the text goes on:

> And the snake, the instructor, said, "With death you shall not die; for it was out of jealousy that he said this to you. Rather your eyes shall open and you shall come to be like gods, recognizing evil and good." And the female spiritual principle was taken away from the snake.

It is interesting to note that in the present passage, even though clearly attributing envy to the Demiurge, there is no interest in explaining the reason behind it. Obviating every attempt to search for a logical explanation, the gnostic rewriting simply explains the prohibition, since the transformation of the narrative frame and actors of the story is explicit enough. "And the carnal woman took from the tree and ate; and she gave to her husband as well as herself ... And their imperfection became apparent in their lack of acquaintance; and they recognized that they were naked of the spiritual element."

The outcome of the transgression is rather different as well. The first thing they realise is their imperfection, namely their lack of acquaintance, and then they notice that they are naked *of the spiritual element*.

CONCLUSIONS

I think that the above analysis sufficiently demonstrates that the interpretation of the Paradise story provided by the *LAE* does not introduce important changes in its biblical model. Admittedly, the motif of God's

---

[33] *Hyp. Arch.* (NHC II,4) 89.31–90.5.

envy as a background to his prohibition to Adam and Eve to eat from the tree of knowledge of good and evil does not appear in the words of the snake of Genesis and represents a clear addition to the text. However, given the two possible interpretations of the snake's accusation, namely God's authoritative denying or envious grudge, *LAE* made use of the latter both because it ideally suited the conceptual context created by Wisdom's assertion that death came into the world through the devil's envy, and because Eve's envy was more appealing to a Hellenistic reader than *hybris* as a reason for her transgression.

Consequently, there is nothing in *LAE*'s version of the story that might allow us to discover behind it the likely, but thus far unproved, attribution of envy to the God of the Old Testament by Marcionites.

Gnostic revisions of the Paradise story, however, present a completely different world of ideas. The appropriation of the motif of envy as a background for God's prohibition, which the gnostic texts dealt with freely endorse, provided them with a convenient support for their own views. On the one hand, it gave them the opportunity to explain both the true cause of human degradation and the need for self-knowledge in order to retrace the steps of devaluation. On the other, the Paradise story offered a perfect opportunity to show on the basis of Genesis itself that the God of the Old Testament could hardly be the loving and merciful God of their creed. This envious God simply did not meet the high requirements of a concept of divinity that was already under the influence of the Platonic-Peripatetic theology.

EL CORDERO DE DIOS EN LA
LITERATURA INTERTESTAMENTAL

Luis Díez Merino

Introducción

Cordero (TH: טלה; Tg: טליא, טלי, טלה; LXX: ἀμνός; Vg: agnus): en la 3a ed. del Koehler-Baumgartner[1] transcribe las formas arameas טלי, טליא encontradas en arameo judaico y samaritano con el significado de "muchacho"; en arameo targúmico también "cordero"; y en arameo egipcio y palmireno: "muchacho", "sirviente"; y, consiguientemente, recuerda la forma del femenino: ταλιθα (Mc 5,41).

M. Sokoloff, en su diccionario de arameo palestino judaico[2] señala la forma טלי, טלייה, con el significado de: (a) "niño", "persona joven" y cita TgN Gen 37,2 (donde el TH tiene נער); 41,12; Ex 33,11; (b) "siervo", y cita el Talmud: "una sierva aramea [gentil]" (TB Aboda Zara 44a[6]).

"Cordero" en esas lenguas se refiere a un animal, que a la vez simboliza la alegría, la docilidad, la inocencia y la mansedumbre.

En el AT ἀμνός (TH כבש) se constata principalmente en el documento sacerdotal y en Ez, por tanto en escritos de orientación cúltico-sacerdotal. Según J. Jeremias ἀμνός responde prevalentemente al término hebreo כבש, pero también, aunque raramente, a צאן, עתוד, אמר, איל שה, רחל, קשיטה.[3]

El término ἀμνός designó, desde un principio, la cría, con frecuencia la cría de un año, el *cordero*, especialmente como animal de sacrificio en numerosos actos de culto. Cuando la referencia cultual quedó en segundo término, el cordero como animal de matanza, el cual es llamado ἀρήν; su diminutivo ἀρνίον designaba en principio al *corderito*, más tarde vino a significar lo mismo que ἀμνός ("cordero").

En el templo se ofrecían corderos como holocausto y como víctima (Lev 9,3; Num 15,5) para reconciliar o purificar al pueblo, o a personas individuales (p.e. leprosos: Lev 14,10).

---

[1] *HALAT*, 359.

[2] M. Sokoloff, *A Dictionary of Jewish Palestinian Aramaic of the Byzantine Period* (Ramat Gan: Bar Ilan University Press, 1990), 225.

[3] J. Jeremias, "ἀμνός," *TWNT* 1:342.

Según Ex 12,5 en la fiesta de la Pascua, como recuerdo de la salida de Egipto, cada familia sacrificaba un cordero añal, macho, sin defecto; y rociaba con su sangre las jambas de la puerta de la casa. Ezequiel, cuando vaticina el nuevo templo, menciona a los corderos como ofrenda para el sacrificio de los sábados y fiestas (Ez 46,4.11).

Con lenguaje metafórico, y en un contexto teológico, ἀμνός designa a Israel y a la comunidad cristiana y se les compara (sobre todo en Mt y Jn) con las ovejas (πρόβατα), y al Siervo de Yahweh, y a Jesús ocasionalmente (Jn y 1Ped), con un cordero (ἀμνός [Jn] y ἀρνίον [Ap]).

1. Interpretación bíblica anticotestamentaria

El cordero se cita en el AT especialmente en los pasajes que se refieren a los sacrificios (p.e. cordero pascual). J. Leal reunió los principales trabajos de investigación referentes a este tema,[4] y al mismo objeto E. May le dedicó su tesis doctoral.[5] El tema del cordero en el AT lo constatamos en dos perspectivas:

1.1. *Siervo de Yahweh*

Jeremías, perseguido por sus enemigos, se comparaba a sí mismo con un «cordero, al que se lleva al matadero» (Jer 11,19). Esta imagen se aplicó durante el exilio al Siervo de Yahweh, quien al morir para expiar los pecados de su pueblo, aparecía «como cordero llevado al matadero, como oveja muda ante los trasquiladores» (Is 53,7); según este texto del DtIs, el paciente y sufrido Siervo de Yahweh es comparado con un cordero que es conducido al matadero y que, ante sus esquiladores, enmudece.

Isaías lo había anunciado proféticamente, si bien no bajo la forma de apelativo, sino más bien como una comparación (Is 53,7). Había comparado al Siervo de Yahweh con el Mesías, cual «da oveja conducida al matadero» y como «al cordero mudo bajo la mano de aquel que le trasquila». Con esto se traspone, por primera vez, la función del animal de sacrificio a una persona.

---

[4] J. Leal, "Exegesis catholica de Agno Dei in ultimis viginti et quinque annis", *VD* 28 (1950): 98–109.

[5] E.E. May, *Ecce Agnus Dei! A Philological and Exegetical Approach to John 1:29, 36* (Washington: Catholic University of America Press, 1947).

El punto de comparación era la paciencia del hombre de dolores, cuyos sufrimientos voluntariamente soportados, serían agradables a Dios, y cuya muerte servirá de rescate para los pecadores.

En este texto de Is 53,7, por una parte, se subrayaba la humildad y la resignación del Siervo, pero también se anunciaba el destino de Cristo, como explicará el apóstol Felipe al eunuco de la reina de Candaces (Act 8,31.35); con esto, por primera vez, la función del cordero como animal de sacrificio se traspone a una persona; y así Act 8,32, citando al Is 53,7 aplica el pasaje al «evangelio de Jesús» (Act 8,35).

Para valorar el sintagma "Cordero de Dios", a propósito de Is 53, tenemos dos interpretaciones:

(a) J. Jeremias remite al vocablo arameo טליא que no solamente significaba "cordero", sino también "muchacho, siervo"; el significado de "siervo" haría inteligible el genitivo: Jesús es el Siervo de Yahweh, y de aquí se comenzaría posteriormente a emplear ἀμνὸς τοῦ θεοῦ.

(b) J. Gess[6] preferiría interpretar el genitivo τοῦ θεοῦ, partiendo de la oración de relativo de Jn 1,29: ὁ αἴρων τὴν ἁμαρτίαν τοῦ κόσμου y comparándola con Is 53,6s: "el cordero (de Dios) que carga con el pecado del mundo"; si se sustituye la palabra "cordero" por "sacrificio", entonces se podría comprender la afirmación del Bautista.

1.2. *El cordero pascual*

1.2.1. *En la tradición judía*

Cuando Dios decidió liberar a su pueblo, que estaba cautivo en Egipto, mandó a los hebreos que inmolasen por familia un cordero «sin mancha, macho, de un año» (Ex 12,5), se debía de comer al anochecer y marcar con su sangre el dintel de la puerta de toda casa hebrea. En virtud de este «signo» el ángel exterminador perdonó a los hebreos cuando vino a herir de muerte a los primogénitos de los egipcios. La inmolación del cordero pascual constituía el centro y era el elemento esencial de la Pascua.

La celebración de la Pascua se prolongaba durante 8 días en el mes de Nisán que comprendía 29 días de la luna de marzo. El día 10 de Nisán se separaba el cordero pascual del rebaño, para empezar su preparación, como para cualquiera acción santa (Ex 19,10; 1Sam 21,5–6).

---

[6] J. Gess, en *Diccionario Teológico del Nuevo Testamento* (editado por L. Coenen et al.; Salamanca: Sígueme, 1983), 3:231.

El cordero debía reunir las condiciones que señalaba la Ley: macho, sin defecto, primal, cordero o cabrito (Lev 22,22). El día 14 de Nisán era inmolado en el Templo entre dos luces, después del sacrificio de la tarde y antes del incienso y de encender las lámparas. Durante la ceremonia los levitas tocaban trompetas y cantaban (Sal 112–117), y cada israelita inmolaba su cordero, y los sacerdotes recogían la sangre y la derramaban al pie del altar de los holocaustos.

La sangre del cordero, cuando estaban en Egipto, les sirvió para marcar las jambas y el dintel de las puertas de las casas, y con esta ceremonia, evitaron que el ángel exterminador hiriera a los primogénitos de los hebreos.

Para degollar a los corderos se les suspendía de unas barras de cedro, que se sostenían en ocho columnas, fijadas en el atrio de los sacerdotes. Pero como eran muchos, también se colgaban de palos que se apoyaban en los hombros de los asistentes. Se abría el vientre de los corderos y se retiraba la grasa, riñones y demás vísceras para ser quemado en el altar. Seguidamente el que ofrecía el cordero lo envolvía en la piel del mismo cordero, y se lo llevaba; no se le podía romper ningún hueso; si se le rompía algún hueso, el que lo había hecho recibía 39 golpes.

El cordero pascual se debía de comer en la misma noche, con panes ácimos y lechugas amargas; nada de él se podía comer crudo, o hervido, sino asado al fuego, tanto la cabeza como las patas y las entrañas; nada debía quedar para el día siguiente, de lo contrario había que quemarlo. Lo debían de comer ceñidos los lomos, calzados los pies, y el báculo en la mano y aprisa, pues era el «paso de Yahweh». Fl. Josefo (Bel.Jud. 6.9.3) llega a decir que en una Pascua se sacrificaron 256.500 corderos.

Llevado a casa, el cordero era asado, y era colocado en dos palos de granado, más resistentes al fuego; el más largo atravesaba todo el cuerpo de arriba abajo, y el otro más corto de espalda a espalda; las patas delanteras estaban extendidas en forma de cruz (M. Nedarim 49,1).

En lo sucesivo la tradición judía fue enriqueciendo el tema primitivo, y dio un valor redentor a la sangre del cordero: «A causa de la sangre de la alianza, y a causa de la sangre de la pascua, yo os he libertado de Egipto[7]».

Merced a la sangre del cordero pascual fueron los hebreos rescatados de la esclavitud de Egipto y pudieron, como consecuencia, llegar a ser

---

[7] Pirqe de-Rabbi Eliezer 29; Cf. Mekilta a Exodo, Ex 12.

una «nación consagrada», «reino de sacerdotes» (Ex 19,6), unidos a Dios mediante una alianza y regidos por la Torah de Moisés.

En el judaísmo tardío es desconocida la imagen del redentor presentado como cordero, y el único paso que se podría citar en su apoyo, parece ser una interpolación cristiana.[8]

1.2.2. *En la tradición cristiana*

La tradición cristiana ha considerado a Cristo como «al verdadero cordero» pascual,[9] y su misión redentora se fue describiendo detenidamente en la catequesis bautismal, como aparece en la 1ª carta de Pedro (1Ped 1,19), y posteriormente en los escritos joánicos (Jn 1,29; Ap 5,6) y en la Carta a los Hebreos.

Esta tradición primitiva vió en Cristo al verdadero cordero pascual, y así lo comprobamos en los orígenes mismos del cristianismo. Así Pablo exhortaba a los fieles de Corinto a vivir como ázimos, «en la pureza y la verdad», ya que «nuestra pascua, Cristo, se ha inmolado» (1Cor 5,7).

Pablo no proponía con esto una enseñanza nueva sobre Cristo cordero, sino que se refería a las tradiciones litúrgicas de la pascua cristiana, y que eran muy anteriores a la fecha en que el Apóstol escribía su 1Cor (55–57 d.C.).

El cordero debía de ser sin tacha (Ex 12,5), lo que los cristianos interpretaron de Jesús, el cual se presentó «sin pecado» (1Ped 1,19; Jn 8,46; 1Jn 3,5; Heb 9,14), y rescató a los hombres al precio de su sangre (1Ped 1,18s; Ap 5,9s; Heb 9,12–15).

Como consecuencia, Jesús ha liberado a los hombres de la «tierra» (Ap 14,3) del mundo malvado, que está entregado a la perversión moral que proviene del culto de los ídolos (1Ped 1,14.18; 4,2s), y así en el futuro podrán evitar el pecado (1Ped 1,15s; Jn 1,29; 1Jn 3,5–9), para formar el nuevo «reino de sacerdotes» y la verdadera «nación consagrada» (1Ped 2,9; Ap 5,9s; cf. Ex 19,6), para ofrecer así a Dios un culto espiritual con una vida irreprochable (1Ped 2,5; Heb 9,14).

De todo esto se sigue el abandono de las tinieblas del paganismo, que les hace pasar a la luz del reino de Dios (1Ped 2,9), y eso está conceptuado como un éxodo espiritual.

Los cristianos, gracias a la sangre del cordero (Ap 12,11), tienen el convencimiento de haber vencido a Satán, cuyo tipo había sido el Faraón,

---

[8] Jeremias, "ἀμνός," 342.
[9] Prefacio de la Misa de Pascua, en el Misal Romano.

y así pueden entonar «el cántico de Moisés y del cordero» (Ap 15,3; 7,9s.14.17; cf. Ex 15), donde se exalta su liberación.

J. Jeremias[10] se pregunta: ¿cómo nació en el NT la representación de Jesús como ἀμνός, o bien, como ἀρνίον? Responde que pueden haber influido en este proceso diversas causas:

(1) Desde los comienzos, la comunidad cristiana vió en Jesús, del mismo modo a como Jesús se vió a sí mismo, reflejando al Siervo de Dios de Is 53. La antigüedad de la presentación de Jesús como παῖς θεοῦ en la comunidad primitiva (Act 3,13; 4,27.30) es clara, pero este apelativo suyo pareció demasiado humilde y fue acogido desfavorablemente y pronto fue evitado, según la opinión de A. von Harnack.[11] No obstante, el Siervo de Dios que sufre pacientemente, es comparado en Is 53,7 a un cordero, y tal comparación está asumida explícitamente como referida a Jesús en Act 8,32 (= Is 53,7): "Fue llevado como oveja al matadero, y como cordero mudo ante el que lo trasquila, así no abre su boca ὡς ἀμνὸς ἐναντίον τοῦ κείραντος αὐτὸν ἄφωνος). En su abatimiento no se le hizo justicia. Su posteridad, ¿quién [la] describirá?, porque arranca su vida de la tierra" (Is 53,5–8 LXX). Así Is 53,7 podría haber sido el origen de la representación de Jesús como ἀμνός.

(2) La crucifixión había tenido lugar en una festividad de la pascua hebrea. Pablo y Juan comparan a Jesús con el cordero pascual: (a) Pablo: "porque nuestro cordero pascual, Cristo, ha sido sacrificado" (1Cor 5,7); (b) Juan: "Pues esto sucedió para que se cumpliera la Escritura: «Ni un hueso suyo será quebrantado (Ex 12,46; Num 9,12; Sal 34,20)»; y también otra Escritura dice: «Verán al que traspasaron (Zac 12,10; Ap 1,7)» (Jn 19,36)". Es verdad que, además de corderos, también estaba permitido sacrificar en la Pascua cabritillos, según consta en la Biblia (Ex 12,3.5), en la Misna (Pesahim 8,2) y en la Tosefta (Pesahim 4,2); sin embargo la costumbre fue la de sacrificar corderos. Por lo mismo la comparación de Jesús con el cordero pascual podría estar en el origen de la designación de Jesús como ἀμνός.

(3) Las dos ideas anteriores pudieron haber ejercido su influencia simultáneamente: Jesús fue Siervo de Dios y humilde como un cordero; y Jesús fue verdadero cordero pascual.

---

[10] Jeremias, "ἀμνός," 342.
[11] A. von Harnack, "Die Bezeichnung Jesu als 'Knecht Gottes' und ihre Geschichte in der alten Kirche," *SPAW* (1926): 212–38.

(4)   La aceptación de Jesús por parte de la comunidad, bajo la figura de Cordero de Dios, posiblemente puede ser también el origen de la misma.

En definitiva, para J. Jeremias,[12] la representación de Jesús como ἀμνός fue una creación de la comunidad cristiana, y esto incidiría en la posibilidad histórica de las palabras del Bautista (Jn 1,29.36: ἴδε ὁ ἀμνὸς τοῦ θεοῦ, con la añadidura de Jn 1,29: ὁ αἴρων τὴν ἁμαρτίαν τοῦ κόσμου). En el texto arameo original de estos dos pasajes se hablaba del Siervo de Dios, posteriormente habrían surgido dificultades sobre la historicidad de estas palabras. Siguiendo a Is 53, el Bautista llamó a Jesús "el Siervo de Dios" que tomaba sobre sí los pecados del mundo, entendiendo que con esto se refería a la expiación vicaria de la pena del pecado. J. Jeremias estudió esa interpretación mesiánica de Is 53.[13]

2. El cordero en el Nuevo Testamento

2.1. *Jesús Cordero*

En el NT Jesús es designado cuatro veces como ἀμνός (Jn 1,29.36; Act 8,32; 1Ped 1,19). El término ἀμνός se aplica primordialmente a Jesucristo, a quien se le adjudica el título «Cordero de Dios», en la acepción de inmolación y de sacrificio propiciatorio. En diversos libros del NT (Jn, Act, 1Ped, y sobre todo Apoc) se identifica a Cristo con un cordero; a Jesús no se le compara solamente con un cordero (Act 8,32; 1Ped 1,19: se hace con la partícula ὡς), sino que Jesús **es** el Cordero de Dios (Jn 1,29.36: ἀμνὸς τοῦ θεοῦ, Cordero de Dios).

P. Joüon[14] dice que el "Cordero de Dios" es un cordero que pertenece a Dios en propiedad, sobre el que tiene derecho; si a esta idea se le acerca el "quitar el pecado", se puede fácilmente concluir que Dios usará de su derecho, y que es por el sacrificio del Cordero a Dios como será quitado el pecado; aquí habría una alusión a Is 53,7. Se puede pensar que los oyentes no comprendieron plenamente en aquel momento la transcendencia de esta palabra misteriosa. Pero hubo alguien que, como Juan, la encontraron muy interesante y la guardaron en la memoria. El "pecado

---

[12] Jeremias, "ἀμνός," 343.
[13] Cf. J. Jeremias, "Erlöser und Erlösung im Spätjudentum und Urchristentum", *Deutsche Theologie* 2 (1929): 106–19.
[14] P. Joüon, *L'Évangile de Notre-Seigneur Jésus-Christ* (Paris: Beauchesne, 1930), 464, n. 29.

del mundo", en singular, o más bien en colectivo, es el pecado como estado: el mundo, desde la caída de Adán está en "el pecado".

A Is 53,7 se refieren los evangelistas cuando recalcan que Cristo «se callaba» delante del Sanhedrín (Mt 26,63) y no respondía a Pilato (Jn 19,9). J. Jeremias[15] indica que tanto Is 53, como la imagen del cordero pascual, pueden haber motivado dicha expresión.

En el Apoc "Cordero de Dios" es una denominación de Jesucristo triunfante, redentor perfecto, sentado por ser Dios en el trono de la divinidad y es esposo de la Iglesia.

El NT y la tradición han interpretado el cordero pascual sin tacha, inmolado sin romperle ningún hueso, y cuya sangre libró del exterminio a los primogénitos israelitas y al pueblo entero de la esclavitud de Egipto, como el símbolo de Jesucristo, el cordero de Dios, sin mancilla, que quita los pecados del mundo, y nos libra de la esclavitud del demonio, con su sangre derramada en la cruz.

Existen, pues, una serie de textos que relacionan el cordero pascual con Jesús: "No le quebrantaréis ningún hueso" (Jn 19,36). "Nuestra Pascua, Cristo ha sido inmolado" (1Cor 5,7). "Habéis sido rescatados... por una sangre preciosa, la del Cordero sin defecto y sin tacha, la sangre de Cristo" (1Ped 1,16ss). "He aquí el Cordero de Dios que quita los pecados del mundo" (Jn 1,29.36): este cordero inmolado es símbolo muy repetido en el Apocalipsis y en la liturgia.

En el contexto de la muerte de Jesús, Juan hace referencia al cordero pascual, con expresa intención de indicar que en Jesús se cumple dicha Escritura: «Pues esto sucedió para que se cumpliera la Escritura: "Ni un hueso suyo será quebrantado (Ex 12,46; Num 9,12; Sal 34,20)" y también otra Escritura dice: "Verán al que traspasaron" (Zac 12,10) [Jn 19,37]». Y en el Ap 1,7 se relaciona, a su vez, con Jesucristo: «Mira, llega entre las nubes, y lo verán todos los ojos, incluso aquellos que le traspasaron; y se lamentarán por él todas las tribus de la tierra». En Jn 19,37 se cita a Zac 12,10 en conexión con la crucifixión de Jesús, pero también se dice que el crucificado es el Juez del mundo, «el Hijo del hombre que llega entre las nubes para juzgar» (Dan 7,13; Mt 24,30; Mc 13,26; Lc 21,27; 1Tes 4,17).

Cuando Jesús está presentado como "cordero" en el NT se entiende en triple aspecto: 1) Act 8,32: hace resaltar su paciencia en el sufrimiento; 2) 1Ped 1,19: con las expresiones "sin defecto y sin mancha" pone de relieve la impecabilidad y perfección del sacrificio de Jesús; 3) Jn 1,29.36:

---

[15] Jeremias, "ἀμνός," 343.

se pone de relieve la fuerza expiatoria de la muerte de Jesús que quita y borra el pecado del mundo.[16]

2.2. *El testimonio del Bautista*

En el EvJn, y en boca del Bautista, se halla en dos ocasiones esta expresión misteriosa para designar a Jesús, como el Mesías:

2.2.1. *«He aquí el Cordero de Dios» (Jn 1,29.36)*

Juan Bautista fue el primero que dio a Jesús el nombre de Cordero: «Viendo a Jesús que venía a él, dice: "He aquí el Cordero de Dios, que quita el pecado del mundo" (ἴδε ὁ ἀμνὸς τοῦ θεοῦ ὁ αἴρων τὴν ἁμαρτίαν τοῦ κόσμου» (Jn 1,29; cf. Is 53,7.12; Heb 9,28).[17]

Si relacionamos Is 53,6s ("cordero que carga con el pecado del mundo") con Jn 1,29 ("el que quita el pecado del mundo"), y sustituimos "cordero" (Is 53,6s) con "sacrificio", entonces se aclara Jn 1,29: todos los sacrificios de los hombres no llegan a eliminar el pecado del mundo; pero Dios entregó a su único Hijo y no lo escatimó (cf. Rom 8,31–32, probablemente alude a Gen 22); así se entiende el contraste de las palabras del Bautista (Jn 1,29) con las que del mismo reproducen los sinópticos sobre el que ha de venir (bieldo, limpieza de la era), pues las palabras de Jn 1,29 presuponen el bautismo de Jesús (Jn 1,32–34); bautismo que significa la aceptación de la cruz, y la entrega de Cristo a la muerte y con ello empieza el tiempo escatológico de la salvación.

La Vg, cuyo texto ha pasado al *ecce Agnus Dei, ecce qui tollis peccata mundi* del rito romano de la Misa, acentúa la afinidad con Isaías sustituyendo el singular por el plural: «…los pecados del mundo».

Posteriormente la escena evangélica se repitió: «Al día siguiente, Juan estaba aún en el mismo sitio con dos discípulos. Al poner los ojos en Jesús, que pasaba, dijo: "He aquí el Cordero de Dios". Y le oyeron los dos discípulos hablar así, y siguieron a Jesús» (Jn 1,35–37): Juan designaba al Mesías y su entorno por una fórmula que no tenía necesidad de explicación.

Se puede decir que ἀμνὸς τοῦ θεοῦ designa el don que Dios ofrece en sacrificio, y designa a Cristo, a quien Dios destinó para cargar con el pecado del mundo.

---

[16] Ibid.

[17] Cf. H. van den Bussche, "Ecce Agnus Dei (Jo 1,29–36)", *Collationes Gandavenses* 32 (1949): 235–41.

2.2.2. «Ni un hueso suyo será quebrantado» (Jn 19,36)

A la muerte de Jesús afirma Juan: «Después de esto, sabiendo Jesús que ya se había cumplido todo, para que se cumpliera la Escritura dijo: "Tengo sed"» (Jn 19,28). Y más adelante: «Y cuando tomó el vinagre, Jesús dijo: "Se ha cumplido"» (Jn 19,30), y precisamente pone en relación a Jesús con el Cordero pascual: «Pues esto sucedió para que se cumpliera la Escritura: "Ni un hueso suyo será quebrandado" (Ex 12,46; Num 9,12; Sal 34,20)»; «y también otra Escritura dice: "Verán al que traspasaron" (Zac 12,10; Ap 1,7)».[18]

2.2.3. Sentido del testimonio del Bautista

Para mejor justipreciar el verdadero sentido de esta palabra, es menester separar el pensamiento del Bautista del de el Evangelista; con esto no pretendemos que se opongan, sino que el Bautista pronuncia estas palabras al comienzo del ministerio de Jesús y a la luz de la teofanía del bautismo, y el Evangelista describe estos términos en circunstancias particulares: a) después de medio siglo de meditación personal; b) a la luz del misterio pascual; c) bajo la iluminación del Espíritu de Pentecostés.

La apelación «Cordero de Dios» tenía en boca del Precursor un sentido determinado, ciertamente derivado de las figuras de la antigua alianza.

2.2.4. Identificación del Cordero

El Cordero de Dios, mostrado por Juan Bautista, había sido a la vez prefigurado por el sacrificio mosaico y predicho por Isaías. Esta explicación parece la mejor, porque la idea de víctima no está ausente en la profecía de Isaías, pues el Mesías sufriente es comparado a un cordero que se inmola y que toma sobre sí las iniquidades de otro. Juan Bautista prefirió usar el título de Cordero al de Siervo.

Dos identificaciones se han ofrecido para interpretar las palabras del Precursor de Jesús: a) una traducción deficiente del arameo, que significase a la vez cordero y a la vez siervo; b) el Bautista se habría referido a Is 53,7 donde se compara al Siervo con «un cordero que es llevado al matadero». Esto segundo habría sido propiciado porque el Bautista habría sido iluminado por el acto de humildad de Jesús, quien habría tratado de confundirse con los pecadores que habría de

---

[18] Cf. May, *Ecce Agnus Dei!*

salvar, poniéndose entre las muchedumbres que se acercaban a ser bautizadas por Juan en el Jordán; el Bautista reconocería en público que aquel hombre, lejos de ser el Rey victorioso que esperaban muchos, se presentaba como el Mesías humilde y desconocido, que tenía una misión expiadora.

El Cordero de Dios, para Juan Bautista, presentaba unas credenciales inequívocas: era víctima inocente, que se ofrecía al dolor; era la víctima universal; era un médico y redentor de los humanos, a los que comunicaba los frutos de su enseñanza y de su muerte mediante el bautismo del Espíritu.

2.2.4.1. El Mesías

Juan Bautista tenía, pues, en mente, al Mesías, justo e inocente, voluntariamente inmolado y quitando el pecado del mundo, después de haberlo tomado a su cargo y haberlo expiado con su sangre. El Cordero que se ha mostrado no es solamente el cordero divino, el Cordero enviado por Dios u ofrecido a Dios; él es el Cordero de Dios, a título de propiedad, el Hijo de Dios que cumplía, con los sufrimientos y la muerte, su misión redentora.

San Jerónimo[19] aplicó al Mesías la palabra del profeta: "emitte agnum dominatorem terrae" (Is 16,1). El Cordero, Señor del mundo, es el Mesías que ha contado entre sus antepasados a Rut, la moabita. A su venida, todo el poder del diablo será destruido y reducido a polvo. Esta interpretación no es más que una acomodación del texto original que, dirigido al rey de Moab, significa: «Enviad al señor de la tierra de Judá los corderos que le debéis como tributo» (cf. 2Re 3,4).[20] Y el mismo Doctor[21] reconocía, con todas las Iglesias, que las palabras que Jer 11,19 decía de sí mismo: «Yo soy como un cordero lleno de mansedumbre que se lleva al matadero» deben ser entendidas como referidas al Mesías del cual dicho profeta era figura. En medio de las persecuciones que ellos soportaron, Jeremías y Jesús son mansos y pacientes como el cordero llevado al matadero.[22]

---

[19] Jerónimo, *Comment. in Isaiam* VI, PL 24:234–35.
[20] J. Knabenbauer, *Commentarius in Isaiam Prophetam* I (Paris, Lethielleux, 1887), 344–45.
[21] J. Knabenbauer, *Commentarius in Jeremiam Prophetam* (Paris: Lethielleux, 1889), 756–57.
[22] Knabenbauer, *Comment. in Jerem.*, 170.

La liturgia romana ha consagrado la aplicación mesiánica de los dos pasajes. Muchas veces, en los días que preceden a Navidad, se coloca en los labios de los lectores el deseo ardiente: «Emitte Agnum, Domine, dominatorem terrae de petra deserti ad montem filiae Sion». En el Jueves Santo, en el Oficio de Tinieblas, se repetía dos veces, aplicándolo a Jesús, la palabra de Jeremías: «Eram quasi agnus innocens; ductus sum ad immolandum, et nesciebam». En la liturgia no se ha olvidado la comparación que Isaías hizo del Salvador con el Cordero inocente y mudo, con la oveja que es degollada sin llorar, y se ha aplicado a Jesús, en los oficios del Jueves Santo y del Sábado Santo. El himno de Laudes, en el tiempo de Pasión, cantaba: «Agnus in Crucis levatur immolandus stipite». Un responsorio del miércoles de la primera semana decía: «Rex noster adveniet Christus quem Joannes praedicavit Agnum esse venturum». Cuando el sacerdote se revestía del alba, decía: «Dealba me, Domine, et munda cor meum, ut in sanguine Agni dealbatus, gaudiis perfruar sempiternis». Después de la fracción del pan consagrado, en la Misa según el rito romano, se dice tres veces, golpeándose el pecho: «Agnus Dei, qui tollis peccata mundi, misere nobis». Fue el Papa Sergio (687–701) quien estableció esta triple invocación.[23] En el momento de la comunión de los fieles, el sacerdote presenta la hostia santa, diciendo: «Ecce Agnus Dei, ecce qui tollit peccata mundi». La triple repetición del «Agnus Dei» concluye todas las letanías («Agnus Dei, qui tollis peccata mundi»).

2.2.4.2. El Siervo de Yahweh

Parece evidente que el Bautista, al llamar a Jesús «Cordero de Dios», se estaba refiriendo al famoso Siervo de Yahweh de los poemas del DtIs (Is 42,1–4; 49,1–7; 50,4–11; 52,13–53,12).

Además de la semejanza de las expresiones con el genitivo posesivo que significa «Siervo de Dios», algo que pertenece a Dios, o sobre el que Dios tiene derecho, se puede comprobar cómo la predicación del Bautista está impregnada del estilo y de las ideas de Isaías. En efecto, el libro de Isaías se muestra como el libro de la consolación (Jn 1,23): «'Yo soy voz de uno que grita en el desierto: rectificad el camino del Señor', como dijo el profeta Isaías (Is 40,3; cf. Lc 3,4)» y además se concluye la presentación de Jesús con otro rasgo que es peculiar del

---

[23] L. Duchesne, *Liber Pontificalis, texte, introduction et commentaire, I* (Paris: de Boccard, 1886), 376.

Siervo: «Él es el Elegido de Dios» (Jn 1,34), aunque figura en la lectura «Hijo de Dios» (Mt 3,17; 17,5: "Éste es mi Hijo querido"; Mt 27,54: "Éste era Hijo de Dios"; Mc 9,7: "Éste es mi Hijo querido"; Lc 9,35: "Éste es mi Hijo elegido".

2.3. *Su actuación*

2.3.1. *Según la interpretación neotestamentaria*
Tanto el Cordero, como el Siervo, tienen una misma misión universal, que es la de abolir el pecado. La manera como se ha de llevar esa actuación, e.d. cómo se obrará la abolición, será interpretada de diversos modos:

(1) El Siervo se mostrará como Siervo-doctor de la Ley de Dios, en especial en la persona de Jesús; pues la misión del Siervo será una enseñanza que permitirá que los hombres conozcan y cumplan la voluntad de Dios, y como consecuencia, evitarán el pecado (Is 42,1–4).
(2) El Siervo será totalmente puro, y proporcionará a los hombres fuerza para que no vuelvan a pecar; por eso la santidad del pueblo de Dios será uno de los caracteres de los tiempos mesiánicos.
(3) El Siervo, afianzado en su inocencia, bautizará en el Espíritu, que él mismo recibió, y comunicará este mismo Espíritu que se transformará en el hombre en principio de vida nueva y de proceder intachable (Is 2,1–9; 32,15–19; 44,3–5; cf. Ex 36,26s).
(4) El Siervo tendrá, ante todo, una misión expiatoria: ha de sufrir y morir por los hombres.

2.3.2. *Según la interpretación qumránica*
En la época de Qumrán, sus moradores y los «pobres de Yahweh» habrían incorporado esa idea del sufrimiento que estaba muy clara en el Déuteroisaías; tal idea habría sido también captada por el último de los profetas canónicos.

2.3.3. *Según la interpretación joánica*
Juan, el evangelista, fue uno de los discípulos que habían seguido las lecciones del Bautista, y después cambió a la escuela de Jesús.

Juan evangelista escuchó el testimonio del Bautista, lo conservó durante toda su vida en la memoria, y lo reinterpretó a la luz del misterio pascual, mediante la iluminación del Espíritu de Pentecostés, y lo inmortalizó en el cordero inmolado que se halla en la entraña del Apocalipsis.

Si nos atenemos a la cronología joánica, el acontecimiento mismo de la muerte habría proporcionado el fundamento a esta tradición. Jesús fue entregado a muerte la víspera de la fiesta de los ázimos (Jn 18,28; 19,14.31), por lo mismo el día de pascua por la tarde (Jn 19,14), en la misma hora en que, de acuerdo con la Ley, se inmolaban en el Templo los corderos pascuales.

Después de la muerte, a Jesús no se le rompieron las piernas como a los otros ajusticiados (Jn 19,33), y precisamente en este hecho ve Juan la realización de una prescripción ritual relativa al cordero pascual (Jn 19,36; cf. Ex 12,46).

Jn establece una estrecha relación entre el Bautismo de Jesús y el misterio de sus sufrimientos expiatorios.[24] El acto por el que el Cordero-Siervo se somete al bautismo entra dentro del secreto del misterio de la salvación. Jesús recibe el bautismo como Mesías sufriente, y en favor de todo el pueblo, prefigurando así el perdón general que llevará a cabo su muerte en la cruz y que "cumplirá toda justicia".

El bautismo de Jesús inicia la actuación de la salvación, y a su vez, prefigura el misterio pascual en sus dos fases: humillación y glorificación, y ya contiene en germen toda la obra salvífica. Para Juan evangelista, cuando el Precursor presenta a Jesús como «Cordero de Dios» que sale de las aguas del Jordán, ya contempla la salvación de la humanidad, mistéricamente anticipada.

3. El Cordero en la Literatura Apócrifa

3.1. *En el Testamento de José*

En el Judaísmo tardío es desconocida la imagen del redentor presentado como un cordero.

El único caso que se aduce es el Testamento de José 19,8–12 donde leemos:

> [Vi que de Judá nacía una doncella, adornada con un vestido de lino.] De ella procedía un *cordero* [*sin mácula*], que a su izquierda tenía algo como un león. Todas las fieras se lanzaron contra él, pero *el cordero* las venció

---

[24] Cf. M.E. Boismard, *Du baptême à Cana (Jean 1,19–2,11)* (LD 18: Paris: Le Cerf, 1956), 41–60.

y las aniquiló bajo sus pies. Se alegraron en él los ángeles, los hombres y toda la tierra. Todo ello ocurrirá a su debido tiempo, en los últimos días. Hijos míos, guardad los mandamientos del Señor y honrad a Judá y a Leví, porque de ellos surgirá para vosotros **el** *cordero* [*de Dios*], que salvará [con su gracia a todos los gentiles y] a Israel. Pues su reino es eterno, nunca pasará; pero mi reino entre vosotros llegará a su fin como cobertizo durante la cosecha, que no subsiste después del verano.[25]

Tanto F. Spitta,[26] como E. Lohmeyer,[27] defienden que la figura del Mesías como un cordero en el Testamento de José proviene de una tradición judaica precristiana.

Hay una expansión del texto eslavo al TestJos 19,12, ciertamente cristiana, que dice:

«Veo –dijo– que ha salido una virgen de Judá, es decir, la santa de la tribu de Judá, la hija de Joaquín, portando un vestido de púrpura: pura y sin error, santa y más que santa. De ella procede –dijo– el *cordero inmaculado*, es decir, el hijo de Dios, manso, humilde, sin maldad ni malicia y que no conoce el pecado. Y a su izquierda (hay) como un león. Ésta es la Palabra de su divinidad, grande, terrible y (bien) señalada, contra la que se lanzan todas las fieras, es decir, vosotros, infelices judíos, que habéis visto al Hijo de Dios que toma un aspecto humilde. Mas todos como fieras salvajes se lanzaron contra él diciendo:—Cogedle, cogedle, crucificadle. ¡Sea su sangre sobre vosotros y vuestros hijos!—*El cordero* los venció –dijo–. Es decir, el Hijo de Dios resucitó de entre los muertos, (ese) de quien vosotros os acordasteis sólo para hacer el mal... Vosotros, pues, hijos míos –dijo–, guardad los mandamientos del Señor y honrad a Judá y a Leví, porque de éstos saldrá para vosotros el *cordero divino*, es decir, de la tribu de Judá y según el orden levítico. Recibirá la hegemonía y salvará por su gracia a todos los pueblos y a Israel. Considéralo tú, Israel, pues no sólo para ti es la salvación, sino para todos los pueblos, hasta el extremo que no nació sólo para salvar a Israel. Nació de una santa virgen y condujo a todos los pueblos a la salvación. Su reino es eterno. Considera que la virgen no anuncia a *otro cordero* y que su reino no parasará nunca.[28]

---

[25] Cf. A. Díez Macho, *Apócrifos del Antiguo Testamento V* (Madrid: Cristiandad, 1987), 148–49. Las palabras que van entre corchetes [ ], según el traductor, son de origen cristiano.

[26] F. Spitta, *Streitfragen zur Geschichte Jesu* (Göttingen: Vandenhoeck, 1907), 187–94.

[27] E. Lohmeyer, *Die Offenbarung des Johannes*, (2a ed.; Tübingen: Mohr, 1953).

[28] Cf. N.S. Tichonravov, *Pamjatniki otrecennoj russkoj literatury I* (San Peterburgo, 1893), 96–232 (223–25).

3.2. *Testamento de Benjamín*

Leemos en el Testamento de Benjamín 3,8: «En ti se cumplirá la profecía del cielo [sobre el cordero de Dios y salvador del mundo: él, sin mácula, será entregado por los infieles; el inocente morirá por los impíos en la sangre de la alianza], con lo que destruirá a Beliar y a sus servidores».[29]

Según el traductor los corchetes [ ] serían de procedencia cristiana. Algunos piensan que el texto primitivo podría referirse a los sufrimientos del "Siervo de Yahweh" (Is 42ss), tal como se puede colegir de la tradición armenia: «se cumplirá la profecía… el inmaculado será profanado por los impíos y el inocente por los malvados». El cordero de Dios es aquel al que se había referido Jn 1,29.

3.3. *Libro I de Henok*

En 1Hen 90,13, cuando nos describe en el 4° período la visión desde los Macabeos hasta el reino mesiánico leemos: «Vi que llegaron los pastores, las águilas, los buitres y los milanos, y gritaron a los cuervos para que despedazaran el cuerpo de aquel *cordero*». Y más adelante en el v. 16: «Vi que llegó el hombre que había escrito los nombres de los pastores y los subía ante el dueño de las ovejas, y lo ayudó, salvó y dejó en claro que habían bajado para ayudar al *cordero*». Y ya comenzado el reino mesiánico, cuando habla de la nueva Jerusalén: «Luego, aquellos tres que vestían de blanco y me habían tomado de la mano, los que antes me habían hecho subir, me hicieron ascender (otra vez), cogido de la mano del *cordero*, y me sentaron entre las ovejas, antes de que fuera el juicio» (v. 31).

4. *Aportación Aramea a la Explicación de* Cordero de Dios

4.1. *Desde la Vorlage aramea del NT*

En la locución ὁ ἀμνὸς τοῦ θεοῦ (Jn 1,29.36) el genitivo expresa de hecho una relación totalmente singular, que se explica solamente con una referencia al arameo; en arameo el término טליא tiene un múltiple significado: *cordero, muchacho/joven* y *siervo*.

---

[29] Díez Macho, *Apócrifos del Antiguo Testamento*, 5:152–53.

Probablemente como base de la expresión griega ὁ ἀμνὸς τοῦ θεοῦ esté la expresión aramea טליא דאלהא, entendida en el sentido de עבד יהוה, opinión que ya había sido propuesta por C.F. Burney[30] y por E. Lohmeyer[31] de modo que Jn 1,29.36 señalaban a Jesús originariamente como Siervo de Dios. Solamente que tenemos extrañamente la traducción de טליא por ἀμνός (en vez de παῖς), resultando la especificación ὁ ἀμνὸς τοῦ θεοῦ.

Es posible que el doble significado de טליא (cordero-siervo) haya tenido parte determinante en la aceptación, y quizá también en el comienzo de la representación de Jesús como ἀμνός (Jn) y como ἀρνίον (Ap). Dicha representación posiblemente nació en un área lingüística mixta (arameo-griega), y así se puede comprender que aparezca exclusivamente en la literatura joánica. De hecho en Act 8,32 y 1Ped 1,19 Jesús es simplemente comparado, pero no representado, como cordero; la representación de Jesús como cordero aparece solamente en la literatura joánica dos veces con el términos ἀμνός (Jn 1,29.36) y 28 veces con ἀρνίον (Ap).

En la comunidad cristiana las palabras del Bautista habrían tomado un nuevo significado cuando Juan, o bien la tradición que él tenía presente, tradujeron טליא דאלהא como ὁ ἀμνὸς τοῦ θεοῦ y representó así a Jesús como el verdadero cordero pascual (cf. Jn 19,36).

4.2. *Desde el Targum*

4.2.1. *El vocablo* טליא

El vocablo en los mss. arameos aparece bajo diversas formas: טליא, טלי, טלה, y la traducción que ofrecía J. Buxtorf[32] "infans, adolescens, puer". En TgSal 37,25: "fui joven (הוית טאלי)"; PsJon Lev 15,2: "hombre joven (נבר טלי)". De José, cuando tenía diecisiete años, se dice: "y era niño (והוא טלה)" (PsJon Gen 37,2); TgGen 41,12: "niño hebreo (טלייא עבראי)"; PsJon Ex 2,6 Moisés era el niño que lloraba: "y el niño lloraba" (בכי טלייא); TgSal 88,16: "desde niño" (מן טליא); TgLam(WT) 4,4: "los niños

---

[30] C.F. Burney, *The Aramaic Origin of the Fourth Gospel* (Oxford: Clarendon Press, 1922), 107–8.

[31] Lohmeyer, *Offenbarung*, 52.

[32] J. Buxtorf, *Lexicon Chaldaicum, Talmudicum et Rabbinicum* (ed. B. Fischer, Leipzig 1869–74), 875.

piden pan" (טליא תבעו לחמא). Su significado es: "cordero, muchacho, joven",[33] pero también "siervo".

4.2.2. El Cántico del Cordero

En el Ms. Kennicott 5 [85],[34] de la Biblioteca Bodleyana de Oxford,[35] descrito por A. Neubauer,[36] aparece un poema arameo en que un cordero tiene un protagonismo; es un ms. sefardí, escrito en Segovia, en el s. XIII.

Dicho ms. transmite una Tosefta Targúmica, en forma de poema acróstico, algo diferente del que se encuentra en otras versiones, y diverso del que figura en la Tosefta que transcribe A. Sperber,[37] quien copia la Tosefta de la Editio Princeps de Leiria.[38] Esta Tosefta figura en Tg1Sam 17,42, y ha sido publicada también por E. van Staalduine-Sulman y precisamente con el título de "Cántico del Cordero".[39]

Este mismo cántico figura en el Ms. 1 de la Universidad de Salamanca, escrito por Alfonso de Zamora en 1532.

Conclusiones

(1) Siguiendo la tradición aramea, el término טליא / אימרא tiene tres ámbitos semánticos: a) cordero, b) muchacho, joven, c) siervo.

(2) Según una Tosefta targúmica que puede fecharse en el s. I–II d.C., en el Judaísmo se conoció la expresión "Cordero de Dios"; aunque figure en un ms. sefardí escrito en Segovia, en el s. XIII, es un poema compuesto en arameo que se añade a Tg1Sam 17,42.

---

[33] E. Klein, *A Comprehensive Etymological Dictionary of the Hebrew Language for Readers of English* (Jerusalem, 1987), 244.

[34] B. Kennicott, *Dissertatio Generalis in Vetus Testamentum Hebraicum; cum variis lectionibus ex codicibus manuscriptis et impressis* (Oxford: Clarendon Press, 1780), 78.

[35] I.B. de Rossi, *Variae Lectiones Veteris Testamenti* (4 vols.; Parma, 1784–1788), I, LXIII.

[36] A. Neubauer, *Catalogue of the Hebrew and Samaritan Manuscripts in the Bodleian Library, Vol. 1* (Oxford: Clarendon, 1886), n° 2329.

[37] A. Sperber, *The Bible in Aramaic. Vol. II: The Former Prophets according to Targum Jonathan* (Leiden: Brill, 1959), 130–31.

[38] *Prophetae Priores*, Leiria 1494.

[39] E. van Staalduine-Sulman, "The Aramaic Song of the Lamb", en *Verse in Ancient Near Eastern Prose* (editado por J.C. de Moor y W.G.E. Watson; AOAT 42: Kevelaer: Butzon & Bercker, 1993), 265–92; eadem, *The Targum of Samuel* (Leiden: Brill, 2002), 366–77.

COLLINS, IO E L'APOCALITTICA;
O ANCHE GLI APOCRIFI?

Paolo Sacchi

1. Ritorno al 1979: il problema di allora era la natura dell'apocalittica e la sua storia

Porgo con grande gioia questo mio studio sull'apocalittica come omaggio all'amico Florentino, che è stato personaggio fondamentale nella ricerca apocalittica soprattutto con gli studi dei suoi rapporti con Qumran.[1]

Nel 1979 si andava chiudendo un periodo della ricerca sull'apocalittica dall'impronta, nell'insieme, pessimistica. Florentino García Martínez così riassumeva nel 1987[2] la situazione in relazione a quell'anno. «Los años 70 han sido testigos de una verdadera revolución copernicana en el estudio de la Apocalíptica. Esta revolución comienza con la publicación en 1970 del libro fundamental de K. Koch[3] y culmina con la publicación en 1979 de *Semeia* 14 editado por Collins».[4]

García Martínez riporta poi una frase tratta da uno studio di Stone (1976): «Finally, it may perhaps be suggested that the terms 'apocalyptic' and 'apocalypticism' be abandoned altogether. They will continue to confuse the issue as they tend to imply an identity between the way of thought they designate and the apocalypses».[5]

---

[1] F. García Martínez, "Orígenes apocalípticos del movimiento esenio y orígenes de la secta qumránica", *Communio* 18 (1985): 353–68; idem, "Essénisme qumrânien: Origines, caractéristiques, héritage", in *Correnti culturali e movimenti religiosi del giudaismo, Atti del V Congresso Internazionale dell'AISG 12–15 novembre 1984* (Roma: Carucci, 1987), 37–57; idem, "Orígenes del movimiento esenio y orígenes qumránicos. Pistas para una solución", in *II Simposio bíblico español* (a cura di V. Collado e V. Vilar; Valencia: Fundación Bíblica Española, 1987), 528–56.

[2] F. García Martínez, "La apocalíptica y Qumrán", in *II Simposio Bíblico Español*, 603–13 (608).

[3] K. Koch, *Ratlos vor der Apokalyptik* (Gütersloh: Gerd Mohn, 1970).

[4] J.J. Collins (curatore e in parte autore), *Apocalypse: The Morphology of a Genre = Semeia* 14 (1979).

[5] M. Stone, "List of Revealed Things in the Apocalyptic Literature", in *Magnalia Dei: The Mighty Acts of God: Essays on the Bible and Archaeology in Memory of G. Ernest Wright* (a cura di F.M. Cross et al.; Garden City, N.Y.: Doubleday, 1976), 414–51 (443).

Nel 1979 uscì il già citato libro a cura di Collins che conteneva anche articoli di suo pugno. Collins si differenziava da Koch in maniera radicale. Mentre Koch e altri cercavano di individuare quali elementi potevano essere indicati come costitutivi dell'apocalittica, per poter individuare con certezza le apocalissi, Collins partì dal principio opposto. Riconosciuto che il termine "apocalisse" era documentato solo in poche e ben tarde apocalissi e che l'uso moderno del termine si era esteso a molte altre opere che gli antichi non classificarono mai come tali, accettò il dato di fatto e cercò solo di individuare quali contenuti avessero le apocalissi—le poche storiche e le molte per convenzione.[6] Gli elementi costanti delle apocalissi, una volta individuati, permettono di arrivare alla seguente definizione, che è stata largamente accettata: « "Apocalypse" is a genre of revelatory literature with a narrative frame-work, in which a revelation is mediated by an otherworldly being to a human recipient, disclosing a transcendent reality which is both temporal, insofar as it envisages eschatological salvation, and spatial insofar as it involves another, supernatural world».[7]

Il metodo di Collins presuppone che gli studiosi abbiano di fatto un'idea di che cosa sia un'apocalisse, perché indicano certe opere come apocalissi. In altri termini il lavoro di Collins mira a prendere e a far prendere coscienza dei contenuti razionali dell'intuizione che è alla base del concetto di apocalisse. Il termine «apocalittica» diventa l'astratto di «apocalisse» inteso come forma letteraria, così come in italiano si può dire che il tale autore ha scritto un romanzo (senso concreto) oppure che il romanzo (senso astratto) è un genere letterario di prosa. È evidente che il termine apocalittica non è nato per indicare solo il genere letterario, perché in questo caso non avremmo avuto bisogno di creare l'astratto «apocalittica». L'uso separato di apocalisse e apocalittica ha potuto alimentarsi in tutte le lingue per il fatto che si tratta di un genere letterario che ha forti connotati di pensiero anche se non unitario. Da qui il problema per lo storico moderno quale fosse il nocciolo del pensiero apocalittico.

Collins ci tiene a precisare che gli elementi da lui raccolti come costitutivi del genere, se presi uno per uno possono essere assenti in qualunque apocalisse, tuttavia vi è un filo conduttore che li unisce e la

---

[6] J.J. Collins, "Toward the Morphology of a Genre", *Semeia* 14 (1979): 1–20 (2) «An "apocalypse" is simply that which scholars can agree to call an "apocalypse"».
[7] Ibid., 9.

cui presenza, non indicata nell'elenco, si può pensare che costituisca il nucleo del pensiero che viene intuito come apocalittico. È questo l'aspetto più interessante della ricerca del Collins e solo ora ne afferro la portata. Scrive a p. 10 del già citato contributo: «The different elements which make up our comprehensive definition of the genre are not associated at random, but are integrally related by their common implications. The key word in the definition is *transcendence* (corsivo mio)».

Nello stesso 1979 uscì anche un mio articolo sull'apocalittica: "Il *Libro dei Vigilanti* e l'apocalittica".[8] Le idee di quest'articolo sono ripetute in forma più sintetica e organica nell'introduzione all'*Enoc Etiopico*, nel primo volume dell'edizione degli apocrifi dell'Antico Testamento uscita nel 1981.[9] La mia impostazione partiva, come quella di Collins, dall'osservazione del fallimento di opere che procedevano come quella di Koch. Anch'io accettavo di studiare le apocalissi nel senso di opere che gli studiosi potevano chiamare apocalissi: mi posi, però, il problema in maniera storica, non letteraria. Collins poteva scrivere che anche se un genere letterario ha una sua dimensione diacronica, tuttavia la sua caratterizzazione è indipendente da considerazioni storiche.[10] Diversamente, la mia impostazione del discorso aveva, come ha tuttora, scopi diversi da quelli di Collins: non volevo definire che cosa costituisca la struttura del genere apocalittico, ma trovare le ragioni della sua formazione ed entrata nella storia. Questa mia impostazione del problema è riconosciuta anche da Collins avere qualche valore: nel 1998 scriveva di me che avevo creato un nuovo metodo, molto originale (highly original), che consiste nel considerare l'apocalittica nel tempo, partendo dall'opera più antica e procedendo verso la più recente e guardandone lo sviluppo seguendo the *underlying problem*. Ora l'*underlying problem* è l'origine del male. «It is to Sacchi's credit that he has highlighted an important motif in apocalyptic literature, especially in the Enochic corpus. But the genre cannot be identified with a single motif or theme, and the early Enoch literature, important though it is, cannot be regarded as normative for all apocalypses».[11]

---

[8] In *Henoch* 1 (1979): 42–98; riprodotto in *L'apocalittica giudaica e la sua storia* (Brescia: Paideia, 1990), 31–78.

[9] P. Sacchi (curatore e in parte autore), *Apocrifi dell'Antico Testamento I* (Torino: UTET, 1981; 3. ed. 2006), 423–61.

[10] J.J. Collins, "Toward the Morphology of a Genre", *Semeia* 14 (1979): 1.

[11] Cf. J.J. Collins, *The Apocalyptic Imagination* (2d ed.; Grand Rapids: Eerdmans, 1998), 10–11. Comprensione più piena del senso della mia opera mostra F. García Martínez in *La apocalíptica y Qumrán*, 611.

In effetti affrontai il problema esattamente nel modo indicato da Collins. Guardai le apocalissi mettendomi nel punto di vista della più antica,[12] cosa che permetteva di comprendere la storia delle apocalissi, ma precludeva la possibilità di creare una teoria sull'origine e formazione del genere letterario dell'apocalisse, che è incentrato sulla rivelazione. Perché la necessità della rivelazione, e della rivelazione nella forma particolare dell'apocalisse, cioè la visione, dove il rivelatore fornisce sempre conoscenza o per la sua natura superiore (un angelo o Dio stesso) o perché elevato a una condizione superiore a quella umana? Il problema della conoscenza in relazione alla salvezza riguarda solo le più tarde apocalissi gnostiche o ha già un peso nella formazione del genere letterario delle apocalissi?

Ritornando alle mie idee di allora, devo dire che davo al genere letterario un'interpretazione essenzialmente crociana:[13] ogni apocalisse aveva la sua forma perché questa era strettamente collegata col suo contenuto, la forma apocalittica era l'aspetto esteriore della spiritualità contenuta nei testi apocalittici. Per me l'esistenza o meno del genere letterario dell'apocalisse aveva scarsa importanza, era solo la forma che emanava dal contenuto e ne completava la comprensione al di là del livello puramente razionale. Aggiungevo poi che questa interpretazione valeva solo per le apocalissi più antiche e per tutte quelle che avessero originalità di pensiero e forza di sentimento. La maggior parte di quelle più tarde poteva bene seguire un modello precedente secondo la moda letteraria. Non mi curai però di stabilire quali fossero queste apocalissi, né il rapporto eventualmente esistente fra moda letteraria e contenuti.

Come elemento base del genere letterario dell'apocalisse posi quello strumento di conoscenza che è la visione. Scrivevo: «Come è naturale, il pensiero di ogni apocalisse è diverso da quello di tutte le altre e l'unico elemento che tiene veramente unite tutte le apocalissi e le contraddistingue è il genere letterario incentrato sulla visione».[14] In realtà la visione non è un elemento puramente letterario: la visione apocalittica è conseguenza di una certa filosofia e interpretazione del

---

[12] In questo contesto non prendo in considerazione il *Libro dell'Astronomia*, le cui idee sul cosmo sono certamente presenti all'autore del *Libro dei Vigilanti*.

[13] Cfr. B. Croce, *Poesia e non poesia* (Bari: Laterza, 1950); ma lo stretto rapporto tra forma e contenuto ho assorbito dalla cultura letteraria dominante al tempo della mia formazione culturale e resta problema letterario massimamente importante, anche se non applicabile direttamente ai problemi della letteratura apocalittica.

[14] Sacchi in Sacchi, *Apocrifi dell'Antico Testamento I*, 446.

mondo, diverse da quelle classiche tramandate dai sadociti e con questi in diretta competizione.[15]

Riprendo l'osservazione fatta nei miei confronti da Collins nel 1998 e concludo che avevo posto il problema solo a metà: mi domandavo se il pensiero dell'apocalisse più antica che possediamo contenesse elementi che poi sarebbero rimasti. In altri termini facevo la storia di una parte del pensiero ebraico a partire dal *Libro dei Vigilanti* piuttosto che cercare di capire le ragioni per cui era nato il *Libro dei Vigilanti* con contenuti così diversi da quelli della tradizione sadocita. Nell'articolo del 1979 mi allargavo infatti anche a opere, purché successive, che non avevano in comune col *Libro dei Vigilanti* né la forma, né la possibile appartenenza a uno stesso movimento. Avendo chiaro che la forma apocalittica esisteva, un po' come Collins, e non avendo nessuna intenzione di definirla, al contrario di Collins, mi trovai ad usare il concetto di apocalittica in due modi diversi: da un lato esso continuava per me ad indicare l'insieme delle apocalissi (senso formale), dall'altro doveva indicare il pensiero del *Libro dei Vigilanti* e quello delle opere che ne dipendevano (senso contenutistico). Scrivo allora che bisognava distinguere fra un'apocalittica in senso formale, cioè l'insieme delle apocalissi, e un'apocalittica in senso nuovo, convenzionale e diverso rispetto al primo, cioè la storia del pensiero del *Libro dei Vigilanti*, cioè di quella corrente di pensiero sorta col *Libro dei Vigilanti* che oggi è detta enochismo.[16]

Scrivevo a p. 446 dell'introduzione all'*Enoc Etiopico*:[17] «Poiché non abbiamo un nome per indicare la corrente di pensiero che nacque dal *Libro dei Vigilanti* e che si incentra sui temi da esso trattati, chiameremo *apocalittica* questa corrente di pensiero». Non avevo dato un nome particolare a questa corrente, ma l'avevo individuata. Continuavo: «Pertanto il termine "apocalittica" viene usato in questa introduzione

---

[15] F. García Martínez in una recensione a J.J. Collins, The *Apocalyptic Imagination* (New York: Crossroad, 1984), critica Collins non per aver considerato l'insieme delle apocalissi un genere letterario, ma per averle considerate solo come un genere letterario: «Su reducción de esta (l'apocalittica) a un simple género literario…le impiden descubrir los ricos y variados elementos que la "imaginación apocalíptica" qumránica aportó en su día al desarrollo de la Apocalíptica» (*RevQ* 12/47 [1986]: 446–48 [448]). E' chiaro che García Martínez usa in questo caso il termine "apocalittica" per indicare una corrente di pensiero. Solo l'impiego di due termini diversi per indicare uno la forma e uno il contenuto possono far uscire da questa oscillazione terminologica che si ripercuote sulla chiarezza di ogni esposizione.

[16] In realtà nella mia apocalittica in senso contenutistico inserivo anche apocalissi tarde che non possono in alcun modo far parte dell'enochismo.

[17] *Apocrifi dell'Antico Testamento I*.

in maniera ambivalente, in quanto può indicare sia il genere letterario, sia il pensiero, sia l'ideologia caratterizzante di un'opera e la tradizione caratterizzata da questa in senso lato. Per evitare confusioni, quando il termine "apocalittica" è usato in senso letterario, il contesto lo farà risaltare chiaramente». In realtà la possibilità di distinguere le due diverse accezioni del medesimo termine è stata illusoria. L'uso del termine "enochismo", che indica chiaramente un gruppo e una teologia,[18] è stato di grande aiuto per il progresso della ricerca in questo campo.

2. Il problema che pongo oggi: qual era la situazione culturale che favorì il sorgere della prima apocalisse

Restando sempre nell'ambito dei miei interessi e, quindi, sul piano della storia, mi pongo adesso il problema volto a comprendere i motivi che condussero qualcuno a scrivere un'opera avente una forma letteraria diversa da quelle usate fino allora. Nel pensiero ebraico anteriore a quello dell'autore del *Libro dei Vigilanti* ci devono essere elementi atti a spiegare perché non abbia trovato nel passato nessuna forma letteraria che gli sembrasse adatta a esprimere le sue idee. Il problema può essere semplificato in questo modo: quali elementi ci sono nella storia del pensiero ebraico anteriore al *Libro dei Vigilanti*, che ne possano spiegare la forma? In questo modo si può sperare di capire per quali esigenze del pensiero di un gruppo di ebrei sorse il genere letterario dell'apocalisse. In concreto si tratta di trovare gli elementi appartenenti alla struttura fondamentale del *Libro dei Vigilanti* che possano avere, da un lato, la loro spiegazione in fenomeni precedenti del pensiero ebraico, dall'altro capire perché per esporre le novità del suo pensiero l'autore del *Libro dei Vigilanti* creò di fatto una nuova forma letteraria. La novità del pensiero trovò la sua espressione in una forma letteraria nuova: perché per esprimere le sue verità, l'autore del *Libro dei Vigilanti* imboccò una via sensibilmente diversa da quelle della tradizione?

---

[18] Cfr. G. Boccaccini, *Oltre l'ipotesi essenica: lo scisma fra Qumran e il giudaismo enochico* (Brescia: Morcelliana, 2003); orig. *Beyond the Essene Hypothesis. The Parting of the Ways between Qumran and Enochic Judaism* (Grand Rapids: Eerdmans, 1998).

3. LA TRASCENDENZA COME SFONDO DEGLI ELEMENTI CARATTERIZZANTI IL *LIBRO DEI VIGILANTI*

Prendo in considerazione gli elementi caratteristici[19] del pensiero del *Libro dei Vigilanti* di fronte al pensiero sadocita cercandoli nelle formulazioni di Collins e mia. Nel 1979[20] posi come elementi caratteristici e innovativi del pensiero della prima apocalisse, cioè del *Libro dei Vigilanti*, l'origine preterumana del male e l'immortalità dell'anima. Sono due concetti che possono essere stati formulati entrambi solo da un autore (o da un ambiente) che credeva nell'esistenza di un mondo diverso e superiore rispetto a quello sensibile nel quale viviamo, un mondo che riguardava l'aldilà, ma che non poteva essere lo sheòl della tradizione. Questo mondo nel quale si inquadrano e al quale si riferiscono le idee dell'autore del *Libro dei Vigilanti*[21] e dominava nella sua fantasia può bene essere indicato come oggetto del senso della trascendenza dell'autore, trascendenza, che è l'elemento apocalittico considerato da Collins la parola chiave delle apocalissi.

Oggi posso aggiungere qualche altro elemento in favore della parola chiave trascendenza, che può servire a descrivere meglio il senso che essa ebbe per l'autore del *Libro dei Vigilanti*: prima di tutto c'è lo slancio mistico, quale è documentato nel cap. 14 (LV) dell'*Enoc Etiopico*. L'ascesa del miste fino alla visione divina attraverso l'esperienza degli estremi opposti è un modo efficace, molto concreto sul piano psicologico, per indicare una realtà che si trova al di là di ciò che è comunemente sensibile e della quale si può parlare solo «con lingua di carne (1H [LV] 14, 2)».

---

[19] F. García Martínez, "Essénisme qumrânien: Origines, caractéristiques, héritage", 37: «La distinction entre origine et caractéristiques est en quelque sorte artificielle. Uniquement à travers les caractéristiques idéologiques différentiatrices d'un certain groupe nous pouvons remonter jusqu'à ses origines».

[20] P. Sacchi, "Il *Libro dei Vigilanti* e l'apocalittica".

[21] Per autore del *Libro dei Vigilanti* intendo l'autore dello strato LV2a: «E' col mito già strutturato nella forma del *Libro di Noè*, che ebbe a che fare l'anonimo iniziatore dell'apocalittica, in pratica l'autore di LV2a, che per brevità chiamerò Ap1», cfr. P. Sacchi, "Storicizzazione e rivelazione: alle origini del giudaismo", *Rivista di Storia e Letteratura Religiosa* 24 (1988): 68–77 (73). Per la mia proposta di stratificazione del *Libro dei Vigilanti* rimando a P. Sacchi, "Per una storia dell'apocalittica", in *L'apocalittica giudaica e la sua storia*, 99–139 (100–102) (ripubblicato dagli *Atti del V Congresso Internazionale dell'Associazione Italiana per lo Studio del Giudaismo*, 9–34) con bibliografia su proposte diverse di stratificazione, cui oggi si può aggiungere G.W.E. Nickelsburg, *1 Enoch 1: A Commentary on the Book of 1 Enoch, Chapters 1–36; 81–108* (Hermeneia; Minneapolis: Fortress Press, 2001).

Il miste è in grado di fare grandi rivelazioni in quanto sale, lui, in cielo, dove Dio stesso o qualche angelo gli parlano e gli danno ordini o gli fanno rivelazioni. Spesso il miste racconta direttamente cose da lui viste. In ogni caso il visionario è il centro del sistema, perché è in grado di rivelare verità che l'uomo comune non può vedere. Il miste ha un contatto diretto col cielo, dove lui è salito, non il sacerdote né chiunque abbia un potere nella società. In questo senso il *Libro dei Vigilanti* si pone al di sopra e al di fuori del culto e della legge. La rivelazione di Enoc è solo per lui e per coloro che l'accettano. Il sadocitismo trasmette una tradizione, che sottolinea sì come solo Mosè parlò «faccia a faccia» con Dio (Num 12,6–8), ma Dio si rivelò in qualche modo a tutto Israele. La tradizione sadocita insiste in più modi sulla partecipazione di tutto il popolo alla rivelazione divina. Si vedano i racconti del Sacerdotale, in particolare quelli dell'Esodo: il popolo ai piedi del Sinai, il patto di Es 24, 3–9, dove tutto il popolo è asperso dal sangue dei vitelli, ecc.

La visione delle apocalissi postesiliche si distingue nettamente da quella dei testi preesilici, per il luogo in cui essa avviene. Anzi il termine visione ha senso solo entro certi limiti, perché l'impressione generale è che il miste non veda con gli occhi dello spirito o in sogno, ma veda concretamente lassù le cose di lassù.

Veniamo all'anima disincarnabile: il concetto ha un senso solo se esiste il mondo superiore, che in qualche modo è quello che le è proprio. D'altra parte, si tratta di un mondo in cui qualcuno almeno può salire col suo corpo, avendo con sé tutti i sensi che permettono la conoscenza in questo mondo e di questo mondo. Si può dire che il mondo superiore è in contatto col nostro e che il trapasso dall'uno all'altro è possibile. Gli angeli peccarono con le donne, perché dal loro mondo potevano vederle. La trascendenza del *Libro dei Vigilanti* ha caratteri, per così dire fisici, marcata dalla volta celeste che divide il nostro mondo da quello superiore, che tuttavia è attiguo al nostro non solo topograficamente, ma per la possibilità degli scambi che esistono fra i due mondi.

Questo mondo superiore in contatto col nostro appare anche in un testo di tradizione sadocita, sicuramente anteriore al *Libro dei Vigilanti*. Questo testo risale ai primissimi anni del postesilio. Nel libro di Zaccaria si racconta (cap. 3) un avvenimento che si colloca fra il 520 e il 515 a.C. Nella guerra civile che seguì al rientro del primo consistente numero di esiliati[22] il sommo sacerdote Giosuè ebbe in un primo momento la

---

[22] Sulla guerra civile scoppiata in Giuda in seguito al rientro in patria di una parte dei deportati da Nabucodonosor, o loro discendenti, cfr. M. Smith, *Gli uomini del ritorno*

peggio, ma poi poté recuperare la sua posizione, in seguito a contatti con Zorobabele e con i capi di Giuda. Di questi avvenimenti non ci sono notizie dirette, ma sono le premesse necessarie per spiegare il fatto di cui il testo fa memoria. Il nostro passo parla della riabilitazione di Giosuè, che non deriva né da un messaggio celeste, né da una visione del profeta: Zaccaria racconta che in cielo si è svolto un processo, nel quale Dio stesso ha assolto Giosuè dalle sue colpe, cosicché può tornare a ricoprire la sua carica. Ho chiamato quella parte del cosmo dove si svolse il processo di Giosuè «mondo di mezzo»,[23] perché si trova fra il luogo dove abita Dio e quello dove abitano gli uomini.

Non si tratta di visioni che facciano vedere a un visionario cose del mondo dello spirito del quale le visioni sono soltanto una metafora da interpretare. È l'uomo stesso che in qualche modo partecipa della vita del mondo superiore; come, non è chiaro, ma il racconto presuppone prima di tutto che il mondo al di sopra del firmamento esista e poi che fra quel mondo e il nostro ci sia una possibilità di intercomunicazione.

4. Ezechiele e il mondo celeste

La più antica testimonianza della credenza nel mondo superiore risale ad Ezechiele.[24] Meglio sarebbe dire che Ezechiele fu lo scopritore di questo mondo. Già in apertura del libro Ezechiele dichiara di aver visto cose che si trovavano al di là della volta celeste. Il mondo celeste di Ezechiele presenta due strati, uno più basso che il cielo (*shammaim*) separa dalla terra e uno più alto dove si trova la Gloria divina. Il cielo inferiore è separato da quello superiore da una seconda volta, chiamata firmamento (*rāqiaʿ*). Il secondo termine, *rāqiaʿ*, richiama chiaramente il testo della Genesi di tradizione sacerdotale. Stando alla tradizione sacerdotale, la terra era coperta, per così dire, da una volta metallica, al di là della quale si trovava l'acqua cosmica: come sta scritto in Gen 1,6, Dio per mezzo del firmamento (*rāqiaʿ*) pose una separazione in

---

(Verona: Essedue), 1984 cap. Ve; orig. *Palestinian Parties and Politics that Shaped the Old Testament* (New York: Columbia University Press, 1971); P. Sacchi, *Storia del Secondo Tempio, Israele fra VI sec. a.C. e I sec. d.C.* (Torino: SEI, 1994; 2. ed. 2000), parte II.

[23] Cfr. P. Sacchi, *Storia del mondo giudaico* (Torino: SEI, 1975), 30–32.

[24] Rapporti fra il pensiero di Ezechiele e le correnti contrarie al sadocitismo sono stati messi in evidenza da B.Z. Wacholder. Vedi "Ezekiel and Ezekielianism as progenitors of Essenianism", in *The Dead Sea Scrolls; Forty Years of Research* (a cura di D. Dimant e U. Rappaport; STDJ 10; Leiden: Brill, 1992), 186–96.

mezzo alle acque, dividendo quelle di sopra da quelle di sotto. Ora Ezechiele innova all'interno della sua stessa tradizione. Davanti ai suoi occhi il cielo si aprì (*nifteḥu haššāmayim*). Lo sguardo di Ezechiele penetrò oltre la volta celeste e poté vedere che al di là di essa non c'era l'acqua superiore, ma c'era il mondo di *elohim*: «E vidi, dice Ezechiele (1,1), *mar'ot 'elohim* visioni di *'elohim*»: *'elohim* è termine abbastanza vago, che non so con precisione che cosa signifchi in questo contesto e di conseguenza di difficile traduzione: di difficile traduzione, perché di difficile interpretazione. Il termine *'elohim* in questo contesto non può significare Dio, perché di Dio Ezechiele percepirà solo la Gloria che abita oltre il firmamento.

In ogni caso, in questo contesto, dove la visione è introdotta da un «il cielo si aprì », *'elohim* indica un mondo diverso da quello terreno, dove non ci sono le stesse forme e non valgono le leggi fisiche che valgono nel nostro: le cose che Ezechiele vede sono impossibili nel nostro mondo, quali gli strani esseri viventi (1,5) e gli strani movimenti delle ruote del carro (Ez 1,17).[25]

Ezechiele vide cose celesti, ma lui stava sulla terra come tutti i profeti che lo avevano preceduto. La novità di Ezechiele non sta nella posizione del veggente, egli vede le cose che vede stando sulla terra, come sulla terra stavano tutti i profeti precedenti. La novità della visione di Ezechiele sta nell'oggetto della visione. Yhwh dei profeti preesilici stava in alto, ma si muoveva fra la terra e la volta celeste:[26] Yhwh volava sulle nubi e si librava nelle folgori, ma non andava al di sopra della volta celeste. Ora il Dio di Ezechiele sta al di sopra del cielo e al di sopra del firmamento.[27] Fra la sfera di Dio e quella dell'uomo sta un «mondo di mezzo», popolato di esseri spirituali. Questo mondo è in contatto da una parte col nostro, dall'altra con la sfera del divino.

La visione delle cose di Ezechiele fu grandiosa non tanto o non solo per avere intuito l'esistenza del mondo dello spirito, ma per aver

---

[25] Per un'interpretazione unitaria del testo di Ezechiele, cfr. M. Greenberg, *Ezechiel 1-20* (AB; Garden City, N.Y.: Doubleday, 1983). W. Eichrodt, *Ezechiele* (Antico Testamento; Brescia: Paideia, 2001), pur accettando la presenza di molte aggiunte, sottolinea l'originalità e la forza della costruzione ezechieliana: (75–76) «Non si deve ridurre la descrizione di Ezechiele, come avviene in molti commentari a una composizione ottenuta scegliendo e sommando elementi già esistenti». A p. 76 parla di un «contenuto spirituale di grande forza espressiva».

[26] Vedi Yhwh che vola sulle nubi portato dai cherubini: 2 Sam 22,11; 2 Re 19,15; Ps 18,11; Ps 68,5. 34 etc.

[27] Per una pluralità di cieli, cfr. Dt 10,14.

«visto» lo stretto rapporto che correva fra le varie parti del cosmo, del quale avvertì profondamente l'unità. Nella terra dell'esilio babilonese la visione delle cose si dilatò in Ezechiele in maniera tale da inserire gli avvenimenti della storia e il culto del dio nazionale in un contesto sempre più ampio che presuppone l'unità del cosmo nella sua interezza e vastità, spaziale e temporale, fisica e storica a un tempo.[28]

Nel pensiero di Ezechiele influì in modo decisivo la cultura scientifica babilonese, non certo quella a carattere religioso:[29] l'unità del cosmo è documentabile nella descrizione del cielo quale si ha negli astrolabi[30] e che si concretizzò nel calendario di 360 giorni fondato sulle stelle, che fu il calendario ebraico più antico a partire dall'esilio:[31] la relazione fra tempo e spazio appare con ogni evidenza e si fonda sul rapporto esistente fra il numero dei giorni e i gradi dell'orizzonte, chiaramente indicati come giorni, perché il cielo si divide in dodici parti corrispondenti ai dodici segni dello zodiaco che trovano il loro corrispondente nel computo del tempo. Spazio e tempo non sono due entità indipendenti l'una dall'altra, ma sono due coordinate che misurano due dimensioni dell'unica realtà cosmica.

Anche il fatto che Ezechiele indichi il giorno della settimana nel quale avvennero alcune delle sue visioni è una conseguenza dell'aver accettato il calendario stellare: tempo e spazio costituiscono un'unità che dipende da Dio. Anche il sabato dell'interpretazione sacerdotale, che passa da giorno medio del mese lunare a memoria del settimo

---

[28] Cfr. L.A. Schökel e J.L. Sicre, *I Profeti* (Roma: Borla, 1984), 767: «La teofania ha una dimensione cosmica».

[29] Cfr. P. Sacchi, "Le origini del giudaismo: tradizione e innovazione", in *Memoria histórica y encrucijada de culturas, Actas del Congreso Internacional de Salamanca 2002* (a cura di J. Campos Santiago y V. Pastor Julián; Salamanca: Asociación Bíblica Española, 2004), 24–48. Sulla cultura scientifica babilonese, cfr. J.J. Glassner, "The Use of Knowledge in Ancient Mesopotamia", in *Civilizations of the Ancient Near East* (a cura di J.M. Sasson; 4 vol.; New York: Scribner's, 1996), 3:1815–24.

[30] Sugli astrolabi, cfr. U. Glessmer, "Horizontal Measuring in the Babylonian Astronomical Compendium MUL.APIN and in the Astronomical Book of 1En', *Henoch* 18 (1996): 259–82.

[31] Per il calendario stellare, cfr. B.L. van der Waerden, "History of the Zodiac, *AfO* 16 (1951–52): 216–30 (218): «There are 12 signs, because there are 12 months in the schematical year of mul Apin. The signs were made of equal length in order to get months of equal duration: they were divided into 30 degrees each because the schematical months were supposed to contain 30 days each». Un calendario con struttura di 360 giorni e mese intercalare, ma con filosofia puramente pratica, è stato scoperto a Ebla: cfr. G. Pettinato, *Ebla, un impero fondato sull'argilla* (Milano: Mondatori, 1979), 141–42.

giorno della creazione,[32] rientra in questo orientamento dell'ambiente dei sacerdoti in esilio.

La visione cosmica delle cose che ebbe Ezechiele è documentata anche dalla sua visione della storia. Dio, come è padrone dello spazio, è padrone anche del tempo. Il passato non deriva il suo valore soltanto dal fatto che è ciò che precede e, quindi, condiziona e in qualche modo causa la forma del futuro, ma dal fatto che il singolo avvenimento può essere ciò che noi chiameremmo il tipo del futuro. In altri termini, il suo valore trascende la storia come semplice concatenazione di fatti. Gli avvenimenti hanno, sì, un senso di per sé, ma ne hanno un altro che trascende la logica umana, perché in qualche modo predisposti da Dio. Passato e futuro diventano così due realtà apparentemente dipendenti l'una dall'altra, ma in realtà controllate e guidate da un termine medio rappresentato dal progetto di Dio sulla storia, che si rivela nelle strutture spazio-temporali del cosmo.[33]

Osea aveva detto che Dio aveva guidato il suo popolo fuori dall'Egitto sotto la guida di un profeta (Os 12,14). Amos aveva predetto punizioni per i grandi peccati di Israele e dei popoli circonvicini (Am 1–2). Isaia aveva predetto la liberazione di Israele dai due re che lo opprimevano in quel momento (Is 7,16); aveva anche previsto, se il passo è suo come mi pare, che dalla stirpe di Yesse sarebbe sorto un re particolare che avrebbe portato la giustizia in Israele (Is 11,1). Sono le radici del messianismo, ma si tratta di un messianismo senza agganci precisi con la storia: Isaia dice solo che ci sarà un certo tempo in cui nascerà un certo discendente di David, dotato di certe qualità.

Ora Ezechiele contempla le vicende di Israele e ne scopre il dipanarsi come un piano di Dio sulla storia che va al di là del singolo periodo, particolarmente di quello in cui il profeta visse. La storia dei peccati di Israele si svolge in tempi lunghissimi: Israele peccò nel deserto; restò di dura cervice nonostante i benefici divini (Ez 20); Dio avrebbe voluto sterminare Israele, ma non lo fece «per riguardo al suo nome» (Ez 20,9). Dio non agisce nella storia solo per retribuire: Dio ha suoi piani che vuole realizzare e che comportano qualche deroga al principio di retribuzione, che resta valido nei princìpi (Ez 20); poiché l'uomo può

---

[32] Sull'interpretazione del sabato come termine che originariamente indicava la luna piena, cfr. A. Lemaire, "Le shabbat à l'époque royale israélite", *RB* 80 (1973): 161–85. Vedi ancora G. Bettenzoli, "Lessemi ebraici di radice –shabat–", *Henoch* 4 (1982): 129–62 e dello stesso, "La tradizione del Shabbat", *Henoch* 4 (1982): 265–93.

[33] Cfr. Sacchi, "Le origini del giudaismo: tradizione e innovazione", 38–41.

vivere solo osservando le leggi (ovviamente giuste, cfr. Ez 20,13), Dio ha dato comandamenti non buoni a Israele (Ez 20,25–26),[34] per provocarne la rovina. La rovina di Israele non è la conseguenza immediata della decisione del tribunale divino, ma è una complessa vicenda storica, che coinvolge anche Dio, che deve abbandonare il suo tempio e andare anche lui in esilio (Ez 10). Il castigo non è più una punizione immediata e diretta, è una serie di avvenimenti negativi per Israele, legati al male stesso che compie e più male compie, più il castigo si affretta, perché è legato alle vicende, lente e complesse della storia, non a una sentenza da eseguirsi immediatamente, in maniera miracolosa. La punizione di Dio non agisce sul singolo caso, ma crea situazioni storiche. Il castigo è legato all'insieme delle vicende. È il male che produce la punizione. Il Dio di Ezechiele non interviene più direttamente nelle vicende umane per difendere il suo popolo o per punirlo, Dio plasma la storia come una volta plasmò il cosmo. Il rapporto fra Dio e la storia diventa simile a quello fra Dio e la creazione.

Il mondo celeste della visione, che possiamo indicare come mondo degli spiriti (il *Libro delle Parabole* chiamerà Dio—secoli dopo—Signore degli spiriti), è presentato da Ezechiele come oggetto reale, non metaforico, e diventò rapidamente, nell'immaginario giudaico, un mondo in stretto contatto con quello terreno, contatto non solo fisico, topografico per così dire, cosa che è ovvia ed era presente già in Ezechiele, ma contatto anche, per così dire, storico, perché nel mondo superiore si pensò che avvenissero cose che si ripercuotevano sul nostro. Fra i due mondi c'erano relazioni continue.

Il cap. 3 di Zaccaria dimostra come alla fine del VI secolo lo scenario del mondo celeste fosse vivo nell'immaginario ebraico. Dopo la riabilitazione di Giosuè le sorti della guerra cambiarono a favore del sacerdote e dei rimpatriati, ma Giosuè non fu generoso come Zorobabele e ai profeti fu messo un prudenziale bavaglio. La profezia fu proibita e punita (Zac 13,3–6): era cosa pericolosa per qualunque establishment, compreso quello di Giosuè. Coloro che credevano nell'esistenza del mondo di mezzo non erano certo fautori dei sadociti di Giosuè. La condanna della profezia condannava coloro che avevano appoggiato Zorobabele. Se in seguito non abbiamo più testi sadociti che parlino esplicitamente di questo mondo e delle sue relazioni col nostro, dipende

---

[34] «Allora io diedi loro perfino comandamenti non buoni, leggi per le quali non potevano vivere.»

dal fatto che il mondo superiore diventò la base della fede di un gruppo
di ebrei dissidenti. Unica eccezione è il racconto del lungo duello sostenuto dall'angelo di Dio contro quello della Persia in Daniele (10,13),
ma siamo ormai in un'altra fase della storia del pensiero ebraico.

5. Nascita del genere letterario dell'apocalisse: o anche della letteratura apocrifa?

Perché un ebreo postesilico, cioè l'autore del *Libro dei Vigilanti*, volendo
comunicare nuove idee, invece di comportarsi come Amos, che aveva
comunicato le sue verità come rivelazioni divine con la formula «Così
dice il Signore», non usò questa via comune ai profeti, ma imboccò
una via completamente diversa?

Un fenomeno di questa portata, che investì la concezione globale
del cosmo e la concezione stessa della conoscenza, non si spiega come
un semplice sviluppo particolare della spiritualità ebraica. Le novità
del *Libro dei Vigilanti* non riguardano solo il pensiero: non c'è solo
l'immortalità dell'anima e l'origine preterumana del male, c'è anche
l'assenza del Tempio e della Legge. Se la credenza nell'immortalità
dell'anima e nell'origine preterumana del male presuppongono solo una
teologia diversa da quella di Gerusalemme, l'assenza del Tempio e della
Legge presuppone un atteggiamento di fronda verso tutte le strutture
politiche e religiose di Israele. Gli elementi nuovi che si aggiungono al
patrimonio culturale dell'autore e gli elementi che scompaiono sono in
stretto rapporto gli uni con gli altri. Le istituzioni non furono criticate
o negate, ma solo ignorate sul piano del pensiero: se il cosmo, che
secondo la creazione sarebbe dovuto essere un ordine, in realtà era un
disordine,[35] questo era dovuto all'opera di forze spirituali perverse che
avevano sconvolto tutto. Tempio e Legge, cioè i cardini delle società e
del mondo, non facevano eccezione.

L'ambiente del *Libro dei Vigilanti* non sostituisce a Yhwh un altro Dio,
ma pone fra la divinità e il mondo esseri spirituali che sconvolgono la
creazione: il mondo di cui abbiamo esperienza è quello dei demoni,
non quello di Dio. Il rapporto con la divinità doveva, perciò, scavalcare
le strutture istituzionali. Così, l'autore del *Libro dei Vigilanti* creò una

---

[35] Sulla complessità dell'opposizione del cosmo come disordine al cosmo come
ordine, cfr. G. Boccaccini, *The Roots of Rabbinic Judaism* (Grand Rapids: Eerdmans,
2002), 91–93.

spiritualità completamente nuova per Israele e forse per qualsiasi società del mondo antico. L'isolamento, più spirituale che fisico, di Qumran ha le sue radici nella spiritualità del primo enochismo.

Una rivoluzione di questo genere lascia pensare che a monte ci fossero non solo problemi del pensiero, ma anche qualche situazione storica particolarmente dura per l'ambiente dell'autore del *Libro dei Vigilanti*. La crisi della profezia, accompagnata dal problema della verità,[36] può spiegare la novità del mezzo espressivo, ma la radicalità dei contenuti con risvolti sociali notevoli sembra avere alle spalle qualche trauma violento.

Certamente, stando alle notizie della Bibbia, profeti continuarono a esistere anche dopo la proibizione di profetare. Questi profeti non furono dalla parte del potere, né quello dei sacerdoti, né quello di un governatore come Neemia che si trovò in urto con la profetessa (o profeta) Noadia. È difficile stabilire quali interessi difendessero, ma certamente con l'affermazione dello stato voluto da Neemia la possibilità di esporre verità per mezzo della profezia doveva essere più impossibile che difficile. Anche la grande profezia della tradizione fu svalutata di fronte al Pentateuco. Mosè solo parlò con Dio «faccia a faccia»; gli altri profeti dovevano sempre interpretare le loro visioni o farle interpretare.[37] L'autore della prima apocalisse scavalcò tutti questi problemi, perché raccontò cose che egli aveva visto personalmente in cielo (quindi cose non interpretate): le caverne dell'occidente esistono, perché sono state viste. La storia preesistente all'autore che narrava degli angeli caduti era storia vera, perché Enoc aveva incontrato personalmente gli angeli in cielo.

Il primo personaggio pseudepigrafico che incontriamo nella storia come autore di queste comunicazioni rivolte agli uomini di cose che esistono e accadono in cielo fu Enoc. L'ambiente in cui sorse la prima

---

[36] Il primo a porsi il problema di come la gente poteva accettare la verità di un profeta piuttosto che di un altro fu Geremia, che percepì la difficoltà che doveva presentarsi alla gente per il fatto che esistevano profeti che profetizzavano cose diverse dalle sue. Egli risolse il problema per mezzo del concetto di segno (Ger 23,33); è lo stesso criterio di Dt. 18,22. Vedi P. Sacchi, "La conoscenza presso gli ebrei da Amos all'essenismo", in *L'apocalittica giudaica e la sua storia*, 220–58 (228).

[37] Vedi Num 12,6–8, che spiega perché il testo della Torah è degno di fede: è autentica parola di Dio. «Ascoltate le mie parole: Se ci sarà tra voi un profeta...mi farò conoscere da lui in visione (*bammar'ah*, gr. ἐν ὁράματι); in sogno parlerò a lui (*bo*); non così il mio servo Mosè. Nella mia casa egli è il più degno di fiducia. Faccia a faccia io gli parlo, per mezzo di concetti chiari (ebr. *umar'eh*, gr. ἐν εἴδει) e non per simboli. Egli può guardare l'aspetto di Yhwh (*temunat YHWH*)».

apocalisse scelse questa figura per esporre i propri convincimenti e per garantirli di veridicità, perché Enoc era personaggio particolarmente credibile in questa materia per la sua vicenda simile a quella di Elia: anche lui fu rapito in cielo e inoltre si doveva occupare di astronomia e astrologia.

Enoc non era un unto, non poteva quindi parlare con una autorità istituzionale, né con quella del re, né con quella del sacerdote. Non poteva nemmeno parlare come profeta: non sarebbe stato credibile. Era, però, in grado di raccontare cose viste: in questo senso chi si fidava di lui acquisiva una conoscenza superiore. In quanto rivelatore di cose viste l'autore del *Libro dei Vigilanti* è l'autore della prima apocalisse, ma in quanto formulatore di un pensiero, che si opponeva all'ordine politico del proprio stato, in questo senso fu l'autore del primo apocrifo. Lo sforzo enochico di avvicinarsi alla grande tradizione ebraica, quale è documentato nel *Libro dei Sogni* e poi in maniera radicale dal libro dei *Giubilei* conferma e testimonia come all'origine l'enochismo fosse un movimento fortemente distaccato dalla società in cui era sorto. Il libro dei *Giubilei*, accettando la Legge di Mosè, conferma che l'enochismo precedente non l'accettava. Ma il libro dei *Giubilei*, accettando la legge mosaica, esce dall'enochismo.[38]

Mi domando quale centro potesse avere una spiritualità come quella del *Libro dei Vigilanti*. L'uomo del primo enochismo apprese di possedere un'anima immortale e guardò il mondo come un grande caos conseguenza dell'alterazione della creazione divina. Queste verità sconvolgenti erano escluse ai più degli ebrei e derise da qualche dotto come Qohelet (3,18–21). Solo gli enochici sapevano che all'estremo occidente c'era una valle destinata ai buoni, dove già stavano le anime dei buoni già defunti. Se Enoc non era un salvatore, ma solo un rivelatore, tuttavia il suo messaggio mostrava l'esistenza di una salvezza diversa da quella tradizionale dei sadociti e immensamente più grande. È possibile che il messaggio di Enoc contenesse la descrizione di questa salvezza nel mondo di là, senza nulla dire dei mezzi per raggiungere questa meta? O l'accettazione della rivelazione era la via stessa per entrare nella valle dei giusti?

---

[38] Per una presentazione globale e schematica della storia dei movimenti religiosi giudaici postesilici secondo la mia interpretazione, cfr. "History of the Earliest Enochic Texts", in *Enoc and Qumran Origins* (a cura di G. Boccaccini; Grand Rapids: Eerdmans, 2005), 402–7. Vedi anche il capitolo sui Giubilei di G. Boccaccini, *Oltre l'ipotesi essenica*, 161–90.

Come dicevo prima, la novità vasta e radicale del pensiero del primo enochismo si può spiegare meglio se a monte ci fu un qualche avvenimento che sia stato vissuto come una tragedia. Fra i pochi avvenimenti relativi al postesilio che la Bibbia sadocita ci ha trasmesso uno potrebbe essere proprio quello che giustifica la radicalità del pensiero enochico. Neemia, probabilmente proprio lui stesso, ci racconta di avere escluso dal servizio del tempio tutti quei sacerdoti che non potevano dimostrare di essere discendenti di deportati (Neh 7,69). Ma non furono solo i sacerdoti non discendenti di deportati ad essere cacciati dalla comunità, se i cittadini convocati nelle assemblee furono soltanto i discendenti dei deportati (Neh 7,5).

Fu in questa situazione storica che nacque e si sviluppò la letteratura di rivelazione, cioè di apocalisse, che, in quanto nata in opposizione al sadocitismo di Gerusalemme, fu probabilmente anche nascosta a Gerusalemme e, parallelamente, dalla tradizione sadocita ignorata e condannata alla *damnatio memoriae*.

Non so quando il termine apocrifo, segreto, abbia cominciato ad essere usato in quel senso di autocompiacimento o di disprezzo con cui è usato anche oggi; molto probabilmente quest'uso è assai tardo. Comunque, una situazione come quella in cui nacque il *Libro dei Vigilanti* aveva tutte le caratteristiche per far nascere una tradizione che in seguito poteva dire se stessa e essere detta apocrifa. La tradizione enochica venne certamente alla luce della vita sociale e politica durante il II sec. a.C., quando tentò un avvicinamento ai sadociti. Il tentativo, che fu reciproco, fallì e solo in seguito nacque l'uso di parole come rivelazione[39] e segreto[40] riferite a quei testi che non appartenevano alla grande tradizione di Israele.

---

[39] Si veda l'*Apocalisse* di Giovanni, dove la parola appartiene sicuramente all'autore e le due apocalissi coeve *Quarto Libro di Ezra* e *Apocalisse Siriaca di Baruc*, nelle quali la parola è nel titolo, ma forse solo inseritavi dalla tradizione.

[40] La parola segreto appare nel titolo dell'*Enoc Slavo* e nell'*incipit* del vangelo gnostico di *Tommaso*.

CANONICAL RECEPTION OF THE DEUTEROCANONICAL AND APOCRYPHAL BOOKS IN CHRISTIANITY

Julio Trebolle

As of today, no satisfactory explanation has been given yet for the inclusion in the Christian canon of the so-called deuterocanonical books, which are absent from the Hebrew Bible. A comparison between these books and the parabiblical and apocryphal writings found at Qumran could, nevertheless, shed some light on this issue. The deuterocanonical books vaunt some pretensions of canonicity. They exhibit, on one hand, a series of features matching those of the apocryphal writings which the Christian tradition picked from the Jewish one, while, at the same time, other works were rejected. Christianity transmitted a series of deuterocanonical and apocryphal Jewish writings, which seems to place it closer to a form of Judaism prior to the Hellenistic crisis and closer to the Aramaic-speaking Diaspora than to Palestinian Judaism of Qumran and New Testament times.

One of the features of this literature incorporated by the Christian tradition is the universalistic perspective. It is represented by figures like Adam, Noah, and the patriarch Abraham, which are preferred to others with a more Israelite or Jewish significance, as Moses, Joshua, or David. It is very meaningful, as I will try to underscore, that the reference to Noah is implicit in the episode on the Apostles' inebriation, once it is connected with the multitude of languages and peoples assembled in Pentecost, as if in a new Babel. Those figures constitute a sequence of models or periods (patriarchal, tribal, and monarchic) as well as of covenants or testaments: Adam, Noah, Abraham, Moses, Joshua, David..., who, in their multiple versions—Jewish, Christian, and Islamic—have forerunners in models from Mesopotamian historiography, which constitutes one of the sources for Jewish apocalyptic.

Such are the hypotheses or suggestions for research which will be presented in this paper, almost without room left for nuances, developments, and notes.[1] At risk of falling into the deceptions forewarned

---

[1] I would like to thank Dr. Andrés Piquer Otero, researcher at Universidad Complutense de Madrid, for the translation of the Spanish original.

in the saying picked by Goethe in his *Wahlverwandschafte*: "latet dolus in generalibus," let this be my tribute to the scholar of Qumran and Hellenistic Judaism, a friend for many years, and above all, the person who is Florentino García Martínez.

1. CANONICAL PRETENSIONS OF THE
DEUTEROCANONICAL BOOKS

Christianity has transmitted a biblical canon which is larger than the Hebrew one. Is it a Jewish heritage or an autonomous Christian development? On one side, Qumran has taken back in time a couple of centuries the origins of the Hebrew canon, whose basic lines could be already identified at the beginning of the second century B.C.E.; on the other hand, the hypothesis according to which the Christian canon reflected an "Alexandrine" one, a feature of the Hellenistic Jewish Diaspora, has been rejected. These two factors have made it even harder to explain the origins of the expanded Christian canon.

If Christians did not inherit from the Jewish Diaspora a canon larger than the Hebrew Bible, it will be necessary to explain why they did not follow the tendency of proto-Rabbinic circles, which limited the number of books in this canon and why they included in their own canon some books which the rabbis ended up forgetting. One could think that Christianity inherited the Hebrew canon of twenty-two/twenty-four books and that the collection of books visible in the LXX version transmitted by the Christian codices constituted simply a *corpus mixtum*, which would not have an equivalent in any putative Jewish canon. One could also bring into the scene the idea—present perhaps among the Essenes—that the canon was not a closed repository, but open to new books. Such could have been the case of *Jubilees* and *Enoch*, as well as of Ps 151A, 151B, 154, 155 and of the canticle which can be found in Sir 51:13–30 and in 11QPsᵃ; all of them could have enjoyed some recognition as authoritative Scriptures among the Qumran group.

It is difficult to conceive of, anyway, an OT Christian canon different from the Hebrew which had no precedent in the Judaism of the Qumran and New Testament era. One of these precedents would be, without any doubt, the quotation in the so-called *Florilegium* (4Q174 1–3 ii 3) from Qumran, which quotes from "the book of the prophet Daniel" (12:10), as also does the gospel of Matthew (24:15), thus ascribing Daniel to the prophetic corpus, a fact which constitutes a marked feature of the

Christian canon. Another Jewish precedent for the Christian canon is the fact that the Greek version of Bar 1:1–3:8 was made by the same translator that produced the Greek text of the book of Jeremiah; this indicates that both books enjoyed the same canonical consideration in some circles.[2]

Deuterocanonical writings compose an interrelated corpus, one that is also connected with the canonical books of Daniel and Esther. So, the Additions to Esther deal with topics similar to those found in the book of Judith, or in Daniel's dreams. Also, the Jewish sources for 1–2 Maccabees can be found in Dan 7–12 and in the *Testament of Moses*. Coincidence is almost literal between Bar 1:15–18 and Dan 9:7–10; it is still discussed whether Baruch is dependent on Daniel, Daniel on Baruch, or both derive from a common source. Often all these texts allude to situations of persecution and, generally speaking, of conflict with religious idolatry, political powers, and prevalent philosophies in the Diaspora settings.

Even if only as a literary fiction, in order to be acknowledged as canonical, a book had to be written prior to the times of King Artaxerxes (465–423 B.C.E.), the moment when, it was believed, the successive chain of inspired prophets was interrupted. That is the case of the book of Daniel, which, though written in the Hellenistic era, is set in the Persian court and times. Thus, the stories of Susanna and Bel and the Dragon and also the Prayer of Azariah and the Song of the Three Young Men are set in Persian or Babylonian times and thereby fulfill the requisite of antiquity necessary for canonical acknowledgement. In the same way, the book of Tobit alludes to the Assyrian period; Judith to the Assyrian and Babylonian empires, which the author confuses and mixes; Baruch and the Letter of Jeremiah are located in the Babylonian exile. In particular, this Letter pretends to be addressed to the exiles at the time of the deportation to Babylon, concretely because it is attacking a kind of idolatry more Babylonian than Greek or Egyptian. Only the book of Wisdom, the latest of them all, is set in Alexandrine Hellenistic circles of the first century C.E. Ben Sira and 1–2 Maccabees are works set around Jerusalem.

---

[2] "It is possible that some Jews at an earlier period also treated I Baruch as an integral part of the Bible but, apart from the later Christian attributions of canonicity, there is no other evidence for this"; cf. E. Schürer, *The History of the Jewish People in the Age of Jesus Christ (175 B.C.–A.D. 135)* (rev. and ed. G. Vermes et al.; 3 vols.; Edinburgh: T&T Clark, 1973–1987), 3:733.

Sapiential texts, Ben Sira and Wisdom are related to Diaspora situations as they confront the problem of "foreign wisdom" in the same way that historiographical books, like 1–2 Maccabees, face the problem of "foreign power": two worlds, those of Greek philosophy and of the Roman empire, which Christianity had to face since its inception, a task which required biblical reference models.

Another evidence of possible pretension of canonical acknowledgement is that, in the same way as the canonical works Esther and Daniel, at least some of the deuterocanonical books were subject to "re-writings" or "re-editions." Such is the case of Ben Sira, Tobit, Susanna, and Bel and the Dragon.

It is very revealing that, among the literature which does not belong to the Hebrew canon, only deuterocanonical books (Tobit, Judith, 2 Maccabees, 3 Maccabees, 4 Maccabees, Susanna, and Baruch) include explicit biblical quotations, nineteen in total, a fact which endows the book with a special status when compared to apocrypha and pseudepigrapha. In the same way that a book being cited as authoritative text in later works—like Qumran and New Testament writings—can be considered evidence of canonicity, the probability that a book contained explicit and authoritative quotations would also endow it with some kind of status of authoritative work. Thus, the canonical gospels contain explicit quotations of the Old Testament, whereas gospels which are considered apocryphal do not have that kind of quotations.

2. Common Features of the Deuterocanonical Books

Regarding the original language of the deuterocanonical books, Ben Sira and 1 Maccabees were written in Hebrew, but Tobit and, probably, the story of Susanna were written in Aramaic, as the fragments discovered in Qumran evidence (cf. Daniel and Susanna, 4Q551). The remaining additions to the book of Daniel were probably also written in Aramaic; its text, partially preserved in Aramaic, was probably written in its entirety in that language. Although the edition of the book was very late, Daniel is one of the most repeated texts in the Qumran library and one of the books most used amongst the first Christians. Several Aramaic writings from Qumran allude to the book of Daniel or are connected to it: *Prayer of Nabonidus* (4Q242), two pseudo-Daniel writings (4Q243–244 and 4Q245), *Aramaic Apocalypse* (or *Apocryphon of Daniel*, 4Q246), *Daniel and Susanna* (4Q551), *Four Kingdoms* (4Q552–553), and *4QpapApocalypse* (4Q489). Also, the work called *Aramaic proto-Esther* shows that the book of Esther also features in the wake of Aramaic narratives. Linguistic reasons support the existence of a Semitic original for the Additions to the book of Esther, with the exception of the two edicts, which where composed in Greek. As for Judith, Jerome says that he made his version from an Aramaic text. Baruch, whose text has been preserved in Greek, was probably written in a Semitic language, especially for 1:1–3:8 and less likely for 4:5–5:9. The book must have been edited in Palestine, because the introduction (1:3–14) was composed in Hebrew. The Letter of Jeremiah could have been written in Hebrew or in Aramaic.[3]

The fact that, with the exception of the book of Wisdom and 2 Maccabees, the deutero-canonical books were written in a Semitic language—a large proportion in Aramaic—could lead us to reorient their perspectives of study, which, until now, was centered in the presumed existence of an Alexandrine Greek canon. The totality of these books is normally located among the Greek Judeo-Hellenistic literature, dominated by the specific weight of the LXX version, the exegetical works of Philo, and the historiography of Flavius Josephus. Nevertheless, when talking about some deuterocanonical books, it is necessary to put the eyes not so much upon the Greek Diaspora, but upon the Aramaic-speaking population, both in the metropolis of Jerusalem, in the Eastern Syro-Babylonian Diaspora, and even in the Egyptian Diaspora at Elephantine. In no case is it possible to speak of a specific Aramaic-language canon. The question is, rather, to acknowledge the importance of the Aramaic and Babylonian tradition in the formation of the Hebrew Canon—from Second Isaiah and the Priestly writing, through Ezra and Nehemiah, up to Daniel. This traditional Aramaic-Babylonian weight has also left its imprint on some of the books which, although they did not enter into the initial Palestinian canon of the Maccabaean period—enjoyed enough recognition among Jewish circles connected with the Eastern Diaspora for the later Judeo-Christian tradition to incorporate them into their deuterocanonical or apocryphal books. The weight of Eastern Judaism was key also for the Aramaic-Targumic tradition and, later, in the *Babylonian Talmud*, Qaraism, and Gaonic Judaism.

Another meaningful common feature of the deuterocanonical books is their finding inspiration or collecting data from extra-biblical Eastern sources. Thus, Tobit is based on tales like the "Fable of the Grateful

---

[3] D.J. Harrington, *Invitation to the Apocrypha* (Grand Rapids: Eerdmans, 1999).

Dead" and "The Devil's Wife." The book of Daniel, whose main character resembles the leading figure in the legend of *Ahiqar*, finds in the *Prayer of Nabonidus* (4Q242) the best evidence for reception of extra-biblical traditions in a biblical book; Daniel's visions pick up Persian, Babylonian, Egyptian, and Canaanite mythological elements.[4] The stories associated to this book (Susanna and Bel and the Dragon) are inspired by folkloric elements. Judith, a tale which originated in the Persian period and was re-written in Hasmonean times, is full of reference to folk-tale topoi, a story applicable to any situation of oppression against Israel. Also, Wisdom picks popular traditions which can also be found in Philo, Josephus, and the Targumim.

3. COMMON FEATURES BETWEEN THE DEUTEROCANONICAL BOOKS
AND THE APOCRYPHAL WRITINGS RECEIVED IN THE
CHRISTIAN TRADITION

The features which have been indicated above for the deuterocanonical texts coincide with those of other parabiblical or apocryphal writings from Qumran: they were written in Aramaic, are related to the Eastern Jewish Diaspora, and pick up mythic or folkloric extra-biblical literary traditions or narratives. That is the case of the *Book of the Watchers* and the *Astronomical Book* (collected in *1 Enoch*), the *Genesis Apocryphon*, and the *Book of the Giants*. Apart from the already-mentioned idiosyncrasies, these books share the feature that their protagonists are characters from Genesis, in particular, pre-Flood ones: Adam and Eve, Cain and Abel, the giants, the angels, Enoch, and Noah; this confers upon them a decidedly universalist perspective. The *Book of the Watchers* has sources of its own when it attributes the leadership of the revolt to Shemichaza or Asael and has no qualms in "resorting to foreign materials" when attempting to "expand Israelite worldviews with prevailing mythical cosmologies, a mix of Israelite, Greek and Babylonian conceptions." The astronomical and geographical elements in the *Astronomical Book* can be traced back to traditions originating in Mesopotamia. The *Genesis Apocryphon* "adds many elements of its own or derived from other extrabiblical sources."[5]

---

[4] J.J. Collins, *Daniel: A Commentary on the Book of Daniel* (Hermeneia; Minneapolis: Fortress Press, 1993), 274–94.
[5] F. García Martínez, "Textos de Qumrán," in *Literatura judía intertestamentaria* (ed. G. Aranda Pérez et al.; Estella: Editorial Verbo Divino, 1996), 129–30.

The distinctive features of these books become clear after a comparison with another group of texts written in Hebrew, where the main characters are specifically-Israelite figures, like Moses or David, and exclusively biblical sources are used, with a tendency to literality and a marked particularistic perspective. This group is composed of the *Sayings of Moses, Moses Apocryphon, Pseudo-Ezekiel, Pseudo-Moses*, and some other texts.[6]

Perhaps it would be possible to differentiate an intermediate group, closer to the first one, constituted by texts written in Aramaic, and related to patriarchal figures before Moses and Aaron, like the *Visions of Amram, Aramaic Testament of Qahat, Aramaic Testament of Levi*, and *Testament of Naphtali*. For example, the *Visions of Amram* carries out a synthesis of traditions that have varied origins about the figures of Michael and Belial, those of Melchizedek and Melchiresha, and of the angel of light and the angel of darkness. The *Aramaic Testament of Levi* is characterized by the abundant usage of materials taken from a source that the author extensively summarizes and reedits.

The book of *Jubilees*, although written in Hebrew and posed as Moses' work, presents features which place it closer to the first group than to the second, because pre-Flood and patriarchal characters are its protagonists; it has extra-biblical connections, and it departs from Pharisaic halakhah, as it is governed by a solar calendar.

A considerable number of texts from the first group—larger than the second—goes back in time to a rather ancient period, the third century B.C.E. and, possibly in some cases, the fourth century during Persian rule. They are, in any case, older than the Hellenistic crisis and the constitution of the Essene community at Qumran: *Genesis Apocryphon, Book of the Watchers* and *Astronomical Book* from *1 Enoch, Book of the Giants, Aramaic Testament of Levi, Aramaic Testament of Qahat*, and *Visions of Amram*. Due to their antiquity, these texts belonged to the literary heritage of Judaism in general, or at least of a wide sector of it, and not to a particular group such as Qumran's. Texts from the second group of equal or comparable antiquity are *Pseudo-Joshua, Pseudo-Moses*, and *Pseudo-Ezekiel*, as well as sections from the *Temple Scroll* and *Ordinances*.

To ancient times—from the perspective of Qumran—go back also the deuterocanonical texts originally written in Aramaic, Tobit (third

---

[6] D. Dimant, "Apocalyptic Texts at Qumran," in *The Community of the Renewed Covenant: The Notre Dame Symposium on the Dead Sea Scrolls* (ed. E. Ulrich and J.C. VanderKam; CJAS 10; Notre Dame, Ind.: University of Notre Dame Press, 1994), 175–91.

or second century B.C.E.), Susanna, and the remaining additions to the book of Daniel. To pre-Qumranic times also belong Ben Sira (ca. 180 B.C.E.), the Letter of Jeremiah, Baruch, and Judith.

It is meaningful to observe which books, among the listed ones, became part of Christian literature as Old Testament apocrypha and which where rejected by the same Christians. Christianity preferably picked up and transmitted books from the first group, that is, books originally written in Aramaic, with pre- and post-Flood patriarchs as main characters, with a universalist slant and set in the background of the Syro-Babylonian Diaspora, whose traditions and folklore cannot but be a source of inspiration. These texts allowed for the development of a universalist perspective and a Christological typology similar to the one presented by Paul in Rom 5:12 and 1 Cor 15:22 (also Phil 2:5–6). The most remarkable cases are the *Book of the Watchers* and the *Astronomical Book*, as well as books connected with biblical patriarchs, like the *Testaments of the Twelve Patriarchs*. The figure of Enoch is key in Jewish apocalyptic, which constituted, as it has been proposed, the Jewish matrix of Christianity. Enoch, the Qur'an's Idris, is one of the prophets who, together with Moses, Abraham, and Noah, compose the series of biblical figures which Islam grants the category of "prophets" (*nabi*). From Jewish apocalyptic literature, Christianity also incorporated the apocryphal *2 Baruch* and *4 Ezra*, which allude to the destruction of Jerusalem. It seems that the reason for this was a desire to bury the hopes for Israel's political restoration, therefore favoring the apocalyptic of universal restoration which Christianity wanted to communicate.

On the other hand, Christianity did not preserve any text from the second group, that is, written in Hebrew, connected to Moses or to clearly Israelite characters, of a more strictly Jewish air, and inspired only in the Bible. It picked up, nevertheless, the texts titled *Martyrdom of Isaiah* and *Paralipomena of Jeremiah* which, although from the Hellenistic era, are set in the times of the respective prophets and hence before the Persian period, through the literary fiction.

Christianity did not preserve, remarkably, any text of legal literature from the sectarian group of Qumran, like the halakhic texts or the *Rule of the Community (Halakhic letter, Temple Scroll, Rule of the Community, Damascus Document, Rule of the Congregation, Ordinances, Rule of Purity, Rule of Damascus, and Rule of War)*. It also discarded Qumran's exegetic literature, namely the Targumim to Leviticus and Job and the distinctive pesharim or biblical commentaries and the thematic midrashim, like *11QMelchizedek* (11Q13).

Judging from the Jewish deuterocanonical and apocryphal literature which Christianity took as its own and transmitted from the very
beginning, the link seems to be stronger with the Judaism prior to the
Hellenistic crisis and the Aramaic Diaspora than with Palestinian Judaism in the times of Qumran and the New Testament. Canonical New
Testament literature, as well as Jewish sources more connected with
first-century C.E. Palestine, are not enough to focus adequately the total
of ideas and representations which Christianity, spread not only through
the Western Jewish Diaspora thanks to Paul's doings, but also through
Syria, Mesopotamia, and Egypt, inherited from this same Judaism of
the Aramaic-speaking Diaspora.

4. Common Emphasis of the Christian Tradition
on Pre-Flood Characters:
Drunk Noah and the Apostles' Inebriation

Due to its universalist projection, Christian literature takes as prime
referents the characters from Genesis prior to the Flood. It is very
meaningful to observe the proportion of the most-quoted OT books in
the NT. The first two are Psalms and Isaiah, but the third one changes
as Christian literature takes shape: In the quotations in Jesus' mouth, it
is the book of the Twelve Minor Prophets; in the total of NT quotes, it
is Deuteronomy, whereas in Paul and the second-century Fathers, it is
already Genesis. Until the third century, the churches could not afford
to have all the books of the OT. Besides the NT, they had the more
frequently used OT books, such as Genesis, Isaiah, and Psalms and,
varying according to circumstances and region, other books used particularly in baptismal instruction. In the third century (Origen, Clement
of Alexandria, Cyprian, and the *Didaskalia*), the picture changes, and
the quotations do not focus so much on the books of Genesis, Isaiah,
and Psalms.[7]

Christian theology of the second and third centuries is basically
constructed upon Genesis and, concretely, on its first four chapters,
around "the divine pre-history before the world..., the great Days of
creation, the epiphany and destiny of protoplastus Adam, the drama
of Paradise, the history of the human race—before and after the Flood

---

[7] F. Stuhlhofer, *Der Gebrauch der Bibel von Jesus bis Euseb: Eine statistische Untersuchung
zur Kanongeschichte* (Wuppertal: R. Brockhaus, 1988), 259.

and the circumcision and the Law."[8] On the other hand, the materials
around Israel's exodus, as well as the history of the people of God until
the days of Jesus, has a typological value in reference to the NT, but
it is not the object of a theological development comparable to that
of the former topics.

If the book of Genesis links Adam and Noah as parallel figures, the
apocryphal literature places a greater emphasis on the relationship
between Enoch and Noah. Some Qumran texts give a special relevance to Noah, particularly regarding his birth, as it is the case of
the two Aramaic versions of his history, in the first chapters of *Genesis
Apocryphon* (1QapGen II) and at the end of *1 Enoch* (106–107; *4QEnoch^c*
[4Q204]). *Birth of Noah^a* (4Q534, also called *Elect of God*) may be an
oracle predicting Noah's birth and mission. The statement in *Aramaic
Levi*, "for thus he found in the writings of the *Book of Noah* concerning the blood" (sec. 57), as well as that of *Jubilees*, "Noah wrote down
everything in a book" (10:1–4), raises the question whether the *Book
of Noah* actually existed. This book could have dealt with the topics of
Noah's birth, sacrificial instructions, and medicine and demonology,
using extra-biblical sources regarding the "birth of the hero" and Noah's
esoteric knowledge.[9] Philo deals with aspects of Noah's life and actions
in *Questions and Answers on Genesis and Exodus*, as well as in *Questions on
Genesis: On Husbandry, On Noah's Work as a Planter, On Drunkenness and on
Sobriety*. Noah also features in biblical retellings such as Pseudo-Philo's
Biblical Antiquities and Josephus' *Jewish Antiquities*.

Jubilees pays more attention to Noah (5:21–10:17) than to Enoch
(4:16–26; 7:38–39). Enoch announces the Flood and has the privilege
of being led to the garden of paradise. He is the first to possess wisdom
and knowledge of writing and astronomy. He is also the first to write

---

[8] A. Orbe, *Introducción a la teología de los siglos II y III* (Rome: Editrice Pontificia Università Gregoriana, 1988), 2.

[9] P.-M. Bogaert, "La personne de Noé dans la littérature juive ancienne de tradition
palestinienne non rabbinique," in *Noé: L'homme universel* (ed. J. Chopineau; vol. 3; Colloque
de Louvain 23 janvier 1978; Bruxelles: Publications de l'Institutum Iudaicum Bruxelles,
1978), 119–47; F. García Martínez, "*4QMess Ar* and the *Book of Noah*," in *Qumran and
Apocalyptic: Studies on the Aramaic Texts from Qumran* (STDJ 9; Leiden: Brill, 1992), 1–44;
M.J. Bernstein, "Noah and the Flood at Qumran," in *The Provo International Conference of
the Dead Sea Scrolls: Technological Innovations, New Texts, and Reformulated Issues* (ed. D.W. Parry
and E. Ulrich; Leiden: Brill, 1999), 199–231; C. Werman, "Qumran and the Book of
Noah," in *Pseudepigraphic Perspectives: The Apocrypha and Pseudepigrapha in Light of the Dead
Sea Scrolls* (ed. E.G. Chazon and M.E. Stone; STDJ 31; Leiden: Brill, 1999), 171–81;
M.E. Stone, "The Book(s) Attributed to Noah," *DSD* 13 (2006): 4–23.

a "testimony" for men and for the Watchers who come to preach to them. Nevertheless, Enoch is nothing but Noah's ancestor. He announces the Flood, but it is Noah who communicates all the astronomic matters connected with the calendar (6:16–38) which had been revealed to Enoch (4:17, 21).

The Christian tradition or *paradosis* based on Jewish traditions divided OT time in periods, finding several covenants within it: Adam's, Noah's, Abraham's, and Moses', as well as Joshua's (regarding the second circumcision). Irenaeus of Lyons acknowledged four covenants or testaments, matching the four gospels: Adam's, Noah's, and Moses', plus a fourth one, represented by the Christian gospel.[10] Another distribution of the four testaments includes Abraham and removes Adam; thus, Noah opens the series of four covenants: Noah, Abraham, Moses, and Jesus the Christ.

In the New Testament, the Letter to the Hebrews (11:1–40) takes some time to consider the figures of faith: Abel, Enoch, Noah, Abraham-Isaac-Jacob, Moses, and Rahab. Then it presents, in a simple list, Gideon, Barak, Samson, Jephthah, David, Solomon, and the prophets. For Matthew, Jesus is another Noah from the outset (1:1–3:17 and 24:38). 1 Peter 3:18–21 speaks of the eight who were saved, Noah's family or, rather, the seven pre-Flood genealogies before Noah. 2 Peter 2:5–6 makes reference to Noah and Lot.

In Acts, the speech put in Stephen's mouth (7:2–53) mentions Abraham, Isaac, Jacob, and Joseph, then Moses, and, finally, Solomon, builder of the Temple, and the later prophets. Also, the speech attributed to Peter in 3:11–26 makes reference to the God of Abraham, Isaac, and Jacob, mentions Moses in the introduction of a quotation from the Pentateuch, and alludes generically to the prophets from Samuel onwards, to finish with a new reference to the covenant established with Abraham and the patriarchs. Also in Paul's speech in Antioch of Pisidia (13:16–41), there are references to Abraham and the patriarchs and also to Moses and David. Acts seem to obviate the figure of Noah. Nevertheless, in my opinion, it is present in two fundamental episodes: the Pentecost scene (2:1–13) and the conversion of the first Gentile, Cornelius (10–11).

The explanations given to the state of inebriation of the apostles are far from satisfactory, as it is the case of the mere reference to Cicero's

---

[10] Orbe, *Introducción a la teología de los siglos II y III*, 380.

expression *ab hora tertia bibebatur, ludebatur* (*Phil.* 2.41.104) or to states
of ecstasy accompanied by drunkenness known from mysteries like
Dionysus'.[11] The inebriation motif serves as a transition into Peter's
speech and also to present in opposition, as often happens in Luke,
two parties in conflict: Jesus' followers or apostles and the "others,"
which take for drunkards those who in fact have been possessed by
the spirit. Nevertheless, the meaning of inebriation is not exhausted
just with those references. It seems to take whole meaning if it is connected with Noah's inebriation. The word μεθύειν (שכר) links both
texts: Noah "drank from the wine and became inebriated" (Gen 9:20)
and "they are loaded with grape-juice"—"it is not that those are
inebriated" (Acts 2:13 Γλεύκους μεμεστωμένοι εἰσίν—15 οὐ γὰρ ὡς
ὑμεῖς ὑπολαμβάνετε οὗτοι μεθύουσιν). Also, the relationship between
drunkenness and glossolalia or multilingualism at Pentecost is given by
the sequence of Genesis in chapters 9–11 and by that in Philo's treatises
De ebrietate, De sobrietate, and *De confusione linguarum.* In the latter, Philo
connects the "Divine Planter" (or *phytourgos theos*) with the dispersion
and expulsion from the city of the world of those who build the city
of Evil and the tower of atheism.[12] The motifs of the tower and the
seventy languages, matching the seventy peoples, appear connected with
the eschatological hope expressed in Isa 2:12–18, "The Eternal One
will set a day...against every tall tower, against every fortified wall."
Then, according to Zephaniah, "I will pour upon the peoples a purified
language so that they all invoke the name of the Eternal one and serve
him with a single mind" (3:9). In Acts, to "everyone's" question, "what
does this mean?" (a question of the *pesher* kind), follows the same kind
of answer: "*This is* what was announced by the prophet Joel: '*And it
will happen* in the last days, God says: *I will pour my spirit upon all flesh...I
will pour my spirit in those days.*'"

Among the signs and portents of "those days" appear fire and smoke.
The scenography of Pentecost has been connected with that of Sinai

---

[11] P.W. van der Horst, "Hellenistic Parallels to the Acts of the Apostles (2.1–47),"
in *Studies on the Hellenistic Background of the New Testament* (ed. idem and G. Mussies;
Utrechtse Theologische Reeks; Utrecht: Faculteit der Godgeleerdheid van de Rijks-
universiteit, 1990), 131–45 (137); L.T. Johnson, *The Acts of the Apostles* (Collegeville,
Minn.: Liturgical Press, 1992), 44.

[12] J.G. Kahn, *De confusione linguarum* (Œuvres de Philon 13; Paris: Le Cerf, 1963),
n. 196.

and with the feast of the Torah,[13] but through the "tongues as of fire," through the speaking in the tongues of the nations, and through the inebriation of the apostles, this episode also takes features of re-creation, signified by the figure of Noah, new Adam, and by a Flood in the form of fire-like tongues upon each of the apostles.

The motif of the apostles being mocked at in Acts also appears in Philo, in allusion to those who "laugh at what happens to others, when they should cry rather than mock (χλευάζειν)" and "he laughed (γελάσας) at what he saw."[14]

The story of Cornelius' conversion is also connected with Noah. It is the narrative of the foundation of the first community in Cae-sarea with a Gentile origin. The vision of the open skies presents the animals of creation: four-legged, reptiles, and birds of the sky (Gen 1:24; Acts 10:12). In Acts 11:6, the bestiary comprises four animals: four-legged land animals, wild beasts, reptiles, and birds, in connec-tion the catalogue of Gen 7:14, where Noah takes into the Ark (*after* his family) wild beasts, domestic species, reptiles, and birds. In this last text, the interest in the pure-impure is connected with a concern for human salvation. The reference to the creation stories of Gen 1 and 7 in these narratives from Acts is clear, as are those regarding other common elements, like the word or voice and the spirit (Gen 1:2; 7:22 "breath of spirit of life"). Luke picks up in the passages of Pentecost and Cornelius different traditions which attempted to relate the genesis of Christian communities to ethnic contacts of a universal character, like those of Gen 9–10, and to food-based symbols of cosmic-biological purity, typical of the times of creation.

5. The Sequence Jesus Christ—David— Abraham—Adam/Noah: Extra-biblical models

I will come back now to the remarks on the Jewish, Christian, and also Islamic tradition of dividing history in periods and covenants marked by the main biblical figures, which, in the case of Christian *paradosis*, are saliently Adam and Abraham. The genealogy in Matt 1:1–17 presents

---

[13] E. Haenchen, *The Acts of the Apostles: A Commentary* (Philadelphia: Westminster Press, 1971), 174.

[14] J. Gorez, *De ebrietate, De sobrietate* (Œuvres de Philon 11–12; Paris: Le Cerf, 1962), nn. 6 and 32 respectively.

"Jesus Christ, son of David, son of Abraham." It answers thus to the mixed constituency of his community of Jewish and Gentile Christians. Matthew's intention is to show that Jesus is the Davidic Messiah. Matthew's genealogy may represent a popular tradition about the royal Davidic lineage, to which the names of Joseph and Jesus have been joined. But Matthew could appeal to Gentile Christian interest by tracing Jesus back to Abraham, whom Jews called "our father," but in whom all the nations of the earth were to be blessed. It was also to Matthew's interest that the four OT women included in his genealogy—Tamar, Rahab, Ruth, and Uriah's wife, Bathsheba—were Gentiles or associated with Gentiles (Uriah's wife), although endowed with the proselyte status granted to such women in Judaism.

On his turn, Luke's list (3:32–38) goes up from Jesus through David and Abraham, back to Adam. Since the Pauline preaching not only related Jesus to Abraham (Gal 3:16) but also drew a parallel between Jesus and Adam (Rom 5:12–21; 1 Cor 15:22,45), Luke may have felt impelled to include both figures in the genealogy. The reference to Jesus as "the son of Adam" immediately precedes the scene in Luke 4:1–13, where Jesus is tempted by Satan, an echo of Adam's struggle with Satan in Eden. There may be another, indirect reference to the Gentiles in the fact that the number of Jesus' ancestors in the Luke list is close to the number of the nations of the world (seventy-two) descended from Noah in Gen 11.[15]

Here I would like to indicate that, in the measure that David represents the figure of the king which institutes monarchy for a people—Israel—, Abraham that of the first nomad—father of peoples—and Adam or Noah that of the first human being—father of humanity—, the sequence David-Abraham-Noah/Adam has old forerunners in Mesopotamian historiography.

Assyrians "constructed history" in three periods: one of "kings who dwelt in tents," one of ancestral tribal leaders, and finally one with the kings of the Assyrian dynasty. That is the historiographical pattern in the Assyrian royal lists upon which the Assyrian monarchy based the legitimacy of its power. Following this Assyrian model, biblical history begins first with the first patriarch, Abraham, from whose children—Isaac and Ishmael—descend Israelites and Ishmaelites (Gen 11–50);

---

[15] R.E. Brown, *The Birth of the Messiah: A Commentary on the Infancy Narratives in Matthew and Luke* (Garden City, N.Y.: Image Books, 1979), 66–91.

later there come tribal leaders or "judges," until David and the kings of the Davidic dynasty (books of *Joshua, Judges, Samuel,* and *Kings*). Israel's neighbors constructed their own history following the same paradigm: after the patriarch Esau/Edom (Gen 36:1–5) come tribal chieftains (36:9–19, 20–30 + 40–41) and, finally, the Edomite kings (36:31–39). Sumerians and Babylonians constructed their own history with pre- and post- Flood mythical characters; their city dynasties were traced back to them. In agreement with this historiographical pattern reflected in the Sumerian royal lists, Genesis initiates human history with a series of characters, from Adam to Noah, who lived centuries of years (1–11).

In this way, the Bible merges the Sumerian and Assyrian historiographical models, placing the former before the latter. The pattern of periods or eras like the "patriarchal era" or "the era of the Judges of Israel" are not simple late inventions of the Bible, regardless of the presence or absence of historical figures in the patriarchal and Judges narratives. The fact is that this periodical division of history in four eras, "pre-Flood," "patriarchal," "tribal," and "monarchic" follows a model whose existence is earlier than biblical historiography.[16]

If monarchic historiography traced its origins back into nomadic or pre-Flood beginnings, apocalyptic historiography, based in a sequence of empires, extended it into a heavenly kingdom as glimpsed in the visions of Daniel and of Revelation. The Babylonian historian Berossus already uses a historiographical model of successive empires, after which the heavenly kingdom would arrive. From a Persian perspective, those three empires had been, namely, Assyria, Media, and Persia. The book of Daniel adapted this conception to biblical history, substituting Assyrians with Babylonians. Later tradition extended this sequence of empires to include the Macedonians and, afterwards, the Romans. The Bible is based, therefore, in two successive historiographies: the first one spans from Genesis to the end of the monarchies, the second one from that end to the apocalyptic visions of Daniel or to Revelations in the Christian Bible. Both historiographical views merge without leaving any kind of mediating vacuum, which history could not admit. The total acquires paradigmatic features typical of a universal history. Apocalyptic

---

[16] In this sense it would be necessary to further comment or modify statements such as Liverani's, Grottanelli's, and others: M. Liverani, "Le 'origini' di Israele: Progetto storico irrealizzabile di ricerca etnogenetica," *RivB* 28 (1980): 9–31; C. Grottanelli, *Kings and Prophets: Monarchic Power, Inspired Leadership, and Sacred Text in Biblical Narrative* (New York: Oxford University Press, 1999), 11–113.

has one of its sources in the Mesopotamian literary models, which biblical historiography imitates.

The model figures of Adam/Noah, Abraham, and David converge in the New Testament into the figure of Jesus. Jesus' genealogies in Luke follow in this respect the pattern of the genealogical lists of Chronicles (1 Chr 1–9) which begin with Adam and are structured around the figures of Abraham, Israel, and David ("These are his [sc. Abraham's] generations," 1:29; "These are Israel's sons," 2:1; "These were David's sons," 3:1).

Moses has no special relevance in the genealogies of Chronicles, in which he features only as one of Levi's offspring; neither has he any reference or entry in the genealogies of Jesus. The Mosaic historiography of Exodus, as well as Deuteronomic legislation, constituted a unit which was independent from monarchic (Genesis and historical books) and apocalyptic historiographies. The figure of Moses and, in particular, the Jewish Law, do not have in Christianity the same paradigmatic value which other, more universal, figures, like Adam or Noah and Abraham, may acquire. Also, Islamic exegesis of the Qur'an Sura 3:93 declares the abrogation of the Jewish Law, which would have been revealed only and specifically to the Israelites as an imposed punishment: "To the children of Israel was lawful all food except what Israel forbade himself before the Torah was revealed. Say: 'Bring the Torah and recite it, if what you say is true.'"[17] This abrogation implies a return to the original covenant established between God and Abraham. In this sense, the exegesis of 3:93 reminds us of some Christian points of view, which considered the Torah as revealed, although already then lacking any legal or canonic power. Some interpretative trends in the Pauline letters (Rom 4 and Gal 3), together with the Jewish-Christian treatise of the *Letter of Barnabas*, already state that the Torah had been revealed only as punishment for the Jews. The Qur'an abrogates the Torah, because the revelation received by the Prophet Muhammad updated the original covenant which was revealed to Abraham. Therefore, it is considered that the revealed Islamic laws and the promises which come along with them are valid for all peoples, like the laws given to Noah, but not like the Torah revealed to the Jews. In Qumran literature and in texts of Hellenistic Judaism, some Jewish antecedents can be

---

[17] A. Ali, *Al-Qur'ān: A Contemporary Translation* (Princeton, N.Y.: Princeton University Press, 1984), 60–61.

found for this primacy of the revelation to Abraham over the Torah of Moses. According to *Pseudo-Jubilees*[b] (4Q226), Abraham's faith led to his acceptance: "Abraham was recognized as faithful to [G]o[d] that he might be accepted. And the Lord blessed [him]" (7 1–2). Similarly, Paul speaks of being "justified by faith and not by doing the works of the Law" Gal 2:16), in contrast to MMT: "And also we have written to you some of the works of the Torah and it shall be reckoned to you as in justice" (4Q398 2 ii 2–3, 7). In similar manner, writings such as *Pseudo-Orphic Fragments, Joseph and Aseneth, Testament of Job, Testament of Abraham, Joseph's Prayer, Books of Adam and Eve* and *2 Enoch* place Jewish identity not so much in the practice of the strictures of the Torah as in new experiences of heavenly revelations linked to those granted to Abraham or to Moses himself. In some Jewish circles the medium of salvation could be not so much the law in its literal form, but rather the heavenly revelation accorded to particular individuals.[18]

---

[18] J.J. Collins, *Between Athens and Jerusalem: Jewish Identity in the Hellenistic Diaspora* (2d ed.; Grand Rapids: Eerdmans, 1999), 210–60.

TEXTOS FUENTE Y TEXTOS CONTEXTUALES
DE LA NARRATIVA EVANGÉLICA

Miguel Pérez Fernández

Los escribas cristianos mostraron la vida de Jesús como cumplimiento de las Escrituras: prácticamente todas las piezas que componen los Evangelios tienen alguna inspiración, a veces expresa, en los textos del AT. En algunos casos, esta referencia pudo ser buscada por el mismo Jesús; otras veces, el escriba parece haber creado una escena evangélica para "actualizar" o "representar" un texto o escena del AT. Tales textos veterotestamentarios son los que denomino *Textos-fuente, Source Texts*.

Por otra parte, con otros muchos textos del AT, la literatura judía extrabíblica (Qumrán, Rabínica, Filón, Josefo, Apócrifos del AT; etc.) es indispensable para contextualizar pasajes evangélicos. Son *textos contextuales privilegiados*, por cuanto son de la Biblia o beben en las mismas fuentes bíblicas que el NT.

Además tenemos otros textos de la literatura helenístico-romana que suelen ser presentados como *background* del NT. Por cuanto no beben en las mismas fuentes bíblicas del NT me permito clasificarlos como *textos contextuales secundarios*. Nos ilustran sobre constantes antropológicas y sociales de las culturas mediterráneas y pueden ser muy útiles desde diversos puntos de vista, teniendo en cuenta que los Evangelios han sido editados en griego para lectores, judíos o gentiles, de habla griega.

El objetivo de este artículo es analizar una perícopa evangélica mostrando esquemáticamente los tres tipos de textos que nos ayudan a mejor comprender el relato del escriba cristiano. Nos fijaremos en la perícopa de Mc 1,21–26, *Un sábado en la sinagoga de Cafarnaúm: la expulsión de un espíritu inmundo*, y nos centraremos en el exorcismo.[1]

---

[1] He elegido este relato por la abundancia de textos qumránicos que nos ayudan a ilustrarlo. Sigo así una preocupación del Prof. García Martínez, manifiesta en numerosos artículos suyos.

1. La estructura

En el relato de Mc el exorcismo (vv. 23–27a) se inserta en una información sobre la enseñanza de Jesús con autoridad (vv. 22 y 27b), de donde resulta que la autoridad de Jesús queda ilustrada no sólo en la enseñanza, sino en el poder sobre los demonios. Tal estructura parece obra del redactor, pues se dejan ver costuras no muy bien disimuladas: el asombro lleno de admiración por el contraste con la enseñanza de los escribas (v. 22), se transforma en espanto en el v. 27. Pero todo el relato lleva el sello característico de Mc en esta jornada, a saber, la prisa y el acontecer frenético: todo ocurre apresuradamente, desde que entran en Cafarnaúm e inmediatamente (εὐθύς) está enseñando en la sinagoga, donde en seguida (εὐθύς) aparece un poseído, hasta que rápidamente (εὐθύς) su fama se divulga.

Es propio de Mc (a quien sigue Lc) la inserción de este exorcismo en el sumario tradicional de la enseñanza. Aunque el exorcismo tenga un origen independiente, Mc muestra la autoridad de la palabra de Jesús por las obras poderosas que la acompañan; en la enseñanza de Jesús se incluye su poder contra los demonios: Jesús enseña no sólo una doctrina, sino también quién es él y con qué poder actúa; y curiosamente esa enseñanza sobre Jesús la proclama el demonio. Con esta inclusión quedan mejor explicadas la admiración, el espanto y la fama.

2. El escenario y los personajes

El escenario está perfectamente montado: un sábado, en la sinagoga de Cafarnaúm. Contexto urbano y sagrado en un día santo. Es programático del Evangelio de Mc que el primer milagro de Jesús se realice en un lugar santo, en el día santo y entre el Santo de Dios y el espíritu inmundo.

En todo el relato sólo se nombra por su nombre a *Jesús* (vv. 24 y 25). En la conclusión (vv. 27–28) se advierte cómo toda la narración está orientada cristológicamente: la novedad de Jesús frente a los escribas, su superioridad frente a los demonios, la fama ante la gente.

Como un coro está *la comunidad sinagogal*, que resalta la autoridad de Jesús frente a los escribas (v. 22), aclama la autoridad de Jesús en la enseñanza nueva y en el poder sobre los espíritus impuros (v. 27), y proclamará la fama de Jesús por toda Galilea (v. 28).

En el exorcismo, quedan *Jesús y el endemoniado solos*. Dos poderes sobrenaturales frente a frente, el Espíritu de Dios en Jesús (Mc 1,10–12) frente al espíritu de Satanás, Jesús frente al mal puro; la derrota de Satanás es la inauguración del Reinado de Dios (cf. Mt 12,28 y Lc 11,20).

3. Textos fuente[2]

—Nah 2,1: "Ve ahí sobre las montañas los pies del *heraldo que anuncia* (מבשר משמיע; LXX εὐαγγελιζομένου καὶ ἀπαγγέλλοντος) la paz. Celebra, ¡oh Judá!, tus fiestas, cumple tus votos, pues no volverá a pasar por ti *el perverso* (בליעל), *ha sido exterminado por completo*".

Beliyyaʿal es nombre del diablo. En el AT aparece como divinidad de los infiernos: "los torrentes de *Beliyyaʿal*" (2 Sam 22,5; Sal 18,5), torrentes destructores, y se usa preferentemente como nombre determinante de personas o cosas para expresar su maldad;[3] en Nah 2,1 encarna la maldad de la ciudad de Nínive. La ubicación de la escena de Mc en "la villa de Nahum" es intencionada; en la expulsión del espíritu impuro, la primera acción salvadora de Jesús, se cumple Nah 2,1: ha llegado el heraldo del Evangelio y *"Beliyyaʿal* ha sido exterminado por completo".[4] La referencia a *Beliyyaʿal* en nuestra perícopa me parece tanto más clara por la única referencia que a él tenemos en el NT: 2 Cor 6,15, "¿Qué sintonía (συμφώνησις) hay de Cristo con Belial?", perfectamente paralela a Mc 1,24: "¿Qué tenemos nosotros contigo, Jesús Nazareno?".

—Mal 3,1–2: "He aquí que envío mi mensajero para que prepare el camino ante mí, y vendrá *de súbito* (ופתאם) a su Templo el Señor…(2) Y ¿quién podrá soportar el día de su venida? *¿Y quién es el que podrá seguir en pie cuando Él se manifieste?*".

La *inmediatez* (εὐθύς) con que Jesús entra en la Sinagoga para enfrentarse con el espíritu inmundo aparece también como el cumplimiento

---

[2] Nos circunscribimos aquí a la búsqueda de textos bíblicos fuente referentes al exorcismo. Por razón de brevedad, dejamos aparte los referentes a la enseñanza nueva.

[3] Dt 13,14; 15,9; Jue 19,22; 20,13; 1 Sm 1,16; 2,12; 10,27; 25,17; 2 Sam 20,1; 22,5; 1 Re 21,10.13; 2 Cr 13,7; Job 34,18; Sal 18,5; 41,9; 101,3; Prov 6,12; 16,27; 19,28; Nah. 1,11; 2,1.

[4] Nah 2,1 es el único texto fuera de Isaías donde se encuentra εὐαγγελιζομένου. La referencia a este texto parece intencionada, pues Mc 1,21–22, en la sinagoga de Cafarnáum, es un calco de Mc 6,1–2, en la sinagoga de Nazaret (cf. comentarios).

de este texto. La alusión a Mal 3,1 no es sorprendente, toda vez que es el texto que abre el Evangelio (Mc 1,2).[5]

—Zac 13,1–2: "En aquel tiempo habrá una fuente abierta para la casa de David y los moradores de Jerusalén para [lavar] el pecado y la impureza (2) Y sucederá en aquel día—oráculo de Yhwh Sebaot— que extirparé del país los nombres de los ídolos y no serán ya mencionados, y asimismo *expulsaré del país a los profetas y el espíritu de impureza* (רוח הטמאה; LXX τὸ πνεῦμα τὸ ἀκάθαρτον)".

Sólo aquí en todo el AT tenemos el sintagma "espíritu de impureza", por lo que resulta muy probable que el evangelista esté pensando en el cumplimiento del oráculo, tanto más cuanto el espíritu impuro carece de nombre en el exorcismo.

—1 Re 17,17–24: "(17) Tras estos sucesos ocurrió que cayó enfermo el hijo de la dueña de la casa [la viuda de Sarepta], y su enfermedad se agravó tanto que ya se quedó sin respiración (18) Dijo entonces ella a Elías: «*¿Qué tengo yo contigo, hombre de Dios* (מה לי ולך איש האלהים? *¿Has venido a mí para recordar mi culpa y matar a mi hijo?*». (19) Elías le contestó: «¡Dame tu hijo!». El tomóle del regazo de ella, le subió al aposento superior, donde él moraba, y le acostó sobre su lecho. (20) Entonces clamó a Yhwh y dijo: «Yhwh, mi Dios, también a la viuda de que soy huésped causarás mal, haciendo morir a su hijo?». (21) Y tendióse sobre el niño tres veces y clamó a Yhwh y dijo. «¡Yhwh mi Dios, vuelva, te ruego, el alma de este niño a su interior!». (22) Yhwh escuchó la voz de Elías, y el alma del niño volvió a su interior y revivió. (23) Entonces Elías tomó al niño, le bajó del aposento superior de la casa y le entregó a su madre, y Elías exclamó: «Ve ahí vivo a tu hijo». (24) La mujer contestó a Elías: «*Ahora sé que eres hombre de Dios y que la palabra de Yhwh es verdad en tu boca*».

Este texto ha sido visto por todos los comentaristas como inspirador o influyente en el relato evangélico. No se trata de ningún exorcismo, pero sí del terror que provoca la presencia de Elías, un hombre de Dios, que viene precedido por la fama del celo que le devora (1 Re 19,10.14), manifiesta en la venganza sobre los profetas de Baal (1 Re 18,40) y

---

[5] Mc 1,2 cita un texto híbrido de Ex 23,20 y Mal 3,1 (cf. comentarios), pero referidos al Bautista. No es extraño que con el mismo texto se haga aquí alusión a Jesús. Las tradiciones de Elías (Mal 3,23–24), muy populares, parece fueron usadas por los primeros narradores cristianos para presentar a Jesús.

sobre los 50 hombres de Ocozías: el hombre de Dios (אִישׁ הָאֱלֹהִים) no puede menos de evocar al fuego de Dios (אֵשׁ הָאֱלֹהִים). Es explicable que el terror de la mujer en el relato de Elías se transfiera al terror del demonio en el relato de Mc. Las similitudes literarias son evidentes: La reacción de la mujer ante Elías (v. 18) es semejante a la del demonio ante Jesús: "¿Qué tenemos nosotros contigo, Jesús nazareno? ¿Viniste a perdernos?" (Mc 1,24); la mujer identifica a Elías como "hombre de Dios" (vv. 18 y 24), y el espíritu inmundo identifica a Jesús como "el Santo de Dios" (Mc 1,24).[6] Pese a las diferencias entre ambos relatos (curación y exorcismo), la atracción se ha realizado porque en ambos casos se trata de mostrar el poder del "hombre de Dios" (Elías) y del "Santo de Dios" (Jesús).

La expresión "Santo de Dios", como la de "hombre de Dios",[7] es propiamente un título profético, que se aplica a Elías, Eliseo y personajes carismáticos: Moisés (Sab 11,1), Aarón, "el santo de Yhwh" (Sal 106,16);[8] designa, pues, a los que Dios consagra, aplicándose también colectivamente al pueblo de Israel, y, en el NT, a los cristianos como pueblo de Dios. En nuestra perícopa, "Santo de Dios" está también en relación con el adjetivo "nazareno", ambos atributos de Jesús en el mismo v. 24. Junto a la forma Ναζαρηνός,[9] que se refiere al origen geográfico, se encuentra también Ναζωραῖος,[10] que al mismo tiempo puede hacer referencia al nazireato: en Jue 13,7 y 16,17 la expresión, referida a Sansón, ναζιραῖον (LXX A) se transforma en ἅγιον θεοῦ en LXX B. Estos textos, conocidos de los escribas cristianos, debieron facilitar la representación de Elías, el hombre de Dios, por Jesús el Nazareno, el Santo de Dios.

---

[6] En ambos casos, la identificación del oponente figura como fórmula defensiva (cf. *infra*). No pueden, por tanto, las palabras del espíritu impuro entenderse como profesión de fe, sino como defensa o intento de anular el poder del conjurador mediante su reconocimiento y la pronunciación de su nombre y título.

[7] *SDt* 342 enumera a las diez personas que reciben en la Biblia el título de "hombre de Dios: Moisés (Dt 33,1; Sal 90,1), Elqanah (1 Sm 2,27); Samuel (1 Sam 9,6); David (Neh 12,24); Semaya (1 Re 12,22), Iddo (1 Re 13,1), Elías (2 Re 1,13), Eliseo (2 Re 4,9), Miqueas (1 Re 20,28), Amós (2 Cr 25,7).

[8] Cf. Ex 29,44.

[9] Mc 1,24; 10,47; 14,67; 16,6; Lc 4,34; 24,19.

[10] Mt 2,23; 26,71; Lc 18,37; Jn 18,5.7; 19,19; Hch 2,22; 3,6; 4,10; 6,14; 22,8; 24,5; 26,9. Es otra forma de designar a los originarios de Nazaret, pero fácilmente, por *remez*, puede referirse al *nazir*, el que se consagra a Dios con el triple voto de no cortarse el cabello, no beber licor y no contaminarse con cadáver (Nm 6,1–8).

4. Textos contextuales privilegiados

(a) *Textos bíblicos*

No hay en la Biblia Hebrea relatos propios de exorcismos. El monoteísmo del AT excluía otros poderes en pie de igualdad con el único Dios. Sin embargo, hay algunos textos que han tenido un desarrollo importante en la tradición exorcista: cuando Saúl es agitado por un mal espíritu se llama a David para que al sonido del arpa el espíritu se marche: 1 Sm 16,23;[11] este texto hace que fórmulas de exorcismo qumránicas se introduzcan en salmos atribuidos a David: 11Q11 (cf. *infra*); *LAB* 60,1 (cf. *infra*) reformula el texto bíblico dando énfasis a la expulsión del mal espíritu. Salomón, por su sabiduría, se convierte, en la tradición judía, en el exorcista por excelencia: era conocedor de proverbios, árboles, plantas y toda clase de animales (1 Re 5,10–13), de donde la confesión que se encuentra en Sab 7,17–21. La creencia en que los demonios podían poseer a una persona (el precedente es Saúl) llegó a ser muy popular, como lo demuestra la historia deuterocanónica de Tobías y Sara: Tob 3,8.17; en el mismo libro se describe todo un ritual exorcista: Tob 6,17s; 8,2–3.

(b) *Textos judíos extrabíblicos*

—Los espíritus perversos e impuros y sus nombres

El espíritu impuro (רוח הטמאה), lit. "espíritu de impureza", es designación que encontramos en la literatura tannaítica. Comentando Dt 18,11–12 (sobre las prácticas cananeas de adivinación y magia, encantamientos y evocación de muertos), *SDt* 173 (a Dt 18,12) lee: "Cuando R. Eliezer llegaba a este versículo [Dt 18,12] decía: «¡Ay de nosotros! Si quien se adhiere a la impureza, *un espíritu impuro* habita en él, se deduce que quien se adhiere a la Šekinah, el espíritu santo habitará en él". La razón de este comentario es que existía la práctica de ir a los cementerios, donde residen los espíritus impuros, para invocar a los muertos (cf. *bSanh* 65b).

---

[11] La sumisión del mal espíritu a Yhwh viene expresamente señalada en la narración bíblica: vv. 14.15.29. Pero es difícil establecer si al mal espíritu supone la creencia en "espíritus demoníacos" o es mera tradición literaria para expresar la tortuosa psicología de Saúl.

La creencia popular en los espíritus perversos e impuros la encontramos ya en el Libro de los Jubileos, donde aparecen estos espíritus, "perversos y creados para destruir", con "Mastema, príncipe de los espíritus": véase *Jub* 10,1–11 y 12,20.[12]

En el libro etiópico de Enoc el ángel Rafael es encargado de encadenar a Azazel y de anunciar la restauración de la tierra corrompida por los vigilantes: *1 En* 10,4–8.

En los TestXII se encuentran numerosas referencias, p.ej., *TestBenjamín* 5,2; *TestNeftalí* 8,4; *TestLeví* 18,12; *TestIsacar* 7,7. Creencia popular es que las pesadillas y malos deseos durante el sueño son debidos a estos espíritus "malvados e impuros" que toman posesión de una persona: *TestSimeón* 4,8–9.[13] A los nombres de Mastema y Satanás, como jefes de los espíritus perversos, se une también el de Belial, Beelzebul, Azazel, Sammael, etc.[14]

Casi cien menciones de Belial hay en los mss. de Qumrán (*DJD* 39:245–46). En el *Documento de Damasco*, Belial es el demonio propio de Israel, siempre sujeto a Dios: CD-A IV 13–15: "*Belial* será enviado contra Israel, como ha dicho Dios por medio del profeta Isaías, hijo de Amoz: «Pánico, fosa y red contra tí, habitante del país» (Is 24,17)…" (cf. CD-A V 18; VIII 2; XII 2; XIX 14).

"El dominio o imperio de Belial" es expresión característica de la Regla de la Comunidad (1QS)[15] y de la Regla de la Guerra (1QM)[16] para designar el período en el que los hijos de Israel se entregan a transgresiones. Frente a los hijos de la luz están los hijos de las tinieblas, "el ejército de Belial" (1QM I 1.13; XV 3; XVIII 1) o "el lote de Belial" (1QS II 5; 1QM I 5; IV 2; XIII 2.12; 4Q257 II 1; 4Q496; 4Q177 III 8; IV 16; 11Q13 II 12), "las hordas de Belial" (1QM XI 8;

---

[12] Cf. también *Jub* 7,27: (Visión de Noé) "Veo que los demonios han comenzado a seduciros, a vosotros y a vuestros hijos, y temo por vosotros, que, tras mi muerte, derraméis sangre humana en la tierra y desaparezcáis también de su faz". En *TestNeft* 5,2: "Si obráis el bien, incluso los espíritus inmundos se apartarán de vosotros y las fieras mismas os temerán".

[13] La actuación en el sueño, es obra de las diablesas (*TanjB Berešit* 17.26.27, final). Sobre los demonios femeninos, *TestSalomón* 4;8.

[14] *TgPsʒ Gn* 3,4.6; 4,1; 5,3. En *TestSalomón* se mencionan numerosos nombres de demonios. Beelzebul en *TestSalomón* 3,6: "Le pregunté (Yo, Salomón): ¿Quién eres tú? El diablo respondió: Yo soy *Beelzebul*, príncipe de los demonios"; ampliamente en *TestSalomón* 6. En la Misnah sólo en *Abot* 5,6 se mencionan a los *mazziqin*, "espíritus dañinos", entre las cosas creadas la víspera del sábado.

[15] 1QS I 18.24; II 19.

[16] 1QM XIV 9; 4Q491 8–10 i 6. También en el Pseudo-Moisés (4Q390 2 i 4), en la *Catena* (4Q177 III 8).

XVIII 3); Belial es el jefe de los espíritus, ángeles de destrucción (1QM XIII 12; 4Q177 III 10; IV 14); los espíritus de Belial pueden dominar en un hombre (CD-A XII 2). En los himnos (*Hodayot*) se usa Belial como en la Biblia Hebrea: nombre determinante de personas o cosas para expresar su maldad: proyectos diabólicos,[17] asamblea diabólica, torrentes traicioneros (1QH[a] X 18.24; XI 30.33; XII 14; XIII 28); Belial es la expresión de la maldad: XI 29; XII 11; Belial es el consejero del corazón de los pervertidos (XIV 24; XV 6). Otras expresiones son "las trampas de Belial" en el *Pešer de Salmos* (4Q171, II 10–11); "los hijos de Belial" en el *Florilegio* (4Q174 I 8) y en el *Rollo del Templo* (11Q19 LV 3); "un hijo de Belial planeará oprimir a mi pueblo" (4Q386 [psEzequiel[b]] II 3); "uno de Belial" en *Testimonia* (4Q175 23); "la mano (el poder) de Belial" (CD VIII 2; XIX 14; 4Q177 IV 12; 5Q13 5 2; 11Q13 II 13.25); "la maquinación malvada y el consejo de Belial" (4QMMT C 29). "No guardar a Belial en el corazón" significa desterrar las obscenidades, mentiras, engaños de la lengua (1QS X 21). Se desprende, pues, que para los qumranitas Belial era el jefe de los espíritus perversos, el principal opresor de Israel, que podía adueñarse de cualquiera.

La mención de Belial (o Beliar) es frecuente en los Testamentos: *TestDan* 5,1; *TestAser* 6,4–5; *TestZabulón* 9,8.

—*Exorcismos en Qumrán*
El *Apócrifo del Génesis* de Qumrán describe a Abraham liberando al faraón de un espíritu maligno, con un ritual más sobrio: oración e imposición de manos:

—1QApGn XX 28–29: "Reza por mí y por mi casa, para que sea expulsado de nosotros ese espíritu perverso. Yo recé [...] (29) e impuse mis manos sobre su cabeza. La plaga fue removida de él; fue expulsado [de él el espíritu] perverso y vivió".

La *Oracion de Nabonida* es un testimonio de la actuación de un exorcista (Daniel) para curar la enfermedad del rey:

—*4QOración de Nabonida* (4Q242): "Palabras de la oración que rezó Nabonida, rey del país de Babilonia, [gran] rey, cuando fue afligido por una inflamación maligna, por decreto del Di[os Altí]simo en Teimán. [Yo, Nabonida], fui afligido [por una inflamación maligna] durante siete

---

[17] También 4Q174 I 8.

años y fui relegado lejos [de los hombres hasta que recé al Dios Altísimo] y mi pecado lo perdonó un exorcista (נזר).[18] Era un [hombre] judío de los desterrados, [el cual me dijo:] Proclama por escrito para que se dé gloria, exal[tación y honor] al Nombre del Di[os Altísimo]…"

Los Cánticos del Sabio de Qumrán es un texto compuesto por el instructor (*maskil*) para exorcizar a los demonios mediante la alabanza a Dios. La obra se componía de una serie indeterminada de salmos de exorcismo.[19] Algunos autores piensan que estos salmos estaban destinados a ser usados como verdadero ritual de exorcismo; otros sugieren que servían para ser recitados con el fin de proteger a la comunidad del influjo de los malos espíritus:[20]

—*4QCánticos del Sabio*ᵃ (4Q510) 1,4ss: "Y yo, el instructor, proclamo la majestad de su esplendor a fin de asustar y aterrorizar a todos los espíritus de los ángeles destructores y los espíritus bastardos, demonios, Lilits, búhos y [chacales]".

Entre los escritos de Qumrán se encuentran otras tres composiciones (*Salmos Apócrifos*) atribuidas a David con fórmulas de conjuro contra los malos espíritus.[21] En ellos se muestra una práctica exorcista ya avanzada: mención de Salomón, interpelación de los demonios, nombres de demonios (entre los cuales Belial y Satán), invocación de los ángeles (entre los cuales Rafael), pregunta agresiva sobre la identidad del demonio, conocimiento de los demonios de las acciones poderosas de Yhwh, temblor y temor de los demonios ante Yhwh:

—*11QSalmos Apócrifos*ᵃ (11Q11)[22] II 2–6: "(2) [De David. Sobre las palabras de conjuro] en nombre de [Yhwh…] (3) […] de Salomón, e

---

[18] *Gazer*, que puede significar "adivino" (Dn 2,27; 4,4; 5,7.11), tiene aquí el sentido de exorcista, según autores de prestigio. De la raíz *gzr*, "decretar", el *gazer* es el que decreta la expulsión del demonio. Importante para la exégesis neotestamentaria sería que el exorcista—si la interpretación es correcta—no expulsa a un demonio, sino que cura la enfermedad y perdona los pecados (Mc 2,2–12).

[19] Los fragmentos que nos han quedado proceden de comienzos del s. I d.C.

[20] Cf. F. García Martínez, "Textos de Qumrán", en *Literatura judía intertestamentaria* (por G. Aranda et al.; Estella: Verbo Divino, 2000), 185–86. "Sectarians believed they could be magically protected from demonic forces by praising God" (L.H. Schiffman, *Reclaiming the Dead Sea Scrolls* [Philadelphia: Jewish Publication Society, 1994], 364).

[21] El manuscrito fue copiado también a comienzos del s. I d.C., pero el texto podría ser anterior a la secta. Cf. García Martínez, "Textos de Qumrán", 186–87.

[22] Damos el texto según la traducción y reconstrucción de García Martínez. La numeración de las columnas está equivocada en la edición española. Cf. F. García Martínez y E.J.C. Tigchelaar, *The Dead Sea Scrolls Study Edition* (Leiden: Brill, 1997–1998).

invocará [el nombre de Yhwh] (4) [para que le libere de toda plaga de los es]píritus, de los demonios, [Lilits,] (5) [búhos y chacales.] Éstos son los demonios, y el príncipe de hostilidad (6) [es Belial] que [domina] sobre el abismo de tinieblas…"

—III 1–11: (1) […Y le dirás: ¿quién] (2) eres? [¿Has hecho tú los cielos y] los abismos [y todo lo que contienen], (3) la tierra y todo lo que hay sobre la tierra? ¿Quién ha he[cho estos signos] (4) y estos prodi[gios sobre la] tierra? Es él, Yhwh, [el que] (5) ha hecho to[do esto por su poder,] conjurando a todos los [ángeles a venir en su ayuda,] (6) a toda semi[lla santa] que está en su presencia, [y el que juzga] a (7) [los hijos del] cielo y [a toda la] tierra por causa de ellos, porque enviaron sobre (8) [toda la tierra] el pecado, y sobre todo hom[bre el mal. Pero] ellos (9) conocen [sus acciones maravillo]sas, que ninguno de ellos [puede hacer ante Yhw]h. Sino que (10) [tiemblan] ante Yhwh, para […y] destruir el alma, (11) [les juzgará] Yhwh y temerán este gran [castigo]…".

—IV 2–12: "(2) […Y enviará un ángel] poderoso y te ex[pulsará] de (3) toda la tierra. […] cielos […](4) Golpeará Yhwh un gol[pe podero]so que es para destruirte [por siempre,] (5) y en el furor de su cólera [enviará] contra tí un ángel poderoso [para ejecutar] (6) todas sus órdenes, [uno] que [no tendrá piedad] contigo, que […] (7) […] sobre todos éstos, que te [arrojará] al gran abismo, (8) [al Šeol] más profundo. Le[jos de la morada de la luz] habitarás, pues es oscuro (9) en extremo el gran [abismo. No dominarás] más sobre la tierra, (10) [sino que estarás encerrado] por siempre. [Maldito serás tú] con las maldiciones del Abadón, (11) [y castigado por] el furor de la ira de Y[hwh. Tú dominarás sobre]las tinieblas por todos (12) [los períodos de] la humillaciones…".

—V 2–13: "(2) que […] los poseídos […] (3) los voluntarios de tu ver[dad, cuando Ra]fael los cura…. *Vacat.* (4) De David. So[bre las palabras de con]juro en nombre de Yhwh. [Invoca en to]do tiempo (5) a los cielos. [Cuando] venga sobre tí Beli[al, tú] le dirás: (6) ¿Quién eres tú, [maldito entre] el hombre y la semilla de los santos? Tu rostro es un rostro (7) de vanidad, y tus cuernos son cuernos de mise[rable]. Tú eres tiniebla y no luz, (8) [ini]quidad y no justicia. [Contra tí,] el jefe del ejército. Yhwh te [encerrará] (9) [en el Še]ol más profundo, [cerrará] las dos puertas de bronce, por [las que] no (10) [atraviesa] la luz. No [te alumbrará la luz del] sol que [se alza] (11) [sobre el] justo para [iluminar su rostro.] Tú le dirás: ¿Acaso [no hay un ángel] (12) [con el jus]to para ir [al juicio cuando] lo maltrata Sa[tán? Y le librará](13) [el espíritu de la ver]dad de las tinie[blas, porque la justi]cia está con él [para sostenerlo en el juicio]".[23]

En la *Regla de la Guerra*, donde los ángeles de Dios[24] librarán la batalla final contra los malos espíritus, y en las *Bendiciones* tenemos fórmulas de execración directas contra Belial:

—*1QRegla de la Guerra* (1QM) XIII 1–5: "(1)...sus hermanos los sacerdotes y los levitas y todos los ancianos de la regla con él. Y bendecirán desde sus posiciones al Dios de Israel y a todas las obras de su verdad, y execrarán (2) allí a Belial y a todos los espíritus de su lote. Tomarán la palabra y dirán: Bendito sea el Dios de Israel en todo su designio santo y en las obras de su verdad, (3) y benditos todos los que le sirven en justicia, quienes le conocen en la fe. *Vacat*. (4) Maldito sea Belial en su designio hostil, sea execrado por su dominio impío. Malditos sean todos los espíritus de su lote en su designio, *Vacat* impío, (5) sean execrados por sus obras de impureza inmunda. Pues ellos son el lote de las tinieblas, y el lote de Dios es para la luz eterna".

—*4QBerakot* (4Q286), frag. 10, col II:[25] "[Los hombres del] (1) consejo de la comunidad dirán, todos juntos: «amén, amén». *vacat*. Y después execrarán a (2) Belial y a todo su lote culpable. Tomarán la palabra y dirán: «Maldito sea Belial en su designio de hostilidad, (3) y sea execrado su servicio culpable. Y malditos sean todos los espíritus de su lote en sus designios impuros, (4) y execrados sean en sus designios de impureza inmunda. Porque [ellos son el lote] de las tinieblas, y su visita será (5) para el foso eterno. Amén, amén». *Vacat*. «Y maldito sea el impío [...] de su dominio, y sean execrados (6) todos los hijos de Belial en todas las iniquidades de sus funciones hasta su exterminación [por siempre. Amén, amén.] *Vacat*. (7) Y [maldito sea...án]gel de la fosa el espí[ritu de la des]trucción en todos los proyectos de tu inclinación (8) [culpable...] y en tu consejo impío. Y execrado seas en el do[minio del] (9) [...]

---

[23] García Martínez ("Textos de Qumrán", 187) menciona otro fragmento arameo breve (4Q560), aún no publicado, donde se pueden identificar fórmulas de conjuro de malos espíritus e interpelaciones a los demonios.

[24] En la guerra escatológica son nombrados los ángeles Miguel, Gabriel, Sariel y Rafael (1QM IX 15–16). El jefe de los ángeles es Miguel, "el príncipe de la luz", que entrega a Belial, ángel de la hostilidad, a la fosa (1QM XIII 10–11).

[25] En la *The Dead Sea Scrolls Study Edition*, frag. 7, col. ii.

con todas las hu[millaciones del Še]ol y con […] (10) […] destrucción […] por la ira destructora de [Dios…] Amén, amén. (11) [Y malditos sean] todos los que obran [sus proyectos im]píos y los que implantan la iniquidad [en sus corazones para conspirar] (12) [contra la alianza de] Dios y para […] y para cambiar los preceptos [de la Ley]»".

—Exorcismos en Flavio Josefo
Flavio Josefo es un testigo importante de la práctica exorcista en su tiempo, considerada como un medio para curar enfermedades. Remonta a Salomón el arte de expulsar demonios (la fama de Salomón está asentada en los datos bíblicos, como ya hemos visto) y describe, como testigo ocular, la práctica exorcista de un tal Eleazar:

—Ant 8.46: "(Salomón) compuso encantamientos para aliviar las enfermedades y dejó la manera de usar los exorcismos mediante los cuales se alejan los demonios para que no vuelvan jamás. Este método curativo se sigue usando mucho entre nosotros hasta el día de hoy. He visto a un hombre de mi propia patria, llamado Eleazar, librando endemoniados en presencia de Vespasiano… La forma de curar era la siguiente: acercaba a las fosas nasales del endemoniado un anillo que tenía en el sello una raíz de una de las clases mencionadas por Salomón, lo hacía aspirar y le sacaba el demonio por la nariz. El hombre caía inmediatamente al suelo y él conjuraba al demonio a que no volviera nunca más, siempre mencionando a Salomón y recitando el encantamiento que había compuesto. Cuando Eleazar quería convencer y demostrar a los espectadores que poseía ese poder, ponía a cierta distancia una copa llena de agua o una palangana y ordenaba al demonio, cuando salía del interior del hombre, que la derramara, haciendo saber de este modo al público que había abandonado al hombre. Hecho esto quedaban claramente expresadas las habilidades y la sabiduría de Salomón".

—Exorcismos en los Apócrifos del AT
El PseudoFilón (*Liber antiquitatum Biblicarum*) transmite la imagen de David exorcista contra el espíritu maligno que ahogaba a Saúl: después de parafrasear 1 Sm 16,14–23 (*LAB* 60,1), continúa con una forma típica de exorcismo:

—LAB 60,3: "Ahora tú, criatura inferior, no seas molesta. Si no, acuérdate del tártaro en que te mueves. ¿No te basta oír el salmo que repito al

son que resuena en tu presencia? ¿No recuerdas que, por una rebelión, vuestro linaje fue fulminado al abismo? Te confundirá *la nueva familia* de que he nacido; de ella, *de mis lomos, nacerá luego el que os subyugará.* Cuando David cantaba, el espíritu no molestaba a Saúl"

La nueva familia es la del propio David, de cuyos lomos nacerá Salomón, el vencedor de los demonios (cf. nota de Alfonso de la Fuente a su traducción española). Algunos autores plantean si la aclamación a Jesús como "hijo de David" cuando cura a un endemoniado ciego y mudo (Mt 12,22–45), no hará referencia al poder de Salomón, el hijo de David. La afirmación de que Jesús es más grande que Salomón (Mt 12,42; Lc 11,31) puede interpretarse con referencia a su poder de expulsar demonios.

En el Libro de las Parábolas de Enoc, tras los nombres y funciones de los ángeles caídos, se anuncia la revelación del nombre del Hijo del Hombre y la aniquilación de los malos espíritus:

—*1 En* 55,4: "Reyes poderosos que habitáis la tierra: habréis de ver a mi Elegido, sentado en el Trono de mi Gloria, juzgar a Azazel, a toda su compañía y toda su hueste en nombre del Señor de los espíritus". *1 En* 69,26–28 puede ser una interpolación cristiana.

En *Testamento de Salomón*, los exorcismos se atribuyen a Salomón, que usa el ritual clásico: pregunta por el nombre del demonio y el anillo de Salomón como amuleto: *TestSalomón* 1,6; 2,1; 3,5. La pregunta por el nombre del demonio, también en *TestSalomón* 4,3; 5,2; 7,3; 8,2; 9,2; 10,1.4; 11,4; 12,1.6; 13,2; 14,2; 15,2; 17,1; 18,2.4; 25,1. El anillo de Salomón, también en *TestSalomón* 1,12; 3,3; 5,11; 7,3; 8,12; 10,7; 12,5 etc. La conminación a callarse, en *TestSalomón* 6,11. El temblor ante la presencia divina, *TestSalomón* 6,8.

—Literatura rabínica

Es explicable que en la tradición rabínica escaseen los exorcismos. Sólo en historias muy fantaseadas encontramos algunos relatos: Una leyenda en torno a R. Simón ben Yojai, famoso por sus milagros y parábolas, y R. Elazar ben Yose, narra un exorcismo:

—*bMeil* 17b: "[Iban hacia Roma R. Simón ben Yojai y R. Elazar ben Yose, cuando el demonio] Ben Temalión les salió al encuentro. «¿Permitís que vaya con vosotros?». R. Simón se puso a llorar y dijo: «La sierva de la casa de mi padre mereció encontrar a un ángel tres veces,[26] y yo ni siquiera una vez. ¡Que suceda el milagro como sea!».[27] Se adelantó [Ben Temalión] y entró en la hija del Emperador. Cuando [R. Simón] llegó dijo: «Ben Temalión, sal; Ben Temalión, sal». Y cuando le gritó, salió".

Entre las numerosas leyendas creadas en torno a Hanina ben Dosa está el encuentro con Igrat, hija de Mahalat, reina de los demonios, que salía las noches de miércoles y sábados con ochenta mil ángeles de la destrucción a perturbar a los trasnochadores. Hanina la despachó con un rotundo: "Si tanto se me estima en el Cielo, te ordeno que nunca vuelvas a pasar por lugar habitado" (*bPes* 112n).

Aunque falten historias más verosímiles, sí se dan elementos típicos de los exorcismos:

En *NmR* se encuentra una anécdota de Yojanán ben Zakkai desmitificadora de las prácticas mágicas exorcistas, incluso del ritual de la vaca roja:

—*NmR* 19,8 a 19,2: "Un idólatra preguntó a Rabban Yohanan ben Zakkai: «Los ritos que vosotros hacéis parecen una cierta magia, pues vosotros traéis una vaca, la quemáis, la trituráis y recogéis sus cenizas. Si uno de vosotros se contamina con un cadáver, lo rociáis dos o tres veces y le decís: estás purificado». R. Yojanán le contestó: «¿Nunca ha entrado en tí el espíritu de la locura?». Respondió: «No». «¿Tú sí has visto a alguien en quien haya entrado el espíritu de la locura?». Contestó: «Sí». Preguntó: «¿Y qué le hacéis?». «Llevamos raíces, las quemamos bajo sus pies, echamos agua sobre el demonio y huye». Le dijo R. Yohanán: «Oigan tus oídos lo que sale de tu boca. Así este espíritu (de locura) es también de impureza, como está escrito: 'Y expulsaré del país a los profetas (locos) y al espíritu de impureza' (Zac 13,2). El agua de la purificación se rocía sobre él y huye». Cuando se hubo marchado (el idólatra), le dijeron sus discípulos: «Maestro nuestro, a éste lo has despachado con una caña,[28] ¿pero cómo nos lo explicas a nosotros?». Les dijo: «¡Por vuestra vida! Ni el cadáver contamina ni el agua purifica, sino que el Santo, bendito sea, dice: Un mandato he mandado, una ley he legislado, tú no puedes violar mi ley, como está escrito: 'éste es el mandato de la Torah'[29] (Nm 19,2)»".

---

[26] Se refiere a Agar (Gn 16 y 21).
[27] Una forma de aceptar el acompañamiento de un ángel, aunque sea demonio.
[28] Con una improvisación o *battuta*.
[29] Referido al ritual de la vaca roja.

Hay que notar las referencias a la victoria definitiva sobre los demonios en la época mesiánica. La relectura targúmica de Gn 3,14–15 sitúa la victoria sobre la serpiente primordial (Sammael en la tradición de *PsJ*) en "el talón (del tiempo)", es decir, en los días del Rey Mesías": *TgN* y *PsJ* Gn 3,15.[30] Además de otros textos ya citados, seleccionamos:

—*SLv* a Lv 26,6 (*Behuqqotai prq 2, W 111a*): "«Os acostaréis sin que nadie os turbe» (Lv 26,6): no tendréis miedo de ninguna criatura. «Y haré desaparecer (*we-hišbatti*) del país la mala bestia» (*ibid.*). R. Yehudah decía: «Los sacará (*ma'abiram*) del mundo». R. Simón decía: «Los reducirá (*mašbitan*) para que no hagan daño». R. Simón decía: «¿Cuándo será (la mala bestia) alabanza de Dios? ¿Cuando ya no haya espíritus dañinos o cuando, aunque haya espíritus dañinos, ya no hagan daño? Has de afirmar que cuando existan espíritus dañinos pero ya no hagan daño». Y en este sentido el texto dice: «Salmo. Canción para el día del sábado (שבת)» (Sal 92,1): para desactivar (*le-mašbit*) del país los espíritus dañinos, los reduce (*mašbitan*) para que no hagan daño".[31]

—*PesR* 36,2: "¿Qué significa «Por tu luz vemos la luz» (Sal 36,10)? ¿Qué luz es la que ve la comunidad de Israel? Es la luz del Mesías, como está dicho: «Y vio Dios que la Luz era buena» (Gn 1,4), lo que quiere decir que el Santo, bendito sea, la contempló en el Mesías y sus obras antes de que el mundo fuera creado, y también que la ocultó (la Luz) al Mesías y su generación bajo el Trono de su Gloria. Dijo Satán ante el Santo, bendito sea: «Señor del mundo, ¿para quién es la luz que escondiste bajo tu Trono de Gloria?». Le contestó: «Para aquél que volverá a confundirte con vergüenza». Le dijo: «Señor del mundo, muéstramelo». Le contestó: «Ven y míralo». Y cuando lo vio, tembló[32] y cayó sobre su rostro diciendo: «Verdaderamente éste es el Mesías que vendrá a hundirme a mí y a todos los príncipes de los pueblos del mundo[33] en

---

[30] Ampliamente en M. Pérez Fernández, *Tradiciones mesiánicas en el Tárgum Palestinense: Estudios exegéticos* (Valencia: Institución San Jerónimo, 1981), 40ss. Sobre Sammael, *PRE* 13 y 14.

[31] La discusión midrásica se basa en el sentido *hif'il* del verbo *šabat*, "dar descanso, desactivar" o meramente "acallar o reducir". El salmo sabático 92 decide: vv. 8.12. El supuesto es que tal reducción se realiza en la edad mesiánica. Sobre la victoria sobre el demonio en la edad mesiánica, cf. *supra 1 En* 55,4; *TestLeví* 18,12; *TestZabulón* 9,8; *TestMoisés* 10,1 etc.

[32] El estremecimiento de los demonios ante Dios o sus enviados es característico.

[33] Los príncipes del mundo es designación de los demonios. Cf. Jn 12,31; 14,30; 16,11.

la gehenna, como está dicho: «Destruirá para siempre a la Muerte,[34] y enjugará el Señor Yhwh las lágrimas de todos los rostros» (Is 25,8). En aquel momento, se estremecieron los pueblos y dijeron ante el Señor del mundo: «¿Quién es éste en cuya poder vamos a caer nosotros? ¿Cuál es su nombre? ¿Cuál su naturaleza?».[35] Les contestó el Santo, bendito sea: «Es el Mesías, y su nombre es Efraím, mi ungido justo»".

5. TEXTOS CONTEXTUALES SECUNDARIOS

—Papiros mágicos

La práctica de exorcismos, encantamientos y magia llegó a hacerse muy popular en todo el oriente helenístico, donde se mezclaron prácticas judías y cristianas con otras de procedencia babilónica y egipcia. A tal sincretismo se llegó por los intercambios de poblaciones y por el movimiento de mercaderes, soldados y predicadores. Así, no es extraño encontrar, en amuletos y conjuros, invocaciones a Jesús o a Yhwh (con nombres deformados o apenas reconocibles) junto a invocaciones a dioses griegos y egipcios. Fue en los dos primeros siglos de la era cristiana cuando la magia llegó a su apogeo: "En ella se refleja la inseguridad religiosa de las masas de esta época, que ya no tenían fe en la ayuda de los antiguos dioses y se refugiaban en la coacción mágica de dioses y démones".[36] La existencia de libros de magia es testificada en Hch 19,19: "Y bastantes de los que habían practicado las artes mágicas, amontonando los libros que habían traído, los quemaban a vista de todos. Y habiendo calculado sus precios, hallaron ser de cincuenta mil monedas de plata". Entre los numerosos amuletos y papiros mágicos resaltamos el *Papiro Mágico de París*, escrito en Egipto en torno al 300 d.C.,[37] donde se pueden apreciar formas y fórmulas típicas de exorcismos que, aquí más desarrollados, ya encontramos en textos anteriores: la preparación del material vegetal curativo, la invocación de los dioses, la inscripción en un metal, la indagación por el nombre del demonio y el mandato al demonio de salir.

---

[34] El midrás entiende "Muerte" como nombre del demonio.
[35] La identificación del demonio es característico de los relatos exorcistas.
[36] J. Leipoldt y W. Grundmann, *El Mundo del Nuevo Testamento* (Madrid: Ediciones Cristiandad, 1973), 1:85.
[37] Texto en A. Deissmann, *Licht vom Osten. Das Neue Testament und die neuentdeckten Texte der hellenistisch-römischen Welt* (4. ed.; Tübingen: Mohr, 1923), 217ss.

6. Conclusión

Continuando la representación de Elías, Jesús—tras la investidura por el Espíritu, la estancia en el desierto y la llamada a los primeros discípulos—e presenta como el profeta carismático (1 Re 17,17–24; Mal 3,1–2), poderoso en palabras y obras (cf. Lc 24,19)—como Elías y también como Moisés (cf. Hch 7,22)—, que arroja a los espíritus impuros (Nah 2,1) y cumple el oráculo de Zac 13,2.

El nombre de Jesús, "el Santo de Dios" o "el Nazireo de Dios", desvelado por el espíritu impuro en fórmula de autodefensa, debe entenderse en el macrotexto marcano como el "Hijo de Dios" del título inicial (1,1), que es el nombre que identifican también los espíritus impuros (3,11), y es la confesión del centurión al final del Evangelio (15,39). Sólo en estos tres lugares usa Mc el título "Hijo de Dios", lo que le da mayor relevancia.

Ya con los precedentes del AT, la praxis exorcista de Jesús le equiparaba a personajes como David, Salomón y el ángel Rafael.

Por otra parte, el testimonio del NT y el de los textos contextuales extrabíblicos muestra que los exorcismos eran práctica común en su tiempo: Mt 12,27–28; Lc 11,17–20; cf. Mc 3,22–27; estos textos afirman indirectamente que la práctica exorcista no era exclusiva de Jesús. Véase también Mc 9,38; Lc 9,49; Mt 7,22. La acusación de mago y endemoniado, que tan frecuentemente se hace a Jesús (Mc 3,22; Mt 9,34; 12,17.24; Lc 11,15–19; Jn 7,20; 8,46.52; 10,20) y que perdurará en la tradición talmúdica posterior confirma la historicidad básica de nuestro relato.

En el contexto de Mc la enseñanza se manifiesta también en el poder de su palabra para expulsar demonios. Si, como hemos comprobado abundantemente, los exorcismos no sorprendían en la época, sí era sorprendente el modo: con la fuerza sólo de su palabra. Entre los textos de exorcismos que hemos recordado, el paralelismo más próximo lo encontramos en Qumrán, donde es la oración—larga y suplicante, por lo general—la que se usa para ahuyentar a Belial; Jesús actúa sólo con un mandato en nombre propio (Mc 1,25; 5,8; 9,25). Nada hay en Jesús de las prácticas mágicas populares.

Por otra parte, la lucha de Jesús con el espíritu impuro tiene un carácter cósmico: es la irrupción del Reino de Dios y, para oídos de muchos judíos, se presentaba como el cumplimiento de la victoria final contra los príncipes de este mundo y finalmente contra la Muerte (cf. *Tg Gn* 3,15; *PesR* 36,2; *SLv* a Lv 26,6). Su forma de hablar hasta contra los vientos (Mc 4,41; en hebreo también רוח) esclarece el alcance cósmico de su lucha contra los espíritus perversos.

LA PARODIA DEL REY AGRIPA Y
EL ESCARNIO DEL *IESUS PATIENS*

Natalio Fernández Marcos

ὅτι θέατρον ἐγενήθημεν τῷ κόσμῳ καὶ ἀγγέλοις καὶ
ἀνθρώποις

(1 Cor 4,9)

El poder del espectáculo y el mimo en la sociedad del imperio romano
ha sido puesto de relieve en una reciente monografía.[1] En la tradición
evangélica de la pasión se narra una escena de cruel tortura psicoló-
gica, el escarnio de Jesús por parte de los soldados romanos antes de
ser conducido al suplicio de la cruz. Está descrita, con variantes, en
los tres sinópticos, el evangelio de Juan y el evangelio de Pedro, que
para algunos especialistas conserva el relato más antiguo de la pasión
mientras que para otros depende de la tradición sinóptica.[2] En todo
caso el relato del escarnio de Jesús se remonta, al parecer, a una tradición preevangélica. Si recoge un núcleo histórico interesa saber qué
indujo a los soldados romanos a llevar a cabo este tipo de burla. Y si
es construcción literaria de los evangelistas en torno a una tradición
de la comunidad, siempre queda el interrogante de esclarecer qué es
lo que llevó a los primeros cristianos a imaginar y describir este tipo
de acción sarcástica por parte de los romanos.

Hay muchas escenas evangélicas construidas sobre pasajes del Antiguo Testamento. La evocación o resonancia de pasajes muy conocidos
de la Escritura ha inducido en los autores del Nuevo Testamento una
construcción análoga pero referida ahora a los dichos y hechos de Jesús
de Nazaret. Lucas, sobre todo, es maestro en la *imitatio* del Antiguo
Testamento a través de la Septuaginta.[3] Sin embargo esta escena no

---

[1] C.A. Frilingos, *Spectacles of Empire. Monsters, Martyrs, and the Book of Revelation* (Philadelphia: University of Pennsylvania Press, 2004).

[2] "What is certain is that there is little exact verbal identity between this Gospel
and the New Testament Gospels; so the most probable hypothesis is that the compiler,
during the middle years of the second century, created his Gospel using both oral and
remembered written sources," concluye F. Lapham, *An Introduction to the New Testament
Apocrypha* (London: T&T Clark, 2003), 90.

[3] Cf. E. Plümacher, *Lukas als hellenistischer Schriftsteller. Studien zur Apostelgeschichte* (Göttingen: Vandenhoeck & Ruprecht, 1972), 38–72. Ver también C. Breytenbach y

parece inspirada en la tradición israelita del siervo sufriente de Yahveh recogida por Isaías, en el salmo 69 o en Sabiduría 2. Ya veremos más adelante si la figura de Sansón, héroe y víctima de los filisteos, según la Septuaginta, puede haber servido de modelo.

Se han buscado paralelos grecorromanos de esta escena en los mimos teatrales, en las fiestas carnavalescas de los Lacios, las Saturnales o las Cronias.[4] Pero ninguno de estos paralelos ofrece una solución satisfactoria. Mi intención es mostrar que la matriz judeo-helenística, y en concreto la parodia del rey Agripa descrita por Filón de Alejandría en su tratado *In Flaccum*, es el relato que mejor ilustra esta escena de la pasión. No hablo de dependencia literaria, en todo caso muy difícil de probar, sino que ambas escenas se iluminan mutuamente porque reflejan el contexto cultural del imperio romano común al mundo mediterráneo de entonces, están conectadas por la proximidad geográfica entre Jerusalén y Alejandría que se acrecienta con las peregrinaciones de los judíos de la diáspora a Jerusalén en las principales fiestas, y están unidas además por la proximidad cronológica, puesto que ambas escenas se sitúan dentro de la misma década, los años 30–40, del s. I d. C.

Veamos en primer lugar la narración de Filón (*Flacc* 36–39) para pasar después a la escena evangélica en sus diversas modulaciones:[5]

> Había un tal Carabas, un demente, no con la demencia salvaje y brutal—pues ésta es peligrosa para los que la padecen y para los de su entorno—sino con la demencia benigna y más suave. Éste vagaba día y noche desnudo por los caminos, sin protegerse ni del calor ni de la helada, un entretenimiento para los niños y muchachos desocupados. Todos a una empujan al desgraciado hasta el gimnasio y lo colocan en un estrado para que todo el mundo pueda verlo. Aplastan una hoja de papiro (βύβλον) y se la colocan sobre la cabeza a modo de diadema (ἀντὶ διαδήματος); le cubren el resto del cuerpo con una estera a modo de clámide (ἀντὶ χλαμύδος); y a modo de cetro uno de ellos le entrega un trozo pequeño de papiro (παπύρου τμῆμα) del país que había visto tirado en el camino. Una vez que había asumido, como en los mimos del teatro (ὡς ἐν θεατρικοῖς

J. Schröter, *Die Apostelgeschichte und die hellenistische Geschichtsschreibung. Festschrift für Eckhard Plümacher zu seinem 65. Geburtstag* (Leiden: Brill, 2004), y, con reservas porque no todas sus intuiciones se verifican y otras requerirían un análisis más preciso sobre los textos griegos de LXX y del Nuevo Testamento, las publicaciones de T.L. Brodie, en particular, *The Birthing of the New Testament. The Intertextual Development of the New Testament Writings* (Sheffield: Phoenix, 2004).

[4] Véase un buen resumen y abundante bibliografía en R.E. Brown, *La muerte del Mesías. Comentario a los relatos de la pasión de los cuatro evangelios. I Desde Getsemaní hasta el sepulcro* (Estella: Verbo Divino, 2005), 1013–31.

[5] Doy mi propia traducción del texto editado por A. Pelletier, *Les oeuvres de Philon d'Alexandrie. 31 In Flaccum. Introduction, Traduction et Notes* (Paris: Le Cerf, 1967), 68–70.

μίμοις), las insignias de la realeza y estaba revestido de rey, unos jóvenes a modo de lanceros con unos palos sobre los hombros lo escoltan por ambos lados imitando la guardia personal. Enseguida otros se adelantan, unos haciendo que lo saludan (ὡς ἀσπασόμενοι), otros simulando que eran juzgados (ὡς δικασόμενοι), otros como si le presentaran quejas sobre los asuntos públicos. A continuación, se oye un grito extraño entre el gentío que le rodeaba y que le llamaba *Marin*—así dicen que llaman al soberano (τὸν κύριον) entre los sirios—pues sabían que Agripa era sirio de raza y que reinaba sobre una parte importante de Siria.[6]

Se trata de un incidente ocurrido en Alejandría con motivo de la visita del rey Herodes Agripa I (10 a. C.–44 d. C.), nieto de Herodes del Grande, de paso hacia Palestina, para tomar posesión del reino que le había otorgado Cayo Calígula. Agripa se había educado en Roma con la familia imperial y era amigo personal de Calígula. En otoño del año 38 vuelve a Palestina a través de Alejandría para poner en orden los asuntos de su reino cliente o vasallo del emperador romano. Se trata del rey que, según los Hechos de los Apóstoles 12,1–23 hizo matar a Santiago, hermano de Juan, metió en prisión a Pedro y estaba furioso con los habitantes de Tiro y Sidón. El autor de los Hechos, siguiendo las convenciones literarias relativas a la muerte del que combate contra Dios o θεομάχος, dice que un ángel del Señor lo golpeó mientras estaba pronunciando un discurso en la sede del tribunal de Cesarea y expiró comido por los gusanos (σκωληκόβρωτος, cf. 12,23).[7] Sin embargo sabemos por Josefo que reinó durante tres años a plena satisfacción de los fariseos debido a su piedad y meticulosa observancia de la Ley mosaica y que murió de repente en una función pública en Cesarea el año 44 (*Ant* 19,343–54).[8] Como consecuencia de su política interna se opuso a la joven comunidad cristiana como aparece reflejado en el libro de los Hechos, pero fue un generoso promotor de la cultura griega.[9]

---

[6] Así se designaba entonces a Palestina como una parte administrativa de la provincia de Siria, cf. *Carta de Aristeas*, 11, 12 y 22.

[7] Contrastan las distintas imágenes que dan del mismo personaje Filón y el autor de los Hechos. Para Filón Herodes Agripa es el que se opone a Flaco, el prefecto de Egipto, auténtico θεομάχος y enemigo de los judíos de Alejandría, mientras que para el autor de los Hechos es el propio Agripa el θεομάχος de la incipiente comunidad cristiana, cf. P.W. van der Horst, "*In Flaccum* and the Book of Acts," en *Philo und das Neue Testament* (ed. R. Deines y K.-W. Niebuhr; WUNT 172; Tübingen: Mohr Siebeck, 2004), 95–105 (98). La misma descripción de la muerte del θεομάχος se aplica a Antioco Epifanés en 2 Mac 9,9.

[8] Cf. Flavio Josefo, *Ant* 19.356–359.

[9] E. Schürer, *The History of the Jewish People in the Age of Jesus Christ (175 B.C.–A.D 135)* (ed. G. Vermes et al.; 3 vol; Edinburgh: T&T Clark, 1973–1987), 1:442–54; y D.R. Schwartz, *Agrippa I: The Last King of Judaea* (TSAJ 23; Tübingen: Mohr Siebeck, 1990).

La parodia del rey Agripa y el escarnio de Jesús son dos escenas que tienen diversos puntos en común que conviene poner de relieve. Ambas ocurren o se localizan en la misma década, una en Alejandría y la otra en Jerusalén y dentro de un mismo contexto: se trata de dos judíos expuestos a la mofa de los gentiles. Filón escribe su tratado *In Flaccum* probablemente entre los años 40–41, es decir, después de la muerte de Jesús, pero antes de que los evangelios y los Hechos se pusieran por escrito a partir de los años sesenta del s. I d. C.

El escarnio de Jesús está recogido en los tres sinópticos, Juan y el evangelio de Pedro. Pero en Lucas la tradición de burla está ubicada en el contexto de la corte de Herodes (Lc 22,63–65 y 23,11–12). En ambos pasajes de Lucas aparece el verbo ἐμπαίζειν, "ser un juguete, objeto de burla". Pero voy a concentrarme en el relato más antiguo, el del evangelio de Marcos 15,16–20, escrito probablemente entre los años 65–70, comentando a continuación las variantes que aparecen en los relatos paralelos de los otros evangelios (Mt 27,27–31a; Jn 19,1–5) y el Evangelio de Pedro 3,6–9. Todos ellos coinciden en el simulacro de entronización real, tal como lo describe Filón en la parodia de Agripa, en los atributos reales y en el comportamiento de los soldados (o el pueblo judío en el Evangelio de Pedro),[10] y, al parecer, reflejan un ritual burlesco bien establecido. El texto de Marcos dice así:[11]

> Los soldados lo llevaron al interior del palacio, es decir al pretorio, y convocan a toda la compañía. Lo visten de púrpura (πορφύραν), trenzan una corona de acanto (ἀκάνθινον στέφανον) y le coronan. Y comenzaron a saludarle: ¡alégrate, rey de los judíos! (χαῖρε, βασιλεῦ τῶν Ἰουδαίων). Y le golpeaban la cabeza con una caña (καλάμῳ) y le escupían, y doblando las rodillas le rendían homenaje (προσεκύνουν αὐτῷ). Y una vez que se habían burlado de él (ἐνέπαιξαν αὐτῷ), le quitaron la púrpura y le pusieron su ropa.

En Mateo la púrpura se transforma en un clámide o manto pequeño de escarlata (χλαμύδα κοκκίνην), la corona que le ponen está hecha de acanto (ἐξ ἀκανθῶν), y además le colocan una caña (κάλαμον) *en su*

---

[10] Es conocido el carácter antijudío del Evangelio de Pedro: "Repeatedly the Jews are represented as unfeeling and cruel, as several non-canonical features of the Gospel illustrate: Jesus is pushed and hustled by the running crowd; it is the Jews, not the Romans, who buffet and scourge Jesus, and mock him with the crown of thorns; and throughout the trial narrative, the chief aim of the compiler of the Gospel seems to be to shift blame for the death of Jesus from the Roman authority to the Jews themselves," cf. Lapham, *An Introduction to the New Testament Apocrypha*, 91.

[11] Traduzco de la NA27.

mano derecha, detalle que aparece recogido en los numerosos *Ecce homo* de nuestra pintura e iconografía. Mateo utiliza el mismo verbo de Marcos, ἐνέπαιξαν, para la burla y el mismo saludo: ¡alégrate, rey de los judíos! Juan emplea también el término "corona de acanto" (στέφανον ἐξ ἀκανθῶν) y para la vestidura emplea la variante "manto de púrpura" (ἱμάτιον πορφυροῦν). Inserta el mismo saludo pero usando el nominativo en función de vocativo[12] (χαῖρε ὁ βασιλεὺς τῶν Ἰουδαίων); y añade que le abofetearon (καὶ ἐδίδοσαν αὐτῷ ῥαπίσματα). Lo que está claro, por los diversos estudios que se han hecho sobre este tipo de coronas y sobre la flora de Palestina, es que en esta escena prevalece el componente de burla por encima del de la tortura física y tormento que ha transmitido la tradición cristiana en torno a la coronación de "espinas".[13]

Por su viveza e interés vale la pena reproducir a continuación la escena del Evangelio de Pedro que completa y modula con nuevos detalles la descripción de los sinópticos. En este evangelio es Herodes, no Pilatos, quien entrega a Jesús al pueblo judío y no a los soldados romanos:[14]

> Y ellos cogieron al Señor y lo empujaban (ὤθουν) mientras corrían y decían: "arrastremos[15] al hijo de Dios puesto que lo tenemos dominado". Y lo vistieron de púrpura (πορφύραν) y lo sentaron en una sede judicial (καθέδραν κρίσεως)[16] y decían: "juzga con justicia (δικαίως κρῖνε), rey de Israel". Y uno de ellos trajo una corona de acanto (στέφανον ἀκάνθινον), y la puso sobre la cabeza del Señor, y otros que estaban junto a él le escupían en la cara, otros le abofeteaban (ἐράπισαν) en las mejillas, otros le pinchaban con una caña (καλάμῳ) y otros le azotaban diciendo: "con este honor queremos honrar al Hijo de Dios".[17]

---

[12] Cf. F. Blass, A. Debrunner, y F. Rehkopf, *Grammatik des neutestamentlichen Griechisch* (15. ed.; Göttingen: Vandenhoeck & Ruprecht, 1979), 147.

[13] Cf. H.St.J. Hart, "The Crown of Thorns in John 19, 2–5," *JTS* 3 (1952): 66–75 (67): "The "crown of thorns" of the Gospels was a caricature of the radiate crown of the divine ruler," y C. Bonner, "The Crown of Thorns," *HTR* 46 (1953): 47–49 (49): "For the present purpose the important residuum of these discussion is, that…mockery, not torture, was the immediate aim of such ceremonies".

[14] Cf. n. 10.

[15] Gr. σύρωμεν, verbo que en toda la Septuaginta sólo aparece en Is 2,2 y Jer 28 (51),44 como lectura de Símaco. Los contactos léxicos entre el Evangelio de Pedro y Símaco ya intrigaron a H.B. Swete, *An Introduction to the Old Testament in Greek* (2. ed.; Cambridge: Cambridge University Press, 1914), 50 n. 4.

[16] Esta alusión al juicio justo parece seguir una tradición próxima a la de Mt 27,19 y Jn 19,13.

[17] T.J. Kraus y T. Nicklas, edd., *Das Petrusevangelium und die Petrusapokalypse. Die griechischen Fragmente mit deutscher und englischer Übersetzung* (Berlin: de Gruyter, 2004), 32–34.

El paralelo entre la descripción del escarnio de Jesús transmitida por los distintos evangelios y la parodia de Agripa en el gimnasio de Alejandría que recurre a Carabas, el tonto callejero disfrazado de rey, no puede ser más elocuente. En ambos casos se trata de un rey, o supuesto rey, de los judíos escarnecido por los gentiles. Agripa I sufre la burla desatada entre los egipcios de Alejandría irritados porque Calígula haya nombrado a un judío rey. Está claro que la acusación contra Jesús fue de signo político. La causa de su muerte (ἡ ἐπιγραφὴ τῆς αἰτίας αὐτοῦ) quedó consignada en la cruz como relata Mc 15,26: ὁ βασιλεὺς τῶν Ἰουδαίων. En ambos casos se da un simulacro de entronización en el que los soldados (o el pueblo judío en el Evangelio de Pedro) invisten a sus personajes con los atributos o insignias reales: corona, vestidura y cetro. En Filón estas insignias se improvisan con una hoja de papiro aplastada (βύβλον), una estera a modo de clámide y como cetro un trozo de papiro del lugar. En la tradición evangélica todos coinciden en que la corona está hecha de acanto (ἀκάνθινον, ἐξ ἀκάνθῶν), el manto es de púrpura o escarlata, y el cetro que se le pone en la mano derecha como precisa Mateo es una caña (κάλαμον).

El segundo acto de la farsa está representado por la formación del simulacro de escolta personal (μιμούμενοι δορυφόρους) en Filón, detalle que falta en los evangelios, el saludo, apenas evocado en Filón ("algunos se adelantaron haciendo que lo saludaban", ὡς ἀσπασόμενοι), pero bien explícito en los evangelios, en donde se menciona el *Ave Caesar*, saludo convencional al emperador: χαῖρε, βασιλεῦ τῶν Ἰουδαίων (Mc 15,18 y Mt 27,29). También se alude en el relato de Filón a otros que se acercaban como para que les hicieran justicia o para presentarle demandas de interés público. Este aspecto del ceremonial está recogido en el Evangelio de Pedro que presenta a Jesús entronizado en una cátedra judicial a la que se acerca el pueblo a pedirle justicia: δικαίως κρῖνε, βασιλεῦ τοῦ Ἰσραήλ. En la farsa de Carabas, surge de entre la multitud un grito extranjero *Marin*, señor en arameo, aludiendo sarcásticamente a la procedencia siro-palestinense de Agripa.

Los evangelistas añaden el elemento de la burla, ἐμπαιγμός,[18] pero solo el Evangelio de Pedro explicita todos los detalles de esa mofa: escupir, abofetear en las mejillas, pinchar u hostigar con la caña, azotar mientras ironizan: "con estas honras queremos honrar al Hijo de Dios."

---

[18] M. Harl, "Un groupe de mots grecs dans le judaïsme hellénistique: à propos d' ἐμπαιγμός dans le psaume 37,8 de la Septante," en *La langue de Japhet. Quinze études sur la Septante et le grec des chrétiens* (Paris: Le Cerf, 1992), 44–58.

Si, como defiende Schmidt,[19] Marcos escribe el relato de la pasión como réplica y adaptación de la procesión triunfal del emperador y convierte la *Via Dolorosa* en una auténtica *Via Sacra* en sentido literal, que relaciona el triunfo con la divinización del emperador, la escena que acabamos de comentar cobraría pleno sentido en este contexto. El homenaje burlesco a Jesús como "rey de los judíos" por parte de los soldados o del pueblo y la misma inscripción de la cruz con el mismo título: ὁ βασιλεὺς τῶν Ἰουδαίων (Mc 15, 26) como causa de la ejecución así lo confirmarían. Es más, la culminación de la burla se realizaría con la crucifixión "entre dos bandidos" (ληστάς), uno a la derecha y otro a la izquierda (Mc 15,27), puesto que en el desfile del triunfo el emperador solía estar flanqueado por los dos generales o familiares que más le habían apoyado. Pero es la escena de la parodia del rey Agripa en la persona del demente vagabundo Carabas la que aporta el contexto más próximo para el escarnio de Jesús. Es el contexto del mimo y teatro callejero en una sociedad ávida del espectáculo en la que los combates del Coliseo y las ejecuciones públicas tanto contribuían a demostrar el poder del estado para asegurar el orden social romano contra todo el que, dentro o fuera del imperio, intentara socavarlo.

Entre las dos escenas, el relato alejandrino de Filón, y la narración de los evangelios se da una proximidad cronológica en cuanto al hecho descrito, la década del 30 al 40 d. C.; una práctica semejante en Jerusalén y Alejandría, el juego del rey en el que todos los espectadores rivalizan por convertirse en actores y participar en la burla degradante; la investidura de la víctima con las insignias de la realeza; el saludo sarcástico y el simulado rendimiento de homenaje así como diversas formas de hostigación y befa. En ambos casos se trata de un judío entregado al escarnio de los gentiles. No hace falta recurrir al contexto del desfile de triunfo romano o el miedo a figurar entre el cortejo de

---

[19] T.E. Schmidt, "Mark 15, 16–32: The Crucifixion Narrative and the Roman Triumphal Procession," *NTS* 41 (1995): 1–18. Si, como parece, el evangelio de Marcos se escribe para una audiencia romana en la persecución de Nerón o poco después, el autor tiene que narrar con sutileza para que los ojos hostiles vean pero no perciban la evocación del triunfo y la exaltación de Jesús en la ignominia de la crucifixión. Ver también J. Marcus, "Crucifixion as Parodic Exaltation," *JBL* 125 (2006): 73–97 (83): "If, as seems likely, the inscription over the cross is historical, it is plausible that it was meant not only to indicate the charge against Jesus but also to continue a mockery that was intrinsic to the process of crucifixion." El componente del sarcasmo es ineludible ya que ni las autoridades romanas ni los soldados pensaban que Jesús fuera realmente rey.

los vencidos y la humillación que ello suponía. En el caso de Carabas
se trata de una experiencia de la vida cotidiana, un ejemplo de mofa
en el contexto cívico de la πόλις y llevado a cabo en el gimnasio. Lo
más que refleja es la crueldad a la que podían llegar las envidias y
conflictos interétnicos entre judíos y egipcios en la crisis alejandrina de
los años cuarenta. Pero también los espectáculos del triunfo romano
con la humillación y tortura de los vencidos y los relatos de martirio
tal como aparecen en Josefo y 2 Macabeos 6–7 tuvieron que causar
enorme impacto en la población.[20]

Decíamos al principio que la escena evangélica del escarnio de Jesús
no parece inspirada en ningún pasaje del Antiguo Testamento, ya fueran
pasajes del Siervo de Yahveh de Isaías, Sabiduría 2 o alguno de los
Salmos que tienen por tema los sufrimientos del justo. Los intérpretes
se inclinan a pensar en un influjo de juegos paródicos, mimos teatrales o fiestas carnavalescas extrabíblicas.[21] Sin embargo es el contexto
judeo-helenístico, y en concreto el paralelo con la escena del gimnasio
narrada por Filón, el que mejor ilumina este relato de la pasión y lo
ancla en una mayor verosimilitud histórica. Lo cual no quiere decir
que los relatos evangélicos no estén intensamente reelaborados, sea cual
sea la tradición sobre la que se asientan. Es más, no descarto, como he
sugerido en otra ocasión,[22] que algunas de las descripciones de la pasión
estén inspiradas en la "pasión" de Sansón en manos de los filisteos, tal
como la describe la Septuaginta antigua. También aquí la burla de los
filisteos con Sansón como víctima a la que previamente le han sacado
los ojos puede haber servido como tema de inspiración e *imitatio* para
los evangelistas. En efecto, es probable que el traductor del libro de los

---

[20] T. Rajak, "Dying for the Law: The Martyr's Portrait in Jewish-Greek Literature,"
en *The Jewish Dialogue with Greece and Rome* (Leiden: Brill, 2001), 99–133. Josefo en *Contra
Apión* 2,233, alude a las escenas de martirio como espectáculo: "Yo, por mi parte, pienso
que algunos de nuestros dominadores nos maltrataban no por odio a los pueblos que
tenían bajo su dominio, sino porque querían contemplar el espectáculo más admirable
(θαυμαστόν τι θέαμα βουλομένους ἰδεῖν)".

[21] Cf. Brown, *La muerte del Mesías*, 1028–31, y R.E. Brown, *El Evangelio de Juan XIII–
XXI* (Madrid: Cristiandad, 1979), 1178–79. Loisy se cuenta entre los que recurren
al texto de Filón para iluminar la escena evangélica del *Ecce homo*. Entiende además
que el nombre de Barrabás sería el mismo de Carabas como forma del título dado
al personaje que representaba aquel papel. Sin embargo, salvo la parcial semejanza
de los nombres, nada hay en común entre el bandido Barrabás y el loco Carabas del
Contra Flaco, cf. Brown, *El Evangelio de Juan XIII–XXI*, 1142.

[22] N. Fernández Marcos, "Héros et victime: Samson dans la LXX," en *L'apport de la
Septante aux études sur l'Antiquité* (ed. J. Joosten y Ph. Le Moigne; Paris: Le Cerf, 2005),
119–33 (128–30).

Jueces, a comienzos del s. II a. C., refleje aspectos del clima creado en el judaísmo por la persecución seleúcida. En todo caso, es posible que experiencias sufridas por los judíos helenísticos, hayan contribuido a la nueva interpretación de Sansón en la LXX como víctima de las naciones gentiles, en este caso de los filisteos. Este rasgo se pone de manifiesto en la traducción de Jueces 16,25 que transforma la escena de diversión del texto hebreo ("¡llamad a Sansón para que nos divierta! y danzó[23] ante ellos") en una escena de burla y tortura: καὶ ἐκάλεσαν τὸν Σαμψων καὶ ἐνέπαιζον αὐτῷ καὶ ἐράπιζον αὐτόν ("y llamaron a Sansón y jugaban con él y lo abofeteaban").

Los sinópticos, a diferencia del Evangelio de Pedro, no disculpan a los romanos en la coronación burlesca sino que, una vez más, recurren al tema de la figura del judío convertido en juguete de los gentiles. Los dos verbos de Sansón escarnecido por los filisteos: ἐμπαίζειν y ῥαπίζειν se utilizan en los relatos evangélicos. ἐμπαίζειν es utilizado por los evangelistas en los pasajes citados y en el anuncio y cumplimiento de la pasión en los tres sinópticos: παραδώσουσιν αὐτὸν τοῖς ἔθνεσιν εἰς τὸ ἐμπαῖξαι (cf. Mt 20,19; 27,29.31.41 y paralelos). ῥαπίζειν aparece en Mt 26,67, el Evangelio de Pedro y el sustantivo de la misma raíz (ῥαπίσματα) en Jn 19,3. El miedo a caer en manos de los gentiles y ser objeto de su escarnio queda patente en el caso de Saúl que prefiere suicidarse por miedo a que los incircuncisos se burlen de él.[24]

En suma, pienso que la parodia del rey Agripa en el gimnasio de Alejandría transmitida por Filón, ilumina como ningún otro texto de la antigüedad la burla de los soldados romanos con Jesús en el pretorio y, de alguna manera, inserta esta escena de la pasión en un contexto histórico, geográfico y cronológico plausible. Pero con independencia de la realidad histórica, siempre de difícil acceso a través de la hermenéutica de los textos antiguos, los evangelios son documentos muy elaborados tanto literaria como teológicamente. Y no excluyo que en este relato de la pasión haya influido la descripción de la mofa de Sansón a manos de los filisteos tal como la cuenta la antigua Septuaginta.

Que estas breves notas sirvan de homenaje a Florentino, infatigable investigador, experto autorizado y entusiasta en Qumrán y el judaísmo del segundo Templo, y siempre caluroso y entrañable amigo.

---

[23] O también "hizo juegos", *pi'el* del verbo פחק.

[24] 1 Sam 31,4: "Desenvaina la espada y atraviésame con ella, no vayan a venir estos incircuncisos, me maten y jueguen conmigo (καὶ ἐμπαίξωσιν ἐν ἐμοί)".

PAGAN AND JEWISH MONOTHEISM ACCORDING TO VARRO, PLUTARCH, AND ST PAUL: THE ANICONIC, MONOTHEISTIC BEGINNINGS OF ROME'S PAGAN CULT—ROMANS 1:19–25 IN A ROMAN CONTEXT

George H. van Kooten

In the opening to his Letter to the Romans, Paul argues that current pagan thinking in Rome and elsewhere in the Graeco-Roman world is a distortion of an aniconic and monotheistic religion originally shared by all.[1] As we shall see, the notion of a monotheistic past resonates particularly with an audience in Rome. By differentiating between the golden age of Roman religion and current practice, Paul presents his own religion as a "logical, i.e. non-ritualistic form of worship" (Rom 12:1–2; cf. 9:4), which restores the ideal. In this way, by invoking the authority of a respectable pagan monotheism in the past, Paul seeks to undermine current polytheistic thinking. At the same time, his approach renders Jewish monotheism less exclusive, as it is not without pagan analogies. This seems to be Paul's double strategy, as in his letter he aims to reduce tensions between Jews and ex-pagans within the Christian communities at Rome.

These tensions were the result of the fact that for the past five years the pagan converts to what we label "Christianity" in Rome had been without the fellowship of their Christian Jews. The latter, together with the non-Christian Jews from the synagogue, had suffered expulsion by Claudius who, according to Suetonius, had expelled the Jews from Rome because they "constantly made disturbances at the instigation of Chrestus" [i.e. of "Christus," Christ] (*Claudius* 25.4).[2] As this had happened in A.D. 49, over these five years the ex-pagan Christians had begun to develop a Christian identity separate from the Jewish Christians. When

---

[1] This paper was first presented at the Pagan Monotheism in the Roman Empire conference at the University of Exeter, 17–20 July 2006. I wish to thank Dr Peter Van Nuffelen (Exeter) and Prof. Gillian Clark (Bristol) for their comments and Dr Maria Sherwood-Smith (Leiden) for her correction of the English.
[2] Translations of classical sources are normally taken from the LCL with occasional small alterations. Translations of biblical quotations are, unless otherwise stated, taken from the REB with occasional alterations.

the former exiles (both non-Christian and Christian Jews) started to
return to Rome after Claudius' death (A.D. 54)[3] and Christian Jews
again met their ex-pagan co-religionists, tensions arose, which Paul set
out to address in his letter.

His answer to these challenges is not simply to bolster the Jewish
monotheistic identity of the returning Christian Jews, but to point at
the pagans' own distant monotheistic golden age. Paul tries to build
common ground between the Jews and pagans, which lies not in *Jewish*
monotheism, but in monotheism as such. It is not surprising then that
Paul sketches the outlines of this monotheism not by reference to the
Jewish scriptures but with the aid of general Greek philosophy.

1. Paul

Although Paul broadens the scope of monotheism beyond Judaism, he is
very critical of paganism insofar as it deviates from original monotheism.
The conduct of pagan polytheists is clearly "indefensible" to him.

> For all that can be known of God (τὸ γνωστὸν τοῦ θεοῦ) lies plain
> before their eyes; indeed God himself has disclosed it to them. Ever
> since the world began his invisible attributes, that is to say his everlasting
> power and deity, have been visible to the eye of reason (τὰ γὰρ ἀόρατα
> αὐτοῦ...νοούμενα καθορᾶται), in the things he has made. Their conduct,
> therefore, is indefensible; knowing God (γνόντες τὸν θεὸν), they have
> refused to honour him as God, or to render him thanks. Hence all their
> thinking has ended in futility (ἐματαιώθησαν ἐν τοῖς διαλογισμοῖς αὐτῶν),
> and their misguided minds (ἡ ἀσύνετος αὐτῶν καρδία) are plunged into
> darkness. (Rom 1:19–21)

Although German protestant scholarship has been very reluctant to
grant that Paul employs Greek natural theology, this is beyond question for those trained in ancient philosophy. Anglo-American biblical
scholars have pointed out this prejudice among German and German-
influenced continental scholars. Commenting on Rom 1:19–20, James
Dunn, for instance, states unequivocally:

> Also clear is the fact that some sort of natural theology is involved
> here.... we still have to speak of a "natural theology"—that is here, of

---

[3] Cf. the fate of Aquila and Prisca/Priscilla according to Acts 18:2, 18, 26; 1 Cor
16:19; and Rom 16:3.

a revelation of God through the cosmos, to humankind as a whole, and operative since the creation of the cosmos...Paul is trading upon...the Greek...understanding of an invisible realm of reality, invisible to sense perception, which can be known only through the rational power of the mind...it is scarcely possible that Paul did not intend his readers to think in terms of some kind of rational perception of the fuller reality in and behind the created cosmos...the extent to which Paul was prepared to build his argument on what was not a traditional Jewish world-view...reveals a breadth and a boldness in his apologetic strategy. (Dunn 1988, 56–58)[4]

Paul is not the first in Judaism to employ this Greek mode of thinking. As is generally acknowledged, the beginning of Romans much resembles the Jewish-Hellenistic work entitled the Wisdom of Solomon. In this first-century B.C. writing, which was included in the Septuagint, the author develops a similar line of thought:

> For all people who were ignorant of God were foolish by nature; and they were unable from the good things that are seen to know the one who exists (καὶ ἐκ τῶν ὁρωμένων ἀγαθῶν οὐκ ἴσχυσαν εἰδέναι τὸν ὄντα), nor did they recognize the artisan while paying heed to his works (οὔτε τοῖς ἔργοις προσέχοντες ἐπέγνωσαν τὸν τεχνίτην); but they supposed that either fire or wind or swift air, or the circle of the stars, or turbulent water, or the luminaries of heaven were the gods that rule the world. If through delight in the beauty of these things people assumed them to be gods, let them know how much better than these is their Lord, for the author of beauty (ὁ τοῦ κάλλους γενεσιάρχης) created them. And if people were amazed at their power and working (δύναμιν καὶ ἐνέργειαν ἐκπλαγέντες), let them perceive from them how much more powerful is the one who formed them. For from the greatness and beauty of created things comes a corresponding perception of their Creator (ἐκ γὰρ μεγέθους καὶ καλλονῆς κτισμάτων ἀναλόγως ὁ γενεσιουργὸς αὐτῶν θεωρεῖται). (Wis 13:1–5; NRSV)

The author clearly shows himself dependent on Greek philosophy.[5] Especially the last line, that "from the greatness and beauty of created

---

[4] Cf. also Fitzmyer 1992, 274: "some commentators have subconsciously reacted by denying the capability of the human mind to attain some knowledge of God. As a result, they have taken refuge in a form of fideism. In doing so, they have been reluctant to admit what Paul himself actually says about natural theology; they deny that God makes himself known in any other manner than in Christ." These commentators are particularly found among the adherents of Luther and Barth. See Wilckens 1978, 118–21.

[5] On this dependence, see in detail Kepper 1999, 170–87; Larcher 1985, 748–67; Winston 1979, 247–57; Gilbert 1973, 13–35; Reese 1970, 50–62; Lange 1936, 293–302.

things their Creator can be perceived *by way of analogy* (ἀναλόγως),"
shows the author's acquaintance with Greek terminology.[6] In a similar
way, Alcinous argues in his *Handbook of Platonism*:

> The second way of conceiving God is that of analogy, as follows: the sun
> is to vision and to visible objects (it is not itself sight, but provides vision to
> sight and visibility to its objects) as the primal intellect is to the power of
> intellection in the soul and to its objects; for it is not the power of intellection
> itself, but provides intellection to it and intelligibility to its objects, illumi-
> nating the truth contained in them. (10.5, 165.20–26; trans. J. Dillon)

Both Paul and the author of the Wisdom of Solomon appear to be well-
versed in the Greek, mainly Platonic and Stoic discussions of "intelligent design," in which the existence of the one God is deduced from
physical reality. For the present purpose it is not necessary to follow
these traditions in detail,[7] nor to focus on the heated discussions between
Platonists and Stoics on the one hand, and Atomists, Materialists, and
Epicureans on the other.[8] Paul and the author of the Wisdom of Solomon should be read in this context.[9] In contrast with Graeco-Roman
philosophers, however, the two Jews are far more critical of the practice
of worshipping images. Although we shall see that Greek philosophers
also criticized this popular custom, they never exhibit the same out-
spokenness as Paul and the author of the Wisdom of Solomon. After
some initial doubts, the latter eventually draws firm conclusions about
those who fail to deduce the Creator from the created things:

> Yet these people are little to be blamed, for perhaps they go astray while
> seeking God and desiring to find him. For while they live among his works,
> they keep searching, and they trust in what they see, because the things
> that are seen are beautiful. Yet again, not even they are to be excused;
> for if they had the power to know so much that they could investigate
> the world, how did they fail to find sooner the Lord of these things? But
> miserable, with their hopes set on dead things, are those who give the
> name "gods" to the works of human hands, gold and silver fashioned

---

[6] See further Reese 1970, 56–58; Winston 1979, 252–53; Gilbert 1973, 25–30;
Larcher 1985, 763–64; Kepper 1999, 179–85.

[7] On "intelligent design" theories in ancient philosophy, see Pease 1941 and Theiler
1965.

[8] Excellent, detailed descriptions by Furley 1999; Mansfeld 1999; Gerson 1990;
Irwin 1989 (see Index s.v. "design, cosmic").

[9] For parallels between Paul and Graeco-Roman philosophy, see also Strecker et al.
1996, 13–21; detailed treatment of Greek philosophical background to Rom 1:20 also
in Cook 1994. See also Guerra 1995, 49–52 and the commentaries on Romans, esp.
Dunn 1988, 56–59, 71 and Fitzmyer 1992, 272–74, 278–81.

with skill, and likenesses of animals, or a useless stone, the work of an ancient hand. (Wis 13:6–10; cf. 13:2 and 13:11–15:19)

Those who worship images are inexcusable. Paul reaches the same conclusions. Those who know God with the eye of reason, but have refused to honour him as God

> boast of their wisdom, but they have made fools of themselves (φάσκοντες εἶναι σοφοὶ ἐμωράνθησαν), exchanging the glory of the immortal God for an image (καὶ ἤλλαξαν τὴν δόξαν τοῦ ἀφθάρτου θεοῦ ἐν ὁμοιώματι εἰκόνος) shaped like mortal man, even for images like birds, beasts, and reptiles... They have exchanged the truth of God for a lie (οἵτινες μετήλλαξαν τὴν ἀλήθειαν τοῦ θεοῦ ἐν τῷ ψεύδει), and have offered reverence and worship to created things instead of to the Creator (καὶ ἐσεβάσθησαν καὶ ἐλάτρευσαν τῇ κτίσει παρὰ τὸν κτίσαντα). (Rom 1:22–23, 25)

Although Paul and the author of the Wisdom of Solomon venture the same Jewish criticism against images, there is nevertheless an important difference. Whereas the author of the Wisdom of Solomon simply describes the pagans as they are (and presumably always have been), Paul, in his description, stresses the fact that the pagans have fallen away from their original knowledge of the one God, have *changed* the glory of the immortal God into an image (καὶ ἤλλαξαν τὴν δόξαν τοῦ ἀφθάρτου θεοῦ ἐν ὁμοιώματι εἰκόνος), and have *altered* the truth of God into a lie (μετήλλαξαν τὴν ἀλήθειαν τοῦ θεοῦ ἐν τῷ ψεύδει).

This clearly implies that Paul postulates an initial golden age of pure, intellectual worship of God without images. He sketches the development of pagan religion as a history of decline, drastically moving away from its original monotheistic and aniconic stance. Originally, the invisible God was visible to the eye of reason in the things he had made, but man has long since exchanged the glory of the immortal God for human and animal images. Paul acknowledges that pagan religion started off well but suffered deterioration. This historiography is remarkably similar to that of the antiquarian of Roman religion, Varro.

2. Varro

2.1. *Varro on pure Roman religious beginnings*

In his book *Antiquitates Rerum Divinarum*, Varro expresses his view that

> for more than 170 years, the Romans of old worshipped the gods without an image. If this practice had remained down to the present day..., the gods would have been worshipped with greater purity...those who first

set up images for the people both diminished reverence and increased error in their cities. (frg. 18 Cardauns; Augustine, *The City of God* 4.31; trans. R.W. Dyson)[10]

The pure, monotheistic era of 170 years mentioned by Varro represents the time-span from the foundation of Rome in 753 B.C. through the first kingship of Romulus and the following kingship of Numa up to the reign of Tarquinius Priscus, the fifth king of Rome (616–579 B.C.), who is reported to have started the building of the temple of Jupiter on the Capitoline.[11] Varro clearly regards the initial period of Rome's religion as aniconic and, for that reason, more pure than the subsequent phase of Rome's religion when images were introduced.[12] Although Varro is able to interpret images in a positive, allegorical way (frg. 225 Cardauns),[13] the development from an aniconic to an iconic religion is seen as a decline of Rome's religious golden age.

By speaking of the first 170 years, Varro also implies the importance of Numa, Rome's legendary second king (715–673 B.C.), who was credited with the fundamental design of Rome's public religion and instituted cults, rituals, priesthoods, and calendars (Ennius, *Annales* 113–119 Skutsch).[14] As we shall see, Plutarch explicitly mentions Numa in connection with the religiously pure period of 170 years. Varro leaves Numa's importance implicit, although he does refer to him in other fragments.[15] In one of them, which was part of his *Curio de cultu deorum*, Varro relates the story of the books of Numa which had been buried with him:[16]

---

[10] Cf. further Augustine, *The City of God* 4.9: "why has he [i.e. the one God] been treated so insultingly at Rome, and among other peoples also, by having an image erected to him? This fact displeased Varro so much that, though he was himself in thrall to the perverse customs of so great a city, he did not in the least hesitate to say and write that those who had set up images for the people had both diminished reverence and increased error"; 7.5: "you [Varro] once soberly judged that those who first set up images for the people diminished the reverence of their citizens and added error, and that the ancient Romans honoured the gods more purely when they were without images."

[11] Cf. O'Daly 1999, 93 n. 34; Cardauns 1976, 2:147, with reference to Pliny, *Natural History* 35.37 for the construction of the Capitoline temple.

[12] On Varro's aniconism, see Van Nuffelen 2007; Lehmann 1997, 182–93; Cancik and Cancik-Lindemaier 2001; Ross-Taylor 1931.

[13] On this see esp. Van Nuffelen 2007.

[14] On Numa's religious reforms, see Hooker 1963; Scheid 1985.

[15] Varro, *Antiquitates Rerum Divinarum*, frgs. 37–38 (Cardauns). Varro, *Curio de cultu deorum* (Cardauns 1976, 1:36, frgs. III–IV; 1:39–40, frg. B).

[16] On Numa's books, see Peglau 2000; Willi 1998; Rosen 1985.

the plough turned up from the ground the king's books, in which were written down the reasons for the sacred institutions. He [a certain Teren- tius] took these to the praetor of the city. He, having perused the first part, referred so important a matter to the Senate. But when the leading senators had read some of the reasons given as to why each part of the sacred rites had been instituted, the Senate declared itself in agreement with the dead Numa, and the assembled fathers, as religious men, required the praetor to burn those same books. (Cardauns 1976, 1:36, frg. III; Augustine, *The City of God* 7.34; trans. Dyson)[17]

Augustine, who preserved this passage, explains the books' destruction by the fact "that the reasons for those rites...were not fit to become known" because "Numa Pompilius had attained to these secrets of the demons by an unlawful curiosity" (7.34).[18] Augustine emphasizes, however, that this demonological interpretation is his own: "Let each man believe as he sees fit; indeed, let every egregious defender of such impiety say whatever mad contentiousness may suggest. For my part, it is enough to point out that" (7.34). As Cardauns has suggested, it is far more likely that Varro himself would have assumed that Numa's books were destroyed because they revealed the philosophical, aniconic founda- tion of Rome's original cults (1960, 27).[19] It is Plutarch who stresses the philosophical nature of the contents of Numa's books (*Numa* 22), but Cardauns is probably right that Varro already held this opinion, although he does not highlight Numa's role in Rome's primeval ani- conic religion.

According to Varro, the reason for the decline of Roman religion was the influence of the poets: "People are on the whole more inclined to follow the poets than the natural philosophers in their beliefs concerning the genealogies of the gods" (frg. 19 Cardauns; Augustine, *The City of God* 4.32).[20] The deterioration of Rome's religion is due to the poets. Their role is contrasted with that of the natural philosophers (*physici*). Here one catches a glimpse of the distinction Varro makes between "physical theology," "mythological theology," and "civic theology" (frgs.

---

[17] Cf. the reports in Livy 40.29; Plutarch, *Numa* 22; and Pliny 13.13.84ff.

[18] See further Cardauns 1976, 1:36, IV = Augustine, *The City of God* 7.35: "Numa himself...was compelled to practise hydromancy, and saw in the water the images of gods, or, rather, the mocking images of demons, from whom he heard what rites he should establish and observe."

[19] Cf. Hagendahl 1967, 2:618–19.

[20] Cf. Augustine, *The City of God* 6.6, 6.1.

7–11 Cardauns; Augustine, *The City of God* 6.5–6). O'Daly briefly summarizes these three types of theology:

> The "genus mythicon" is found in myth and especially in literature. It is anthropomorphic in tendency. The "genus civile" has to do with worship rites, and sacrifices: it enshrines the beliefs to which Varro does not subscribe, but whose [social] utility he commends. The "genus physicon" is philosophical, and deals with the origins, identity, and nature of the gods in a speculative and often controversial way: but it is more appropriate to a school than to the public arena (6.5). Yet Varro approves of this third kind of discourse. (1999, 103)[21]

In his regret that "people are on the whole more inclined to follow the poets than the natural philosophers," Varro expresses his own preference for natural philosophy. For this reason, in Augustine's words,

> it is not by his own judgment that he follows the institutions established by the city of Rome. For he does not hesitate to confess that, if he were founding the city anew, he would consecrate the gods, and give them names, according to the principles of nature (*ex naturae potius formula*) rather than following what is done now. As it is, however, finding himself among a people already ancient, he says that he must adhere to the names and titles of the gods traditionally received from antiquity, and that the purpose of his writing and study is to encourage people to worship the gods rather than to despise them. (frg. 12 Cardauns; Augustine, *The City of God* 4.31)[22]

Ideally speaking, religion should be physical, defined "according to the principles of nature." Yet, the Roman religion no longer accords with this ideal type of theology, since it has deteriorated. The ideal, physical theology consists of a monotheistic understanding of God as the "soul of the world": "The only men who have truly understood what God is are those who have believed Him to be the soul of the world, governing it by movement and reason" (frg. 13 Cardauns; Augustine, *The City of God* 4.31). This one God is Jupiter, "the king of all the gods and goddesses" (frg. 14 Cardauns; Augustine, *The City of God* 4.9), "the supreme God," as Augustine interprets Varro (*The City of God* 19.22). Although identified as "Jupiter," the name of the supreme God is unimportant

---

[21] Cf. also Hagendahl 1967, 2:610–17.

[22] Cf. Augustine, *The City of God* 6.4: "if he were himself founding a new city, he would have written according to the rule of nature, but since he found himself to be a member of an old one, he could do nothing but follow its custom" (trans. Dyson).

to Varro:[23] "Varro believes that he [i.e. Jupiter] is worshipped, though called by another name, even by those who worship one God only, without an image" (frg. 15 Cardauns; Augustine, *The City of God* 4.9). Although Persians, Scythians and others were believed to have aniconic cults,[24] Varro also points to the Jews as a present-day example of those who, unlike the Romans, have preserved their pure, original religion and "worship one God only, without an image." Varro's estimation of Jewish monotheism will be treated in detail in the next section.

2.2. *Varro on the Jews*

(a) *References to the Jews in Varro*
In the fragment in which he praises the purity of aniconic religion, from which Rome had lapsed after 170 years, Varro also refers to the Jews:

> For more than 170 years, the Romans of old worshipped the gods without an image. "If this practice had remained *down to the present day*," he [Varro] says, "the gods would have been worshipped with greater purity" (*castius dii observarentur*). In support of this opinion, he cites, among other things, the testimony of *the Jewish nation*. (frg. 18 Cardauns; Augustine, *The City of God* 4.31)

The Jews are referred to as a present-day example of pure, uncontaminated aniconic religion. As we shall see presently, Varro's high estimation of the Jews was already preceded by that of philosophers before him, and others followed suit. The Jews are also mentioned in other passages in Varro. He identifies the God of the Jews as "Jupiter,"[25] but also gives his name as "Iao," the Greek form of "Yahweh."[26] It was

---

[23] On the issue of the interchangeability of the name of the supreme God according to ancient philosophers, see Celsus apud Origen, *Against Celsus* 5.41 and Van den Berg 2006.

[24] Cf. Cardauns 1976, 2:146: "bildloser Kult bei Persern, Skythen, Serern und anderen: Herod. 1.131 und 4.59; Strabo 15C 732; Celsus ap. Orig. 7.62 (zit. Heraklit VS 22 B5); Dino ap. Clem. Alex. Protr. 5 p. 65.1; Diog. Laertius prooem. 6 und 9; Cic. Rep. 3.14; Tac. Germ. 9. Zur Literatur vgl. fr. 18."

[25] Frg. 16 Cardauns; Augustine, *Harmony of the Gospels* 1.22.30, 31, 42: "Varro... thought that the God of the Jews was Jupiter...; when he observed that the Jews worshipped the supreme God, he could not think of any object under that title other than Jupiter himself...but we revere that Jupiter of whom Maro says that 'All things are full of Jove' [Vergil, *Eclogues* 3.5.60], that is to say, the spirit of life that vivifies all things. It is not without some reason, therefore, that Varro thought that Jove was worshipped by the Jews" (trans. S.D.F. Salmond, Nicene & Post-Nicene Fathers series).

[26] Frg. 17 Cardauns = Lydus, *De mensibus* 4.54. Apart from Varro, in the first century B.C. Diodorus Siculus, too, gives the Jewish God's name as "Iao" (Diodorus, *Library of*

the aniconic religion directed towards this god that Varro praised. In this he followed philosophers like Theophrastus and Hecataeus of Abdera before him.

(b) *Varro's predecessors*

Theophrastus is only in part a precursor to Varro. He characterizes the Jews as "philosophers by race" because of their behaviour during sacrifices, but says nothing of their aniconic cult: "During this whole time, being philosophers by race, they converse with each other about the deity, and at night-time they make observations of the stars, gazing at them and calling on God by prayer" (Theophrastus [372–288/7 B.C.] apud Porphyry, *On Abstinence* 2.26; Stern, No. 4). A full concurrence with Varro is exhibited by Hecataeus of Abdera (ca. 300 B.C.). Commenting on the figure of Moses, Hecataeus portrays the cult which Moses established as aniconic:

> Moses, outstanding both for his wisdom and his courage...established the temple that they hold in chief veneration, instituted their forms of worship and ritual, drew up their laws and ordered their political institutions...But he had no images whatsoever of the gods made for them, being of the opinion that God is not in human form; rather the Heaven that surrounds the earth is alone divine, and rules the universe. (Hecataeus of Abdera apud Diodorus Siculus 40.3.1–4; Stern, No. 11)

This passage from Hecataeus shows that Varro was not the first to appreciate the Jews for their aniconic and monotheistic cult. In the past, scholars have also referred to Posidonius as a forerunner of Varro, but the Posidonian origins of the passages in Strabo and Tacitus adduced to this end are not conclusive. I shall therefore ascribe them to Strabo and Tacitus themselves and treat them below. Nevertheless, it is clear that Varro formed part of a tradition of authors who were favourable towards Jewish aniconic and monotheistic cult.

(c) *Varro's successors*

One of the most important representatives of the tradition after Varro is Strabo. As I have just briefly indicated, there seem to be no grounds

---

History 1.94.1–2; Stern, No. 58). To judge from the surviving evidence, Varro and Diodorus are the first Graeco-Roman authors to mention "Iao." On Graeco-Roman views on the name and identity of the Jewish God, see, extensively, Van Kooten 2006.

to assume that Strabo is dependent on Posidonius. According to Strabo, again in a passage on Moses,

> Moses…was accompanied by many people who worshipped the Divine Being (τὸ θεῖον). For he said, and taught, that the Egyptians were mistaken in representing the Divine Being by the images of beast and cattle…; and that the Greeks were also wrong in modelling gods in human form. For, according to him, God is this one thing alone that encompasses us all and encompasses land and sea—the thing which we call heaven, or universe, or the nature of all that exists (καὶ τὴν τῶν ὄντων φύσιν). What man, then, if he has sense, could be bold enough to fabricate an image of God resembling any creature amongst us? Nay, people should leave off all image-carving and…should worship God *without an image*. (ἔδους χωρίς; 16.2.35; Stern, No. 115)[27]

The passage shows that Varro's high esteem for Judaism did not remain an exception. Like Varro, Strabo compares Jewish aniconism with Graeco-Roman image-centred religion.

Another relevant passage is the one in Tacitus' *Histories* in which he not only points to the aniconic nature of Jewish religion, but also to the fact that, consequently, the Jewish God is conceived of "with the mind only":

> The Jews…conceive of one god only, and that with the mind only ("Iudaei *mente sola* unumque numen intellegunt"): they regard as impious those who make from perishable materials representations of gods in man's image; that supreme and eternal being is to them incapable of representation and without end. Therefore they set up no statues in their cities, still less in their temples. (Tacitus, *Histories* 5.5.4; Stern, No. 281)[28]

This passage is particularly relevant to our discussion of the beginning of Paul's Letter to the Romans. It shows that the Jews do what, in Paul's

---

[27] Strabo 16.2.35 in the context of 16.2.35–37. Edelstein and Kidd's edition of Posidonius, frg. 279 only includes Strabo 16.2.43, but not the passage before. See Edelstein and Kidd, 1:244 = frg. 279 = Strabo 16.2.42–43; 2.2:951–53 (952): "There is nothing to link [Strabo 16.2.]35–39 with the citation of Posidonius in [Strabo 16.2.]43… There is nothing else explicitly in the Moses fragment with Posidonius"; and 3:354–55, with special attention to the disputed nature of the extent of this fragment (Norden: Strabo 16.2.34–43; Jacoby, frg. 70: 16.2.34–35; Reinhardt: 16.2.35–39; Theiler, frg. 133: 16.2.35–39). Despite the previous scholarly consensus about the Posidonian background of the passage, according to Edelstein and Kidd "Posidonius is only mentioned for a specific point in 43." For this reason I follow Edelstein and Kidd's minimalist approach and treat the passage in 16.2.35 as Strabo's own.

[28] Tacitus, *Histories* 5.5.4 is not included among the fragments of Posidonius in Edelstein and Kidd. *Pace* Theiler 1982, 2:283.

view, was also characteristic of pagan physical religion in the past, i.e. "conceive of one god only, and that with the mind only (*mente sola*)." As Paul puts it: "Ever since the world began, God's invisible attributes, that is to say his everlasting power and deity, have been visible with the νοῦς in the things he has made" (Rom 1:20).

This overview may suffice to show that Varro's high appreciation of Jewish aniconic religion was no exception among Graeco-Roman philosophers.[29] Among Graeco-Roman authors, however, Varro is the exception in tracing Roman religion itself back to aniconic beginnings. In this, he is followed by Plutarch, who also taught at Rome and who referred to Varro (Βάρρων) by name in various writings. Plutarch seems to be dependent on Varro in his passages about the origin of Rome's religion.[30]

3. Plutarch on pure Roman religious beginnings with Numa

Plutarch's remarks about Rome's originally aniconic religion are found in his *Life of Numa*.[31] Unlike Varro, Plutarch explicitly connects this phase with the figure of Numa. Numa Pompilius, requested to become king of Rome after Romulus' ascension into heaven (2–6), sets out to "soften the [recently founded] city," "as iron is softened in the fire, and to change its harsh and warlike temper into one of greater gentleness and justice. For if a city was ever in what Plato calls a 'feverish' state, Rome certainly was at that time" (7–8 at 8.1). Numa achieves this softening effect by means of religion. He "calls in the gods to aid and assist him" (8.2). Plutarch does not repeat Varro's comparison between Rome's original aniconic cult and the contemporary cult of the Jews.

---

[29] See further Livy in *Scholia in Lucanum* 2.593: "nor is any image found there, since they do not think that God partakes of any figure" (Stern, No. 133); and Cassius Dio, *Historia Romana* 37, 17.2: "they do not honour any of the usual gods, but show extreme reverence for one particular divinity. They never had any statue of him, even in Jerusalem itself, but believing him to be unnameable and invisible, they worship him in the most extravagant fashion on earth" (Stern, No. 406).

[30] On Plutarch's dependence on Varro, cf. also Cardauns 1976, 2:147: "Bei Plutarch Numa 8 ist die Notiz aus Varro [about the time-span of 170 years of aniconic cult in Rome; frg. 18] in einen Bericht eingeschoben, der vielleicht aus Kastor v. Rhodos stammt (v. Borries 64ff.)."

[31] On Plutarch's Numa, see Buchheit 1991 and 1993; De Blois and Bons 1992.

Rather, he points to the alleged Pythagorean background of Numa's religious institutions:

> Furthermore, his [Numa's] ordinances concerning images are altogether in harmony with the doctrines of Pythagoras. For that philosopher maintained that the first principle of being was beyond sense or feeling, was invisible and uncreated, and discernible only by the mind. And in like manner Numa forbade the Romans to revere an image of God which had the form of man or beast. Nor was there among them in this earlier time any painted or graven likeness of Deity, but while for the first hundred and seventy years they were continually building temples and establishing sacred shrines, they made no statues in bodily form for them, convinced that it was impious to liken higher things to lower, and that it was impossible to apprehend Deity except by the intellect. (*Numa* 8.7–8; trans. B. Perrin)

Plutarch clearly takes over from Varro the information about the time-span of 170 years of aniconic cult, but he renders the role of Numa explicit and adds the remarks about the Pythagorean nature of Numa's philosophical convictions.[32] Plutarch stresses that iconic reverence for God is inappropriate as the first principle of being is considered, by Pythagoras, as "beyond sense or feeling, invisible and uncreated, and discernible only by the mind" (οὔτε γὰρ ἐκεῖνος αἰσθητὸν ἢ παθητόν, ἀόρατον δὲ καὶ ἄκτιστον καὶ νοητὸν ὑπελάμβανεν εἶναι τὸ πρῶτον; *Numa* 8.7). Paul's language in Rom 1 closely resembles this mode of thinking. According to Paul, too, God's invisible attributes (τὰ ἀόρατα) become visible when reflected upon by the *nous* (νοῦς): τὰ γὰρ ἀόρατα αὐτοῦ...νοούμενα καθορᾶται (Rom 1:20).

Plutarch exceeds Varro by portraying Numa's Pythagorean background, but at the same time he de-emphasizes the subsequent degeneration when Rome's cult became iconic. Varro remarks that "if this [aniconic] practice had remained down to the present day..., the gods would have been worshipped with greater purity," and that "those who first set up images for the people both diminished reverence and increased error in their cities" (frg. 18 Cardauns; Augustine, *The City of God* 4.31); Plutarch, on the other hand, does not sketch this degeneration but simply states that Numa, following Pythagoras' views on God, "forbade the Romans to revere an image of God which had the form of man or beast." The Romans "made no statues in bodily

---

[32] On Numa and Pythagoras, see Panitschek 1990 and Prowse 1964.

form for them, convinced that it was impious to liken higher things to lower, and that it was impossible to apprehend Deity except by the intellect" (νόησις): οὔτε ἐφάπτεσθαι θεοῦ δυνατὸν ἄλλως ἢ νοήσει (Plutarch, *Numa* 8.8). Unlike Varro and several other Graeco-Roman philosophers,[33] Plutarch does not explicitly criticize the use of images and limits himself to noting the philosophical background of Numa's religious legislation.

For that reason, he probably also drops Varro's reference to the Jews' exemplary maintenance of their aniconic cult.[34] Moreover, such a reference to contemporary Jews was compatible with Varro's programme, but was probably out of place in Plutarch's biography of Numa, who was part of a twin biography of Lycurgus on the Greek side, followed by Numa on the Roman side, and concluded with a comparison between the two. As such, a reference to the Jews would have been compatible with Plutarch's elaboration of the Pythagorean background of Numa's ideas, as several philosophers in Antiquity voiced the opinion that, eventually, Pythagoras himself was dependent on the Jews.[35] In any case, compared with Varro, Plutarch is less interested in the decline of aniconic religion after Numa.

---

[33] For pagan criticism of images, see also Cardauns 1976, 2:146–47: "Zum bildlosen Kult bei Barbaren und Juden vgl. fr. 15–17; die philosophische Kritik an den Götterbildern ist bekanntlich alt: Xenophanes VS 21B 15; Heraklit VS 22B 5, B 128; Antisthenes ap. Clem. Alexandr. Protr. 46c, strom. 5 p. 601A; Zeno de Rep. SVF 1.264ff.; Chrysipp SVF 2.1076; Diogenes Babylonius SVF 3.33.... Ablehnung der Götterbilder durch Varro findet sich noch fr. 22.... Dennoch hat er RD SVI eine allegorische Deutung der Bilder gegeben (fr. 225)." See also Stern 1974, 1:207.

[34] For Plutarch on the Jews in other writings, see Plutarch, *De Iside et Osiride* 363D (Typhon and the Jews); *De superstitione* 169C (Jewish scruples on the Sabbath); *Regum et imperatorum apophthegmata* 184E–F (armistice on a Jewish festival); *Quaestiones convivales* 669C, 669E, 670D, 671C (who the god of the Jews is); *De Stoicorum repugnantiis* 1051E (Jewish preconceptions of the gods).

[35] On Pythagoras and the Jews, see Burnyeat 2006, 140–41 n. 6: "The idea that Plato's philosophy, and Pythagoras' too, derives from the Jews goes back to a commentary on the Pentateuch (standardly dated 2nd cent. BC) by the Jewish Peripatetic Aristobulus, who claims they studied the *Exodus* story and 'our' law in translation (Eusebius, *Praeparatio Evangelica* 9.6.6, followed by Numenius' λόγιον; 13.12.1). Pythagoras' borrowing of Jewish (and Thracian) ideas is already found in the third-century biographer Hermippus, quoted in Josephus, *Contra Apionem* 1.165. Such claims are but one symptom of a widespread ancient tendency (anxiously combated in the opening chapters of Diogenes Laertius) to find foreign origins for Greek philosophy. By the early modern period some were ready to believe that Pythagoras was himself a Jew: J.B. Schneewind, *The Invention of Autonomy: A History of Modern Moral Philosophy*, Cambridge 1998, 536–40." See also Van Kooten 2006, 121–26 on Pythagoras, the descendants of Mochos and the Jews.

4. Ideas of Decline

Before returning to Paul's view on pagan aniconic religion, I shall just pause to reflect on the type of historiography that Varro invokes in his description of the fate of Rome's religion. His historiography espouses the model of a golden age and subsequent decline. In this model, after a period of over 170 years the Roman religion ceased to be aniconic and became less pure, as, under the influence of the poets, religion ceased to be organized according to the principles of nature, true reverence to the gods diminished, and error increased.[36]

A similar historiography, positing religious decline after a golden age, is also employed by Theophrastus and Posidonius. According to Theophrastus, between the animal-like primeval era and the beginning of moral degeneration there was a rational golden age (Theophrastus, frg. 584 Fortenbaugh, 2:405ff.). Posidonius, too, expresses the belief that after a golden age of Stoic perfection, religion and morals declined (Posidonius, frg. 284; Edelstein and Kidd, 1:248–52 text; 2.2:960–71 comm.; 3:359–66 transl.).[37] Theophrastus and Posidonius apply their historiography to the history of mankind in general. Varro, however, makes a very specific statement about the degeneration of *Roman* religion. It is interesting to note that Strabo is equally specific about such a degeneration when he deals with the history of *Jewish* religion and sketches its development into superstition. We have already seen Strabo's great admiration for Moses and his institution of a Jewish religion in which the Divine Being is worshipped without an image as the nature of all that exists (16.2.35). However, Strabo is far from positive about Moses' successors:

> His successors for some time abided by the same course, acting righteously and being truly pious toward God; but afterwards, in the first place, superstitious men were appointed to the priesthood, and then tyrannical people; and from superstition arose abstinence from flesh, from which it is their custom to abstain even today, and circumcisions…and other observances of the kind. (16.2.37)[38]

---

[36] Cf., however, Van Nuffelen 2007, who argues that, although Varro regarded the initial phase as "purer," at the same time he admitted the possibility of the allegorical interpretation of images and of interpreting the *theologia civilis* in line with the *theologia naturalis*.

[37] See also Dölle-Oelmüller 2004.

[38] This similarity between Strabo and Varro causes Cardauns to assume that Posidonius is the source of Varro's views, taking it for granted that Strabo, too, is dependent

Both Strabo and Varro employ the historiography of decline. Strabo does so to account for particular Jewish customs such as abstinence from pork and the practice of circumcision, Varro to explain the introduction of iconic cult in Rome.

5. CONCLUSION

Paul makes use of a Varronian view of the development of Roman religion in his Letter to the Romans. After 170 years of pure aniconic cult, the Romans started to worship with images. As a result, the Roman religion lost something of its initial purity, because by erecting images, the people both diminished reverence and increased error in their cities (frg. 18 Cardauns).

Paul emphasizes this transition from aniconic cult to the worship of images by stating that the worshippers changed the glory of the immortal God into an image (καὶ ἤλλαξαν τὴν δόξαν τοῦ ἀφθάρτου θεοῦ ἐν ὁμοιώματι εἰκόνος; Rom 1:23). Like Varro, he stresses the error which results from this, saying that they altered the truth of God into a lie (μετήλλαξαν τὴν ἀλήθειαν τοῦ θεοῦ ἐν τῷ ψεύδει; Rom 1:25). Although Plutarch does not explicitly speak of degeneration, he implies it by stating that Numa forbade the Romans to revere images and instilled in his people the conviction "that it was impious to liken higher things to lower, and that it was impossible to apprehend Deity except by the intellect" (οὔτε ἐφάπτεσθαι θεοῦ δυνατὸν ἄλλως ἢ νοήσει; (Numa 8.7–8).

The same view is expressed by Paul when he speaks about the *decline* of Roman religion. By inaugurating images in their cult, the Roman religion has become impious, because the Romans offer reverence and worship to created things instead of to the Creator (καὶ ἐσεβάσθησαν καὶ ἐλάτρευσαν τῇ κτίσει παρὰ τὸν κτίσαντα; Rom 1:25). This type of worship diminishes the perception of the invisible God by the mind (Rom 1:20). For this reason, Paul contrasts the Romans' pagan religion with his own, which he characterizes as a logical form of worship, a λογικὴ λατρεία, which consists in the transformation of one's mind

---

on Posidonius. See Cardauns 1976, 2:146: "Für Posidonius als Quelle Varos kann sprechen, dass bei Strabo eine Entstellung der reinen Lehre des Moses angenommen wird und Varro diese Vorstellung mit der ältesten römischen Religion verbindet." It is far from sure, however, that Strabo is dependent on Posidonius here. See above.

(*nous*): μεταμορφοῦσθε τῇ ἀνακαινώσει τοῦ νοὸς (Rom 12:1–2). What Paul suggests is that by accepting his Jewish-Christian monotheistic convictions, the Romans have not so much crossed the boundary into Judaism, as reverted to their own originally aniconic religion.[39] This seems to be his strategy to solve the tensions about identity which were marring relations between the Jews and ex-pagans within the Christian communities of Rome. In some way, he seems to put the two groups on an equal footing, by granting the pagans a glorious past of which Christianity is the restoration.

BIBLIOGRAPHY

Buchheit, V. 1991. Plutarch, Cicero und Livius über die Humanisierung Roms durch König Numa. *Symbolae Osloenses* 66: 71–96.

Buchheit, V. 1993. Numa-Pythagoras in der Deutung Ovids. *Hermes* 121: 77–99.

Burnyeat, M.F. 2006. Platonism in the Bible: Numenius of Apamea on *Exodus* and Eternity. Pages 139–168 in *The Revelation of the Name YHWH to Moses: Perspectives from Judaism, the Pagan Graeco-Roman World, and Early Christianity.* Edited by G.H. van Kooten. TBN 9. Leiden: Brill.

De Blois, L., and J.A.E. Bons. 1992. Platonic philosophy and Isocratean virtues in Plutarch's Numa. *Ancient Society* 23: 159–88.

Cancik, H., and H. Cancik-Lindemaier. 2001. The Truth of Images: Cicero and Varro on Image Worship. Pages 43–61 in *Representation in Religion: Studies in Honor of Mosche Berasche.* Edited by J. Assmann and A.I. Baumgarten. Numen 89. Leiden: Brill.

Cardauns, B. 1960. *Varros Logistoricus über die Götterverehrung (Curio de cultu deorum): Ausgabe und Erklärung der Fragmente.* Würzburg: Konrad Triltsch.

Cardauns, B. 1976. *M. Terentius Varro Antiquitates rerum divinarum* (Abhandlungen der Geistes- und Sozialwissenschaftlichen Klasse: Einzelveröffentlichung). 2 vols. Wiesbaden: Franz Steiner.

Cook, J.G. 1994. The Logic and Language of Romans 1,20. *Bib* 75: 494–517.

Dölle-Oelmüller, R. 2004. Zeitalter: goldenes. Pages 1262–65 in *Historisches Wörterbuch der Philosophie.* Vol. 12. Edited by Joachim Ritter, Karlfried Gründer, Gottfried Gabriel, and Rudolf Eisler. Basel: Schwabe.

Dunn, J.D.G. 1988. *Romans 1–8.* Dallas, Tex.: Word.

Edelstein, L., and I.G. Kidd. 1972–1999. *Posidonius.* Cambridge Classical Texts and Commentaries 13–14, 36. Cambridge: Cambridge University Press.

Fitzmyer, J.A. 1992. *Romans.* New York: Doubleday.

Furley, D. 1999. Cosmology. Pages 412–51 in *The Cambridge History of Hellenistic Philosophy.* Edited by K. Algra, J. Barnes, J. Mansfeld, and M. Schofield. Cambridge: Cambridge University Press.

Gerson, L. 1990. *God and Greek Philosophy: Studies in the Early History of Natural Theology.* London: Routledge.

Gilbert, M. 1973. *La critique des dieux dans le Livre de la Sagesse (Sg 13–15).* Rome: Biblical Institute Press.

---

[39] On other apologetic early Christian views on Roman religion, see Rüpke 2006.

Guerra, A.J. 1995. *Romans and the Apologetic Tradition.* Cambridge: Cambridge University Press.

Hagendahl, H. 1967. *Augustine and the Latin Classics.* 2 vols. Studia Graeca et Latina Gothoburgensia 20; Göteborg: Acta Universitatis Gothoburgensis.

Hooker, E.M. 1963. Significance of Numa's Religious Reforms. *Numen* 10: 87–132.

Irwin, T. 1989. *Classical Thought.* Oxford: Oxford University Press.

Kepper, M. 1999. *Hellenistische Bildung im Buch der Weisheit.* Berlin: de Gruyter.

Lange, S. 1936. The Wisdom of Solomon and Plato. *JBL* 55: 293–302.

Larcher, C. 1985. *Le Livre de la Sagesse ou la Sagesse de Salomon.* Paris: Librairie Lecoffre.

Lehmann, Y. 1997. *Varron: Théologien et philosophe romain.* Collection Latomus 237. Bruxelles: Latomus.

Mansfeld, M. 1999. Theology. Pages 452–78 in *The Cambridge History of Hellenistic Philosophy.* Edited by K. Algra, J. Barnes, J. Mansfeld, and M. Schofield. Cambridge: Cambridge University Press.

O'Daly, G. 1999. *Augustine's "City of God": A Reader's Guide.* Oxford: Oxford University Press.

Panitschek, P. 1990. Numa Pompilius als Schüler des Pythagoras. *Grazer Beiträge* 17: 49–65.

Pease, A.S. 1941. Caeli Enarrant. *HTR* 34: 163–200.

Peglau, M. 2000. Varro und die angeblichen Schriften des Numa Pompilius. Pages 441–50 in *Hortus litterarum antiquarum: Festschrift für H.A. Gärtner zum 70. Geburtstag.* Edited by A. Haltenhoff and F.-H. Mutschler. Bibliothek der klassischen Altertumswissenschaften. Neue Folge 2. Reihe 109. Heidelberg: Winter.

Prowse, K.R. 1964. Numa and the Pythagoreans: A Curious Incident. *Greece & Rome* 11: 36–42.

Reese, J.M. 1970. *Hellenistic Influence on the Book of Wisdom.* Rome: Biblical Institute Press.

Rosen, K. 1985. Die falschen Numabücher. *Chiron* 15: 65–90.

Ross-Taylor, L. 1931. Aniconic Worship among the Early Romans. Pages 305–14 in *Classical Studies in Honor of John C. Rolfe.* Edited by G.D. Hadzsits. Philadelphia: University of Pennsylvania Press.

Rüpke, J. 2006. Römische Religion in christlicher Apologetik. Pages 209–23 in *Texte als Medium und Reflexion von Religion im römischen Reich.* Edited by D.E. von der Osten, J. Rüpke, and K. Waldner. Potsdamer Altertumswissenschaftliche Beiträge 14. Stuttgart: Franz Steiner.

Scheid, J. 1985. Numa et Jupiter ou les dieux citoyens de Rome. *ASSR* 59: 41–53.

Skutsch, O. 1985. *The Annals of Q. Ennius: Edited with Introduction and Commentary.* Oxford: Oxford University Press.

Stern, M. 1974–1984. *Greek and Latin Authors on Jews and Judaism: Edition with Introduction, Translation and Commentary.* Publications of the Israel Academy of Sciences and Humanities; Section of Humanities = Fontes ad res Judaicas spectantes. 3 vols. Jerusalem: Israel Academy of Sciences and Humanities.

Strecker, G., U. Schnelle, and G. Seelig, eds. 1996. *Neuer Wettstein: Texte zum Neuen Testament aus Griechentum und Hellenismus.* Vol. 2. Berlin: de Gruyter.

Theiler, W. 1965. *Zur Geschichte der teleologischen Naturbetrachtung bis auf Aristoteles.* Second edition. Berlin: de Gruyter.

Theiler, W. 1982. *Die Fragmente/Poseidonios.* Texte und Kommentare: Eine altertumswissenschaftliche Reihe 10. 2 vols. Berlin: de Gruyter.

Van den Berg, R.M. 2006. Does It Matter To Call God Zeus? Origen, *Contra Celsum* I 24–25 Against the Greek Intellectuals on Divine Names. Pages 169–83 in *The Revelation of the Name YHWH to Moses: Perspectives from Judaism, the Pagan Graeco-Roman World, and Early Christianity.* Edited by G.H. van Kooten. TBN 9. Leiden: Brill.

Van Kooten, G.H. 2006. Moses/Musaeus/Mochos and his God YHWH, Iao, and Sabaoth, Seen from a Graeco-Roman Perspective. Pages 107–38 in *The Revelation of the Name YHWH to Moses: Perspectives from Judaism, the Pagan Graeco-Roman World, and Early Christianity*. Edited by G.H. van Kooten. TBN 9. Leiden: Brill.

Van Nuffelen, P. 2007. Varro's *Divine Antiquities*: Roman Religion as an Image of Truth. Forthcoming.

Wilckens, U. 1978. *Römer 1–5*. Vol. 1 of *Der Brief an die Römer*. Zürich: Benziger.

Willi, A. 1998. Numa's Dangerous Books: The Exegetic History of a Roman Forgery. *MH* 55: 139–73.

Winston, D. 1979. *The Wisdom of Solomon*. Garden City, N.Y.: Doubleday.

THE MYSTERY OF ISRAEL'S SALVATION: A RE-READING OF ROMANS 11:25–32 IN LIGHT OF THE DEAD SEA SCROLLS

Albert L.A. Hogeterp

1. INTRODUCTION

Close to the end of his theological exposition about Israel (Rom 9–11), Paul envisages the ultimate salvation of all Israel in Rom 11:25–32 as a "mystery." It is usually agreed in scholarship that the basic theological connotations to the Pauline concept μυστήριον stem from a Jewish, in particular apocalyptic, background,[1] not from a broader Hellenistic horizon of meaning.[2] Our understanding of this background or rather context of dialogue, if we conceive of Paul's theology in terms of a dialogue,[3] merits reconsideration in light of recent discussion about

---

[1] See, e.g., R.E. Brown, *The Semitic Background of the Term "Mystery" in the New Testament* (FBBS 21; Philadelphia: Fortress, 1968); C.E.B. Cranfield, *A Critical and Exegetical Commentary on the Epistle to the Romans* (ICC 32; Edinburgh: T&T Clark, 1979), 2:573; J.D.G. Dunn, *Romans 9–16* (WBC 38B; Dallas: Word Books, 1988), 678; J.A. Fitzmyer, *Romans: A New Translation with Introduction and Commentary* (AB 33; New York: Doubleday, 1992), 621. See, however, the divergent view of D. Sänger, "Rettung der Heiden und Erwählung Israels: Einige vorläufige Erwägungen zu Römer 11.25–27," *KD* 32 (1986): 99–119 (115) on Rom 11:25: "kein Mysterium im genuinen Sinn—etwa so, wie wir es in der jüdischen Apokalyptik, im Qumran, im Rabbinat oder auch in 1.Kor 15.51 finden."

[2] The "religionsgeschichtlich" approach, which compared the concept μυστήριον in the New Testament and Paul in particular to extra-biblical Hellenistic usage, has been extensively refuted in earlier scholarship. See e.g. M.N.A. Bockmuehl, *Revelation and Mystery in Ancient Judaism and Pauline Christianity* (WUNT II/36; Tübingen: Mohr Siebeck, 1990), 223 and n. 7, who mentions a study by K. Prümm, "Mystères," *DBSup* 6 (1960): 1–225 (180); D.A. Carson, "Mystery and Fulfillment: Toward a More Comprehensive Paradigm of Paul's Understanding of the Old and the New," in *Justification and Variegated Nomism. II. The Paradoxes of Paul* (ed. idem et al.; WUNT II/181; Tübingen: Mohr Siebeck, 2004), 393–436 (413 and nn. 51–52), who observes that the essays by D. Deden, "Le 'Mystère' Paulinien," *ETL* 13 (1936): 405–42, and by G. Bornkamm, "Μυστήριον, μυέω," *TDNT* 4:802–28, have "decisively over-thrown" this religionsgeschichtlich approach. Note also the distinction of pagan "mysteries and initiations," μυστήρια καὶ τελεταί, from God's wisdom in Jewish literature (e.g. Wis 14:15,23; Josephus, *Ag Ap.* 2.189).

[3] Cf. J.D.G. Dunn, *The Theology of Paul the Apostle* (London: T&T Clark, 1998), 23–26, who puts forward the model of dialogue for the study of Paul's Letters on historical, theological, and existential levels.

wisdom and apocalypticism as well as new evidence about apocalyptic thought in the Second Temple period, in particular that of the Dead Sea Scrolls. The evaluation of Paul's thought of salvation in relation to eschatology can now be undertaken in light of newly published Qumran texts, which discuss divine mysteries in both sapiential and apocalyptic settings. Scholarly discussion about Qumran apocalypticism and the relation between wisdom and apocalypticism owes much to Florentino García Martínez,[4] and it is in honour to him that I write this article. The momentous increase in publication of both sectarian and non-sectarian Qumran texts since the 1990s, including texts with an apocalyptic or eschatological outlook, further adds evidence to a Jewish horizon of thought contemporary to Paul.

It is the thesis of this article that, while a "Sonderweg for Israel" stands rightly criticised,[5] a close reading of Paul's theological thought and a re-reading of this passage in light of the Scrolls may fine-tune our understanding of Paul's salvific message for both Jewish and Gentile believers, rather than one taking precedence over the other.[6] Since the focus of Rom 11:25–32 is on all Israel's salvation, a re-reading in comparison with Qumran texts could add new and relevant angles of thought about mystery and revelation, salvation and the final age.

2. Mystery and Revelation

The mystery which Paul wants his readers to understand follows the questions and answers in which the apostle has engaged his readers so

---

[4] See F. García Martínez, *Qumran and Apocalyptic: Studies on the Aramaic Texts from Qumran* (STDJ 9; Leiden: Brill, 1992); idem, ed., *Wisdom and Apocalypticism in the Dead Sea Scrolls and in the Biblical Tradition* (BETL 168; Leuven: Peeters, 2003). On wisdom and apocalypticism, see further J.J. Collins, "The Eschatologizing of Wisdom in the Dead Sea Scrolls," in *Sapiential Perspectives: Wisdom Literature in Light of the Dead Sea Scrolls* (ed. idem et al.; STDJ 51; Leiden: Brill, 2004), 49–65; B.G. Wright and L.M. Wills, eds., *Conflicted Boundaries in Wisdom and Apocalypticism* (SBLSymS 35; Leiden: Brill, 2006).

[5] See R. Hvalvik, "A 'Sonderweg' for Israel: A Critical Examination of a Current Interpretation of Romans 11.25–27," *JSNT* 38 (1990): 87–107.

[6] Contra Hvalvik, "A 'Sonderweg' for Israel," 99, whose interpretation appears to amount to a swing of the pendulum to the other side, not that of a "Sonderweg" for Israel, but to the position that "the salvation of the Gentiles will take place *prior* to and will be a *condition* for the salvation of 'all Israel.'" In my view, this interpretation does not follow from Rom 11:25–26a, since "coming in" (εἰσέρχεσθαι) is not identical with "being saved" (σῳζέσθαι), nor is "being grafted in" identical with salvation in Paul's thought (cf. Rom 11:17–24). Perhaps "coming in" may be connected with a share in riches (Rom 11:12.17) and "spiritual blessings" (Rom 15:27).

far in Rom 9–11, having explicitly addressed the reader as his interlocutor at some points (e.g. Rom 9:19–20; 11:13, 19, 25a). In this and other respects, Rom 9–11 is a clear specimen of theological conversation or dialogue.[7] We may therefore suppose some kind of connection with preceding theological reflection, and it is a debated question to what extent and in which way what Paul is about to tell his readers is "new or unknown." However, the conceptualisation of "mystery" does entail something which had hitherto been hidden from human perception and which is now revealed.[8] In biblical tradition, divine mystery occurs in both sapiential (Wis 2:22; Sir ℵ^{suppl} 3:19) and apocalyptic settings (Dan 2:18, 19, 27–30, 47; Dan Th 4:6). These two settings are both relevant for the understanding of Rom 11:25–32.

The focus of Paul's μυστήριον on Israel's future destiny in terms of ultimate salvation and divine mercy presupposes an eschatological perspective.[9] Romans 1:18–2:16 provides a general eschatological setting of announced divine judgement. Romans 9–11 provides further indications of an apocalyptic-eschatological perspective through imagery of determinism and dualism (Rom 9:22–23) and of "life from the dead," i.e. resurrection (Rom 11:15). The notion of salvation in Rom 11:25–26 is part of salvific thought in Romans and comprises an eschatological component (see section on "Salvation and the Final Age" below).[10] An additional argument could be drawn from Rom 16:25–27 if we

---

[7] Apart from a dialogue with the reader as imagined interlocutor, Rom 9–11 also presents an intensive intertextual dialogue with Scripture; cf. Fitzmyer, *Romans*, 539: "The argument in this part of Romans becomes heavily scriptural"; R.B. Hays, *Echoes of Scripture in the Letters of Paul* (New Haven: Yale University Press, 1989), 34–83 (61–70) ("Intertextual Echo in Romans"). A third domain of dialogue, as we will see, is that with exegetical tradition about Israel in light of contemporary Jewish literature.

[8] It seems doubtful whether parallels from 1 Cor 10:1 and 12:1, which Hvalvik ("A 'Sonderweg' for Israel," 99) adduces to illuminate the "disclosure formula" οὐ θέλω ὑμᾶς ἀγνοεῖν, are helpful to illuminate the content of that which is disclosed, the μυστήριον. In this connection, 1 Cor 2:6–10 provides a clearer parallel, referring to the disclosure of divine wisdom "hidden and in the form of a mystery," ἐν μυστηρίῳ (1 Cor 2:7).

[9] See Bockmuehl, *Revelation and Mystery*, 24–41 (35–40) on eschatological mysteries in apocalyptic literature; J.J. Collins, *The Apocalyptic Imagination: An Introduction to Jewish Apocalyptic Literature* (BRS; Grand Rapids: Eerdmans 1998), 13 on ancient apocalypticism as "a worldview in which supernatural revelation, the heavenly world, and *eschatological judgment* played essential parts."

[10] Cf. Dunn, *The Theology of Paul the Apostle*, 461–532, whose chapter about "The Process of Salvation" presupposes an "eschatological tension" (461–98) in Paul's salvific thought, including passages from Romans in his discussion of evidence, and then turns to "Israel (Romans 9–11)" (499–532).

understand this as an amplification of Paul's understanding of mystery.[11] Romans 16:25–27 distinguishes between what was "kept secret for long ages" and what "is now disclosed." These considerations give the apocalyptic understanding of the term "mystery" its pertinence for our passage.

Besides the apocalyptic dimension, the sapiential setting of thought is not far removed from this passage either. Paul implicitly contrasts human and divine wisdom when he aims to turn the readers away from "being wise in their own conceits" and closes this exposition in Rom 11:33–36 with a hymn on God's wisdom. This hymn gives praise to divine providence, and as such it may be compared to sapiential texts and sapiential hymnic literature.[12] The question of how sapiential and apocalyptic dimensions may relate to each other can be better understood when we also take into account ancient Jewish exegetical tradition.[13]

The confluence of sapiential and apocalyptic/eschatological dimensions in the revelation of divine mystery finds its most versatile expression beyond biblical tradition not so much in the literature of Hellenistic Diaspora Judaism,[14] but in Palestinian Jewish texts.[15] This is not to deny the social reality and thought world of the Hellenistic environment in which Paul wrote his Letters.[16] Yet, recent discussion has brought to

---

[11] According to Dunn (*The Theology of Paul the Apostle*, 526 and n. 132), God's ultimate purpose with Israel and the nations, as expounded in Rom 9:25–32, is "spelled out more clearly in the addendum in Rom 16:25–26."

[12] Wisdom of Solomon, Sirach, 4Q411 (*4QSapiential Hymn*). Cf. 1QH^a V 20, 30–31; IX 9–22; XVII 23.

[13] See the earlier incentive by E.E. Johnson, *The Function of Apocalyptic and Wisdom Traditions in Romans 9–11* (SBLDS 109; Atlanta: Scholars Press, 1989) to criticise a wisdom/apocalypticism dichotomy, interpreting Rom 9–11 instead in light of a confluence of apocalyptic and wisdom traditions (160–64).

[14] See Bockmuehl, *Revelation and Mystery*, 69–81 (81) on Philo's "philosophical-mystical" understanding of divine revelation and 82–92 on Josephus' prophetic and providential understanding of divine revelation, stressing the point that this understanding is "decidedly non-eschatological" with the example of *B.J.* 6.310 (87). On 93–103 (102) ("The Ancient Versions"), Bockmuehl notes the "reluctant use of mystery language" in the Septuagint beyond its Hebrew *Vorlage*.

[15] Brown, *Semitic Background*, includes discussion of *1 Enoch, 4 Ezra, 2* and *3 Baruch*, Sirach, and, in particular, Qumran literature (22–30), in relation to the Semitic background of the New Testament μυστήριον.

[16] See now T. Engberg-Pedersen, ed., *Paul Beyond the Judaism/Hellenism Divide* (Louisville: Westminster, 2001), which includes essays on Pauline Christianity and Hellenistic philosophy (e.g. S.K. Stowers, 81–102; and H. Tronier, 165–96), while yet presenting important caveats (100–101) and concluding that Paul's "basic interpretive framework is a distinctly apocalyptic one" (196).

light new connections between Pauline terms in, among other places, Romans and the theological discourse of Palestinian Judaism, such as "works of the Law," ἔργα νόμου (Rom 3:20, 28), justification (Rom 4:1–8), and "life from the dead," ζωὴ ἐκ νεκρῶν, i.e. resurrection (Rom 11:15).[17] Paul's Roman audience would not have been outsiders to such discourse in view of Paul's personal notes about practical and spiritual matters related to Jerusalem (Rom 15:19, 25–27, 31) and of the Jewish as well as apostolic affiliations of certain converts (Rom 16:7, 11, 21).[18] The "mystery" of all Israel's salvation in Rom 11:25–32 makes part of Paul's dialogue with Palestinian Jewish discourse.

The literature of Qumran, with its large repository of both sectarian and non-sectarian texts, provides ample evidence of exegetical Jewish tradition about divine mystery and revelation contemporary to Paul. The discussion of Qumran literature by Markus Bockmuehl illustrates an understanding of divine mysteries and their revelation in these texts which, rightly so, is to an important extent apocalyptic.[19] Yet, E. Elizabeth Johnson has succinctly noted that elements from both sapiential and apocalyptic tradition occur in Qumran sectarian texts which disclose divine mysteries, namely in the Serekh ha-Yahad (1QS), the War Scroll (1QM), the Hodayot (1QH), and the Pesher to Habakkuk (1QpHab).[20]

---

[17] On "works of the Law" and מעשי התורה in 4QMMT C 27 as well as justification and ונחשבה לך לצדקה in 4QMMT C 31, see e.g. M.G. Abegg, "4QMMT, Paul, and 'Works of the Law,'" in *The Bible at Qumran: Text, Shape, and Interpretation* (ed. P.W. Flint; SDSS; Grand Rapids: Eerdmans, 2001), 203–16. On "life from the dead," cf. 4Q521 2 ii 12 (מתים יחיה) and 7+5 ii 6 (המחיה את מתי עמו). Cf. the survey by J.A. Fitzmyer, "Paul and the Dead Sea Scrolls," in *The Dead Sea Scrolls after Fifty Years: A Comprehensive Assessment* (vol. 2; ed. P.W. Flint and J.C. VanderKam; Leiden: Brill, 1999), 599–621, including examples from both longstanding and recent discussion.

[18] See P. Lampe, "The Roman Christians of Romans 16," in *The Romans Debate* (ed. K.P. Donfried; Revised and Expanded Edition; Edinburgh: T&T Clark, 1991), 216–30 (224–27), for discussion of "Jewish Christians-Gentile Christians" and "Immigrants-Natives of Rome," including some "who belonged to the first Palestinian apostles and had been Christians already before Paul" (226; see Rom 16:7).

[19] Cf. Bockmuehl, *Revelation and Mystery*, 42–56 (53–56) on "Revelation of Mysteries," referring to the theological mystery רז "as primarily an 'apocalyptic' designation of the divine plan and order of salvation." Cf. J.J. Collins, *Apocalypticism in the Dead Sea Scrolls* (The Literature of the Dead Sea Scrolls; London: Routledge, 1997) on the sectarian Qumran worldview as standing in and elaborating on the apocalyptic tradition.

[20] Johnson, *Function of Apocalyptic and Wisdom Traditions*, 95–102 includes the sectarian evidence of 1QS IX 17–19a; XI 5–8; 1QM X 9b–11a; 1QHᵃ IX 21–22; 1QpHab VII 1–5 into her survey. Curiously, 1Q27 (1QMysteries) is absent in her discussion.

Since the 1990s, the availability of a whole set of newly published Qumran texts which mention divine mysteries and their revelation has prompted discussion about the evolution of the Danielic concept רז for divine mystery and the interrelationship between wisdom and apocalypticism. Parallel to this, a broader discussion about "boundary lines" between wisdom and apocalypticism in ancient Judaism and early Christianity has been going on since the mid-1990s.[21] A concrete example with regard to Qumran texts is the renewed discussion of what the term רז נהיה, variously translated as "the mystery to be/come"[22] or "the mystery of existence,"[23] may stand for in different settings.[24] The immediate context where the term occurs and the overall character of the composition play a part in determining the sense of רז נהיה. In the sectarian setting of 1QS XI 2–4, the רז נהיה has apocalyptic affiliations of divine judgement and revelation (cf. 1QS IV 23–25), even though, as Johnson has demonstrated, sapiential elements are not far removed from this passage either (1QS XI 5–8).[25] 1Q/4QMysteries appears more detached from a clearly recognizable sectarian setting and has been associated with sapiential literature, albeit with apocalyptic elements like visionary revelation and dualism.[26] Besides 1Q26 (1QInstruction), which does not mention the רז נהיה, the newly available evidence of 4QInstruction brings various additional occurrences of the term in a sapiential setting into the discussion. Scholarly evaluation of the evidence of 4QInstruction indicates that its usage of רז נהיה includes

---

[21] See Wright and Wills, *Conflicted Boundaries*, starting with the article by G.W.E. Nickelsburg, "Wisdom and Apocalypticism in Early Judaism: Some Points for Discussion," 17–37, and being followed up by articles on apocryphal, pseudepigraphical, and Qumran literature on the early Jewish side and literature of the New Testament and Apostolic Fathers on the early Christian side.

[22] "Mystère futur" in *DJD* 1:102–4; translation of the term as it occurs in 1Q27 (Book of Mysteries) by Brown, *Semitic Background*, 28, while Brown translates the same term רז נהיה in 1QS XI 3–4 as "the mystery to be" (24); D.J. Harrington, "The *rāz nihyeh* in a Qumran Wisdom Text (1Q26, 4Q415–418, 423)," *RevQ* 17/65–68 (1996): 549–53.

[23] F. García Martínez and E.J.C. Tigchelaar, *The Dead Sea Scrolls Study Edition* (Leiden: Brill), 1:67 and 97; 2:663, 847, 849, 851, 853, 855, 859, 861, 869, 871, 875, 877, 879, 887, 889.

[24] See F. García Martínez, "Wisdom at Qumran: Worldly or Heavenly?" in idem, *Wisdom and Apocalypticism*, 1–15 (9 n. 34).

[25] 1QS XI stresses a revelation about both "what always is" (5) and "every period to come" (8–9).

[26] Cf. E.J.C. Tigchelaar, "Your Wisdom and Your Folly: The Case of 1–4QMysteries," in García Martínez, *Wisdom and Apocalypticism*, 68–88 (83) who refers to 1Q27 1 I as "the apocalyptic introduction."

both predestined origins of the ways of the world and eschatology.[27] The רז נהיה, therefore, incorporates notions of revelation about divine providence in creation and history and future-eschatological destiny. These texts represent a stream of tradition in which sapiential and apocalyptic-eschatological dimensions are interrelated.

This stream of tradition is not isolated from other Palestinian Jewish literature, even though the term רז נהיה is not found there. Passages at the end of the so-called "Epistle of Enoch"[28] comprise references to a mystery which further presuppose the interrelatedness of wisdom and apocalypticism.[29] The "Epistle of Enoch" at large addresses issues of both eschatological judgement (e.g. *1 En.* 102:4–104:8) and wisdom (*1 En.* 92:1; 93:8, 10; 98:1, 9; 99:10; 101:8). *1 Enoch* 103:2 mentions "this mystery" which comprises revealed knowledge from heavenly tablets and a writing of "what must be" or "of necessity,"[30] namely the rewards of the afterlife prepared for the souls of the pious. On the other hand, *1 En.* 104:10–105:2, a part of the Epistle which has a doxological conclusion, comprises a "second mystery" that "to the righteous and pious and wise my books will be given for the joy of righteousness and much wisdom."[31] The sapiential aspects of this "second mystery" indicate that both wisdom and apocalyptic eschatology tie in with the Epistle's conceptualisation of mystery. In scholarly discussion, Sir 42:19 and 48:25 have further been adduced as complementary evidence of revealed knowledge of what is to be in a sapiential setting.[32]

It stands to reason that both sapiential (divine providence and wisdom) and apocalyptic dimensions (future-eschatological destiny) of mystery in

---

[27] Harrington, "The *rāz nihyeh* in a Qumran Wisdom Text," 549–53 (552); J.J. Collins, "The Mysteries of God: Creation and Eschatology in 4QInstruction and the Wisdom of Solomon," in García Martínez, *Wisdom and Apocalypticism*, 287–305 (290); M.J. Goff, "Wisdom, Apocalypticism, and the Pedagogical Ethos of 4QInstruction," in Wright and Wills, *Conflicted Boundaries*, 57–67 (61).

[28] The Epistle of Enoch is variously designated as comprising *1 Enoch* 91–107 (E. Isaac, "1 [Ethiopic Apocalypse of] Enoch," in *OTP* 1:5–89 [7]), *1 Enoch* 91–108 (Johnson, *Function of Apocalyptic and Wisdom Traditions*, 81), or *1 Enoch* 92–105 (G.W.E. Nickelsburg and J.C. VanderKam, *1 Enoch: A New Translation* [Minneapolis: Fortress, 2004], 139–63). Note that various Aramaic fragments of this Epistle have been preserved in Qumran texts 4Q204 (4QEn^c ar) 5 i–ii and 4Q212 (4QEn^g ar) II–V.

[29] Johnson, *Function of Apocalyptic and Wisdom Traditions*, 79–90 (81) discusses the evidence of the Epistle only in the most general terms, focussing more on the evidence of *1 Enoch* 1–36, 37–71, and 72–82.

[30] Nickelsburg and VanderKam, *1 Enoch*, 159.

[31] Nickelsburg and VanderKam, *1 Enoch*, 163.

[32] Collins, "The Mysteries of God," 289.

Palestinian Jewish discourse, as illustrated by Qumran literature, play in the background to Paul's concept of "mystery" in Rom 11:25, for the mystery of all Israel's salvation presupposes a process of salvation which is not only future-oriented, but part of salvation history.

Let us now return to the question of what the core of the mystery as disclosed by Paul in Rom 11:25 is. Some commentators maintain that the ultimate salvation of all Israel would hardly be a mystery to the apostle with his Jewish background.[33] Yet, much depends on the immediate context of theological reflection to which one relates Rom 11:25–32. Depending on whether one takes the theological question if God rejected his people (Rom 11:1)[34] or if Israel's stumbling means ultimate failure (Rom 11:11)[35] as one's lead for interpreting what follows, up to and including Rom 11:25–32, this also determines presuppositions about the divine mystery that all Israel will be saved. In my view, Rom 11:25–32 takes up elements from previous argument in Rom 11, such as the partial hardening of Israel (Rom 11:7) and the coming in/being grafted in of the Gentiles (Rom 11:11, 17–24). Yet, besides the figurative amplification through the imagery of the olive tree (Rom 11:17–24), the major connection of Paul's concept of "mystery" appears to be with Rom 11:11–16, as I will point out below.

The overall passage of Rom 11:11–16 is concerned with the issue of salvation (Rom 11:11, 14) and is interrelated with Paul's understanding of the mission to Jews and Gentiles. At various points, Paul hints at Israel's divine acceptance and salvation (Rom 11:12b, 14–15). Specific points of connection of Rom 11:25–32 with Rom 11:11–16 have been noted in previous scholarship, such as with Israel's acceptance followed by apocalyptic imagery of "life from the dead" in Rom 11:15[36] and

---

[33] E.g. D. Zeller and B. Mayer as referred to by Hvalvik, "A 'Sonderweg' for Israel," 100 n. 89; Fitzmyer, *Romans*, 622 calls it Paul's "conviction about the lot of his former coreligionists (which) is thus formalized."

[34] Dunn, *Romans 9–16*, 632 designates Rom 11:1–32 as a section about "The Mystery of God's Faithfulness"; Johnson, *The Function of Apocalyptic and Wisdom Traditions in Romans 9–11*, 160–63; Fitzmyer, *Romans*, 602–36 designates Rom 11:1–36 as a section on "Israel's Failure: It is partial and temporary."

[35] According to the view of J. Lambrecht ("Israel's Future According to Romans 9–11: An Exegetical and Hermeneutical Approach," *FS Jan Kerkhofs* [1989]: 319–36; repr. in *Pauline Studies: Collected Essays* [BETL 115; Leuven: Peeters, 1994], 33–54), Rom 9:6–10:21 and 11:1–10 constitute answers to two central questions whether the word of God failed (Rom 9:6) and whether God rejected his people (Rom 11:1), while Rom 11:11–32 tackles the question whether Israel's stumbling means definite failure.

[36] Johnson, *Function of Apocalyptic and Wisdom Traditions*, 160–63; R.H. Bell, *The Irrevocable Call of God: An Inquiry into Paul's Theology of Israel* (WUNT 184; Tübingen: Mohr Siebeck, 2005), 251–53.

with the "a fortiori argument" in Rom 11:12.[37] The "full inclusion" of Israel, το πλήρωμα αὐτῶν, into the gospel message of salvation in Rom 11:12 appears to be the mirror image of the "full inclusion" of the Gentiles in Rom 11:25 (τὸ πλήρωμα τῶν ἐθνῶν), which makes part of the Pauline mystery of ultimate salvation of all Israel. Even more striking is the parallel with Rom 11:15. This parallel informs us that in Paul's theology the ultimate salvation of all Israel is preceded by and made conditional on the paradoxically salutary effects of both Israel's temporary failure (Rom 11:12) and rejection (Rom 11:15a)[38] and its acceptance as the elected people of God. It is therefore not the salvation of the Gentiles[39] which is the condition for Israel's ultimate salvation, but a vision of reconciliation of the world, in which both Israel and other peoples have a place, which precedes future (re)acceptance imagined in terms of "life from the dead," ζωὴ ἐκ νεκρῶν (Rom 11:15b). It has been asked why Paul did not use the more explicit term ἀνάστασις here, assuming that Paul does indeed have resurrection in mind.[40] Yet, this term is more specifically related to Christ's resurrection (1 Cor 15;[41] Rom 1:4; 6:5; Phil 3:10), while in Rom 11:15 the general notion of Israel's acceptance through faith (cf. Rom 11:20–23) is at issue rather than the more specific Pauline terminology of fellowship with Christ.

Since we can identify "all Israel" with the Jewish people as the elected people of God,[42] the core of the mystery which Paul discloses in Rom 11:25–32 appears to be the contrast between the present situation of partial unbelief of Israel and the ultimate divine plan of salvation as he envisages it. The way in which the apostle envisages all Israel's

---

[37] Bell, *The Irrevocable Call of God*, 253–56.

[38] In connection with the question of rejection (Rom 11:1, 11a) and with regard to Rom 11:25–27, Brown, *Semitic Background*, 50 has noted a parallel in *4 Ezra* 10:38–39.

[39] When Paul writes in Rom 11:11 that "salvation has come to the Gentiles," ἡ σωτηρία τοῖς ἔθνεσιν, this means that salvation through the gospel message has come into the reach of the Gentiles, not that it is in the possession of Gentile converts, for this depends on mercy on God's side in the end (Rom 11:30–32) and is determined by the act of standing fast through faith on the human side (Rom 11:20–22).

[40] Bell, *The Irrevocable Call of God*, 254.

[41] On a possible connection between the disclosure of "mystery" in 1 Cor 15:51–55 and Rom 11:25–27, see Bockmuehl, *Revelation and Mystery*, 170–75, who categorises both as examples of disclosure of "new doctrine," and Carson, "Mystery and Fulfillment," 419 who notes about Rom 11:25–27 and 1 Cor 15:50–55 that "in both passages the apostle Paul discloses an element of new teaching which he calls a μυστήριον."

[42] On πᾶς Ἰσραήλ and its Semitic overtones, see, e.g., Cranfield, *Romans IX–XVI*, 577 who refers to biblical texts and *m. Sanh.* 10; Fitzmyer, *Romans*, 623 who calls it a "corporate expression"; Bell, *The Irrevocable Call of God*, 260–65 includes various rabbinic texts in his discussion of the term.

salvation, taking into account both Rom 11:11–16 and 11:25–32, inter-
sects significantly with biblical tradition as well as apocalyptic discourse
contemporary to Paul. The idea of rejection parallel to reconciliation
of the world and acceptance parallel to life from the dead (Rom 11:15)
could be Pauline elaboration on prophetic ideas in Isaiah. For Isaiah
54–56 conveys both the assurance that salvation will come for Israel
in its affliction and the vision of other peoples joining themselves to
the Lord. As part of the "Isaiah Apocalypse" (Isa 24–27), Isa 26:19
conceptualises God's aid to his people in distress in terms of apocalyptic imagery that "your dead shall live." Daniel 12:1–3 envisages
the deliverance of "your people" through the apocalyptic imagery of
resurrection, and 4Q521 envisages divine agency which makes the
dead live (2 ii 12; 7+5 ii 6) as well as it gives reason for the earth and
all Israel, כל ישראל, to rejoice (2 iii 4–5).

It is with this theological discourse that Paul is in dialogue when he
discloses the mystery of all Israel's salvation. The parameters of salvation, as they are elaborated in both theological and christological terms
in Rom 11:25–32, will concern us in the next section. A few observations
on revelation of mystery are still in place here. Different suggestions
have been made with regard to the nature of Pauline revelation in this
passage: "revelation by a vision" (S. Kim) or "revelation by exegesis"
(M.N.A. Bockmuehl; R.H. Bell).[43] If not restricted to the vision "on the
road to Damascus," the two may not by definition be mutually exclusive. In a recent study, Armin Lange stressed the mantic dimension to
scriptural interpretation in apocalyptic texts and the pesharim.[44]

3. Salvation and the Final Age

As we already noted, salvation is related to history up to the present as well as to eschatology. The notion of salvation should first be

---

[43] See discussion of literature by Carson, "Mystery and Fulfillment," 422 and nn.
81–82. Bell, *The Irrevocable Call of God*, 256–57 and n. 84 refers to the Qumran text
1QpHab VII 4–5 as background to revelation as "discovered through the study of
scripture" (257).

[44] A. Lange, "Interpretation als Offenbarung: Zum Verhältnis von Schriftauslegung
und Offenbarung in apokalyptischer und nichtapokalyptischer Literatur," in García
Martínez, *Wisdom and Apocalypticism*, 17–33. Cf. R.G. Wooden, "Guided by God: Divine
Aid in Interpretation in the Dead Sea Scrolls and the New Testament," in *Christian
Beginnings and the Dead Sea Scrolls* (ed. J.J. Collins and C.A. Evans; Grand Rapids: Baker
Academic, 2006), 101–20.

understood in its historical context, before we turn to the relation of salvation to the final age in Rom 11:25–32. In Romans 11:5, Paul observes that "at the present time there is a remnant, chosen by grace" (RSV), while subsequently contrasting Israel's temporary and partial failure through hardening to the achievement of the "elect," ἡ ἐκλογή (Rom 11:7). The notion of election recurs in Rom 11:28 and is then related to the Jewish people of Israel "for the sake of the forefathers," διὰ τοὺς πατέρας. Romans 11:29 establishes the point that God's gifts and God's call are irrevocable.

Various aspects of this salvific thought which lays its foundation in biblical history can be understood against the background of Jewish exegetical tradition contemporary to Paul. The idea of election and separate position of a remnant also occurs in Qumran theological thought, which relates this to God's remembrance of "the covenant with the forefathers," ברית ראשנים (CD A I 4–5 // 4QDᶜ [4Q268] 1 11–12). A sapiential Qumran text, 4Q185, presents wisdom as God's gift to Israel with which God "has saved all his people," וכל עמו נאל (1–2 ii 10), wisdom which was given a man "to his fathers" and is to be given in inheritance to descendants (1–2 II 14–15). Even the dichotomy in Rom 11:28, which juxtaposes the image of Israel as regards the gospel as "enemies for your sake," ἐχθροὶ δι' ὑμᾶς, to the image of Israel as regards election as beloved for the sake of the forefathers, comprises elements of admonition which may not be unrelated to intra-Jewish discourse. The language of juxtaposition in terms of beloved versus enemy also occurs in contemporary Jewish literature. In a context of admonition to do good (lines 3–6), 4Q525 10 5 (4QBeatitudes) refers to "enemy and friend," אויב ואוהב, after which the text insist that "G[od] will not justify all flesh," [ל]א יצדק אל בשר וכול.[45]

The issue of all Israel's salvation as it relates to the final age pre-supposes both theological and christological lines of thought in Rom 11:25–32. For Paul mentions the gospel in Rom 11:28a and disobedience in Rom 11:30–32 (cf. Rom 10:14–21 at v. 21), on the one hand, while stressing God's irrevocable gifts and call as well as divine mercy, on the other. The question is along which theological and christological lines the future-oriented notion of covenant in the scriptural proof-texts of Rom 11:26b–27 should be interpreted.

---

[45] Text and translation from García Martínez and Tigchelaar, *Dead Sea Scrolls Study Edition*, 2:1054–55.

In Rom 11:26b–27, Paul adduces proof-texts for the revelation that all Israel will be saved after partial hardening has brought about the coming in of the full number of Gentiles. This passage reads as follows: "The Redeemer will come from Zion, he will banish ungodliness from Jacob. And this will be my covenant with them when I take away their sins" (after RSV). The scriptural proof-texts are from Isa 59:20–21a and Isa 27:9. The connection between the mystery of all Israel's salvation (Rom 11:25–26a) and the biblical proof-texts (Rom 11:26b–27) has received both theological and christological interpretations.[46] It is a debated question whether the future-oriented activity of the Redeemer-figure, ὁ ῥυόμενος, who stands for the Lord God in Isa 59, should be interpreted as an implicit reference to Jesus Christ, and if so, to the Parousia.[47]

I would be inclined to argue that Paul's use of proof-texts in Rom 11:26b–27 represents converging christological and theological lines of thought for the following reasons. The one other instance in Rom 9–11 where Paul refers to Zion is another Isaianic proof-text in Rom 9:33, which has both christological (stumbling block) and theological significance (divine agency in laying this stone in Zion). The envisioned salvation as enacted by the Redeemer could be associated with Christ (cf. 1 Thess 1:10) as well as with God (cf. 2 Cor 1:9–10). Paul's use of the language of Scripture does not further specify the identity of the divine agency, thereby possibly including but not necessarily specifically limited to the Parousia. The apostle does presuppose that redemption from sin is through Jesus Christ (cf. Rom 3:21–26). The convergence of christological and theological lines of thought is also implied by intertwined references to the "gospel of God" (Rom 1:1; 15:16) and

---

[46] Fitzmyer, *Romans*, 618–20 surveys three positions: (1) theological, (2) christological and specifically related to the Parousia of Christ, and (3) christological but not limited to the Parousia.

[47] The interpretation that all Israel will be saved "at the Parousia" has been defended by e.g. Cranfield, *Romans IX–XVI*, 577–78; Bockmuehl, *Revelation and Mystery*, 173; Lambrecht, "Israel's Future According to Romans 9–11," 46; K. Kuula, *The Law, the Covenant and God's Plan: Vol. 2 Paul's Treatment of the Law and Israel in Romans* (PFES 85; Helsinki: The Finnish Exegetical Society, 2003), 336–45 (337–38); Carson, "Mystery and Fulfillment," 393–436 (420); Bell, *The Irrevocable Call of God*, 266. Fitzmyer, *Romans*, 620 interprets the christological interpretation of ὁ ῥυόμενος more generally as related to deliverance and (new) covenant through the ministry, death, and resurrection of Jesus Christ. Hvalvik, "A 'Sonderweg' for Israel," 101 concludes that the Parousia-interpretation "must be labelled speculation," arguing that christological presuppositions about Israel's salvation rather consist in the condition of faith (Rom 11:20–23).

to the "gospel of Christ" (Rom 15:19) and by the eschatological vision of 1 Cor 15:20–28. Concomitantly, the concept of covenant in Rom 11:26–27 includes notions of both continuity from the forefathers to the end of time (Rom 11:28b) and of "new covenant" instituted through Jesus Christ.[48]

Messianic interpretation of Isa 59:20 was not alien to ancient Judaism, as the parallel with *b. Sanh* 98a noted by several scholars may indicate.[49] Yet, this is a late antique parallel, and Second Temple Jewish evidence attests to a wide variety of messianic ideas.[50] In Qumran literature, one clear instance of redemption for Israel identifies the Redeemer, גוֹאֵל, with God (4Q176 8–11 7–10).

4. CONCLUSION

Close reading of Rom 11:25–32 in connection with preceding passages, in particular Rom 11:11–16, gives insight into Paul's conceptualisation of salvation as a process related to past, present, and future, including the final age. In the present of Paul's perspective, "salvation has come to the Gentiles" (Rom 11:11) while a "remnant, chose by grace" stands out against a hardening of part of Israel (Rom 11:5, 7, 25). Yet, the biblical past of Israel's forefathers provides a signpost of assurance that God's call is irrevocable (Rom 9:4–5; 11:28–29). Due to the interrelatedness of perspectives on Jews and Gentiles in the Pauline gospel mission, the destiny of Israel in terms of temporary and partial hardening (Rom 11:25) mirrors reconciliation of the world (Rom 11:15a), while its ultimate salvation (Rom 11:26a) mirrors the apocalyptic imagery of life from the dead (Rom 11:15b).

A re-reading of Rom 11:25–32 in light of the Dead Sea Scrolls makes it clear that Paul's revelation of mystery stands close to a Palestinian Jewish stream of tradition in which sapiential and apocalyptic dimensions are interrelated. This can be demonstrated from Qumran texts

---

[48] E.J. Christiansen, *The Covenant in Judaism and Paul: A Study of Ritual Boundaries as Identity Markers* (AGJU 27; Leiden: Brill, 1995), 225–32, having compared Rom 11:26–27 with Rom 9:4–5 and 9:33, stresses that it is Paul's concern "to maintain an interpretation of Christ as promise *within* Israel's covenant relationship."

[49] Cranfield, *Romans IX–XVI*, 578 and n. 1; Bell, *The Irrevocable Call of God*, 266 n. 129.

[50] See e.g. J.J. Collins, *The Scepter and the Star: The Messiahs of the Dead Sea Scrolls and Other Ancient Literature* (New York: Doubleday, 1995).

published since the 1990s, discussion about רז נהיה, and comparison
with other ancient Jewish literature. My discussion of Qumran texts
provides further evidence that there are more intra-Jewish aspects of
Pauline thought in Rom 11:25–32 than have hitherto been assumed.
In this respect, Paul's mystery of Israel's ultimate salvation may be
understood as a dialogue with contemporary Jewish discourse.

ON THE HELLENIZATION OF CHRISTIANITY
ONE EXAMPLE: THE SALVATION OF GENTILES IN PAUL

Antonio Piñero

The question of the hellenization of Christianity is very ancient, but it began to be seriously debated since the Protestant Reformation as the new confessions, ideologically and sociologically opposed to Rome, discovered that there were diverse theological levels in the New Testament and that not all the writings contained therein fit into the same ideological, primitive pattern that would fundamentally correspond to Jesus and to Paul. Modern discussion on the "Frühkatholizismus" inside the New Testament raises the same question of the hellenization of Christian theology: a primitive, ideal theology—without ecclesiology, sacraments, hierarchy, dogma, etc., which would be that of Jesus and Paul—that was corrupted by the contact with Hellenism and was transformed into a new hellenized one. This corruption was mainly caused by the followers of the apostle Paul, the authors of Ephesians, Colossians, the Pastoral Epistles, and of 2 Peter. Though the leading liberal, protestant theologian Adolf von Harnack supported that such a Frühkatholizismus did not exist in the New Testament,[1] Ernst Käsemann sustained the opposite view,[2] which has since then influenced the current Protestant view on the subject: Christian theology was certainly hellenized in the late writings of the New Testament. Käsemann was indeed following the steps of the former History of Religions School, which since the end of the nineteenth century has defended a remarkable influence of Greek popular religion on New Testament authors and on their most important theological conceptions.[3]

---

[1] *What is Christianity* (trans. T.B. Saunders; introd. by R. Bultmann; New York: Harper, 1957), 190. Trans. of *Das Wesen des Christentums* (Leipzig: Hinrichs, 1900).

[2] *Essays on New Testament Themes* (SBT 41; London: SCM, 1964), 95–107. Trans. of *Exegetische Versuche und Besinnungen 1* (Göttingen: Vandenhoeck & Ruprecht, 1960).

[3] See A. Piñero and J. Peláez, *The Study of the New Testament: A Comprehensive Introduction* (Tools for Biblical Study 3; Leiden: Deo, 2003), 38ff.; trans. of *El Nuevo Testamento. Introducción al estudio de los primeros escritos cristianos* (Córdoba: El Almendro, 1995).

Amongst Catholic NT interpreters, the positions on the issue of the hellenization of Christianity are diverse. Clearly influenced by Protestant theology, most of them sustain that the beginnings of a certain hellenization of Christian theology is apparent in Ephesians, Colossians, and rather less so in Hebrews. In these writings, Hellenistic elements of thinking clearly appear which serve a creative Christian theology. The influence of the mystery religions, especially on Ephesians and Colossians, is admitted with many doubts, and it is generally sustained that it does not seem satisfactory to speak of a massive influence of these religions on the formation of the late New Testament theology. But a partial influence is not excluded, especially in the language and in some literary images. It is still thought that the real hellenization of Christianity begins, in fact, with the Apologists of the second century, with the gnosis, and with the speculative theology of Clement of Alexandria and Origen.

In this brief contribution, we want to defend a return to previous positions—considered already overcome by some NT scholars—of the History of Religions School on the issue of the hellenization of Christianity, because the actual discussion of the problem of New Testament "Frühkatholizismus" does not seem to enter into the core of the matter. I will give only one example, Paul's doctrine on salvation of Gentiles, to illustrate our case: some brief considerations on the core of this doctrine lead us to a position closer to the "Religionsgeschichtliche Schule."

1. The core of Paul's doctrine on the salvation of Gentiles

In our opinion, Paul's doctrine on the salvation of Gentiles, as Jesus of Nazareth's conception of the arrival of the Kingdom, is only well understood if framed in the theology of the "Restoration of Israel." This seems to be deduced from some Pauline convictions: Paul was persuaded that he was not creating a new religion, but only elevating Israel to perfection, that the end of the world was immediate, and that the complete and real Israel had to confront God's definitive judgment, according to the view of the Scriptures.

We know that the beginning of the Pauline, personal religious thought was marked by a divine "call" (not a "conversion"!) to take part in the group of believers in Jesus as the messiah. This "call" is described three times (9:1–19; 22:5–16; 26:12–18) in Acts—every time with different connotations and even some contradictions. The call was probably a kind of ecstatic or visionary experience (cf. 2 Cor 12:1–4): Paul was always persuaded that God had given him a special revelation (Gal 1:11–12) similar to these granted to the former prophets of Israel (Gal 1:15–16). This revelation transformed him into an apostle of Jesus, exactly as those who accompanied him in his ministry. Paul feels very proud of it and fiercely defends his title of "apostle" (see 2 Cor 2:14–7:4). Paul understands "apostle" as the envoy chosen by God to preach the Gospel with absolute authority. As an apostle, Paul has been worthy of God's confidence, and he is an example for the Christians to imitate.

For our present purposes, we can summarise the content of the essential theological features of this "call"—a content which was outlined and eventually perfected by Paul—as follows:

(1) In spite of the fact of his apparent failure at the cross, Jesus is the real Messiah. His death is to be interpreted as an expiatory sacrifice accepted by God.

(2) This event inaugurates the messianic, preparatory time for the final salvation of humanity and for the definitive restoration of God's power over it.

(3) There is now a new divine plan for salvation; it begins an age of grace; the promise to Abraham is fulfilled; Jesus the Messiah is the redeemer of Israel. But he is not a redeemer, as the average Jews would understand it, but *the* redeemer *of the complete, restored Israel, which in the last times will accept in its bosom a certain amount of converted Gentiles.* The eschatological people of God, now completed, formed of Jews and of a *certain number* of Gentiles, were being assembled by God just in those moments, thanks to Jesus' work.

(4) Consequently, the chosen ones—formerly sinners but then justified by their faith in Jesus—have to hurry to fulfil God's plan for the last time: (a) it is necessary to preach in order to persuade all of Israel to accept Jesus as the messiah; (b) the number of Gentiles, predetermined by God to join all of God's people, is to be carried out through *conversion*, so that the end of the world can come about.

(5) The end of the world is very close. The remaining time is scarce. Soon, very soon, Jesus will come as the ultimate judge of the living and the dead. At this moment, God's sovereignty will be restored. This implies the end of the present world, and the inauguration of a divine, otherworldly, and eternal reign.

This "gospel" was completed and perfected by Paul during years of maturity in contact with the tradition of Jesus received in the Christian communities of Damascus and especially Antioch and by his own reflection on Jesus. It is to be concluded, from Acts 9:28–29 and Gal 1–2, that Paul gets to work immediately after his call and tries intensely to spread his own, new view of Jesus and salvation in the end of the world amongst the people who he had brutally pursued before.

What made Paul—a member of a minuscule Jewish sectarian group, who was waiting for the immediate end of the world—preach the message of salvation *also to Gentiles*? The reason may be in a certain continuity of the Jewish-Christian theology of the Hellenists (Acts 6) mixed with Jesus' doctrine. We had indirectly defined Jesus before as a prophet of the restoration of Israel. One feature of this restoration theology, deeply oriented towards the end of times, was the conception that God had decided to incorporate *a certain number of Gentiles into the Jewish faith* at the time when such a restoration was being carried out. The prophets of Israel since the exile—especially the Third Isaiah—had clearly proclaimed it (Isa 58:1–8; 60:3–7, 10–14; 66:18–24): some Gentiles would also take part in the future glory of the messianic Israel.

This conception was the reason why many members of the Hellenists' group—amongst them Paul himself—were forced to attain the greatest possible amount of conversions from paganism before the end of the world…in agreement with a divine plan that had previously determined the exact amount of Gentiles to be converted. *It was not necessary therefore to convert all the pagans, but to achieve the number previously determined by God for the coming end of the world* (cf. Rom 11:25). Paul founded a few communities in Asia and Europe (in which the converted Gentiles would reach perhaps 0.5 percent of the total pagan population of the Roman Empire), but *he thought he had already fulfilled his mission in those areas*. After having converted a few people here and there, Paul thought he should go to the end of the world, to the extreme West, Hispania, to gain a few more believers. Initially, the amount of people converted to the new Israel mattered little: it was in God's hand.

It is important to know that this conception was the basis for a new missionary movement in Israel. But this movement would eventually forget the theory of the conversion of "a precise number of Gentiles decided by God" and would change to the idea of "God's will is to convert as many people as possible," and finally "all Gentiles are to be converted."

Therefore Paul began to preach to convince his fellow Jewish citizens that Jesus was *the* messiah and that it was necessary for a few Gentiles to join the true Israel, because this conversion was part of a divine plan—according to his theology of Israel's restoration. Luke's Acts tell us that the Apostle, when arriving to a new city, first went to the Jews, visited their synagogues, and preached that Jesus was the messiah of Israel. Only when he was not successful did he turn his gaze towards the Gentiles.

Unfortunately, the divine plan failed in its first part: there was no way of convincing Israel to accept Jesus as the messiah. It was therefore necessary to revise the plan. Paul noticed, then, that God's intention was more complicated: a certain amount of Gentiles should first enter into the Kingdom; later—only as a consequence of the Jewish-Christian mission to the Gentiles—Israel would be jealous of it, would accept Jesus, and would be saved (Rom 11:13–16; [11:26: "*This way* Israel will be saved"]). The revision of the plan, in Rom 8:28–11:36 confirms its previous existence and proves beyond any doubt the eschatological context—the restoration of Israel—of Paul's thought.

As a consequence of the general psychological "*law of the slightest effort*," Paul tried to get as easily, and quickly as possible, the amount of converted Gentiles that had to take part in the complete Israel of the end of times. Therefore, Paul first oriented his message of "Jesus as the messiah/saviour of Israel and of the Gentiles" toward those "fearful of God" (φοβούμενοι τὸν θεόν): the group of common pagans gathered around the synagogues. They were Gentiles, because they had not been circumcised. Paul's effort to convince them can be compared to the attempts of a good trade man who tries to sell his product to a hard market. His goods—message—were: "Jesus is indeed the Jewish messiah, but also the universal saviour; God had revealed that at the end of times some Gentiles (later, all!) were to be converted to the faith of Israel, because they were equal to the Jews for the sake of salvation." The religious market where these "goods" were to be sold was the oriental Mediterranean, where other "sellers" of religious ideas were swarming: followers of the mystery religions, travelling philosophers in search of disciples, street preachers of oriental religions. Paul confronted their preaching with a simple but interesting message: *Jesus, the only Saviour, as the Son of the only God, offered a better, simpler salvation than theirs... and for nothing...*

Judaism—and also the Jewish-Christians—of the first century A.D. had thought of two possibilities for the Gentiles to be saved, so that they could go into the restored Israel in accordance with God's plan for the end of times:

(1) A traditional and simple one: Gentiles have to convert to Judaism, that is to say, they must become proselytes by means of circumcision and the observance of the complete Law: all the saved, Gentiles and Jews, must obey the Law.

(2) A second system, also traditional but connected to a broader mental framework and with conceptions defended also by Judaism perhaps for centuries: Gentiles could be saved in a sort of second class salvation, not being necessary for them to be fully converted to Judaism. It was only indispensable for them to fulfil the so called "Laws of Noah," based on the alliance established by God with this patriarch and his lineage (Gen 9:3–13). The most important of these precepts were: Not to blaspheme; not to adore false gods; not to commit sexual sins; not to kill; not to steal; not to eat meat together with its blood. Chapter 15 of Acts reveals to us the existence of a way of imagining the admission of Gentiles into a Jewish-Christian group that considered themselves to be the true Israel. It seems possible that this position was very close to Peter's mental stance on the issue at time of the "Antioch controversy" (Gal 2): Jews are to be saved under the Law; Gentiles not circumcised are to be saved under the rules of Noah. The chosen ones are now divided in two different communities, but at the end of times, they will become only one.

But there was a third possibility of salvation... that of Paul's. God had revealed to him that the new divine plan for salvation was *to make it as easy as possible for the Gentiles to take part in the restored Israel in the end of times* (the "messianic era" that lasted from the sacrificial death of Christ to his coming as universal judge). Paul's thought on the issue was: Until Jesus' appearance on earth, salvation was to be achieved in two ways:

(1) for the Jews: the observance of Mosaic law;
(2) for the Gentiles: the recognition of God's existence and the fulfilment of the natural law, which was the same thing as observing the Decalogue (Rom 1–2).

After Jesus' coming to the world ("the fullness of times": Gal 4:4) and after his redeeming sacrifice, God's revelation to Paul confirmed that there were easier conditions for salvation:

(1) *The observance of the Law was not already an indispensable requirement.* In opposition to his contemporary Judaism, Paul defended a revolutionary idea: now God does not demand the fulfilment of a ritual Law, but "the law of love" reinforced by Jesus (Gal 5:13–14; see Gal 6:2). *Therefore, the Law of Moses does not have any soteriological efficiency for the Gentiles.* No one can be saved by the mere fulfilment of the Law of Moses, not even a Jew (Galatians) or at least, not a Gentile (Romans). Nor is it necessary for the Gentiles to observe Noah's rules *as such* (for example, the ingestion of meat together with blood, which is no part of the "natural law").

(2) *Circumcision is not already a necessary exigency for salvation either.* The Jewish tradition going back to Moses (Exod 4:24–26) declared circumcision as the indispensable condition to be part of God's chosen people, the people of His covenant. Paul sustained the opposite: for the Gentiles, the time has come for *spiritual circumcision*, not a physical one, but one achieved by an act of faith (see Phil 3:3).

The public defence of this new divine plan for salvation, revealed to him, places Paul's teachings opposite those of Judaism. In Galatians and Romans he outlined the contour of this divine plan, intended first for the salvation of the Gentiles, but also concerned with the core of Judaism. A human being that claims that his sins are to be pardoned—i.e. that he is to be saved—by the performance of acts due to his own human power—being circumcised, for example, or "doing the works of the law"—will act in vain. After his coming, only Jesus takes away the sins of humanity and reconciles it with God, thanks to the expiatory sacrifice of his death. To obtain the benefits of this reconciliation, every human being has to accept God's will and present Him with *an act of faith based on the value of this sacrifice*. Abraham is an example of acceptance of God's will and of this act of faith. Therefore, Abraham is the father of Israel and the Patriarch to whom God had promised that: "In his seed, humanity would be saved." *By an equivalent act of faith, every human being receives the benefits of the promise made to Abraham.*

This Pauline approach to salvation, according to God's latest plan revealed to his Apostle, may be synthesized in the following scheme:

Before Christ's arrival	After Christ's arrival
Circumcision in the flesh	Spiritual circumcision: Or justification by faith
Carnal law of Moses	Spiritual law of love and freedom in Christ
Insistence on covenant theology	Insistence on promise theology

(Insistence on fulfilling the
  laws of the covenant)
	(Insistence on the benefits
	  of God's promise to Israel)

All the Gentiles who heard Paul (almost all "fearful of God," who knew the Jewish theology well) felt that this new divine plan for salvation, revealed through Paul, was sensational and amazing and provided agreeable consequences:

(1) It was not necessary to be circumcised.
(2) It was not necessary to fulfil the law of Moses, especially the complicated rules of purity and meals (The Mishnah records a total of 613 precepts that the pious Jew must observe).
(3) It was not necessary to fulfil the laws of Noah, which did not coincide with the Decalogue or the rules of natural law.
(4) It was only required to be spiritually circumcised by an act of faith and to observe "the law of love"—certainly with all its consequences—as proclaimed by Christ.

It is to be observed, that this contraposition of "carnal and spiritual" is not a Jewish one, but rather corresponds to a clear vulgar platonic / gnostic mental framework.

Similarly, it is to be observed that justification by faith as the main act of salvation is after all an intellectual act. For a normal, first-century Jew, for whom Judaism and salvation was a matter of "orthopraxis" (i.e. a matter of observance of certain laws) and not of "orthodoxy" (i.e. not a matter of sustaining certain dogmatic issues—contrast the religious "dogmas" of an Essene and a Sadducean!), this conception of salvation ought to be exceedingly surprising: a hellenistic Greek conception, not a Jewish one!

Furthermore, the new divine plan of Gentile salvation contained an ace of the highest value: a full response to the spiritual anxieties of part of the religious spirits in the Roman Empire that longed for salvation and immortality. According to Paul, this ace was: all the rites and ceremonies designed, for instance, by the mystery religions, for conquering immortality at a huge cost were offered by Christianity easier and cheaper... for nothing! The ceremonies of *baptism* (to submerge in Christ's death and to emerge from the water participating in the eternal life with Him) and of the *Eucharist* (a sort of theophagy: taking part of the body and the blood of Christ) performed the same functions as the expensive rites of initiation of the mystery religions: in Eleusis, for example, they consisted of two acts separated by months; the several degrees of Isis initiations (remember Apuleius) needed to be repeated. It was necessary for many to spend a great deal of time away from home in boarding houses and also to pay the expenses of the sanctuary. On the contrary, in Christianity, everything was simple, easy... and besides, at no cost! The success among the "fearful of God" and the pagans was, in general, insured!

To sum up: Paul offered the following ideas to the Gentiles (and also to the Jews) concerning salvation:

(1) The only God, God of Israel and of the world, creator, legislator, provident, judge of the universe, has sent his Son, Jesus Christ, to the world submersed in sin. Up to this moment, the fulfilment of the law of Moses for the Jews or of the natural law for the pagans were the normal ways of salvation established by Him.

(2) After the expiatory sacrifice of the cross, God has cancelled the sin of the world and has reconciled it with Him. God has brought Jesus back to life and has placed him at his side. The covenant and the promise have been fulfilled; Israel is restored. To benefit from this sacrifice and from this reconciliation, it is indispensable for mankind to perform an act of faith in what God has done by means of Jesus the Messiah / Saviour of Israel and of the world. This *act of faith is a spiritual circumcision* and allows men to take part in the restored Israel, whose forefather is Abraham. The *carnal law of Moses has been replaced by Christ's spiritual law of love and freedom*. Salvation and immortality, which were offered expensively and laboriously by the rites of initiation of the mystery religions of Hellenism, are offered by the Messiah / Saviour in a free, easy, and simple way thanks to the faith and to the rites of Baptism and Eucharist.

(3) The remaining time until the end and until the complete fulfilment of God's plan of salvation of humanity is very scarce. These brief moments are to be employed in completing the restoration of Israel.

God has decided that at the end of the world, some Gentiles should also join His chosen people in an easy way: circumcision and the observance of the law of Moses are not necessary for them as means of salvation. Now, by the acceptance of Jesus by Israel and by the conversion of the Gentiles, the promise made by God to Abraham is fulfilled.

2. Assessment of the Pauline contribution to the doctrine of salvation of Gentiles

It seems that this new Pauline offer of salvation for some (and later for all) Gentiles is a real contribution to the conformation of the theoretical basis of future Christianity. In short: it meant the transformation of Jesus' message of the imminent arrival of God's kingdom (a kingdom of Jewish messianic features, full of spiritual but also material effects in the land of Israel) into a message of universal salvation, which implies an otherworldly "kingdom" (a conception more in accordance to an orphic-platonic understanding of the future world than to a Jewish understanding). A conception of Israel's restoration, in which the participation of *a certain number of Gentiles* was included, by easy internal logic, soon turned into a message of: "All gentiles converted to the final Israel will be welcome." Salvation was open to all, because the converted Gentiles completed the (enlarged) number of the chosen people to be saved before the final moments of history. This step forward will be more explicit in the Pauline "school": Colossians and Ephesians present a concept of a Christian Church with cosmic dimensions.

The shift from a Jewish kingdom to universal salvation was probably already made by the mission of the Hellenistic Jewish community, but it was Paul who shaped it more precisely and gave it an almost definite form with a strong theological foundation. The Apostle scarcely speaks of God's kingdom in his letters. Indeed, this expression appears a few times in them, but it does not have the same content as in Jesus' preaching, as recorded by the Synoptic Gospels. Instead, Paul writes about a salvation act of God performed in a preceding time (not in the future!) through the vicarious death of His Son, a sacrifice whose benefits are for humanity as a whole, Jews and Gentiles alike. It was a question of the possibility of an easy salvation for all, without exception.

On the other hand, this radical change of perspective can be seen as natural, if considered from the point of view of the historical setting of Christianity's expansion in the Roman Hellenistic Empire. The particular Christian theology on salvation, the one developed in the Pauline churches, not in the Jewish-Christian community in Jerusalem, was formed:

(1) Upon the interpretation of Jesus' death as a vicarious sacrifice. This conception is not Jewish but Graeco-Roman. The victim of this sacrifice—Jesus—must be human and divine at the same time: human in order for the victim to be able to represent humanity before God; divine in order for the victim to placate God who is irritated by sins. This conception implies the divine status of Jesus (pre-existence) and the incarnation. Both of these concepts are impossible in a Jewish mental framework, but very comprehensible in a mystic-pagan one.

(2) In confrontation—especially in the provinces of the Empire—with a theology of the Emperor as a divine being who functions as a peace and salvation giver.

(3) In confrontation with other salvation theologies, especially of the mystery religions.

It is fully understandable that a strictly Jewish messianism (which implied a conception of the liberation and restoration of Israel, the immediate coming of God's kingdom to Israel that would involve a theocracy upon the land of God, the crushing of the Gentiles' yoke upon Israel thanks to God's decisive intervention in the imminent, final moments of the world) would not have attracted anyone in the Roman Empire, nor have the slightest possibility of success among the candidates for conversion, except in the narrow geographical frame of Judea, Samaria, and Galilee. It would only have been interesting to someone who had already decided to convert to Jewish faith. On the contrary, the explicit transformation of the Jewish message of the kingdom of God in Israel into a kerygma of universal salvation through the faith in Christ (divine, redeemer, granter of immortality, saviour) made it possible for the new form of Judaism presented by the Pauline Christians to be successful. Furthermore, salvation ought to be open to all, because the substantial unity and equality of mankind was an established doctrine spread everywhere at this time by the Stoics.

The adaptation to the environment also explains why the messianic title "The Son of the Man"—incomprehensible for those who were not Aramaic speakers—was practically suppressed from Paul's letter.

To designate Jesus, the Apostle will preferably use other titles such as
"Son of God" (*divi filius*) and especially "The Lord" in an absolute
sense. For the sake of strategy, in his letters Paul does not often repeat
the title of Jesus as the messiah of Israel (with the notable exception of
Rom 1:1–6: his audience was in a great part Jews), but he disguises the
term "messiah"—"anointed one," "Christ"—as almost a proper name,
Jesus Christ, which nevertheless preserves its connotations of messiah.
This Pauline shift of emphasis allows the image of Jesus to successfully
compete with the representations of "divinities-son" worshipped in the
mystery religions throughout the Empire. Once again, Paul's attempt
was to proclaim Jesus to his audience as the true redeemer and universal
saviour, who had come to defeat other divinities in the Roman Empire
with a better offer of salvation.

The Hellenistic environment of Paul also explains why he—who
knows about the historical Jesus more than it seems at first—softens
Jesus' radical ethics ("interim ethics," according to E. Schweizer) conceived for the time before the coming of the Kingdom. The Apostle
accepts divorce in the case of a mixed marriage (1 Cor 7:15); he does
not expressly discredit the familiar bonds if they obstruct the preaching
of the Kingdom (contrast Mark 1:16 to 1 Cor 7: Paul is rather indifferent
to the family). We do not find in Paul vitriolic speeches against the rich
(as in Jesus, for instance Mark 10:25); Paul recommends payment of
taxes and encourages obedience to the civil authority (Rom 13; contrast
to Luke 23,); he admonishes working all the time (1 Thess 4:11–12) and
allows the missionaries to live off a sort of salary obtained from their
preaching of the gospel (contrast Luke 10:3–4 to 1 Cor 9:4–5).

The elimination of the salvation value of the Mosaic Law undergoes
a similar evolution. Initially, the Pauline argument against the necessity
of observing the entire Mosaic Law must have been a simple elimination of barriers arranged by God to facilitate the Gentiles' flow to the
renewed and final Israel. In Romans, however, as the Pauline thought
achieves its maturity, the suppression of the observance of the Law
(7:1–25) transforms itself into a wonderful reality of freedom to the
liking of his Hellenistic readers, especially the Stoic ones. The "justice
of God" yields the following effects on the existence of mankind: the
believer is free of sin (chapter 5); he is liberated from death (chapter
6); Christian life is characterised by the "freedom of the sons of God,"
by a life in the Spirit whose final destiny is the glory (chapter 8). The
human being, that seemed to be immersed in sin, is elevated to being
the son of God and to reign with Him (Rom 5:17).

Also in agreement with his spiritual environment, Paul incorporates gnostic motives (not Gnosticism!) into his interpretation of Jesus' message. This is another Pauline contribution to the hellenization of the theological Jewish Christian thought: gnostic terms and expressions helped him to deepen and elucidate what was considered by him to be the nuclear truths of his "Gospel." We are speaking now of gnostic motives, observable in the first century A.D., and not of a more or less formed gnostic system (in Christianity this will not happen until the middle of the second century). In tight synthesis, the most prominent features of gnostic terms or conceptions in Paul's writings may be outlined as follows:

(1) An anthropology of gnostic / platonic traits: mankind is composed not only of soul and body, but body, soul, and spirit. Consequently, the human beings can be divided into "spiritual" / "psychic" / "carnal" / corporeal according to their understanding and acceptance of the truths of the revelation (1 Cor 3:1, etc.). As before observed, the contraposition "carnal / spiritual" plays an essential role in his doctrine of Gentiles' salvation.

(2) The conception of the Christian's struggle against the evil, archontic powers as a cosmic drama (2 Cor 2:6, etc.).

(3) The equality of substance between the Redeemer and the spirit of the saved. The conception that baptised Christians form a body together with Christ will develop later based on this equality of substance. Thanks to this—and only for this—, it is possible for the Church to be the body or the members and for Christ to be the head (Rom 12:4ff; 1 Cor 12:12–27).

(4) A radical division between matter and spirit. Paul's lack of appreciation for marriage has its foundation (besides other reasons, as the nearing end of mundane history) in the deep division between the spiritual and material world, a duality that dominates his thought. Only the first deserves attention; the second one is inferior, bad, ephemeral, and perishable (1 Cor 7).

Some scholars, however, support that in Paul there is not even the slightest trace of gnostic motives, but only a simple use of terms or vocabulary of his gnostic adversaries, those that he blames for their ideas. He would attack them—it is claimed—with the same weapons. This interpretation seems inappropriate to us. It should rather be affirmed that Paul does not only use the terms of his dialectical enemies, but also his concepts. If Pauline Christianity can express its message

to its audience by means of certain concepts that we do not doubt to
designate as gnostic, it is because a certain identity exists among this
Pauline Christianity and the ideas on salvation of Paul's adversaries,
whom can be called gnostic.

Paul, even being conscious of the novelty of his conceptions on salvation and on Jesus, does not think at all that he is laying the foundations
of a new religion. Paul is persuaded to be absolutely loyal to the faith of
Israel and to its Sacred Book. He does not question God's covenant with
Israel: though Jesus Christ is not accepted by Jews, he is the fulfilment
of the ancient Scriptures as the real messiah and saviour of Israel; in
Phil 3:3 Paul names the Christian the "real circumcised," that is to say,
the true Israel. In spite of his strong diatribe against the Law in Galatians, Paul accepts in Romans, that this Law has an enormous moral
value for the Jews, that these may continue to observe it, and—if they
want—they may continue to perform circumcision. Jewish-Christian
theology is not at all a new religion, but only a revivification of Judaism. There is only a spiritual olive tree, and the Gentiles are branches
grafted to it. If any branch of this olive tree breaks off (the actual Israel
who does not believe in the messiah Jesus), it will be re-grafted in it at
the end of the time. After the death and resurrection of the messiah,
Jewish-Christianity is the only possible Judaism.

Nevertheless, a new religion will develop from the Pauline conceptions on salvation, a religion that in a few hundred years will have its
own corpus of sacred Scriptures. It is not one of the interests of this
brief article to raise the highly debated question about the "founder"
of Christianity, since it is a complex topic. It may even be said that
Christianity was never a static, but a dynamic reality, a syncretic and
even a contradictory one; therefore, this reality could never have had
one single founder. Though this observation may be true, there are
moments in the evolution of Christianity in which transcendental,
constituent steps were made. And Paul made the first and important
one. Since Christianity is first of all an ideological phenomenon, that
is, doctrinal matters occupy an absolutely principal position in it, it
seems clear that Paul holds a pre-eminent position at least among the
plurality of founders.

3. THE HISTORICAL PLACE OF PAUL'S CHRISTIANITY

The historical place of Paul's religious thought can be deduced from
his theology of salvation. If the ideas on salvation of mankind by

Jesus of Nazareth are contrasted with the doctrine of salvation by his follower Paul, it does not seem to be an exaggeration to maintain that the preaching of the latter means a radical splitting off from Jesus' gospel, inasmuch as:

(1) Paul interprets the figure of the historical Jesus in a very different way than the latter conceived himself. Jesus viewed himself as a normal human being, though with a special relationship with God; on the contrary, Paul considered him a divine being, a pre-existent one. The deification of Jesus was for a Jewish and Greek mentality analogous to the thinking of Greek polytheistic culture, which was familiar with human sons of gods and with divine entities not only populating the invisible world but also acting in the human world.

(2) Paul modifies the conception of a Jewish Messiah, whose task of salvation was fundamentally restricted to Israel, proclaiming Jesus as a universal saviour, a redeemer of all without exception.

(3) Paul affirms that the reconciliation of Israel with God will not be an act in the future (the coming of the Kingdom), but an act that already happened in the past at the cross.

(4) Paul announces that God has changed the conditions and requirements for the salvation of Gentiles, which are very different from those supposed to be of Jesus. The most outstanding points are: the justification by faith and the consistent denial of the salvation value of the law of Moses. Now, all Gentiles can be saved.

According to these elements, the historical place of Paul's thought could be a very hellenized branch of Judaism characterised by two specific differences: (1) the divinity / pre-existence of Jesus, the messiah; (2) a new doctrine of salvation for the Gentiles. Such categories fit very well into the religious and philosophic Hellenistic thought (Jesus Christ as a sort of divine hypostasis) and into the religious thought of its Hellenistic environment in which salvation or mystery religions (Jesus Christ as universal saviour) were developing.

This statement does not mean that Paul and his predecessors *were devoting themselves to copying* the theological characteristics of some of the Hellenistic religions, but it means that Paul was persuaded that Jesus had all the trappings and titles granted to Hellenistic salvation divinities...and even more fully. Therefore, it could be rightly proclaimed that these titles were his own. And Paul owed this global re-interpretation of the doctrine, figure, and Jesus' mission to a "call," a divine vision granted to him.

4. Some consequences on the general question of the
Hellenization of Christianity

From the above said and from the conviction that Jesus' religion was
very different from Paul's religion,[4] it can be deduced:

(1) Paul's religion, his presentation of Jesus to the Gentiles as the
    universal saviour and as a divine being, a pre-existent one, would
    only be understandable in the framework of a very hellenized Jew-
    ish thought, which could probably understand a language of "a
    second power in heaven" and of a "second God." This "Judaism"
    intended to be a response to the religious desires of Gentiles in the
    Roman Empire, a Judaism even more hellenized than presumed by
    M. Hengel in his works *Judentum und Hellenismus* and especially *The
    "Hellenization" of Judaea in the First Century after Christ.*[5] The utilisa-
    tion by Paul of a vocabulary and concepts related to the gnosis, the
    confrontation to complicated Jewish salvation requirements, and the
    response to the deep longings of the mystery religions have seri-
    ously modified in Paul a "normal" Jewish-Christian understanding
    of Jesus. The vocabulary and concepts of the milieu have deeply
    conditioned his re-interpretation of Jesus. It was an unacceptable
    view for the strictest Jewish-Christianity (for instance: that of the
    Church of Jerusalem). Therefore, a rigid opposition arose against
    him. It was so during his whole life (the Judaizer's opposition as
    described in Galatians and Philippians), and it will be so after his
    death (the denigration of Paul's figure as Simon the Magus, the
    false Prophet of the *Pseudo-Clementines*).
(2) Paul's preaching on Jesus and on the salvation of Gentiles can be
    characterised as a religious system essentially Hellenistic, though at
    the same time deeply Jewish. The main act of salvation, justifica-
    tion by faith, is a merely intellectual act (although granted by divine
    grace, of course).
(3) It can be affirmed that Paul's thought on the salvation of Gentiles
    constitutes one of the first steps of Christian theology or simply of
    Christianity. Accordingly, it could be said that the question of the

---

[4] G. Vermes, *The Religion of Jesus the Jew* (Minneapolis: Fortress, 1993); H. Maccoby,
Paul and Hellenism (London: SCM, 1991).
[5] *Judentum und Hellenismus* (Tübingen: Mohr, 1969); *The "Hellenization" of Judaea in
the First Century after Christ* (London: SCM, 1989).

Hellenization of Christianity is badly formulated if it is understood as "first existed Christianity, and then it was hellenized." It was not so, and it could not be so. In its own birth, Christian theology was deeply Jewish and deeply Hellenic. It was Hellenic, or it was not: Christianity is born already hellenized. "Hellenization" was probably for Paul a voluntary act: Paul purposely intended to inculturate the Word into the Greek-Roman world. Paul proclaimed to Gentiles his faith in Jesus and the message of their salvation in terms they could understand...and this faith was in turn profoundly shaped by this culture.

(4) Christian theology, or at least the principal branch that has come to us, is characterised from the same moment of its birth as a re-reading, as a re-interpretation of Jesus' actions and sayings in the light of the firm belief in his resurrection. Proper Christian theology was born in a deeply hellenized milieu that does not fit with the primitive community of Jerusalem as the book of Acts portrays it. This re-reading or re-interpretation of the figure and mission of Jesus is carried out by diverse criteria according to the mentality of the different groups in which it was born. The birth of Christianity is then an exegetical or interpretative phenomenon according to categories that are not only Jewish, but also Greek.

(5) Paul's disciples, the authors of Colossians, Ephesians, 2 Thessalonians, Pastoral Epistles, were faithful to the decisive impulse of their master and continued his line of thought in essential areas for theology such as ecclesiology, Christology, community life, etc., starting from Greek Hellenistic conceptions more than Jewish ones.

(6) The reflections synthetically exposed in this article do not represent any innovation at all, but a return—probably cyclical—to already defended positions, a long time ago, by the History of Religions School, positions perhaps unjustly forgotten by some.

(7) It is necessary to eliminate the negative connotation of the words "Hellenization of Christianity," in any case if they should be understood as a compromise of authentic New Testament teaching.

"IN ADAM":
1 COR 15:21–22; 12:27 IN THEIR JEWISH SETTING*

Menahem Kister

Paul contrasts Adam with Christ twice in 1 Cor 15. The context in both passages is the resurrection, but the nuances of the contrast between Adam and Christ are rather different in each. Another passage in which Paul addresses the topic of Adam and Christ is Rom 5:12–21. The relationship between Adam and Christ varies significantly in each of these passages. Both, however, have their source in contemporary Judaism, to which Paul gives a peculiar christological twist. I have dealt with the other two passages elsewhere;[1] here I shall confine myself to the first passage in 1 Cor 15, which reads:

> (21) For as by a man (came) death, by a man (has come) also the resurrection of the dead. (22) For as in Adam (ἐν τῷ Ἀδάμ) all die, so also in Christ shall all be made alive (ζῳοποιηθήσονται)

The analogy between Adam and the Messiah, an eschatological figure, is not surprising: the conception that all humankind will reenter Eden in the eschatological period occurs as early as *1 En.* 25:5. Additionally, according to the "doctrine of the two spirits," when God will renew His works in the *eschaton*, the elect, whose bodies will be changed, will retain "all the glory of Adam (or: of humankind)" (1QS IV 20–25). When eschatology became Christology, it was almost inevitable that the figures of Adam and Christ would be compared. What is unique to this passage, however, is the statement that all the believers are made alive "in Christ" and that, analogically, all human beings die not only *because* of Adam's sin, but "in Adam."[2]

---

* I thank Mr. Michael Guggenheimer for improving the English style of this article.
[1] M. Kister, "Romans 5:12–21 against the Background of Tannaitic Torah-Theology and Hebrew Usage" (forthcoming); idem, "'First Adam' and 'Second Adam' according to Paul (1 Cor 15) in the Light of Midrashic Exegesis and Hebrew Usage" (forthcoming).
[2] To be sure, the preposition ἐν could theoretically be interpreted as synonymous with διά, thus taking on the instrumental sense of the Hebrew preposition *be*. Such an interpretation, however, seems quite unlikely, both because of the redundancy thus

The conception of being "in Christ" is fundamental to Paul's theology. Being "in Adam" may well be a "backwards" reflection of the
christological conception (to use Sanders' terminology), Paul's Christology being reflected in his anthropology (the latter is less important
in Paul's theological system than the former).[3] The conceptual background of Paul's notion that all Christians are members of the Body
of Christ, as he explicitly says in 1 Cor 12:12, 27, is rather obscure and
therefore problematic. The idea that a community is an organism and
that its members can be viewed metaphorically as the organs of one
body occurs in Hellenistic[4] and Jewish[5] sources; the novelty in Paul's
idea is that the individuals are conceived of not only as members of
the community, but also as members of *Corpus Christi*, i.e., of the body
of Christ Himself.[6] To be sure, Seneca says that the Roman empire is
Nero's body, while arguing that Nero is its soul;[7] this analogy (rather
different from the Christian conception), though interesting, does not
settle the intriguing question as to what could be the origin or the
cultural context of Paul's idea that the believers exist *in Christ* and that
they are members of Christ.

---

created and because the words ἐν Χριστῷ have a definite meaning in Pauline terminology, a meaning which is to be expected to apply to ἐν τῷ Ἀδάμ as well.

[3] "Paul does not go to Adam to see how he is connected with Christ; he goes to Christ
to see how *He* is connected to Adam" (K. Barth, *Christ and Adam: Man and Humanity in
Romans 5* [Edinburgh: Oliver & Boyd, 1956], 17); similarly O. Michel, *Der Brief an die
Römer* (5th ed.; KEK; Göttingen: Vandenhoeck & Ruprecht, 1978), 194 (both concerning
Rom 5); E.P. Sanders, *Paul and Palestinian Judaism: A Comparison of Patterns of Religion*
(Philadelphia: Fortress, 1977), 453–63. On the general phenomenon of understanding
the figure of Adam in Judaism and Christianity either through the Sinai revelation or
the advent and passion of Christ, see G.A. Anderson, *The Genesis of Perfection: Adam and
Eve in Jewish and Christian Imagination* (Louisville: Westminster, 2001).

[4] For parallels in classical literature, see the passages noted by H. Lietzmann, *An
die Korinther I–II* (4th ed.; Tübingen: J.C.B. Mohr, 1949), 62 (commentary to 1 Cor
12:12).

[5] For some Jewish parallels to this concept in the literature of the Second Temple
period, see M. Kister, "Physical and Metaphysical Measurements Ordained by God in
the Literature of the Second Temple Period," in *Reworking the Bible: Apocryphal and Related
Texts at Qumran* (ed. E.G. Chazon et al.; STDJ 58; Leiden: Brill, 2005), 153–76. Cf. also
Tanhuma Nizavim 2 where the expression כל איש ישראל (Deut 29:9) is interpreted as
indicating that the entire Nation of Israel, regardless of rank, is one body (cf. 1 Cor
12:12–30). For a detailed comparison of this midrashic passage to Rom 5:15–19, see
Kister, "Romans 5:12–21."

[6] As emphasized by J.A.T. Robinson, *The Body: A Study in Pauline Theology* (London:
SCM, 1952), 49–67 (49–50 n. 1; 59–60 n. 1).

[7] Seneca, *Clem.* 1.5.1, cited by M.V. Lee, *Paul, the Stoics, and the Body of Christ* (SNTSMS
137; Cambridge: Cambridge University Press, 2006), 35–38.

A Semitic origin to this conception, namely, the so-called "Hebrew conception of corporate personality,"[8] was suggested as a possible source for Paul's notion concerning both Christ and Adam. The use of collective nouns in the Bible was considered as reflecting this ancient conception. It has been noted by many commentators that the word *adam* in the Bible means both Adam and "humankind." It should be added that the word *adam* in the collective sense ("humankind") occurs also in the Dead Sea Scrolls (יאמרו האדם, 4Q385 4 2–3).[9] Linguistic usage, however, can be misleading: languages include fossilized expressions, and the speakers of a language are often unaware of their cultural significance. Do we have evidence for the existence of the conception of a corporate personality in the late Second Temple period?

A revealing text, in which the borderline between an ancestor and his descendants (i.e., his tribe) is blurred in a way that can be interpreted as reflecting the conception of corporate personality, is found in a newly published fragment from Qumran, which reads:

> And in all this Joseph was cast into lands…and fools [i.e., the Samaritans] were dwelling [in their land] and making for themselves a high place on a high mountain [i.e., Gerizim]…words of deceit they spoke to provoke Levi and Judah and Benjamin…And in all this Joseph [was given] into the hands of foreigners, who were devouring his strength and breaking all his bones until the time of the end for him. And he cried out [and aloud] he called to mighty God to save him from their hand and he said, "My father and my God, do not abandon me…[they took] my land from me and from all my brothers who have joined me." (4Q372 1 10–20)[10]

The use of the singular here is remarkable. The time described in this fragment is the exile of the Ten Tribes and the settlement of the Samaritans in the territories of the tribe of Joseph. But the tribe of Joseph is, in fact, the body of Joseph the eponym. This tribe is described as

---

[8] H.W. Robinson, "The Hebrew Conception of Corporate Personality," *BZAW* 66 (1936): 49–61; idem, *The Cross in the Old Testament* (London: SCM, 1955), 77. For a similar view concerning the Hebrew Bible, see A.R. Johnson, *The One and the Many in the Israelite Conception of God* (Cardiff: University of Wales, 1961). Against Robinson's theory, see J.W. Rogerson, "The Hebrew Conception of Corporate Personality: A Re-Examination," *JTS* N.S. 21 (1970): 1–16.

[9] D. Dimant, *DJD* 30:37, following the reading and interpretation of M. Kister and E. Qimron, "Observations on 4QSecond Ezekiel (4Q385 2–3)," *RevQ* 15/60 (1992): 601. Note the plural form of the verb.

[10] E. Schuller and M.J. Bernstein, *DJD* 28:167–69, published as 4QNarrative and Poetic Composition[b].

Joseph's "bones," and its exile is described as "breaking his bones."[11] A long prayer in the *singular* seemed appropriate to the writer. For our purposes, therefore, it suffices to say that what might be a remnant of an ancient conception was still operative in the pre-Maccabean or early Maccabean period. Even if we take a minimalist assumption and regard the usage in this fragment as a manner of speech, it should always be kept in mind that ancient conceptions may become figures of speech as easily as figures of speech can become mythical ideas.[12]

Similar expressions concerning biblical heroes are rather well attested in midrashic literature, much later than Paul's time.[13] In some rabbinic traditions, Adam's relation to humankind is also expressed in this way.[14] According to a *midrash* included in two versions of the *Tanhuma* literature (*Exodus Rabbah* and the printed edition of the *Tanhuma*),[15] the souls of all human beings were on various parts of Adam's body.

---

[11] Cf. the midrashic interpretation of the words "He has worn away my flesh and my skin, He has broken my bones" (Lam 3:4): "'my flesh'—indicates the public; 'my skin'—refers to the Sanhedrin, who cover Israel as the skin covers the body; 'my bones' (עצמותי)—indicates the great persons (עצומי)" (*Lam. Rab. ad loc.*). The first verse of this chapter, "I am the man who has known affliction" is interpreted as referring to כנסת ישראל, "Israel." Despite the affinities between the *Joseph Apocryphon* and this midrash, the point that the "body and the bones" are those of the *eponym* is not made in the midrash.

[12] M. Kister, "Observations on Aspects of Exegesis, Tradition, and Theology in Midrash, Pseudepigrapha, and Other Jewish Writings," in *Tracing the Threads: Studies in the Vitality of Jewish Pseudepigrapha* (ed. J.C. Reeves; SBLEJL 6; Atlanta: Scholars Press, 1994), 16.

[13] Cf., for instance, *Gen. Rab.* 53:14 (Theodor-Albeck, 537), where the phrase "*a man* (אדם) that is going to kill Your children (= Israel)" refers to the Ishmaelites (*y. Ta'an.* 4:5 [69b]). In numerous midrashim, "Jacob" stands for the Jewish people. These passages (and others) are further evidence of the vitality of such a notion of "corporate personality," at least in the broad sense of this category. The argument, expressed by New Testament scholars (e.g., Rogerson, "The Hebrew Conception"), that this concept represents an ancient mode of thinking and therefore cannot be used to construe Paul's thinking, does not seem convincing.

[14] Similarly also in Syriac literature, see Brock's statement: "It is characteristic of St. Ephrem's essentially Semitic understanding of the Biblical narrative that he is able to move rapidly to and fro between the individual and the collective, between Adam and humanity as a whole" (S.P. Brock, *St. Ephrem the Syrian: Hymns on Paradise* [Crestwood, N.Y.: St Vladimir's Seminary Press, 1990], 70). Admittedly, Ephrem might be influenced by Paul's thinking.

[15] עד שאדם הראשון מוטל נולם הראה לו הקב"ה כל צדיק וצדיק שעתיד לעמוד ממנו יש שהוא תלוי בראשו של אדם ויש שהוא תלוי בשערו ויש שהוא תלוי במצחו ויש בעיניו ויש בחטמו ויש בפיו ויש באזנו (*Exod. Rab.* 40:3 // *Tanhuma*, *Ki Tissa*, 12). "While Adam was still a *golem*, God showed him every righteous person that would descend from him; some hung on Adam's hair and others on his head; some on his forehead, on his eyes, nose, mouth, ear" (S.M. Lehrman, trans., *Midrash Rabbah: Exodus* [London: Soncino, 1983], 462 with slight alteration).

W.D. Davies has suggested that this midrash is reminiscent of Paul's system, especially of 1 Cor 12:12–30.[16] Fitzmyer objects to this comparison; he writes: "Davies should have paid more attention to the dates of rabbinic passages to which he alludes...Is there any clear reference in pre-Christian Jewish literature to such a notion as the incorporation of all human beings in Adam?"[17] *Midrash Tanhuma* is a late source,[18] but it should be remembered that the idea that one's descendants are incorporated in oneself is nothing but a continuation of ancient conceptions.[19] Although an ancient parallel to the notion of the incorporation of all human beings in *Adam* is still unknown, the notion of the incorporation of Joseph's descendants in Joseph supplies sufficient evidence for the existence of this notion in pre-Christian Jewish literature. Moreover, these notions were not entirely new to this period, but rather the continuation of even earlier, more ancient conceptions. These conceptions could easily have been conflated with Hellenistic ideas in Jewish and Pauline thinking.

It is beyond the scope of the present article to decide whether Paul's idea that every Christian is included in Christ (1 Cor 12:12–30) was *based* on the notion of "corporate personality" of one's descendants; it is certainly not identical with it: after all, Christ is not the ancestor of his believers. A modest conclusion would be that 1 Cor 15:22 is better understood in the light of this Jewish notion.

Elsewhere, I compared Rom 5:12–21 with rabbinic material[20] and noted that, while in the Jewish passages the point is that the righteous deeds and sins of an ancestor *affect* his descendants, without a clearcut border between the generations, in Rom 5:12–21 there is a shift of ancestral relations to the relations of Christ and his believers. The cultural presumption underlying this conception is that, in a sense, there

---

[16] P. Billerbeck and H.L. Strack, *Kommentar zum Neuen Testament aus Talmud und Midrasch* (Munich: Beck, 1922–1928), 3.174; W.D. Davies, *Paul and Rabbinic Judaism: Some Rabbinic Elements in Pauline Theology* (London: S.P.C.K., 1984), 55.

[17] J.A. Fitzmyer, *Romans: A New Translation with Introduction and Commentary* (AB: New York: Doubleday, 1993), 412.

[18] For ancient traditions in the *Tanhuma*, see M. Bregman, "Early Traditions and Sources in the *Tanhuma-Yelamdenu* Literature," *Tarbiz* 60 (1991): 269–74 [Hebrew].

[19] Elsewhere in midrashic literature it is stated that Moses died because of Adam's sin, as an embryo of an imprisoned woman is born (and grows up) in prison (*Eccl. Rab.* 7:13). This may be considered a vivid illustration of Paul's theological statement "in Adam all die": all future humankind is included in an embryonic manner in Adam. For another variation of this conception cf. also Heb 7:9–10.

[20] Kister, "Romans 5:12–21."

is no clear ontological border between the ancestor and his descendants. But it is hardly justifiable to introduce in Rom 5:12–21 the concept of "corporate personality"; this is only verified by the comparison to the Jewish parallels to this passage. In our passage, however, this conception is taken one step further, to the notion that the descendants of one ancestor, Adam, and the believers in Christ constitute a "corporate personality." There is no hint in the Epistle to the Romans that human beings die "*in* Adam" (1 Cor 15:22), although Romans was written a short time after 1 Corinthians.

The two passages referring to Adam and Christ in 1 Cor 15 share the conception that Christ is "life giving," in contrast to Adam in the context of resurrection. However, the differences between the two passages in this chapter are substantial. According to vv. 21–22, all people are "in Adam," whereas believers gain eternal life "in Christ." Verses 45–49 of the same chapter, on the other hand, emphasize the *ontological* contrast between Adam and Christ and the eschatological dimension of the latter, which lie at the core of this chapter. As I have demonstrated elsewhere,[21] vv. 45–49 are a Christianized version of Jewish ideas, modes of thought, and exegesis. The ontological contrast of Adam and Christ scarcely fits Rom 5:12–21 and should not be read into 1 Cor 15:21–22.[22] It might be argued that Paul did not try to amalgamate in these epistles clusters of Jewish ideas derived from different Jewish sources. Be that as it may, the one component that is dominant in all three Pauline passages is the transference of conceptions concerning ancestor-descendant relations to Christ and His believers.

---

[21] Kister, "'First Adam' and 'Second Adam.'"

[22] See E. Brandenburger, "Alter und neuer Mensch, erster und letzter Adam-Anthropos," in *Vom alten zum neuen Adam: Urzeitmythos und Heilsgeschichte* (ed. W. Strolz; Freiburg: Herder, 1986), 205–17.

HANANIAH BEN HEZEKIAH BEN GARON, THE EIGHTEEN DECREES AND THE OUTBREAK OF THE WAR AGAINST ROME

Günter Stemberger

Little is known about Hananiah (in some texts Haninah) ben Hezekiah ben Garon (or Gurion). He is supposed to have lived late in the Second Temple period and to have belonged to the school of Shammai.[1] In the Mishnah he is mentioned only once (*m. Šabb.* 1:4; parallel *t. Šabb.* 1:16); Eleazar (or Eliezer) ben Hananiah ben Hezekiah ben Garon (mentioned in *Sifre Deut* 294 and *Mek. Baḥodesh* 7) might have been his son. A baraita in *b. Šabb.* 13b attributes to him the writing of *Meg. Taʿan.* and special efforts for the book of Ezekiel:

> *Our rabbis have taught on Tannaite authority*: Who wrote the Scroll That Lists Days on Which It Is Forbidden to Fast? It was Hananiah b. Hezekiah and his colleagues, who valued the days on which they were released from troubles
>
> ...
>
> Said R. Judah [said Rab], "That man is to be remembered for good, by name of Hananiah b. Hezekiah, for if it were not for his efforts, the book of Ezekiel would have been hidden away, for its words contradict the words of the Torah. "What did he do to save the situation? He took up three hundred barrels of oil with him to an upper room and stayed there until he had ironed out all the problems."[2]

Neither tradition is found in earlier rabbinic texts; the introduction of the passage as baraita does not guarantee its early origin. As to the book of Ezekiel, it is not included in the rabbinic discussions about biblical books that (do not) render the hands unclean. Although the vision of the divine chariot in Ezek 1 was considered as problematic for public reading or general study because of its esoteric interpretations (*m. Ḥag.* 2:1; *m. Meg.* 4:10), the book as such was never excluded from public

---

[1] See J. Neusner, *The Rabbinic Traditions about the Pharisees Before 70* (3 vols.; Leiden: Brill, 1971), 1:416; I. Ben-Shalom, *The School of Shammai and the Zealots' Struggle Against Rome* (Jerusalem: Bialik, 1993), 235–36 [Hebrew].

[2] Translations of rabbinic texts follow those of Jacob Neusner, slightly adapted where necessary.

reading in the synagogue. Problems which arose in the interpretation of particular texts were solved over time, but certainly not through the efforts of one single person. That Hananiah was reduced to writing the earlier traditions contained in the Scroll of Fasts seems to be confirmed by the scholion to *Meg. Ta'an.* on Adar 28, which, however, names the followers of R. Eliezer ben Haninah (Hananiah). This tradition is mostly accepted, although the intention behind this action is disputed.[3] I assume that both traditions adapt stories about the biblical king Hezekiah, who in the Bavli is mentioned several times together with his followers (חזקיה וסיעתו), as is here Hananiah ben Hezekiah and his followers. King "Hezekiah and his followers wrote Isaiah, Proverbs, Canticles and Kohelet" (*b. B. Bat.* 15a); *ARN A* 1 interprets Prov 25:1 *"Also those are the proverbs of Solomon, which the men of Hezekiah, king of Judah, copied"* to mean that they spelled out their meaning and thus saved them together with Canticles and Kohelet from being hidden away. As King Hezekiah and his men are credited with writing down a book and saving biblical books from being hidden away, so are Hananiah ben Hezekiah and his men. The parallels are too obvious to be fortuitous. I therefore would not use these texts as historically trustworthy traditions.[4]

But let us turn to the only tradition about Hananiah ben Hezekiah which is found already in the Mishnah and is further developed in both Talmudim, i.e. the Eighteen Decrees.

1. THE MAIN TEXTS

1.1. *In* m. Šabb. *1:4 we read:*

These are some of the laws which they stated in the upper room of Hananiah b. Hezekiah b. Garon when they went up to visit him. They took a vote, and the House of Shammai outnumbered the House of Hillel. And eighteen rules did they decree on that very day.

---

[3] See V. Noam, *Megillat Ta'anit: Versions, Interpretation, History: With a Critical Edition* (Jerusalem: Ben-Zvi, 2003), 132 (text), 334–36 (discussion) [Hebrew]. Noam rightly doubts the interpretation, offered by Heinrich Graetz, that the Scroll was written down directly before the outbreak of the war against Rome and was intended to encourage the people to fight.

[4] For these traditions see G. Stemberger, "Il contributo delle baraitot babilonesi alla conoscenza storica della Palestina prima del 70 d.C.," in *Il Giudaismo palestinese dal I secolo a.C. al I secolo d.C.* (ed. P. Sacchi; AISG Testi e Studi 8; Bologna: Fattoadarte 1993), 213–29 (223–25). This article also includes an earlier version of the following analysis of the Eighteen Decrees.

"These are some of the laws" is sometimes referred to as what is said before in 1:1–3, laws regarding the Sabbath and one purity law. Thus, for example, Maimonides says in his commentary on the passage or, among modern authors, I. Ben-Shalom.[5] But normally in the Mishnah, אלו introduces an enumeration that follows, e.g. *m. Ber.* 8:1, *m. Pe'ah* 1:1, *m. Šeb.* 5:6. In our case, this would be 1:5–8, a list of five laws in which the Shammaites differ from the Hillelites. All concern the Sabbath, or more precisely actions set before the Shabbat but which continue to take their effect during the Sabbath; the last two of them concern non-Jews: Is it permitted to help them in an action or to charge them with work which they will continue on the Sabbath? This second solution corresponds to the normal usage of the Mishnah and is more probable. But whatever solution we choose, Sabbath laws are the main subject, and only part of the eighteen decrees are enumerated. There is no full list of the eighteen decrees. What else was decided there, we do not know. Purity laws might have been included, since immediately before our passage we read: "A male Zab should not eat a meal with a female Zab, because it leads to transgression;" cooperation with Gentiles might also have been a topic when we consider the end of the list (but only marginally since the main concern is the effect of an action of a Jew, even if continued by a Gentile).

1.2. *T. Šabb.* 1:16–17 offers the same text as *m. Šabb.* 1:4 (quoted above) and adds the following comment:

> And that day was as harsh for Israel as the day on which the golden calf was made.
> R. Eliezer says, "On that day they overfilled the *se'ah* measure."
> R. Joshua says, "On that day they smashed the *se'ah* measure. For so long as the measure is full and one puts more into it, in the end it will give up part of what [already] is in it."

The text continues with another halakhah (uncleanness through over-shadowing) on which they voted and where the House of Shammai outnumbered the House of Hillel. The following disputes between the two Houses all concern the Sabbath law; they no longer mention taking votes and who outnumbered whom.

The Tosefta hardly adds to our knowledge as to what the Eighteen Decrees actually contained. 1:18–19 adds two halakhot on which they

---

[5] Ben-Shalom, *School of Shammai*, 253.

voted "on that day" and where the House of Shammai outnumbered
the House of Hillel: One is a purity law (*m. ʾOhal.* 16:1, in the Mishnah
not a dispute between the Houses), the second a Sabbath law (*m. Miqw.*
4:1, where it is also said that in this matter the House of Shammai
outnumbered the House of Hillel; but the Mishnah does not contain the
reference to the eve of Sabbath at dusk[6] and does not date the event).
The combination of Sabbath and purity laws is in line with what we
know from *m. Šabb.* 1:1–3; it is, however, strange that only these two
halakhot are offered as a kind of appendix to the tradition about the
vote in the house of Hananiah b. Hezekiah. More importantly the text
offers an evaluation of the victory of the House of Shammai. The
comparison with the day on which the golden calf was made is taken
up in both Talmudim on this passage (more on which later); elsewhere
it is to be found in rabbinic literature only in *Sop.* 1:7 (cf. *Sefer Torah*
1:8), where it is applied to the day when the Torah was translated into
Greek: "For the Torah could not be adequately translated." This seems
to imply that a necessarily inadequate translation leads to a violation
of the Torah as at Mount Sinai and agrees with the comments made
by R. Eliezer and R. Joshua, who both express the fear that exaggerated halakhic rigorosity will endanger the observance even of the most
essential halakhot.

Thus far we know only that at a certain occasion in the upper room
of Hananiah b. Hezekiah b. Gurion, the House of Shammai outnumbered the House of Hillel when they voted on eighteen rules. The
context makes it clear that these rule belonged to the fields of Sabbath
and purity laws. If the two laws mentioned in *t. Šabb.* 1:18–19 really
belong to the eighteen decrees—at least the first one (*m. Miqw.* 4:1) is
highly problematic—, we would know at least two concrete items that
fit the general context. As to the time when this event occurred, the
persons and groups involved point to some date in the first century,
most likely before 70.

1.3. The Palestinian Talmud (*y. Šabb.* 1, 7, 3c–d) makes a great effort
to explain *m. Šabb.* 1:4. The gemara adds the text of *t. Šabb.* 1:16–17
(without introducing it as a quotation, as is frequent when the Mishnaic
lemma is immediately followed by a text of the Tosefta) and expands
the comments made there by R. Eliezer and R. Joshua. Only Joshua is

---

[6] MS Erfurt of the Tosefta also omits this passage.

here absolutely negative regarding the halakhic decisions taken in the house of Hananiah b. Hezekiah. Most interesting is what follows:

> R. Joshua Onayya taught (תני), "The disciples of the House of Shammai took positions down below and killed disciples of the House of Hillel [before they went upstairs]."
> It has been taught (תני): Six of them went upstairs, and the rest of them took positions against them with swords and spears.

R. Joshua of Ono occurs in rabbinic literature only in the Yerushalmi, always as tradent of tannaitic traditions; he is supposed to have lived in the third century. There is no indication from where he might have received this information on this violent clash between disciples of the two schools with several casualties. The following baraita does not speak of people killed at this occasion, but only of people taking their stand at the entry, obviously to prevent other people from going upstairs. Both units do not seem to be based on historical traditions (not documented elsewhere); they may rather be regarded as attempts to explain how it could happen that at this occasion the House of Shammai outnumbered the usually victorious House of Hillel. The violence may have been derived from the comparison of this day with the day when the golden calf was made. In the Tosefta the point of comparison probably was the breaking of the tablets of the Torah (Exod 32:19), as the comments made by R. Eliezer and R. Joshua suggest. The tradition offered by R. Joshua of Ono rather refers to Exod 32:17: "There is the sound of war in the camp" and even more so to 27: "Each man strap a sword to his side. Go back and forth through the camp from one end to the other, each killing his brother and friend and neighbour."

The Yerushalmi continues with an attempt to identify the eighteen decrees:

> [A] It has been taught: Eighteen rules did they decree, in eighteen matters they formed the majority, and concerning eighteen matters they disputed. These are the matters on which they issued decrees: (1) Bread prepared by Gentiles, (2) their cheese, (3) their oil, (4) and their daughters; (5) their semen (6) and urine; (7) the laws governing one who has suffered a nocturnal emission; (8) the laws covering the uncleanness of Gentile territory.
> [B] There we have learned: These render heave offering unfit: (1) He who eats food unclean in the first remove; (2) and he who eats food unclean in the second remove; (3) he who drinks unclean liquid; (4) he whose head and the greater part of whose body enter drawn water; (5) one who was clean, on whose head and the greater part of whose body three logs of drawn water fall; (6) a holy book; (7) hands; (8) a tebul-yom;

(9) and food (10) and utensils which have been made unclean by unclean liquids [*m. Zabim* 5:12].

The baraita in (A) mentions three groups of eighteen halakhot. "Decreed" (גזרו) here does not refer to the halakhot where the House of Shammai obtained the majority, but to those on which there was unanimity. It is not clear whether the following list ("These are the matters...") still is part of the baraita or not. The following text of *m. Zabim* 5:12 seems to be quoted to arrive at eighteen halakhot. The combination of the two lists obviously is secondary. In the text of the Mishnah, we have anonymous halakhah, not points of dispute between the two schools. Both lists concentrate on purity laws, not on laws of the Sabbath, as the context of *m. Šabb.* 1:4 suggests. This reinforces a shift of interest which began already in the Tosefta. The first list concentrates on the separation of Jews and Gentiles; the list is composite: three items of forbidden food, three of personal impurities; the last two items differ stylistically from the rest (adding הלכות). As parallels in *b. Šabb.* 17b and *b. 'Abod. Zar.* 36a ("their bread and their oil, their wine and their daughters") show, shorter lists were filled up in the course of time. The second list concerns exclusively the Jewish community, the priestly gifts (terumah), and what makes them impure.

The topic of the separation from non-Jews is completely foreign to *m. Šabb.* 1. *M. Šabb.* 1:7–9 forbids selling anything to a Gentile on the eve of the Sabbath, lifting up a burden onto his back, or giving him work to do. But the aim of these laws is not separation, but avoiding Jewish cooperation in the violation of the Sabbath rest by non-Jews.

The Yerushalmi continues with an objection of the Rabbis of Caesarea who see (in the preceding lists?) only seven decrees where the Shammaites outnumbered the Hillelites (or agreed with them? The text is not clear) and supplement them with a Sabbath law and five purity laws, all taken directly from the Mishnah. Only if we count the last one (*m. Toh.* 4:1: "Concerning six matters of doubt...") as six do we arrive at eighteen items altogether. The whole passage does not quote traditions, but is one more attempt to arrive at a list of eighteen halakhot. But after an additional law in the name of R. Yose b. R. Bun, the text continues:

> These are the first ten decrees. As to the rest of them, they derive from that which R. Simeon b. Yohai has taught: On that day they made a decree against (1) their bread, (2) cheese, (3) wine, (4) vinegar, (5) brine, (6) muries; (7) what they brew, (8) pickle, (9) salt; (10) pounded wheat, (11)

groats, and (12) grits; [the decree further was made against] (13) their language and (14) their testimony; (15) gifts given by them [for Temple offerings]; (16) [marriage with] their sons and (17) their daughters; and (18) [accepting] their firstlings.

It is not clear what they count as the first ten decrees. The list in the name of R. Simeon b. Yohai has some points of contact with the first list of halakhot quoted in [A]: their bread, their cheese, their oil (here: wine), their daughters. For most commentators, the list of Simeon b. Yohai is the most original tradition; if this is really the case, the connection with the preceding text would be only a secondary problem. The following discussion in the gemara (3c–d) does not deal with Simeon's list, but the list quoted in [A] with its eight decrees against non-Jews and their products. This suggests that all that comes between this earlier list and its discussion is a later insertion.

The list attributed to R. Simeon b. Yohai is coherent; the common aim of the eighteen halakhot is the separation from non-Jews by forbidding a number of their food products, social, and legal contacts (language, testimony, intermarriage, gifts). The first twelve items occur also in *m. ʿAbod. Zar.* 2:3–6, although in a completely different order; there already they are grouped together in lists, introduced by the heading: "These things of Gentiles are prohibited" (2:3, 6). The first eight items also occur in *t. ʿAbod. Zar.* 4:8–13, again in a different sequence. The list apparently is a variant of lists known to the redactors of Mishnah and Tosefta and may be old. As to the items 13–18 of Simeon's list, they might have been put together to fill up the number of eighteen.

"Their language" (13) probably refers to *m. Sotah* 9:14: "In the war against Qitos they decreed... that a man should not teach Greek to his son." "Their testimony" (14) might refer to *m. B. Qam.* 1:3: "[Assessment of the compensation for an injury to be paid is] on the basis of evidence given by witnesses who are freemen and members of the covenant." One could also point to *m. Yebam.* 16:5, where R. Judah b. Baba says with regard to someone casually saying that somebody has died: "In the case of an Israelite, this is valid only if he intended to give testimony. And in the case of a Gentile, if he intended to give testimony, his testimony is not valid." "Their gifts" (15: מתנותיהן) is normally understood to refer to the refusal of sacrifices offered by non-Jews (thus also Neusner's translation: "gifts given by them [for Temple offerings]") and connected with the events of the year 66, when it was decided no longer to accept sacrifices for the welfare of the emperor; but, it might quite as well refer to the prohibition to accept gifts from Gentiles on the occasion of their festivals. *M. 'Abod. Zar.* 1:1 prohibits only business dealings with Gentiles three days before their festivals, but *y. 'Abod. Zar.* 1:1, 39b assumes in the story about Yudan Nesiah and the Roman officer that the patriarch may not benefit from the gift he received from the Roman. There is no rabbinic text that explicitly forbids the acceptance of gifts from Gentiles for sacrifices. *M. Šeqal.* 7:6 explicitly states that whole-offerings sent by a Gentile from abroad together with their drink-offerings have to be offered up together; if he did not send a drink-offering, it has to be provided from the public funds.[7] If the prohibition of their sons (16) and their daughters (17) refers to marriages, this would be strange since it is already found in Deut 7:3, as *y. Šabb.* 1:7, 3d remarks. Thus it could not be part of the eighteen decrees, unless it is understood in a more general meaning, forbidding all close social contacts with non-Jews. The last item, "their firstlings" (18), is very strange since non-Jews certainly are not expected to offer first fruits. Liebermann suggests that it might refer to the first fruits of a field which has been sold to a Gentile.[8]

The interpretation of single points remains uncertain. But it seems clear that a list of twelve food laws, which where intended to separate Jews from Gentiles, was expanded later on. A common historical background for the whole list is suggested only by the introductory words "on that day" (בו ביום), which rabbinic texts most commonly connect with the day of the deposition of Rabban Gamaliel in Yavneh. But once we consider the individual halakhot, they clearly derive from quite different situations—a fact noted already in the gemara; many of them are much earlier than the episode in the upper room of Hananiah b. Hezekiah b. Garon.[9] If the list of eighteen decrees offered in the name of Simeon b. Yohai really goes back to him, the most probable intention of the list is a collection of rules severely limiting contacts of Jews with non-Jews in the years after the Bar Kokhba revolt. But this, too, must remain in the field of speculation.

---

[7] S. Liebermann, *Hayerushalmi Kiphshuto, I.1* (Jerusalem, 1934), 45, thinks that the prohibition to accept sacrifices from Gentiles was only a temporary measure and thus left no trace in rabbinic literature except in an addition to *Pesiq. Rab.* (Friedmann 192). Liebermann interprets our passage in agreement with H. Graetz as referring to the events of 66. Ben-Shalom (*School of Shammai*, 270) leaves it open if the passage is to be understood of sacrifices in the Temple or of every gift offered by a Gentile to a Jew.

[8] Liebermann, *Hayerushalmi*, 45, with reference to *b. Git.* 47b. *M. Git.* 4:9 on which this passage is based, speaks of a Jew who buys from a Gentile a field, which originally had been Jewish property: He has to bring the first fruits.

[9] See the discussion of the single decrees in Ben-Shalom, *School of Shammai*, 267–70.

1.4. The Babylonian Talmud comments on our passage in *b. Šabb.* 13b–17b. After a brief discussion about the correct reading of the Mishnah, "these are" or "and these are" (אלו or ואלו) and, consequently, whether the eighteen decrees include the foregoing or refer only to what comes afterwards, the text offers traditions that associate Hananiah ben Hezekiah with the Scroll of Fasts and the book of Ezekiel. The gemara tries to identify the eighteen halakhot. As in the Yerushalmi, *m. Zabim* 5:12 is quoted, a list of what renders heave-offering unfit. After a discussion of this list, R. Judah is quoted in the name of Samuel: "Eighteen matters did they issue as decrees, and concerning eighteen matters they differed." The objection that it has been taught that they came to an agreement is countered with the answer: "That day they differed; the next day they came to an agreement." Halakhic differences between Shammai and Hillel are quoted on the basis of *m. 'Ed.* 1:1–3 and *m. Ḥag* 2:2; one more difference concerns the question whether grapes gleaned for the wine press have been rendered susceptible to uncleanness. Only after a long discussion of related halakhot, the text returns in 16b to the question as to what else was included in the eighteen halakhot. *M. Miqw.* 4:1 (do utensils left under the waterspout render the immersion pool unfit or not) and *m. 'Ohal.* 16:1 (movables as thick as an ox goad bring uncleanness as tents) are quoted and discussed. The text then continues (17a):

> Any more enactments [among the eighteen]?
> He who gleans grapes for the wine press—Shammai says, "The grapes have been rendered susceptible to uncleanness." Hillel says, "The grapes have not been rendered susceptible to uncleanness." But Hillel concurred with Shammai.
> Said Hillel to Shammai, "How come grapes have to be vintaged in a state of cultic cleanness but olives don't have to be gathered in a state of cultic cleanness?" He said to him, "So if you get me really mad, I'll make a decree of uncleanness also in the matter of gathering olives, too."
> They plunged a sword into the schoolhouse, saying, "Let anyone come in who wants, but no one is going to get out of here," and on that day, Hillel sat humble before Shammai like just another disciple. And that day was as hard for Israel as the day on which the golden calf was made [*t. Šabb.* 1:16].
> Well, Shammai and Hillel made this decree, but they wouldn't take it from them, and then their disciples came along and made the same decree, and they took it from them.

Only the introduction and the end of the passage are in Aramaic; the central part on the dispute between Hillel and Shammai is in Hebrew, but is not introduced as a baraita. The text seems to be based on the comparison of the Tosefta with the day when the golden calf was made; it also seems to know the baraita of the Yerushalmi that the access to the room where the vote took place was controlled by armed people. There we have already noted how the first baraita speaking of several disciples of the House of Hillel being killed in the violent encounter contrasts with the second baraita in the name of R. Joshua of Ono, where the weapons serve only to keep people away from the vote, but no actual bloodshed is mentioned. In the Bavli, the scene becomes even more innocuous: Everybody may enter the room, but nobody may leave it. The rabbis are only bystanders, witnesses of the dispute between Hillel and Shammai, but they do not vote on the halakhah.

The scene is closely related with a passage in *b. Sanh.* 94b on the biblical king Hezekiah:

> "And it shall come to pass in that day that his burden shall be taken away from off your shoulders and his yoke from off your neck, and the yoke shall be destroyed because of the oil" (Isa 10:27):
>
> Said R. Isaac Nappaha, "The yoke of Sennacherib will be destroyed because of the oil of Hezekiah, which he would kindle in the synagogues and school houses."
>
> What did [Hezekiah] do? He affixed a sword at the door of the school house and said, "Whoever does not take up study of the Torah will be pierced by this sword."
>
> They searched from Dan to Beer Sheba and found no ignoramus, from Gabbath to Antipatris and found no boy or girl, no man or woman, not expert in the laws of uncleanness and cleanness.

The most obvious parallel between this passage and the scene with Hillel and Shammai is the sword at the entrance of the house of study. But contrary to Hillel and Shammai who do not agree on questions of ritual purity, in the days of King Hezekiah every child is expert in the laws of uncleanness and cleanness. As mentioned already earlier, rabbinic traditions on Hananiah b. Hezekiah are closely connected with traditions about the biblical king Hezekiah and are clearly influenced by them.

The scene in *b. Šabb.* 17a has become a dispute between Shammai and Hillel themselves and not one between their schools. Hillel himself is here represented as sitting before Shammai like just another disciple. This personalization clearly shows a late stage in the development of the tradition, where elements of the events in the upper room of Hananiah b. Hezekiah are transferred to Hillel and Shammai. The scene thus becomes irrelevant for the interpretation of the Mishnah. The Aramaic commentary adds that the halakhic decision of Shammai to which Hillel submits has been repeated by their disciples. The text clearly cannot be used for any historical reconstruction.

The Bavli then continues the search for the eighteen decrees. Samuel states: "That the produce of food in the status of heave-offering is itself in the status of heave-offering, was enacted on that day, too" (17b). *M. Šabb.* 24:1 ("He who was overtaken by darkness on the road gives his purse to a gentile") is also said to have been enacted on that day. Only now do we encounter parts of the list quoted in the Yerushalmi:

> The decrees against Gentile bread, oil, wine, and women all are among the eighteen decrees...Said R. Nahman bar Isaac, "They decreed that a Gentile child imparts uncleanness that is in the status of flux uncleanness, so that Israelite children won't get into the habit of playing with him by reason of sodomy."

The list of the Bavli is no longer connected with the Sabbath halakhah. Its reconstruction proceeds only with great difficulty; the traditions behind it are very fragmentary. The anti-Gentile tendency of two lists in the Yerushalmi comes to the fore only at the end of the discussion when the clearly traditional sequence bread, oil, wine, and daughters of the Gentiles is mentioned, but strikingly not as a baraita, but as the saying of an otherwise unknown master. The anti-Gentile bias of the Yerushalmi does seem to be an answer to certain regional and time bound problems of Palestinian Judaism, possibly after the Bar Kokhba revolt or even later. It is hard to see what older traditions are behind the Yerushalmi.

2. THE EIGHTEEN DECREES AND JEWISH HISTORY

It is only after this brief analysis of the rabbinic traditions on the eighteen decrees that I want to turn to their use in the reconstruction of the history of the last years before the destruction of the Temple, as proposed by H. Graetz[10] and followed by many historians since.[11] Graetz based himself on the version of the Yerushalmi, more precisely on the tradition

---

[10] H.H. Graetz, *Geschichte der Juden von den ältesten Zeiten bis auf die Gegenwart* (11 vols; 5th ed.; Leipzig: Friese, 1905), 3.2:805–13.

[11] See, e.g., S. Zeitlin, "Les 'dix-huit mesures,'" in *Studies in the Early History of Judaism* (4 vols; New York: Ktav, 1973–1978), 4:412–26; repr. from *REJ* 68 (1914); M. Hengel, *Die Zeloten: Untersuchungen zur jüdischen Freiheitsbewegung in der Zeit von Herodes I. bis 70 n. Chr.* (AGSU 1; Leiden: Brill, 1961), 204–11; A. Kasher, *Jews and Hellenistic*

in the name of R. Joshua of Ono regarding the bloody clash between the supporters of the schools of Hillel and Shammai in which several Hillelites were killed. He accepted the list of the eighteen decrees offered in the name of Simeon b. Yohai as authentic and identified (Eleazar b.) Hananiah b. Hezekiah b. Garon with Eleazar the son of the high priest Ananias, who as captain of the Temple in 66 persuaded the authorities to accept no more sacrifices from foreigners, thus stopping also the sacrifices for the emperor's well-being (Josephus, *B.J.* 2.409–410). He thus identified "their gifts" in Simeon's list of the eighteen decrees as sacrifices offered by foreigners, more specifically the sacrifice for the emperor. The other measures in his interpretation were also intended as a strict line of demarcation between Jews and non-Jews. The victory of the Shammaites, who were very close to the Zealots, thus signalled the outbreak of the Great War against Rome.[12]

This reconstruction is based on a highly selective and historicistic reading of the Yerushalmi. But when the traditions about the eighteen decrees are considered in their entirety, the statement about the violent clash between the two schools seems not to be based on historical traditions, but on the statement of the Tosefta that compared the day when the eighteen decrees were decided with the day when the golden calf was made. This comparison puzzled later rabbis; in Exod 32 they found the basis for this comparison—a battle within the Israelite camp where the Levites killed so many Israelites with the sword. It was a solution which in the very context of the Yerushalmi was mitigated by another proposal: Nobody was killed; the weapons served only to prevent Hillelites from taking part in the vote. As we have seen, in the next step the sword was reduced to a pure symbol in the interpretation of the Bavli.

Cities in Eretz-Israel (TSAJ 21; Tübingen: Mohr, 1990), 266–68; Ben-Shalom, *School of Shammai*, 252–72.

[12] J.N. Epstein, "Sifre Zutta Parashat Para," *Tarbiz* 1 (1929): 46–78; repr. in idem, *Studies in Talmudic Literature and Semitic Languages* (2 vols.; Jerusalem: Magnes, 1983–1988), 2.1:141–78, thought to find confirmation of the position proposed by Graetz in a text not yet known to Graetz, a Genizah fragment of *Sifre Zutta* (ed. Horovitz 310), which in the context of a discussion of purity laws states: "The House of Shammai had Edomite disciples. In that hour they said to them…" (.שמי לבית אדומים תלמידים היו). לחן אמרו השעה באותה) (p. 70 = 165, reading corrected with M. Kahana, *The Genizah Fragments of the Halakhic Midrashim* [Part I, Jerusalem: Magnes 2005], 220, line 17). Epstein (p. 52f. = 147f) identified the Edomite disciples as zealots from the South of the country whom he thinks to have been very close to the Shammaites. "In that hour" is referring to the time when the eighteen halakhot were decided. Liebermann (*Hayerushalmi*, 38), accepts Epstein's interpretation. In reality, it is an extreme over-interpretation, which is possible only if Graetz' reconstruction is taken for granted.

The identification of the eighteen decrees is equally problematic. In the context of the Mishnah, we have to think of Sabbath laws, possibly combined with purity laws. The anti-Gentile tendency of these laws is assumed only in the Yerushalmi where several efforts are made to identify these halakhot on the basis of lists of halakhot in the Mishnah. This line of interpretation, which even in the Yerushalmi is not the only one, in the Bavli recedes again to the background. The understanding of "their gifts" as sacrifices offered by Gentiles is not the natural meaning of the expression. But it became the cornerstone of the historical reconstruction—a very weak cornerstone indeed. Only on the basis of this identification was it possible to date the meeting in the upper room of Hananiah b. Hezekiah b. Garon in the year 66 C.E. at the outbreak of the war against Rome. Without this identification, an earlier date would be quite as possible as a later one. It thus becomes impossible to derive from these texts about the eighteen halakhot details about the history of the revolt against Rome or the attitude of certain Pharisaic groups towards the revolt and their tendency to join the Zealots. The Mishnaic text is problematic. The efforts to interpret it have led to a number of hypotheses in the Talmudim. They have to be considered as literary developments, but not as remnants of solid historical traditions.

RELIGIÓN Y PODER EN EL JUDAÍSMO RABÍNICO: PARÁBOLAS DE "UN REY DE ESTE MUNDO"

Luis F. Girón Blanc

El judaísmo rabínico o judaísmo talmúdico, que acaba siendo el judaísmo triunfante tras las desgracias que asolaron a los judíos habitantes de Palestina en los siglos I y II del cómputo de los cristianos, recoge tradiciones muy antiguas y enraíza con el Israel anterior al exilio y con el inmediato al regreso de Babilonia. Pero se encuentra con unas circunstancias socio-políticas muy diferentes.

Tras la ocupación romana en el 64 aC los que ostenten el nombre de reyes no serán más que unos títeres en manos de los romanos. La jefatura del sacerdocio que durante la dinastía de los Hasmoneos coincidirá frecuentemente en la persona del rey, quedará definitivamente separada y el final será la implantación de lo que podemos denominar la dinastía herodiana tras el nombramiento-proclamación de Herodes el Grande como rey el año 37 aC tras vencer al último rey hasmoneo, Antígono, con ayuda de los romanos.

Herodes el Grande no era ni siquiera judío de origen, sino idumeo de una familia conversa y a su muerte, en torno al cambio de era, el territorio se dividirá entre sus hijos y parientes. Aquellos reyes, reyezuelos y tetrarcas no tenían ningún reconocimiento por parte del pueblo y eran más bien odiados por su carácter de títeres del ocupante romano.

La controversia en pro y en contra de la realeza en el antiguo Israel había sido enconada, apoyada básicamente en la defensa a ultranza que algunos hacían de que el único rey de Israel es Dios, Adonai. Los primeros reyes se nos presentarán en el texto bíblico elegidos por Dios como sus representantes y ungidos como reyes por mandato divino; y la promesa hecha a David concederá este mismo carácter a sus descendientes, cualquiera que sea el método o las intrigas por las que asciendan al trono. Y se nos dirá también que dejan de ser reyes, por muerte, cuando pierden el favor divino.

Pero en la época del cambio de era todo esto queda ya muy lejos. Curiosamente durante el siglo I volverá a ser el jefe de los sacerdotes, el Sumo Sacerdote, el que se arrogue una buena parte de la representación del pueblo ante los romanos, sabedores el uno y los otros de la capacidad de movilización que tenían los planteamientos religiosos trufados de nacionalismo. Y por su parte las autoridades romanas del lugar tratarán de mantener las riendas precisamente teniendo metafóricamente maniatado al Sumo Sacerdote. Recordemos que esas autoridades custodiaban los ropajes litúrgicos que el Sumo Sacerdote debía vestir en la solemnidad de *Yôm Kippur* y podían no entregárselos para la celebración. Aunque no quede constancia de que eso llegara nunca a suceder, la amenaza y la posibilidad eran bien reales.

Con la destrucción del Templo en el año 70 desaparece totalmente la influencia sacerdotal y serán los maestros o rabíes los que tomen el relevo con el Patriarca—Príncipe o Presidente, *Nasi'*—en la cúspide de su estructura jerárquica. En teoría no se trata de un puesto político, sino religioso-académico, pero la realidad será muchas veces distinta. El relato legendario que nos presenta a Rabí Yojanán ben Zakai negociando personalmente con Vespasiano nos da la pauta de este cambio.

En estas circunstancias la literatura que llamamos rabínica o tal-múdica recurrirá con frecuencia a la figura de un rey para explicar, interpretar y en última instancia bajar al nivel de lo cotidiano las actitu-des, sentimientos y actuaciones que se atribuyen a Dios o se proyectan en él, del cual el rey es en última instancia representante. Y lo hará también con frecuencia de forma precisa para evitar malentendidos con la expresión "un rey terrenal", que algunos traducen como un "rey de este mundo" y que literalmente suele decir un "rey de carne y sangre" que es la forma hebrea de expresar lo que en español se dice "de carne y hueso".

No se trata, pues, tanto de las relaciones específicas entre la religión y el poder, sino más bien del concepto que la religión, el judaísmo tal-múdico en este caso, tiene del poder, en cuanto que emanado de Dios; las obligaciones que esta "realidad" impone al gobernante, y las que de rechazo corresponden a Dios. Los planteamientos teocráticos provienen de una teología, pero a su vez la generan y la desarrollan.

(1) La primera parábola que vamos a ver es realmente audaz en su planteamiento:

> Se parece a dos atletas que estaban luchando cuerpo a cuerpo ante el rey. Si el rey hubiera querido habría parado la lucha, pero no quiso separarlos. Uno de ellos acorraló al otro y lo mató, mientras la víctima

gritaba: que se presente demanda contra el rey que no ha impedido mi asesinato. (*Gén Rab* 22,9)[1]

Según esto, el gobernante es responsable del mal que hacen los súbditos si pudiendo hacerlo no lo evita. En este caso se está comentando la muerte de Abel a manos de Caín y se culpa a Dios de ello; es más, según la audaz lectura que se propone del texto, el propio Dios se autoinculpa porque en vez de "la sangre de tu hermano clama ante mí (*'elay*)" (Gén 4,10) el comentarista le hace decir "la sangre de tu hermano clama *contra* mí (*'alay*)".

El atrevimiento de la interpretación hace decir al rabino que la propone: Duro resulta este asunto para decirlo e imposible de explicar.

(2) En la siguiente parábola vemos que el rey, por encargo divino, organiza la sociedad y espera que todos colaboren, de la misma manera que Dios, Rey del universo, da a cada uno sus capacidades de todo tipo y espera que las pongan en juego.

Pusieron un ejemplo. ¿A qué se parece este asunto?—A un rey de este mundo que tenía dos siervos a los que apreciaba muchísimo, y a cada uno le entregó un saquito de grano y un manojo de lino. ¿Qué creéis que hizo el que era listo?—Tomó el lino y tejió un paño, y molió el grano, tamizó la harina, la amasó, horneó una torta y la colocó en una bandeja, cubriéndola con el paño, hasta que viniera el rey. Pero el necio no hizo nada. Al cabo de unos días vino el rey y les dijo: A ver, hijos míos, traedme lo que os dí. Sacó el primero la torta de harina sobre la bandeja con el paño que la cubría y el otro sacó el grano en una cesta y el haz de lino sobre ella. ¡Ay qué vergüenza! ¡Ay qué bochorno! ¡Dime! ¿Cuál de ellos agradó más?—El que sacó la bandeja con la torta de harina. (*Seder Eliyahu Zuta* 2)[2]

En este caso la responsabilidad es una cuestión personal y se mueve en un terreno tan ambiguo como "el de agradar al rey", por eso el comentarista la usa en un terreno meramente "religioso" sin ninguna proyección política, y la explica: Dios dio la Torá y los judíos deben estudiarla y profundizar en ella.

---

[1] Ver M. Ayali y L. F. Girón, *Te voy a contar un cuento…* (Madrid: Palas Atenea Ediciones, 1992), 136.

[2] Ayali y Girón, *Te voy a contar*, 138.

(3) El poder absoluto del rey, se dice en la siguiente parábola, tiene sus ventajas, y cumplir sus decretos o simplemente no hacer lo que el rey no quiere que se haga o no ha dicho que se haga, puede tener su premio.

> La situación se parece al caso de un manzano que se levantaba en el huerto del rey y los labradores querían cortarlo. Les dijo el príncipe: Si el rey se entera os cortará la cabeza. Al cabo de unos días hacía sol y no sabían dónde protegerse. Se colocaron bajo el manzano, a su sombra, y comieron de sus frutos. (*Mid. Yelammedenu* a Gén 42,1)[3]

El texto es muy escueto y parece que sólo el temor al disgusto del rey retiene a los súbditos de actuar, con el consiguiente aunque inesperado y no pretendido beneficio posterior, pero en realidad el ejemplo está aplicado en el comentario al plan que tienen los hermanos del José bíblico de matarlo por celos y envidia—lo cual parece objetivamente malo, y contrario a los derechos humanos, diríamos hoy, y no una mera arbitrariedad del rey—; y más tarde, frustrado el plan, este José significará la continuidad y la supervivencia del pueblo de Israel; de forma que el contexto aporta una connotación moral a la acción aparentemente inocua de cortar el manzano. Vuelve a utilizarse el recurso al rey para hacer teología.

(4) Un Dios dotado de los defectos que pueden percibirse en el rey tendrá que ser llamado al orden en la siguiente parábola:

> Dijo Rabí Berekyá en nombre de R. Leví: Se parece a un rey que tenía una viña y la arrendó a un labrador. Cuando producía buen vino decía, qué bueno es el vino de mi viña, y cuando producía mal vino decía, qué malo es el vino de mi labrador. Y éste le dijo: Majestad, cuando el vino es bueno hablas del "vino de mi viña" y cuando es malo del "vino de mi labrador". Tanto si es bueno como si es malo, el vino es tuyo.
>
> Así, primero dijo Dios a Moisés: "Saca a mi pueblo de Egipto" (Ex 3,10); pero cuando los israelitas se postraron ante el becerro le dijo: "Baja del monte porque se ha pervertido tu pueblo". (Ex 32,7). Entonces dijo Moisés a Dios: ¡Señor del Universo! ¡Cuando pecan son mi pueblo y cuando guardan tus preceptos son tuyos! ¡tanto pecador como cumplidor, Israel es tuyo! (*Pesiqta Rab Kahana* 16)[4]

El rey, hombre al fin y al cabo, trata de apropiarse de lo bueno y desentenderse de lo malo, y según el texto, Dios también, de forma que Moisés

---

[3] Ayali y Girón, *Te voy a contar*, 146.
[4] Ayali y Girón, *Te voy a contar*, 148.

tiene que recordarle su responsabilidad, de alguna manera semejante a lo que veíamos en la primera de las parábolas, con la diferencia de que allí se trataba de una cuestión social, el asesinato de Abel por Caín, es decir una cuestión entre hombres de la que el gobernante no puede desentenderse, y menos aún Dios; y aquí se trata de una cuestión de menores consecuencias sociales entre el pueblo y Dios.

Las tres parábolas siguientes tratan el tema de la justicia, pero desde planteamientos muy distintos en cada una de ellas.

(5) Es característica del rey, o incluso una exigencia, que sea sabio, sobre todo en el momento de impartir justicia. Y el ejemplo bien conocido es del famoso juicio de Salomón. La siguiente parábola aporta un caso de sabiduría, de forma que no se puede engañar al rey.

> Dijo Rabbí Yehudá al emperador Antonino: Te voy a poner un ejemplo; ¿A qué se parece este asunto?—A un rey de este mundo que tenía un huerto magnífico con brevas estupendas y puso allí dos guardianes, uno cojo y el otro ciego. Dijo el cojo al ciego: veo unas brevas estupendas en el huerto, súbeme a hombros y las cogeremos para comerlas. Montó el cojo sobre los hombros del ciego, las cogieron y se las comieron. Al cabo de unos días vino el rey y les preguntó: ¿Dónde están las brevas estupendas?—contestó el cojo: ¡Pues yo no tengo pies para llegar a ellas!; y el ciego: ¡Pues yo no tengo ojos para verlas! ¿Qué creéis que hizo el rey?—Montó al cojo sobre los hombros del ciego y los castigó conjuntamente. (*bSanh* 91ab)[5]

El ejemplo tiene sentido y fin en sí mismo como retrato de un buen gobernante sabio que no se deja engañar, pero como casi siempre el contexto lo pone en relación con cuestiones teológicas y se refiere a Dios en el marco de una polémica sobre la retribución después de la muerte y la resurrección. En la cosmovisión judía, ni el cuerpo inanimado ni el ánimo que lo vivifica podrían ser objeto de juicio, pues nada pueden hacer por separado, como el cojo y el ciego. Luego para el supremo juicio, que se da por supuesto, habrá que reunirlos de nuevo, y por ello el ejemplo termina diciendo: Así el Santo, bendito sea, toma el ánima, vuelve a colocarla en el cuerpo y los juzga conjuntamente.

(6) El mismo tema de la justicia pero desde una perspectiva diferente puede analizarse en la siguiente parábola. Se habla de un rey,

---

[5] Ver Ayali y Girón, *Te voy a contar*, 152.

representante o trasunto de Dios, que aplica un sistema de justicia individualizada y personalizada, quizá la única verdadera justicia que es la que puede ofrecer una trato desigual a los desiguales, salvando siempre, diríamos hoy, los principios básicos en que todos los seres humanos son iguales.

> ¿A qué se pareció el caso de Rabbí Abún?—A un rey que tenía una viña y contrató muchos jornaleros para cultivarla. Había entre ellos uno que se esmeraba más que ninguno en el trabajo, incluso demasiado. ¿Qué creéis que hizo el rey?—Lo cogió del brazo y se puso a pasear con él arriba y abajo. Al caer la tarde vinieron los obreros a cobrar, y también vino aquel, y el rey le pagó el jornal completo. Los demás comenzaron a murmurar diciendo: Hemos trabajado todo el día y éste tan sólo dos horas, pero el rey le ha pagado el jornal completo.—Les contestó el rey: ¿Por qué murmuráis? Sabed que éste en dos horas de dedicación ha hecho más que vosotros en todo el día. (*Qoh Rab* 5,11)[6]

Se puede considerar arbitraria la actuación del rey, aunque quizá no lo sea tanto si la comparamos con una práctica laboral bien extendida en nuestra sociedad, conocida como "contrato por obra". Si elucubramos un poco, el "contrato por obra" lleva al trabajo "a destajo" y este, con mucha frecuencia, al exceso de horas y a la explotación. La justicia de este rey se manifiesta precisamente en eso. En una parábola muy semejante en el Nuevo Testamento cristiano puede notarse que allí sí que se resalta al arbitrariedad: "¿no voy a poder hacer yo con lo mío lo que quiera?" (Mt 20,1–16), aunque pueda tener también allí una lectura incluso más socializante que la de aquí: "cada uno según su capacidad y a cada uno según su necesidad".

En cualquier caso el contexto de esta parábola rabínica es muy concreto y también muy teológico, y se presenta como *laudatio* fúnebre y a modo de explicación (!!!) por la muerte prematura de un joven maestro rabínico, porque termina diciendo: Rabbí Abún había aprendido más Torá en veintiocho años que cualquier discípulo veterano en cien años.

(7) También de preocupación por la justicia nos habla la siguiente parábola, aunque el rey no sea aquí realmente el protagonista, sino solamente el que tranquiliza al protagonista y no sólo no lo castiga sino que le paga el salario.

---

[6] Ver Ayali y Girón, *Te voy a contar*, 156.

> Se parece a uno que iba vendiendo paja y al pasar por delante del huerto del rey vió unos haces de zarzas y se detuvo a cogerlos. El rey apareció de repente y lo vió, y él intentó esconderse. Le dijo el rey: ¿Por qué te escondes? hubiera necesitado unos obreros que las recogieran, y puesto que las has recogido tú, toma tu salario. (*Gén. Rab.* 44,4)[7]

Sólo el contexto nos puede aclarar el sentido de este ejemplo, más allá de los aspectos puramente prácticos que son evidentes. Nos va a plantear un caso de preocupación "a posteriori" por lo que hoy llamaríamos los "efectos colaterales" de una acción bélica. Abraham estaba pesaroso por si entre los que habían muerto a manos de sus tropas en la guerra contra Kedarlaomer (Gén 14) se habrían encontrado algunos inocentes. Y la interpretación rabínica, que pone tan buenos sentimientos en Abraham, tranquiliza a los oyentes apoyándose en que Dios le dice en otro lugar: "No temas, Abraham" (Gén 15,1), es decir, no te preocupes porque estaban ya cortados para ser retirados y tú simplemente hiciste el trabajo, del mismo modo que el que retiró los hacer de zarzas.

(8) Finalmente una parábola que ofrece el trasfondo justificador a todo lo dicho y a muchas cuestiones más que podrían decirse al hilo de otras parábolas de "un rey de este mundo".

> Contaban una parábola: ¿A qué se parece esto?—A un rey que entró en la ciudad y dijo a la gente: Voy a reinar sobre vosotros.—Le contestaron: Nada bueno has hecho por nosotros para reinar sobre nosotros. ¿Qué hizo?—Les construyó una muralla, les llevó agua e hizo las guerras a favor de ellos. Entonces les dijo: Voy a reinar sobre vosotros; y le contestaron: ¡Sí, Sí!. (*Mek bahodes* 4 a Ex 12,2)[8]

Encontramos aquí una curiosidad inesperada. Parece que la de este rey es una monarquía parlamentaria, o al menos sujeta al refrendo del pueblo que le pide hechos antes de aceptarle como tal, diríamos que "tiene que trabajárselo". Y no está tan descaminada la intuición puesto que, como siempre, se trata de una analogía y la relación de Dios con el pueblo de Israel es fruto de un pacto. Por eso cuando a la hora de establecer el pacto, antes de especificar las cláusulas del contrato, que son lo que se conoce como "los diez mandamientos", se diga aquello de

---

[7] Ver Ayali y Girón, *Te voy a contar*, 158.
[8] Traducción de A. Salvatierra en "Los Mesalim. Parábolas de Mekilta de R. Yismael". Texto de *Mek Bahodes* 4 en J.Z. Lauterbach, *Mekilta de-Rabbi Ishmael: a critical edition* (3 vols.; Philadelphia: Jewish Publication Society of America, 1933–1935), 2:229–30.

"Yo soy Adonai, tu Dios" (Ex 12,2), los israelitas lo aceptarán, porque como dice el texto del comentario:

> El Omnipresente había sacado a Israel de Egipto, les había separado las aguas del mar, había hecho bajar el maná y las codornices sobre ellos y brotar el manantial de la roca y había combatido las guerras de Amaleq por ellos, y entonces dijo: Voy a reinar sobre vosotros, y le contestaron: ¡Sí, sí!.

En resumen, había dado pruebas de que podía ser ventajoso aceptarlo como Dios/rey y eso animaba a la contraparte a aceptar el pacto, con sus correspondientes obligaciones.

EL TARGUM DE ABDÍAS

Josep Ribera-Florit

0. LA VISIÓN JUDAICO-RABÍNICA DEL PROFETA

El libro apócrifo *Vitae prophetarum*[1] describe la personalidad de Abdías parcamente, pero da ya las pautas para las leyendas midrásicas posteriores sobre este profeta, cuyo texto es el más breve de todos los profetas escritores. Según *Vitae Prophetarum* Abdías era originario de Siquem, del distrito de Bet Harán. Fue discípulo de Elías y compartió con él el sufrimiento y la huida a causa de la persecución de Jezabel. Se le identifica con el mayordomo de palacio de Acab (1Re 2–16) y el tercer capitán de los cincuenta militares en tiempos de Ocozías, sucesor de Acab (2Re 1,13–15). Después dejó de ser oficial del rey para iniciar su predicación profética.[2]

Estas breves indicaciones se amplían en los textos midrásicos y talmúdicos, y se enfocan a veces de diversa forma. Siguiendo la tradición midrásica, el profeta Abdías era de origen idumeo y profetizó contra los edomitas. Muy a pesar suyo se vio obligado a ello por los setenta y un miembros del sanedrín celestial. Una *hagadá* lo considera prosélito, supervisor de la primera división del paraíso, perteneciente a los prosélitos. Formaba parte de los altos cargos del rey Acab (1Re 18,3), a quien acusó por su impiedad. Su esposa se llamaba Será, hija de Ašer, catalogada entre las mujeres de valor. Abdías gastó su fortuna para mantener a los cien profetas escondidos por él durante la persecución de Jezabel (1Re 18,4), lo que ocasionó unas deudas, a las que tuvo que hacer frente su viuda; ésta apeló en el cementerio al temeroso de Dios; y entre los cuatro temerosos de Dios mencionados por una voz celestial (Abraham, Jonás, Job y Abdías) sobresalía el último en su temor al Señor. Entonces la viuda fue ayudada milagrosamente por el profeta Eliseo para saldar la deuda (el milagro de las vasijas de aceite,

---

[1] De esta obra conservada en griego, probablemente del s. I dC, recientemente ha hecho una edición crítica A.M. Schwemer, *Studien zu den frühjüdischen Prophetenlegenden: Vitae Prophetarum* (2 vols; TSAJ 49–50; Tübingen: Mohr Siebeck, 1995–1996), 2:43–47; *Synopse zu den Vitae Prophetarum*, esp. 36*–38*.

[2] Cf. *OTP* 2:379–99, (392–99, texto de Abdías).

2Re 4,1–7). Posteriormente Abdías profetizó bajo Josafat, siendo contemporáneo de otros profetas (Isaías, Miqueas). Fue discípulo de Elías con los profetas Miqueas, Jonás y Eliseo. Isaías y Abdías, el más extenso y el más breve de los profetas escritores, vaticinaron en muchos lugares (setenta y un lugares, siendo uno de ellos el de los filisteos).[3]

Con estas pinceladas la tradición judía realza la figura de Abdías a pesar de la brevedad de su profecía. Lo sitúa dentro del grupo de prosélitos de origen idumeo en la época de Elías y, como discípulo de éste, lo parangona con otros profetas como Miqueas, Jonás y Eliseo e incluso Isaías.

0.1. *El uso sinagogal del profeta Abdías*

Sin duda en el Israel exílico y postexílico la sinagoga, sobre todo en la diáspora, representa el centro del culto y formación del pueblo en el conocimiento y práctica de la Torá, junto con otros textos bíblicos que le acompañan o sustituyen. Entre éstos cabe mencionar las *haftarot*, o perícopas normalmente de los Profetas, que completan la lectura sagrada de la Sinagoga y sirven para introducir un comentario del Rabí. Ciertamente, no todos los Profetas fueron recitados en la sinagoga, pero entre algunos privilegiados hay el profeta Abdías que, por su brevedad, se leía entero.

Tenemos a nuestra disposición algunos documentos que nos indican con qué *seder* se completaba este profeta. En el ciclo trienal palestinense, el más antiguo que conocemos, la perícopa Gn 32,4ss e Is 31,11ss se completaba con Abdías; también se leía después de Dt 2,2ss y Jon 2,2ss. A la recitación en hebreo seguía la versión targúmica, que paulatinamente se convirtió en el texto de Abdías de que hoy disponemos.[4]

1. El texto del Targum de Abdías (Tg Abd)

El texto tal cual ha llegado a nosotros parece que forma parte del Targum de los Profetas Menores que, según las opiniones de los expertos

---

[3] Cf. L. Ginsberg, *The Legends of the Jews* (7 vols.; Philadelphia: The Jewish Publication Society of America, 1909–1946). Sobre los aspectos de la vida de Abdías según las tradiciones judías consúltense los siguientes apartados: 6:345 n. 7; 6:344–45; 1:21–22; 5:258 n. 271; 6:321 n. 23; 6:355 n. 20; 5:195 n. 72; 4:240–41; 6:345 n. 7; 6:356 n. 20; 6:343 n. 1; 6:375 n. 104.

[4] Sobre la recitación de la Biblia según la tradición palestinense, cf. C. Perrot, *La Lecture de la Bible dans la Synagogue* (Hildesheim: Gerstenberg, 1973).

actuales, tiene ya antecedentes en el período del 70 al 135 d.C. y per-
tenecería en la forma cercana a la actual a los ss. IV–V d.C.[5]

Para la edición del texto arameo me he basado, hasta que no haya
una edición crítica aceptable, en el ms. Or. 1474 del Museo Británico,
con la sigla *z*, el cual, a pesar de tratarse de un texto más tardío (s. XVI)
que el ms. Or 2211 editado por A. Sperber,[6] conserva elementos orientales más significativos que este último. De hecho no me consta ningún
fragmento conocido de este Tg en masora babilónica. Se encuentra un
fragmento de Ab 4–18 en la colección *Antonin* de San Petersburgo 819,
clasificado por I. Yeivin como Eb 25 y cuya calidad es ínfima (BRI),
que equivaldría a un texto yemenita como el Ms Or 1474. Según el
estudio del arameo targúmico de Eb 25 se aprecia que se trata de
una vocalización muy defectiva completada por mano tiberiense y,
probablemente, por un *naqdán* palestinense. Restos babilónicos claros
son el v. 4 *'amar*, el v. 5 *meš'arin*, el v. 15 *kol, da'atid*, el v. 7 *'enaš*, el v.
10 *mḥaṭof*; hay confusión de *pataḥ* y *qameṣ* en el v. 9 *guibarāk* y en el v.
15 *kmā'*. Restos probablemente palestinenses son el v. 9 *mĕqṭal, mkarĕka*
y el v. 15 *'amĕmaya', kĕma'*.

He añadido en el texto arameo y en la versión castellana las variantes
más significativas de los manuscritos cotejados por Sperber: El ms. Or
2211 del Museo Británico, publicado por Sperber como texto base, y al
que le he dado la sigla *s*. El ms. Or 1470 del Museo Británico, que son
unas *haftarot* leídas dos veces al año; contiene el Tg Abd entero; lleva
la sigla 5. El Ms. p. 116 de la Biblioteca Montefiore del colegio judío
de Londres; lleva la sigla *c*. El conocido Codex Reuchlinianus (a. 1105)
de la *Badische Landesbibliothek* de Karlsruhe de Alemania, con la sigla *f*.[7]
Otros códices importantes de la tradición tiberiense, no estudiados por
Sperber, son el Codex Urbinati de la Biblioteca Vaticana y procedente
de la familia italiana Urbina, escrito en 1294, catalogado con la sigla
u; y el Codex Solger, depositado en la *Stadtbibliothek* de Nuremberg

---

[5] Es muy difícil en un texto tan breve como el del Tg Abdías sacar conclusiones
determinantes en cuanto a la lengua aramea y a la fecha de su composición, por ello
me remito a la introducción de la obra de K.J. Cathcart y R.P. Gordon, *The Targum of
the Minor Prophets. Translated with a Critical Introduction, and Notes.* (Wilmington: Delaware,
1989), 10–19 y la obra más reciente de S.P. Carbone y G. Rizzi, *Habaquq, Abdia, Nahum,
Sofonia. Lettura hebraica, greca e aramaica.* (Bologna: Dehoniane, 1998), 198–233.

[6] A. Sperber, *The Bible in Aramaic. Volume III, The Latter Prophets According to Targum
Jonathan.* (Leiden: Brill, 1962), 433–35.

[7] Sperber, *Bible in Aramaic. Vol. III*, X, indica con 7 variantes de *f* las diferentes n.s
margínales del Codex Reuchlinianus.

(Alemania) fechado según parece en 1292. Este códice bilingüe, hebreo y arameo targúmico, consta de 7 mss, siendo el ms. 5 el que comprende además de otros libros bíblicos, los Profetas Menores y entre ellos Abdías; lo he indicado con la sigla *so*. Luego he comparado el texto base con la Primera Biblia Rabínica de Venecia 1515–1517, que lleva la sigla *b*; la Segunda de Venecia 1524–25, con la sigla *g*, y la políglota de Amberes de 1569–73, con la sigla *o*. Así tenemos a nuestra disposición una importante representación de la tradición oriental babilónica y la occidental tiberiense del Tg.

En cuanto a las variantes vocálicas de los mss. que están a nuestro alcance, constatamos que algunas veces tienen repercusión semántica: en v. 3 *šere* (perfecto *pe'al* en el ms. *s*) e *yišre* (imperfecto en el ms. *so*) el ms *z* lo lee *šare* (participio); en el v. 5 el ms *c* no lee *dingabu*, forma sencilla *pe'al*, sino *dingibbu* intensivo *pa'el* ("robar, despojar").

Respecto a las variantes consonánticas, las más importantes (indicadas en el texto) son una muestra de que en realidad este texto oficial fue en general bastante homogéneo, por lo que son poco significativas. A veces resulta que las variantes encontradas en algún ms. o edición suponen que su traducción targúmica sigue literalmente al TM. Las variantes más importantes del texto targúmico de Abdías se hallan en el mss *u*, *c* y en el impreso *o*. Tanto las técnicas de traducción como el método derásico empleado por el Targum se usan siempre en función de una exégesis que podríamos clasificarla de aclaratoria y actualizante.

2. Hermenéutica

La hermenéutica comprende las técnicas de traducción judías, muchas de ellas comunes a las versiones antiguas, y el llamado método derásico.[8]

2.1. *Técnicas de traducción*

En este breve texto se pueden encontrar varios de los elementos característicos de la forma de traducir del Tg que, en muchas ocasiones,

---

[8] Cf. J. Ribera-Florit, "The Use of the Derash Method in the Targum of Ezekiel", en *The Interpretation of the Scripture in Early Judaism and Christianity. Studies in Language and Tradition* (ed. C. Evans et al.; Sheffield: Sheffield Academic Press, 2000), 406–22.

coincide con el método seguido por las traducciones antiguas griega, siríaca, *Vetus latina* y *Vulgata*.

En cuanto a cambios gramaticales, por concordancia sintáctica, el Tg en el v. 6 cambia el plural del TM (*nepašu* "han sido registrados") por el singular (*itbeleš* "ha sido registrado"). Escoge el pasivo en lugar del activo como acaece en el v. 21, donde *mešezebin* puede entenderse como activo y, como pasivo, *šafʿel*; sin embargo, por el contexto, a pesar de que el TM tiene forma activa, debería preferirse la pasiva como sugiere Sperber.[9] De hecho en el v. 14 se usa la misma forma para traducir un término pasivo (*šeridayw* "sus escapados") por otro pasivo *mešezebohi* "sus salvados", Tg). Otro cambio evidente es el empleo de tiempo finito (*tešawe* "pusieras", v. 4) en vez del infinitivo del TM (*sim* "poner"). Asimismo, encontramos el paso de una frase asindética (*al tereʾ* "no veas" del TM, v. 12) a una sindética (*wedehazitah* "y contemplarás", Tg). Finalmente, en el v. 11 aparece un *qere-ketib* (*šaʿaro* es el *ketib* en vez del *qere šarayw*, al que sigue el Tg).

2.2. *Recursos contextuales*

El Tg se vale de unos recursos en función de la clarificación del TM, difícil de entender. Así la palabra *ndmh* del v. 5, que parece tener el sentido de "destruir, ser destruida", el Tg la lee *nrdm* en el sentido de "estar sosegada" por entenderla como "dormida". El término *laḥmak*, "tu pan" (v. 7), de difícil comprensión en el contexto, sugiere al Tg una paráfrasis: "los que comen en tu mesa".[10] Al nombre *mazor* (v. 8) del TM, que significa "herida", el Tg prefiere *maṣod* "trampa"; todas las versiones antiguas coinciden en el cambio de este último término, lo cual podría sugerir una *Vorlage* distinta del TM. Siendo la frase del TM incompleta *al tišlaḥnah* (v. 13) nada fácil de entender, el Tg le añade un acusativo: "has alargado *tu mano*". Por otra parte, el Tg recurre a figuras retóricas, ausentes a veces en el TM como, por ejemplo, la paranomasia *ḥaṭofin keqaṭofin* "salteadores como vendimiadores" (v. 5).

---

[9] A. Sperber, *The Bible in Aramaic. Volume IV B: The Targum and the Hebrew Bible.* (Leiden: Brill, 1973), 74.
[10] Así lo interpretan también Símmaco y Vulgata.

2.3. *Recursos léxicos*

El verbo *tbr* "quebrantar" (vv. 12,13), de uso frecuente en el Tg, se emplea para sustituir palabras sinónimas del TM (*nkr, ʿbd, ʾyd, rʾhn ʾyd*). El vocablo *purʿanut* (v. 16) es un término también muy característico del Tg para indicar el castigo justiciero, la venganza divina, sobre todo contra las naciones, enemigas de Israel. Asimismo la expresión *beqarib yomaʾ daʿatid le mete min qodam yyy* "cerca está el día que está por llegar procedente del Señor" (v. 15) es común en el Tg de los Profetas para indicar la proximidad de un acontecimiento normalmente de índole escatológica.[11]

2.4. *El método derásico*

El llamado método *derás* es uno de los recursos más frecuentes empleados muchas veces en la exégesis judía para actualizar conceptos de textos bíblicos. Para ello se recurre a diversos cambios.

2.4.1. *Cambios semánticos*

El concepto de profeta es sobre todo de transmisor del mensaje divino que, para el Tg, es un mensaje profético (*nebuʾah*, v. 1), de ahí que substituya a *ḥazon* "visión" del TM. A Edom, que para el Tg es sinónimo de Roma,[12] se le atribuye connotaciones propias: es débil en lugar de pequeño (v. 2),[13] en su corazón hay maldad en vez de arrogancia (v. 3); no engaña sencillamente, sino que extravía (*ʿty*) con su poder fascinante hacia la idolatría (vv 3 y 7). Por dos veces alude a las águilas de Edom-Roma, en la glosa del v. 3 y en la traducción literal del v. 4. Para personalizar más el significado simbólico del águila, afirma que "mora" en vez de "anida" en las alturas, de las que el Señor por su Palabra la hará bajar.[14]

Otro recurso derásico es el empleo frecuente del genérico "tiempo" en lugar del concreto "día" (vv. 8,12), menos cuando se refiere al día

---

[11] Cf. Tgs Is 2,12; 13,6; Ez 30,3; Jo 2,1.11; 3,4; 4,14; Am 5,18.20; Ab 15; Sof 1,14; Zac 14,1; Mal 3,23.

[12] Según el Talmud Bablí *ʿAbodah Zarah* 10a R. Josef aplicó Abdías 1 a Roma. La misma alusión encontramos en Lv Rabba 13,5; Nm Rabba 15,17; cf. Cathcart y Gordon, *The Targum of the Minor Prophets*, 99, n. 3.

[13] En cuanto a la interpretación judía de Esaú como débil, cf. Cathcart y Gordon, *The Targum of the Minor Prophets*, 99, n. 4.

[14] En Tg Os 1,1 se habla claramente del águila grabada en sus estandartes como símbolo del ejército romano.

del Señor escatológico (v. 15). El uso del todo por la parte: "puertas" se convierte en "ciudades" (v. 11); o de lo concreto en vez de lo abstracto: *tebunah* "inteligencia" se entiende por "todo varón que tiene inteligencia"; el nombre topográfico de "Teman" se generaliza como "los habitantes del Sur" (v. 9).[15] Todo el v. 19 está repleto de complementos, que concretan el texto genérico del TM. el Tg cambia la frase *har 'Esau* "monte de Esaú" por "fortaleza de Esaú (vv. 9,10,19 y 21)[16] y sólo conserva *har*, "monte", al referirse al monte santo de Sión (v.17).

El uso de la figura rabínica denominada *tarte mašma'*, "doble sentido", está también presente en el Tg. Así con la palabra *ḥelo* del TM v. 11, que se entiende como "ejército y riquezas", el Tg recurre al segundo significado. Más frecuente es la práctica de la ley rabínica denominada *al tiqre*, "no leas", por la que *nidmah* el Tg lo deriva de *dmh* (v. 5); *ḥty* "desmayarse", pasa a *ḥtt*, "romper" (v. 9),[17] y *mazor*, "herida",[18] se cambia por *maṣod*, "trampa" (v. 7).

2.5. *Interpretación de metáforas*

Anunciando el desmoronamiento de Edom, el Tg hace realista la metáfora de "vendimiadores" identificándolos con "salteadores" (v. 6). En otros pasajes el Tg Ab expone el sentido real de las metáforas: el poder del fuego, el vigor de la llama y la debilidad de la paja (v. 18). El Tg da del v. 18 a la figura del fuego y de la paja que se quema y es devorada un sentido histórico guerrero: *"dominarán y matarán"*. En los vv. 12–14 la exégesis pide un cambio, así las afirmaciones negativas, empleadas como recurso retórico (ruega al oyente que no lo haga), el Tg las convierte en afirmaciones positivas como de algo que se ha hecho: "has visto, te has alegrado…".

A su vez el Tg evita o comenta las repeticiones y sinónimos del TM. Así, en el v. 11 *zarim* y *nekarim* se cambian por "naciones y extranjeros". A veces añade glosas en función de clarificar la frase (*"del que tienes necesidad"*, v. 9).

---

[15] Es común al Tg la versión del nombre topográfico Temán por el genérico "el Sur", cf. Jr 49,7.20; Ez 25,13; Am 1,12; Hab 3,3.

[16] También encontramos este cambio en Tg Am 4,1.

[17] De hecho ambas raíces se encuentran en mss. hebreos; Gen Rabba 89,6 cita ambas interpretaciones.

[18] *LXX*, *Pesitta* y *Vulgata* traducen *mazor* por "emboscada", con un sentido similar a la interpretación targúmica.

3. Exégesis

Si la exégesis targúmica se ha de basar sobre todo en las variantes y paráfrasis respecto al TM, hay que tener en cuenta que en textos tan breves, y tal vez también en otros, el ensamblaje de la traducción literal y la interpretada es muy estrecho y en estos casos la versión literal tiene, en un contexto retocado, un sentido distinto o añadido al original, y se puede considerar como una interpretación.[19]

3.1. *Actualización histórica*

La literalidad y la interpretación están íntimamente conectadas en el ejemplo siguiente. El Tg entiende Edom, en un sentido traslaticio, como símbolo de Roma y, sin cambiar la palabra, le da por *tarte mašmaʿ* el doble sentido: el del Edom (antiguo adversario de Judá) y el actualizado de Roma, el Edom actual, enemigo de Israel. Lo mismo sucede con el sinónimo Esaú, del que resalta sobre todo su fortaleza (vv. 8,19,21); seguramente por relacionarlo con Petra, la capital de Edom.

3.2. *Actualización geográfica.*

Consiste en la traducción actualizada de topónimos: Teman (v. 9) y Negeb (v. 20) los convierte en el genérico Sur.[20] Sefarad del v. 20, que probablemente se refiere en el TM a Sardis, capital de Lidia (Asia Menor), el Tg lo actualiza en Ispamia (*Pesitta* lee "Hispana"), que es el nombre de la región romana que luego se identificará con la Sefarad medieval.[21]

---

[19] Cf. L. Smolar y M. Aberbach, *Studies in Targum Jonathan to the Prophets* (New York: KTAV, 1983), donde los autores presentan una visión sobre las actualizaciones halá-quicas, históricas y teológicas del Tg de los Profetas.

[20] Sobre la versión de los Tgs de los Profetas de Temán y Negev por "Sur", cf. *Studies in Targum* Jonathan, 124.

[21] En cuanto a las diversas interpretaciones del TM y del Tg de Separad, cf. Car-bone y Rizzi, *Habaquq*, 224–25, n. 100. Según J. Padró en uno de los *wadis* de la zona montañosa de Tebas se encontraron unos graffiti en copto, de comienzos de la era cristiana, en que se habla de "Apa, el hombre de Espania", cf. "Espania en Egipto", *AuOr* 17–18 (1999–2000): 483–92 (= *Homenaje a G. Del Olmo Lete*).

3.3. *Actualización teológica*

3.3.1. *El concepto de la Divinidad en el Tg Abdias*

La frase, característica del TM, *Adonai Yahweh* (v. 1) se convierte en *YYY Elohim* "El señor Dios", manteniendo el término hebreo *Elohim* para el único Dios. Esta traducción es común a todos los Tgs a fin de hacer resaltar la existencia única del Dios de Israel.[22]

En el empleo de los atributos substitutivos de la divinidad se resalta la función justiciera de la Palabra divina (*memri*, v. 4). En el v. 18 el Tg hace hincapié en la restauración de Israel y en el castigo de sus enemigos no simplemente porque el Señor lo ha dicho, sino porque lo ha decretado mediante su Palabra. Es también común a los Tgs traducir *ne'um yahweh*, "oráculo de Yahvé", por *'amar yyy*, "ha dicho el Señor" (v. 8).

3.3.2. *Israel, el pueblo elegido*

El Tg Ab acentúa los abusos de Edom-Roma contra Jacob-Israel y, en concreto, contra Jerusalén (vv. 10,11), descritos detalladamente en los vv. 12–14. Por otra parte, el Tg insiste en la cercanía del día del juicio definitivo contra los enemigos de Israel (v. 15) recurriendo a la imagen simbólica de beber la copa del castigo justiciero (v. 16).[23]

A su vez expone, a modo de premio definitivo por las vejaciones que ha sufrido Israel, el retorno de éste al Monte Santo y la recuperación de las riquezas perdidas, con el dominio sobre sus enemigos: los escapados serán los triunfadores (tal vez éste sea el *tarte mašma*' del verbo *mešezebin*). El Tg atribuye la santidad del monte de Sión a los supervivientes "y serán santos" como influencia de la sacralidad del templo (v. 17);[24] son los separados, los escogidos, lo cual implica la reunión del gran Israel esparcido entre las ciudades de Efraim, Benjamín, Samaria, y la zona de Gilead (v. 19).[25]

Roma, el enemigo de Israel por excelencia, se simboliza con Edom y Esaú; el Tg carga las tintas y de la soberbia pasa a la perversidad de

---

[22] Cf. J. Ribera-Florit, *Targum de Ezequiel. Introducción, traducción crítica y notas* (Biblioteca midrásica 27; Estella: Verbo Divino, 2004), 41–42.

[23] Tal expresión, con una evidente connotación escatológica, es frecuente en el Tg de los Profetas; cf. Carbone y Rizzi, *Habaquq, Abdia*, 218–19, n. 70.

[24] Esta santidad del Monte Sión está claramente expresada en Tg Jo 4,17.

[25] Por razones de actualización los "campos y tiendas" del texto bíblico tienden en el período helénico-romano a urbanizarse y convertirse en "ciudades"; cf. Smolar y Aberbach, *Studies in Targum Jonathan*, 99–100.

corazón (v. 3); Edom no engaña sencillamente sino que extravía a Israel hacia la idolatría (t°). La imagen del águila expresa el orgullo en creerse que se halla en el olimpo de los dioses; pero detrás de este símbolo marcial está la imagen del culto al emperador romano. La acusación directa y positiva de su ataque a Israel (vv. 12–14) es un signo más del recurso targúmico para acentuar la vileza de los enemigos de Israel. La frase "la copa de la venganza" o del "castigo justiciero" (*pur'anut*, v. 16) es otro de los tópicos del Tg para hacer hincapié en la justicia vindicativa del Señor contra los enemigos de Israel.

3.3.3. *Escatología.*

El Tg Ab proyecta todo cuanto se describe de la salvación de Israel en un futuro próximo y definitivo.[26] Una frase del acontecimiento normalmente escatológico es la targúmica *yoma de 'atid lemete*, "el día que está por llegar" (v. 15). La venganza divina contra las naciones llevará a la recuperación final de las tribus de Israel que culminará con la manifestación del reino universal del Señor, duradero para siempre como glosan algunos mss. o impresos (el ms. de la Biblioteca Montefiore con la sigla *c* y la políglota de Amberes catalogada como *o*).[27]

4. Conclusión

Evidentemente, en una obra tan reducida como la del profeta Abdías no se puede sino descubrir unas pinceladas sobre el método targúmico, aplicado muy brevemente a este profeta. Tanto en la traducción como en el contenido del Tg Ab se constata que el targumista sigue las pautas de los otros profetas Menores. Aparece claro la imagen del Dios único existente con el marchamo hebreo de *Elohim*. Israel, el pueblo escogido y ultrajado por los enemigos de Dios, queda compensado con una prueba definitiva de la elección divina: con el agrupamiento del Israel esparcido por el exilio y el dominio sobre sus enemigos, Edom y Esaú, es decir Roma, en el tiempo escatológico cercano, cuando se

---

[26] Para una visión global de la escatología en los Tgs, cf. J. Ribera-Florit, "La escatología en el targum Jonatán (Tg Jon) y su relación con el targum palestinense (Tg Pal)", en *II Simposio Bíblico Español* (eds. V. Collado Bertomeu y V. Vilar Hueso; Valencia: Fundación Bíblica Español, 1987), 487–99.

[27] Sobre la revelación del reino de Dios en la literatura targúmica, cf. J. Ribera-Florit, *El Targum de Isaías. Versión crítica, introducción y notas* (Valencia: Instituto San Jerónimo, 1988), 50–51.

manifestará plenamente el reino de Dios. Una vez más, el Tg Abd es un ejemplo obvio de la literatura targúmica aplicada a los Profetas.

Anotaciones respecto a la traducción castellana

Como ya he indicado en la *Introducción*, el texto arameo usado como texto básico ha sido el del ms. 1474 (z) de la Biblioteca Oriental de Londres, que creo que es de categoría superior en relación con la tradición babilónica al ms Or 2211 (*s*), publicado por Sperber.

En la versión castellana he procurado ser lo más fiel posible al texto arameo, aunque a veces la idiosincrasia de la lengua castellana exige unas variantes propias de una lengua occidental. Por esta razón, alguna vez he añadido alguna palabra entre paréntesis para hacer más comprensible la frase.

Aunque algunos traductores evitan traducir el atributo *memrá*, he preferido, como he hecho en otras traducciones, verterlo por "Palabra" refiriéndome a la Palabra divina.

Las palabras en itálica indican las variantes más importantes del Tg con respecto al Texto Masorético (TM).

Las variantes indicadas en las notas se refieren a las que se encuentran en los diversos mss e impresos cotejados y que difieren del texto base.

Or 1474   Abdías

א

1   נְבוּאַת עוֹבַדְיָה¹ כְּדְנַן אֲמַר יְיָ אֱלֹהִים לֶאֱדוֹם בְּסוֹרָא² שְׁמַעְנָא מִן קֳדָם יְיָ
וְאִזְּנָד בְּעַמְמַיָּא³ שְׁלִיחַ קוּמוּ וְנִתְּעַתַּד עֲלַהּ לִקְרָבָא:

2   הָא חֲלָשׁ יְהַבְתָּךְ⁴ בְּעַמְמַיָּא בְּסִיר אַתְּ לַחְדָּא:

3   רִשַּׁע לִבָּךְ אַטְעְיָךְ⁵ דְּאַתְּ דָּמֵי לְנִשְׁרָא דְּשָׁרֵי⁷⁶ בִּשְׁנֵי כֵּיפָא בְּרוֹמָא מוֹתְבֵיהּ
אֲמַר בְּלִבֵּיהּ מָן יַחְתִנַּנִי לְאַרְעָא:

4   אִם תְּרִים כְּנִשְׁרָא וְאִם בֵּינֵי כּוֹכְבַיָּא תְּשַׁוֵּי מְדוֹרָךְ מִתַּמָּן בְּמֵימְרִי⁸ אֲחֲתִנָּךְ
אֲמַר יְיָ:

5   אִם נַבּוֹבִין אֲתוֹ עֲלָךְ אִם בָּזוֹזֵי⁹ לֵילְיָא אֵיכְדֵין הֲוֵיתָא דְמוּךְ עַד דְּנַבּוֹ
מִסָּתְּהוֹן אִם קְטוֹפִין כָּקְטוֹפִין אֲתוֹ עֲלָךְ הֲלָא מַשְׁאֲרִין לָךְ עוֹלְלָן:

6   אֵיכְדֵין אִתְבְּלֵישׁ עֵשָׂו אִתְגְּלִיוֹ מַטְמוֹרוֹהִי:

7   מִן תְּחוּמָא אַגְלְיוּךְ כָּל אֱנָשׁ קְיָמָךְ אַטְעְיוּךְ יְכִילוּ לָךְ אֱנָשׁ שְׁלָמָךְ אָכְלֵי
פְּתוֹרָךְ שַׁוִּיאוּ תְּקָלָא תְּחוֹתָךְ דַּלֵית בֵּהּ¹⁰ סָכְלְתָנוּ:

8   הֲלָא בְּעִדָּנָא הַהוּא אֲמַר יְיָ וְאוֹבֵיד חַכִּימִין מֵאֱדוֹם וְכָל נְבַר דְּבֵיהּ
סָכְלְתָנוּתָא¹¹ מִטּוּרָא¹² ¹³ דְּעֵשָׂו:

9   וְיִתְבְּרוּן נִבָּרָךְ¹⁴ דְּרוֹמָא בְּדִיל דְּיִשְׁתֵּיצֵי נְבַר דְּבֵיהּ צוֹרְכָא
מִטּוּרָא¹⁵ דְּעֵשָׂו מִקְּטוֹל:

10   מֵחֲטוֹף אֲחוּךְ יַעֲקֹב תְּחַפִּנָּךְ¹⁶ בַּהְתָא וְתִשְׁתֵּיצֵי לְעָלַם:

11   בְּיוֹם מְקָמָךְ מִקֳּבֵיל בְּיוֹמָא דְּבַזּוֹ עַמְמַיָּא¹⁷ נִכְסוֹהִי וְנוּכְרָאִין עֲלוּ בְּקִרְווֹהִי
וְעַל יְרוּשְׁלֵם רְמוֹ עַדְבִין אַף אַתְּ¹⁸ כְּחַד מִנְּהוֹן:

12 וְדַחֲזֵיתָא בְּיוֹמָא דְאָתֹוךְ דָאוֹתֹוךְ בְּיוֹם תַּבְרֵיהּ וְדַחֲדֵיתָא לִבְנֵי יְהוּדָה בְּיוֹם תַּבְרְהוֹן
וְדָאַסְנִיתָא לְמַלָּלָא דְרַבְרְבָן בְּעִידָן[19] עָקָא:

13 דַעֲלָתָא[20] בְּתַרְעֵי עַמִּי בְּיוֹם תַּבְרְהוֹן דַחֲזֵיתָא אַף אַת בְּבִשְׁתֵיהּ בְּיוֹם תַּבְרֵיהּ
וְדָאוֹשִׁיטָא יְדָךְ בְּנִכְסוֹהִי בְּיוֹם תַּבְרֵיהּ:

14 וּדְקַמְתָּא עַל פָּרְקָא לְשֵׁיצָאָה יָת מְעָרְקוֹהִי וּדְמַסְרְתָּא מְשֵׁיזֹבוֹהִי בְּעִדָּן עָקָא:

15 אֲרֵי קָרִיב יוֹמָא דַעֲתִיד לְמֵיתֵי מִן קֳדָם יְיָ עַל כָּל עַמְמַיָּא כְּמָא דַעֲבַדְתָּא
יִתְעֲבֵידָ[21] לָךְ גְּמֻלָךְ יְתוּב בְּרֵישָׁךְ:

16 אֲרֵי כְּמָא דַחֲדֵיתוּן עַל מֵחַת טוּרָא דְקוּדְשִׁי כֵּן[22] יִשְׁתּוֹן כָּל עַמְמַיָּא בַּס
פֻּרְעָנוּתְהוֹן תְּדִירָא וְיִשְׁתּוֹן וְיִסְתַּלְעֲמוּן וִיהוֹן כַּד לָא הֲווֹ:

17 וּבְטוּרָא דְצִיּוֹן תְּהֵי שֵׁיזָבָא וִיהוֹן קַדִּישִׁין וְיַחְסְנוּן דְּבֵית[23] יַעֲקֹב[24] נִכְסֵי עַמְמַיָּא
דַהֲווֹ מַחְסְנִין לְהוֹן:

18 וִיהוֹן דְּבֵית יַעֲקֹב תַּקִּיפִין כְּאֶשָּׁתָא וּבֵית[25] יוֹסֵף חֲסִינִין כְּשַׁלְהֲבִיתָא וּבֵית[26]
עֵשָׂו חַלָּשִׁין כְּקַשָּׁא וְיִשְׁלְטוּן בְּהוֹן וִיקַטְּלוּנוּן וְלָא יְהֵי שֵׁיזָבָא לְבֵית עֵשָׂו אֲרֵי
בְּמֵימְרָא דַייָ נְזַר כֵּן:

19 וְיַחְסְנוּן[27] יָתְבֵי דָרוֹמָא יָת כַּרְכָא דְעֵשָׂו וְיָתְבֵי שְׁפִילְתָא יָת אֲרַע פְּלִשְׁתָּאֵי וְיַחְסְנוּן
יָת קִרְוֵי אֶפְרָאִם וְיָת קִרְוֵי שֹׁמְרוֹן וּדְבֵית בִּנְיָמִין יַחְסְנוּן[28] יָת[29] יָתְבֵי אֲרַע
גִּלְעָד:

20 וְגָלוּת עַמָּא הָדֵין לִבְנֵי[30] יִשְׂרָאֵל דִּבְאֲרַע כְּנַעֲנָאֵי[31][32]
עַד צָרְפַת וְגָלוּת דִּירוּשְׁלֶם בִּסְפַמְיָא[33] יַחְסְנוּן יָת קִרְוֵי אֲרַע דְרוֹמָא:

21 וְיִסְּקוּן מְשֵׁיזְבִין[34] בְּטוּרָא דְצִיּוֹן לְמִדַּן יָת כַּרְכָא[35] דְעֵשָׂו וּתְהֵי מַלְכוּתָא דַייָ[36]
עַל כָּל יָתְבֵי אַרְעָא[37]

---

1 [1] Añade: הוּא עֹובָדְיָה דְּדָר בֵּין תְּרֵין רַשִׁיעַיָּא בֵּין אַחְאָב וְאִיזֶבֶל וְלָא עֲבַד כְּעֹובָדֵיהֹון
וְלָא הַלֵּיךְ בְּנִמֹוסֵיהֹון וְאִתְנַבֵּי עַל עֵשָׂו רַשִׁיעָא דְּדָר בֵּין תְּרֵין צַדִּיקַיָּא בֵּין יִצְחָק
וְרִבְקָה לָא עֲבַד כְּעֹובָדֵיהֹון וְלָא הַלֵּיךְ בְּנִמֹוסֵיהֹון u;
[2] שמועא o; [3] En vez de בעממא se lee מִן קֳדָם יְיָ u

2 [4] Añade עשׂו רשׁיעא a u

3 [5] Añade עֵשָׂו רַשִׁיעָא u; [6] דִשְׁרֵי s; [7] דִישְׁרֵי so

4 [8] Elimina בְּמֵימְרֵי b g o

5 [9] בְּזֹוזֵי u

7 [10] בֵיהּ c

8 [11] וְסוּכְלְתָנִיָא c; [12] Añade רַבָּא u; [13] Cambia por מְטוּרָא f

9 [14] Añade יָתְבֵי b g o c; [15] Añade רַבָא u o

10 [16] Variante fonética תַּחְפְּנָךְ u

11 [17] Elimina עממיא 5; [18] Añade עשׂו רשׁיעא השׁיב u c

12 [19] Cambia por בְּיוֹם o

13 [20] וְדַעֲלָתָא b g o u c

15 [21] Precede כֵּן 5

16 [22] Elimina כֵּן s

17 [23] Cambia por בֵּית c u; [24] Elimina יעקב b g

18 [25] Cambia por וּדְבֵית b g o; [26] Cambia por וּדְבֵית b g o

19 [27] Elimina וְיַחְסְנוּן b g o f c; [28] Elimina יַחְסְנוּן b g o f c u; [29] Añade קִרְוֵי s

20 [30] Cambia por לִדְבֵי 5 b g o f; [31] Cambia por דִּי בַאֲרַע כְּנַעֲנָאֵי u; [32] Cambia por דִּי בַאְסְפַמְיָא יָת אֲרַע כְּנַעַן c; [33] יַחְסְנוּן יָת אֲרַע כְּנַעַן c

21 [34] Cambia por פְּרִיקַיָּא u; [35] Añade רבא o u; [36] Añade בְּקָרִיב o;
[37] Añade וּתְהֵי מַלְכוּתָא דַייָ קַיָּם לְעָלַם וְעָלְמֵי עָלְמַיָּא o

Traducción castellana

1.- *Profecía* de Abdías.[28] Así ha dicho el Señor *Dios* acerca de Edom. *Una buena noticia*[29] hemos escuchado procedente del Señor y un mensajero entre las naciones[30] ha sido enviado: levantaos, coloquémonos contra él en orden de batalla.

2.- He aquí que[31] te hecho *débil*, entre las naciones eres muy despreciable.

3.- *La maldad* de tu corazón te *ha extraviado*,[32] *ya que tú te pareces al águila que posa*[33] en las hendiduras del roquedal y cuya morada es la altura, (el águila) que ha dicho en su corazón: ¿Quién me hará bajar a tierra?

4.- Aunque remontes como el águila y aunque en las estrellas pusieras *tu morada*, de allí *por mi Palabra*[34] te haré bajar, *ha dicho el Señor*.

5.- Si vinieron ladrones a ti, si salteadores[35] nocturnos ¿cómo *estabas dormida para que* te hayan robado según lo que precisaban? *Si vinieren salteadores como* vendimiadores a ti, ¿acaso no te dejarían rebusco?

6.- ¡Como ha sido registrado Esaú, *se han descubierto* sus tesoros ocultos!

7.- *Del* territorio te *han desterrado* todos tus aliados, te *han descarriado*, han prevalecido sobre ti tus hombres confederados, *tus comensales* te han tendido lazo debajo de ti, sin que haya en *ti*[36] conocimiento.

8.- ¿Acaso en aquel *entonces, ha dicho el Señor*, no eliminaré a los sabios de Edom y a *todo hombre que tenga* inteligencia[37] de *la fortaleza*[38] de Esaú?

---

[28] Añade: "Él es Abdía, que mora entre los dos malvados: entre Acab y Jezabel, pero no obra según sus acciones ni camina según sus leyes, sino que profetiza contra Esaú, el malvado que habita entre dos justos: entre Isaac y Rebeca; no actúa según sus acciones ni camina conforme a sus leyes", *u*.

[29] "noticia", *o*.

[30] En vez de "entre las naciones" lee: "por parte del Señor", *u*.

[31] Añade: "oh malvado Esaú", *u a*.

[32] Añade: "oh malvado Esaú", *c*.

[33] "que ha posado", *s*; "que posará", *so*.

[34] Elimina "por mi Palabra", *b g o*.

[35] Variante de "salteadores", *u*.

[36] "en él", *c*.

[37] "y todo hombre que haya allí y sea inteligente", *c*.

[38] Añade: "grande", *u*; lee: "de la montaña", *f*.

9.- Y se aterrarán tus valientes[39] *del Sur, y* será eliminado por la muerte de *la fortaleza*[40] de Esaú el varón del que tienes necesidad.

10.- Por la violencia contra tu hermano Jacob te cubrirá[41] la vergüenza y serás destruido para siempre.

11.- En el día en que te mantenías distante, en el día en que *las naciones*[42] *saquearon sus riquezas* y los extranjeros penetraron en *sus ciudades* y echaron suertes sobre Jerusalén, también tú fuiste[43] como uno de ellos.

12.- *Porque* tú has visto el día de tu hermano, el día de su *quebranto y* te has alegrado a costa *de los hijos* de Judá en el día de su ruina y *has proferido muchas* altanerías en el *tiempo*[44] de su angustia.

13.- Has franqueado[45] las puertas de mi pueblo en el día de su desgracia y te has fijado también[46] en su infortunio en el día de su quebranto y *has alargado tu mano* en su hacienda en el día de su ruina;

14.- *y porque* te has colocado en la encrucijada para exterminar a sus fugitivos *y* has entregado a sus evadidos en el *tiempo* de la angustia,

15.- cierto que está próximo el día *que está por llegar procedente* del Señor contra todas las naciones y conforme hiciste[47] se te hará; tu acción *se* revertirá en tu cabeza.

16.- Pues como *os habéis alegrado por el golpe* contra el monte santo, así[48] beberán siempre todas las naciones *la copa de su venganza*, beberán, *tragarán* y serán cual si no hubieran sido.

17.- Pero en la montaña de Sión estarán los escapados, y *serán santos* y *los de* la casa de Jacob[49] recobrarán las riquezas *de las que las naciones se habían apoderado*.

---

[39] Añade: "los habitantes", *b g o c.*
[40] "de la gran fortaleza", *o u.*
[41] Variante fonética de "te cubrirá", *u.*
[42] Elimina "las naciones", *5.*
[43] Añade: "también tú, Esaú malvado fuiste considerado", *c.*
[44] "en el día", *o.*
[45] "ya que has franqueado", *b g o u c.*
[46] "has fijado y tú has puesto en su infortunio", *u.*
[47] Añade: "así", *5.*
[48] Elimina "así", *s.*
[49] "la casa de Jacob", *c u.* Elimina "de Jacob", *b g.*

18.- Y los de la casa de Jacob serán *poderosos como* el fuego y la casa de José[50] *vigorosa como* la llama, pero la casa de Esaú[51] *débil como* la paja, a ellos *dominarán y matarán* y no habrá escapatoria para la casa de Esaú, pues *por la Palabra del* Señor ha sido *decretado así.*

19.- *Los habitantes del Sur* poseerán *la fortaleza* de Esaú y *los de* la Sefelá, *el país de* los filisteos, y tomarán posesión de[52] *las ciudades* de Efraim y de *las ciudades* de Samaría, y *los de la casa de* Benjamín[53] poseerán[54] Gilead.

20.- Los deportados de este *pueblo*, perteneciente a los hijos de Israel[55], que *están en el país de los*[56] cananeos[57] hasta Sarefat, y los deportados de Jerusalén *que están en España,*[58] poseerán las ciudades *del país del Sur.*

21.- Y subirán libertados[59] al monte Sión para juzgar a *la fortaleza*[60] de Esaú, entonces *se manifestará* el reino del Señor[61] *sobre todos los habitantes de la tierra.*[62]

---

[50] Añade: "los de la casa de José", *b g o.*
[51] Añade: "los de la casa de Esaú", *b g o.*
[52] Elimina "tomarán posesión de", *b g o f c*
[53] Añade: "ciudades de los moradores", *s.*
[54] Elimina: "poseerán", *b g o f c.*
[55] "de los hijos de Israel", *5 b g o f.*
[56] "En el país de los cananeos, *u.*
[57] "Poseerán la tierra de Canaán", *c.*
[58] Lit. en arameo *dbispamia, z.* "en Ispamia", *c o f.*
[59] "los salvados" sinónimo, *u.*
[60] Añade: "a la gran fortaleza", *o.*
[61] Añade: "pronto", *o.*
[62] Añade: "y será el reino del Señor estable por siempre, por los siglos de los siglos", *o.*

PEREGRINUS' CHRISTIAN CAREER

Jan N. Bremmer

One of the more fascinating figures for the history of Christianity and Judaism in the middle of the second century undoubtedly is the pagan philosopher Peregrinus of Parion, a port situated in Mysia on the eastern entrance of the Hellespont.[1] His spectacular suicide in A.D. 165 led the ancient social satirist Lucian to dedicate a "debunking" pamphlet, *De morte Peregrini*, to his life. As Peregrinus stayed for a while in Palestine where he joined a Christian congregation, this "biography" may be also of some interest to my esteemed colleague, as he himself, more recently, also has started to work on the crossroads of Judaism and Christianity. It would transcend the available space to write a commentary on the whole of the pamphlet, however interesting that would be, and therefore I will mainly limit myself to the chapters that discuss Peregrinus' career as a Christian (11–13, 16) or that suggest a Christian influence (40). My principal aim is to ask what Lucian's views, if taken seriously, tell us about the nature of Peregrinus' congregation and Lucian's knowledge thereof. Lucian had traveled widely between Greece and Samosata in Commagene, where he was born around A.D. 120. He was also well read and had a keen eye for the more outrageous figures of his time. He thus may be an interesting case by which to ascertain what knowledge a contemporary pagan intellectual had of the new religion.[2]

---

[1] For all testimonia see P. Frisch, *Die Inschriften von Parion* (Bonn: Habelt, 1983), 47–96.

[2] For our purpose the most important studies are: D. Plooij and J. Koopman, *Lucianus: de dood van Peregrinus* (Utrecht: Ruys, 1915), which is much more useful than J. Schwartz, *Lucien de Samosate: Philopseudès et De morte Peregrini* (Paris: Les Belles Lettres, 1951), but overlooked by all the more recent notable contributions: H.D. Betz, "Lukian von Samosata und das Christentum," *NovT* 3 (1959): 226–37; repr., with "Nachtrag," in *Hellenismus und Urchristentum* (Tübingen: Mohr Siebeck, 1990), 10–21; C.P. Jones, *Culture and Society in Lucian* (Cambridge, Mass.: Harvard University Press, 1986), 117–32; M.J. Edwards, "Satire and Verisimilitude: Christianity in Lucian's Peregrinus," *Historia* 38 (1989): 89–98; D. Clay, "Lucian of Samosata: Four Philosophical Lives (Nigrinus, Demonax, Peregrinus, Alexander Pseudomantis)," *ANRW* 2/36.5:3406–50 (3430–38); P. Pilhofer et al., *Lukian: der Tod des Peregrinos: Ein Scharlatan auf dem Scheiterhaufen* (SAPERE 9; Darmstadt: Wissenschaftliche Buchgesellschaft, 2005), whose text I follow; J. König,

Lucian starts his treatise with a description of Peregrinus' suicide, which the latter staged himself during the Olympian Games of A.D. 165. In this beginning we already hear different voices: there is praise by a fellow Cynic, Theagenes (4), but also blame by an unknown bystander who related that, in his youth, Peregrinus had been caught *in flagrante* "in Armenia" (9),[3] had committed himself to paederasty (9),[4] and had even strangled his father (10), parricide being perhaps the worst crime in Greek culture.[5] Consequently, he had to leave Parion and to wander from city to city. This is of course information from Lucian, which has to be taken with a pinch of salt, as Parion erected a statue for Peregrinus,[6] presumably shortly after his death.

It is immediately after this introduction, which clearly suggests an extremely roguish and criminal character, that Lucian continues in chapter 11 with Peregrinus' attraction to, as Lucian ironically remarks,[7] the "wondrous wisdom of the Christians" in Palestine. It is interesting to see that Lucian already calls the followers of Jesus by the name of "Christians," as this particular name was not yet generally accepted at his time.[8] Lucian does not mention anything about the catechumenate, which was already quite developed in the time of Justin Martyr. Like Cyprian's, Peregrinus' catechumenate may have been unusually short.[9] His status as a philosopher may well have speeded up the process.

"The Cynic and Christian Lives of Lucian's *Peregrinus*," in *The Limits of Ancient Biography* (ed. B. McGing and J. Mossman; Swansea: The Classical Press of Wales, 2006), 227–54.

[3] Is this a mistake made by Lucian, whose town of birth, Samosata, was not that far from ancient Armenia, whereas Parion was nowhere near? Cf. K. Rigsby, "Peregrinus in Armenia," *CQ* 54 (2004): 317–18.

[4] In the course of time, paederasty had become less and less acceptable, see Lucian, *Amores*, 28; F. Buffière, *Éros adolescent: la pédérastie dans la Grèce antique* (Paris: Belles Lettres, 1980), 485–90.

[5] J.N. Bremmer, "Oedipus and the Greek Oedipus Complex," in *Interpretations of Greek Mythology* (ed. idem; 2d ed.; London: Routledge, 1988), 41–59 (45–53).

[6] Athenagoras, *Leg.* 26.4–5. For the possible appearance of the statue see R.R.R. Smith, "Cultural Choice and Political Identity in Honorific Portrait Statues in the Greek East in the Second Century A.D.," *JRS* 88 (1998): 56–93.

[7] Jones, *Culture and Society*, 121 n. 19.

[8] For the origin and gradual acceptance of the name "Christians," see J.N. Bremmer, *The Rise and Fall of the Afterlife* (London: Routledge, 2002), 103–8, 175–78, overlooked by T. Hegedus, "Naming Christians in Antiquity," *SR* 32 (2004): 173–90.

[9] Justin, *1 Apol.* 61; Pontius, *Vita Cypriani* 2–3; cf. A. Stewart-Sykes, "Catechumenate and Contra-Culture: the social process of catechumenate in third-century Africa and its development," *St. Vladimir's Theological Quarterly* 47 (2003): 289–306.

The mention of Palestine indicates that Peregrinus was one of those contemporary wandering philosophers who moved through the Mediterranean. Wandering was especially a well-known characteristic of Cynicism, and Peregrinus may already have been attracted to that movement before his conversion, as he became a Cynic later.[10] In Palestine he associated himself with τοῖς ἱερεῦσιν καὶ γραμματεῦσιν αὐτῶν, "their priests and scribes." Although these titles do occur separately in pagan associations, their combination is not attested there: pagan examples of these titles therefore hardly provide a persuasive parallel.[11] Betz notes that priests may be assumed for early Christianity and that Christian scribes are already mentioned in Matthew (13:52; 23:34), but neither category is mentioned in second-century Christianity,[12] whereas the New Testament always uses the combination οἱ ἀρχιερεῖς καὶ οἱ γραμματεῖς.[13] It is only once that we find οἱ ἱερεῖς καὶ γραμματεῖς τοῦ ἱεροῦ in an enumeration of Jewish offices in Flavius Josephus.[14] In fact, we know that, at the time, the scribes functioned as copyists of Torah scrolls and as teachers of children, whereas the priests remained authorities on Jewish law also after the destruction of the Temple in A.D. 70.[15] It is perhaps their contemporary relevance that indicates that these titles were apparently taken over by the leaders of the Christian congregation. In any case, it strongly suggests that Peregrinus had joined one of the Judaeo-Christian congregations that existed, not surprisingly, in Palestine and Syria.[16]

The association with the Christians was clearly a success, as in no time Peregrinus became an important person in the congregation: προφήτης καὶ θιασάρχης καὶ ξυναγωγεὺς (11). How do we analyse these terms? Betz suggests a certain hierarchy in these terms, but this is hardly obvious. Moreover, like Plooij and Koopman, Schwartz and Jones, he is inclined to see a Christian phenomenon behind this mention of a

---

[10] S. Montiglio, "Wandering Philosophers in Classical Greece," *JHS* 120 (2000): 86–105.

[11] Contra Pilhofer, *Lukian*, 59.

[12] Contra Betz, "Lukian," 229 n. 5.

[13] Matt 2:4; 16:21; 20:18; etc.

[14] Josephus, *Ant.* 12.142; note also τοὺς ἀρχιερεῖς καὶ τοὺς ἱερεῖς καὶ τοὺς γραμματεῖς in *Protevangelium Jacobi* 6.

[15] C. Hezser, *The Social Structure of the Rabbinic Movement in Roman Palestine* (Tübingen: Mohr Siebeck, 1994), 467–75 (scribes), 480–89 (priests).

[16] See most recently R. Kimelman, "Identifying Jews and Christians in Roman Syria-Palestine," in *Galilee through the Centuries* (ed. E.M. Meyers; Winona Lake: Eisenbrauns, 1999), 301–33.

"prophet."[17] However, the term should not be taken out of context but looked at as part of the enumeration. When we approach the problem from that angle, it is immediately clear that Lucian uses *prophêtês* in the meaning of "manager of an oracle,"[18] as the other two terms also suggest the leadership of a religious institution. A *thiasarchês* was the head of a *thiasos*, a term most often used for a Dionysiac association,[19] but not necessarily so: *thiasoi* of Jews,[20] of Heracles,[21] of the Mater Oureia (*Supplementum Epigraphicum Graecum* [= *SEG*] 41.1329A.4), of the Agathodaimôn (*SEG* 48.1120), and of the Theos Hypsistos (*CIRB* 1259) are well attested. Curiously, *thiasarchês* seems to be a *hapax legomenon* and occuring only here, and also the related verb *thiasarcheô* seems to occur only once.[22] Finally, a *synagôgeus* was the founder or chairperson of a religious or professional association.[23] The term can be used in a context of affinity to Judaism, but not necessarily so.[24] Jones states that Lucian sees "Christianity through Greek eyes" and points out that these terms have no place in early Christianity.[25] That is certainly true, but Lucian is not concerned here with an exact description of the structure of a Christian congregation. He evidently wants to show Peregrinus' prominent position within the Christian community by quoting prominent positions in religious institutions familiar to his readership.[26]

---

[17] Contra Plooij and Koopman, *Lucianus*, 67; Schwartz and Jones, *Culture and Society*, 122.

[18] J.N. Bremmer, "Prophetes IV," *DNP* 10:421–22; add now the personal name "Prophetes," in F. Rumscheid, "Inschriften aus Milas im Museum Bodrum," *Epigrafia Anatolica* 37 (2004): 43–61 (43–47); A. Busine, "The Officials of Oracular Sanctuaries in Roman Asia Minor," *ARG* 8 (2006): 275–316, *passim*.

[19] A.-F. Jaccottet, *Choisir Dionysos: Les associations dionysiaques ou la face cachée du dionysisme* (2 vols.; Kilchberg: Akanthus, 2003), 2: *passim*, cf. index s.v.

[20] See the passages collected by J. Scheid, "Communauté et communauté: Réflexions sur quelques ambiguïtés d'après l'exemple des thiases de l'Égypte romaine," in *Les communautés religieuses dans le monde gréco-romain* (ed. N. Belayche and S. Mimouni; Turnhout: Brepols, 2003), 61–74 (66 n. 31); add *Corpus inscriptionum regni Bosporani* [= *CIRB*] 1260–61, 1277–87, 1289; Philo, *Prob.* 85 (Essenes).

[21] *Inscriptiones Graecae* II² 2345; *SEG* 51.224; S.D. Lambert, "Thiasoi of Heracles and the Salaminioi," *ZPE* 125 (1999): 93–130.

[22] *Orientis Graeci inscriptiones selectae* 529.5 = *Inscriptiones antiquae orae septentrionalis Ponti Euxini* I.2 425.11.

[23] F. Poland, "Synagogeus," in *RE* 4A.2 (1932), 1316–22.

[24] F. Sokolowski, *Lois sacrées de l'Asie Mineure* (Paris: E. de Boccard, 1955), no. 80.10 (Sabbatistai), but see also *I. Delos* 1641 b 6; *I. Istros* 193 (= *SEG* 1.330); *SEG* 24.1055 (Moesia), 34.695 (Tomis).

[25] Jones, *Culture and Society*, 122.

[26] This is not understood by Pilhofer, *Lukian*, 58–60, 102.

It is highly interesting that Peregrinus uses his position to interpret and explain some of the books of the Christians as well as to write many himself. The interpretation will have taken place in the Sunday services, as Justin Martyr (*Apol.* 1.67) relates: "On the day called the day of the sun there is an assembly of all those who live in the towns or in the country, and the memoirs of the apostles or the writings of the prophets are read for as long as time permits. Then the reader ceases, and the president speaks, admonishing and exhorting us to imitate these excellent examples." This reading of the Scriptures and early authoritative followers of Christ, such as Paul, is attested in the earliest Christian writings, as the apostle Paul already says in the First Letter to the Thessalonians (5:27): "I adjure you by the Lord that this letter be read to all the brothers and sisters." We can follow these exhortations to read in the Letter to the Colossians (4:16), the book of Revelation (1:3) and the First Letter to Timothy (4:13) where the congregation is admonished "to give attention to the public reading of scripture, to exhorting, to teaching." Apparently, it was the most important person in the congregation who commented on the Scriptures, which is exactly the position ascribed to Peregrinus by Lucian. The fact that Peregrinus also wrote books can have only added to his prominence. These need not have been big books, but perhaps more like the many letters written by people like Paul, pseudo-Pauls, and Ignatius. Another possibility would be apologies, as a fragmentary papyrus may still preserve a reference to "[*Pere*]*grinus' Apologies.*"[27] However this may be, unfortunately, none of these writings has survived.

Peregrinus' prominent position went so far that "they looked at him like a god and used him as a lawgiver and called him *prostatês*, thus after him whom they also worship, the man who was crucified in Palestine because he introduced that new mystery cult into the world." It is, I think, absolutely unthinkable that a Christian community could have worshipped Peregrinus as a god.[28] Lucian possibly uses the expression here to indicate that the faithful saw him in the line of the great philosophers, such as Plato and Pythagoras, who attracted the term

---

[27] *P. Ross. Georg.* 1 no. 22, cf. Pilhofer, *Lukian*, 98–100.
[28] But see Herm. *Vis.* 1.7, cf. A. Hilhorst, "Erotic Elements in the 'Shepherd' of Hermas," in *Groningen Colloquia on the Novel* (vol. 9; ed. H. Hofmann and M. Zimmerman; Groningen: Forster, 1998), 193–204 (199–200).

"divine" in the course of time.[29] On the other hand, and perhaps more likely, we know that some sophists could elicit from the audience strong emotions, and in the case of the sophist Prohairesios the public licked his chest (!), kissed his hands and feet, but also called him "god" after a successful performance.[30] Perhaps Lucian's "report" has to be seen in this light. It is certainly more difficult to see why Peregrinus should have been made use of as a "lawgiver," but, perhaps, he received the title in imitation of Christ (below). *Prostatês* is a title that occurs in several Jewish communities,[31] and it seems not improbable that Lucian refers here to the fact that the Jewish priests of this period still could have an important legal function in society before being displaced by the rabbis in this respect in later antiquity.[32]

Yet however important Peregrinus was, he was only second after Jesus, "whom they still worship, the man who was crucified in Palestine because he introduced that new cult into the world." The concluding part of the first "Christian" chapter shows that Lucian knew of Jesus and his crucifixion, but it also gives an insight as to how he looked at Christianity. He calls Christianity a *teletê*, which means that he considers it a type of mystery cult. This terminology is not totally strange, as Celsus too compared Christianity to "the other *teletai*" (Origen, *Cels.* 3.59). And indeed, several Christians, orthodox and heterodox, had been struck by the similarity of some elements of the Christian ritual, such as baptism and the Eucharist, with those of the mysteries.[33] Undoubtedly, it is this resemblance that made early Christians inveigh against the mysteries, those of Eleusis of course, but also less famous ones.[34]

But why would Lucian think that Jesus was killed because he had introduced a new cult? The answer is perhaps somewhat surprising. In 399 B.C. the Athenians had charged Socrates as follows: "Socrates does wrong by not acknowledging the gods the city acknowledges, and

---

[29] See now D.S. du Toit, *Theios anthropos: zur Verwendung von theios anthrôpos und sinnverwandten Ausdrücken in der Literatur der Kaiserzeit* (Tübingen: Mohr Siebeck, 1997).

[30] Eunapios 489, cf. M. Korenjak, *Publikum und Redner: Ihre Interaktion in der sophistischen Rhetorik der Kaiserzeit* (Munich: Beck, 2000), 96–100.

[31] W. Ameling, *Inscriptiones Iudaicae Orientis Vol. II Kleinasien* (Tübingen: Mohr Siebeck, 2004), 93, overlooked by Pilhofer, *Lukian*, 61–62.

[32] Hezser, *Social structure*, 482–83.

[33] Ignatius, *Eph.* 12.2; Justin, *1 Apol.* 29.2; Irenaeus, *Haer.* 1.21.3; Clement of Alexandria, *Strom.* 3.27.1.5. C. Auffarth, "'Licht vom Osten': Die antiken Mysterienkulte als Vorläufer, Gegenmodell oder katholisches Gift zum Christentum," *ARG* 8 (2006): 206–26 interestingly studies some of the consequences of this relationship.

[34] Justin, *1 Apol.* 54 and 66.4; *Dial.* 70, 78; Tertullian, *Cor.* 15, *Bapt.* 5, *Praescr.* 40.

introducing other, new powers (*daimonia*). He also does wrong by cor-
rupting the young."[35] The trial of Socrates still poses several questions,
but many Athenians apparently saw Socrates as somebody who had
introduced new divinities.[36] This had not escaped Justin Martyr, who
noted that Socrates was condemned on the charge of "introducing new
divinities (*daimonia*)" and compared him to Jesus: Justin clearly knew the
official Athenian charge.[37] Had Lucian read Justin, whose *First Apology*
had appeared little over a decade before Lucian wrote his *Peregrinus*?
The idea may look preposterous, but recent research has plausibly
argued that in his *True Histories* Lucian used the Apocalypse of John
in his picture of the City of the Blessed and the *Apocalypse of Peter* in
his passage on the Isle of the Damned.[38] Lucian may well have read
more Christian literature than we are used to expect.

The Christians also called Peregrinus a "new Socrates," as we read in
the next chapter. The bestowing of this title has been doubted by Plooij
and Koopman, but they overlooked the fact that Christian martyrs are
compared to Socrates more than once. In fact, the Smyrnean martyr
Pionius compared himself not only to Socrates but also to Aristides
and Anaxarchus, other pagan "saints."[39] Socrates was of course not
only innocently condemned to death but also a famous philosopher.
We can see here one of the stratagems of the early Church in regards
to the pagan opposition: by relating Jesus and their own martyrs to
pagan examples of virtue, the early Christians removed them from the
criminal sphere and claimed the moral high ground.[40]

---

[35] Favorinus *apud* Diogenes Laertius 2.40, trans. Parker (next note); note also
Xenophon, *Mem.* 1.1.1, *Apol.* 10; Plato, *Apol.* 24b8–c1, *Eutyphr.* 3b; Philodemus, *Piet.*,
1696–1697 Obbink.

[36] For the charge and the trial see now R. Parker, *Athenian Religion* (Oxford: Oxford
University Press, 1996), 199–207; P. Millett, "The Trial of Socrates Revisited," *European
Review of History* 12 (2005): 23–62.

[37] Justin, *1 Apol.* 5; cf. J.M. Pfättisch, "Christus und Sokrates bei Justin," *TQ* 90
(1908): 503–23.

[38] P. von Möllendorff, *Auf der Suche nach der verlogenen Wahrheit: Lukians* Wahre
Geschichten (Tübingen: Narr, 2000), 318–21 (Apocalypse of John), 427–30 (*Apocalypse
of Peter*).

[39] *Martyrium Pionii* 17; cf. J.N. Bremmer and J. den Boeft, "Notiunculae martyrologicae
III," *VC* 39 (1985): 110–30 (120–22).

[40] See A. Harnack, *Reden und Aufsätze* (2 vols.; 2d ed.; Giessen: Töpelman, 1906),
17–49 ("Sokrates und die alte Kirche," 1901), criticized by J. Geffcken, *Sokrates und
das alte Christentum* (Heidelberg: Winter, 1908); E. Benz, "Christus und Sokrates in der
alten Kirche," *ZNW* 43 (1950/51): 195–224; K. Döring, *Exemplum Socratis* (Wiesbaden:
Steiner, 1979), 143–61; T. Baumeister, "'Anytus und Meletus können mich zwar töten,
schaden jedoch können sie mir nicht': Platon, Apologie des Sokrates 30c/d bei Plutarch,

In chapter 12 we hear that Peregrinus' prominence attracted the attention of the Roman authorities: "Then he became arrested for that reason and was thrown into prison." Which "reason" is not quite clear, and it is not excluded that some Christians have censored the text, as has happened also in some other passages.[41] As attempts to liberate Peregrinus from prison proved to be unsuccessful, he was well looked after in prison. He was visited by γράδια, χήρας τινὰς καὶ παιδία ὀρφανά, "old women, some widows and orphaned children."[42] The combination of old women and widows also occurs in the *Apocryphal Acts of John*, where the apostle is pictured being surrounded by widows and old women, who lived off alms from the church and accused John of keeping back the majority of the gifts he had received and of enriching himself at their expense.[43] Widows and old women were important groups in the early Church, and Lucian's information is a welcome confirmation of the Christian sources in this respect.[44]

Those in charge in the congregation even had bribed the guards to let them sleep inside with Peregrinus. Betz has some doubts about this bribery,[45] but bribing wardens was very normal in antiquity,[46] as it still is in many a poor country. In fact, visits of imprisoned fellow Christians are well attested in the *Acta martyrum*.[47] In addition, "all kinds of

---

Epiktet, Justin Martyr und Clemens Alexandrinus," in *Platonismus und Christentum* (ed. H.-D. Blume and F. Mann; Münster: Aschendorff, 1983), 58–63. This literature clearly escaped Clay, "Lucian," 3437 n. 74.

[41] Cf. Plooij and Koopman *ad loc.*

[42] For this type of asyndeton (A, B and C) in Greek see J.D. Denniston, *The Greek Particles* (2d ed; Oxford: Oxford University Press, 1954), 289–90 (with thanks to Stefan Radt). Like A.M. Harmon in the Loeb translation, Pilhofer, *Lukian*, 23 translates with "alte Witwen und Waisenkinder," and sees these as deaconesses (62–63).

[43] Cf. E. Junod and J.-D. Kaestli, *Acta Iohannis* (vol. 1; Turnhout: Brepols, 1983), 114–115.

[44] See most recently R.B. Siola, "*Viduae* e *coetus viduarum* nella Chiesa primitiva e nella normazione dei primi imperatori cristiani," in *Atti dell'Accademia Romanistica Costantiniana: VIII convegno internazionale* (Naples, 1990), 367–426; J.-U. Krause, *Witwen und Waisen im Römischen Reich* (4 vols.; Stuttgart: Steiner, 1994–1995); J.N. Bremmer, "Pauper or Patroness: The Widow in the Early Christian Church," in *Between Poverty and the Pyre: Moments in the History of Widowhood* (ed. idem and L.P. van den Bosch; London: Routledge, 1995), 31–57; V. Recchia, *Lettera e profezia nell'esegesi di Gregorio Magno* (Bari: Edipuglia, 2003), 107–36 ("Le vedove nella letteratura istituzionale dell'antico cristianesimo e nella tipologia biblica").

[45] Betz, "Lukian," 231.

[46] J.N. Bremmer, ed., *The Apocryphal Acts of Paul and Thecla* (Kampen: Kok, 1996), 48 n. 45; J.-U. Krause, *Gefängnisse im Römischen Reich* (Stuttgart: Steiner, 1996), 305–8.

[47] P. Pavón, "Régimen de vida y tratamiento del preso durante los tres primeros siglos del Imperio," in *Carcer: Prison et privation de liberté dans l'Antiquité classique* (ed. C. Bertrand-Dagenbach et al.; Paris: E. de Boccard, 1999), 105–13 (111–12) ("Las visitas").

foods were brought to him, their holy scriptures were read, and...he was called a new Socrates (see above) by them." Material help to the imprisoned was quite common among the early Christians and must have been one of the means to keep up morale. We hear of this charity already in the *Letters* of Ignatius, in Tertullian, and in the *Letters* of Cyprian. Tertullian even warned against too great a care, as apparently some people preferred to go to jail in order to be well looked after.[48] As the Roman government hardly provided food to its prisoners,[49] it is natural that the Christians made up for this deficiency. In the *Passio Perpetuae* (17.1), the prisoners celebrated the *agape*, a special meal that enhanced early Christian sociability, but that was already on the way out in Perpetua's time.[50] Lucian's mention of food may well have included such a special meal.[51]

In addition to this material assistance, the Christians read *logoi hieroi* to him. In Philo, these refer to the Torah and divinely inspired words or thoughts, whereas in the Church Fathers they refer to the Old and New Testament.[52] In the case of Peregrinus we probably have to think of the Scriptures too. The late Keith Hopkins (1934–2004) suggested that early Christianity spread at an amazing rate despite the fact that "many or most Christian communities (and *a fortiori* even more house cult-groups) simply did not have among them a single sophisticated reader or writer."[53] Yet this passage is one more argument against this assumption.[54] Everything we know seems to point to Christianity being a movement connected and maintained by the written word. This use of the written word must go back to the earliest times of Christianity, as appears from the many exhortations to read from the Scriptures, which we quoted above. And it is highly interesting that Peregrinus himself

---

[48] Ignatius, *Trall.* 12, *Eph.* 2, *Magn.* 15, *Smyrn.* 9.12; Tertullian, *Mart.* 1.1, *Jeiun.* 12.3 (warning); Cyprian, *Sent.* 5.1, 7.1.1, 12.2, 14.2.

[49] Pavón, "Régimen de vida," 110–11 ("La alimentación").

[50] Tertullian, *Marty.* 2, *Or.* 28, *Bapt.* 9.4, *Jejun.* 17; E. Dekkers, *Tertullianus en de geschiedenis der liturgie* (Brussels: De Kinkhoren, 1947), 48; H. Pétré, *Caritas* (Louvain: Spicilegium Sacrum Lovaniense, 1948), 64–65; W.-D. Hauschild, "Agapen I," *TRE* 1:748–53.

[51] Betz, "Lukian," 14 also refers to Acts 16:34, but that is a different meal.

[52] A. Henrichs, "*Hieroi Logoi* and *Hierai Bibloi*: The (Un)written Margins of the Sacred in Ancient Greece," *HSCP* 101 (2003): 207–66 (241–42).

[53] K. Hopkins, "Christian Number and Its Implications," *JECS* 6 (1998): 185–226 (213).

[54] In this paragraph I repeat and elaborate a point made in my "The Social and Religious Capital of the Early Christians," *Hephaistos* 24 (2006): 269–78 (271–72). See now also L.W. Hurtado, *The Earliest Christian Artifacts: Manuscripts and Christian Origins* (Grand Rapids: Eerdmans, 2006).

wrote letters to "almost all the famous cities" (41) before his death. He called these letters and their carriers "underworld messengers" and "underworld runners," a terminology that seems to have been inspired by the *Letters* of Ignatius, which Peregrinus probably read during the Christian phase of his life.[55]

Hopkins also takes too little account of the Jewish contribution to early Christianity, which must have positively influenced the level of early Christian literacy.[56] It is true that the Dead Sea Scrolls are the main surviving texts from the period before the destruction of the Temple, but it seems highly unlikely that the Qumran community was the only one or the only religious movement that put its thoughts and ideals into writing:[57] we only need to think of the Second Temple Jewish literature that was written in the same time as the New Testament. Moreover, the reading of the Torah and the Septuagint will have required a certain amount of literacy as well. Christian literacy, then, will have been more widespread than Hopkins suggests. In fact, Christian literacy and its pervasive use of letter writing must have been an important contribution to the rise of orthodoxy,[58] as only in this way could a certain standard of unanimity be maintained.[59]

In prison, Peregrinus was visited not only by the members of his congregation, but, as chapter 13 relates, people came even "from the

---

[55] Ignatius, *Smyrn.* 11 and *Polc.* 7, cf. K. Waldner, "Ignatius' Reise von Antiochia nach Rom: Zentralität und lokale Vernetzung im christlichen Diskurs des 2. Jahrhunderts," in *Zentralität und Religion* (ed. H. Cancik et al., Tübingen: Mohr Siebeck, 2006), 95–121 (118). Pilhofer (*ad loc.*) objects that Lucian hardly will have read the letters of Ignatius. This is perhaps true, if not necessarily so, but Peregrinus will have read them, as he must have familiarised himself with important Christian writings.

[56] See the considerations by H.Y. Gamble, *Books and Readers in the Early Church* (New Haven: Yale University Press, 1995), 1–41; note also I. Henderson, "Early Christianity: Textual Representation and Ritual Extension," in *Texte als Medium und Reflexion von Religion im römischen Reich* (ed. D.E. von der Osten et al.; Stuttgart: Steiner, 2006), 81–100.

[57] Contra C. Hezser, *Jewish Literacy in Roman Palestine* (TSAJ 81; Tübingen: Mohr Siebeck, 2001), 426, and eadem, "Jewish Literacy and the Use of Writing in Late Roman Palestine," in *Jewish Culture and Society under the Christian Roman Empire* (ed. R. Kalmin and S. Schwartz; ISACR 3; Leuven: Peeters, 2003), 149–95 (151–52); see also P.S. Alexander, "Literacy among Jews in Second Temple Palestine: Reflections on the Evidence from Qumran," in *Hamlet on a Hill: Semitic and Greek Studies Presented to Professor T. Muraoka on the Occasion of his Sixty-Fifth Birthday* (ed. M.F.J. Baasten and W. Th. van Peursen; OLA 118; Leuven: Peeters, 2003), 3–24.

[58] See now H.-J. Klauck, *Ancient Letters and the New Testament* (Waco: Baylor University Press, 2006).

[59] For interesting reflections on Christian literacy, see also G. Stroumsa, "Early Christianity: A Religion of the Book?" in *Homer, the Bible and Beyond* (ed. M. Finkelberg and G.G. Stroumsa; JSRC 2; Leiden: Brill, 2003), 153–73.

cities of Asia Minor," and all contributed substantial amounts of money. Lucian is clearly impressed by these signs of compassion and interest. He adds that the Christians immediately come into action in such a case. We may perhaps speculate that such imprisonments were still fairly uncommon and therefore the cause of such a focus of people and means on one particular person. On the other hand, Lucian would not overlook the possibility to slander Peregrinus and thus adds that he was making quite an income from his imprisonment.

It is more interesting that he continues with: "these poor creatures have convinced themselves that they will be completely immortal and live for ever, which is the reason why most of them despise death and voluntarily give them themselves up." It is clear from these words that Lucian himself had little sympathy for the Christian point of view. At the same time, though, he shows himself reasonably well informed about Christian doctrine and practice. It is not surprising that he had noted the Christian belief in the "life ever after," as the persecutions had promoted the belief in immortality.[60] Moreover, the reactions of philosophers, such as Marcus Aurelius and Celsus, and the Greek novels show that empty tombs and the resurrection exerted great fascination on pagan intellectuals, as Glen Bowersock has argued in an innovative study.[61] In other words, many pagans had noted that the Christians believed in the immortality of the soul *and* the body, which was a revolutionary Christian innovation.[62] This new belief probably contributed to the Christian proclivity for voluntary martyrdom, and the available evidence seems to show that indeed a considerable number of Christians became martyrs of their own accord.[63]

Lucian continues with the observation that "their first lawgiver persuaded them that they would be all brothers from one another" after having rejected the Greek gods and worshiped *aneskolopismenon ekeinon*

---

[60] Bremmer, *The Rise and Fall of the Afterlife*, 70.

[61] G.W. Bowersock, *Fiction as History: Nero to Julian* (Berkeley: University of California Press, 1994), 99–119.

[62] As is persuasively argued by V. Schmidt, "Lukian über die Auferstehung der Toten," *VC* 49 (1995): 388–92.

[63] Cf. C. Butterweck, *"Martyriumssucht" in der Alten Kirche? Studien zur Darstellung und Deutung frühchristlicher Martyrien* (Tübingen: Mohr, 1995); A.R. Birley, "Voluntary Martyrs in the Early Church: Heroes or Heretics?" *Cristianesimo nella Storia* 27 (2006): 99–127; G. de Ste. Croix, *Christian Persecution, Martyrdom, and Orthodoxy* (ed. M. Whitby and J. Streeter; Oxford: Oxford University Press, 2006), 152–200.

sophistên, "that crucified sophist."[64] The "lawgiver" clearly is Christ, whose transmission of the law is often portrayed in early Christianity.[65] The designation "brother" is also defended by Tertullian in his *Apology* (39.8–10), and the somewhat later *Octavius* by Minucius Felix has the opponent of Christianity state that: "hardly have they met when they love each other, throughout the world uniting in the practice of a veritable religion of lusts. Indiscriminately they call each other brother and sister, thus turning even ordinary fornication into incest by the intervention of these hallowed names" (9.2, trans. G.W. Clarke). Although accusations of Christian atheism are still relatively rare at the time,[66] the rejection of the Greek gods well fits the fact that in the same years we already see the Christians called "atheists" in the descriptions of the deaths of Polycarp and the Lyonese martyrs.[67] However, it is rather surprising that Lucian calls Christ a "sophist." Unfortunately, we cannot be certain about the exact connotation of the term in this context, as it is sometimes used favourably and sometimes unfavourably by Lucian. If we look at the contemporary sophists, who were rhetors and teachers of younger pupils,[68] often moving from one place to the next,[69] it is not difficult to see that Lucian could have interpreted Jesus' activities in this particular manner.[70]

Lucian concludes chapter 13 with noting that they have all things in common and that their gullibility leads them to be robbed by char-

---

[64] For some observations, if not always plausible, on *aneskolopismenon* (the verb is also used in ch. 11), see J. Schwartz, "Du *Testament de Lévi* au *Discours véritable de Celse*," *RHPR* 40 (1960): 126–45 (126–29).

[65] Contra Pilhofer *ad loc.*, cf. R. Hvalvik, "Christ Proclaiming His Law to the Apostles: The *Traditio Legis*-Motif in Early Christian Art and Literature," in *The New Testament and Early Christian Literature in Greco-Roman Context* (ed. J. Fotopoulos; NovTSup 122; Leiden: Brill, 2006), 404–37.

[66] J.J. Walsh, "On Christian Atheism," *VC* 45 (1991): 255–77.

[67] Cf. J.N. Bremmer, "Atheism in Antiquity," in *The Cambridge Companion to Atheism* (ed. M. Martin; Cambridge: Cambridge University Press, 2006), 11–26 (21–22).

[68] On the sophists see most recently G.W. Dobrov, "The Sophist on his Craft: Art, Text, and Self-Construction in Lucian," *Helios* 29 (2002): 173–92; B. Puech, *Orateurs et sophistes grecs dans les inscriptions d'époque impériale* (Paris: J. Vrin, 2002); B.E. Borg, ed., *Paideia: The World of the Second Sophistic* (Berlin: de Gruyter, 2004); T. Whitmarsh, *The Second Sophistic* (Oxford: Oxford University Press, 2005).

[69] C. Lüth, "Anstößige Intellektuelle: Die Sophisten als Fremde und Wanderlehrer," in *Xenophobie, Philoxenie: vom Umgang mit Fremden in der Antike* (ed. U. Riemer and P. Riemer; Stuttgart: Steiner, 2005), 157–76.

[70] See also L. Pernot, "Christianisme et sophistique," in *Papers on Rhetoric* (vol. 4; ed. L.C. Montefusco; Rome: Herder, 2002), 245–62 (246–50); G.H. van Kooten, *Het evangelie: "Dwaasheid voor de Grieken"? Christus en Herakles in de antieke opiniepeilingen* (Groningen: Faculteit der Godgeleerdheid en Godsdienstwetenschap, 2006), 15.

latans. In Acts (2:42–47; 4:32–37) Luke presents the same image, and this *Brüderlichkeitsethik* confirms one of Max Weber's insights, viz. that when people first come together on the basis of religious views, they are more closely associated with one another than with their "normal" associates, such as relatives or neighbours, and thus will help each other in case of material needs.[71] Yet none of our sources points to such a sharing of goods in the later second century. As Lucian seems quite well informed about the Christians, as we have seen so far, it is not impossible that, directly or indirectly, he had received some idealising information about the Christians. However this may be, Lucian clearly intends to mock the Christians because of their gullibility and he notes that they fall victim to any "charlatan and huckster" that comes among them.[72] From the *Didache* (12) we learn that the Christians themselves were also aware of this risk and even had coined the word *Christemporos*, "he who uses Christ to make a gain."

This first phase of Peregrinus' Christianity is concluded with his release from prison by "the governor of Syria, a man who enjoyed philosophy" (14). Pilhofer (*ad loc.*) wonders how a Syrian governor can free a prisoner in Palestine, but the answer is simple: the Roman province was called *Syria Palaestina* (Samaria, Judea, Idumea) since Hadrian.[73] Unfortunately, Lucian does not provide a name for the governor. An excellent candidate would have been T. Flavius Boethus, who was consul in, probably, 161 and a good friend of Galen.[74] However, Lucian's chronology of Peregrinus makes this less plausible, as Boethus can hardly have been in Palestine before the second half of 163. On the other hand, Lucian's chronology is demonstrably incorrect, as he lets Peregrinus return to Paros as a Cynic before his apostasy from Christianity.[75] Without further information or new discoveries, this particular event in Peregrinus' career cannot be completely clarified, just as we cannot locate his Christian episode in a specific period of time. The mention of the "priests and scribes" as well as all the help from Asia

---

[71] M. Weber, *Gesammelte Aufsätze zur Religionssoziologie* (3 vols.; Tübingen: Mohr: 1920–1921), 1:536–73.

[72] The same combination in Lucian, *Dial. mort.* 5.

[73] M. Avi-Yonah, *RE: Suppl. XIII* (Munich: Druckenmüller, 1973), 322–23.

[74] *Prosopographia Imperii Romani*² F 0229; V. Nutton, "[II 13] F. Boethus," *DNP* 4:460, to be corrected in the light of W. Eck et al., "Ein Militärdiplom aus der Provinz Dacia Porolissensis," *ZPE* 100 (1994): 577–91 (584–86) = *Roman Military Diplomas* III.177.

[75] Thus, rightly, Jones, *Culture and Society*, 123.

Minor probably suggest a time around A.D. 150 or earlier, rather than later, in the second century.

The action of the governor does suggest, however, that Peregrinus had been imprisoned in Caesarea Maritima, the capital of the province and the seat of the Roman governor's praetorium. In fact, this city could well have been the place where Peregrinus had settled. It was big, prosperous, and typically the place where a person like Peregrinus might have expected an audience for his teachings.[76] We have virtuallly no information about its Christian congretations in the middle of the second century, but in the third century there was a lot of contact between a scholar like Origen and the Jewish rabbis. We do not, though, get the impression of the existence of a Judaeo-Christian type of church in Caesarea at that time.[77]

After his release from prison, Peregrinus returned to Parion, where he appeared as a Cynic in front of the local assembly: "He wore his hair long by now, had dressed himself in a dirty cloak, had slung a satchel over his shoulder and had a walking stick in his hand" (15). Subsequently, he acted as a *philosophe provocateur* in Egypt, Rome, and Greece—a worthy imitator of the Cynic Diogenes. Several scholars have seen a close connection between the Cynics and Jesus,[78] but that debate need not detain us here. In fact, there is little indication that in the middle of the second century Christians converted to Cynicism or *vice versa*.[79] Peregrinus is our only example.[80] It is true that both groups had a negative view of worldly wealth, but the Christians had

---

[76] L.I. Levine, *Caesarea under Roman Rule* (Leiden: Brill, 1975); K.G. Holum et al., ed., *Caesarea Papers 2: Herod's Temple, the Provincial Governor's Praetorium and Granaries, the Later Harbor, a Gold Coin Hoard, and Other Studies* (JRASup 35; Portsmouth, R.I., 1999); Y. Turnheim and A. Ovadiah, *Art in the Public and Private Spheres in Roman Caesarea Maritima: Temples, Architectural Decoration and Tesserae* (Rome: Bretschneider, 2002).

[77] See the studies of M. Murray (Jews), R.S. Ascough (Christians), and R.A. Clements (Origen and the Jews) in *Religious Rivalries and the Struggle for Success in Caesarea Maritima* (ed. T.L. Donaldson; Waterloo: Wilfrid Laurier University Press, 2000).

[78] See most recently P.R. Eddy, "Jesus as Diogenes? Reflections on the Cynic Jesus Thesis," *JBL* 115 (1996): 449–69; D. Seeley, "Jesus and the Cynics Revisited," *JBL* 116 (1997): 704–12; H.D. Betz, *Antike und Christentum* (vol. 4 of *Gesammelte Aufsätze*; Tübingen: Mohr Siebeck, 1998), 32–56 ("Jesus and the Cynics: Survey and Analysis of a Hypothesis," 1994).

[79] See the survey by S.G. Wilson, "Rivalry and defection," in *Religious Rivalries in the Early Roman Empire and the Rise of Christianity* (ed. L. Vaage; Waterloo: Wilfrid Laurier University Press, 2006), 51–71.

[80] C.P. Jones, "Cynisme et sagesse barbare: le cas de Pérégrinus Proteus," in *Le Cynicisme ancien et ses prolongements* (ed. M.-O. Goulet-Cazé and R. Goulet; Paris: PUF, 1993), 305–17.

a negative image of the Cynics,[81] and we know of the persecution of Christians by Cynics, such as Justin by the Cynic Crescens.[82] In the end we cannot get into the mind of Peregrinus, however much we would have liked that.

In his report of Peregrinus' philosophic career, Lucian locates his apostasy after the renunciation of his goods. In fact, he suggests a certain connection between the two, as Peregrinus now needed the Christians to live a prosperous life: "He left home, then, for the second time, to roam about, possessing an ample source of funds in the Christians, through whose ministrations he lived in unalloyed prosperity" (16: trans. Harmon, LCL). Apparently, Peregrinus acted as one of those wandering apostles and prophets about whom we hear more in early Christianity and against whom the *Didache* strongly warned: "And when the apostle goes away, let him take nothing but bread until he finds somewhere shelter. If he asks for money, he is a false prophet" (11). Despite these warnings, Peregrinus clearly—or so Lucian suggests—managed to convince enough Christians on his travels to have a good life. The notice in the *Didache* nicely fits Celsus' description of begging prophets in Phoenicia and Palestine, who wander through towns and villages handing out apocalyptic (in our sense of the word!) oracles. Celsus claims that he himself was an eye-witness to these prophets and had showed them up as frauds. We need not immediately believe this claim, and Origen does indeed a pretty good job in refuting his opponent.[83] Yet even if Celsus had only read about them, the value of his information remains considerable, as it is the only late source actually still mentioning wandering prophets. Evidently, the wandering teachers and prophets of the New Testament had managed to survive well into the second century in Syria Palestine.[84]

This period of his career seems to have come to an abrupt halt when it was discovered that he ate from forbidden food (16). The nature of this food has been variously explained. Some suggest that Peregrinus

---

[81] See M.-O. Goulet-Cazé, "Le cynisme à l'époque impériale," *ANRW* 2/36.4:2720–2833 (2788–2800); G. Dorival, "L'image des Cyniques chez les Pères grecs," in Goulet-Cazé and Goulet, *Le Cynicisme ancien*, 419–43; Van Kooten, *Het evangelie: 'Dwaasheid voor de Grieken'?*

[82] Justin, *2 Apol.* 3, cf. Dorival, "L'image des Cyniques," 421–22.

[83] Origen, *Contra Celsum* 7.9, 11.

[84] For these itinerant teachers see most recently the interesting study by D. Horrell, "Leadership Patterns and the Development of Ideology in Early Christianity," *Sociology of Religion* 58 (1997): 323–41.

had eaten from the food of Hekate on the crossroads.[85] This is very unlikely, as it would imply a Cynic type of acting during his enjoying of Christian support. Others think of the eating of sacrifical meat, which was already a bone of contention in the time of Paul.[86] As a third possibility, it has been suggested that the reference may be "to non-kosher food, the more so since the Christians with whom he had been in contact in Palestine may well have been Judaeo-Christians who kept the Jewish laws, a phenomenon that was still very common in the second century."[87] This suggestion would well fit our conclusion that Peregrinus had joined a kind of Judaeo-Christian congregation, but, unfortunately, Lucian does not offer a certain clue, and we have to leave the precise reason open.

With Peregrinus' apostasy we have come to the end of his Christian episode. However, there is perhaps one more connection with Christianity. After Peregrinus' spectacular self-immolation at the stake during the Olympic Games of A.D. 165, Lucian continues as follows his report: "As I was going away to the *panegyris*,[88] I met a grey man, who, by Zeus, looked reliable with his beard and dignified appearance. About Proteus (as Peregrinus was called later in his career) he told, among other things, that after his cremation he saw him in white clothing only a short time before and that he had just now left him walking cheerfully about the Echo Colonnade, wearing a wreath of wild olive." And he continued: "To top it off, he added the vulture, swearing that he himself had seen it flying up from the pyre, which I myself had only just let fly, while it was laughing about the stupidity and foolishness of the people" (40).

This is a fascinating and sophisticated passage, in which Lucian seems to make fun of more than one group of people. Just before this encounter, in chapter 39, he had told that after Peregrinus' death he had helped to spread some false rumours to those people who seemed

---

[85] Harmon et al., *Lucien, ad loc.* For these suppers of Hekate see S.I. Johnston, "Crossroads," *ZPE* 88 (1991): 217–24.

[86] Acts 15:29; 21:25; 1 Cor 8:7, cf. Pilhofer ad loc., who follows here Wilhelm Nestle's edition of *De morte Peregrini* (Munich, 1925).

[87] P.W. van der Horst, review of Pilhofer et al., *Lukian*, *Bryn Mawr Classical Review* (2005): 11.16.

[88] A fair was a standard part of Greek festivals, cf. L. de Ligt and P.W. de Neeve, "Ancient periodic markets: Festivals and fairs," *Athenaeum* 66 (1988): 391–416; M. Wörrle, *Stadt und Fest im kaiserzeitlichen Kleinasien* (Munich: Beck, 1988), 209–15; C. Chandezon, "Foires et panégyries dans le monde grec classique et hellénistique," *REG* 113 (2000): 70–100; R. Basser, "Is the Pagan Fair Fairly Dangerous? Jewish-Pagan Relations in Antiquity," in Vaage, *Religious Rivalries*, 73–84.

stupid enough to believe them: "that when the pyre was lit and Proteus had thrown himself upon it, there first happened a big earthquake while the ground bellowed. Then a vulture flew up from the midst of the flames and went off to heaven, loudly saying with a human voice: 'I left the earth, but I go to the Olympus.'"

These fictitious details clearly draw on traditional motifs.[89] Caesar's and Jesus' death were also accompanied by an earthquake, of which bellowing is a standard part,[90] and oaths and/or witnesses regarding the trustworthiness of the ascension are attested in the cases of Augustus, Drusilla, Jesus, and Iphigeneia.[91] The vulture, already in antiquity an unpleasant bird,[92] is clearly a way of making fun of the custom of releasing an eagle from the flames of an imperial cremation in the case of emperors and, albeit somewhat later, of peacocks in the case of empresses. This is contested by Christopher Jones, who argues that the eagle was also associated with the souls of private persons.[93] Yet, we do not hear of such a custom in the case of private cremations, and there can be little doubt that the imperial ascension was by far the most impressive version of this tradition.[94] Lucian was clearly not the only one who had his thoughts about the imperial deification, which was still practised in his time: his contemporary Justin Martyr too questions the witness that saw "the burning Caesar" rise to heaven from the flames of his pyre.[95] The words spoken by the vulture have long been recognised as probably coming from a lost tragedy. But it is important to note that the most likely speaker of these lines is Heracles,[96] and

---

[89] For still valuable references to the older literature, see O. Weinreich, "De dis ignotis quaestiones selectae," *ARW* 18 (1915): 1–52 (35–38).

[90] Caesar: Virgil, *Georg.* 1.475; Ovid, *Metam.* 15.798. Jesus: Matt 27:51.

[91] Augustus: Suetonius, *Aug.*, 100; Dio 56.45.2. Drusilla: Seneca, *Apol.* 1; Dio 59.11.4, cf. I. Gradel, *Emperor Worship and Roman Religion* (Oxford: Oxford University Press, 2002), 295–97. Jesus: Acts 1:9–11. Iphigeneia: Euripides, *Iph. aul.*, 1608, which, interestingly, probably dates from Late Antiquity, cf. M.L. West, "Tragica V," *BICS* 28 (1981): 61–78 (74–76).

[92] W. Speyer, "Geier," in *RAC* 9:430–68 (452–54).

[93] Jones, *Culture and Society*, 129.

[94] See now Gradel, *Emperor Worship*, 291–95 (eagle), and, with extensive bibliography, I. Gradel and P. Karanastassi, "B. Roman apotheosis," in *Thesaurus cultus et rituum antiquorum* (vol. 2; Los Angeles: J. Paul Getty Museum, 2004), 186–212 (196–97, 203) (eagle and peacock).

[95] Jusin Martyr, *1 Apol.* 21.3.

[96] See R. Kannicht and B. Snell, *Tragicorum Graecorum fragmenta, Vol. 2: fragmenta adespota* (Göttingen: Vandenhoeck & Ruprecht, 1981), 92 on fragment 290a.

this is the more fitting as Peregrinus himself had said that "one who has lived like Heracles should die as Heracles" (33).[97]

Yet, by stating that he himself had made up all these details, Lucian also undercuts the testimony of the old man that he had seen Peregrinus walking around. Like with Jesus and Mohammed, the deceased was not met on the place of his death or disappearance but at some, sometimes considerable, distance.[98] Christopher Jones has argued that the material is fully pagan and should be explained in reference to the appearance of "Plutarch's description of Romulus appearing after his death in shining armor and with cheerful face."[99] Although the "cheerful face" is not in Plutarch's text,[100] the wreath is clearly derived from the wreath of the Olympic victors, and the Roman model of Julius Proculus, who claimed to have met Romulus after his death,[101] is not impossible. On the other hand, it is difficult to see why Lucian would have wanted to make fun of the return of Romulus, who hardly played a role in the contemporary world of the Second Sophistic. That is why influence of the New Testament seems more likely. In his already mentioned fascinating discussion of the attraction of the resurrection in contemporary society, Glen Bowersock also included Lucian's description of Peregrinus' resurrection, which, as he notes, perfectly fits this interest.[102] Lucian's description, then, not only mocked Roman imperial practice but also Christian belief in the resurrection.

It is time to conclude. It is clear that Lucian was not uninformed about Christianity, which he also mentions in his *Alexander of Abounoteichos* (25, 38), as he demonstrates knowledge of a number of details about its doctrines, practices and writings.[103] Evidently, he knew just as much,

---

[97] For the Cynic and Christian canonisations of Heracles, see R. Höistad, *Cynic Hero and Cynic King: Studies in the Cynic Conception of Man* (Uppsala: s.n., 1948); M. Simon, *Hercule et le christianisme* (Paris: Les Belles Lettres, 1955).

[98] As argued by E.J. Bickerman, *Studies in Jewish and Christian History. Part 3* (AGJU 9.3; Leiden: Brill, 1986), 78; repr. in idem, *Studies in Jewish and Christian History: A New Edition in English including The God of the Maccabees* (2 vols.; ed. A. Tropper; Leiden: Brill, 2007), 2:721–22.

[99] Jones, *Culture and Society*, 129, comparing Plutarch, *Rom.* 28.1.

[100] It has indeed disappeared in Jones, "Cynisme," 315.

[101] For this episode see J.N. Bremmer and N. Horsfall, *Roman Myth and Mythography* (London: University of London, Institute of Classical Studies, 1987), 45–46.

[102] Bowersock, *Fiction as History*, 115–16; see also König, "Cynic and Christian Lives," 230.

[103] The judgement of G. Bagnani, "Peregrinus Proteus and the Christians," *Historia* 4 (1955): 107–12 (111), "Lucian's ignorance of Christianity and Christian doctrine is really monumental," seems to me monumentally misguided. For a more balanced

if not rather more, about Christianity as many modern intellectuals about, say, Mormons, Pentecostals, or Christianity itself. That is all we can reasonably ask of him. Unfortunately, we do not know anything about his knowledge of the Jews. He may have encountered them in his home city Samosata,[104] or elsewhere, but he clearly did not find them interesting enough to write about. There is then no reason to doubt him when he mentions that the Palestinian Christians had "priests and scribes," which suggests, as we have seen, a Judaeo-Christian congregation. These communities have recently attracted much attention, as contemporary Jews and Christians reflect about the parting of the ways with its fateful consequences.[105] The Christian career of Peregrinus will be looked for in vain in these studies. Does it not deserve a place?[106]

---

judgement see P. de Labriolle, *La Réaction païenne: Étude sur la polémique antichrétienne du Ier au Ve siècle* (2d ed.; Paris: Artisan du livre, 1948), 100–107.

[104] J. Rist, "Paul von Samosata und Zenobia von Palmyra: Anmerkungen zu Aufstieg und Fall eines frühchristlichen Bischofs," *Römische Quartalschrift* 92 (1997): 145–61 (154–57).

[105] From the enormous literature see most recently G.P. Luttikhuizen, "Vroegchristelijk Jodendom," in *Jodendom en vroeg christendom: continuïteit en discontinuïteit* (ed. T. Baarda et al.; Kampen: Kok, 1991), 163–89; D. Boyarin, *Border Lines: The Partition of Judaeo-Christianity* (Philadelphia: University of Pennsylvania Press, 2004); S. Mimouni, *Les chrétiens d'origine juive dans l'Antiquité* (Paris: Michel, 2004); J.D.G. Dunn, *The partings of the ways: between Christianity and Judaism and their Significance for the Character of Christianity* (2d ed.; London: SCM, 2006); D. Jaffé, *Le Talmud et les origines juives du christianisme: Jésus, Paul et les judéo-chrétiens dans la littérature talmudique* (Paris: Le Cerf, 2007).

[106] I am most grateful to Werner Eck, Ton Hilhorst, and Peter van Minnen for information and comments as well as to Kristina Meinking for correcting my English.

MONISM AND DUALISM IN JEWISH-MYSTICAL AND GNOSTIC ASCENT TEXTS

Gerard P. Luttikhuizen

A variety of texts from the ancient world depict human beings escaping the constraints of their physical existence even before death and ascending to a supernal realm.[1] This essay, which I am happy to offer to my friend and distinguished colleague Florentino García Martínez, will discuss and compare two bodies of ancient esoteric literature in which the ascent theme is prominently present—a group of late antique or medieval Jewish mystical writings commonly referred to as *Hekhalot* texts[2] and some of the early Christian gnostic texts which were recovered in Egypt in 1945. In my analysis of the relevant texts, I shall address such questions as who the subject or protagonist of the ascension is, how the journey on high is imagined and depicted, and what its ultimate goal is regarded as. In this way I hope to throw some light onto the distinct features of these two literary corpora as well as onto the possible relationship between them.

This is not a new topic of study. Ever since academic research into ancient Judaism began in the 19th century, scholars have drawn attention to what they regarded as gnostic trends of thinking in the Jewish culture of late antiquity, notably in early Jewish mysticism. I will begin by briefly reviewing some of the more relevant and influential studies. It will appear that until recently, "Gnosticism" and "mysticism" were two words for more or less the same religious phenomenon.

GNOSTICISM AND JEWISH MYSTICISM IN PAST RESEARCH

1. Heinrich Graetz, *Gnosticismus und Judenthum*

The first scholarly publication devoted to this subject was Heinrich Graetz's critical investigation of "gnostic" tendencies in Mishnaic

---

[1] Himmelfarb, "The Practice of Ascent."
[2] The *Hekhalot* texts are the literary basis for the study of *Merkavah* mysticism. For the meaning of these Hebrew terms see below.

and Talmudic teachings, *Gnosticismus und Judenthum* (1846). For Graetz and for several generations of scholars after him who had no access to the authentic gnostic sources which we now have at our disposal, "Gnosticism" or "gnosis"—Graetz and others used the two terms interchangeably—was a fairly loose term referring to a variety of syncretistic religious speculations in late antiquity and thereafter. It is worth quoting Graetz's characterization of what he considered as diverse forms of "Gnosticism":

> In allen diesen verschiedenen Weisen herrscht…immer *ein* Grundton vor: mit Hülfe mystischer Erkenntnisweisen und ekstatischer Beschauungen in die Lichtregion der Gottheit aufgenommen zu werden.[3]

Graetz insisted that these mystical ways of thinking and experiencing divine truths developed from pagan origins and thus were alien—if not dangerous and destructive—to the Jewish religion.[4] On the other hand, he observed how time and again "gnostic" ideas managed to infiltrate Judaism.[5] He therefore distinguished gnostic and non-gnostic manifestations of Judaism and felt free to speak of "Jewish Gnosticism" and "Jewish gnostics."

2. Moritz Friedländer, *Der vorchristliche jüdische Gnosticismus*

Almost half a century later, Moritz Friedländer published a book that he programmatically titled *Der vorchristliche jüdische Gnosticismus* (1889). In line with Graetz and others, Friedländer regarded cosmogonical and theosophical doctrines as the main characteristics of "Gnosticism."[6] His new proposal was that these doctrines were based on allegorical interpretations of the Jewish Scriptures. In sharp contrast with Graetz,

---

[3] Graetz, *Gnosticismus und Judenthum*, 3.
[4] For this reason Graetz had no special interest in gnostic origins. Manuel Joel, another influential Jewish scholar, basically accepted Graetz's interpretation but pointed more explicitly to the Greek philosophical (Platonic and Pythagorean) roots of early gnostic speculations. Cf. his detailed discussion in *Blicke in die Religionsgeschichte*, 103–70.
[5] In *Gnosticismus und Judenthum*, Graetz wished to prove that gnostic ideas had already penetrated Judaism in the Mishnaic period, despite the fact that they were rejected by prominent rabbis. In "Die mystische Literatur in der gaonischen Epoche," published thirteen years later, Graetz draws attention more specifically to *Hekhalot* writings, arguing that they are "degenerate" texts produced in the post-Talmudic period under the influence of certain Islamic mystical speculations.
[6] *Der vorchristliche jüdische Gnosticismus*, 45.

he therefore argued that "Gnosticism" was an originally Jewish current of thought.

It is probable that according to Friedländer, the theosophical teachings of "Gnosticism" included mystical themes such as heavenly ascent and visions of God.[7] However, where he refers to gnostic doctrines based on allegorical biblical interpretations, he seems to have primarily been thinking of doctrines relating to the origin of the world and human beings and to the earliest history of humanity—the "descent myth" rather than the "ascent myth," as described below.

Friedländer suggested that his Jewish Gnosticism originated in the Diaspora community of Alexandria out of the interaction between Jews and their Hellenistic-pagan environment. He hypothesized that in the pre-Christian era, Jewish gnostics developed in two separate directions. The first movement, which he called "orthodox" or "conservative"— represented by Philo—remained faithful to the Law. Friedländer had a high opinion of this form of "Jewish Gnosticism" since, he argued, "Gnosticism was a very appropriate and in fact indispensable means to transform Judaism into a universal religion."[8] Because he recognized some of the main features of this originally Alexandrian Jewish Gnosticism in Palestinian Jewish mystical traditions, Friedländer guessed that in the course of time, it also moved to the Jewish homeland.[9]

Friedländer also discerned a "radical" gnostic movement.[10] In his view, these radical gnostics became "heretical"—even in the pre-Christian era—, because their allegorical approach to the Scriptures eventually led them to distance themselves from the biblical Creator and his Law.

---

[7] Friedländer referred to *Merkavah* passages "in the earliest Mishnah-teachings," cf. below, n. 9.

[8] In *Die religiösen Bewegungen*, vi, Friedländer clarifies his position in claiming that the Judaism of the Diaspora "preserved the universalistic traditions of the prophets, which were wide-spread at the time of the Maccabees, whereas the traditions of the Pharisees were the more recent ones, artificially implanted into the Law by a then dominant nationalism." Cf. Brenner, "Gnosis and History," esp. 46 and 51.

[9] *Der vorchristliche jüdische Gnosticismus*, 49: "Unbestreitbare Thatsache bleibt jedenfalls, dass die kosmogonischen und theosophischen Mysterien selbst in Palästina, und in den Kreisen der hervorragendsten Gestzeslehrer, schon im ersten christlichen Jahrhundert, wo das Christenthum noch nicht erkennbar aus dem Rahmen des Judenthums herausgetreten, und von einer christlichen Gnosis auch nicht die geringste Spur vorhanden sein konnte, in vollster Blüte stand"; on p. 46 and 56–62 Friedländer refers to *Maasseh-Bereshith* and *Maasseh-Merkavah* passages "bei den ältesten Mischna-Lehrern."

[10] *Der vorchristliche jüdische Gnosticismus*, 5–8 and passim. For this radical movement Friedländer referred to Philo, *Migr.* 89 (where Philo mentions people who regard the written laws as symbols of spiritual teachings but in fact hold these laws in contempt), Eusebius, *Praep. ev.* VII 10, and a few other patristic sources.

He therefore also designated the heretics in question as "antinomians."[11] The important thing is that Friedländer detected similarities between this hypothetical pre-Christian Jewish Gnosticism and such gnostic-Christian sects as the Ophites, the Cainites, the Sethians or Sethites, and the Melchizedekians known to him from patristic reports. A characteristic feature these sects had in common with his pre-Christian Jewish Gnosticism was their critical attitude towards the Jewish Scriptures.[12] Furthermore, Friedländer pointed to the fact that their "idols" were Old Testament figures—the serpent, Cain, Seth, and Melchizedek.[13] In his opinion, Jesus would have entered into the doctrines of these sects at a later stage in their development.

For a comparatively long period, Friedländer's suggestions were ignored or even brushed aside.[14] To a certain extent this was due to the strong position of the *religionsgeschichtliche Schule* in the first half of the 20th century and its "orientalizing" approach to gnostic as well as biblical texts and traditions. Influential scholars such as Wilhelm Bousset and Richard Reitzenstein found ever-increasing numbers of indications of Babylonian, Persian, and other non-Jewish oriental antecedents of gnostic ideas and mythological motifs.[15] However, at least from the mid-20th century onwards, Friedländer's suggestions began to be taken more seriously.[16]

---

[11] *Der vorchristliche jüdische Gnosticismus*, 6: "noch vor der Entstehung des Christenthums (hat es) in der Diaspora eine jüdische Partei...gegeben, welche das Ceremonialgesetz unter Anwendung der allegorischen Auslegung aufgelöst (...und) sich selbst ausserhalb des Verbandes des nationalen Judenthums und der jüdischen Gemeinde gestellt (hat)."

[12] *Der vorchristliche jüdische Gnosticismus*, 17: "Diese 'christlichen' Häretiker verraten sich auf den ersten Blick als die Nachkommen der von Philo gerügten, das 'Gesetz' geringachtenden Radicalen der jüdischen Diaspora"; 27: "Sie sind Kinder der jüdischen Diaspora und zwar der allegorischen Schule Alexandria's, deren radicalsten Flügel sie bildeten."

[13] *Der vorchristliche jüdische Gnosticismus*, 27.

[14] As Scholem (*Jewish Gnosticism*, 3) observes, "many scholars, not always justifiably, have been poking fun" at the writings of Friedländer. On his own part, he allows that "quite a grain of truth has been overshadowed by many inconsequential and misleading statements" in Friedländer's writings (ibid., 9); cf. Brenner, "Gnosis and History," 52.

[15] Bousset, "Himmelsreise"; idem, *Hauptprobleme*; Reitzenstein, *Das iranische Erlösungsmysterium*; idem, *Studien*; cf. King, *What is Gnosticism?* 71–109.

[16] Cf. Birger Pearson's statement: "The evidence continues to mount that Gnosticism is not, in its origins, a Christian heresy, but that it is, in fact, a Jewish heresy. Friedländer's arguments tracing the origins of Gnosticism to a Hellenized Judaism are very strong indeed, and are bolstered with every passing year by newly discovered or newly studied texts, the Nag Hammadi Coptic Gnostic Libary providing the bulk of this evidence" ("Friedländer Revisited," 26).

3. Gershom Scholem, *Jewish Gnosticism, Merkabah Mysticism,* and *Talmudic Tradition*

The writings of Gershom Scholem mark the beginning of contemporary research of *Merkavah* and *Hekhalot* mysticism. In accordance with Graetz and Friedländer, Scholem treated Jewish mysticism as a form of Gnosticism. In *Jewish Gnosticism, Merkabah Mysticism, and Talmudic Tradition* (1st edition 1960), he states:

> Gnosticism (is a) convenient term for the religious movement that proclaimed a mystical esotericism for the elect based on illumination and the acquisition of a higher knowledge of things heavenly and divine.[17]

In his earlier book, *Major Trends in Jewish Mysticism* (1941), Scholem had already expressed his opinion that "the ascent of the soul from the earth, through the spheres of the hostile planet-angels and rulers of the cosmos, and its return to its divine home in the 'fullness' of God's light" was the central idea of Gnosticism.[18]

In his appreciation of "Gnosticism" and his view of the relationship between "Gnosticism" and Jewish mysticism, he agreed much more with Friedländer than with Graetz. Apparently, this difference of opinion with Graetz firstly concerned the definition of Judaism. Against Graetz's narrow concept of ("legitimate" or "normative") Judaism and his description of classical rabbinic Judaism as entirely rational and logical, Scholem emphasized the pluralistic and heterogeneous character of Judaism and maintained that the ancient Jewish mystical texts were the products of the very same culture that created the Mishnah and the Talmud. In his view, "Jewish Gnosticism" originated within the heart of Palestinian Judaism and not, as Friedländer suggested, from the interaction between Diaspora Jews and their pagan environment.[19] Scholem did not have any difficulty with the term "rabbinical Gnosticism" as a designation of ancient Jewish mysticism.[20]

---

[17] *Jewish Gnosticism*, 1.

[18] *Major Trends*, 49. Scholem might have adopted this idea from Anz, *Zur Frage*, 9–58: "Die Lehre vom Aufstieg der Seele als die gnostische Zentrallehre"; cf. also Bousset, "Himmelsreise," 20.

[19] But Scholem did not assume that all forms of "Gnosticism" originated from Jewish roots, as Friedländer did, for he reckoned with a broad gnostic trend of thinking, of which "Jewish Gnosticism" was just a "branch"; cf. *Major Trends*, 65; *Jewish Gnosticism*, 10.

[20] See e.g. *Major Trends*, 47.

Scholem's detailed philological and religious-historical studies of Jewish mystical texts were, and still are, lauded and heavily criticized at the same time.[21] Some of the issues in question will be discussed below. With regard to his qualification of Jewish mysticism as a form of Gnosticism, reference is made to the criticism voiced by Hans Jonas:[22]

> a Gnosis merely of the heavenly palaces, of the mystical ascent, the ecstatic vision of the Throne, of the awesome secrets of the divine majesty—in short: a *monotheistic* Gnosis of the *mysterium numinosum et tremendum*, important as it is in its own right, is a different matter [different, that is, from Gnosticism, G.L.].[23]

Midway through the 20th century—more or less in the same period that Scholem and Jonas published their seminal studies—research into gnostic currents of thought and into ancient Judaism received new impulse thanks to the great manuscript discoveries in the deserts of Egypt and Judea. Earlier definitions of ancient Judaism and Gnosticism were questioned, and ideas about the nature and extent of contact between these two phenomena were reconsidered—as were those on the gnostic character of Jewish mysticism.

In total conformity with Hans Jonas' judgement, the general opinion among scholars of ancient Gnosticism today is that it makes no sense to stretch the definition of Gnosticism so far as to include *Hekhalot* and *Merkavah* mysticism.[24] One of the consequences of the more delimited definition is that the question of the relationship between Gnosti-

---

[21] Cf. the detailed discussion of Scholem's studies by Deutsch, *Gnostic Imagination*; and Lesses, *Ritual Practices*, 25–28.

[22] Hans Jonas, who was well acquainted with Gershom Scholem, is generally regarded as the founding father of recent research of ancient gnosticism. His stature within this field of research can be compared to that of Scholem in the study of early Jewish mysticism.

[23] "Response to G. Quispel's 'Gnosticism and the New Testament,'" 293. For a similar criticism by a scholar of ancient Judaism see Flusser, "Scholem's recent book on Merkabah Literature."

[24] Following the recent manuscript discoveries, the variety of texts, ideas, and religious currents commonly designated as gnostic appears to have been so wide that it is barely possible to encompass them all in one descriptive category. A possible solution is to distinguish subcategories of gnostic texts. Martin Schenke's ("Phenomenon and Significance") identification of a group of "Sethian" texts is accepted in several studies. A common feature of these texts is the prominent role assigned to the biblical figure of Seth. In *Gnostic Revisions*, 2–3, I propose a broader category of "demiurgical-Gnostic" texts. The distinct feature of these texts is their radical theological dualism: not only is the creator and ruler of this world distinguished from a fully transcendent and hypercosmic true God, as in some ancient philosophies, but the demiurgical God is also viewed as an evil figure.

cism and Judaism lost much of its relevance to scholars of ancient Judaism.[25]

There have been attempts made to distinguish between "gnosis" and "Gnosticism." For instance, it has been proposed to use the term "gnosis" as a general designation of esoteric or intuitive knowledge of divine mysteries and "Gnosticism" as a more specific designation of certain late antique schools of religious thought.[26] However, these attempts do not seem to have been very successful. The main reason could be that historians of religion are inclined to connect "gnosis" with the ideas of the ancient gnostics. Viewed this way, there is no gnosis outside Gnosticism. But of course, historians of religion are not alone in employing this terminology. Much broader notions of "gnosis" and "Gnosticism" are still current in other areas, such as psychology,[27] philosophy,[28] and literary criticism[29] and in discussions of various forms of modern spirituality.

Jewish and Gnostic Ascent Texts

1. *Descent and Ascent Mythology*

It is possible to differentiate two complementary basic patterns in the mythologies of various ancient cultures—the so-called *katabasis* or descent pattern, and the *anabasis* or ascent pattern. Alan Segal, who discusses these mythological structures in his article "Heavenly Ascent in Hellenistic Judaism, Early Christianity and their Environment," associates the descent pattern with "cosmologies, theophanies or angelophanies and prophetic mediation" and the ascent pattern

---

[25] For discussions of this relationship by contemporary scholars of ancient Judaism see Gruenwald, "Jewish Merkavah Mysticism"; and idem, *From Apocalypticism to Gnosticism*; Alexander, "Comparing"; idem, "Jewish Elements"; Dan, *Jewish Mysticism in Late Antiquity*, ch. 1: "Jewish Gnosticism?"

[26] Cf. the "terminological and conceptual agreement" proposed as a result of the international congress on the Origins of Gnosticism (Messina 1966), in Bianchi, *Le Origini dello Gnosticismo*, XXVI; and the critical reaction by Rudolph in his handbook *Gnosis: The Nature and History of Gnosticism*, 56–57 (*Die Gnosis*, 65). Cf. also Markschies, *Gnosis: An Introduction*, 13–16.

[27] Notably in studies based on the analytical psychology of Carl Jung. See Hoeller, *The Gnostic Jung*.

[28] Cf. e.g. Sloterdijk and Macho, *Weltrevolution der Seele*; Hanratty, *Studies in Gnosticism*; Koslowski, *Philosophische Religion*.

[29] Cf. Perkins, "Epilogue: Gnosis and the Modern Spirit"; Smith, "The Modern Relevance of Gnosticism."

with "ascensions, ecstatic ascents, journeys to heaven and the heavenly journey of the soul."[30]

Different versions of the gnostic descent myth, or the myth of origins, narrate how God's original unity disintegrated and how, as a result, a portion of the divine substance fell into the world, where it was detained by the demiurgical God and his powers. As a rule, they also mention spiritual helpers sent down from the divine realm to bring the truth to the first human beings and their progeny. In effect, this myth explains the present situation of humanity as the outcome of a conflict between good and evil powers.[31] The gnostic ascent myth, on the other hand, concerns the return of the lost spiritual substance to its divine source. We shall see how this ultimate return could be anticipated in visionary ascents.

In the Hebrew Bible we find various expressions of the descent pattern (creation narratives, stories about the origin of evil, accounts of divine revelations mediated by angels and prophets), while ascent stories are rare.[32] In fact, the only clear example of a heavenly journey is the ascension of Elijah in the whirlwind in 2 Kgs 2:11 (cf. the brief report of God's taking Enoch away in Gen 5:24). In non-canonical and post-biblical Jewish traditions, ascent stories became much more popular. Ascensions are told of Enoch[33] and Moses—who according to biblical tradition mounted Sinai and saw God "face-to-face"—and of several other biblical heroes, including Adam, Abraham, Levi, Baruch, Phinehas, and Isaiah.[34] The ascent theme took a particular shape in various *Hekhalot* texts. In this literature, the journey on high is presented as a recurring experience of living people.[35] The writings that undisputedly belong to this corpus are *Hekhalot Rabbati* ("the Greater Palaces"), *Hekhalot Zutarti* ("the Lesser Palaces"), *Ma'aseh Merkavah* ("the Works of the Chariot"), and the so-called *Hebrew*, or *Third*, *Book of Enoch*. They all deal, among other things, with the mystic's journey through

---

[30] "Heavenly Ascent," 1340.

[31] This is elaborated in my *Gnostic Revisions of Genesis Stories*, 44–58.

[32] In biblical tradition, God reveals himself by descending to the recipients of his message rather than by bringing the messenger to the divine realm. Idel, *Ascensions on High in Jewish Mysticism*, 24.

[33] García Martínez, *Qumran and Apocalyptic*, 72 with n. 83, argues that the roots of *Merkavah* mysticism can somehow be connected with early Enochic mystical speculations.

[34] Segal, "Heavenly Ascent," 1352–68; Himmelfarb, *Ascent to Heaven*.

[35] Cf. Bousset, "Himmelsreise," 5, and the classification suggested by Culianu, *Psychanodia*, 5–15.

the heavenly *hekhalot* ("palaces" or "halls") to reach the *Merkavah*, the divine Chariot.[36]

2. *The Sources*

In the last twenty to thirty years, increased attention has been paid to *Hekhalot* literature.[37] Virtually all the relevant texts have become easily accessible in synoptic editions prepared by Peter Schäfer and his research team.[38] It is unnecessary to recall the growth in our knowledge of ancient gnostic texts and ideas following the discovery and publication of the Nag Hammadi collection of books.[39] Thanks to the progress in scholarship in both fields, a comparison of Jewish-mystical and gnostic ascent texts can be based on more solid ground. By way of introduction, the literary character and the possible time and place of origin of the relevant Jewish and gnostic texts will be presented first.

The earliest textual witnesses to *Hekhalot* literature are the ninth-century manuscript fragments from the Cairo Geniza. The bulk of the texts are contained in large manuscripts produced in Europe in the late Middle Ages. However, the texts inscribed in these manuscripts might be much older. As we have seen, Gershom Scholem believed that their essential content stems from the first and second centuries C.E. Several scholars have challenged this early dating, in particular Peter Schäfer.[40] It would seem that the majority of contemporary experts hypothesize that some of the *Hekhalot* traditions may go back to third and fourth-century mystical circles in Palestine, but it has also been pointed out in recent studies that Babylonian traditions must have been of central importance in the development of *Merkavah* mysticism.[41]

The *Hekhalot* corpus includes various literary genres and diverse traditions—accounts of ascensions, magical prescriptions and cosmological

---

[36] Ideas about the divine Chariot were inspired by Ezekiel's Throne-vision, as described in Ezek 1; cf. Isa 6, Dan 7, *1 En.* 14. Some of the Qumran texts, notably the *Songs of the Sabbath Sacrifice* (4Q400–407 and 11QShirShabb), contain detailed descriptions of liturgical ceremonies in the heavenly temple but do not report individual ascensions nor do they include prescriptions for heavenly journeys. Cf. Newsom, *Songs*, 17; Davila, "Heavenly Ascent," 479–80.

[37] See Karr, "Notes on the Study of Merkabah Mysticism."

[38] Schäfer et al., *Synopse.*

[39] See Scholer, *Nag Hammadi Bibliography*, continued in the journal *Novum Testamentum.*

[40] Schäfer relegates the texts to the Gaonic period (the end of the sixth to the middle of the eleventh century, a dating already suggested by Heinrich Graetz), "Aim and Purpose"; cf. Halperin, *Faces.*

[41] See e.g. Davila, *Descenders to the Chariot*, esp. 20–22; Arbel, *Beholders.*

expositions, descriptions of angelic figures and heavenly rituals, speculations of the nature and the appearance of God, and other topics,
interwoven with songs, prayers, and incantations. Owing to the fluc-
tuating and sometimes disorderly and fragmentary character of their
content, they can hardly be described as clearly composed "books."
Schäfer prefers to speak of them as "macroforms."[42]

Aspects of the above *Hekhalot* texts will be compared here with three
gnostic treatises from the Nag Hammadi collection that are likewise
concerned with pre-mortal ascensions, namely *Zostrianos* (Codex VIII,1),
Marsanes (Codex X), and *Allogenes* (Codex XI,3). The manuscripts date
from the mid-fourth century.[43] The Coptic texts contained in the codices
are translations of Greek texts. As we shall see below, there is good reason to assume that the originals of *Zostrianos* and *Allogenes* were composed
sometime before 269. The possibility that the gnostic texts in question
are considerably older than the oldest parts of the *Hekhalot* corpus must
be considered. Unfortunately, the surviving texts, in particular those of
Zostrianos and *Marsanes*, are in a very bad physical condition. More than
half of their pages are lost or seriously damaged.

3. Hekhalot *Texts*

3a. *The subject or protagonist of the ascension*
The *Hekhalot* texts claim to transmit the teachings of reputed rabbinic
teachers such as Rabbi Akiva, Rabbi Ishmael, and Rabbi Nehunia ben
ha-Kanah. The sages relate how they ascended on high and reached the
divine realm. Their reports of previous heavenly journeys are alternated
with detailed instructions informing the addressees on what to do to
follow the lead of the teacher and also embark on a heavenly journey.
The texts are pseudepigraphic for, *pace* Scholem, there can be little
doubt that they were written several centuries after the lifetimes—i.e.
the early second century C.E.—of these rabbis.

That we are dealing with pseudepigraphic and fictional texts is also
clear from the fact that their message differs on essential points from
what we know about the actual teaching of the rabbinic authorities

---

[42] "Die Handschriften zur Hekhalot-Literatur," 214–15; idem, *Hidden and Manifest
God*, 6.
[43] This can be inferred from the dates and names mentioned on papyrus scraps that
were pasted inside the covers of the codices. Cf. Barns et al., *Nag Hammadi Codices*.

in question.[44] In basic agreement with the ancient Scriptures, the rabbis described meetings with God as the result of divine rather than human initiative, while the *Hekhalot* texts declare that anyone fulfilling the proper requirements would be able to ascend and reach the divine realm. Furthermore, the rabbis insisted that all truth is contained in the Scriptures and in the interpretations given orally by Moses, whereas the *Hekhalot* texts claim to reveal a direct route to coming into contact with the divine, without any reference to Scripture and tradition.[45] The alleged authorization by classical sages cannot mask the radical differences from rabbinic tradition.[46]

The ascending mystic is seen as a representative of Israel, "an emissary of the earthly congregation."[47] After his visit to the highest palace, he is supposed to descend and give testimony of the things seen and heard. A few passages claim that all Jewish people are able to engage in the "matter of the *Merkavah*" and ascend on high.[48] However, in point of fact, this is a theoretical possibility alone as the texts make clear that only highly qualified individuals can initiate a heavenly ascent. The requirements not only include a sufficient level of education, spiritual development and moral integrity but also the willingness to exercise various ascetical practices and to train in magical-theurgic and trance-inducing techniques. Mention is made of fasts and special diets, bodily postures and ritual cleansings, repetition of prayers and adjurations, recitation of divine names, etc. The effect of these practices is discussed in a conversation between two Babylonian scholars (ca. 1000 C.E.). One of the rabbis states:

> one who possesses the qualities described in the books and who wants to behold the *Merkavah* and the palaces (*hekhalot*) of the angels on high, must follow certain procedures. He must fast a certain number of days, put his

---

[44] Schäfer, "Aim and Purpose," 293 ("we are concerned here with a type of *pseudepigraphical literature* which is related to rabbinic literature in a way similar to that by which the biblical pseudepigrapha are related to the Bible"); cf. Dan, *Jewish Mysticism*, 92.

[45] Elior, "The Concept of God in Hekhalot Literature," 99: "The divine form and the structure of the celestial realms, rather than God's will and commandments vis-a-vis mankind, interest the mystic."

[46] Schäfer, "Aim and Purpose," 293; Dan, *Jewish Mysticism*, 98. Cf. Alexander, "Response" (to P. Schäfer)," 79–83.

[47] Schäfer, "Aim and Purpose," 288; idem, *Hidden and Manifest God*, 143. Cf. *Hekh. Rabbati*, section 248, where the mystic is addressed as "son of the beloved seed" (apparently for the sake of clarity one manuscript adds: "of Abraham").

[48] Arbel, *Beholders*, 34, who refers to sections 181 (81?), 204, 247, 335, 421, and 572 in Schäfer's *Synopse*.

head between his knees, and whisper many hymns and praises...so he can glimpse into their inner rooms (i.e. inside the palaces), as one who sees the seven palaces with his own eyes, entering from one palace into the other and seeing what is in it.[49]

These mystical methods were supposed to lead to an elevated spiritual consciousness, enabling the *Merkavah* seekers to surpass their limited human capacities. At the end of their ecstatic ascent, they could experience a direct understanding of veiled divine realities. It should be observed that the texts do not presuppose an ontological duality in the human being. They do not state that only a higher part—the soul, mind, or spirit—ascends on high, while the other components of the person remain behind.[50] Instead of assuming a duality in the human being, *Hekhalot* texts point to a duality—in fact an immense distance—between the human and the divine.

3b. *How is the journey on high imagined?*

Note, first of all, that several texts, in particular *Hekhalot Rabbati*, paradoxically refer to the ascent to heaven as a *descent* ("descent to the Chariot," *yeridah la-Merkavah*). Accordingly, those embarking on a heavenly ascent were referred to as *descenders* (*yordei Merkavah*).[51] Gershom Scholem explains this terminology from the synagogical practice to "descend" to the Torah shrine.[52] Other explanations have also been proposed, but unfortunately they all remain hypothetical.[53]

The *Merkavah* mystics had no special interest in the lower universe as the texts suggest that the "descenders" crossed the spheres of the planets and the fixed stars and started their journey immediately in the celestial realm above the firmament. Otherwise, the heavenly world

---

[49] Quoted by Scholem, *Major Trends*, 49; Schäfer, *Hidden and Manifest God*, 153–54; Arbel, *Beholders*, 32.

[50] Idel, *Ascensions on High*, 28–33 and 56–58, conjectures that a kind of astral body is meant.

[51] Cf. the titles of the studies by Kuyt, *The 'Descent' to the Chariot*, and Davila, *Descenders to the Chariot*.

[52] *Jewish Gnosticism*, 20, n. 1.

[53] In a later publication, Scholem explains the term from the practice of the mystics "to reach down in themselves in order to perceive the chariot" ("Kabbalah," col. 494); according to Joseph Dan, the expression reflects Song of Songs 6:11, "I went down to the nut orchard" (*Jewish Mysticism*, 40, n. 1); Halperin connects the term with the descent of the Israelites to the Red Sea (*Faces*, 226–27); Wolfson argues that the term only refers to the last phase of the ascension, where the traveller is seated near the throne of glory ("Yeridah la-Merkavah"; cf. the critical discussion of Wolfson's proposal by Kuyt, *The 'Descent' to the Chariot*, esp. 372–74.

resembled the cosmos below the firmament in so far as it was imagined as a structure of superimposed layers of increasing holiness, all of them more or less equal in size and shape.[54] The mystics are likely to have imagined the world above as an immense structure with the features of a temple as well as a royal palace. The highest heaven, the palace of the divine Chariot, is also depicted as a concrete and tangible space, rather than as a transcendent and unlimited realm.[55]

Hekhalot texts present the process of a gradually increasing awareness of transcendent truths as a voyage towards the divine realm. The journey is pictured with the help of various biblical, extra-biblical apocalyptic, and Near Eastern mythological concepts and modes of expression.[56] In some of the texts, several stages of the ascent are distinguished. During the first stage, where the mystic tries to free himself of all the restrictions of human existence, he often faints or falls backwards. The later stages of the ascent also appear to be difficult and even dangerous as mighty and terrifying angelic guardians or "gatekeepers" try to prevent unworthy voyagers from approaching the Godhead. *Hekhalot Rabbati* describes the gatekeepers of the seventh palace as follows:

> At the entrance to the seventh palace stand and rage all mighty ones, ruthless, powerful, and hard, terrible, and frightening, higher than mountains and sharper than hills...Bolts of lightning come from their eyes, channels of fire from their noses, and torches of coal from their mouths. They are adorned (with) helmets and armors, lances and spears...Their horses are horses of darkness, horses of the shadow of death, horses of gloom, fire, blood, hail, iron, fog...And a cloud is over their heads, dripping blood over their heads and the heads of their horses. This is the mark and measurement of the guardians at the entrance to the seventh palace, and such is the entrance of each palace.[57]

Although their frightening appearance and armor might suggest otherwise, the gatekeepers were not seen as demonic figures. On the contrary, they acted on behalf of God in defending the heavenly palaces against intruders. The aspirant ascenders were advised to take certain instruments of protection with them—"seals" on which secret divine

---

[54] Lesses, *Ritual Practices*, 13, and the literature mentioned there.
[55] Arbel, *Beholders*, 75–86.
[56] Arbel, *Beholders*, chs. 3 and 4.
[57] Schäfer, *Synopse*, section 213. Cf. idem, "Aim and Purpose," 251; idem, *Hidden and Manifest God*, 33.

names were engraved.[58] When the mystic showed the correct seal to the guardians they would let him in and help him continue on his way to the divine Throne.

Large portions of the *Hekhalot* texts consist of technical guides or manuals for mystics. It is clearly implied in these instructions that the heavenly ascent could be performed more than once.[59] A few texts relate how an enlightened teacher describes what he experiences in the other world while remaining among his disciples.[60] It is also reported that attendants called an ascender back from his heavenly journey to answer their questions.[61]

3c. *The goal of the ascension*

There is some divergence of opinion in recent scholarship about the goal of the heavenly journeys as they are described in *Hekhalot* texts.[62] For the purpose of this study, it may suffice to state that the prospect of a direct encounter with God in his glory must have been at least one of the motivating forces behind the ascents and a supreme goal in itself.[63] However, what were the mystics supposed to see, and how did they imagine the encounter with God?

Firstly, the God of the *Merkavah* mystics is the biblical Creator and Master of the universe. Much emphasis is placed on God's kingly aspect. As a rule, he is portrayed as a mighty, anthropomorphic sovereign of enormous dimensions, clothed in garments of light, and wearing a royal crown. God is seated on his Chariot-Throne in the seventh heavenly palace, while numerous angels glorify him, exalting his name and accepting his absolute authority. It is possible to see the account of God's immense bodily dimensions as a paradoxical attempt to express the idea of his imperceptible transcendence. Anyhow, other texts of the same corpus affirm that God is in fact totally imperceptible and

---

[58] For the meaning of the seals, see Lesses, *Ritual Practices*, 317–23.

[59] Schäfer suggests that the ascension to heaven was primarily conceived and practiced as "a ritual, so to speak a liturgical act" ("Aim and Purpose," 294).

[60] Cf. *Hekh. Rabbati*, sections 198–228, and *Ma'aseh Merkavah*, section 582, discussed by Swartz, *Mystical Prayer*, 22–23, and Idel, *Ascensions on High*, 32: "the assumption of a double presence...may have something to do with the concept of a spiritual body" (ibid.; "a sort of astral body," cf. above n. 51).

[61] Arbel, *Beholders*, 76. It was already noted above that the descender was supposed to return and give testimony to his community.

[62] Schäfer and others emphasize the magical aspects of the "ascent ritual" and consider the adjuration of angelic powers as its main goal.

[63] Cf. Chernus, "Visions of God," esp. 124; Wolfson, *Speculum*, 81–84.

beyond human imagination.[64] It may be noted that these two seemingly conflicting conceptions of God could already be found in biblical and rabbinic traditions.[65] The *Hekhalot* corpus does not yet distinguish between God's true essence and his appearance in anthropomorphic form, as later kabbalistic speculation would do.[66] As Elliot Wolfson notes, "the ancient Jewish mystics lived with the paradox of assuming the visibility of the essentially invisible God."[67]

Gershom Scholem stresses that a total union with the Divine is absent in early Jewish mystical texts.

> The Creator and His creature remain apart, and nowhere is an attempt made to bridge the gulf between them or to blur the distinction. The mystic who in his ecstasy has passed through all the gates, braved all the dangers, now stands before the throne; he sees and hears—but that is all.[68]

The final words of this statement perhaps need some qualification. Wolfson rightly observes that according to many *Hekhalot* texts, upon his arrival in the seventh palace the mystic is said to be seated on a throne before God. Wolfson interprets this "enthronement" as a form of angelification[69] but underlines that this does not make the mystic divine or equal to God's glory. *Hekhalot* literature is rooted in "Yahwistic dualism," as Wolfson calls it.[70] The distinction between God and his creature is of an ontological nature and therefore insurmountable. Only in the kabbalistic texts of the later Middle Ages do we find notions such as the mystic's total self-annihilation and subsequent immersion in God—"as a drop of water within the sea"—and the integration of

---

[64] Arbel, *Beholders*, 126, speaks of a mythological model of "transcendent anthropomorphism," which in her view is embedded in ancient Near Eastern traditions and found later, in more restricted form, in various biblical and apocalyptic sources. Sometimes the dimensions are so large that they are in fact infinite and immeasurable (ibid., 129). Elior, "The Concept of God," argues that what the traveller actually sees is the *Merkavah* rather than God himself.

[65] In contrast to the anthropomorphism of God found in various biblical texts, Deut 4:12, 15–16 emphasizes that the Israelites did not see (could not see?) God but only heard his voice.

[66] Chernus, "Visions of God," 145; Wolfson, *Speculum*, 107.

[67] *Speculum*, 90. See also Schäfer, *Hidden and Manifest God*, 139–41.

[68] *Major Trends*, 56.

[69] *Speculum*, 83–84.

[70] *Speculum*, 84, n. 46.

all things in God's infinite Being.[71] Here the *unio mystica* is believed to overcome God's otherness.

The awareness of God's sublime and solemn majesty may have prevented the *Merkavah* mystics from describing their relationship with God in the language of love,[72] although Wolfson points to a few passages where, as he suggests, erotic terminology is used.[73] It is probable that this language was influenced by the traditional concept of God's love for Israel and Israel's love for God,[74] since, as previously noted, the mystic was believed to represent God's people. The loving relationship between God and his community can be imagined as a communion but certainly not as a dissolution of the duality of God and man.

4. *Gnostic Ascent Texts*

4a. *The subject or protagonist of the ascension*

Three treatises in the Nag Hammadi collection of books relate the visionary ascent of Zostrianos, Marsanes, and Allogenes respectively. Zostrianos was believed to be the great-grandfather or great-uncle of the founder of the Zoroastrian religion, Zoroaster/Zarathustra.[75] The role attributed to him testifies to the widespread ancient idea that religious seers of old, such as Hermes Trismegistos, Zoroaster, and Moses, had extraordinary information about divine truths.[76] It is not clear from the damaged text of *Marsanes* whether this book likewise presents its hero as an ancient prophetical figure.[77] The Greek name "Allogenes," meaning "Foreigner" or "One of another race," is a generic rather

---

[71] Cf. Idel, *Kabbalah*, esp. 67–70; idem, "Universalization and Integration."

[72] Scholem, *Major Trends*, 55: "What there is of love in the relationship between the Jewish mystic and his God belongs to a much later period."

[73] *Speculum*, 98–105, esp. 104, n. 139: "Contrary to Scholem's generalization that there is no love between God and the Merkavah mystic, it is possible that the very moment of visual encounter is an erotic experience. The sexual component may be implied in the terminology 'beloved' employed to refer to the mystic." Cf. Deutsch, *Gnostic Imagination*, 132–35.

[74] Schäfer, "Aim and Purpose," 289; idem, *Hidden and Manifest God*, 149.

[75] Clement of Alexandria, *Stromateis* 5.103.2–4; Arnobius, *Adv. nationes* 1.52. Cf. Turner, *Sethian Gnosticism*, 294–95, n. 29.

[76] Layton, *Gnostic Scriptures*, 122.

[77] It has been hypothesized that the name "Marsianos" is of Syrian origin. Pearson, *Nag Hammadi Codices IX and X*, 232–33, recognizes in the first part of the name (*mar*) the Aramaic/Syriac word for "master."

than a proper name.[78] Because gnostics saw themselves as people of another, i.e. divine, race,[79] it is not unlikely that Allogenes is imagined as a timeless model figure rather than as an ancient seer. Otherwise, his role as a mediator of divinely revealed teachings is comparable to that of Zostrianos and Marsanes in the other two books. Allogenes delivers his revelatory messages to his "son" Messos. The teachings of the books are worded in the first person.

In his biography of the Neo-Platonist philosopher Plotinus, Porphyry writes that Plotinus was engaged in a polemic against gnostic Christians who "produced revelations by Zoroaster and Zostrianos and Nicotheos and Allogenes and Messos and other such people."[80] If Porphyry's information means that the gnostics in question possessed early Greek texts of the books of *Zostrianos* and *Allogenes* known to us from fourth-century Coptic translations, the original compositions must be dated back to some point before 269 C.E., when Plotinus left Rome (he was active in Rome as a philosophical teacher between 244 and 269 and died in 270). First consider a passage of the opening section of *Zostrianos*:

> After I parted in mind (νοῦς) from the corporeal darkness within me and the psychic chaos and the feminine desire [that is] in the darkness—as I did not have to do with it—and after I had discovered the boundlessness of my material (nature) and reproved the dead creation within me and the divine ruler of the perceptible world, I powerfully preached wholeness to those with alien parts.[81]

Two features of this passage deserve special attention. According to Zostrianos it was his mind (νοῦς) that traveled on high. This account presupposes a particular anthropology—the human being is composed of two or perhaps three parts—body, soul, and mind. Only the highest component is able and worthy to ascend. Note further that Zostrianos speaks in the past tense about his ascent. After his return he summoned potential gnostics to seek the divine truth in the same way as he did.[82] It is important to observe this as it means his teachings are not so much

---

[78] Epiphanius, *Pan.* 40.7.2–5, writes that the gnostic Archontics used "Allogenes" as another name for Seth (cf. Gen 4:25). To the best of this author's knowledge, this identification is not confirmed by any extant gnostic source. Allogenes seems to be the central figure of the last document inscribed in the Codex Maghagha (Codex Tchacos). We have to await its publication.

[79] Jonas, *Gnostic Religion*, 49–51.

[80] *Vita Plotini* 16. Cf. Layton, *Gnostic Scriptures*, 184.

[81] VIII 1.10–21.

[82] Allogenes leaves this task to Messos.

concerned with the final redemption—the *post mortem* ascent of the soul—as with the question of how self-recognition and perfect insight into ultimate reality can be achieved.[83] Insomuch as *Zostrianos, Marsanes*, and *Allogenes* report the visionary ascents of their heroes, these gnostic texts can be paralleled with the relevant *Hekhalot* accounts.

More than once, Zostrianos insists that those who endeavor to seek the spiritual truth must withdraw from their material body and its psychic accretions, apparently because attention to the body and the emotions is believed to darken the mind and distract from focusing on stability, simplicity, and unity. Indeed, the surviving pages are replete with negative statements about the body, the material world, and its creator and ruler.[84] In the sermon which concludes his book, Zostrianos repeats:

> Awaken your divine part as divine, and strengthen your sinless elect soul. Mark the passing of this world and seek the immutable ingenerateness... You have come to escape your bondage. Release yourselves, and that which has bound you will be dissolved.[85]

While the body will disappear ("that which has bound you will be dissolved" or "nullified"), the spiritual part of the seer is destined to be assimilated with the divine.[86] Allogenes, too, relates that at the moment of his ascension he had to leave behind his body (his "garment, ἔνδυμα):

> After <I> had been seized by an eternal Light out of the garment that clothed me, and had been taken up to a holy place whose likeness cannot be revealed in the world, then, through a great blessedness I saw all those things about which I had heard.[87]

Only after a person's earthly confines have been escaped through ascension to a "holy place" can direct knowledge of the divine truth be achieved. In the preserved pages of *Marsanes*, the separation from

---

[83] King, *Revelation of the Unknowable God*, 2 and passim.

[84] The material world and the body are associated with darkness, changeability (VIII 5.9), powerlessness (26.9–11), pain and suffering (46.2–15), bondage (46.15–30), multiplicity and boundlessness (46.5f.), death (123.6–8), ignorance (130.7), and perishability. The creator-God is condemned (1.16–190; 9.12–15; 128.7–14; 131.23f). Cf. Sieber, *Nag Hammadi Codex VIII*, 13.

[85] VIII 130.18–24 and 131.10–12.

[86] Zostrianos states that it is possible for a certain type of human to part "from all these matters" and "having withdrawn into God, to become divine" (44.18–22); at p. 53.18f. Zostrianos affirms: "I became divine."

[87] XI 58.26–37: "about which I had heard" refers to the first main part of the book in which Allogenes is prepared for his ascent by several revelations.

the body is not reported. However, expressions such as "incorporeal spheres," "incorporeal beings," and "incorporeal substance" are encountered several times. This anthropological dualism is quite common in gnostic texts. An interesting parallel to the above passages of *Zostrianos* and *Allogenes* occurs in the first *Apocalypse of James* (NHC 5.3) where Christ summons James:

> Cast away from yourself…this bond of flesh, which encircles you. Then you will reach Him-who-is (the transcendent God). And you will no longer be James; rather you will be The-One-who-is.[88]

In their statements about the earthly condition of humankind, these gnostic texts are explicitly dualistic. However, they add that the spiritual part is the only thing that counts. Even before death, the body should be escaped from since the corporeal components are completely unrelated to a person's true identity. Ultimately, everything related to the body will be reduced to nothing while the spiritual core is preserved and will be united with the only One who truly is.

4b. *How is the journey on high imagined?*
The three gnostic books depict the journey on high as an escape from duality and as a search for unity. On the one hand, they do so with the help of philosophical concepts ultimately based on Plato's doctrine on the soul's progress to ever-higher levels of comprehension (*Symposium* 210a–212a) in order to attain true knowledge of that which really is (*Phaedrus* 247b–e).[89] On the other hand, the ascent is described in religious language. Only to a small degree is the progress in knowledge presented as the result of discursive reasoning. For the greater part it is dependent upon the reception of revelations from divine helpers. They explain what the voyager sees, and they guide him on his way to higher forms of knowledge.[90] In addition, the gnostic books describe the ascent as a process of gradual initiation. At each stage, Zostrianos receives one or more metaphorical baths in celestial water.[91] Anointments in *Allogenes* seem to have a similar function.[92]

---

[88] V 27. 3–10.
[89] For a detailed comparison with ancient philosophical speculations see Turner, *Sethian Gnosticism*, esp. 693–743; idem, "Platonizing"; Finamore, "Iamblichus."
[90] King, *Revelation of the Unknowable God*, 6–8.
[91] VIII 4.21–7.22; 25.10–20; 53.15–54.1; 62.12–14.
[92] XI 52.13–15.

The role of the angelic helpers ("powers" or "glories") is made clear in the following passage of *Zostrianos*, speaking of the souls seeking to escape from the bonds of the body.

> Powers have been appointed for their (the souls') salvation, and these same ones are in this place. And...there stand at each [aeon] certain glories so that one who is in the [world] might be saved together with [them]. The glories are perfect living thoughts (νόημα). They cannot perish because [they are] models (τύπος) of salvation; each one will be saved by them. And being a model (oneself) one will receive strength by it, and having that glory as a helper (βοηθός), one thus passes through the world (κόσμος) and through [every] aeon.[93]

First the souls pass through the cosmic world and then through the various realms above the firmament. As far as we can assess from the extant portions of their texts, the gnostic books under discussion reveal little interest in the cosmic stages of the journey on high. The very damaged second page of *Marsanes* seems to distinguish thirteen levels (designated as "seals").[94] This spatial structure serves as a very long bridge between matter and pure spirit, multiplicity and unity, and ignorance and true knowledge, respectively. It is also an attempt to explain the multiplicity of the universe from the one divine source. In *Marsanes* the first three spheres are viewed as "material" realms. The fourth sphere is probably imagined as "incorporeal" and "divine." The other "seals" are connected with increasingly abstract entities or "aeons."

The lack of interest in the passage of the soul through the cosmic—planetary and zodiacal—spheres is a particular feature of *Zostrianos*, *Marsanes*, and *Allogenes*. Numerous other gnostic and non-gnostic texts specify in great detail the dangers that threaten the soul when it ascends through these spheres, usually described as the realms of hostile powers. The three books have this almost exclusive interest in otherworldly realities in common with the *Hekhalot* writings.

The higher stages of the ascent reflect the structure of the divine hierarchy. Viewed from above, each aeon is a somewhat less than perfect representation of the former or parent aeon. From the point of view of the ascender, each level represents one stage upwards on the way to complete knowledge and salvation. In *Zostrianos* and *Allogenes*, "the

---

[93] VIII 46.16–31.
[94] Turner, *Sethian Gnosticism*, 111 with n. 22.

all-glorious Youel" prepares the ascender for the reception of the final revelation of the highest realities.[95]

The central figure in the *pleroma* ("fullness") or divine world is Barbelo.[96] She is regarded as the first and only externalization of God's self-contemplating thought and therefore as the principle of all knowledge and salvation.

> (She is) a thought of the perfect mind (νοῦς) of the Light that causes immortal souls to acquire knowledge.[97]

While the Invisible Spirit remains undivided, Barbelo divides into three aeons, designated by abstract names—Kalyptos, Protophanes, and Autogenes. Each of these major aeons in turn has a multitude of constituent parts, often designated as powers, glories, or luminaries. The luminaries of the Barbelo aeon reveal the highest levels of divine Being to the ascender. The ascent through their aeons requires a gradual shift from discursive knowledge to contemplative knowledge and silent intuition. Through this process the mind of the gnostic becomes assimilated to ever-higher ontological levels.[98]

4c. *The goal of the ascension*

In *Allogenes*, Barbelo's luminaries teach the ascender that it is impossible to know the Unknowable. Accordingly, they command him to stop when he approaches the highest level of knowledge, because, they caution, seeking the unknowable God would only disturb him (61.25–39). This episode introduces a traditional definition of God's transcendence with the help of abstractions and negations (the *via negativa*).[99] However, before warning the seer, the luminaries told him that he would receive a "first revelation of the Unknowable" (59.27–30). This revelatory knowledge—designated paradoxically as "ignorant knowledge" (64.10–11; cf. 59.30–32)—enabled the gnostic to reach the completely

---

[95] The name of this angelic figure is likely to have been adopted, directly or indirectly, from a Jewish tradition. Cf. Scholem, *Major Trends*, 68; King, *Revelation of the Unknowable God*, 46. See also below, n. 107.

[96] The name "Barbelo" has not yet been explained satisfactorily.

[97] *Zostr.* VIII 29.17–20.

[98] Turner, *Sethian Gnosticism*, 652f. While Allogenes and Marsanes reach the highest level, Zostrianos does not seem to travel farther than the first levels of the Barbelo Aeon.

[99] Cf. the discussion of various "negative theologies" in Luttikhuizen, *Gnostic Revisions*, 112–16.

transcendent God—provided, that is, that he was prepared to abandon
all efforts to understand.

> Do not [know] him, for that is impossible. And if through an enlightened
> thought (ἔννοια) you should know him: be ignorant of him.[100]

This passage of *Allogenes* shows that the author was aware of the
theoretical problem raised by the idea of reaching perfect knowledge
of God's unknowable transcendence. In *Allogenes* and in the other two
treatises, the highest phase of the ascender's search for knowledge is
described as a contemplative vision. In this vision, the gnostic loses
the awareness of his individuality. What the seer experiences are only
ineffability, tranquility, silence, and stability.[101]

Closely connected with the pursuit of perfect knowledge of ultimate
reality was the gnostic's desire to unite with the Divine. Apparently,
this goal could not be achieved by the protagonists of the three books.
After all, they were only temporary residents of the otherworldly realm.
It may be taken for granted that complete union with God was the
ultimate goal of the soul's *post mortem* ascension.

5. *Comparison*

So far, the characteristic features of the ascension have been examined
within their own literary and conceptual frames, respectively, in *Hekhalot*
texts and in three gnostic texts on visionary ascents. In conclusion, I
will summarize the most striking similarities and dissimilarities, pay-
ing special attention to agreements and disagreements in the religious
thought structure expressed or presupposed in the texts.

5a. *The subject or protagonist of the ascension*
In the gnostic treatises, the journey on high is reserved for the highest
part of the human being. The physical body and the irrational parts
of the soul are left behind. In the *Hekhalot* corpus we do not find clear
traces of a similar anthropological dualism. Apparently, the entire

---

[100] XI 60.8–12.

[101] Turner, *Sethian Gnosticism*, 666–669. The expression "standing at rest" is often used
to denote the stability of the supernal realm in contrast with the chaos and turmoil of
the physical world, cf. *Zostr.* VIII 78.15f; 81.12f; 82.13–15; *Allog.* XI 46.13f; 59.20–23;
60.4, 28–37; 66, 31f; Middle-Platonic authors and Plotinus used quite similar terminology to denote the experience of stability and tranquillity in a mystical withdrawal to
transcendent reality. See Williams, "Stability"; idem, *Immovable Race*.

human person is believed to ascend to the celestial world. Perhaps we may compare the ascender and his journey in *Hekhalot* texts to people and their actions as we see them in our dreams. In any event, the *Merkavah* mystics do not seem to have reflected upon the physical nature of the ascender.[102] It is interesting to recall the uncertainty in this respect expressed by the apostle Paul when he speaks of his visionary journey to the third heaven: "in the body or out of the body, I cannot tell" (2 Cor 12:2 and 3).[103]

5b. *How is the journey on high imagined?*

The ascension through the realms beyond the starry sky is imagined in quite different ways.[104] Whereas the seekers of the *Merkavah* entered into successive, more or less concrete "halls" or "palaces," all of them guarded by mighty "gatekeepers," the soul or mind of the gnostic had to adapt itself to increasingly abstract levels of existence. In general, the imagery of the *Hekhalot* texts builds on biblical, ancient Near Eastern, and Mesopotamian mythology,[105] while the ascent model of the three gnostic treatises had its roots in later-Platonic ontology and epistemology.

Remarkably enough, the gnostic travelers were somehow guided by angelic beings, while the *Merkavah* seekers seem to have traveled alone. This is striking, because the role of the revealer figures in gnostic ascent texts is vaguely reminiscent of the traditional function of the *angelus interpres* in apocalyptic writings, the more so because some of them bear Hebrew-sounding names.[106] As we have seen, the spiritual progress of the gnostic ascender was dependent on his reception of divine revelations.

---

[102] As we noted above, n. 51, Idel suggests that the mystic travelled in an astral body.

[103] However, note that Paul did not ascend on his own initiative and after serious preparation, as the *Merkavah* mystics reportedly did. Rather, he experienced a sudden rapture to Paradise. Cf. Schäfer, "New Testament and Hekhalot Literature"; and Roukema, "Paul's Rapture."

[104] Like the *Hekhalot* texts, the three gnostic treatises neglect the cosmic phase of the journey on high.

[105] Arbel, *Beholders*, ch. 4 ("Mystical Journeys in Mythological Language").

[106] Compare the name and the role of "the all-glorious Youel" in *Zostrianos* and *Allogenes* to the angel Yaoel in the *Apocalypse of Abraham* (discussed by Himmelfarb, *Ascent to Heaven*, 61–66). The function and the names of angelic helpers in gnostic texts deserve closer examination. For the time being I refer to Bohak, "Hebrew, Hebrew Everywhere?" and Van der Horst, "'The God who Drowned the King of Egypt.'"

To an extent, the action of Barbelo's luminaries in *Allogenes* is comparable to that of the gatekeepers in *Hekhalot* texts. Both groups of celestial powers caution the traveler when he nears the final goal of his journey. However, they had different reasons for doing so. In the *Hekhalot* writings, the guardians of the heavenly palaces act as defenders of God's holiness, whereas Barbelo's powers remind the gnostic of God's fully transcendent and therefore unknowable nature.

5c. *The goal of the ascension*

The three gnostic ascent texts do not present the journey on high as the final return voyage of the soul or spirit to its divine origin. In these books, the ascent is basically a quest for perfect knowledge. Interestingly, this epistemological concern can also be found in *Hekhalot* texts, since the heavenly voyage of the *Merkavah* seeker can be regarded as a search for hidden celestial mysteries.[107] It is worth mentioning in this connection that the gnostic and the Jewish ascenders returned from their journey in order to share their experiences with those deemed "worthy."

However, these similarities are of a rather superficial and general character. Jewish and gnostic ascenders aspired to see or comprehend quite different things. The ultimate goal of the *Merkavah* mystics was apparently to join in the celestial glorification of God's majesty[108] and so perhaps to confirm Israel's trust in God, whereas the gnostics wished to attain perfect knowledge of ultimate reality and of themselves in anticipation of their final salvation.

When the *Merkavah* mystic worshipped God's glory in the highest heaven, he was as close to God as possible but must nevertheless have been aware of the ontologically infinite distance between God and his creature, whereas gnostics started from the conviction that the innermost core of their being was not created by a demiurgical God but originated from, and was consubstantial with, the metacosmic unknowable God. When attempting to obtain true knowledge of ultimate reality, they were searching for the source of their own existence.

---

[107] Note that they did not share the apocalyptic interest in the mysteries of history and in eschatological issues. Attention was focused on God's presence in his celestial temple-like palace.

[108] Cf. Schäfer, "Aim and Purpose," 286.

BIBLIOGRAPHY

Alexander, P.S. "Comparing Merkavah Mysticism and Gnosticism: An Essay in Method." *JJS* 35 (1984): 1–18.

———. "Jewish Elements in Gnosticism and Magic c. C.E. 70–c. C.E. 270." Pages 1054–78 in *The Cambridge History of Judaism, III: The Early Roman Period*. Cambridge: Cambridge University Press, 1990.

———. "Response" (to P. Schäfer). Pages 79-83 in *Gershom Scholem's "Major Trends in Jewish Mysticism": 50 Years After*. Edited by J. Dan and P. Schäfer. Tübingen: Mohr, 1993.

Anz, W. *Zur Frage nach dem Ursprung des Gnostizismus*. Leipzig: Hinrichs, 1897.

Arbel, V.D. *Beholders of Divine Secrets: Mysticism and Myth in the Hekhalot and Merkavah Literature*. Albany: State University of New York Press, 2003.

Barns, J.W.B., G.M. Brown, and J.C. Shelton. *Nag Hammadi Codices: Greek and Coptic Papyri from the Cartonnage of the Covers*. NHS 16. Leiden: Brill, 1981.

Bianchi, U. *Le Origini dello Gnosticismo*. SHR 12. Leiden: Brill, 1967.

Bohak, G. "Hebrew, Hebrew Everywhere? Notes on the Interpretation of *Voces Magicae*." Pages 69–82 in *Prayer, Magic, and the Stars in the Ancient and Late Antique World*. Edited by Scott B. Noegel et al. University Park, PA: Pennsylvania State University Press, 2003.

Bousset, W. "Die Himmelsreise der Seele." *Archiv für Religionswissenschaft* 4 (1901): 136–69, 229–73. Repr. Darmstadt: Wissenschaftliche Buchgesellschaft, 1971. [Page references to the 1971 edition]

———. *Hauptprobleme der Gnosis*. Göttingen: Vandenhoeck & Ruprecht, 1907.

Brenner, M. "Gnosis and History: Polemics of German-Jewish Identity from Graetz to Scholem." *New German Critique* 77 (1999): 45–60.

Chernus, I. "Visions of God in Merkabah Mysticism." *JSJ* 13 (1982): 123–46.

Culianu, I.P. *Psychanodia, I: A Survey of the Evidence Concerning the Ascension of the Soul and its Relevance*. EPRO 99. Leiden: Brill, 1983.

Dan, J. *Jewish Mysticism in Late Antiquity*. Vol. 1. North Vale, NJ: Jason Aronson, 1998.

Davila, J.R. "Heavenly Ascent in the Dead Sea Scrolls." Pages 461–85 in *The Dead Sea Scrolls After Fifty Years*. Edited by P.W. Flint and J.C. VanderKam. Leiden: Brill, 1999.

———. *Descenders to the Chariot: The People behind the Hekhalot Literature*. JSJSup 70. Leiden: Brill, 2001.

Deutsch, N. *The Gnostic Imagination: Gnosticism, Mandaeism, and Merkabah Mysticism*. BSJS 3. Leiden: Brill, 1995.

Elior, R. "The Concept of God in Hekhalot Literature." Pages 97–120 in *Binah*. Vol. 2. Edited by J. Dan. New York: Praeger Publishers, 1989.

Finamore, J.F. "Iamblichus, the Sethians, and *Marsanes*." Pages 225–57 in *Gnosticism and Later Platonism* Edited by J.D. Turner and R. Majercik. Atlanta: SBL, 2000.

Flusser, D. "Scholem's Recent Book on Merkabah Literature." *JJS* 11 (1960): 59–68.

Friedländer, M. *Der vorchristliche jüdische Gnosticismus*. Richmond: Gregg Publishers, 1972. Repr. Göttingen: Vandenhoeck & Ruprecht, 1989.

———. *Die religiösen Bewegungen innerhalb des Judentums im Zeitalter Jesu*. Berlin: Reimer, 1905.

García Martínez, F. *Qumran and Apocalyptic: Studies on the Aramaic Texts from Qumran*. STDJ 8. Leiden: Brill, 1992.

Graetz, H. *Gnosticismus und Judenthum*. Krotoschin: Monasch, 1846. Repr. Richmond: Gregg Publishers, 1971.

———. "Die mystische Literatur in der gaonischen Epoche." *Monatschrift für Geschichte und Wissenschaft des Judenthums* 8 (1859): 115–18, 140–44.

Gruenwald, I. "Jewish Merkavah Mysticism and Gnosticism." Pages 41–55 in *Studies in Jewish Mysticism*. Edited by J. Dan and F. Talmage. Cambridge, Mass.: Association of Jewish Studies, 1982.

——. *From Apocalypticism to Gnosticism*. Frankfurt am Main: Peter Lang, 1988.

Halperin, D. *The Faces of the Chariot: Early Jewish Responses to Ezekiel's Vision*. TSAJ 16. Tübingen: Mohr, 1988.

Hanratty, G. *Studies in Gnosticism and in the Philosophy of Religion*. Portland, OR: Four Courts Press, 1997.

Himmelfarb, M. *Ascent to Heaven in Jewish and Christian Apocalypses*. New York: Oxford University Press, 1993.

——. "The Practice of Ascent in the Ancient Mediterranean World." Pages 123–37 in *Death, Ecstasy, and Other Worldly Journeys*. Edited by J.J. Collins and M. Fishbane. Albany: State University of New York Press, 1995.

Hoeller, S.A. *The Gnostic Jung and the Seven Sermons to the Dead*. Madras: Theosophical Publishing House, 1982.

Idel, M. *Kabbalah: New Perspectives*. New Haven: Yale University Press, 1988.

——. "Universalization and Integration: Two Conceptions of Mystical Union in Jewish Mysticism." Pages 59–86 in *Mystical Union in Judaism, Christianity, and Islam*. Edited by M. Idel and B. McGinn. New York: Continuum, 1999.

——. *Ascensions on High in Jewish Mysticism*. Budapest: CEU Press, 2005.

Joel, M. *Blicke in die Religionsgeschichte zu Anfang des zweiten christlichen Jahrhunderts*. Vol. 1. Breslau: Schottlander, 1880.

Jonas, H. *The Gnostic Religion: The Message of the Alien God and the Beginnings of Christianity*. 2d ed. Boston: Beacon Press, 1958.

——. "Response to G. Quispel's 'Gnosticism and the New Testament.'" In *The Bible in Modern Scholarship*. Edited by J.P. Hyatt. Nashville: Abingdon Press, 1965.

Karr, D. "Notes on the Study of Merkabah Mysticism and Hekhalot Literature in English." http://www.digital-brilliance.com/kab/karr/mmhie.pdf.

King, K.L. *Revelation of the Unknowable God*. Santa Rosa, Calif.: Polebridge, 1995.

——. *What is Gnosticism?* Cambridge, Mass.: Harvard University Press, 2003.

Koslowski, P., ed. *Philosophische Religion: Gnosis zwischen Philosophie und Religion*. München: Wilhelm Fink Verlag, 2006.

Kuyt, A. *The 'Descent' to the Chariot*. TSAJ 45. Tübingen: Mohr, 1995.

Layton, B. *The Rediscovery of Gnosticism*. SHR 41. Vol. 2. Leiden: Brill, 1981.

——. *The Gnostic Scriptures*. Garden City, NY: Doubleday, 1987.

Lesses, R.M. *Ritual Practices to Gain Power*. HTS 44. Harrisburg, Pa.: Trinity Press, 1998.

Luttikhuizen, G.P. *Gnostic Revisions of Genesis Stories and Early Jesus Traditions*. NHMS 58. Leiden: Brill, 2006.

Markschies, C. *Gnosis: An Introduction*. London: T&T Clark, 2003.

Newsom, C. *Songs of the Sabbath Sacrifice: a Critical Edition*. HSS 27. Atlanta: Scholars Press, 1985.

Pearson, B.A. "Friedländer Revisited: Alexandrian Judaism and Gnostic Origins." *Studia Philonica* 2 (1973): 23–39. Repr. Pages 10–28 in *Gnosticism, Judaism, and Egyptian Christianity*. Minneapolis: Fortress, 1990.

——. *Nag Hammadi Codices IX and X*. NHS 15. Leiden: Brill, 1981.

Perkins, P. "Epilogue: Gnosis and the Modern Spirit." Pages 205–17 in *The Gnostic Dialogue: The Early Church and the Crisis of Gnosticism*. New York: Paulist Press, 1980.

Reitzenstein, R. *Das iranische Erlösungsmysterium*. Bonn: Marcus & Weber, 1921.

——. *Studien zum antiken Synkretismus aus Iran und Griechenland*. Leipzig: Teubner, 1926.

Roukema, R. "Paul's Rapture to Paradise in Early Christian Literature." Pages 267–83 in *The Wisdom of Egypt: Jewish, Early Christian, and Gnostic Essays in Honour of Gerard P. Luttikhuizen*. AJEC 59. Edited by A. Hilhorst and G.H. van Kooten. Leiden: Brill, 2005.

Rudolph, K. *Gnosis: The Nature and History of Gnosticism.* San Francisco: HarperCollins, 1987. Reprint of *Gnosis: The Nature and History of Gnosticism.* Edinburgh: T&T Clark, 1980. Translation of *Die Gnosis: Wesen und Geschichte einer spätantiken Religion.* Leipzig: Koehler & Amelang, 1977.

Schäfer, P. *Synopse zur Hekhalot-Literatur.* TSAJ 2. Tübingen: Mohr, 1981.

———. "Die Handschriften zur Hekhalot-Literatur." Pages 154–233 in *Hekhalot-Studien.* TSAJ 19. Tübingen: Mohr, 1988.

———. "New Testament and Hekhalot Literature: The Journey into Heaven in Paul and in Merkavah Mysticism." Pages 234–49 in *Hekhalot-Studien.* TSAJ 19. Tübingen: Mohr, 1988.

———. "Aim and Purpose of Early Jewish Mysticism." Pages 277–95 in *Hekhalot-Studien.* TSAJ 19. Tübingen: Mohr, 1988.

———. *The Hidden and Manifest God: Some Major Themes in Jewish Mysticism.* Albany: State University of New York Press, 1992.

Schenke, H.-M. "The Phenomenon and Significance of Gnostic Sethianism." Pages 588–616 in *The Rediscovery of Gnosticism.* Vol. 2. Edited by B. Layton. Leiden: Brill, 1981.

Scholem, G. *Major Trends in Jewish Mysticism.* New York: Schocken, 1941. Repr. of the 3d ed., 1960.

———. *Jewish Gnosticism, Merkabah Mysticism, and Talmudic Tradition.* 2d ed. New York: The Jewish Theological Seminary of America, 1965.

———. "Kabbalah." Col. 489–653 in *Encyclopaedia Judaica* 10. Jerusalem: Keter, 1972.

Scholer, D.M. *Nag Hammadi Bibliography.* 2 vols. Leiden: Brill, 1971 and 1997.

Segal, Alan. "Heavenly Ascent in Hellenistic Judaism, Early Christianity and their Environment." Pages 1333–94 in *ANRW* II 23, 2. Edited by H. Temporini. Berlin: de Gruyter, 1980.

Sieber, J.H. *Nag Hammadi Codex VIII.* NHS 31. Leiden: Brill, 1991.

Sloterdijk, P., and T. Macho. *Weltrevolution der Seele: Ein Lese- und Arbeitsbuch der Gnosis von der Spätantike bis zur Gegenwart.* 2 vols. 3d ed. Gütersloh: Artemis & Winkler. 1993.

Smith, R. "The Modern Relevance of Gnosticism." Pages 532–49 in *The Nag Hammadi Library in English.* Edited by J.M. Robinson. 3d ed. Leiden: Brill, 1988.

Swartz, M.D. *Mystical Prayer in Ancient Judaism.* TSAJ 28. Tübingen: Mohr, 1992.

Turner, J.D. "The Setting of the Platonizing Sethian Treatises in Middle Platonism." Pages 179–224 in *Gnosticism and Later Platonism.* Edited by J.D. Turner and R. Majercik. Atlanta: SBL, 2000.

———. *Sethian Gnosticism and the Platonic Tradition.* Leuven: Peeters, 2001.

Van der Horst, P.W. "'The God who Drowned the King of Egypt': A Short Note on an Exorcistic Formula." Pages 135–39 in *The Wisdom of Egypt: Jewish, Early Christian, and Gnostic Essays in Honour of Gerard P. Luttikhuizen.* AJEC 59. Edited by A. Hilhorst and G.H. van Kooten. Leiden: Brill, 2005.

Williams, M.A. "Stability as a Soteriological Theme in Gnosticism." Pages 819–29 in *The Rediscovery of Gnosticism.* Vol. 2. Edited by B. Layton. Leiden: Brill, 1982.

———. *The Immovable Race: A Gnostic Designation and the Theme of Stability in Late Antiquity.* NHS 29. Leiden: Brill, 1985.

Wolfson, E. "Yeridah la-Merkavah: Typology of Ecstasy and Enthronement in Ancient Jewish Mysticism." Pages 13–44 in *Mystics of the Book.* Edited by R.A. Herrera. New York: Peter Lang 1993.

———. *Through a Speculum that Shines: Vision and Imagination in Medieval Jewish Mysticism.* Princeton, NJ: Princeton University Press, 1994.

THE PRESTIGE OF HEBREW IN THE CHRISTIAN WORLD OF LATE ANTIQUITY AND MIDDLE AGES

Ton Hilhorst

In his Letter 108, which is in fact a *Life* of the Roman aristocrat Paula, Saint Jerome has the following to say about the heroine's linguistic accomplishments:

> I shall tell also something else, which may seem incredible to her emulators: The Hebrew language, which I myself, with much toil and sweat from my early years on, partly acquired, and which by continuous training I do not let alone so as not to be let alone by it, she wished to learn; and she succeeded so well that she sang the Psalms in Hebrew and pronounced the language without any Latin peculiarities (*Epist.* 108.26 [CSEL 55.344–345]).

Let us admire in our turn the subtlety of the hermit of Bethlehem. Indeed, he is singing the praises of Paula's capacities, in this case her command of Hebrew, and our first impression is that in this respect she easily beat Jerome, who was famous for his familiarity with just that language. But first of all, he draws attention to his own ability as much as to hers, and secondly, on reflection, her achievement amounts to little more than being able to pronounce the Hebrew text of the Psalms without a Latin accent. In fact, we do not hear about her being able to read, let alone speak, Hebrew, whereas Jerome himself—the reader is tacitly invited to realize—at least had a reading knowledge of the language sufficient for him to translate the Hebrew Bible into Latin. Whatever the case, Paula and Jerome belonged to the extremely few Christians in the Graeco-Roman world who were, up to a point, familiar with Hebrew. Generally speaking, knowledge of Hebrew, and Aramaic, was extinct in the Early Church, except for its Oriental, Aramaic-, and Syriac-speaking part. On the other hand, Christians were well aware of the fact that they were the spiritual children of the Israelites, that the older and larger part of Scripture had been written in Hebrew, and that Jesus and his disciples were Palestinian Jews who conversed in that language. This lent a stature to Hebrew that was never to be forgotten. In this paper to honour a dear friend whose knowledge of Hebrew no doubt surpasses Paula's and even Jerome's, we cannot discuss this subject in all its bearings. We will deal with a number of topics current among Greek- and Latin-speaking Christians who were unacquainted with Semitic languages; these topics, it is hoped, will suffice to give an idea of the lasting prestige of Hebrew in the Christian world until the Renaissance.

Let me begin, however, with two preliminary remarks. First of all, as is well known, Hebrew was not an uncomprehended, though venerable, tongue from the beginning of Christianity. Even if we cannot exclude that Jesus and his circle knew some Greek, it is obvious that their native language was a Semitic one. But what Semitic language? The days are gone when we were confident that that language was exclusively Aramaic, Hebrew being extinct as a living language, so conclusive was the evidence brought us by the discoveries of the Dead Sea Scrolls with their mass of manuscripts in Hebrew. In addition, the Bar Kokhba letters from the third decade of the second century, which were found in Murabba'at in or shortly after 1950, revealed that their writers used Greek, Aramaic, and Hebrew, without preferring any one of these languages for a specific use. So it became difficult to deny the Hebrew language any life in the centuries around the turn of the era, although it remained difficult to pinpoint the extent to which and the function in which Hebrew was used in those centuries.[1] One at least of the older arguments for Hebrew having sunk into oblivion, namely

---

[1] Studies on the topic are numerous; they include H.P. Rüger, "Zum Problem der Sprache Jesu," *ZNW* 59 (1968): 113–22; J. A. Fitzmyer, S.J., "The Languages of Palestine in the First Century A.D.," *CBQ* 32 (1970): 501–31; repr. in *A Wandering Aramean: Collected Aramaic Essays* (SBLMS 25; Missoula, Mont.: Scholars Press, 1979), 29–56; and repr. in *The Semitic Background of the New Testament: Combined Edition of Essays on the Semitic Background of the New Testament and A Wandering Aramean: Collected Aramaic Essays* (BRS; Grand Rapids: Eerdmans, 1997), 29–56, 296–97; J. Barr, "Which Language Did Jesus Speak?—Some Remarks of a Semitist," *BJRL* 53 (1970–1971): 9–29; J.C. Greenfield, "The Language of Palestine: 200 B.C.E.–200 C.E.," in *Jewish Languages: Theme and Variations: Proceedings of Regional Conferences of the Association for Jewish Studies Held at the University of Michigan and New York University in March–April 1975* (ed. H.H. Paper; Cambridge, Mass.: Association for Jewish Studies, 1978), 143–54; repr. in *'Al Kanfei Yonah: Collected Studies of Jonas C. Greenfield on Semitic Philology* (ed. S.M. Paul et al.; Leiden: Brill, 2001), 376–87; E. Schürer, *The History of the Jewish People in the Age of Jesus Christ (175 B.C.–A.D 135)* (rev. and ed. G. Vermes et al.; 3 vols.; Edinburgh: T&T Clark, 1973–1987), 2:20–29; H.B. Rosén, "Die Sprachsituation im römischen Palästina," in *Die Sprachen im römischen Reich der Kaiserzeit. Kolloquium vom 8. bis 10. April 1974* (ed. G. Neumann and J. Untermann; Beihefte BJb 40; Cologne: Rheinland-Verlag, 1980), 215–39; S. Weitzman, "Why Did the Qumran Community Write in Hebrew?" *JAOS* 119 (1999): 35–45; N.R.M. de Lange, review of J.J. Collins and G.E. Sterling, eds., *Hellenism in the Land of Israel*, *BJGS* 28 (2001): 27–29; U. Wagner-Lux, "Iudaea," *RAC* 19 (2001): 63–130 (67–70).

the use of targums to make the Hebrew Scriptures understandable, still held water; and Joseph Fitzmyer, to whom we owe an expert survey of the languages of first-century A.D. Palestine, while stating that "pockets of Palestinian Jews also used Hebrew," immediately adds that its use was not widespread; "the emergence of the targums supports this."[2]

In the New Testament, traces of the Semitic stage of the primitive Christian community have maintained themselves in the Hebrew and Aramaic words and phrases and, less clearly, grammatical Semitisms— but no serious scholar nowadays would still hold the view propagated at the time by C.C. Torrey (1863–1956) that all four gospels were written at first in Palestinian Aramaic. No compositions in either Aramaic or Hebrew from the earliest stages of Christianity have survived; Semitic-language Christian texts that have come down to us started to be produced with the rise of Syriac literature, followed much later by literature in Palestinian Christian Aramaic.

A second observation which is in order before embarking on our round trip is of a terminological nature. The Semitic languages mentioned in this essay, Hebrew, Aramaic, and Syriac, are referred to in modern Greek as ἑβραϊκός, ἀραμαϊκός, and συριακός, respectively; likewise, modern academic Latin speaks of *Aramaicus* (or, more sophisticatedly, *Chaldaicus*), *Hebraicus*, and *Syriacus*. We should beware, however, of thinking that this usage is in conformity with the ancient one. Ἀραμαϊκός and *Aramaicus* simply do not exist in ancient and medieval Greek and Latin; the words are learned formations based on אֲרָמִית.[3] Χαλδαϊκός / Χαλδαΐζω / Χαλδαϊστί and *Chaldaice* are used to designate either Hebrew or Aramaic.[4] Ἑβραϊκός / Ἑβραϊκῶς / Ἑβραΐς / Ἑβραΐζω / Ἑβραϊσμός / Ἑβραϊστί and *Hebraeus / Hebraicus / Hebraice* may denote either Hebrew or Aramaic or both; it is left to the context to reveal which language is meant.[5] Συριατικός / Συριάζω / Συρίζω / Συριστί and *Syriacus / Syriace / Syrus* are used either for Aramaic or for

---

[2] Fitzmyer, "The Languages of Palestine," 531; cf. also G. Bardy, *La question des langues dans l'Église ancienne* (Études de Théologie Historique; Paris: Beauchesne, 1948), 3.

[3] But the noun Ἀραμαῖοι is used in Josephus, *Ant.* 1.144: Ἀραμαίους δὲ Ἄραμος ἔσχεν, οὓς Ἕλληνες Σύρους προσαγορεύουσιν.

[4] In Philo the stem Χαλδα- denotes Hebrew, cf. Ch.-K. Wong, "Philo's Use of *Chaldaioi*," *SPhilo* 4 (1992): 1–14; unfortunately, the author does not distinguish between nouns, adjectives, verbs, and adverbs.

[5] See the generous documentation in T. Zahn, *Einleitung in das Neue Testament* (3d ed.; vol. 1; Leipzig: Deichert, 1906), 15–16, 18–19. Cf. also K.G. Kuhn and W. Gutbrod, *TDNT* 3:365–67, 372–75, 389–91; trans. of *TWNT* 3:367–68, 374–76, 391–92; Fitzmyer, "The Languages of Palestine," 526–27; M. Hengel, "Zwischen Jesus und

that branch of Aramaic which we call Syriac. Συριστί is the Septuagint equivalent of Hebrew ארמית (4 Kgdms 18:26; 2 Esd 4:7; Isa 36:11; Dan 2:4). This ambiguity has consequences for our discussion. Even if the authors of our texts knew which language they had in mind while using a specific term, later readers were, generally speaking, not in a position to decide which language was meant; they assumed that there was a *sermo Hebraicus*, a *sermo Chaldaicus*, and a *sermo Syrus*, unaware of the fact that the first two designations might mean either Hebrew or Aramaic and the last either Aramaic or Syriac. Describing here the views and traditions of these later readers, we can only act in their spirit and naïvely use the term Hebrew for the words beginning with Ἑβρα- / *Hebra-*, Chaldean for those beginning with Χαλδα- / *Chalda-*, and Syriac for those beginning with Συρ- / *Syr-*.

1. The status of Hebrew

1.1. *Primordial language*

Readers of Gen 11:1 knew that up to the building of the tower of Babel "the whole earth had one language." That language was taken by Jews and Christians to be Hebrew.[6] Hebrew was the primordial language, the mother of all languages, *linguam Hebraicam omnium linguarum esse matricem*, as Jerome, *Comm. Soph.* 3.14–18 (CCSL 76A.708), has it. The author of the *Pseudo-Clementine Recognitions*, 1.30.5 (GCS p. 25), has still another title of honour for it: it is the *diuinitus humano generi data Hebraeorum lingua*. The *Apocalypse of Paul*, ch. 30 of the Latin version, even has the guiding angel say that Hebrew is "the language of God and angels," not quite absurdly, given the fact that God's speaking to angels and men is mentioned in the Bible and that Paul, 1 Cor 13:1, refers to the "tongues of men and of angels," but more sophisticated views are conceivable, such as Augustine's discussion of the matter in *Civ.* 16.6.1. Different aspects are touched upon in Isidore of Sevilla's *Etymologies* 9.1.11–12:

Paulus: Die «Hellenisten», die «Sieben» und Stephanus (Apg 6, 1–15; 7, 54–8, 3)," *ZTK* 72 (1975): 151–206 (168–72).

[6] For Jewish sources see M. Maher, M.S.C., *Targum Pseudo-Jonathan: Genesis: Translated, with Introduction and Notes* (The Aramaic Bible IB; Edinburgh: T&T Clark, 1992), 49 n. 3. Christian authors repeat the opinion time and again, see A. Borst, *Der Turmbau von Babel: Geschichte der Meinungen über Ursprung und Vielfalt der Sprachen und Völker* (4 vols.; Stuttgart: Anton Hiersemann, 1957–1963), *passim* (see 1946 n. 204).

It is hard to determine what sort of language God spoke at the beginning of the world, when he said, "Be light made," for there were not yet any languages. Or again, it is hard to know with what language he spoke afterwards to the outer ears of humans, especially as he spoke to the first man, or to the prophets, or when the voice of God resounded in bodily fashion when he said, "Thou art my beloved Son." It is believed by some that the language in these places was that single one which existed before the diversity of tongues. As for the various language communities, it is rather believed that God speaks to them in the same language that the people use themselves, so that he may be understood by them. Indeed, God speaks to humans not through an invisible substance, but through a bodily creature, through which he even wished to appear to humans when he spoke. Now the Apostle says, "If I speak with the tongues of men, and of angels." Here the question arises, with what tongue do angels speak? But Paul is saying this by way of exaggeration, not because there are tongues belonging to angels (trans. S.A. Barney et al.).

The building of the tower of Babel, we read in Gen 11:7–9, induced the Lord to confuse the language of men that they might not understand one another's speech. Genesis does not pronounce upon the consequences this had for the survival of Hebrew. This topic is addressed in the *Little Genesis*, the book of *Jubilees*. In 12:25–26 of that book, God orders his angel to open Abram's mouth and ears so that he might hear and speak the language which had ceased from the mouth of all the sons of men from the day of the fall of the tower. The angel carries out the assignment and begins "to speak with him in Hebrew, in the tongue of creation."[7] George Syncellus, *Ecloga* 185, refers to this passage in *Jubilees*. In a competing Jewish tradition, Eber, eponym of the Hebrews (Gen 10:21), is the only one of Noah's descendants to have kept the knowledge of Hebrew and passed it on to his descendants, because he had not participated in the construction of the tower.[8] This tradition is assumed in patristic literature and repeated by medieval Christian authors.[9] The fact that Eber is mentioned among Christ's ancestors (Luke 3:35) may have favoured its acceptation in the Christian world.

---

[7] Cf. K. Müller, "Die hebräische Sprache der Halacha als Textur der Schöpfung: Beobachtungen zum Verhältnis von Tora und Halacha im Buch der Jubiläen," in *Bibel in jüdischer und christlicher Tradition: Festschrift für Johann Maier zum 60. Geburtstag* (ed. H. Merklein et al.; BBB 88; Frankfurt am Main: Anton Hain, 1993), 157–76.

[8] Cf. L. Ginzberg, *The Legends of the Jews* (7 vols.; Philadelphia: Jewish Publication Society of America, 1909–1939), 2:214; 5:205.

[9] John Chrysostom, *Hom. 30 in Gen.* (PG 53.279); Pseudo-John Chrysostom, *Synopsis* (PG 56.315, 318); Augustine, *Civ.* 16.11; Peter Comestor, *Scholastic History*, Genesis c. 41 (CCCM 191.79). Cf. Borst, *Der Turmbau von Babel*, 207, 282, 301–2, 304, 320, 347,

We do not need to review other traditions about a primordial language, but it should be noted that from time to time the Aramaic or Syriac rather than the Hebrew language is assigned the honour of being the primitive language, both in Judaism and Christianity.[10] Quite understandably, in the Christian world this opinion is found chiefly in Syrian texts. Thus, the *Cave of Treasures*, which its latest commentator dates to the late sixth or early seventh century,[11] affirms in 24.10–11:

> And in the days of Peleg all the tribes and families of the children of Noah gathered together, and went up from the East. And they found a plain in the land of Sên'ar, and they all sat down there; and from Adam until this time they were all of one speech and one language. They all spake this language, that is to say, Sûryâyâ (Syrian), which is Ârâmâyâ (Aramean), and this language is the king of all languages. Now, ancient writers have erred in that they said that Hebrew was the first language, and in this matter they have mingled an ignorant mistake with their writing. For all the languages there are in the world are derived from Syrian, and all the languages in books are mingled with it (trans. E.A.W. Budge).

Earlier, the erudite Syrian Theodoret of Cyrrhus (ca. 393–ca. 460), in his *Quaestiones in Genesim* 60–61 (56–57 Fernández Marcos and Sáenz-Badillos), maintained that Syriac was the oldest language: Hebrew was no one's mother tongue, but was learned as a second language in order to be able to read the Bible, which was written in that language.

1.2. *The three principal languages*

Hebrew was not used in the Christian world in either daily speech or liturgy, but as the language used in creation and preserved with God's chosen people, it enjoyed such authority that it counted as one of the three principal languages: Hebrew, Greek, and Latin. Many Church Fathers took this idea to be visualized in the suprascription of the cross of Christ, particularly in the version of John 19:19–20, which runs: "Pilate also wrote a title and put it on the cross; it read,

---

443–44, 446, 692, 718, 740, 753, 760, 780, 795. Theodoret of Cyrrhus, *Quaestiones in Genesim* 62 (57–58 Fernández Marcos and Sáenz-Badillos) challenges this idea.

[10] See M. Grünbaum, *Neue Beiträge zur semitischen Sagenkunde* (Leiden: Brill, 1893), 63; Ginzberg, *Legends of the Jews*, 5:206; W. Speyer, *Bücherfunde in der Glaubenswerbung der Antike: Mit einem Ausblick auf Mittelalter und Neuzeit* (Hypomnemata 24; Göttingen: Vandenhoeck & Ruprecht, 1970), 75; Borst, *Der Turmbau von Babel*, 193, 254, 263–65, 271, 276, 279, 281–82, 287–91, 332, 333, 335, 337, 343 D. Dimant, this volume, 203.

[11] A. Toepel, *Die Adam- und Seth-Legenden im syrischen* Buch der Schatzhöhle: *Eine quellenkritische Untersuchung* (CSCO 618; Subsidia 119; Leuven: Peeters, 2006), 6.

'Jesus of Nazareth, the King of the Jews.' Many of the Jews read this title, for the place where Jesus was crucified was near the city; and it was written in Hebrew, in Latin, and in Greek." Jerome refers to this in a letter to Heliodorus, *Epist.* 60.4 (CSEL 54.553): "Before Christ's resurrection, God was known in Judah only…But now the voices and writings of all nations proclaim the passion and resurrection of Christ. I say nothing of the Jews, the Greeks, and the Romans, peoples which the Lord had dedicated to his faith by the title written on his cross." In a similar vein, Prudentius, *Apotheosis* 376–385, has Pilate unwittingly order the proclamation of Christ's rule in the trilingual suprascription of the cross. The reason why exactly these three languages had this right of precedence was formulated earlier by Hilary, *Instructio psalmorum* 15 (CSEL 22.13): the mystery of God's will and the expectation of the blessed Kingdom were preached most of all in these three languages. Augustine, *Tract. ep. Jo.* 117.4 (CCSL 36.653), offered an explanation specifying the importance of the different languages: Hebrew qualified because of the Jews glorying in the Law of God (cf. Rom 9:4), Greek because of the wisdom of the Gentiles, and Latin because of the world dominion of the Romans. Later on, Isidore, *Etymologies* 9.1.3, tags a practical lesson onto it: these three languages are indispensable tools for the study of Scripture. Of course this is theory for the time being: few medieval scholars in the Latin West knew Greek, and almost none Hebrew. But it was of the utmost importance that the view was entertained at all. In the meantime, as a substitute for a real philological use of Greek and Latin, in early medieval Ireland a habit developed to denote important concepts in equivalent terms taken or would-be taken from each of the three languages. Bernhard Bischoff interpreted this habit as an attempt to vie with Jerome, who so easily drew from his linguistic accomplishments to elucidate the texts of the Bible. But J.W. Smit may well be right to assume that "what might, viewed superficially, be regarded among the Irish as a vain flaunting of knowledge was perhaps for them a more or less sacred obligation," a tribute to the idea of what was called, from Isidore onward, the *tres linguae sacrae*.[12]

---

[12] B. Bischoff, "Das griechische Element in der abendländischen Bildung des Mittelalters," *ByzZ* 44 (1951): 27–55 (29–32); repr. in *Mittelalterliche Studien: Ausgewählte Aufsätze zur Schriftkunde und Literaturgeschichte* (vol. 2; Stuttgart: Anton Hiersemann, 1967), 246–75 (248–51); R.E. McNally, S.J., "The 'Tres Linguae Sacrae' in Early Irish Bible Exegesis," *TS* 19 (1958): 395–403; J.W. Smit, *Studies on the Language and Style of Columba the Younger*

This idea would seem to be sacrosanct in itself, but again the author of the *Cave of Treasures* undauntedly challenges it in favour of his Syriac language. In 53.20–25 he declares:

> And when Joseph brought Him down from the Cross, he took away that inscription which was spread out above His head, that is to say, over the head of the Cross of Christ, because it had been written by Pilate in Greek, and Latin, and Hebrew. And why did Pilate write it in no word of the Syrians? Because the Syrians participated in no way whatsoever in the [shedding of the] blood of Christ. And Pilate, a wise man and a lover of the truth, did not wish to write a lie as wicked judges do, but he did according to what is written in the Law of Moses. Pilate wrote in the inscription [the names of the languages of] those who condemned the innocent in the order in which the slayers of Christ laid their hands upon Him, and he hung the writing above Him. Herod was a Greek, Caiaphas was a Hebrew, and Pilate a Roman (trans. E.A.W. Budge).[13]

2. LANGUAGE OF THE PRIMITIVE CHRISTIAN COMMUNITY

2.1. *Jesus and his followers*

Jesus and his followers will have had Aramaic for their daily speech, although we cannot rule out his use of Hebrew in certain circumstances and even of some Greek. The gospels do not mention explicitly the language Jesus used, but the readers could have certainty on that point, because he was cited in the original Aramaic language both in Mark 5:41: "Talitha, kum, which means, Little girl, I say to you, arise,"[14] in Mark 7:34: "Ephphatha, that is, Be opened," and in Mark 15.34: "Eloi, Eloi, lama sabachthani?, which means, My God, my God, why have you deserted me?," the latter passage, a quotation of Ps 22(21):2, appearing in a form closer to the Hebrew also in Matt 27:46. And John 20.16, in a highly dramatic scene, has Mary Magdalene saying to Jesus in Hebrew (Ἑβραϊστί): "Rabbuni!—which means Master."

(Columbanus) (Amsterdam: Hakkert, 1971), 143–45; Borst, *Der Turmbau von Babel*, 465–70. For the idea of the three sacred languages see Borst, *Der Turmbau von Babel*, 320, 396, 454, 468–69, 478, 504, 507, 555, 611, 613, 649, 651, 790, 794, 800, 806–807, 815, 817, 839, 842, 859, 861, 892, 938.

[13] Cf. A. Su-Min Ri, *Commentaire de la* Caverne des Trésors: *Étude sur l'histoire du texte et de ses sources* (CSCO 581; Subsidia 103; Louvain: Peeters, 2000), 491–93.

[14] "I say to you" is an addition to the translation of κουμ. For the variant reading κουμι cf. J. Barr, "Hebrew, Aramaic and Greek in the Hellenistic Age," in *CHJ* 2:79–114 (97); B.M. Metzger, *A Textual Commentary on the Greek New Testament* (2d ed.; Stuttgart: Deutsche Bibelgesellschaft, 1994), 74–75.

The Acts of the Apostles state in so many words that Paul heard Jesus saying to him τῇ Ἑβραΐδι διαλέκτῳ (26:14): "Saul, Saul, why are you persecuting me?" And also Paul himself is put on stage speaking to the people in Jerusalem in Hebrew, an act which favourably impresses the audience (Acts 21:40; 22:2).[15] What is more, Paul himself cites the Aramaic "Marana tha," "The Lord is coming" (1 Cor 16:22).[16] All these pieces of Hebrew and Aramaic reflect the earliest stage of the Christian movement, which was Semitic-speaking.

Later compositions, which cannot be supposed to have been produced in communities still using Hebrew and Aramaic, are anxious to show their awareness that Jesus and the primitive Christian community spoke Hebrew. Thus, in the second-century *Martyrdom of Paul* 5 (*AAA* I 115), the Apostle's execution is described as follows: "And turning toward the east, Paul lifted up his hands to heaven and prayed at length; and after having conversed in Hebrew with the fathers during prayer he bent his neck" (trans. J.K. Elliott). These "fathers," according to M. Erbetta, are the great figures of the Old Testament, Paul's forefathers.[17] The scene then distantly recalls Jesus' talk with Moses and Elijah on the mountain (Matt 17:3 and parallels); nevertheless, the conversation with Old Testament personalities here is somewhat surprising. Therefore, some other witnesses to the text leave this detail out or state instead that Paul prayed in Hebrew. Possibly the reading of the Vatopedi 79 manuscript is the original one: κοινολογησάμενος ὁμοῦ πᾶσιν τὸν τῆς σωτηρίας λόγον τῇ Ἑβραίων φωνῇ πρὸς πάντας τοὺς ἀδελφοὺς καὶ πατέρας, "after having spoken to all the word of salvation [Acts 13:26] in the language of the Hebrews, to all the brethren and fathers." According to that reading the "brethren and fathers" are the assembled Christians of Rome (cf. Acts 22:1), supposed to speak Hebrew in everyday life, and the reviser whose version we cited initially may have meant them rather than Old Testament celebrities.

---

[15] Cf. I. Czachesz, *Commission Narratives: A Comparative Study of the Canonical and Apocryphal Acts* (SECA 8; Leuven: Peeters, 2007), 72, 83.

[16] Cf. *Did.* 10.6 μαρὰν ἀθά, "Lord, come!"

[17] M. Erbetta, *Atti e Leggende* (vol. 2 of *Gli apocrifi del Nuovo Testamento*; Turin: Marietti, 1966), 288 n. 9. For this meaning of πατήρ, cf. F.W. Danker, *A Greek-English Lexicon of the New Testament and Other Early Christian Literature* (3d ed.; Chicago: University of Chicago Press, 2000), s.v. 2 and 5b; G.W.H. Lampe, *A Patristic Greek Lexicon* (Oxford: Clarendon Press, 1961–1968), s.v. A6, neither of whom mentions our passage. Cf. also L. Vouaux, *Les Actes de Paul et ses lettres apocryphes: Introduction, textes, traduction et commentaire* (Documents pour servir à l'étude des origines chrétiennes: les apocryphes du Nouveau Testament; Paris: Letouzey et Ané, 1913), 307, 309.

Praying in Hebrew is also told of Matthew in chapter 22 (*AAA* II 1.249) of the *Martyrdom of Matthew*, written ca. 400: "And so he gazed into heaven, prayed for a long time in Hebrew, commended all his brethren to the Lord, and saying 'Peace be with you' he died."

The Hebrew language is an important issue in the third-century *Acts of Thomas*. In ch. 1 of that text, the apostles portion out the regions of the world as mission territories, and by lot India falls to Thomas. He makes difficulties, saying: "How can I, a Hebrew, go among the Indians to proclaim the truth?" implying that he was able to speak only in Hebrew. Nevertheless he goes, and the accent on his Hebrew speaking prepares a further scene, which happens when Thomas is on his way to India. Landing in the "royal city" of Andrapolis,[18] he attends the marriage of the king's daughter. There he sings a profound song, which the wedding guests fail to understand, "as he was a Hebrew and his words were spoken in Hebrew" (chs. 3–8). There is, however, a flute-girl present, "a Hebrew by race," who does understand; she has also heard how Thomas predicted a divine punishment for a cupbearer who had struck Thomas. When the punishment comes true, she is able to point out that it was foretold by Thomas, who must be, she concludes, "either God or God's apostle." This makes the king ask Thomas to come with him and pray for his daughter (chs. 8–9).

We also find the feature of the use of Hebrew in later texts. Thus, there is the eyewitness account of the finding of St Stephen's relics in A.D. 415 by a priest Lucian. Although he knows from a monk that the hill where he suspects the grave of the saint to be is wrong, he proceeds to just that place:

> Nevertheless, we went first to the hill and after digging till the third hour, we found a monolithic gravestone, inscribed with Hebrew characters. We sent for a Hebrew, who read the characters and said to us: "This writing says thus: This is the place of the lamentation of the righteous" [cf. Acts 8:2]. And so we left and went to the spot where he [namely Gamaliel] had appeared us that night. We dug and found everything manifestly according to what was shown us: their relics, and their inscription running thus:

---

[18] For this city, Sandaruk in the Syriac version, see P.-H. Poirier and Y. Tissot in *Écrits apocryphes chrétiens* (ed. F. Bovon and P. Geoltrain; vol. 1; Bibliothèque de la Pléiade 442; [Paris]: Gallimard, 1997), 1333; A.F.J. Klijn, *The Acts of Thomas: Introduction, Text, and Commentary* (2d rev. ed.; NovTSup 108; Leiden: Brill, 2003), 24.

"Cheliel, Nazoami, Gamaliel, son Habibos," Hebrew names, but written in Greek characters. Cheliel means Stephanus, Nazoami Nicodemus.[19]

Still later, the *Life of Martha*, written between 1187 and 1220, in a moving attempt to come through authentically, has Martha addressing Jesus with the Hebrew divine names *Adonay* and *Heli*.[20]

In this connexion, another tradition deserves to be mentioned. It was generally agreed that Jesus, just like Socrates, had written nothing, leaving aside the mysterious "writing with his finger on the ground" (John 8:6, 8). Nevertheless, Eusebius in his *Hist. eccl.* 1.13.5 relates a correspondence in Syriac (τῆς Σύρων φωνῆς) between Abgar, king of Edessa, and Jesus, preserved in the archives of Edessa. Eusebius declares to have translated the letters himself into Greek (*Hist. eccl.* 1.13.5, 22); he writes them out in his account.[21] We cannot be sure, however, whether the mention of Syriac is meant here to stress that the documents were in Jesus' mother tongue; Eusebius might also have included this detail to show that they came from the Syrian city of Edessa.

One should not underestimate the lasting popularity of these stories. They were copied, reworked, and translated into a number of languages and were, for example, presented again in the large hagiographical collections of the thirteenth century.[22]

---

[19] For the Greek text, see N. Franco, "L'Apocalisse del prete Luciano di Kaphar Gamala e la versione di Avito," *Roma e l'Oriente* 4 (1914): 291–307 (306). I have followed H. Leclercq, "Étienne (Martyre et sépulture de saint)," in *Dictionnaire d'archéologie chrétienne et de liturgie* 5.1 (Paris: Letouzey, 1922), 645 n. 1 in reading δικαύγων as δικαίων. For the name Χελιήλ denoting Stephen, cf. the Septuagint rendering of כליל by στέφανος in Lam 2:15 and Ezek 28:12.

[20] The *Life* is in B. Mombritius, *Sanctuarium seu Vitae Sanctorum: Novam hanc editionem curaverunt duo monachi Solesmenses* (vol. 2; Paris: Fontemoing, 1910), 231–40; cf. ibid. 236 l. 44, 237 ll. 41–46, 238 ll. 13–14. Cf. also A. Boureau, ed., *Jacques de Voragine, La Légende dorée* (Bibliothèque de la Pléiade 504; [Paris]: Gallimard, 2004), 1312–13.

[21] Cf. the treatment by H.J.W. Drijvers in W. Schneemelcher, *Gospels and Related Writings* (vol. 1 of *New Testament and Apocrypha*; Cambridge: James Clarke, 1991), 492–99; trans. of *Neutestamentliche Apokryphen in deutscher Übersetzung* (vol. 1; Tübingen: Mohr [Siebeck], 1987), 389–95. Augustine, *Cons.* 1.9.14–15 (PL 34.1049), challenges the claim of some people that Jesus had written books on the art of performing miracles.

[22] For *Martyrdom of Paul* 5 cf. Bartholomew of Trent, *Liber epilogorum in gesta sanctorum* 217 (169 Paoli); Jacobus de Voragine, *The Golden Legend* 85.97 (581 Maggioni), adds "As soon as his head bounded from his body, it intoned, in Hebrew and in a clear voice, 'Jesus Christ,' the name that had been so sweet to him in life and that he had pronounced so often" (85.99; trans. G. Ryan). For *Acts of Thomas* 8, cf. J. de Mailly, *Abbreuiatio in gestis et miraculis sanctorum* 5.18; Bartholomew of Trent, *Liber epilogorum* 16 (30 Paoli); Jacobus de Voragine, *The Golden Legend* 5.25–26 (54 Maggioni). Also the finding of Stephen's tomb is in Bartholomew of Trent 255 (206–7 Paoli) and Jacobus

2.2. *Hebrew origin of Greek and Latin texts*

If Hebrew (including Aramaic) was the language of the primitive Christian community, texts dating to that period should have been formulated in that language as well. This topic, and in particular the *ipsissima uerba Iesu*, has been studied down to the finest detail and does not belong to our discussion, which is on ideas rather than facts. But there is an aspect that belongs to both approaches, and that is the putative Hebrew original of works that have come down to us in Greek or Latin.

The most important of these is without a doubt the Gospel according to Matthew.[23] About A.D. 130, Papias, a bishop of Hierapolis in Asia Minor, composed a work entitled *Expositions of the Oracles of the Lord*, fragments of which survive in quotations of Irenaeus and Eusebius. In one of these fragments, transmitted in Eusebius, *Hist. eccl.* 3.39, he has the following to say on Matthew: "Now Matthew made an ordered arrangement of the oracles in the Hebrew language (Ἑβραΐδι διαλέκτῳ), and each one translated (or: interpreted) it as he was able." This view of an originally Semitic version of Matthew has been rejected by most biblical scholars, since that Gospel is held to have been made up from two already Greek documents, Mark and the lost source known as Q. But Papias's statement has been repeated many times by the Church Fathers, and there are no dissident views among them on this question. Thus, Irenaeus 3.1.1 observes: "Matthew also among the Hebrews published a written gospel in their own dialect, when Peter and Paul were preaching in Rome and founding the church there." And Eusebius, *Hist. eccl.* 5.10.3, mentions that the Apostle Bartholomew had brought the gospel according to Matthew to India and left there "the writing of Matthew in Hebrew letters."[24] Jerome, in his *Vir. ill.* 3, even asserts that he has seen and copied it with the Nazarenes in Beroea:

---

de Voragine 108 (711–713 Maggioni), but the appearance of the Hebrew inscription is only indirectly indicated there by translating the exotic proper names.

[23] The question has been discussed many times, e.g. by A. Wikenhauser and J. Schmid, *Einleitung in das Neue Testament* (6th ed.; Freiburg: Herder, 1973), 230–34. Cf. also W. Horbury, "The Hebrew Matthew and Hebrew Study," in *Hebrew Study from Ezra to Ben-Yehuda* (ed. W. Horbury; Edinburgh: T&T Clark, 1999), 122–31.

[24] See W.D. Davies and D.C. Allison, *A Critical and Exegetical Commentary on the Gospel according to Saint Matthew* (vol. 1; Edinburgh: T&T Clark, 1988), 8. I have quoted from their translations there.

Matthew who was called also Levi, and who from a publican became an Apostle, composed the Gospel of Christ in Hebrew letters and words first in Judea, on account of those from the circumcision who had believed; who later translated it into Greek is not sufficiently certain. The Hebrew itself is kept to this day in the Caesarean library which Pamphilus the martyr diligently assembled. I also got the opportunity from the Nazareans to copy this volume, which they use in Beroea, a city in Syria. In it, it should be noted that wherever the evangelist, either of his person or of the Lord Saviour, brings forth the testimony of the old scriptures he does not follow the authority of the Seventy translators, but the Hebrew. From which, these are two: "Out of Egypt have I called my son," and "He shall be called a Nazarean."[25]

Also some of the Jewish-Christian gospels, such as the *Gospel according to the Hebrews* and the *Gospel according to the Nazaraeans*, are said to be written in the Hebrew language. On the former, Jerome, *Pelag.* 3.2 (PL 23.597B), explicitly states that it is written in the Syro-Chaldaic tongue but in Hebrew characters: *In euangelio iuxta Hebraeos, quod Chaldaico quidem Syroque sermone sed Hebraicis litteris scriptum est.* These gospels have come down to us only in short fragments, none of them in Hebrew or Aramaic.[26]

In later periods, the pretension of a Hebrew origin works as a device to prove authenticity. Thus, there is a collection of Latin Acts of apostles, now usually known as *Virtutes Apostolorum*, which claims to be written originally in Hebrew by the otherwise unknown Abdias of Babylon. It probably was produced in Ireland or France in the sixth century.[27]

More well-known is the *Acts of Pilate*, a work originally written in Greek and usually dated to the fifth or sixth century. The relevant information is given in the prologue: One Ananias, who introduces himself as an officer of the praetorian guard and as a νομομαθής, i.e. learned in the (Jewish or Roman?) law, declares: "Having searched for the reports made at that period in the time of our Lord Jesus Christ which the Jews committed to writing under Pontius Pilate, I found these

---

[25] The quotations are from Matt 2:15 and 2:23 respectively; the former is taken from Hos 11:1, the latter cannot be found in the Old Testament, see Davies and Allison, *A Critical and Exegetical Commentary on the Gospel according to Saint Matthew*, 275.

[26] See A.F.J. Klijn, *Jewish Christian Gospel Tradition* (VCSup 17; Leiden: Brill, 1992), 3–43; J.K. Elliott, *The Apocryphal New Testament: A Collection of Apocryphal Christian Literature in an English Translation* (Oxford: Clarendon Press, 1993), 3–9; D.A. Bertrand in Bovon and Geoltrain, *Écrits apocryphes chrétiens*, 433–63.

[27] See M. Geerard, *Clauis apocryphorum Noui Testamenti* (Corpus Christianorum; Turnhout: Brepols, 1992), 158–59; S. Döpp and W. Geerlings, eds., *Lexikon der antiken christlichen Literatur* (3d ed.; Freiburg: Herder, 2002), 1.

acts in the Hebrew language and according to God's good pleasure
I translated them into Greek" (trans. J.K. Elliott). At the end of the
prologue, however, the author of these acts turns out to be Nicodemus
known from Saint John's Gospel: "The things that Nicodemus recorded
after the passion of the Lord upon the cross and delivered unto the
chief priests and the rest of the Jews. This same Nicodemus drew up
his records in the Hebrew language" (trans. J.K. Elliott, revised).[28]

Furthermore, there is the *Gospel of Pseudo-Matthew*, an adaptation of
the *Protevangelium of James* and compiled in Latin, presumably, as his
latest editor argues, in the first quarter of the seventh century.[29] In a
branch of its transmission, a prologue has been added posing as a correspondence between bishops Chromatius and Heliodorus, on the one
hand, and Jerome, on the other. It is too long to quote verbatim, but
we may summarize it as follows. The bishops have heard it said that
Jerome has found a "Hebrew volume written by the hand of the most
blessed evangelist Matthew" containing the account of "the infancy
of the Virgin Mother and of our Saviour" and ask him to translate it
from Hebrew into Latin. Jerome accepts but makes them understand
that it is no small matter they ask of him. Indeed, he explains, Saint
Matthew himself did not want the document to be published, otherwise he would have added it to his gospel. On the contrary, he wrote
it in Hebrew and put it under the care of people who never gave it
to anyone for translation. But now that heretics with evil intentions
have made it public, Jerome has decided not to add it to the canonical Scriptures, but to translate it to unmask the fraud of the heretics.[30]
Needless to say, the Hebrew original of the *Gospel of Pseudo-Matthew*
has never been found.

The procedure remains popular in the Middle Ages. The *Life of Martha*, already mentioned, purports to be written in Hebrew by Martha's
maidservant Marcilia or Marcilla and translated into Latin by Syntex,
one of Martha's companions.[31] Even later, namely from the sixteenth

---

[28] The witnesses to the text show serious discrepancies, cf. e.g. F. Scheidweiler in
Schneemelcher, *Gospels and Related Writings*, 535 n. 4.
[29] J. Gijsel in idem and R. Beyers, eds., *Libri de Nativitate Mariae. Pseudo-Matthaei
Evangelium: Textus et commentarius cura Jan Gijsel. Libellus de nativitate sanctae Mariae: Textus
et commentarius cura Rita Beyers* (CCSA 9; Turnhout: Brepols, 1997), 67.
[30] *Ibid.*, 278–85.
[31] Cf. Mombritius, *Sanctuarium seu Vitae Sanctorum*, 239 ll. 44–46: *Marcilla uero post beatam
Martham decem annis uixit; cuius uitam non paruo lumine Haebraicae edidit. Deinde ego Syntex
ipsam multa praetermittens Latine transcripsi.*

century, we have a letter by Mary to the citizens of Messina, preserved in Latin but claiming again to be written in Hebrew, and an Italian but supposedly originally Hebrew *Sententia Pilati*, in which Pilate formulates the sentence condemning Jesus to the death by crucifixion.[32]

2.3. Finds of Hebrew texts

Sporadically, we also hear of ancient documents recovered or preserved not in a Greek or Latin translation, but in their original Hebrew form.

In 1947 the first discovery of what are now known as the Dead Sea Scrolls was made. This discovery had at least two—possibly fictitious, but not improbably real—precedents. Origen, in dealing with the *Quinta* and *Sixta* of the Hebrew Bible, mentions that the latter was "found together with other Hebrew and Greek books in a jar in the vicinity of Jericho, in the time of the reign of Antoninus, son of Severus." Antoninus is Caracalla, emperor from 211 to 217.[33] We do not hear what texts "the other books" contained, nor who was the one who found them—it may have been Origen himself, although he does not expressly say so. The second case is the account of the Nestorian Patriarch Timotheus I (726–819) in a letter to Sergius, Metropolite of Elam. The Patriarch has heard from trustworthy people that some ten years earlier books have been found in a cave near Jericho. A hunter's dog had got into the cave, and so the books had been discovered. The texts they contained were Old Testament books and other Hebrew writings.[34]

Less sure, to say the least, is the historicity of a find narrated by the fifth-century Greek church historian Sozomen. In a sense, it is the continuation of the episode on the prophet Zechariah in 2 Chr 24:20–22, where we find the account of the murder of the prophet by command of King Joash. The prophet's last words there run, "May the Lord see and avenge!" The fulfilment of this wish is described by Sozomen at the close of his *Church History*, 9.17 (GCS 50.407–408). In that chapter, Zechariah himself appears to a slave whom he orders to

---

[32] For the latter two examples see Speyer, *Bücherfunde*, 41 n. 35, 106 n. 47.

[33] Cf. Speyer, *Bücherfunde*, 143; N. Fernández Marcos, *The Septuagint in Context: Introduction to the Greek Version of the Bible* (Leiden: Brill, 2000), 156–57. For the storage in a jar see Speyer, *Bücherfunde*, 48 n. 21, 67, 68, 143 n. 6; E. Tov, *Scribal Practices and Approaches Reflected in the Texts Found in the Judean Desert* (STDJ 54; Leiden: Brill, 2004), 42–43.

[34] Cf. Speyer, *Bücherfunde*, 143–44; H. Stegemann, *Die Essener, Qumran, Johannes der Täufer und Jesus: Ein Sachbuch* (Herder/Spektrum 4249; Freiburg: Herder, 1993), 100–102.

dig there and there, where he will find certain marvellous objects. The slave obeys, and together with the objects finds the body of the prophet and in addition the mortal remains of a royal child. As no one knew who the child was, an abbot, a namesake of the prophet, found an ancient document, written in Hebrew, in which was explained that the child was the son of King Joash and that he had passed away seven days after the murder of the prophet, obviously as a punishment for the king. The latter, conscious of guilt, buried the child under the feet of the prophet.[35]

A final example takes us as far as the year 1763. Leopold Mozart on his great tour with his family has reached Mainz, from where he writes one of his many letters to his friend and sponsor Lorenz Hagenauer in Salzburg. He mentions a dinner at the house of Baron von Dalberg and makes a casual remark on the age of the von Dalberg line: it goes back to such a distant past that in some document the ancestor of the family mentions as a piece of news that a carpenter's son, who had posed as the Messiah, was sentenced to crucifixion.[36] This document was a letter in Hebrew, in which this ancestor, named Conradus a Cajo Marcello, as a Roman officer in charge reports to a fellow-officer Christ's death on the cross. The document is lost, but in 1844 the family archives still possessed an authenticated copy of it.[37] Once again, we find the use of Hebrew to evoke the time of Christ, even though we might have expected Roman officers to correspond in Latin.

3. Use of Hebrew

3.1. *Magic*

For all its fame as the very first language, or as the language of Jesus himself, Hebrew was a foreign and unspoken idiom among Christians. Nonetheless, bits of Hebrew kept the awareness of its existence alive.

---

[35] See Speyer, *Bücherfunde*, 85–87, and cf. Matt 23:35.

[36] The passage runs as follows: "Diese Familie ist so alt, daß man einen Brief von zusammgerolltem Zeuge, so einer Baumrinde ähnlich ist vorzeiget, auf welcher ein Herr v Dalberg unter anderen als eine Neuigkeit berichtet, daß ein Zimmermanns Sohn, der sich für den Messias ausgegeben, zum Kreuzgalgen seye verdamt worden" (W.A. Bauer and O.E. Deutsch, *Mozart, Briefe und Aufzeichnungen: Gesamtausgabe* [vol. 1; Kassel: Bärenreiter, 1962], 83). It is not clear whether Leopold Mozart saw the document himself.

[37] J.H. Eibl, *Mozart, Briefe und Aufzeichnungen: Gesamtausgabe* (vol. 5; Kassel: Bärenreiter, 1971), 69.

In this section, we will cast a glance at some situations where this might occur. First of all, I want to point to an area which was by no means exclusively Christian, but was a common playing field of the different groups that made up the society of late Antiquity, namely magic.

In the Bible, there is no lack of disapproval of magical practices. Deuteronomy 18:10–12 thunders: "There shall not be found among you any one who makes his son or his daughter pass through the fire, any one who practises divination, a soothsayer, or an augur, or a sorcerer, or a charmer, or a medium, or a wizard, or a necromancer. For whoever does these things is an abomination to the Lord." And Rev 21:8 ensures that for sorcerers as well as for other categories of sinners "their lot shall be in the lake that burns with fire and sulphur, which is the second death." But from the same Bible it appears how ubiquitous sorcery was; and the very prohibitions showed its vitality. This situation remained unaltered in the later Christian world. It follows that Christians were often confronted, willingly or otherwise, with magic, and consequently we are entitled to extend our investigation to the written manifestations of magic to find out which role, if any, Hebrew plays in it.

The evidence is of a twofold nature. On the one hand, we have occasional utterances in patristic literature; on the other, there is the mass of non-literary texts of magical papyri and curse tablets. Two features are conspicuous in this material. As regards content, the texts are highly syncretistic: they are pervaded with elements not only from Greek or Roman religion, but also from Oriental religions: Egyptian, Jewish, Syrian, and other, and also biblical, including the New Testament. As to the form, the magical character of the formulas is often enhanced by the presence of *uoces magicae*, unintelligible words known in everyday speech as abracadabra.[38] One might suppose that Hebrew plays a considerable role in this material, the more so because Jewish

---

[38] Cf. H.S. Versnel, "The Poetics of the Magical Charm: An Essay in the Power of Words," in *Magic and Ritual in the Ancient World* (ed. P. Mirecki and M. Meyer; RGRW 141; Leiden: Brill, 2002), 105–58. For the abundant literature on the different aspects of ancient magic, we may refer e.g. to the bibliographies in *Der Neue Pauly* added to 3.363–365 Defixio; 3.1076–77 Ephesia Grammata; 7.662–672 Magie, Magier; 12/2.697–700 Zauberpapyri; 12/2.701–704 Zauberworte. As for the word *abracadabra*, this is more ancient than is generally known, cf. Serenus Sammonicus (late second, third or fourth c. A.D.), *Liber medicinalis* 51.4: *Inscribes chartae quod dicitur abracadabra.*

magicians were very active in the Roman world.[39] And yet, the harvest is rather moderate. We find a frequent use first of biblical divine names such as Αδωναι, Ιαω, or Σαβαωθ and furthermore a habit of forming proper names, especially of angels, ending on the Hebrew -ōth or -ēl.[40] The *uoces magicae* are a tricky subject. The number of unmistakably Hebrew or Aramaic words is limited. On the other hand, the long lists of magical words compiled by students of the field may contain Semitic terms, provided one feels justified to restore the corrupted word forms to their shape in the supposed source language.[41] As for the names, they are also to be found in gnostic texts, and Jerome, in a letter to the widow of one Lucinius, praises her husband (*Epist.* 75.3 [CSEL 55.32]) "who, when the filthy heresy of Basilides raged in Spain... upheld in all its purity the faith of the church and altogether refused to embrace Armagil, Barbelon, Abraxas, Balsamum, and the absurd Leusibora." "Such are," he continues, "the portentous names which, to excite the minds of unlearned men and weak women, they pretend to draw from Hebrew sources, terrifying the simple by barbarous combinations which they admire the more the less they understand them" (trans. W.H. Fremantle).

3.2. *Semitic formulas*

Fascination with Hebrew betrays itself also in the bringing up of formulas in Hebrew or (in fact) Aramaic. Christians knew of course the New Testament sayings mentioned above: "Talitha, kum," "Ephphatha," "Eloi, Eloi, lama sabachthani," "Rabbuni," "Marana tha." But

---

[39] G. Lacerenza, "Jewish Magicians and Christian Clients in Late Antiquity: The Testimony of Amulets and Inscriptions," in *What Athens Has to Do with Jerusalem: Essays on Classical, Jewish, and Early Christian Art and Archaeology in Honor of Gideon Foerster* (ed. L.V. Rutgers; Interdisciplinary Studies in Ancient Culture and Religion 1; Louvain: Peeters, 2002), 393–419 (395–401).

[40] P.S. Alexander, "Jewish Elements in Gnosticism and Magic *c.* CE 70–*c.* CE 270," in *CHJ* 3:1052–78 (1072); G. Bohak, "Hebrew, Hebrew Everywhere? Notes on the Interpretation of *Voces Magicae*," in *Prayer, Magic, and the Stars in the Ancient and Late Antique World* (ed. S. Noegel et al.; Magic in History; University Park: Pennsylvania State University Press, 2003), 69–82.

[41] W.M. Brashear, "The Greek Magical Papyri: an Introduction and Survey; Annotated Bibliography (1928–1994)," *ANRW* 2.18.5: 3380–3684, offers a "Glossary of *Voces Magicae*" of twenty-eight pages (3576–3603), in which he indicates for each term the comments on its linguistic origin by earlier scholars. The onus of their assertions, however, he leaves to them; indeed, he himself seems to be sceptical in most cases of a Hebrew origin. Cf. also Bohak, "Hebrew, Hebrew Everywhere?" *passim*.

new ones appear in post-biblical texts. To give an idea of them, we will cite here six examples and discuss them as succinctly as possible. In their textual transmission, instability is the rule, not surprisingly given the incomprehensible language; usually, it has proven impossible to reconstruct the supposed Semitic form, either because corruption has disfigured it too much or because such a form never existed. We offer the formulas as they appear in Greek versions, although in some cases the versions in other languages may be more original.

(1) A document, written originally in Greek early in the fifth century, narrates the finding of the Cross according to the so-called Judas Kyriakos version. Helena, we read, forces the Jews to reveal where it had been buried, keeping a Jew named Judas in a dry well until he indicates the spot. After seven days he is prepared to do so, but not knowing exactly where it is, he prays "in Hebrew": ακρααк ραβριμι λαμμεδδωχ αζζαηλ ζωθφεν φαυθιου βαρουκκαθα αδωναιε ελωι μνανε δασφιδων βαρουχατα σιαμωρ ιλημ αδωναβειρ αδωναι βελενων καθα ελωειμαχηλ δαδαυα δαμε*ω ελχμαρω ιροβαιστρηλ αζαζιρ αβρα*νω καθα αμην. These words are subsequently translated into Greek.[42]

(2) In the years around 375, Epiphanius of Salamis compiled his *Panarion* or *Refutation of all the Heresies*. Chapter 19 of that work, on the sect of the Osseans, is mainly devoted to a "false prophet" called Elxai. Among the many details Epiphanius relates of the book written by him, the following passage, 19.4.3–4 (GCS 25.221), is of special relevance to our subject: "But what deceitful and empty talk he utters later in the book? He says this: 'Let nobody search for the meaning but only speak in prayer the following words.' Apparently the words that follow have been taken from the Hebrew language, as we have at least partly understood since his phantasies make no sense. For he says that one should say this: αβαρ ανιδ μωιβ νωχιλε δαασιμ ανη δαασιμ νωχιλε μωιβ ανιδ αβαρ σελαμ." Apart from the last one, these words are arranged in a mirror image form. Epiphanius offers a Greek rendering, but a more convincing interpretation is reached by reading the first six words from right to left, as suggested in 1858 by two scholars

---

[42] E. Nestle, "Die Kreuzauffindungslegende: Nach einer Handschrift vom Sinai," *ByzZ* 4 (1895): 319–45 (328); the asterisks denote illegible characters. Cf. ibid., 342–45, where the words, less accurately, it seems, are given again, together with those of other witnesses. Cf. also H.J.W. Drijvers and J.W. Drijvers, *The Finding of the True Cross: The Judas Kyriakos Legend in Syriac: Introduction, Text and Translation* (CSCO 565; Subsidia 93; Louvain: Peeters, 1997), 64 n. 20.

independently of each other.[43] Gerard Luttikhuizen points out that it is
the translator of the Aramaic (which must be the sense of "Hebrew"
here) who decided to leave the words of the formula untranslated and
who added the warning not to try to find the meaning of the words;
after all, the Aramaic formula, which in this case can be deciphered
in a satisfactory way, offered no problems to an Aramaic readership.[44]
I am less sure of his idea that the letters had been inverted already
in the original Aramaic version; the translator could content himself
with transliterating letter for letter, since the direction of letters in the
Semitic languages is opposite to the one in Greek. In any case, the
formula had a chequered career: drawn up as a meaningful sentence
in the original Aramaic, it was converted into an enigmatic mantra by
the translator and subsequently deciphered (correctly or incorrectly)
by Epiphanius; so the translator proceeded against the wishes of the
author, and Epiphanius against those of the translator.

(3) A curious use of the device is found in the *Apocalypse of Paul*,
whose date of composition is often, though not universally, assumed to
be the end of the fourth century. Although there is a version in Greek,
the language in which it was originally written, the old Latin translation
is reputed to be closer to the original text. In its chapter 30, Paul asks
the angel who guides him what is the meaning of Alleluia, whereupon
the text continues (Paul speaking; text of the Paris manuscript): "And
he said to me, 'Alleluia is Hebrew, the language of God and angels,
for the meaning of Alleluia is this: *tecel cat marith macha*.' And I said,
'Sir, what is *tecel cat marith macha*?' And the angel answered and said to
me, '*Tecel cat marith macha* is: Let us all bless him together'" (trans. J.K.
Elliott).[45] It may be the case that the Greek, which heavily abbrevi-
ates and offers the formula only once, has preserved the original form
better: θεβελ μαρημαθα;[46] cf. the Arnhem manuscript: *thebaemarigmata*,
but it remains curious that the foreign word *Alleluia* is explained by

---

[43] See G.P. Luttikhuizen, *The Revelation of Elchasai: Investigations into the Evidence for
a Mesopotamian Jewish Apocalypse of the Second Century and its Reception by Judeo-Christian
Propagandists* (TSAJ 8; Tübingen: Mohr [Siebeck], 1985), 100–101, 124–25, 193.

[44] Luttikhuizen, *The Revelation of Elchasai*, 125.

[45] In the extant Greek, the formula runs: θεβελ μαρημαθα, quoted once. For the
Latin text forms, see T. Silverstein and A. Hilhorst, *Apocalypse of Paul: A New Critical
Edition of Three Long Latin Versions* (Cahiers d'Orientalisme 21; Geneva: Patrick Cramer
1997), 134–35.

[46] Cf. C.-C. Kappler and R. Kappler ad loc. in Bovon and Geoltrain, *Écrits apocryphes
chrétiens*, 808.

an again incomprehensible formula, which in its turn is translated in plain language. Is the motive the underlining of the mysteriousness of the angel's disclosure?

(4) In the *Martyrdom of Matthew*, dated ca. 400, the Apostle is seized by the pagan king, who wants to destroy him by fire. The moment the execution will be carried out, Matthew raises his eyes to heaven and shouts (ch. 21; *AAA* II 1.245): Αδωναι ελωι σαβαωθ μαρμαρι μαρμουνθ, words translated as a prayer for help directed to God, Father of Jesus Christ. This prayer is, as we might expect, heard immediately. No language is mentioned in the text, but since one of the Apostles is portrayed, we may safely suppose that the formula is meant as Hebrew; the words Ἀδωναΐ, ἐλωΐ, and σαβαώθ point in the same direction.

(5) The *Questions of Bartholomew* cannot be dated within narrow limits; its date is estimated, Elliott remarks, between the second and sixth centuries.[47] In its second chapter, Mary on being asked by the apostles "how she conceived the incomprehensible" begins by saying a prayer which in the Greek text runs as follows (2.13): Ελφουζα...ολωθ και μια θεσσαι λισο αδοναι ρερουνβαυβελθ βαρβουρ θαρασου ερουρα εδεθ ερροσε......θεοθεα αρνενιοθ ανεβ..ας ευαργθ μαρμαριγε εοφφος θυριαμουχ ευσβαρ...π...This formula is followed by a translation which is much longer than Mary's exotic words. As in the other formulas, there is much confusion in the form of the formula. Again, no language is explicitly mentioned, but since it is Mary who is speaking, Hebrew must be meant, although there are hardly more recognizable Hebrew words than αδοναι.

(6) The *Acts of Pilate*, i.e. the first sixteen chapters of the *Gospel of Nicodemus*, is now dated by specialists to the fourth century.[48] Hebrew formulas occur twice here. In 1.4 Pilate asks the Jews who are assembled before him what "the children of the Hebrews" cried out in Hebrew

---

[47] Elliott, *The Apocryphal New Testament*, 652. But cf. also J.-D. Kaestli in Bovon and Geoltrain, *Écrits apocryphes chrétiens*, 263: "Notre texte est en tout cas antérieur au Concile d'Éphèse de 431 et à l'essor de la dévotion à la « Mère de Dieu »." I quote from the edition in Aurelio de Santos Otero, *Los evangelios apócrifos: Colección de textos griegos y latinos, versión crítica, estudios introductorios y comentarios e ilustraciones* (BAC 148; Madrid: Editorial Católica 1956), 576–608.

[48] R. Gounelle and Z. Izydorczyk, *L'Évangile de Nicodème ou Les Actes faits sous Ponce Pilate (recension latine A) suivi de La Lettre de Pilate à l'empereur Claude* (Apocryphes 9; [Turnhout]: Brepols, 1997), 118. A. Daguet-Gagey, "Le procès du Christ dans les *Acta Pilati*: Étude des termes et *realia* institutionnels, juridiques et administratifs," *Apocrypha* 16 (2005): 9–34 (33) even opts for a date "du premier ou du deuxième tiers du IVe s." I quote from the edition in Santos Otero, *Los evangelios apócrifos*, 426–500.

when Jesus, sitting on an ass, entered Jerusalem (Matt 21:1–9 and parallels). The Jews answer by quoting the words: Ὡσαννα μεμβρομη βαρουχαμμα αδονα (followed by a translation), in which we can recognize parts of the Hebrew text of Ps 118:25–26. The translation which the Jews add on Pilate's request seems to be influenced by the New Testament account, since it renders Ὡσαννά by Σῶσον δή, which is in accordance with the Septuagint translation of the Psalm text, but add a vocatival ὁ ἐν τοῖς ὑψίστοις, which reminds us of Matt 21:9 and Mark 11:10. Much more could be said on the passage; in any case it is highly interesting that the unknown author who, we may suppose, used the New Testament account, added to it the Hebrew text of Ps 118:25–26. A similar procedure is followed in 11.1, where the last words Jesus speaks in Luke 23:46 are given in the Hebrew of Ps 31:6: βαδδαχ εφκιδ ρουελ, before they are cited in Luke's Greek translation.

These formulas have something in common with those we find in magical texts: to a Greek ear they were composed of *uoces barbarae* which were to impress the audience. But on the other hand, they were diametrically opposed to each other: whereas the magical formulas were consciously left obscure and indeed possibly were not taken at all from any existing language, the utterances presented here are always provided with a translation; the hearer has to be aware of the fact that these words, spoken in the incomprehensible but at any rate venerable Hebrew tongue, are full of meaning. The epithet venerable may be less appropriate in the case of the Jew who is compelled to show the place where the Cross is buried (above, item [1]), but even there we are supposed to understand that meaningful words are being spoken. Further study of these formulas is asked for, complicated as it may be given the diverse skills needed, from familiarity with Hebrew and Aramaic to experience in the remote corners of textual criticism, but a first requirement is an enlargement of the collection of items.[49] Let me just mention the famous, if borderline, case of Dan 5:25, where the words Mene, Tekel, and Parsin were already enigmatic in the original text and remained so in the translations, beginning with the Septuagintal Μανη θεκελ φαρες. But also here it is crucial that the words are interpreted: the exotic form serves to inspire awe, but the explanation shows that they were not just meant as abracadabra.

---

[49] Some more instances are mentioned by J.-D. Kaestli in Bovon and Geoltrain, *Écrits apocryphes chrétiens*, 275.

3.3. *Liturgy*

There is another area in which the faithful came into contact with the Hebrew language, and that is worship. It is true that as soon as Christianity spread outside Palestine it went on in Greek, even in its cultic gatherings. On the other hand, certain Hebrew or Aramaic terms, acclamations, and formulas that had been inherited from its Jewish origin or had developed during the very first period of the Church had such a firm foothold that they were to stay even in new linguistic environments. We cannot understand this phenomenon as long as we think of language merely as a means of communication; and it was certainly possible for the Greek language with its dislike of foreign elements to produce normal equivalents for such expressions as μαμωνᾶς, ἀββᾶ, πάσχα, and μαράνα θά. But the language of liturgy has a natural tendency to sacral stylization, a tendency which may manifest itself by the use of foreign linguistic elements.[50] To mention the most common of these elements: in every celebration of the Mass and in several other liturgical contexts the words *amen, alleluia, sabaoth,* and *hosanna* are heard. But uncommon elements did not need to be frequently used to make a lasting impression. A telling example of this from a later period may be found in the matins for the last three days of Holy Week, the Tenebrae. From the eighth century onward, during this service the biblical book of Lamentations was sung, complete with the names of the letters of the Hebrew alphabet, the plaintive performance of which did not miss its effect on sensitive minds.[51]

It would not be difficult to produce a plethora of statements on the Semitic words preserved in liturgy. Two of them may stand for them all. Gregory the Great, pope from 590 to 604, was well aware of his success in the mission to England. In his *Moralia in Iob*, 27.11.21 (CCSL 143B.1346), he exults at the worldwide spread of the Christian faith: "For behold, it has penetrated the hearts of almost all peoples; behold, it has united the formerly separated East and West in one faith; behold,

---

[50] See C. Mohrmann, *Liturgical Latin: Its Origins and Character* (London: Burns & Oates, 1959), 17–23.

[51] As already observed by Sicard of Cremona (ca. 1155–1215), *Mitrale* 6.11 (PL 213.298): *tres primae de Ieremia propheta lamentationes, quae non tam legendo quam plangendo recitantur.* Sicard subsequently explains the meaning of each of the letters of the Hebrew alphabet. Cf. A. Hollaardt, o.p., "Klaagliederen," *Liturgisch Woordenboek* (vol. 2; Roermond: Romen, 1965–1968), 1348–49; B. Stäblein and M. Marx-Weber, "Lamentatio," *Die Musik in Geschichte und Gegenwart: Sachteil* (vol. 5; 2d ed.; Kassel: Bärenreiter, 1996), 893–904.

the tongue of Britain, which was unable to mutter anything but barbarous sounds, has long begun to re-echo the Hebrew *Alleluia* in praise
of God." The second quotation is a remark found more than once in
the liturgists of the high Middle Ages, who connect the use of Hebrew
in the Mass with the topos of the three sacred languages we discussed
earlier. Thus John Beleth (ca. 1108–ca. 1183) in *Summa de ecclesiasticis
officiis* 98p (CCCM 41A.180) declares: "And note that whereas there are
many kinds of languages, three are the principal ones: first the Latin
because of its nobility and the rule of the Roman empire, second the
Greek because of its wisdom, and third the Hebrew, which is the mother
of languages. In these three languages the title of the Lord on the cross
was written, for which reason these three are sung in the mass: in Greek
Kyrieleison, in Hebrew *Alleluia*, in Latin: self-evident."[52]

3.4. *Knowledge of Hebrew*

In the Greek- and Latin-speaking Church, the familiarity with Hebrew
rapidly diminished and was virtually extinct within two or three generations after Jesus' public ministry. Origen, it is true, in the fourth and
fifth decades of the third century put up a monumental performance
by producing the Hexapla, in which the Hebrew text, the Hebrew text
transliterated into Greek characters, and the four Greek translations
of the Hebrew Bible were arranged in parallel columns, but his own
knowledge of the Hebrew language was poor, not to say lacking.[53]
Jerome was the great exception and his biblical commentaries, and
many of his letters, are interspersed with explanations from Hebrew
grammar and vocabulary. So the Church Fathers and their medieval
successors had a mine of information at their disposal, which, however,
far from stimulating further study of the language had the effect of
making the effort superfluous. In the centuries after Jerome, we find
many remarks on Hebrew in biblical commentaries and other works,
but as a rule they have been copied from Jerome. Jerome himself more
than once consulted learned Jews about this or that Hebrew word or
expression; this example was followed in the centuries to come, although

---

[52] Cf. also *Summa* 35b (CCCM 41A.64–65), where he explains the words *Alleluia,
Amen, Sabaoth,* and *Osanna*; Sicardus, *Mitrale* 3.2 (PL 213.96); Jacobus de Voragine, *Golden
Legend* 178.22–26 (1284 Maggioni).
[53] See Fernández Marcos, *The Septuagint in Context,* 204–6.

we cannot always be sure whether we have to do here with facts or fabrications.[54]

There was not, however, an absolute separation from the Jews and their language, and a curious, if hardly representative, instance of Christian study of the Hebrew language may find a place here. Saint Willibald, the first bishop of Eichstätt, in 723 made a pilgrimage to the Holy Land. One of his later successors, Reginold, who held the chair from 966 to 989, was famous not only for his mastery of music and knowledge of Greek and Latin, but also for his command of Hebrew. For the feast of Saint Willibald, he composed a sequence which in its use of languages followed the territories Willibald travelled on his way to Palestine and back: Latin (Italy), Greek (Greece), Hebrew (Palestine), Greek (Greece), Latin (Italy). The text of this piece of "virtuosité puérile," as dom Morin has called it, has been preserved in a MS in Munich, all three languages in Roman letters and, as we might expect, not without serious corruptions.[55]

The Crusades gave a new impetus to the study of Hebrew, and from the twelfth century onward, the language was learned by a handful of scholars. The Council of Vienne in 1311 ordered the establishment of chairs for Hebrew, Arabic, and Chaldee at the universities of Paris, Oxford, Bologna, and Salamanca. But a much more powerful impulse for Hebrew studies came from humanism; not intending to pursue that history further, we shall end by mentioning the name of John Reuchlin (1455–1522), the author of *De rudimentis Hebraicis* from 1506, in which he introduced many technical terms that have remained in use down to the present day.[56]

---

[54] Cf. H. Schreckenberg, *Die christlichen Adversus-Judaeos-Texte und ihr literarisches und historisches Umfeld (1.–11. Jh.)* (3d ed.; Europäische Hochschulschriften 23.172; Frankfurt am Main: Peter Lang, 1995), 333, 495, 507, 511.

[55] G. Morin, O.S.B., "Une étrange composition liturgique de l'évêque d'Eichstätt Reginold en l'honneur de s. Willibald," *Historisches Jahrbuch* 38 (1917): 773–75. Cf. B. Bischoff, *Mittelalterliche Studien: Ausgewählte Aufsätze zur Schriftkunde und Literaturgeschichte* (vol. 2; Stuttgart: Hiersemann, 1967), 270.

[56] A comprehensive survey of Christian study of Hebrew, especially before the Renaissance, is still a desideratum; in the meantime, cf. B. Altaner, "Zur Kenntnis des Hebräischen im Mittelalter," *BZ* 21 (1933): 288–308, and, for particular scholars and movements, the relevant contributions in W. Horbury, ed., *Hebrew Study from Ezra to Ben Yehuda*; G. Veltri and G. Necker, eds., *Gottes Sprache in der philologischen Werkstatt: Hebraistik vom 15. bis zum 19. Jahrhundert* (SEJ 11; Leiden: Brill, 2004).

4. Conclusion

The subject examined in this essay with seven-league strides certainly deserves a book-sized study. But even so, the picture seems to be clear. It was definitely not philosemitism that inspired the interest in the Hebrew language—the contrary would probably be nearer to the truth. But reality has innumerable faces, and reciprocal attitudes between Jews and Christians have varied in times, places, and, of course, individuals. If, however, we insist upon stating generalities, a striking and indeed unique factor in bringing about the high esteem of the Hebrew language is the Bible. A certain parallel might be found in the deep respect the Romans had for the Greek language, disdaining as they were at the same time the *Graeculi* of their own time. But for all their admiration of Hellas, there was no single book or corpus of texts set apart as God's word as there was with Christians in their veneration of Holy Scripture. Two objections against these views come to mind: the role of the Bible seems unimportant in the case of magic; and if the status of Hebrew for Christians was so dominant, it is strange that so few Christians and even Christian theologians felt the need to learn that language. As for magic, this is true up to a point. Hebrew as an exotic Oriental language lent itself to garnishing charms and curses, just like, say, Egyptian or Persian. All the same it is mainly the biblical names of God and names of angels that form the contribution of Hebrew to the magical texts. As for the lack of competence in Hebrew among Christians, even highly educated ones, we should keep in mind that the desire to be able to read valuable texts in the original language is a modern attainment. Greeks did not deign to look at any other language than their own, Romans were virtually bilingual for a couple of centuries, but Augustine already felt ill at ease in Greek, and later generations relapsed into monolinguality. If this was the case with two languages as intimately linked as Greek and Latin, we should not be amazed at finding that Hebrew was lost as a known language. Nevertheless, the awareness of there being a Hebrew language, the bearer of God's own words in their original form, was never lost, and so the prerequisite was in place for the rebirth of Hebrew studies.[57]

---

[57] I want to thank Jan Bremmer, Carolien Hilhorst-Böink, Gerard Luttikhuizen, and Jacques van Ruiten for their careful responses to an earlier draft of this paper; Jan Smit for giving his opinion on a specific issue; and Annemieke ter Brugge for providing literature not available in Dutch libraries.

BIBLIOGRAPHY OF FLORENTINO GARCÍA MARTÍNEZ

BOOKS

As author or co-author:

1   Delcor, M., y F. García Martínez. *Introducción a la Literatura Esenia de Qumrán*. Academia Cristiana. Madrid: Cristiandad, 1982.
2   González Echegaray, J., J. Asurmendi, F. García Martínez, L. Alonso Schökel, J. Trebolle Barrera. *La Biblia en su entorno*. Vol. 1 of *Introducción al Estudio de la Biblia*. Estella: Verbo Divino, 1990.
3   García Martínez, F. *Qumran and Apocalyptic: Studies on the Aramaic Texts from Qumran*. STDJ 9. Leiden: Brill, 1992. (2d ed. 1994)
4   García Martínez, F. *Textos de Qumrán*. Estructuras y Procesos / Serie Religión. Madrid: Editorial Trotta, 1992. (2a, 3a, 4a ed. 1993; 5a ed. 2000)
5   García Martínez, F., y J. Trebolle Barrera. *Los Hombres de Qumrán: Literatura, estructura social y concepciones religiosas*. Estructuras y Procesos / Serie Religión. Madrid: Editorial Trotta, 1993. (2a ed. 1997)
6   García Martínez, F. *The Dead Sea Scrolls Translated: The Qumran Texts in English*. Leiden: Brill, 1994. (2d ed. 1996)
7   García Martínez, F., en A.S. van der Woude. *De Rollen van de Dode Zee: Ingeleid en in het Nederlands vertaald. Deel 1. Wetsliteratuur en Orderegels. Poëtische teksten*. Kampen: Kok 1994. (2e ed. 1998)
*   González Echegaray, J., J. Asurmendi, F. García Martínez, L. Alonso Schökel, e J. Trebolle Barrera. *La Bibbia nel suo contesto*. Introduzione allo studio della Bibbia 1. Brescia: Paideia, 1994. (Italian translation of 2)
*   González Echegaray, J., J. Asurmendi, F. García Martínez, L. Alonso Schökel, J.M. Sánchez Caro, J. Trebolle Barrera. *A Bíblia e seu contexto*. Introdução ao estudo da Bíblia 1. São Paulo: Ave Maria edições, 1994. (Portuguese translation of 2)
*   García Martínez, F. *Textos de Qumran: Edição fiel e completa dos Documentos do Mar Morto*. Petrópolis: Vozes, 1995. (Portuguese translation of 4)
*   García Martínez, F., and J. Trebolle Barrera. *The People of the Dead Sea Scrolls: Their Writings, Beliefs and Practices*. Leiden: Brill, 1995. (English translation of 5)
8   García Martínez, F., en A.S. van der Woude. *De Rollen van de Dode Zee: Ingeleid en in het Nederlands vertaald. Deel 2. Liturgische teksten, eschatologische teksten, exegetische literatuur, para-bijbelse literatuur en overige geschriften*. Kampen: Kok, 1995.
9   Qimron, E. *The Temple Scroll: A Critical Edition with Extensive Reconstructions*, with Bibliography by F. García Martínez. Judean Desert Studies. Beer Sheva: Ben-Gurion University of the Negev Press, 1996.
*   García Martínez, F. *The Dead Sea Scrolls Translated: The Qumran Texts in English*. 2d ed. Grand Rapids, Mich.: Eerdmans, 1996. (Revised edition of 6)
10 García Martínez, F., and D.W. Parry. *A Bibliography of the Finds in the Desert of Judah 1970–95: Arranged by Author with Citation and Subject Indexes*. STDJ 19. Leiden: Brill, 1996.
11 Aranda Pérez, G., F. García Martínez, y M. Pérez Fernández. *Literatura Judía Intertestamentaria*. Vol 9 of *Introducción al Estudio de la Biblia*. Estella: Verbo Divino, 1996. (2a ed. 2000)
*   García Martínez, F., e J. Trebolle Barrera. *Gli uomini di Qumran: Letteratura, struttura sociale e concezioni religiose*. Studi Biblici 113. Brescia: Paideia, 1996. (Italian translation of 5)
*   García Martínez, F. *Testi di Qumran*. Biblica 4. Edizione italiana a cura di

C. Martone. Brescia: Paideia, 1996. (Italian translation of 4)

* García Martínez, F., e J. Trebolle Barrera. *Os Homens de Qumran: Literatura, estrutura e concepções religiosas.* Petropolis: Vozes, 1996. (Portuguese translation of 5)

12 García Martínez, F., and E.J.C. Tigchelaar. *The Dead Sea Scrolls Study Edition. Volume One. 1Q1–4Q273.* Leiden: Brill, 1997.

13 García Martínez, F., E.J.C. Tigchelaar, and A.S. van der Woude. *Qumran Cave 11.II: 11Q2–18, 11Q20–31.* Discoveries in the Judaean Desert 23. Oxford: Clarendon Press, 1998.

14 García Martínez, F., and E.J.C. Tigchelaar. *4Q274–11Q31. The Dead Sea Scrolls Study Edition. Volume Two. 4Q274–11Q31.* Leiden: Brill, 1998.

* Aranda Pérez, G., F. García Martínez, e M. Pérez Fernández. *Letteratura giudaica intertestamentaria.* Introduzione allo studio della Bibbia 9. Brescia: Paideia, 1998. (Italian translation of 11)

* García Martínez, F., and E.J.C. Tigchelaar. *The Dead Sea Scrolls Study Edition.* 2 vols. Leiden: Brill, 2000. (revised edition of 12 and 14)

* Aranda Pérez, G., F. García Martínez, e M. Pérez Fernández. *Literatura Judaica Intertestamentária.* Vol. 9 of *Introdução ao Estudio da Bíblia.* São Paolo: Ave Maria, 2000. (Portuguese translation of 11)

15 García Martínez, F. *Qumranica Minora I. Qumran Origins and Apocalypticism.* Edited by E.J.C. Tigchelaar. STDJ 63. Leiden: Brill, 2007.

16 García Martínez, F. *Qumranica Minora II. Thematic Studies on the Dead Sea Scrolls.* Edited by E.J.C. Tigchelaar. STDJ 64. Leiden: Brill, 2007.

As editor or co-editor:

1 García Martínez, F., C.H.J. de Geus, en A.F.J. Klijn, red. *Profeten en Profetische Geschriften.* Kampen: Kok, [1987].

2 García Martínez, F., et É. Puech (sous la direction de). *Études Qumrâniennes: Mémorial Jean Carmignac.* Paris: Gabalda, 1988. (= *RevQ* 13/49–52)

3 García Martínez, F., ed. *The Texts of Qumran and the History of the Community: Proceedings of the Groningen Congress on the Dead Sea Scrolls (20–23 August 1989). Vol. I. Biblical Texts.* Paris: Gabalda, 1989. (= *RevQ* 14/54)

4 García Martínez, F., ed. *The Texts of Qumran and the History of the Community: Proceedings of the Groningen Congress on the Dead Sea Scrolls (20–23 August 1989). Vol. II. Non-Biblical Texts.* Paris: Gabalda, 1990. (= *RevQ* 14/55)

5 García Martínez, F., ed. *The Texts of Qumran and the History of the Community: Proceedings of the Groningen Congress on the Dead Sea Scrolls (20–23 August 1989). Vol. III. The History of the Community.* Paris: Gabalda, 1990. (= *RevQ* 14/56)

6 Puech, É., et F. García Martínez (sous la direction de). *Mémorial Jean Starcky. Textes et études qumrâniens I.* Paris: Gabalda, 1991. (= *RevQ* 15/57–58)

7 Puech, E., et F. García Martínez (sous la direction de). *Mémorial Jean Starcky. Textes et études qumrâniens II.* Paris: Gabalda, 1992. (= *RevQ* 15/59)

8 Bremmer, J.N., and F. García Martínez, eds. *Sacred History and Sacred Texts in Early Judaism: A Symposium in Honour of A. S. van der Woude.* Kampen: Kok Pharos, 1992.

9 García Martínez, F., A. Hilhorst, and C.J. Labuschagne, eds. *The Scriptures and the Scrolls: Studies in Honour of A.S. van der Woude on the Occasion of his 65th Birthday.* VTSup 49. Leiden: Brill, 1992.

10 García Martínez, F., A. Hilhorst, J.T.A.G.M. van Ruiten, and A.S. van der Woude, eds., *Studies in Deuteronomy. In Honour of C.J. Labuschagne on the Occasion of his 65th Birthday.* VTSup 53. Leiden: Brill, 1994.

11 Brooke, G.J., ed. with F. García Martínez, *New Qumran Texts and Studies: Proceedings of the First Meeting of the International Organization for Qumran Studies, Paris 1992.* STDJ 15. Leiden: Brill, 1994.

12 García Martínez, F., et É. Puech (sous la direction de). *Hommage à Jozef T. Milik.* Paris: Gabalda, 1996. (= *RevQ* 17/65–68)
13 Bernstein, M., F. García Martínez, and J. Kampen, eds. *Legal Texts and Legal Issues: Proceedings of the Second Meeting of the International Organization for Qumran Studies, Cambridge 1995. Published in Honour of Joseph M. Baumgarten.* STDJ 23. Leiden: Brill, 1997.
14 García Martínez, F., ed. *Los Manuscritos de Qumrán.* Reseña Bíblica 19. Estella: Verbo Divino, 1998.
15 García Martínez, F., and E. Noort, eds. *Perspectives in the Study of the Old Testament and Early Judaism: A Symposium in Honour of Adam S. van der Woude on the Occasion of His 70th Birthday.* VTSup 73. Leiden: Brill, 1998.
16 García Martínez, F., and G.P. Luttikhuizen, eds. *Interpretations of the Flood.* TBN 1. Leiden: Brill, 1998.
17 Schiffman, L.H., and J.C. VanderKam, eds. in chief; G.J. Brooke, J.J. Collins, F. García Martínez, E.M. Schuller, E. Tov and E. Ulrich, eds. *Encyclopedia of the Dead Sea Scrolls.* 2 vols. New York: Oxford University Press, 2000.
18 Falk, D.K., F. García Martínez, and E.M. Schuller, eds. *Sapiential, Liturgical and Poetical Texts from Qumran. Proceedings of the Third Meeting of the International Organization for Qumran Studies, Oslo 1998. Published in Memory of Maurice Baillet.* STDJ 35. Leiden: Brill, 2000.
19 García Martínez, F. ed. *Wisdom and Apocalypticism in the Dead Sea Scrolls and in the Biblical Tradition.* BETL 168. Leuven: Peeters, 2003.
20 García Martínez, F., and G.P. Luttikhuizen, eds. *Jerusalem, Alexandria, Rome: Studies in Ancient Cultural Interaction in Honour of A. Hilhorst.* JSJSup 82. Leiden: Brill, 2003.
21 García Martínez, F., en E. Tigchelaar, red. *Fragmenten uit de woestijn: De Dode-Zeerollen opnieuw bekeken.* Zoetermeer: Meinema, 2003.
23 García Martínez, F., and M. Vervenne, eds. *Interpreting Translation: Studies on the LXX and Ezekiel in Honour of Johann Lust.* BETL 192. Leuven: Peeters, 2005.
24 García Martínez, F., A. Steudel, and E. Tigchelaar, eds. *From 4QMMT to Resurrection: Mélanges qumraniens en hommage à Émile Puech.* STDJ 61. Leiden: Brill, 2006.

ARTICLES

as author or co-author:

1 García Martínez, F. "El mundo de los Apócrifos del Antiguo Testamento." *Tierra Santa* 51 (1976): 246–51.
2 García Martínez, F. "Penitencia de Adán y Eva." *Tierra Santa* 51 (1976): 252–57.
3 García Martínez, F. "El mundo de los Apócrifos del Antiguo Testamento. 2: Enoc." *Tierra Santa* 51 (1976): 276–83.
4 García Martínez, F. "El mundo de los Apócrifos del Antiguo Testamento. 3: Abraham." *Tierra Santa* 52 (1977): 4–11.
5 García Martínez. F. "Nuevas lecturas de 11QtgJob." *Sefarad* 36 (1976): 241–49.
6 García Martínez, F. "El Rollo del Templo. Traducción y notas." *EstBíb* 36 (1977): 247–92.
7 García Martínez, F. "El mundo de los Apócrifos del Antiguo Testamento. 4: Los 12 Patriarcas (1–2)." *Tierra Santa* 52 (1977): 58–63, 99–103.
8 García Martínez, F. "El mundo de los Apócrifos del Antiguo Testamento. 5: José y Asenet." *Tierra Santa* 52 (1977): 147–53.
9 García Martínez, F. "El mundo de los Apócrifos del Antiguo Testamento. 6: Moisés." *Tierra Santa* 52 (1977): 168–74.
10 García Martínez, F. "El mundo de los Apócrifos del Antiguo Testamento. 7: Ajicar (1–2)." *Tierra Santa* 52 (1977): 211–16, 266–73.

11   García Martínez, F. "El mundo de los Apócrifos del Antiguo Testamento. 8: Salomón." *Tierra Santa* 52 (1977): 298–305.

12   García Martínez, F. "El mundo de los Apócrifos del Antiguo Testamento. 9: Isaías y Jeremías." *Tierra Santa* 52 (1977): 356–61.

13   Bagatti, B., y F. García Martínez. "Presentación." (por García Martínez). Pages 4–5 in "La Vida de Jesús en los Apócrifos del Nuevo Testamento". *Tierra Santa* 53 (1978): 4–10.

14   Bagatti, B., y F. García Martínez. "La Vida de Jesús en los Apócrifos del Nuevo Testamento. 1: Apocrifos de la Pasión." *Tierra Santa* 53 (1978): 53–63.

15   Bagatti, B., y F. García Martínez. "La Vida de Jesús en los Apócrifos del Nuevo Testamento. 2: La Resurrección." *Tierra Santa* 53 (1978): 118–29.

16   Bagatti, B., y F. García Martínez. "La Vida de Jesús en los Apócrifos del Nuevo Testamento. 3: La Vida Pública según el Evangelio de Tomás." *Tierra Santa* 53 (1978): 154–66.

17   Bagatti, B., y F. García Martínez. "La Vida de Jesús en los Apócrifos del Nuevo Testamento. Observaciones sobre el pensamiento del Evangelio de Tomás." *Tierra Santa* 53 (1978): 241–46.

18   Bagatti, B., y F. García Martínez. "La Vida de Jesús en los Apócrifos del Nuevo Testamento. 4: La Asunción de Maria según el Pseudo Melitón." *Tierra Santa* 53 (1978): 279–88.

19   Bagatti, B., y F. García Martínez. "La Vida de Jesús en los Apócrifos del Nuevo Testamento. 5: La Infancia según el Evangelio del Pseudo Tomás." *Tierra Santa* 53 (1978): 316–24.

20   Bagatti, B., y F. García Martínez. "La Vida de Jesús en los Apócrifos del Nuevo Testamento. 6: La Natividad según el Protoevangelio de Santiago." *Tierra Santa* 53 (1978): 358–67.

21   Puech, É., et F. García Martínez. "Remarques sur la colonne XXXVIII de 11 Q tg Job." *RevQ* 9/35 (1978): 401–7.

22   García Martínez, F. "El Pesher: Interpretación profética de la Escritura." *Salmanticensis* 26 (1979): 125–39.

23   García Martínez, F. "4QpNah y la Crucifixión. Nueva hipótesis de reconstrucción de 4Q169 3–4 i, 4–8." *EstBíb* 38 (1979–1981): 221–35.

24   García Martínez, F. "4Q Or Nab. Nueva síntesis." *Sefarad* 40 (1980): 5–25.

25   García Martínez, F. "4Q Mes. Aram. y el Libro de Noé." *Miscelánea conmemorativa del aniversario del Instituto Español Bíblico y Arqueológico (Casa de Santiago) de Jerusalén.* Edición preparada por R. Aguirre Monasterio y F. García Lopez. *Escritos de Biblia y Oriente, Salmanticensis* 28 (1981): 195–232.

26   García Martínez, F. "Bibliographie." *RevQ* 11/41 (1982): 119–59.

27   García Martínez, F. "Salmos Apócrifos en Qumran." *EstBíb* 40 (1982): 197–220.

28   García Martínez, F. "Bibliographie." *RevQ* 11/42 (1983): 295–320.

29   García Martínez, F. "4Q 246: ¿Tipo del Anticristo o Libertador escatológico?" Pages 229–44 in *El Misterio de la Palabra: Homenaje a profesor L. Alonso Schökel.* Editan V. Collado y E. Zurro. Madrid: Cristiandad, 1983.

30   García Martínez, F. "Notas al margen de 4QpsDaniel Arameo." *Aula Orientalis* 1 (1983): 193–208.

31   García Martínez, F. "Bibliographie." *RevQ* 11/43 (1983): 461–78.

32   García Martínez, F. "Las Tablas Celestes en el Libro de los Jubileos." Pages 333–49 in *Palabra y Vida: Homenaje a José Alonso Díaz en su 70 cumpleaños.* Editan A. Vargas-Machuca y G. Ruiz. Madrid: Ediciones Universidad Pontificia Comillas, 1984.

33   García Martínez, F. "El Rollo del Templo y la halaká sectaria." Pages 611–22 in *Simposio Bíblico Español (Salamanca, 1982).* Editado por N. Fernández Marcos, J. Trebolle, y J. Vallina. Madrid: Editorial de la Universidad Complutense, 1984.

34   García Martínez, F. "La Novedad de Qumrán." Pages 45–69 in *De Abrahán a*

Maimónides. II. Para entender a los Judíos. Bajo la dirección de J. Peláez del Rosal. Cuadernos de Cultura Hebrea 2. Córdoba: El Almendro, 1984.

35 García Martínez, F. "4 Q 'Amram B I,14: ¿ Melki-reša' o Melki-ṣedeq?" *RevQ* 12/45 (1985): 111–14.

36 García Martínez, F. "Bibliographie." *RevQ* 12/45 (1985): 129–60.

37 García Martínez, F. "¿Judas Macabeo, Sacerdote Impío? Notas al margen de 1Q pHab viii, 8–13." Pages 169–81 in *Mélanges bibliques et orientaux en l'honneur de M. Mathias Delcor.* Sous la direction de A. Caquot, S. Legasse, et M. Tardieu. AOAT 215. Kevelaer: Butzon & Bercker, 1985.

38 García Martínez, F. "Orígenes apocalípticos del movimiento esenio y orígenes de la secta qumránica." *Communio* 18 (1985): 353–68.

39 García Martínez, F. "Bibliographie." *RevQ* 12/46 (1986): 293–315.

40 García Martínez, F. "La 'Nueva Jerusalén' y el Templo Futuro de los MSS. de Qumrán." Pages 563–90 in *Salvación en la Palabra: Targum—Derash—Berith. En Memoria del profesor A. Díez Macho.* Edición preparada por D. Muñoz León. Madrid: Cristiandad, 1986.

41 García Martínez, F. "El Rollo del Templo *(11 Q Temple).* Bibliografía Sistemática." *RevQ* 12/47 (1986): 425–40.

42 García Martínez, F. "Bibliographie." *RevQ* 12/47 (1986): 455–80.

43 García Martínez, F. "Encore l'Apocalyptique." *JSJ* 17 (1986): 224–32.

44 García Martínez, F. "Escatologización de los Escritos proféticos en Qumrán." *EstBíb* 44 (1986): 101–16.

45 García Martínez, F. "Profeet en profetie in de geschriften van Qumran." Pages 119–32 in *Profeten en Profetische Geschriften.* Onder redaktie van F. García Martínez, C.H.J. de Geus, en A.F.J. Klijn. Kampen: Kok, 1986.

46 García Martínez, F. "Bibliografie van prof. dr. A.S. van der Woude." Pages 167–73 in *Profeet en Profetische Geschriften.* Onder redaktie van F. García Martínez, C.H.J. de Geus, en A.F.J. Klijn. Kampen: Kok, 1986.

47 García Martínez, F. "Les traditions apocalyptiques à Qumrân." Pages 201–35 in *Apocalypses et Voyages dans l'Au-delà. Études annexes de la Bible de Jérusalem.* C. Kappler et collaborateurs. Paris: Le Cerf, 1987.

48 García Martínez, F. "Le Livre d'Isaïe à Qumrân. Les Textes, l'influence." *Le Monde de la Bible* 49 (1987): 43–44.

49 García Martínez, F. "Estudios Qumránicos 1975–1985: Panorama crítico (I)." *EstBíb* 45 (1987): 125–205.

50 García Martínez, F. "Estudios Qumránicos 1975–1985: Panorama crítico (II)." *EstBíb* 45 (1987): 361–402.

51 García Martínez, F. "Essénisme Qumrânien: Origines, caractéristiques, héritage." Pages 37–57 in *Movimenti e correnti culturali nel Giudaismo. Atti del congresso tenuto a S. Miniato dal 12 al 15 novembre 1984.* A cura di B. Chiesa. Rome: Carducci, 1987.

52 García Martínez, F. "Orígenes del movimiento esenio y orígenes qumránicos: Pistas para una solución." Pages 527–56 in *II Simposio Bíblico Español (Córdoba, 1985).* Edición preparada por V. Collado Bertomeu y V. Villar Hueso. Valencia: Fundación Bíblica Española, 1987.

53 García Martínez, F. "La Apocalíptica y Qumrán." Pages 603–13 in *II Simposio Bíblico Español (Córdoba, 1985).* Edición preparada por V. Collado Bertomeu y V. Villar Hueso. Valencia-Córdoba: Fundación Bíblica Española, 1987.

54 García Martínez, F. "Les limites de la communauté: pureté et impureté à Qumrân et dans le Nouveau Testament." Pages 111–22 in *Text and Testimony. Essays on New Testament and Apocryphal Literature in Honour of A.F.J. Klijn.* Edited by T. Baarda, A. Hilhorst, G.P. Luttikhuizen, and A.S. van der Woude. Kampen: Kok, 1988.

55 García Martínez, F. "Bibliographie de M. l'Abbé Jean Carmignac." Pages 9–20 in *Mémorial Jean Carmignac.* Sous la direction de F. García Martínez et É. Puech. Paris: Gabalda, 1988. (= *RevQ* 13/49–52)

56   García Martínez, F. "L'interprétation de la Torah d'Ezéchiel dans les MSS. de Qumrân." Pages 441–52 in *Mémorial Jean Carmignac*. Sous la direction de F. García Martínez et É. Puech. Paris: Gabalda, 1988. (= *RevQ* 13/49–52)

57   García Martínez, F. "Qumran Origins and Early History: A Groningen Hypothesis." *Folia Orientalia* 25 (1988): 113–36.

58   García Martínez, F. "Estudios Qumránicos 1975–1985: Panorama crítico (III)." *EstBíb* 46 (1988): 325–74.

59   García Martínez, F. "Estudios Qumránicos 1975–1985: Panorama crítico (IV)." *EstBíb* 46 (1988): 527–48.

60   García Martínez, F. "Il problema della purità: la soluzione qumranica." Pages 169–91 in *Israele alla ricerca di identità tra il III sec. a.C. e il I sec. d.C. Atti del V Convegno di studi veterotestamentari*. A cura di G.L. Prato. Bologna: Dehoniane, 1989. (= *Ricerche Storico Bibliche* 1)

61   García Martínez, F., and E.J.C. Tigchelaar. "The *Books of Enoch (1 Enoch)* and the Aramaic Fragments from Qumran." *RevQ* 14/53 (1989): 131–46.

62   García Martínez, F., and E.J.C. Tigchelaar. "*1 Enoch* and the Figure of Enoch: A Bibliography of Studies 1970–1988." *RevQ* 14/53 (1989): 149–74.

63   García Martínez, F. "Lista de MSS procedentes de Qumrán." *Henoch* 11 (1989): 149–232.

64   García Martínez, F. "Estudios Qumránicos 1975–1985: Panorama crítico (V)." *EstBíb* 47 (1989): 93–118.

65   García Martínez, F. "Estudios Qumránicos 1975–1985: Panorama crítico (VI)." *EstBíb* 47 (1989): 225–67.

66   García Martínez, F. "La represión fraterna en Qumrân y Mt 18,15–17." *Filología Neotestamentaria* 2 (1989): 23–40.

67   García Martínez, F. "Significado de los Manuscritos de Qumrán para el conocimiento de Jesucristo y del Cristianismo." *Communio* 22 (1989): 331–42.

68   García Martínez, F. "Qumran Origins and Early History: A Groningen Hypothesis." *Sprawozdania z posiedzeń komisji naukowych: Polska Akademia Nauk.* Tom 31/1 (1989): 79–82.

69   García Martínez, F., and A.S. van der Woude. "A 'Groningen' Hypothesis of Qumran Origins and Early History." Pages 521–41 in *The Texts of Qumran and the History of the Community: Proceedings of the Groningen Congress on the Dead Sea Scrolls (20–23 August 1989). Vol. III. The History of the Community.* Edited by F. García Martínez. Paris: Gabalda, 1990. (= *RevQ* 14/56)

70   Asurmendi J., y F. García Martínez. "Historia e instituciones del pueblo bíblico: Introducción." Pages 119–27 in *Introducción al Estudio de la Biblia. La Biblia en su entorno.* Vol. 1. Estella: Verbo Divino, 1990.

71   García Martínez, F. "Desde Alejandro Magno hasta la segunda revuelta judía." Pages 241–365 in *Introducción al Estudio de la Biblia. La Biblia en su entorno.* Vol. 1. Estella: Verbo Divino, 1990.

72   García Martínez, F. "Entorno literario del Nuevo Testamento." Pages 391–410 in *Introducción al Estudio de la Biblia. La Biblia en su entorno.* Vol. 1. Estella: Verbo Divino, 1990.

73   García Martínez, F. "Tradiciones apocalípticas en Qumrán: 4QSecond Ezekiel." Pages 303–21 in *Biblische und Judaistische Studien: Festschrift für Paolo Sacchi.* Herausgegeben von A. Vivian. Judentum und Umwelt 29. Frankfurt: P. Lang, 1990.

74   García Martínez, F. "Los MSS de Qumrán y el Cristianismo." Pages 239–50 in *Jesucristo Hoy: Cursos de verano en El Escorial 1989.* Madrid: Universidad Complutense, 1990.

75   García Martínez, F. "Traditions communes dans le *IV Esdras* et dans les MSS de Qumrân." Pages 287–301 in *Mémorial Jean Starcky. Textes et études qumrâniens I.* Sous la direction de É. Puech et F. García Martínez. Paris: Gabalda, 1991. (= *RevQ* 15/57–58)

76 García Martínez, F. "Sources et rédaction du *Rouleau du Temple*." *Henoch* 13 (1991): 219–32.

77 García Martínez, F. "Algunas aportaciones al conocimiento del Judaísmo del Segundo Templo de los textos no-bíblicos de Qumrán recientemente publicados." Pages 161–68 in *III Simposio Bíblico Español*. Edición preparada por J. Carreira das Neves, V. Collado Bertomeu, y V. Vilar Hueso. Valencia: Fundación Bíblica Española, 1991.

78 García Martínez, F. "4QSecond Ezekiel y las tradiciones apocalípticas." Pages 477–88 in *III Simposio Bíblico Español*. Edición preparada por J. Carreira das Neves, V. Collado Bertomeu, y V. Vilar Hueso. Valencia: Fundación Bíblica Española, 1991.

79 García Martínez, F. "Resultados y Tendencias: Congreso internacional sobre los Manuscritos del Mar Muerto." *Sefarad* 51 (1991): 417–35.

80 García Martínez, F. "Nuevos textos no bíblicos procedentes de Qumrán." *EstBíb* 49 (1991): 97–134.

81 García Martínez, F. "¿La apocalíptica judía como matriz de la teología cristiana?" Pages 177–99 in *Orígenes del cristianismo. Antecedentes y primeros pasos*. Edición preparada por A. Piñero. Córdoba: El Almendro—Madrid: Universidad Complutense, 1991.

82 García Martínez, F. "Las fronteras de «lo bíblico»." *Scripta Theologica* 23 (1991): 759–84.

83 García Martínez, F. "Damascus Document: A Bibliography of Studies 1970–1989." Pages 63–83 in *The Damascus Document Reconsidered*. Edited by Magen Broshi. Jerusalem: Israel Exploration Society, 1992.

84 García Martínez, F. "Los Manuscritos de Qumrán." *El Ciervo* 41 (1992): 6–14.

85 García Martínez, F. "The Last Surviving Columns of *11QNJ*." Pages 178–92, pl. 3–9 in *The Scriptures and the Scrolls: Studies in Honour of A.S. van der Woude on the Occasion of his 65th Birthday*. Edited by F. García Martínez, A. Hilhorst, and C.J. Labuschagne. VTSup 49. Leiden: Brill, 1992.

86 García Martínez, F. "A Bibliography of A.S. van der Woude." Pages 228–68 in *The Scriptures and the Scrolls: Studies in Honour of A.S. van der Woude on the Occasion of his 65th Birthday*. Edited by F. García Martínez, A. Hilhorst, and C.J. Labuschagne. VTSup 49. Leiden: Brill, 1992.

87 García Martínez, F. "Texts from Qumran Cave 11." Pages 18–26 in *The Dead Sea Scrolls. Forty Years of Research*. Edited by D. Dimant and U. Rappaport. STDJ 10. Leiden: Brill, 1992.

88 García Martínez, F. "11QTemple^b: A Preliminary Publication." Pages 363–91, pl. 667–673 in *The Madrid Qumran Congress. Proceedings of the International Congress on the Dead Sea Scrolls, Madrid 18–21 March, 1991. Vol. 2*. Edited by J. Trebolle Barrera and L. Vegas Montaner. STDJ 11. Leiden: Brill; Madrid: Editorial Complutense, 1992.

89 García Martínez, F. "The Temple Scroll: A Systematic Bibliography 1985–1991." Pages 393–403 in *The Madrid Qumran Congress: Proceedings of the International Congress on the Dead Sea Scrolls, Madrid, 18–21 March 1991. Vol. 2*. Edited by J. Trebolle Barrera and L. Vegas Montaner. STDJ 11. Leiden: Brill; Madrid: Editorial Complutense, 1992.

90 García Martínez, F. "Le *IV Esdras* et les MSS de Qumrân." Pages 81–90 in *RASHI 1040–1990. Hommage à Ephraïm E. Urbach. Congrès européen des Études juives*. Textes édités par G. Sed-Rajna. Patrimoines. Judaïsme. Paris: Le Cerf, 1993.

91 García Martínez, F. "Notas al margen de *The Dead Sea Scrolls Uncovered*." *RevQ* 16/61 (1993): 123–50.

92 García Martínez, F. "Los Mesías de Qumrán. Problemas de un traductor." *Sefarad* 53 (1993): 345–60.

93 García Martínez, F. "Nuevos Textos Mesiánicos de Qumrán y el Mesías del Nuevo Testamento." *Communio* 26 (1993): 3–31.

94 García Martínez, F. "Los hombres del Mar Muerto." *El Ciervo* 42 (1993): 5–11.

95 García Martínez, F. "Messianische Erwartungen in den Qumranschriften." *Jahrbuch für Biblische Theologie* 8 (1993): 171–208.

96 García Martínez, F. "Dos notas sobre *4QMMT.*" *RevQ* 16/62 (1993): 293–97.

97 García Martínez, F. "De la découverte à la publication." *Le Monde de la Bible* 86 (1994): 6–8.

98 García Martínez, F. "Une secte dans le Judaïsme de l'époque." *Le Monde de la Bible* 86 (1994): 24–27.

99 García Martínez, F. "Les manuscrits du Désert de Juda et le Deutéronome." Pages 63–82 in *Studies in Deuteronomy: In Honour of C.J. Labuschagne on the Occasion of his 65th Birthday.* Edited by F. García Martínez, et al. VTSup 53. Leiden: Brill, 1994.

100 García Martínez, F. "Los Manuscritos del Mar Muerto: balance de hallazgos y de cuarenta años de estudios." Pages 15–33 in *Los Manuscritos del Mar Muerto: balance de hallazgos y de cuarenta años de estudios.* Edición preparada por A. Piñero y D. Fernández-Galiano. En torno al Nuevo Testamento 18. Córdoba: El Almendro, 1994.

101 García Martínez, F. "Los Manuscritos del Mar Muerto y el mesianismo cristiano." Pages 189–206 in *Los Manuscritos del Mar Muerto: balance de hallazgos y de cuarenta años de estudios.* Edición preparada por A. Piñero y D. Fernández-Galiano. En torno al Nuevo Testamento 18. Córdoba: El Almendro, 1994.

102 García Martínez, F. "¿Fin del Mundo o Transformación de la Historia? La Apocalíptica Intertestamentaria," *Communio* 27 (1994): 3–33.

103 García Martínez, F. "Los Himnos de Qumrán y Los Salmos bíblicos: Convergencias y Divergencias." *Reseña Bíblica* 6 (1995): 53–62.

104 García Martínez, F. "De handschriften van de Dode Zee." *Hermeneus* 67 (1995): 139–50.

105 García Martínez, F. "Les manuscrits de Qumrân et les "frontières" de la Bible." Pages 63–76 in *Recueil de travaux de l'association des études du Proche-Orient Ancien-Collected Papers of the Society for Near Eastern Studies.* Vol. 4. Faculté de théologie. Montréal: Université de Montréal, 1995.

106 García Martínez, F. "A Classified Bibliography." Pages 95–121 in *The Temple Scroll: A Critical Edition with Extensive Reconstructions.* Edited by E. Qimron. With Bibliography by F. García Martínez. Judean Desert Studies. Beer Sheva: Ben-Gurion University of the Negev Press, 1996.

107 García Martínez, F. "Nouveaux livres sur les manuscrits de la Mer Morte." *JSJ* 27 (1996): 46–74.

108 García Martínez, F. "Le Document de Damas à Qumrân." *Le Monde de la Bible* 98 (1996): 33.

109 García Martínez, F. "4QMMT in a Qumran Context." Pages 15–27 in *Reading 4QMMT: New Perspectives on Qumran Law and History.* Edited by J. Kampen and M.J. Bernstein. SBLSymS 2. Atlanta: Scholars Press, 1996.

110 García Martínez, F. "Two Messianic Figures in the Qumran Texts." Pages 14–40 in *Current Research and Technological Developments on the Dead Sea Scrolls: Conference on the Texts from the Judean Desert, Jerusalem, 30 April 1995.* Edited by D.W. Parry and S.D. Ricks. STDJ 20. Leiden: Brill, 1996.

111 García Martínez, F. "Calendarios en Qumrán (I)." *EstBíb* 54 (1996): 327–48.

112 García Martínez, F. "Bibliographie qumrânienne de Józef Tadeusz Milik." Pages 11–20 in *Hommage à Józef T. Milik.* Sous la direction de F. García Martínez et É. Puech. Paris: Gabalda, 1996. (= *RevQ* 17/65–68)

113 García Martínez, F., and E.J.C. Tigchelaar. "Psalms Manuscripts from Qumran Cave 11: a Preliminary Edition." Pages 73–107 in *Hommage à Józef T. Milik.* Sous la direction de F. García Martínez et E. Puech. Paris: Gabalda, 1996. (= *RevQ* 17/65–68)

114   García Martínez, F. "Calendarios en Qumrán (II)." *EstBíb* 54 (1996): 523–52.

115   García Martínez, F. "Regla de la Comunidad." Pages 134–45 in *The Dead Sea Scrolls: Rule of the Community*. Edited by J.H. Charlesworth. Photographic Multilanguage Edition. Philadelphia: American Interfaith Institute, 1996.

116   García Martínez, F. "Los manuscritos del Mar Muerto: Qumrán entre el Antiguo y el Nuevo Testamento." Pages 33–52 in *Actas de las IX Jornadas Bíblicas 1996*. Edición a cargo de Jesús Campos Santiago. Zamora: ABE, 1996.

117   García Martínez, F. "A Bibliography of Joseph M. Baumgarten." Pages xix–xxv in *Legal Texts and Legal Issues: Proceedings of the Second Meeting of the International Organization for Qumran Studies, Cambridge 1995. Published in Honour of Joseph M. Baumgarten*. Edited by M. Bernstein, F. García Martínez, and J. Kampen. STDJ 23. Leiden: Brill, 1997.

118   García Martínez, F. "Messianic Hopes in the Qumran Writings." Pages 115–75 in *LDS Perspective on the Dead Sea Scrolls*. Edited by D.W. Parry and D.M. Pike. Provo, Utah: FARMS, 1997.

119   García Martínez, F. "Qumran: le ultime scoperte e lo stato delle pubblicazioni." Pages 11–47 in *Qumran e le origini cristiane: Atti del VI Convegno di studi neotestamentari (L'Aquila, 14–17 settembre 1995)*. A cura di R. Penna. Bologna: Dehoniane, 1997. (= *Ricerche storico bibliche* 9/2)

120   García Martínez, F. "Les grandes batailles de Qumrân." *Le Monde de la Bible* 107 (1997): 5–10.

121   García Martínez, F. "The Heavenly Tablets in the Book of Jubilees." Pages 243–60 in *Studies in the Book of Jubilees*. Edited by M. Albani, J. Frey, and A. Lange. TSAJ 65. Tübingen: Mohr Siebeck, 1997.

122   García Martínez, F. "Interés de los manuscritos del Mar Muerto para judíos y cristianos." *El Olivo* 21/46 (1997): 23–44.

123   García Martínez, F. "Interpretación de la Biblia en Qumrán." *Fortunatae: Revista Canaria de Filología, Cultura y Humanidades Clásicas* 9 (1997): 261–86.

124   García Martínez, F. "Apocalypticism in the Dead Sea Scrolls." Pages 162–92 in *The Origins of Apocalypticism in Judaism and Christianity*. Vol. 1 of *The Encyclopedia of Apocalypticism*. Edited by J.J. Collins. New York: Continuum, 1998.

125   García Martínez, F. "Cincuenta Años de polémicas." *Reseña Bíblica* 19 (1998): 5–14.

126   García Martínez, F. "Una Biblioteca de literatura religiosa." *Reseña Bíblica* 19 (1998): 15–28.

127   García Martínez, F. "Los manuscritos de Qumrán y el Judaísmo." *Reseña Bíblica* 19 (1998): 39–46.

128   García Martínez, F. "¿El Nuevo Testamento en Qumrán?" *Reseña Bíblica* 19 (1998): 59–63.

129   García Martínez, F., and E.J.C. Tigchelaar. "Bibliography of the Dead Sea Scrolls." *RevQ* 18/71 (1998): 459–90.

130   García Martínez, F. "Los esenios de Qumrán y su relación con el cristianismo." *Vida Nueva* 2.156 (1998): 23–29.

131   García Martínez, F. "Apocalyptiek in de Dode Zee rollen." Pages 68–103 in *Visioenen aangaande het einde: Apocalyptische geschriften en bewegingen door de eeuwen heen*. Onder redactie van J.W. van Henten en O. Mellink. Zoetermeer: Meinema, 1998.

132   García Martínez, F. "The History of the Qumran Community in the Light of Recently Available Texts." Pages 194–216 in *Qumran Between the Old and New Testaments*. Edited by F.H. Cryer and T.L. Thompson. JSOTSup 290. Sheffield: Sheffield Academic Press, 1998.

133   García Martínez, F., and E.J.C. Tigchelaar. "Bibliography of the Dead Sea Scrolls." *RevQ* 18/72 (1998): 605–39.

134   García Martínez, F. "New Perspectives on the Study of the Dead Sea Scrolls." Pages 230–48 in *Perspectives in the Study of the Old Testament and Early Judaism: A*

Symposium in Honour of Adam S. van der Woude on the Occasion of His 70th Birthday.
Edited by F. García Martínez and E. Noort. VTSup 73. Leiden: Brill, 1998.

135　García Martínez, F. "Biblical Interpretation in Qumran." Pages 40–42 in
International Catholic Bible Commentary. Edited by W. Farmer. Collegeville, Minn.:
Liturgical Press, 1998.

136　García Martínez, F. "More Fragments of 11QNJ." Pages 186–98 in *The Provo
International Conference on the Dead Sea Scrolls: Technological Innovations, New Texts, and
Reformulated Issues.* Edited by D.W. Parry and E. Ulrich. STDJ 30. Leiden: Brill,
1999.

137　García Martínez, F. "Interpretations of the Flood in the Dead Sea Scrolls."
Pages 86–108 in *Interpretations of the Flood in Jewish and Christian Tradition.* Edited
by F. García Martínez and G.P. Luttikhuizen. TBN 1. Leiden: Brill, 1998.

138　García Martínez, F. "Ben Sira: A Bibliography of Studies, 1965–1997." Pages
233–52 in *Masada VI. Yigael Yadin Excavations 1963–1965: Final Reports.* Jerusalem:
Israel Exploration Society, 1999.

139　García Martínez, F. "Debates recientes en torno a los manuscritos de Qumrán."
Pages 55–79 in *Paganos, judíos y cristianos en los textos de Qumrán.* Coordinador
J. Trebolle Barrera. Biblioteca de Ciencias Bíblicas y Orientales 5. Madrid:
Trotta, 1999.

140　García Martínez, F. "Aplicación de técnicas actuales al análisis de los manuscritos
de Qumrán." Pages 93–108 in *Paganos, judíos y cristianos en los textos de Qumrán.*
Coordinador J. Trebolle Barrera. Biblioteca de Ciencias Bíblicas y Orientales 5.
Madrid: Trotta, 1999.

141　García Martínez, F. "Literatura jurídico-religiosa de Qumrán." Pages 155–79 in
Paganos, judíos y cristianos en los textos de Qumrán. Coordinador J. Trebolle Barrera.
Biblioteca de Ciencias Bíblicas y Orientales 5. Madrid: Trotta, 1999.

142　García Martínez, F. "The Temple Scroll and the New Jerusalem." Pages 431–60
in *The Dead Sea Scrolls after Fifty years: A Comprehensive Assessment. Vol. 2.* Edited by
P. W. Flint and J.C. VanderKam. Leiden: Brill, 1999.

143　García Martínez, F. "Man and Woman: Halakhah Based upon Eden in the
Dead Sea Scrolls." Pages 95–115 in *Paradise Interpreted: Representations of Biblical
Paradise in Judaism and Christianity.* Edited by G. P. Luttikhuizen. TBN 2. Leiden:
Brill, 1999.

144　García Martínez, F. "Priestly Functions in a Community without Temple."
Pages 303–19 in *Gemeinde ohne Tempel: Community without Temple. Zur Substituierung
und Transformation des Jerusalemer Tempels und seines Kults im Alten Testament, antiken
Judentum und frühen Christentum.* Herausgegeben von B. Ego, A. Lange, und
P. Pilhofer. WUNT 118. Tübingen: Mohr Siebeck, 1999.

145　García Martínez, F., and J. Trebolle Barrera. "Qumran Scholarship: A European
Perspective." Pages 129–41 in *The Dead Sea Scrolls at Fifty: Proceedings of the 1997
Society of Biblical Literature Qumran Section Meetings.* Edited by R.A. Kugler and E.M.
Schuller. SBLEJL 15. Atlanta: Scholars Press, 1999.

146　García Martínez, F. "Fifty Years of Research on the Dead Sea Scrolls and Its
Impact on Jewish Studies." Pages 235–51 in *Biblical, Rabbinical, and Medieval Studies.*
Vol. 1 of *Jewish Studies at the Turn of the Twentieth Century: Proceedings of the 6th EAJS
Congress, Toledo, July 1998.* Edited by J. Targarona Borrás and A. Sáenz-Badillos.
Leiden: Brill, 1999.

147　García Martínez, F. "More Fragments of 11QNJ". Pages 186–198 in *The Provo
International Conference on the Dead Sea Scrolls. Technological Innovations, New Texts, and
Reformulated Issues.* Edited by D.W. Parry and E.C. Ulrich. STDJ 30. Leiden:
Brill, 1999.

148　García Martínez, F. "Il Rotolo del Tempio e la Nuova Gerusalemme: Quanti
esemplari possediamo?" *Henoch* 21 (1999): 253–83.

149　García Martínez, F. "Las tradiciones sobre Melquisedec en los manuscritos de
Qumrán." *Biblica* 81 (2000): 70–80.

150 García Martínez, F. "Les grandes batailles de Qumrân." Pages 119–30 in *Aux origines du Christianisme*. Textes présentés par P. Geoltrain. Folio/Histoire. Paris: Gallimard, 2000.

151 García Martínez, F. "New Jerusalem." Pages 606–10 in *Encyclopedia of the Dead Sea Scrolls*. Edited by L.H. Schiffman and J.C. VanderKam. New York: Oxford University Press, 2000.

152 García Martínez, F. "Temple Scroll." Pages 927–33 in *Encyclopedia of the Dead Sea Scrolls*. Edited by L.H. Schiffman and J.C. VanderKam. New York: Oxford University Press, 2000.

153 García Martínez, F. "1Q Genesis Apocryphon." *Schrift* 187 (2000): 21–24.

154 Tigchelaar, E.J.C., and F. García Martínez. "4Q208–209 4QAstronomical Enoch[a–b] ar: Introduction." Pages 95–103 in *Qumran Cave 4.XXVI Cryptic Texts and Miscellanea, Part 1*. DJD XXXVI. Edited by P.S. Alexander, et al. Oxford: Clarendon Press, 2000.

155 Tigchelaar, E.J.C., and F. García Martínez. "4Q208 4QAstronomical Enoch[a] ar." Pages 104–31, pls III–IV in *Qumran Cave 4 XXVI Cryptic Texts and Miscellanea, Part 1*. DJD XXXVI. Edited by P.S. Alexander, et al. Oxford: Clarendon Press, 2000.

157 Tigchelaar, E.J.C., and F. García Martínez. "4Q209 4QAstronomical Enoch[b] ar." Pages 132–71, pls V–VII in *Qumran Cave 4 XXVI Cryptic Texts and Miscellanea, Part 1*. DJD XXXVI. Edited by P.S. Alexander, et al. Oxford: Clarendon Press, 2000.

158 García Martínez, F. "Multiple Literary Editions of the Temple Scroll?" Pages 364–371 in *The Dead Sea Scrolls Fifty Years after their Discovery: Proceedings of the Jerusalem Congress, July 20–25, 1997*. Edited by L.H. Schiffman, E. Tov, and J.C. VanderKam. Jerusalem: Israel Exploration Society, 2000.

159 García Martínez, F. "Sapiential, Liturgical and Poetical Texts from Qumran." Pages 1–11 in *Sapiential, Liturgical and Poetical Texts from Qumran: Proceedings of the Third Meeting of the International Organization for Qumran Studies, Oslo 1998. Published in Memory of Maurice Baillet*. Edited by D.K. Falk, F. García Martínez, and E.M. Schuller. STDJ 35. Leiden: Brill, 2000.

160 García Martínez, F. "Sektarische composities: de Regel van de gemeenschap (*Serek ha-Jahad*)." *Schrift* 191 (2000): 151–54.

161 García Martínez, F. "L'Apocalyptique à Qumrân." *Tranversalités, Revue de l'Institut Catholique de Paris* 75 (2000): 183–200.

162 García Martínez, F. "Adam Simon van der Woude." *Henoch* 22 (2000): 364–66.

163 García Martínez, F. "Influjos de la religión persa en el pensamiento de la comunidad de Qumrán." Pages 153–82 in *Religions de l'Antic Orient*. Editado por M.L. Sánchez León. Palma: Universitat de les Illes Balears, 2000.

164 García Martínez, F. "The Great Battles Over Qumran." *Near Eastern Archaeology* 63:3 (2000): 124–30.

165 García Martínez, F. "The Temple Scrolls." *Near Eastern Archaeology* 63:3 (2000): 172–74.

166 García Martínez, F. "La figure de Melki-Sedeq et le messianisme qumrânien." Pages 45–50 in *Józef Tadeusz Milik et Cinquantenaire de la découverte des manuscrits de la mer Morte de Qumrân*. Collectif sous la direction de Dariusz Duglosz et Henryk Ratajczak. Varsovie: Centre Scientifique de l'Académie Polonaise des Sciences à Paris, 2000.

167 García Martínez, F. "Adam Simon van der Woude (1927–2000)" (avec un supplément à sa bibliographie). *RevQ* 19/76 (2000): 500–505.

168 García Martínez, F. "Adam Simon van der Woude, 1927–2000." *JSJ* 32 (2001): 1–4.

169 García Martínez, F. "Discoveries in the Judaean Desert: Textes Légaux (I)." *JSJ* 32 (2001): 71–89.

170   García Martínez, F. "Colloquium Biblicum Lovaniense 2002." *RevQ* 20/77 (2001): 165–67.

171   García Martínez, F. "Schriftuitleg in Qumran." Pages 76–79 in *Internationaal Commentaar op de Bijbel*. Onder redactie van E. Eynikel, E. Noort, T. Baarda, en A. Denaux. Kampen: Kok, 2001.

172   García Martínez, F. "Interpretación de la creación en el Judaísmo antiguo." Pages 115–35 in *Religions del món antic: La creació*. Dirigit per M.L. Sánchez León. Palma de Mallorca: Universitat de les Illes Balears, 2001.

173   García Martínez, F. "The Sacrifice of Isaac in 4Q225." Pages 44–57 in *The Sacrifice of Isaac: The Aqedah (Genesis 22) and its Interpretations*. Edited by E. Noort and E. Tigchelaar. TBN 4. Leiden: Brill, 2002.

174   García Martínez, F. "¿Ángel, Hombre, Mesías, Maestro de Justicia? El problemático 'yo' de un poema qumránico." Pages 103–31 in *Plenitudo Temporis. Miscelánea Homenaje al prof. Dr. Ramón Trevijano Etcheverría*. Coordinadores J.J. Fernández Sangrador y S. Guijarro Oporto. Bibliotheca Salmanticensis 249. Salamanca: Universidad Pontificia de Salamanca, 2002.

175   García Martínez, F. "Old Texts and Modern Mirages: The "I" of Two Qumran Hymns." *ETL* 78 (2002): 321–39.

176   García Martínez, F. "Wisdom and Apocalypticism in the Dead Sea Scrolls and in the Biblical Tradition." *ETL* 78 (2002): 536–49.

177   García Martínez, F. "Guerra e pace in prospettiva eschatologica e apocalittica." Pages 47–64 in *Pace e Guerra nella Bibbia e nel Corano*. A cura di P. Stefani e G. Menestrina. Brescia: Morcelliana, 2002.

178   Ellens, J.H., and F. García Martínez. "Enochians and Zadokites." Pages 147–53 in *The Origins of Enochic Judaism: Proceedings of the First Enoch Seminar: University of Michigan, Sesto Fiorentino, Italy June 19– 23, 2001*. Edited by G. Boccaccini. Torino: Zamorani, 2002. (= *Henoch* 24)

179   García Martínez, F. "Magic in the Dead Sea Scrolls." Pages 13–33 in *The Metamorphosis of Magic from Late Antiquity to the Early Modern Period*. Edited by J.N. Bremmer and J.R. Veenstra. GSCC 1. Leuven: Peeters, 2002.

180   García Martínez, F. "La fascination des chrétiens pour Qumrân." Pages 119–23 in *Les manuscrits de la mer Morte*, par F. Mébarki et É. Puech, Rodez: Les Éditions du Rouergue, 2002.

181   García Martínez, F. "Eve's Children in the Targumim." Pages 27–45 in *Eve's Children: The Biblical Stories Retold and Interpreted in Jewish and Christian Traditions*. Edited by G.P. Luttikhuizen. TBN 5. Leiden: Brill, 2003.

182   García Martínez, F. "Greek Loanwords in the *Copper Scroll*." Pages 119–45 in *Jerusalem, Alexandria, Rome: Studies in Ancient Cultural Interaction in Honour of A. Hilhorst*. Edited by F. García Martínez and G. P. Luttikhuizen. JSJSup 82. Leiden: Brill, 2003.

183   García Martínez, F. "Introduction." Pages xiii–xxxiv in *Wisdom and Apocalypticism in the Dead Sea Scrolls and in the Biblical Traditions*. Edited by F. García Martínez. BETL 168. Peeters: Leuven, 2003.

184   García Martínez, F. "Wisdom at Qumran: Wordly or Heavenly?" Pages 1–15 in *Wisdom and Apocalypticism in the Dead Sea Scrolls and in the Biblical Tradition*. Edited by F. García Martínez. BETL 168. Peeters: Leuven, 2003.

185   García Martínez, F. "Caín, su padre, y el origen del Mal." Pages 17–35 in *Palabra, prodigio, poesía. In memoriam P. Luis Alonso Schökel, S.J.*. Analecta Biblica 151. Rome: Pontificio Istituto Biblico, 2003.

186   García Martínez, F. "Iranian influences in Qumran?" Pages 37–49 in *Apocalyptic and Eschatological Heritage: The Middle East and Celtic Realms*. Edited by M. McNamara. Dublin: Four Courts Press, 2003.

187   García Martínez, F. "De Dode-Zeerollen en het Nieuwe Testament." Pages 111–31 in *Fragmenten uit de woestijn: De Dode-Zeerollen opnieuw bekeken*. Onder redactie van F. García Martínez en E. Tigchelaar. Zoetermeer: Meinema, 2003.

188   García Martínez, F., and E. Tigchelaar. "De sektarische gemeenschap van de
      Regel van de Gemeenschap." Pages 133–44 in *Fragmenten uit de woestijn: De Dode-Zeerol-
      len opnieuw bekeken.* Onder redactie van F. García Martínez en E. Tigchelaar.
      Zoetermeer: Meinema, 2003.
189   García Martínez, F. "Abraham y los dioses: Los caminos del monoteísmo en la
      religión judía." Pages 75–94 in *Religions del Món Antic: Entre politeisme i monoteisme.*
      Dirigit per M.L. Sánchez León. Palma: Universitat de les Illes Balears, 2003.
190   García Martínez, F. "André Dupont-Sommer et les manuscrits de la mer Morte."
      Pages 1421–34 in *Hommage rendu à André Dupont-Sommer. Séance du 14 novembre
      2003.* Institut de France. Comptes rendus de l'Académie des Inscriptions et des
      Belles-Lettres, Paris: Institut, 2003.
192   García Martínez, F. "Querelle sur le messianisme." *Le Monde de la Bible* 151
      (2003) : 18–23.
193   García Martínez, F. "Ces manuscrits qui parlent de magie." *Le Monde de la Bible*
      151 (2003) : 34–37.
194   García Martínez, F. "Sodom and Gomorrah in the Targumim." Pages 83–96
      in *Sodom's Sin: Genesis 18–19 and its Interpretations.* Edited by E. Noort and
      E. Tigchelaar. TBN 7. Leiden: Brill, 2004.
195   García Martínez, F. "Apocryphal, Pseudepigraphical and Para-Biblical Texts
      from Qumran." *RevQ* 21/83 (2004): 365–78.
196   García Martínez, F. "Dualismo y el origen del mal." Pages 103–18 in *Para
      comprender los manuscritos del mar Muerto.* Coordinador J. Vázquez Allegue. Estella:
      Verbo Divino, 2004.
197   García Martínez, F. "Calendarios de Qumrán." Pages 157–75 in *Para comprender
      los manuscritos del mar Muerto.* Coordinador J. Vázquez Allegue. Estella: Verbo
      Divino, 2004.
198   García Martínez, F. "La memoria inventada: El 'otro' en los manuscritos de
      Qumran." Pages 49–71 in *Congreso internacional: "Biblia, memoria histórica y encrucijada
      de culturas." Actas.* Editado por J. Campos Santiago y V. Pastor Julián. Zamora:
      ABE, 2004.
199   García Martínez, F. "The Texts of the XII Prophets at Qumran." *Old Testament
      Essays* 17/1 (2004): 103–19.
200   García Martínez, F. "Samma'el in Pseudo-Jonathan and the Origin of Evil."
      JNSL 30 (2004): 19–41.
201   García Martínez, F. "Emerging Christianity and Second Temple Judaism: A
      «Qumranic» Perspective." *RCatT* 29 (2004): 255–67.
203   García Martínez, F. "Creation in the Dead Sea Scrolls." Pages 49–70 in *The
      Creation of Heaven and Earth. Re-interpretations of Genesis I in the Context of Judaism,
      Ancient Philosophy, Christianity, and Modern Physics.* Edited by George H. van Kooten.
      TBN 8. Leiden: Brill, 2005.
204   García Martínez, F. "La Genèse d'Alexandrie, les Rabbins et Qumrân." Pages
      21–41 in *The Wisdom of Egypt. Jewish, Early Christian, and Gnostic Essays in Honour
      of Gerard P. Luttikhuizen.* Edited by A. Hilhorst and G.H. van Kooten. AJEC 59.
      Leiden: Brill, 2005.
205   García Martínez, F. "Johan Lust: Academic Bibliography." Pages xvii–xliii in
      Interpreting Translation: Studies on the LXX and Ezekiel in Honour of Johan Lust. Edited
      by F. García Martínez and M. Vervenne. BETL 192. Leuven: Peeters, 2005.
206   García Martínez, F. "The Apocalyptic Interpretation of Ezekiel in the Dead
      Sea Scrolls." Pages 163–76 in *Interpreting Translation. Studies on the LXX and Ezekiel
      in Honour of Johan Lust.* Edited by F. García Martínez and M. Vervenne. BETL
      192. Leuven: Peeters, 2005.
207   García Martínez, F. "Comparing the Groups Behind Dream Visions and Daniel:
      A Brief Note." Pages 45–46 in *Enoch and Qumran Origins: New Light on a Forgotten
      Connection.* Edited by G. Boccaccini. Grand Rapids, Mich.: Eerdmans, 2005.
208   García Martínez, F. "Response: The Groningen Hypothesis Revisited." Pages

310–16 in *Enoch and Qumran Origins: New Light on a Forgotten Connection.* Edited by G. Boccaccini. Grand Rapids, Mich.: Eerdmans, 2005.

209   García Martínez, F. "La Bible d'Alexandrie au miroir de Qumrân." *RevQ* 86/22 (2005): 253–68.

210   García Martínez, F. "Lo stato attuale degli studi qumranici: cambiamenti e prospettive." Pages 205–11 in *Il Messia tra memoria e attesa.* A cura di G. Boccaccini. Brescia: Morcelliana, 2005.

211   García Martínez, F. "Marginalia on 4QInstruction." *DSD* 13 (2006): 24–37.

212   García Martínez, F. "De Dode-Zeerollen en het Nieuwe Testament." Pages 161–78 in *Weten in woorden en daden: Lessen voor de eenentwintigste eeuw.* Onder redactie van B. Raymaekers en G. van Riel. Leuven: Universitaire Pers, 2006.

213   García Martínez, F. "Divine Sonship at Qumran: Between the Old and the New Testament." Pages 109–32 in *Biblical Traditions in Transmission: Essays in Honour of Michael A. Knibb.* Edited by C. Hempel and J.M. Lieu. JSJSup 111. Leiden: Brill, 2006.

214   García Martínez, F. "La conception de «l'autre» dans le *Document de Damas.*" Pages 37–50 in *Qoumrân et le judaïsme du tournant de notre ère. Actes de la Table Ronde, Collège de France, 16 novembre 2004.* Sous la direction de A. Lemaire et S.C. Mimouni. Collection de la *Revue des Études juives.* Paris-Louvain: Peeters, 2006.

215   García Martínez, F. "Qumrán en el siglo XXI: Cambios y perspectivas después de 50 años de estudios," *MEAH.* Sección de Hebreo 55 (2006): 309–34.

216   García Martínez, F. "Qumran en el siglo XXI: Cambios y perspectivas después de 50 años de estudios." *Anales de teología de la Universidad Católica de la Santísima Concepción* 8.2 (2006): 5–21.

*   García Martínez, F. "Metamorfosis de una prohibición: La magia en los Manuscritos de Qumrán." In *Religions del Món Antic: La Màgia.* Editado por M.L. Sánchez León. Palma de Mallorca: Universitat de les Illes Balears, 2006.

*   García Martínez, F. "Divine Sonship at Qumran and in Philo." *SPhilo* 19 (2007) forthcoming.

*   García Martínez, F. "Balaam in the Dead Sea Scrolls." In *Balaam's Prophecy.* Edited by G.H. van Kooten and J.T.A.G.M. van Ruiten. TBN 10. Leiden: Brill, forthcoming.

*   García Martínez, F. "Hagar in Targum Pseudo-Jonathan." In *Hagar.* Edited by G. H. van Kooten. TBN 11. Leiden: Brill, forthcoming.

*   García Martínez, F. "Defining Identities." In *Defining Identities: We, You and the Others in the Dead Sea Scrolls.* Edited by F. García Martínez and M. Popović. STDJ. Leiden: Brill, forthcoming.

INDEX OF ANCIENT SOURCES

Old Testament Pseudepigrapha

RABBINIC JUDAISM

INDEX OF MODERN AUTHORS